The Handbook of
Speech Production

Blackwell Handbooks in Linguistics

This outstanding multi-volume series covers all the major subdisciplines within linguistics today to offer a comprehensive survey of linguistics as a whole.
To see the full list of titles available in the series please visit www.wiley.com/go/linguistics-handbooks

The Handbook of Contemporary Syntactic Theory
Edited by Mark Baltin & Chris Collins

The Handbook of Historical Linguistics
Edited by Brian D. Joseph & Richard D. Janda

The Handbook of Second Language Acquisition
Edited by Catherine J. Doughty & Michael H. Long

The Handbook of Applied Linguistics
Edited by Alan Davies & Catherine Elder

The Handbook of Pragmatics
Edited by Laurence R. Horn & Gregory Ward

The Handbook of Speech Perception
Edited by David B. Pisoni & Robert E. Remez

The Handbook of the History of English
Edited by Ans van Kemenade & Bettelou Los

The Handbook of English Linguistics
Edited by Bas Aarts & April McMahon

The Handbook of World Englishes
Edited by Braj B. Kachru, Yamuna Kachru, & Cecil L. Nelson

The Handbook of Educational Linguistics
Edited by Bernard Spolsky & Francis M. Hult

The Handbook of Clinical Linguistics
Edited by Martin J. Ball, Michael R. Perkins, Nicole Müller, & Sara Howard

The Handbook of Pidgin and Creole Studies
Edited by Silvia Kouwenberg & John Victor Singler

The Handbook of Language Teaching
Edited by Michael H. Long & Catherine J. Doughty

The Handbook of Phonetic Sciences, Second Edition
Edited by William J. Hardcastle, John Laver, & Fiona E. Gibbon

The Handbook of Language and Speech Disorders
Edited by Jack S. Damico, Nicole Müller, & Martin J. Ball

The Handbook of Language Contact
Edited by Raymond Hickey

The Handbook of Computational Linguistics and Natural Language Processing
Edited by Alexander Clark, Chris Fox, & Shalom Lappin

The Handbook of Language and Globalization
Edited by Nikolas Coupland

The Handbook of Hispanic Sociolinguistics
Edited by Manuel Díaz-Campos

The Handbook of Language Socialization
Edited by Alessandro Duranti, Elinor Ochs, & Bambi B. Schieffelin

The Handbook of Phonological Theory, Second Edition
Edited by John A. Goldsmith, Jason Riggle, & Alan C. L. Yu

The Handbook of Intercultural Discourse and Communication
Edited by Christina Bratt Paulston, Scott F. Kiesling, & Elizabeth S. Rangel

The Handbook of Hispanic Linguistics
Edited by José Ignacio Hualde, Antxon Olarrea, & Erin O'Rourke

The Handbook of Historical Sociolinguistics
Edited by Juan M. Hernández-Campoy & J. Camilo Conde-Silvestre

The Handbook of Conversation Analysis
Edited by Jack Sidnell & Tanya Stivers

The Handbook of English for Specific Purposes
Edited by Brian Paltridge & Sue Starfield

The Handbook of Bilingualism and Multilingualism, Second Edition
Edited by Tej K. Bhatia & William C. Ritchie

The Handbook of Language Variation and Change
Edited by J. K. Chambers, Peter Trudgill, & Natalie Schilling

The Handbook of Spanish Second Language Acquisition
Edited by Kimberly L. Geeslin

The Handbook of Chinese Linguistics
Edited by C.-T. James Huang, Y.-H. Audrey Li, & Andrew Simpson

The Handbook of Language, Gender, and Sexuality, Second Edition
Edited by Susan Ehrlich, Miriam Meyerhoff, & Janet Holmes

The Handbook of Language Emergence
Edited by Brian MacWhinney & William O'Grady

The Handbook of Bilingual and Multilingual Education
Edited by Wayne E. Wright, Sovicheth Boun, & Ofelia Garcia

The Handbook of Discourse Analysis, Second Edition
Edited by Deborah Tannen, Heidi E. Hamilton, & Deborah Schiffrin

The Handbook of English Pronunciation
Edited by Marnie Reed & John M. Levis

The Handbook of Classroom Discourse and Interaction
Edited by Numa Markee

The Handbook of Korean Linguistics
Edited by Lucien Brown & Jaehoon Yeon

The Handbook of Speech Production
Edited by Melissa A. Redford

The Handbook of Narrative Analysis
Edited by Anna De Fina & Alexandra Georgakopoulou

The Handbook of Contemporary Semantic Theory, Second Edition
Edited by Shalom Lappin & Chris Fox

The Handbook of Portuguese Linguistics
Edited by W. Leo Wetzels, Sergio Menuzzi, & João Costa

The Handbook of Translation and Cognition
Edited by John W. Schwieter & Aline Ferreira

The Handbook of Linguistics, Second Edition
Edited by Mark Aronoff & Janie Rees-Miller

The Handbook of Dialectology
Edited by Charles Boberg, John Nerbonne, & Dominic Watt

The Handbook of Technology and Second Language Teaching and Learning
Edited by Carol A. Chapelle & Shannon Sauro

The Handbook of Psycholinguistics
Edited by Eva M. Fernández & Helen Smith Cairns

The Handbook of Advanced Proficiency in Second Language Acquisition
Edited by Paul A. Malovrh & Alessandro G. Benati

The Handbook of Speech Production

Edited by

Melissa A. Redford

WILEY Blackwell

This paperback edition first published 2019
© 2015 John Wiley & Sons, Inc.

Edition history: John Wiley and Sons, Inc. (hardback, 2015)

All rights reserved. No part of this publication may be reproduced, stored in a retrieval system, or transmitted, in any form or by any means, electronic, mechanical, photocopying, recording or otherwise, except as permitted by law. Advice on how to obtain permission to reuse material from this title is available at http://www.wiley.com/go/permissions.

The right of Melissa A. Redford to be identified as the author of the editorial material in this work has been asserted in accordance with law.

Registered Office
John Wiley & Sons, Inc., 111 River Street, Hoboken, NJ 07030, USA

Editorial Office
9600 Garsington Road, Oxford, OX4 2DQ, UK

For details of our global editorial offices, customer services, and more information about Wiley products visit us at www.wiley.com.

Wiley also publishes its books in a variety of electronic formats and by print-on-demand. Some content that appears in standard print versions of this book may not be available in other formats.

Limit of Liability/Disclaimer of Warranty
While the publisher and authors have used their best efforts in preparing this work, they make no representations or warranties with respect to the accuracy or completeness of the contents of this work and specifically disclaim all warranties, including without limitation any implied warranties of merchantability or fitness for a particular purpose. No warranty may be created or extended by sales representatives, written sales materials or promotional statements for this work. The fact that an organization, website, or product is referred to in this work as a citation and/or potential source of further information does not mean that the publisher and authors endorse the information or services the organization, website, or product may provide or recommendations it may make. This work is sold with the understanding that the publisher is not engaged in rendering professional services. The advice and strategies contained herein may not be suitable for your situation. You should consult with a specialist where appropriate. Further, readers should be aware that websites listed in this work may have changed or disappeared between when this work was written and when it is read. Neither the publisher nor authors shall be liable for any loss of profit or any other commercial damages, including but not limited to special, incidental, consequential, or other damages.

Library of Congress Cataloging-in-Publication Data
The handbook of speech production / edited by Melissa A. Redford. – 1
    pages cm. – (Blackwell handbooks in linguistics)
   Includes bibliographical references and index.
   ISBN 978-0-470-65993-9 (hardback) | ISBN 978-1-119-02914-4 (paperback)
1. Speech–Handbooks, manuals, etc.   2. Oral communication–Handbooks, manuals, etc.
3. Speech acts (Linguistics)–Handbooks, manuals, etc.   4. Psycholinguistics–Handbooks, manuals, etc.   I. Redford, Melissa A., editor.
  P95.H36 2015
  612.7'8–dc23
                                                                        2014048347

Cover Design: Wiley
Cover Image: an abstract painting © clivewa/Shutterstock

Set in 10/12pt Palatino by SPi Global, Pondicherry, India

Printed in the UK

Contents

Notes on Contributors	vii
Acknowledgments	xii

1	Introduction MELISSA A. REDFORD	1
Part I	**The Speech Mechanism**	**11**
2	Speech Breathing Across the Life Span and in Disease JESSICA E. HUBER AND ELAINE T. STATHOPOULOS	13
3	Mechanisms of Voice Production BRAD H. STORY	34
4	Supralaryngeal Articulators in the Oropharyngeal Region KIYOSHI HONDA	59
5	Jaw and Lips PASCAL H.H.M. VAN LIESHOUT	79
6	Velopharyngeal Function in Speech Production: Some Developmental and Structural Considerations DAVID J. ZAJAC	109
Part II	**Coordination and Multimodal Speech**	**131**
7	Interarticulatory Coordination: Speech Sounds PHILIP HOOLE AND MARIANNE POUPLIER	133
8	Rhythm and Speech FRED CUMMINS	158
9	Auditory-Visual Speech Processing: Something Doesn't Add Up ERIC VATIKIOTIS-BATESON AND KEVIN G. MUNHALL	178
10	Multimodal Speech Production LUCIE MÉNARD	200

Part III Speech Motor Control — 223

11. Motor Equivalence in Speech Production — 225
    PASCAL PERRIER AND SUSANNE FUCHS
12. Orofacial Cutaneous Function in Speech Motor Control and Learning — 248
    TAKAYUKI ITO
13. Auditory Feedback — 267
    JOHN HOUDE AND SRIKANTAN NAGARAJAN
14. Speech Production in Motor Speech Disorders: Lesions, Models, and a Research Agenda — 298
    GARY WEISMER AND JORDAN R. GREEN
15. Process-Oriented Diagnosis of Childhood and Adult Apraxia of Speech (CAS and AOS) — 331
    BEN MAASSEN AND HAYO TERBAND

Part IV Sequencing and Planning — 351

16. Central Tenets of the Frame/Content Theory of Evolution and Acquisition of Speech Production — 353
    PETER F. MACNEILAGE
17. The Acquisition of Temporal Patterns — 379
    MELISSA A. REDFORD
18. Insights for Speech Production Planning from Errors in Inner Speech — 404
    GARY S. DELL AND GARY M. OPPENHEIM
19. Prosodic Frames in Speech Production — 419
    STEFANIE SHATTUCK-HUFNAGEL
20. Fluency and Disfluency — 445
    ROBIN J. LICKLEY

Part V Language Factors — 475

21. Insights from the Field — 477
    DIDIER DEMOLIN
22. Language Effects on Timing at the Segmental and Suprasegmental Levels — 505
    TAEHONG CHO
23. Cross-Language Differences in Acquisition — 530
    JAN R. EDWARDS, MARY E. BECKMAN, AND BENJAMIN MUNSON
24. Effects of Language on Motor Processes in Development — 555
    LISA GOFFMAN

Index of Authors — 578
Index of Subjects — 592

Notes on Contributors

Mary E. Beckman is a Distinguished Humanities Professor of Linguistics, Ohio State University, USA. She is the author of *Stress and Non-Stress Accent* (1986), co-author of *Japanese Tone Structure* (with Janet Pierrehumbert, 1988), and co-editor of *Between the Grammar and Physics of Speech* (with John Kingston, 1990).

Taehong Cho is a Professor of Phonetics in the Department of English Language and Literature, and the director of the Phonetics and Psycholinguistics Lab at Hanyang University, Seoul, Korea. He earned his PhD degree in phonetics at the University of California at Los Angeles (UCLA) and worked at the Max Planck Institute for Psycholinguistics. His main research interest is in the interplay between prosody, phonology, and phonetics in speech production and its perceptual effects in speech comprehension. He is currently serving as Associate Editor of *Journal of Phonetics* (Elsevier) and is book series editor for "Studies in Laboratory Phonology" (Language Science Press).

Fred Cummins has a background in linguistics, computer science, and cognitive science. His thesis work (Indiana University, 1997) saw the development of an experimental tool, speech cycling, that revealed some generic organizational principles that constrain repeated movements of the speech articulators. Subsequent work has looked at the properties of synchronous speech. This focus has recently extended to joint speech, as found in prayer, protest, sports stadiums, and beyond. His approach is characterized by the use of dynamic systems concepts to found a non-representationalist account of behavior.

Gary S. Dell obtained his PhD in Psychology from the University of Toronto in 1980. He has since held academic positions at Dartmouth College, the University of Rochester, and the University of Illinois at Urbana-Champaign, USA, where he is currently chair of the Cognitive Science Group of the Beckman Institute. His research interests include language production, learning, and neural network models.

Didier Demolin is Professor of Experimental Phonetics, Phonology, and Linguistics at the Université de Paris 3-Sorbonne Nouvelle, France, and researcher at the

Laboratoire de Phonétique et Phonologie (CNRS-Paris3). He has done extensive fieldwork on various Sub-Saharan and South American languages. He is a member of the Academia Europaea.

Jan R. Edwards is a Professor in the Department of Communication Sciences and Disorders at the University of Wisconsin-Madison, USA. Her research examines interactions between vocabulary growth and phonological acquisition in both typically developing children and children with speech and language disorders as well as cross-linguistic phonological acquisition and the impact of dialect mismatch on academic achievement. She has co-authored numerous journal articles and book chapters on this research.

Susanne Fuchs was awarded a PhD from Queen Margaret University College, Edinburgh, UK. Currently, she is working at the ZAS in Berlin. She is interested in experimental phonetics and speech motor control, using a variety of methods (electrophalatography, articulography, intraoral pressure measures, Respitrace). She is co-editor of the book series "Speech Production and Perception" (Peter Lang).

Lisa Goffman is a Professor in the Department of Speech, Language, and Hearing Sciences at Purdue University. The major objective of her research program is to provide an empirical foundation for understanding language development and disorders, one that incorporates findings about shared language and motor substrates.

Jordan R. Green is Professor of Communication Sciences and Disorders at the MGH Institute of Health Professions and director of the Speech and Feeding Disorders Lab. His research focuses on disorders of speech production, oromotor skill development for early speech and feeding, and quantification of speech motor performance.

Kiyoshi Honda is currently a Research Professor at Tianjin University School of Computer Science and Technology, who continues to work on physiology of speech production and experimental phonetics. His recent publications include anatomical reviews on articulatory muscles and vocal tract visualization studies using MRI.

Philip Hoole is Senior Lecturer at the Institute of Phonetics and Speech Processing, Munich University. His main research interests include linguistic phonetics, speech motor control, and laryngeal articulation.

John Houde did his PhD work at the Massachusetts Institute of Technology on sensorimotor adaptation in speech production. He then did postdoctoral training at the University of California San Francisco, where he has remained and is currently Associate Professor in the Department of Otolaryngology – Head and Neck Surgery.

Jessica E. Huber PhD, CCC-SLP, is a Professor in the Department of Speech, Language, and Hearing Sciences at Purdue University, USA. Her research emphasis is the effects of aging and motor disorders on speech production. Her current research examines the effectiveness of treatments for impairments of speech (with special focus on the respiratory system), balance, and cognitive changes as a result of Parkinson's disease and aging.

Takayuki Ito has been senior research scientist in Haskins Laboratories since 2005 and Adjunct Professor at the University of Connecticut, USA, since 2011. He earned his PhD at Chiba University, Japan, in 1999. His research interests are in somatosensory processing in speech production and perception.

Robin J. Lickley is Reader in Speech Sciences at the Clinical Audiology, Speech and Language (CASL) Research Centre at Queen Margaret University, Edinburgh, UK, and Honorary Fellow of the College of Science and Engineering at the University of Edinburgh. His research interests include production and perception of typical and clinical disfluency, speech articulation, and prosody.

Ben Maassen is Professor of Dyslexia and Clinical Neuropsychology, Centre for Language and Cognition (CLCG), University of Groningen, Netherlands, with a background in cognitive neuropsychology and speech-language pathology. His main research areas are dyslexia, neurogenic and developmental speech disorders in children, electrophysiological processes, perception-production modeling, and speech-related cognitive dysfunctions.

Peter F. MacNeilage is Professor Emeritus of Psychology, University of Texas at Austin, USA. He has written over 120 papers about the evolution of complex output systems. He is the author of two theories: The Frame/Content theory of evolution of speech production and the Postural Origins theory of evolution of primate handedness.

Lucie Ménard completed her doctoral degree at GIPSA-lab, Grenoble, in the field of Speech Sciences. She is currently a Full Professor of Phonetic Sciences and the director of the Phonetics Laboratory at the Université du Québec à Montréal, Canada. She is also affiliated with Ste-Justine Pediatric Hospital Research Center in Montreal. She has developed an expertise in the development of speech production and perception in various sensory conditions. She uses experimental techniques such as ultrasound imaging, articulography, and acoustic analysis. Prior to her academic career, she participated in the development of the Canadian French text-to-speech system at Bell Laboratories/Lucent Technologies.

Kevin G. Munhall is a Professor of Psychology at Queen's University in Canada with cross-appointments in the Department of Otolaryngology and the Linguistics program. His current work focuses on conversation, auditory feedback, and audiovisual perception.

Benjamin Munson is a Professor in the Department of Speech-Language-Hearing Sciences at the University of Minnesota, Twin Cities, USA. He has co-authored more than 70 articles and chapters on phonological development, sociophonetics, and speech science.

Srikantan Nagarajan did his MS and PhD work in Biomedical Engineering at Case Western Reserve University, USA, and holds a postdoctoral fellowship from the University of California, San Francisco, where he is currently a Professor in the Department of Radiology and Biomedical Imaging. His research interests are in Neural Engineering with a focus on speech motor control and brain plasticity.

Gary M. Oppenheim obtained his PhD in Psychology from the University of Illinois at Urbana-Champaign in 2011. Following a postdoctoral fellowship at the Center for Research in Language at the University of California, San Diego, Gary is now a Lecturer in Psychology at Bangor University in Wales and an Adjunct Assistant Professor of Psychology at Rice University in Texas, USA. His research interests include language production, computational modeling, heuristics, and learning.

Pascal Perrier was awarded a PhD from Grenoble University. He is a Professor at Grenoble INP/GIPSA-lab, France. His research interests include speech motor control and orofacial biomechanics. He worked with the ZAS in Berlin, the Speech Group at MIT, and the JAIST in Ishikawa, Japan. He is co-editor of the book series "Speech Production and Perception" (Peter Lang).

Marianne Pouplier is Principal Investigator at the Institute of Phonetics and Speech Processing, Munich University, Germany. Her main research interests include the phonetics-phonology interface and speech production.

Melissa A. Redford is Professor of Linguistics at University of Oregon, USA, with a broad cognitive sciences background. She received her PhD in Psychology at the University of Texas and completed an NRSA Individual Postdoctoral Fellowship in Computer Science, also at the University of Texas, before joining the faculty at the University of Oregon in 2002. Her research focuses on the development and structure of the speech plan and on the parameters that control rate, rhythm, emphasis, and style changes in spoken language.

Stefanie Shattuck-Hufnagel is a Principal Research Scientist at the Research Laboratory of Electronics (RLE) at the Massachusetts Institute of Technology, USA. She received her PhD in cognitive psychology from MIT in 1975, and was Assistant Professor of Psychology at Cornell University before joining RLE in 1980. She investigates the cognitive structures and processes involved in speech production planning, particularly at the level of speech sound sequencing, as well as related aspects of utterance production planning such as speech-accompanying gesture, phonological development, and clinical manifestations of phonological and phonetic disorders.

Elaine T. Stathopoulos is a Professor in the Department of Communicative Sciences and Disorders at the University at Buffalo, USA. Stathopoulos's major area of study is in the human developmental and life span trends for respiratory and laryngeal function during speech production.

Brad H. Story received his BS degree in Applied Physics from the University of Northern Iowa in 1987. He worked as an engineer for the Donaldson Company in Minneapolis, Minnesota from 1987 to 1991. He received his PhD degree in Speech Science from the University of Iowa in 1995 and was employed from 1996 to 2000 as a research scientist at the WJ Gould Voice Research Center, Denver Center for the Performing Arts in Denver, Colorado. Since 2000, he has been on faculty in the Department of Speech, Language, and Hearing Sciences at the University of Arizona, in Tucson, USA. His research interests are in computational modeling of the speech production system, speech perception, acoustics, and signal processing.

Hayo Terband is a speech researcher collaborating with speech-language pathologists, neurologists, audiologists, psychologists, and neurophysiologists. His research revolves around the developmental process of the speech production and perception system in both normal and disordered development. Besides fundamental research, he also works on clinical applications and initiated the development and implementation of a process-oriented method for diagnostics and treatment planning of developmental speech disorders, a collaborative project between six Dutch university institutions.

Pascal H.H.M. Van Lieshout is a Professor in the Department of Speech-Language Pathology at the University of Toronto, Canada, a Canada Research Chair (II) in Oral Motor Function, and director of the Oral Dynamics Laboratory. He studies dynamical principles in oral motor control in normal and disordered speech, including stuttering.

Eric Vatikiotis-Bateson studied philosophy and physics (St. John's College, Maryland), ethnographic film making (Anthropology Film Centre, New Mexico), and linguistics and neuroscience (Indiana University). After eight years at Haskins Laboratories (Connecticut) as a PhD student and staff scientist, he moved to ATR International, Japan, to examine the production, perception, and associated brain functions of multimodal communication in complex environments, especially spoken language processing. He is now a Professor of Linguistics and Cognitive Systems at the University of British Columbia, Canada.

Gary Weismer is Oros Bascom Professor and Chair of the Department of Communication Sciences and Disorders, University of Wisconsin-Madison, USA. His research interests include normal speech production processes, models, and theories, and their application to motor speech disorders.

David J. Zajac is an ASHA Fellow and Associate Professor in the Craniofacial Center, Department of Dental Ecology, University of North Carolina at Chapel Hill, USA. His main research interests are in normal aspects of speech production and cleft palate speech.

Acknowledgments

The *Handbook* reflects a collaboration between researchers who agreed to contribute their time, intellect, and expertise to the project, and the editors at Wiley-Blackwell who imagined the project. I was fortunate to mediate between these two groups of people, and have learned a great deal from each and from the process of editing the *Handbook* itself. Danielle Descoteaux, the Acquisitions Editor, gave me the opportunity to do this work and I am grateful to her for that and for her confidence in my abilities. I am also grateful to the many researchers who accepted my invitation to participate in this project and saw their contribution through. It was my pleasure to make the acquaintance of some for the first time and to get to know others a little better. With respect to the work itself, I would like to acknowledge a number of colleagues – Eric Vatikiotis-Bateson, Susanne Fuchs, Pascal Perrier, Vsevolod Kapatsinski, Mary Beckman, and Ben Munson – who provided good advice and constructive feedback on different aspects of the project at different stages in its realization. Julia Kirk, the Project Editor, shepherded me through the administrative aspects of the editorial process; not a small task either. At one point in time, graduate students in my lab read many of the chapters that were contributed to the Handbook. Our group debriefings helped me to hone my expectations for the chapters, and so I am grateful to Wook Kyung Choe, Zahra Foroughifar, Erin Maloney, Paul Olejarczuk, and Hema Sirsa for their efforts and insights. David Bebee helped me significantly with many editorial details. A grant from the Eunice Kennedy Shriver National Institute of Child Health and Human Development (Award Number R01HD061458) provided me time to work on the project. Finally, Sergei Bogdanov kept me sane with his good humor and unfailing support during the nearly five years this project took from conception to completion.

Melissa A. Redford
Eugene, Oregon

1 Introduction

MELISSA A. REDFORD

1.1 Speech production: What it is and why it matters

Speech is the principal mode used to convey human language – a complex communication system that creates cohesion (and division) among us; a system that allows us to structure and build knowledge and social-cultural practices through time. Speech is an activity, defined at its core by an acoustic signal that is generated by the speaker and transduced by the listener. Activities unfold through time, and so does speech. When speech is defined in terms of the signal, it is as a time-varying acoustic waveform, amplitude and frequency modulated. The modulations are due to movements of the speech organs (articulators) in service of the message to be conveyed. Since there is no way to move except through time, the generation of speech constrains how the message is structured: the output must be roughly linear, even though the complex thoughts and feelings we want to communicate are not.

The relationship between complexity and the quasi-linearity of action was famously explored by Karl Lashley (1951). Lashley's concern was to explain "the existence of generalized schemata of action which determine the sequence of specific acts, acts which in themselves or in their associations seem to have no temporal valence (122)." To do so, Lashley devoted over half of his presentation, intended for an audience of neuroscientists, to language. He argued, based on the evidence from language, that the control structures he sought to define (i.e., schemata) must be hierarchical in their organization:

> I have devoted so much time to the discussion of the problem of syntax, not only because language is one of the most important products of human cerebral action, but also because the problems raised by the organization of language seem to me to be characteristic of almost all other cerebral activities. There is a series of hierarchies of organization; the order of vocal movements in pronouncing the word, the order of words in the sentence, the order of sentences in the paragraph, the rational order of paragraphs in a discourse.
>
> (1951: 121)

The Handbook of Speech Production, First Edition. Edited by Melissa A. Redford.
© 2015 John Wiley & Sons, Inc. Published 2019 by John Wiley & Sons, Inc.

Thus, well before Chomsky's (1959) equally famous critique of Skinner's (1957) book, *Verbal Behavior*, Lashley argued that the hierarchical structure of language implied hierarchical representations of language. No doubt that ideas about hierarchical structure and representations were in the intellectual ether of the time, so the issue here is not so much who was first to insist on the importance of these, but instead to note that Lashley linked such representations to action. In so doing, he suggested an interdependency between language and speech that is underappreciated in modern linguistics and psychology.

Insofar as thoughts and feelings are to be externalized and shared between people, they must be structured so that they can be realized in time (i.e., in a serial order). Pinker and Bloom (1990: 713) noted as much when thinking about the evolution of language: "grammars for spoken languages must map propositional structures onto a serial channel." Pinker and Bloom suggest that from this constraint many of the features that Lashley found so intriguing about language follow. Just as Lashley began his paper with reference to "an unpronounceable Cree word" that is analyzed into a "verbal root *tusheka*, 'to remain,' and the various particles which modify it" to produce the meaning "may it remain with you" (1951: 112–113), Pinker and Bloom referred to complex verbal morphology in Native American languages when listing the various devices by which propositions are mapped onto a serial channel: "(v)erb affixes also typically agree with the subject and other arguments, and thus provide another redundant mechanism that can convey predicate-argument relations by itself (e.g., in many Native American languages such as Cherokee and Navajo)" (1990: 713). For Lashley, the fact that particular subsequences within a long Cree word had particular meanings that contributed to a larger one suggested that the "generalized schemata of action" could be conceived of as a hierarchical structure, with smaller units embedded in larger ones. Since the argument was based on language, it is reasonable to conclude that meaning structures action. But what if we were also to emphasize that the units exist to make action possible? With such an emphasis, we might just as well conclude that action structures meaning.

The focus on grammar in the study of language has relegated speech production and perception to the periphery of what is fundamental about language. Speech is merely the dominant mode of communication. Grammar is central. Grammar is structure. But if, as suggested here, the structure that our communication system takes is due in large part to its dominant mode of transmission, then other questions emerge: To what extent are speech and language representations independent? From a developmental perspective it is hard to see exactly where the divide should be drawn since the proximal target of early language acquisition is the ability to produce a sound shape that is linked to some meaning (i.e., a word or construction). Later on, the child must figure out how to link stored units (words) into longer and longer sequences (sentences) that will be "read off" by some speech production mechanism as fluent speech. Shouldn't the speech production mechanism then contribute to how these sequences are chunked for output? Or does linguistic structure (e.g., syntax) wholly determine the chunking, thereby driving the development of the mechanism? And what of the action sequences that are the realization of fluent speech? Is the plan (generalized schemata) that guides extended action defined by units that are independent of action? If so, then how is sequential action executed?

There cannot be layers of abstract linguistic representations all the way down, so to speak, since at some point explicit motor commands are needed to instantiate movements that produce an acoustic signal. The instantiation of planned actions is considered the execution stage of speech production. At this stage, it is generally assumed that the plan is coded as a sequence of realizable motor goals, which are not executed individually during fluent speech, but instead in practiced sequences, that is, as "motor programs" (Keele 1968). Still, the goals themselves are usually considered the critical link between the plan and actual movement. So, what precisely are speech motor goals? There is no current consensus on this question other than to point to those vocal tract configurations that, after centuries of work in phonetics, we have come to associate with particular speech sounds. But whether it is the vocal tract configurations or the sounds themselves that define the goals, depends on your theory. If it is the former, the goal is a motor command (or set of commands) that realize(s) a specific vocal tract constriction (e.g., gesture). If it is the latter, the goal is a specific, acoustically defined set of features. Acoustic goals require an extra step in execution because they must be translated into motor commands with reference to an auditory-motor map set up during development. Nonetheless, most of the contributors to this Handbook who address motor control directly assume acoustic goals since these may allow for speech movements that are more adaptable to the speech context. No matter how the goals are defined, the question that animates research on speech execution is what kinds of feedback and feedforward processes are involved in making sure that the goals are achieved. The stunning complexity of speech action entails that this question be explored from many angles; competing hypotheses regarding the nature of goals ensures that this happens.

The concept of motor goals and their association with particular vocal tract configurations/speech sounds might suggest to the reader that every aspect of speech production is centrally controlled. This is highly unlikely, though, given the evidence that neurotypical adults will spontaneously adapt to certain unanticipated perturbations of the speech articulators (see Chapter 11). Many suggest, including several contributors to this Handbook, that articulatory coordination, which gives rise to particular vocal tract configurations, emerges from dynamical principles. This does not say that the configurations (or their acoustic consequences) can't be goals. It merely says that their achievement cannot depend entirely on central control. But those who advocate a dynamical systems approach to movement coordination are also often wary of goals and the language of control (e.g., Chapter 8). Similar to our earlier question about where to draw the boundary between language and speech representations, these researchers wonder where to draw the boundary between executive function and dynamics. Put another way, we all acknowledge that speech is an intentional activity, but the field has not yet determined where top-down control yields to emergent behavior.

It will hopefully be clear by this point that questions about dynamics, control, and even speech planning cannot be seriously addressed absent a detailed appreciation of speech action. Consider, once again, another extract from Lashley's (1951) paper:

> Pronunciation of the word "right" consists first of retraction and elevation of the tongue, expiration of air and activation of the vocal cords; second, depression of the tongue and jaw; third, elevation of the tongue to touch the dental ridge, stopping of vocalization, and forceful expiration of air with depression of the tongue and jaw. These movements have no intrinsic order of association. Pronunciation of the word "tire" involves the same motor elements in reverse order.
>
> (116)

Leaving aside the oversimplification of articulatory movements described here and the lack of reference to biomechanical linkages within and across time, it is decidedly *not* the case that "the word 'tire' involves the same motor elements [as 'right'] in reverse order." In actual fact, interarticulatory coordination varies substantially by position and context, and especially by position within a syllable (see Chapter 7). There is no sound for which this may be more true than the English *r* that Lashley inadvertently made prominent by having it occur in both syllable-onset and syllable-offset position in his example.

Although Lashley's (1951) true goal was to demonstrate the recombinatorial (i.e., generative) nature of language, his description of vocal action is highlighted here to argue that a misunderstanding of the details of speech has both theoretical and practical consequences. A specific consequence of Lashley's misunderstanding is that it suggests a one-to-one relationship between articulatory configurations and phonemes ("letters" in Lashley's words), which in turn suggests a long-discredited model of execution that proceeds phoneme-by-phoneme. Lashley may have rescued himself from a commitment to the most naive version of such a model by also noting that "letters" are embedded in a "word" and thereby given context. But embedding movements in a context is not quite the same as understanding that interarticulatory coordination is never independent of context. The nuance is important. If taken seriously, it suggests a theory of speech production that is built up from biomechanics, goals, and motor programs. It also suggests *language* representations, such as those proposed in Articulatory Phonology (Browman and Goldstein 1986), that are very different from the familiar atemporal units assumed in modern phonological theory and by Lashley himself. Of course, it is possible to appreciate the details of articulation and reject the types of representation proposed in Articulatory Phonology (a number of contributors to this Handbook do); but, by doing so, one incurs the responsibility of proposing models to bridge the hypothesized divide between speech and language (see Chapter 19 for an example of how this might be achieved).

In summary, Lashley (1951) emphasized that behavior is planned action and argued that the plan for complex behaviors – read serially ordered actions – is best described by hierarchical models, where smaller units of action are embedded in larger ones. I accept this as true, but have also suggested that there are substantial benefits to looking at the relationship between the plan and the behavior from the other direction: where it is the constraints on behavior – the anatomy of its realization and its fundamental temporality – that define the units of action and so contribute to structuring a plan that must also encode meaning. When viewed in this way, speech production is no longer peripheral to language; it is central to its understanding. The chapters in this Handbook are intended to provide readers with a broad base of knowledge about speech production research, models, and theories from multiple perspectives so that they may draw their own conclusions on the relationship between speech and language.

1.2 Organization of the Handbook

This Handbook is organized from the most concrete aspect of speech production to its most abstract; from an emphasis on the physical to an emphasis on the mental. Between these poles we consider the organization and control of speech behavior with reference to dynamical principles and underlying neural structures. All of the chapters engage with behavior; many focus on kinematics, some adopt a computational approach, and some a cross-linguistic one. Because speech production is a skill that takes over a decade to acquire and is easily disrupted by injury or disease, many contributions were solicited from researchers who would engage with a particular topic in speech production from a developmental and/or clinical perspective. Gary Weismer and Jordan Green (Chapter 14), referencing Bernstein and Weismer (2000), argue that "speech production and perception models/theories should have the capacity to predict and/or explain data from *any* speaker or listener, regardless of his or her status as 'normal' or communicatively-impaired." They worry explicitly about the practice of refining speech production models and theories "for 'normal' speakers, with minimal attention paid to speakers with communicative disorders" and, I would add, to development. In addition to the inherent explanatory weakness that results from such practice, models and theories that are perfectly tuned to the typical adult speaker also subvert an important function of basic science: to build a foundation for applied scientific advances. Simply put, individuals with disordered speech and children with immature speech skills provide important data on speech behavior that models and theories of speech production should incorporate for intellectual reasons as well as for practical ones. The organization of the Handbook accommodates this point of view by interleaving chapters focused on disorder and/or development with chapters focused on typical adult behavior.

Whether from a clinical, developmental, or typical adult perspective, each chapter in this Handbook addresses some important aspect of speech production. Many contributions focus on theory, and either suggest revisions to dominant frameworks or extend existing ones. Many contributions also make clear the applied consequences of basic research on speech production; several others focus on questions related to the speech–language divide. The following overview of the chapters in each Part is provided to better orient the reader to the specific content covered in the Handbook.

1.2.1 The speech mechanism

Our anatomy, physiology, and resultant biomechanics define the action that is used to create speech. Phonation is dependent on the constant airstream supplied by the lungs. The waveform generated by vibrations of the vocal folds is further modulated by pharyngeal constrictions, by the movement of the tongue and lips which are biomechanically linked to the jaw, and by virtue of acoustic coupling (or not) with the nasal cavity. The five chapters in Part I provide the reader with a detailed understanding of the action of all of these articulators. But each of these chapters does much more than describe the many muscles involved in speech movement. Pascal van Leishout (Chapter 5) adopts a comparative perspective to present the anatomy and physiology of the lips and jaw in the context not only of speech, but also of the other oral-motor functions to which they are adapted. He concurs with MacNeilage (Chapter 16) and others that "the way we use oral anatomical structures in our communications has been adapted from their original primary use, namely to support feeding and breathing." Brad Story (Chapter 3) and Kiyoshi Honda (Chapter 4) make explicit connections to acoustic theory in their respective chapters on voice production and on the tongue and pharynx. Their chapters are also aimed at updating our understanding of the mechanism: Story provides us with a modern view of the vocal folds as a self-oscillating system, describing computational models of phonation that formalize this view; Honda invites us to jettison our simple tube-model understanding of vocal tract resonances and to consider the contribution of hypopharyngeal cavities to the acoustics of speech (and singing), providing us with compelling 3D MRI images to make his point. Jessica Huber and Elaine Stathopoulos (Chapter 2) and David Zajac (Chapter 6) connect us to language – utterances and oral versus nasal sounds, respectively – while also providing us with information about speech breathing and the velopharyngeal port/nasal cavity: Huber and Stathopoulos document important changes in lung capacity and breath control that occur across the lifespan and in elderly speakers with Parkinson's disease; Zajac documents structural changes in the development of the upper vocal tract and velopharyngeal function in child and adult speakers with typical morphology as well as in those with cleft palate.

1.2.2 Coordination and multimodal speech

The articulators come together, moving into and out of the configurations we associate with specific speech sounds, over and over again through time. Individuals come together to exchange speech, first as the perceiver then as the generator, over and over again through time. This coordination of articulatory movement within and across individuals has consequences for our understanding of speech production processes, as the contributors to Part II of this Handbook make clear. Philip Hoole and Marianne Pouplier (Chapter 7), Fred Cummins (Chapter 8), Eric Vatikiotis-Bateson and Kevin Munhall (Chapter 9) consider coordination at different levels of analysis from the perspective of dynamical systems. Hoole and Pouplier focus on interarticulatory coordination at the level of the segment and across segments, showing how timing patterns vary systematically by language and by syllable position within a language. Moreover, they embed their discussion of these phenomena within an Articulatory Phonology framework, providing the reader with a sense of the theory; its primitives, emergent units, and the coupling dynamics referenced to account for positional effects. Cummins explores rhythm in speech and language; a phenomenon that binds movement through time and speakers in dialogue. He reviews the various historical attempts to test the rhythm class hypothesis, and argues that "the vigorous pursuit of a classificatory scheme for languages on rhythmic grounds alone has probably enjoyed an undue amount of attention, with little success." He advocates that we consider studying phenomena that relate more intuitively to what we might identify as having high degrees of temporal structure, including choral speaking and dyadic interactions. Vatikiotis-Bateson and Munhall consider the speaker–listener dyad in more detail. They review results from behavioral and computational work to show that articulatory movement "simultaneously shapes the acoustic resonances of the speech signal and visibly deforms the face," that speech intelligibility increases if visual information about speech is provided, but that fairly low quality information is sufficient for the increase. From these results, Vatikiotis-Bateson and Munhall argue that we need to develop a better sense of the role of redundancy in production and perception, but offer the hypothesis that redundancies in the visual channel may facilitate the perceiver's spatial and temporal alignment to speech events by multiple means such as highlighting prosodic structure. Lucie Ménard (Chapter 10) also explores audio-visual processing, but from a developmental perspective and within an information-processing framework. She argues, based on work with sensory deprived individuals, that motor goals are multimodal – built up from experience with the acoustic and visible aspects of the signal.

1.2.3 *Speech motor control*

Motor goals are the principal focus of chapters in Part III. Pascal Perrier and Susanne Fuchs (Chapter 11) provide an extensive introduction to the concept of a goal with reference to motor equivalence, which they define as the "capacity of the motor system to adopt certain (different movement) strategies depending on external constraints." They also link motor equivalence to the concept of "plasticity" and to the workings of the central nervous system (CNS). Takayuki Ito (Chapter 12) and John Houde and Srikantan Nagarajan (Chapter 13) discuss the role of sensory feedback in speech motor control with Ito focused on somatosensory information and Houde and Nagarajan on auditory information. Both contributors review findings from feedback perturbation experiments, and both adopt a neuroscientific approach to explain these findings. Whereas Ito concentrates on contributions from the peripheral nervous system, Houde and Nagarajan elaborate a CNS model of control based on internal auditory feedback (efferent copy) and an external feedback loop that allows for the correction of errors in prediction based on incoming sensory information. Gary Weismer and Jordan Green (Chapter 14) are also very focused on the CNS, but their objective is to understand whether the "execution" stage of speech production – classically thought to be disrupted in dysarthria – is truly separable from the "planning" stage of speech production. They conclude, based on clinical and experimental data from individuals with dysarthria and apraxia of speech (a "planning" disorder), that the anatomical and behavioral boundary between the two stages is poorly defined. Ben Maassen and Hayo Terband (Chapter 15) appear to confirm Weismer and Green's point regarding fuzzy boundaries by noting that childhood apraxia of speech, a developmental rather than acquired disorder, may be localized "at the level of phonetic planning, and/or motor programming, and/or motor execution, including internal and external self-monitoring systems." They also make the important point that whether the primary deficit is localized in planning or execution, this *motor* disorder has consequences for *language* representation.

1.2.4 Sequencing and planning

Sequencing and planning are at the interface of speech motor processes and the language representations we associate with meaning. It is here that we grapple most directly with Lashley's (1951) serial order problem as applied to speech. Peter MacNeilage (Chapter 16) addresses the problem within an evolutionary framework. He starts with an oral-motor function – chewing – that precedes speech in evolutionary time and hypothesizes that the movements associated with this function were exapted for speech: once coupled with phonation, the up-down jaw movements of chewing yield an amplitude modulated waveform reminiscent of the ones that linguistic systems segment and categorize as consonant–vowel sequences. In Chapter 17, I think about continuities and junctures in development and what these imply for the acquisition of prosodically related temporal patterns. I argue that the acquisition of temporal patterns is due both to the refinement of speech motor skills and the development of a plan, which is suggested to emerge at the transition from vocal play to concept-driven communication. Gary Dell and Gary Oppenheim (Chapter 18), Stefanie Shattuck-Hufnagel (Chapter 19), and Robin Lickley (Chapter 20) all assume a plan based on units that are more closely tied to the abstract representations postulated in most modern linguistic theories. Dell and Oppenheim make an explicit argument against Articulatory Phonology type representations, in favor of atemporal units. Their evidence comes from the finding that the speech errors of inner speech are less subject to the phonemic similarity effects found in the speech errors of overt speech. Shattuck-Hufnagel is less concerned with the specific identity of segment-sized units, and more interested in the macro-structure of the speech plan. She argues, following Lashley (1951), that planning is hierarchically organized and proposes that prosodic structures, from the intonational phrase to the metrical foot, provide successive frames for planning and execution. In her view, we move from abstract linguistic representation to motor commands as we iterate through the prosodic hierarchy. Finally, Lickley (Chapter 20) considers what happens when there are disruptions at any level in the planning and execution process by describing different kinds of disfluencies and repair strategies. He argues that understanding these in typical speech is critical to being able to define and understand disfluencies that result from developmental or acquired disorders.

1.2.5 *Language factors*

Although many chapters in the Handbook provide evidence for the argument that speech contributes to our understanding of language, this does not contradict the importance of the more widely recognized contribution of language to our understanding of speech and its acquisition. The chapters in this final Part of the Handbook directly address this contribution. Didier Demolin (Chapter 21) makes a strong case for cross-language investigations of speech sound production. He argues that a mainstay of phonetic sciences for over 100 years, the International Phonetic Alphabet (IPA), is based on limited language data and so may improperly circumscribe the capabilities of the human speech production mechanism. Fieldwork studies on speech production provide us with a clearer sense of what is possible, allowing for better documentation and preservation of minority languages. An understanding of diversity and variation also informs theories of sound change. Like Demolin, Taehong Cho (Chapter 22) addresses cross-linguistic diversity. Cho reviews the literature on timing effects at the segmental and suprasegmental level to argue for a phonetic component to the grammar, noting that "fine-grained phonetic details suggest that none of the putative universal timing patterns can be accounted for in their entirety by physiological/biomechanic factors." Jan Edwards, Mary Beckman, and Ben Munson (Chapter 23) are interested in the effects of language-specific sound patterns and social meaning on speech production and phonological acquisition. They review findings from their παιδολογος project and other cross-linguistic research, demonstrating the importance of the social group in speech and language acquisition. They also show that cross-cultural variation in speech sound acquisition is best understood with reference to specific acoustic differences in how the "same" phoneme is produced in different languages and varieties. Finally, Lisa Goffman (Chapter 24) returns to our theme of the fuzzy divide between speech and language to investigate the effects of lexical, morphological, and syntactic structures on the acquisition of speech motor skills. She notes that "though there is little question that [a] more domain specific view is dominant in framing how research on language acquisition has been approached, there have long been powerful suggestions that motor and other factors also play a crucial role in how children approach the language learning task." The studies on speech kinematics in children that she reviews in her chapter indicate that the reverse is also true: language factors affect the acquisition of timing control and articulatory precision in children.

1.3 Conclusion

The *Handbook of Speech Production* is designed to provide the reader with a broad understanding of speech production. Leading international researchers have contributed chapters that review work in their particular area of expertise, outline important issues and theories of speech production, and detail those questions that require further investigation. The contributions bring together behavioral, clinical, computational, developmental, and neuropsychological perspectives on speech production with an emphasis on kinematics, control, and planning in production. The organization of the Handbook is from the most concrete aspects of speech production to its most abstract. Such an organization is designed to encourage careful reflection on the relationship between speech and language, but alternate pathways through the Handbook are always possible. The brief overview of content provided in this Introduction was meant to show how the chapters create a coherent whole, but it will hopefully also help you, the reader, design a personal pathway through the Handbook if that is your wish.

REFERENCES

Bernstein, Lynne E. and Gary Weismer. 2000. Basic science at the intersection of speech science and communication disorders. *Journal of Phonetics* 28: 225–232.

Browman, Catherine P. and Louis M. Goldstein. 1986. Towards an articulatory phonology. *Phonology Yearbook* 3: 219–252.

Chomsky, Noam. 1959. A review of B.F. Skinner's *Verbal Behavior*. *Language* 35: 26–58.

Keele, Steven W. 1968. Movement control in skilled motor performance. *Psychological Bulletin* 70: 387–403.

Lashley, Karl S. 1951. The problem of serial order in behavior. In L.A. Jeffress (ed.), *Cerebral Mechanisms in Behavior*, 112–131. New York: John Wiley & Sons, Inc.

Pinker, Steven and Paul Bloom. 1990. Natural language and natural selection. *Behavioral and Brain Sciences* 13: 707–784.

Skinner, Burrhus F. 1957. *Verbal Behavior*. New York: Appleton-Century-Crofts.

Part I The Speech Mechanism

2 Speech Breathing Across the Life Span and in Disease

JESSICA E. HUBER AND
ELAINE T. STATHOPOULOS

2.1 Introduction

It is human nature to have an irrepressible need to speak, but we must manage the communicative/cultural/linguistic needs with our need to ventilate and maintain a homeostatic environment for important internal organs (Bunn and Mead 1971; Hoit, Lansing, and Perona 2007). Normal speech breathing has been described in the literature for many years, as far back as the early 1800s. First, it was described in a context for elocutionists, pedagogues, actors, and/or singers, and these early descriptions of speech breathing were based on anecdotal observations of the movement of the singer's rib cage and/or abdomen (Guttmann 1882). With the advent of technology like the body plethysmograph, inductance coils, linearized magnetometers, and most recently, respitrace inductance coils, it has been possible to describe breathing during speech more thoroughly and accurately. Much of the early data obtained from sensing devices was based on the adult male, and was largely descriptive in nature. Since the 1980s, researchers have focused on the study of speech breathing across the life span, in males and females, as well as in individuals with neurologically-based disorders.

Observation of speech breathing/movement of the chest wall across the life span and during disease states provides a strong paradigm for discussion of the underlying components affecting the work of the respiratory system. The work of breathing can account for how the respiratory system responds to changes in task and challenges (i.e., ventilation vs. speech vs. exercise) and it can account for how underlying anatomical and physiological components (i.e., muscles, bones, cartilage, and movement, viscosity, elasticity, compliance, and airway resistance) affect breathing. We know that one of the most obvious anatomical changes, body size, is an important factor affecting respiratory control during speech. Further, there are many other physiological effects of development, aging, and disease that affect the cardiovascular, pulmonary, muscle and joint, and skeletal systems (Cerny and Burton 2001). The task of speech production, by necessity, responds to both respiratory ventilatory demands as well as cognitive-linguistic demands. The respiratory system is always responding to what we want to say, but it can't help but be limited by its anatomical and physiological constraints.

In this chapter, we describe the highly complex movements involved in speech breathing, and the subtle and not so subtle differences across the life span, between female and male speakers, and in individuals with Parkinson's disease. We will also discuss how speakers actively coordinate linguistic factors such as breath pauses and length of utterance with respiratory patterns. Changes in speech breathing patterns are intricately tied to changes in anatomy and physiology of the respiratory system as we develop throughout our life span and with disease. Our speech breathing patterns will be viewed through the perspective of the work (efficiency) of breathing. The respiratory system strives to exchange air for ventilation in the most efficient and effortless manner, and it will adapt to different activities like exercise – and in the case of the present interest, to speech. Further, the respiratory system will function as efficiently as possible, regardless of our age, sex, or disease state.

2.2 Kinematic overview of the breathing cycle

Breath support for speech involves a balance between active and passive forces within the respiratory system. The lung and thorax can be modeled as one unit (hereafter referred to as the lung-thorax unit) since they are coupled to one another by pleural pressure, a negative pressure in the space between the parietal pleura covering the inner surface of the rib cage and the visceral pleura covering the outer surface of the lungs. The lungs and the thorax are both elastic structures which, by definition, resist being moved from their rest position and exert a force to return to rest. In the respiratory system, passive forces are generated by the lung-thorax unit returning to rest and are called recoil pressures. Since the recoil pressures are generated by the elastic nature of the lung-thorax unit, anything which changes their elasticity will change the air pressures generated. For example, as we will discuss later, in older adults, the lungs lose elasticity and become more compliant, resulting in lower recoil pressures. This also occurs in individuals with emphysema although to a much larger degree. Pulmonary fibrosis decreases lung compliance, resulting in more recoil pressure. Further, in people with Parkinson's disease, axial rigidity may increase (Cano-de-la-Cuerda et al. 2011), potentially leading to an increase in the rigidity of the rib cage and lower recoil pressures.

The rest position of the lung-thorax unit is located near or at the end-expiratory level, the point in the respiratory cycle at the end of a tidal (quiet) expiration. When we inspire above end-expiratory level, a positive recoil pressure is generated by the lung-thorax unit's return to end-expiratory level and we expire. When we expire below end-expiratory level, a negative recoil pressure is generated by the lung-thorax unit's return to rest and we inspire. As we move farther from rest, to higher and lower lung volumes, recoil pressures increase (Rahn et al. 1946).

Active forces in the respiratory system are generated by the respiratory muscles. The main role of the respiratory system in speech is to provide the correct pressure drive to the larynx (called subglottal pressure) to meet the demands of our communication task. Thus, we balance the active forces generated with the recoil forces which are present as lung volume changes throughout the speech breathing cycle to ensure we are generating adequate subglottal air pressure for speech.

Hixon and colleagues' early classic work on speech breathing in adult males has weathered the years (Hixon 1976; Hixon, Goldman, and Mead 1973). Their basic tenets of normal speech breathing include the fact that we breathe in a mid-lung volume range so that our speech breathing is efficient. Breathing at the mid-lung volume range allows us to take advantage of the natural mechanics of the respiratory system and to not oppose our own natural elastic recoil forces. During speech, the pattern of breathing involves a quick inspiration followed by a long, slow expiration. Quick inspirations are important for reducing pause times, allowing us to maintain our turn in a speaking exchange. The primary muscle for inspiration is the diaphragm. The abdominal muscles (rectus abdominus, external oblique, internal oblique, and transverse abdominus) play a role during inspiration. They contract to move the diaphragm to its rest length, the length at which it can produce the greatest force and the quickest force. The abdominal muscles also provide a base of support for rib cage expansion during inspiration (Hixon 1973, 1976). When we are expiring, we control the flow of air from the lungs to lengthen the expiratory period and thus lengthen the time we can speak. We use the external intercostal muscles to check the descent of the rib cage, reducing the recoil pressure and slowing flow output from the respiratory system (Draper, Ladefoged, and Whitteridge 1959). We also use expiratory muscles (internal intercostals and abdominal muscles) to add respiratory pressures to continue to speak below end-expiratory level.

The respiratory muscles are innervated from the spinal nerves, starting in the high cervical spine region (cervical nerve 3) to the high lumbar region (lumbar nerve 1). Any damage to innervation to the respiratory muscles can lead to muscle paresis and paralysis and result in difficulty controlling the respiratory system for speech. In patients with high cervical spinal cord injury, a ventilator is commonly required as most/all of the innervation to the respiratory muscles can be affected. In patients with lower cervical spinal cord lesions, inspiration is often adequate since innervation to the diaphragm is not affected. However, these patients cannot control the expiratory phase and tend to produce much shorter utterances and lower vocal intensity (Hoit, Banzett, et al. 1990).

Work of breathing is an important concept to consider when examining changes to speech breathing across the life span. Conceptually, work of breathing relates to how much effort it takes to move air volume into the lungs for the purpose of oxygen and CO_2 exchange, and ventilation is considered to be efficient when this exchange occurs with minimum effort (Levitzky 2007). At the end of a resting breath exhalation or end-expiratory level, there is a corresponding lung capacity called functional residual capacity, when the recoil forces of the lung to collapse and of the thorax to expand are balanced in the linked lung-thorax unit. At functional residual capacity, no inspiratory and expiratory muscular forces are required to maintain this lung volume. Thus, this lung volume is referred to as the "relaxed" state of the lung-thorax unit. The further we expand or compress the respiratory system away from the relaxed position, the more effort it takes to breathe. During exercise, and by extension, speech, there is more "energy cost" to breathe as compared to rest breathing, but we attempt to stay as close to functional residual capacity as possible (Cerny and Burton 2001). In the speech literature, this concept of work of breathing has been popularly referred to as the mid-lung volume range and, more recently, the "mid-range of the vital capacity for speech production" (Hixon, Weismer, and Hoit 2008: 33). Since there must be a change in volume and pressure to accomplish inhalation, the primary work to be done during rest breathing is the effort of creating a pressure change between the lungs and atmosphere allowing air to flow into the lungs. In addition to elastic/recoil characteristics affecting the work of breathing, another factor affects how much effort or muscular force it takes to inhale and exhale during speech. This factor includes resistance to airflow (size of the airways) and tissue resistance (pulmonary resistance; viscous forces within tissues as they slide over each other) (Cerny and Burton 2001; Levitzky 2007). Rate of respiration (frequency of breathing in 60 seconds) can be adjusted to affect the work of breathing. There is a very complex relationship between work of breathing and breathing frequency. But put simply, assuming the same minute volume (amount of air inhaled and exhaled in one minute), if you increase your frequency of breathing, you decrease work of breathing. This is because by breathing more frequently and therefore more shallowly, respiration occurs closer to the lung-thorax rest position/functional residual capacity. Any factors which affect the elastic structures of the lung-thorax unit or the size of the airways and/or the compliance of the airways will affect the work of breathing. Keeping in mind the factors associated with the work of breathing, it is possible to extend this knowledge to speech breathing throughout development and aging, and to individuals who are affected by a disease process. Of course, in speech breathing, we must consider not only the forces applied to inspire, but those used for expiration and those needed to control the rate of expiration. During speech, we engage inspiratory and expiratory muscles continuously through the breath cycle (Hixon et al. 2008). Last, respiratory patterns need to be coordinated with linguistic factors during speech breathing.

2.3 Anatomical and physiological changes of the respiratory system across the life span

Before describing speech breathing patterns across the life span, it is necessary to describe some general developmental characteristics of the human body that could affect the speech breathing apparatus. One of the most obvious factors that could affect respiratory function is body size. Bigger bodies will generally yield bigger respiratory systems and larger lung volumes (McDowell et al. 2008). Body height increases in a fairly linear manner from birth through 14 years of age (Sorkin, Muller, and Andres 1999). There are no differences in height between boys and girls until 14 years. After 14 years, girls plateau, and boys continue to gain in height until their early 20s. Height begins to decline when women are in their third decade of life, while height in men starts declining in the beginning of the fourth decade. Similarly, body weight increases in a fairly linear manner from birth through 14 years of age. There are no substantial differences in weight between boys and girls until 14 years. After 14 years, girls continue small increases in weight, while men continue to gain weight until about the fourth decade of life. Weight loss begins to occur in women and men between 60 and 69 years of age, and continues to decline in the seventh and eighth decades of life. Examination of growth charts for lung length and lung width substantiate the fact that larger respiratory systems develop as a function of age and body size: both lung length and width increase in a linear manner until about 13–14 years of age (Polgar and Weng 1979; Zeman and Bennett 2006). As was true for the other structures, girls' lung growth patterns stabilize at about 14 years old, while the lungs of boys continue to grow until age 18–20 years (Polgar and Weng 1979).

Now, we will consider several respiratory physiological components that are important to speech breathing. Vital capacity is the volume of air which can be exchanged in the lungs, and is formally defined as the maximum amount of air which can be exhaled after a maximum inhalation. Forced vital capacity is similar except the individual is asked to expire as forcefully as possible after maximal inspiration. Vital capacity size follows very closely to the general body growth patterns (see Figure 2.1a). Vital capacity increases dramatically from birth to about 15 years of age for both girls and boys. Males reach peak forced vital capacity around age 27 years whereas females reach their peak around age 20 years (Knudson et al. 1976). Young men experience a plateau in forced vital capacity to age 26 years, but young women do not experience a plateau in function and instead show slowly declining capacity to about age 45 years (Sherrill et al. 1992). At age 46, the loss in forced vital capacity is accelerated in women (Sherrill et al. 1992). Men also show a decline in forced vital capacity starting at age 45 (Behrens 1956; Ferris, Whittenberger, and Gallagher 1952; Sherrill et al. 1992; Verschakelen and Demedts 1995).

Residual volume is the volume of air which is left in the lungs after a forceful expiration. Examination of residual volume across the life span shows a continuous increase for both males and females as a function of age, from about age 6–65 years (see Figure 2.1b) (Behrens 1956; Brozek 1960; Hibbert, Couriel, and Landau 1984; Seccombe et al. 2011).

Static recoil pressure is generated passively within the lungs by the lung-thorax unit's physical properties. Since the lung-thorax unit is an elastic structure, it exerts a force to return to its balanced resting position when it is moved from rest. Respiratory physiologists measure the rest position of the lung-thorax unit as end-expiratory level or functional residual capacity. Static recoil pressure shows a U-shaped curve (Knudson et al. 1977; Mansell, Bryan, and Levison 1977). Recoil pressure data show lower values at both young and older ages. There is a substantial linear increase in recoil pressure until about age 12 years, a peak/plateau between 12 and 18 years, and then substantial decline from ages 20–75 years (see Figure 2.1c). As we age, the compliance of the chest wall decreases, and the

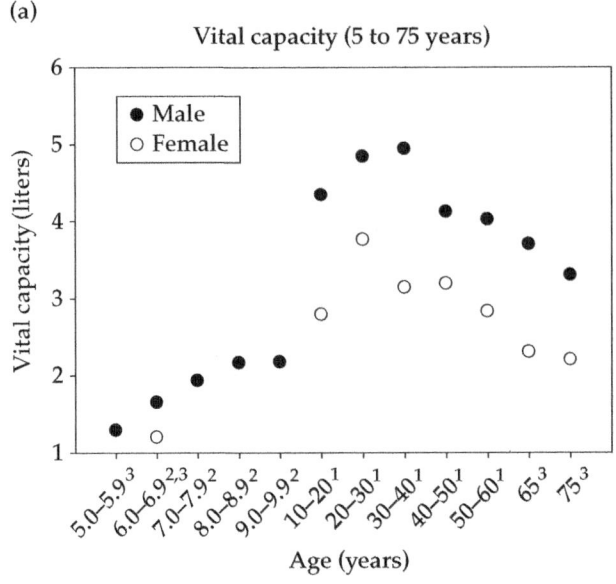

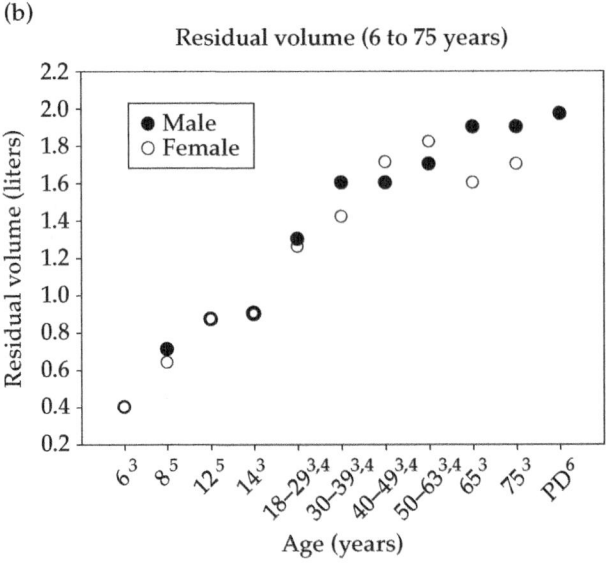

Figure 2.1 Respiratory function. (a) Vital capacity across the lifespan ([1]Verschakelen and Demedts 1995; [2]Ferris, Whittenberger, and Gallagher 1952; [3]Behrens 1956); (b) Residual volume across the lifespan ([3]Behrens 1956; [4]Brozek 1960; [5]Hibbert, Couriel, and Landau 1984; [6]Seccombe et al. 2011) (cont'd over);

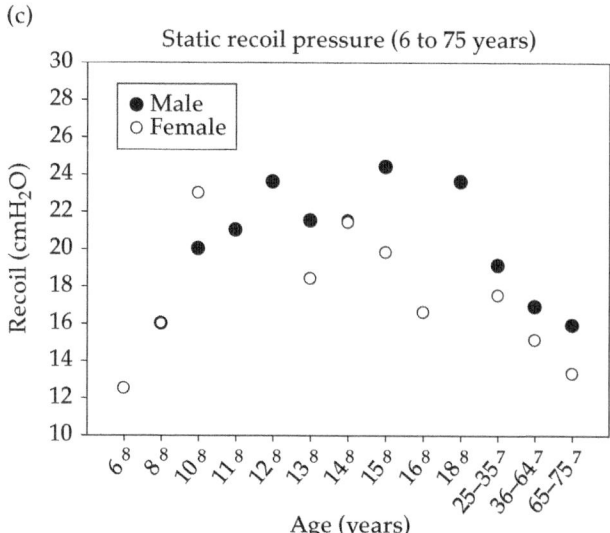

Figure 2.1 (cont'd) (c) Recoil pressure across the lifespan ([7]Knudson et al. 1977; [8]Mansell, Bryan, and Levison 1977).

compliance of the lungs may increase (Frank, Mead, and Ferris 1957; Mittman et al. 1965). These tissue changes result in a decrease in vital capacity, an increase in residual volume, and lower elastic recoil forces (Enright et al. 1995; Knudson et al. 1976; Pfitzenmeyer et al. 1993; Sherrill et al. 1992) (see Figure 2.1a–c). From the limited available data, there do not appear to be a sex differences in children younger than 11 years, but men show higher static recoil pressure at each age group compared to women (see Figure 2.1c). However, men may experience a greater loss of lung elasticity, particularly between ages 45 and 58 years, than women (Bode et al. 1976), resulting in lower static recoil pressures. There is some feeling that an increased large airway elastic recoil force (trachea) may help compensate for the loss of lung elasticity in older aged individuals, so that the overall resistance to air flow may increase only slightly in old age (Gibellino et al. 1985).

Finally, with typical aging, inspiratory and expiratory muscle strength is reduced (Berry et al. 1996; Black and Hyatt 1969; Enright et al. 1994). Although changes in expiratory muscle force can be impacted by decreased elastic recoil pressures, changes to inspiratory muscle force are not likely related to changes in recoil pressure (Ringqvist 1966). Further, it has been shown that the force generated by the diaphragm decreases with age (Tolep and Kelsen 1993). Tolep and Kelsen report that measurement of diaphragmatic strength would not be impacted by elastic recoil pressure or by differences in fitness or nutrition between the older and younger adults. However, reduced muscle strength and chest wall compliance with aging may result in a reduction in superior and inferior chest wall expansion which has been correlated with reduced vital capacity and forced expiratory volume (Pfitzenmeyer et al. 1993). Loss of muscle strength with aging may not be equivalent for men and women. The loss of inspiratory muscle strength may be larger in women (Berry et al. 1996; Black and Hyatt 1969; Enright et al. 1994). Also, inferior expansion of the chest wall is more impaired in older women than in older men (Pfitzenmeyer et al. 1993). Further, sex differences in age-related changes to physiology are likely to result in different changes to speech breathing for males and females throughout the life span.

These anatomical and physiological changes have consequences for speech breathing. Evaluating the two ends of the continuum, we see that the very young and old have somewhat restricted respiratory function values and possibly more airway resistance. Both the young and old have smaller vital capacities, and lower recoil forces compared to young and middle-aged adults. In addition, older adults have larger residual volumes. The combination of smaller usable air volumes, lower recoil pressures, higher airway resistance, and lower muscle pressures suggest that children and the elderly may have to do more respiratory work to accomplish the same speech tasks as typical young adults. Thus these anatomical and physiological changes in the lungs and chest wall will affect how the respiratory system is used to generate, maintain, and modulate subglottal air pressure during speech production.

2.4   Typical speech breathing across the life span

Our knowledge about speech breathing has increased in the last 30 years and now includes more objective data on girls and boys of all ages, younger and older women and men, and individuals with neuromuscular disorders such as those with Parkinson's disease. However, before exploring the data about speech breathing, it is helpful to discuss some of the conventions of measurement. First, respiratory patterns are generally discussed relative to percents of lung, rib cage, and abdominal volumes (Hoit and Hixon 1987; Stathopoulos and Sapienza 1997). This convention allows comparison across individuals of varied sizes, from a four-year-old female to a 20-year-old male, for example. Thus, in this chapter, we discuss lung volume data relative to percent vital capacity. Further, measurements are commonly made in reference to end-expiratory level, the rest position of the lung-thorax unit. This makes it easier to develop hypotheses about the types of muscle forces being applied to the system (inspiratory and expiratory).

Utterance length is defined as the number of syllables or words produced on one speech breath. In this chapter, we use data regarding the number of syllables produced. Lung volume at utterance initiation is the percent of vital capacity in the lungs, relative to end-expiratory level, when speech is initiated. Lung volume at utterance termination is the percent of vital capacity in the lungs, relative to end-expiratory level, when speech is terminated. Lung volume excursion for the utterance is the percent of vital capacity expended across the speech utterance (initiation minus termination). Vital capacity expended per syllable is the lung volume excursion divided by the number of syllables in the utterance. This measure reflects both respiratory support and laryngeal valving.

Much of what we know about the development of speech breathing is from rather limited data. One systematic study (Stathopoulos and Sapienza 1997), combined with two other studies (Hoit, Hixon, et al. 1990; Stathopoulos and Sapienza 1994), provide data which can produce a coherent "picture" of how younger children breathe while they are producing speech. Figure 2.2a depicts some distinctive lung volume differences between young speakers and their older counterparts. For the younger age groups of 4, 6, and 8 years, it can be seen that speech is produced using higher lung volume initiations than the older children and young adults. Younger children also use lower lung volume terminations (Stathopoulos and Sapienza 1997). As a result of higher lung volume initiations and lower lung volume terminations, children use a greater lung volume excursion (in percent vital capacity), in spite of the fact that they produce shorter utterances than young and older adults (Hoit and Hixon 1987; Hoit et al. 1989; Hoit, Hixon, et al. 1990; Huber 2007, 2008) (see Figure 2.2c). Since children's pulmonary compliance is lower than adults' (De Troyer et al. 1978; Lanteri and Sly 1993), children's lower recoil forces may allow them to terminate speech at lower lung volumes without an undue amount of expiratory muscle force, reducing the work of breathing at low lung volumes (Russell and Stathopoulos 1988).

Teenagers between 12 and 14 years show important developmental changes marking the period when speech breathing transitions to adult speech breathing. One major change has to do with the lung volume excursion that is used to produce speech utterances. The teenage children show a marked decrease in how much vital capacity they use to produce an utterance. This can be seen by smaller (or shorter) bars in Figure 2.2a and is also depicted in Figure 2.2b as lower percent vital capacity used for each syllable. Second, the utterance terminations are higher, indicating that teenagers terminate their utterances closer to the end-expiratory level as in the "typically" described (adult) mid-lung volume range (see Figure 2.2a; EEL = end-expiratory level). This occurs at the same time that teenagers start producing significantly more syllables per breath group (see Figure 2.2c). Further, sex differences are apparent in teenagers and young adults. Young men use lower lung volume initiations and terminations as compared to young women (Huber 2007; Huber, Chandrasekaran, and Wolstencroft 2005; Stathopoulos and Sapienza 1997).

Sex differences in respiratory patterns do not appear to be present until after puberty. Sex differences at younger ages are more commonly reported in percent vital capacity expended per syllable than in respiratory patterns. For children and teenagers, females use a greater percent of their vital capacity per syllables than males (Hoit, Hixon, et al. 1990) (see Figure 2.2b). However, there are no sex differences in percent vital capacity expended per syllable in adulthood, for either young or older adults (Hoit and Hixon 1987; Hoit et al. 1989; Huber and Darling 2011) (see Figure 2.2b).

Moving on to the older developmental age continuum, many studies have demonstrated significant changes in respiratory support for speech with typical aging. As compared to young adults, older adults initiate and terminate speech at higher lung volumes, use larger lung volume excursions, and use a greater percent of their lung volume per syllable (Huber 2008; Huber and Spruill 2008; Hoit and Hixon 1987; Hoit et al. 1989; Sperry and Klich 1992) (see Figure 2.2a and b). Older

22 The Speech Mechanism

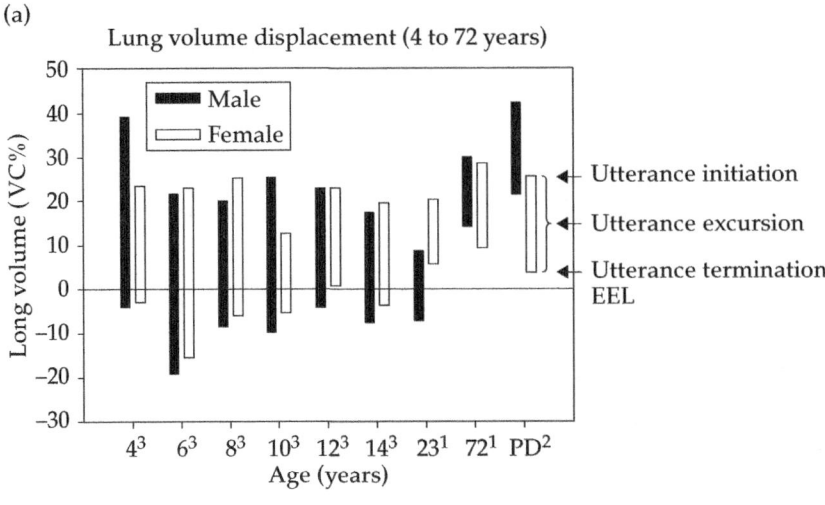

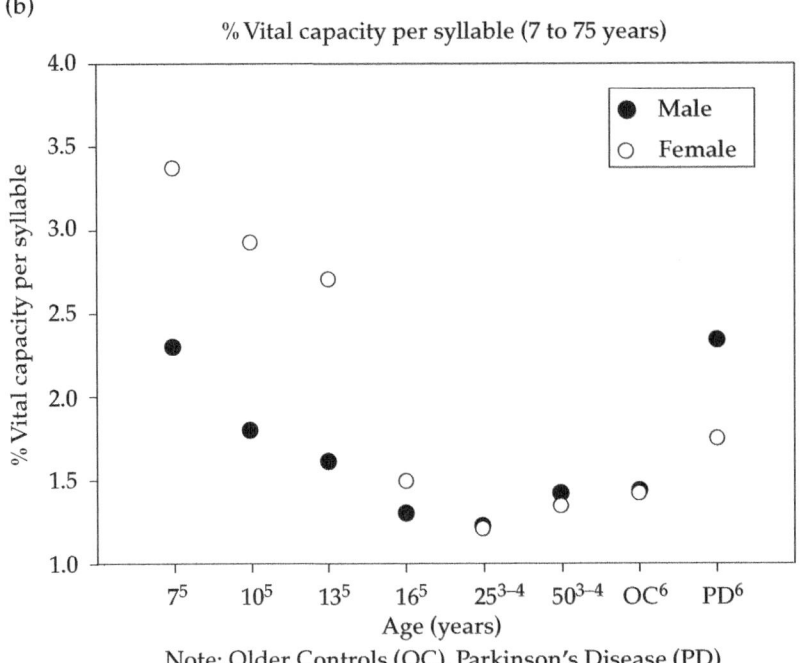

Figure 2.2 Speech breathing. (a) Lung volume initiations, terminations, and excursions across the lifespan ([1]Huber 2008; [2]Sadagopan and Huber, 2007; [3]Stathopoulos and Sapienza 1997); (b) Percent vital capacity expended per syllable across the Lifespan ([3]Hoit and Hixon 1987; [4]Hoit et al. 1989; [5]Hoit, Hixon, et al. 1990; [6]Huber and Darling 2011) (cont'd over);

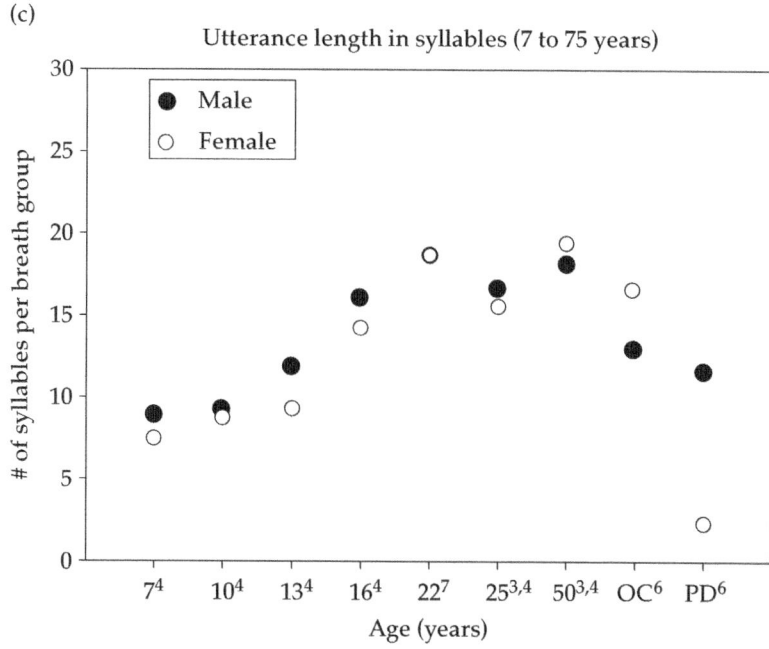

Note: Older Controls (OC), Parkinson's Disease (PD)

Figure 2.2 (cont'd) (c) Utterance length across the lifespan ([7]Huber 2007; [6]Huber and Darling 2011; [3]Hoit and Hixon 1987; [4]Hoit et al. 1989).

women inspire more often and more deeply when reading a standard passage than young women (Sperry and Klich 1992; Russell, Cerny, and Stathopoulos 1998). Compensating for reduced recoil pressure by initiating speech at a higher lung volume is logical from the perspective of work of breathing. It allows older adults to take advantage of the higher recoil pressures available at higher lung volumes to generate adequate subglottal pressure for speech and may result in larger lung volumes available for speech. Sex differences in respiratory kinematics are less prominent in older adults than are typically seen for young adults (Hoit et al. 1989; Huber 2008) (see Figure 2.2a).

2.4.1 *Utterance length and linguistic considerations*

Several studies have provided evidence indicating that both young and older adults plan speech breathing for the length of the upcoming utterance (Huber 2008; Sperry and Klich 1992; Winkworth et al. 1994), suggesting the importance of utterance length as a control mechanism for speech breathing. Due to the physiological changes to the respiratory system with typical aging, older adults have lower vital capacity and lower muscle forces, and thus less usable air volume to support speech. These changes are likely to lead to more work of breathing, particularly when the system is taxed. One natural way the respiratory system is taxed during everyday speech is through the production of longer utterances. Previous studies have shown that older adults, particularly men, produce shorter utterances than young adults during reading, monologue, and conversation tasks (Hoit and Hixon 1987; Huber 2008; Sperry and Klich 1992) (see Figure 2.2c). The production of shorter utterances with typical aging may be a compensatory mechanism for changes in respiratory physiology. Because of these changes, age-related differences in respiratory function for speech may be greater when older adults produce longer utterances. For example, while both young and older women increased the amount of air inhaled and exhaled as utterance length increased (Sperry and Klich 1992; Winkworth et al. 1994), the difference between older and younger adults was more pronounced for longer utterances than for shorter utterances due to a larger increase in volume inspired and expired by older adults (Sperry and Klich 1992). Further, Huber (2008) found greater differences in utterance length between older and younger adults during spontaneous speech, in particular when the utterances were longer.

Producing shorter utterances allows older adults to take more frequent breaths which may compensate for changes to the respiratory system, reducing the work of breathing, but more frequent breath pauses may have unintentional linguistic consequences. In speech, pauses are used to mark the ends of prosodic phrases, changes in intonation, and syllable duration (Schirmer et al. 2001; Steinhauer 2003). Typical adults produce longer pauses at major prosodic boundaries (e.g., boundary of a group of intonational phrases) than at minor ones (e.g., boundary for a single intonational phrase) (Price et al. 1991). Prosodic boundaries typically coincide with syntactic boundaries (Price et al. 1991; Warren 1996) with the longest pauses often occurring at major syntactic boundaries (e.g., after independent and dependent clauses) (Price et al. 1991). Similarly, it has been shown that both young and older adults take more breaths at major syntactic boundaries than at minor syntactic boundaries (e.g., after a prepositional phrase) (Grosjean and Collins 1979; Wang et al. 2005; Winkworth et al. 1994). However, older adults take fewer breaths at major syntactic boundaries and more breaths at minor syntactic boundaries than young adults (Huber et al. 2012). Taking breaths at fewer major boundaries and more minor boundaries causes utterances to be chunked into smaller linguistic units, degrading linguistic cues embedded within the speech signal. Listeners may perceive older adults as less competent if they pause to breathe more often while speaking. In summary, data examining the interaction between speech breathing and syntax suggest that higher-level functions (particularly cognitive load and linguistic complexity) alter respiratory support for speech. Further, as we will discuss next, there are data to support that the perception of task or goal of speech affects respiratory support for speech.

2.4.2 *Effects of vocal intensity*

Another way the respiratory system is taxed during everyday speech production is when louder speech is required. In noisy rooms or when talking across a distance, speakers increase their vocal intensity to ensure they are clearly heard and understood. Further, requiring speakers to alter their vocal intensity is an important research paradigm from a speech physiology perspective. First, asking speakers to change their vocal intensity allows us to examine the underlying physiological alterations to the respiratory, laryngeal, and supralaryngeal systems necessary to support speech. Second, using developmental/life span and disease-state paradigms to assess vocal intensity allows a more robust interpretation of the underlying anatomical and physiological constraints placed on the mechanism. Last, each speaker's ability to make these underlying physiological changes is crucial to being able to produce normal-sounding voice. Increasing vocal intensity requires the generation of higher subglottal air pressures and the respiratory system has a primary role in this (Finnegan, Luschei, and Hoffman 2000). Understanding how the respiratory system responds to common speaking challenges like increasing vocal intensity has significant implications for being able to build age- and sex-appropriate models of speech production, as well as application for how to remediate voice and speech disorders.

Young children, teenagers, and young adults all show active respiratory support when speakers increase their vocal intensity (Hixon et al. 1973; Huber 2007; Stathopoulos and Sapienza 1993, 1997). All of these groups have been shown to use larger lung and rib cage volume excursions as intensity increased (Stathopoulos and Sapienza 1997). The larger volume excursions can be explained by a shift to overall higher lung and rib cage volumes. This is an effective mechanism – initiating utterances at higher lung volumes takes advantage of inherent recoil pressures which are higher at higher lung volumes (Hixon et al. 1973) and nicely decreases the work of breathing. It is also evident that this pattern is used more by the older groups of children and the adults. Twelve to 14-year-old children terminated their utterances above end-expiratory level and used a pattern that was quite similar to the adult pattern for increasing sound pressure level (Stathopoulos and Sapienza 1997). The younger children's rib cage volume terminations extended further below end-expiratory level during high intensity speech, and this difference may be related to the fact that they have greater chest wall compliance (Stathopoulos and Sapienza 1993).

Older adults do not show the same patters as young adults in response to speaking at higher vocal intensities. During a reading task, older adults did not significantly change lung volume or rib cage volume initiations or terminations at high vocal intensities (Sadagopan and Huber 2007). During an extemporaneous speech task, older adults did not change lung volume initiations but used significantly lower lung volume terminations (Huber 2008; Huber and Darling 2011). Older adults use a rather high lung volume for comfortable intensity speech. It may be difficult for them to further increase lung volume initiations, above the level used at comfortable intensity. It may be less work to use more expiratory muscle force and lower lung volume terminations.

2.5 Effects of Parkinson's disease on the respiratory system

Studies comparing individuals with Parkinson's disease to age- and sex-matched control speakers have demonstrated that Parkinson's disease has a significant effect on both speech and non-speech respiratory function. Studies of pulmonary function in individuals with Parkinson's disease have demonstrated disease-related reductions in forced vital capacity and forced expiratory volume in one second and increases in residual volume (De Pandis et al. 2002; Inzelberg et al. 2005; Sabate et al. 1996; Seccombe et al. 2011; Weiner et al. 2002) (see Figure 2.1a and b). Further, reductions in inspiratory and expiratory muscle strength have been reported in individuals with Parkinson's disease (Haas, Trew, and Castle 2004; Inzelberg et al. 2005; Sabate et al. 1996; Seccombe et al. 2011). Decreases in lung capacity and respiratory muscle strength may worsen with disease progression and may be, at least partially, due to physical changes to the respiratory system, including increased rigidity (Haas et al. 2004; Polatli et al. 2001; Sabate et al. 1996). Also, one study demonstrated impairments in the control of breathing (Seccombe et al. 2011), which was hypothesized to be related to early brainstem involvement in individuals with Parkinson's disease, as suggested by Braak's model of Parkinson's disease progression (Braak and Del Tredici 2008; Braak et al. 2004). The brainstem is hypothesized to be important for neurological control of lower-level breathing functions. In summary, individuals with Parkinson's disease have a less compliant or stiffer respiratory system, reduced elasticity, and reduced muscle forces. All of these changes increase the work of breathing, and these patients are very likely to find speech breathing more effortful.

2.6 Effects of Parkinson's disease on speech breathing

Studies have reported a large number of changes to respiratory support for speech associated with Parkinson's disease, including higher and lower lung volume initiations and terminations, larger abdominal initiations, smaller rib cage volume initiations, larger rib cage excursions, more variability of respiratory movements, and larger percent of their lung volume per speech breath and per syllable as compared to typical older adults (Bunton 2005; Huber and Darling 2011; Sadagopan and Huber 2007; Huber et al. 2003; Lethlean, Chenery, and Murdoch 1990; Murdoch et al. 1989; Solomon and Hixon 1993) (see Figure 2.2a and b). However, respiratory kinematic findings related to Parkinson's disease have not been consistent across studies, and a large amount of variability across subjects has been reported (Bunton 2005; Huber et al. 2003). Significant variability is also present in measurements of utterance length. Some studies have reported that individuals with Parkinson's disease produced shorter utterances than age-matched control subjects in reading and extemporaneous speech (Huber and Darling 2011; Solomon and Hixon 1993) (see Figure 2.2c), but Bunton (2005) reported a large amount of variability in utterance length across speakers with Parkinson's disease. Breath pausing is also affected in individuals with Parkinson's disease. Although individuals with Parkinson's disease do not take fewer breaths at major boundaries or more breaths at minor boundaries, individuals with Parkinson's disease were demonstrated to take more breaths at locations unrelated to syntax than age- and sex-matched control participants (Huber et al. 2012).

In the data from individuals with Parkinson's disease, there may be a sex difference in respiratory patterns with men with Parkinson's disease using lower lung volume initiations and terminations than women with Parkinson's disease

(Huber and Darling 2011) (see Figure 2.2a). Also, there is a potential sex difference in the individuals with the disease, with men showing larger percent vital capacity expended per syllable than women (see Figure 2.2b). However, it is not clear if the differences demonstrated in the data are truly sex differences or if they relate to differences in the severity of disease symptoms or speech impairments. In the Huber and Darling (2011) study, the men with Parkinson's disease were more severe than the women with Parkinson's disease. However, sex differences have been reported in how Parkinson's disease affects articulation, voice, and prosody, so it is possible that there are differences in the effects on the respiratory system between men and women (Doyle et al. 2005; Hertrich and Ackermann 1995; Lyons et al. 1998; MacPherson, Huber, and Snow 2011; Rahn et al. 2007). There do not appear to be large sex differences in utterance length at any age (see Figure 2.2c).

In general, these findings suggest that, for individuals with Parkinson's disease, respiratory support for speech may reflect stiffer respiratory muscles (resulting in lower lung volume initiations and terminations) or weaker expiratory muscles (resulting in shorter utterances and higher lung volume initiations and terminations). Some of the variability across studies may be due to different speech tasks being examined as different speech tasks likely require different cognitive and planning demands (Huber 2007; Huber and Darling 2011; Mitchell, Hoit, and Watson 1996). However, variability across studies is also likely due to differences in disease severity of the patients being examined. Since respiratory function declines with disease progression, it is not unexpected that the effects on respiratory support would be more pronounced as disease severity increased.

Recent data from speakers with Parkinson's disease have been collected in Huber and Stathopoulos's laboratories and these data are insightful when describing how neurologically impaired people use their respiratory systems for speech production at increased vocal intensities. Some mildly to moderately impaired speakers with Parkinson's disease use their respiratory systems much like speakers with typical voice and speech. When speaking at higher vocal intensities, their lung and rib cage volume ranges are higher, and they also use abdominal muscles to help support their respiratory function. As for typical adults, the data indicate the presence of abdominal muscle contraction for both comfortable and high intensity speech. On the other hand, some speakers with Parkinson's disease show a marked divergence from normal speakers. While lung and rib cage volume ranges increase when speaking at high vocal intensities as do other typical speakers, their use of abdominal muscles is quite limited. The speakers with Parkinson's disease tend to show larger abdominal positions during speech. The mechanism for this abdominal position is complex, but our interpretation of the position of the abdominal wall is as follows. When the diaphragm contracts and flattens during inhalation prior to a speech utterance, it pushes downward and outward on the abdominal contents, thereby displacing the ventral muscular abdominal wall outward. With no active control of the abdominal muscles to counteract the displacement, the anterior wall will be pushed outward beyond the relaxed position. In short, some speakers with Parkinson's disease were not able to use their abdominal muscles to support speech breathing at either comfortable or high vocal intensities (Huber et al. 2003; Sadagopan and Huber 2007; Solomon and Hixon 1993).

2.7 Summary and future directions

Future research should broaden our understanding of the role of the respiratory system in speech. It is clear we need to know more about how disease (like cerebral palsy, multiple sclerosis, chronic obstructive pulmonary disorders) affects respiratory support for speech. But we also need to know more about how the respiratory system behaves in different conditions, specifically those which mimic everyday life. For example, we need a better understanding of how cognitive demands affect respiratory support for speech. Further, speech is a task which is commonly coupled with other motor behaviors such as walking and standing and reaching. Given that our respiratory muscles are also involved in upright balance and that balancing also requires significant cognitive resources (Andersson et al. 2002; Brauer, Wollacott, and Shumway-Cook 2001; Fraizer and Mitra 2008), it is likely that respiratory support for speech may change during a dual-task like talking and walking.

Another important area for examination is the efficacy of treatment for improving respiratory support for speech. For example, Sapienza and colleagues have demonstrated the significant effects of expiratory muscle strength training on cough and swallow in individuals with Parkinson's disease (Sapienza 2008; Sapienza et al. 2011; Pitts et al. 2009; Pitts et al. 2008), but it is not clear how well this treatment affects speech production. This type of therapy has strong potential for improving respiratory support for speech in individuals with respiratory weakness, like those with spinal cord injury or Parkinson's disease or even in typically aging older adults. More research needs to identify specific mechanisms for improving respiratory support in a variety of clinical populations.

In summary, the relationships between anatomy, physiology, and work of breathing result in changes to speech breathing patterns across the life span and in individuals with Parkinson's disease. Data from studies like those cited and proposed are critical for informing theories of human cognition and its interaction with physiological processes, and at the same time have important implications for treatment.

REFERENCES

Andersson, Gerhard, Jenni Hagman, Roya Talianzadeh, Alf Svedberg, and Hans Christian Larsen. 2002. Effect of cognitive load on postural control. *Brain Research Bulletin* 58(1): 135–139.

Behrens, Charles F. 1956. In W. Spector (ed.), *Handbook of Biological Data*. Philadelphia, PA: W.B. Saunders.

Berry, Jean K., Candice A. Vitalo, Janet L. Larson, Minu Patel, and Mi Ja Kim. 1996. Respiratory muscle strength in older adults. *Nursing Research* 45(3): 154–159.

Black, Leo F. and Robert E. Hyatt. 1969. Maximal respiratory pressures: Normal values and relationships to age and sex. *American Review of Respiratory Disease* 99: 696–702.

Bode, Frederick R., James Dosman, Richard R. Martin, Heberto Ghezzo, and Peter T. Macklem. 1976. Age and sex differences in lung elasticity and in closing capacity in nonsmokers. *Journal of Applied Physiology* 41(2): 129–135.

Braak, Heiko and Kelly Del Tredici. 2008. Cortico-basal ganglia-cortical circuitry in Parkinson's disease reconsidered. *Experimental Neurology* 212: 226–229.

Braak, Heiko, Estifanos Ghebremedhin, Udo Rub, Hansjurgen Bratzke, and Kelly Del Tredici. 2004. Stages in the development of Parkinson's disease-related pathology. *Cell and Tissue Research* 318(1): 121–134.

Brauer, Sandra G., Marjorie Wollacott, and Anne Shumway-Cook. 2001. The interacting effects of cognitive demand and recovery of postural stability in balance-impaired elderly persons. *The Journals of Gerontology, Series A: Biological Sciences and Medical Sciences* 56: M489–496.

Brozek, Josef. 1960. Age differences in residual lung volume and vital capacity in normal individuals. *Journal of Gerontology* 15: 155–160.

Bunn, Jack C. and Jere Mead. 1971. Control of ventilation during speech. *Journal of Applied Physiology* 31(6): 870–872.

Bunton, Kate. 2005. Patterns of lung volume use during an extemporaneous speech task in persons with Parkinson's disease. *Journal of Communication Disorders* 38: 331–348.

Cano-de-la-Cuerda, Roberto, Lydia Vela-Desojo, Juan C. Miangolarra-Page, Yolanda Macias-Macias, and Elena Munoz-Hellin. 2011. Axial rigidity and quality of life in patients with Parkinson's disease: A preliminary study. *Quality of Life Research* 20 (6): 817–823.

Cerny, Frank J. and Harold Burton. 2001. *Exercise Physiology for Health Care Professionals*. Champaign, IL: Human Kinetics.

De Pandis, Maria F., A. Starace, Francesco Stefanelli, P. Marruzzo, I. Meoli, G. De Simone, R. Prati, and Fabrizio Stocchi. 2002. Modification of respiratory function parameters in patients with severe Parkinson's disease. *Neurological Sciences* 23(2): S69–70.

De Troyer, Andre, Jean-Claude Yernault, Marc Englert, Daniel Baran, and Manuel Paiva. 1978. Evoluation of intrathoracic airway mechanics during lung growth. *Journal of Applied Physiology* 44(4): 521–527.

Doyle, Philip, Adele S. Raade, Annette St. Pierre, and Seema Desai. 2005. Fundamental frequency and acoustic variability associated with production of sustained vowels by speakers with hypokinetic dysarthria. *Journal of Medical Speech-Language Pathology* 3(1): 41–50.

Draper, M.H., Peter Ladefoged, and David Whitteridge. 1959. Respiratory muscle in speech. *Journal of Speech and Hearing Research* 2(1): 16–27.

Enright, Paul L., Alex B. Adams, Peter J.R. Boyle, and Duane L. Sherrill. 1995. Spirometry and maximal respiratory pressure references from healthy Minnesota 65- to 85-year-old women and men. *Chest* 108: 663–669.

Enright, Paul L., Richard A. Kronmal, Teri A. Manolio, Marc B. Schenker, and Robert E. Hyatt. 1994. Respiratory muscle strength in the elderly. *American Journal of Respiratory and Critical Care Medicine* 149(2): 430–438.

Ferris, Benjamin G., James L. Whittenberger, and James R. Gallagher. 1952. Maximum breathing capacity and vital capacity of male children and adolescents. *Pediatrics* 9: 659–670.

Finnegan, Eileen M., Erich S. Luschei, and Henry T. Hoffman. 2000. Modulations in respiratory and laryngeal activity associated with changes in vocal intensity during speech. *Journal of Speech, Language, and Hearing Research* 43: 934–950.

Fraizer, Elaine V. and Subhobrata Mitra. 2008. Methodological and interpretive issues in posture-cognition dual-tasking in upright stance. *Gait and Posture* 27(2): 271–279.

Frank, N. Robert, Jere Mead, and Benjamin G. Ferris, Jr. 1957. The mechanical behavior of the lungs in healthy elderly persons. *Journal of Clinical Investigation* 36: 1680–1687.

Gibellino, Francesca, Dencho P. Osmanliev, A. Watson, and Neil B. Pride. 1985. Increase in tracheal size with age: Implications for maximal expiratory flow. *American Review of Respiratory Disease* 132(4): 784–787.

Grosjean, Francois and Maryann Collins. 1979. Breathing, pausing and reading. *Phonetica* 36: 98–114.

Guttmann, Oskar. 1882. *Gymnastics of the Voice: A System of Correct Breathing in Singing and Speaking, Based Upon Physiological Laws*. Albany, NY: The Voice Press.

Haas, Bernhard M., Marion Trew, and Paul C. Castle. 2004. Effects of respiratory muscle weakness on daily living function, quality of life, activity levels and exercise capacity in mild to moderate Parkinson's disease. *American Journal of Physical Medicine and Rehabilitation* 83: 601–607.

Hertrich, Ingo and Hermann Ackermann. 1995. Gender-specific vocal dysfunctions in Parkinson's disease: Electroglottographic and acoustic analyses. *Annals of Otology, Rhinology, and Laryngology* 104: 197–202.

Hibbert, Marienne E., Jonathan M. Couriel, and Louis I. Landau. 1984. Changes in lung, airway and chest wall function in boys and girls between 8 and 12 years. *Journal of Applied Physiology* 57: 304–308.

Hixon, Thomas J. 1973. Respiratory function in speech. In F.D. Minifie, T.J. Hixon, and F. Williams (eds.), *Normal Aspects of Speech, Hearing and Language*. Englewood Cliffs, NJ: Prentice Hall.

Hixon, Thomas J. 1976. Dynamics of the chest wall during speech production: Function of the thorax, rib cage, diaphragm and abdomen. *Journal of Speech and Hearing Research* 19: 297–356.

Hixon, Thomas J., Michael D. Goldman, and Jere Mead. 1973. Kinematics of the chest wall during speech production: Volume displacements of the rib cage, abdomen and lung. *Journal of Speech and Hearing Research* 16(1): 78–115.

Hixon, Thomas J., Gary Weismer, and Jeannette D. Hoit. 2008. *Preclinical Speech Science: Anatomy, Physiology, Acoustics, Perception*. San Diego, CA: Plural Publishing.

Hoit, Jeanette D. and Thomas J. Hixon. 1987. Age and speech breathing. *Journal of Speech and Hearing Research* 30: 351–366.

Hoit, Jeannette D., Robert W. Lansing, and Kristen E. Perona. 2007. Speaking-related dyspnea in healthy adults. *Journal of Speech, Language, and Hearing Research* 50: 361–374.

Hoit, Jeannette D., Robert B. Banzett, Robert Brown, and Stephen H. Loring. 1990a. Speech breathing in individuals with cervical spinal cord injury. *Journal of Speech and Hearing Research* 33: 798–807.

Hoit, Jeannette D., Thomas J. Hixon, M.E. Altman, and W.J. Morgan. 1989. Speech breathing in women. *Journal of Speech and Hearing Research* 32(2): 353–365.

Hoit, Jeannette D., Thomas J. Hixon, Peter J. Watson, and Wayne J. Morgan. 1990b. Speech breathing in children and adolescents. *Journal of Speech and Hearing Research* 33: 51–69.

Huber, Jessica E. 2007. Effects of cues to increase sound pressure level on respiratory kinematic patterns during connected speech. *Journal of Speech, Language, and Hearing Research* 50: 621–634.

Huber, Jessica E. 2008. Effects of utterance length and vocal loudness on speech breathing in older adults. *Respiratory Physiology and Neurobiology* 164(3): 323–330.

Huber, Jessica E. and Meghan Darling. 2011. Effect of Parkinson's disease on the production of structured and unstructured speaking tasks: Respiratory physiologic and linguistic considerations. *Journal and of Speech, Language, and Hearing Research* 54(1): 33–46.

Huber, Jessica E. and John Spruill III. 2008. Age-related changes to speech breathing with increased vocal loudness. *Journal of Speech, Language and Hearing Research* 51 (3): 651–668.

Huber, Jessica E., Bharath Chandrasekaran, and Jay J. Wolstencroft. 2005. Changes to respiratory mechanisms during speech as a result of different cues to increase loudness. *Journal of Applied Physiology* 98: 2177–2184.

Huber, Jessica E., Meghan Darling, Elaine J. Francis, and Dabao Zhang. 2012. Impact of typical aging and Parkinson's disease on the relationship among breath pausing, syntax and punctuation. *American Journal of Speech-Language Pathology* 21: 368–379.

Huber, Jessica E., Elaine T. Stathopoulos, Lorraine O. Ramig, and Sandi L. Lancaster. 2003. Respiratory function and variability in individuals with Parkinson disease: Pre- and post-Lee Silverman Voice Treatment. *Journal of Medical Speech-Language Pathology* 11(4): 185–201.

Inzelberg, Rivka, Nana Peleg, Puiu Nisipeanu, Rasmi Magadle, Ralph L. Carasso, and Paltiel Weiner. 2005. Inspiratory muscle training and the perception of dyspnea in Parkinson's disease. *Canadian Journal of Neurological Sciences* 32: 213–217.

Knudson, Ronald J., Dumont F. Clark, Timothy C. Kennedy, and Dwyn E. Knudson. 1977. Effect of aging alone on mechanical properties of the normal adult human lung. *Journal of Applied Physiology: Respiration, Environmental and Exercise Physiology* 43(6): 1054–1062.

Knudson, Ronald J., Ronald C. Slatin, Michael D. Lebowitz, and Benjamin Burrows. 1976. The maximal expiratory flow-volume curve. *American Review of Respiratory Disease* 113: 587–600.

Lanteri, Celia J. and Peter D. Sly. 1993. Changes in respiratory mechanics with age. *Journal of Applied Physiology* 74(1): 369–378.

Lethlean, Jennifer B., Helen J. Chenery, and Bruce E. Murdoch. 1990. Disturbed respiratory and prosodic function in Parkinson's disease: A perceptual and instrumental analysis. *Australian Journal of Human Communication Disorders* 18(2): 83–97.

Levitzky, Michael G. 2007. *Pulmonary Physiology*. New York: McGraw-Hill.

Lyons, Kelly E., Jean P. Hubble, Alexander I. Troster, Rajesh Pahwa, and William C. Koller. 1998. Gender differences in Parkinson's disease. *Clinical Neuropharmacology* 21(2): 118–121.

MacPherson, Megan K., Jessica E. Huber, and David P. Snow. 2011. The intonation-syntax interface in the speech of individuals with Parkinson's disease. *Journal of Speech, Language, and Hearing Research* 54: 19–32.

Mansell, Anthony L., A. Charles Bryan, and Henry Levison. 1977. Relationship of lung recoil to lung volume and maximum expiratory flow in normal children. *Journal of Applied Physiology: Respiration, Environmental and Exercise Physiology* 42(6): 817–823.

McDowell, Margaret A., Cheryl D. Fryar, Cynthia L. Ogden, and Katherine M. Flegal. 2008. *Anthropometric Reference Data for Children and Adults: United States, 2003–2006*. Hyattsville, MD: National Center for Health Statistics.

Mitchell, Heather L., Jeannette D. Hoit, and Peter J. Watson. 1996. Cognitive-linguistic demands and speech breathing. *Journal of Speech, Language, and Hearing Research* 39: 93–104.

Mittman, Charles, Norman H. Edelman, Arthur H. Norris, and Nathan W. Shock. 1965. Relationship between chest wall and pulmonary compliance with age. *Journal of Applied Physiology* 20: 1211–1216.

Murdoch, Bruce E., Helen J. Chenery, Simon Bowler, and John C.L. Ingram. 1989. Respiratory function in Parkinson's subjects exhibiting a perceptible speech deficit: A kinematic and spirometric analysis. *Journal of Speech and Hearing Disorders* 54: 610–626.

Pfitzenmeyer, Pierre, Laurent Brondel, Philippe d'Athis, Serge Lacroix, Jean Pierre Didier, and Michel Gaudet. 1993. Lung function in advanced age: Study of ambulatory subjects aged over 75 years. *Gerontology* 39: 267–275.

Pitts, Teresa, Donald Bolser, John Rosenbek, Michelle Troche, and Christine Sapienza. 2008. Voluntary cough production and swallow dysfunction in Parkinson's disease. *Dysphagia* 23: 297–301.

Pitts, Teresa, Donald Bolser, John Rosenbek, Michelle Troche, Michael S. Okun, and Christine Sapienza. 2009. Impact of expiratory muscle strength training on voluntary cough and swallow function in Parkinson disease. *Chest* 135(5): 1301–1308.

Polatli, M., A. Akyol, O. Cildag, and K. Bayulkem. 2001. Pulmonary function tests in Parkinson's disease. *European Journal of Neurology* 8: 341–345.

Polgar, George and Tzong R. Weng. 1979. The functional development of the respiratory system from the period of gestation to adulthood. *American Review of Respiratory Disease* 120(3): 625–695.

Price, Patti J., Mari Ostendorf, Stefanie Schattuck-Hufnagel, and Cynthia Fong. 1991. The use of prosody in syntactic disambiguation. *Journal of the Acoustical Society of America* 90: 2956–2970.

Rahn, Douglas A., Maggie Chou, Jack J. Jiang, and Yu Zhang. 2007. Phonatory impairment in Parkinson's disease: Evidence from nonlinear dynamic analysis and perturbation analysis. *Journal of Voice* 21: 64–71.

Rahn, Hermann, Arthur B. Otis, Leigh E. Chadwick, and Wallace O. Fenn. 1946. The pressure-volume diagram of the thorax and lung. *American Journal of Physiology* 146(6): 161–178.

Ringqvist, Torsten. 1966. The ventilatory capacity in healthy subjects: An analysis of causal factors with special reference to the respiratory forces. *The Scandinavian Journal of Clinical and Laboratory Investigation* 18(88): 1–179.

Russell, Bridget A., Frank J. Cerny, and Elaine T. Stathopoulos. 1998. Effects of varied vocal intensity on ventilation and energy expenditure in women and men. *Journal of Speech, Language, and Hearing Research* 41: 239–248.

Russell, Nancy K. and Elaine T. Stathopoulos. 1988. Lung volume changes in children and adults during speech production. *Journal of Speech and Hearing Research* 31: 146–155.

Sabate, Magdalena, Isidro Gonzalez, Felix Ruperez, and Manuel Rodriguez. 1996. Obstructive and restrictive pulmonary dysfunctions in Parkinson's disease. *Journal of Neurological Sciences* 138: 114–119.

Sadagopan, Neeraja and Jessica E. Huber. 2007. Effects of loudness cues on respiration in individuals with Parkinson's disease. *Movement Disorders* 22: 651–659.

Sapienza, Christine M. 2008. Respiratory muscle strength training applications. *Current Opinion in Otolaryngology and Head and Neck Surgery* 16: 216–220.

Sapienza, Christine, Michelle Troche, Teresa Pitts, and Paul Davenport. 2011. Respiratory strength training: Concept and intervention outcomes. *Seminars in Speech and Language* 32(1): 21–30.

Schirmer, Annett, Kai Alter, Sonja A. Kotz, and Angela D. Friederici. 2001. Lateralization of prosody during language production: A lesion study. *Brain and Language* 76: 1–17.

Seccombe, Leigh M., Hugh L. Giddings, Peter G. Rogers, Alastair J. Corbett, Michael W. Hayes, Matthew J. Peters, and Elizabeth M. Veitch. 2011. Abnormal ventilatory control in Parkinson's disease: Further evidence for non-motor dysfunction. *Respiratory Physiology and Neurobiology* 179: 300–304.

Sherrill, D.L., M.D. Lebowitz, R.J. Knudson, and B. Burrows. 1992. Continuous longitudinal regression equations for pulmonary function measures. *European Respiratory Journal* 5: 452–462.

Solomon, Nancy P. and Thomas J. Hixon. 1993. Speech breathing in Parkinson's disease. *Journal of Speech and Hearing Research* 36: 294–310.

Sorkin, John D., Denis C. Muller, and Reubin Andres. 1999. Longitudinal change in height of men and women: Implications for interpretation of the body mass index. *American Journal of Epidemiology* 150(9): 969–977.

Sperry, Elizabeth E. and Richard J. Klich. 1992. Speech breathing in senescent and younger women during oral reading. *Journal of Speech and Hearing Research* 35: 1246–1255.

Stathopoulos, Elaine T. and Christine M. Sapienza. 1993. Respiratory and laryngeal measures of children during vocal intensity variation. *Journal of the Acoustical Society of America* 94(5): 2531–2543.

Stathopoulos, Elaine T. and Christine M. Sapienza. 1994. Comparison of maximum flow declination rate: Children vs. adults. *Journal of Voice* 8(3): 240–247.

Stathopoulos, Elaine T. and Christine M. Sapienza. 1997. Developmental changes in laryngeal and respiratory function with variations in sound pressure level. *Journal of Speech, Language, and Hearing Research* 40: 595–614.

Steinhauer, Kimberly M. 2003. Electrophysiological correlates of prosody and punctuation. *Brain and Language* 86: 142–164.

Tolep, Kenneth and Steven G. Kelsen. 1993. Effect of aging on respiratory skeletal muscles. *Clinics in Chest Medicine* 14: 363–378.

Verschakelen, Johny A. and Maurits G. Demedts. 1995. Normal thoracoabdominal motions: Influence of sex, age, posture and breath size. *American Journal of Respiratory and Critical Care Medicine* 15: 399–405.

Wang, Yu-Tsai, Raymond D. Kent, Joseph R. Duffy, and Jack E. Thomas. 2005. Dysarthria in traumatic brain injury: A breath group and intonational analysis. *Folia Phoniatrica et Logopaedica* 57: 59–89.

Warren, Paul. 1996. Prosody and parsing: An introduction. *Language and Cognitive Processes* 11: 1–16.

Weiner, Paltiel, Rivka Inzelberg, Avi Davidovich, Puiu Nisipeanu, Rasmi Magadle, Noa Berar-Yanay, and Ralph L. Carasso. 2002. Respiratory muscle performance and the perception of dyspnea in Parkinson's disease. *Canadian Journal of Neurological Sciences* 29: 68–72.

Winkworth, Alison L., Pamela J. Davis, Elizabeth Ellis, and Roger D. Adams. 1994. Variability and consistency in speech breathing during reading: Lung volumes, speech intensity and linguistic factors. *Journal of Speech and Hearing Research* 37: 535–556.

Zeman, Kirby L. and William D. Bennett. 2006. Growth of the small airways and alveoli from childhood to the adult lung measured by aerosol-derived airway morphometry. *Journal of Applied Physiology* 100(3): 965–971.

3 Mechanisms of Voice Production

BRAD H. STORY

3.1 Introduction[1]

The aim of this chapter is to provide an overview of laryngeal anatomy and physiology, characteristics of vocal fold motion, transformation of vocal fold vibration to sound, and mechanisms of vocal fold vibration. Throughout the chapter computational models have been used for demonstration purposes to generate examples of vocal fold motion and resulting waveforms representing various quantities.

3.2 Laryngeal anatomy and physiology

The rigid structure of the larynx is formed primarily by four cartilages, the thyroid, cricoid, and two arytenoids (Figures 3.1 and 3.2). The cricoid cartilage is shaped like a signet ring set on its side with the signet portion most posterior. It is located just above the most superior tracheal ring. The thyroid cartilage is characterized by two wide plate-like structures called the laminae that extend posteriorly from their vertex (called the thyroid prominence) in a V-shape. This cartilage sits atop the cricoid and articulates with it via the inferior cornua that extend inferiorly from the laminae. Two arytenoid cartilages, shaped somewhat like pyramids, rest on the superior surface of the posterior portion of the cricoid (signet), one on the left side and one on the right. One leg of each arytenoid points anteriorly toward the thyroid prominence and is called the vocal process. This is the point of insertion for the thyroarytenoid muscle which originates near the vertex of the thyroid cartilage. Medial to the thyroarytenoid muscle on both left and right sides are layers of ligament and mucosal tissue, which together comprise the vocal folds (Hirano 1974).

In Figure 3.2a, the vocal folds are shown widely separated, or *abducted*, at the vocal process creating an open space between them called the *glottis*. This is a typical

---

The Handbook of Speech Production, First Edition. Edited by Melissa A. Redford.
© 2015 John Wiley & Sons, Inc. Published 2019 by John Wiley & Sons, Inc.

Mechanisms of Voice Production 35

(a) Midsagittal view

(b) Perspective view

- Arytenoid cartilage (*hidden*)
- Thyroid cartilage
- Location of the vocal folds (*hidden*)
- Cricothyroid muscle
- Cricoid cartilage
- Larynx
- Trachea
- Trachea

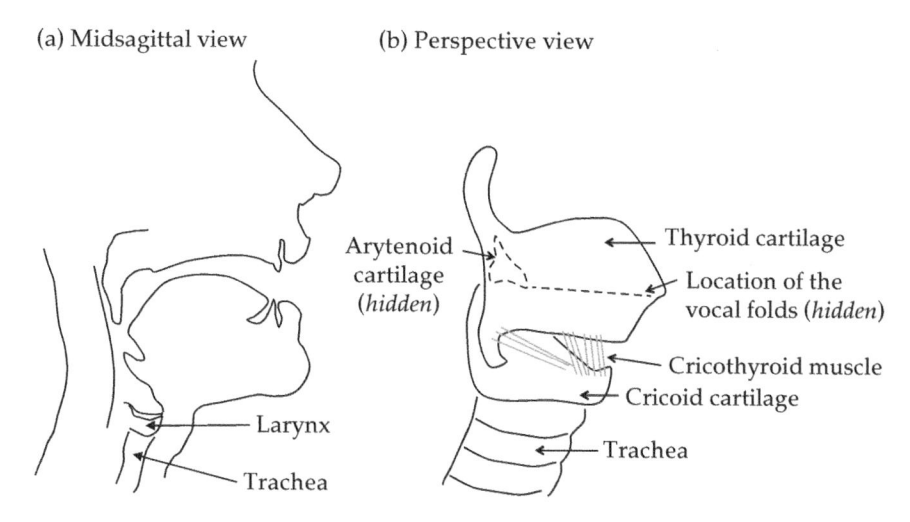

Figure 3.1 Schematic diagrams of speech production anatomy. (a) Midsagittal view of the upper portion of the trachea, larynx, and vocal tract. (b) Perspective view of laryngeal cartilages and cricothyroid muscle. The dashed lines represent structures hidden in the view by cartilage.

(a) Axial view: abducted
- Thyroid prominence
- Thyroarytenoid muscle
- Ligament
- Mucosa
- Glottis
- Cricoid cartilage
- Thyroid cartilage
- Vocal process
- Arytenoid cartilages

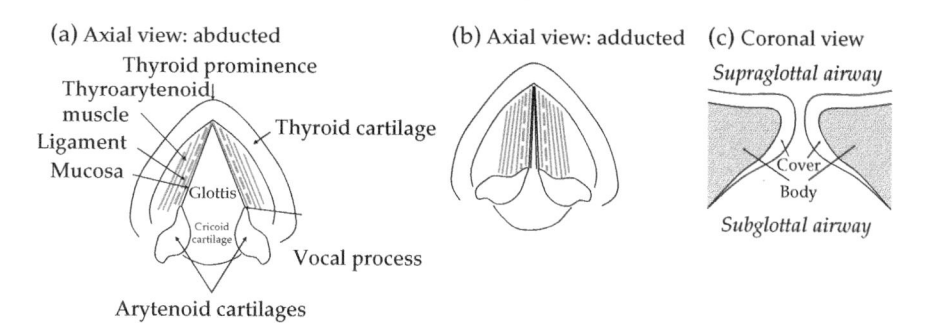

(b) Axial view: adducted

(c) Coronal view
- *Supraglottal airway*
- Cover
- Body
- *Subglottal airway*

Figure 3.2 Diagrams of the larynx and vocal folds. (a) Superior view of larynx when the vocal folds are abducted, as during respiration. (b) Superior view of larynx when the vocal folds are adducted, as during phonation. (c) Division of the vocal fold into the cover and body portions (based on Hirano 1974).

configuration during respiration and for developing pressure in the supraglottal airspace for consonant production (e.g., for stops, fricatives, and affricates). Abductory maneuvers are executed and maintained by contraction of the posterior cricoarytenoid muscle (not shown in the figure). In preparation for phonation (or for breath-holding), the arytenoids can be rotated and translated medially by contracting the lateral cricoarytenoid and interarytenoid muscles (also not shown in the figures). These contractions have the effect of moving the vocal fold surfaces toward each other, or *adducting* them, to reduce or eliminate the glottal airspace, as shown in Figure 3.2b.

Contraction of the thyroarytenoid muscle tends to slide the arytenoids anteriorly, decreasing the distance between the vocal processes and the thyroid prominence, and consequently shortening the vocal folds. The cricothyroid muscles originate on the anterior surface of the cricoid cartilage and insert on the inferior edge of the thyroid laminae. Their contraction tends to rotate the cricoid and thyroid cartilages toward each other, having the effect of increasing the distance between the vocal processes and the thyroid prominence, thereby lengthening the vocal folds. Thus, the thyroarytenoid and cricothyroid muscles are effectively configured as an agonist/antagonist pair and their relative degree of activation can precisely adjust the overall length of the vocal folds. More detailed descriptions of the effect of laryngeal muscle contractions can be found in Zemlin (1998), Titze (1994), and Hixon, Weismer, and Hoit (2008).

The internal structure of the vocal folds is often described by the cover-body concept (Hirano 1974). It suggests that the vocal folds can be roughly divided into two tissue layers (Figure 3.2c) with different mechanical properties. The cover layer is comprised of pliable, non-contractile mucosal tissue that serves as a sheath around the body. In contrast, the body layer consists of muscle fibers (thyroarytenoid) and some ligamentous tissue. Other more detailed schemes have been used to describe the layers of tissue in the vocal folds (see Titze 1994 for a summary), but the cover-body scheme is particularly useful for purposes of studying the vibratory characteristics of the vocal folds.

In summary, the cartilages of the larynx form a structure that supports and houses the vocal folds. When differentially contracted, the intrinsic laryngeal musculature can move the cartilages relative to one another in order to open and close the glottis through abductory and adductory maneuvers, respectively, as well as to modify the length and mechanical properties of the vocal fold tissue. It is important to note that these movements are executed on a time scale similar to the other articulators such as the tongue, lips, jaw, and velum, and do not in themselves generate *vibratory* motion of the vocal folds, and hence, do not produce sound. Vibration, which causes a portion of the vocal folds to move back and forth hundreds of time per second and produces sound, occurs when the configuration of the medial surface of vocal folds, their mechanical properties, and the aerodynamic conditions surrounding them is sufficient to initiate and sustain self-oscillation.

3.3 Kinematics of vocal fold vibration

In this section the kinematics of vocal fold motion during vibration will be described without consideration of how the vibration occurs. The physical mechanisms of oscillation will be explained in a later section, and are somewhat easier to understand with prior knowledge of the kinematic patterns. For production of sound, the movement of the medial surfaces of the vocal folds is of primary importance because they modulate the airspace between them, giving rise to an acoustic excitation that can be formed into speech. A simplified 3D view of the medial

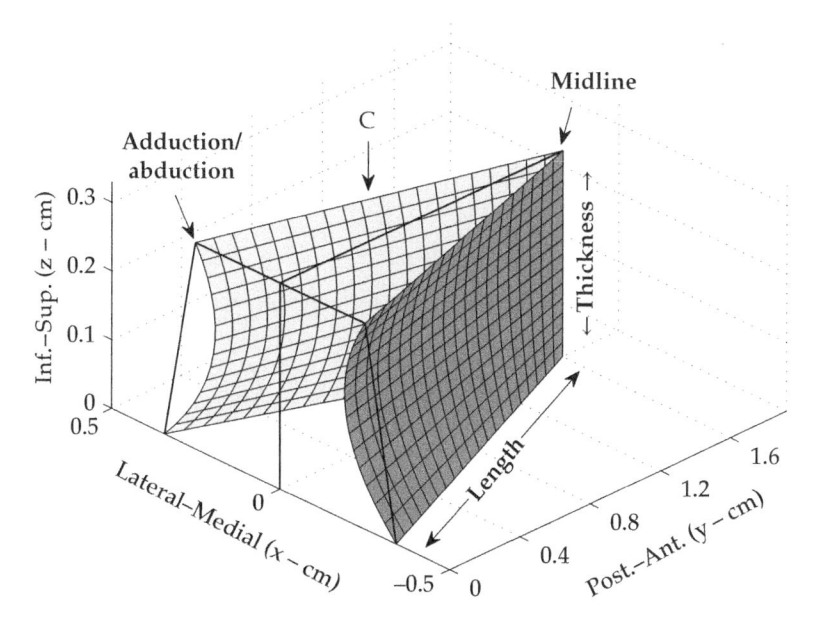

Figure 3.3 3D representation of the medial surfaces of the vocal folds based on the kinematic model of Titze (1984, 2006).

surfaces is shown in Figure 3.3 based on Titze (1984, 2006), and is configured here to be representative of an adult male. The posterior-anterior dimension represents the vocal fold length, whereas the thickness is represented on the inferior-superior dimension. The point labeled "Adduction/abduction" is where the vocal processes of the arytenoid cartilages would be located; adductory or abductory maneuvers can be conceived as moving this point medially or laterally, respectively.

Observations of the vibrating vocal folds with stroboscopic techniques or high-speed film/video have shown that the cover tissue supports a surface wave that propagates from the inferior to superior portions of the vocal fold cover (a summary of vocal fold observation techniques can be found in Moore 1991). This wave is typically referred to as the *mucosal wave* or *vertical phase difference* and is most clearly observed in the coronal plane (e.g., Figure 3.2c). Vocal fold motion in this plane (along the axis of airflow) was first viewed with X-ray techniques (Hollien and Moore 1968), studies of excised larynges (Baer 1975), and more recently with observations of excised hemilaryngeal vibration using videostroboscopy (Jiang and Titze 1993) and high-speed video (Berry, Montequin, and Tayama 2001; Doellinger, Berry, and Berke 2005; Doellinger and Berry 2006).

An idealized cycle of vocal fold vibration in the coronal plane denoted by C in Figure 3.3 is demonstrated in the series of time-frame plots of Figure 3.4. In the first time frame ($t=1$) the vocal folds on the left and right sides are just barely in contact, the airway is closed, and the direction of tissue motion is outward away from midline as indicated by the arrows. The next two frames ($t=2$ and $t=3$) indicate large lateral movement of the inferior portion of cover surface and similar but

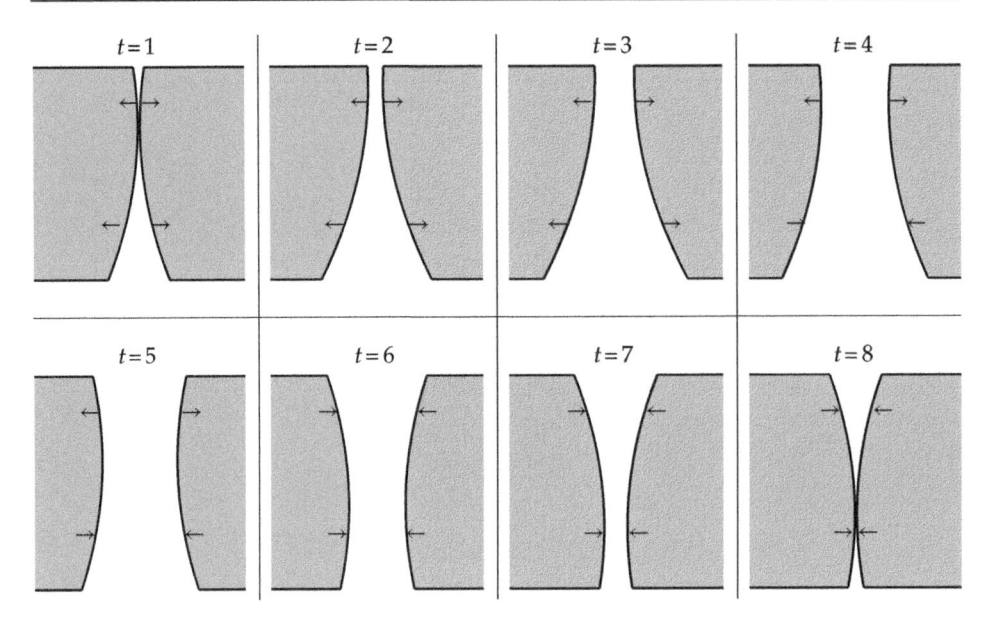

Figure 3.4 Diagram showing eight frames of an idealized cycle of vocal fold vibration in the coronal plane denoted by C in Figure 3.3. Note that the lower portion of the vocal folds leads the upper portion creating a wave-like motion on the vocal fold surface. This is called the mucosal wave.

smaller lateral displacement of the upper portion which breaks contact between the left and right sides, thereby opening the airway. Once the maximum lateral displacement is achieved ($t=4$), the lower portion of the vocal folds begins to move medially (note that the direction of the arrows has switched) while the upper portion continues its outward motion ($t=5$). In frames $t=6$ and $t=7$ the upper portion of the vocal fold has changed its direction of motion and now follows the lower portion toward the midline. Eventually, the lower portions on the left and right sides collide with each other and again close the airway ($t=8$). Medial displacement continues as the upper portions also collide as in the first frame $t=1$. The entire process repeats itself cyclically at the fundamental frequency of vibration (F0).

Note that the lateral displacement of the upper (superior) portion of each vocal fold is not in phase with the lower portion. That is, the lower part of the vocal fold leads the upper, creating wave-like motion in the cover from bottom to top. A simplified view of the vibration pattern is shown in Figure 3.5 where the surface of a single vocal fold is represented as thin plate capable of both rotation and lateral displacement. The mucosal wave, indicated by the rotation of plate, can be conceived as "riding" on the overall back and forth movement of the tissue. These patterns are the two basic vibrational *eigenmodes* or natural modes of the vocal fold tissue system with regard to the motion in the coronal plane (Titze 1976, 2006; Berry and Titze 1996); vibration patterns in the transverse plane can also be

Mechanisms of Voice Production 39

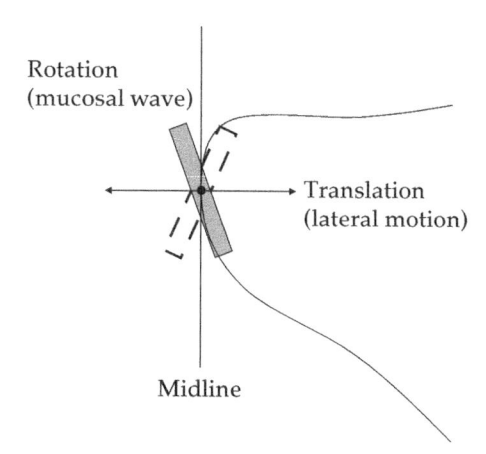

Figure 3.5 Simplification of vocal fold motion. The rotation of the thin plate is intended to account for the mucosal wave while lateral motion represents overall lateral motion.

represented with eigenmodes (Titze 2006; Berry and Titze 1996). A specific pattern of vibration can be considered to be a combination of these two eigenmodes (Berry 2001). In the context of the 3D representation of the medial surfaces in Figure 3.3, each coronal section along the vocal fold length will, to some degree, exhibit a pattern of motion similar to the time frame plots in Figure 3.4, except that the anterior sections will typically lead those that are located successively posterior. This results in a zipper-like closure of the glottis when viewed from above the vocal folds.

As the vocal folds move together medially and then move apart laterally, they repeatedly close and open the glottis, respectively. This pattern of modulating the airway at the location of the vocal folds can be quantified with a *glottal area* waveform. An example is shown in the upper panel of Figure 3.6a in which the glottal area remains at zero for the first several milliseconds and then rapidly increases to a peak value of $0.075 \, cm^2$ before decreasing back to zero. In this particular case, the opening and closing pattern of the glottal area repeats every 0.01 seconds, or equivalently at a frequency of 100 cycles per second (Hz). Also as the vocal folds move together and apart, their medial surfaces come into contact for a period of time and then separate. A waveform denoting the amount of contact over successive cycles of vibration is shown in the lower panel of Figure 3.6, where the contact area has been normalized to a peak value of one. The reciprocal nature of this signal with the glottal area is apparent as the contact area is initially high while the glottal area is zero. As the contact area decreases there is a point at which the glottal area becomes nonzero and begins to rise. The sets of vertical lines traversing both plots indicate a part of the vibratory cycle where the glottis is open and contact area is low (solid lines), and another part where the glottis is closed (or mostly so) and the contact area is large (dashed lines). This example was set up such that closure of the glottis would be achieved during the portion of the vibratory cycle where tissue contact is maximized. If, however, the setting of the vocal process (i.e., "Abduction/

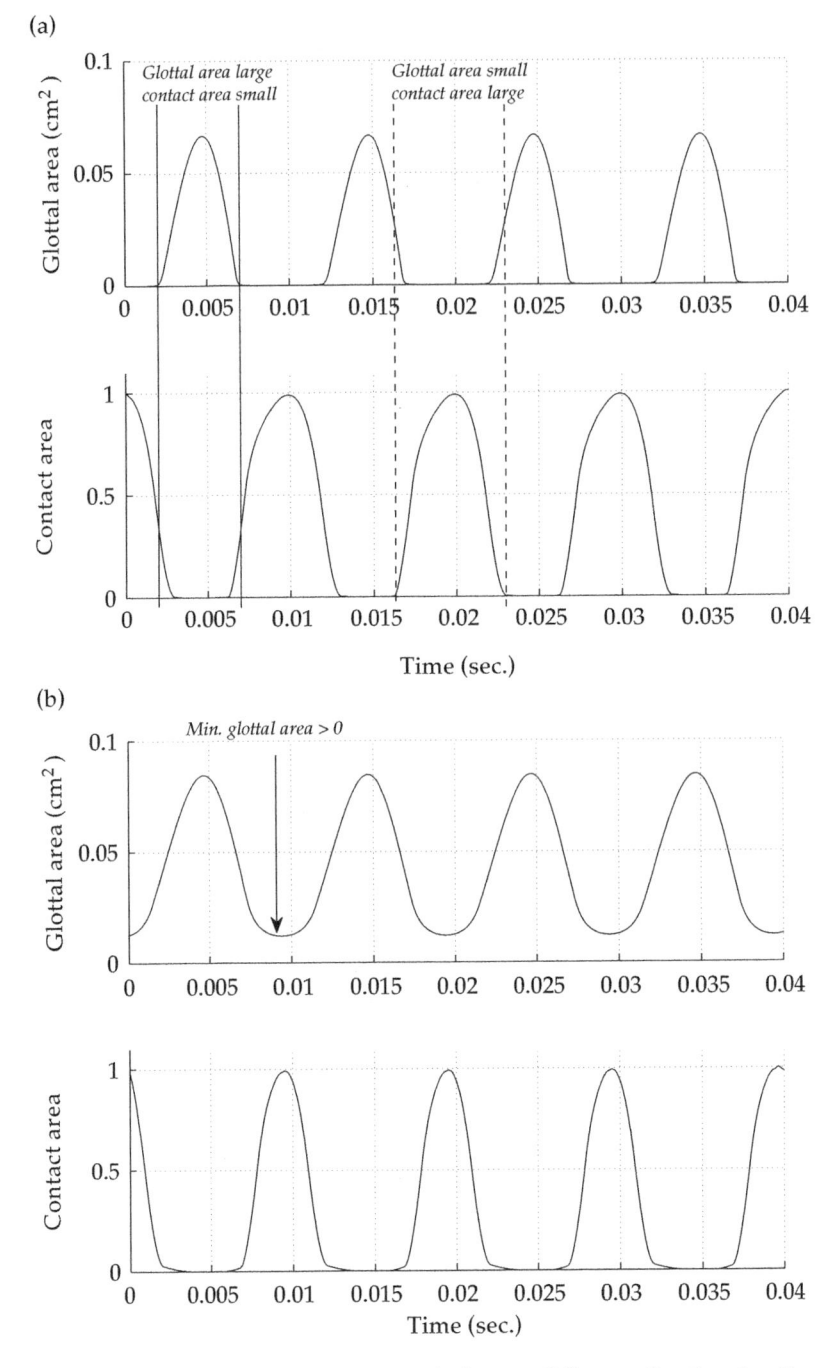

Figure 3.6 Glottal area and contact area signals for two different vibrational patterns of the vocal folds. (a) Typical vibration with distinct closed and open phases. (b) Vibration with no glottal closure; may generate characteristics of a breathy voice.

adduction" point in Figure 3.3) is considerably distant from the midline, the glottis may never truly close. Shown in Figure 3.6b are glottal area and contact area waveforms produced with such a configuration. Although the glottal area varies cyclically at a frequency of 100 Hz much like in Figure 3.6a, it has a nonzero value at all points in time indicating that the glottis never fully closes. The contact area waveform also takes a somewhat different temporal shape, with the primary change being a shortened duration of tissue contact.

Although the glottal area is of most interest relative to sound production, an electrical analog of the contact area is more easily obtained from human talkers in a laboratory or clinical environment. The electroglottograph (EGG) allows for a noninvasive measurement of contact area with an electrode array that is held in contact with the skin at the location of the thyroid lamina (Fourcin and Abberton 1971). This device passes a low amplitude, alternating current through the larynx; as the vocal folds vibrate, they modulate the conductivity of the electrical (tissue) path between the two electrodes, effectively producing a contact area analog. Due to its reciprocal nature with the glottal area, the EGG signal can be used to assess some aspects of voice production (e.g., Rothenberg and Mahshie 1988; Orlikoff 1991; Henrich et al. 2004, 2005). A signal representative of the glottal area can also be obtained with a combination of a light source located on the supraglottal or subglottal side of the vocal folds, and a photosensor on the opposite side. As the vocal folds vibrate, the light passing through the glottis is modulated and the photosensor generates a signal proportional to the modulation, thus producing an analog to the glottal area. Called a photoglottograph (PGG), this instrument is somewhat more invasive than the EGG since ideally both the light source and sensor are located within the pharynx and trachea, respectively (Rothenberg and Mahshie 1988; Zemlin 1959; Sonneson 1959). There have been some designs that have used an external light source and sensor with some success (Druker 1999), but in general the PGG tends be less used than the EGG.

3.4 Acoustics of vocal sound production

The purpose of setting the vocal folds into vibration is, of course, to produce sound that provides the excitation of the vocal tract resonances for vowel production and voiced consonants. This section provides an overview of how the vibratory motion of the vocal folds is transformed into a sound source, and how that sound is shaped into speech.

Understanding sound production can be facilitated by "installing" the medial surface model of the vocal folds into a simplified system of airways representative of the trachea, pharynx, and oral cavity, the latter two comprising the "vocal tract." This is shown in Figure 3.7 where, for sake of clarity, the vocal fold surfaces are displayed in magnified form and offset to the right of their actual location in the system. The vocal tract is configured in this case as a neutral vowel. At the inferior end of the trachea is the variable P_L, and represents the static pressure supplied by the respiratory system (L = lungs). When the vocal folds are separated and the

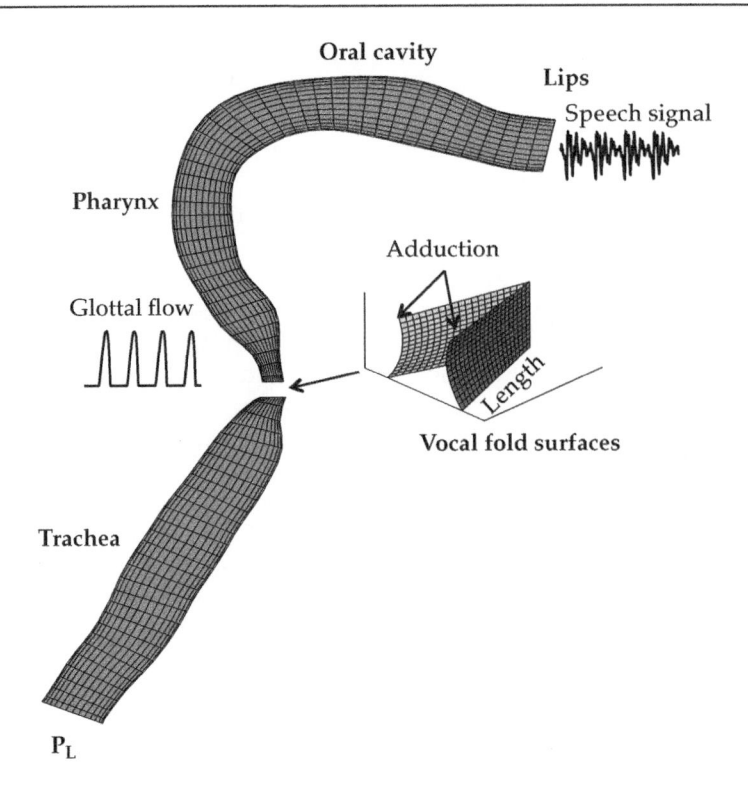

Figure 3.7 Schematic diagram of the airway system for speech production. The vocal folds, which are shown magnified, would be located where the arrow points and produce the glottal flow signal shown to the left. The flow pulses excite acoustic wave propagation in the vocal tract and produce the output (radiated) pressure waveform shown at the lips.

glottis open, this pressure will drive air through the glottis and generate a *glottal flow*. If the vocal processes are in an abducted position and no vibration occurs, the glottal flow will be essentially a steady outward movement of air from the lungs. During vibration, however, the vocal fold surfaces cyclically and rapidly open and close the glottis, allowing air to flow during the period of time when the glottal area is nonzero and halting flow during the periods when the glottis is closed. The result is a glottal flow waveform that is a train of flow pulses, as demonstrated by the plot offset to the left in Figure 3.7, and serves as the primary acoustic excitation for vowels and voiced consonants. The amplitude and shape of the glottal flow pulses are influenced by the magnitude of P_L and the temporal pattern of the glottal area waveform, as well as by the moment-to-moment variations in acoustic pressure just superior and inferior to the glottis.

The glottal flow initiates acoustic wave propagation in both the trachea and vocal tract. The reflected and transmitted pressures throughout the system shape the glottal flow excitation according to the natural resonance frequencies of the airways, but primarily those of the vocal tract. The pressure generated at the lip termination radiates outward into free space and is the "speech waveform" or "speech signal" because it now carries information relative to the shape of the vocal tract.

The glottal flow and output pressure signals are shown in more detail in Figure 3.8a. The thick solid line in the upper panel is the glottal flow waveform and shows the train of air pulses generated by the opening of the closing of the glottis shown previously in Figure 3.6a. A typical characteristic of the glottal flow relative to the glottal area waveform is the rightward skew in time. This is due to the acoustic inertance (or mass-like property) of the air in the vocal tract delaying the increase in flow as the glottis opens (Fant 1960, 1979; Flanagan 1968; Rothenberg 1973, 1981; Titze 1984). Also shown in the upper panel of Figure 3.8a is the time derivative of the glottal flow; it has been scaled in amplitude so that its temporal pattern can be easily compared to the glottal flow but is not displayed with the appropriate units of cm^3/s^2. As an indicator of change, this waveform clearly demonstrates the points in time during a vibratory cycle at which the glottal flow is rapidly increasing or decreasing. The large negative "peaks" are the points of maximum flow declination, and constitute the primary acoustic excitation during a glottal cycle. A secondary excitation occurs when the flow initially increases just as the glottis opens. The acoustic output pressure radiated at the lips is shown in the lower panel of Figure 3.8a. Because the radiation impedance is effectively a

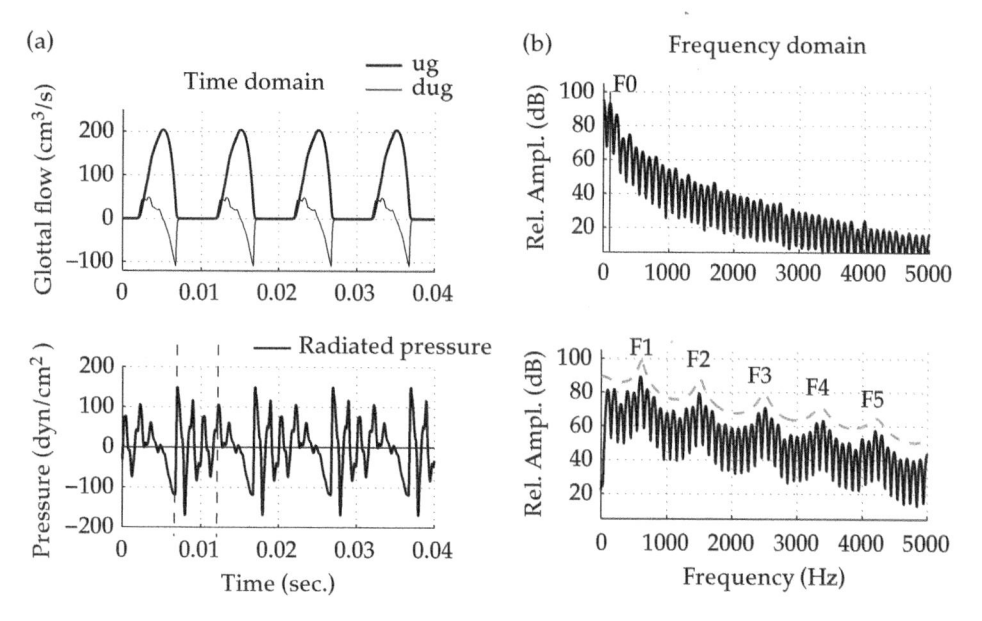

Figure 3.8 Waveforms and spectra that demonstrate the source-filter representation of speech production. (a) Time-domain waveforms; the upper panel shows glottal flow (ug) and its derivative (dug) (scaled to fit on the same plot), and the bottom panel contains the output pressure waveform. (b) The upper panel is the glottal flow spectrum and the lower panel is the output pressure spectrum. The F0 and formants are marked in each panel.

differentiator, the pressure waveform has characteristics similar to that of the flow derivative except that it oscillates during the period of time that the glottis is closed (i.e., when the flow and derivative waveforms are zero). One such oscillatory period is indicated by the vertical dashed lines, and results from the acoustic filtering properties of the vocal tract resonances. Thus, the glottal flow can be considered the sound *source* for vowels and voice consonants, whereas the vocal tract is the *filter* that transforms the source waveform into the final speech signal.

The spectra of the glottal flow and output pressure waveforms are shown in Figure 3.8b. The components of the flow spectrum in the upper panel with the highest amplitudes are the fundamental frequency (F0) and the second harmonic (2F0); the other harmonics are reduced in amplitude by roughly 12 dB per octave. Although the frequencies of the harmonics in the output pressure spectrum (lower panel) are the same as in the flow spectrum, their amplitudes rise and fall with frequency. The regions of the spectrum where the amplitude is prominent are the *formants* and are the result of the vocal tract resonances transforming the flow into an output pressure. The gray dashed line is the spectral envelope whose peaks are marked as the formants F1–F5.

3.5 The vocal folds as a self-oscillating system

In previous sections, the general characteristics of vocal fold motion during vibration were described, as well as the acoustic characteristics produced by that motion as it interacts with flow and pressure. These descriptions were presented under the assumption that the vocal folds were, in fact, already in vibration. The purpose of this section is to provide an overview of *why the vocal folds vibrate*. That is, what mechanical and aerodynamic conditions are necessary to allow the vocal folds to sustain a repeating oscillatory cycle of medial and lateral motion?

That the vocal folds are capable of converting a steady stream of airflow into vibratory tissue motion, and subsequently producing an acoustic wave, puts them into a category of physical systems that support *self-sustained oscillation*. A early attempt at describing the process was Van den Berg's (1958) "Myoelastic-aerodynamic theory of voice production" which was an empirical investigation of the interaction of vocal fold tissue elasticity and aerodynamic forces. The oscillatory mechanisms were described in terms of tissue elasticity and the so-called Bernoulli effect. That is, high air velocity through a narrow glottis would create a negative pressure that would "suck" the vocal folds together, after which a build-up of subglottal pressure would blow the vocal folds apart (move them laterally) and start the process again. Subsequent theoretical studies, however, have assigned a secondary role to the Bernoulli effect and have formed the current view that the vocal folds may oscillate whenever an asymmetry exists between the aerodynamic driving forces produced within the glottis during the lateral and medial movement phases of a vibratory cycle (Ishizaka and Matsudaira 1972; Titze 1976, 1988; Stevens 1977). This asymmetry is facilitated by (1) the mucosal wave, which creates a time delay with respect to the upper and lower portions of the vocal folds because of the alternating convergent and divergent glottal shape, and (2) the inertial acoustic loading presented by the vocal tract which creates a time delay between the build-up and release of supraglottal pressure and glottal opening/closing. Both of these mechanisms have the effect of decreasing the aerodynamic driving forces during the glottal closing phase and increasing them during the opening phase.

Although self-sustained oscillation is a complex process, the two mechanisms of vocal fold oscillation can be explained in large part under simplified conditions of idealized air flow and no collision of the vocal folds (Titze 1983, 1988, 1994). These may seem like severe limitations, but the mechanisms involved in the simplified case exist even when the more complex details of the system are included. In the next two subsections each mechanism is explained separately.

3.5.1 Alternating convergence and divergence of the glottis

Shown in Figure 3.9a are two representative convergent and divergent configurations of the glottis (in the coronal plane) that could occur during a vibratory cycle. In either case, a generalized force exerted on the vocal fold tissue can be represented as the mean intraglottal pressure over the medial surfaces based on the Bernoulli energy law (Titze 1983, 1988). Under conditions of no vocal fold collision and idealized flow in the glottis the intraglottal pressure P_g can be written as

$$P_g = \left(1 - \frac{a_2}{a_1}\right)(P_s - P_i) + P_i \tag{3.1}$$

where a_1 and a_2 are the cross-sectional areas at the glottal entry and exit, respectively, P_s is the subglottal pressure, and P_i is the input pressure to the vocal tract (Titze 1994). Eqn. 3.1 shows that the vocal folds are driven by the sum of the vocal tract input pressure P_i and the *transglottal pressure* $(P_s - P_i)$ scaled by the glottal shaping factor $(1 - a_2/a_1)$. For purposes of illustration, the situation can be further simplified such that $P_i \approx 0$, so that the mean intraglottal pressure becomes

$$P_g = \left(1 - \frac{a_2}{a_1}\right) P_s \tag{3.2}$$

This equation shows that when the tissue is moving laterally and the glottis is convergent $(a_1 > a_2)$, P_g will be greater than zero. That is, the force exerted on the medial surfaces is in the same direction as their motion. As the folds move outward, restoring forces within the tissue grow in increasing opposition to the motion and cause them rotate into a divergent configuration $(a_1 < a_2)$ and begin their movement back toward the glottal midline. As soon as the glottis becomes divergent, P_g will switch to a negative value, again exerting a force on the tissue in the direction of motion.

This sequence of events is demonstrated in Figure 3.9b where hypothetical variations of a_1 and a_2 for a single cycle of vibration are plotted as the solid and dashed

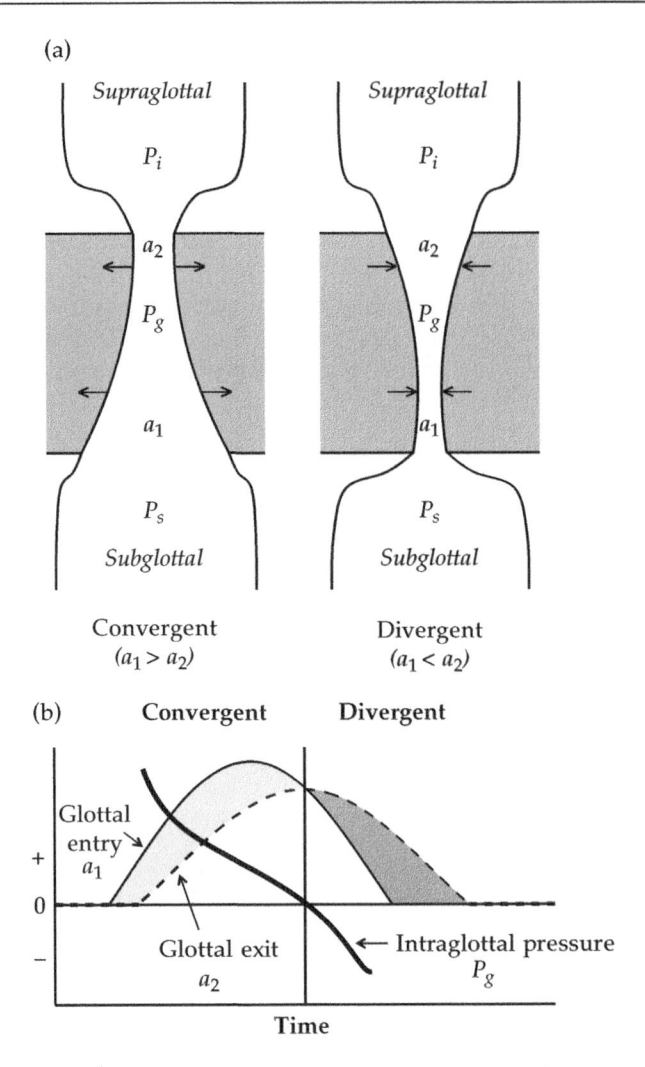

Figure 3.9 Demonstration of the vibration mechanism based on alternating convergent/divergent glottal shape. (a) Coronal view of the glottis and vocal folds in the convergent and divergent conditions. (b) Time-dependent glottal entry and exit areas superimposed with the intraglottal pressure.

lines, respectively. The portion of the cycle for which $a_1 > a_2$ is shown in light gray, whereas the $a_1 < a_2$ portion is shown in darker gray. The intraglottal pressure P_g calculated with Eqn. 2 is plotted as the thick black line (it has been scaled so that it can easily be compared to the glottal area signals) and can be seen to be positively-valued while the glottis is convergent and becomes negative during the time the glottis is divergent. Furthermore, P_g is highest when the vocal folds first separate and then decreases over the remainder of the cycle. This means that the intraglottal pressure provides a large "push" on the vocal fold surfaces during the time that they are beginning their lateral excursion, and then "gets out of the way" as they move toward their maximum displacement. On the return path, the reduced and negative intraglottal pressure may provide some assistance in accelerating the vocal folds toward the midline.

This asymmetric pattern of intraglottal pressure during the open glottis part of the vibratory cycle was confirmed by Jiang and Titze (1993) who measured P_g directly in an excised larynx in which one vocal fold was replaced with a plexiglas plate embedded with a pressure transducer. Scherer et al. (2001) and Li et al. (2006) have investigated the intraglottal pressure distributions for a wide variety of glottal configurations and found that driving pressures are correlated with angle of glottal convergence. Using both a synthetic, physical model of the vocal folds and a computational model, Thomson, Mongeau, and Frankel (2005) also showed that the variation of the glottal shape from convergence to divergence generates a temporal asymmetry in the mean intraglottal pressure.

3.5.2 *Inertance of the vocal tract*

The second mechanism that can create an asymmetric driving force on the vocal fold surfaces is due to the inertive or mass-like properties of the supraglottal air column (i.e., the vocal tract). To simplify the explanation, the alternating pattern of convergence and divergence will be removed and replaced with an assumed square glottis as shown in Figure 3.10a such that $a_1 = a_2$. Eqn. 3.2 now reduces to

$$P_g = P_i \tag{3.3}$$

suggesting that the vocal folds are driven by only the vocal tract input pressure P_i. This may seem like an odd result because the subglottal pressure, and hence the transglottal pressure, is *not* involved in sustaining the vibration of the folds. The airflow through the glottis (typically referred to as glottal flow or U_g), however, is driven by the transglottal pressure, thus involving P_s in generation of the airflow waveform. As the vocal fold surfaces move laterally the glottal flow increases, and decreases when they move medially (see Figure 3.10a). The input pressure P_i is then determined by the rate of change of the glottal flow (i.e., flow derivative) multiplied by the vocal tract inertance I

$$P_i = I \frac{dU_g}{dt} \tag{3.4}$$

For a cylindrical tube approximation of the vocal tract, the inertance can be calculated as

$$I = \frac{\rho l}{A} \tag{3.5}$$

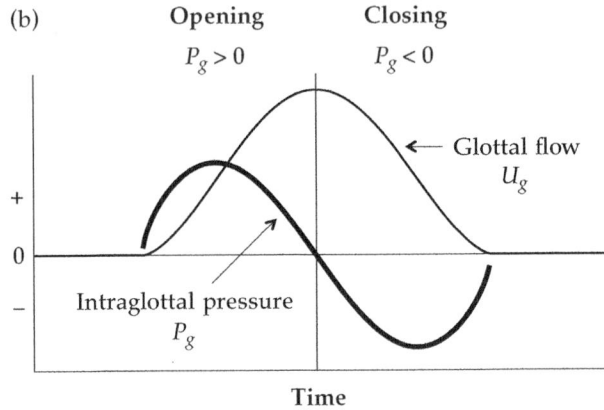

Figure 3.10 Demonstration of the vibration mechanism based on vocal tract inertance. (a) Coronal view of a rectangular glottis and vocal folds as they move laterally (left panel) and medially (right panel). (b) Time-dependent glottal airflow superimposed with the intraglottal pressure.

where ρl is air density, l is the length, and A is the cross-sectional area of the vocal tract.

As the glottal flow increases during the opening phase, the rate of change will be positive ($dU/dt > 0$) and will result in a positive value of P_i; during the closing phase the flow derivative is negative resulting in a negative P_i. Since the intraglottal pressure is equal to P_i, according to Eqn. 3.3, the vocal folds will be driven by positive pressure during the time they move laterally, and by negative pressure when they move medially. This can be seen in Figure 3.10b where a hypothetical glottal flow signal is shown by the thin line, and an idealized intraglottal pressure based on the flow derivative is shown by the thick line. Early in the opening phase P_g rises to a peak value and then decreases over most of the duration of the cycle. Much like the effect of the alternating convergence and divergence, the intraglottal pressure due to the vocal tract inertance provides a "push" at the early part of lateral excursion before decreasing and becoming negatively-valued to assist the return movement toward midline.

3.5.3 Two mechanisms in concert

For a real talker, the mechanisms of glottal convergence/divergence and vocal tract inertance are both more or less available whenever phonation is produced. Although it is a simplified version of the pressure calculation, Eqn. 1 includes the effects of both mechanisms: the glottal geometry is included in the first term and the vocal tract input pressure, determined by the rate of change of the flow, is included in both terms. It has been shown that either an alternating pattern of glottal convergence and divergence, or vocal tract inertance can create sufficient conditions for sustained vocal fold oscillation. The negative driving pressure observed in the glottal closing phase, regardless of the mechanism of vibration, appears similar to the "Bernoulli effect" explanation in which the vocal folds are "sucked" together. It is not necessary, however, for P_g to become negative during the return phase toward midline. In fact, flow tends to detach from the duct walls in a divergent configuration to form a jet, causing P_g to be roughly equal to the value of the vocal tract inlet pressure P_i (Titze 2006) which may be either positive or negative depending on the tract configuration. The important point is that the intraglottal pressure generated when the vocal fold motion is in the lateral direction must be greater than the intraglottal pressure on the return path, thus creating the necessary asymmetric driving force over a cycle of vibration. In contrast, the "Bernoulli effect" explanation would generate identical forces on both the lateral and medial portions of the glottal cycle, and could not sustain oscillation (i.e., the suction force would be present on both the lateral excursion and medial return paths of the cycle).

Both mechanisms operating simultaneously can be studied with a computational model that allows self-oscillation to be initiated and sustained. As an example, a three-mass model (Story and Titze 1995) can be used to include the effect of the cover-body vocal fold structure in which a "body" mass is positioned lateral to two masses representing the cover tissue (see Figure 3.11a). The cover masses are both connected to the body mass via spring and damper systems that

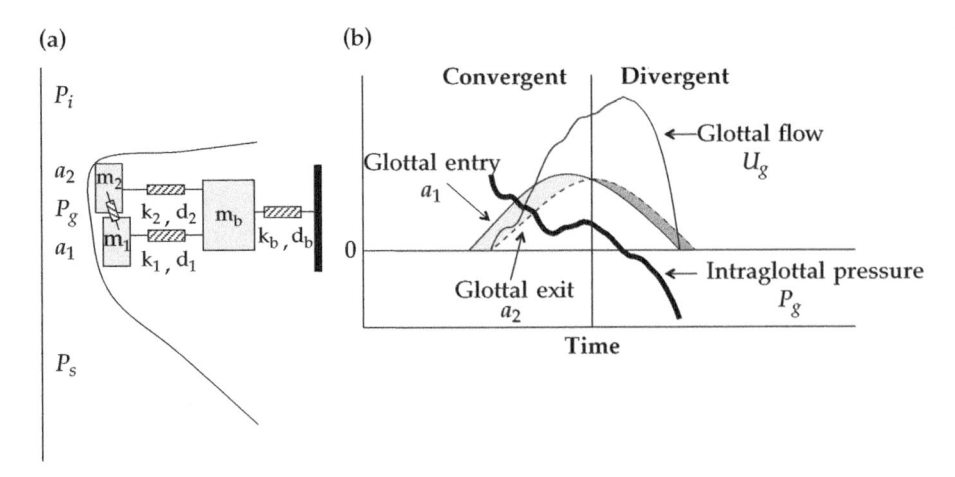

Figure 3.11 Demonstration of two vibration mechanisms in concert. (a) The three-mass model of the vocal folds (Story and Titze 1995) which represents the mucosal wave, lateral motion, coupling between the cover and body, and vocal tract inertance (when coupled to a vocal tract). (b) Time-dependent glottal entry and exit areas, and glottal airflow, superimposed with the intraglottal pressure.

represent stiffness of the cover tissue as well as the effective coupling stiffness between the body and cover. The body mass, in turn, is connected to a rigid lateral boundary with another spring and damper system. This accounts for the effective stiffness of the body which is dependent on the level of contraction of the muscle tissue. To account for shear forces in the cover, the two cover masses are coupled to each other with another spring-damper element. When coupled aerodynamically and acoustically to the tracheal airway on the subglottal side, and to the vocal tract on the supraglottal side (Titze 2002), the model can be (computationally) set into vibration.

With the vocal tract shape configured to be a uniform tube of cross-sectional area 3 cm² (not shown), the model produces the four quantities shown in Figure 3.11b for one cycle of vibration. The glottal entry and exit areas, a_1 and a_2, at the location of each of the two cover masses are again plotted such that the convergent and divergent phases of the cycle are apparent. The glottal flow, U_g, based on the minimum of a_1 and a_2 as well as P_s and $P_{i'}$ is shown as the thin line in Figure 3.11b. It rises slowly, and with ripple, to a peak before sharply decreasing; the delay in achieving peak flow relative to the temporal pattern of the glottal areas is due to the vocal tract inertance. The intraglottal pressure P_g, shown as the thick line, decreases over the course of the open glottis part of the cycle, but does contain some small peaks and valleys due to acoustic interaction with vocal tract resonances. In addition, P_g does *not* become negative at the point when the glottal shape switches from convergent to divergent as in Figure 3.9, but rather remains positive until the glottal flow reaches its peak value. Other configurations of the vocal tract may generate somewhat different patterns of U_g and P_g but, in any case, the important point is that the intraglottal pressure pattern over time is configured such that it pushes the tissue outward, and then decreases over the remainder of the cycle to allow it to return to the midline and start a new cycle. In addition, the build-up of the glottal flow to its peak value lags behind the peak in glottal area because of the time required to accelerate the air column of the vocal tract (Rothenberg 1981; Titze 1988).

This example points to an aspect of voice production that is sometimes overlooked. The delay of the peak glottal flow relative to the peak in glottal opening, and the presence of "ripple" on both the glottal flow and intraglottal pressure waveforms, indicates that the vocal tract and trachea can have a significant influence on the characteristics of the voice excitation signal itself. In fact, the ripple that can be observed on the opening phase of the glottal flow is essentially an imprint of the vocal tract resonances, and will thus contain spectral information from both the voice source and vocal tract. It is typical, however, to represent speech production as a linear combination of an excitation signal (i.e., glottal flow) and the vocal tract filter. A key assumption of a linear system approach is that the filter (i.e., the vocal tract and trachea) does not influence or modify the source, rather it can only enhance or suppress the amplitudes of the spectral components produced by the source. Although the effect of the vocal tract on the glottal flow has been recognized for a long time (cf. Fant 1979; Rothenberg 1981; Titze 1988, 2004; Titze and Story 1997), it is only recently that a *nonlinear source-filter theory* has been formally stated that explicitly addresses various types of nonlinear interaction of the voice production components and the vocal tract (Titze 2008). The theory defines a "Level 1" interaction as the dependency of the glottal flow pulse shape on subglottal and supraglottal acoustic pressures, and a "Level 2" interaction as the flow dependency (Level 1) plus the effects of vocal tract inertance on the mechanical modes of tissue vibration.

In light of this new theoretical view, it is perhaps most accurate to consider the mechanisms of vocal sound production as existing along a continuum. At one end of the continuum the sound generated by vocal fold vibration is weakly coupled to the resonances of the vocal tract such that the output is a linear combination of their respective acoustic characteristics, whereas at the other end there is strong nonlinear coupling of the vibratory source to the vocal tract resonances. To adequately express phonetic properties in the output, such as formants, the *linear* case requires that the vibratory source produce sound that is rich in either harmonic or broadband energy, or both. In contrast, the *nonlinear* case allows for the possibility of an harmonically rich source signal to be generated even when the vibration pattern of the vocal folds (e.g., glottal area) is so simple that it may contain only a few harmonics (Titze 2008).

3.5.4 Registers

The two mechanisms of oscillation contribute to any type of self-sustained vibratory motion of the vocal folds, but the actual tempo-spatial patterns of vibration produced can give rise to a variety of vocal qualities. One such quality descriptor is the *register* which, for speaking, typically refers to the *pulse, modal,* and *falsetto* registers (Hollien 1974). In general, the pulse register (also called vocal fry) is characterized as vibration with a very low fundamental frequency (<70 Hz; Keidar 1986) such that a listener hears each glottal cycle as a separate burst of energy. It may also include period doublings or irregularities. Production of such low frequencies would presumably require that the intrinsic laryngeal muscles be activated at fairly low levels to minimize the tension within the tissue layers (cf. Lowell and Story 2006). Most speech is typically produced in the modal register, which can be characterized as a sound that is continuous (not pulse-like) and harmonically rich. This is achieved when the vocal fold vibration causes the airflow through the glottis to rapidly decrease during the closing phase of each vibratory cycle; the example shown previously in Figure 3.8 would be characteristic of modal register. Falsetto register produces a vibratory pattern for which most of the acoustic energy is in the first few harmonic components, thus giving a "fluty" quality. Generally, falsetto occurs at fairly high fundamental frequencies and cut off of the glottal flow is less rapid than in modal register.

Although the terminology of registers is common in the literature on phonetics, speech science, and singing, there is much that is not known about how they are produced and perceived. For example, Titze (1994) presents two hypotheses concerning the transition from modal to falsetto registers. The first hypothesis suggests that the rapid change between registers, often referred to as a voice break, is influenced by the acoustic resonances of the subglottal system. The second, alternative hypothesis is that the transition is due to rapid decrease in activation of the thyroarytenoid muscle. Both are plausible, but need to be further tested with experimental and computational studies.

3.6 Computational models of phonation

The three-mass model used in the previous section is one of many models of vocal fold vibration that have been proposed throughout the past four decades or so. These range from simple to complex, and allow for investigations of various aspects of phonation.

One of the earliest computational models was reported by Flanagan and Landgraf (1968) in which the vocal fold tissue (of either the right or left side) was lumped into a single mass and allowed to have only lateral displacement. With its single-degree of freedom this model cannot represent the mucosal wave unless it is allowed a rotational degree of freedom (Liljencrants 1991; Titze and Story 2002). As a result, coupling to the acoustic inertance of the vocal tract is essential to create a condition where the tissue velocity and the intraglottal pressure are in phase and hence initiate and sustain oscillation.

Shortly after the introduction of the one-mass model, a slightly more complex version was proposed that represented a single vocal fold by two masses in the coronal (vertical) dimension (Ishizaka and Matsudaira 1972; Ishizaka and Flanagan 1972). The two degrees of freedom afforded by the two-mass model allow for the mucosal wave to be represented as well as overall lateral tissue displacement. While it is admittedly a crude discretization of the real tissue structure, it provides appropriate conditions for oscillation to occur with or without a coupled vocal tract inertance. Because of its simplicity and reasonable agreement with physiologic data, the two-mass model has been widely used in simulation/synthesis studies of vocal fold vibration (cf. Steinecke and Herzel 1995; Mergell, Herzel, and Titze 2000; Wong et al. 1991; Lucero 1996; Lucero and Koenig 2005). It is noted that a modified one-mass model has recently been described by Fulcher et al. (2006) and enhanced by Zanartu, Mongeau, and Wodicka (2007) that generates intraglottal pressure distributions similar to the two-mass model by imposing time-varying fluid dynamic considerations. Zanartu et al. (2007) utilized this model to study the effects of both the subglottal and supraglottal systems on vocal fold vibration.

A limitation of both the one-mass and two-mass models is that their discretization of tissue in the coronal plane does not capture the known layered structure of the vocal folds (Hirano 1974). In the two-mass model (Ishizaka and Flanagan 1972), the lower mass is made thicker (vertical dimension in the coronal plane) and more massive than the upper mass in an effort to simulate the effects of the body layer. However, since this arrangement does not allow for a coupled oscillation of both the cover and body layers, the two-mass model is essentially a "cover" model rather than a "cover–body" model. It was this limitation that motivated the introduction of a three-mass model (Story and Titze 1995) that was intended to include the effect of the cover- body vocal fold structure but also maintain the simplicity of a low–dimensional system. In addition to coupled oscillation of the cover and body layers, the advantage of the three-mass configuration is that physiologically realistic control parameters characterizing the cover and body tissue are more easily determined (than with the two-mass approach) when the discretization imposed by the model more closely follows anatomical boundaries. For example, a contraction of the thyroarytenoid muscle (muscle in the "body") will increase the stiffness of the body but may not necessarily stiffen the cover. Titze and Story (2002) developed an extensive set of "rules" that allow transformation of specified laryngeal muscle activation levels (primarily for the thyroarytenoid and cricothyroid muscles) to values of model parameters such as masses and stiffnesses.

Other more complex models have been developed to simulate the layered vocal fold structure and also account for the vibrational patterns in the transverse plane. For example, the two-mass approach was modified such that a single vocal fold could be represented by eight coupled transverse sections, each with two masses in the coronal plane that had both lateral and vertical degrees of freedom (Titze 1973, 1974). This model allows for simulation of the vibrational pattern of the vocal folds in both the coronal and traverse planes. Recently, Yang et al. (2010) described a lumped-element multi-mass model that permits motion in three dimensions, allowing for simulation of complex tissue trajectories. A further step up in computational complexity came with a continuum mechanics model (Titze and Talkin 1979) and a more recent finite-element model (Alipour, Berry, and Titze 2000) both of which provide a precise physiological and mechanical representation of the tissue layers of the vocal folds without lumping large anatomical regions into a few mass elements. Their large number of degrees of freedom allows for detailed study of the complex vibratory pattern observed in human vocal folds. Interestingly, however, these complex models, capable of producing many modal vibration patterns, have shown that vocal fold vibration is largely dominated by only two or three modes of vibrations (Berry and Titze 1996), similar to movement patterns shown in Figures 3.4 and 3.5. Thus, the lumped-element models seem to capture enough of the vibratory characteristics to serve as a useful research tool if fine detail is unnecessary.

The medial vocal fold surface configuration shown previously in Figure 3.3 is also representative of a type of computational model. It is not a self-oscillating system, but rather one in which the kinematic characteristics of vocal fold vibration can be imposed on the medial surfaces. That is, the translational and rotational components of vibration are driven at a prescribed fundamental frequency and amplitude, and results in a pattern of glottal opening and closing that is dependent on the settings of vocal fold adduction, bulging, length, and thickness (Titze 1984, 2006). When combined with aerodynamic and acoustic considerations similar to those of the self-oscillating models, glottal flow is produced in time-synchrony with the vibratory pattern. A kinematic model is useful for relating physiologic aspects of voice production to both acoustic output and perception by listeners because the parameters of the model can be precisely controlled. For example, Samlan and Story (2011) recently reported a study in which variations of the medial surface parameters were related to acoustic measures often used to characterize *breathiness*. Samlan (2012) has taken this a step farther and studied the effects of left–right vibratory asymmetries on characteristics of glottal flow, acoustic output, and perceptual response.

3.7 Summary

The vocal folds are soft tissue structures contained within the cartilaginous framework of the larynx, and serve as the primary generator of sound for vowels as well as a pressure controller for many consonants. Their location in the neck and their function of generating and controlling sound makes the vocal folds the natural point of division between the subglottal and supraglottal airways. When adducted, motion of the vocal fold tissue is initiated and sustained over time by the *steady* air flow and pressure supplied by the lower respiratory system. The tissue motion is characterized by a translational component that captures the medial/lateral excursion, and a rotational component that produces an alternating pattern of glottal convergence and divergence (i.e., mucosal wave). The convergence and divergence of the glottis, as well as the inertive characteristics of the supraglottal vocal tract, are both mechanisms that facilitate vocal fold vibration by assuring that the intraglottal driving pressure is in phase with the tissue velocity. Once in vibration, the vocal folds effectively convert the steady air flow from the lungs into a series of flow pulses by periodically opening and closing the air space between the vocal folds, thus providing the excitation of the vocal tract. The acoustic resonances of the vocal tract and trachea, however, can influence the production of the glottal flow signal itself, suggesting that speech is produced by a nonlinear interaction of the voice source and airway resonances.

Although much has been learned about the mechanisms of voice production, most of our knowledge has been, largely by necessity, derived from experiments and modeling studies that treat the vocal folds as an independent generator of sound. Future research needs to be directed toward an understanding of vocal fold vibration as an interactive component of the speech production system as a whole, and on time scales representative of words, phrases, and sentences. For example, more needs to be known about how vibration is initiated and sustained for the brief periods of time between production of consonants during connected speech. This may involve investigating the characteristics of an abduction/adduction maneuver that allows for both optimal production of a stop consonant and start-up of vocal fold vibration for a following vowel, or finding out what effects tissue characteristics and muscle activation levels have on vocal fold vibration during a vocal tract occlusion as in production of a voiced stop or fricative. There is also much yet to be understood about how the nonlinear interaction of the vocal folds and the vocal tract contribute to connected speech. Perhaps such an interaction is more important in children's speech production systems than for adults. Finally, there are many future studies that need be carried out to aid in understanding voice disorders and possible treatments. Experiments and simulation studies of vocal fold lesions, tissue scarring, asymmetric vocal fold vibration due to paralysis, neurological influences such as tremor, and therapeutic interventions are all needed to further our knowledge of human voice production.

NOTE

1 This work was supported by grants R01 DC04789 and R01 DC011275 from the National Institutes on Deafness and Other Communication Disorders.

REFERENCES

Alipour, Fariborz, David A. Berry, and Ingo R. Titze. 2000. A finite-element model of vocal fold vibration. *Journal of the Acoustical Society of America* 108(6): 3003–3012.

Baer, Thomas. 1975. Investigation of phonation using excised larynges. PhD dissertation, Massachusetts Institute of Technology.

Berry, David A. 2001. Mechanisms of model and nonmodal phonation. *Journal of Phonetics* 29: 431–450.

Berry, David A. and Ingo R. Titze. 1996. Normal modes in a continuum model of vocal fold tissues. *Journal of the Acoustical Society of America* 100: 3345–3354.

Berry, David A., Douglas W. Montequin, and Niro Tayama. 2001. High-speed digital imaging of the medial surface of the vocal folds. *Journal of the Acoustical Society of America* 110(5): 2539–2547.

Doellinger, Michael and David A. Berry. 2006. Visualization and quantification of the medial surface dynamics of an excised human vocal fold during phonation. *Journal of Voice* 20(3): 401–413.

Doellinger, Michael, David A. Berry, and Gerald S. Berke. 2005. Medial surface dynamics of an in vivo canine vocal fold during phonation. *Journal of the Acoustical Society of America* 117(5): 3174–3183.

Druker, David. 1999. Vocal fold kinematics of voice types: Data and modeling. PhD dissertation, University of Iowa.

Fant, Gunnar. 1960. *The Acoustic Theory of Speech Production*. Paris: Mouton.

Fant, Gunnar. 1979. Glottal source and excitation analysis. *Speech Transmission Laboratory Quarterly Progress and Status Reports* 20(1): 85–107.

Flanagan, James L. 1968. Source-system interaction in the vocal tract. *Annals of the New York Academy of Sciences* 155: 9–17.

Flanagan, James L. and Lorinda Landgraf. 1968. Self-oscillating source for vocal tract synthesizers. *IEEE Transactions on Audio Electroacoustics* AU-16: 57–64.

Fourcin, Adrian J. and Evelyn Abberton. 1971. First applications of a new laryngograph. *Medical and Biological Illustration* 21(3): 172–182.

Fulcher, Lewis P., Ronald C. Scherer, Artem Melnykov, Vesela Gateva, and Mark E. Limes. 2006. Negative Coulomb damping, limiting cycles, and self-oscillation of the vocal folds. *American Journal of Physics* 74(5): 386–393.

Henrich, Nathalie, Christophe d'Alessandro, Boris Doval, and Michele Castellengo. 2004. On the use of the derivative of electroglottographic signals for characterization of nonpathological phonation. *Journal of the Acoustical Society of America* 115(3): 1321–1332.

Henrich, Nathalie, Christophe d'Alessandro, Boris Doval and Michele Castellengo. 2005. Glottal open quotient in singing: Measurements and correlation with laryngeal mechanisms, vocal intensity, and fundamental frequency. *Journal of the Acoustical Society of America* 117(3): 1417–1430.

Hirano, Minoru. 1974. Morphological structure of the vocal cord as a vibrator and its variations. *Folia Phoniatrica* 26: 89–94.

Hixon, Thomas J., Gary Weismer, and Jeannette D. Hoit. 2008. *Preclinical Speech Science: Anatomy, Physiology, Acoustics, Perception*. San Diego, CA: Plural.

Hollien, Harry. 1974. On vocal registers. *Journal of Phonetics* 2: 125–143.

Hollien, Harry and G. Paul Moore. 1968. Stroboscopic laminography of the larynx during phonation. *Acta Oto-laryngologica* 65: 209–215.

Ishizaka, Kenzo and James L. Flanagan. 1972. Synthesis of voiced sounds from a two-mass model of the vocal cords. *Bell Systems Technical Journal* 51(6): 1233–1268.

Ishizaka, Kenzo and M. Matsudaira. 1972. *Fluid Mechanical Considerations of Vocal Cord Vibration*. Santa Barbara, CA: Speech Communications Research Laboratory.

Jiang, Jack Jiaqi and Ingo R. Titze. 1993. A methodological study of hemilaryngeal phonation. *Laryngoscope* 103: 872–882.

Keidar, Anat. 1986. Vocal register change: An investigation of perceptual and acoustic isomorphism. PhD dissertation, University of Iowa.

Li, Sheng, Ronald C. Scherer, MingXi Wan, SuPin Wang, and HuiHui Wu. 2006. The effect of glottal angle on intraglottal pressure. *Journal of the Acoustical Society of America* 119(1): 539–548.

Liljencrants, Johan. 1991. A translating and rotating mass model of the vocal folds. *Speech Transmission Laboratory Quarterly Progress and Status Reports* 32(1): 1–18.

Lowell, Soren Y. and Brad H. Story. 2006. Simulated effects of cricothyroid and thyroarytenoid muscle activation on adult-male vocal fold vibration. *Journal of the Acoustical Society of America* 120(1): 386–397.

Lucero, Jorge C. 1996. Chest- and falsetto-like oscillations in a two-mass model of the vocal folds. *Journal of the Acoustical Society of America* 100(5): 3355–3359.

Lucero, Jorge C. and Laura L. Koenig. 2005. Simulations of temporal patterns of oral airflow in men and women using a two-mass model of the vocal folds under dynamic control. *Journal of the Acoustical Society of America* 117(3): 1362–1372.

Mergell, Patrick, Hanspeter Herzel, and Ingo R. Titze. 2000. Irregular vocal-fold vibration: High-speed observation and modeling. *Journal of the Acoustical Society of America* 108(6): 2996–3002.

Moore, Paul, 1991. A short history of laryngeal investigation. *Journal of Voice* 5(3): 266–281.

Orlikoff, Robert F. 1991. Assessment of the dynamics of vocal fold contact from the electroglottogram: Data from normal male subjects. *Journal of Speech and Hearing Research* 34: 1066–1072.

Rothenberg, Martin. 1973. A new inverse-filtering technique for deriving the glottal airflow waveform during voicing. *Journal of the Acoustical Society of America* 53: 1632–1645.

Rothenberg, Martin. 1981. Acoustic interaction between the glottal source and the vocal tract. In Kenneth N. Stevens and Minoru Hirano (eds.), *Vocal Fold Physiology*, 305–328. Tokyo: University of Tokyo Press.

Rothenberg, Martin and James M. Mahshie. 1988. Monitoring vocal fold abduction through vocal fold contact area. *Journal of Speech and Hearing Research* 31: 338–351.

Samlan, Robin A. 2012. Kinematic modeling of asymmetric vocal fold vibration. PhD dissertation, University of Arizona.

Samlan, Robin A. and Brad H. Story. 2011. Relation of structural and vibratory kinematics of the vocal folds to two acoustic measures of breathy voice based on computational modeling. *Journal of Speech, Language, and Hearing Research* 54(5): 1267–1283.

Scherer, Ronald C., Daoud Shinwari, Kenneth J. DeWitt, Chao Zhang, Bogdan R. Kucinschi, and Abdollah A. Afjeh. 2001. Intraglottal pressure profiles for a symmetric and oblique glottis with a divergence angle of 10 degrees. *Journal of the Acoustical Society of America* 109(4): 1616–1630.

Sonneson, Bertil. 1959. A method for studying the vibratory movements of the vocal cords: A preliminary report. *Journal of Laryngology and Otology* 73: 732–737.

Steinecke, Ina and Hanspeter Herzel. 1995. Bifurcations in an asymmetric vocal-fold model. *Journal of the Acoustical Society of America* 97(3): 1874–1884.

Stevens, Kenneth N. 1977. Physics of laryngeal behavior and larynx modes. *Phonetica* 34: 264–279.

Story, Brad H. and Ingo R. Titze. 1995. Voice simulation with a body-cover model of the vocal folds. *Journal of the Acoustical Society of America* 97(2): 1249–1260.

Thomson, Scott L., Luc Mongeau, and Steven H. Frankel. 2005. Aerodynamic transfer of energy to the vocal folds. *Journal of the Acoustical Society of America* 118(3): 1689–1700.

Titze, Ingo R. 1973. The human vocal cords: A mathematical model, part I. *Phonetica* 28: 129–170.

Titze, Ingo R. 1974. The human vocal cords: A mathematical model, part II. *Phonetica* 29: 1–21.

Titze, Ingo R. 1976. On the mechanics of vocal fold vibration. *Journal of the Acoustical Society of America* 60: 1366–1380.

Titze, Ingo R. 1983. Mechanisms of sustained oscillation of the vocal folds. In Ingo R. Titze and Ronald C. Scherer (eds.), *Vocal Fold Physiology: Biomechanics, Acoustics, and Phonatory Control*, 349–357. Denver, CO: Denver Center for the Performing Arts.

Titze, Ingo R. 1984. Parameterization of the glottal area, glottal flow, and vocal fold contact area. *Journal of the Acoustical Society of America* 75(2): 570–580.

Titze, Ingo R. 1988. The physics of small amplitude oscillation of the vocal folds. *Journal of the Acoustical Society of America* 83(4): 1536–1552.

Titze, Ingo R. 1994. *Principles of Voice Production.* Englewood Cliffs, NJ: Prentice Hall.

Titze, Ingo R. 2002. Regulating glottal airflow in phonation: Application of the maximum power transfer theorem to a low dimensional phonation model. *Journal of the Acoustical Society of America* 111(1): 367–376.

Titze, Ingo R. 2004. A theoretical study of F0–F1 interaction with application to resonant speaking and singing voice. *Journal of Voice* 18(3): 292–298.

Titze, Ingo R. 2006. *The Myoelastic Aerodynamic Theory of Phonation.* Iowa City, IA: National Center for Voice and Speech.

Titze, Ingo R. 2008. Nonlinear source-filter coupling in phonation: Theory. *Journal of the Acoustical Society of America* 123(5): 2733–2749.

Titze, Ingo R. and Brad H. Story. 1997. Acoustic interactions of the voice source with the lower vocal tract. *Journal of the Acoustical Society of America* 101(4): 2234–2243.

Titze, Ingo R. and Brad H. Story. 2002. Rules for controlling low-dimensional vocal fold models with muscle activation. *Journal of the Acoustical Society of America* 112(3): 1064–1076.

Titze, Ingo R. and David T. Talkin. 1979. A theoretical study of the effects of various laryngeal configurations on the acoustics of phonation. *Journal of the Acoustical Society of America* 66: 60–74.

Van den Berg, Janwillem. 1958. Myoelastic-aerodynamic theory of voice production. *Journal of Speech and Hearing Research* 1: 227–244.

Wong, Darrell, Mabo R. Ito, Neil B. Cox, and Ingo R. Titze. 1991. Observation of perturbations in a lumped-element model of the vocal folds with application to some pathological cases. *Journal of the Acoustical Society of America* 89(1): 383–394.

Yang, Anxiong, Jorg Lohscheller, David A. Berry, Stefan Becker, Ulrich Eysholdt, Daniel Voigt, and Michael Dollinger. 2010. Biomechanical modeling of the three-dimensional aspects of human vocal fold dynamics. *Journal of the Acoustical Society of America* 127(2): 1014–1031.

Zanartu, Matias, Luc Mongeau, and George R. Wodicka. 2007. Influence of acoustic loading on an effective single mass model of the vocal folds. *Journal of the Acoustical Society of America* 121(2): 1119–1129.

Zemlin, Willard. 1959. A comparison of a high-speed cinematographic and a transillumination photo-conductive technique in the study of the glottis during voice production. Master's thesis, University of Minnesota.

Zemlin, Willard. 1998. *Speech and Hearing Science: Anatomy and Physiology*, 4th edn. Needham Heights, MA: Allyn and Bacon.

4 Supralaryngeal Articulators in the Oropharyngeal Region

KIYOSHI HONDA

4.1 Introduction

Speech production in humans largely relies on changes in the supralaryngeal airway, called the vocal tract, to create the phonetic quality of speech sounds. The changing shape of the vocal tract is due to physiological functions of the supralaryngeal articulators. This chapter first describes the anatomy and function of these articulators in the oropharyngeal region (section 4.2), and then outlines a few basics of vocal-tract shape in relation to speech spectra (section 4.3).

The supralaryngeal articulators constitute an integrated motor system for speech production, which is so unique that it cannot be accounted for by simple analogy to other motor systems and is thus resistant to simulation by computers or mimicry by robotics. The uniqueness of the system is due to several reasons including that the motor organs for speech are comprised mainly of muscle, their primary role is to regulate vocal-tract resonance, and their movements are difficult to visualize. This uniqueness has led to the specialized study of speech production. Speech researchers have invented instruments for the observation of speech movement to interpret the structure–function relationship between movement and the acoustic realization processes and to test hypotheses regarding this relationship in experiments and through simulations. In recent years, three-dimensional visualization techniques have been used to reexamine the acoustic function of the supralaryngeal articulators with a few interesting results. In this chapter, a contemporary vision of the articulators is attempted by exploring in detail the anatomy and physiology of the tongue and pharynx. This exploration is followed by notes on recent efforts toward physiological modeling.

Movements of the supralaryngeal articulators affect the shape of the vocal tract from the glottis to the lips. This airway, which excludes the nasal cavity, is often called the main vocal tract. Since the eighteenth century, it has been known that

---

The Handbook of Speech Production, First Edition. Edited by Melissa A. Redford.
© 2015 John Wiley & Sons, Inc. Published 2019 by John Wiley & Sons, Inc.

vocal tract shaping is a key to understanding the acoustic stage of speech production, especially vowel production. Early studies resulted in a debate regarding theories on vowel production that persisted into the twentieth century (Fletcher, 1929). In the middle of the twentieth century, Chiba and Kajiyama (1942) employed state-of-art instruments to reach two solid conclusions regarding vowel production: the vowel acoustics are determined by vocal-tract shape, and vowel spectra can be calculated from vocal-tract area function. Their foundational work stimulated speech research in 1950s (Dunn 1950; Stevens, Kasowski, and Fant 1953), ultimately giving rise to the modern source-filter theory, further developed by Fant (1960) into the acoustic theory of speech production.

Modern acoustic theory continues to focus on vowels. But this has meant that the shape of the vocal tract is often simplified in concept so that it can be modeled as a uniaxial tube for linear transmission of sound. In practice, the vocal tract is not only a vowel emitter but also a generator of voice quality and of the unique characteristics of an individual's speech. In light of these additional characteristics, classical views of the vocal tract need to be updated to reveal speech production processes as a whole. In this chapter, the acoustic role of the vocal tract in speech production is reviewed with a few new observations incorporated from visualization studies of the vocal tract.

4.2 Oropharyngeal articulators

The supralaryngeal articulators include organs comprised of muscle (tongue, lips, velum, and pharyngeal wall) and of rigid structures (upper and lower jaws, teeth, palate, hyoid bone, and cervical spine). The muscles in the region are characterized by their unique functions in tissue deformation, resulting not only in changes to muscle length but also in changes to muscle thickness by virtue of muscle shortening. The rigid structures provide a foundation for the muscles, limit the extent of tissue deformation, and define the remainder of the cavity spaces. This section describes the anatomy of the tongue and pharynx involved in the control of speech articulation. Other components of supralaryngeal articulation are described elsewhere in this volume.

4.2.1 *The tongue and its muscles*

The tongue is often called "the hand in the mouth," not only for its skilled movements but also for its phylogenetic origins, which parallel that of the hand muscles. The tongue is an organ composed entirely of muscle with no rigid effecters. Tissue deformation is accomplished by a muscular network, which provides the basis of articulatory movement of the tongue. The human tongue is grossly fungiform with a stem and hat. Its volume is roughly about 100 cm^3 with large individual variation. The size of the tongue is not always proportional to the size of the oral and

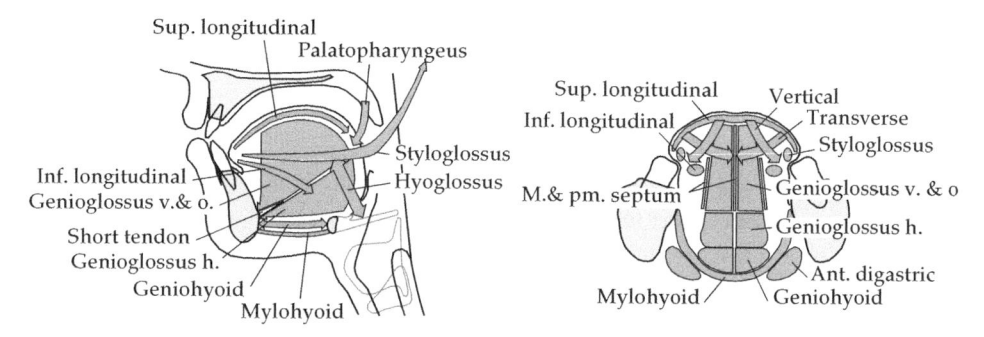

Figure 4.1 Schematic drawing of the extrinsic, intrinsic, and floor muscles of the tongue in sagittal (left) and coronal (right) views.

pharyngeal cavities, which results in a certain articulatory idiosyncrasy: tongue body movement during speech tends to be more rapid and distant for the microlingual cases than for the macrolingual ones. The tongue is conventionally divided into three parts: the base (bottom part), body (upper round part) and blade (free anterior part). The tongue tissue is composed of the mucosal layer, muscles, fibrous tissues, and salivary glands. The tongue surface is covered by a layer of numerous papillae on the oral surface and by adenoid tissue on the pharyngeal surface. The ventral surface of the blade includes the fraenum, sublingual ridge, and orifices of the ducts of the salivary glands.

The muscles of the tongue play a central role in realizing speech articulation by their combined actions. Figure 4.1 illustrates the extrinsic, intrinsic, and floor muscles of the tongue with arrow patterns that represent their functional interpretations. Table 4.1 and Table 4.2 list an anatomical summary of those muscles with divisions of the muscles, their origins, insertions, and functions. The anatomical literature on the tongue is abundant, and descriptions largely agree for the muscles (Abd-el-Malek 1939; Takemoto 2001) with some differences in detail (e.g., the origin of the inferior longitudinal muscle). The tongue muscles are separated by fibrous tissues that include three septa (median, paramedian, and lateral) and a tendon (short tendon of the tongue). They are anatomical landmarks used to identify the muscles or subdivisions.

The tongue has two connections to bony structures, the mandible and hyoid bone. The hyoid bone is a U-shaped bone composed of three parts: the body, greater horn, and lesser horn. The body is located at the posterior corner of the tongue base and anchored by the supra- and infra-hyoid muscles. The hyoid bone supports the tongue base, provides muscle attachments, suspends the thyroid cartilage, connects the epiglottis, and maintains the shape of the pharyngeal cavity. The hyoid bone is advanced by the protractor muscles such as the genioglossus and geniohyoid muscles when producing high vowels or high-pitched voices (Honda 1983). This protraction force is counterbalanced by the middle constrictor muscle. Reciprocal vertical movement of the hyoid bone and the mandible has been observed during speech (Westbury 1988).

Table 4.1 Extrinsic and intrinsic tongue muscles: origin, insertion, and function.

	Origin	Insertion	Function
Genioglossus	**Horizontal part** from the lower surface of the short tendon of the tongue; **oblique** and **vertical parts** from the upper surface of the short tendon	**Horizontal part** toward the pharyngeal surface of the tongue; **oblique** and **vertical parts** toward the oral surface along the midline	Protractor of the back tongue, compressor of the mid tongue, and depressor of the front tongue
Styloglossus	From the anterior and lateral surface of the styloid process and the stylomandibular ligament	**Posterior (extralingual) part** to the side of the tongue; **anterior (intralingual) part** to the tongue tip	Retractor of the tongue
Hyoglossus	**Ceratoglossal** and **basioglossal parts** from the greater horn and the body of the hyoid bone; **chondroglossal part** from the lesser horn and the body	To the side of the tongue blending with the styloglossus and inferior longitudinal, with the anterior fibers reaching the tongue tip	Depressor of the tongue
Palatoglossus	From the anterior surface of the velum	To the sides of the tongue	Depressor of the velum
Sup. longitudinal	From the submucous layer of the tongue base	To the submucous layer of the tongue tip	Retractor and elevator of the tongue tip
Inf. longitudinal	From the fibrous tissue near the tongue base	To the submucous layer of the tongue tip	Retractor and depressor of the tongue tip
Transverse	From the median fibrous septum	To the lateral margin of the tongue (superior to the inferior longitudinal)	Transverse contractor of the tongue
Vertical	From the submucous layer of the tongue tip and dorsum	To the submucous layer of the ventral surface of the tongue	Transverse expander of the tongue

Table 4.2 Oral floor and suprahyoid muscles: origin, insertion, and function.

	Origin	Insertion	Function
Geniohyoid	From the inferior mental spine on the inner surface of the mandible	To the anterior surface of the body of the hyoid bone	Protractor of the hyoid bone and depressor of the mandible
Mylohyoid	From the mylohyoid line along the inner surface of the mandible	**Anterior part** to the median raphe; **posterior part** to the body of the hyoid bone	Elevator of the tongue floor
Stylohyoid	From the styloid process of the temporal bone	To the greater horn of the hyoid bone	Elevator of the hyoid bone
Digastric	**Anterior part** from the mandible; **posterior part** from the mastoid process of the temporal bone	Both parts to the intermediate tendon near the lesser horn of the hyoid bone	Depressor of the mandible and elevator of the hyoid bone

4.2.1.1 Extrinsic tongue muscles The extrinsic tongue muscles are defined as a group of muscles that arise from external bony structures and insert into the soft tissue of the tongue. According to this definition, the palatoglossus muscle should be considered one of the extrinsic muscles of the tongue even though its function and innervation differ from others. Instead, following its function and innervation, the palatoglossus is better regarded as one of the velar muscles. The exclusion of the palatoglossus suggests that the extrinsic muscles are better defined by function than by anatomy.

The *genioglossus* (GG) is the largest muscle in the tongue. Its muscle fibers radiate from the mandible to a wide area of the tongue surface. Anatomically, this is a triangular muscle, attached by the short tendon of the tongue, which roots on the superior genial tubercle of the mandible and supplies fiber attachments to the muscle (see also section 4.2.3.1). The muscle fibers arising from the inferior aspect of the short tendon run almost horizontally toward the posterior tongue surface (referred to as GGh), and those arising from the superior aspect run obliquely and vertically spreading toward the tongue dorsum along the midline (referred to as GGo and GGv, respectively). The GGh also plays a role as an anterior pharyngeal dilator by advancing the pharyngeal surface of the tongue.

The *styloglossus* (SG) travels a long course from the styloid process on the skull base to enter the side of the tongue near the tonsillar bed and further advances to the tongue apex. The SG also sends a branch toward the hyoid bone.

The bilateral segments of the intralingual part of the SG form anterior and posterior slings of fibers that meet together at the midline. It is assumed that the anterior sling retracts the tongue tip or blade to bunch up the tissue behind, while the posterior sling draws the tongue body backward. (See section 4.2.3.2 for detail.)

The *hyoglossus* (HG) is a flat muscle that arises from the hyoid bone vertically along the side of the tongue, and it runs beneath the dorsal surface toward the midline. The HG lowers the tongue body by pulling down the side of the tongue. Its anterior fibers run parallel with the anterior fibers of the SG, possibly cooperating as a retractor of the tongue blade.

4.2.1.2 *Intrinsic tongue muscles* The intrinsic tongue muscles are four muscles located entirely within the tongue tissue: the superior longitudinal, inferior longitudinal, transverse, and vertical. It is common to note that, while the extrinsic muscles serve to position the tongue, the function of the intrinsic tongue muscles is to deform the shape of the tongue. Nonetheless, such dichotomy of functional difference between the extrinsic and intrinsic tongue muscles may not be realistic (Schwenk 2001).

The *superior longitudinal* (SL) runs beneath the oral and pharyngeal surfaces of the tongue. The SL has short range fibers that overlap with each other to form a long and wide muscle sheath. The function of this sheath possibly varies from region to region. It is clear, though, that the anterior part of the SL elevates the tip and sides of the tongue. The *inferior longitudinal* (IL), a short band of muscle running near the inferior tongue surface, also serves to retracts the tongue tip and to curl it inferiorly.

The *transverse* (T) radiates from the median fibrous septum to the side of the tongue. The anterior part of this muscle helps to depress the oral surface of the tongue. By contrast, the anterior part of the *vertical* (V), which altogether spans from the dorsum to the lateral inferior surface of the tongue, helps to elevate the oral surface of the tongue. Both muscles together compress the tongue tissue to advance the tongue tip.

4.2.1.3 *Oral floor and suprahyoid muscles* Two muscles form the floor of the mouth: the geniohyoid lies immediately below the tongue, and the mylohyoid covers the oral floor. These muscles are surrounded by two other suprahyoid muscles: the digastric and stylohyoid.

The *geniohyoid* (GH) is a narrow muscle that connects the mandibular symphysis and hyoid bone anteroposteriorly. The GH functions to lower the mandible for a wide jaw opening, and to protract the hyoid bone for increasing voice fundamental frequency. The muscle is also an anterior pharyngeal dilator. The *mylohyoid* (MH) is a muscle sheath spreading left to right like a basket to hold the tongue. The MH is convex in the coronal view, supporting the oral floor when the tongue makes contact with the palate during the articulation of palatal or velar consonants.

The *digastric* is two fleshy portions of muscle called the anterior belly of the digastric (ABD) and the posterior belly of the digastric (PBD), which are united by the intermediate tendon. The tendon is connected with the hyoid bone by a loop of fascia, by which the two bellies function as an active jaw opener in speech articulation. The *stylohyoid* (SH) is a long slender muscle that is thought to elevate the hyoid bone while constricting the pharynx.

4.2.2 Pharyngeal wall

The geometry of the pharyngeal wall is largely determined by the muscles located in the pharynx wall. Although conventional lateral or midsagittal views of the speech organs demonstrate no dramatic changes of the pharynx during speech, transverse motion images obtained by cine-MRI elucidate rapid changes of the pharyngeal cavity, repeatedly expanding during inhalation and constricting during utterances. Given this active expansion and constriction of the pharynx during speech, the pharyngeal wall can be regarded as an independent articulatory organ. However, the actions of the pharyngeal wall have not been well explored. Further research is needed to explore their roles during speech. In this section, the muscular components that control the pharyngeal wall are briefly described with reference to the constrictor muscles and to the internal muscles (see Figure 4.2 and Table 4.3).

4.2.2.1 Pharyngeal constrictor muscles The pharyngeal constrictor muscles are a group of muscles that surround the entire pharynx in a semicircular fashion. They are divided into three parts by their position within the pharynx: the superior, middle, and inferior constrictor muscles. The muscles overlap with each other

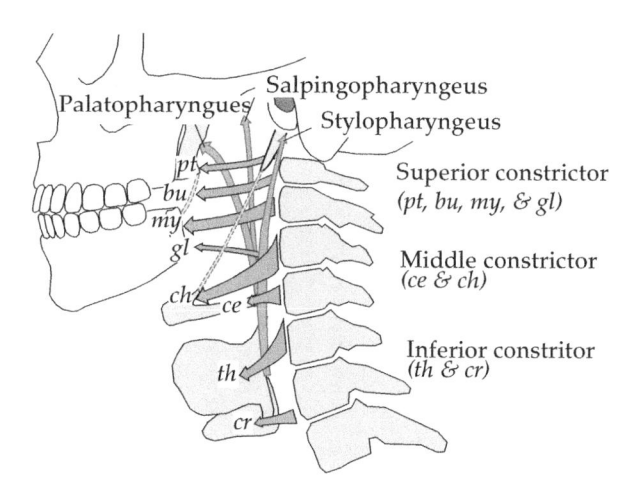

Figure 4.2 Pharyngeal constrictor and internal pharyngeal muscles. Four parts of the superior constrictor are pterygopharyngeal (pt); buccopharyngeal (bu); mylopharyngeal (my); and glossopharyngeal (gl). Parts of the middle constrictor are ceratopharyngeal (ce); and chondropharyngeal (ch). Parts of the inferior constrictor are thyropharyngeal (th); and cricopharyngeal (cr).

Table 4.3 Pharyngeal constrictor and internal pharyngeal muscles: origin, insertion, and function.

	Origin	Insertion	Functions
Sup. Constrictor	Four parts from the post-sphenoidal region (**pterygopharyngeal** and **buccopharyngeal parts**) and the mandibular region (**mylopharyngeal** and **glossopharyngeal parts**)	To the median raphe of the pharynx and pharyngeal tubercle	Constrictor of the velopharyngeal port
Mid. Constrictor	Two parts from the hyoid bone and ligaments (**ceratopharyngeal** and **chondropharyngeal parts**)	To the median raphe of the pharynx	Elevator and retractor of the hyoid bone
Inf. Constrictor	Two parts from the laryngeal cartilages (**thyropharyngeal** and **cricopharyngeal parts**)	To the median raphe of the pharynx	Elevator of the thyroid cartilage
Stylo-pharyngeus	From the medial side of the base of the styloid process	To the pharyngeal submucosa and the rear border of the thyroid cartilage	Elevator of the larynx and dilator of the pharynx
Palato-pharyngeus	From the posterior margin of the hard palate and the palatine aponeurosis of the soft palate	**Longitudinal part** to the rear border of the thyroid cartilage and the hypopharyngeal submucosa; **transverse part** to the midline at the pharyngeal isthmus	Elevator of the larynx and depressor of the velum
Salpingo-pharyngeus	From the inferior part of the cartilage of the Eustachian tube	To the posterior fasciculus of the palatopharyngeus muscle	Elevator of the larynx and opener of the Eustachian tube

such that the edges of each are nestled into the other with the superior constrictor being innermost and the inferior one outermost.

The *superior pharyngeal constrictor* controls the size of the opening of the velopharyngeal port from the sides, which assists in velopharyngeal closure. The upper (pterygopharyngeal) part of this muscle sometimes produces a bulge on the posterior wall near the velopharyngeal port, called Passavant's ridge.

The *middle pharyngeal constrictor* radiates widely from the hyoid bone to the pharyngeal wall. This muscle not only constricts the pharynx, but also retracts the hyoid bone functioning as an antagonist to the protractor muscles of the hyoid bone.

The *inferior pharyngeal constrictor* narrows the hypopharyngeal cavity during glottal constriction gestures in speech (e.g., initial or final glottalization, whispering, etc.), and its cricopharyngeal part is a sphincter of the esophageal entrance.

4.2.2.2 Internal pharyngeal muscles The internal pharyngeal muscles are a group of muscles that descend vertically along the entire pharynx. As a group, they are thought to elevate the larynx and shorten the pharynx. Each also has its own function related to its attachment points.

The *stylopharyngeus* passes between the superior and middle constrictor muscles and can be a lateral dilator of the pharynx because of its oblique course from the styloid process. The *palatopharyngeus* forms the palatopharyngeal arch behind the palatine tonsils and is thought to narrow the pharynx at the fauces and lower the velum. The *salpingopharyngeus* opens the entrance of the auditory tube by its contraction.

4.2.3 Physiological models of articulation

Computational modeling of articulatory movement has been attempted by many researchers for a variety of purposes including to better understand phonetic realization (Fujimura and Kakita 1979), the physics of soft tissue and muscle movement (Wilhelms-Tricarico 1995), or neuromuscular control (Perkell 1996; Gérard et al. 2003), as well as to improve speech synthesis (Dang and Honda 2001) or clinical evaluation of articulatory disorders (Fujita et al. 2007). Physiologically-based articulatory modeling requires a broad knowledge of the precise anatomy of articulatory organs and realistic muscle functions, knowledge of the neuromuscular organization in the peripheral and central nervous system, and an understanding of the best computational techniques for modeling. There are three main types of articulatory models: the geometrical model that determines vocal-tract shapes from arbitrary changes in the position of articulatory organs (Rubin, Baer, and Mermelstein 1981), the statistical model that is based on the analysis of articulatory relevant components from observation of vocal tract motions (Harshman, Ladefoged, and Goldstein 1977; Maeda 1990), and the physiological model that simulates the process from muscle contraction to speech articulation (Perkell 1996), and which is aimed at generating vocal-tract shapes to synthesize dynamic characteristics of speech sounds due to coarticulation. This section comments on some common problems or misinterpretations of tongue anatomy found in existing articulatory models. The goal is to encourage modeling improvements based on a more complete analysis of the muscles in question.

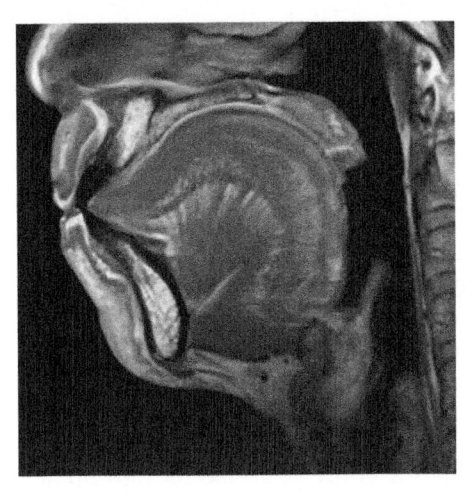

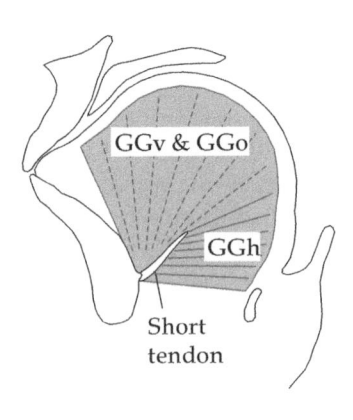

Figure 4.3 Midsagittal MRI of the tongue, showing the short tendon as a bright spur originating from the superior genial tubercle of the mandible. The radial pattern of the median fibrous septum suggests muscle fiber radiation from the tendon.

4.2.3.1 Genioglossus as a triangular muscle In many physiological articulatory models developed in the past, the genioglossus muscle (GG) is functionally segmented into a few divisions according to the angles of radiating muscle fibers. This is based on two common notions that the GG is anatomically a single muscle having no subdivisions and that the GG arises from the superior genial tubercle of the mandible. Thus, in many models, three divisions (anterior, middle, and posterior parts) are arbitrarily determined, and the GG fibers attach on the mandible broadly beyond the genial tubercle. The uncertainty of the GG's subdivision and attachment results in the varied treatment of this muscle across models according to what is convenient for model simulation.

The GG is a triangular muscle having a central tendon, called the short tendon of the tongue (Kahane and Folkins 1984), and recent literature states often that the GG fibers arise from the short tendon (e.g., Standring 2008). These observations suggest that the short tendon is the possible anatomical structure that divides the GG fibers into two segments. Figure 4.3 shows a midsagittal slice from a high-resolution MRI with the tongue volume at rest. The short tendon being surrounded by the fatty tissue can be visualized as the bright spur that stretches from the genial tubercle into the tongue tissue. The radiation of the GG fibers is seen in the brightness pattern of the median fibrous septum: the horizontal part of the muscle (GGh) arises from the inferior side of the tendon, and the rest from the superior side. Thus, the short tendon offers an anatomical structure for the dense fibers of the GG to radiate from a small region. Note that, in the figure, the vertical and oblique parts (GGv and GGo, respectively) are named not for anatomical but for functional divisions according to the orientation of fiber radiation.

Evidence of the subdivision of the GG is also inferred from the pattern of endplate distribution to the muscle. Mu and Sanders (2010) suggest a possible neuroanatomical division of the GG: the motor nerve endplates on the GGh show a dual attachment pattern, while those in the other parts are singular. This finding may be related to the electromyographic finding that the GGh generates signals of much higher voltage than the rest of the muscle during the production of high vowels (Baer, Alfonso, and Honda 1998). Further investigation is necessary to resolve the question on this muscle.

4.2.3.2 Styloglossus as a pure retractor muscle The styloglossus muscle is commonly believed to draw the tongue body back and upward. This interpretation of the muscle as a retractor and elevator of the tongue body is due to the oblique orientation of the posterior (extralingual) part of the muscle. In many models, this extralingual part of the styloglossus is a set of strands from the styloid process of the temporal bone (e.g., Dang and Honda 2001). Changes in orientation of this part take place in model simulation, as the insertion point into the tongue body rises and falls for articulation. In reality, the extralingual part of the styloglossus is bounded by the parapharyngeal soft tissues. The bundle of fibers that enters the tongue is located next to the middle pharyngeal constrictor medially, the median pterygoid muscle laterally, and the submandibular gland inferiorly. Those surrounding tissues limit the mobility of the muscle bundle at the pharyngeal region. Thus, the contraction of the styloglossus results only in retraction of the tongue tissue near the insertion point, and the upward component of movement toward the styloid process is almost lost (Takano and Honda 2007). It is also worth noting that the styloglossus does more than merely retract the tongue. The bundle of fibers that forwards into the tongue blade also anchors the action of the anterior (intralingual) part of the tongue. Contraction of the styloglossus therefore also helps to retract the tongue tip and elevate the tongue dorsum by tissue bunching.

4.2.3.3 Regional functional variation of intrinsic muscles Since electromyographic access to the intrinsic muscles is limited, physiologically informed articulatory models may provide the best means for understanding the action of these muscles. Nonetheless, the anatomy suggests that the function of these muscles may vary from region to region across the tongue.

The superior longitudinal, transverse, and vertical muscles form a thick layer of muscle tissue beneath the oral and pharyngeal surfaces of the tongue. This muscle layer may deform the tongue in various manners, depending on the locations of the muscle fibers. The regional differential activation of muscle fibers is supported by the dendritic distribution of the distal motor nerves from the internal branch of the hypopharyngeal nerve to those muscles. The superior longitudinal muscle is composed of many short-range fibers overlapping with each other longitudinally along the tongue surface (Slaughter, Li, and Sokoloff 2005), allowing perhaps for segregated function. For example, the elevation of the tongue tip may be produced mainly by the anterior fibers alone. The transverse and vertical muscles form a band of laminar units with the genioglossus muscles that also distribute longitudinally from the tip to the base of the tongue (Takemoto 2001). The narrowing for the tongue blade for the apical contact of the tongue tip with side pathways (e.g., in /l/-sound) may be made by the anterior segments of those muscles.

Table 4.4 Peak amplitudes sampled from ensemble average EMG data recorded during word utterances with 11 English vowels (Baer et al. 1988). The values for HG in parenthesis indicate negative peak values because this muscle shows suppression pattern in front vowels.

	i	I	e	ɛ	æ	a	ɔ	o	ʊ	u	ʌ
GGa	.85	.6	.7	.6	1.0	.5	.4	.4	.45	.4	.4
GGp	1.0	.35	.6	.25	.4	.1	.15	.3	.2	.6	.15
HG	(.25)	(.45)	(.25)	(.45)	(.5)	1.0	.9	.95	.7	.85	.8
SG	.15	.2	.1	.25	.3	.35	1.0	.85	.4	.8	.35

4.2.3.4 Motor organization of tongue muscles in vowel production Our knowledge about the motor organization of the tongue muscles in speech production is limited because of the technical difficulty in obtaining physiological data. Thus, ideas about neuromuscular control of the tongue remain largely speculative. The few electromyographic (EMG) studies of tongue muscles during speech production that do exist nonetheless provide valuable first order information that helps inform our speculation. Table 4.4 is a numerical summary of the ensemble-average EMG data recorded from the extrinsic muscles (genioglossus, styloglossus, and hyoglossus) for 11 English vowels (Baer et al. 1988). The data for the genioglossus were recorded from the horizontal and oblique parts, labeled as GGp and GGa, respectively. A cursory look at these data, focusing on the four cardinal vowels, suggests that each vowel is produced by co-contraction of two pairs of muscles. In particular, the vowel /i/ is produced by GGa and GGp, the vowel /u/ by GGp and SG, the vowel /ae/ by GGa and HG, and vowel /a/ by HG and SG. Co-contraction of the GGa and GGp for vowel /i/ is likely necessary to maintain a midline groove on the oral surface of the tongue, which is necessary to achieve the vowel formants associated with /i/ (Fujimura and Kakita 1979).

Motor control for tongue deformation that involves two pairs of antagonistic muscles is agreement with factor analysis studies on tongue deformation (Maeda and Honda 1994). Converging evidence such as this suggests that an understanding of neuromuscular control of the tongue will be provided as physiological models are advanced in conjunction with electrophysiological studies of the muscles involved.

4.3 Vocal tract and its resonances

The vocal tract is defined here as the airway from the hypopharynx to the labial vestibule, which includes the oral cavity and mesopharynx. The oral vestibule is bounded from the oral cavity by the teeth. The mesopharynx is bordered by the palatoglossal arch anteriorly and the aryepiglottic ridge inferiorly, and it contains the tonsillar fossa and epiglottic vallecula. The hypopharynx is composed of the supraglottic laryngeal cavity and the bilateral cavities of the piriform fossa.

The vocal tract undergoes a developmental change in length, which is characterized by the disproportionate elongation of the pharynx during maturation and by the lowering of the larynx with aging after maturation. A monotonic growth pattern describes the developmental change in vocal-tract length (VTL). Measured at rest in the supine position, the VTL is roughly 10 cm at age 3 years, and 14 and 15.5 cm in young adult females and males, respectively (Fitch and Giedd 1999). Changes in vocal-tract length during speech involve two factors: passive variation due to varying vocal-tract midline length, which is shorter for open vowels and longer for close vowels; and active variation due to raising or depressing the larynx and/or spreading or protruding the lips. For example, the high back vowel /u/ in English results in one of the longest vocal-tract configurations, with a low larynx position that lengthens the hypopharynx and lip protrusion that creates a long labial vestibule. The vocal tract also changes in length along with the rise and fall of voice fundamental frequency in speech due to laryngeal functions for voicing.

The vocal tract is the space where the final stage of speech production takes place. Movement of the supralaryngeal articulators alters the shape of this space, which results in spectral modification of sounds by air column resonance. This vocal-tract resonance is described below based on two common accounts: standing wave and multiple reflection. This is followed by discussion of additional acoustic effects due to boundary conditions and side cavities that are not part of the textbook descriptions but nonetheless influence resonances in the low and high frequencies.

4.3.1 Modeling the vocal tract

In acoustics of speech production, the vocal tract has been modeled as concatenated cylinders. In the simplest form of the models, the vocal tract is treated as a uniform tube being closed at one end and open at the other with a flange. This form of a tube is called the "closed tube" in contrast to the "open tube" with both ends open. Multiple standing waves can be set up in this tube; the interference patterns establish the position of the nodes and anti-nodes, which determine resonance patterns that are equivalent to a set of formants with particular frequency intervals. To account for formant-cavity affiliations, two-tube models for vowels and three-tube models for consonants have been proposed. When the vocal tract is modeled as two tubes with a narrow back tube and a wide front one, the resonance mode in each tube resembles that of a uniform closed tube, where each tube resonates nearly independently to produce two formants at similar frequencies, as in the case for the vowel /a/. When the vocal tract is modeled as a wide back tube and a narrow front one, a different treatment is necessary. In this situation, the back and front tubes resemble the cavity and neck of a Helmholtz resonator, respectively, which emits a resonant sound at a much lower frequency than that expected from the length of the uniform tube. This resonance corresponds to the first formant of the vowel /i/. Meanwhile, the front tube resonates as an open tube producing high-frequency resonance, which corresponds to the second formant of this vowel.

Although the two-tube model of the vocal tract is useful to contrast the low back and high front vowel, it fails to predict formant values in vowels that are created with two constrictions, such as the high back vowel /u/. Accordingly, multi-tube models have been employed to provide a phonetic account for a wider range of vowels and to model consonants with resonances, such as liquids and nasals (Fant 1960; Stevens 2000). Altogether, these somewhat more complex models have contributed to an understanding of the acoustic-phonetic realization of the lower three formant frequencies in vowels and vowel-like consonants.

Better approximations of vocal-tract resonances have been achieved by modeling the vocal tract as an acoustic tube with numerous cylinders, each with a constant unit length (Story, Titze, and Hoffman 1996; Clément et al. 2007; Mokhtari et al. 2007). The acoustic output in the frequency domain (i.e., the transfer function) is computed using a transmission-line analog of the vocal tract. The transmission-line model assumes multiple reflections of acoustic waves in a tube between its closed and open ends and wherever the cylinder changes in shape. The cross-sectional areas of the cylinders along the vocal tract (i.e., the area function) can be estimated from two-dimensionally projected vocal-tract shapes (Sundberg et al. 1987; Maeda 1990) or measured directly from three-dimensionally visualized vocal tracts (Baer et al. 1991; Story et al. 1996). Unlike the simpler tube models described above, these area function models no longer suggest a simple account of formant-cavity affiliation. Instead, the relationship between vocal tract regions and formant frequencies need clarification by the sensitivity functions for formants (Mrayati, Carré, and Guérin 1988). The sensitivity function describes the effect of a small change in area or length applied to a region of interest on each formant frequency.

For even more accurate estimates of the vocal-tract transfer function, many additional parameters and effects should be incorporated in the transmission-line model. For example, Figure 4.4 illustrates a few relevant cavities that affect vocal-tract resonances, which are not typically factored in to area function models. These

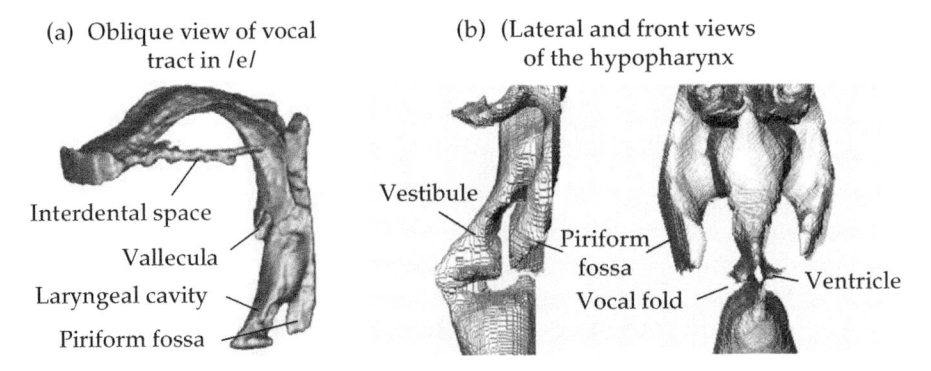

Figure 4.4 Vocal tract and its side cavities reconstructed from 3D MRI. (a) Oblique view of the vocal tract in /e/. (b) Lateral and front views of the hypopharyngeal cavity in /a/ (Honda et al. 2004). Reprinted by kind permission of The Institute of Electronics, Information, and Communication Engineers (IEICE).

cavities include the bilateral piriform fossae, which are located in the hypopharyngeal cavity near the larynx, and are open during speech production (Dang and Honda 1997). Other small side cavities are the interdental space and epiglottic vallecula, which change their form along with tongue articulation (Takemoto, Mokhtari, and Kitamura 2010). The sublingual cavity (not shown in the figure) is another functional side cavity of the vocal tract that varies with tongue-blade positioning for consonant production. Several of these cavities contribute resonances at the lower and higher frequencies as discussed below.

4.3.2 Vocal tract resonances in the lower frequencies

It is common to note that vowel formants vary systematically with vocal-tract length between the two boundaries: the glottis and lips. Acoustically, the boundaries of the vocal tract are less clear. The closed end of the vocal tract is not necessarily the glottis because the vocal tract divides into three cavities in the hypopharynx. According to the multiple reflection account of vocal-tract resonance, acoustic waves are thought to reflect near the orifice of the laryngeal cavity and above the bottom of the piriform fossa, which suggests distributed closed-end boundaries. The open end of the vocal tract for reflecting waves is even more ambiguous. This is because the shape/position of the lips and teeth complicate the open-end location or deform the wave front. Thus, the boundaries for reflecting acoustic waves in the vocal tract do not always conform to the anatomical boundaries, and the acoustically equivalent length of the vocal tract differs from the physical length measured from anatomical images. Here, the boundary effects at the both ends of the vocal tract (hypopharynx and labial vestibule) and other effects in the middle of the vocal tract at the velum and the teeth are discussed. These effects should be incorporated in future acoustic models of speech production to generate more accurate estimates of the vocal-tract transfer function.

A common simplifying assumption in tube models concerns the boundary effect at the glottis, which is taken to be the closed end of the vocal tract or tube. In reality, the glottis is repeatedly opening and closing, thereby producing the phonatory source for vocalic sounds (see Story, this volume, Chapter 3). This action at the glottis has acoustic consequences that are not consistent with the hermetically closed end assumed in simple tube models. In particular, during the open glottal phase, acoustic coupling takes place with the subglottal airway. The effect is to raise the first formant (F1) frequency in high vowels. In addition, the glottis possibly transmits the resonances of the subglottal system into the vocal tract. The second subglottal resonance, which occurs at about 1500 Hz, often interacts with the second formant (F2) in the transition between vowel /i/ and /a/ (Lulich 2010).

The second adjustment that is needed to acoustic-phonetic models of vowel production concerns the boundary effect at the lips, modeled as the open end of the tube, where sound radiates into an open field. The plane wave, which travels along the vocal tract as volume velocity variation, transforms into the spherical pressure wave at the lips by losing the DC component. At the boundary, the wave partially reflects back into vocal tract, but this reflection takes place at a certain point beyond the physical end of the vocal tract because the plane wave bulges a little outward from the lips. This open-end boundary effect is equivalent to a slight elongation of the tube, and the magnitude of the effect depends mainly on the diameter of the open end at the lips. The excess tube length has been estimated from experiments to be in the range of 0.3D~0.4D in a tube with a large flange, where D is the diameter. This open-end effect is a low-frequency approximation, and it diminishes at higher frequencies. In addition, this well-known treatment for the open end of the tube does not always accurately model the physics of real vocal tracts. For example, the sound wave interacts with the closed teeth in close vowels and radiates at the side wedges of the lips in open vowels. These complications lead to the conclusion that the coefficient for the open end correction should to be adjusted in models to reflect the geometry of the lip end of the vocal tract.

Other structures in the vocal tract give rise to additional lower-frequency effects that are not accounted for by current acoustic-phonetics models of vowel production. The first structure to consider is the velum. In high vowels and voiced obstruents, the cavity behind the constriction demonstrates sound pressure variation of the larger amplitude than in other sounds. The augmented pressure variation transmits into the nasal cavity via soft-tissue vibration of the velum, which amplifies sound output from the nostrils in lower frequencies. Another structure to consider is the interdental space between the upper and lower teeth. In high vowels the space forms side branches off the oral cavity, while in low vowels the space is entirely included into the oral cavity. The changing length of the side branch formed by the interdental space during speech is sometimes captured as a traveling anti-resonance on a spectrograph between open and close vowels.

4.3.3 *Vocal-tract resonance at higher frequencies*

While vocal-tract resonances at lower frequencies are relevant to phonetic quality of vowels, resonances at higher frequencies add another acoustic dimension to speech, such as voice quality and individual vocal characteristics. To the best of our current knowledge, the structures responsible for the appearance of anti-resonance and extra-resonance are the piriform fossa and laryngeal cavity. Those hypopharyngeal cavities not only modify the closed-end boundary but also determine spectral shapes at higher frequencies.

The piriform fossae are located in the hypopharynx near the larynx bilaterally above the entrance of the esophagus. These are non-negligible side cavities in the vocal tract that are always open during speech production. The cavities are known to cause one or two deep zero(s) between 4 and 5 kHz in male voices (Dang and Honda 1997; Takemoto et al. 2013) and thus provide a source for certain higher-frequency spectral patterns in speech.

The supraglottic laryngeal cavity is formed by the bilateral small recesses above the vocal folds called the laryngeal ventricles and a narrow conduit called the laryngeal vestibule that opens into the wide pharynx. The structure of this cavity resembles a Helmholtz resonator and is relatively stable in shape across vowels. The cavity is also acoustically independent from the rest of the vocal tract. It generates a resonance peak at a stable frequency region, which is around 3 kHz in male voice, and was referred to as the laryngeal resonance in early studies (Chiba and Kajiyama 1942). This resonance may be observed as the fourth formant, though it may often overlap with nearby formant peaks. This regional resonance exhibits a unique on-off pattern during each cycle of vocal-fold vibration because it rapidly decays at the open phase of the glottis, which differs from the pattern of gradual amplitude decay observed in other formants (Kitamura et al. 2006). While the peak of the laryngeal cavity resonance is evident in a male voice, it is not clear whether it also appears in a female voice. Future studies are needed to understand this sex difference, but two possible reasons for the difference are advanced here. The laryngeal cavity may be irrelevant in the female voice either because the female laryngeal cavity is wide enough to couple with the pharyngeal cavity, or because the female glottis is slightly open, leading to even more rapid decay in the resonance than is observed in the male voice. The sex difference observed for the laryngeal cavity resonance is parallel to the sex difference observed for the so-called singers' formant (Sundberg 1974): the singers' formant is found in male voice, but not in female voice in singing. It may be that in the female voice, ringing sounds are produced by vocal-tract resonances with expanded hypopharyngeal cavities.

In sum, together the piriform fossa and laryngeal cavity account for the spectral patterns above 2.5 kHz that are observed in mature male voices, whether speaking or singing. These characteristics include a large spectral tilt, a prominent peak at 3 kHz and deep zero(s) around 4–5 kHz. Human hearing is highly sensitive in the frequency region near 3 kHz, even though this is higher than that which conveys vowel quality information. The spectral patterns generated in this region are also stable in the face of changing vocal tract shapes. Given our sensitivity to information in this region, and the dearth of linguistic information that is conveyed by these higher frequencies, it is reasonable to conjecture that the hypopharyngeal cavity resonances provide high-frequency cues to that add to voice quality information or convey individual identities via speaker-to-speaker differences in the vocal characteristics.

4.4 Summary

This chapter described the anatomy and physiology of the supralaryngeal articulators in the oropharyngeal cavities as well as the geometry and resonances of the main vocal tract. Anatomy and physiology provide a basis for understanding human behavior. Not surprisingly, the complexity of the vocal organs and their organization into a speech production system is reflective of the complexity of human speech. The most active articulators in the oropharyngeal region include the tongue and pharyngeal wall, and so the muscles of these organs were described in detail. A few remarks were added regarding the need to incorporate a detailed understanding of tongue muscle geometry and function to improve computational models of articulatory action. That said, there remains a gap in our understanding of articulatory muscle function. Electromyography and finer tissue imaging are critical research methods that will be useful for helping to bridge this gap in future studies. The supralaryngeal organs function together to shape acoustic processes in the vocal tract, which are also informed by additional effects and structures that are not commonly considered in standing wave accounts of vowel production. While some of these structures contributed to effects in the lower frequency range and so help to determine vowel quality, others contribute to effects in the higher frequency range and may account for other important information and qualities that are conveyed in speech, such as individual vocal characteristics or the varying vocal qualities of speech and singing.

REFERENCES

Abd-el-Malek, Shafik. 1939. Observations on the morphology of the human tongue. *Journal of Anatomy* 73: 201–210.

Baer, Thomas, Peter J. Alfonso, and Kiyoshi Honda. 1988. Electromyography of the tongue muscle during vowels in /əpVp/ Environment. *Annual Bulletin of the Research Institute of Logopedics and Phoniatrics* 22: 7–20.

Baer, Thomas, John C. Gore, L. Carol Gracco, and Patrick W. Nye. 1991. Analysis of vocal tract shape and dimensions using magnetic resonance imaging: Vowels. *Journal of the Acoustical Society of America* 90: 799–828.

Chiba, Tsutomu and Masato Kajiyama. 1942. *The Vowel, Its Nature and Structure*. Tokyo: Tokyo-Kaiseikan.

Clément, Philippe, Stéphane Hans, Dana M. Hartl, Shinji Maeda, Jacqueline Vaissière, and Daniel Brasnu. 2007. Vocal tract area function for vowels using three-dimensional magnetic resonance imaging: A preliminary study. *Journal of Voice* 21: 522–530.

Dang, Jianwu and Kiyoshi Honda. 1997. Acoustic characteristics of the piriform fossa in models and humans. *Journal of the Acoustical Society of America* 101: 456–465.

Dang, Jianwu and Kiyoshi Honda. 2001. A physiological model of a dynamic vocal tract for speech production. *Acoustical Science and Technology* 22: 415–425.

Dunn, Hugh K. 1950. The calculation of vowel resonances, and an electrical vocal tract. *Journal of the Acoustical Society of America* 22: 740–753.

Fant, Gunnar. 1960. *Acoustic Theory of Speech Production*. The Hague: Mouton.

Fitch, W. Tecumseh and Jay Giedd. 1999. Morphology and development of the human vocal tract: A study using magnetic resonance imaging. *Journal of the Acoustical Society of America* 106: 1511–1522.

Fletcher, Harvey. 1929. *Speech and Hearing*. New York: D. Van Nostrand.

Fujimura, Osamu and Yakita Kakita. 1979. Remarks on quantitative description of the lingual articulation. In Bjorn Lindblom and Sven Öhman (eds.), *Frontiers of Speech Communication Research*, 17–24. London: Academic Press.

Fujita, Satoru, Jianwu Dang, Noriko Suzuki, and Kiyoshi Honda. 2007. A computational tongue model and its clinical application. *Oral Science International*, November: 97–109.

Gérard, Jean-Michael, Reiner Wilhelms-Tricarico, Pascal Perrier, and Yohan Payan. 2003. A 3D dynamical biomechanical tongue model to study speech motor control. *Recent Research Developments in Biomechanics* 1: 49–64.

Harshman, Richard, Peter Ladefoged, and Louis Goldstein. 1977. Factor analyses of tongue shapes. *Journal of the Acoustical Society of America* 62: 693–707.

Honda, Kiyoshi. 1983. Relationship between pitch control and vowel articulation. In D.M. Bless and J.H. Abbs (eds.), *Vocal Fold Physiology*, 286–299. San Diego, CA: College-Hill Press.

Honda, Kiyoshi, Hironori Takemoto, Tatsuya Kitamura, Satoru Fujita, and Sayoko Takano. 2004. Exploring human speech production mechanisms by MRI. *IEICE Transactions on Information and Systems* E87-D: 1050–1058.

Kahane, Joel C. and John W. Folkins. 1984. *Atlas of Speech and Hearing Anatomy*. Columbus, OH: Charles E. Merrill.

Kitamura, Tatsuya, Hironori Takemoto, Seiji Adachi, Parham Mokhtari, and Kiyoshi Honda. 2006. Cyclicity of laryngeal cavity resonance due to vocal fold vibration. *Journal of the Acoustical Society of America* 120: 2239–2249.

Lulich, Steven. M. 2010. Subglottal resonances and distinctive features. *Journal of Phonetics* 38: 20–32.

Maeda, Shinji. 1990. Compensatory articulation during speech: Evidence from the analysis and synthesis of vocal-tract shapes using an articulatory model. In W.J. Hardcastle and A. Marchal (eds.), *Speech Production and Speech Modelling*, 131–149. Dordrecht: Kluwer Academic Publishers.

Maeda, Shinji and Kiyoshi Honda. 1994. From EMG to formant patterns of vowels: The implication of vowel spaces. *Phonetica* 51: 17–19.

Mokhtari, Parham, Tatsuya Kitamura, Hironori Takemoto, and Kiyoshi Honda. 2007. Principal components of vocal-tract area functions and inversion of vowels by linear regression of cepstrum coefficients. *Journal of Phonetics* 35: 20–39.

Mrayati, Mohammed, René Carré, and Bernard Guérin. 1988. Distinctive regions and modes: A new theory of speech production. *Speech Communication* 7: 257–286.

Mu, Liancai and Ira Sanders. 2010. Human tongue neuroanatomy: Nerve supply and motor endplates. *Clinical Anatomy* 23: 777–791.

Perkell, Joseph S. 1996. Properties of the tongue help to define vowel categories: Hypotheses based on physiologically-oriented modeling. *Journal of Phonetics* 24: 3–22.

Rubin, Philip, Thomas Baer, and Paul Mermelstein. 1981. An articulatory synthesizer for perceptual research. *Journal of the Acoustical Society of America* 50: 1180–1192.

Schwenk, Kurt. 2001. Extrinsic versus intrinsic lingual muscles: A false dichotomy. *Bulletin of the Museum of Comparative Zoology* 156: 219–235.

Slaughter, Kate, H. Li, and Alan J. Sokoloff. 2005. Neuromuscular organization of the superior longitudinalis muscle in the human tongue. 1. Motor endplate morphology and muscle fiber architecture. *Cells Tissues Organs* 181: 51–64.

Standring, Susan. 2008. *Gray's Anatomy: The Anatomical Basis of Clinical Practice*, 40th Edition. London: Churchill Livingstone.

Stevens, Kenneth. N. 2000. *Acoustic Phonetics*. Cambridge, MA: The MIT Press.

Stevens, Kenneth N., Stanley Kasowski, and Gunnar Fant. 1953. An electrical analog of the vocal tract. *Journal of the Acoustical Society of America* 25: 734–742.

Story, Brad H., Ingo R. Titze, and Eric A. Hoffman. 1996. Vocal tract area functions from magnetic resonance imaging. *Journal of the Acoustical Society of America* 100: 537–554.

Sundberg, Johan. 1974. Articulatory interpretation of the "singing formant." *Journal of the Acoustical Society of America* 55: 838–844.

Sundberg, Johan, C. Johansson, Herman Wilbrand, and Christer Ytterbergh. 1987.

From sagittal distance to area: A study of transverse, vocal tract cross-sectional area. *Phonetica* 44: 76–90.

Takano, Sayoko and Kiyoshi Honda. 2007. An MRI analysis of the extrinsic tongue muscles during vowel production. *Speech Communication* 49: 49–58.

Takemoto, Hironori. 2001. Morphological analysis of the human tongue musculature for three-dimensional modeling. *Journal of Speech, Language, and Hearing Research* 44: 95–107.

Takemoto, Hironori, Parham Mokhtari, and Tatsuya Kitamura. 2010. Acoustic analysis of the vocal tract during vowel production by finite-difference time-domain method. *Journal of the Acoustical Society of America* 128: 3724–3738.

Takemoto, Hironori, Seiji Adachi, Parhoam Mokhtari, and Tatsuya Kitamura. 2013. Acoustic interaction between the right and left piriform fossae in generating spectral dips. *Journal of the Acoustical Society of America* 134: 2955–2964.

Takemoto, Hironori, Seiji Adachi, Tatsuya Kitamura, Parham Mokhtari, and Kiyoshi Honda. 2006. Acoustic roles of the laryngeal cavity in vocal tract resonance. *Journal of the Acoustical Society of America* 120: 2228–2238.

Westbury, John R. 1988. Mandible and hyoid bone movements during speech. *Journal of Speech, Language, and Hearing Research* 31: 405–416.

Wilhelms-Tricarico, Reiner. 1995. Physiological modeling of speech production: Methods for modeling soft-tissue articulators. *Journal of the Acoustical Society of America* 97: 3085–3098.

FURTHER READING

Chiba, Tsutomu and Masato Kajiyama, M. 1942. *The Vowel, Its Nature and Structure*. Tokyo: Tokyo-Kaiseikan. The historical achievement of this work lies in the authors' insight and theoretical construction to resolve long-standing questions about vowels. Modern readers will be attracted by the authors' scientific approach to building a concept by experimental and analytical work. Knowledge of the debate on vowel theories at the period of this monograph is also helpful in understanding the acoustic process of vowel production in depth.

Honda, Kiyoshi. 2007. Physiological processes of speech production. In J. Benesty, M. Sondhi, and Y. Huang (eds.), *Springer Handbook of Speech Processing*, 7–26. Heidelberg: Springer-Verlag. Readers will find more illustrations that are not included in this chapter, including schematic anatomical figures of the voice and speech organs, resonance of side cavities, and techniques for instrumentation.

Sundberg, Johan. 1987. *The Science of the Singing Voice*. Dekalb: Northern Illinois University Press. This book is not merely on singing voices but also on vocal-tract contributions to producing voice quality. The singers' formant results from fine adjustment of the vocal tract near the larynx. The author's articles elsewhere are also helpful to find the role of the vocal tract in determining the varied aspects of vocal sounds.

Zemlin, Willard R. 1998. *Speech and Hearing Science: Anatomy and Physiology*, 4th edn. Needham Heights, MA: Allyn and Bacon. It cannot be overstated that anatomy is the basis of all human activities including speech production. Any modeling studies must be faithful to human anatomy. Otherwise, efforts for speech production modeling would only be meaningless. This publication tells us standard descriptions on anatomy and physiology with many details, such as anthropological terminology as landmark points on rigid structures.

5 Jaw and Lips

PASCAL H.H.M. VAN LIESHOUT

Hear; for I will speak of excellent things; and the opening of my lips shall be right things
(Proverbs 8:6, King James bible)

5.1 Introduction

Oral structures like lips and jaw have always drawn a strong attention in people's mind, likely because they are so clearly and visibly engaged in producing speech as well as expressing our emotional states. This is obvious from the many idioms and proverbs that include a reference to these structures, as for example, "The lips of the righteous feed many: but fools die for want of wisdom" or "he snatched victory from the jaws of defeat." These structures have also fascinated people in a more academic way, from surgeons who need to repair cleft lips in children born with such an affliction to speech scientists, who wish to understand the mechanisms by which the lips and jaw move and coordinate in producing speech and in other oral motor functions. In this chapter, I will review the various aspects by which lips and jaw can be characterized, starting with their anatomical and physiological features, and then highlighting their specific roles in different oral motor functions such as chewing, swallowing, and perhaps most importantly in the context of this volume, speech production. I will take this broad perspective since the use of lips and jaw in speech production from an evolutionary point of view is a rather recent oral motor behavior in comparison to the far older existing functions of chewing, swallowing, and facial expressions that humans as a species share with other primates. Speech is unique to humans and has specific characteristics that will differentiate it from other oral motor functions, as will be discussed in this chapter, but understanding its origins and relationship to these other oral motor functions is crucial for those who wish to study it. In this sense, I will follow the lead from pioneers in this area, like Philip Lieberman, John Locke, Peter MacNeilage, and James Lund, highlighting the fact that speech did not come out of the blue during the development of the human species. From this review, I hope that readers will understand that the fascination with these oral structures is not only well deserved but also reflects still a bit of a mystery around their involvement in the various complex oral motor functions we perform on a daily basis.[1]

5.2 Anatomy and physiology

As argued by Lieberman, "The evolution of speech was driven by Darwinian natural selection, the opportunistic use of existing structures adapted for another purpose, and mutations on regulatory genes that had far-reaching consequences" (2007: 52). He believes that some form of auditory communication must have existed even before humanoids (*Homo sapiens*) developed the anatomical-acoustic capability to produce quantal vowels (somewhere between 50,000 and 90,000 years ago). In Lieberman's view this is intrinsically related to the descent (and reshaping) of the tongue into the pharynx, together with the corresponding changes in neck length and the angle between the horizontal and vertical parts of the vocal tract only found in humans as opposed to other primates. As these developments converged onto the human vocal tract in its current state it should be no surprise that it is unique in many of its anatomical and physiological features, including the musculature that is involved in moving and shaping its components (Kent 2004).

Obviously, having the right "equipment" as such is not sufficient to produce speech. There is also a need for a "control" system (for lack of a better word) that allows these components to move in some orchestrated way to produce repeatable strings of vocal tract actions that lead to identifiable modifications in acoustic patterns to which meaning can be attached. Non-human primates have the capability to produce sound, but it is claimed to be restricted to so-called stereotypical patterns (Hauser 1996; Lieberman 2007) used to express certain emotional and sexual states (e.g., anger, threat, submission) or environmental threats/opportunities (e.g., snake/fruit nearby).

Regardless of these ongoing discussions about the origins of human speech and language, there is little doubt among those who study the biology of our oral system that the way we use oral anatomical structures in our communications has been adapted from their original primary use, namely to support feeding and breathing. This is quite evident for the structures that are focused on in this chapter, the lips and lower jaw (mandible). In the next sections, I will detail some of their anatomical and physiological characteristics and highlight those features that are unique to our species when compared to other members of the hominidae.

5.2.1 Upper lip and lower lip

The main body of the lips is formed by the orbicularis oris muscle, which has a complex multilayered structure. It attaches to the dermis of the upper and lower lip by means of a thin superficial musculo-aponeurotic system (SMAS), consisting of fat and connective tissue (Rogers et al. 2009). Embryonically, the upper fibers develop from the infraorbital lamina and the lower fibers develop from the mandibular lamina. Upper and lower fibers can be further separated into left and right anterior pars marginalis and posterior pars peripheralis, which meet at the vermillion border. Thus, one can divide the lips into eight muscular parts that converge at their respective left or right modiolus (see Figure 5.1, labeled A–H). Contraction of the fibers in the peripheral part leads to lip elevation (upper) or lip depression (lower), whereas contraction of the marginal parts acts directly upon the parts covered by the vermillion, moving the body of the lips closer to the surface of the teeth as in compression or inversion. In general, these parts work together for the flexible shaping of the lips in the production of various speech sounds, facial expressions, or during feeding. The pars peripheralis segments of the upper lip are the largest in size and attach to various other muscles involved in facial expression as indicated in Figure 5.1. With respect to the pars marginalis, a study on 11 adult Korean tissue samples (Hwang, Kim, and Hwang 2007) showed the thickness to vary between 1.1 and 2.0 mm.

In terms of more general physical dimensions of the lips, a study by Janson and Ingervall (1982) showed for a group of 50 children between 7 and 14 years of age

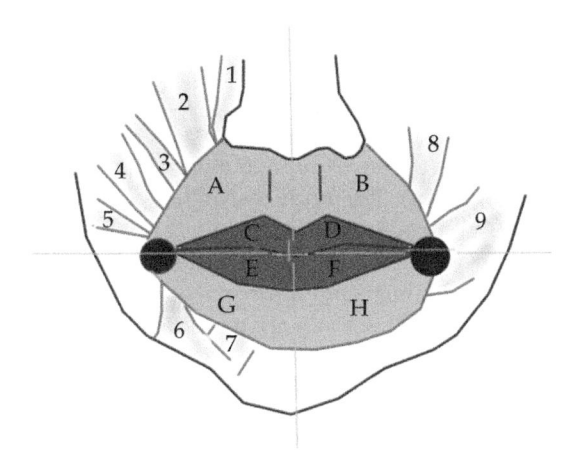

Figure 5.1 Schematic depiction of human orbicularis oris muscle fibers and extrinsic lip muscles that attach to it. Lighter grey section shows the boundaries of the pars peripheralis (posterior) and the dark grey section shows the boundaries of the pars marginalis (anterior). The modiolus on the left and right side of the mouth is shown in small black circles. To identify the eight muscular parts, a crosshair is drawn on top of the figure, with the individual parts labeled by a letter (A–H). The extrinsic muscles shown on the right side of the face in this figure are close to the surface, whereas the ones shown on the left are more deeply located: 1. levator labii superioris alaeque nasi; 2. levator labii superioris (quadratus labii superioris); 3. zygomaticus minor; 4. zygomaticus major; 5. risorius; 6. depressor anguli oris (triangularis); 7. depressor labii inferioris (quadratus labii inferioris); 8. levator anguli oris (caninus); 9. buccinator. Modified from Rogers et al. (2009: Figure 1). Reprinted with permission of John Wiley & Sons, Inc.

an average height range of 19–30 mm for upper lip and a range of 33.5–52.5 mm for lower lip, with an upper lip thickness varying between 7.5 and 16 mm and the lower lip thickness showing a slightly larger range of 11.5–17 mm. A more recent study (Rogers et al. 2009) shows that transverse, longitudinal, and oblique fibers are found throughout the upper fiber segments, both in human and chimpanzee (*Pan troglodytes*). However, transverse fibers appeared to be more numerous in the pars peripheralis as opposed to the more equal distribution of longitudinal fibers across the peripheral and marginal segments. Unlike previous reports mentioned in their paper, Rogers and colleagues provide evidence for a clear pars marginalis layer in their chimpanzee tissue samples. However, humans and chimpanzees do differ in their average fiber diameter (larger in chimpanzees) and the ratio between connective tissue vs. muscle tissue (lower in chimpanzees). According to these authors, this implies a stronger force-generating capacity in the upper lip for chimpanzees. Given the more extensive use of the lips as an instrument to manipulate food or other objects in chimpanzees, this seems to fit the different ecological needs of the two species. Another interesting feature reported in this study is the thicker dermis found for human lips, which provides for a fuller and thus more visible appearance of these structures. It is tempting to associate this increase in visibility with the role lips play in visual speech perception in humans as part of facial expressions.

5.2.1.1 Blood supply Lip muscles like all organs in our body depend on blood supply in order to receive oxygen and dispose of metabolic waste products. Changes in vascularization due to trauma or surgery can impact on their functionality (Archontaki et al. 2010). For both researchers and clinicians dealing with patients with speech impairments, having a good knowledge of blood supply to oral structures facilitates understanding difficulties with speech and swallowing functions after extensive reconstructive surgery or facial trauma.

The upper lip receives its blood supply mainly from the superior labial artery (SLA), which originates from the facial artery (Figure 5.2). In most cases there is also supply through alar and septal branches (Al-Hoqail and Meguid 2008; Crouzet et al. 1998; Mağden et al. 2004). Based on 14 cadaveric samples, Mağden and colleagues found that the SLA length ranged from 29 to 85 mm (with a mean length of 45.4 mm) with a mean external diameter of 1.3 mm at its origin. In 10 of 14 samples there was a bilateral representation of the SLA, with unilateral representations equally distributed left or right. However, the anatomical distribution was found to be highly variable across individuals.

For the lower lip, the main blood supply comes from the inferior labial artery (ILA), also shown in Figure 5.2, which branches off the facial artery, with additional supply from the horizontal and vertical labiomental arteries (Al-Hoqail and Meguid 2008; Crouzet et al. 1998; Edizer et al. 2003; Kawai et al. 2004). According to Edizer and colleagues, the mean length of the ILA was 52.3 mm with a range of 16–98 mm, based on 14 samples. This means it is slightly longer than the SLA. The mean external diameter at the origin was found to be 1.2 mm, which is smaller than the value of 1.8 mm reported by others (Al-Hoqail and Meguid 2008). As with

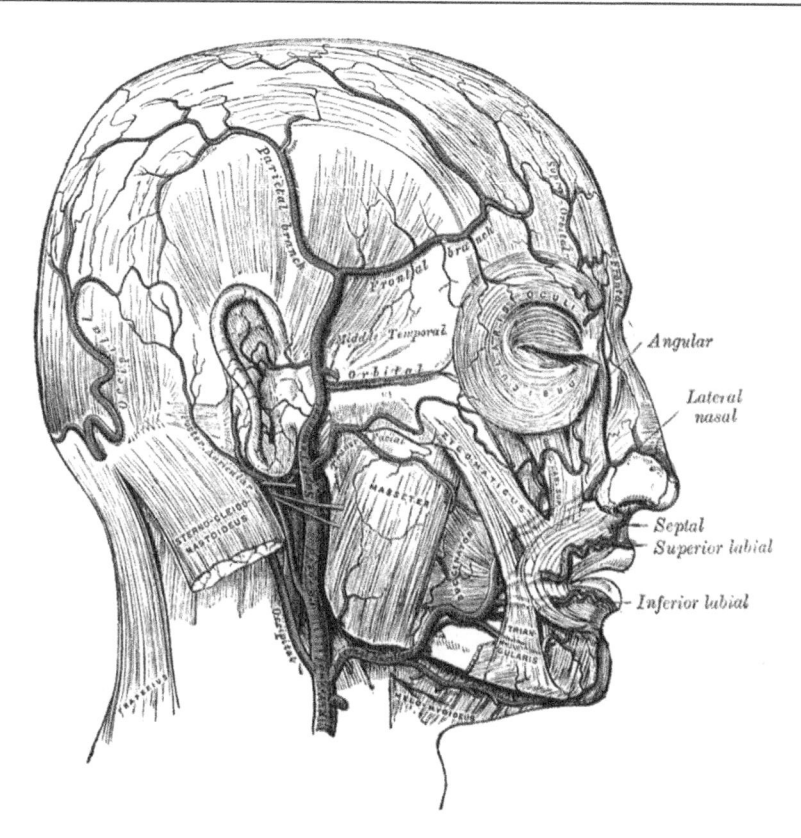

Figure 5.2 Superficial blood supply to face, including lip and mandibular region. Wikimedia Commons, http://en.wikipedia.org/wiki/File:Gray508.png; *Gray's Anatomy of the Human Body*, 20th US Edition, 1918.

the upper lip region, the anatomical distribution of arterial supply was found to be highly variable across individuals.

The arterial vessels supplying facial structures, in general, show diffuse cross-connections at the same site of the face and across the midline, thus creating links between internal and external carotid systems. A similar configuration is seen by and large for the facial veins. With respect to lymphatic systems, the upper lip drains into the submandibular lymphatic nodes, whereas the lower lip drains into the submental nodes (Bentsianov and Blitzer 2004).

5.2.1.2 Nerve supply Since humans basically share the same facial musculature with other primates (Diogo et al. 2009), it might seem that nerve supply would also be similar among the primates. However, recent studies using a special technique to visualize facial and sensory nerves in adult macaque fascicularis monkeys (Lee et al. 2008) and humans cadavers (Liu et al. 2010) showed that humans

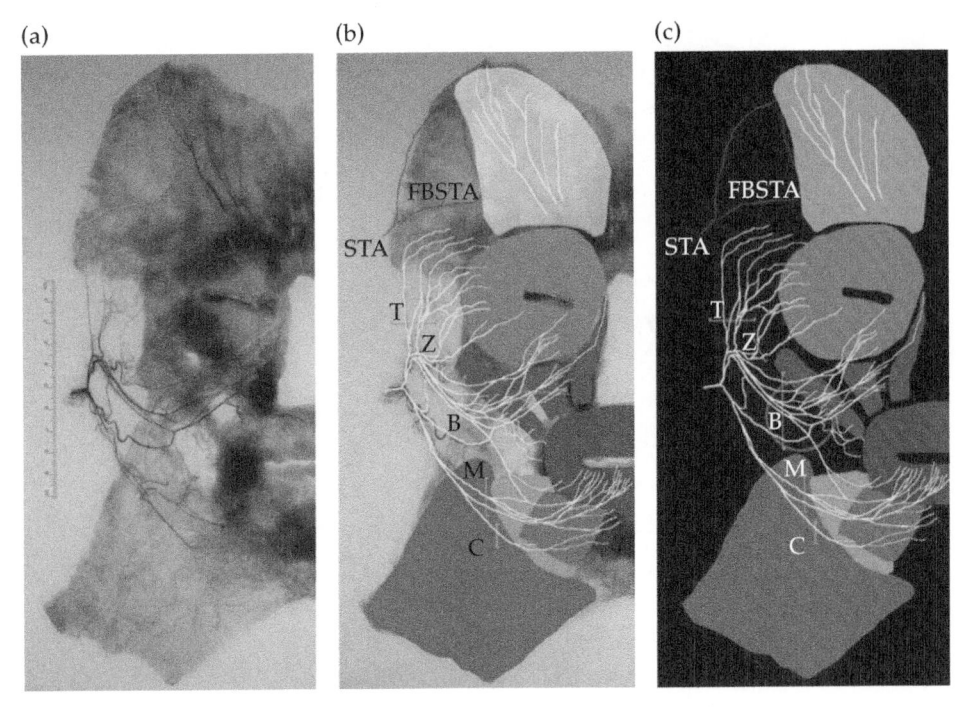

Figure 5.3 A schematic depiction of facial nerve branches in a human using a modified Sihler's staining technique (a), shown from the inside of the face. (b) shows the five separate main branches of the facial nerve: T (temporal), Z (zygomatic), B (buccal), M (marginal mandibular), and C (cervical). STA, superficial temporal artery; FBSTA, front branch of STA. (c) shows the same information as (b), but also identifies the mesh-like nerve plexus lateral to the zygomaticus major, formed by the buccal branches of the facial nerve (red circle). Modified from Liu et al. (2010: Figure 7). Reprinted with permission of John Wiley & Sons, Inc.

have a more complex pattern of facial and sensory nerves (see Figure 5.3). This includes the formation of a mesh-like nerve plexus lateral to the zygomatic major muscle and many cross-connections within a facial half (but never across the face), especially in the mid-face regions supplied by the buccal branches of the facial nerve (Liu et al. 2010). This was interpreted as a direct consequence of a finer and more complex differentiation of the musculature in humans in this region compared to macaques in support of the complex facial expressions used in human communication (Liu et al. 2010).

Knowledge about the innervation of the facial musculature and sensory nerves that provide feedback to the neural control system is important for research and clinical applications. Understanding the consequences of peripheral nerve lesions due to trauma, surgery, disease, congenital, or idiopathic causes provides realistic expectations regarding nerve regeneration and functional outcomes of speech therapy and other types of interventions (e.g., electrical stimulation). Although this kind of information is still incomplete, promising techniques are available that can preserve the finer details and structure of these delicate tissues in a way that is more similar to their layout in vivo (Liu et al. 2010).

The facial muscles are embryologically derived from the second pharyngeal arch (hyoid arch) and innervated by branches of the seventh cranial nerve, or facial nerve (Bentsianov and Blitzer 2004; Zemlin 1998; Liu et al. 2010). Specifically, the orbicularis oris superior (OOS) and other muscles of the face that act upon the upper lip (i.e., levator labii alaeque nasi; levator anguli oris; levator labii superioris; zygomaticus minor and major; and risorius) are innervated by the buccal branch of the facial nerve (n. VII). Cadaveric studies on 17 Korean adults (Hwang et al. 2006) showed that the buccal branch travels inferior to the zygomaticus major and minor and levator labii superioris (LLS), with its ramification point located between the zygomaticus minor and LLS at on average 14.5 mm (SD = 8.6 mm) lateral and 26.6 mm (SD = 4.2 mm) superior to the corner of the mouth. From there, branches radiate at an angle of about 70 degrees into the pars peripheralis and pars marginalis of the upper lip. This was confirmed in the study by Liu and colleagues (2010) who found that rami of the facial nerve branches all entered their target muscles at a right angle, except for the upper lip. This was similar to what was found in macaques (Lee et al. 2008).

The orbicularis oris inferior (OOI) and other muscles that act upon the lower lip (depressor labii inferioris; depressor anguli oris; mentalis) are innervated by the marginal mandibular branch of the facial nerve (Zemlin 1998: Liu et al. 2010). According to a study based on 50 samples (Al-Hayani 2007), the marginal mandibular nerve may have up to three branches, all progressing deep into the depressor anguli oris muscle (and other lower lip muscles). Although in all cases branches could run below or above the lower border of the mandible, if there were three branches the lower one was always found below. If it runs below, the site where it crosses the border to run its course toward the lower lip muscles is quite variable and not systematically related to the location of the inferior facial artery. When a branch runs above the lower border of the mandible, it exits the parotid gland across the masseter muscle covered by the superficial layer of the parotid fascia. Below the border it runs intrafascially in the upper part of the neck (Al-Hayani 2007).

Sensory information from the upper lip is carried by the maxillary branch (V2) of the trigeminal nerve (n. V), whereas the mandibular branch (V3) of the same nerve provides access to sensory information of the lower lip (Siemionow, Gharb, and Rampazzo 2011). More details on the mandibular branch will be provided in the section on the mandible below. The maxillary branch is a pure sensory nerve. One of its main branches, the infraorbital nerve, provides sensory innervation of the maxillary teeth through the superior alveolar nerves, before splitting into four branches after passing through the infraorbital foramen: inferior palpebral, external and internal nasal, and superior labial nerves, which supply sensory information from eyelid, nose, cheek, and upper lip. Other branches from the maxillary nerve include the palatine nerves, from which the anterior part (greater palatine nerve) provides sensory information from the roof of the mouth, soft palate, tonsils, and lining of the nasal cavities, with occasional branches supplying molar and pre-molar maxillary teeth (Rodella et al. 2012).

5.2.2 Mandible

The mandible, or lower jaw, is a bony structure consisting of a horizontal and vertical part (Figure 5.4). The horizontal structure makes up most of its volume and is called the body or corpus, whereas the vertical structure is referred to as the ramus. At the front, the left and right parts of the body are fused in the middle at the mental symphysis, which at the lower border forms a triangular projection (mental protuberance) often bounded on the lateral sides by the mental tubercles. The upper tooth-bearing side of the body of the mandible is referred to as the alveolar arch, which contains individual sockets for each tooth (dental alveolus), separated by interalveolar septa. Where the posterior border of the ramus meets the inferior border of the body, there is the so-called angle of the mandible, which in adults reaches a near 90-degree inclination. On the top of the ramus, we find the coronoid process and the head and neck of the condylar process, separated by the mandibular notch. The coronoid process serves as an attachment for the temporalis muscle, whereas the head of the condylar process articulates with the temporal bone to create the temporo-mandibular joint (Zemlin 1998).

During evolution, the human mandible has seen a dramatic reduction in prognathism (degree of protrusion relative to a predetermined imaginary line in the frontal plane of the skull) and length, as well as changes in number and size of teeth, resulting in a relatively flat face and (among other factors) giving rise to our uniquely bended vocal tract shape with a near equal-sized horizontal oral cavity and vertical pharyngeal cavity (Anderson, Thompson, and Popovich 1975; Lieberman 2007). Such evolutionary changes are also manifested in significant differences among primates in symphyseal inclination (angle between the principal axis of the symphysis and alveolar plane) and bicanine width (crosswise distance between the bottommost points of the canine crypts), which has been related to how the overall species-specific size of the mandible needs to accommodate the formation of dentition (Fukase 2012). However, a general support for the idea that mandibular dimensions across hominins and other primates reflect tooth dimensions (simply put, bigger teeth need bigger jaws) was not confirmed in a recent study (Plavcan and Daegling 2006). However, these authors did find that across different primate species canine tooth size was correlated with mandibular depth in males, be it that such effects are more likely to occur beyond a certain canine size. Most likely, changes in size and shape of the mandible during the development of hominins were the result of a variety of factors, including biomechanical changes in occlusal load distribution and variations in tooth dimensions in what is likely to be a response to functional adaptations in lifestyle and diet (Plavcan and Daegling 2006). Interestingly, the study by Anderson and colleagues (1975) found a positive relationship between body weight, mandibular prognathism and length (i.e., larger body weight tends to come with longer and more prognatic jaws) in a sample of over 200 Caucasian males and females, mostly from Anglo-Saxon origin

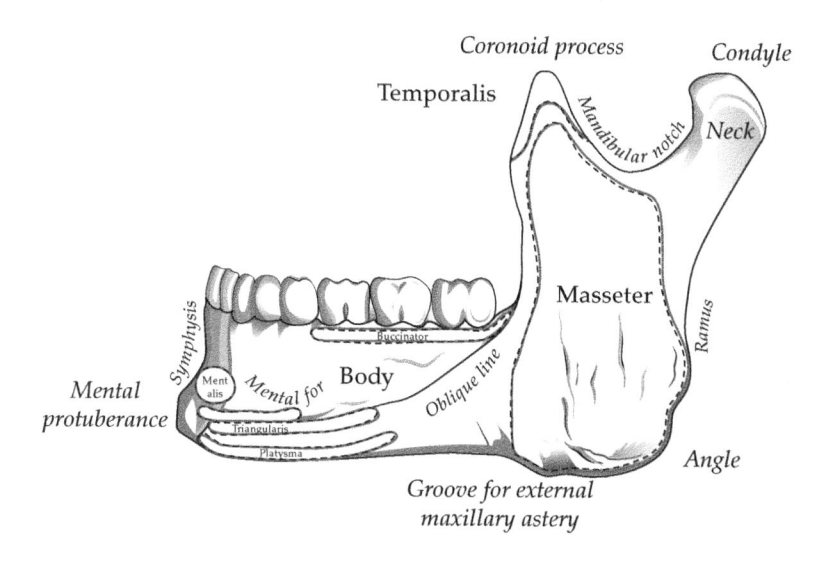

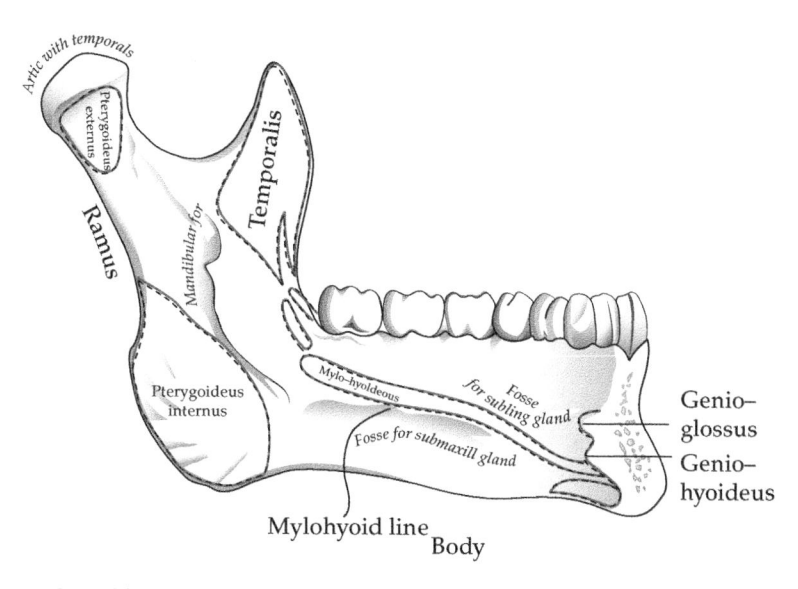

Figure 5.4 Mandible and areas of muscular attachments. Wikimedia Commons, http://en.wikipedia.org/wiki/File:Gray176.png and http://en.wikipedia.org/wiki/File:Gray177.png; *Gray's Anatomy of the Human Body*, 20th US Edition, 1918.

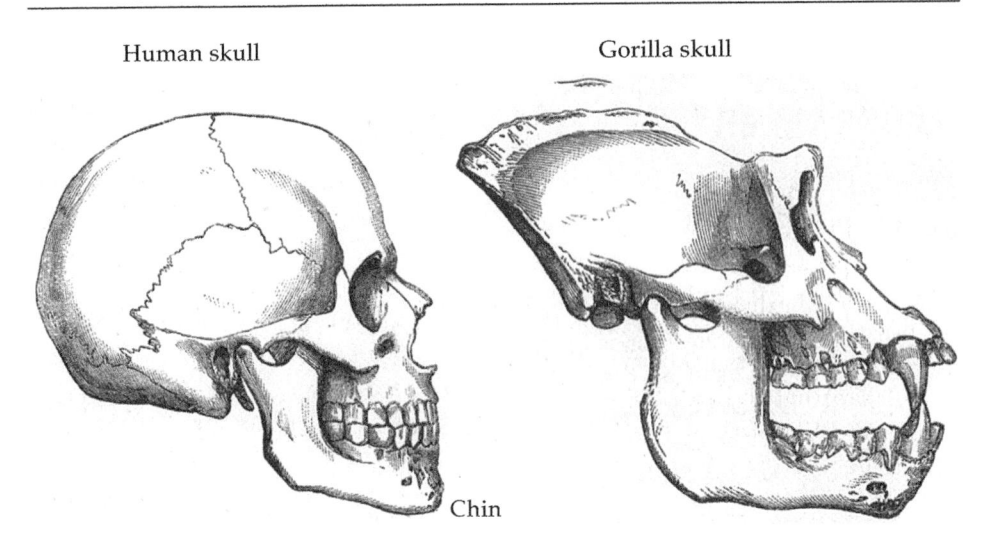

Figure 5.5 Skulls of adult specimens of a human and gorilla. Courtesy of University of Wisconsin Digital Collections.

and derived from lateral cephalograms taken at the age of 16 as part of the Burlington Growth Centre database. These authors speculated about a possible relationship between environmental challenges (lack of sufficient food), reductions in body weight/size to enhance survival, and accompanying changes in mandibular geometry in our ancestors.

A recent paper by Daegling (2012) reviewed the existing literature on the possible role of speech on the development of the modern human mandible. In essence, the human mandible has two characteristic features that distinguish it from other hominoids. First, there is the hypertrophy of cortical bone (also known as compact bone, which forms the outer shell of most bones) in the mandibular corpus. Second, there is the chin or anterior basal swelling of the mandibular symphysis. The latter feature is clearly shown in comparing the skull of a human with that of a gorilla as depicted in Figure 5.5. Section 5.3.1 provides some more detail about the relevance of these differences in oral motor functions that require substantial force generation as in chewing.

The mandible is a large, dense and very strong bone. A study by Zhang, Peck, and Hannam (2002) using CT scans to estimate jaw mass properties from eight adult human mandibles, reported an estimated mass of 102.32 g (SD = 18.33) and an average bone density of $1.72\,g/cm^3$ (SD = 0.02). The mass estimates ignored soft tissue components, which could increase the actual mass by roughly a factor of four. Moments of inertia were found to be smallest around the jaw's lateral axis, and largest around its vertical axis. In other words, it requires less muscle rotational force (torque) to accelerate the jaw for open-close movements than for lateral excursions (see also Shiller, Houle, and Ostry 2005). The center of mass is located in the midsagittal plane between second and third molars, in the upper third part

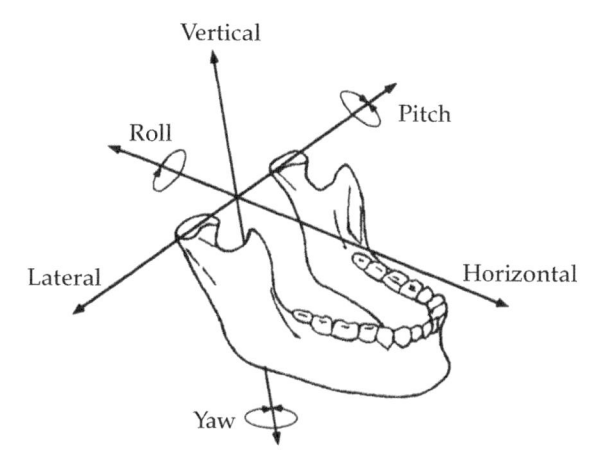

Figure 5.6 Translational and rotational components of mandibular motion. Vatikiotis-Bateson and Ostry (1995: Figure 1). Reproduced Courtesy of Elsevier.

of the distance between occlusal plane and lower border of the mandible. Mandibular length (3D distance between condylion and gnathion) in the samples used by Zhang and colleagues (2002) varied roughly between 110 and 124 mm and correlated with mass estimates.

Moving the mandible is primarily a responsibility of the muscles involved in mastication and speech but passive structures may restrict certain movements. In a review on the dynamics of the mandibular system, Koolstra (2002) lists several reasons why it is relatively underrepresented in research compared to other parts of the human musculoskeletal system. In essence, these reasons come down to the fact that the mandible and its associated structures form a complex system with many muscles of different size, shape, and with an architecture acting on structurally complex temporo-mandibular joints (TMJ) allowing for six degrees of freedom (see also Vatikiotis-Bateson and Ostry 1995) as illustrated in Figure 5.6. In addition, access to these muscles through electromyographic (EMG) recordings is limited in human participants (see Davies et al. 2012; Kawakami et al. 2012 for some recent alternative approaches).

The mandible articulates with the skull in such a way that the head of the condylar process rotates and translates along the surface of the mandibular fossa and articular eminence of the temporal bone. Both condylar and temporal bone surfaces are covered by cartilage. In addition, since the shapes of the temporal and mandibular joint surfaces are quite different, the presence of a separate cartilage disk reduces friction and increases stability. The disk is able to not only follow the movements of the condylar head, but also has some freedom to rotate on the condylar head. This flexibility is largely responsible for the extended degrees of freedom in the TMJ (Koolstra 2002; Zemlin 1998).

The mandibular system not only has the capacity to support very different oral motor functions (as in chewing and speech), it also shows kinematic redundancy, which means that the same movement outcome can be generated by a great variety of muscle contraction patterns (Koolstra 2002; Vatikiotis-Bateson and Ostry 1995). For each muscle acting upon the mandible, it can create (when activated unilaterally) a translational movement along its principal line of action and at the same time a rotation around the axis perpendicular to that and running through the jaw's center of gravity. For example, contraction of a muscle that will move the jaw upward will at the same time induce a rotation around the x-axis (front-back). As such, these two movement components are not independent and for that particular line of action represent a single degree of freedom. In other words, the degrees of freedom in any muscle system depends on the available number of independent lines of action, which for the jaw system is much higher than the six degrees of freedom associated with jaw movement and this explains the kinematic redundancy mentioned above (see Koolstra 2002: Figure 4). The actual movement of the jaw reflects the net combination of linear and angular accelerations induced by all active and passive forces acting on this structure.

The muscles that act upon these complex joints are traditionally separated in jaw elevators and jaw depressors. The jaw elevators consist of the masseter, temporalis, and medial pterygoid muscles, and the jaw-depressor group is formed by the geniohyoid, mylohyoid, and digastric muscles. The lateral pterygoid muscle with its two heads is involved in both jaw protrusion and opening movements. The elevator muscles have a clear pennate structure with large cross-sectional areas and short fibers, well suited to generate large forces. In contrast, the depressor muscles and lateral pterygoid muscle show a more parallel structure, thus able to contract over longer distances using less force (Zemlin 1998).

In order to understand the different contractile characteristics of these muscles and the resulting forces that drive the motion of the jaw, it is important to be aware of the differences in fiber type composition and fiber cross-sectional area.

The temporalis, masseter, and pterygoid muscles show an abundance of hybrid fibers, with a large number expressing MyHC-I (MyHC = Myosin Heavy Chain components, which basically determine the speed of motor unit contraction), MyHC-fetal, and MyHC-cardiac alpha isoforms (these are functionally equivalent proteins but encoded by a different gene). In addition, their type I fibers show a larger cross-sectional area than type II fibers (note: type I fibers have lower contraction velocities than type II fibers, but are less prone to fatigue). The temporalis also shows overall larger fibers and a different fiber type composition compared to the other two muscles. In contrast, mylohyoid, geniohyoid, and digastric muscles showed less hybrid fibers without a clear difference in cross-sectional areas for type I versus type II fibers. They contain less of the MyHC-I, MyHc-fetal, and MyHC-cardiac alpha isoforms and more of the MyHC-IIA type (Korfage et al. 2005a, 2005b; Korfage and Van Eijden 2000). Korfage and colleagues (2005a, 2005b) also found intramuscular differences in fiber type composition, and in another study reported that medial and lateral pterygoid muscles do not differ from each other in myosin isoform composition, despite their different roles in mastication (Korfage, Brugman, and Van Eijden 2000). Overall, it is suggested by the differences in fiber type composition that jaw closing muscles are more optimized to operate in a slower and smooth force-generating manner, whereas the jaw opening muscles are more optimized for faster movements. The latter are also structurally less complex in terms of activation, fiber type composition, and muscular architecture (Korfage et al. 2005b).

Muscle contractions induce a change in tension through actin-myosin cross-bridging, which can lead to muscle shortening, lengthening, or no change in length. The amount of force generated by jaw muscles is determined by the specific strength of isometric contraction in relation to the length of the muscle (force–length relationship) and the speed by which they can change their length (force–velocity relationship). Examples of how such principles can play a role in protective mechanisms (limiting maximum jaw opening or deceleration of jaw closing during forceful biting) can be found in Koolstra (2002). As a proper understanding of muscle contributions to jaw movement is extremely difficult to achieve through human experimentation, biomechanical models have been used as alternative means with some success (see Peck and Hannam 2007 for a recent review). In particular, for speech it is important to account for the biomechanical influences caused by soft tissue deformations and interactions with bony structures on both passively induced and active movements generated by specific neural control signals. Passive factors in jaw movement are mostly related to influences due to the shape of articulator surfaces in TMJ, the presence of reactive forces due to TMJ loading, restraining (protective) forces from TMJ ligaments, and passive stretch of muscles. Such passive forces are considered most important at the boundaries of active movements and when the jaw movements show lateral deviations (Koolstra 2002).

Although there are several biomechanically plausible models proposed for speech and other oral motor functions, I will highlight one specific model because it included simulations of biomechanical influences and neural control signals on multiple vocal tract components, including jaw (Sanguineti, Laboissière, and Ostry 1998). This model, based on X-ray data from a young female speaker, incorporated two degrees of freedom for the mandible (sagittal orientation and translation). The mandibular inertia was fixed at $0.0042\,\text{kg}\,\text{m}^2$ and its mass at 1 kg (Laboissière, Ostry, and Feldman 1996), which may be a bit high given the mass estimate of 102.32 g (SD = 18.33) reported in a study by Zhang and colleagues (2002). In addition, most of the other physical parameters in this model were estimated based on a small number of studies in humans and animals, which obviously introduces some simplifications to the complex nature of the system. For example, the model included a single jaw opener and jaw closer component, which each represented the effects of all individual muscles that act upon the jaw. In spite of these simplifications, the simulations reproduced clear effects of jaw movement (protrusion/retraction, rotation) on tongue position found in real data. The authors also reported that the individual commands for movement of model components gave rise to the same position changes regardless of the initial configuration of the vocal tract, suggesting that commands are independent and can be combined in a linear fashion to generate any type of movement. Obviously, much more modeling work remains to be done, and advances in technology and a better understanding of individual variations in jaw geometry and muscle activation dynamics will lead to further improvements.

5.2.2.1 Blood supply With respect to the vascularization of the mandibular structures, the main vessel supplying blood to the body of the mandible is the inferior alveolar artery (Ø 280 micron), which originates from the maxillary artery (a major branch from the external carotid artery). The inferior alveolar artery splits off in two branches, with the incisor branch supplying a capillary network in support of dental pulp, alveolar bone, interalveolar septi, and periodontal membranes, and the mental branch exiting through the mental foramen supplying the chin, eventually connecting to the inferior labial and submental arteries (Zemlin 1998).

The inferior alveolar artery splits off the mylohyoid branch at the point where it enters the foramen in order to supply the mylohyoid muscle. The condyloid and coronoid processes have their own blood supply. The condyloid process capillaries are fed by arteries (Ø 120 micron) from the temporo-mandibular joint and lateral pterygoid muscle, whereas the coronoid process is supplied by slightly smaller vessels (Ø 70 micron) originating from the temporalis muscle. Larger size vessels (Ø > 250 microns) originating from the inferior alveolar artery in the incisive area of the mandible branch off to the geniohyoid, genioglossus, and anterior digastric muscles. The veins in this area follow their own course, providing an effective venous drainage system especially around the interalveolar septi (Bentsianov and Blitzer 2004; Castelli 1963; Loukas et al. 2008).

5.2.2.2 Nerve supply Both the depressor and elevator muscles of mastication are innervated by the motor fibers of the trigeminal nerve, the largest cranial nerve (see Figure 5.3). The trigeminal nerve provides sensation for the entire face except for a small area around the mandibular angle and the auricular lobe, which is innervated by the great auricular nerve (Siemionow et al. 2011). The trigeminal nerve splits into three major branches distal from the trigeminal ganglion: the ophthalmic branch (V1; sensory only), the maxillary branch (V2; sensory only), and the largest one, the mandibular branch (V3; sensory and motor). The latter first splits into a small branch called the nervus spinosus, which innervates the dura mater and mucous lining of the mastoid cells, a recurrent meningeal branch and the medial pterygoid nerve (including motor nerves to tensor tympani and tensor veli palatini muscles). A further division creates a smaller anterior part, which is mostly motor, and a larger posterior part. The anterior part continues as masseteric nerve, deep temporal nerve, long buccal nerve, and lateral pterygoid nerve. The posterior part continues as the auricolotemporal nerve, lingual nerve, and the inferior alveolar nerve. The latter further splits off the mylohoid nerve – this also involves the anterior belly of digastric muscles, and sensory fibers innervating mandibular teeth; (Rodella et al. 2012) – and after passing through the mental foramen, it terminates in the mental and incisive nerves. The sensory fibers innervate the skin and mucous membrane of the cheeks, ear, the lining of the external auditory meatus and tympanic membrane, the temporo-mandibular joint, the parotid gland, and the skin in the temporal region and covering the side of the head above the ears, the auricle, the anterior two-thirds of the tongue, as well as the mandibular teeth and associated gingiva, together with the skin and mucosa of the lower lip and the chin. For many of these nerves there is considerable anatomical variation in terms of extra branches, interconnections between nerves (e.g., between lingual and inferior alveolar or mylohyoid nerve), their relationship to principal arteries, and associated variations in the number (and in some cases locations) of mandibular accessory foramina and canals (Rodella et al. 2012; see also Liang et al. 2009; Siemionow et al. 2011). Such anatomical variations may complicate surgical procedures, administration of anesthesia, and potentially trigger certain trigeminal pain conditions (Rodella et al. 2012; Siemionow et al. 2011).

5.3 Role of lips and jaw in oral motor functions

Following the basic review on the structural aspects of the lips and mandible, we turn now to three specific oral motor functions of these articulators. The main focus will be on speech, as this is typically considered to be the most complex oral motor function we can perform, but we start with other primary oral motor functions of these articulators, chewing and swallowing, since these functions are likely to underlie the evolution of speech behavior (see, e.g., MacNeilage, this volume, Chapter 16). As highlighted above, the lips and jaw also contribute significantly to facial expression, but this primary function is not addressed in the current chapter due to limited space.

5.3.1 Chewing

The main purpose of chewing is to break down food into smaller particles using predominantly the (pre)molars. These particles when mixed with saliva will create a softer bolus that is easier to swallow. The smaller particles also enable early digestive processes in the way enzymes in the saliva[2] (e.g., amylase which breaks down starch and lipase fat) can do their work more efficiently due to the effective increase in net contact surface area.

In a detailed recent review, van der Bilt (2011) summarizes the main features of chewing. Typically it is characterized by a fast and slow closing component: the fast closure is the initial lower jaw closing movement until the teeth contact the bolus at which point the closing action slows down in order to compact and fragmentize the food parts, applying carefully adjusted force to the jaw in relation to the physical properties of the bolus (e.g., more muscle activity is found with harder foods). Masticatory performance (i.e., the ability to grind or mix test samples after a fixed number of chewing cycles) is negatively influenced by loss of (pre)molars and dentures and shows a large variation across healthy individuals. Dental status and number of teeth also seem strong indicators for self-reported masticatory ability, although objective performance tests and subjective assessments of mastication function are poorly correlated. People in general seem consistent in the number of cycles they use across different types of food, leading to fast (few cycles) and slow (many cycles) swallowers, and this number may or may not correlate to chewing performance depending on the type of food. However, those who show good masticatory performance tend to swallow smaller food particles in general (van der Bilt 2011).

As mentioned, dental status and number of teeth are important factors in determining chewing efficiency. Another relevant factor is (maximum) voluntary bite force, which is higher for males (ranging between 306 N(ewton) and 878 N unilaterally and between 491 N and 1110 N bilaterally across different studies) compared to females (ranging between 234 N and 690 N unilaterally and between 442 N and 615 N bilaterally across different studies) and tends to decrease with age (van der Bilt 2011). It has been argued that modern humans lack a strong bite force compared to other members of the hominidae family due to smaller jaw muscles and a lighter overall skull construction, but a recent study by Wroe and colleagues (2010) using a three-dimensional finite element analysis technique actually showed this not to be true. In comparing skulls and lower jaw models of an adult human female with those of four other adult female members of the hominidae family (the common chimpanzee, gorilla, orangutan, and white-handed gibbon) as well as with virtual reconstructions of fossil remains of two early hominins (*Australopithecus africanus* and *Paranthropus boisei*), their findings show that in principle modern humans can generate bite forces that are comparable to those of similar-sized other members of the hominidae (note that bite force correlates with body mass), while using less muscular force from the mandibular closing muscles and without causing more mechanical stress in the skull. These authors also concluded that "the human mandible may in fact be better adapted than those of other hominids to resist stresses developed under the specific loadings applied here, which are designed to simulate peak transitory bite forces" (2010: 3584). However, such efficiency may be restricted to rotational jaw movements compared to translation as needed for powerful sustained chewing (Wroe et al. 2010). In other words, we can crack the occasional nut (with proper healthy dentition), but we should not engage in chewing tough materials for a relatively long time.

Saliva is another important factor for chewing (as mentioned above) and its flow (0.16–4.55 mL min^{-1} across studies using mechanical stimulation) is assumed to be triggered by the impact of chewing on gingival mechanoreceptors, even at low force levels. Saliva flow rate has not been found to be a strong predictor for the number of chewing cycles, but obviously, people with high flow rates will tend to show a better bolus status (moist and slippery) prior to swallowing (for more details see van der Bilt 2011).

Although the jaw plays the most important role in chewing, the lips are also quite active. Orbicularis oris (superior or OOS and inferior or OOI) EMG activity has been reported to vary as a function of the duration of the chewing cycle, size of the bolus, and whether or not the lips are in contact with each other during chewing (van der Bilt 2011). Most of orbicularis activity is found during the opening part of the chewing cycle (van der Bilt 2011; see also Hanawa et al. 2008; Ingervall 1978; Ingervall and Hedegård 1980), which is assumed to serve the purpose of keeping the lips closed to avoid bolus spillage. Buccinator muscle activity is also seen during the opening phase of the chewing cycle (van der Bilt 2011; Hanawa et al. 2008), probably used to position bolus content between the dental arches in preparation of the upward movement of the lower jaw by masseter muscle and other jaw elevators. Larger boluses seem to enhance the effects by inducing greater amounts of activity in all muscles, as well as showing some changes in the relative timing and duration of muscle activity periods (Hanawa et al. 2008; Schieppati, Di Francesco, and Nardone 1989). In sum, with respect to the lips during chewing, the literature suggests that their contribution is important for keeping food inside the mouth during especially the open phase and that their activities may differ as a function of inherent (or acquired) orofacial morphological variations.

In terms of neural control, chewing is invoked by input to jaw muscle motoneurons from different levels (Lund 1991). Cortical areas involved in chewing seem to be most active during food intake, which is interpreted as setting the stage for the first bite (Sessle 2011). In mammals, these areas are involved in controlling the output of the central pattern generator (CPG), located in the brainstem, to adapt these patterns to changes in bolus resistance for controlling bite force. This is clearly shown in changes in jaw muscle activity, jaw amplitude, and cycle duration as food becomes smaller in size and softer due to mixing with saliva over the course of a sequence of chewing cycles. The CPG itself generates the basic rhythmic activity of the jaw opening and closing during chewing (van der Bilt 2011; Lund and Kolta 2006). The fact that normal chewing behavior is not stereotypical and shows variation from cycle to cycle in response to changes in food status and other factors, suggests that the CPG output is modified based on information related to the position and velocity of the jaw, the forces acting upon the jaw and teeth, and the length and contraction velocity of the involved muscles (see Lund 2011 for a review).

The sensory role in jaw muscle control was clearly shown in a study on human participants using a jaw perturbation paradigm (Abbink et al. 1998). Here it was found that on average peripherally triggered (muscle spindle-based) muscle activity occurred 25 ms after presentation of the (unexpected) load in both digastric and masseter muscles. If the load was expected, both muscles showed an increase in EMG activity preceding the load onset. This increase in EMG activity prior to loading was followed within 120 ms by an even stronger reflex-based increase in both muscles, although the relative increase was much higher for the masseter, suggesting a stronger response ability in this closing muscle to jaw perturbations. Muscle spindle feedback from jaw closers is typically suppressed during jaw opening and jaw reflexes in general are modulated during different phases of the chewing cycle, with stronger responses closer to occlusion (see also Kubota and Masegi 1977).

5.3.2 *Swallowing*

During swallowing, the lips perform basically the same function as during chewing, namely to create a seal between them to prevent spillage of food while it is manipulated inside the mouth. A study by Ding and colleagues (2002) indicated that while OOI activity starts earlier than OOS (on average by 133 ms; SD 106 ms) and leads the onset of the swallowing sequence, the OOS was found to be typically the first muscle to start the final swallowing stage. These authors also reported no significant difference in EMG activity during normal swallows between OOI and OOS, unlike what is reported for speech (see section 5.3.3). In comparing (healthy aging) older and younger individuals, a recent study showed no group differences in lip pressure and lip pressure variation, but there was evidence for reduced lip pressure and increased variation for seniors who show signs of dysphagia (Tamura et al. 2009).

With respect to jaw movements, earlier work by Hiiemae and colleagues (1996) identified distinct jaw movements for the different stages in swallowing, with an increase in chewing cycles during stage I transport (initial bite and moving bolus from incisors to (pre)molars) as a function of bolus type (more cycles with harder food). During stage II transport, jaw movements for chewing alternate with jaw cycles for intermittent swallows, which on average had longer durations due to increased durations of jaw opening (see also van der Bilt 2011). During final clearance swallows, jaw movements were found to be very irregular.

Clearly, there is a complex relationship between jaw and tongue movements during swallowing as shown in consistent patterns of tongue movement relative to jaw movement with high correlations for in particular the vertical dimension of tongue and jaw movements. Palmer, Hiiemae, and Liu (1997) provide a detailed description of these patterns, starting with a maximum gape during food ingestion followed by fairly cyclic movements except during the already mentioned clearance phase prior to the final swallow, where the jaw basically positions the tongue. The authors related differences in early and middle/late cycles to food consistency, which also affected jaw movement amplitudes (smaller for softer foods). Jaw opening was found to be correlated with a downward motion of the anterior tongue, which is consistent with the findings of Matsuo and Palmer (2010) showing a relative stronger influence of jaw on anterior tongue movement compared to posterior tongue movement in swallowing. The same authors found overall lower correlations for speech and this agrees with earlier work by Hertrich and Ackermann (2000) who also found that for speech the relationship between jaw and tongue movements seems less constrained and shows strong phonetic and individual influences. In the study by Matsuo and Palmer (2010), horizontal movements of the tongue showed little influence from jaw movements, but more so from hyoid movements, which also had a stronger influence on posterior tongue position.

Another study investigated the coupling between different segments of the tongue with jaw in more detail, based on a very large sample of swallows for thin and honey-thick liquids with both discrete and continuous swallows using electromagnetic articulography (Steele and Van Lieshout 2008). The findings showed a relatively consistent pattern of tongue–jaw coupling across the repeated swallows, but with sufficient flexibility to accommodate differences in bolus consistency. However, more recently the same group (Steele, Van Lieshout, and Pelletier 2012) reported on tongue segment sequences and found a remarkable absence of any dominant pattern in thin liquid discrete swallows, suggesting a high degree of flexibility in how different parts of the tongue contribute to liquid bolus transport across individuals and even within individuals.

In sum then, for swallowing the lips perform an important function in keeping the bolus in place, and assisting the tongue in its main role to position food for mastication (in between occlusal surfaces) and moving it from the anterior to the posterior end of oral cavity, and further downward once it passes into the oropharynx. The jaw forms a functional synergy with the tongue during swallowing, next to playing a different role in chewing (see section 5.3.1). Mostly its influence pertains to vertical movements of the front of the tongue, although other parts of the tongue are functionally linked as well (van der Bilt 2011).

5.3.3 Speech production

What about the role of jaw and lips in speech production? There are in fact, many studies that have investigated the characteristics of these movements (and associated muscle activations) in a variety of tasks. This review takes a developmental and evolutionary perspective on the question.

From a developmental perspective, it is relevant to know how lips and jaw are coordinated in early stages of (pre)speech and at what point their patterns of interaction reflect the use of highly efficient coordinative structures that is typically witnessed in the articulation of normal speaking adults. To address this question, Green and colleagues (2000) performed a cross-sectional study with 1, 2, and 6 year-old children as well as a group of adults, using video registrations of facial markers on upper lip, lower lip, and jaw during the production of bisyllabic words with bilabial consonants (*baba*, *papa*, and *mama*). Their premise was based on three key concepts: differentiation, integration, and refinement. *Differentiation* refers to the process of modifying existing (more general) behaviors toward more task-specific functions, often on the basis of the development of stronger independence among formerly tightly "coupled" structures. *Integration* on the other hand refers to a process whereby new functional units are created by incorporating a (new) behavior into existing (stable) behaviors. *Refinement* is the ongoing modification of existing behaviors toward a more adult-like model. Their findings indicated that the jaw was the most significant contributor to oral closure for the 1 and 2 year-olds (with the strongest overall jaw contribution for the 1 year-olds) and more equal contributions for lower lip and jaw were found for 6 year-olds and adults. The upper lip contribution in general was very small for all groups, which to some extent contrast with the stronger involvement of upper lip in other oral motor functions (chewing, swallowing), as described in sections 5.3.1 and 5.3.2. In general, spatial (correlation coefficients) and temporal (lags) indices indicated stronger coherence among the structures with an increase in age. The authors interpreted their findings as being in support of the concepts proposed by MacNeilage (1998; see also this volume, Chapter 16) who argues that the jaw and lips initially act as a single uniform control unit in early stages of babbling (essentially, the lower lip follows the jaw), but then will show a differentiation ("release") of the upper and lower lip movements toward more independent actions in support of labial gestures, and this process shows further tuning toward the complex sound productions found at later stages.

In a later study, Green, Moore, and Reilly (2002) confirmed their initial findings showing a non-uniform development in the control of jaw and lips, with the latter reaching adult-like patterns much later than the former (see also Smith 1995). The same group also looked at chewing development (Green et al. 1997) and noticed how the more fixed coordination pattern between jaw muscles found for four children between 1 and 4 years during chewing would be less suitable for speech. This seems an interesting contrast with a recent study which used a principal component approach for tongue movements in speech and swallowing and found that the feeding model created by the authors was more general in nature and suitable to reconstruct speech-related tongue articulations (Serrurier et al. 2012).

Differences in the stability of lip movement during development have been shown in a series of studies (Goffman and Smith 1999; Smith and Goffman 1998). Moreover, they were able to demonstrate that variability in lower lip movements was conditioned by changes in linguistic complexity both in adults and children, but more strongly so for the latter group (Maner, Smith, and Grayson 2000; see also Dromey and Benson 2003). Such differences seem to reflect changes in neural control as opposed to changes in movement patterns induced by adaptations to the size or shape of the orofacial structures, as lower lip and jaw movement amplitudes were not found to vary with size when comparing adults with children (Riely and Smith 2003). This seems in contrast to the findings on the relationship between deep masseter muscle activity and mandibular symphysis size/shape found for chewing (Vinyard et al. 2011). In the study by Riely and Smith (2003), children did show temporal differences (lower peak velocities) with adult speakers, which the authors interpreted as the consequence of a more feedback-driven control strategy.

The notion that feedback plays a strong role in the development of control of speech movements was emphasized by Barlow and Estep (2006), highlighting how sensory modulation shapes the assembly and output of CPGs in patterned output behaviors, perhaps similar to how such networks are used in the control of other oral motor functions. Such a modulation can be envisioned in terms of entrainment between afferent input and efferent output of neural networks (Barlow and Estep 2006; Van Lieshout 2004; Williamson 1998) and based on this principle, our lab has conducted several studies to determine to what extent changes in movement output (and as we assume, by consequence, sensory input) may influence motor control stability. These studies uniquely demonstrated that the coordination between individual articulators or synergies (a.k.a. gestures; Goldstein, Byrd, and Saltzman 2006) is influenced by movement amplitude which most likely can be associated with a certain critical but idiosyncratic amplitude threshold (Namasivayam and Van Lieshout 2011; Namasivayam and Van Lieshout 2008; Namasivayam et al. 2009; Terband et al. 2009; Van Lieshout, Hulstijn, and Peters 2004; Van Lieshout, Rutjens, and Spauwen 2002; Van Lieshout et al. 2007). In several of these studies, it was interesting to notice how only changes in upper lip movement seem influential on coordination stability in the production of bilabial gestures. One could argue that lower lip movements are more critical in the expression of linguistic contrast (Barlow and Rath 1985; Maner et al. 2000), which would free up the upper lip to modify its contribution in the expression of bilabial gestures for motor control stabilization purposes. The smaller contribution for upper lip found in the study by Green and colleagues (2000) may thus not only reflect the physically more limited movement range for this articulator, but also its more flexible role in speech, as opposed to its more constrained contribution during chewing and swallowing.

What about lip and jaw movements during speech production in terms of general kinematic features? How much and how fast can they move? The Riely and Smith (2003) study showed that lower lip movement ranges for two sentence tasks ("buy Bobby a puppy" and "mommy bakes pot pies") were around 8 mm for 5 year-olds (N=30) and 9 mm for young adults (N=30), with peak velocities on average at 146 mm/s for the children and 222 mm/s for adults. In contrast, a study on 15 healthy adult speakers (Tasko and McClean 2004) found lower lip and mandibular displacements for a sentence, paragraph reading, and monologue task, produced at different rates and/or loudness levels, to be very small at around 2 mm, whereas the upper lip was moving on average at 1.5 mm. The differences across studies could easily have resulted from the use of different stimuli. Given the more natural speech context in the Tasko and McClean study, it may confirm that casual speech typically shows more reduced speech movement ranges along the hypo/hyperspeech continuum as suggested by Lindblom (1983). Peak speeds in the Tasko and McClean study also showed a strong similarity between the lips (around 20 mm/s for lower lip/jaw vs. 15 mm/s for upper lip), whereas opening/closing durations varied around 130 ms for both lips and close to 150 ms for the jaw. Changes in these parameters across rate and loudness manipulations varied for the different articulators. As one would expect, rate variations induced systematic changes in movement durations (shorter durations for faster rates), but only small and often non-significant changes in movement displacement. Movement speed was found to be slower in the slow rate condition. Confirming an earlier report by Dromey and Ramig (1998), the data showed a trend for louder speech to be associated with larger movement ranges and higher peak speeds whereas softer speech showed the reverse pattern.

With respect to mandibular movements, a study on 40 Brazilian Portuguese speaking adult participants during a picture naming task (Bianchini and de Andrade 2006), showed a sagittal opening range of 12.77 mm (frontal: 11.21 mm). Forward movements were small (1.22 mm) whereas backward movements showed a greater displacement (5.67 mm). Sideward movements were very small to both the right (1.49 mm) and left (1.59 mm). The limitations in sideward and forward/backward movements relative to superior/inferior movements can be explained by biomechanical restrictions on the former movement dimensions for both speech and chewing (Shiller et al. 2005; Zhang et al. 2002).

In terms of the forces that can be generated by the lips during speech, Barlow and Rath (1985) measured maximum voluntary closing force (MVCF) separately for upper and lower lip in 15 male and 15 female adults. For male participants upper lip MVCF ranged between 1.85 N and 6.87 N (Mean = 4.44 N) and for females it was found to be between 1.15 N and 5.07 N (Mean = 3.35 N). For lower lip these values were higher, with a range between 7.20 N and 22.06 N (Mean = 14.13 N) for males and between 3.44 N and 17.61 (Mean = 8.98 N) for females. Clearly, lower lip forces were significantly higher in both groups compared to upper lip and males in general produced greater forces with both lips compared to female participants. In a different study, Barlow and Muller (1991) looked at the relationship between interangle span (as an indicator for muscle length) and maximum voluntary contraction (MVC), estimating both passive (due to tension of the stretched elastic lower face tissue) and active components (due to work performed by contractile elements in the muscles) from the total resultant interangle forces. Again, there were two groups of adult participants (15 males and 15 females). First, interangle force (both passive and active) increased with interangle span. Passive force was not found to be different between men and women and ranged from near 0 at rest position to close to 1.5 N at a maximum interangle span of 70 mm. Active force generation did indicate a gender difference, especially at larger interangle spans, with males and females showing an average active force generation of close to 5 N at rest position and going up to about 20 N for males and 13 N for females at a maximum interangle span of 70 mm. Exponential functions explained a significant portion (R^2 values above 90%) of the relationship between interangle span and both passive and active force generation.

How do we know the lips and jaw work together as a control unit? Most of the evidence in favor of this notion comes from studies where either lower lip or jaw are prevented from either moving at all (static perturbation) or from continuing its normal trajectory (dynamic perturbation). Perturbation paradigms became very popular in the late 1970s and early 1980s and showed that in general the lips work toward a common goal (lip closure in the case of bilabial stops), such that if the lower lip is prevented from doing so (in time), both lips show a compensatory attempt to overcome the potential negative effects on achieving their goal (e.g., Abbs and Gracco 1984; Folkins and Zimmermann 1982; Kelso et al. 1984). This compensation has been found to be specific to the type of speech task (Shaiman 1989). This paradigm was later extended to investigate coordination across oral and laryngeal structures (Munhall, Löfqvist, and Kelso 1994; Saltzman et al. 1998) with a similar outcome; namely, that within and across systems, control is targeted toward achieving task specific goals as exemplified in the concept of coordinative structures or gestures (Browman and Goldstein 1992; Goldstein et al. 2006). A more recent study indicated that such compensatory responses may differ for younger and older participants (Marzullo et al. 2010), such that younger people do better on these manipulations and neural activation patterns differ across the age groups. Younger people may do better because their sensory systems are not affected by age, even though during regular speech such age-related differences may not become evident in the control of speech articulators (Bennett, Van Lieshout, and Steele 2007). The perturbation paradigm has also been used with patient populations, for example in stuttering individuals, showing that although they accommodate for these perturbations, they do so in a different way than non-stuttering individuals (Namasivayam, Van Lieshout, and De Nil 2008).

In sum then, published data support the notion that lips and jaw form a functional control unit that can display a tremendous amount of flexibility in achieving specific speech task goals, even different from using the same structures in non-speech tasks (Bose and Van Lieshout 2012). Their movements in general may be relatively small (and often fast) when compared to other oromotor functions like chewing and swallowing, which may provide some challenges for keeping their execution stable, especially in light of potential limitations due to disease or increasing age.

5.4 Summary and conclusions

This chapter was written to review the anatomy and function of lips and jaw. Obviously, it is impossible to completely cover the extensive literature on this topic in a single paper. One might be surprised initially that there is actually so much literature on these structures, but I hope that in presenting this overview, the reader has gained a new and hopefully better understanding of the richness and complexity of these structures at the anatomical, physiological, and behavioral levels. At the end of this chapter, I would argue that their attraction as objects of high visibility, their role in shaping and visualizing speech sounds, as well as in grinding our food and facilitating its digestion earns them a prominent place in human phylogeny and ontogeny. Despite the rich literature, there is still much to learn about their contributions to speech and other oromotor functions. For example, how are their movements and especially their coordination patterns shaped by both sensory and motor contributions across the lifespan and to what extent can we separate the influence of higher and lower order control networks from the naturally occurring biomechanical constraints/opportunities (Perrier, Ma, and Payan 2005; Sanguineti et al. 1998; Shiller et al. 2005)? How did humans adapt these oral structures to speech over the time course of evolution and how do infants learn to control them going from early-stage feeding behaviors to babbling to adult-like speech? Lips and jaw serve different oromotor functions and developmental patterns are not only non-linear, but also influenced by contextual demands and vulnerable to structural and neurological damage (e.g., Smith 2006; Terband et al. 2011; Van Lieshout, Rutjens, and Spauwen 2002). Knowing more about control principles for lips and jaw in these oromotor functions will hopefully also improve our understanding of how these are changed by disease and traumatic lesions, which in turn may lead to refined diagnostic and treatment procedures.

NOTES

1 The work was made possible in part by funding from the Canada Research Chair program. I wish to further acknowledge the valuable contribution of Dr. Peter Alfonso who commented on an earlier version of this manuscript.
2 Saliva has also an important antimicrobial function (see Tenuvuo 2002 for a brief review).

REFERENCES

Abbink, Jan Hendrik, Andries van der Bilt, Fred Bosman, and Hilbert W. van der Glas. 1998. A comparison of jaw-opener and jaw-closer muscle activity in humans to overcome an external force counteracting jaw movement. *Experimental Brain Research* 118(2): 269–278.

Abbink, Jan Hendrik, Andries van der Bilt, Fred Bosman, and Hilbert W. van der Glas. 1999. Speed-dependent control of cyclic open-close movements of the human jaw with an external force counteracting closing. *Journal of Dental Research* 78(4): 878–886.

Abbs, James H. and Vincent L. Gracco. 1984. Control of complex motor gestures: Orofacial muscle responses to load perturbations of lip during speech. *Journal of Neurophysiology* 51(4): 705–723.

Al-Hayani, A. 2007. Anatomical localisation of the marginal mandibular branch of the facial nerve. *Folia Morphologica (Praha)* 66(4): 307–313.

Al-Hoqail, Rola A. and E.M.A. Meguid. 2008. Anatomic dissection of the arterial supply of the lips: An anatomical and analytical approach. *Journal of Craniofacial Surgery* 19(3): 785–794.

Anderson, D.L., Gordon W. Thompson, and Frank Popovich. 1975. Evolutionary dental changes. *American Journal of Physical Anthropology* 43(1): 95–102.

Archontaki, Maria, Athanasios Athanasiou, Spyros D. Stavrianos, Dimitris P. Korkolis, Gregory Faratzis, Flora Papadopoulou, Georgios Kokkalis, and Alexander D. Rapidis. 2010. Functional results of speech and swallowing after oral microvascular free flap reconstruction. *European Archives of Otorhinolaryngology* 267(11): 1771–1777.

Barlow, Steven M. and Meredith Estep. 2006. Central pattern generation and the motor infrastructure for suck, respiration, and speech. *Journal of Communication Disorders* 39(5): 366–380.

Barlow, Steven M. and Eric M. Muller. 1991. The relation between interangle span and in vivo resultant force in the perioral musculature. *Journal of Speech and Hearing Research* 34(2): 252–259.

Barlow, Steven M. and Erick M. Rath. 1985. Maximum voluntary closing forces in the upper and lower lips of humans. *Journal of Speech and Hearing Research* 28(3): 373–376.

Bennett, Janice W., Pascal H.H.M. Van Lieshout, and Catriona M. Steele. 2007. Tongue control for speech and swallowing in healthy younger and older subjects. *International Journal of Orofacial Myology* 33: 5–18.

Bentsianov, Boris and Andrew Blitzer. 2004. Facial anatomy. *Clinics in Dermatology* 22(1): 3–13.

Bianchini, Esther M.G. and Cláudia R.F. de Andrade. 2006. A model of mandibular movements during speech normative pilot study for the Brazilian Portuguese language. *Cranio: The Journal of Craniomandibular Practice* 24(3): 197–206.

Bose, Arpita and Pascal Van Lieshout. 2012. Speech-like and non-speech lip kinematics and coordination in aphasia. *International Journal of Language & Communication Disorders* 47(6): 654–672.

Browman, Catherine P. and Louis Goldstein. 1992. Articulatory phonology: An overview. *Phonetica* 49(3–4): 155–180.

Castelli, W. 1963. Vascular architecture of the human adult mandible. *Journal of Dental Research* 42: 786–792.

Crouzet, C., Henri Fournier, Xavier Papon, Nejmeddine Hentati, Patrick Cronier, and Ph.H. Mercier. 1998. Anatomy of the arterial vascularization of the lips. *Surgical and Radiologic Anatomy* 20(4): 273–278.

Daegling, David J. 2012. The human mandible and the origins of speech. *Journal of Anthropology* 2: 1–14.

Davies, Joel C., Marc Charles, David Cantelmi, Bernard Liebgott, Mayoorendra Ravichandiran, Kajeandra Ravichandiran, and Anne M. Agur. 2012. Lateral pterygoid muscle: A three-dimensional analysis of neuromuscular partitioning. *Clinical Anatomy* 25(5): 576–583.

Ding, Ruiying, Charles R. Larson, Jeri A. Logemann, and Alfred W. Rademaker. 2002. Surface electromyographic and electroglottographic studies in normal subjects under two swallow conditions: Normal and during the Mendelsohn maneuver. *Dysphagia* 17(1): 1–12.

Diogo, Rui, Bernard A. Wood, Mohammed A. Aziz, and Anne Burrows. 2009. On the origin, homologies and evolution of primate facial muscles with a particular focus on hominoids and a suggested unifying nomenclature for the facial muscles of the Mammalia. *Journal of Anatomy* 215(3): 300–319.

Dromey, Christopher and April Benson. 2003. Effects of concurrent motor, linguistic, or cognitive tasks on speech motor performance. *Journal of Speech, Language, and Hearing Research* 46(5): 1234–1246.

Dromey, Christopher and Lorraine O. Ramig. 1998. Intentional changes in sound pressure level and rate: Their impact on measures of respiration, phonation, and articulation. *Journal of Speech, Language, and Hearing Research* 41(5): 1003–1018.

Edizer, Mete, Orhan Mağden, Volkan Tayfur, Amaç Kiray, Ipek Ergür, and Atay Atabey. 2003. Arterial anatomy of the lower lip: A cadaveric study. *Plastic and Reconstructive Surgery* 111(7): 2176–2181.

Folkins, John W. and Gerald N. Zimmermann. 1982. Lip and jaw interaction during speech responses to perturbation of lower-lip movement prior to bilabial closure. *Journal of the Acoustical Society of America* 71(5): 1225–1233.

Fukase, Hitoshi. 2012. Interspecies difference in placement of developing teeth and its relationship with cross-sectional geometry of the mandibular symphysis in four primate species including modern humans. *American Journal of Physical Anthropology* 147(2): 217–226.

Goffman, Lisa and Anne Smith. 1999. Development and phonetic differentiation of speech movement patterns. *Journal of Experimental Psychology: Human Perception and Performance* 25(3): 649–660.

Goldstein, Louis, Dani Byrd, and Elliott Saltzman. 2006. The role of vocal tract gestural action units in understanding the evolution of phonology. In Michael A. Arbib (ed.), *Action to Language via the Mirror Neuron System*, 215–249. Cambridge: Cambridge University Press.

Green, Jordan R., Christopher A. Moore, and Kevin J. Reilly. 2002. The sequential development of jaw and lip control for speech. *Journal of Speech, Language, and Hearing Research* 45(1): 66–79.

Green, Jordan R., Christopher A. Moore, Masahiko Higashikawa, and Roger W. Steeve. 2000. The physiologic development of speech motor control lip and jaw coordination. *Journal of Speech, Language, and Hearing Research* 43(1): 239–255.

Green, Jordan R., Christopher A. Moore, Jacki L. Ruark, Paula R. Rodda, Wendy T. Morvée, and Marcus J. VanWitzenburg. 1997. Development of chewing in children from 12 to 48 months: Longitudinal study of EMG patterns. *Journal of Neurophysiology* 77(5): 2704–2716.

Hanawa, Soshi, Akito Tsuboi, Makoto Watanabe, and Keiichi Sasaki. 2008. EMG study for perioral facial muscles function during mastication. *Journal of Oral Rehabilitation* 35(3): 159–170.

Hauser, Marc D. 1996. Neurobiological design and communication. In Marc

D. Hauser, *The Evolution of Communication*, 111–266. Cambridge, MA: The MIT Press.

Hertrich, Ingo and Hermann Ackermann. 2000. Lip-jaw and tongue-jaw coordination during rate-controlled syllable repetitions. *Journal of the Acoustical Society of America* 107(4): 2236–2247.

Hiiemae, Karen, Michael R. Heath, Gillian Heath, Ender Kazazoglu, Joseph Murray, Darren Sapper, and Kevin Hamblett. 1996. Natural bites, food consistency and feeding behaviour in man. *Archives of Oral Biology* 41(2): 175–189.

Hwang, K., D.J. Kim, and S.H. Hwang. 2007. Musculature of the pars marginalis of the upper orbicularis oris muscle. *Journal of Craniofacial Surgery* 18: 151–154.

Hwang, Kun, Sheng Jin, SeHo Hwang, and InHyuk Chung. 2006. Innervation of upper orbicularis oris muscle. *Journal of Craniofacial Surgery* 17(6): 1116–1117.

Ingervall, Bengt. 1978. Activity of temporal and lip muscles during swallowing and chewing. *Journal of Oral Rehabilitation* 5(4): 329–337.

Ingervall, Bengt and Björn Hedegård. 1980. An electromyographic study of masticatory and lip muscle function in patients with complete dentures. *Journal of Prosthetic Dentistry* 43(3): 266–271.

Janson, Tomas and Bengt Ingervall. 1982. Relationship between lip strength and lip function in posture and chewing. *European Journal of Orthodontics* 4(1): 45–53.

Kawai, Kenichiro, Nobuaki Imanishi, Hideo Nakajima, Sadakazu Aiso, Masao Kakibuchi, and Ko Hosokawa. 2004. Arterial anatomy of the lower lip. *Scandinavian Journal of Plastic and Reconstructive Surgery and Hand Surgery* 38(3): 135–139.

Kawakami, Shigehisa, Naoki Kodama, Naoto Maeda, Shunichi Sakamoto, Kazuhiro Oki, Yoshinobu Yanagi, Jun-Ichi Asaumi, Teruta Maeda, and Shogo Minagi. 2012. Mechanomyographic activity in the human lateral pterygoid muscle during mandibular movement. *Journal of Neuroscience Methods* 203(1): 157–162.

Kelso, J.A. Scott, Betty Tuller, Eric Vatikiotis-Bateson, and Carol A. Fowler. 1984. Functionally specific articulatory cooperation following jaw perturbations during speech: Evidence for coordinative structures. *Journal of Experimental Psychology: Human Perception and Performance* 10(6): 812–832.

Kent, Ray D. 2004. The uniqueness of speech among motor systems. *Clinical Linguistics and Phonetics* 18(6–8): 495–505.

Koolstra, Jan Harm. 2002. Dynamics of the human masticatory system. *Critical Reviews in Oral Biology and Medicine* 13(4): 366–376.

Korfage, Joannes A.M. and Theo M.G.J. Van Eijden. 2000. Myosin isoform composition of the human medial and lateral pterygoid muscles. *Journal of Dental Research* 79(8): 1618–1625.

Korfage, Joannes A.M., Peter Brugman, and Theo M.G.J. Van Eijden. 2000. Intermuscular and intramuscular differences in myosin heavy chain composition of the human masticatory muscles. *Journal of the Neurological Sciences* 178(2): 95–106.

Korfage, Joannes A.M., Jan Harm Koolstra, Geerling E.J. Langenbach, and Theo M.G.J. Van Eijden. 2005a. Fiber-type composition of the human jaw muscles: (Part 1) Origin and functional significance of fiber-type diversity. *Journal of Dental Research* 84(9): 774–783.

Korfage, Joannes A.M., Jan Harm Koolstra, Geerling E.J. Langenbach, and Theo M.G.J. Van Eijden. 2005b. Fiber-type composition of the human jaw muscles: (Part 2) Role of hybrid fibers and factors responsible for inter-individual variation. *Journal of Dental Research* 84(9): 784–793.

Kubota, Kinziro and Toshiaki Masegi. 1977. Muscle spindle supply to the human jaw muscle. *Journal of Dental Research* 56(8): 901–909.

Laboissière, Rafael, David J. Ostry, and Anatol G. Feldman. 1996. The control of multi-muscle systems: Human jaw and hyoid movements. *Biological Cybernetics* 74(4): 373–384.

Lee, ShuJin, Aymeric Y.T. Lim, IvorJiun Lim, ThiamChye Lim, and Robert W.H. Pho. 2008. Innervation of the face studied using modifications to Sihler's technique in a primate model. *Plastic and Reconstructive Surgery* 121(4): 1188–1205.

Liang, Xin, Reinhilde Jacobs, Livia S. Corpas, Patrick Semal, and Ivo Lambrichts. 2009. Chronologic and geographic variability of neurovascular structures in the human mandible. *Forensic Science International* 190(1): 24–32.

Lieberman, Philip H. 2007. The evolution of human speech: Its anatomical and neural bases. *Current Anthropology* 48(1): 39–66.

Lindblom, Björn. 1983. Economy of speech gestures. In Peter F. MacNeilage (ed.), *The Production of Speech*, 217–245. New York: Springer Verlag.

Liu, Antang, Dazhi Yu, Gang Chen, Ruishan Dang, YingFan Zhang, WenJun Zhang, BenLi Liu, and Hong Jiang. 2010. Profiling of innervations of mimetic muscles in fresh human cadavers using a modified Sihler's technique. *Muscle and Nerve* 42(1): 88–94.

Loukas, Marios, Christopher R. Kinsella Jr., Theodoros Kapos, Richard S. Tubbs, and, Srinivasa Ramachandra. 2008. Anatomical variation in arterial supply of the mandible with special regard to implant placement. *International Journal of Oral and Maxillofacial Surgery* 37(4): 367–371.

Lund, James P. 1991. Mastication and its control by the brain stem. *Critical Reviews in Oral Biology and Medicine* 2(1): 33–64.

Lund, James P. 2011. Chew before you swallow. In Jean Pierre Gossard, Réjean Dubuc, and Arlette Kolta (eds.), *Breathe, Walk and Chew: The Neural Challenge: Part II*, 219–228. Amsterdam: Elsevier.

Lund, James P. and Arlette Kolta. 2006. Brainstem circuits that control mastication: Do they have anything to say during speech? *Journal of Communication Disorders* 39(5): 381–390.

Ma, LuYao, Huawei C. Li, Akiko Amono-Kusumoto, Willy Wong, and Pascal Van Lieshout. 2008. Assessing the intrinsic relationship between facial motion and acoustics in patients with Parkinson's disease. *Canadian Acoustics / Acoustique Canadienne* 37(3): 192–193.

MacNeilage, Peter F. 1998. The frame/content theory of evolution of speech production. *Behavioral and Brain Sciences* 21(4): 499–546.

Mağden, Orhan, Mete Edizer, Atay Atabey, Volkan Tayfur, and Ipek Ergür. 2004. Cadaveric study of the arterial anatomy of the upper lip. *Plastic and Reconstructive Surgery* 114(2): 355–359.

Maner, Kimberly J., Anne Smith, and Liane Grayson. 2000. Influences of utterance length and complexity on speech motor performance in children and adults. *Journal of Speech, Language, and Hearing Research* 43(2): 560–573.

Marzullo, Ana Carolina de Miranda, Osmar Pinto Neto, Kirrie J. Ballard, Donald A. Robin, Lauren Chaitow, and Evangelos A. Christou. 2010. Neural control of the lips differs for young and older adults following a perturbation. *Experimental Brain Research* 206(3): 319–327.

Matsuo, Kolchiro and Jeffrey B. Palmer. 2010. Kinematic linkage of the tongue jaw and hyoid during eating and speech. *Archives of Oral Biology* 55(4): 325–331.

Munhall, Kevin G., Anders Löfqvist, and J.A. Scott Kelso. 1994. Lip-larynx coordination in speech: Effects of mechanical perturbations to the lower lip. *Journal of the Acoustical Society of America* 95(6): 3605–3616.

Namasivayam, Aravind Kumar and Pascal Van Lieshout. 2008. Investigating speech motor practice and learning in people who stutter. *Journal of Fluency Disorders* 33(1): 32–51.

Namasivayam, Aravind Kumar and Pascal Van Lieshout. 2011. Speech motor skill and stuttering. *Journal of Motor Behavior* 43(6): 477–489.

Namasivayam, Aravind Kumar, Pascal Van Lieshout, and Luc De Nil. 2008. Bite-block perturbation in people who stutter: Immediate compensatory and delayed adaptive processes. *Journal of Communication Disorders* 41(4): 372–394.

Namasivayam, Aravind Kumar, Pascal Van Lieshout, William E. McIlroy, and Luc De Nil. 2009. Sensory feedback dependence hypothesis in persons who stutter. *Human Movement Science* 28(6): 688–707.

Palmer, Jeffrey B., Karen M. Hiiemae, and Jianmin Liu. 1997. Tongue-jaw linkages in human feeding: A preliminary videofluorographic study. *Archives of Oral Biology* 42(6): 429–441.

Peck, Christopher C. and Alan G. Hannam. 2007. Human jaw and muscle modelling. *Archives of Oral Biology* 52(4): 300–304.

Perrier, Pascal, Liang Ma, and Yohan Payan. 2005. Modeling the production of VCV sequences via the inversion of a biomechanical model of the tongue. In *Proceedings of the 9th European Conference on Speech Communication and Technology*, 1040–1043. International Speech Communication Association.

Plavcan, J. Michael and David J. Daegling 2006. Interspecific and intraspecific relationships between tooth size and jaw size in primates. *Journal of Human Evolution* 51(2): 171–184.

Riely, Rachel R. and Anne Smith. 2003. Speech movements do not scale by orofacial structure size. *Journal of Applied Physiology* 94(6): 2119–2126.

Rodella, Luigi F., Barbara Buffoli, Mauro Labanca, and Rita Rezzani. 2012. A review of the mandibular and maxillary nerve supplies and their clinical relevance. *Archives of Oral Biology* 57(4): 323–334.

Rogers, Carolyn R., Mark P. Mooney, Timothy D. Smith, Seth M. Weinberg, Bridget M. Waller, Lisa A. Parr, Beth A. Docherty, and Anne M. Burrows. 2009. Comparative microanatomy of the orbicularis oris muscle between chimpanzees and humans: Evolutionary divergence of lip function. *Journal of Anatomy* 214(1): 36–44.

Saltzman, Elliot, Anders Löfqvist, Bruce Kay, Jeffrey Kinsella-Shaw, and Philip Rubin. 1998. Dynamics of intergestural timing: A perturbation study of lip-larynx coordination. *Experimental Brain Research* 123(4): 412–424.

Sanguineti, Vittorio, Rafael Laboissière, and David J. Ostry. 1998. A dynamic biomechanical model for neural control of speech production. *Journal of the Acoustical Society of America* 103(3): 1615–1627.

Schieppati, Marco, G. Di Francesco, and Antonio Nardone. 1989. Patterns of activity of perioral facial muscles during mastication in man. *Experimental Brain Research* 77(1): 103–112.

Serrurier, Antoine, Pierre Badin, Anna Barney, Louis-Jean Boë, and Christophe Savariaux. 2012. The tongue in speech and feeding: Comparative articulatory modelling. *Journal of Phonetics* 40(6): 745–763.

Sessle, Barry J. 2011. Face sensorimotor cortex: Its role and neuroplasticity in the control of orofacial movements. In Jean Pierre Gossard, Réjean Dubuc, and Arlette Kolta (eds.), *Breathe, Walk and Chew: The Neural Challenge: Part II*, 71–82. Amsterdam: Elsevier.

Shaiman, Susan. 1989. Kinematic and electromyographic responses to perturbation of the jaw. *Journal of the Acoustical Society of America* 86(1): 78–88.

Shiller, Douglas M., Guillaume Houle, and David J. Ostry. 2005. Voluntary control of human jaw stiffness. *Journal of Neurophysiology* 94(3): 2207–2217.

Siemionow, Maria, Bahar B. Gharb, and Antonio Rampazzo. 2011. The face as a sensory organ. *Plastic and Reconstructive Surgery* 127(2): 652–662.

Smith, Anne. 2006. Speech motor development: Integrating muscles, movements, and linguistic units. *Journal* of *Communication Disorders* 39(5): 331–349.

Smith, Anne and Lisa Goffman. 1998. Stability and patterning of speech movement sequences in children and adults. *Journal of Speech, Language, and Hearing Research* 41(1): 18–30.

Smith, Bruce L. 1995. Variability of lip and jaw movements in the speech of children and adults. *Phonetica* 52(4): 307–316.

Steele, Catriona M. and Pascal H.H.M. Van Lieshout. 2008. The dynamics of lingual-mandibular coordination during liquid swallowing. *Dysphagia* 23(1): 33–46.

Steele, Catriona M., Pascal H.H.M. Van Lieshout, and Cathy A. Pelletier. 2012. The influence of stimulus taste and chemesthesis on tongue movement timing in swallowing. *Journal of Speech, Language, and Hearing Research* 55(1): 262–275.

Tamura, Fumiyo, Tomoko Fukui, Takeshi Kikutani, Reiko Machida, Mitsuyoshi Yoshida, Takeyoshi Yoneyama, and Akira Hamura. 2009. Lip-closing function of elderly people during ingestion: Comparison with young adults. *The International Journal of Orofacial Myology* 35: 33–43.

Tasko, Stephen M. and Michael D. McClean. 2004. Variations in articulatory movement with changes in speech task. *Journal of Speech, Language, and Hearing Research* 47(1): 85–100.

Tenuvuo, Jorma O. 2002 Antimicrobial agents in saliva: Protection for the whole body. *Journal of Dental Research* 81(12): 807–809.

Terband, Hayo, Ben Maassen, Pascal Van Lieshout, and Lian Nijland. 2011. Stability and composition of functional synergies for speech movements in children with developmental speech disorders. *Journal of Communication Disorders* 44(1): 59–74.

Terband, Hayo, Frits Van Brenk, Pascal Van Lieshout, Lian Nijland, and Ben Maassen. 2009. Stability and composition of functional synergies for speech movements in children and adults. In *Proceedings of the 10th Annual Conference of the International Speech Communication Association*, 788–791. International Speech Communication Association.

Van der Bilt, Andries. 2011. Assessment of mastication with implications for oral rehabilitation: a review. *Journal of Oral Rehabilitation* 38 (10): 754–780.

Van Lieshout, Pascal H.H.M. 2004. Dynamical systems theory and its application in speech. In Ben A.M. Maassen, Ray D. Kent, Herman F.M. Peters, Pascal H.H.M. Van Lieshout, and Wouter Hulstijn (eds.), *Speech Motor Control in Normal and Disordered Speech*, 51–82. Oxford: Oxford University Press

Van Lieshout, Pascal H.H.M., Wouter Hulstijn, and Herman F.M. Peters. 2004. Searching for the weak link in the speech production chain of people who stutter: A motor skill approach. In Ben A.M. Maassen, Ray D. Kent, Herman F.M. Peters, Pascal H.H.M. Van Lieshout, and Wouter Hulstijn (eds.), *Speech Motor Control in Normal and Disordered Speech*, 313–356. Oxford: Oxford University Press.

Van Lieshout, Pascal H.H.M., Christel A.W. Rutjens, and Paul H.M. Spauwen. 2002. The dynamics of interlip coupling in speakers with a repaired unilateral cleft-lip history. *Journal of Speech, Language, and Hearing Research* 45(1): 5–19.

Van Lieshout, Pascal H.H.M., Arpita Bose, Paula A. Square, and Catriona M. Steele. 2007. Speech motor control in fluent and dysfluent speech production of an individual with apraxia of speech and Broca's aphasia. *Clinical Linguistics and Phonetics* 21(3): 159–188.

Vatikiotis-Bateson, Eric and David J. Ostry 1995. An analysis of the dimensionality of jaw motion in speech. *Journal of Phonetics* 23(1–2): 101–117.

Vinyard, Christopher J., Susan H. Williams, Christine E. Wall, Alison H. Doherty, Alfred W. Crompton, and William L. Hylander. 2011. A preliminary analysis of correlations between chewing motor patterns and mandibular morphology across mammals. *Integrative and Comparative Biology* 51(2): 260–270.

Williamson, Matthew M. 1998. Neural control of rhythmic arm movements. *Neural Networks* 11(7–8): 1379–1394.

Wroe, Stephen, Toni L. Ferrara, Colin R. McHenry, Darren Curnoe, and Uphar Chamoli. 2010. The craniomandibular mechanics of being human. *Proceedings of the Royal Society B: Biological Sciences* 277(1700): 3579–3586.

Zemlin, Willard R. 1998. *Speech and Hearing Science*, 4th edn. Needham Heights, MA: Allyn and Bacon.

Zhang, Futang, Christopher C. Peck, and Alan G. Hannam 2002. Mass properties of the human mandible. *Journal of Biomechanics* 35(7): 975–978.

6 Velopharyngeal Function in Speech Production
Some Developmental and Structural Considerations

DAVID J. ZAJAC

6.1 Introduction

The velopharyngeal (VP) port and nasal cavity form a continuous airway as part of the supralaryngeal subsystem of speech production. The VP port functions as an aerodynamic-acoustic valve to separate the oral and nasal cavities during non-nasal speech segments and to couple the oral and nasal cavities during nasal speech segments. When coupled to the oral cavity, the nasal cavity functions primarily as an acoustic resonator. The VP port and nasal cavity consist of complex muscular-skeletal structures that undergo significant changes with growth of the individual from birth to adulthood. Despite structural changes, VP function remains remarkably stable throughout the lifespan. VP and nasal structures, however, are susceptible to embryologic disruptions that can result in significant birth defects such as cleft lip and/or palate. These defects can significantly affect growth of structures and impact function.

This chapter reviews VP function during speech production in individuals with and without structural anomalies with a focus on aerodynamic events. The chapter begins with a brief overview of instrumental procedures used to study VP function. Pressure-flow assessment is emphasized given the focus on speech aerodynamics. Following this, normal VP function for nasal consonants, oral consonants, and vowels are reviewed. Current evidence of age-related changes in VP function from infancy to senescence is then presented. Finally, some effects of VP dysfunction secondary to cleft palate on speech production are considered.

The Handbook of Speech Production, First Edition. Edited by Melissa A. Redford.
© 2015 John Wiley & Sons, Inc. Published 2019 by John Wiley & Sons, Inc.

6.2 Instrumental assessment of VP function

6.2.1 Direct methods

Following Lubker and Moll (1965), most researchers distinguish between "direct" and "indirect" methods of assessing VP function. Direct methods provide actual observations of structure and/or function. Direct methods include imaging techniques such as single-frame radiographs (e.g., lateral cephalograms), high-speed cinefluorography, multiview videofluorography, fiberoptic nasoendoscopy, and magnetic resonance imaging (MRI). Detailed descriptions of these and other direct techniques are available in many excellent sources (e.g., Baken and Orlikoff 2000; Hixon, Weismer, and Hoit 2008; Krakow and Huffman 1993; Moon 1993: Skolnick and Cohn 1989; Williams, Henningsson, and Pegoraro-Krook 1997). Typically, direct methods have not been employed in large-scale studies of normal speakers given both the risk of exposure to ionizing radiation associated with X-rays, and the invasiveness of procedures that involve endoscopy. Direct imaging techniques, however, are routinely used with individuals who have craniofacial anomalies as part of diagnostic evaluations and for management planning. Although single-frame radiographs were popular with early clinicians and researchers, a significant disadvantage of this procedure is that information is limited to static positions of the articulators during production of prolonged vowels and/or continuant consonants. As noted by Williams et al. (1997: 351), VP function "during the production of isolated sounds is not predictive of VP function during connected speech." Because of this limitation, the popularity of single-frame radiographs has been supplanted by procedures such as videofluorography and nasoendoscopy that allow assessment of continuous speech.

The use of MRI techniques to study VP structure and function has gained popularity with some researchers (e.g., Bae et al. 2011; Ettema et al. 2002; Ha et al. 2007; Tian and Redett 2009). An advantage of MRI is the acquisition of high-quality images without the use of ionizing radiation. Because of slow imaging rates, early MRI studies – similar to single-frame radiographic studies – were limited to examining static configurations of VP structures either at rest or during prolongation of isolated sounds. An additional disadvantage of MRI is the noise associated with the scanner that makes speech recordings impracticable, at least for acoustic analysis. Recent advancements in technology, however, are overcoming these limitations. Bae et al. (2011) achieved an effective scanning rate of 30 images per second that is equivalent to standard video recording. These investigators also used a fiber optic microphone with internal noise attenuation that is compatible with MRI. Using this technology, Bae et al. were able to obtain simultaneous speech recordings during MRI scans that enabled them to determine formant amplitude and bandwidth of nasalized vowels in relation to lingual and velar positions.

6.2.2 Indirect methods

In contrast to direct techniques, indirect assessment procedures provide information about some effect of VP function. Indirect techniques include photodetection (e.g., Dalston 1982; Moon and Lagu 1987), mechanical transduction of velar movement (e.g., Bell-Berti and Krakow 1991; Horiguchi and Bell-Berti 1987), accelerometry (e.g., Horii 1983), aerodynamics (e.g., Thompson and Hixon 1979; Warren and Dubois 1964; Zajac 2000), and acoustic analysis (e.g., Curtis 1969; Kataoka et al. 2001; Philips and Kent 1984; Schwartz 1968). Detailed descriptions of these and other indirect techniques are found in several of the previously cited sources (e.g., Baken and Orlikoff 2000; Hixon et al. 2008; Krakow and Huffman 1993; Moon 1993).

A brief treatment of basic aerodynamic principles and assessment techniques is provided below for several reasons. First, speech production essentially consists of the generation of a pressurized air stream in the vocal tract. Second, the VP port functions primarily as an aeromechanical valve to direct the air stream into the oral or nasal cavities. Third, as discussed later in this chapter, two primary symptoms of VP dysfunction are reduced oral air pressure and nasal air escape during production of obstruent consonants. Aerodynamic techniques, therefore, are ideally suited to study both normal VP function and dysfunction. These techniques are also noninvasive and relatively easy to use, even with young children.

6.2.3 The pressure-flow method

Warren and colleagues were among the first researchers to systematically apply aerodynamic principles to study VP function (Warren 1964a, 1964b; Warren and DuBois 1964). They developed a technique for estimating the minimal cross-sectional area of the VP port that has subsequently become known as the "pressure-flow method." Using a plastic model of the upper vocal tract, Warren and DuBois (1964) showed that the minimal cross-sectional area of the VP port could be estimated by simultaneously measuring the pressure drop across the port along with the volume rate of airflow through the port. They calculated the cross-sectional area of the port using a modification of Bernoulli's equation that included a correction factor (k) for unsteady or turbulent airflow. Warren and DuBois chose an average value of $k = .65$ for the "orifice equation." This value was derived from tests using short tubes to model the VP port that varied in cross-sectional area:

$$\text{Orifice area (cm}^2) = U / k (2 \times \Delta P / p)^{1/2}$$

where U = rate of airflow in mL/s, ΔP = differential pressure in dynes/cm², and p = density of air ($.001 \, \text{g/cm}^3$).

Yates, McWilliams, and Vallino (1990) noted that accuracy of pressure-flow estimates of VP port size is dependent upon the value of the flow coefficient k, used to correct for turbulent airflow. The value of k varies as a function of inlet geometry of the orifice. Yates et al. pointed out that a k value approaching .99 may be more representative of rounded inlets that are likely to be present in the human VP anatomy. If so, then estimates of VP orifice size may be overestimated by 20–30% when using a k value of .65. Because the exact shape of the VP port is unlikely to be determined for a given speaker, Yates et al. did not suggest a change in the value of k.

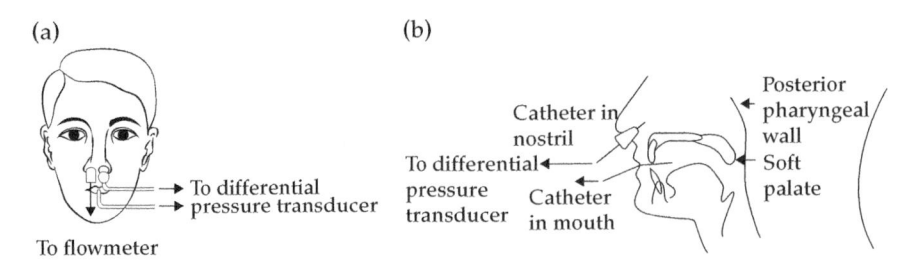

Figure 6.1 Front (a) and side (b) views of air pressure catheters and flow tube placement for the pressure-flow method (Warren 1976: 113).

Application of the pressure-flow method to speakers is rather straightforward (Figure 6.1). Differential pressure across the VP port is obtained by detecting oral and nasal cavity air pressures. Oral pressure is detected by placing the open end of a small catheter behind the lips of a speaker. The catheter is connected to a calibrated differential air-pressure transducer. During production of a bilabial stop consonant, a stagnation pressure is created in the oral cavity that is continuous with pressure below the VP port. Nasal pressure is detected by passing another small catheter through a cork or foam plug that is secured in one nostril of the speaker. The nasal catheter is attached to a second differential air-pressure transducer. By occluding the nostril, a stagnation pressure is created in the nasal cavity that is continuous with pressure above the VP port. Differential pressure across the VP port is simply determined as the difference between oral and nasal air pressure. The volume rate of airflow through the VP port is obtained by inserting a larger, snug-fitting flow tube into the other nostril of the speaker. The nasal flow tube is coupled to a heated and calibrated pneumotachometer.[1]

The pressure-flow method is ideally suited to studying nasal and oral stop consonants, especially the bilabial consonants /m/, /b/, and /p/. Because of a closed oral cavity, no special orientation of the pressure-detecting catheter is required for these sounds. As noted by Baken and Orlikoff (2000), perpendicular orientation of the catheter is necessary for detection of static air pressure in a moving air stream during production of fricatives. It must be noted that the pressure-flow method is not well suited to estimate the size of the VP port during production of vowels. This occurs because oral air pressure is relatively low – close to atmospheric levels – and accurate detection of pressure is problematic.

6.3 Normal VP function

6.3.1 *VP function during nasal and oral obstruent consonants*

The VP port functions primarily as an aeromechanical-acoustic valve during speech production to signal phonological contrasts between nasal and oral sound segments. During production of an oral obstruent consonant, the velum elevates in a superior-posterior direction and contacts the posterior pharyngeal wall to separate the nose from the mouth (Graber, Bzoch, and Aoba 1959). Conversely, during production of a nasal segment, the velum lowers to some extent to open the VP port and allow the nasal cavity to function as an acoustic resonator.[2] As reviewed later in this chapter, the extent of velar elevation and amount of contact with the posterior pharyngeal wall (if any) vary as a function of phonetic context, particularly for vowels. The primary muscle that elevates the velum is the levator veli palatini (Bell-Berti 1976; Bosma 1953; Dickson 1975; Fritzell 1969; Lubker 1968). The superior pharyngeal constrictor muscle may also assist in closure by displacing the posterior and lateral pharyngeal walls forward and medially to form sphincter-like closure around the elevated velum (Graber et al. 1959; Iglesias, Kuehn, and Morris 1980). Additional muscles of the oral and pharyngeal cavities assist in controlling precise positioning of the velum during speech segments.

Early radiographic studies showed that complete closure of the VP port typically occurs for obstruent consonants with little variability (Graber et al. 1959; Moll 1962). Graber et al. (1959) used high-speed, fine-focused lateral radiographs to study changes in VP structures during production of the consonants /p/, /b/, /f/, /w/, and /m/ in 44 adult speakers. They reported that the VP port was "consistently closed" for the consonants /p/, /b/, /f/, and /w/. While the glide /w/ was produced with a closed VP port, Graber et al. noted that velar length was reduced for this sound as compared to the obstruent consonants. Graber et al. also reported that the nasal consonant /m/ was produced with closure-like activity. They described the VP port configuration for /m/ as a "close-ready position" that was more similar to closure than resting position. Moll (1962) also reported little variation in velar height or VP closure across the obstruent consonants /t/, /d/, /s/, /z/, /tʃ/, and /dʒ/ in various vowel contexts.

6.3.2 Aerodynamic characteristics of nasal and oral stop consonants

Many studies have described the VP port as a highly efficient aeromechanical valve during production of nasal and oral stop consonants (Emanuel and Counihan 1970; Hoit et al. 1994; Thompson and Hixon 1979; Zajac 2000; Zajac and Mayo 1996). Emanuel and Counihan (1970) studied oral and nasal airflow of the stops /p/, /b/, /t/, /d/, /k/, and /g/ produced by 25 men and 25 women. Oral and nasal airflows were detected using a partitioned face mask with hot-wire anemometers embedded in the mask. Hot-wire anemometers consist of fine wires that are heated and change temperature due to changes in airflow. Speakers produced all combinations of the stops with the vowels /i/ and /a/ in CV, VCV, and VC syllables. Emanuel and Counihan reported that all speakers produced all stops with mean rates of nasal airflow that did not exceed 30 mL/s – the highest rate of nasal airflow observed for any single stop was 72 mL/s. These findings showed that the speakers achieved highly consistent VP closure during stop consonant production, similar to radiographic studies. Low rates of nasal airflow (i.e., under

30 mL/s) reported by Emanuel and Counihan may occur due to minor bounce-like displacements of the velum in the presence of airtight closure (Lubker and Moll 1965; Thompson and Hixon 1979). While the occurrence of nasal airflow at a rate of 72 mL/s may not be associated with velar bounce, this value most likely reflects a relatively small VP opening that would not distort the perceptual quality of a stop consonant (see findings of Zajac and Mayo 1996 reported below).

Thompson and Hixon (1979) studied nasal airflow during production of nasal consonants and oral stops produced by 92 typically developing boys and girls aged 3–18 years and 20 men and women aged 18–37 years. Nasal airflow was obtained using a nasal mask and pneumotachometer. The speakers produced CV and VCV syllables in a carrier phrase that included /ti/, /di/, /ni/, /iti/, /idi/, and /ini/. Each syllable was repeated seven times with the middle three productions analyzed. Thompson and Hixon reported that nasal airflow was present during the nasal consonants of all speakers and absent during the oral stops for all but one of the speakers. Mean rates of nasal airflow determined at the midpoint of /n/ for the CV and VCV syllables for all speakers were 88.8 mL/s (range = 46.0–273.0) and 94.2 mL/s (range = 30.0–266.0), respectively.

Zajac and Mayo (1996) used the pressure-flow method to study nasal and oral consonants produced by 21 men and 21 women without palatal anomalies who ranged in age from 18 to 37 years. All speakers exhibited perceptually normal resonance as determined by the investigators. They produced the word *hamper* five times during a single breath group using self-determined rate and loudness. Estimates of VP port size were obtained at peak nasal airflow associated with the /m/ segments and peak oral air pressure associated with the /p/ segments of the middle three productions of each word.[3] Zajac and Mayo reported that mean estimates of VP port area during the /m/ segment of *hamper* for the men and women were approximately 18 and 22 mm^2, respectively (Table 6.1). In contrast, mean estimates of VP port area during the /p/ segment of *hamper* were less than 1.0 mm^2 for both sexes, reflecting essentially complete closure.[4] The largest mean estimate of VP port area during /p/ was only 3.4 mm^2 and was associated with a mean rate of nasal airflow that was 76 mL/s. Although Zajac and Mayo reported relatively large variability of VP port areas for the /m/ segment, there was no overlap with /p/ segments. That is, as seen in Table 6.1, the largest VP area for /p/ did not exceed the smallest VP area for /m/ for any speaker.

6.3.3 VP function during vowel production

6.3.3.1 Vowel height In contrast to obstruent consonants, vowel production does not always occur with complete VP closure. Moll (1962) reported that low vowels had a greater tendency to be produced with lower velar height and some opening of the VP port as compared to high vowels. Specifically, Moll reported that almost 40% of low vowels produced by 10 adult speakers had some opening of the VP port as compared to less than 15% of high vowels. Subsequent studies have also reported differences between high and low vowels relative to velar height

Table 6.1 Means, standard deviations (SD), and low and high values of oral air pressure (Po), nasal air flow (Un), and estimated velopharyngeal (VP) areas of /m/ and /p/ produced during *hamper* by male and female adult speakers (Zajac and Mayo 1996).

Variable	Males (n = 21)				Females (n = 21)			
	Mean	SD	Low	High	Mean	SD	Low	High
Po (cm H_2O)								
/m/	1.5	0.9	0.2	4.1	1.1	0.5	0.1	2.3
/p/	5.9	1.6	3.8	9.1	4.7	1.0	2.5	7.2
Un (mL/s)								
/m/	149	73	47	280	129	37	69	216
/p/	20	21	2	76	10	8	1	30
VP area (mm^2)								
/m/	17.5	9.9	4.5	42.7	22.2	10.1	8.6	42.5
/p/	0.9	1.0	0.1	3.4	0.6	0.5	0.0	2.4

(Bell-Berti 1980; Lubker 1968), VP closing force (Kuehn and Moon 1998; Moon, Kuehn, and Huisman 1994), and nasal airflow (Young et al. 2001).

Bell-Berti (1993) called attention to the fact that velar position varies much more greatly with phonetic context than suggested by binary linguistic descriptions of low velar height for nasal segments and high velar height for oral segments. Bell-Berti summarized various studies that showed: (1) nasal consonants have the lowest velar position, (2) low vowels have a somewhat higher position, (3) high vowels have a still higher position, and (4) obstruent consonants have the highest velar position. In addition, Bell-Berti noted that liquid consonants such as /l/ are produced with lower velar height than obstruent consonants, and oral vowels between obstruent consonants have reduced velar height as compared to the consonants.

Differences in velar height between high and low vowels have been explained by two rather dissimilar mechanisms – biomechanical and acoustic-perceptual. Because palatoglossus and palatopharyngeus have origins below the velum, these muscles may oppose velar elevation during vowels produced with a lowered mandible (Bell-Berti 1976; Lubker 1968; Moll 1962). The acoustic-perceptual explanation is influenced by early acoustic findings of House and Stevens (1956). They used electrical analog models to show that high vowels were perceived as more nasal than low vowels for a given VP coupling area. Thus, speakers may volitionally close the VP port to a greater extent during production of high vowels to avoid the perceptual consequences of excessive nasality (Hixon et al. 2008). These explanations raise several interesting questions that currently lack definite answers. Do typically developing young children exhibit consistent velar height differences for high and low vowels at the time of vowel emergence or do they require practice and acoustic feedback to develop such differences? Also, if acoustic feedback is necessary to develop velar height differences, are young children with cleft palate at a disadvantage given that Eustachian tube dysfunction and conductive hearing loss occur almost universally?

6.3.3.2 Vowel nasalization The phenomenon of vowel nasalization has long interested researchers. Radiographic studies have shown that vowels produced adjacent to nasal consonants have lower velar height and some amount of VP opening (Lubker and Moll 1965; Moll 1962). Moll (1962) also noted that larger VP openings tended to occur during vowels that preceded rather than followed nasal consonants. Moll and colleagues proposed a "binary" theory of velar control to account for vowel nasalization (Moll and Daniloff 1971; Moll and Shriner 1967). According to this theory, the speech motor control program specifies non-nasal consonants as closed, nasal consonants (and utterance endings) as open, and vowels as neutral (or unspecified). Given a "look ahead" model, vowels preceding a nasal consonant assume an open VP configuration. Kent, Carney, and Severeid (1974) acknowledged the attractiveness of this theory but noted that it made predictions that did not occur in English. More important, Kent et al. reported velar movement and timing patterns of speakers that were not predicted by the model. Using cinefluorography, they showed that velar elevation actually started during certain vowels that were specified as open according to a binary model (e.g., vowels within a CVNC sequence). Kent et al. concluded that "a fairly rigid time program" must exist for velar articulation.

Bell-Berti and colleagues also emphasized temporal constraints on velar function to explain vowel nasalization (Bell-Berti 1993; Bell-Berti and Krakow 1991). They proposed a "coproduction" account of velar control where distinct spatial targets were specified for each phonetic segment in a string. While the segment's core spatial target does not change, Bell-Berti (1993: 72) noted that "its realization may *appear* to change as it overlaps more and less with the onsets and offsets of other segments." Bell-Berti emphasized that such interactions occur over relatively short intervals and that careful observation of the velum was needed to detect the changing spatial configurations.

6.3.4 Aerodynamic characteristics of nasalized vowels

Thompson and Hixon (1979) reported differences in anticipatory and carryover nasal airflow during production of the VNV sequence /ini/. They reported that all speakers exhibited nasal airflow during the second vowel of /ini/ (mean = 43 mL/s, range = 8–120 mL/s) but that only 47 speakers exhibited nasal airflow during the initial vowel (mean = 29 mL/s, range = 3–80 mL/s). Thompson and Hixon also reported that of the 47 speakers who exhibited nasal airflow during the first vowel of /ini/, approximately 70% were female. They attributed this finding to biomechanical differences in VP function between men and women (e.g., McKerns and Bzoch 1970).[5]

Anticipatory and carryover nasal airflow during production of the VNV sequence /ini/ was also studied by Zajac, Mayo, and Kataoka (1998). They used

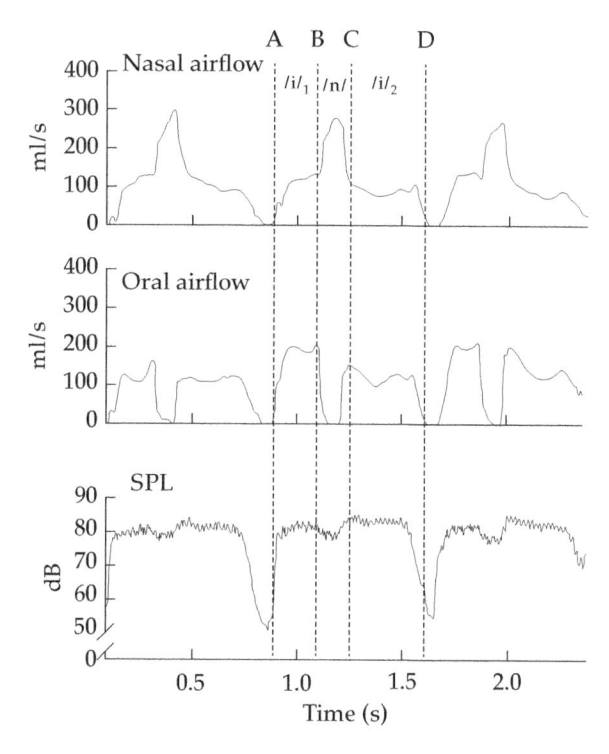

Figure 6.2 Nasal airflow, oral airflow, and sound pressure level (SPL) of /ini/ produced three times by an adult male (Zajac, Mayo, and Kataoka 1998).

a partitioned, circumferentially-vented pneumotachograph face mask to obtain oral and nasal airflow from 20 adult speakers, 10 men and 10 women. Speakers produced /ini/ in a carrier phrase with equal stress on both syllables and with contrastive stress placed on the second syllable. In contrast to Thompson and Hixon (1979), Zajac et al. found no obvious sex effects relative to anticipatory nasal airflow. More significant, all speakers except one woman exhibited onset of anticipatory nasal airflow for the first vowel of /ini/ that coincided with onset of oral airflow for the vowel (Figure 6.2). Similar patterns of simultaneous onsets of oral and nasal airflow for the first vowel of /ini/ and /ana/ were reported by Young et al. (2001). As seen in Figure 6.2, distinct patterns of nasal airflow occur during production of /ini/. Nasal airflow abruptly increases during the beginning of the first vowel, reaches a plateau at the midpoint of the vowel, and then peaks during the nasal consonant. Nasal airflow during the second vowel of /ini/ decreases in a mirror-like image of the first vowel. Although Zajac et al. (1998) did not obtain velar movement data, the multi-staged patterns of nasal airflow that they found are consistent with a coproduction model of velar control that posits the overlapping of core spatial targets of neighboring segments.

6.4 Age-related changes in VP structure and function

6.4.1 Developmental changes in VP structures

At birth, the size, shape, and position of structures of the upper vocal tract of the human infant are ideal to facilitate sucking behavior. The larynx is relatively high, the pharynx is relatively short, the epiglottis approximates the velum, the tongue occupies a relatively anterior position in the oral cavity, and the buccal pads are relatively large (Kent and Murray 1982; Kummer 2008). The close proximity of the epiglottis to the velum has led researchers to characterize the infant as an obligate nasal breather (Sasaki et al. 1977). Structures of the upper vocal tract begin to change at four to six months of age as the larynx descends, the velum and epiglottis separate, the pharynx lengthens, and the posterior aspect of the tongue lowers (Sasaki et al. 1977; Vorperian et al. 2005). These physical changes are thought to be obligatory precursors to the emergence of babbling in the infant (Vorperian et al. 2005).

Vorperian et al. (2005) used MRI to determine the growth rate of the vocal tract and related structures in 63 pediatric cases from birth to approximately six years of age. They reported continuous growth for most structures during the period studied "with a somewhat more rapid growth during approximately the first 18 months of life" (344). The hard palate showed an accelerated growth pattern with 80% of its adult size achieved by 18 months. The velum showed a more gradual pattern of growth with only 65% of its adult size achieved by 18 months (Vorperian et al. 2005: 342, Figure 9). Subtelny (1957) also reported a "marked and consistent" growth of the velum from birth to approximately 18 to 24 months of age followed by a relative plateau until approximately four to five years of age.

Lymphoid tissue in the nasopharynx (adenoids) also undergoes considerable growth during the first two years of life. Adenoid tissue is part of the immune system and functions to detect antigens entering the upper airway (Brodsky et al. 1988). At birth, little adenoid tissue is present. Adenoid tissue undergoes rapid growth during infancy with clear hypertrophy by two years of age (Handelman and Osborne 1976). Growth continues at a slower rate throughout childhood and peaks at approximately 10 years of age. If a child has large adenoids, then closure of the VP port may actually involve velar-adenoidal contact (Hixon et al. 2008; Kummer 2008). The adenoids begin to atrophy during adolescence and most tissue is generally absent by 16 years of age (Handelman and Osborne 1976; Subtelny and Baker 1956).

Closure of the VP port during the period of adenoid atrophy is typically maintained by adolescents without palatal anomalies as the VP structures easily adapt to gradual changes in nasopharyngeal depth. Most children can even adapt to sudden surgical removal of the adenoids with only transient VP dysfunction. Following adenoidectomy, children typically compensate by increasing velar length and height and/or increasing pharyngeal wall activity to maintain closure (Neiman and Simpson 1975). As reviewed later, if a child has underlying structural anomalies such as submucous cleft palate, then persistent VP dysfunction is likely to occur following adenoidectomy.

6.4.2 VP function in infants and toddlers

Relatively little information is available concerning VP function during early vocalizations of infants. As reviewed by Hixon et al. (2008), acoustic-perceptual studies have suggested that the VP port is open for cry and non-cry vocalizations until about four months of age and then closure begins to occur for oral sounds at four to six months of age. Given that infants typically begin canonical babbling of CV syllables at approximately six or seven months of age (Oller and Eilers 1988), it appears reasonable to expect that VP closure might occur with emergence of obstruent consonants that require a buildup of oral air pressure.

In a preliminary study, Thom et al. (2006) studied six infants longitudinally from two to six months of age using a novel and relatively simple method to identify closure of the VP port. They inserted a double-barrel nasal cannula into the nares of the infants to detect changes in ram (impact) pressure as air exits the nose. This technique, unlike the pressure-flow method, does not provide estimates of VP port size but only binary information relative to the port being open or closed. Thom et al. studied cries, screams, windups, whimpers, laughs, raspberries, and syllables that consisted of either isolated vowels or vowel-consonant combinations. In contrast to previous studies, Thom et al. reported that cries and screams – along with raspberries – were produced with VP closure at all ages. Laughs, whimpers, and windups prior to cries were produced with an open VP port. Thom et al. reported that the percentage of syllables produced with closure of the VP port during some portion of the breath group increased from approximately 20% at two months of age to 65% at six months of age. Thus, Thom et al. did not find evidence to support the expectation that oral sound segments would be produced with consistent VP closure by six months of age. As noted by Hixon et al. (2008), however, Thom et al. did not distinguish between syllables that contained only vowels and those that contained consonants and vowels. This may have influenced the findings given that young infants typically produce mostly vowels.

Zajac et al. (2011) used nasal ram pressure to investigate VP closure during production of stop consonants by toddlers with and without repaired cleft palate. They studied four typically developing toddlers without cleft palate who were 22–26 months of age. A stop was considered to be produced with VP closure if nasal ram pressure was zero (atmospheric) during the segment. Zajac et al. reported that all four children exhibited closure of the VP port during at least 90% of stops produced. Although based on a limited number of toddlers, these findings suggest that consistent VP closure occurs during production of stop consonants by at least two years of age.

6.4.3 VP function in preschool and school-aged children

As reviewed previously, Thompson and Hixon (1979) investigated nasal airflow during production of nasal and oral consonants by 92 typically developing boys and girls aged 3–18 years. They reported the occurrence of nasal airflow during /n/ by all children and the absence of nasal airflow during oral consonants by all but one of the children. Although this study was cross-sectional in nature, the findings suggest that once established, young children are able to maintain closure of the VP port for obstruent consonants throughout adolescence and the period of adenoid atrophy.

Zajac (2000) also investigated VP function during production of nasal and oral consonants in a cross-sectional study that involved 181 children ranging in age from 6 to 16 years. The pressure-flow technique was used to obtain oral air pressure, nasal air pressure, nasal airflow, and to estimate the minimal cross-sectional area of the VP port during production of the /m/ and /p/ segments in the syllables /mi/, /pi/, and /pa/ and the word *hamper*. The children were grouped into four age ranges: 6–8 years (n=47), 9–10 years (n=71), 11–12 years (n=41), and 13–16 years (n=22). Zajac reported that nasal airflow and estimated VP areas for the nasal consonant /m/ typically increased across the age groups. Mean nasal airflow increased from 87 mL/s for the 6 to 8 year-olds to 158 mL/s for the 13–16 year-olds. Zajac attributed these findings to larger dimensions of the upper airways in the older children. In contrast to the /m/ consonant, mean nasal airflow during production of /p/ in *hamper* was less than 10 mL/s for the three youngest age groups and was only 14 mL/s for the 13–16 year-olds. The single highest rate of nasal airflow during production of /p/ among the 13–16 year-olds was 70 mL/s. This corresponded to a VP port size of only 2.1 mm^2. These findings, like those of Thompson and Hixon (1979), suggest that children easily adapt to physical changes in the VP mechanism during adolescence and the period of adenoid atrophy.

Although children appear to develop adult-like VP function for nasal and oral consonants relatively early, do they also exhibit adult patterns of nasal coarticulation during vowel production? Thompson and Hixon (1979) reported an age effect relative to anticipatory coarticulation for the syllable /ini/. Specifically, Thompson and Hixon found a "moderate trend" for a greater proportion of the oldest children (15–18 years of age) to exhibit nasal airflow at the midpoint of the initial vowel in /ini/ than the youngest children (3–6 years of age). They interpreted this finding to suggest that the youngest children had not yet achieved the skill level of adult speakers relative to motor control during anticipatory nasal coarticulation. Zajac (2000), however, reported data that do not support this view. Zajac determined a measure of anticipatory coarticulation by calculating the ratio of nasal air volume that preceded /m/ in *hamper* to the nasal air volume of the entire word. He found no differences among any of the age groups of children studied or between the children and adult speakers previously studied by Zajac and Mayo (1996). Thus, at least for the word *hamper*, children appear to be similar to adults relative to velar control of anticipatory nasal airflow.

6.4.4 VP function in older adults

Does VP function deteriorate with advanced age? Intuitively, one may believe that this happens given that most bodily functions tend to decline with advancing age. Relative to voice production, it is known that laryngeal structures undergo changes in advanced age that affect fundamental frequency (F_0). Hixon et al. (2008)

summarized studies that typically showed a gradual rise for men and a gradual fall for women in F_0 beginning in the fifth or sixth decade of life. The rise in F_0 for men may be related to muscle atrophy and the general loss of mass while the fall in F_0 for women may be related to an increase in edema (see Hixon et al. for a review).

At least one study has provided evidence that VP function deteriorates with advanced age. Hutchinson, Robinson, and Nerbonne (1978) used the Nasometer (KayPENTAX, Inc.) to study 60 men and women aged 50–80 years during reading of various passages. The Nasometer is an acoustic device that computes the ratio of nasal to oral-plus-nasal sound energy (termed "nasalance") as a correlate of perceived nasality. Hutchinson et al. reported significantly increased nasalance during reading of a passage that contained no nasal phones compared to a sample of younger adults aged 18–37 years. Based on these findings, Hutchinson et al. suggested that VP function became less competent with age.

Two subsequent studies, however, have not found evidence that VP function declines with age. Hoit et al. (1994) obtained nasal airflow using a mask and pneumotachograph during speech production of 10 men and 10 women in each of four age groups: 20–30, 40–50, 60–70, and 80+ years of age. The speakers produced the same speech samples as used by Thompson and Hixon (1979). Hoit et al. (1994: 297) reported that "it was rare to find nasal air flow during productions of oral utterance samples in any of the four age groups studied." Zajac (1997) also investigated VP function in 21 older speakers aged 68–83 years (10 men, 11 women) as compared to 42 younger speakers aged 18–37 years (21 men, 21 women). He used the pressure-flow method to obtain nasal airflow and to estimate VP port size during the /p/ segment of *hamper*. Similar to Hoit et al. (1994), Zajac (1997) reported essentially complete VP closure for all speakers regardless of age.

Hoit et al. (1994) explained the apparent discrepancy between acoustic and aerodynamic studies of elderly speakers to "sympathetic vibration" of the air mass in the nasal cavity. As noted by Hoit et al., acoustic nasalance is affected by many factors other than VP port opening. Even in the presence of complete VP closure, acoustic energy can transfer through palatal structures and excite the air mass in the nasal cavity (Bundy and Zajac 2006; Gildersleeve-Neumann and Dalston 2001). Hoit et al. (1994) noted that less dense palatal structures would facilitate greater transfer of acoustic energy, and that some VP muscles atrophy with age (Tomoda et al. 1984). Thus, while it appears that acoustic integrity of VP structures may deteriorate with advanced age, aerodynamic integrity does not.

6.5 Impact of structural anomalies on VP function

Structural anomalies can have significant impact on VP function during speech production. Structural defects can be present from birth as the result of embryologic disruptions that result in cleft lip and/or palate or can occur throughout life as the result of surgical interventions for other conditions (e.g., tonsillectomy, adenoidectomy, and/or removal of oropharyngeal tumors). Cleft palate with or without cleft lip is the most frequently occurring facial birth defect in the United States with an estimated prevalence of 1-in-500 to 1-in-750 live births (CDC 2006). A complete cleft of the hard and soft palate disrupts both feeding and development of communication in an infant. Until the palate is surgically repaired, the generation of either negative oral air pressure for sucking or positive oral air pressure for consonant production is unlikely, if not impossible.[6] Typically, most infants in the United States undergo surgical repair of palatal clefts at 9–12 months of age. The rationale for this timing has been largely influenced by studies that have shown rapid growth of the palate during the first 18–24 months of life (e.g., Subtelny 1957; Vorperian et al. 2005) and clinical reports of restricted growth of the palate following cleft surgery.

It is estimated that VP dysfunction occurs in approximately 20–30% of children following surgical repair (Kuehn and Moller 2000; Kummer 2008; Peterson-Falzone, Hardin-Jones, and Karnell 2001). Typically, the cause of VP dysfunction is a velum that is too short to completely contact the posterior pharyngeal wall.[7] In cases of severe dysfunction characterized by large VP gaps, a child may be unintelligible and speech limited to production of vowels, nasal consonants, and/or glottal stops. In cases of mild to moderate VP dysfunction, a child may be intelligible but exhibit varying degrees of hypernasality, audible nasal air escape, and/or weak oral air pressure. Typically, additional palatal surgery is required when children exhibit moderate to severe VP dysfunction.

VP dysfunction can also result following adenoidectomy. This surgery is typically performed in young children – often in combination with tonsillectomy – after four to five years of age for upper airway obstruction and/or recurring ear infections (Kummer 2008). Persistent VP dysfunction with hypernasality, defined as lasting longer than 12 months, has been estimated to occur in 1-in-1500 cases following adenoidectomy (Donnelly 1994). The likelihood of VP dysfunction increases substantially if conditions such as reduced muscle tone and/or submucous cleft palate also are present. It has been reported, for example, that approximately 29% of cases of persistent VP dysfunction following adenoidectomy were associated with submucous cleft palate (Croft, Shprintzen, and Ruben 1981).

The following sections review several aspects of VP dysfunction, mostly in speakers with repaired cleft palate. The focus is first on oral air pressure and nasal airflow during production of stop consonants, and then on some acoustic-perceptual characteristics of nasal air escape.

6.5.1 *Oral air pressure in speakers with VP dysfunction*

One of the most common symptoms of VP dysfunction is weak or reduced oral air pressure during production of stop consonants. The extent of the loss of oral air pressure varies directly with the size of the VP gap (Dalston et al. 1988; Warren et al. 1989). Dalston et al. (1988) used the pressure-flow method to study 267 speakers with varying degrees of VP dysfunction ranging in age from 4 to 58 years. Most of the speakers (93%) had cleft palate with or without cleft lip. They produced repetitions of the word *hamper* and estimates of VP port size were calculated for the /p/ segment. The speakers were categorized into five groups based upon VP port size:

Table 6.2 Means and standard deviations (SD) of oral air pressure during production of the syllable /pi/ as a function of age by speakers with repaired cleft palate and controls (modified from Zajac 2003).

	Oral Air Pressure (cm H_2O)					
	Controls			Cleft Palate		
Age group	N	Mean	SD	N	Mean	SD
5–8	47	8.0	2.2	54	9.2	3.0
9–12	112	7.6	2.1	56	7.9	2.0
13–16	22	6.3	1.3	46	7.8	2.3
≥18	42	6.0	1.4	20	5.1	1.9

(1) "adequate" speakers had VP areas less than 5 mm², (2) "adequate-borderline" speakers had VP areas from 5 to less than 10 mm², (3) "borderline-inadequate" speakers had VP areas from 10 to less than 20 mm², (4) "inadequate" speakers had VP areas from 20 to 80 mm², and (5) "grossly inadequate" speakers had essentially equal oral and nasal air pressures that precluded accurate gap size estimates. Dalston et al. reported that peak oral air pressure associated with the /p/ segment of *hamper* decreased dramatically across the five groups of speakers: 6.7 (SD = 2.4), 4.5 (SD = 1.9), 4.1 (SD = 1.7), 3.5 (SD = 2.0), and 3.0 (SD = 1.3) cm H_2O, respectively.

Zajac (2003) investigated peak oral air pressure of the /p/ segment in the syllable /pi/ produced by speakers with and without repaired cleft palate. He studied 176 speakers with cleft palate ranging in age from 5 to 51 years and compared them to 218 speakers without cleft palate ranging in age from 6 to 37 years. The latter speakers were previously studied by Zajac and Mayo (1996) and Zajac (2000). Zajac (2003) grouped the speakers into four age categories: (1) 5–8 years, (2) 9–12 years, (3) 13–16 years, and (4) 18+ years (adults). As seen in Table 6.2, there was a clear age effect on oral air pressure in that the youngest children, regardless of cleft status, exhibited higher levels of oral air pressure than the adults. Because the speakers used self-determined loudness levels, this finding might reflect the fact that the youngest children simply spoke louder than the adults. A more significant finding, however, is that the children with repaired cleft palate produced higher levels of oral air pressure than their counterparts without cleft palate. The differences in oral air pressure between children with and without cleft palate were significant ($p < .05$) in the 5–8 and 13–16 year-old age groups. For the adults, the findings were reversed in that adults with repaired cleft palate produced lower levels of oral air pressure than adults without cleft palate.

Why would children with repaired cleft palate use greater oral air pressure than children without cleft palate? One explanation may be that they increased respiratory effort as a compensatory strategy to help achieve VP closure. As reported below, most of the children with repaired cleft palate exhibited adequate

VP closure as reflected by the lack of significant nasal airflow. It is also possible that increased respiratory effort may have developed in response to chronic conductive hearing loss during early periods of speech acquisition. The opposite – but expected – finding of reduced oral air pressure by the adults with repaired cleft palate is most likely explained by their VP status. That is, most of the adult speakers had borderline-inadequate or inadequate VP closure as compared to the children.

6.5.2 Nasal airflow in speakers with VP dysfunction

Another primary symptom of VP dysfunction is nasal air emission during production of obstruent consonants. Warren et al. (1989) presented evidence to show that the extent of nasal airflow is also directly related to size of the VP gap. They used the pressure-flow method to study 107 speakers with repaired cleft palate ranging in age from approximately 5–58 years. All speakers produced repetitions of the word *hamper* and were categorized into four groups based upon VP port size during the /p/ segment: (1) 0–4.9 mm^2, (2) 5–9.9 mm^2, (3) 10–19.9 mm^2, and (4) 20+ mm^2. Warren et al. reported that mean nasal airflow at the point of peak oral air pressure during production of /p/ increased systematically across the four groups: 32 (SD=25), 102 (SD=34), 149 (SD=51), and 313 (SD=188) mL/s, respectively.[8]

6.5.3 Acoustic-perceptual characteristics of nasal air emission

The acoustic-perceptual characteristics of nasal air emission vary across speakers who exhibit VP dysfunction. Nasal air escape may or may not be audible depending upon the overall respiratory effort level of the speaker, size of the VP port opening, and patency of the nasal cavity. Audible nasal air escape is more likely to occur during production of voiceless obstruent consonants as these sounds are typically produced with higher levels of oral air pressure. Peterson-Falzone et al. (2001) described audible nasal air escape as the sound that occurs if one were to "forcibly" exhale through the nose. This type of audible nasal air escape is typically associated with speakers who have large VP gaps and excessive hypernasality. A more distinctive "nasal rustle" was identified in patients who exhibited relatively small VP gaps by Kummer, Curtis, Wiggs, Lee, and Strife (1992). They described nasal rustle as a louder and more distorting form of turbulence that is "due to the friction of the air being forced through a small velopharyngeal gap" (155).

We have often encountered children with repaired cleft palate who present with audible nasal air emission that appears similar to the description of nasal rustle. The most salient perceptual characteristic of this type of emission includes a periodic, raspberry-like sound that is relatively low in frequency. This distinctive sound may be due to vibration of either the free edge of the velum and/or tissue of the posterior pharyngeal wall, similar to vocal-fold vibration. Indeed, Trost (1981) described "flutter-like" vibration of a relatively closed VP port in a radiographic study of speakers who produced posterior nasal fricatives. These sounds are learned phonemic substitutions for fricatives that are produced by stopping oral airflow while forcing nasal airflow through a constricted VP port that results in a flutter like quality.

6.6 Conclusions and some future challenges

The VP port functions as a remarkably efficient aeromechanical valve in speech production throughout the life span. Although research findings are limited, children as young as two years of age appear to demonstrate adult-like control of VP port closure, at least for stop consonants. Children without palatal anomalies also appear to have little difficulty in adjusting to changes in nasopharyngeal anatomy during the growth spurt of the adolescent years. Even in advanced old age, the aerodynamic integrity of the VP valve appears stable. Congenital birth defects such as cleft palate, however, can significantly alter VP function. Speakers with severe VP dysfunction typically exhibit reduced oral air pressure, nasal air escape, and hypernasality. Even speakers with less severe VP dysfunction may present with perceptual symptoms of nasal air escape. While much is known about normal VP function, additional research is needed to describe the early developmental course of VP closure relative to phonetic context and nasal coarticulation in young children. Research is also needed to better understand the complex interactions that may occur between structural anomalies, conductive hearing loss, and VP function in children with repaired cleft palate.

NOTES

1. Baken and Orlikoff (2000: 490) state that the pressure-flow method "does not take account of nasal resistance" and, therefore, estimates of VP port area are actually "equivalent" estimates of the nasal-velopharyngeal airway. This was true of the original procedure described by Warren and DuBois (1964) in that differential pressure across both the VP port and nasal cavity was obtained using a single balloon-tipped catheter positioned in the oropharynx. Warren (1964b), however, modified the pressure-flow approach to directly obtain differential pressure across the VP port as illustrated in Figure 6.1.
2. By design, this chapter does not review acoustic characteristics of nasal consonants and/or nasalized vowels. Excellent summaries of this information can be found in Baken and Orlikoff (2000), Hixon et al. (2008), and many other sources.
3. Pressure-flow estimates of VP port size are most reliable when made at peak nasal airflow where the rate of change in flow is minimal. Mean estimates of VP port size for /p/ in a nasal-plosive sequence, therefore, may have increased variability due to the rapid change in air flow from the nasal to the plosive segment.
4. Complete VP closure was considered to occur if the mean VP opening for a speaker was 1.0 mm^2 or less. This somewhat arbitrary criterion was selected because Zajac (2000) reported that rates of nasal airflow associated with VP areas of 1.0 mm^2 or less typically did not exceed 10–20 mL/s, and Hoit et al. (1994) reported that low rates of nasal airflow

in the range of 10–20 mL/s may occur in the presence of airtight VP closure due to bounce-like movements of the velum.

5. McKerns and Bzoch (1970) suggested that males and females exhibit different configurations of VP closure as determined by videofluoroscopy. While some subsequent studies have reported sex differences in some aspects of VP function, the overall consensus is that no major sex differences exist. See Hixon et al. (2008) for a review of findings.

6. Some infants with incomplete clefts of the secondary palate that involve only the soft palate may be able to suck normally and/or produce stop consonants, especially the velar stops, with lingual assistance to occlude the cleft.

7. Although some authors have advocated use of the terms "insufficiency" to refer to structural/tissue causes of VP dysfunction and "incompetency" to refer to neuromuscular cause of VP dysfunction, the more generic term "dysfunction" is used throughout the chapter.

8. Warren (1967) reported a strong correlation between VP port size and the rate of nasal airflow in speakers with VP gaps up to 20 mm^2. When VP gaps exceed this value, especially 40 mm^2, the rate of nasal air is most likely limited by the size of the nasal cavity.

REFERENCES

Bae, Youkyung, David P. Kuehn, Charles A. Conway, and Bradley P. Sutton. 2011. Real-time magnetic resonance imaging of velopharyngeal activities with simultaneous speech recordings. *Cleft Palate-Craniofacial Journal* 48: 695–707.

Baken, R.J. and Robert F. Orlikoff. 2000. *Clinical Measurement of Speech and Voice*, 2nd edn. San Diego, CA: Singular.

Bell-Berti, Fredericka. 1976. An electromyographic study of velopharyngeal function in speech. *Journal of Speech and Hearing Research* 2: 225–240.

Bell-Berti, Fredericka. 1980. A spatial-temporal model of velopharyngeal function. In Norman J. Lass (ed.), *Speech and Language: Advances in Basic Research and Practice*, vol. 4. New York: Academic Press.

Bell-Berti, Fredericka. 1993. Understanding velic motor control: Studies of segmental context. In Marie K. Huffman and Rena A. Krakow (eds.), *Phonetics and Phonology: Nasals, Nasalization, and the Velum*. San Diego, CA: Academic Press.

Bell-Berti, Fredericka and Rena A. Krakow. 1991. Anticipatory velar lowering: A coproduction account. *Journal of the Acoustical Society of America* 90: 112–123.

Bosma, James F. 1953. A correlated study of the anatomy and motor activity of the upper pharynx by cadaver dissection and by cinematic study of patients after maxillo-facial surgery. *Annals of Otology, Rhinology, and Laryngology* 62(1): 51–72.

Brodsky, Linda, Linda Moore, John F. Stanievich, and Pearay L. Ogra. 1988. The immunology of tonsils in children: The effect of bacterial load on the presence of B- and T-cell subsets. *Laryngoscope* 98: 93–98.

Bundy, Emily and David J. Zajac. 2006. Estimation of transpalatal nasalance during production of voiced stop consonants by non-cleft speakers using an oral-nasal mask. *Cleft Palate-Craniofacial Journal* 43: 691–701.

Centers for Disease Control and Prevention (CDC). 2006. Improved national prevalence estimates for 18 selected major birth defects: United States

1999–2001. *Morbidity and Mortality Weekly Report* 54(51/52): 1301–1305.

Croft, Charles B., Robert J. Shprintzen, and Robert J. Ruben. 1981. Hypernasal speech following adenotonsillectomy. *Otolaryngology – Head and Neck Surgery* 89: 179–188.

Curtis, James. 1969. The acoustics of nasalized speech. *Cleft Palate Journal* 6: 380–396.

Dalston, Rodger D. 1982. Photodetector assessment of velopharyngeal activity. *Cleft Palate Journal* 19: 1–8.

Dalston, Rodger D., Donald W. Warren, Kathleen E. Morr, and Lynn R. Smith. 1988. Intraoral pressure and its relationship to velopharyngeal inadequacy. *Cleft Palate Journal* 25: 210–219.

Dickson, David R. 1975. Anatomy of the normal velopharyngeal mechanism. *Clinics in Plastic Surgery* 2(2): 235–248.

Donnelly, Martin J. 1994. Hypernasality following adenoid removal. *Irish Journal of Medical Science* 163: 225–227.

Emanuel, Floyd W. and Donald T. Counihan. 1970. Some characteristics of oral and nasal air flow during plosive consonant production. *Cleft Palate Journal* 7: 249–260.

Ettema, Sandra L., David P. Kuehn, Adrienne L. Perlman, and Noam Alperin. 2002. Magnetic resonance imaging of the levator veli palatini muscle during speech. *Cleft Palate-Craniofacial Journal* 39: 130–144.

Fritzell, Björn. 1969. The velopharyngeal muscles in speech: An electromyographic and cineradiographic study. *Acta Otolaryngologica,* Supplement 250: 1–81.

Gildersleeve-Neumann, Christina E. and Rodger D. Dalston. 2001. Nasalance scores in noncleft individuals: Why not zero? *Cleft Palate-Craniofacial Journal* 38: 106–111.

Graber, Thomas M., Kenneth R. Bzoch, and Tsuneo Aoba. 1959. A functional study of the palatal and pharyngeal structures. *Angle Orthodontist* 29: 30–40.

Ha, Seunghee, David P. Kuehn, Mimis Cohen, and Noam Alperin. 2007. Magnetic resonance imaging of the levator veli palatini muscle in speakers with repaired cleft palate. *Cleft Palate-Craniofacial Journal* 44: 494–505.

Handelman, Chester S. and George Osborne. 1976. Growth of the nasopharynx and adenoid development from one to eighteeen years. *Angle Orthodontist* 46: 243–259.

Hixon, Thomas J., Gary Weismer, and Jeannette D. Hoit. 2008. *Preclinical Speech Science: Anatomy, Physiology, Acoustics, Perception*. San Diego, CA: Plural Publishing.

Hoit, Jeannette D., Peter J. Watson, Kimberly E. Hixon, Patricia McMahon, and Cynthia L. Johnson. 1994. Age and velopharyngeal function. *Journal of Speech and Hearing Research* 37: 295–302.

Horiguchi, Satoshi and Fredericka Bell-Berti. 1987. The Velotrace: A device for monitoring velar position. *Cleft Palate Journal* 24: 104–111.

Horii, Yoshiyuki. 1983. An accelerometric measure as a physical correlate of perceived hypernasality in speech. *Journal of Speech and Hearing Research* 26: 476–480.

House, Arthur S. and Kenneth N. Stevens. 1956. Analog studies of the nasalization of vowels. *Journal of Speech and Hearing Disorders* 21: 218–232.

Hutchinson, J.M., K.L. Robinson, and M.A. Nerbonne. 1978. Patterns of nasalance in a sample of normal gerontologic subjects. *Journal of Communication Disorders* 11(6): 469–481.

Iglesias, Aquiles, David P. Kuehn, and Hughlett L. Morris. 1980. Simultaneous assessment of pharyngeal wall and velar displacement for selected speech sounds. *Journal of Speech and Hearing Research* 23(2): 429–446.

Kataoka, Ryuta, Donald W. Warren, David J. Zajac, Robert Mayo, and Richard Lutz. 2001.The relationship between spectral characteristics and perceived hypernasality in children. *Journal of the Acoustical Society of America* 109: 2181–2189.

Kent, Raymond D. and Ann D. Murray. 1982. Acoustic features of infant vocalic utterances at 3, 6, and 9 months. *Journal of the Acoustical Society of America* 72: 353–365.

Kent, Raymond D., Patrick J. Carney, and Larry R. Severeid. 1974. Velar movement and timing: Evaluation of a model for binary control. *Journal of Speech and Hearing Research* 17: 470–488.

Krakow, Rena A. and Marie K. Huffman. 1993. Instruments and techniques for investigating nasalization and velopharyngeal function in the laboratory: An introduction. In Marie K. Huffman and Rena A. Krakow (eds.), *Phonetics and Phonology: Nasals, Nasalization, and the Velum*. San Diego, CA: Academic Press.

Kuehn, David P. and Karlind T. Moller. 2000. Speech and language issues in the cleft palate population: The state of the art. *Cleft Palate-Craniofacial Journal* 37(4): 348–383.

Kuehn, David P. and Jerald B. Moon. 1998. Velopharyngeal closure force and levator veli palatini activation levels in varying phonetic contexts. *Journal of Speech, Language, and Hearing Research* 41: 51–62.

Kummer, Ann. 2008. *Cleft Palate and Craniofacial Anomalies: Effects on Speech and Resonance*, 2nd edn. San Diego, CA: Singular.

Kummer, Ann W., Cindy Curtis, Melissa Wiggs, Linda Lee, and Janet L. Strife. 1992. Comparison of velopharyngeal gap size in patients with hypernasality, hypernasality and nasal emission, or nasal turbulence (rustle) as the primary speech characteristic. *The Cleft Palate-Craniofacial Journal* 29: 152–156.

Lubker, James F. 1968. An electromyographic-cinefluorographic investigation of velar function during normal speech production. *Cleft Palate Journal* 5: 1–18.

Lubker, James F. and Kenneth L. Moll. 1965. Simultaneous oral-nasal air flow measurements and cinefluorographic observations during speech production. *Cleft Palate Journal* 2: 257–272.

McKerns, David and Kenneth R. Bzoch. 1970. Variations in velopharyngeal valving: The factor of sex. *Cleft Palate Journal* 7: 652–662.

Moll, Kenneth L. 1962. Velopharyngeal closure on vowels. *Journal of Speech and Hearing Research* 17: 30–77.

Moll, Kenneth L. and Raymond G. Daniloff. 1971. Investigation of the timing of velar movements during speech. *Journal of the Acoustical Society of America* 50: 678–684.

Moll, Kenneth L. and Thomas H. Shriner. 1967. Preliminary investigation of a new concept of velar activity during speech. *Cleft Palate Journal* 4: 58–69.

Moon, Jerald B. 1993. Evaluation of velopharyngeal function. In Karlind T. Moller and Clark D. Starr (eds.), *Cleft Palate: Interdisciplinary Issues and Treatment for Clinicians by Clinicians*. Austin, TX: Pro-Ed.

Moon, Jerald B. and Rajendra Lagu. 1987. Development of a second-generation phototransducer for the assessment of velopharyngeal activity. *Cleft Palate Journal* 24: 240–243.

Moon, Jerald B., David P. Kuehn, and Jessica J. Huisman. 1994. Measurement of velopharyngeal closure force during vowel production. *Cleft Palate-Craniofacial Journal* 31: 356–363.

Neiman, Gary S. and Robert K. Simpson. 1975. A roentgencephalometric investigation of the effect of adenoid removal upon selected measures of velopharyngeal function. *Cleft Palate Journal* 12: 377–389.

Oller, D. Kimbrough and Rebecca E. Eilers. 1988. The role of audition in infant babbling. *Child Development* 59: 441–449.

Peterson-Falzone, Sally, Mary Hardin-Jones, and Michael Karnell. 2001. *Cleft*

Palate Speech, 3rd edn. St. Louis, MO: Mosby Elsevier.

Philips, Betty Jane and Raymond D. Kent. 1984. Acoustic-phonetic descriptions of speech production in speakers with cleft palate and other velopharyngeal disorders. In Norman Lass (ed.), *Speech and Language: Advances in Basic Research*, vol. 11, 113–168. New York: Academic Press.

Sasaki, Clarence T., Paul A. Levine, Jeffrey T. Laitman, and Edmund S. Crelin, Jr. 1977. Postnatal descent of the epiglottis in man: A preliminary report. *Archives of Otolaryngology* 103: 169–171.

Schwartz, Martin F. 1968. Acoustics of normal and nasal vowel production. *Cleft Palate Journal* 5: 125–138.

Skolnick, M. Leon and Ellen R. Cohn. 1989. *Videofluoroscopic Studies of Speech in Patients with Cleft Palate*. New York: Springer-Verlag.

Subtelny, J. Daniel. 1957. A cephalometric study of the growth of the soft palate. *Plastic and Reconstructive Surgery* 19: 49–62.

Subtelny, J. Daniel and Herbert K. Baker. 1956. The significance of adenoid tissue in velopharyngeal function. *Plastic and Reconstructive Surgery* 17: 235–250.

Thom, Stacey A., Jeannette D. Hoit, Thomas J. Hixon, and Alice E. Smith. 2006. Velopharyngeal function during vocalization in infants. *Cleft Palate-Craniofacial Journal* 43: 539–546.

Thompson, Amy E. and Thomas J. Hixon. 1979. Nasal air flow during normal speech production. *Cleft Palate Journal* 16: 412–420.

Tian, Wei and Richard J. Redett. 2009. New velopharyngeal measurements at rest and during speech: Implication and applications. *Journal of Craniofacial Surgery* 20: 532–539.

Tomoda, Koichi, Sotokichi Morii, Toshio Yamashita, and Tadami Kumazawa. 1984. Histology of human Eustachian tube muscles: Effects of aging. *Annals of Otology, Rhinology, and Laryngology* 93: 17–24.

Trost, Judith E. 1981. Articulatory additions to the classical description of the speech of persons with cleft palate. *Cleft Palate Journal* 18: 193–203.

Vorperian, Houri K., Raymond D. Kent, Mary J. Lindstrom, Cliff M. Kalina, Lindell R. Gentry, and Brian S. Yandell. 2005. Development of vocal tract length during early childhood: A magnetic resonance imaging study. *Journal of the Acoustical Society of America* 117: 338–350.

Warren, Donald W. 1964a. Velopharyngeal orifice size and upper pharyngeal pressure-flow patterns in normal speech. *Plastic and Reconstructive Surgery* 33: 148–161.

Warren, Donald W. 1964b. Velopharyngeal orifice size and upper pharyngeal pressure-flow patterns in cleft palate speech: A preliminary study. *Plastic and Reconstructive Surgery* 34: 15–26.

Warren, Donald W. 1967. Nasal emission of air and velopharyngeal function. *Cleft Palate Journal* 16: 279–285.

Warren, Donald W. 1976. Aerodynamics of speech production. In N.J. Lass (ed.), *Contemporary Issues in Experimental Phonetics*, 105–137. New York: Academic Press.

Warren, Donald W. and Arthur DuBois. 1964. A pressure-flow technique for measuring velopharyngeal orifice area during continuous speech. *Cleft Palate Journal* 1: 52–71.

Warren, Donald W., Rodger M. Dalston, Kathleen Morr, and William Hairfield. 1989. The speech regulating system: Temporal and aerodynamic responses to velopharyngeal inadequacy. *Journal of Speech and Hearing Research* 32: 566–575.

Williams, William N., Gunilla Henningsson, and Maria I. Pegoraro-Krook. 1997. Radiographic assessment of velopharyngeal function for speech. In Kenneth R. Bzoch (ed.), *Communicative Disorders Related to Cleft Lip and Palate*, 4th edn. Austin, TX: Pro-Ed.

Yates, Cambell C., Betty Jane McWilliams, and Linda D. Vallino. 1990. The pressure-flow method: Some fundamental concepts. *Cleft Palate Journal* 27: 193–198.

Young, Lisa H., David J. Zajac, Robert Mayo, and Celia R. Hooper. 2001. Effects of vowel height and vocal intensity on anticipatory nasal airflow in individuals with normal speech. *Journal of Speech, Language, and Hearing Research* 44: 52–60.

Zajac, David J. 1997. Velopharyngeal function in young and older adult speakers: Evidence from aerodynamic studies. *Journal of the Acoustical Society of America* 102: 1846–1852.

Zajac, David J. 2000. Pressure-flow characteristics of /m/ and /p/ production in speakers without cleft palate: Developmental findings. *The Cleft Palate-Craniofacial Journal* 37(5): 468–477.

Zajac, David J. 2003. Pressure-flow characteristics of speakers with repaired cleft palate. Paper presented at the Annual Meeting of the American Cleft Palate-Craniofacial Association, Asheville, NC.

Zajac, David J. and Robert Mayo. 1996. Aerodynamic and temporal aspects of velopharyngeal function in normal speakers. *Journal of Speech and Hearing Research* 39(6): 1199–1207.

Zajac, David J., Robert Mayo, and Ryuta Kataoka. 1998. Nasal coarticulation in normal speakers: A re-examination of the effects of gender. *Journal of Speech, Language, and Hearing Research* 41: 503–510.

Zajac, David J., John van Aalst, Linda Vallino, and Joseph Napoli. 2011. Nasal ram pressure as an indicator of velopharyngeal closure during stop consonants in 2 year-olds following palate repair. Paper presented at the Annual Meeting of the American Cleft Palate-Craniofacial Association, San Juan, PR.

Part II Coordination and Multimodal Speech

7 Interarticulatory Coordination
Speech Sounds

PHILIP HOOLE AND MARIANNE POUPLIER

7.1 Introduction

There is probably no speech utterance that involves only a single organ of the vocal tract. In a sense, full coverage of the topic of interarticulatory coordination therefore requires coverage of speech production in its entirety, and it is important at the beginning of this chapter to outline how we intend to define a task of manageable proportions. Thinking in terms of the three processes defined by Catford (2001), initiation, phonation, and articulation, we will focus on articulation, defined as the process of modifying an airstream. So we will not go into areas such as the coordination of respiratory and phonatory activity, nor the patterns of coordinated movement that are required for non-pulmonic initiation. We will, however, be devoting a section to laryngeal-oral coordination in which we treat the alternation between voicing and voicelessness as articulatory behavior of the larynx.

A basic distinction in articulation is that between temporal and spatial aspects. We will be looking at interarticulatory coordination above all in its temporal aspects. Spatial aspects, namely how multiple articulators collaborate to achieve some functional goal, are dealt with by Perrier and Fuchs in Chapter 11 of this volume under the title of motor equivalence, a key theoretical issue in speech motor control.

Even from the temporal point of view, we will not attempt to cover one big area, namely timing issues with respect to coarticulation. Coarticulation necessarily involves issues of interarticulatory coordination. For example, when investigating the extent of anticipatory labial coarticulation, the activity of the lips in the articulation of some sound must be referenced in time to the activity of some other speech organ, or perhaps to some acoustic goal. Since good reviews of coarticulation are readily available, and full coverage of this topic would involve discussion of a multitude of acoustic studies, we refer the reader to the relevant sources (e.g., Farnetani and Recasens 2010).

Turning now to the structure of the chapter itself, the most fundamental division we will be making is between the coordination of multiple articulators in the articulation of single segments (section 7.2) versus coordination of multiple articulators in the articulation of multiple segments (section 7.3). In section 7.2, attention will be paid to influences on timing patterns when, for example, the tongue and jaw or the lips and jaw are coordinated to form a constriction. Attention will also be paid to a particularly clear case in which interarticulatory timing has linguistic relevance, namely laryngeal-oral timing in various forms of the voicing distinction. We thus also need to distinguish between cases where multiple articulators contribute to a single gesture in a single segment and those where the different articulators also involve different gestures (gesture is used here in the sense of a constriction in the vocal tract). We will also review the influence of syllable position on multiple-gesture segments.

In section 7.3, which focuses on the case of the coordination of multiple articulators across multiple segments, we examine the timing of consonant sequences, such as the movements of tongue-dorsum and tongue-tip for /kl/, and also the timing of consonant-vowel sequences. Discussion will again focus on the role of syllable position in determining timing patterns. We will also consider the influence of the segmental properties of the elements in a sound sequence, such as voicing or place order, as well as language-specific preferences for specific coordination patterns.

It is worth mentioning at this point that the traditional term "segment" we have used here is often regarded by proponents of gestural theories (e.g., Task Dynamics, Articulatory Phonology) as the epiphenomenal expression of underlying coordination patterns. Regarding gestures as the basic units ("atoms") of articulatory representation, "segment" is simply a convenient term for multigestural ("molecular") structures with a particularly high degree of cohesiveness. Evidence for this view comes from, for example, Saltzman et al. (1998) and Saltzman, Löfqvist, and Mitra (2000), who analyzed phase-resetting in a perturbation paradigm and found stronger intergestural "glue" within than between segments. Along these lines, Pouplier (2011) has recently noted that a consonant cluster is not fundamentally different from a single consonantal segment given that closure and release can be modeled by separate but coupled dynamic building blocks, as in the split-gesture dynamics approach of Nam, Goldstein, and Saltzman (2009).

7.2 Coordination of multiple articulators for single segments

7.2.1 Multiple articulators for a single gesture

A considerable body of work has looked at the coordination of multiple articulators to form a specific vocal tract constriction, such as lip-closure, from the point of view of the cohesiveness of the component movements. A high level of cohesiveness in coordination patterns provides evidence for the existence of higher-level functional groupings of the articulators. These functional grouping are often referred to as coordinative structures following Turvey (1977, 1990) and Bernstein (1967). Such groupings are considered necessary to understand how speakers manage the potentially very large number of degrees of freedom in the vocal apparatus (Kelso, Saltzman, and Tuller 1986). Moreover, coordinative structures form the substrate for the spatial tradeoffs characteristic of motor equivalence (Perrier and Fuchs, this volume, Chapter 11).

For the particularly well-researched lip-jaw complex considerable evidence has been found for consistent interarticulatory timing patterns. For lip closing movements the typical pattern has been for peak velocities to occur in the temporal order (1) upper lip, (2) lower lip, (3) jaw (e.g., Gracco 1988). The tightness of the coordination is generally more precise for oral closure than for oral opening (Gracco 1988; Kollia, Gracco, and Harris 1995). This variation in tightness of coordination provides one example of the observation that movements into and out of a constriction are quite asymmetric, which in turn has led to the proposal that the closure and opening phase of a gesture are best modeled as separately controlled movements (Browman 1994; Nam 2007; Harrington, Fletcher, and Roberts 1995).

Interarticulatory coordination can also be influenced by the precise identity of the target sounds even when the articulators involved are basically the same. For example, Mooshammer, Hoole, and Geumann (2006) looked in particular at the influence of manner of articulation on tongue-jaw coordination. The results showed a substantial degree of consistency in that the jaw almost always reached its target position for the consonant later than the tongue tip. The more interesting feature of the results came from some subtle but consistent timing differences between the consonants: the sibilants showed a symmetrical tongue-jaw coordination pattern, meaning late location of jaw target onset and early location of jaw target offset within the encompassing tongue target phase. In contrast, the voiceless plosive /t/ showed an asymmetrical pattern with very late attainment of the jaw target, but also a late location of jaw target offset close to tongue target offset. These differences in coordination can be readily understood in terms of the different aerodynamic and acoustic requirements of the sounds involved. The sibilant fricatives require a stable, high position of the jaw centered on the oral constriction phase in order to ensure generation of turbulence. The critical location for voiceless plosives is at the release of the constriction where a high jaw position can help to support a salient burst. Interestingly, for other consonants (e.g., voiced plosive, nasal, lateral), where none of these constraints so obviously apply, Mooshammer et al. found more variability (i.e., not such a clear preference) for either the symmetrical or asymmetrical timing pattern. These results indicate that, in spite of stable timing patterns for many multi-articulator constriction gestures, these patterns are not totally stereotypic. Instead, they can be modulated to fulfill differing aerodynamic and acoustic demands.

Given that speech motor control obviously exhibits a whole range of very precise timing relationships, a question arises as to the most appropriate framework in which to express these relationships.

One answer is simply based on what kinematic measures exhibit the most stable patterns. For example, various studies have suggested that timing relationships expressed in terms of the time-points of peak velocities are more stable than position-based ones, such as attainment of target position (see Kollia et al. 1995, for discussion).

A more controversial answer is that temporal invariance in coordination patterns can be captured using a phase-plane representation. For example, when cyclical movements of the jaw are plotted with velocity as a function of position then a roughly circular pattern in this two-dimensional representation is traced out. Characteristic time-points in the movement of another articulator, such as the lip, can then be expressed as an angle in this plane (see, e.g., Kelso et al. 1986; Nittrouer et al. 1988, for more details on procedures). The original hypothesis, based on other work in motor control and the characterization of dynamic systems (Kelso et al. 1986) was that stability in interarticulatory timing might express itself as a phase-angle that remains constant over manipulations such as stress and rate. However, the balance of later work indicates that systematic changes in phase-angle probably occur (e.g., Nittrouer et al. 1988 and Shaiman, Adams, and Kimelman 1995, for lip-jaw; Nittrouer 1991, for tongue-jaw).

7.2.2 *Multiple articulators for multiple gestures*

In this section we first compare the degree of interarticulator cohesion within versus between gestures, then move on to look at effects of syllable position on multiple-gesture segments, and then at within and cross-language patterns of laryngeal-oral coordination.

7.2.2.1 Inter- vs. intragesture cohesion With regard to the degree of interarticulator cohesion within versus between gestures, we can return to Kollia et al. (1995). This paper takes as its point of departure the many findings on interarticulator coordination for the lip-jaw complex and integrates velar movement into the analyses. The question then asked is: How cohesive is the interarticulator timing for lip-velum or jaw-velum (for example during lip closing and velum closing for /b/) in comparison to the intragestural lip-jaw case discussed in the previous section? Kollia et al. found that for the two closing movements associated with /b/ in the sequence /mabnab/, intergestural (velum-jaw, velum-upper lip) cohesion was clearly weaker than intragestural cohesion when estimated from time-points of peak velocities. However, the interpretation of this result is not entirely straightforward since velar raising is probably influenced not only by the /b/ but also, if only weakly, by the preceding /a/. Thus, intergestural cohesion may have an inherently more complex and variable velocity profile than intragestural cohesion. Support for this interpretation comes from the fact that, when the analysis was based on peak position rather than peak velocity timing, the intragestural advantage was much less evident, albeit the correlations were overall weaker when based on peak positions (peak velar position in this sound sequence is more easily attributed to a single segment than is peak velocity). By contrast, for the oral and velar opening movements in the /bna/ part of the sequence, the peak velocity that referenced velum-jaw coordination suggested tighter cohesion than for jaw-upper lip coordination. A transition such as that from /b/ to /n/ is probably a good example of where tight intergestural coordination is required and possible. Kollia et al. also suggest that compared to peak positions "peak velocity relations may be more illustrative of critical or constrained timing relations" (1323).

A study by Gracco and Löfqvist (1994) followed a somewhat similar approach to that of Kollia et al. (1995), but focused on the intergestural coordination of oral and laryngeal movements. Specifically, they looked at the temporal cohesion of jaw lowering and glottal closing in the movement from /s/ to the vowel in words like "supper," and of lower lip raising and glottal opening from the vowel to /p/. At a gross level of analysis, timing patterns showed evidence of stable organization in both cases. The time-point of peak glottal closing velocity always preceded peak jaw lowering velocity, while the time-point of peak lip raising velocity always preceded peak glottal opening velocity. When detailed correlation analyses were used to assess temporal cohesion between gestures, it emerged that correlations between oral and glottal time-points were noticeably lower for the oral opening movements. At first glance, this suggests a similar intergestural pattern of coordination to the intragestural pattern of coordination already noted above (less cohesion for oral opening movements, section 7.2.1). However, the authors emphasize that the intergestural cohesion level they found was remarkably high compared to results reported in other studies for intragestural lip-jaw coordination in opening movements (intergestural cohesion is typically lower than intragestural cohesion, Saltzman et al. 1998, 2000). Assessment of the conclusion is not entirely straightforward, though, because Gracco and Löfqvist did not explicitly measure lip-jaw cohesion in their study. Nevertheless, the results may indicate that intergestural cohesion can be as high as that involved in forming a single constriction.

7.2.2.2 Influence of syllable position on multi-gesture segments We will first consider the effects of syllable position on multi-gesture segments with respect to the coordination of the oral and velar gestures in nasal consonants. These particular multi-gesture segments have been the object of some clear and influential results with respect to syllable position. They thus provide a good starting point for discussing generalizations in interarticulatory coordination for a much wider range of multi-gesture segments. Liquids have also been a particular focus in studies that investigate the effect of syllable position on interarticulatory coordination. In fact, liquids might be construed as the tip of an iceberg consisting of everything that would fall under the traditional phonetic terms of secondary and double articulation.

In an influential paper, Krakow (1999) reports results from an investigation into the coordination of lips and velum in the nasal /m/ in American English. Critically, she also embedded the empirical work in a wide-ranging review of articulatory evidence for syllabic structure. The basic timing result for lip-velum coordination was that in syllable-initial position the velum and the lower lip moved more or less in synchrony. That is, the end of the velar lowering movement for /m/ roughly coincided with the beginning of the lip-raising movement for the oral closure. In contrast, in syllable-final position, the velar movement was timed much earlier. Specifically, the end of the velar lowering movement roughly corresponded to the *beginning* of the lip closing movement. This basic timing pattern was recently confirmed by Byrd et al. (2009), who also gave an interesting overview of how the coupling relations among the articulators could be modeled.

Given Krakow (1999) and Byrd et al.'s (2009) results, it is quite clear that syllable position can have striking effects on articulatory coordination. The much more difficult issue is the extent to which such findings are generalizable from lip-velum coordination to other patterns of interarticulatory coordination. Both Byrd et al. and Krakow make the link to other multi-gesture segments. Byrd et al. formulated the link as follows:

> Strikingly, there appear general parallels (see also Browman and Goldstein, 1992; Krakow, 1999) in the effect of syllable structure on nasals, glides, and liquids – namely, that in onset position the primary oral constriction gesture target precedes or is synchronous with the secondary (non-primary constriction) gesture target (i.e., the pharyngeal gesture for [r], dorsal for [l], or velum for nasals), whereas in coda, the secondary gesture target occurs far earlier, during the preceding vocalic nucleus.
>
> (2009: 98)

However, one could ask whether these "parallels" are not just a fortuitous coincidence of specific properties of certain sounds in a particular dialect of English. For example, the fact that English has no contrastive vowel nasalization may allow early velar lowering before the post-vocalic nasal, which then just happens to meet a preferred timing pattern for dark /l/. Certainly, it is not obvious to us that it is attractive to regard the velar gesture for /m/ as "secondary" in the same sense as velarization for dark /l/ (or as "wider" as suggested in Browman and Goldstein 1995: 25). In particular, there do indeed seem to be well-documented differences in the timing of nasals across languages. French (Cohn 1993) and the Australian aboriginal language Arrernte (Butcher 1999) both show synchronous coordination of the oral and velar constrictions in both onset and coda. In the case of French, this could be explained by the need to maintain a difference between oral and nasal vowels, as these constitute phonologically contrastive units. Arrernte, on the other hand, has no oral-nasal vowel contrast. Cross-linguistic variety in the coordination patterns for the multiple lingual gestures has also been reported for liquids by Gick et al. (2006), as discussed in more detail below. These cross-language differences underscore a fact which will come up again in section 7.3; namely, that of systematic language-specific differences in articulatory organization.

Although the range of possible patterns for liquids and other sound categories will be discussed in detail immediately below, it is first worth emphasizing that Krakow (1999) did not confine herself to the basic syllable-initial/final contrast in discussing the empirical findings. Instead, she highlighted a whole range of timing issues that the basic finding led to. For example, in considering why Cantonese (Wang 1995) did not show the same pattern as English, Krakow considered whether fast/casual speech could lead to re-syllabification of final consonants:

> In casual (or fast) speech, the pattern characteristic of the final consonant (whether /m/ or /l/) was subject to a shift in the direction of that for the initial consonant. It appears that this shift is more likely to occur when the consonant is word-medial than -marginal. On the other hand, the syllable-initial consonants (/m/ and /l/) remained relatively stable with respect to their inter-articulator timing, regardless of the style or rate of speech.
> (Krakow 1999: 43)

In this way, Krakow makes the important point that not only timing itself, but also the *stability* of timing can be position dependent: there is less stability in the coda (a point that will also be relevant later in coordination of segment sequences). The question of whether syllable affiliation is better seen as gradient or discrete is currently still under discussion (e.g., Scobbie and Pouplier 2010: 252).

Let us now consider a wider range of multi-gesture segments. A good point of departure is the extensively cited paper of Sproat and Fujimura (1993) on the component gestures of American English /l/ (extensive discussion in Krakow 1999, who also reproduces one of the main figures). In many dialects of English, /l/ is considered light in onsets and dark in codas. The assumption is that the latter allophone involves an additional gesture of the dorsum, traditionally referred to as velarization. Note, though, that recent work claims that liquids are generally composed of two gestures (see Proctor 2011: Recasens 2012). In the variety of American English investigated by Sproat and Fujimura, there was clear dorsal activity for the onset /l/s as well. The striking finding, if /l/ is regarded as inherently multi-gestural, is that the gestural timing showed a very clear dependence on position of /l/ in the syllable. Target achievement for the dorsal movement tended to precede target achievement for the apical movement in final position, but to follow it in initial position. If we consider the dorsal component of /l/ articulation a vocalic gesture, then we might regard the positional effect as one in which the vocalic gesture is attracted toward the syllable nucleus while the consonantal apical gesture is associated with the syllable margin.

Browman and Goldstein (1995) looked at the pattern of multi-gesture coordination for /l/ as synchronous in initial position and asynchronous in final position. They pointed to the fact that in Sproat and Fujimura's (1993) data the amount by which the dorsum led the tip in final position was greater in absolute terms than the amount by which it followed the tip in initial position (averaged over subjects about 60ms vs. 30ms).

In addition to illustrating effects of syllable position, Sproat and Fujimura's (1993) data illustrate very elegantly how the timing for syllable final laterals can vary over a whole continuum of values depending on the segmental and prosodic context. This variation probably represents a syllable-related timing feature that goes well beyond laterals and nasals.

We indicated above some general reservations about regarding the velar gesture in a nasal and the dorsal gesture in a liquid as somehow similar in status (e.g., secondary, more open). To this general reservation, one could now add the observation that the dorsal gesture for dark /l/ in English is probably not secondary in the same sense as, for example, palatalization in Russian or Serbo-Croat. The dorsal component of /l/ is very often much more resistant to reduction than the coronal component (cf. Scobbie and Pouplier 2010). It is also important to realize that the gestural constellation referenced in Sproat and Fujimura's (1993) investigation is probably just one of quite a large number of possibilities that could be found for liquids within and across language. Consider, for example, languages with a dorsal retraction gesture only in final position (e.g., two speakers of Quebec French in Gick et al. 2006), or only a clear /l/ with a raised tongue body or potentially no secondary gesture at all (e.g., German, Romanian: Marin and Pouplier 2014; Recasens, Fontdevila, and Pallarès 1995), or a dorsal gesture both initially and finally but timed synchronously with the coronal gesture in both positions (two speakers of Serbo-Croat, Gick et al. 2006). The latter case is particularly interesting because of the presence of palatalization in the Serbo-Croat sound system. The Serbo-Croat /l/ investigated by Gick et al. was the non-palatalized liquid. The presence of a palatalized variant might lead to constraints on interarticulatory coordination. Unfortunately, little about the effects of secondary articulations on intergestural coordination is currently known (but see Zsiga 2003, on a timing comparison of English and Russian).

In point of fact, "classical" secondary articulations like palatalization have indeed themselves hardly been investigated in terms of interarticulatory coordination. A rare exception to this generalization is a study by Kochetov (2006). Kochetov examined the labial and dorsal gestures for Russian /pʲ/ in initial and final position (also comparing it with the phonemic sequences /pj/ and /jp/). As in the studies discussed above there was an effect of syllable position. Moreover, the general direction of the effect was the same in the sense that the dorsal gesture was timed earlier relative to the labial gesture in final position compared to initial position. However, there was also one substantial difference: the gestures were more synchronous in final than initial position. Kochetov raised the important issue of gestural recoverability as a constraint on interarticulatory timing. For initial /pʲ/ the observed slight delay of the dorsal gesture relative to the labial gesture is advantageous in ensuring firstly that the dorsal gesture is not completely obscured by the more anterior, more constricted labial gesture, and also that it contributes to probably very salient perceptual differences in the burst properties of palatalized vs. non-palatalized /p/. The notion of perceptual recoverability will also be a major issue in our discussion of segment sequences below.

Russian is actually a very interesting language for investigating recoverability constraints because, as Kochetov's (2006) data show, the dorsal component of /pʲ/ cannot be delayed to such an extent as to lead to confusion with /pj/. Kochetov suggests that the syllable-position-dependent timing pattern for /pʲ/ is more similar to findings of Gick (2003) for the English approximant /w/ than most of the nasal and liquid findings outlined above (the approximant also showed greater asynchronicity in initial than final position). Once again we would be inclined to not push any parallels too far because of the controversial phonological status of coda /w/ in English. However, the case of /w/ does provide a convenient link to a further gap in our understanding. If /w/ is regarded in traditional terms as a labial-velar double articulation, then one might ask whether it has any similarities in timing with the only other doubly articulated consonant of appreciable frequency, namely the corresponding plosive /kp/ (not found in English, of course, but quite common in West African languages). Here the current balance of evidence would seem to be that the labial component is timed slightly later than the dorsal component (see in particular Ladefoged and Maddieson 1996: 338). This is the opposite pattern to that found by Gick for /w/ in initial position. But this comparison must be seen as tentative in the extreme because to our knowledge articulatory timing for /w/ and /kp/ has not yet been compared within the same language.

As for avenues for future research in this area, one sound that is likely to attract increasing attention is American English /r/. This sound is a classic case of a multi-gestural segment, but most likely with three constrictions (labial, palatal, pharyngeal). Timing investigations into the articulation of this sound have been difficult until recently because the pharyngeal component is not observable with traditional tools, such as electromagnetic articulography (EMA). But with the increasing availability and frame-rates of ultrasound and real-time MRI, this situation is clearly changing (see, e.g., Campbell et al. 2010). In spite of the recent availability of techniques that can be used to study American English /r/, we would like to suggest that it might be more fruitful to focus on secondary articulations of the traditional type exemplified by Kochetov's (2006) investigation. The reason for this is that secondary articulations are extremely pervasive and linguistically rich whereas American English /r/ (and perhaps its Mandarin counterpart) is a genuinely exotic sound (even if a large number of speakers happen to have it in their repertoire).

7.2.2.3 Laryngeal-oral coordination for single segments The combination of plosive articulation with the laryngeal abduction-adduction movement illustrates particularly well how intimately interarticulatory timing is bound up with linguistic distinctions. By varying the timing of the glottal gesture from early to late, one can move through the categories voiceless pre-aspirated, voiceless unaspirated, voiceless aspirated, and voiced aspirated. Cross-linguistically, less use seems to be made of the pre-aspirated category than of the other three categories, even though it is a well-known feature of Icelandic (see Hoole and Bombien 2010, for recent data and discussion). Hindi is an example of a language that contrasts voiceless unaspirated, voiceless aspirated, and voiced aspirated (plus normal voiced) stops. Accordingly, several studies on Hindi that have used fiberoptics and transillumination provide convenient illustrative material of the timing relationships between glottal and oral gestures (e.g., Kagaya and Hirose 1975: Figure 1; Benguerel and Bhatia 1980: Figures 1–2; Dixit 1989: Figures 1–4). Of course, the timing relationships are not all that is different across these three categories. For example, the voiceless aspirated category generally has a longer, larger movement than the other two; the voiced aspirated category is also striking for the particularly strong suppression of cricothyroid activity (cf. Dixit and MacNeilage 1980). Nonetheless, appropriate timing is clearly a key feature of the distinction between the voiceless unaspirated, voiceless aspirated, and voiced aspirated categories.

Of course, undoubtedly the single most famous index of interarticulatory coordination of any kind is the Voice Onset Time (VOT) measure introduced in Lisker and Abramson's (1964) seminal work. Because it can be conveniently measured in the acoustic signal, it has found widespread use not only as a measure of language differences, but also to investigate the development of timing skills in first and second language acquisition (e.g., Lowenstein and Nittrouer 2008; Flege et al. 1998) and the disintegration of coordinated behavior in speech pathology (e.g., Hoole, Schröter-Morasch, and Ziegler 1997; Ackermann and Hertrich 1997; Auzou et al. 2000). Although we will not attempt to review the vast literature on VOT, we will look briefly at one specific VOT-related issue where instrumental data of laryngeal kinematics is particularly relevant: this is the common finding that VOT varies fairly systematically with place of articulation in plosives, with VOT for /p/ generally being shorter than /t, k/ (for reviews see, e.g., Docherty 1992; Cho and Ladefoged 1999).

VOT variation as a function of place of articulation is an interesting case study in interarticulatory coordination. One simple explanation for a shorter VOT in /p/ is that the later oral release relative to the glottal abduction-adduction cycle falls out passively from differences in occlusion duration, since it is also well known that /p/ tends to have a longer oral occlusion phase. Evidence has indeed been found in the literature that the duration of the interval from peak glottal opening to release of the plosive is inversely related to the duration of the occlusion (e.g., Jessen 1999; further data and review in Hoole 2006; Hoole and Bombien 2014), but this may not be the only explanation for longer VOT in /t/ than /p/ since there is also evidence that the duration of the glottal gesture is not constant over all places of articulation, and a longer glottal gesture duration may in some cases also contribute to longer VOT in /t/. Nevertheless, speakers and languages may try to get as much mileage as possible out of a fairly constant duration of the glottal abductory-adductory cycle (cf. Weismer 1980; Shipp 1982); for example, there appears to be a cross-language tendency that long aspiration phases are associated with short occlusion phases and vice versa (Hutters 1985; recently Bombien and Hoole 2013), and the occlusion duration of voiceless fricatives is typically longer than that of aspirated voiceless plosives (fricatives are normally neither pre- nor post-aspirated).

We close this section on laryngeal-oral coordination with a brief look at differences across manner of articulation, specifically plosives vs. fricatives. Here the timing of the start of glottal abduction is of more interest than the timing of peak glottal opening since the latter, as just seen, is mainly conditioned by the control of aspiration for plosives, so plosives and fricatives differ radically but trivially in many languages. It turns out that an earlier onset of glottal abduction for fricatives (relative to the formation of the oral occlusion) is an extremely stable feature of interarticulatory coodination. For example, it is a consistent feature of the many early studies on a variety of languages conducted by Löfqvist and colleagues (e.g., Löfqvist and Yoshioka 1984; Löfqvist and McGarr 1987) and is probably the most consistent timing pattern in extensive data for German (Hoole 2006; Hoole and Bombien 2014). The stability of this relationship is probably because resistance to airflow at the glottis must be reduced quickly and early in the occlusion phase for fricatives in order to allow sufficient air-pressure build-up to drive the noise source. This is in contrast to plosives, where precise control of the aerodynamic conditions is probably more critical at the release rather than at the formation of the occlusion.

7.3 Coordination of multiple articulators for multiple segments

In this section, we will focus on the articulatory coordination of multiple gestures over longer extents of time, resulting in the articulation of successive segments. As before, we will subdivide the present section with respect to the coordination of supraglottal articulators (7.3.1) versus laryngeal-oral coordination (7.3.2).

7.3.1 Supraglottal coordination for multiple segments

First, we will address consonant-consonant (CC) and consonant-vowel (CV) timing, which brings us again into the realm of the syllable since the timing of successive segments is to a significant degree determined by syllabic structure. In keeping with the Articulatory Phonology framework adopted in this chapter, our focus in this discussion will be the Coupled Oscillator Model of Syllable Structure (COMS), which is described more completely in Goldstein and Pouplier (2014). We will also consider how timing that is conditioned by syllable position interacts with other factors known to affect CC timing, such as voicing and place of articulation.

In the previous section, we noted that, at least in English, the multiple, segment-internal gestures of liquids and nasals show differential timing patterns in syllable onset and coda position: in onset position the target plateaus of the two gestures are timed to coincide, in coda position the gestures occur more sequentially, and the earlier gesture overlaps substantially with the vowel. The coda timing pattern leads to an audible vowel darkening/rhotacization in case of liquids and vowel nasalization in the case of nasals. Importantly, these effects truly pertain to the syllable, as shown in Krakow (1993). Specifically, she found that the intervening syllable boundary prevents early lowering of the velum during the preceding vowel in the case of *see$me* compared to *seem$E*.

The observations about the differential timing of segment-internal gestures in onset and coda position have been the basis for the Articulatory Phonology model of syllable structure, namely, COMS (Browman and Goldstein 1988, 2000; Goldstein, Byrd, and Saltzman 2006; Nam et al. 2009; Kelso et al. 1986). In this model, syllabic organization is hypothesized to emerge from the specific coupling relationships between consonants and vowels. In onset position, each consonantal gesture is coupled in-phase to the vowel and anti-phase to the other onset consonant(s), if present. In coda position, VC and CC coupling is exclusively anti-phase. Thus, for onsets, the temporal midpoint of the onset cluster as a whole (i.e., the "c-center") maintains an invariant timing relationship to the vowel, irrespective of how many consonants the onset comprises. Coda clusters, on the other hand, form a "chain" rather than a "loop" (for more details, see Goldstein and Pouplier 2014). Modeling studies support the hypothesis that the difference in underlying coupling topology gives rise to the known differences in (C)CV versus VC(C) timing (Nam and Saltzman 2003). However, we have already seen in the case of liquids and nasals that the assumption of strictly anti-phase coupling for codas is probably not tenable cross-linguistically. Accordingly, more recently, the postulate that languages only ever make use of in-phase and anti-phase coupling relationships has been relaxed somewhat such that the notion of an eccentric phase has been used to characterize any phase relationships other than an in-phase relationship (see, e.g., Goldstein and Pouplier 2014).

Whereas much of the work on CV timing goes back to the pioneering studies on coarticulation by Öhman (1966, 1967) and Kozhevnikov and Chistovich (1965; for an overview of theories and data on coarticulation see Farnetani and Recasens 2010), empirical support for the COMS hypothesis that onsets are characterized by in-phase coupling between a consonant and vowel comes from a study on American English by Löfqvist and Gracco (1999), who showed that in simple consonant-vowel syllables with bilabial stops the lip movements for the bilabial closure and the tongue movements for the vowel constriction are initiated approximately synchronously (within 25 ms of one another, across speakers and vowel contexts). Similar data have been reported for Catalan, German, and Italian (Mücke et al. 2012; Niemann et al. 2011).

As for onset clusters, the c-center timing pattern described by COMS has been by and large confirmed for a variety of languages: English (Nam et al. 2009; Marin and Pouplier 2010), French (Kühnert, Hoole, and Mooshammer 2006), Georgian (Goldstein, Chitoran, and Selkirk 2007), Italian (Hermes, Mücke, and Grice 2013), Mandarin (Gao 2008), German (Pouplier 2012), and Romanian (Marin 2013). Yet exceptions to the general rule have also been reported. Romanian and Georgian may serve here to illustrate cases in which other factors seem to partly override syllable position-specific timing effects. We will also briefly discuss Slovak, which has been reported to not follow a c-center timing pattern at all.

With respect to Romanian, there are two exceptional patterns which we will consider here, one concerning onset clusters (Marin 2013) and the other one liquids in coda position (Marin and Pouplier 2014). Firstly for onsets, Marin has found that clusters fall into two groups: s-initial clusters (/sp, sk, sm/) adhere to the c-center pattern, while stop-initial clusters (/kt, kn, ks, ps/) are timed in a fashion more akin to sequential coda-timing, contrary to the predictions of COMS. One factor which separates the two groups is lexical frequency, with the latter group being of low lexical frequency (borrowings from Slavic or Greek). Marin hypothesized that there may be a causal relationship between a low lexical frequency and the lack of a complex c-center coupling topology. Specifically, she hypothesizes that the "default" onset pattern only emerges with sufficient learning and that low lexical frequency items are in fact not produced as complex onsets. The precise coupling topology that best describes the Romanian pattern will have to be addressed on the basis of modeling studies.

The other exceptional pattern in Romanian concerns the timing of liquids in coda position. Marin and Pouplier (2010) had earlier confirmed the predictions of COMS for American English codas with the exception of liquids (/-lk, -lp/; see also Katz 2012). These liquid+plosive clusters failed to exhibit the sequential timing pattern predicted by COMS; the surface timing measurements were more in line with what is expected for onsets (vowel shortening or increasing vowel overlap with increasing syllable margin complexity). Pouplier (2012) came to the conclusion that this might be related to the strong velarization of English /l/ (see above), with the dorsal gesture having a close affinity to the nucleus. This conclusion was motivated in part by data showing that German /l/ is not velarized, in contrast to American English /l/, and indeed German coda /l/ clusters behaved exactly as predicted by COMS in terms of strictly sequential timing (Pouplier 2012). However, Marin and Pouplier (2014) compared the English and German pattern to Romanian, which, like German, does not have a velarized /l/ and should therefore be expected to be similar to German. Indeed Romanian coda /l/ clusters behaved like German, yet Romanian coda /r/ clusters patterned with American English /l/ in terms of a more onset-like timing pattern. The Romanian rhotic is realized as a trill. Trills are produced with a dorsal constriction similar to the one for velarized /l/ (Proctor 2011; Recasens 2013); therefore Marin and Pouplier point out that this "special" timing pattern seen in American English dark /l/ (and /r/, Katz 2012) and Romanian /r/ may simply be a measurement issue since the measures performed in these studies do not take the dorsal gesture into account. They argue that the temporal characteristics of the dorsal gesture constituted a confounding factor in previous analyses, in terms of the duration of the dorsal gesture itself as well as in terms of possible intergestural timing change between dorsal and tongue tip gesture in clusters. Relatedly, Gick et al. (2006) found considerable variability in the intrasegmental organization of liquids across languages, and suggest that the unexpected diversity in timing may be part of arbitrary, grammatical parameter settings that languages display. This study points to the possibility that language-specific timing differences for the multigesture segments may interact with syllable-position specific timing relations.

Due to the greater degrees of freedom inherent in the COMS for codas (less coupling relations are specified) there may also be a greater potential for language-specific effects to emerge in coda position compared to onset position. That said, onset clusters also show considerable variation in timing patterns. For example, Georgian onset clusters present another exception to the basic COMS pattern. This Caucasian language has come to be known for a place order effect, first described by Chitoran, Goldstein, and Byrd (2002) and Chitoran and Goldstein (2006). Chitoran and colleagues found that the relative order of place of articulation of the two consonants of a cluster is a significant determinant of articulatory timing. In

Georgian, onset clusters with place of articulation ordered from front-to-back, such as in /bg/, show more overlap than corresponding back-to-front clusters (here: /gb/). The place-order effect also exists in other languages (French: Kühnert et al. 2006; German: Bombien et al. 2010, Pouplier 2012; Korean and Russian: Kochetov, Pouplier, and Son 2007; Moroccan Arabic: Gafos et al. 2010). Importantly, there is some evidence that global onset coordination for these two cluster types is not the same, with back-to-front onset clusters deviating from the COMS pattern (Goldstein et al. 2008), although a systematic analysis is missing. Yet there is still another layer of complexity. For example, Gafos et al. (2010) argued, on the basis of data from two Moroccan Arabic speakers, that the emergence of a place-order effect may be speaker-specific and may vary with the degree of consonantal overlap characteristic for a given speaker. They assume that timing patterns with inter-speaker variability are not part of the phonological plan, and that only consistent speaker behavior (e.g., overlap in homorganic vs. heteroganic clusters) should be taken as an index of phonologically controlled timing. With respect to the place-order effect, Gafos et al. suggested that is not phonological and emerges only if overlap impacts on perceptibility. For speakers who time their consonants far enough apart, the consonants will be recoverable in either order. However, their argument for a perceptual basis to the place-order effect is not uncontroversial (Kühnert et al. 2006; Chitoran and Goldstein 2006), and given that their study comprises only two speakers, it awaits further corroboration. Along these lines, it should also be noted that the word-initial Moroccan Arabic consonant sequences of the Gafos et al. study probably do not form onset clusters (Shaw et al. 2009), in contrast to the unequivocally tautosyllabic status of these word-initial clusters in Georgian.

But there is more to cluster timing than place order. For example, Bombien and colleagues (Bombien, Mooshammer, and Hoole 2013; Bombien et al. 2010; Hoole et al. 2013) have shown for German data that even within the same place order, there may be systematic differences in overlap. For example, the onset cluster /kn-/ shows less CC overlap compared to /kl-/ even though both are back-to-front clusters. Like Gafos et al. (2010), Bombien and colleagues assumed that perceptual constraints, driven in turn by the aerodynamic requirements of each specific sound in the cluster, can govern cluster timing. Unfortunately, the relationship between onset cluster and vowel was not investigated so we do not know whether the different timing patterns result in different coordination patterns with the vowel analogously to the Georgian place-order effect.

Another factor known to affect CC overlap is voicing. Bombien and Hoole (2013) investigated how CC timing differs in French and German as a function of the voicing specification of C1 (cf. Pouplier 2012 for an interaction of voicing and place order in German). When C1 is voiced in a C1C2 onset cluster, the consonants show more overlap for German. French clusters, however, are consistently similar to the German voiceless pattern, irrespective of the voicing status of C1. This is quite surprising given that voiced stops in French have negative VOT, while in German voiced stops are rather voiceless unaspirated.

The cross-language variation in timing patterns described above strongly suggests that languages differ systematically in how much they allow their consonants to overlap (Kochetov et al. 2007; Cho, this volume, Chapter 22; Zsiga 2003). If this is the case, then one might expect that the timing patterns described by COMS interact with language-specific patterns. Pouplier and Beňuš (2011) made this suggestion in the context of Slovak timing in syllables with syllabic consonants.

Slovak is a language in which word onset clusters that are phonologically analyzed as true tautosyllabic onset clusters nonetheless fail to exhibit the c-center pattern predicted by COMS. This may be related to the fact that Slovak allows for syllabic consonants (e.g., *smrt*, "death"). Pouplier and Beňuš (2011) present data showing that syllables with a consonantal nucleus are generally timed differently from syllables with a vocalic nucleus, which suggests that in-phase coupling between onset and nucleus may only be possible at all if the nucleus is a vowel: Slovak C-C onset nucleus sequences were found to be less overlapped than C-V onset nucleus sequences. It could be that this difference emerges as follows. When onset consonant and vowel sequences are timed synchronously at movement onset, the vowel will extend temporally beyond the consonant, due to the slower movement parameterization of vowels compared to consonants. When the nucleus is a consonant, there is no such asymmetry in movement dynamics between onset and nucleus, therefore in-phase coupling would endanger perceptual recovery.

The Slovak data once more underscore the reality of considerable language-specific effects in intersegmental timing. These effects have led to the proposal that Articulatory Phonology be incorporated into a formal phonological model such as Optimality Theory (Prince and Smolensky 2008), in order to be able to formalize the arbitrary choices that languages make with respect to articulatory timing (for work in this area see Gafos 2002; Gafos and Beňuš 2006; Davidson 2006). This modification would also allow us to formalize in a predictive fashion how perceptual constraints may impact articulatory timing, even though much more experimental work is required to uncover this relationship.

There have been only a few other concrete suggestions to date how to modify the basic assumptions of COMS in order to capture the range of empirically observed timing relations across speakers and languages. With respect to inter-speaker variability, Goldstein et al. (2008) suggested that such variability is due to variations in coupling strength and/or articulator weights. For instance, they argued that sequential onset effects could arise in a C1C2V sequence when C1 is less tightly coupled to the vowel compared to C2 in a particular speaker's production. This kind of speaker-to-speaker variation is seen as a natural by-product of a self-organizing system, and is therefore not phonological. With respect to cross-language variability, Browman and Goldstein (2000) suggested that anti-phase V-C coupling in coda may be generally weaker than in-phase C-V coupling in onset, and discuss the incorporation of coupling strength as a means to think about the phonological notion of syllable weight in gestural terms (see also Nam 2007). Arguably, it also provides a basis for the kind of language-specific effects we saw for liquids to emerge in coda position. Also, on the topic of cross-language variability in timing relations, there are the cases of timing differences between cluster types, such as the already mentioned place order effect, which is phonologically relevant in Georgian (see Chitoran et al. 2002). Goldstein et al. (2008) proposed that the back-to-front and front-to-back clusters are differentiated in Georgian by the coupling of the consonantal release gesture. For a front-to-back cluster, only the closure, but not the release gestures of C1 in a C1C2 are coupled in-phase to the vowel, resulting in more overlap compared to back-to-front clusters in which it is the *release* of C1 and closure of C2 that are coupled in-phase to the vowel.

Another route to achieve a greater variety of coupling topologies is discussed by Goldstein et al. (2008) in the context of English /l/. The proposal is that "secondary" gestures (our reservations about this term have already been expressed above) such as the tongue body gesture of English /l/ may not be directly coupled to the vowel. In that case, only the tongue tip gesture would bear a direct relation to the vowel (in-phase coupling), the tongue body gesture would be linked to the tongue tip gesture only. Note that this proposal arguably acknowledges the segment as a unit of speech production, a topic on which there has been little consensus among Articulatory Phonology proponents (see for discussion Browman and Goldstein 1986; Saltzman and Munhall 1989; Byrd et al. 2009; Hoole 2006).

Overall, the detailed ramifications of the various proposals for modifications to the basic COMS model will have to be worked out by modeling studies in combination with more comprehensive datasets, but the list of factors affecting CC and CV timing is long, and we have covered only a few. Moreover, language-specific temporal settings can be expected to interact with basic COMS patterns in a complex fashion.

In concluding this section, we would like to point out that higher-order prosodic boundaries, such as feet or prosodic words, likewise have an effect on articulatory organization. There is, however, relatively little work on articulatory coordination in this area. The interested reader is referred to, among others, Cho (2006), Saltzman et al. (2008), Byrd and Choi (2010), Hoole et al. (2008), and Tilsen (2009). There are also effects of stress on interarticulatory and intergestural organization. Relevant studies on these effects include de Jong, Beckman, and Edwards (1993) and Harrington et al. (1995). Finally, there is recent work on tonal alignment and its effects on the c-center timing pattern of the supralaryngeal articulators. The interested reader is referred to Gao (2008) and Mücke et al. (2012).

7.3.2 *Laryngeal-oral coordination for multiple segments*

In this section we will look briefly at two areas that in our opinion present interesting challenges to our understanding of how laryngeal-oral coordination relations are most appropriately specified: clusters that have a sonorant as their last element (e.g., /pl/); and sequences of purely voiceless consonants.

For clusters with sonorants, we will concentrate on syllable-initial consonants, comparing the articulation of the cluster with that of the simple voiceless onset, for example, /pl/ with simply /p/. For sounds with a clear devoicing gesture, it is intuitively appealing to specify laryngeal-oral coordination with respect to the timing of peak glottal opening. Thus, for languages like English or German, with clearly aspirated plosives in initial position, Browman and Goldstein (1986) formulate the following two rules: (1) If a fricative gesture is present, coordinate the peak glottal opening with the midpoint of the fricative. (2) Otherwise, coordinate the peak glottal opening with the release of the stop gesture.

We have already seen in section 7.2.2.3 that some fine-tuning of rule (2) may be required, in that the interval from peak glottal opening to oral release may vary with place of articulation. But if we start from the naive assumption that the devoicing gesture "belongs" to the /p/, then whether a vowel or /l/ follows the /p/ should be irrelevant to the timing, making any shift in the timing of peak glottal opening rather surprising.

In fact, there is a reasonable amount of evidence that shifts in timing of peak glottal opening do occur. Hoole (2006) investigated quite a wide range of onsets that contrasted in terms of the presence or absence of an /l/ as last element (not just /p/ vs. /pl/, but also longer sequences such as /ʃp/ vs. /ʃpl/). Fairly consistent timing differences were found, particularly when expressed as the time within the glottal abduction-adduction cycle at which the release of the last non-sonorant consonant in the onset occurred (i.e., the release of the /p/ in /p vs. pl/ as well as in /ʃp vs. ʃpl/). The shift is always in the direction of the oral release being relatively earlier in the glottal cycle for Cl or CCl onsets (compared to the corresponding simple C or CC onsets). Further evidence that such timing shifts are frequently – even if not invariably – present can be found in Jessen (1999), Tsuchida, Cohn, and Kumada (2000), and Hoole and Bombien (2014).

Although it is clear from the data presented above that timing shifts occur, it is much less clear whether there is a single organizational principle underlying these shifts. For example, it is conceivable that timing shifts occur because the duration of the glottal abduction-adduction movement remains essentially constant, while oral occlusion durations shorten in the more complex onsets with final sonorant (cf. section 7.2.2.3). While this pattern can indeed be found, it does not appear to be the only one. For example, Hoole (2006) found that the laryngeal movement was sometimes even lengthened. Faced with a variety of movement patterns, Hoole suggested that the unifying principle might be the acoustic goal of the speaker: typically, VOT is longer in the onsets terminated by a sonorant than in those without. Assuming that this represents planned behavior by the speaker (i.e., assuming that it is not purely attributable to aerodynamic conditions, cf. Docherty 1992), then there are quite a range of laryngeal-oral coordination patterns that would fulfill this goal. Crucially, this means that coordination may then be better expressed in terms of fulfilling the acoustic or communicative demands of the onset as a whole rather than with respect to a specific segment (for a similar conclusion reached from a more phonological perspective see, e.g., Kehrein and Golston 2004). This in turn points toward an issue that is too large to deal with here; namely, how interarticulatory coordination is affected by the status of the segments and syllables within the prosodic hierarchy (but see, e.g., Cho, this volume, Chapter 22).

Turning now to sequences of purely voiceless consonants, Löfqvist (1990) summarized the observable kinematics of laryngeal behavior as follows: "sounds requiring a high rate of airflow, such as fricatives and aspirated stops, are produced with a separate gesture" (296). The interesting issue with regard to understanding gestural coordination in voiceless sequences is to determine whether the number of gestures observable at the articulatory surface corresponds to the underlying gestural input. Munhall and Löfqvist (1992) investigated this question for a single sequence /s#t/, embedded in the phrase "kiss Ted" (i.e., with a word boundary), over a wide range of stress and speech rate conditions. They showed that the observable kinematic behavior ranged from two clearly distinct gestures at the slowest rates to a single-peaked pattern at the fastest. On this basis, they argued that it may be preferable to assume the presence of two underlying gestures in onset clusters like /#st/, where almost invariably only a single-peaked movement is actually observable. In this respect, their account differs from Browman and Goldstein (1986) who assume that English syllable onsets show only a single glottal gesture, where the timing of that gesture is captured in the two rules given at the beginning of this section.

The Munhall and Löfqvist (1992) study conveniently allows us to recall the concept of gestural dominance that is undoubtedly of considerable importance in understanding gestural coordination generally, and as it is applied to laryngeal-oral coordination. As discussed in Saltzman and Munhall (1989), if one assumes that fricatives dominate glottal timing more strongly than plosives do, and that dominance can be enhanced in initial position, then this may allow a single-peaked pattern at the surface to be reconciled with two underlying gestures in the input. The concept of dominance is also relevant for Browman and Goldstein's (1986) account as well, since the high dominance value for the fricative determines the order of the two rules given above. That said, we note that rather similar shifts in the timing of peak glottal opening in the /s/ of /st/ compared to single /s/ can also be found for /sl/ vs. /s/ (Hoole 2006). This makes it difficult to argue that the timing shift in /st/ is caused by an additional, albeit weak, gesture for /t/ perturbing the location of peak glottal opening away from the midpoint of the fricative, since in /sl/ there is no obvious reason to assume any competition between /s/ and /l/ for control of the glottal articulator.

Similarly to the account proposed in the first part of this section for obstruent-sonorant sequences, Hoole (2006) has argued that laryngeal-oral coordination in complex syllable onsets of purely voiceless consonants is also best understood as fulfilling constraints imposed by the aerodynamic demands of the onset as a whole. For example, in a sequence of voiceless fricative+plosive there is a very strong constraint that glottal abduction must be initiated promptly as the fricative constriction is formed; however, there are only very weak constraints as to where glottal adduction is completed. Even if adduction is completed well before the plosive occlusion is released there is no danger that the plosive will inadvertently become voiced because intraoral pressure will prevent vocal fold vibration. The aerodynamic explanation suggests that peak glottal opening may not be the crucial timing parameter and accounts for the quite radical departures from the timing rules proposed by Browman and Goldstein (1986), which are not that difficult to find (see Goldstein 1990, for further discussion).

Summarizing this section on laryngeal-oral coordination it can be said that laryngeal kinematics are attractive to study because the movement patterns are well suited to studying issues such as gestural blending. Even though we now have a wealth of information going back many years, the area remains an interesting one because it also indicates that interarticulatory coordination does not proceed segment by segment; larger structures must be taken into account. This conclusion is reminiscent of the conclusion to section 7.3.1.

7.4 Conclusion

Although we hope to have shown that a good understanding of many aspects of articulatory timing already exists, it should equally be clear that there still remains much to do. Two major unresolved issues are to understand how segmental effects interact with higher-level prosodic effects, and to join this understanding with an understanding of how individual languages develop preferred timing patterns.

REFERENCES

Ackermann, Herman and Ingo Hertrich. 1997. Voice onset time in ataxic dysarthria. *Brain and Language* 56(3): 321–333.

Auzou, Pascal, Canan Ozsancak, Richard J. Morris, Mary Jan, and Francis Eustache. 2000. Voice onset time in aphasia, apraxia of speech and dysarthria: A review. *Clinical Linguistics Phonetics* 14(2): 131–150.

Benguerel, André-Pierre and Tej K. Bhatia. 1980. Hindi stop consonants: An acoustic and fiberoscopic study. *Phonetica* 37: 134–148.

Bernstein, Nikolaj A. 1967. *The Coordination and Regulation of Movements*. Oxford: Pergamon Press.

Bombien, Lasse and Philip Hoole. 2013. Articulatory overlap as a function of voicing in French and German consonant clusters. *Journal of the Acoustical Society of America* 134: 539–550.

Bombien, Lasse, Christine Mooshammer, and Philip Hoole (2013). Articulatory coordination in word-initial clusters of German. *Journal of Phonetics* 41: 546–561.

Bombien, Lasse, Christine Mooshammer, Philip Hoole, and Barbara Kühnert. 2010. Prosodic segmental effects on EPG contact patterns of word-initial German clusters. *Journal of Phonetics* 38(3): 388–403.

Browman, Catherine. 1994. Lip aperture and consonant releases. In P. Keating (ed.), *Papers in Laboratory Phonology III: Phonological Structure and Phonetic Form*, 331–353. Cambridge: Cambridge University Press.

Browman, Catherine and Louis Goldstein. 1986. Towards an Articulatory Phonology. *Phonology Yearbook* 3: 219–252.

Browman, Catherine and Louis Goldstein. 1988. Some notes on syllable structure in Articulatory Phonology. *Phonetica* 45(2–4): 140–155.

Browman, Catherine and Louis Goldstein. 1992. Articulatory phonology: An overview. *Phonetica* 49: 155–180.

Browman, Catherine and Louis Goldstein. 1995. Gestural syllable position effects in American English. In F. Bell-Berti and L.J. Raphael (eds.), *Producing Speech: Contemporary Issues (for Katherine Safford Harris)*, 19–33. Woodbury, NY: AIP Press.

Browman, Catherine and Louis Goldstein. 2000. Competing constraints on intergestural coordination and self-organization of phonological structures. *Bulletin de la Communication Parlée* 5: 25–34.

Butcher, Andrew R. 1999. What speakers of Australian aboriginal languages do with their velums and why: The phonetics of the nasal/oral contrast. In J.J. Ohala, Y. Hasegawa, M. Ohala, D. Granville, and A.C. Bailey (eds.), *Proceedings of the XIVth International Congress of Phonetic Sciences*, 479–482.

Byrd, Dani and Susie Choi. 2010. At the juncture of prosody, phonology and phonetics: The interaction of phrasal and syllable structure in shaping the timing of consonant gestures. *Laboratory Phonology*, 10: 31–60.

Byrd, Dani, Stephen Tobin, Erik Bresch, and Shrikanth Narayanan. 2009. Timing effects of syllable structure and stress on nasals: A real-time MRI examination. *Journal of Phonetics* 37: 97–110.

Campbell, Fiona, Bryan Gick, Ian Wilson, and Eric Vatikiotis-Bateson. 2010. Spatial and temporal properties of gestures in North American English /r/. *Language and Speech* 53(1): 49–69.

Catford, John Cunnison. 2001. *A Practical Introduction to Phonetics*. Oxford: Oxford University Press.

Chitoran, Iona and Louis Goldstein. 2006. Testing the phonological status of perceptual recoverability: Articulatory evidence from Georgian. Poster presented at the 10th Conference on Laboratory Phonology, Paris.

Chitoran, Iona, Louis Goldstein, and Dani Byrd. 2002. Gestural overlap and recoverability: Articulatory evidence from Georgian. *Laboratory Phonology* 7: 419–448.

Cho, Taehong. 2006. Manifestation of prosodic structure in articulatory variation: Evidence from lip kinematics in English. *Laboratory Phonology* 8: 519–548.

Cho, Taehong and Peter Ladefoged. 1999. Variation and universals in VOT: Evidence from 18 languages. *Journal of Phonetics* 27: 207–229.

Cohn, Abigail. 1993. The status of nasalized continuants. In M. Huffman and R. Krakow (eds.), *Phonetics and Phonology V: Nasals, Nasalization, and the Velum*, 329–367. Orlando, FL: Academic Press.

Davidson, Lisa. 2006. Phonotactics and articulatory coordination interact in phonology: Evidence from non-native production. *Cognitive Science* 30(5): 837–862.

de Jong, Kenneth, Mary E. Beckman, and Jan Edwards. 1993. The interplay between prosodic structure and coarticulation. *Language and Speech* 36(2–3): 197–212.

Dixit, R. Prakash. 1989. Glottal gestures in Hindi plosives. *Journal of Phonetics* 17: 213–237.

Dixit, R. Prakash and Peter F. MacNeilage. 1980. Cricothyroid activity and control of voicing in Hindi stops and affricates. *Phonetica* 37: 397–406.

Docherty, Gerard J. 1992. *The Timing of Voicing in British English Obstruents*. Berlin: Foris.

Farnetani, Edda and Daniel Recasens. 2010. Coarticulation and connected speech processes. In W.J. Hardcastle, J. Laver, and F.E. Gibbon (eds.), *The Handbook of Phonetic Sciences*, 2nd edn., 316–352. Oxford: Wiley-Blackwell.

Flege, James E., Elaina M. Frieda, Amanda C. Walley, and Lauren A. Randazza. 1998. Lexical factors and segmental accuracy in second-language speech production. *Studies in Second Language Acquisition* 20: 155–188.

Gafos, Adamantios I. 2002. A grammar of gestural coordination. *Natural Language and Linguistic Theory* 20: 269–337.

Gafos, Adamantios I. and Štefan Beňuš. 2006. Dynamics of phonological cognition. *Cognitive Science* 30(5): 905–943.

Gafos, Adamantios I., Philip Hoole, Kevin Roon, and Chakir Zeroual. 2010. Variation in timing and phonological grammar in Moroccan Arabic clusters. *Laboratory Phonology* 10: 657–698.

Gao, Man. 2008. Tonal alignment in Mandarin Chinese: An Articulatory Phonology account. PhD dissertation, Yale University.

Gick, Bryan. 2003. Articulatory correlates of ambisyllabicity in English glides and liquids. In J. Local, R. Ogden, and R. Temple (eds.), *Papers in Laboratory Phonology 6: Constraints on Phonetic Interpretation*, 222–236. Cambridge: Cambridge University Press.

Gick, Bryan, Fiona Campbell, Sunyoung Oh, and Linda Tamburri-Watt. 2006. Towards universals in the gestural organization of syllables: A cross-linguistic study of liquids. *Journal of Phonetics* 34: 49–72.

Goldstein, Louis. 1990. On articulatory binding: Comments on Kingston's paper. In J. Kingston and M.E. Beckman (eds.), *Papers in Laboratory Phonology 1: Between the Grammar and Physics of Speech*, 445–450. Cambridge: Cambridge University Press.

Goldstein, Louis and Marianne Pouplier. 2014. The temporal organization of speech. In V. Ferreira, M. Goldrick, and M. Miozzo (eds.), *The Oxford Handbook of Language Production*, 210–227. Oxford: Oxford University Press.

Goldstein, Louis, Dani Byrd, and Elliot Saltzman. 2006. The role of vocal tract gestural action units in understanding the evolution of phonology. In M. Arbib (ed.), *From Action to Language: The Mirror Neuron System*, 215–249. Cambridge: Cambridge University Press.

Goldstein, Louis, Ioana Chitoran, and Elisabeth Selkirk. 2007. Syllable structure as coupled oscillator modes: Evidence from Georgian vs. Tashlhiyt Berber. *Proceedings of the XVIth International Congress of Phonetic Sciences, Saarbrücken*, 241–244.

Goldstein, Louis, Hosung Nam, Elliot Saltzman, and Ioana Chitoran. 2009. Coupled oscillator planning model of speech timing and syllable structure.

In G. Fant, H. Fujisaki, J. Shen (eds.), *Frontiers in Phonetics and Speech Science. Festschrift for Wu Zongji,* 239–249. Beijing: Commercial Press.

Gracco, Vincent L. 1988. Timing factors in the coordination of speech movements. *The Journal of Neuroscience* 8: 4628–4639.

Gracco, Vincent L. and Anders Löfqvist. 1994. Speech motor coordination and control: Evidence from lip, jaw and laryngeal movements. *The Journal of Neuroscience* 14(11): 6585–6597.

Harrington, Jonathan, Janet Fletcher, and Corinne Roberts. 1995. Coarticulation and the accented/unaccented distinction: Evidence from jaw movement data. *Journal of Phonetics* 23: 305–322.

Hermes, Anne, Doris Mücke, and Martine Grice (2013). Gestural coordination of Italian word initial clusters – the case of impure "s". *Phonology* 30(1): 1–25.

Hoole, Philip. 2006. Experimental studies of laryngeal articulation. Habilitationsschrift, Ludwig-Maximilians Universität München. http://www.phonetik.uni-muenchen.de/~hoole/pdf/habilpgg_chap_all.pdf (accessed November 29, 2014).

Hoole, Philip and Lasse Bombien. 2010. Velar and glottal activity in Icelandic. In S. Fuchs, P. Hoole, C. Mooshammer, and M. Zygis (eds.), *Between the Regular and the Particular in Speech and Language*, 171–204. Frankfurt am Main: Peter Lang.

Hoole, Philip and Lasse Bombien. 2014. Laryngeal-oral coordination in mixed-voicing clusters. *Journal of Phonetics* 44: 8–24.

Hoole, Philip, Heidrun Schröter-Morasch, and Wolfram Ziegler. 1997. Patterns of laryngeal apraxia in two patients with Broca's aphasia. *Clinical Linguistics and Phonetics* 11: 429–442.

Hoole, Philip, Lasse Bombien, Barbara Kühnert, and Christine Mooshammer. 2009. Intrinsic and prosodic effects on articulatory coordination in initial consonant clusters. In G. Fant,

H. Fujisaki, J. Shen (eds.), *Frontiers in Phonetics and Speech Science. Festschrift for Wu Zongji*, 275–286. Beijing: Commercial Press.

Hoole, Philip, Marianne Pouplier, Štefan Beňuš, and Lasse Bombien. 2013. Articulatory coordination in obstruent-sonorant clusters and syllabic consonants: Data and modelling. In L. Spreafico and A. Vietti (eds.), *Proceedings of Ratics3*, pp. 81–97. Bolzano: Bolzano University Press.

Hutters, Birgit. 1985. Vocal fold adjustments in aspirated and unaspirated stops in Danish. *Phonetica* 42: 1–24.

Jessen, Michael. 1999. Redundant aspiration in German is primarily controlled by closure duration. In *Proceedings of the XIVth International Congress of Phonetic Sciences*, 993–996.

Kagaya, Ryohei and Hajime Hirose. 1975. Fiberoptic, electromyographic and acoustic analyses of Hindi stop consonants. *Annual Bulletin, Research Institute of Logopedic and Phoniatrics* 9: 27–46. University of Tokyo.

Katz, Jonah. 2012. Compression effects in English. *Journal of Phonetics* 40: 390–402.

Kehrein, Wolfgang and Chris Golston. 2004. A prosodic theory of laryngeal contrasts. *Phonology* 21(3): 325–357.

Kelso, J.A. Scott, Elliot L. Saltzman, and Betty Tuller. 1986. The dynamical perspective on speech production: Data and theory. *Journal of Phonetics* 14: 29–59.

Kochetov, Alexei. 2006. Syllable position effects and gestural organization: Evidence from Russian. *Laboratory Phonology* 8: 565–588.

Kochetov, Alexei, Marianne Pouplier, and Minjung Son. 2007. Cross-language differences in overlap and assimilation patterns in Korean and Russian. *Proceedings of the XVIth International Congress of Phonetic Sciences, Saarbrücken*, 1361–1364.

Kollia, H. Betty, Vincent L. Gracco, and Katherine S. Harris. 1995. Articulatory organization of mandibular, labial and velar movements during speech. *Journal of the Acoustical Society of America* 98: 1313–1324.

Kozhevnikov, Valerii A. and Ludmilla Chistovich. 1965. *Speech, Articulation and Perception*. Washington, DC: Joint Publications Research Service.

Krakow, Rena A. 1993. Nonsegmental influences on velum movement patterns: Syllables, sentences, stress and speaking rate. In M.K. Huffman and R.A. Krakow (eds.), *Nasals, Nasalization and the Velum*, 87–116. San Diego, CA: Academic Press.

Krakow, Rena A. 1999. Physiological organization of syllables: A review. *Journal of Phonetics* 27: 23–54.

Kühnert, Barbara, Philip Hoole, and Christine Mooshammer. 2006. Gestural overlap and c-center in selected French consonant clusters. In H.C. Yehia, D. Demolin, and R. Laboissière (eds.), *Proceedings of the 7th International Seminar on Speech Production, UFMG Belo Horizonte*, 327–334.

Ladefoged, Peter and Ian Maddieson. 1996. *The Sounds of the World's Languages*. Oxford: Blackwell.

Lisker, Leigh and Arthur S. Abramson. 1964. A cross-language study of voicing in initial stops: Acoustic measurements. *Word* 20: 384–422.

Löfqvist, Anders. 1990. Speech as audible gestures. In W.J. Hardcastle and A. Marchal (eds.), *Speech Production and Speech Modelling*, 289–322. Dordrecht: Kluwer Academic.

Löfqvist, Anders and Vincent L. Gracco. 1999. Interarticulator programming in VCV sequences: Lip and tongue movements. *Journal of the Acoustical Society of America* 105(3): 1864–1876.

Löfqvist, Anders and Nancy McGarr. 1987. Laryngeal dynamics in voiceless consonant production. In T. Baer, C. Sasaki, and K.S. Harris (eds.), *Laryngeal Function in Phonation and Respiration*, 391–402. Boston, MA: College-Hill Press.

Löfqvist, Anders and Hirohide Yoshioka. 1984. Intrasegmental timing: Laryngeal-oral coordination in voiceless consonant production. *Speech Communication* 3: 279–289.

Lowenstein, Joanna H. and Susan Nittrouer. 2008. Patterns of acquisition of native voice onset time in English-learning children. *Journal of the Acoustical Society of America* 124(2): 1180–1191.

Marin, Stefania. 2013. The temporal organization of complex onsets and codas in Romanian: A gestural approach. *Journal of Phonetics* 41(3–4): 211–227.

Marin, Stefania and Marianne Pouplier. 2010. Temporal organization of complex onsets and codas in American English: Testing the predictions of a gestural coupling model. *Motor Control* 14(3): 380–407.

Marin, Stefania and Marianne Pouplier. 2014. Articulatory synergies in the temporal organization of liquid clusters in Romanian. *Journal of Phonetics* 42: 24–26.

Mooshammer, Christine, Philip Hoole, and Anja Geumann. 2006. Inter-articulator cohesion within coronal consonant production. *Journal of the Acoustical Society of America* 120(2): 1028–1039.

Mücke, Doris, Hosung Nam, Anne Hermes, and Louis Goldstein. 2012. Coupling of tone and constriction gestures in pitch accents. In P. Hoole, L. Bombien, M. Pouplier, C. Mooshammer, and B. Kühnert (eds.), *Consonant Clusters and Structural Complexity*, 205–229. Berlin: Mouton de Gruyter.

Munhall, Kevin and Anders Löfqvist. 1992. Gestural aggregation in speech: Laryngeal gestures. *Journal of Phonetics* 20: 111–126.

Nam, Hosung. 2007. Syllable-level intergestural timing model: Split-gesture dynamics focusing on positional asymmetry and moraic structure. In J. Cole and J.I. Hualde (eds.), *Papers in Laboratory Phonology*, vol. 9, 483–506. Berlin: Mouton de Gruyter.

Nam, Hosung and Elliot Saltzman. 2003. A competitive, coupled oscillator model of syllable structure. In M.-J. Solé, D. Recasens, and J. Romero (eds.), *Proceedings of the XVth International Congress of Phonetic Sciences, Barcelona, Spain*, 2253–2256.

Nam, Hosung, Louis Goldstein, and Elliot Saltzman. 2009. Self-organization of syllable structure: A coupled oscillator model. In F. Pellegrino, E. Marisco, I. Chitoran, and C. Coupé (eds.), *Approaches to Phonological Complexity*, 299–328. Berlin: Mouton de Gruyter.

Niemann, Henrik, Doris Mücke, Hosung Nam, Louis Goldstein, and Martine Grice. 2011. Tones as gestures: The case of Italian and German. *Proceedings of the XVIIth International Congress of Phonetic Sciences*, Hongkong, 1486–1489.

Nittrouer, Susan. 1991. Phase relations of jaw and tongue tip movements in the production of VCV utterances. *Journal of the Acoustical Society of America* 90(4): 1806–1815.

Nittrouer, Susan, Kevin Munhall, J. Scott Kelso, and Betty Tuller. 1988. Patterns of interarticulator phasing and their relation to linguistic structure. *Journal of the Acoustical Society of America* 84: 1653–1661.

Öhman, Sven E. 1966. Coarticulation in VCV utterances: Spectrographic measurements. *Journal of the Acoustical Society of America* 39(1): 151–168.

Öhman, Sven E. 1967. Numerical model of coarticulation. *Journal of the Acoustical Society of America* 41(2): 310–320.

Pouplier, Marianne. 2011. The atoms of phonological representations. In Marc van Oostendorp, Keren Rice, Beth Hume, and Colin Ewen (eds.), *The Blackwell Companion to Phonology*, 107–129. Oxford: Wiley-Blackwell.

Pouplier, Marianne. 2012. The gestural approach to syllable structure: Universal, language- and cluster-specific aspects. In S. Fuchs, M. Weirich, D. Pape, and

P. Perrier (eds.), *Speech Planning and Dynamics*, 63–96. Berlin: Peter Lang.

Pouplier, Marianne and Štefan Beňuš. 2011. On the phonetic status of syllabic consonants: Evidence from Slovak. *Journal of Laboratory Phonology* 2(2): 243–273.

Prince, Alan and Paul Smolensky. 2008. *Optimality Theory: Constraint Interaction in Generative Grammar.* Oxford: Wiley-Blackwell.

Proctor, Michael. 2011 Towards a gestural characterization of liquids: Evidence from Spanish and Russian. *Laboratory Phonology* 2(2): 451–485.

Recasens, Daniel. 2012. A cross-language acoustic study of initial and final allophones of /l/. *Speech Communication* 54: 368–383.

Recasens, Daniel. 2013. Coarticulation in Catalan dark /l/ and the avleolar trill: General implications for sound change. *Language and Speech* 56(1): 45–68.

Recasens, Daniel, Jordi Fontdevila, and Maria Dolors Pallarès. 1995. Velarization degree and coarticulatory resistance for /l/ in Catalan and German. *Journal of Phonetics* 23: 37–52.

Saltzman, Elliot and Kevin G. Munhall. 1989. A dynamical approach to gestural patterning in speech production. *Ecological Psychology* 1: 333–382.

Saltzman, Elliot, Anders Löfqvist, and Subhobrata Mitra. 2000. "Glue" and "clocks": Intergestural cohesion and global timing. In M.B. Broe and J.B. Pierrehumbert (eds.), *Papers in Laboratory Phonology V: Acquisition and the Lexicon*, 88–101. Cambridge: Cambridge University Press.

Saltzman, Elliot, Hosung Nam, Jelena Krivokapic, and Louis Goldstein. 2008. A task-dynamic toolkit for modeling the effects of prosodic structure on articulation. In P.A. Barbosa and S. Madureira (eds.), *Proceedings of the Speech Prosody 2008 Conference, Campinas, Brazil,* 175–184.

Saltzman, Elliot, Anders Löfqvist, Bruce Kay, Jeff Kinsella-Shaw, and Philip Rubin. 1998. Dynamics of intergestural timing: A perturbation study of lip-larynx coordination. *Experimental Brain Research* 123: 412–424.

Scobbie, James and Marianne Pouplier. 2010. The role of syllable structure in external sandhi: An EPG study of vocalisation and retraction of word final English /l/. *Journal of Phonetics* 38: 240–259.

Shaiman, Susan, Scott Adams, and Mikael Kimelman. 1995. Timing relationships of the upper lip and jaw across changes in speaking rate. *Journal of Phonetics* 23: 119–128.

Shaw, Jason A., Adamantios I. Gafos, Philip Hoole, and Chakir Zeroual. 2009. Dynamic invariance in the phonetic expression of syllable structure: A case study of Moroccan Arabic consonant clusters. *Phonology* 26: 187–215.

Shipp, Thomas. 1982. Aspects of voice production and motor control. In S. Grillner, B. Lindblom, J. Lubker, and A. Persson (eds.), *Speech Motor Control,* 105–112. Oxford: Pergamon Press.

Sproat, Richard and Osamu Fujimura. 1993. Allophonic variation in English /l/ and its implications for phonetic implementation. *Journal of Phonetics* 21(3): 291–311.

Tilsen, Sam. 2009. Multitimescale dynamical interactions between speech rhythm and gesture. *Cognitive Science* 33: 839–879.

Tsuchida, Ayako, Abigail Cohn, and Masanobu Kumada. 2000. Sonorant devoicing and the phonetic realization of [spread glottis] in English. *Working Papers of the Cornell Phonetics Laboratory* 13: 167–181.

Turvey, Michael T. 1977. Preliminaries to a theory of action with reference to vision. In R. Shaw and J. Bransford (eds.), *Perceiving, Acting and Knowing: Toward an Ecological Psychology,* 211–265. Hillsdale, NJ: Lawrence Erlbaum Associates.

Turvey, Michael T. 1990. Coordination. *American Psychologist* 45(8): 938–953.

Wang, Qi Emily. 1995. Are syllables units of speech motor organization? A kinematic analysis of labial and velar gestures in Cantonese. PhD dissertation, University of Connecticut.

Weismer, Gary. 1980. Control of the voicing distinction for intervocalic stops and fricatives: Some data and theoretical considerations. *Journal of Phonetics* 8: 427–438.

Zsiga, Elizabeth C. 2003. Articulatory timing in a second language: Evidence from Russian and English. *Studies in Second Language Acquisition* 25(3): 399–432.

8 Rhythm and Speech

FRED CUMMINS

8.1 Laying the foundations: The many senses of rhythm

In a jazz band, the rhythm section of drum and bass provides a regular framework around which the soloists dance and weave, at times conspiring with the beat, at times pulling away from it in playful or passionate exchange. Rhythm is both the regular grid that provides structure, and the use of that grid to generate, satisfy, or frustrate expectation in time. Whether we use the term "rhythm" in a narrow or extended sense, its use creates a tension between two poles. With the first, we immediately evoke a sense of periodicity, of regularity and recurrence, that serves to heighten expectations and to tie events to particular points in time or space. With the other, we develop the potential for creative expression that lifts off from the grid, and that expresses itself by not being perfectly regular, by omitting the predictable, and switching in the unexpected. Events and accents are interpreted against a background of regularity evoked by an underlying period. Rhythm is more than mere clock time, the invariant sequence of evenly spaced intervals, and yet of such regularity is rhythm born.

It is in music that the concept of rhythm, as distinct from mere periodicity, is at home. In a musical representation of the well known "shave-and-a-haircut – two bits!" motif (Figure 8.1), we can distinguish between the rhythmic pattern of the specific phrase, and the interpretation of this pattern as based on a sequence of evenly spaced (isochronous) beats, which in turn admit of grouping into relatively stronger and weaker positions. Figure 8.1 (right) shows a metrical grouping built over a sequence of eight beats. The numbers indicate the relative rhythmic strength at each point in the sequence. These strengths serve to tune expectation about future events, to focus attention at specific points in time, and to provide a sense of compositional structure to a note sequence (Huron 2006; Large and Riess Jones 1999).

The Handbook of Speech Production, First Edition. Edited by Melissa A. Redford.
© 2015 John Wiley & Sons, Inc. Published 2019 by John Wiley & Sons, Inc.

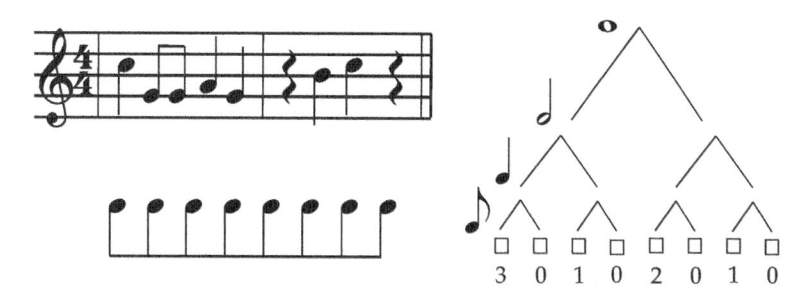

Figure 8.1 Musical representation of the well-known "shave-and-a-haircut – two bits!" motif and beat structure (left) with its metrical interpretation (right).

Speech is continuous with music, but most speech is not musical. When we discuss rhythm in speech, we are not applying a musical concept in an entirely novel domain. The voice is a valued instrument from opera to hip hop. Moving from music, there are intermediate forms of vocal activity in group recitations, prayers, chants, and protest calls that share many of the characteristics of musical performance. These are all collective activities, requiring coordinated timing across individuals. Most forms of choral speaking or recitation employ familiar texts and they are repeated many times, resulting in a highly stylized form of prosody. The characteristic cadences of the American Pledge of Allegiance, for example, will be familiar to many.

The speech of an individual may be rhythmically exaggerated too. Auctioneers often use an idiosyncratic form of patter intended to maintain a constant stream of speech, even when propositional content is limited (Kuiper 1992). Livestock auctioneer competitions provide amusing examples aplenty. Parents reading nursery rhymes to infants will exaggerate rhythm too, using the expectation generated by a strong meter to modulate the attention of the child (Bergeson and Trehub 2002). Trouvain and Barry (2000) provide a thorough analysis of the timing characteristics of the excited speech of race horse commentators. In all cases, rhythmic modulation of the speech goes hand in hand with the modulation of other prosodic characteristics, including speech melody, intensity, and voice quality.

The term "rhythm" has been liberally applied with respect to speech. This chapter will focus primarily on senses of the term that remain close to the musical sense of events critically located in continuous time. It will not treat of the phonology of meter, which understands rhythm as consisting in the atemporal but sequential ordering of strong and weak elements arranged into hierarchical structures (Liberman and Prince 1977). Poetics too must be passed over (Abercrombie 1965), and with it, the formerly canonical art of rhetoric, now sadly in decline.[1]

8.2 The isochrony debate

The manifest similarities between speech and music have led to many attempts to find common underlying principles. One of the first is Joshua Steele's *An Essay towards Establishing the Melody and Measure of Speech to be Expressed and Perpetuated by Peculiar Symbols* (1775). Although Steele was concerned mainly with links between the pitch of speech and musical melody, he employed a form of musical notation that also ascribed durations to individual syllables. These gave expression to an underlying assumption, shared by many since, that the impression of near-regular rhythm in speech might be derivable from musical models, and specifically, that some event sequence, such as the onsets of stressed syllables, might be found to be evenly spaced in time. Daniel Jones made this explicit, when he said: "there is a general tendency to make the stress-points of stressed syllables follow each other at equal intervals of time, but ... this general tendency is constantly interfered with by the variations in the number and nature of the sounds between successive stress-points" (1918/1956).

An early instrumental study by Classé (1939) served to lend support to this eminently plausible intuition about English speech rhythm. He had subjects read texts (taken from Daniel Jones) into a device called a kymograph that produced a trace of the intensity variation of the speech wave. He measured the intervals between successive syllable onsets (see below), and arrived at findings that were both illuminating and unsurprising. Even spacing between successive stressed syllables emerged as a tendency in the recordings – a tendency greatly encouraged when the lexical material was written with an ear to rhythm, when successive intervals contained phonetically matched segments and syllables, and when they had relatively similar grammatical construction. Any such tendency was disrupted by inter-sentence breaks. This was much as Daniel Jones had surmised, and is to be expected on the basis of English phonology, in which we find both full and greatly reduced syllables, in approximate alternation.

8.2.1 Measurement issues

In his measurements, Classé demonstrated a robust phonetician's instinct that the onsets of stressed syllables are important events in the perception of rhythmic progression in spoken utterances. The onsets he measured were indexed, not by the first occurrence of acoustic energy, but by the mid-point in the rise of the amplitude envelope displayed in the kymograph trace.

Determining precisely when something happens is possible only for idealized punctate events of no duration. Real world events take time, and the identification of a moment at which the event is perceived to happen, or to start, is a non-trivial matter. Morton, Marcus, and Frankish (1976) reported that sequences of alternating syllables such as /ba-ma-ba-ma/ were not perceived as isochronous if they were arranged with even spacing from one syllable acoustic onset to the next. To be perceived as evenly spaced, it was necessary for the /ba-ma/ inter-onset interval to be systematically smaller than for /ma-ba/. They introduced the term P-center to describe the perceptual moment of occurrence of a syllable, analogous to the musical notion of a beat.

Subsequent work has demonstrated that the P-center does not correspond to any simple acoustic or articulatory feature, although the rise time, or period of increasing amplitude at the onset, critically affects the perception of the P-center (Scott 1993; De Jong 1994). The P-center can be thought of as an estimate of the beat

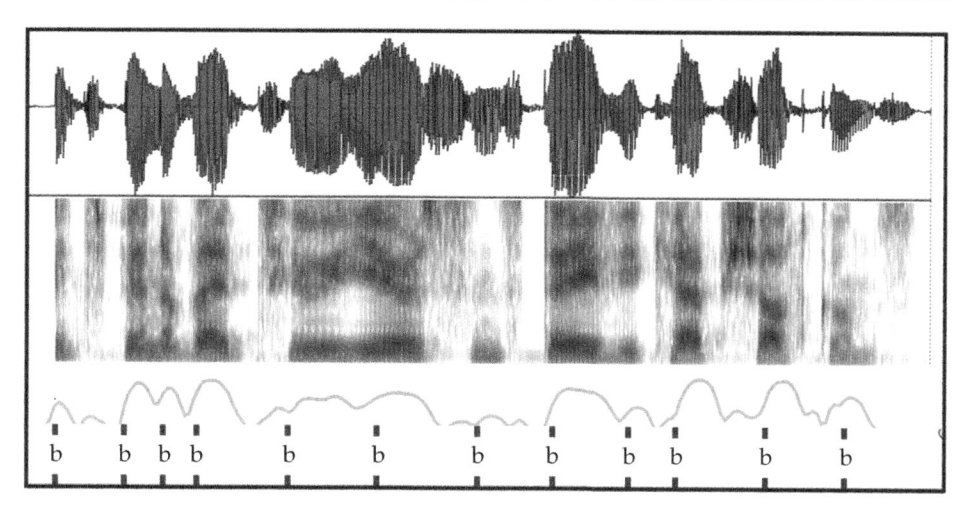

Figure 8.2 P-center estimates are placed at the mid-point of local rises in a smoothed amplitude envelope (bottom) of the filtered signal (top).

location associated with a syllable, and the concept extends naturally to musical tones as well (Vos and Rasch 1981).

A simple algorithm to calculate a P-center estimate, based on prior work by Scott (1993), is provided in Cummins and Port (1998). It is illustrated in Figure 8.2. Speech is first bandpass filtered with cut off frequencies chosen to largely exclude energy directly attributable to the fundamental frequency, and to fricative noise. P-center estimates are placed at the mid-points of local rises in the smoothed amplitude envelope of the filtered signal. This algorithm generates estimates based on the physical characteristics of the signal, and the care of the phonetician is still required to assess the relevance of such estimates to the perception of rhythmically salient events.

8.2.2 Stress-timing and syllable-timing

As texts vary, so too does the rhythm of the speech they generate. Lloyd James (1940) observed that two kinds of temporal regularity are notable in speaking, which he dubbed machine gun and Morse code styles. It should be noted that these were transitory aspects of speech, and could both be found within the speech of an individual. Kenneth Pike (1945) renamed these patterns as syllable-timed and stress-timed speech, respectively. Those familiar with Martin Luther King's "I have a dream" speech can find reasonably clear examples of each of these in the two phrases "[will be able to] SPEED UP THAT DAY" (syllable timing) and "BLACK men and WHITE men, JEWS and GENtiles, PROTestants and CATHolics" (stress timing).

In the 1960s, these two impressionistic labels acquired a new use, being interpreted as features of whole languages, rather than specific utterances. David Abercrombie generated an enduring linguistic myth when he made the strong typological claim:

> As far as is known, every language in the world is spoken with one kind of rhythm or with the other. In the one kind, known as a syllable-timed rhythm, the periodic recurrence of movement is supplied by the syllable-producing process: the chest-pulses, and hence the syllables, recur at equal intervals of time – they are isochronous. French, Telugu, Yoruba illustrate this mode of co-ordinating the two pulse systems: they are syllable-timed languages. In the other kind, known as a stress-timed rhythm, the periodic recurrence of movement is supplied by the stress-producing process: the stress-pulses, and hence the stressed syllables, are isochronous. English, Russian, Arabic illustrate this other mode: they are stress-timed languages.
>
> (Abercrombie 1967: 97)

This remarkable, and demonstrably false, claim has attracted an undue amount of attention, and has been unquestioningly accepted in some quarters, such that it is regularly repeated as a factual assertion about languages. Despite the slight measurement issues that arise due to uncertainty about the exact location of a beat or pulse (see above), it is a matter of no great difficulty to test Abercrombie's assertion on a linguistic sample. This has been done many times (Classé 1939; Shen and Peterson 1962; Bolinger 1965; O'Connor 1968; Nakatani, O'Connor, and Aston 1981; Crystal and House 1990), and each and every such study has falsified the claim, though many have sought to maintain something of the essence of the claim by appealing to unobservable "perceptual isochrony" (Lehiste 1977; Donovan and Darwin 1979), or by positing an intermediate position between syllable- and stress-timing for specific languages (Balasubramanian 1980; Major 1981; de Manrique and Signorini 1983; Miller 1984). Perhaps the most thorough debunking of the isochrony hypothesis, as Abercrombie's clam has come to be known, was provided by Dauer (1983), who measured inter-stress intervals from readings of texts in English, Thai, Spanish, Italian, and Greek. She found no more inter-stress isochrony in English than in any of the other languages. All languages measured showed a weak tendency for stresses to recur regularly, much as Classé had found in 1939. Dauer persuasively argued that impressionistic accounts of "rhythmic" differences among the languages probably had to do with a variety of factors affecting signal variability, including differences in syllable structure, vowel reduction, and the phonetic realization of stress, rather than with the temporal patterning of stressed syllable onsets. Tellingly, she noted:

> The concept of syllable-timing was originally developed by English speakers to describe a kind of rhythm that is opposite to that of English, that is, it has been defined primarily negatively. However, the label has not been widely accepted by native speakers of those languages described as such.
>
> (Dauer 1983: 60)

A third "rhythm class" has sometimes been claimed, also based on notions of an isochronous timing unit, but in this case it is the Japanese mora, rather than the syllable or stress foot, that has traditionally been claimed to be of equal duration (Port, Dalby, and O'Dell 1987; Han 1994). The mora is often coextensive with the syllable, as in the simple CV form (e.g., ke, ya, etc.). Geminate consonants and long vowels contain two morae, and a nasal may also be a whole mora, so that, for example, Honda has two syllables, but three morae (ho-n-da), and the place name Tokyo has two syllables, but four morae (to-o-kʲo-o). Traditional Japanese pedagogy had maintained that morae were of equal duration, and this had been roundly disputed by phoneticians (Beckman 1982). Port et al. demonstrated that words with increasing numbers of morae increase in duration by almost constant increments as morae were added, so that the locally computed average duration of a mora remained constant, with non-local variation in timing distributed over several morae contributing to the net effect. Thus the intuition about even mora timing rested, not on isochrony, but on a statistical property of morae in combination.

One possible reason for the sustained controversy about notional isochrony in speech has been the non-trivial issue of the domain in which isochrony might be observed. Proponents of the direct realist approach to perception have suggested that listeners directly perceive articulatory events, "seeing through," as it were, the acoustic signal to the generative acts from which they arise (Fowler 1979). Articulatory studies have failed to produce evidence for isochrony in this domain however (De Jong 1994). Others have suggested that isochrony is not to be found in the physical signal at all (acoustic or articulatory), but is rather best understood as a perceptual phenomenon (Lehiste 1977). This suggestion seems to remove the hypothesis from the remit of empirical inquiry. Scott, Isard, and de Boysson-Bardies (1985) found that the tendency to perceive events as more regular than they are was generic, not specific to any language or to speech, and so could not be used to support an isochrony hypothesis for English.

Two issues have become confused in this debate. There is first a question of whether speech is rhythmic in the specific sense of providing a sequence of events that are evenly spaced in time. This question, which must usually be answered in the negative, can only be approached on the basis of some specific sample of speech, which may or may not satisfy some criterion of representativeness of a specific language (or dialect, or speaking style, or genre). The second issue is whether languages (abstract entities such as English, Tamil, etc.) fall into two or three distinct classes based on some acoustic properties that might loosely be called "rhythm." This second hypothesis, let us call it the rhythm class hypothesis, has had further development beyond matters pertaining to isochrony.

8.3   The rhythm class hypothesis

Despite the absence of evidence for isochrony in speech, many researchers have sought to defend the supposed dichotomy on grounds other than temporal patterning (Bertinetto 1988). Ramus, Nespor, and Mehler (1999) presented some novel phonetic measures that they thought might justify a presumed classification of languages into stress-timed and syllable-timed families. The authors were heavily committed to the two-way classification, and they had shortly before demonstrated that French newborn infants could discriminate between low-pass filtered speech in Japanese and English, but not between Dutch and English. They could also discriminate between the sets {English, Dutch} and {Spanish, Italian}, but not between the sets {English, Spanish} and {Dutch, Italian}. Of course, these discrimination results in no way confirm that languages fall into two groups, but they are certainly compatible with such a hypothesis, if it were to be established on independent grounds. They arrived at two (correlated) variables, defined over an utterance: the proportion of vocalic intervals (%V) and the standard deviation of the duration of consonantal intervals (ΔC).

Results from eight languages are shown in Figure 8.3 (top). These stem from four speakers per language, reading five short declarative sentences each. At first glance, there appear to be two distinct clusters, and one outlier. The clusters group

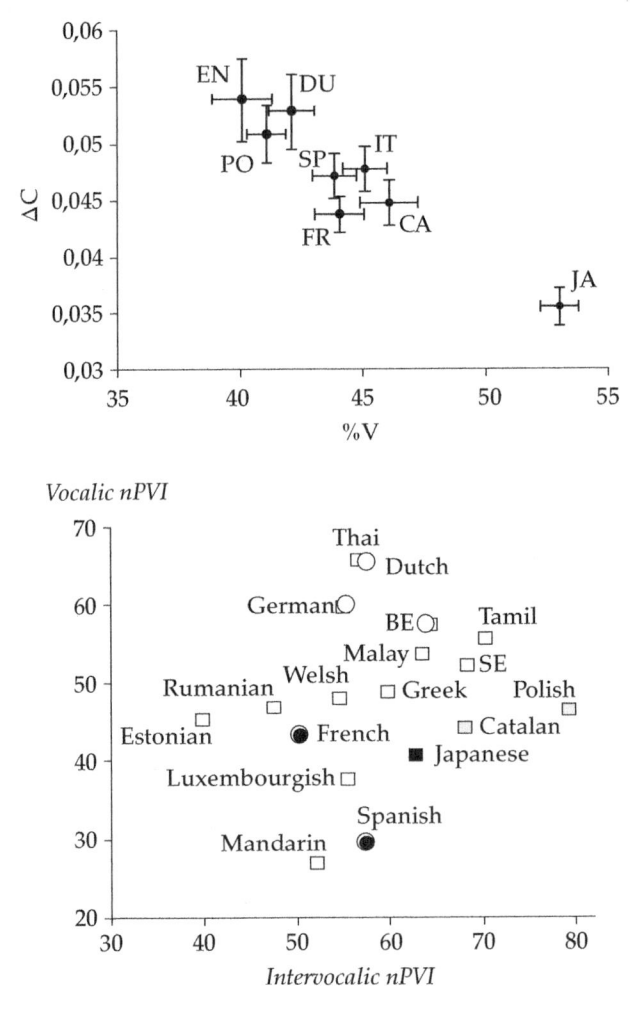

Figure 8.3 Rhythm metrics have been used to discriminate between speech data from different languages. Results from Ramus et al. (1999) and Grabe and Low (2002) are shown in the left and right panels, respectively. Reprinted by permission of De Gruyter.

languages claimed to be stress-timed (English, Dutch, Polish) together, while the so-called syllable-timed languages (French, Spanish, Italian, Catalan) form a second group. Japanese (mora timed) is satisfyingly distant from both groups.

With similar motivation, Grabe and Low (2002) employed a measure of local timing variability originally developed by Francis Nolan, the Pairwise Variability Index, or PVI, that quantifies the degree to which successive units (often, but not necessarily, syllables) differ in duration. Two variants were employed: the raw index (rPVI):

$$\text{rPVI} = \left[\sum_{k=1}^{m-1} |d_k - d_{k+1}| / (m-1) \right] \qquad (8.1)$$

and a normalized form, that uses the average interval length within each pair as a normalization factor:

$$\text{nPVI} = 100 \left[\sum_{k=1}^{m-1} \left| \frac{d_k - d_{k+1}}{(d_k + d_{k+1})/2} \right| / (m-1) \right] \qquad (8.2)$$

where m is the number of items contained in an utterance, and d_k is the duration of the kth item. The nPVI measure was applied to vowel durations, and the rPVI to the intervals between vowel onsets.

Figure 8.3 (bottom) shows comprehensive results for 18 languages, with data from a single speaker for each language reading set texts in a recording booth. One can read what one likes into the resulting distribution. The authors claimed that the data "support a weak categorical distinction between stress-timing and syllable-timing ... [but] ... there is considerable overlap between the stress-timed and the syllable-timed group and hitherto unclassified languages" (Grabe and Low 2002: 538). Nolan, from whom the PVI originally stems, has recently applied the measure at both syllable and foot level for four languages (Estonian, English, Mexican Spanish, and Castilian Spanish) (Nolan and Asu 2009). Five speakers of each read a short text to provide the data. There were serious methodological problems in defining units, especially the foot, in comparable fashion across language. Despite these, the author argued that syllable-timing and stress-timing were orthogonal dimension, such that a given language might exhibit characteristics of either, both, or neither.

Several related metrics have subsequently been proposed, any of which might serve to locate languages in a low-dimensional "rhythm-space." Galves et al. (2002) proposed a sonority-based measure that obviated the need for manual annotation of the speech material. Gibbon and Gut (2001) contributed another, and Wagner and Dellwo (2004) provided yet another variant on the PVI in the service of more or less the same goals. Common to all these approaches is the use of a small (sometimes very small) corpus of read text as the source material that is held to represent the language in question, without consideration of variation within a language. Common to them all is also a rather refined sense of the term "rhythm" that seems to lie quite distant from the core of the term in its musical sense.

The task of identifying objective correlates of speech rhythm is complicated by the fact that perceived temporal properties of speech are influenced by many factors in ways still poorly understood. These include the role of perceived pitch, the presence and strength of accents, and prominences more generally, the duration and distribution of pauses, and the complex effects of speech rate (Dellwo and Wagner 2003; Zvonik and Cummins 2002; Trouvain and Barry 2000; Farnetani and Kori 1990). Arvaniti (2009, 2012) has persuasively argued that studies employing rhythm metrics typically assess the merits of their approach by appeal to the degree to which they support the existing and presumed classification of specific languages. They are typically not at all robust to inter-speaker variation, or elicitation method, rending their utility in contributing to the rhythm class debate problematic at best.

Several theoretical approaches to speech have suggested that the production and the perception of speech may be very intimately intertwined. This gave rise to the venerable Motor Theory of Speech Perception (Liberman and Mattingly 1985) which posited shared representations, and, with different motivation, to the theory of Articulatory Phonology (Fowler et al. 1980; Browman and Goldstein 1995), which entertains the notion that the abstract units of linguistic contrast that give rise to phonological systematicity are one and the same thing as units of movement, or phonetic gestures. Recent neuroscientific evidence has provided strong evidence that the neural substratum for the production of goal-directed action is not separable from the means by which such actions are perceived (Rizzolatti and Arbib 1998; Goldstein, Byrd, and Saltzman 2006).

Collectively, these approaches and insights suggest that the generation of rhythmic speech may have implications for how speech is perceived. Rhythmic expectation can be construed as a means by which listeners predict what is coming up in the speech signal, and rhythm would thus play a role in the allocation of scarce attentional resources to specific, rhythmically salient, moments in time (Large and Riess Jones 1999). This kind of role for rhythmic structure in speech has been suggested to facilitate the parsing of the speech stream (Cutler and Mehler 1993), and the acquisition of both first (Morgan 1996) and, perhaps, second languages (Wenk 1985).

Whether chasing isochrony, or seeking to underwrite a classification of languages into two or three classes, much of the discussion about rhythm in speech has moved away from the sense of rhythm that is grounded in real time performance, and that is best exemplified by the compulsion to tap one's foot along with a tune. It is to such performative considerations that we now turn.

8.4 Rhythm and fluency

Alterations to speech rhythm are frequently noted in a wide range of speech pathologies, and as a supervening symptom in many kinds of movement and psychological disorders. When the word "rhythm" is employed here, it is typically the case that an extended sense of the term is meant, that overlaps greatly with the notion of "fluency," and that does not admit of a simple operationalization. Prosodically altered speech that gives rise to the perception of altered rhythm may exhibit changes in the distribution and duration of pauses, in the timing of segments or supra-segmental units, in the degree of reduction in unstressed syllables, in the features of the intonational contour, especially in the way in which prominences are signaled, and more besides. Although durational measurements may be employed to illustrate changes in "rhythm," it is clear that the impression of altered speech rhythm does not derive from a single factor alone. Likewise, rhythm is unlikely to be affected in isolation in any given pathology (see, e.g., the multiple alterations found in so-called foreign accent syndrome; Kurowski, Blumstein, and Alexander 1996). Impressionistic labels of "stress-timing" or "syllable-timing" are frequently used to characterize speech with global prosodic alteration, for example, in autistic or schizophrenic individuals (Paul et al. 2008; Goldfarb et al. 1972), or after brain trauma (Knight and Cocks 2007). The literature is heavily biased toward reports of cases in which English is the principal language, which may explain why reports of a change toward syllable-timing are common, but reports of a change from syllable-timing to stress-timing are virtually nonexistent. It has been pointed out that the labels probably do not refer to well-defined language types, and their use in cases of pathological prosody may instead reflect a deviation from canonical, fluent, and expressive speech.

Any sense of rhythm in continuous speech demands that the speech be fluent. This is true of other forms of movement too, and there are many parallels to be drawn between rhythmically disturbed, or dysfluent, speech, and dysfluent movement in other domains. Stuttering provides a domain in which the fluency of speech is threatened, due to difficulties in both the initiation of speech, and its fluent continuous production (Starkweather 1987). Initiation difficulties frequently lead to long pauses, or to multiple attempts to start a single utterance, or a single prosodic unit such as a syllable. This can give rise to repetition, which can also be seen as a frustrated attempt to move on to the next unit of production. Once speech is initiated, characteristic rhythmic disturbances include the prolongation of segments (Yaruss 1997). Stuttering is not simply a timing problem, as evidenced, for example, by a study by Max and Yudman (2003) in which stutterers and non-stutterers performed at entirely equivalent levels in a task that required synchronization of either finger taps or spoken syllables with a metronome. Yet stutterers have been found to display subtle differences compared to non-stutterers on a variety of coordinative tasks, including imitative and shadowing tasks (Starkweather 1987; Nudelman et al. 1987; Williams and Bishop 1992). In many respects, the coordinative and rhythmic problems displayed by stutterers are similar to gross movement deficits seen in patients with Parkinson's disease. This neurological disease, typically linked to pathology of the dopamine system, is readily recognized by the characteristic movement tremor, gait difficulties, and dysfluencies of sufferers. Parkinson's patients frequently display freezing, in which a desired movement, such as walking, is inhibited. For both Parkinson's and stuttering patients, a wide variety of non-specific forms of intervention can help to overcome movement problems (Andrews et al. 1982). These can include moving/speaking at an altered tempo, typically a slower tempo, or by changing the context of production, for example, by getting a frozen walker to step "over" an imaginary stick, or by getting a stutterer to sing, instead of speak.

The study of dysfluency in speech points to the deep relation that obtains between rhythm, fluency, and the coordination of movement. Of the many senses in which the term "rhythm" is applied, one central use is to distinguish between movement sequences that are fluid, skilled, and effortless, in contrast to those which seem disjointed, clumsy, or effortful. Some further insight into rhythm in speech is revealed by consideration of the characteristics of skilled movement, in which rhythm may be usefully viewed as an emergent and gradient phenomenon.

8.5 Rhythm as an emergent phenomenon

In the study of coordinated movement, one of the most profound insights of the last hundred years has been the realization that generic dynamical principles underlie the self-organization of complex systems into simpler, task-specific assemblies suited to specific behavioral goals like walking, reaching, etc. (Latash 2008). Thus, in studying locomotion in the jellyfish, the millipede, the ape, and the bird, common principles can be found, such as the recruitment of multiple body parts into phase-locked coordinative domains in which each limb/effector adopts a fixed cyclic offset with respect to the others (Grillner 1981). A model of this form of coordination had been developed in great detail by Scott Kelso and colleagues, taking the two hands as effectors, and constraining movement such that two fingers are wagged at identical frequencies (Haken, Kelso, and Bunz 1985; Kelso 1995). Just as with multi-legged gaits, the simultaneous cycling of these two effectors can only be performed in a stable fashion when the fingers adopt one of two simple phase relations: either they cycle in synchrony (in phase) or in syncopated (anti-phase) manner. As with gaits, the relative stability of the two forms of coordination depends on rate, and characteristic transitions from the less stable (syncopated) pattern to the more stable (in phase) pattern reliably occur at fast rates. For our present purposes, the importance of this well-studied and modeled system is that it suggests that multiple parts of the body, when performing a periodic task, will spontaneously adopt specific stable configurations, and will shift discretely from one pattern to the other. This is a generic dynamical principle of biomechanical self-organization, and it has been tested in the speech domain as well, despite the manifest dissimilarities between the effectors of locomotion and the articulators of the vocal tract.

In the speech cycling experimental paradigm, a short phrase is repeated in time with an auditory metronome. A canonical example is the targeted speech cycling reported in Cummins and Port (1998), where a short phrase, such as "big for a duck," is repeated along with a series of alternating high and low tones. The high tone sequence cues phrase onset, while the low tone provides a temporal target for the onset of the final stressed syllable (duck). It is quickly apparent that cyclic

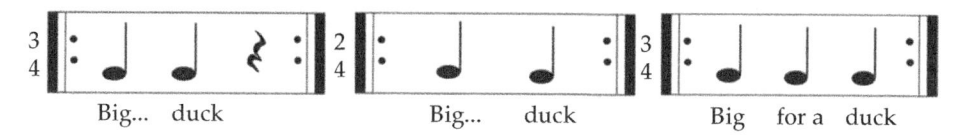

Figure 8.4 Schematic of three stable rhythm patterns produced during the repetition of the phrase *big for a duck*.

repetition like this is highly constrained, and the constraint lies in the temporal relationship between the sequence of syllables, and their organization into larger units, here the foot and the phrase. When the phase (relative time) of the low tone is varied from trial to trial, it becomes clear that some positions of the stressed syllable onset within the repeating phrase cycle are relatively natural, and can be maintained in a stable fashion, while others cannot be so produced. Figure 8.4 shows a schematic representation of the three stable patterns that are found. The last of the three (with a medial phase of 0.66) is less frequent, while the second (phase = 0.5) is the most stable, and the most likely to occur at fast rates. This work suggests that the rhythmic constraints that are apparent in repetitive speech production are of a kind with rhythmic constraints on cyclic movement of the limbs, for example, in juggling, walking, or dancing, and that the temporal patterns arise from generic dynamical principles of self-organization in complex systems, rather than from specific properties of the articulators. It also shows that under appropriate task constraints, speech can, indeed, be produced isochronously.

The idea that speakers/listeners may become mutually entrained to each other during conversational interaction has been suggested on several accounts (Richardson, Dale, and Kirkham 2007; Cummins 2009b, 2009a). Using transcranial magnetic stimulation to reveal weak excitation in muscles, Fadiga et al. (2002) found that there was a highly specific modulation of tongue activation as a function of the speech being perceived by a listener. That is to say, the speech production mechanisms of the listener were being selectively activated, or entrained, by the speech being produced by another. Condon and Sander (1974) observed that the movements of neonates became synchronized with the speech of the mother. Shockley, Santana, and Fowler (2003) documented entrainment in postural sway among standing conversational participants who were engaging in a collaborative speech task.

An experimental variant on choral speaking has been introduced by Cummins (2009b). In a synchronous speech task, two subjects read a prepared text together, attempting to remain in synchrony. This task proves to be easy to do, and on average, asynchrony of approximately 40 ms is observed, rising to a mean asynchrony of 60 ms at phrase onsets (Cummins 2003). Practice does not seem to greatly improve performance (Cummins 2003). The ability of speakers to maintain such tight temporal alignment in the absence of any underlying periodic structure or beat sequence poses something of a challenge, and suggests that entrainment among speakers may provide an alternative way of conceptualizing the role of rhythm in speech. Rhythm thus plausibly has an alternative characterization as a means by which bodily movement becomes entrained across individuals. This view of rhythm also seems to be continuous with its role in music and dance (Cummins 2009a).

8.6 Models

In modeling the form and function of rhythm in speech, two large classes of model can be discerned, and these two classes shadow a long-standing debate in the literature of speech production and motor control more generally about the degree to which temporal structure is controlled (extrinsic, or clock, timing models) or is emergent (intrinsic timing) (Keller 1990; Thelen 1991). Some of this debate has a somewhat anachronistic feel to it today, as we are somewhat more accustomed to working with a plurality of modeling approaches, without insisting on the primacy of one over the other (Lubker 1986). At the heart of the debate, however, lies the important issue of whether time is a controlled variable, measured in the process of perception, and doled out in the act of production, or whether temporal structure is an emergent property of suitably constrained and parameterized dynamical systems.

Models that regard time as a controlled variable typically include a role for a clock, or time- keeping process. One of the most influential of these is the timing model of Wing and Kristofferson (1973) in which a central timekeeper is distinguished from peripheral movement processes. This model has been widely applied in simple repetitive tasks, such as finger tapping. A timekeeper component of this kind is an important element in the EXPLAN model developed by Howell and colleagues, specifically to model dysfluency in speech production, as in stuttering (Howell and Au-Yeung 2002). The explicit computation of temporal intervals has long been a mainstay of rule-based approaches to speech synthesis (Allen, Hunnicutt, and Klatt 1987). Including clock or timekeeper components within a model allows one to dictate temporal patterns of arbitrary complexity. In this sphere, rhythmic patterns are privileged primarily because they are simpler than other patterns.

Models in which time is explicitly metered in production or measured in perception belong squarely in the class of cognitivist computational models that represented a preeminent orthodoxy within the cognitive sciences throughout the last few decades of the twentieth century. A large field of alternative accounts has since become prominent, emphasizing the embeddedness of the organism in an environment, the ineliminable role of the body in any perceptual or active processes, and the emergence of domains of lawfulness that transcend the boundaries between brains, bodies, and the world. These are often referred to (somewhat inaccurately) as embodied or enactive theories of cognition, and the tools and concepts of dynamical systems theory find application where cognitivist models employ rule-based transformations over abstract representations. The coordination dynamics of Scott Kelso, and its application in the speech cycling paradigm, were already mentioned above (Kelso 1995; Cummins and Port 1998). A good primer on the basic concepts of dynamical systems is found in Norton (1995).

The emergence of temporal structure, without explicit metering of time, is a characteristic of dynamical systems models. Here, model components are typically oscillatory systems with intrinsic periods, which may be modified in interaction with other such systems. When self-sustaining oscillators interact weakly, they will tend to coordinate their activity, bringing their frequencies into relatively simple relative timing relations, such as 1:1, 2:3, etc. The principles by which oscillating systems tend to coordinate and adopt relatively simple mutual temporal relations are entirely generic, and depend on their dynamical properties, rather than their material substrate (Pikovsky, Rosenblum, and Kurths 2001). Oscillator models provide a natural platform for capturing rhythmic patterning, and they have been widely used in speech studies (O'Dell and Nieminen 1999; Barbosa 2002; Nam and Saltzman 2003). Although these models generate a wide variety of rhythmic phenomena, a limitation in their application to speech has been the absence of clearly defined periodic patterns in actual speech production.

There remains a tension between intrinsic and extrinsic timing approaches that mirrors a larger debate within cognitive science. The computational approaches arising from decades of work within artificial intelligence and cognitive psychology are currently being challenged from a number of quarters by approaches to understanding behavior as a property of embodied beings embedded lawfully in structured environments. This is a very large debate that goes beyond our present concerns.

8.7 Open questions in the study of speech rhythm

The many themes that arise in the study of rhythm ensure that there will always be a rich variety of phenomena to be studied, and a correspondingly plurality in theoretical and modeling approaches employed. This can be confusing to the newcomer, and it is incumbent on researchers within any of these many fields to make explicit their understanding of central concepts such as rhythm, meter, entrainment, coupling, and more. The equation of mere periodicity with the richer set of phenomena deserving of the term "rhythm" constitutes a clear source of conceptual confusion throughout the literature which future work would do well to avoid. Some of the principal areas that have hitherto defined the study of rhythm in speech include the classification of languages, the characterization of speaking styles, the role of rhythm in dysfluencies, and the way in which coordination emerges in speaking. Many of these will continue to be fruitful areas of inquiry, although one might surmise from the above discussion that the vigorous pursuit of a classificatory scheme for languages on rhythmic grounds alone has probably enjoyed an undue amount of attention, with little success.

A large area of recent interest arises from studying rhythm and timing at the dyadic level, or, more generally, as a property of multi-party interaction. If an informal use of the term may be allowed, rhythms emerge in conversational interaction; they arise, are sustained, and disappear again in the ebb and flow of attention and activity among participants. The dynamics of turn-taking has long been hypothesized to be guided by rhythmic principles (Couper-Kuhlen 1993), although empirical studies of the timing of turns has yet to deliver a robust account that is grounded in quantitative observation (Bull 1996). Part of the difficulty encountered lies in the great degree of temporal variability exhibited by pauses in speech (Trouvain and Barry 2000; Zvonik and Cummins 2002), and recent investigation of turn-taking when speakers overlap may open new avenues here (Wlodarczak, Simko, and Wagner, 2012). Beyond turn-taking, the employment of dynamical models may allow the characterization of collective temporal phenomena that are poorly, if at all, identifiable when speech is considered one individual at a time. Synchronized speech represents one emerging topic in this field (Cummins 2012). It is somewhat perplexing that the ubiquitous phenomenon of joint, or choral, speaking has received so little attention by empirical studies, especially when one considers the deep integration of collective speaking practices in educational institutions, houses of worship, sports stadia, and street protests throughout the world.

With the rise of interest in the role of movement in rhythmic behaviors, the study of rhythm in speech is increasingly taking stock of the rich body of work on gestures and whole-body involvement in speaking (McNeill 1992; Goldin-Meadow 1999). Manual gestures, facial movements, even gaze and blinking are potentially co-implicated in the temporal patterning that is speaking (Cassell et al. 1994; Leonard and Cummins 2011; Cummins 2011), and much remains to be uncovered about how these disparate streams are integrated within and across individuals.

Finally, although the approach here has tried to stay close to the core sense of "rhythm" that is home in the domain of music and dance, there is much to be done in fleshing out the continuum that exists between the spoken word and the use of the voice in a musical context. Parallels between music and speech may range from the merely metaphorical to the literal. Anniruddh Patel has contributed a very varied set of studies that have contributed to our understanding of the way in which musical and speech rhythm might relate to one another (Patel et al. 1998; Patel and Daniele 2003), but much remains to be done.

NOTE

1   The notion of "cognitive rhythms" that arose in the 1960s might bear mention in passing, if only to warn newcomers to the field that that particular construct is not theoretically sound and is no longer part of the state of the art (Henderson, Goldman-Eisler, and Skarbek 1966; Goldman-Eisler 1967; Jaffe, Breskin, and Gerstman 1972; Kowal and O'Connell 1985).

REFERENCES

Abercrombie, D. 1965. A phonetician's view of verse structure. In *Studies in Phonetics and Linguistics* 16–25. Oxford: Oxford University Press.

Abercrombie, D. 1967. *Elements of General Phonetics*. Chicago, IL: Aldine.

Allen, J., M. Hunnicutt, and D. Klatt. 1987. *From Text to Speech: The MITalk System.*

Cambridge: Cambridge University Press.

Andrews, G., P. Howie, M. Dozsa, and B.E. Guitar. 1982. Stuttering: Speech pattern characteristics under fluency-inducing conditions. *Journal of Speech and Hearing Research* 25: 208–216.

Arvaniti, A. 2009. Rhythm, timing and the timing of rhythm. *Phonetica* 66(1–2): 46–63.

Arvaniti, A. 2012. The usefulness of metrics in the quantification of speech rhythm. *Journal of Phonetics* 40(3): 351–373.

Balasubramanian, T. 1980. Timing in Tamil. *Journal of Phonetics* 8: 449–467.

Barbosa, P.A. 2002. Explaining cross-linguistic rhythmic variability via a coupled-oscillator model of rhythm production. In *Proceedings of Speech Prosody 2002, Aix-en-Provence*, 163–166.

Beckman, M. 1982. Segment duration and the "mora" in Japanese. *Phonetica* 39: 113–135.

Bergeson, T. and S. Trehub. 2002. Absolute pitch and tempo in mothers songs to infants. *Psychological Science* 13(1): 72–75.

Bertinetto, P.M. 1988. Reflections on the dichotomy "stress" vs. "syllable" timing. *Quaderni del Laboratorio di Linguistica* 2: 59–84 (Scuola Normale Superiore di Pisa).

Bolinger, D. 1965. Pitch accent and sentence rhythm. In I. Abe and T. Kanekiyo (eds.), *Forms of English: Accent, Morpheme, Order*, 139–180. Cambridge, MA: Harvard University Press.

Browman, C.P. and L. Goldstein. 1995. Dynamics and articulatory phonology. In R.F. Port and T. van Gelder (eds.), *Mind as Motion*, 175–193. Cambridge, MA: MIT Press.

Bull, M.C. 1996. An analysis of between-speaker intervals. In *Proceedings of the Edinburgh Linguistics Department Conference '96*, 18–27.

Cassell, J., C. Pelachaud, N. Badler, M. Steedman, B. Achorn, T. Becket, B. Douville, S. Prevost, and M. Stone. 1994. Animated conversation: Rule-based generation of facial expression, gesture and spoken intonation for multiple conversational agents. In *Proceedings of the 21st Annual Conference on Computer Graphics and Interactive Techniques*, 413–420.

Classé, A. 1939. *The Rhythm of English Prose*. Oxford: Basil Blackwell.

Condon, W.S. and L.W. Sander. 1974. Synchrony demonstrated between movements of the neonate and adult speech. *Child Development* 45: 456–462.

Couper-Kuhlen, E. 1993. *English Speech Rhythm*. Philadelphia, PA: John Benjamins.

Crystal, T.H. and A.S. House. 1990. Articulation rate and the duration of syllables and stress groups in connected speech. *Journal of the Acoustical Society of America* 88(1): 101–112.

Cummins, F. 2003. Practice and performance in speech produced synchronously. *Journal of Phonetics* 31(2): 139–148.

Cummins, F. 2009a. Rhythm as an affordance for the entrainment of movement. *Phonetica* 66(1–2): 15–28.

Cummins, F. 2009b. Rhythm as entrainment: The case of synchronous speech. *Journal of Phonetics* 37(1): 16–28.

Cummins, F. 2011. Gaze and blinking in dyadic conversation: A study in coordinated behavior among individuals. *Language & Cognitive Processes*. 27(10): 1525–1541.

Cummins, F. 2012. Periodic and aperiodic synchronization in skilled action. *Frontiers in Human Neuroscience* 5: 170.

Cummins, F. and R.F. Port. 1998. Rhythmic constraints on stress timing in English. *Journal of Phonetics* 26(2): 145–171.

Cutler, A. and J. Mehler. 1993. The periodicity bias. *Journal of Phonetics* 21: 103–108.

Dauer, R.M. 1983. Stress-timing and syllable-timing reanalyzed. *Journal of Phonetics* 11: 51–62.

De Jong, K.J. 1994. The correlation of p-center adjustments with articulatory and acoustic events. *Attention, Perception, & Psychophysics* 56(4): 447–460.

de Manrique, A.M.B. and A. Signorini. 1983. Segmental duration and rhythm in Spanish. *Journal of Phonetics* 11: 117–128.

Dellwo, V. and P. Wagner. 2003. Relations between language rhythm and speech rate. In *Proceedings of the 15th International Congress of Phonetics Sciences*, 471–474.

Donovan, A. and C.J. Darwin. 1979. The perceived rhythm of speech. In *Proceedings of the Ninth International Congress of Phonetic Sciences*, vol. 2, 268–274.

Fadiga, L., L. Craighero, G. Buccino, and G. Rizzolatti. 2002. Speech listening specifically modulates the excitability of tongue muscles: A TMS study. *European Journal of Neuroscience* 15(2): 399–402.

Farnetani, E. and S. Kori. 1990. Rhythmic structure in Italian noun phrases: A study on vowel durations. *Phonetica* 47: 50–65.

Fowler, C. 1979. Perceptual centers in speech production and perception. *Attention, Perception, & Psychophysics* 25(5): 375–388.

Fowler, C.A., P. Rubin, R. Remez, and M. Turvey. 1980. Implications for speech production of a general theory of action. In B. Butterworth (ed.), *Language Production*, 373–420. San Diego, CA: Academic Press.

Galves, A., J. Garcia, D. Duarte, and C. Galves. 2002. Sonority as a basis for rhythmic class discrimination. In *Proceedings of Speech Prosody 2002*, Aix-en-Provence.

Gibbon, D. and U. Gut. 2001. Measuring speech rhythm. In *Proceedings of the Seventh European Conference on Speech Communication and Technology*.

Goldfarb, W., N. Goldfarb, P. Braunstein, and H. Scholl. 1972. Speech and language faults of schizophrenic children. *Journal of Autism and Developmental Disorders* 2(3): 219–233.

Goldin-Meadow, S. 1999. The role of gesture in communication and thinking. *Trends in Cognitive Sciences* 3(11): 419–429.

Goldman-Eisler, F. 1967. Sequential temporal patterns and cognitive processes in speech. *Language and Speech* 10: 122–132.

Goldstein, L., D. Byrd, and E. Saltzman. 2006. The role of vocal tract gestural action units in understanding the evolution of phonology. In M.A. Arbib (ed.), *Action to Language via the Mirror Neuron System*, 215–249. Cambridge: Cambridge University Press.

Grabe, E. and E. Low. 2002. Durational variability in speech and the rhythm class hypothesis. *Laboratory Phonology* 7.

Grillner, S. 1981. Control of locomotion in bipeds, tetrapods, and fish. In V.B. Brooks (ed.), *Handbook of Physiology, Motor Control*. Baltimore, MD: Williams and Wilkins.

Haken, H., J.A.S. Kelso, and H. Bunz. 1985. A theoretical model of phase transitions in human hand movement. *Biological Cybernetics* 51: 347–356.

Han, M.S. 1994. Acoustic manifestations of mora timing in Japanese. *Journal of the Acoustical Society of America* 96: 73–82.

Henderson, A., F. Goldman-Eisler, and A. Skarbek. 1966. Sequential temporal patterns in spontaneous speech. *Language and Speech* 9: 207–216.

Howell, P. and J. Au-Yeung. 2002. The EXPLAN theory of fluency control applied to the diagnosis of stuttering. In E. Fava (ed.), *Clinical Linguistics: Theory and Applications in Speech Pathology and Therapy*, 75–94. Amsterdam: John Benjamins.

Huron, D. 2006. *Sweet Anticipation: Music and the Psychology of Expectation*. Cambridge, MA: MIT Press.

Jaffe, J., S. Breskin, and L.J. Gerstman. 1972. Random generation of apparent speech rhythms. *Language and Speech* 15: 68–71.

Jones, D. 1956. *An Outline of English Phonetics*, 8th edn. Cambridge: Heffer. First published in 1918.

Keller, E. 1990. Speech motor timing. In W.J. Hardcastle and A. Marchal (eds.), *Speech*

Production and Speech Modelling, 343–364. Dordrecht: Kluwer Academic.

Kelso, J.A.S. 1995. *Dynamic Patterns*. Cambridge, MA: MIT Press.

Knight, R. and N. Cocks. 2007. Rhythm in the speech of a person with right hemisphere damage: Applying the pairwise variability index. *International Journal of Speech-Language Pathology* 9(3): 256–264.

Kowal, S.H. and D.C. O'Connell. 1985. Cognitive rhythms reluctantly revisited. *Language and Speech* 28(1): 93–95.

Kuiper, K. 1992. The oral tradition in auction speech. *American Speech* 67(3): 279–289.

Kurowski, K., S. Blumstein, and M. Alexander. 1996. The foreign accent syndrome: A reconsideration. *Brain and Language* 54(1): 1–25.

Large, E.W. and M. Riess Jones. 1999. The dynamics of attending: How people track time-varying events. *Psychological Review* 106(1): 119–159.

Latash, M. 2008. *Synergy*. Oxford: Oxford University Press.

Lehiste, I. 1977. Isochrony reconsidered. *Journal of Phonetics* 5: 253–263.

Leonard, T. and F. Cummins. 2011. The temporal relation between beat gestures and speech. *Language and Cognitive Processes* 26(10): 1457–1471.

Liberman, A.M. and I.G. Mattingly. 1985. The motor theory of speech perception revised. *Cognition* 21: 1–36.

Liberman, M. and A. Prince. 1977. On stress and linguistic rhythm. *Linguistic Inquiry* 8: 249–336.

Lloyd James, A. 1940. *Speech Signals in Telephony*. London: Pitman.

Lubker, J. 1986. Articulatory timing and the concept of phase. *Journal of Phonetics* 14: 133–137.

Major, R.C. 1981. Stress-timing in Brazilian Portuguese. *Journal of Phonetics* 9: 343–351.

Max, L. and E.M. Yudman. 2003. Accuracy and variability of isochronous rhythmic timing across motor systems in stuttering versus nonstuttering individuals. *Journal of Speech, Language, and Hearing Research* 46: 146–163.

McNeill, D. 1992. *Hand and Mind: What Gestures Reveal about Thought*. Chicago, IL: University of Chicago Press.

Miller, M. 1984. On the perception of rhythm. *Journal of Phonetics* 12: 75–83.

Morgan, J.L. 1996. A rhythmic bias in preverbal speech segmentation. *Journal of Memory and Language* 35(5): 666–688.

Morton, J., S. Marcus, and C. Frankish. 1976. Perceptual centers (P-centers). *Psychological Review* 83(5): 405–408.

Nakatani, L.H., K.D. O'Connor, and C.H. Aston. 1981. Prosodic aspects of American English speech rhythm. *Phonetica* 38: 84–106.

Nam, H. and E. Saltzman. 2003. A competitive, coupled oscillator model of syllable structure. In *Proceedings of the 15th International Congress of Phonetic Sciences*, 2253–2256.

Nolan, F. and E. Asu. 2009. The pairwise variability index and coexisting rhythms in language. *Phonetica* 66(1–2): 64–77.

Norton, A. 1995. Dynamics: An introduction. In R.F. Port and T. van Gelder (eds.), *Mind as Motion: Explorations in the Dynamics of Cognition*, 45–68. Cambridge, MA: Bradford Books/MIT Press.

Nudelman, H.B., K.E. Herbrich, B.D. Hoyt, and D.B. Rosenfield. 1987. Dynamic characteristics of vocal frequency tracking in stutterers and nonstutterers. In H.F.M. Peters and W. Hulstijn (eds.), *Speech Motor Dynamics in Stuttering*, 162–169. New York: Springer.

O'Connor, J.D. 1968. The duration of the foot in relation to the number of component sound-segments. *Technical Progress Report* 3: 1–6 (Phonetics Laboratory, University College London).

O'Dell, M. and T. Nieminen. 1999. Coupled oscillator model of speech rhythm. In *Proceedings of the XIVth International Congress of Phonetic Sciences*, vol. 2, 1075–1078.

Patel, A. and J. Daniele. 2003. An empirical comparison of rhythm in language and music. *Cognition* 87(1): B35–B45.

Patel, A., I. Peretz, M. Tramo, and R. Labreque. 1998. Processing prosodic and musical patterns: A neuropsychological investigation. *Brain and Language* 61(1): 123–144.

Paul, R., N. Bianchi, A. Augustyn, A. Klin, and F. Volkmar. 2008. Production of syllable stress in speakers with autism spectrum disorders. *Research in Autism Spectrum Disorders* 2(1): 110–124.

Pike, K.L. 1945. *The Intonation of American English*. Ann Arbor: University of Michigan Press.

Pikovsky, A., M. Rosenblum, and J. Kurths. 2001. *Synchronization: A Universal Concept in Nonlinear Sciences*. Cambridge: Cambridge University Press.

Port, R.F., J. Dalby, and M. O'Dell. 1987. Evidence for mora timing in Japanese. *Journal of the Acoustical Society of America* 81(5): 1574–1585.

Ramus, F., M. Nespor, and J. Mehler. 1999. Correlates of linguistic rhythm in the speech signal. *Cognition* 73(3): 265–292.

Richardson, D., R. Dale, and N. Kirkham. 2007. The art of conversation is coordination. *Psychological Science* 18(5): 407.

Rizzolatti, G. and M.A. Arbib. 1998. Language within our grasp. *Trends in Neuroscience* 21(5): 188–194.

Scott, D., S. Isard, and B. de Boysson-Bardies. 1985. Perceptual isochrony in English and in French. *Journal of Phonetics* 19: 351–365.

Scott, S.K. 1993. P-centers in speech: An acoustic analysis. PhD thesis, University College London.

Shen, Y. and G.G. Peterson. 1962. Isochronism in English. In *Studies in Linguistics*, Occasional Papers 9, 1–36. Buffalo, NY: University of Buffalo.

Shockley, K., M. Santana, and C. Fowler. 2003. Mutual interpersonal postural constraints are involved in cooperative conversation. *Journal of Experimental Psychology: Human Perception and Performance* 29(2): 326–332.

Starkweather, C.W. 1987. *Fluency and Stuttering*. Englewood Cliffs, NJ: Prentice Hall.

Steele, J. 1775. *An Essay towards Establishing the Melody and Measure of Speech to be Expressed and Perpetuated by Peculiar Symbols*. London: Printed by W. Bowyer and J. Nichols, for J. Almon.

Thelen, E. 1991. Motor aspects of emergent speech: A dynamic approach. In N.A. Krasnegor, D.M. Rumbaugh, R.L. Schiefelbusch, and M. Studdert-Kennedy (eds.), *Biological and Behavioral Determinants of Language Development*, 339–362. Hillsdale, NJ: Lawrence Erlbaum Associates.

Trouvain, J. and W.J. Barry. 2000. The prosody of excitement in horse race commentaries. In *Proceedings of ISCA Workshop (ITRW) on Speech and Emotion, Belfast*.

Vos, J. and R. Rasch. 1981. The perceptual onset of musical tones. *Perception and Psychophysics* 29(4): 323–335.

Wagner, P. and V. Dellwo. 2004. Introducing YARD (Yet Another Rhythm Determination) and reintroducing isochrony to rhythm research. In *Speech Prosody 2004, International Conference*. ISCA.

Wenk, B. 1985. Speech rhythms in second language acquisition. *Language and Speech* 28(2): 157–175.

Williams, H.G. and J.H. Bishop. 1992. Speed and consistency of manual movements of stutterers, articulation-disordered children, and children with normal speech. *Journal of Fluency Disorders* 17: 191–203.

Wing, A.M. and A.B. Kristofferson. 1973. Response delays and the timing of discrete motor responses. *Perception and Psychophysics* 14(1): 5–12.

Wlodarczak, M., J. Simko, and P. Wagner. 2012. Temporal entrainment in overlapped speech: Cross-linguistic study. In *Proceedings of the 13th Annual Conference of the International Speech Communication Association, 2012, Portland, OR*.

Yaruss, J.S. 1997. Clinical measurement of stuttering behaviors. *Contemporary Issues in Communication Science and Disorders* 24: 33–44.

Zvonik, E. and F. Cummins. 2002. Pause duration and variability in read texts. In *Proceedings of the ICSLP, Denver, CO*, 1109–1112.

FURTHER READING

The following works provide a variety of entry points to the diverse senses of rhythm as applied in speech research. Most are broader in topic and should help to situate rhythm research with respect to other, related, fields.

Couper-Kuhlen, E. 1993. *English Speech Rhythm*. Philadelphia, PA: John Benjamins. This work is rich in following intuitions about the role of rhythm in conversation, though somewhat light on empirical investigation.

Dauer, R.M. 1983. Stress-timing and syllable-timing reanalyzed. *Journal of Phonetics* 11: 51–62. Not a book, but if you only ever read one text on the isochrony debate, this would be a good choice.

Huron, D. 2006. *Sweet Anticipation: Music and the Psychology of Expectation*. Cambridge, MA: MIT Press. This book is primarily about music, but it makes explicit links to speech, and to rhythm in speech.

Kelso, J.A.S. 1995. *Dynamic Patterns*. Cambridge, MA: MIT Press. This book summarizes one of the best worked-out examples of the application of dynamical systems modeling to human behavior. Relatively little on speech, but provides a good foundation with which to tackle subsequent work in dynamical modeling of speech.

McNeill, D. 1992. *Hand and Mind: What Gestures Reveal about Thought*. Chicago, IL: University of Chicago Press. Focuses on the form and function of gestures, which are increasingly important as embodied theories of speech production and perception gain traction.

Patel, A.D. 2008. Music, Language, and the Brain. NY: Oxford University Press. Teases out and makes explicit links between music and speech, with special attention to the form and role of rhythm.

9 Auditory-Visual Speech Processing
Something Doesn't Add Up

ERIC VATIKIOTIS-BATESON AND
KEVIN G. MUNHALL

9.1 Introduction

The multimodal production and multisensory perception of speech have received much research attention in the past 60 years since Sumby and Pollack's landmark demonstration that being able to see a talker's face in noisy acoustic conditions dramatically improves speech intelligibility (Sumby and Pollack 1954). Myriad studies have pursued various conceptual lines about the production and processing of multisensory information in the context of diverse tasks applied to clinical populations and hordes of undergraduate psychology students, and in technical applications for multimedia and speech technology. Previously, we have reviewed the progress in auditory-visual speech processing, particularly with respect to the production and perception of time-varying speech behavior (Munhall and Vatikiotis-Bateson 1998, 2004; Vatikiotis-Bateson and Munhall 2012a, 2012b). In this chapter,[1] we examine what has been learned about auditory-visual speech processing (AVSP) from the potentially disturbing perspective that we still do not have a cogent story for how the visual enhancement of speech intelligibility works. Examining the neural underpinnings of AVSP is, of course, a promising and increasingly well-worn path toward working out a suitable story. However, before turning to neurophysiology to account for behavior, we think it worthwhile to critically review what we have and have not learned from behavioral studies of the production and perception of multimodal speech. In particular, the research questions that have been asked were based on premises and assumptions about language and cognition that may need to be rethought before the observed results can begin to make sense, and should be reexamined

The Handbook of Speech Production, First Edition. Edited by Melissa A. Redford.
© 2015 John Wiley & Sons, Inc. Published 2019 by John Wiley & Sons, Inc.

and possibly reframed or discarded entirely before looking for answers in the neural processes of the brain. In the following, we first summarize the findings about which we are confident. Then, we discuss findings that either lead to conflicting interpretations and/or cast doubt on the meta-theoretical premises and assumptions that shaped the way the research questions were formulated. We conclude the chapter with a tentative prescription for future studies based on new questions about AVSP.

9.2 What we think we know and think we understand

In our own studies of the production and perception of multimodal speech, carried out over the past 20 years, we have discovered or confirmed a number of facts about which there appears to be little controversy insofar as the results have proven to be robustly replicable across myriad differences in experimental methodology and design. How they all fit together and should be interpreted is a more difficult problem and is taken up in sections 9.3 and 9.4.

9.2.1 Causal and functional linkages in multimodal speech production

Configuring the vocal tract through time simultaneously shapes the acoustic resonances of the speech signal and visibly deforms the face, primarily through the motions of the jaw and shaping of the lips. That is, what happens in the vocal tract during speech production *physically* determines the audible and visible signals that result from that process. Simply recognizing that the face *defines* the sidewalls of the vocal tract should lead one to expect a tight, causal coupling between the vocal tract and the face. We demonstrated this coupling with analyses of kinematic (vocal tract and face) and acoustic data for speakers of Japanese and English published in the mid-to-late 1990s with Takaaki Kuratate, Philip Rubin, and Hani Yehia (Vatikiotis-Bateson and Yehia 1996b; Yehia, Kuratate, and Vatikiotis-Bateson 1999; Yehia, Rubin, and Vatikiotis-Bateson 1998).

In these studies, analyses of Japanese and English sentence production showed that measures of two-dimensional (2D: midsagittal height and protrusion) position of the jaw, lips, and four flesh points on the anterior tongue surface correspond closely with measures from the three-dimensional (3D) positions of markers – usually 17 or 18 – arranged on the chin, lips, and other regions of the face below the eyes (see Figure 9.1). Calculated as a multivariate correlation averaged over the span of medium-length sentences (20+ syllables), the correspondence between the measures made in the vocal tract and on the face was strong enough to estimate more than 80% of the face motion behavior from vocal-tract articulation. Similarly, but not quite as efficiently, about 65% of the spectral acoustics could be estimated from vocal-tract articulation, with the

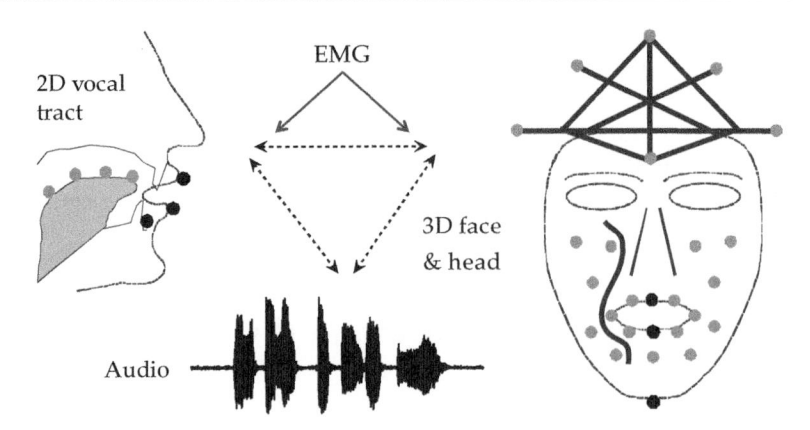

Figure 9.1 Schematic of physiological and acoustic production measures: muscle activity (EMG), 2D vocal-tract motion, 3D face motion, 6D head motion, and the audio acoustics. The arrows indicate the various cross-domain analyses that have been carried out.

frequencies in the vicinity of the second formant band (F2: 1500–2500 Hz) estimated at 80% accuracy or better. This last finding is not surprising since F2 corresponds most closely with the shape of the front oral cavity, which is where the electromagnetic tongue markers were located (for details about the EMMA system, see Perkell et al. 1992).

Applying the elementary principle that two things that are each similar to a third should be similar to each other (i.e., if $a \approx c$ and $b \approx c$, then $a \approx b$), these analyses also showed that 3D face motion could be estimated from the spectral components of the acoustics at about 95% accuracy or better using nonlinear estimation techniques (Yehia et al. 1999; Yehia, Kuratate, and Vatikiotis-Bateson 2002). In these analyses, the correspondence between face motion and acoustics was given a significant boost by small deformations in the face that were likely due to structured fluctuations of intraoral air pressure (see Carter, Shadle, and Davies 1996).[2] Although small in terms of the effect on signal variance, these structural fluctuations have proven highly effective in subsequent synthesis of speech based on nonlinear estimates of time-varying acoustic spectral parameters from facial markers located bilaterally on the cheeks (see Figure 9.1).

In a subsequent study of Japanese and English sentence production, in which no movement-restricting vocal tract measures were made, a *functional* linkage was identified between the rigid body (6D) motion of the head and the fundamental frequency (F0) of the speech acoustics (Yehia et al. 2002).[3] Correlation analysis showed that, as F0 increases, the head tends to tilt upward and away from the chest; and downward (chin closer to the chest) as F0 decreases. That the linkage can be decoupled with practice supports the notion that this is a functional linkage rather than something primarily structural. For example, while most people have difficulty damping or reversing the relation – try it for yourself – trained singers have no problem decoupling head motion and F0.

Another functional correspondence between head motion and the speech acoustics is the tendency for head motion to increase with acoustic amplitude (intensity). In early motion studies where head motion was an undesirable artifact, the head was usually constrained by a headband of some sort. This had the unpleasant effect of reducing the talker's vocal amplitude. As reported by Tom Scholte (Department of Film and Theatre, University of British Columbia) and confirmed repeatedly by others involved in theatre, decoupling head motion and vocal amplitude is a basic component in training actors to project their voices at higher amplitudes while maintaining the visual demeanor appropriate to the much lower amplitude appropriate to, say, face-to-face interaction. On the other hand, the repeated observation that acoustic amplitude (root mean square: RMS) also correlates with movement amplitude of vocal tract and facial motion suggests a physical, rather than functional, coupling (Barbosa et al. 2006; Barbosa, Yehia, and Vatikiotis-Bateson 2008; Yehia et al. 2002).

9.2.2 Visible actions relevant to speech intelligibility are everywhere

In one of our early forays into AVSP, we conducted a study whose aim was to determine where Japanese or English listeners direct their eyes (foveate) during audiovisual perception and the extent to which their eye motion patterns change under different auditory and visual conditions (Vatikiotis-Bateson et al. 1998). We recorded the eye movement behavior of perceivers watching video monologues presented with a range of amplitudes of auditory masking noise (a multilingual party recorded in a Japanese kitchen) and at image sizes ranging from normal (for face-face interaction at approximately 1 meter inter-talker distance) to much larger than normal. Simple questions at the end of each trial such as "Did he say '*peep*' or '*beep*'?" served to index the stimulus intelligibility while focusing perceiver attention on phonetic aspects of the talker's speech rather than on other factors such as the talker's sincerity or happiness (Eigsti et al. 1995). The basic findings of the Vatikiotis-Bateson et al. (1998) study were that, even under conditions of the highest masking noise and largest image projection, perceivers foveate more on the eyes and less on the mouth than previously believed. Also, eye movement patterns – specifically saccades between the eyes and the mouth – change little, if at all, even when the noise levels are high and the image size so large that the eyes and mouth cannot both be viewed within the relatively high-acuity region of the perifovea.

It was clear from pretesting, aimed at determining the appropriate noise levels for auditory-only conditions (Vatikiotis-Bateson, Eigsti, and Yano 1994), that being able to see the face enhances intelligibility. This was expected from Sumby and Pollack's (1954) earlier research, at least when the faces are displayed at sizes appropriate for face-to-face interaction. What was surprising was that the same enhancement was observed even at the largest image sizes, when perceivers could not simultaneously foveate on the eyes and keep the mouth in sharp focus. This led to two questions that were pursued in subsequent production and perception studies:

- How much spatial and temporal acuity (or resolution) are needed for visual enhancement of speech intelligibility to occur?
- Where is the linguistically relevant information located?

Based on what we thought we knew in the 1990s about the role of eye motion in optimizing visual acuity – namely, that spatial acuity was highest at the fovea and temporal acuity was highest at the visual periphery (Carpenter 1988) – our results for perceiver eye motion during distorted visual and noise-degraded auditory speech perception suggested two alternative hypotheses about the location of visual information on the face. First was the hypothesis that linguistically relevant visual speech information is distributed widely across the face, rather than merely in the vicinity of the mouth. Earlier analysis of orofacial production data supported this hypothesis (Vatikiotis-Bateson and Yehia 1996b). For semi-spontaneous production of short sentences and phrases, the correspondence between two sets of 3D facial motion markers was extremely high (see Figure 9.1 for delineation of the two marker sets). The inner set consisted of five markers placed around the right-hand perimeter of the lips (sagittal midline of the upper and lower lips, the right-hand corner of the lips, and two markers midway between the midline and corner on each lip). The outer consisted of five markers away from the mouth on the right side of the face (two on the lower face and three on the cheeks). Marker motion for the inner set was highly predictable, $85\% < r^2 < 99\%$, from motion of the outer set.

The alternative hypothesis, based on the acclaimed temporal acuity of visual periphery, was that temporal information is more important than spatial information for the visual enhancement of speech intelligibility. This made sense, given perceivers' strong performance recovering speech information presented at high levels of auditory masking noise and at large image sizes, where foveating on the stimulus talker's eyes put the mouth region 10–11 degrees away from the foveal center.

As it turned out, neither hypothesis about how perceivers make use of temporal and spatial information in visible speech was borne out by subsequent studies.

9.2.3 Very little visual information is required for perception

In a series of SPeech-In-Noise (SPIN) studies, Munhall and colleagues showed that perceivers retrieve relevant visual speech information at low spatial and temporal resolutions (dePaula et al. 2003, 2006; Munhall, Jozan, et al. 2004; for overview, see Munhall and Vatikiotis-Bateson 2004). These studies showed that perceivers could retrieve visual speech information presented in noise at cumulative (lowpass filtered) spatial frequencies as low as 5 cycles per face (cpf), using a Chebchev filter (dePaula et al. 2006), and at 7 cpf, using one-octave passband filtered images for a range of center resolutions of 3–44 cps (Munhall, Jozan, et al. 2004).

To determine the lower bound on temporal resolution of the visual information, dePaula et al. (2006) used Gaussian filtering of the image sequence to show that intelligibility of semantically unpredictable sentences (based on specialized topics and vocabulary) did not begin to degrade until temporal resolution fell to 6–9 Hz (depending on listener). These values are substantially lower than the 14–16 Hz previously reported by Vitkovich and Barber (1994). We attribute the discrepancy to the fact that Vitkovich and Barber used frame decimation which, by removing frames from the image sequence, reduces the frame rate and increases the duration of the black gaps between frames. These gaps, as they get larger, could disrupt processing of the visual information. The Gaussian filter used by dePaula et al. (2006), on the other hand, reduced the temporal resolution without reducing the frame rate, which remained at 30 fps. One drawback to the Gaussian filter method is that smearing the reduced temporal information across 30 fps also reduces the spatial information represented in each frame, making it difficult to determine the exact contribution of temporal resolution to perceptual performance.

Finally, in their study of spatial resolution requirements for visual enhancement of speech intelligibility, Munhall, Jozan, et al. (2004) also showed that the effectiveness of visual speech information in enhancing the intelligibility of speech produced with noise-masked acoustics is not affected by the relative size of the talker's image on the perceiver's retina. They rigorously tested talker–perceiver distances between 1 m and more than 3 m and found no degradation in perception. At the time, Munhall, Jozan, et al. inferred from this finding that the visual enhancement must be cognitive rather than physical.

9.3 What we know, but do not understand

In this section we discuss different pieces of research whose results are solid enough, but which have not yet lent themselves to tidy interpretation, especially when it comes to connecting the results of production studies with multisensory perception studies. For example, as discussed in section 9.2.1, the motion of the head correlates well with F0 and to a lesser extent with acoustic amplitude. One would hope that perceivers take advantage of such strong production linkages, and it appears that they do; but, as we discuss in section 9.3.1 below, more questions are raised than answered by the finding that being able to see the head's motion during speech contributes substantially to the perceived intelligibility of audiovisual stimuli consisting of talking head animations and noise-degraded acoustics.

Even more unsettling, we have not been able to determine crucial orofacial landmarks for measuring facial motion relevant to audiovisual production-perception. Discovering where the relevant information is on the face was one of the original reasons for launching this entire research paradigm in the early 1990s. One motivation for examining perceiver eye movement during multisensory speech production was the hope that where perceivers foveate would help us identify ideal locations for marker placement. Subsequently, we manipulated marker placements and dimensionality and found that various locations, such as the cheeks and non-midsagittal placements on the lips, made specific contributions to the correspondence with the spectral acoustics (from movement of the cheeks) and the position of the tongue (from movement of the non-midsagittal lips); but we found nothing that clearly contributed to audiovisual speech perception. To make matters worse, it turns out that all of the motion in a large region of interest (ROI) such as the head and face can be reduced to one time-varying magnitude with little loss of relevant information about the spatiotemporal organization of the speech behavior. We discuss this latter issue further in section 9.3.2.

Finally, the idea that speech production is a nonlinear, distributed process is not new. One of the most successful attempts to link speech performance and linguistic structure, Articulatory Phonology (for early overview, see Browman and Goldstein 1986), construes speech production as a symphony of semi-independent articulatory events, temporally orchestrated to attain serialized linguistic goals. Indeed, were it not for the predominant conceptual dependence on the notion that the continuous speech stream must be decomposable into strings of contrastive phoneme segments, the fact that information crucial to speech perception is distributed over substantial spans of signal would not be surprising at all. In section 9.3.3, we discuss one aspect of the distributed timing of events specific to the production and (non)perception of the labial viseme; in part because it further emphasizes the disconnect between information contained in speech signals and how perceivers access that information, and partly because we want to emphasize that human perception performance should not be used as a gold standard for building artificial perception systems.

9.3.1 Head motion provides crucial information for audiovisual perception

It is well known that the head is an active and important component of communicative interaction, providing paralinguistic information (see Trager 1958) including emphasis and indications of listener attention, comprehension, disagreement, and the like. The finding that head motion correlates well with F0 suggests that the head potentially provides perceivers redundant information that might otherwise be lost when the acoustic signal is severely degraded. This is important because F0 may contribute segmental information about vowel identity – insofar as different sonorants have different intrinsic F0 ranges (e.g., Ewan 1979; Vilkman et al. 1989; Katz and Assmann 2001) – and conveys substantial prosodic information about stress and intonation via its modulation over the course of an utterance.

We say the head *potentially* provides information to perceivers because the existence of such redundancies or any of the other measured correlations in the production data is no guarantee that perceivers actually detect and make use of them. This is why we went to so much effort to create a talking head animation system that could be used to create synthesized stimuli from time-varying physiological and acoustic data for perceptual evaluation (Kuratate, Yehia, and

Vatikiotis-Bateson 1998). In a study designed both to determine the linguistic validity of the animated stimuli for perceivers and to examine the extent to which head motion influences audiovisual speech perception, Munhall, Jones, and colleagues (2004) presented talking head animations in auditory noise-masking for three conditions: the motion of the face and the head synthesized from recorded kinematics of these structures, the motion of the face without head motion, and motion of the face and head with doubled amplitudes, but no change in movement times (thereby doubling the velocity of all motions.)[4]

The intelligibility results for Japanese semantically unpredictable sentences, presented with noise-masked acoustics, are shown in Figure 9.2. As shown, intelligibility was reliably better for all three talking head conditions than for noisy audio alone. The best results were obtained for the head + face condition, which was the most natural of the video conditions. Distorting the spatiotemporal acoustics disrupted audiovisual intelligibility the most. The results for normal face motion without head motion were closer to the results for the distorted kinematics than for the combination of face, head, and noisy audio.

The talking head animation system provided a first demonstration that seeing rigid body motion of the head enhances speech intelligibility substantially. It simply is not possible to produce natural, communicative speech without head motion, and certainly the face motion alone condition is not natural insofar as no typical speaker holds the head completely still while producing speech at normal

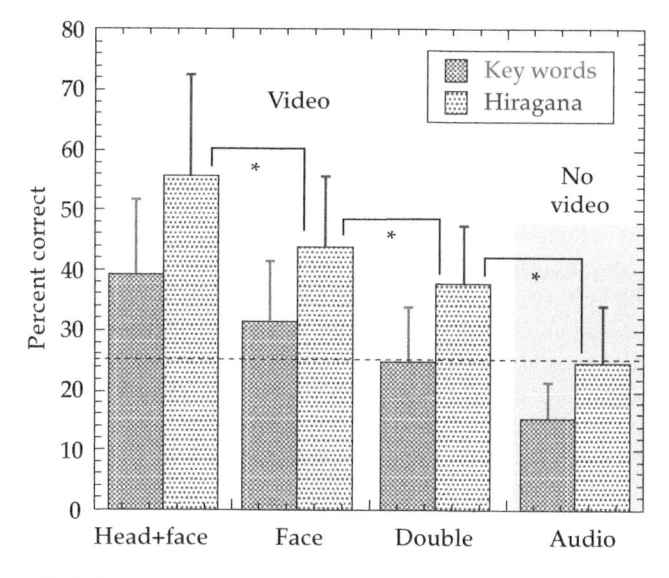

Figure 9.2 Intelligibility of semantically unpredictable sentences (Japanese) presented in acoustic masking noise for one, noise-masked audio control and three audiovisual conditions (head + face, double, face presented with noise-masked audio). Results are shown for the percent correct of key words and syllables (hiragana). Modified from Munhall, Jones, et al. (2004: Figure 3).

levels. As for why head motion enhances intelligibility, this study does not help provide a real answer. With the exception mentioned before of some possible vowel quality information gleaned from inherent F0, there is surely no substantial segmental information accessible by monitoring head motion. Instead, it is more likely that head motion plays one or more roles in conveying speech prosody. Modulation of head motion in rhythmically tuned chunks, such as the stress foot in English, prominence peaks, etc., could help perceivers align to the multisensory speech signal, which in turn could enhance auditory and/or visual perception. That is, the head's role in audiovisual perception could be indirectly a matter of helping listeners find the signal(s) from which they need to glean speech information. A visual analog to this is watching telephone poles from the side window of a fast-moving car or train. If you track the motion of the poles with your head and eyes, you obtain much more information about the poles than when you stare straight out the window and let them whiz across your retina.

In sum, while there is no question that head motion enhances audiovisual speech intelligibility, we do not have much idea about how this enhancement is achieved. We suspect that the visible head motion alone may contribute to entraining listeners to the modulated acoustic signal, but this is not sufficient to induce observable enhancement of speech intelligibility (suggested by the failure of animations containing only head motion and degraded acoustics to improve intelligibility: Hill and Vatikiotis-Bateson 2005). More likely, listeners require the combined motion of the head and face *and* their knowledge of the specific language prosody to align to the signal. We return to the question of perceiver alignment to production in section 9.3.3.

9.3.2 *Crucial orofacial landmarks are difficult to determine (almost anything works)*

When Yehia and colleagues originally calculated the multivariate correspondences within and across measurement domains (Vatikiotis-Bateson and Yehia 1996a; Yehia et al. 1998; Yehia et al. 1999, 2002), their concern was first to get high-resolution spatiotemporal measures for as many physiological channels as possible, especially for the face and head. Once obtained, they used filtering and dimensionality reduction techniques, such as principal component analysis (PCA), to optimize the complexity of the data. This approach made sense at the time, because speech-related signals had never been examined this way before. There was also a craze, encouraged by new technology for acquiring high-resolution signals in abundance, for oversampling time-varying spatiotemporal data. In the end, this work established that cross-domain estimations between vocal-tract articulation, face and head motion, and acoustics are temporally fitted to the rate of opening and closing the vocal tract (under 9 Hz), and that the within-domain spatial complexity can be reduced to five or six orthogonally independent components for vocal tract and orofacial motion and 10 components for the spectral acoustics (plus two more for F0 and amplitude).

The reduction in complexity to five or six components for vocal-tract and orofacial motion is consistent with the finding discussed in section 9.2.3 above that perceivers require very little detail in the visual stream to enhance utterance intelligibility. The low dimensionality of visual speech information coupled with the finding that linguistically relevant information appears to be distributed all over the face led Barbosa and colleagues to conduct a more careful consideration of what needs to be measured and where. In a series of studies beginning with his PhD thesis, Barbosa showed that 2D measures were just as good as 3D measures for within- and cross-domain analysis (Barbosa 2004). This finding facilitated the transition from tethered marker or difficult-to-calibrate passive marker systems to physically non-invasive, video-based recovery of visible 2D motion (Barbosa and Vatikiotis-Bateson 2006; Barbosa et al. 2006; Barbosa, Yehia, and Vatikiotis-Bateson 2003). These studies varied the number, placement, and physical characteristics (e.g., size, color, whether painted or pasted on) of markers and tested different algorithms for marker tracking.

Finally, we compared markerless motion measures derived from video using Horn and Schunk's (1981) optical flow algorithm with those obtained using marker-based systems. Although it seemed absurd at first, test after test showed that most analyses spanning multiple measurement domains, in which the correspondence between domains is the primary interest, can be carried out with little or no change in outcome using only one ROI for the entire head and face. Specifically, there is almost no difference in estimation power between measuring 25 individual markers on the face and head, and summing the changes of pixel intensity, converted by optical flow analysis to changes of position (i.e., velocities) between one image frame and the next, into one time-series of all the motion within an ROI (Barbosa et al. 2008). Even though many analyses are improved by keeping the horizontal (x) and vertical (y) components of the optical flow distinct, analyses focused on computing continuous correspondence with other measured behaviors do equally well or better by conflating the x and y components to one, time-varying, Euclidean amplitude (Barbosa et al. 2012).

By way of contrast, consider the work done in the 1970s and 1980s by Paul Ekman and others leading to the Facial Action Coding System (FACS: Ekman and Friesen 1978). The aim of that work was not to model an individual's time-varying behavior across a range of speaking contexts via analysis of image sequences; rather the aim was to establish consistent locations and number of landmarks across sets of isolated images for different people expressing specially concocted emotions such as happiness, sadness, and anger (Ekman 1989; Ekman and Friesen 1978; Ekman, Friesen, and Ellsworth 1972). In the 1990s, the Institute of Electrical and Electronics Engineers (IEEE), and other international bodies concerned with developing standards for digital video, finally settled on a set of nearly 70 facial landmarks taken from FACS to incorporate into MPEG-4, currently the prevalent video compression format used in science, technology, and commercial applications, including mesh-based animations (e.g., Tekalp and Ostermann 2000). Although industrial MPEG-4 animations tend not to receive rigorous perceptual evaluations of the sort applied to the talking head animation system developed by

Kuratate and colleagues (2005, 1998), the low dimensionality and the demonstrated low spatial and temporal resolution required for most multimodal analyses and particularly multisensory perception suggest that the FACS codes of MPEG-4 are more than sufficient, possibly even excessive, for most research applications.

9.3.3 The temporal distribution of linguistically relevant audiovisual information

Almost anyone who has studied speech phenomena that straddle the boundary between phonetics and phonology has heard of anticipatory and carryover coarticulation in which some attribute such as nasalization of stop consonants, /m, n, ŋ/, or rounding of high back vowels, /u, o/ in English, is observable for some amount of time before and/or after the presumed production of the associated phoneme. That is, whether the velar port, connecting the oral and nasal cavities is open or closed does not interfere with the identification of other phonemes that have no nasal counterpart (e.g., Bell-Berti et al. 1979). Similarly, lip rounding, which has been treated as a secondary feature for English vowels classified as high and back, does not interfere with the production of most other consonants and vowels (e.g., Bell-Berti and Harris 1982). In both of these examples, the audible and visible (if there are any) components of the production co-occur continuously before, during, and possibly after their supposed phonemic moment.

A quite different example of temporal distribution involves a temporal dislocation of the acoustic consequences from the articulation that produces them; that is, in many contexts and languages, plosive stops such as /p, t, k, b, d, g/ have no acoustic realization during the articulation of the consonant and are audible only after stop release during the transition to the onset of the vowel and possibly during the transition from a preceding vowel into the stop closure (Catford 1977). From the perspective of audiovisual production and perception, this becomes quite interesting because the temporal dislocation between the visible articulation of a bilabial plosive, /p, b/, and its auditory consequence is roughly 150–200 ms (Abry, Lallouache, and Cathiard 1996; Cathiard, Lallouache, and Abry 1996). In other words, perceivers must align with multimodal signal components displaced substantially in time.

Munhall and colleagues (Munhall et al. 1996; Munhall and Tohkura 1998) examined a version of the temporal alignment problem using McGurk effect stimuli (McGurk and MacDonald 1976). The McGurk effect, also known as the "fusion illusion," pertains to the mandatory integration of mismatched visual and auditory speech stimuli, resulting in a percept different from either of the original stimuli. Munhall and colleagues showed that perceivers could fuse auditory /ba/ and visual /ga/ stimuli to perceive something like [da] across substantial temporal dislocations. Interestingly, the tolerance for temporal dislocation was much greater when the audible component followed the visible component. This asymmetry accommodates the increased temporal displacement that occurs when perceivers are further away from a sound source. It also fits the causal sequence of a physical (e.g., vocal tract) event having acoustic consequences, rather than the other way around: just as we do not expect thunder to precede lightning, we do not expect sound to precede movement.

Another way to consider the temporal distribution of audiovisual events is that the distributed presentation of related and/or redundant events facilitates perception by providing perceivers a better opportunity to align to the multisensory stream. This is what we proposed in section 9.3.1 for the prosodic role of head motion. Because related and/or redundant event streams are primarily a consequence of how the physical system is organized and behaves, there is no guarantee that perceivers will, in fact, develop or commit the cognitive resources needed to take full advantage of the opportunity these time-varying events provide. As a preliminary test of the potential mismatch between production events and perception, several students designed an audiovisual production and perception study to test the extent to which /p, b, m/ can be distinguished via computational analysis of the visible face and head motion, even if not perceptually (Abel et al. 2011). The three bilabial stops form the classic labial viseme in which the component sounds are not visually distinguishable (Woodward and Barber 1960). In earlier work, the high confusability of these stops was tested on static key frames, rather than on image sequences (for overview, see Bruce and Young 1986); but the student study showed that viseme-internal differences cannot be perceived even when presented in short image sequences excised either from nonsense VCV sequences (e.g., aba, ama, apa) or from different positions in sentential utterances such as, "it was the sabby/sammy/sappy that went to the store." This is not to say that perceivers are entirely insensitive to differences between the bilabial stops. Most subjects in the student study had more difficulty correctly identifying the visibly and audibly most neutral /b/ productions than one or both of the other two labials. This response bias suggests a kind of viseme-internal discrimination that is simply too weak to reliably differentiate the bilabial stops.

The story is quite different when the production data are considered. Applying optical flow analysis (Barbosa et al. 2008; Horn and Schunk 1981) to a single ROI that encompassed the entire head and face showed reliable differences in the time course and amplitude of motion within the ROI associated with the three labial stops. Similar to the temporal distribution of nasality discussed previously, stop-specific differences in visible motion spanned substantial stretches of signal that included, for example, the transitions from the vowel preceding the word, sabby, into the initial /s/, from the /s/ to /ae/, from the /ae/ to /b/, and from /b/ to /i/. These differences were reliable for both talkers and confirmed the much earlier observation that the voicing of a final obstruent in simple CVCs such as [baeb] and [baep] influences the kinematics of both the CV and VC transitions (Kelso et al. 1984; Vatikiotis-Bateson and Kelso 1984).

In sum, this study provides a clear example of perceivers not being able to exploit differences contained within the production data. That is, the perception results confirmed the visual confusability expected of the three stops comprising the labial viseme, even though the head and face motion contained measurable, temporally distributed differences associated with the three labial stops. On a happier note, these results demonstrate that, despite the inability of human perceivers to distinguish the visible differences between labial stops, a machine recognition system would have no trouble.

9.4 Recommendations for future studies

In the 20 years that we have been involved with audiovisual speech research, we have had some remarkable success that just scratches the surface of our original question about what the visual channel contributes to speech perception. Our results certainly have raised many more questions than we are likely to answer in what remains of our careers. Rather than try to enumerate these as a shopping list, we describe several broad lines of inquiry that we believe could greatly increase our understanding of auditory-visual speech processing. Rigorous future research is needed to

- attain a better understanding of the role of redundancy in both the production and perception of speech,
- take a much closer look at brain function during audiovisual speech perception,
- assess the role of spatiotemporal coordination in the production and perception of audiovisual speech.

9.4.1 Redundancy in AVSP

Redundancy is essential to the successful operation of many systems, both natural and artificial. Vertebrates are equipped bilaterally with pairs of limbs, sensory organs, two brain hemispheres, along with pairs of some other internal organs (lungs, kidneys, etc.). Artificial systems, in which the consequences of system failure are deemed unacceptable, such as the flight controls that keep airplanes in the air, are replicated – many times in the case of commercial aircraft – with independent systems that can be called into service when a primary system fails. Yet, in science, systems are modeled by specifying the smallest number of parameters needed to characterize or simulate the system's structure and/or observed behavior. What gives? Why is it that in many branches of scientific inquiry, optimization is synonymous with maximum parsimony, and the modeling process incorporates greater complexity only when it is demonstrably necessary?

Language research has suffered from this minimalist approach to optimization. For example, phonemics, whose business in the first half of the twentieth century was to describe and classify the sounds of a language, relied heavily on establishing the set of linguistically contrastive elements, or phonemes, whose descriptions included two types of feature sets: *distinctive* features which contributed to distinguishing one phoneme from all others, and *descriptive* features which collated all of a phoneme's known attributes (Jakobson, Fant, and Halle 1951/1963). By the time Chomsky and Halle's *Sound Pattern of English* was published (1968), descriptive features were beginning to be called redundant features with the negative implication that they were not needed for linguistic analysis, and certainly not for specifying the paradigmatic contrasts within a particular phoneme inventory (for the cybernetic/information theoretic precursor to this formalization, see Ashby 1956). In contrast, a vast amount of speech research has focused on discovering the why and how of sounds interacting syntagmatically – in the speech stream as it unfolds in time. Indeed, without recognizing it as such, much of the research on speech synthesis and recognition, where coarticulation and other processes such as dissimilation span multiple segments, has had to depend at least as much on the descriptive attributes of sounds as on their contrastive features.

In audiovisual speech research, determining what is redundant in the acoustic and visible signal streams has never been systematically investigated. In large part, this has to do with the difference of perspective distinguishing production and perception research. As one would expect, most research proceeds from an observation of behavior to questions about how the behavior came about and what effects it has on other behavior. In other words, the initial perspective is perceptual. In spoken language, there is another important bias, namely, that speech is primarily an acoustic/auditory phenomenon. There is no question that whatever contribution is made by the visual channel, it is secondary to that of the auditory stream. Early recognition that there might be useful visual information most certainly arose in contexts of hearing deficits and situations where environmental noise masked speech acoustics. It is then not surprising that early audiovisual research by Quentin Summerfield treated the visual stream as a source of information that complemented the more fragile aspects of the acoustics, such as rapid transitions in higher frequency acoustics and their relation to visible changes in vocal tract configuration. Initially, Summerfield (1979) proposed that the complementarity of different sensory channels might be orchestrated cognitively, but he backed away from this view later (Summerfield 1987). The definition and status of complementarity in audiovisual perception has evolved along lines more amenable to the research described in this chapter (e.g., Grant and Seitz 2000).

The work by Yehia and colleagues, discussed earlier, exploring the correspondences between the various audible and visible signal domains was by definition largely dependent on redundancy between the domains. That the motion of the head and face can be used to synthesize more or less intelligible speech acoustics, and the acoustics can be used to synthesize very accurate head and face motion, leaves little doubt about the importance of redundancy in audiovisual production. Furthermore, we know that much of the audiovisual correspondence stems from a common source – vocal tract articulation. The other major sources of redundancy are due to the functional coupling of the head to vocalization, which is itself not entirely decoupled from the vocal tract dynamics despite the mathematically convenient fantasy about the independence of the vocal *source* at the larynx and the vocal tract *filter* (Fant 1960).

Indeed, in speech production, complementarity implies *uncorrelated* signal components, but this simply has not been examined. Similarly, in speech perception, complementarity arising from redundant multimodal production of the sort discussed here needs to be distinguished from complementarity created by selectively attending to and combining otherwise unrelated signal events. Doing so might, for example, better inform us about the processes underlying various phonetic and non-phonetic forms of convergence and divergence that occur as a result of speaker interaction (e.g., Kim, Horton, and Bradlow 2011; Pardo 2006).

9.4.2 Brain function and AVSP

In the late 1990s, we began to look more closely at the perception side of auditory-visual speech processing. Callan and colleagues (2002, 2004) designed one of the first series of studies examining brain behavior during audiovisual speech perception. Using electroencephalography (EEG) and functional magnetic resonance imaging (fMRI), these studies established a linkage between motor activation and multisensory perception (Callan et al. 2002) and delivered early evidence that visible speech activates auditory areas even when presented without an acoustic signal, while the reverse – activation of visual signals from only auditory stimulation – does not occur (Callan et al. 2004).

A possible interpretation of these findings harkens back to our earlier discussion of the role of visual speech information in speech perception, the notion that the auditory stream is primary, and to the body of evidence our extended group has collected showing how minimal the requirements are for visual enhancement of speech intelligibility to occur. Specifically, the primary function of visual speech information may be to increase the sensitivity of the auditory system. Perhaps coincidentally, it is commonly observed that, when a speaker suddenly becomes visible during a noisy acoustic presentation, the speech signal is perceived to suddenly become louder and clearer. Whether or not such observations are related to somewhat nebulous differences in the activation of the auditory system, the possibility that visual speech information boosts the gain of the auditory system deserves closer attention. Doing so would not only tie together many of the loose ends in our research, as discussed in this chapter, but would also put an entirely different perspective on other longstanding issues, such as the relevance of auditory-visual integration in speech processing (e.g., Massaro and Cohen 1983; Robert-Ribes, Schwartz, and Escudier 1995).

9.4.3 Spatiotemporal coordination in audiovisual speech

An underlying theme of this chapter has been a general concern about how spatial and temporal coordination operates at various levels of observation within and between individuals during communicative interaction. Our discussion in sections 9.3.1 and 9.3.3 about how perceivers must first align with multimodal signals in order to actually retrieve relevant speech information is but one piece of this concern. Another issue is how perceivers, who are also typically producers of the languages they perceive, manage the re-characterization of event timing at different levels of observation. For example, if we accept for a moment the multi-tiered orchestration of articulatory events proposed by Articulatory Phonology, the timing of gestural scores is clearly quite different from the temporal scheme of the subsequent acoustic signal. Aided by literacy (and perhaps some linguistic training), we readily discern a much more linear stream of events, consisting of modulated rises and falls in acoustic amplitude coinciding generally with opening and closing the vocal tract, which in turn signal syllable nuclei, different manners of consonant production, and the like.

Our own work on multimodal speech production readily coincides with the gestural score approach outlined by Articulatory Phonology. We have demonstrated that the strong correspondences between vocal tract, orofacial, and acoustic signals described in section 9.2.1 capture at least some of what is needed to bridge between production and perception. In particular, we have synthesized fairly complex and appropriate acoustics from the motion signals of the face and head, and have done an even better job in the other direction, from acoustics to visible motion, due to the greater richness of the measured acoustic signal compared to the motion signals being estimated (for discussion, see Yehia et al. 2002). However, these analyses are computational and driven entirely by time-varying signals; they do not involve phonemes or any other construct hypothesized to be associated with linguistically tuned perception. From the computational perspective, this is probably a good thing. Recent advances in machine recognition of continuous speech using deep belief networks (Hinton, Osindero, and Teh 2006) have outperformed phoneme-constrained approaches to automatic speech recognition (ASR) that combine phoneme-aligned Hidden Markov Models (HMMs) and Gaussian Mixture Models (GMMs).

Despite the success of the various signal-based computational approaches in bridging between measurement domains without having to rely on constructs such as phonemes, we worry that the organization and timing of multimodal events is not only physical, but also cognitive; as is perception. Multisensory perception suggests sensitivity in the visual domain to the multi-tiered timing of the jaw, lips, head, and even changes in intra-oral air pressure. Even though the subsequent acoustic signal is related to articulatory behavior in a straightforward, if somewhat complex way, the acoustics may activate a different temporal structure in the auditory system. If so, how are these different timing regimes managed? We think this will be a difficult question to answer until more is known about the nature of and connection between physical and cognitive constraints on production and perception.

Because biological systems are anything but efficient and parsimoniously given to singular descriptions, it may be that there is no formalizable connection between the physical and cognitive aspects of speech processing. This could partially explain why perception does not always fully exploit the output of production. Unlike the iterative algorithm in a computational analysis that can take as long as it needs to process a speech event, the perceptual system has one shot at a unique signal perceived in a unique context. Cognition is notoriously efficient at making error-prone predictions about novel events. The work of Abel et al. (2011) shows clearly that there are reliable differences in the production of the different English labial stops that are distributed over relatively long temporal spans, but also that perceivers cannot quite grasp these differences, at least not to the point of pushing the correct button key during an experiment. Of course, there may be other extenuating factors that need to be examined; for example, the tipping point for successful detection may be how familiar the talker is to the perceiver. If the perceiver has prior experience, analogous to the iteratively applied computational algorithm, the perceptual system may do a much better job of aligning to and processing novel instances. Another factor may be that idiosyncratic differences in production are more or less easily parsed by perceivers who are themselves representative of both production and perception asymmetries. It is well known that some talkers produce more readily intelligible speech than others, but we do not yet know what makes one talker more intelligible than another.

9.5 Conclusion

In this chapter we have presented an overview of research on auditory-visual speech processing with which we have been directly involved for the last 20 years. We attempted to identify questions that are either raised by the research and/or must be addressed to clarify the interpretation of results. The findings discussed in section 9.2 are ones about which we are fairly confident because they have proven to be readily replicable and depend little, if at all, on the persistence of any particular theoretical perspective. The studies discussed in section 9.3 are ones that have produced provocative results whose interpretations more actively demand further exploration of questions, such as those raised in section 9.4. More specifically, the past 20 years have seen a general acceptance of the notion that the analysis of spoken communication, like any behavior, must acknowledge that much of its structure is context-specific and variable in time. In this chapter, we push one step further by proposing that production and perception may interface with the same dynamical system, but they do so differently, and that this difference needs to be understood before we can make pronouncements about, for example, the visual contribution to speech intelligibility in noisy acoustics.

NOTES

1   The work reported here was supported primarily by ATR International (Japan) and secondarily by Canadian Tri-Council grants from the Social Sciences and Humanities Research Council (SSHRC) and the National Science and Engineering Research Council (NSERC), the Canada Research Chairs program, and the Canada Foundation for Innovation (CFI). Many students and colleagues have contributed substantially and generously to this research program through the years, too many to list here, but particular thanks goes to the late Yoh'ichi Tohkura, without whose vision and support this research would never have been undertaken.
2   The Optotrak (NDI, Inc.) measures position changes accurately at 0.1 mm, well within the resolution range of the structured light measurement techniques used by Carter et al. (1996) to correlate facial deformation with intraoral air pressure.

3   The three-dimensional motion of rigid objects such as the head or skeletal segments (e.g., arms and legs) consists of six geometric degrees of freedom: three translations defining position and three rotations defining orientation; that is, one translation and one rotation for each of the three Cartesian axes. Unlike deformable objects such as the tongue or lips, the position and orientation of any point on the object has a fixed relation to the position and orientation of every other point on the object; so the entire object can be treated as a single six-dimensional point. For greater detail, see Vatikiotis-Bateson and Ostry (1995).

4   Velocity = distance / time. Therefore, doubling the motion amplitude for the same time period, doubles the speed (velocity) of motion as well.

REFERENCES

Abel, Jennifer, Adriano V. Barbosa, Alexis Black, Connor Mayer, and Eric Vatikiotis-Bateson. 2011. The labial viseme reconsidered: Evidence from production and perception. In Y. Laprie and I. Steiner (eds.), *9th International Seminar on Speech Production (ISSP)*, 337–344. CD-ROM.

Abry, Christian, Mohamed-Tahar Lallouache, and Marie-Agnes Cathiard. 1996. How can coarticulation models account for speech sensitivity to audio-visual desynchronization? In D. Stork and M. Hennecke (eds.), *Speechreading by Humans and Machines*, vol. 150, 247–256. Berlin: Springer-Verlag.

Ashby, W. Ross. 1956. *An Introduction to Cybernetics*. London: Chapman and Hall.

Barbosa, Adriano V. 2004. A study on the relations between audible and visible speech. PhD dissertation, Federal University of Minas Gerais, Belo Horizonte, Brazil.

Barbosa, Adriano V. and Eric Vatikiotis-Bateson. 2006. Video tracking of 2D face motion during speech. In F. Gebali and R. Ward (eds.), *IEEE Symposium of Signal Processing and Information Technology – ISSPIT 2006*, 1–6. Vancouver: IEEE.

Barbosa, Adriano V., Hani C. Yehia, and Eric Vatikiotis-Bateson. 2003. Modeling the relation between speech acoustics and 3D face motion. *Technical Report of the Institute of Electronics, Information, and Communication Engineers* 102(735): 13–18.

Barbosa, Adriano V., Hani C. Yehia, and Eric Vatikiotis-Bateson. 2008. Linguistically valid movement behavior measured non-invasively. In R. Goecke, P. Lucey, and S. Lucey (eds.), *Proceedings of the International Conference on Auditory-Visual Speech Processing 2008*, 173–177.

Barbosa, Adriano V., Rose-Marie Dechaine, Eric Vatikiotis-Bateson, and Hani C. Yehia. 2012. Quantifying time-varying coordination of multimodal speech signals using correlation map analysis. *Journal of the Acoustical Society of America* 131(3): 2162–2172.

Barbosa, Adriano V., Hani C. Yehia, Philip Rubin, and Eric Vatikiotis-Bateson. 2006. Relating the audible and visible components of speech. In H.C. Yehia, D. Demolin, and R. Laboissière (eds.), *Proceedings of the 7th International Seminar on Speech Production – ISSP 2006*, 119–126.

Bell-Berti, Fredericka and Katherine S. Harris. 1982. Temporal patterns of coarticulation: Lip rounding. *Journal of the Acoustical Society of America* 71: 449–454.

Bell-Berti, Fredericka, Thomas Baer, Katherine S. Harris, and Seiji Niimi. 1979. Coarticulatory effects of vowel quality on velar elevation. *Phonetica* 36: 187–193.

Browman, Catherine P. and Louis Goldstein. 1986. Towards an articulatory phonology. *Phonology Yearbook* 3: 219–252.

Bruce, Vicki and Andy W. Young. 1986. Understanding face recognition. *British Journal of Psychology* 77: 305–327.

Callan, Daniel E., Jeffrey A. Jones, Kevin Munhall, Akiko M. Callan, Christian Kroos, and Eric Vatikiotis-Bateson. 2004. Neural processes underlying perceptual enhancement by visual speech gestures. *NeuroReport* 14(17): 2213–2218.

Callan, Daniel E., Jeffrey A. Jones, Kevin G. Munhall, Christian Kroos, Akiko M. Callan, and Eric Vatikiotis-Bateson. 2002. Mirror neuron system activity and audiovisual speech perception. Paper presented at the Eighth International Conference on Functional Mapping of the Human Brain, Sendai, Japan.

Carpenter, Roger H.S. 1988. *Movement of the Eyes*, 2nd edn. London: Pion.

Carter, John N., Christine H. Shadle, and Colin J. Davies. 1996. On the use of structured light in speech research. Paper presented at the 1st ESCA Tutorial and Research Workshop on Speech Production Modeling: From Control Strategies to Acoustics and 4th Speech Production Seminar: Models and Data, Autrans, France.

Catford, John C. 1977. *Fundamental Problems in Phonetics*. Bloomington: Indiana University Press.

Cathiard, Marie-Agnes, Mohamed-Tahar Lallouache, and Christian Abry. 1996. Does movement on the lips mean movement in the mind? In D. Stork and M. Hennecke (eds.), *Speechreading by Humans and Machines*, vol. 150, 211–219. Berlin: Springer-Verlag.

Chomsky, Noam and Morris Halle. 1968. *The Sound Pattern of English*. New York: Harper and Row.

dePaula, Hugo, Hani C. Yehia, Douglas Shiller, Gregoire Jozan, Kevin G. Munhall, and Eric Vatikiotis-Bateson. 2003. Linking production and perception through spatial and temporal filtering of visible speech information. Paper presented at the Fifth International Seminar on Speech Production, ISSP5, Macquarie University, Australia.

dePaula, Hugo, Hani C. Yehia, Douglas Shiller, Gregoire Jozan, Kevin G. Munhall, and Eric Vatikiotis-Bateson. 2006. Analysis of audiovisual speech intelligibility based on spatial and temporal filtering of visual speech information. In J. Harrington and M. Tabain (eds.), *Speech Production: Models, Phonetic Processes, and Techniques*, 135–147. London: Psychology Press.

Eigsti, Inge-Marie, Eric Vatikiotis-Bateson, Sumio Yano, and Kevin G. Munhall. 1995. Effects of listener expectation on eye movement behavior during audiovisual perception. *Journal of the Acoustical Society of America* 97: 3286.

Ekman, Paul. 1989. The argument and evidence about universals in facial expressions of emotion. In H. Wagner and A. Monstead (eds.), *Handbook of Social Psychophysiology*, 143–146. Chichester: John Wiley & Sons Ltd.

Ekman, Paul and Wallace V. Friesen. 1978. *Manual for the Facial Action Coding System*. Palo Alto, CA: Consulting Psychologists Press.

Ekman, Paul, Wallace V. Friesen, and Phoebe Ellsworth. 1972. *Emotion in the Human Face: Guidelines for Research and a Review of Findings*. New York: Pergamon Press.

Ewan, William G. 1979. Can intrinsic vowel F0 be explained by source/tract coupling? *Journal of the Acoustical Society of America* 66: 358–362.

Fant, Gunnar. 1960. *Acoustic Theory of Speech Production*. The Hague: Mouton.

Grant, Ken W. and Philip F. Seitz. 2000. The use of visible speech cues for improving auditory detection of spoken sentences. *Journal of the Acoustical Society of America* 108: 1197–1208.

Hill, Harold and Eric Vatikiotis-Bateson. 2005. Using animations to investigate the perception of facial speech. Paper presented at the ATR Symposium of Cross-Modal Processing of Faces and Voices, ATR Human Information Science Labs, Japan.

Hinton, Geoffrey E., Simon Osindero, and Yee-Whye Teh. 2006. A fast learning algorithm for deep belief nets. *Neural Computation* 18: 1527–1554.

Horn, Berthold K.P. and Brian G. Schunk. 1981. Determining optical flow. *Artificial Intelligence* 17: 185–203.

Jakobson, Roman, Gunnar Fant, and Morris Halle. 1951/1963. *Preliminaries to Speech Analysis: The Distinctive Features and Their Correlates.* Cambridge, MA: MIT Press.

Katz, William F. and Peter F. Assmann. 2001. Identification of children's and adults' vowels: Intrinsic fundamental frequency, fundamental frequency dynamics, and presence of voicing. *Journal of Phonetics* 29(1): 23–51.

Kelso, J.A. Scott, Betty Tuller, Eric Vatikiotis-Bateson, and Carol A. Fowler. 1984. Functionally specific articulatory cooperation following jaw perturbations during speech: Evidence for coordinative structures. *Journal of Experimental Psychology: Human Perception and Performance* 10: 812–832.

Kim, Midam, William S. Horton, and Ann R. Bradlow. 2011. Phonetic convergence in spontaneous conversations as a function of interlocutor language distance. *Laboratory Phonology* 2(1): 125–156.

Kuratate, Takaaki, Eric Vatikiotis-Bateson, and Hana C. Yehia. 2005. Estimation and animation of faces using facial motion mapping and a 3D face database. In J.G. Clement and M.K. Marks (eds.), *Computer-Graphic Facial Reconstruction*, 325–346. Amsterdam: Academic Press.

Kuratate, Takaaki, Hana Yehia, and Eric Vatikiotis-Bateson. 1998. Kinematics-based synthesis of realistic talking faces. In D. Burnham, J. Robert-Ribes, and E. Vatikiotis-Bateson (eds.), *International Conference on Auditory-Visual Speech Processing 1998*, 185–190.

Massaro, Dominic W. and Michael M. Cohen. 1983. Evaluation and integration of visual and auditory information in speech perception. *Journal of Experimental Psychology: Human Perception and Performance* 9: 753–771.

McGurk, Harry and John MacDonald. 1976. Hearing lips and seeing voices. *Nature* 264: 746–748.

Munhall, Kevin G. and Yoh'ichi Tohkura. 1998. Audiovisual gating and the time course of speech perception. *Journal of the Acoustical Society of America* 104: 530–539.

Munhall, Kevin G. and Eric Vatikiotis-Bateson. 1998. The moving face during speech communication. In R. Campbell, B. Dodd, and D. Burnham (eds.), *Hearing by Eye II: Advances in the Psychology of Speechreading and Auditory-Visual Speech*, 123–139. Hove, UK: Psychology Press.

Munhall, Kevin G. and Eric Vatikiotis-Bateson. 2004. Spatial and temporal constraints on audiovisual speech perception. In G. Calvert, C. Spence, and B. Stein (eds.), *The Handbook of Multisensory Processes*, 177–188. Cambridge, MA: MIT Press.

Munhall, Kevin G., P. Gribble, L. Sacco, and M. Ward. 1996. Temporal constraints on the McGurk effect. *Perception and Psychophysics* 58(3): 351–362.

Munhall, Kevin G., Jeffrey A. Jones, Daniel E. Callan, Takaaki Kuratate, and Eric Vatikiotis-Bateson. 2004. Visual prosody and speech intelligibility: Head movement improves auditory speech perception. *Psychological Science* 15(2): 133–137.

Munhall, Kevin G., Gregoire Jozan, Christian Kroos, and Eric Vatikiotis-Bateson. 2004. Spatial frequency requirements for audiovisual speech perception. *Perception and Psychophysics* 66(4): 574–583.

Pardo, Jennifer S. 2006. On phonetic convergence during conversational interaction. *Journal of the Acoustical Society of America* 119(4): 2382–2393.

Perkell, Joseph S., Marc Cohen, Mario A. Svirsky, Melanie Matthies, Inaki Garabieta, and Michel Jackson. 1992.

Electromagnetic midsagittal articulometer (EMMA) systems for transducing speech articulatory movements. *Journal of the Acoustical Society of America* 92: 3078–3096.

Robert-Ribes, Jordi, Jean-Luc Schwartz, and Pierre Escudier. 1995. A comparison of models for fusion of the auditory and visual sensors in speech perception. *Artificial Intelligence Review* 9: 323–346.

Sumby, William H. and Irwin Pollack. 1954. Visual contribution to speech intelligibility in noise. *Journal of the Acoustical Society of America* 26: 212–215.

Summerfield, Quentin. 1979. Use of visual information for phonetic perception. *Phonetica* 36: 314–331.

Summerfield, Quentin. 1987. Some preliminaries to a comprehensive account of audiovisual speech perception. In B. Dodd and R. Campbell (eds.), *Hearing by Eye: The Psychology of Lipreading*, 3–52. Hillsdale, NJ: Lawrence Erlbaum Associates.

Tekalp, A. Murat and Joern Ostermann. 2000. Face and 2-D mesh animation in MPEG-4. *Signal Processing: Image Communication* 15(4–5): 387–421.

Trager, George L. 1958. Paralanguage: A first approximation. *Studies in Linguistics* 13: 1–13.

Vatikiotis-Bateson, Eric and J.A. Scott Kelso. 1984. Remote and autogenic articulatory adaptation to jaw perturbations during speech. *Journal of the Acoustical Society of America* 75: S23–24.

Vatikiotis-Bateson, Eric and Kevin G. Munhall. 2012a. Empirical perceptual-motor linkage of multimodal speech. In G. Bailly, P. Perrier, and E. Vatikiotis-Bateson (eds.), *Advances in Auditory and Visual Speech Perception*, 346–367. Cambridge: Cambridge University Press.

Vatikiotis-Bateson, Eric and Kevin G. Munhall. 2012b. Time-varying coordination in multisensory speech processing. In B. Stein (ed.), *The New Handbook of Multisensory Processing*, 421–434. Cambridge, MA: MIT Press.

Vatikiotis-Bateson, Eric and David J. Ostry. 1995. An analysis of the dimensionality of jaw motion in speech. *Journal of Phonetics* 23: 101–117.

Vatikiotis-Bateson, Eric and Hani C. Yehia. 1996a. Physiological modeling of facial motion during speech. *Transactions Technical Committee Psychological Physiological Acoustics* H-96-65: 1–8.

Vatikiotis-Bateson, Eric and Hani C. Yehia. 1996b. Synthesizing audiovisual speech from physiological signals. Paper presented at the Acoustical Society of America and Acoustical Society of Japan Third Joint Meeting, 2–6 December, 1996, Honolulu, HI.

Vatikiotis-Bateson, Eric, Inge-Marie Eigsti, and Sumio Yano. 1994. Listener eye movement behavior during audiovisual perception. Paper presented at the International Conference on Spoken Language Processing (ICSLP-94), Yokohama, Japan.

Vatikiotis-Bateson, Eric, Inge-Marie Eigsti, Sumio Yano, and Kevin G. Munhall. 1998. Eye movement of perceivers during audiovisual speech perception. *Perception and Psychophysics* 60(6): 926–940.

Vilkman, Erkki, Olli Aaltonen, Ilkka Raimo, Paula Arajärvi, and Hanna Oksanen. 1989. Articulatory hyoid-laryngeal changes vs. cricothyroid muscle activity in the control of intrinsic F0 of vowels. *Journal of Phonetics* 17: 193–203.

Vitkovich, Melanie and Paul Barber. 1994. Effects of video frame rate on subjects' ability to shadow one of two competing verbal passages. *Journal of Speech, Language, and Hearing Research* 37: 1204–1210.

Woodward, Mary F. and Carroll G. Barber. 1960. Phoneme perception in lipreading. *Journal of Speech and Hearing Research* 3: 212–222.

Yehia, Hani C., Takaaki Kuratate, and Eric Vatikiotis-Bateson. 1999. Using speech acoustics to drive facial motion.

Paper presented at the 14th International Congress of Phonetic Sciences, San Francisco, CA.

Yehia, Hani C., Takaaki Kuratate, and Eric Vatikiotis-Bateson. 2002. Linking facial animation, head motion, and speech acoustics. *Journal of Phonetics* 30(3): 555–568.

Yehia, Hani C., Philip E. Rubin, and Eric Vatikiotis-Bateson. 1998. Quantitative association of vocal-tract and facial behavior. *Speech Communication* 26: 23–44.

10 Multimodal Speech Production

LUCIE MÉNARD

In face-to-face conversation, speech is produced and perceived through various modalities. Movements of the lips, jaw, and tongue, for instance, modulate air pressure to produce a complex waveform perceived by the listener's ears. Visually salient articulatory movements (of the lips and jaw) also contribute to speech identification in acoustically degraded conditions (Sumby and Pollack 1954; Summerfield 1979) and in non-degraded conditions (Arnold and Hill 2001). The seminal McGurk effect (McGurk and MacDonald 1976) shows how high-level speech perception integrates auditory and visual features. This phenomenon occurs when a listener hears a stimulus such as /pa/ while watching a discordant visual stimulus such as /ka/. For most subjects, the resulting percept is a fusion of both modalities (i.e., /da/). Although many studies have been conducted on the role of visual components in speech perception, much less is known about their role in speech production. However, many studies have emphasized the important relationship between speech production and speech perception systems. If perceived visual and auditory cues are not independent but instead act in synergy and complement each other (Robert-Ribes et al. 1998), they must be involved in the speech production process. In this chapter, we explore the effects of auditory and visual feedback on speech production.[1]

10.1 The link between speech production and speech perception

During the last five decades, a large body of evidence has been found that supports the existence of a functional link between action and perception in speech (Galantucci, Fowler, and Turvey 2006). Many behavioral and neurophysiological studies have been conducted, and they can be grouped according to their primary

---

The Handbook of Speech Production, First Edition. Edited by Melissa A. Redford.
© 2015 John Wiley & Sons, Inc. Published 2019 by John Wiley & Sons, Inc.

focus: (1) how production mechanisms are involved in speech perception, or (2) how perception mechanisms are involved in speech production.

10.1.1 Speech production is involved in speech perception tasks

A first set of experiments explored how speech perception processes are influenced by production tasks. In the classical selective adaptation paradigm, Cooper, Billings, and Cole (1976) and Cooper, Blumstein, and Nigro (1975) asked speakers to produce reiterated syllables such as /pa/. When they were subsequently asked to identify similar syllables (e.g., /pa/) on a continuum, the participants perceived fewer ambiguous instances of this syllable. More recently, Sams, Mottonen, and Sihvonen (2005) studied the influence of participants' own articulation and observation of others' articulation on the perception of acoustic stimuli. Four conditions were tested: "audiovisual," "mirror," "articulation," and "control" conditions. In the audiovisual condition, participants had to identify /pa/ or /ka/ syllables presented auditorily and visually. Some stimuli were concordant (the auditorily presented syllable was similar to the visually presented syllable) and others were discordant, typical of the McGurk effect (the auditory syllable /pa/ was dubbed onto the visual syllable /ka/). This audiovisual condition was contrasted with a mirror condition in which participants had to identify the syllable while watching themselves in a mirror silently articulating a syllable (/pa/ or /ka/) in synchrony with the acoustic syllable that was transmitted through earphones. As in the audiovisual condition, for some tokens, the subjects articulated /ka/ while hearing /pa/. In the articulation condition, subjects performed a perceptual task similar to that in the mirror condition, but without watching themselves in a mirror. Lastly, the control condition involved performing a similar task, but without synchronously articulating a syllable. As expected, the results showed that the percent correct identification of /pa/ was altered by seeing a discordant /ka/ consonant. More importantly, in this study the observation of the participants' own articulation resulted in similar patterns to the ones while subjects were seeing others' articulation. Silently producing a /ka/ syllable while listening to a /pa/ syllable (mirror condition) deteriorated the perception of the syllable compared to the articulation condition. Thus, perception was significantly affected by the production system.

The strong linkages between motor and sensory systems have also been confirmed by the discovery of mirror neurons in the macaque's brain and its homologue in the human brain (as described in the review by Rizzolatti, Fogassi, and Gallese 2001). In the speech domain, mirror neurons found in the macaque ventral premotor cortex and the anterior inferior parietal lobule are a subset of neurons that fire both when producing a phonological unit and when passively watching or listening to the same unit (Kohler et al. 2002). Following the discovery of mirror neurons, many studies have shown how cortical circuits and areas activated during the production of speech gestures play a fundamental role in the perception of the same gestures. A detailed description of these studies is beyond the scope of this chapter. Representative results will be summarized here.

Cortical areas known to be involved in speech production tasks (the left inferior frontal gyrus, the ventral premotor cortex, and the primary motor cortex) have been found to be activated in speech perception (e.g., Pulvermuller et al. 2006; Skipper, Nusbaum, and Small 2005; Wilson and Iacoboni 2006). Studies using transcranial magnetic stimulation (TMS) have demonstrated that motor-evoked potentials related to the lips and tongue are enhanced during passive speech listening and viewing if the perceived stimuli involve the same articulators (e.g., Fadiga et al. 2002; Watkins, Strafella, and Paus 2003). Watkins et al. (2003) recorded electromyographic (EMG) activity of the lip muscle (orbicularis oris) under various perceptual conditions. Motor-evoked potentials (MEPs) in the lip muscle elicited by TMS were measured in four conditions: (1) listening to speech, (2) listening to non-verbal sounds, (3) viewing speech-related lip movements, and (4) viewing eye and brow movements. In all conditions, subjects were viewing (conditions 1 and 2) or listening to (conditions 3 and 4) white noise. It was found that the size of the MEPs in the speech perception conditions was significantly greater than in the non-speech perception conditions. Seeing or listening to speech enhanced excitability of the motor units involved in speech production. Focusing explicitly on a speaker's perception of his or her own speech, Curio et al. (2000) conducted a MEG study and observed a delay of the M100 response in the left hemisphere relative to the right hemisphere when a subject was repeating vowels, a pattern that was not observed when a subject listened to the vowels.

Skipper et al. (2005, 2007) found various patterns of activity in the frontal motor areas involved in speech production during the audiovisual perception of different syllables. Finding these patterns led to the development of a model of speech production in which multisensory representations are a key component, since they interact with phonetic identification. Mirror neurons allow the mapping of heard and observed speech articulation to abstract representations of action (motor commands) that would have been activated had the listener produced those actions. Those actions are then mapped to predicted (multi)sensory consequences, through forward mapping models. These internally generated sensory signals act as different hypotheses against which incoming sensory input is compared. Multisensory information thus constrains phonetic interpretation. When the discrepancy between the hypotheses and the incoming signal is too large (e.g., in a degraded speech condition), the motor system is recruited.

Skipper's model has to be distinguished from the motor theory of speech perception (Liberman 1957; Liberman and Mattingly 1985; Galantucci et al. 2006; Liberman and Whalen 2000) in which speech perception automatically involves speech gestures. The motor theory's general claim is that perceiving speech involves perceiving the intended articulatory gestures through specialized processes devoted to speech. This theory was developed in part to account for the fact that the acoustic signal is highly variable and thus cannot be invariantly related to speech goals. Related to the motor theory, the direct realism theory (Fowler 1986) states that gestures are recovered from speech, but no specialized modules are required. According to this view, the knowledge the speaker has of movement laws interacts with the perception of the same movement ("procedural knowledge of action," Viviani and Stucchi 1992). Gestural theorists claim that the role of visual cues (by which access to gestures is direct) in speech perception confirms the primacy of articulatory gestures.

In the speech production field, the view that primary invariant units are articulatory in nature is central to articulatory phonology (Browman and Goldstein 1989, 1992). According to this theoretical framework, vocal tract constriction actions can be decomposed into discrete units referred to as gestures. Those constrictions are formed by six articulators: lips, tongue tip, tongue body, tongue root, velum, and larynx. Gestures are represented by mass-spring dynamical systems, such as in the task dynamics model (Saltzman and Munhall 1989). A dynamic system is specified in terms of its target, stiffness, and damping. Thus, gestures are internally specified for movements. When two gestures are activated sequentially, differences in gestural parameterization, for instance, may give rise to overlapping movements of articulatory organs, referred to as coarticulation. Gestures are combined with each other into larger sequences by specifying phase relations. Specific parameters involved in gestural specification can be found in Browman and Goldstein (1990) and Saltzman and Byrd (2000).

10.1.2 Speech perception is involved in speech production tasks

Another set of experiments has explored the link between production and perception by measuring the effects of various perceptual tasks on speech production. Related to the activity of mirror neurons described earlier, imitation is an experimental paradigm revealing how speakers interact with perceived listeners to adjust their perceptuo-motor links. In the very first hours of life, humans imitate facial movements such as lip protrusion, tongue protrusion, and mouth opening (Meltzoff 2002; Meltzoff and Moore 1977). In an experiment aimed at investigating whether or not babies were using visual cues to imitate speech sounds, Legerstee (1990) presented 30 infants aged 3–4 months old with the sounds /a/ and /u/. For one half of the group, the vowels were dubbed onto the face of an adult uttering the same sounds (matched condition). For the other half, the vowel sounds were dubbed onto the face of an adult uttering the opposite vowel (mismatched condition). Results revealed that infants produced significantly more /a/-like and /u/-like vowels in the matched condition than in the mismatched condition. Thus, perceived auditory and visual cues are used to produce vowel-like sounds early in life. In adults, Gentilucci and Bernardis (2007) investigated how lip kinematics and voice spectra of participants uttering phoneme strings are affected by seeing a face or hearing a voice utter the same phonemes. They found that the participants' lip closures and lip apertures changed to match those that were visually presented by actors. These results suggest that there is a direct link between the production of a speech gesture (lip movement) and its visual perception.

From a different, but somewhat related, perspective, perturbation experiments have helped elucidate the role of feedback in speech production. Using artificial perturbations, such as bite-blocks inserted between the teeth or a lip tube inserted between the lips, movements of the jaw or the lips, respectively, were blocked during the production of various phonemes (Gay, Lindblom, and Lubker 1981; Savariaux, Perrier, and Orliaguet 1995; Savariaux et al. 1999; Ménard et al. 2008). It was shown that speakers changed their articulatory strategies to adapt to the new perturbed conditions. Based on auditory feedback of their own production, the speakers developed new perceptuo-motor links to produce acoustic-auditory goals typical of the non-perturbed sound. Similar findings were revealed in experiments using structural modifications of the vocal tract, such as artificial palates (Thibeault et al. 2011; Aasland, Baum, and McFarland 2006; McFarland, Baum, and Chabot 1996). Speakers also adapted to perturbation of their own auditory feedback, in sensorimotor-adaptation experiments (Houde and Jordan 2002; Jones and Munhall 2005; Shiller et al. 2009). Villacorta, Perkell, and Guenther (2007) even showed that a speaker's ability to adapt is related to his or her perceptual acuity; speakers with better discrimination acuity showed better compensation in sound production. Together, these studies emphasize the primacy of auditory-acoustic targets over articulatory gestures.

The above-mentioned experimental data led researchers to propose purely auditory theories of speech perception (Diehl, Lotto, and Holt 2004). In contrast with the motor theory of speech perception, auditory theories postulate that perceiving speech does not involve articulatory gestures, but rather involves invariant auditory or multisensory representations. The speech goals would consist of regions within an auditory-perceptual space. The exact nature of this space is, however, controversial. It has been claimed that perceptual goals can explain the covariance of different production strategies, to enhance auditory distinctiveness (Lotto, Holt, and Kluender 1997).

Building on a similar view, auditory-based theoretical frameworks of speech production have been proposed, in part to account for the motor equivalence phenomenon, according to which different articulatory gestures are related to a given perceptuo-acoustic pattern. If different articulatory gestures are related to the perception of a similar phonetic category, invariant parameters associated with phonemes are not articulatory gestures but rather are auditory parameters. According to this sensory-based view (Perkell et al. 2000), speech goals related to phonemic units are multidimensional regions in auditory and somatosensory spaces. Articulatory movements produced to reach these goals are controlled through feedback and feedforward control mechanisms. Auditory feedback is used during the speech acquisition period to acquire these goals and during adulthood to maintain them. In adults, feedforward commands are activated to control speech production. Feedback control mechanisms are recruited to correct for mismatches between expected and produced multisensory consequences. Perkell's theory has been formalized within a neural computational model of speech production (Guenther, Ghosh, and Tourville 2006), the directions into velocities of articulators (DIVA) model. This model has provided a fruitful framework for testing hypotheses in speech development and hearing deprivation. To support this view, several lines of evidence have been found in favor of a close link between a speaker's own production and perception of sounds. For instance, Fox (1982) showed that speakers' auditory perception scores were correlated with their produced formant values for cardinal vowels. Similar correlations between subjects' perceptual scores and produced formants or articulatory dimensions were found for other speech sounds (Bell-Berti et al. 1979; Frieda et al. 2000; Newman 2003). More recently, from the perspective of an auditory-based theory of speech motor control, Perkell and colleagues have addressed the issue of the relationships between sensory acuity and produced speech contrasts. A first study (Perkell, Guenther, et al. 2004) was conducted on the /ɑ/–/ʌ/ and /u/–/ʊ/ contrasts produced by 19 American English speakers. The authors' main hypothesis was that speakers who produce greater contrasts between vowels in both pairs are those who have higher auditory perceptual acuity. In the production domain, vowel contrast was calculated as the Euclidean distances between vowels, in the F1 versus F2 space (in mels) and in the tongue position articulatory space. Perceptual acuity corresponded to the peak discrimination score of an ABX discrimination task of a continuum of synthetic vowels. The results confirmed the hypothesis, in that speakers with higher peak discrimination scores produced vowels with greater contrasts (in both articulatory and acoustic spaces). A similar relationship was found for the /s/ versus /ʃ/ contrast (Perkell, Matthies, et al. 2004; Ghosh et al. 2010). Together, those studies point to the important role of perceptual processes in speech production.

Another theory, the perception for action control theory (PACT: Schwartz et al. 2012), posits that perceptual processes and procedural knowledge of speech actions are both involved in the planning and recovering of speech units. According to PACT, speech goals correspond to multisensory perceptuo-motor units. In the course of speech development, perception and action are tightly linked, and speech perception necessarily involves procedural knowledge of the speech production mechanisms. Furthermore, perceptual mechanisms provide gestures with auditory, visual, and somatosensory templates that guide and maintain their development.

10.2 Speech production in sensory deprived conditions

The previous section demonstrated how multimodal speech production and perception are tightly linked to each other. In the present section, we describe how speech production mechanisms are affected when perceptual processes are altered, such as in sensory-deprived conditions (deafness and blindness). For the sake of clarity and conciseness, summaries of results from a subset of studies are presented.

Since produced phonemes are also perceived through multimodal cues (including auditory and visual cues), examining speech production when one modality is missing requires a description of the nature of those auditory and visual cues. Which phonemic contrasts can be recovered from the auditory channel, and which ones can be recovered from the visual channel? Figure 10.1 provides a schematized view of three vowel features (height, place of articulation, and

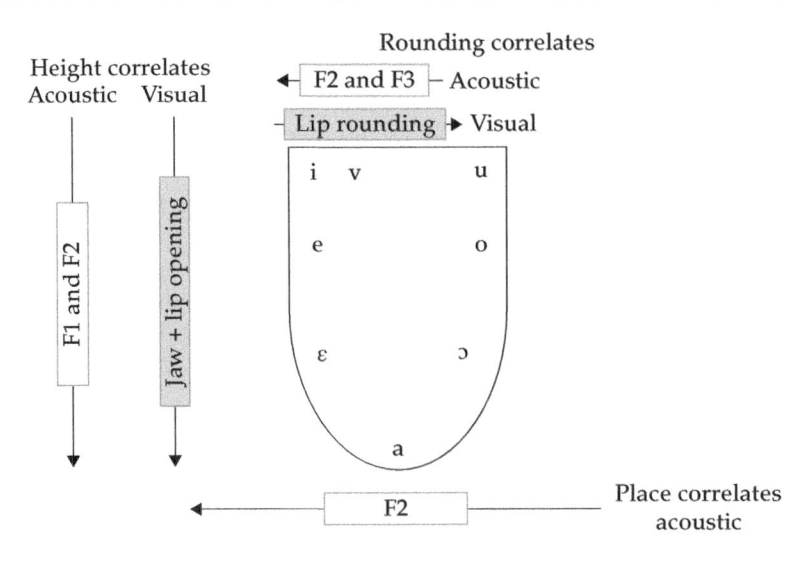

Figure 10.1 Acoustic and visual correlates of vowel features of height, place of articulation, and rounding.

rounding), with their corresponding acoustic and visual correlates. Note that we focus here on the lower part of the speaker's face (lips and jaw). Munhall and Vatikiotis-Bateson (1998) have shown that other visual cues (such as eyebrows) can be involved in speech perception.

As can be seen from Figure 10.1, producing rounding contrasts (involving the lips) is more visible than producing place-of-articulation contrasts (involving the tongue). Regarding the height dimension, however, various gestures can be recruited to achieve specific contrasts, in complementary ways (Maeda 1990; Perkell et al. 1993; Perkell and Nelson 1985). For instance, contrasts between high and low vowels can be implemented mainly through variations in jaw positions, the tongue being passively carried. In contrast, jaw position can remain relatively stable while the tongue is actively elevated or depressed. These articulatory maneuvers yield various visual effects, jaw movement being visible while tongue movement is not (apart from tongue tip displacements, partially visible when the mouth is opened). The strength of their visible correlates thus varies according to the contributions of the lips and the jaw.

In the auditory channel, mandatory for the acquisition of speech, height contrasts are mainly related to F1, whereas place-of-articulation contrasts are mainly related to F2. Rounding is associated with F2 and F3. Note that due to biomechanical links between the jaw and the tongue, for very open vowels, front-back contrasts of the tongue are limited, and thus, front and back vowels are more centralized than they are for high vowels (trapezoid shape of the vowel system). As a result, open vowels involve more F1 and F2 changes compared to high vowels.

Formant values are, however, largely dependent on each speaker's vocal tract length. To account for the important between-speaker variability, normalization

Table 10.1 Auditory and visual robustness to noise for French vowel features (summary of Robert-Ribes et al. 1998).

	less robust		more robust
Auditory channel	rounding	place of articulation	height
Visual channel	place of articulation	height	rounding

experiments have been conducted to find combinations of acoustic cues that would act as invariant parameters related to phonological features. These studies have been conducted within auditory-based accounts of speech perception. The proposed acoustic dimensions usually correspond to linear combinations of spectral peaks and F0 (Ménard et al. 2002; Traunmüller 1981; Syrdal and Gopal 1986; Hoemeke and Diehl 1994; Fant 1983). In French, for instance, Ménard et al. (2002) have proposed that height contrasts are related to the value of F1-F0, in bark. Perceived place of articulation correspond to F2-F1 (in bark), whereas perceived rounding is related to F2', a weighted sum of F2, F3, and F4. Those parameters can in turn be interpreted as constraints in the production domain. Regarding English vowel normalization, Syrdal and Gopal (1986) interpreted their boundaries as limits within which formants can be spaced from each other, thus limiting production variability. In producing a high front rounded vowel, for instance, the speaker's task would consist of producing formant and F0 values in appropriate regions of the vowel space, such that phonemic targets are reached.

These produced multimodal correlates are relevant in speech perception. Robert-Ribes et al. (1998) investigated the contribution of auditory and visual information in the identification of French vowels. Analyses aimed to identify which phonological features were best transmitted through each channel. Based on perceivers' percent correct identification of vowels in various signal-to-noise ratios, a multimodal robustness scale of vocal features was proposed, as shown in Table 10.1. The table reveals that audition and vision are complementary: some vocal features are more robust in one modality, but less so in the other modality. In acoustic-auditory terms, height and place of articulation are more easily identified in noise than rounding, the latter being better identified through the visual modality.

10.2.1 Speech production and hearing impairment

It is well documented that severe or profound deafness significantly alters phoneme inventory and accuracy. When no auditory speech cues are accessible, speakers must rely on other sensory modalities, one of which is vision.

10.2.1.1 A developmental perspective Infants with congenital or early (acquired before the age of 3 months) profound deafness show distinct patterns of vocal development compared to their hearing peers. During the first 6 months of life, deaf infants produce significantly more glottal sequences than hearing infants (Koopmans-van Beinum, Clement, and van den Dikkenberg-Pot 2001; Oller 1991). Whereas hearing infants enter the canonical babbling phase between 6 and 10 months of age, deaf infants do not start babbling before the second year of life (Oller 2006; Koopmans-van Beinum et al. 2001). However, other types of early vocalizations are very similar between both groups.

Hearing aids and cochlear implants provide children with a means of restoring some degree of auditory feedback. Children who use amplification methods such as hearing aids develop speech perception and production abilities (Smith 1975) but still demonstrate considerable delays. The importance of those delays depends on the severity of the deafness. Since the mid-1980s, cochlear implantation has become available. Large-scale studies of vocal development have demonstrated the dramatic increase in speech perception abilities in cochlear-implanted children compared to hearing-aid users (e.g., Kirk 2000; Nikolopoulos, Archbold, and O'Donoghue 2006). As a consequence, speech production abilities (and, more generally, language abilities) improve (e.g., Geers 2006; Svirsky et al. 2000). Various methods are employed to collect speech samples produced by cochlear-implanted children: play situations between a child and an adult, syllable repetition, or picture naming tasks. The resulting samples differ in many respects and comparisons between studies require caution (Morrison and Shriberg 1992; Bouchard, Ouellet, and Cohen 2008). General trends are nevertheless found: after implantation, children gradually increase their vocal repertoire and improve the accuracy of their articulatory strategies recruited to produce phonemes (Bouchard et al. 2008). The extent to which these trends are observable depends on several factors: communication mode, socioeconomic status, age at onset of deafness (Geers 2006), age at diagnosis (Yoshinaga-Itano 2000), pre-implant residual-hearing (Tye-Murray, Spencer, and Woodworth 1995), and age at implantation (although there are contradictory results, e.g., Bouchard et al. 2008). Regarding the phonetic repertoire, it has been shown that after cochlear implantation, children produce a significantly wider range of vowels and consonants, as evaluated by perceptual judgments (transcriptions) and acoustic analysis. Before implantation, centralized vowels are usually found. After several months of implant use, the vowel space expands to include front vowels and variations in height degrees (Ertmer 2001; McCaffrey et al. 1999). Other studies have shown that prelingually deaf children implanted during childhood (between 2.9 and 7 years of age) also improve vowel accuracy (Ertmer et al. 1997; Tye-Murray and Kirk 1993; Tobey, Geers, and Brenner 1994). Those patterns contrast with those of Warner-Czyz and Davis (2008), who found similar accuracy and error patterns in cochlear-implanted children compared with their normal-hearing peers.

Regarding the development of consonants, with the restoration of some acoustic feedback provided by the implant, a wider variety of consonants are produced: whereas labials and nasals are initially more frequent, coronal and dorsal places of articulation emerge, as well as fricatives and glides (Blamey, Barry, and Jacq 2001; Ertmer and Mellon 2001). Tobey et al. (1991) and Tye-Murray et al. (1995) note that phonemes (such as labials) that are articulated with a visible place of articulation are more frequent and more likely to be produced accurately than phonemes that are produced with a less visible place of articulation. Owens and Blazek (1985) introduced the concept of "viseme," which is defined as a group of vowels or consonants that have similar visual correlates (e.g., lip shapes).

Effects of hearing loss are also observable in acoustic analyses (e.g., Angelocci, Kopp, and Holbrook 1964; Monsen 1976; Osberger 1987; Kent et al. 1987; Osberger and McGarr 1982). In general, hearing-impaired speakers have higher values of F0, F1, and F2, associated with more variability in those measures. When some acoustic feedback is restored through cochlear implantation, produced acoustic values become closer to those of control subjects with no hearing impairment.

The effects of restoring some auditory feedback through cochlear implantation have also been investigated by examining articulatory dynamics. Goffman, Ertmer, and Erdle (2002) reported on kinematic variability for /m/, /p/, /f/, and /n/ in a 7-year-old child who became progressively deaf after 3 years of age and was implanted at 7 years of age. Analyses of lower-lip and jaw trajectories over several repetitions of the target phonemes embedded in carrier sentences revealed that kinematic variability before implantation was slightly higher than that of typically developing children. Shortly after receiving his implant, the child's produced variability increased and gradually decreased after 6 months of implant use. Thus, restoring auditory feedback at first degraded articulatory movements related to speech targets. Some experience with the implant was needed in order to improve speech production. More recently, we have used ultrasound imaging to investigate the articulatory strategies underlying speech intelligibility in deaf English-speaking children who received cochlear implant before age 2. Results showed that auditory feedback deprivation caused a global tongue fronting when articulating vowels (Turgeon et al. 2014).

10.2.1.2 Speech production in hearing-impaired adults Within the framework of an auditory-based motor theory of speech production, Perkell and colleagues investigated the role of auditory feedback in postlingually deaf speakers with cochlear implants (e.g., Lane et al. 2007; Matthies et al. 2008; Matthies et al. 1994; Ménard et al. 2007). Two dependent variables were measured, in acoustic dimensions: contrast distance and vowel dispersion. Contrast distance is defined as the Euclidean distance between two vowels, in F1 versus F2 space. Vowel dispersion is defined as the mean of the Euclidean distances for a given vowel, in the formant space, between each repetition and the target mean of all repetitions. Adult speakers who become profoundly deaf postlingually continue to produce intelligible speech for years following hearing loss, but they do experience some gradual degradation of their speech. Compared to normal-hearing speakers, postlingually deaf speakers produce decreased spectral contrast distances among vowels (Vick et al. 2001; Perkell et al. 2001; Svirsky and Tobey 1991), increased vowel dispersion (Lane et al. 2005) and increased vowel duration (Lane et al. 1995). After a year of cochlear implant use, contrast distances, vowel dispersion, and vowel duration decreased in the direction of normative values, in these studies.

At the articulatory and muscular level, deafness has been found to affect jaw movement and tongue-muscle activity. McGarr, Kobayashi, and Honda (1984), in a study of one deaf speaker and one normal-hearing control subject, report that the activation of the genioglossus and jaw position were not different in low versus high vowels in the deaf speaker, in contrast to the control subject. Stress placement also differed between both subjects. The timing of the geniohyoid and digastric muscle movements differed between the control subject and the deaf subject. McGarr, Löfqvist, and Story (1986) later documented jaw kinematics in three deaf participants and concluded that stress versus unstressed correlates were not systematically produced by deaf subjects.

10.2.2 Speech production and visual impairment

In contrast with knowledge of auditory feedback, much less is known about the influence of visual feedback on articulatory movements. The ability to produce speech contrasts involving visible articulators such as the lips and the jaw has been demonstrated for hearing-impaired listeners. Although the visual modality is crucial for these speakers, the fact that congenitally blind speakers learn to produce correct speech sounds suggests that visual cues are not mandatory in the control of speech movements. Nevertheless, some studies, mainly developmental, have shown differences in produced speech between blind and sighted subjects.

If the speaker's sensory-motor targets associated with phonemes are built during the speech acquisition period through various sensory modalities provided by the articulators (Locke and Pearson 1992; Schwartz et al. 2012), then some vowel features in blind speakers might be more strongly associated with non-visual cues than others. For example, rounding contrasts likely involve visual-based templates. How do motor strategies recruited in speech production relate to such a sensory template? In the rest of this section, we examine how speech production in congenitally blind speakers compares with speech production in sighted speakers.

10.2.2.1 A developmental perspective As reported by Kuhl and Meltzoff (1982), Legerstee (1990), and Rosenblum, Schmuckler, and Johnson (1997), by the age of 4 months, sighted babies demonstrate strong capacities to associate sounds with corresponding visual representations of the lips. Babies also imitate labial movements of sounds that are visually presented. It is therefore clear that at the language acquisition stage, babies establish relationships between auditory parameters and visual events. As Elstner (1983) states, visual impairment deprives the child from an important source of information. Such deprivation could have consequences on the strategies used to develop language (Reynell 1978; McConachie 1990) and more specifically to produce phonological targets. Lewis (1975) reported that at the pre-babbling stage, there was less imitation of lip gestures by a blind baby than by sighted babies. Blind babies also show longer babbling phases, as well as delays in the production of the first words (Burlingham 1961; Warren 1977). Elstner (1983) and Mills (1987) presented various studies showing phonological delays and phonetic-phonological disorders in older children. In a study of syllables produced by a congenitally blind 2-year-old German child, Mills (1983) reported a higher number of phonological confusions between groups of visually dissimilar consonants (labial /b/ vs. velar /k/) for the blind child compared to two English-speaking sighted children. These data must, however, be interpreted with caution, since they come from a single child. Mills (1987) extended her study to three blind speakers and found comparable results. As reported by Elstner (1983), it is difficult to study homogeneous populations of blind speakers because observed differences in speech production abilities between blind and sighted groups might be related to the presence of uncontrolled variables such as additional motor control disorders or language disorders unrelated to the visual impairment.

In a few studies focusing on phonological awareness, contradictory results were found. Lucas (1984) reported a similar percentage of correct responses in blind and sighted children in an imitation task. Thomas et al. (2000), however, found differences in responses from 8 visually impaired children aged 6.5–9.5 years and 8 age-matched control subjects. In a non-word repetition task, the visually impaired children had significantly higher errors on phoneme contrasts based on visible place of articulation such as /p/ and /k/. Prost et al. (2002) further studied access to phonological targets and found similar results.

In perhaps the most directly relevant study, Göllesz (1972) collected EMG data from 13-year-old and 14-year-old blind Hungarian male speakers uttering vowels. Data was also collected from sighted control subjects. Despite reduced labial dynamics in blind speakers compared to sighted speakers, as measured by the degree of EMG activation, no significant differences were observed in the acoustic signals. These results suggest that visual impairment leads speakers to adopt different control strategies for the visible labial articulators. Some compensatory abilities of the other articulators are also likely involved to offset the limited *ability* of the lips to reach the acoustic targets.

10.2.2.2 Speech production in visually impaired adults A crucial point to address when comparing speech production between sighted and blind speakers is auditory acuity. Indeed, it is well documented that auditory perception abilities of congenitally blind subjects differ from those of sighted subjects (Miller 1992; Stankov and Spilsbury 1978; Starlinger and Niemeyer 1981; Niemeyer and Starlinger 1981; Lucas 1984; Hugdahl et al. 2004; Gougoux et al. 2004). Many studies have also shown how cortical areas devoted to vision in sighted subjects are active in blind speakers during speech perception tasks (e.g., Collignon et al. 2011; Arnaud et al. 2011). Since the ability to perceive speech is related to the amount of contrast produced between two sounds (e.g., Perkell, Guenther, et al. 2004), this between-group difference related to auditory discrimination abilities may entail differences at the production level. Furthermore, apart from differences in discrimination abilities between congenitally blind speakers and sighted speakers, deprivation from visual information might also induce differences in the control of the speech articulators (especially the visible ones). To the best of our knowledge, very few studies have addressed speech production abilities in speakers with visual impairments. We will discuss a few studies conducted in our laboratory (Dupont and Ménard 2005; Leclerc 2007; Leclerc et al. 2006; Ménard et al. 2013; Ménard et al. 2009; Ménard, Leclerc, and Tiede 2014) that aimed to investigate speech production in blindness.

In a first study (Ménard et al. 2009), 12 congenitally blind adults (6 males and 6 females) and 12 sighted adult control subjects (6 males and 6 females) produced 10 repetitions of the 10 French oral vowels (/i y u e ø o ɛ œ ɔ a/). Participants' auditory acuity was evaluated through AXB discrimination tests of synthesized vowels along five continua: /i/ versus /e/, /e/ versus /ɛ/, /ɛ/ versus /a/ (representing the height contrast), /y/ versus /u/ (representing the place-of-articulation contrast, and /i/ versus /y/ (representing rounding). Blind speakers had significantly higher peak discrimination scores than sighted speakers for the /e/–/ɛ/ and the /ɛ/–/a/ contrasts. The difference in peak discrimination scores for the /i/–/y/ continuum did not reach significance ($p < .07$) but the observed pattern is similar to the significant one noted for the /e/–/ɛ/ and /ɛ/–/a/ contrasts, with blind speakers having higher peaks than sighted speakers.

At the acoustic level, produced contrast distances, measured by the value of average vowel space (AVS), were significantly higher for sighted speakers than for blind speakers. Thus, vowels were spaced farther apart for sighted speakers than for blind participants, despite the higher auditory discrimination scores obtained by the latter group. According to Perkell, Guenther, et al. (2004), speakers who are better at discriminating vowel pairs produce vowels that are spaced farther apart in the acoustic and articulatory spaces. The inverse patterns found here do not disconfirm Perkell's hypotheses, but rather suggest that the effects of congenital visual deprivation are greater than the effects of higher auditory acuity.

To further investigate lip–tongue relationships, the contributions of upper lip protrusion and tongue shape/position in the implementation of three French phonological vowel contrasts mainly involving those articulators (rounding, place of articulation, rounding and place of articulation combined) were examined in a follow-up study (Ménard et al. 2013). It had previously been shown, at least in French (Schwartz et al. 1993) and in English (Perkell et al. 1993), that lip and tongue gestures act in synergy, which likely enhances the lengthening effect of the lip protrusion gesture on the front cavity. Such maneuvers would in turn result in F2 lowering, the main acoustic correlate of rounded and back vowels compared to unrounded or front vowels. Since one gesture (lip protrusion) is highly visible compared to the other (tongue displacement), we hypothesized that the absence for blind speakers of the visual cues associated with lip movements would result in a reduced magnitude of lip protrusion. However, we further hypothesized that tongue displacement would be observed to compensate for the reduced lip protrusion, in order to achieve a similar speech goal.

First, it was found that lips and tongue were involved in the implementation of the rounding contrast, but the magnitude of the variance in upper lip protrusion (in cm) between those vowel pairs was significantly greater for sighted participants than for blind participants. Regarding the place of articulation feature, tongue front-back position differences between those pairs were significantly greater for congenitally blind speakers than for their sighted peers. However, the contribution of upper lip protrusion was reduced for the blind speakers, suggesting a trade-off relationship. The analysis of vowel pairs involving contrasts in both rounding and place of articulation (/i/-/u/, /e/-/o/, and /ɛ/-/ɔ/) showed that sighted participants had a larger range of upper lip protrusion compared to blind participants. The reverse pattern was found for tongue curvature and front-back position of the tongue, for which the blind group produced a greater variation in articulatory position.

The role of congenital visual deprivation on phonemic representations of French vowels was further investigated through manipulations of prosodic focus. Contrastive focus has been reported to increase perceptual saliency and to enhance phonemic distinctiveness. In order to achieve greater contrasts, speakers would use articulatory strategies that are more tightly linked to the perceptual speech target. Two groups of nine speakers were recorded while producing the vowels /i/, /y/, /u/, and /a/ in three consonantal contexts (/b/, /d/, and /g/) and in two prosodic conditions (contrastive focus and neutral). Both subject groups produced acoustic correlates of focus, but the articulatory strategies they used differed. At the acoustic level, this study showed that both sighted and congenitally blind speakers used increased values of F0, RMS, and duration to signal prosodic contrastive focus in French. At the articulatory level, lip geometry was affected differently by the prosodic condition: the internal lip area values were significantly increased under focus for all consonantal contexts in sighted speakers, while they were not significantly increased for blind speakers. As for upper lip protrusion, prosodic condition was found to affect only the vowel /y/ in sighted speakers.

The findings presented thus far suggest that the lack of visual cues resulting from congenital blindness significantly influenced the articulatory strategies used by speakers to produce speech targets. According to the perception for action control theory (PACT) described in Schwartz et al. (2012), speech goals correspond to multisensory perceptuo-motor units. In the course of speech development, perception and action are tightly linked, and speech perception necessarily involves procedural knowledge of speech production mechanisms. Furthermore, perceptual mechanisms provide gestures with auditory, visual, and somatosensory templates that guide and maintain their development. The fact that visual deprivation triggers different production strategies strongly supports the view that perception and production are co-structured. In the course of speech development, blind speakers do not integrate lip movements as a component of the speech task for some phonological features as strongly as sighted speakers do. Indeed, for the latter, seeing the lips might act as a constraint on lip movements; since this articulator has auditory and visual correlates (among others), its weight during speech development could be more important than that of less visible articulators such as the tongue. Blind speakers, in contrast, would not be affected by such constraints and, apart from variability in robustness to noise (MacLeod and Summerfield 1990), articulatory movements would have comparable perceptual correlates. The speech template is thus incomplete in blind speakers, compared to sighted speakers. The production of phonological contrasts that basically involve lengthening the front cavity does not necessarily involve lip protrusion when this articulator cannot be seen.

10.3 Conclusion

In this chapter, we explored the link between multimodal feedback and speech production. Evidence supporting the fact that production mechanisms are closely related to multimodal speech perception was presented. Studies conducted with sensory deprived populations (deaf and blind) showed that acoustic and articulatory correlates of produced phonemes were directly influenced by the speaker's access to vision and audition.

NOTE

1. This work was supported by the Social Sciences and Humanities Research Council of Canada, the Natural Sciences and Engineering Research Council of Canada, and the Canadian Foundation for Innovation. Thanks to Marlene Busko for copy-editing the paper.

REFERENCES

Aasland, Wendy, Shari R. Baum, and David H. McFarland. 2006. Electropalatographic, acoustic and perceptual data on adaptation to a palatal perturbation. *Journal of the Acoustical Society of America* 119: 2372–2381.

Angelocci, Angelo A., George A. Kopp, and Anthony Holbrook. 1964. The vowel formants of deaf and normal-hearing eleven- to fourteen-year-old boys. *Journal of Speech and Hearing Disorders* 29: 156–170.

Arnaud, L., Lucie Ménard, Marc Sato, and Vincent Gracco. 2011. Auditory speech processing and predictive coding in the visual cortex of congenitally blind adults. Paper presented at the annual meeting of the Organization for Human Brain Mapping, Quebec City, Canada.

Arnold, Paul and Fiona Hill. 2001. Bisensory augmentation: A speechreading advantage when speech is clearly audible and intact. *British Journal of Psychology* 92: 339–355.

Bell-Berti, Fredericka, Lawrence J. Raphael, David B. Pisoni, and James R. Sawusch. 1979. Some relationships between speech production and perception. *Phonetica* 36: 373–383.

Blamey, Peter J., Johanna G. Barry, and Pascale Jacq. 2001. Phonetic inventory development in young cochlear implant users 6 years postoperation. *Journal of Speech, Language, and Hearing Research* 44: 73–79.

Bouchard, M.-Eve, Christine Ouellet, and Henri Cohen. 2008. Speech development in prelingually deaf children with cochlear implant. *Language and Linguistics Compass* 3(1): 1–18.

Browman, Catherine P. and Louis Goldstein. 1989. Articulatory gestures as phonological units. *Phonology* 6: 201–251.

Browman, Catherine P. and Louis Goldstein. 1990. Gestural specification using dynamically-defined articulatory structures. *Journal of Phonetics* 18: 299–320.

Browman, Catherine P. and Louis Goldstein. 1992. Articulatory phonology: An overview. *Phonetica* 49(3–4): 155–180.

Burlingham, Dorothy. 1961. Some notes on the development of the blind. *Psychoanalytic Study of the Child* 16: 121–145.

Collignon, Oliver, Gilles Vandewalle, Patrice Voss, et al. 2011. Functional specialization for auditory-spatial processing in the occipital cortex of congenitally blind humans. *Proceedings of the National Academy of Sciences of the USA* 108: 4435–4440.

Cooper, William E., Dumont Billings, and Ronald A. Cole. 1976. Articulatory effects on speech perception: A second report. *Journal of Phonetics* 4: 219–232.

Cooper, William E., Sheila E. Blumstein, and Georgia Nigro. 1975. Articulatory effects on speech perception: A preliminary report. *Journal of Phonetics* 3: 87–98.

Curio, Gabriel, Georg Neuloh, Jussi Numminen, Veikko Jousmaki, and Riitta Hari. 2000. Speaking modifies voice-evoked activity in the human auditory cortex. *Human Brain Mapping* 9: 183–191.

Diehl, Randy L., Andrew J. Lotto, and Lori L. Holt. 2004. Speech perception. *Annual Review of Psychology* 55: 149–179.

Dupont, Sophie and Lucie Ménard. 2005. Vowel production and perception in French blind and sighted adults. Paper presented at the Congress of the Acoustical Society of America, Vancouver, BC, Canada.

Elstner, W. 1983. Abnormalities in the verbal communication of visually-impaired children. In A.E. Mills (ed.), *Language Acquisition in the Blind Child*, 18–41. London: Croom Helm.

Ertmer, David J. 2001. Emergence of a vowel system in a young cochlear implant recipient. *Journal of Speech, Language, and Hearing Research* 44: 803–813.

Ertmer, David J. and Jennifer A. Mellon. 2001. Beginning to talk at 20 months: Early vocal development in a young cochlear implant recipient. *Journal of Speech and Hearing Research* 44: 192–206.

Ertmer, David J., Karen I. Kirk, Susan Todd Sehgal, Allyson I. Riley, and Mary Joe Osberger. 1997. A comparison of vowel production by children with multichannel cochlear implants or tactile aids: Perceptual evidence. *Ear and Hearing* 18: 307–315.

Fadiga, Luciano, Laila Craighero, Giovanni Buccino, and Giacomo Rizzolatti. 2002. Speech listening specifically modulates the excitability of tongue muscles: A TMS study. *European Journal of Neuroscience* 15: 399–402.

Fant, Gunnar. 1983. Feature analysis of Swedish vowels – a revisit. *Speech Transmission Laboratory: Quarterly Progress and Status Reports* 2–3: 1–19.

Fowler, Carol A. 1986. An event approach to a theory of speech perception from a direct-realist perspective. *Journal of Phonetics* 14: 3–28.

Fox, Robert A. 1982. Individual variation in the perception of vowels: Implications for a perception-production link. *Phonetica* 39: 1–22.

Frieda, Elaina M., Amanda C. Walley, James E. Flege, and Michael E. Sloane. 2000. Adults' perception and production of the English vowel /i/. *Journal of Speech, Language, and Hearing Research* 43: 129–143.

Galantucci, Bruno, Carol A. Fowler, and Michael T. Turvey. 2006. The motor theory of speech perception reviewed. *Psychonomic Bulletin and Review* 13: 361–377.

Gay, Thomas, Bjorn Lindblom, and James Lubker. 1981. Production of bite-block vowels: Acoustic equivalence by selective compensation. *Journal of the Acoustical Society of America* 69: 802–810.

Geers, Ann E. 2006. Factors influencing spoken language outcomes in children following early cochlear implantation. *Advances in Otorhinolaryngology* 64: 50–65.

Gentilucci, Maurizio and Paolo Bernardis. 2007. Imitation during phoneme production. *Neuropsychologica* 45(3:. 608–615.

Ghosh, Satrajit, Melanie Matthies, Edwin Maas, et al. 2010. An investigation of the relation between sibilant production and somatosensory and auditory acuity. *Journal of the Acoustical Society of America* 128: 3079–3087.

Goffman, Lisa, David J. Ertmer, and Christa Erdle. 2002. Changes in speech production in a child with a cochlear implant: Acoustic and kinematic evidence. *Journal of Speech, Language, and Hearing Research* 45: 891–901.

Göllesz, Viktor. 1972. Über die lippenartikulation der von geburt an blinden [About the lip articulation of the blind from birth]. In S. Hirschberg, G.Y. Szépe, and E. Vass- Kovoics (eds.), *Papers in Interdisciplinary Speech Research, Speech Symposium*, 85–91. Budapest: Akadémiai Kiado.

Gougoux, Frederic, Franco Lepore, Maryse Lassonde, Patrice Voss, Robert J. Zatorre, and Pascal Belin. 2004. Pitch discrimination in the early blind. *Nature* 430: 309–310.

Guenther, Frank H., Satrajit S. Ghosh, and Jason A. Tourville. 2006. Neural modeling and imaging of the cortical interactions underlying syllable production. *Brain and Language* 96: 280–301.

Hoemeke, Kathryn A. and Randy L. Diehl. 1994. Perception of vowel height: The role of F1–F0 distance. *Journal of the Acoustical Society of America* 96: 661–674.

Houde, John F. and Michael I. Jordan. 2002. Sensorimotor adaptation of speech I: Compensation and adaptation. *Journal of Speech, Language, and Hearing Research* 45: 295–310.

Hugdahl, Kenneth, Maria Ek, Fiia Takio, et al. 2004. Blind individuals show enhanced perceptual and attentional sensitivity for identification of speech sounds. *Cognitive Brain Research* 19: 28–32.

Jones, Jeffrey A. and Kevin G. Munhall. 2005. Remapping auditory-motor representations in voice production. *Current Biology* 15(19): 1768–1772.

Kent, Raymond D., Mary Joe Osberger, Ronald Netsell, and Carol G. Hustedde. 1987. Phonetic development in identical twins differing in auditory function. *Journal of Speech and Hearing Disorders* 52: 64–75.

Kirk, Karen I. 2000. Challenges in the clinical investigation of cochlear implant outcomes. In J.K. Niparko, K.I. Kirk, N.K. Mellon, A.M. Robbins, B.L. Tucci, and B.S. Wilson (eds.), *Cochlear Implants: Principles and Practices*, 225–259. Philadelphia, PA: Lippincott, Williams & Wilkins.

Kohler, Evelyne, Christian Keysers, M. Alessandra Umiltà, Leonardo Fogassi, Vittorio Gallese, and Giacomo Rizzolatti. 2002. Hearing sounds, understanding actions: Action representation in mirror neurons. *Science* 297: 846–848.

Koopmans-van Beinum, Florien J., Chris J. Clement, and I. van den Dikkenberg-Pot. 2001. Babbling and the lack of auditory speech perception: A matter of coordination? *Developmental Science* 4: 61–70.

Kuhl, Patricia K. and Andrew N. Meltzoff. 1982. The bimodal perception of speech in infancy. *Science* 218(4577): 1138–1141.

Lane, Harlan, Jane Wozniak, Melanie Matthies, Mario Svirsky, and Joseph Perkell. 1995. Phonemic resetting vs. postural adjustments in the speech of cochlear implant users: An exploration of voice-onset time. *Journal of the Acoustical Society of America* 98: 3096–3106.

Lane, Harlan, Margaret Denny, Frank Guenther, et al. 2005. Effects of bite blocks and hearing status on vowel production. *Journal of the Acoustical Society of America* 118: 1636–1646.

Lane, Harlan, Melanie L. Matthies, Frank H. Guenther, et al. 2007. Effects of short and long-term changes in auditory feedback on vowel and sibilant contrasts. *Journal of Speech, Language, and Hearing Research* 50: 913–927.

Leclerc, Annie. 2007. Le rôle de la vision dans la production de la parole: Étude articulatoire et acoustique des voyelles orales du français québécois produites par des locuteurs voyants et aveugles. Mémoire de maîtrise en Linguistique, Université du Québec à Montréal.

Leclerc, Annie, Jerome Aubin, Lucie Ménard, Annie Brasseur, Amelie Brisebois, and Mark Tiede. 2006. Lip protrusion and tongue position in French vowels produced by blind speakers and sighted speakers. Paper presented at the CRLMB Student Research Day, Centre for Research on Language, Mind and Brain, McGill University, Montréal, Quebec.

Legerstee, Maria. 1990. Infants use multimodal information to imitate speech sounds. *Infant Behavior and Development* 13: 343–354.

Lewis, Morris Michael. 1975. *Infant Speech: A Study of the Beginnings of Language.* New York: Arno Press.

Liberman, Alvin M. 1957. Some results of research on speech perception. *Journal of the Acoustical Society of America* 29: 117–123.

Liberman, Alvin M. and Ignatius G. Mattingly. 1985. The motor theory of speech perception revised. *Cognition* 21: 1–36.

Liberman, Alvin M. and Doug H. Whalen. 2000. On the relation of speech to language. *Trends in Cognitive Science* 4: 187–196.

Locke, John L. and Dawn M. Pearson. 1992. Vocal learning and the emergence of phonological capacity: A neurobiological approach. In C.A. Ferguson, L. Menn, and C. Stoel-Gammon (eds.), *Phonological Development: Models, Research, Implications,* 91–129. Timonium, MD: York Press.

Lotto, Andrew J., Lori L. Holt, and Keith R. Kluender. 1997. Effect of voice quality on perceived height of English vowels. *Phonetica* 54: 76–93.

Lucas, Sally Anne. 1984. Auditory discrimination and speech production in the blind child. *International Journal of Rehabilitation Research* 7(1): 74–76.

MacLeod, Alison and Quentin Summerfield. 1990. A procedure for measuring auditory and audiovisual speech-reception thresholds for sentences in noise: Rationale, evaluation and recommendations for use. *British Journal of Audiology* 24: 29–43.

Maeda, Shinji. 1990. Compensatory articulation during speech: Evidence from the analysis and synthesis of vocal-tract shapes using an articulatory model. In W.J. Hardcastle and A. Marchal (eds.), *Speech Production and Speech Modelling,* 131–149. Dordrecht: Kluwer Academic.

Matthies, Melanie L., Mario A. Svirsky, Harlan L. Lane, and Joseph S. Perkell. 1994. A preliminary study of the effects of cochlear implants on the production of sibilants. *Journal of the Acoustical Society of America* 96: 1367–1373.

Matthies, Melanie L., Frank H. Guenther, Margaret Denny, et al. 2008. Perception and production of /r/ allophones improve with hearing from a cochlear implant. *Journal of the Acoustical Society of America* 124: 3191–3202.

McCaffrey, Helen A., Barbara L. Davis, Peter F. MacNeilage, and Deborah von Hapsburg. 1999. Multichannel cochlear implantation and the organization of early speech. *Volta Review* 101: 5–28.

McConachie, Helen. 1990. Early language development and severe visual impairment. *Child: Care, Health, and Development* 16(1): 55–61.

McFarland, David H., Shari R. Baum, and Caroline Chabot. 1996. Speech compensations to structural modifications of the oral cavity. *Journal of the Acoustical Society of America* 100: 1093–1104.

McGarr, Nancy S., Noriko Kobayashi, and Kiyoshi Honda. 1984. Electromyographic and kinematic measures of articulatory coordination in a deaf speaker. *Journal of the Acoustical Society of America* 75: S23.

McGarr, Nancy S., Anders Löfqvist, and Robin Seider Story. 1986. Jaw kinematics in hearing-impaired speakers. *Journal of the Acoustical Society of America* 80: S79.

McGurk, Harry and John MacDonald. 1976. Hearing lips and seeing voices. *Nature* 264: 746–748.

Meltzoff, Andrew N. 2002. Elements of a developmental theory of imitation. In A.N. Meltzoff and W. Prinz (eds.), *The Imitative Mind: Development, Evolution, and Brain Bases*, 19–41. Cambridge: Cambridge University Press.

Meltzoff, Andrew N. and M. Keith Moore. 1977. Imitation of facial and manual gestures by human neonates. *Science* 198: 75–78.

Ménard, Lucie, Annie Leclerc, and Mark Tiede. 2014. Articulatory and acoustic correlates of contrastive focus in congenitally blind adults and sighted adults. *Journal of Speech, Language, and Hearing Research* 57: 793–804.

Ménard, Lucie, Sophie Dupont, Shari R. Baum, and Jerome Aubin. 2009. Production and perception of French vowels by congenitally blind adults and sighted adults. *Journal of the Acoustical Society of America* 126: 1406–1414.

Ménard, Lucie, Pascal Perrier, Christophe Savariaux, Jerome Aubin, and Melanie Thibeault. 2008. Compensation strategies for a lip-tube perturbation of French [u]: An acoustic and perceptual study of 4-year-old children. *Journal of the Acoustical Society of America* 124: 1192–1206.

Ménard, Lucie, Jean-Luc Schwartz, Louis-Jean Boë, Sonia Kandel, and Nathalie Vallée. 2002. Auditory normalization of French vowels synthesized by an articulatory model simulating growth from birth to adulthood. *Journal of the Acoustical Society of America* 111: 1892–1905.

Ménard, Lucie, Corinne Toupin, Shari Baum, S. Drouin, Jerome Aubin, and Mark Tiede. 2013. Acoustic and articulatory analysis of French vowels produced by congenitally blind adults and sighted adults. *Journal of the Acoustical Society of America* 134(4): 2975–2987.

Ménard, Lucie, Marek Polak, Margaret Denny, et al. 2007. Interactions of speaking condition and auditory feedback on vowel production in postlingually deaf adults with cochlear implants. *Journal of the Acoustical Society of America* 121(6): 3790–3801.

Miller, L. 1992. Diderot reconsidered: Visual impairment and auditory compensation. *Journal of Visual Impairment and Blindness* 86(5): 206–210.

Mills, Anne E. 1983. *Language Acquisition in the Blind Child: Normal and Deficient*. San Diego, CA: College-Hill Press.

Mills, Anne E. 1987. The development of phonology in the blind child. In B. Dodd and R. Campbell (eds.), *Hearing by Eye: The Psychology of Lip-Reading*, 145–163. London: Lawrence Erlbaum Associates.

Monsen, Randall B. 1976. Second formant transitions of selected consonant-vowel combinations in the speech of deaf and normal-hearing children. *Journal of Speech and Hearing Research* 19: 279–289.

Morrison, Judith A. and Lawrence D. Shriberg. 1992. Articulation testing versus conversational speech sampling. *Journal of Speech and Hearing Research* 35: 259–273.

Munhall, Kevin G. and Eric Vatikiotis-Bateson. 1998. The moving face during speech communication. In R. Campbell, B. Dodd, and D. Burnham (eds.), *Hearing by Eye II: The Psychology of Speechreading and Audiovisual Speech*. Hove, UK: Psychology Press.

Newman, Rochelle S. 2003. Using links between speech perception and speech production to evaluate different acoustic metrics: A preliminary report. *Journal of the Acoustical Society of America* 113: 2850–2860.

Niemeyer, W. and I. Starlinger. 1981. Do the blind hear better? Investigations on auditory processing in congenital or early acquired blindness. II: Central functions. *Audiology* 20: 510–515.

Nikolopoulos, Thomas P., Sue M. Archbold, and Gerard M. O'Donoghue. 2006. Does cause of deafness influence outcome after cochlear implantation in children? *Pediatrics* 118: 1350–1356.

Oller, D. Kimbrough. 1991. Computational approaches to transcription and analysis in child phonology. *Journal for Computer Users in Speech and Hearing* 7: 44–59.

Oller, D. Kimbrough. 2006. Vocal language development in deaf infants: New challenges. In P. Spencer and M. Marschark (eds.), *The Spoken Language Development of Deaf and Hard-of-Hearing Children*, 2–41. Oxford: Oxford University Press.

Osberger, Mary Joe. 1987. Training effects on vowel production by two profoundly hearing-impaired speakers. *Journal of Speech and Hearing Research* 30: 241–251.

Osberger, Mary Joe and Nancy S. McGarr. 1982. Speech production characteristics of the hearing impaired. In N. Lass (ed.), *Speech and language: Advances in Basic Research and Practice*, vol. 8, 221–283. New York: Academic Press.

Owens, Elmer and Barbara Blazek. 1985. Visemes observed by hearing-impaired and normal-hearing adult viewers. *Journal of Speech and Hearing Research* 28(3): 381–393.

Perkell, Joseph S. and Winston L. Nelson. 1985. Variability in production of the vowels /i/ and /a/. *Journal of the Acoustical Society of America* 77: 1889–1895.

Perkell, Joseph S., Melanie L. Matthies, Mario A. Svirsky, and Michael I. Jordan. 1993. Trading relations between tongue-body raising and lip rounding in production of the vowel /u/: A pilot "motor equivalence" study. *Journal of the Acoustical Society of America* 93: 2948–2961.

Perkell, Joseph S., Frank H. Guenther, Harlan Lane, et al. 2000. A theory of speech motor control and supporting data from speakers with normal hearing and with profound hearing loss. *Journal of Phonetics* 28: 233–272.

Perkell, Joseph, Frank H. Guenther, Harlan Lane, et al. 2001. Planning and auditory feedback in speech production. Presented at the 4th International Speech Motor Conference, Nijmegen, The Netherlands.

Perkell, Joseph S., Frank H. Guenther, Harlan Lane, et al. 2004. The distinctness of speakers' productions of vowel contrasts is related to their discrimination of the contrasts. *Journal of the Acoustical Society of America* 116: 2338–2344.

Perkell, Joseph S., Melanie L. Matthies, Mark Tiede, et al. 2004. The distinctness of speakers' /s/–/ʃ/ contrast is related to their auditory discrimination and use of an articulatory saturation effect. *Journal of Speech, Language, and Hearing Research* 47: 1259–1269.

Prost, Véronique, R. Espesser, Carine Sabater, Karine Thomas-Bartalucci, and Véronique Rey. 2002. Entraînement de la conscience phonologique d'enfants déficients visuels: Quel support temporophonologique? Presented at the XXIVèmes Journées d'Étude sur la Parole, Nancy, France.

Pulvermuller, Friedemann, Martina Huss, Ferath Kherif, Fermin Moscoso del Prado Martin, Olaf Hauk, and Yury Shtyrov. 2006. Motor cortex maps articulatory features of speech sounds. *Proceedings of the National Academy of Sciences of the USA* 103: 7865–7870.

Reynell, Joan. 1978 Development patterns of visually handicapped children. *Child: Care, Health and Development* 4: 291–303.

Rizzolatti, Giacomo, Leonardo Fogassi, and Vittorio Gallese. 2001. Neurophysiological mechanisms underlying the understanding and imitation of action. *Nature Reviews Neuroscience* 2: 661–670.

Robert-Ribes, Jordi, Jean-Luc Schwartz, Tahar Lallouache, and Pierre Escudier. 1998. Complementarity and synergy in bimodal speech: Auditory, visual, and audio-visual identification of French oral vowels in noise. *Journal of the Acoustical Society of America* 103(6): 3677–3689.

Rosenblum, Lawrence D., Mark A. Schmuckler, and Jennifer A. Johnson. 1997. The McGurk effect in infants. *Perception and Psychophysics* 59(3): 347–357.

Saltzman, Elliot and Dani Byrd. 2000. Task-dynamics of gestural timing: Phase windows and multifrequency rhythms. *Human Movement Science* 19: 499–526.

Saltzman, Elliot L. and Kevin G. Munhall. 1989. A dynamical approach to gestural patterning in speech production. *Ecological Psychology* 1(4): 333–382.

Sams, Mikko, Riikka Mottonen, and Toni Sihvonen. 2005. Seeing and hearing others and oneself talk. *Cognitive Brain Research* 23: 429–435.

Savariaux, Christophe, Pascal Perrier, and Jean-Pierre Orliaguet. 1995. Compensation strategies for the perturbation of the rounded vowel [u] using a lip-tube: A study of the control space in speech production. *Journal of the Acoustical Society of America* 98: 2428–2442.

Savariaux, Christophe, Pascal Perrier, Jean-Pierre Orliaguet, and Jean-Luc Schwartz. 1999. Compensation strategies for the perturbation of French [u] using a lip tube. II: Perceptual analysis. *Journal of the Acoustical Society of America* 106: 381–393.

Schwartz, Jean-Luc, Anahita Basirat, Lucie Ménard, and Marc Sato. 2012. The Perception for Action Control Theory (PACT): A perceptuo-motor theory of speech perception. *Journal of Neurolinguistics* 25: 336–354.

Schwartz, Jean-Luc, Denis Beautemps, Christian Abry, and Pierre Escudier. 1993. Inter-individual and cross-linguistic strategies for the production of the [i] vs. [y] contrast. *Journal of Phonetics* 21: 411–425.

Shiller, Douglas, Marc Sato, Vincent L. Gracco, and Shari R. Baum. 2009. Perceptual recalibration of speech sounds following speech motor learning. *Journal of the Acoustical Society of America* 125(2): 1103–1113.

Skipper, Jeremy I., Howard C. Nusbaum, and Steven L. Small. 2005. Listening to talking faces: Motor cortical activation during speech perception. *NeuroImage* 25: 76–89.

Skipper, Jeremy I., Virginie Van Wassenhove, Howard C. Nusbaum, and Steven L. Small. 2007. Hearing lips and seeing voices: How cortical areas supporting speech production mediate audiovisual speech perception. *Cerebral Cortex* 17: 2387–2399.

Smith, Clarissa R. 1975. Residual hearing and speech production in deaf children. *Journal of Speech and Hearing Research* 18: 795–811.

Stankov, Lazar and Georgina Spilsbury. 1978. The measurement of auditory abilities of blind, partially sighted, and sighted children. *Applied Psychological Measurement* 2(4): 491–503.

Starlinger, I. and W. Niemeyer. 1981. Do the blind hear better? Investigations on auditory processing in congenital or early acquired blindness. I: Peripheral Functions. *Audiology* 20: 503–509.

Sumby, William H. and Irwin Pollack. 1954. Visual contribution to speech intelligibility in noise. *Journal of the Acoustical Society of America* 26(2): 212–215.

Summerfield, Quentin. 1979. Use of visual information for phonetic perception. *Phonetica* 36: 314–331.

Svirsky, Mario A. and Emily A. Tobey. 1991. Effect of different types of auditory stimulation on vowel formant frequencies in multichannel cochlear implant users. *Journal of the Acoustical Society of America* 89: 2895–2904.

Svirsky, Mario A., Amy M. Robbins, Karen Iler Kirk, David B. Pisoni, and Richard T. Miyamoto. 2000. Language development in profoundly deaf children with cochlear implants. *Psychological Science* 11(2): 153–158.

Syrdal, Ann K. and Hundrai S. Gopal. 1986. A perceptual model of vowel recognition based on the auditory representation of

American English vowels. *Journal of the Acoustical Society of America* 79: 1086–1100.

Thibeault, Melanie, Lucie Ménard, Shari R. Baum, Gabrielle Richard, and David H. McFarland. 2011. Articulatory movements during speech adaptation to palatal perturbation. *Journal of the Acoustical Society of America* 129(4): 2112–2120.

Thomas, K., V. Prost, Robert Espesser, and V. Rey. 2000. Capacité phonologique implicite et explicite chez les malvoyants. Presented at the 13e Journées d'Étude sur la Parole, Aussois, France.

Tobey, Emily, Ann Geers, Chris Brenner. 1994. Speech production results: Speech feature acquisition. *The Volta Review* 96: 109–129.

Tobey, Emily A., Susan Pancamo, Steven J. Staller, Judy A. Brimacombe, and Anne L. Beiter. 1991. Consonant production in children receiving a multichannel cochlear implant. *Ear and Hearing* 12: 23–31.

Traunmüller, Hartmut. 1981. Perceptual dimension of openness in vowels. *Journal of the Acoustical Society of America* 69: 1465–1475.

Turgeon, Christine, Lucie Ménard, Pamela Trudeau-Fisette, Marie Bellavance-Courtemanche, and Elizabeth Fitzpatrick. 2014. Speech production in children with cochlear implant. Poster presented at Hearing Across the Lifespan, Italy, June 5–7.

Tye-Murray, Nancy and Karen Iler Kirk. 1993. Vowel and diphthong production by young users of cochlear implants and the relationship between the phonetic level evaluation and spontaneous speech. *Journal of Speech and Hearing Research* 36: 488–502.

Tye-Murray, Nancy, Patricia E. Spencer, and George Woodworth. 1995. Acquisition of speech by children who have prolonged cochlear implant experience. *Journal of Speech and Hearing Research* 38: 327–337.

Vick, Jennell C., Harlan Lane, Joseph S. Perkell, Melanie L. Matthies, John Gould, and Majid Zandipour. 2001. Covariation of cochlear implant users' perception and production of vowel contrasts and their identification by listeners with normal hearing. *Journal of Speech, Language, and Hearing Research* 44(6): 1257–1267.

Villacorta, Virgilio M., Joseph S. Perkell, and Frank H. Guenther. 2007. Sensorimotor adaptation to feedback perturbations of vowel acoustics and its relation to perception. *Journal of the Acoustical Society of America* 122: 2306–2319.

Viviani, Paolo and Natale Stucchi. 1992. Biological movements look uniform: Evidence of motor-perceptual interactions. *Journal of Experimental Psychology: Human Perception and Performance* 18: 603–623.

Warner-Czyz, Andrea D. and Barbara L. Davis. 2008. The emergence of segmental accuracy in young cochlear implant recipients. *Cochlear Implants International* 9(3): 143–166.

Warren, David H. 1977. *Blindness and Early Childhood Development*. New York: American Foundation for the Blind.

Watkins, Kate E., Antonio P. Strafella, and Tomas Paus. 2003. Seeing and hearing speech excites the motor system involved in speech production. *Neuropsychologia* 41: 989–994.

Wilson, Stephen M. and Marco Iacoboni. 2006. Neural responses to non-native phonemes varying in producibility: Evidence for the sensorimotor nature of speech perception. *NeuroImage* 33: 316–325.

Yoshinaga-Itano, Christine. 2000. Development of audition and speech: Implication for early intervention with infants who are deaf or hard of hearing. *The Volta Review* 100: 213–234.

Part III Speech Motor Control

11 Motor Equivalence in Speech Production

PASCAL PERRIER AND SUSANNE FUCHS

11.1 What is motor equivalence in speech production?

Motor equivalence is a very important property of motor control in animals and in humans. It can be roughly defined as the capacity to achieve the same motor task differently. Motor equivalence is observed in our everyday life: we can grasp an object on the ground by bending over or by crouching down; we can paint a wall while holding the brush in our right or left hand; we can turn on the light by pushing the switch with our finger or with our elbow. These simple examples illustrate well the power of motor equivalence in motor control: motor equivalence offers freedom to the motor system and this freedom can be used to deal with various kinds of additional constraints. Lifting a heavy object from the ground is more efficient if it is done using the legs rather than the back; painting alternately with the right and left hand is less exhausting than painting continuously with the same hand; turning on the light with the elbow enables us to hold an object in our hands at the same time. This capacity of the motor system to adapt certain strategies depending on external constraints is called "plasticity" of the motor system. The plasticity of the motor system allows the Central Nervous System to fulfill the intended motor task properly, while integrating constraints. These constraints can be, for instance, the search for efficiency, as in lifting an object using our legs rather than using our back, or the need for the parallel execution of other motor tasks. Plasticity is also the basis for motor rehabilitation when the peripheral motor system is damaged and certain body parts take over for others.

Motor equivalence exists in speech production. A typical and well-known example of motor equivalence is the ability to communicate efficiently with listeners either while speaking with a free-moving jaw (the normal way of speaking) or while speaking with a pencil wedged between the upper and lower teeth restraining the jaw in a fixed position. Motor equivalence in speech has been clearly documented in

The Handbook of Speech Production, First Edition. Edited by Melissa A. Redford.
© 2015 John Wiley & Sons, Inc. Published 2019 by John Wiley & Sons, Inc.

a number of experimental studies. For example, Hughes and Abbs (1976) studied interarticulatory variability of /æ, i, ɛ/ vowels during repetitive productions of CV syllables in native speakers of American English. They observed that for the same distance between the lower and upper lips, different individual positions of the lower lip, upper lip, and jaw were reached. Variations in the position of one of these articulators were counterbalanced by coordinated variations of the two other articulators, in order to keep the distance between the lips at a constant value. This is a motor equivalence strategy, one that uses the property that various interarticulatory configurations can lead to the same interlabial distance. Interlabial distance was assumed to be the motor goal of the task. Similarly, Maeda (1990) observed the variability of the jaw and tongue dorsum positions during the production of /i/ and /a/ in various phonetic contexts for native speakers of French. He reported that jaw height and tongue dorsum front-back position cooperated to ensure the achievement of the required vocal-tract shape for each vowel. The vocal-tract shape was assumed to be the motor goal. The common observation for both vowels was that insufficient jaw height was counterbalanced by a more anterior positioning of the tongue, and, reciprocally, a high jaw position was associated with a more posterior tongue positioning. For vowel /i/, the more anterior positioning was associated with an elevation of the tongue with respect to the jaw when the jaw was low. This was presumably done in order to keep the constriction small and anterior enough. For vowel /a/, a more anterior tongue positioning was presumably required in order to prevent the reduction of the pharyngeal area, which is associated with a low jaw.

Motor equivalence has also been found at the level of the vocal-tract shape to achieve an acoustic goal (e.g., Perkell et al. 1993). Perkell and colleagues analyzed a large number of repetitions of the rounded vowel /u/ in native speakers of American English. They observed a significant negative correlation between tongue raising, which determines the size of the constriction inside the vocal tract, and lip rounding, which determines the size of the constriction at the lips. A narrow constriction at the lips was associated with a more open constriction in the vocal tract, and vice versa. These two constrictions are the major factors determining the frequency of the second maximum of amplitude in the spectrum (second formant or F2) of the vowel /u/. A low value of this frequency is the most important characteristics of /u/ from an auditory point of view. This acoustic property was therefore considered to be the motor goal. The narrower both constrictions are, the lower the second formant. The negative correlation observed by Perkell and colleagues is consistent with the idea of motor equivalence. If one of these constrictions is too large (a property that tends to increase F2), the other constriction is adjusted accordingly.

Kelso and Tuller (1983) summarized motor equivalence as follows: "Within limits, people (and animals) can achieve the same 'goal' through a variety of kinematic trajectories, with different muscle groups and in the face of ever-changing postural and biomechanical requirements" (217). This description is interesting because it contains the two most important key words that refer to the main issues that are addressed in motor equivalence studies in speech production.

The first key word is "*goal.*" The relative invariance of the goal across different motor strategies is a basic requirement for the existence of motor equivalence. The definition of the goal determines whether motor equivalence exists or not for a given motor task. One of the peculiarities of speech production, as compared to other human motor tasks, is that the goal is not physical but cognitive in nature. Basically, in speech production the goal is the meaning of the message that is transmitted to the listeners. By defining the goal in this way, we can see a huge variety of possibilities for motor equivalence in speech production. In this context, motor equivalence not only includes equivalences in terms of "muscle recruitments" or "kinematic trajectories" but also in terms of lexical and semantic features. Studies of motor equivalence in speech production have not considered all these possibilities. Rather, they have strongly reduced the scope of investigation by considering goals at a phonological level. The tasks investigated have concentrated on the production of a phoneme or of phoneme sequences and so on motor goals associated with the production of a phoneme, or of a short sequence of phonemes. The three examples of experimental studies cited above illustrate well the complexity of even this restricted problem of phoneme production. In these studies, goals have been defined either in the articulatory domain or in the acoustic domain. This point will be further developed in section 11.3.1.

The second key word is "*variety.*" Motor equivalence enables motor tasks to be achieved in a variety of ways. In speech, articulatory and acoustic variability is frequently observed across phonetic contexts and/or speaking styles, and in this respect it is called "coarticulation." Understanding what the degrees of freedom are for the speech motor system and how these degrees of freedom are taken into account by the Central Nervous System is crucial for explaining and predicting coarticulation phenomena. Thus, studies of motor equivalence in speech production are important for studies of interarticulatory coordination underlying coarticulation phenomena. This point will be further developed in section 11.3.2.

Methodologically, motor equivalence in speech has often been investigated via experimental studies. Sometimes these experimental studies have been associated with modeling work, and experimental data have been compared to the results of simulations. The basic idea underlying the design of experimental studies is to generate variability in the realization of the same goal. In normal speech, variability can be generated by varying phonetic context or speaking style (speaking rate, level of clarity, prosodic patterns, etc.). It can be also induced by introducing perturbations to the production-perception loop. The latter approach allows an investigation of the motor task. It has been used in the majority of studies on motor equivalence. The next section is concerned with the presentation of the general experimental methodology of these studies.

11.2 Methodology for studying motor equivalence in speech

The majority of experimental studies of motor equivalence phenomena in general, and of speech production in particular, have used perturbation paradigms. The basic idea underlying these paradigms is to provide significant changes to the conditions in which the motor task is achieved. These applied changes disturb the way in which motor strategies are used to fulfill the respective motor task under normal conditions. In the absence of motor equivalence, perturbations would definitely prevent the subjects from fulfilling the motor task. When motor equivalence strategies exist for a given task, perturbations are an efficient way of studying the link between coordinated articulators or the perception-action loop. In addition, perturbations allow investigations of the degrees of freedom for a given task and how the Central Nervous System is interacting with the external world to preserve the achievement of the motor goal. Perturbation studies differ with respect to the level they apply to. They can be classified in three ways:

- Perturbations that limit the degrees of freedom of the motor system;
- Perturbations that change the physical conditions of speech production;
- Perturbations that change feedback information.

More details are given below for these three kinds of perturbations.

11.2.1 *Perturbations that limit the number of degrees of freedom*

Perturbations that limit degrees of freedom prevent the use of one or more degrees of freedom in the fulfillment of the speech production task. The perturbation can be static (i.e., constant for the duration of the motor task) or variable in time (i.e., applied at selected time points and for a certain duration). By looking at the way the Central Nervous System uses the remaining degrees of freedom to achieve the task, it is possible to gather interesting information about degrees of freedom in general, about the nature of the goal that is preserved, and about the process underlying the development of motor equivalent strategies in the restricted space of the remaining degrees of freedom.

A number of phonetic studies on different languages have shown that jaw position can vary during the production of vowels. This observation, together with the fact that speaking is possible with an object maintained between the teeth, has led to the conclusion that jaw opening is a degree of freedom that can be manipulated in vowel production. The first motor equivalence studies in speech were applied to the jaw. One of the most popular static perturbations of jaw opening has been a bite-block (Lindblom, Lubker, and Gay 1979; Gay, Lindblom, and Lubker 1981). Bite-blocks are small rigid blocks, a few millimeters in depth and width, that are inserted between the lower and upper teeth of the subject. This perturbation constrains the jaw to stay at a constant position during the production of speech. Depending on the height of the block, the jaw is fixed either at a high position (bite-block height 3–5 mm) or at a low position (bite-block height 20–25 mm). Another perturbation of the jaw consists in applying resistive loading to the articulator during the closing movement of a bilabial stop (Folkins and Abbs 1975; Kelso et al. 1984). The loading prevents the jaw continuing its upward movement toward the position usually reached under normal conditions in the bilabial stop. However, as long as the loading is not too strong, this perturbation does not prevent the achievement of the labial closure that is required for bilabial stops. Since the labial closure is the result of the combined influences of the jaw, the upper lip and the lower lip positions, the limited amplitude of the jaw can be compensated for by increasing the amplitude of the movements of the lower and upper lips.

A similar unexpected perturbing force can be applied to the lower lip, rather than to the jaw, in bilabial stops (Gracco and Abbs 1985) or in bilabial fricatives (Gomi et al. 2002). Again the bilabial closure or constriction can be achieved by a downward shift of the upper lip.

Acoustic models of speech production (Fant 1960) have shown that the position and size of the constriction within the vocal tract, and the shape of the lips (spread or rounded) are the two main factors influencing the spectral characteristics (the formants) that are relevant for the perception of vowels. These models have also shown that for the vowels /u/ and /ʊ/ two different constriction patterns are possible in the vocal tract. A constriction in the palato-velar region is possible in association with a small lip area, or a constriction in the velo-pharyngeal region can be used in combination with a larger lip area. For these vowels, lip opening is one of the degrees of freedom. Perturbation of the lip opening has been manipulated by Savariaux, Perrier, and Orliaguet (1995) and Savariaux et al. (1999). The perturbation consists of using a 25-mm-diameter tube to prevent the achievement of the small lip area required for rounded lips. Based on the acoustic theory of speech production, it is possible to produce a vowel in the presence of this perturbation by constricting the velo-pharyngeal region of the vocal tract. Thus, this is an appropriate paradigm to study motor equivalence.

11.2.2 Perturbations that change the physical conditions of speech production

A second kind of perturbation consists in modifying the physical conditions of speech production. The idea underlying these paradigms is quite different from the preceding one. It is not a matter of restricting the degrees of freedom in the speech production system, but of changing the way the articulators interact with the vocal-tract boundaries or of changing the dynamical constraints, i.e. the forces applied to the articulators. Under these perturbed conditions, the Central Nervous System has to face the fact that the usual motor control strategies do not produce the expected effects, either in the articulatory or in the acoustic domain. The ultimate goal of the task, the production of a phoneme or of a short sequence of phonemes, does not change, but new strategies have to be found to reach this goal. In that sense it is a motor equivalence problem. However, these perturbations involve a level of adaptation other than the perturbations described in section 11.2.1, since a new mapping between articulators and acoustics or between applied forces and articulatory dynamics has to be taken into account. Available motor equivalence strategies for normal speech may not be used to the same extent. The Central Nervous System has to explore new possibilities for motor equivalence and to elaborate new motor control strategies in order to reach the same goals as under normal conditions. The purpose of this kind of perturbation studies is to observe how the Central Nervous System explores motor plasticity in the articulatory and acoustic domains to preserve the achievement of the speech goals. These studies provide information on the nature of the goal, the plasticity of the motor system, and on the way new strategies can be developed.

A first example for this type of perturbation is the modification of the morphology of the vocal tract. When the morphology of the vocal tract changes, articulatory movements do not shape vocal-tract cavities in the same way as under normal conditions. Consequently, the relationship between articulatory movements and acoustics also changes. Perturbations of the vocal-tract morphology are classically introduced with artificial palates of different thicknesses (McFarland, Baum, and Chabot 1996) or different shapes (Brunner, Hoole, and Perrier 2011) or with a dental prosthesis in which the upper incisors are longer than under normal conditions (Jones and Munhall 2003). These perturbations are static. Unexpected and time-variable perturbations have also been provided using an inflatable artificial palate (Honda, Fujino, and Kaburagi 2002).

A more complex perturbation to the speech production apparatus consists in applying a time-varying force field to the jaw. The intensity of the force field varies in time as a function of the velocity of the jaw movement: the faster the movement, the stronger the force field. No force is applied both at the beginning and at the end of the movement, since the velocity is zero at these positions. Rather, the force field modifies the mechanical conditions for the displacement between these two extreme positions (Tremblay, Shiller, and Ostry 2003). Thanks to the existence of motor equivalence at the level of muscle activations underlying a given jaw movement, the Central Nervous System can develop new motor strategies to resist against the influence of the external force field, and ensure the achievement of the goal.

11.2.3 *Perturbations that change feedback information*

The third kind of perturbation does not affect the speech production system itself. It modifies the way the Central Nervous System can assess whether motor goals are reached by altering orosensory (tactile and/or somatosensory) or auditory feedback. Motor equivalence strategies with altered feedback are different from strategies that are used under normal conditions, since the entire production-perception system is taken into account, and goals are defined in sensory rather than in physical terms. Altered feedback perturbation provides information on the motor control processes underlying the use of motor equivalence strategies, on the role of feedback in the selection of motor equivalence strategies, and on the nature of the speech production goals in the sensory domain.

Altered orosensory feedback is frequently produced by applying an anesthetic that reduces the amplitude of orosensory feedback, though anesthesia has the drawback of effects that are hard to control in their extent. Anesthesia has been applied to the temporomandibular joint, which provides information on jaw position, and to the oral mucosa, which provides tactile feedback information (Kelso and Tuller 1983). Recently, Ito and Ostry (2010) perturbed the kinesthetic information provided by the cutaneous receptors in the skin of the face. These receptors provide information on the stretching of the skin, which is influenced by the positioning of the jaw and by the spreading or protrusion of the lips in natural speech. Perturbing this feedback information modifies the perception of the positions of these speech articulators.

Altered auditory feedback can also be used to perturb the production-perception system. Further details are given in Chapter 13 of this book. A common perturbation consists in restricting the availability of auditory information by presenting very loud white noise (classically 80–90 dB) to the subjects via headphones (Kelso and Tuller 1983; Brunner et al. 2011). This perturbation should be used with caution since it is known to induce significant changes in speech articulation, according to the well-known "Lombard effect" (Summers et al. 1988). Another perturbation, more complex to implement, is altering the spectral characteristics of the speech signal. This perturbation can affect the formant values of vowels in whispered speech (Houde and Jordan 1998) or in normal speech (Purcell and Munhall 2006a), the spectral center of gravity of fricatives (Shiller et al. 2009), or the fundamental frequency (Jones and Munhall 2002). In all these experiments, natural auditory feedback due to acoustic wave propagation in the air and to bone conduction of acoustic vibrations has to be masked. This is why the perturbed auditory feedback is presented to the subjects via headphones and at a relatively high intensity level (again 80–90 dB).

All the perturbation paradigms described in this and the previous two subsections are used to study motor equivalence in speech production with the following two aims. First, to investigate either the nature of the speech motor goals, or the motor control processes underlying the use of the degrees of freedom to organize interarticulatory coordination. Second, to study the role of feedback in speech motor control. Hence, the data recorded during these experiments are acoustic signals, articulatory movements, vocal-tract geometries, and muscular activations (using electromyography). Recently, brain activations have also been recorded to look at the cortical correlates of the adaptation mechanisms (Tourville, Reilly, and Guenther 2006). Acoustic signals are in general analyzed in the spectral domain to investigate aspects of the spectral envelope. This envelope provides information on the spectral maxima (e.g., formants) and the distribution of the energy in the frequency domain. The measured acoustic properties in the spectral domain often reflect auditory cues to the perception of phonemes. This is why we will use the terms acoustic and auditory interchangeably in this chapter.

11.3 What can be inferred from motor equivalence studies?

Motor equivalence phenomena are interesting in speech production research because they are an efficient way of addressing fundamental issues: the nature of speech goals and the interarticulatory coordination underlying speech variability due to coarticulation and variations in speaking style. Major contributions to these topics will be developed below.

11.3.1 The nature of the goals

Since the end of the 1970s, numerous studies have investigated the nature of speech goals. Speech production consists in moving the orofacial articulators in order to provide appropriate changes in the vocal-tract shape. The vocal-tract shape determines the resonance modes of the vocal tract which are excited by the acoustics associated with vocal-fold vibrations and turbulent air flow. These resonance modes are the major factors that determine the spectral peaks of the acoustic speech signal, and these spectral peaks are the main cues used by the auditory speech perception system. In addition, it is known that speech can be perceived, at least partly, in the absence of an acoustic signal or with a highly degraded signal, when listeners can see the face of the speaker and the movements of the orofacial articulators. This multimodal (i.e., motor, articulatory, and acoustic) nature of the speech production process has led to a debate about the nature of the goals in speech production. The debate was particularly strong in the 1980s in phonetics and phonology, and has now been taken up in the neuroscience domain. In the phonetics-phonology literature the question was: Are goals specified in terms of articulatory movements (Fujimura 1986), in terms of vocal-tract shapes (Fowler 1986), or in terms of spectral characteristics (Stevens 1972)?

A major difficulty in the investigation of speech goals is the fact that in normal speech production the characteristics that are measurable for one speaker, in terms of muscle activations, articulatory positions, vocal-tract shapes, and spectral properties, are quite strongly related for a given sequence of phonemes. To disentangle these links, experimental paradigms generating motor equivalencies are efficient because they generate variability in one domain, but not necessarily in another. In all the experimental studies on motor equivalence, the methodology is based on the following assumption: When variability occurs in speech production, goals correspond to the least variable properties across conditions; properties that are significantly more variable are the degrees of freedom of the task.

There are numerous studies of motor equivalence that investigate the nature of goals in speech production. Some of these have been cited in section 11.2 to illustrate different experimental paradigms. There exist many others that could be acknowledged here. However, we will focus in this section on only a few that illustrate well, from our point of view, the challenges and approaches of these studies.

11.3.1.1 Bite-block experiment: Motor goals for vowels are the acoustically most significant characteristics of the vocal-tract geometry Gay et al. (1981) studied five native speakers of Swedish during the production of the long vowels /i, a, u, o/ in a series of VVV sequences. Subjects were asked to produce these sequences either under normal conditions or with a bite-block. For the closed vowels /i, u, o/ the bite-block was high (22.5 mm) and for the open vowel /a/ it was low (2.5 mm). The task was to produce the vowels with the same quality across the normal and the bite-block conditions. Lateral X-ray views of the vocal tract were recorded.

These data allowed measurements of individual articulatory positions and the shape of the vocal tract in the mid-sagittal plane of the head. The acoustic signal was recorded and analyzed. According to simulations with an articulatory model of the vocal tract, changes in jaw position due to the insertion of the bite-block should have induced a significant change in the formant patterns if there was no compensatory change in tongue position. The results of the study were consistent for all subjects: differences in formant patterns between the normal and the bite-block condition were much smaller than differences that would have occurred in the absence of compensatory strategy; this was true even in the first trial. The smallest variation in the articulatory domain occurred in the region of maximum constriction in the vocal tract. Cross-dimensional deviations increased with an increase in distance away from the point of maximum constriction. The authors concluded that the goal of vowel production is defined in terms of formant patterns and that this goal was "coded neurophysiologically in terms of area-function related information and is specified with respect to the acoustically most significant area-function features, the points of constriction along the length of the tract" (1981: 809).

Gay et al.'s (1981) study would prove very important in discarding the hypothesis that speech production goals could be specified in terms of absolute position of the articulators in the vocal tract. The results showed the importance of the acoustic domain in specifying goals. That said, perturbations using a bite-block do not allow for testing whether vowel goals are specified in terms of constrictions in the vocal tract or in terms of formant patterns in the acoustic domain. A bite-block perturbs the usual articulatory positions associated with the production of the vowel, but it does not prevent speakers from attaining the usual geometric shape of the vocal tract associated with the usual formant pattern of this vowel. To test whether vowel goals are specified in terms of vocal-tract constriction or formant pattern, Savariaux et al. (1995) conducted a study using a perturbation of the usual geometric shape of the vocal tract. This study is described next.

11.3.1.2 Lip-tube experiment: Vowel goals are auditory under vocal-tract related constraints Savariaux et al. (1995) perturbed the production of the French /u/, pronounced in isolation, by introducing a 25-mm-diameter tube between the lips of 11 native speakers of French. The tube, henceforth called a *lip tube*, induced a large increase in lip area, without altering the jaw position much. The subjects were asked to produce an /u/ with the lip tube. Immediately after the insertion of the lip tube the subjects received a training session. In this session the subjects had the lip tube in place and were allowed to produce /u/ 19 times in order to compensate for the perturbation, if they felt that compensation was needed. At the end of the training session, the subjects were asked to produce /u/ once again with the lip tube in place using the strategy they considered to be the best among the 19 preceding training trials. Compensatory strategies were analyzed in the articulatory domain with lateral X-ray views.

The production of /u/ in French is normally achieved with very rounded and protruded lips and a high and back tongue position, generating a vocal-tract constriction in the palato-velar region. However, the acoustic theory of vowel production (Fant 1960) predicts that the same (F1, F2) pattern can also be produced with open lips and with a vocal-tract constriction in the velo-pharyngeal region.

An analysis of the acoustic signal in terms of fundamental frequency and formant patterns (F1, F2, F3) was performed, and perceptual tests were run for 10 of the 11 subjects to evaluate the perceptual quality of the vowel /u/ produced under perturbed conditions (Savariaux et al. 1999). Results were as follows. First, in contrast to the observations of Gay et al. (1981), none of the subjects could compensate for the lip tube perturbation in the first trial. Compensation was not achieved immediately, but after a number of trials in the training session. Second, during the training sessions all the subjects shifted the formant pattern (F1, F2) of their /u/ in direction of the pattern produced without the perturbation. Third, the extent of this compensation was highly variable across subjects. For four subjects, the perception tests revealed full compensation, for three subjects partial compensation, and for three subjects no compensation at all. The articulatory data indicated that only one subject radically moved the vocal-tract constriction from the palatal to the velo-pharyngeal region. The other subjects moved their tongue backward, but to a lesser extent. Those who improved the perceptual quality also changed their fundamental frequency.

These observations support the hypothesis that the goal of vowel /u/ is specified in the auditory domain in terms of formant frequencies with some additional influence of fundamental frequency. However, variability in the extent of compensation across subjects shows that speakers use also orosensory feedback to compensate for a perturbation, that the role of this feedback is speaker-specific, and that it may rely on speaker-specific vocal-tract properties.

11.3.1.3 Dental prosthesis: Goals for sibilants are auditory Jones, and Munhall (2003) investigated the contribution of auditory feedback in adapting to a dental prosthesis during the production of the fricative /s/ in Canadian English. The dental prosthesis lengthened the upper incisors between 5 and 6 mm, without affecting the bite of the six speakers in the study. In contrast to the bite-block and the lip tube, this perturbation did not prevent the subjects from producing their usual constriction in the vocal tract, nor did it hinder proprioceptive or tactile feedback in the vocal tract.

In the production of /s/, the noise source arises from a jet of air, generated by the vocal-tract constriction, hitting the surface of the front teeth (Shadle 1989). The resulting noise excites resonances mainly in the small front cavity located between the constriction and the lips, which maximizes spectral energy in the high frequencies (above 5 kHz). According to Jones and Munhall (2003), lengthening the upper incisor teeth induces an effect that is comparable to the enlargement of the front cavity. In the absence of a correction, the larger cavity results in lowering the frequency of maximum spectral energy, such that /s/ will sound more like /ʃ/.

Jones and Munhall's (2003) experimental session consisted of two sub-sessions. Each of these sub-sessions consisted of 15 blocks of 10 repetitions of /tas/ under four different conditions: (C1) normal condition; (C2) without the dental prosthesis in the mouth and with masked auditory feedback consisting of white noise; (C3) with the prosthesis in the mouth and with masked auditory feedback; (C4) with the prosthesis in the mouth and with normal auditory feedback. The ordering of the 15 blocks was as follows: C1, C2, C3, C4, C3, four alternations (C4–C3), C2, C1. The acoustic production of /s/ was evaluated by measuring the center of gravity of the spectrum and the ratio between the slope of the spectral envelope below 2.5 kHz and the slope between 2.5 and 8 kHz. Perception tests were also run with 16 listeners.

Results were as follows. In the first block of condition C3 (no auditory feedback), the acoustic production of /s/ was altered by the dental prosthesis, and the spectral impact conformed to the theoretical prediction: /s/ sounded more like /ʃ/. When auditory feedback was available, a trend for improvement was found in the slope ratio. The perception tests also revealed that utterances were of significantly higher quality when auditory feedback was available during the production than when it was masked. In addition, the perception tests showed that the sounds produced in the presence of auditory feedback improved over several repetitions with training. This was not the case when auditory feedback was masked.

The observation that compensatory strategies are developed when a dental prosthesis is in place, together with the findings from the perception test, which show the role of auditory feedback in the development of such strategies, supports the hypothesis of an auditory goal for the sibilant /s/.

11.3.1.4 Velocity-dependent force fields: Articulatory components are part of the goals Tremblay et al. (2003) applied a velocity-dependent force field to the jaw during speech and non-speech mandibular movements. The force was applied in the mid-sagittal plane of the head along an axis parallel to the occlusal plane and in the direction of jaw protrusion (methodology described above in section 11.2.2). Three different conditions were tested with native speakers of English: productions of the utterance /siat/ in slow and clear speech; articulation of the same utterance slowly and clearly without vocalization (silent speech); non-speech jaw movement that matched the amplitude and duration of the two speech conditions. For each condition the session started with 20 repetitions of the task without perturbation, it continued with 20 repetitions with perturbations of the jaw, and finally the perturbation was removed and the task was again repeated 20 times. The movement of the jaw in the mid-sagittal plane was recorded together with the acoustic signal. The first two formant frequencies (F1, F2) were measured to characterize the produced speech sequence in the auditory domain.

Results were as follows. In the first trials following the introduction of the force field, a noticeable modification of the motion path of the jaw was observed for all subjects and for the three conditions. After training, an adaptation to the perturbation was observed for the two speech conditions (silent and vocalized speech), but not for the non-speech condition. After a few trials, the motion path of the jaw during speech became similar to the one produced without the perturbation, and differences in the (F1, F2) patterns were minimal. In addition, perceptual tests indicated that listeners could not systematically distinguish between speech stimuli with and without perturbations. These last two results suggest that the compensation to force field after training was not guided by any goal in the auditory domain. No similar compensatory effects were observed after training in the non-speech condition.

Since speech and non-speech movements used the jaw in very similar ranges of displacement and duration, the differences observed between speech and non-speech conditions cannot be attributed to any peripheral phenomenon, such as muscle mechanics or jaw dynamics. Rather, the differences must have their origins in the motor control strategies underlying the speech and non-speech movements. According to Tremblay et al. (2003), the different strategies reflect differences in the specification of the goals. For the speech task, time-varying somatosensory feedback during movement is part of the specification of the goal, while this is not the case for non-speech movements.

11.3.1.5 Auditory feedback perturbation: Articulation is modified to reach auditory goals Purcell and Munhall (2006b) studied the effect of perturbating auditory feedback during the production of the vowel /ɛ/ in "head" in 10 native speakers of English. The perturbation consisted of either a positive or a negative shift of the first formant F1. After a first phase where the subjects produced the word "head" without any perturbation, F1 was gradually shifted within a range of +/− 200 Hz in 50 successive steps of 4 Hz. At the end of this gradual shift, the subjects were asked to repeat the word 15 times again. The formant patterns were measured continuously during three phases of production: no perturbation, positive and negative shifts in F1. On average, the subjects provided changes to F1 in the opposite direction of the shift. However, compensation was never complete. In addition, subjects did not change their production immediately after the shift started. A minimal shift was necessary, which was on average 76 Hz. This value is well above the psychoacoustic threshold (around 20 Hz for vowel /ɛ/, according to Kewley-Port 2001), where spectral differences start to be perceived.

In summary, the Purcell and Munhall (2006b) experiment confirms that vowel goals are in the auditory domain and that speakers change their articulation and corresponding vocal-tract shapes if they do not generate the expected auditory goal. The threshold value and the incomplete compensation at the end of the shift phase suggest that compensation is related to a phonetic goal (i.e., a region in the acoustic space) and not to a psychoacoustic threshold.

11.3.1.6 Time-varying inflated palate: Speech goals are articulatory and auditory Honda et al. (2002) designed a time-varying perturbation of the palate based on a balloon glued onto a thin artificial palate. The balloon could be inflated or deflated within a maximum of 60 ms by external air pressure through a lead tube. The maximum thickness of the palate (inflated balloon) was 5 mm, and the minimum thickness (deflated balloon) 1 mm. The perturbation was applied to two native speakers of Japanese during utterances containing repetitions of the syllables /ʃa/ or /tʃa/, and was done in two different ways. In one session, the artificial palate was mainly deflated and became randomly inflated in 20 percent of the utterances; in another session, the pattern was similar with the inflated palate as the basic condition and deflation as the random perturbation. The perturbation was applied just before the first syllable of each utterance and was maintained throughout the utterance. Each session was run twice, first with auditory feedback available, and then with auditory feedback masked by pink noise. Articulatory data were recorded in the mid-sagittal plane and perception tests were run. The listeners' task was to identify the consonant in the syllable. The articulatory data recorded in the random inflation and deflation conditions were compared with productions in the steady-state deflated palate condition.

The results were as follows. The random deflation of the palate generated very few errors. The impact of the perturbation was much stronger when the palate was randomly inflated: we will therefore concentrate on this perturbation. For both subjects, the first syllable was incorrectly produced and incorrectly perceived under the perturbed condition, but the second syllable was significantly improved on these measures compared to the first. The articulatory data revealed that compensatory adjustments of the tongue position started within 75 ms and 150 ms after the contact onset between tongue and palate in the first syllable. In the authors' opinion, this latency is too short to enable the processing of auditory feedback at a cortical level. In addition, in the first two syllables no difference could be noted in the perception tests between the condition with auditory feedback available and the condition with masked auditory feedback. Hence, we interpret these results as evidence that the compensatory response to the inflation of the palate is driven initially by tactile feedback rather than by auditory feedback. Significant differences between the two conditions, with and without auditory feedback, started in the third syllable and they were maintained up to the end of the utterance. With auditory feedback available, the quality of the consonant improved rapidly. Thus, from the middle of the utterance onward no significant difference could be found in the identifications of the sounds pronounced with and without perturbation. With masked auditory feedback, no additional improvement in production was noticed after the second syllable.

In summary, Honda et al.'s (2002) results suggest that important characteristics of the goal are specified in terms of the proximity of the tongue and the palate, which is monitored by tactile feedback. The results also suggest that auditory feedback is necessary if the goal is to be reached with the required accuracy. This supports the idea of speech goals specified both in articulatory and acoustic terms, with a predominant requirement in the acoustics.

11.3.1.7 Summary Since the pioneering work of Gay et al. (1981), numerous studies have investigated motor equivalence phenomena in speech production in order to understand the nature of speech production goals. As the selection of studies we have described exemplifies, our interpretation of this rich literature is that speech goals have components both in the acoustic/auditory and in the articulatory/motor domains. The studies by Gay et al. (1981), Savariaux et al. (1995), Jones and Munhall (2003), and Purcell and Munhall (2006b) clearly show that in response to various perturbations subjects change their usual articulatory strategies and their usual vocal-tract shapes to generate the expected acoustic/auditory properties. To our knowledge, there exists no example of speech perturbations in the articulatory/motor domain that do not cause subjects to use compensatory strategies if the perturbations prevent them from achieving the acoustic component of the speech goal. In addition, compensatory strategies systematically tend to make acoustic properties closer to those produced under normal speaking conditions. We are also not aware of any examples of experiments where subjects keep their articulatory/motor strategies constant, while the acoustics are modified to a significant extent. Hence, speech goals must be primarily acoustic in nature.

However, goals are also defined in the articulatory/motor domain. Tremblay et al. (2003) showed that if speech acoustics are not altered, then preferred articulatory patterns exist. Honda et al. (2002) found evidence in support of the predominant role of tactile feedback in the first stage of a compensatory response to randomly applied palatal perturbations. They also showed that accurate compensation requires auditory feedback in a second stage. Savariaux et al.'s (1995) results suggest that, in the absence of any possibility of reaching the acoustic/auditory goal, subjects use their preferred vocal-tract shape to produce /u/. Our interpretation of these perturbation studies is that speech goals have both articulatory/motor and acoustic/auditory components, but that there is a hierarchy between these two components: both components of the goals can influence the emergence of compensation strategies, but the articulatory/motor component is influential only if its achievement is compatible with the achievement of the acoustic/auditory component.

Our interpretation of the results from perturbation studies is compatible with a recent experimental study by Feng, Gracco, and Max (2011). Their eight subjects, all native speakers of English, were asked to produce CVC sequences under four conditions, where V was either /e/ or /æ/. The conditions were a normal speaking condition, a condition with a perturbation of the auditory feedback corresponding to a positive shift of the first formant F1, a condition with a vertical force field applied to the jaw either upward or downward, and a condition with both the auditory feedback perturbation and the force field perturbation.

The results were as follows. Subjects systematically compensated for both auditory feedback and force field perturbations when they were applied separately. When the perturbations were applied together, subjects systematically compensated for the auditory feedback perturbation, but they compensated for the force field only in the cases where the compensation was compatible with the achievement of the acoustic goal. This experiment clearly supports our conclusion: speech goals are auditory and articulatory, but auditory first.

A more recent experimental study by Lametti, Nasir, and Ostry (2012) has tempered the strength of our conclusion. Here again the authors combined a perturbation of the auditory feedback (shift of the first formant) with a perturbation of the somatosensory feedback (alteration of the jaw path with a robotic device). Seventy-five native speakers of English were recorded during the production of the words "had" and "head." They were distributed among five sub-groups according to five different experimental conditions: (1) speech production with jaw perturbation only; (2) speech production with auditory perturbation only; (3) speech production with both auditory and jaw perturbations simultaneously; (4) speech production with an auditory perturbation in the first half of the trials and with a jaw perturbation in the second half of the trials ; (5) speech production with a jaw perturbation in the first half of the trials and with an auditory perturbation in the second half of the trials. In group 3 (both perturbation at the same time), some of the subjects compensated more for the auditory perturbation than for the somatosensory perturbation (in agreement with Feng et al. 2011), but others compensated more for the somatosensory perturbation than for the auditory perturbation (in opposition with Feng et al. 2011). Similar results were obtained with the subjects of groups 4 and 5, for which the perturbations were applied sequentially and in different orders. These results suggest that the predominance of a modality could be strongly speaker-dependent: for some speakers acoustic could be first, as we hypothesized; but for other speakers, articulation could be first.

Further studies will be necessary to assess the possible predominance of the acoustic component of the speech goal more precisely, and to evaluate whether it applies in the same way to all sounds in all languages. Motor equivalence will continue to be an excellent paradigm for this purpose. However, a refinement of the data analysis could be necessary. In this regard, the concept of "Uncontrolled Manifold" proposed by Scholz and Schöner (1999) could be useful. For a given motor task, some motor commands do not vary much across repetitions. For this reason, they are assumed to be related to the fundamental goal of the task. Some other motor commands, less closely related to the achievement of the goal, can vary more. All the possible values of these less strictly controlled motor commands define a subspace of the motor command space. Scholz and Schöner (1999) assumed that this subspace has a continuous structure that they called "Uncontrolled Manifold" (UCM). Each UCM is attached to a specific motor goal, and UCMs change across motor goals. For a given motor task, UCMs correspond to the subspace defined by the degrees of freedom of the task, as introduced in section 11.1. The subspace that is orthogonal to the UCM attached to a motor goal, corresponds to motor commands whose variations induce a change of the motor goal value. Scholz and Schöner (1999) suggested that, in order to assess whether a motor goal is constant across repetitions of the task, it is useful to look at the structure of the variance within the UCM that is related to the motor goal. If the variance is mainly within the UCM, it can be concluded that the motor goal is preserved across the repetitions of the task. If the variance is orthogonal to the UCM, it can be concluded that the motor goal varies across repetitions. The computation of the UCM requires the existence of a model of the motor system in the brain, which enables a general description between motor commands and motor goals. Depending on the nature of the motor commands, this can be more or less complex. If motor commands can be assumed to be the measurable positions of the articulators in speech production studies, the proposed estimation of the variance could be calculated quite easily from experimental data. If motor commands are assumed to be muscle-related commands, the implementation could be complex and could require the use of physiological models of the orofacial articulators to infer motor commands from experimental data. A critical analysis of the use of UCM in speech motor control has been presented in Saltzman, Kubo, and Tsao (2006).

11.3.2 Motor control strategies for interarticulatory coordination

The concept of motor equivalence has also been used to study motor control strategies that enable coordination between articulators. Motor equivalence phenomena are interesting in this regard because they give insight into how degrees of freedom are selected in various conditions to reach a motor goal. There is an ongoing debate between the concept of "coordinative structures" and the "prediction-error-correction" principle.

The concept of *"coordinative structures"* (Bernstein 1977) considers that, for a given motor task, the degrees of freedom of the motor system are not controlled individually, but within more global functional units, called "coordinative structures." Coordinative structures are not inherent to the speech production system. They are functional units and are used to achieve a specific motor task (Saltzman 1986, 1991).

The *"prediction-error-correction"* principle assumes that motor equivalence strategies are developed on the basis of a model that takes into account the conditions under which the motor system moves and predicts the output of the system from the motor commands. The predicted output is compared with characteristics of the desired goal, and an error is computed. If the error is significant, as would be the case in a perturbation where a degree of freedom is inhibited, correction is provided using the predictive model. This principle is based on three important hypotheses: (1) a predictive model exists in the Central Nervous System; (2) the Central Nervous System can compute an error; (3) the predictive model is able to adjust the motor commands to reduce the error. The concept of *"internal model"* introduced by Kawato, Furukawa, and Suzuki (1987) in motor control research provided support for this principle on the basis of neurophysiological data (see for details Wolpert, Miall, and Kawato 1998).

In an experiment presented by Kelso et al. (1984), a native speaker of English was asked to repeat the utterances "a /bæb/ again" and "a /bæz/ again" several times under normal and perturbed conditions. The perturbation was a sudden loading applied to the jaw during the closing gesture of the second consonant. This perturbation was applied randomly across repetitions of the utterances, in such a way that the subject could not predict when it would occur. When it occurred, the perturbation was systematically triggered at the same point of the upward trajectory of the jaw. The perturbation prevented the jaw from reaching the vertical position used in the absence of perturbation. In a first run of the experiment, the movements of the jaw and lips were recorded. In a second run, muscle activations were recorded with electromyography. The activation of the orbicularis oris superior generates a lowering of the upper lip, that of orbicularis oris inferior generates an elevation of the lower lip, and the posterior part of the genioglossus enables the elevation of the tongue required for the production of /z/. In both runs, the acoustic signal was recorded.

Results were as follows. The subject was able to systematically compensate for the perturbation, and compensation started rapidly after the onset of the perturbation, with an average latency of 20 ms. Compensation was phoneme specific. A downward shift of the upper lip was observed for the bilabial stop /b/. No change in upper lip movement was noticed for the alveolar fricative /z/, instead there was a stronger activation of the genioglossus. Overall, the results were compatible with the framework of coordinative structures: the very rapid compensation within a time interval shorter than the time required for feedback processed at a cortical level, supports the hypothesis of a functional coupling. The phoneme specific responses are evidence in support of the hypothesis that the functional coupling is oriented toward the achievement of a specific goal that is defined in terms of closure either at the lips, for /b/, or in the alveolar region, for /z/.

Another motor equivalence study that supports the concept of coordinative structures was conducted by Kelso and Tuller (1983). These authors ran a bite-block experiment similar to the one of Gay et al. (1981) but with speakers of English and, more importantly, with a strong reduction in orosensory and auditory feedback. Orosensory feedback was reduced with anesthesia and auditory feedback was masked by a loud white noise (see section 11.2.3 for details). The results showed that subjects were able to compensate for bite-block perturbations very rapidly, and with a similar accuracy as reported in Gay et al. (1981). Kelso and Tuller (1983) argued that there is no way to compute an error between the current state of the motor system and the desired goal for the Central Nervous System in the absence of feedback. Thus, the capacity to compensate in the absence of feedback contradicts the "prediction-error-correction" principle. Kelso and Tuller concluded that the very rapid compensatory responses support a functional coupling of the articulators.

From this selection of studies, it can be concluded that evidence in support of coordinative structures lies mainly in the great rapidity of the response to perturbation and in the efficiency of compensation in the absence of feedback. These two pieces of evidence were quite convincing at the time of the experiments. But this was before the concept of an *internal model* was introduced to the field of speech motor control (Bailly, Laboissière, and Schwartz 1991).

The internal model hypothesis assumes that two models of the motor system exist in the brain: a forward internal model that provides an approximation of the output of the motor system; and an inverse model that can find the motor commands appropriate to the achievement of the task on the basis of a computation of costs (for a tutorial in the context of speech production see Perrier 2012). Once a forward model is assumed, the rapidity of response to perturbation and the ability to compensate in the absence of feedback no longer provide evidence only in favor of coordinative structures. Once developed, a forward model provides the Central Nervous System with a reliable approximation of biological feedback, this is the so-called internal feedback. Internal feedback can be processed very rapidly (within 20 ms) by the Central Nervous System, and the Central Nervous System can then rely on this, rather than on biological feedback, in ongoing control. Thus, an internal model can explain why compensations are possible in the absence of feedback.

Numerous experiments involving motor equivalence strategies in response to perturbations have provided support for the internal model hypothesis, especially when they have shown the existence of after-effects. After-effects correspond to the fact that compensation strategies developed during the production of speech with perturbation are still used for a time after the perturbation has been removed. After-effects suggest that new mechanisms have been learned and stored in the brain (Shadmehr and Mussa-Ivaldi 1994). Whether these mechanisms are linked with motor memory or a generalized model of the motor system is still a debated issue (Conditt, Gandolfo, and Mussa-Ivaldi 1997; Purcell and Munhall 2006b). However, they are often interpreted as evidence that new internal models are acquired when speech production conditions change (Houde and Jordan 1998). Internal models can be in the form of coordinative structures, but they can also be more complex and deliver internal feedback. After-effects were found in force field perturbations (Tremblay et al. 2003) and in auditory feedback perturbations (Houde and Jordan 1998; Purcell and Munhall 2006b; Cai et al. 2011). There is still uncertainty over the exact nature of the learning that takes place, whether it involves a simple motor memory, a complete generalized model of the speech production system, or something in between. Depending on the nature of the learning, it is possible to assume or to contest that the Central Nervous System is able to compensate accurately and rapidly in response to perturbations using a "prediction-error-correction" principle. Current experimental studies of motor equivalence mechanisms in the presence of perturbations are mainly focused on investigating the nature and complexity of the representations of the speech motor system that are stored in the brain.

11.4 Conclusion

Motor equivalence, the capacity to achieve the same motor task in different ways, is an exceptional capacity of the motor system. It allows flexibility in general and adaptability under certain circumstances. Since the physical conditions in which a certain motor task has to be fulfilled can vary, different solutions may be possible. These solutions depend on both speaker-specific morphology and biomechanics in human speech production, and on the inner and outer conditions that define the effort that must be expended to solve the task. Most studies on motor equivalence in speech production use short term perturbation paradigms. This methodology allows investigation of the goals of speech, a fundamental concept that is crucial to the understanding of speech motor control. The results from perturbation experiments strongly suggest that speech goals are specified in both the articulatory/motor and the acoustic/auditory domains. Many results also suggest the preeminence of the acoustic/auditory goal when a perturbation makes reaching both articulatory and acoustic goals impossible. Current work aims to investigate and clarify the proposed preeminence of acoustic/auditory goals over articulatory/somatosensory goals.

Motor equivalence also contributes to the generation of hypotheses regarding neural principles that underlie speech motor control, such as the coupling of coordinative structures or the prediction-correction-error principle (internal model). Motor equivalence may to a large extent reflect motor learning. Current works using perturbations of the production-perception loop in speech communication is being used to investigate the nature of the learnt representations of the speech production system in the brain.

REFERENCES

Bailly, Gérard, Rafael Laboissière, and Jean-Luc Schwartz. 1991. Formant trajectories as audible gestures: An alternative for speech synthesis. *Journal of Phonetics* 19: 9–23.

Bernstein, Nikolai A. 1967. *The Coordination and Regulation of Movements.* London: Pergamon Press.

Brunner, Jana, Phil Hoole, and Pascal Perrier. 2011. Adaptation strategies in perturbed /s/. *Clinical Linguistics, and Phonetics* 25(8): 705–724.

Cai, Shanqing, Satrajit S. Ghosh, Frank H. Guenther, and Joseph S. Perkell. 2011. Focal manipulations of formant trajectories reveal a role of auditory feedback in the online control of both within-syllable and between-syllable speech timing. *Journal of Neuroscience* 31: 16483–16490.

Conditt, Michael A., Francesca Gandolfo, and Ferdinando A. Mussa-Ivaldi. 1997. The motor system does not learn the dynamics of the arm by rote memorization of past experience. *Journal of Neurophysiology* 78: 554–560.

Fant, Gunnar. 1960. *Acoustic Theory of Speech Production.* The Hague: Mouton.

Feng, Yongqiang, Vincent L. Gracco, and Ludo Max. 2011. Integration of auditory and somatosensory error signals in the neural control of speech movements. *Journal of Neurophysiology* 106(2): 667–679.

Folkins, John W. and James H. Abbs. 1975. Lip and jaw motor control during speech: Responses to resistive loading of the jaw. *Journal of Speech and Hearing Research* 18: 207–220.

Fowler, Carol A. 1986. An event approach of the study of speech perception from a direct-realist perspective. *Journal of Phonetics* 14: 3–28.

Fujimura, Osamu. 1986. Relative invariance of articulatory movements: An iceberg model. In Joseph S. Perkell and Dennis H. Klatt (eds.), *Invariance and Variability in Speech Processes*, 226–242. Hillsdale, NJ: Lawrence Erlbaum Associates.

Gay, Thomas, Björn Lindblom, and James Lubker. 1981. Production of bite-block vowels: Acoustic equivalence by selective compensation. *Journal of the Acoustical Society of America* 69(3): 802–810.

Gomi, Hiroaki, Masaaki Honda, Takayuki Ito, and Emi Z. Murano. 2002. Compensatory articulation during bilabial fricative production by regulating muscle stiffness. *Journal of Phonetics* 30: 261–279.

Gracco, Vincent L. and James H. Abbs. 1985. Dynamic control of the perioral system during speech: Kinematic analyses of autogenic and nonautogenic sensorimotor processes. *Journal of Neurophysiology* 54(2): 418–432.

Honda, Masaaki, Akinori Fujino, and Tokihiko Kaburagi. 2002. Compensatory responses of articulators to unexpected perturbation of the palate shape. *Journal of Phonetics* 30: 281–302.

Houde, John F. and Michael I. Jordan. 1998. Sensorimotor adaptation in speech production. *Science* 279: 1213–1216.

Hughes, Marie Olive and James A. Abbs. 1976. Labial-mandibular coordination in the production of speech: Implications for the operation of motor equivalence. *Phonetica* 33(3): 119–221.

Ito, Takayuki and David J. Ostry. 2010. Somatosensory contribution to motor learning due to facial skin deformation. *Journal of Neurophysiology* 104: 1230–1238.

Jones, Jeffery A. and Kevin G. Munhall. 2002. The role of auditory feedback during phonation: Studies of Mandarin tone production. *Journal of Phonetics* 30: 303–320.

Jones, Jeffery A. and Kevin G. Munhall. 2003. Learning to produce speech with an altered vocal tract: The role of auditory feedback. *Journal of the Acoustical Society of America* 113(1): 532–543.

Kawato, Mitsuo, Kazunori Furukawa, and Ryoji Suzuki. 1987. A hierarchical neural-network model for control and learning of voluntary movement. *Biological Cybernetics* 57: 169–185.

Kelso, J.A. Scott and Betty Tuller. 1983. "Compensatory articulation" under conditions of reduced afferent information: A dynamic formulation. *Journal of Speech and Hearing Research* 26: 217–224.

Kelso, J.A. Scott, Betty Tuller, Eric Vatikiotis-Bateson, and Carol A. Fowler. 1984. Functionally specific articulatory cooperation following jaw perturbations during speech: Evidence for coordinative structures. *Journal of Experimental Psychology: Human Perception and Performance* 10(6): 812–832.

Kewley-Port, Diane. 2001. Vowel formant discrimination II: Effects of stimulus uncertainty, consonantal context, and training. *Journal of the Acoustical Society of America* 110(4): 2141–2155.

Lametti, Daniel R., Sazzad M. Nasir, and David J. Ostry. 2012. Sensory preference in speech production revealed by simultaneous alteration of auditory and somatosensory feedback. *Journal of Neuroscience* 32(27): 9351–9358.

Lindblom, Björn, James Lubker, and Thomas Gay. 1979. Formant frequencies of some fixed-mandible vowels and a model of speech motor programming by predictive simulation. *Journal of Phonetics* 7: 147–161.

Maeda, Shinji. 1990. Compensatory articulation during speech: Evidence from the analysis and synthesis of vocal-tract shapes using an articulatory model. In William J. Hardcastle and Alain Marchal (eds.), *Speech Production and Speech Modeling*, 131–149. Dordrecht: Kluwer Academic.

McFarland, David H., Shari R. Baum, and Caroline Chabot. 1996. Speech compensation to structural modifications of the oral cavity. *Journal of the Acoustical Society of America* 100(2): 1093–1104.

Perkell, Joseph S., Melanie L. Matthies, Mario A. Svirsky, and Michael I. Jordan. 1993. Trading relations between tongue-body raising and lip rounding in production of the vowel /u/: A pilot "motor equivalence" study. *Journal of the Acoustical Society of America* 93(5): 2948–2961.

Perrier, Pascal. 2012. Gesture planning integrating knowledge of the motor plant's dynamics: A literature review from motor control and speech motor control. In Susanne Fuchs, Melanie Weirich, Daniel Pape, and Pascal Perrier (eds.), *Speech Planning and Dynamics*, 191–238. Frankfurt am Main: Peter Lang.

Purcell, David W. and Kevin G. Munhall. 2006a. Compensation following real-time manipulation of formants in isolated vowels. *Journal of the Acoustical Society of America* 119(4): 2288–2297.

Purcell, David W. and Kevin G. Munhall. 2006b. Adaptive control of vowel formant frequency: Evidence from real-time formant manipulation. *Journal of the Acoustical Society of America* 120(2): 966–977.

Saltzman, Elliot. 1986. Task dynamic coordination of the speech articulators: A preliminary model. *Experimental Brain Research Series* 15: 129–144.

Saltzman, Elliot. 1991. The task dynamic model in speech production. In Herman F.M. Peters, Wouter Hulstijn, and C. Woodruff Starkweather (eds.), *Speech Motor Control and Stuttering*, 37–52. Amsterdam: Elsevier Science.

Saltzman, Elliot, Masayoshi Kubo, and Cheng-Chi Tsao. 2006. Controlled variables, the uncontrolled manifold method and the task-dynamic model of speech production. In Pierre Divenyi, Steven Greenberg, and Georg Meyer (eds.), *Dynamics of Speech Production and Perception*, 21–31. Amsterdam: IOS Press.

Savariaux, Christophe, Pascal Perrier, and Jean-Pierre Orliaguet. 1995. Compensation strategies for a lip-tube perturbation of the rounded vowel [u]. *Journal of the Acoustical Society of America* 98(5): 2428–2442.

Savariaux, Christophe, Pascal Perrier, Jean-Pierre Orliaguet, and Jean-Luc Schwartz. 1999. Compensation strategies for the perturbation of French [u] using a lip tube. II: Perceptual analysis. *Journal of the Acoustical Society of America* 106(1): 381–393.

Scholz, John P. and Gregor Schöner. 1999. The uncontrolled manifold concept: Identifying control variables for a functional task. *Experimental Brain Research* 126: 289–306.

Shadle, Christine H. 1989. Articulatory-acoustic relationships in fricative consonants. In William J. Hardcastle and Alain Marchal (eds.), *Speech Production and Speech Modeling*, 211–240. Dordrecht: Kluwer Academic.

Shadmehr, Reza and Ferdinando A. Mussa-Ivaldi. 1994. Adaptive representation of dynamics during learning of a motor task. *Journal of Neuroscience* 14(5): 3208–3224.

Shiller, Douglas M., Marc Sato, Vincent L. Gracco, and Shari B. Baum. 2009. Perceptual recalibration of speech sounds following speech motor learning. *Journal of the Acoustical Society of America* 125(2): 1103–1113.

Stevens, Kenneth N. 1972. The quantal nature of speech: Evidence from articulatory-acoustic data. In Edward E. David, Jr. and Peter B. Denes (eds.), *Human Communication: A Unified View*, 51–66. New York: McGraw-Hill.

Summers, Walter van, David B. Pisoni, Robert H. Bemacki, Robert I. Pedlow, and Michael I. Stokes. 1988. Effects of noise on speech production: Acoustic and perceptual analyses. *Journal of the Acoustical Society of America* 84(3): 917–928.

Tourville, Jason A., Kevin J. Reilly, and Frank H. Guenther. 2006. Neural mechanisms underlying auditory feedback control of speech. *NeuroImage* 39: 1429–1443.

Tremblay, Stéphanie, Douglas M. Shiller, and David J. Ostry. 2003. Somatosensory basis of speech production. *Nature* 423: 866–869.

Wolpert, Daniel M., R. Chris Miall, and Mitsuo Kawato. 1998. Internal models in the cerebellum. *Trends in Cognitive Sciences* 2(9): 338–347.

FURTHER READING

Grimme, Britta, Susanne Fuchs, Pascal Perrier, and Gregor Schöner. 2011. Limb versus speech motor control: A conceptual review. *Motor Control* 15(1): 5–33. Provides a comparison of methods and issues, including motor equivalence, in limb motor control and speech motor control research.

Guenther, Frank H., Michelle Hampson, and Dave Johnson. 1998. A theoretical investigation of reference frames for the planning of speech movements. *Psychological Review* 105(4): 611–633. Presents an extensive modeling work addressing the issues of speech goals, internal models, and motor equivalence.

Latash, Mark L., Mindy F. Levin, John P. Scholz, and Gregor Schöner. 2010. Motor control theories and their applications. *Medicina* (Kaunas) 46(6): 382–392. Presents a theoretical framework to study motor control issues, including motor equivalence, without internal models and using a combination of theories, namely the Uncontrolled Manifold concept and the Equilibrium-Point-Hypothesis.

Munhall, Kevin, Ewen G. MacDonald, S.K. Byrne, and I. Johnsrude. 2009. Talkers alter vowel production in response to real-time formant perturbation even when instructed not to compensate. *Journal of the Acoustical Society of America* 125(1): 384–390. Presents experimental results showing an automaticity of the compensation in the auditory domain when auditory feedback is altered.

Rochet-Capellan, Amélie, Lara Richer, and David J. Ostry. 2012. Non-homogeneous transfer reveals specificity in speech motor learning. *Journal of Neurophysiology* 107: 1711–1717. Presents the results of experiments using auditory feedback perturbations, which suggest that for speech production the relation between motor commands and spectral patterns is learnt locally in the acoustic space.

Sakata, Jon T. and Michael S. Brainard. 2009. Social context rapidly modulates the influence of auditory feedback on avian vocal motor control. *Journal of Neurophysiology* 102(4): 2485–2497. Shows that in the presence of auditory feedback perturbation birds, when they are singing, develop compensatory strategies, and the extent of the compensation is modulated by the social context of the song production.

Tremblay, Stéphanie, Guillaume Houle, and David J. Ostry. 2008. Specificity of speech motor learning. *Journal of Neuroscience* 28(10): 2426–2434. Presents the results of force field perturbation experiments that suggest for speech production that the Central Nervous System learns task-specific, instead of generalized, representations of the relations between motor commands and movements.

Vahdat, Shahabeddin, Mohammad Darainy, Theodore E. Milner, and David J. Ostry. 2011. Functionally specific changes in resting-state sensorimotor networks after motor learning. *Journal of Neuroscience* 31(47): 16907–16915. Presents the results of an fMRI study in which a network of brain regions has been found, which is active during motor perturbation experiments and can be associated with motor learning.

12 Orofacial Cutaneous Function in Speech Motor Control and Learning

TAKAYUKI ITO

12.1 Introduction

Cutaneous afferents in the skin are known to be a source for kinesthetic information (sense of motion) in motor control (McCloskey 1978; Proske and Gandevia 2009). Because the skin deforms in various ways for a given movement, cutaneous afferents associated with skin deformation related to motion can provide kinesthetic information of the corresponding movement in sensorimotor control processing. However, the prevailing view is that kinesthetic information comes largely from proprioceptors and accordingly attention to cutaneous afferents has been more limited (Proske and Gandevia 2009). Indeed most of the literature on cutaneous receptors focuses on their role in pain, thermal sensation, and touch, rather than on kinesthesia or sensation of motion (McGlone and Reilly 2010).

Given that cutaneous mechanoreceptors are relatively dense in the facial skin as well as the skin over the hand (comparable to the skin over the trunk and limb system) (Halata and Munger 1983; Munger and Halata 1983), somatosensory signals arising from cutaneous afferents in the facial skin can play a crucial role in speech motor control compared with the other skeletal system, such as the limb system (Connor and Abbs 1998; Ito and Gomi 2007; Ito and Ostry 2010; Johansson et al. 1988a). In addition, they are potentially valuable in understanding the kinesthetic role of cutaneous information because many orofacial structures, and notably the perioral system, lack muscle proprioceptors (Folkins and Larson 1978; Stål et al. 1987, 1990) and cannot make up for this through visual input for control of articulatory motion. For these reasons, the face represents a model system for examining the kinesthetic role of cutaneous afferents. Knowing the functional role of facial skin deformation can thus offer a new way of understanding orofacial somatosensory function in speech processing.

This chapter focuses on the kinesthetic role of orofacial cutaneous afferents in speech processing and how somatosensory signals arising from cutaneous

---

The Handbook of Speech Production, First Edition. Edited by Melissa A. Redford.
© 2015 John Wiley & Sons, Inc. Published 2019 by John Wiley & Sons, Inc.

afferents in the facial skin contribute to speech motor control and learning. Section 12.2 summarizes anatomical and physiological foundations in the facial proprioceptive system in comparison with limb proprioception and addresses the importance of cutaneous afferents in facial motor control. Section 12.3 describes the neural activity of orofacial cutaneous afferents in speech motion based on physiological studies using microelectrode recording. Sections 12.4 and 12.5 describe the functional role of cutaneous afferents in speech motor control and learning in terms of kinesthetic function. Section 12.6 considers the contribution of the somatosensory system to the processing of speech sounds from the aspect of orofacial cutaneous function. Together these sections link concepts of orofacial cutaneous afferents and provide a basis for the kinesthetic role of orofacial cutaneous afferents in speech processing.

12.2 Anatomical and physiological foundations of the orofacial somatosensory system

The sensory organs for proprioception have been primarily investigated for the limb skeletal system. There has been limited attention directed to orofacial proprioception including cutaneous mechanoreceptors. Indeed, common understanding to date is that muscle proprioceptors (muscle spindles and tendon organs) are the main source for the sense of motion needed for motor control of the various skeletal systems. Given strong evidence of the importance of muscle spindles and tendon system for the sense of motion, the following questions arise: Does the orofacial system behave in the same way as limb proprioception? Are muscle proprioceptors the main source of kinesthetic information in speech motor control? To facilitate comparison with the orofacial system, we begin addressing these questions by introducing the basic physiological function of muscle proprioceptors associated with reflex. The overall aim of this section is to describe specifics of orofacial proprioception based on the current findings.

12.2.1 Orofacial muscle proprioceptors

Muscle proprioceptors (muscle spindles and tendon organs) are sensory organs in muscles that provide the sense of motion (McCloskey 1978; Proske and Gandevia 2009). Muscle spindles are the mechanoreceptors in muscles that detect a change of muscle contraction (or stretch). The role of muscle spindles in sensorimotor control can be seen in various reflexes. A representative example is the stretch reflex that maintains the same limb posture when the limb is suddenly flexed or extended due to external disturbance (Marsden, Merton, and Morton 1972). Muscle length change due to sudden stretch is coded in the discharge of muscle spindles as motor error. Since spindle afferents monosynaptically connect to motor neurons in the spinal cord, the motor error signal arising from muscle spindles directly drives compensatory activation in the motor neurons. This additional discharge in the motor neurons results in a contraction of the stretched muscle to maintain the same muscle length. Because its functional and neural characteristics have been well investigated, the stretch reflex is an effective means to assess muscle spindle function for scientific hypothesis testing or clinical diagnosis. Physiological characteristics of muscle spindles are also exemplified by the tonic vibration reflex (TVR). TVR induces additional muscle contraction (increasing generated force) when vibratory stimulation is applied to a muscle or tendon. Vibratory stimulation of a muscle stimulates muscle spindles in the absence of an obvious muscle stretch.

Another representative proprioceptor is the tendon organs that connect skeletal muscle to bone. Tendon organs are known to provide information of muscle tension force in order to protect muscles from excessively heavy loads. Like muscle spindles, the reflex called the tendon reflex illustrates a kinesthetic function of tendon organs. The tendon stretch reflex is commonly elicited in clinical examinations by tapping the tendon with a rubber hammer. Interestingly, vibratory stimulation to the tendon organs causes an illusionary perceptual sensation, that is, the feeling that the stimulated muscle is being stretched (Goodwin, McCloskey, and Matthews 1972). This illusionary sensation is used as a mean to investigate muscle proprioceptive function in motion (Cordo et al. 1995).

The fundamental functions of muscle proprioceptors including reflex function have been examined in the orofacial system to determine whether proprioceptive function in the orofacial system is the same as in the limb system. In the speech articulatory system, the lip, tongue and jaw are the main articulators to determine the specific vocal tract shape for the production of vowels and consonants. Here we discuss muscle proprioceptors of the lip and jaw mainly because the lip and jaw motion are always accompanied by facial skin deformation.

Lip motion is achieved by a combination of multiple muscle contractions (orbicularis oris superior and inferior, buccinators, risorius, major and minor zygomaticus, depressor anguli oris, levator labii superior and inferior, mentalis). Each muscle works separately or together for specific lip motion (O'Dwyer et al. 1981). For example, orbicularis oris superior and inferior predominantly control lip protrusion and rounding. Unlike the other skeletal muscles, lip motion is the result of adding the directional forces from a combination of several muscle contractions. Hence no skeletal movement is involved in lip motion.

Several studies have attempted to assess whether lip muscles have muscle proprioceptors. Anatomical studies (Stål et al. 1987, 1990) showed no evidence of muscle spindles in several lip muscles: orbicularus oris, buccinators, major and minor zygomaticus. Neilson et al. (1979) approached physiologically the existence of muscle spindles by examining the stretch reflex. They stretched the lip in a variety of ways to make sudden muscle stretches and recorded electromyography from most lip muscles (orbicularis oris, major zygomaticus, levator labii inferior, depressor anguli oris, depressor labii inferioris, mentalis, and buccinator). No evidence of stretch reflex was observed, suggesting an absence of muscle spindles. Folkins and Larson (1978) examined tonic vibration reflex, that is, the other typical reflex driven by muscles spindles. When vibratory stimulation was applied to the lip, no additional force was found in measurement of the lip force using a force transducer, consistent with the absence of muscle spindles.

In addition to the lack of muscle spindles, there is no report of tendon organs in the lip muscles. Since the lip is not a system for generating skeletal motion like the limb system, one end of the muscle or its entire body does not connect to the skull or mandible bone directly. Rather, the lip muscles are intermingled with each other to make a connection (McClean and Smith 1982). In particular, multiple lip muscles are concentrated at the corners of the mouth. These anatomical and physiological findings provide no evidence for muscle proprioceptors in lip muscles, and in fact suggest their absence and the need for an alternative source of proprioceptive information for lip movement.

The jaw is a system similar to the limb system in that muscle contraction generates skeletal motion. But one difference from the limb system is that the jaw has asymmetrical requirements for force generation between opening and closing motions, whereas the limb system has approximately symmetrical requirements for flexion and extension movement. Jaw closing requires precise force control with a large force for mastication of a variety of foods, but relatively imprecise control with much less force is sufficient for jaw opening. This asymmetrical functional requirement may directly be seen in the configuration of muscle proprioceptors. Jaw closing muscles, particularly the masseter and temporalis, have rich muscle spindles, although there is a relatively smaller number of spindles in lateral pterygoid (Kubota and Masegi 1977). Moreover, the muscles spindles in the masseter are larger and more complex than in limb muscles (Eriksson, Butler-Browne, and Thornell 1994). This might be due to the precise control needed for mastication.

Muscle spindles in the jaw closing muscles typically show the same reflexes driven by muscle proprioceptors as the limb muscles. They induce stretch reflexes called the jaw-jerk reflex (Lund et al. 1983; Miles, Flavel, and Nordstrom 2004) and the tonic vibration reflex (Eklund and Hagbarth 1966). These reflexes suggest that muscle spindles in the jaw closing muscles play a role in providing kinesthetic information like those in the limb system as servo control mechanisms shown in Lamarre and Lund (1975). On the other hand, spindles may not be essential source of sensory information during jaw opening because muscle spindles are rarely present in jaw opening muscles (digastricus, mylohyoid, geniohyoid, and lateral pterygoid). Lennartsson (1979) found only a few muscle spindles in digastricus, but not in all muscles that were investigated in this study or in all individuals. They concluded that the muscle spindles in jaw opening muscles are not an essential source of sensory input. The tonic stretch reflex was also examined in the digastric muscles. The muscle response changed, depending on motor parameters such as joint torque and jaw orientation, despite the fact that there are few or no muscle spindles in these jaw opening muscles (Ostry et al. 1997). This suggests that there must be an alternative source of proprioceptive inputs other than muscle spindles for jaw opening.

The proprioception of the tongue muscles is not yet well studied, however it might also have different characteristics from the proprioceptors in the limb system, which is described in textbooks. In the extrinsic tongue muscle (e.g., the genioglossus), proprioceptive information seems to be available from muscle spindles that have been found (Cooper 1953). However, like the muscles of the lips, tongue extrinsic muscles do not show any evidence of a stretch reflex (Neilson et al. 1979), suggesting that muscle spindles in the tongue may not work in the same way as in the limb systems. Different from the lip muscles, tongue extrinsic muscles are connected to the mandibular symphysis by the short tendon (Takano and Honda 2007), although its sensory function is not known yet.

To summarize, current anatomical and physiological evidence shows that the orofacial system is not the same as the limb system with respect to sensing motion. In particular, a paucity of muscle proprioceptors in perioral muscles strongly suggests the contribution of some other source of proprioceptive inputs, such as cutaneous afferents.

12.2.2 *Orofacial skin receptors*

Cutaneous mechanoreceptors are relatively densely innervated in facial skin compared to skin over other parts of the body (Halata and Munger 1983; Munger and Halata 1983), and the corners of the mouth is the most densely innervated area in the face (Johansson et al. 1988a; Nordin and Hagbarth 1989). Like the skin on the palm of one's hand, the oral and perioral regions have outstanding tactile spatial acuity as determined by two-point discrimination task (Weinstein 1968). In fact, there is an anatomical difference between facial skin and the skin over other parts of the body. In general knowledge of skin receptors, there are several types of mechanoreceptor – Ruffini corpuscles, Meissner corpuscles, Merkes disk receptors, and Pacini corpuscles, hair follicle fibers, and free nerve endings. Interestingly, the Pacini corpuscles, which are well represented in the fingertips and the palm of the hand where they are responsible for detection of high-frequency vibrations, are absent in the facial skin. In microelectrode recording of cutaneous afferents of peri- and intra-oral tissue, no afferents show response properties similar to typical Pacinian-corpuscle afferents (Johansson et al. 1988b). This is supported by physiological tests using vibro-tactile stimulation showing that Pacinian-type frequency sensitivity is absent in the face (Barlow 1987). However, it is not clear yet how the lack of Pacini corpuscles in facial skin affects facial skin sensory processes including the sense of motion. Whereas there is anatomical difference from the skin over other parts of the body, facial cutaneous afferents are similar to the afferent types described in the human hand in terms of the rate of adaptation to constant or static stimulation (Trulsson and Johansson 2002). These are consist with three types of afferents: fast adapting, and slowly adapting (Type I and Type II) afferents. In the facial skin and the transitional zone of the lip, a majority of the afferents are slowly adapting (Johansson et al. 1988b).

Sensory inputs arising from facial cutaneous mechanoreceptors are conveyed through the trigeminal nerve. The trigeminal nerve has three major branches: the ophthalmic nerve, the maxillary (or infraorbital) nerve, and the mandibular nerve. These branches innervate separate facial areas. Roughly, the ophthalmic nerve is for the upper part of the face: the scalp, forehead, upper eyelid, and nose. The maxillary nerves are for the middle part of the face: cheek, lower eyelid, and upper lip. The mandibular nerve is for the lower part of the face: the lower lip and jaw.

The ophthalmic and maxillary nerves are purely sensory. The mandibular nerve has both sensory and motor functions. Since the maxillary nerve and the mandibular nerve are mostly involved in the sense of speech motion, only the cutaneous afferents arising from these two nerves are discussed in this chapter.

The mandibular nerve controls motor function in the jaw muscles. The fact that this one nerve has both motor and sensory function is similar to the nerves that innervate limb muscles. The similarity between jaw closing muscles and limb muscles is reflected in the fact that the stretch reflex, which is transmitted via monosynaptic loop in the skeletal muscles. As noted above, though, this reflex is evident only in the jaw closing muscles.

Different from the jaw closing muscles, two physically separate nerves, the facial nerve and trigeminal nerve, innervate the lip region for motor function and for sensory function respectively. These two nerves originate from separate nuclei in the spinal cord, suggesting a lack of monosynaptic connection from sensory afferents to motor neurons. The lack of monosynaptic connection is also consistent with the lack of spindle-like receptors or function in the perioral system.

Orofacial cutaneous afferents are polysynaptically connected to the facial motor system in the subcortical level. A typical example is perioral reflex seen in one of the lip muscles (orbicularis oris). Brief tapping on the lip is a common method to evoke the perioral reflex (Bratzlavsky 1979). Stretching the lip lateral to the oral angle also induces the reflex in the lip muscles (Ito and Gomi 2007; Larson et al. 1978; McClean and Smith 1982). The latency of the perioral reflex (approximately 16 ms: McClean and Clay 1994; Smith et al. 1985b) is approximately twice as long as the jaw-jerk reflex (approximately 8 ms: Murray and Klineberg 1984). Given that the jaw-jerk reflex is driven via monosynaptic loop, the approximately doubled perioral latency despite almost the same travel distance indicates that the perioral reflex spends more time due to going through multiple neural connections.

The function of the perioral reflex in orofacial motor control is still controversial. The amplitude of the perioral reflex is slightly suppressed prior to speech production (McClean and Clay 1994), but not during sustained phonation (Smith et al. 1985b). The effect of cutaneous afferents arising from the lip (or sensory nerve of the lip) is not limited only to the orbicularis oris. Air-jet stimulation of the lip or electrical stimulation to orofacial tactile nerves induces inhibitory responses in jaw closing muscles (Di Francesco, Nardone, and Schieppati 1986; Okdeh, Lyons, and Cadden 1999). Stretching the facial skin lateral to the oral angle also induces a similar inhibitory response in the jaw closing muscle (Ito and Ostry 2010). This indicates a neural connection of facial cutaneous afferents to the motor system of two main articulators in the subcortical level.

12.3 Cutaneous activation in facial motion

Lip and jaw motion is normally accompanied by facial skin deformation, which occurs broadly in the overall lower facial area in several tasks: lip protrusion, chewing, and speaking (Connor and Abbs 1998). The range of skin strain in response to lower lip motion is greater than the threshold of skin strain in cutaneous mechanoreceptors (a minimal strain sensitivity of 0.0125 is reported in Edin 1992). Facial skin deformation during various movement tasks was of sufficient magnitude to elicit discharge from cutaneous mechanoreceptors. In addition, displacement of the lower lip can be estimated from the amount of skin stretch in the lower facial area. Displacement of facial skin deformation during speech motion can also be used to estimate corresponding tongue motion and speech acoustics (Vatikiotis-Bateson et al. 1999; Yehia, Rubin, and Vatikiotis-Bateson 1998).

Actual activation of facial cutaneous mechanoreceptors during motion has been observed in microelectrode recording of facial sensory nerve. Cutaneous mechanoreceptive afferents in the infraorbital nerve, which innervate the middle part of the face, discharge due to the deformation of the facial skin associated with various phases of voluntary lip and jaw motion, including speaking motions (Johansson et al. 1988a; Nordin and Thomander 1989). In speech tasks, cutaneous afferents show biphasic activity prior to the production of the explosive sound /p/ or /b/ (Johansson et al. 1988a). The first phase of the biphasic activation corresponds to the lip closing motion in a bilabial articulation. The second phase relates to the air pressure build up for explosive sounds. This activation has been observed in the cutaneous afferents that have their receptive fields close to the corners of the mouth. Cutaneous mechanoreceptors from the corners of the mouth also discharge during lip protrusion in non-speech tasks (Nordin and Thomander 1989). In chewing, discharge of cutaneous mechanoreceptors shows a biphasic discharge per one jaw cycle; the equivalent of a single jaw opening and closing motion (Johansson et al. 1988a; Nordin and Thomander 1989). Externally applied skin stretch, in the absence of actual speech articulator motion, also induces similar cutaneous activation (Nordin and Hagbarth 1989; Nordin and Thomander 1989). When the skin above the upper lip is stretched in the lateral direction by pulling an adhesive tape attached outside the receptive field, a dynamic on and off discharge is clearly induced. Static deformation induces less discharge.

Detailed kinesthetic characteristics of cutaneous discharge pattern associated with motion-related skin deformation have been examined in limb studies. Finger skeletal motion is relatively easier to map onto nerve activation associated with skin deformation than facial motion. Cutaneous mechanoreceptors in the dorsal skin of the hand discharge due to flexion and extension of the finger (Edin and Abbs 1991). Directional responses to these joint movements have been seen in the response of the cutaneous mechanoreceptors, which have the characteristic of slowly adapting to continuous stimulation. Flexion motion induces greater activity in slowly adapting mechanoreceptors than extension motion. Velocity sensitivity has also been examined in the finger extensor muscles (extensor digitorum). In a recording of slowly adapting mechanoreceptors and muscle spindles, discharge patterns of both types of receptors was proportional to velocity of ramp flexion movements (Grill and Hallett 1995). This finding is consistent even with a wider area of skin deformation during motion. The response of slowly adapting cutaneous afferents in the thigh reveals both dynamic and static aspects of knee joint movements (Edin 2001). The same group of slowly adapting units also discharge due to manually applied skin stretch. These results suggest peripheral cutaneous activation pattern in response to motion-related skin deformation effectively encodes direction and velocity information.

In addition to peripheral neural responses, cortical responses associated with motion-related skin deformation have also been studied in direct cortical recording in an awake monkey. Skin deformation in an arm movement task generated tactile activity in primary somatosensory cortex (Cohen, Prud'homme, and Kalaska 1994; Prud'homme, Cohen, and Kalaska 1994). This indicates that skin strain due to motion induces the discharge of cutaneous afferents that is similar to other stimulations to the skin (painful, thermal, and touch stimulations). Activity in primary somatosensory cortex supports the idea that cutaneous afferents play a kinesthetic role in motor control.

Further quantitative analysis using a different type of cutaneous stimulation to facial skin have provided more understanding of how tactile information is decoded during cortical processing. Brush stimuli applied to the facial and finger hairy skins induce direction-dependent activation patterns in microelectrode recording of cutaneous afferents (Edin et al. 1995). Brush stimulation in the same direction shows a consistent spatial pattern of cutaneous activation and the stimulation in another direction shows a different consistent pattern. However, a consistent pattern of activation may not be used to detect motion information such as direction and velocity, since it is necessary to process the activation in the temporal domain in order to obtain velocity information, but not in the special domain as observed in here. Instead of special pattern consistency, it is likely that velocity and direction information from a moving tactile stimulus is coded by the mean firing rate in the population of excited mechanoreceptors (Essick and Edin 1995).

Facial cutaneous mechanoreceptors respond to motion of the skin the same way as other cutaneous mechanoreceptors respond to motion in the finger and arm. Since the activation patterns of cutaneous afferents register dynamical characteristics of movement, the cutaneous mechanoreceptors can code the kinesthetic information needed for motor control. The skin at the corners of the mouth may be especially important to motor control because cutaneous mechanoreceptors are the most densely innervated there and show activation in response to movement of the speech articulators. This idea is further discussed in the following section.

12.4 Cutaneous contribution in speech motor control

The kinesthetic role of cutaneous mechanoreceptors in the speech motor system has been assessed in a study that investigated the compensatory speech adjustments (Ito and Gomi 2007). The quick compensatory response examined was that of the upper lip motion during the production of the bilabial fricative consonant /φ/. Precise lip constriction is required in bilabial fricative consonants to achieve the production of fricative noise. When jaw position is unexpectedly shifted downward by an external force disturbing lip constriction, the upper lip quickly compensates by an additional downward shift in order to achieve an intact labial aperture (Gomi et al. 2002). This quick compensatory motion is driven by two mechanisms in sequence. A mechanical component due to muscle linkage (Gomi et al. 2002; Ito, Gomi, and Honda 2004) works for the initial phase and a transcortical reflex works for the following phase (Ito, Kimura, and Gomi 2005). While the mechanical component due to muscle linkage is planned in advance for the motion, the transcortical reflex is driven by sensory error signals due to the sudden position change of the jaw (or the lower lip). Although muscle spindles are rich in the jaw closing muscles, if orofacial cutaneous mechanoreceptors contribute to providing motion information for the jaw together with muscle spindles, the compensatory reflex should be induced by orofacial skin deformation associated with the jaw motion in the absence of actual jaw position change. To test this hypothesis, Ito and Gomi (2007) disrupted participants' production of the bilabial fricative by pulling the skin lateral to the oral angle downward while jaw position was held constant. As expected, the compensatory reflex was induced. The compensatory reflex of the upper lip in response to facial skin stretch suggests that cutaneous mechanoreceptors can provide sensory error signals that are associated with jaw motion. In this way, we find that orofacial cutaneous afferents contribute directly to speech motor control.

Although deformation of the facial skin is more or less distributed in the broad area of the lower face during speech motion (Connor and Abbs 1998), cutaneous mechanoreceptors in the skin lateral to the oral angle might be predominantly responsible for the detection of speech articulatory motion. This idea has already been suggested in the previously mentioned physiological observations of neural recording that cutaneous mechanoreceptors lateral to the oral angle are activated in jaw motion (Johansson et al. 1988a) and the area around the oral angle is the most densely innervated (Johansson et al. 1988b; Nordin and Hagbarth 1989). To test this idea, facial skin stretch perturbations were applied at several sites other than lateral to the oral angle and the area of the facial skin predominantly involved in lip compensatory reflex was examined (Ito and Gomi 2007). There was no evidence for induction of the compensatory reflex in the facial skin except that lateral to the oral angles. This indicates that the skin stretch lateral to the oral angle plays a predominant role in detecting jaw motion. The facial skin stimulation to the same area also modifies the lip motion over the course of training and the perception of speech sounds, both of which are discussed in the following sections. Taken together these suggest the mechanoreceptors may be narrowly tuned in the facial skin lateral to the oral angle to detect lip and jaw articulatory motion.

Kinesthetic contribution of cutaneous mechanoreceptors is also apparent in limb studies. These studies have examined how the stimulation associated with skin deformation induces sensations of limb location and motion. Skin stretch is carefully applied without producing any position change in the manipulated limb. In the index finger, when skin strain patterns that are usually associated with finger flexion or extension were applied in the absence of passive position change, the movement-related skin strains were correctly perceived as flexion or extension motion depending on the pattern of skin stretch even when both skin and deeper tissues were anesthetized (Edin and Johansson 1995). Other examples of the skin stretch effect were seen in movement illusions due to tendon vibratory stimulation. When vibratory stimulation are applied at the wrist, where there are tendon organs for finger muscles, without producing actual finger flexion we nonetheless feel the sensation that the finger is gradually being flexed. When the same tendon vibration is applied in combination with a stretch of finger skin, we feel a greater sensation of motion than the case of tendon vibration alone (Collins, Refshauge, and Gandevia 2000). This illusionary effect is not limited to the finger but is also observed in the forearm and leg (Collins et al. 2005). These results suggest that stretching the skin can cause motion-related sensation and that cutaneous mechanoreceptors provide the information of motion.

Skin stretch stimulation is presumably limited to activation of cutaneous mechanoreceptors, particularly in the facial system. Supportive evidences have been examined by observing the effect on the jaw muscle spindles. Jaw muscle spindles are known to be sensitive to muscle length change because the jaw-jerk reflex has been readily induced using percutaneous indentation as small as 1 mm to the masseter (Smith, Moore, and Pratt 1985). There is however no excitatory reflex when the percutaneous stimulus is delivered in a motion parallel to the skin surface on the masseter exactly above the location where the jaw-jerk reflex can be induced by indentation. Similarly the skin stretch lateral to the oral angle does not show any indication of the jaw-jerk reflex; rather it shows an inhibitory reflex that is generally induced by facial cutaneous stimulation, such as by air-puff or electrical stimulation (Ito and Ostry 2010). This suggests skin stretch stimulation affects only cutaneous mechanoreceptors and not muscle spindle activation.

Electrical stimulation is an alternative method for stimulating cutaneous mechanoreceptors. Electrical stimulation to spindle afferent nerves produces an illusory sensation of movement and distorts their position in the absence of overt movement (Gandevia 1985). Likewise, electrical stimulation to the cutaneous sensory afferents induces motion illusions (Collins and Prochazka 1996). However the sensation of motion due to electrical stimulation is less than that of stretching the skin. Thus, stretching the skin may be a more effective tool for investigating the kinesthetic role of cutaneous mechanoreceptors than electrical stimulation.

In addition to studies on skin stretching, the contribution of facial cutaneous mechanoreceptors in speech motor control is also apparent in studies that deliver mechanical perturbations to the lip. Given that lip muscles lack muscle spindles, if motion error information is transmitted then it must be transmitted through orofacial cutaneous afferents. In Gracco and Abbs (1985), mechanical perturbation was applied to the lower lip during the production of bilabial explosive sounds /p/ or /b/, producing a sudden depression of the lower lip just before lip closure. This sudden depression of the lower lip was immediately compensated by the additional downward movement of the upper lip. The compensatory movement resulted in intact lip closure and accurate production of the plosive sound.

Although cutaneous afferents presumably play a predominant role in detecting motor error due to mechanical lip perturbation, the contribution of muscle spindle in the jaw closing muscles cannot be ruled out because the jaw is also involved in producing lower lip position. To rule out such contributions, Shaiman and Gracco

(2002) conducted a study in which they perturbed the upper lip during production of plosive /p/ and labio-dental fricative /f/. The perturbation to the upper lip induced compensatory motion in both upper and lower lip for the production of /p/, but no compensatory motion for the production of /f/ because the upper lip is not involved in its production. Since upper lip motion, unlike lower lip motion, is independent of jaw motion, cutaneous mechanoreceptors are the only available sensory organs for detecting motor errors. Given the evidence of task dependent compensatory motion, the conclusion is that somatosensory information associated with skin deformation contributes to the adjustment of speech articulatory motion in multiarticulatory coordination.

12.5 Orofacial cutaneous contribution to speech learning

Just like acoustic information, somatosensory information is important to speech motor learning. Tremblay, Shiller, and Ostry (2003) showed that motor errors due to external force are corrected over the course of training independent of speech sounds. For the production of a high–low vowel sequence /i/–/a/, the jaw trajectory shows an almost straight line in normal production. Tremblay et al. applied a velocity-dependent perturbation force perpendicular to the movement direction with amplitude proportional to the velocity of motion during production of the /i/–/a/ sequence in a speech motor learning task. At the beginning of training, the jaw trajectory followed a curved line in the protrusion direction because the perturbation force peaked at the mid-point of jaw opening. After a number of repetitions with the jaw perturbation, the jaw trajectory eventually returned to the original approximately straight line. Since the produced vowel sounds did not change over the course of the adaptive motion change, the results suggest that motor error correction works independently of acoustic output. This conclusion is further supported by work with profoundly deaf patients, who show the same adaptive change in motion even when their cochlear implants were off (Nasir and Ostry 2009). Together these studies suggest that somatosensory goals are set independently of acoustic goals to some extent.

Some individuals even seem to rely more heavily on somatosensory than auditory feedback during speech production (Lametti, Nasir, and Ostry 2012). When the jaw perturbation mentioned above is applied together with altered auditory feedback, individuals adapt to either just one or both sensory modulations. Interestingly some individuals preferentially adjusted to somatosensory modulation alone, ignoring audition.

Whereas jaw perturbation studies demonstrate the crucial role of somatosensory function in speech motor learning, they are unable to dissociate the contribution of cutaneous from proprioceptive receptors because jaw motion, uniquely in the orofacial system, also relies on the contribution of muscle proprioceptors. Given that muscle and joint receptors are absent in perioral muscles, the face represents a model system for examining the role of cutaneous afferents in motor learning.

As might be expected, deforming the facial skin over the course of training induces motor adaptive change in speech production. Ito and Ostry (2010) applied gentle facial skin stretch in a regular adaptation paradigm using a speech production task. For the production of /w/ in "wood," in which the lips are required to protrude more than for the production of the following /u/ vowel, robotic devices gently stretched the facial skin lateral to the oral angle and backward in the periods just before the onset of the target speech gesture. When the amplitude of upper lip protrusion was tracked over the course of training, the findings were that upper lip protrusion was gradually increased over the course of the training. This change was maintained as an after-effect in the trials that followed facial skin deformation. As with the other speech motor learning studies (Nasir and Ostry 2008; Tremblay, Houle, and Ostry 2008; Tremblay et al. 2003), the somatosensory learning process did not affect the acoustic output.

Progressively increasing lip protrusion in response to skin stretch is in contrast to the studies of motor learning that have used jaw motion perturbation (Nasir and Ostry 2008; Tremblay et al. 2008, 2003) in that facial skin stretch was applied in a direction opposite to the upcoming movement. It could be that the opposing stimulus resulted in sensory input that led the nervous system to underestimate lip position. Consequently, the actual motion may have been consistently evaluated as smaller than the intended one, and motor commands may have been updated to progressively to yield larger movement.

Separate from the adaptive change of lip protrusion, the Ito and Ostry (2010) study also showed a compensatory response due to backward skin stretch. In order to overcome a backward skin stretch, the lip has to be driven with greater force than usual to attain the same lip protrusion target. Since the skin stretch perturbation was removed before the production of the target /w/, the greater compensatory force simply resulted in greater lip protrusion than usual. This compensatory lip protrusion was evident at the beginning and end of training. In the first trial of training, the amplitude of lip protrusion was suddenly increased by some amount. This same amplitude difference was also observed when the skin stretch was removed in the first trial after training, and the gradual adaptive increase over the training remained. The findings of initial change and after-affects suggest that the online compensatory process might be driven separately in any adaptation process.

Ito and Ostry (2010) also assessed the generalization of learning using the facial skin stretch paradigm to determine whether the pattern of adaptation acquired in the context of the training task transferred to other speech movements that involved lip motion of different amplitudes. The consonant /h/ was used for the transfer task as it involves a different pattern of lip protrusion than the production of /w/. In this test, training was carried out using the same production of /w/ in "wood" as previously. A similar gradual change in the production of /w/ was observed over the course of the training. However, when the transfer task /h/ in "hood" was produced immediately after the training (in the absence of skin stretch perturbation), only a limited amplitude of the trained lip protrusion was transferred. This is consistent with the findings from a jaw perturbation speech motor learning study (Tremblay et al. 2008).

Results from these studies indicate that somatosensory inputs arising from facial skin deformation and jaw perturbation contribute to speech motor learning. The findings document the involvement of cutaneous afferent information in motor learning in the orofacial system. The progressive increase due to somatosensory error suggests that the nervous system produces motor commands with the expectation that sensory input correctly signals kinematic error.

12.6 Somatosensory function in speech perception

Speech perception is not the simple processing of auditory signals, but a complicated process involving the integration of multiple sensory inputs. For example, visual information from a speaker's face can enhance or interfere with accurate auditory perception. In a noisy environment, looking at a talker's face greatly improves the perception of speech sounds (Sumby and Pollack 1954). In the McGurk effect (McGurk and MacDonald 1976), when the auditory component of one sound (e.g., /ba/) is paired with the visual component of another sound (e.g., /ga/), a third sound can be perceived (e.g., /da/). Besides visual inputs, interactions between auditory and somatosensory information may be relevant to the neural processing of speech, since speech processes and certainly speech production involve auditory information as well as inputs that arise from the muscles and tissues of the vocal tract.

This idea is addressed from a somatosensory aspect using facial skin stretch. When the facial skin is stretched while people listen to words in the absence of any volitional speech motion, it alters the sounds they hear (Ito et al. 2009). For example, in Ito et al. (2009), listeners made a forced-choice identification of the words *"head"* or *"had"* when one of 10 possibilities on a continuum between *"head"* and *"had"* was presented. During this identification task, the skin lateral to the oral angles was pulled either upward, downward, or backward. Systematic perceptual variation was induced, which depended on the direction of skin stretch. When the skin was pulled upward, the sound was identified as *"head"* more than *"had."* This tendency was reversed when the skin was pulled downward. There was no evidence for perceptual change when the skin was pulled backward. Considering that difference of articulatory motion between *"head"* and *"had"* is characterized by the vertical position of the jaw and tongue, the perception of speech sounds is altered by speech-like patterns of skin stretch in a manner that reflects the way in which auditory and somatosensory effects are linked in speech production. Somatosensory inputs affect the neural processing of speech sounds and show the involvement of the somatosensory system in the perceptual processing of speech.

A reverse effect is also true in that speech sounds can alter the perception of facial somatosensory inputs associated with skin deformation (Ito and Ostry 2012). Ito and Ostry investigated whether speech influences the perception of amplitude between two sequential facial skin deformations that would normally accompany speech production. The skin stretch was applied at the lateral to the oral angle in upward direction. The auditory stimuli *"head"* or *"had"* were timed to coincide with the skin stretch. The main manipulation was the order in which the speech sounds were presented for the two sequential stretches. In one condition, the word *"head"* was presented with the first skin stretch, and the word *"had"* was presented with the second skin stretch. In the other condition, the opposite order was used. Somatosensory judgment was that the force with the skin stretched during the sound *"had"* was greater even though the actual force was the same for both speech stimuli. Moreover, somatosensory judgments were not affected when the skin deformation was delivered to the forearm or palm or when the facial skin deformation accompanied non-speech sounds. This suggests that the modulation of orofacial somatosensory processing by auditory inputs is specific to speech and likewise to facial skin deformation. The perceptual modulation in conjunction with speech sounds shows that speech sounds specifically affect neural processing in the facial somatosensory system and suggest the involvement of the somatosensory system in both the production and perceptual processing of speech.

This might be also examined in the interaction between speech perception and overt speech production although somatosensory and motor function are equally involved in the case of actual speech production. Similar to the McGurk effect in which incongruent visual stimulation modifies the perception of a speech sound, our own motion itself can affect the perception of speech sounds (Sams, Möttönen, and Sihvonen 2005). In this study, while listening to one series of sounds (e.g., *"pa"*), the speaking motion associated with an incongruent sound (e.g., *"ka"*) was produced silently. The presented sound was mostly perceived as a third sound (*"ta"*) or the articulated sound (e.g., *"ka"*). Although the amplitude of the effect induced by silently speaking is smaller than that produced through visual feedback, the sensorimotor process in speech production clearly interacts with the perception of speech sounds. As an opposite effect, somatosensation during speech motion is also changed as a consequence of altered auditory feedback. When the spoken voice was amplified by external manipulation during a sustained voiced sound, /u/, participants reported a throbbing sensation over the lip and laryngeal regions (Champoux, Shiller, and Zatorre 2011).

Apart from the kinesthetic role of orofacial cutaneous afferents, the tactile sense from the other body part also contributes to the perception of speech sounds by detecting information movement associated with speaking. Tadoma method has been developed for deaf-blind individuals as a tactile communication method (see Reed et al. 1985 for review). In Tadoma, a hand is placed on the talker's face in order to monitor actions associated with speech production. Performance is roughly equivalent to that of normal listening in noise. In addition, perceptual modulation like the McGurk effect can be observed if the information detected by the hands is incongruent with that which is detected by audition (Fowler and Dekle 1991).

A passive tactile sense might aid in perceiving speech sounds in daily-life situations. For example, some speech sounds like /p/ produce tiny bursts of aspiration. Gick and Derrick (2009) showed that when listeners feel a puff of air, delivered to the hand or neck while hearing either aspirated (/pa/ and /ta/) or unaspirated sounds (/ba/ and /da/), syllables heard simultaneously with air puffs were more likely to be heard as aspirated than as unaspirated sounds.

The contribution of tactile sensation in speech perception is used in hearing aid devices. As might be expected given the success of the Tadoma method, tactile sensations delivered to the fingers improve the performance of speech perception in normal and hearing-impaired individuals (Auer, Bernstein, and Coulter 1998; Cowan et al. 1990). Accordingly, there are devices designed for the hand. These devices provide speech information such as formants and amplitude using either or both electro-tactile stimulation or vibro-tactile stimulation in conjunction with auditory information. Attempts have also been made to support speech perception via tactile devices alone (Galvin et al. 1999).

12.7 Conclusions

This chapter described the kinesthetic role of cutaneous afferents in orofacial motion and speech processing. Although the neural mechanisms and functions are not yet fully understood, the importance of facial cutaneous afferents in speech motor control and learning is clear because we accurately detect orofacial movements in spite of a lack of muscle proprioceptors in most perioral muscles. Specifically, orofacial cutaneous mechanoreceptors show a particular discharge pattern in response to facial motion, including motions involved in speaking. Accordingly, stretching the skin is an effective tool for investigating somatosensory function in speech processing. Studies using somatosensory modulation associated with facial skin deformation demonstrate the kinesthetic role of cutaneous afferents in speech motor control and learning. In particular, cutaneous mechanoreceptors are narrowly tuned at the skin lateral to the oral angles. In addition to their role in speech production, cutaneous afferents associated with articulatory motion also affect the perception of speech sounds. Speech sounds may possibly serve to tune the motor system, including kinesthetic processing, during language acquisition and vice versa.

REFERENCES

Auer, Edward T., Jr., Lynne E. Bernstein, and David C. Coulter. 1998. Temporal and spatio-temporal vibrotactile displays for voice fundamental frequency: An initial evaluation of a new vibrotactile speech perception aid with normal-hearing and hearing-impaired individuals. *Journal of the Acoustical Society of America* 104: 2477–2489.

Barlow, Steven M. 1987. Mechanical frequency detection thresholds in the human face. *Experimental Neurology* 96: 253–261.

Bratzlavsky, Marc. 1979. Feedback control of human lip muscle. *Experimental Neurology* 65: 209–217.

Champoux, François, Douglas M. Shiller, and Robert J. Zatorre. 2011. Feel what you say: An auditory effect on somatosensory perception. *PLoS ONE* 6: e22829.

Cohen, Dan A.D., Michel J. Prud'homme, and John F. Kalaska. 1994. Tactile activity in primate primary somatosensory cortex during active arm movements: Correlation with receptive field properties. *Journal of Neurophysiology* 71: 161–172.

Collins, David F. and Arthur Prochazka. 1996. Movement illusions evoked by ensemble cutaneous input from the dorsum of the human hand. *Journal of Physiology* 496(3): 857–871.

Collins, David F., Kathryn M. Refshauge, and Simon C. Gandevia. 2000. Sensory integration in the perception of movements at the human metacarpophalangeal joint. *Journal of Physiology* 529(2): 505–515.

Collins, David F., Kathryn M. Refshauge, Gabrielle Todd, and Simon C. Gandevia. 2005. Cutaneous receptors contribute to kinesthesia at the index finger, elbow, and knee. *Journal of Neurophysiology* 94: 1699–1706.

Connor, Nadin P. and James H. Abbs. 1998. Movement-related skin strain associated with goal-oriented lip actions. *Experimental Brain Research* 123: 235–241.

Cooper, Sybil. 1953. Muscle spindles in the intrinsic muscles of the human tongue. *Journal of Physiology* 122: 193–202.

Cordo, Paul, Victor S. Gurfinkel, Leslie Bevan, and Graham K. Kerr. 1995. Proprioceptive consequences of tendon vibration during movement. *Journal of Neurophysiology* 74: 1675–1688.

Cowan, Robert S., Peter J. Blamey, Karyn L. Galvin, Julia Z. Sarant, Joseph I. Alcántara, and Graeme M. Clark. 1990. Perception of sentences, words, and speech features by profoundly hearing-impaired children using a multichannel electrotactile speech processor. *Journal of the Acoustical Society of America* 88: 1374–1384.

Di Francesco, G., Antonio Nardone, and Marco Schieppati. 1986. Inhibition of jaw-closing muscle activity by tactile air-jet stimulation of peri- and intra-oral sites in man. *Archives of Oral Biology* 31: 273–278.

Edin, Benoni B. 1992. Quantitative analysis of static strain sensitivity in human mechanoreceptors from hairy skin. *Journal of Neurophysiology* 67: 1105–1113.

Edin, Benoni. 2001. Cutaneous afferents provide information about knee joint movements in humans. *Journal of Physiology* 531: 289–297.

Edin, Benoni B. and James H. Abbs. 1991. Finger movement responses of cutaneous mechanoreceptors in the dorsal skin of the human hand. *Journal of Neurophysiology* 65: 657–670.

Edin, Benoni B. and Niclas Johansson. 1995. Skin strain patterns provide kinaesthetic information to the human central nervous system. *Journal of Physiology* 487(1): 243–251.

Edin, Benoni B., Gregory K. Essick, Mats Trulsson, and Kurt A. Olsson. 1995. Receptor encoding of moving tactile stimuli in humans. I: Temporal pattern of discharge of individual low-threshold mechanoreceptors. *Journal of Neuroscience* 15: 830–847.

Eklund, Göran and Karl-Erik Hagbarth. 1966. Normal variability of tonic vibration reflexes in man. *Experimental Neurology* 16: 80–92.

Eriksson, Per-Olof, Gill S. Butler-Browne, and Lars-Eric Thornell. 1994. Immunohistochemical characterization of human masseter muscle spindles. *Muscle Nerve* 17: 31–41.

Essick, Gregory K. and Benoni B. Edin. 1995. Receptor encoding of moving tactile stimuli in humans. II: The mean response of individual low-threshold mechanoreceptors to motion across the receptive field. *Journal of Neuroscience* 15: 848–864.

Folkins, John W. and Charles R. Larson. 1978. In search of a tonic vibration reflex in the human lip. *Brain Research* 151: 409–412.

Fowler, Carol A. and Dawn J. Dekle. 1991. Listening with eye and hand: Cross-modal contributions to speech perception. *Journal of Experimental Psychology: Human Perception and Performance* 17: 816–828.

Galvin, Karyn L., Peter J. Blamey, Michael Oerlemans, Robert S. Cowan, and Graeme M. Clark. 1999. Acquisition of a tactile-alone vocabulary by normally hearing users of the Tickle Talker. *Journal of the Acoustical Society of America* 106: 1084–1089.

Gandevia, Simon C. 1985. Illusory movements produced by electrical stimulation of low-threshold muscle afferents from the hand. *Brain* 108(4): 965–981.

Gick, Bryan and Donald Derrick. 2009. Aero-tactile integration in speech perception. *Nature* 462: 502–504.

Gomi, Hiroaki, Takayuki Ito, Emi Z. Murano, and Masaaki Honda. 2002. Compensatory articulation during bilabial fricative production by regulating muscle stiffness. *Journal of Phonetics* 30: 261–279.

Goodwin, Guy M., D. Ian McCloskey, and Peter B.C. Matthews. 1972. Proprioceptive illusions induced by muscle vibration: Contribution by muscle spindles to perception? *Science* 175: 1382–1384.

Gracco, Vincent L. and James H. Abbs. 1985. Dynamic Control of perioral system during speech: Kinematic analysis of autogenic and nonautogenic sensorimotor processes. *Journal of Neurophysiology* 54: 418–432.

Grill, Stephen E. and Mark Hallett. 1995. Velocity sensitivity of human muscle spindle afferents and slowly adapting type II cutaneous mechanoreceptors. *Journal of Physiology* 489(2): 593–602.

Halata, Zdenek and Bryce L. Munger. 1983. The sensory innervation of primate facial skin. II: Vermilion border and mucosa of lip. *Brain Research* 286: 81–107.

Ito, Takayuki and Hiroaki Gomi. 2007. Cutaneous mechanoreceptors contribute to the generation of a cortical reflex in speech. *Neuroreport* 18: 907–910.

Ito, Takayuki and David J. Ostry. 2010. Somatosensory contribution to motor learning due to facial skin deformation. *Journal of Neurophysiology* 104: 1230–1238.

Ito, Takayuki and David J. Ostry. 2012. Speech sounds alter facial skin sensation. *Journal of Neurophysiology* 107: 442–447.

Ito, Takayuki, Hiroaki Gomi, and Masaaki Honda. 2004. Dynamical simulation of speech cooperative articulation by muscle linkages. *Biological Cybernetics* 91: 275–282.

Ito, Takayuki, Toshitaka Kimura, and Hiroaki Gomi. 2005. The motor cortex is involved in reflexive compensatory adjustment of speech articulation. *Neuroreport* 16: 1791–1794.

Johansson, Roland S., Mats Trulsson, Kurt Â. Olsson, and James H. Abbs. 1988a. Mechanoreceptive afferent activity in the infraorbital nerve in man during speech and chewing movements. *Experimental Brain Research* 72: 209–214.

Johansson, Roland S., Mats Trulsson, Kurt Â. Olsson, and Karl-Gunnar Westberg. 1988b. Mechanoreceptor activity from the human face and oral mucosa. *Experimental Brain Research* 72: 204–208.

Kubota, Kinziro and Toshiaki Masegi. 1977. Muscle spindle supply to the human jaw muscle. *Journal of Dental Research* 56: 901–909.

Lamarre, Y. and James P. Lund. 1975. Load compensation in human masseter muscles. *Journal of Physiology* 253: 21–35.

Lametti, Daniel R., Sazzad M. Nasir, and David J. Ostry. 2012. Sensory preference in speech production revealed by simultaneous alteration of auditory and somatosensory feedback. *Journal of Neuroscience* 32: 9351–9358.

Larson, Charles R., John W. Folkins, Michael D. McClean, and Eric M. Muller. 1978. Sensitivity of the human perioral reflex to parameters of mechanical stretch. *Brain Research* 146: 159–164.

Lennartsson, Bertil. 1979. Muscle spindles in the human anterior digastric muscle. *Acta Odontologica Scandinavica* 37: 329–333.

Lund, James P., Yves Lamarre, Gilles Lavigne, and G. Duquet. 1983. Human jaw reflexes. *Advances in Neurology* 39: 739–755.

Marsden, Charles D., Patrick A. Merton, and H.B. Morton. 1972. Servo action in human voluntary movement. *Nature* 238: 140–143.

McClean, Michael D. and John L. Clay. 1994. Evidence for suppression of lip muscle reflexes prior to speech. *Experimental Brain Research* 97: 541–544.

McClean, Michael D. and Anne Smith. 1982. The reflex responses of single motor units in human lower lip muscles to mechanical stimulation. *Brain Research* 251: 65–75.

McCloskey, Douglas I. 1978. Kinesthetic sensibility. *Physiological Reviews* 58: 763–820.

McGlone, Francis and David Reilly. 2010. The cutaneous sensory system. *Neuroscience & Biobehavioral Reviews* 34: 148–159.

McGurk, Harry and John MacDonald. 1976. Hearing lips and seeing voices. *Nature* 264: 746–748.

Miles, Timothy S., Stanley C. Flavel, and Michael A. Nordstrom. 2004. Stretch reflexes in the human masticatory muscles: A brief review and a new functional role. *Human Movement Science* 23: 337–349.

Munger, Bryce L. and Zdenek Halata. 1983. The sensory innervation of primate facial skin. I: Hairy skin. *Brain Research* 286: 45–80.

Murray, Gregory M. and Iven J. Klineberg. 1984. Electromyographic recordings of human jaw-jerk reflex characteristics evoked under standardized conditions. *Archives of Oral Biology* 29: 537–549.

Nasir, Sazzad M. and David J. Ostry. 2008. Speech motor learning in profoundly deaf adults. *Nature Neuroscience* 11: 1217–1222.

Nasir, S.M. and D.J. Ostry. 2009. Auditory plasticity and speech motor learning. *Proceedings of the National Academy of Sciences, USA* 106: 20470–20475.

Neilson, Peter D., Gavin Andrews, Barry E. Guitar, and Peter T. Quinn. 1979. Tonic stretch reflexes in lip, tongue and jaw muscles. *Brain Research* 178: 311–327.

Nordin, Magnus and Karl-Erik Hagbarth. 1989. Mechanoreceptive units in the human infra-orbital nerve. *Acta Physiologica Scandinavica* 135: 149–161.

Nordin, Magnus and Lars Thomander. 1989. Intrafascicular multi-unit recordings from the human infra-orbital nerve. *Acta Physiologica Scandinavica* 135: 139–148.

O'Dwyer, Nicolas J., Peter T. Quinn, Barry E. Guitar, Gavin Andrews, and Peter D. Neilson. 1981. Procedures for verification of electrode placement in EMG studies of orofacial and mandibular muscles. *Journal of Speech and Hearing Research* 24: 273–288.

Okdeh, Atef M., Mervyn F. Lyons, and Samuel W. Cadden. 1999. The study of jaw reflexes evoked by electrical stimulation of the lip: The importance of stimulus intensity and polarity. *Journal of Oral Rehabilitation* 26: 479–487.

Ostry, David J., Paul L. Gribble, Mindy F. Levin, and Anatol G. Feldman. 1997. Phasic and tonic stretch reflexes in muscles with few muscle spindles: Human jaw-opener muscles. *Experimental Brain Research* 116: 299–308.

Proske, Uwe and Simon C. Gandevia. 2009. The kinaesthetic senses. *Journal of Physiology* 587: 4139–4146.

Prud'homme, Michel J., Dan A.D. Cohen, and John F. Kalaska. 1994. Tactile activity in primate primary somatosensory cortex during active arm movements: Cytoarchitectonic distribution. *Journal of Neurophysiology* 71: 173–181.

Reed, Charlotte M., William M. Rabinowitz, Nathaniel I. Durlach, Louis D. Braida, Susan Conway-Fithian, and Martin C. Schultz. 1985. Research on the Tadoma method of speech communication. *Journal of the Acoustical Society of America* 77: 247–257.

Sams, Mikko, Riikka Möttönen, and Toni Sihvonen. 2005. Seeing and hearing others and oneself talk. *Cognitive Brain Research* 23: 429–435.

Shaiman, Susan and Vincent L. Gracco. 2002. Task-specific sensorimotor interactions in speech production. *Experimental Brain Research* 146: 411–418.

Smith, Anne, Christopher A. Moore, and Carol A. Pratt. 1985a. Distribution of the human jaw stretch reflex response elicited by percutaneous, localized stretch of jaw-closing muscles. *Experimental Neurology* 88: 544–561.

Smith, Anne, Christopher A. Moore, David H. McFarland, and Christine M. Weber. 1985b. Reflex responses of human lip muscles to mechanical stimulation during speech. *Journal of Motor Behavior* 17: 148–167.

Stål, Per, Per-Olof Eriksson, Anders Eriksson, and Lars-Eric Thornell. 1987. Enzyme-histochemical differences in fibre-type between the human major and minor zygomatic and the first dorsal interosseus muscles. *Archives of Oral Biology* 32: 833–841.

Stål, Per, Per-Olof Eriksson, Anders Eriksson, and Lars-Eric Thornell. 1990. Enzyme-histochemical and morphological characteristics of muscle fibre types in the human buccinator and orbicularis oris. *Archives of Oral Biology* 35: 449–458.

Sumby, W.H. and Irwin Pollack. 1954. Visual contribution to speech intelligibility in noise. *Journal of the Acoustical Society of America* 26: 212–215.

Takano, Sayoko and Kiyoshi Honda. 2007. An MRI analysis of the extrinsic tongue muscles during vowel production. *Speech Communication* 49: 49–58.

Tremblay, Stéphanie, Guillaume Houle, and David J. Ostry. 2008. Specificity of speech motor learning. *Journal of Neuroscience* 28: 2426–2434.

Tremblay, Stéphanie, Douglas M. Shiller, and David J. Ostry. 2003. Somatosensory basis of speech production. *Nature* 423: 866–869.

Trulsson, Mats and Roland S. Johansson. 2002. Orofacial mechanoreceptors in humans: Encoding characteristics and responses during natural orofacial behaviors. *Behavioural Brain Research* 135: 27–33.

Vatikiotis-Bateson, Eric, Takaaki Kuratate, Myuki Kamachi, and Hani Yehia. 1999. Facial deformation parameters for audiovisual synthesis. Paper presented to the Auditory-Visual Speech Processing, Santa Cruz, CA, USA, 1999.

Weinstein, Sidney. 1968. Intensive and extensive aspects of tactile sensitivity as function of body part, sex and laterality. In D.R. Kenshalo (ed.), *The Skin Senses*, 195–222. Springfield, IL: Thomas.

Yehia, Hani, Philip Rubin, and Eric Vatikiotis-Bateson. 1998. Quantitative association of vocal-tract and facial behavior. *Speech Communication* 26: 23–43.

FURTHER READING

Siemionow, Maria, Bahar B. Gharb, and Antonio Rampazzo. 2011. The face as a sensory organ. *Plastic and Reconstructive Surgery* 127: 652–662.

13 Auditory Feedback

JOHN HOUDE AND SRIKANTAN NAGARAJAN

Auditory feedback has a unique role in speech production. As compared with somatosensory perception (tactile, proprioceptive), audition is the sensory modality by which we perceive not only our own speech, but also the speech of others. Thus, by extension, auditory feedback tells us most directly whether others are likely to perceive our own productions as what we intended them to convey. It is not surprising, therefore, that speakers monitor their sound output and that this auditory feedback exerts a powerful influence on their speech. However, it is only recently, through advances in digital signal processing (DSP) technology, computational modeling, and functional neuroimaging methods that we have begun to understand how auditory feedback influences speech production.

13.1 Introduction

Audition is certainly important for learning to speak, since it is almost impossibly difficult for deaf children to learn to speak (Levitt et al. 1980; Oller and Eilers 1988; Ross and Giolas 1978; Smith 1975). However, after the basic speech motor control skill has been learned, the role of audition in speaking becomes less clear. In the absence of auditory feedback, speaking is only selectively disrupted. In postlingually deafened speakers, the control of pitch and loudness degrades rapidly after hearing loss, yet their speech will remain intelligible for decades (Cowie and Douglas-Cowie 1992; Lane et al. 1997). This deafness condition can also be simulated in normal hearing speakers: if masking noise is made loud enough (an extreme example of the Lombard effect) it will block a speaker's ability to hear him/herself. Yet speakers can produce intelligible (albeit loud) speech under these conditions (Lane and Tranel 1971; Lombard 1911). But this does not mean auditory feedback is not used after speaking is learned. At the highest levels of language production, speakers clearly monitor the words and phonemes they are saying, as

---

The Handbook of Speech Production, First Edition. Edited by Melissa A. Redford.
© 2015 John Wiley & Sons, Inc. Published 2019 by John Wiley & Sons, Inc.

well as the meaning conveyed by them (Levelt 1989). Syllable production also appears to be sensitive to auditory feedback, since delayed auditory feedback (DAF) of roughly a syllable's production time (100–200 ms) seems most effective at disrupting speech (Fairbanks 1954; Lee 1950; Yates 1963).

More recently, the advent of realtime DSP has enabled researchers to examine how speakers respond to alterations of specific features of their audio feedback. The newer experiments have revealed two classes of responses to auditory feedback alterations: (1) *compensation* in response to altered auditory feedback, when speakers make immediate compensatory responses in their ongoing speech; and (2) *adaptation* in response to consistently altered feedback, when speakers adjust subsequent productions and continue with compensatory responses even once the altered feedback is removed.

13.2 Compensation and adaptation

13.2.1 *Compensation and the efference copy hypothesis*

One of the main reasons these newer classes of altered feedback experiments have been so revealing is that, unlike the earlier DAF experiments, the new experiments alter feedback in ways speakers can compensate for. With DAF, there is nothing speakers can do to cancel out the effects of the feedback delay; they can only slow their speech to minimize its disfluent effects. From this, we learned mainly that auditory feedback *does* affect ongoing speech, not *how* it is used in ongoing speech. However, it was immediately clear from the earliest experiments that when speakers can compensate for a feedback alteration, they do. Investigations of the so-called *sidetone amplification effect* found that speakers lower their speech volume when given amplified audio feedback of their speech (Chang-Yit, Pick, and Siegel 1975). This effect may in fact be a general feature of audio-motor coordination, as the effect was also shown in guitar playing (Johnson et al. 1978). Somewhat later, researchers were able to alter the pitch of speakers' feedback and found this caused compensatory pitch changes (Elman 1981).

With the advent of realtime DSP methods, more recent studies have been able to examine the latencies and transfer functions of these compensatory phenomena. Kawahara used trains of pseudo-randomly occurring brief perturbations of speakers' pitch feedback to make inferences about the frequency-domain transfer function characterizing speakers' responses (Kawahara 1993). Larson and colleagues instead characterized these pitch responses in the time domain and found that speakers begin to make compensatory adjustments within 100–200 ms after perturbations of their pitch feedback (Burnett et al. 1998; Burnett, Senner, and Larson 1997). More recently, similar response latencies have been seen when speakers compensate for perturbations of amplitude of their speech feedback (Bauer et al. 2006; Heinks-Maldonado and Houde 2005), as well as for perturbations of the formants in their ongoing auditory feedback (Niziolek 2010; Purcell and Munhall 2006b; Tourville, Reilly, and Guenther 2008).

That the speech motor control system exhibits compensation is of great theoretical importance. In compensation, we see the system responding to a feedback alteration by adjusting its output to bring feedback closer to what it was before the alteration. This suggests the system has a target feedback sensation it seeks to achieve and that it compares incoming feedback with that target; if the two differ, corrective motor commands are issued. At a basic level, this is the classic description of feedback control. But if replace the term "target feedback" with "expected feedback," we see that compensation is also consistent with the *efference copy hypothesis*, which attempts to explain how reafference of self-generated sensations might be filtered out of the sensory stream. To accomplish such sensory filtering, it was hypothesized that internal feedback ("efference copy") of the neural commands generating motor actions might also generate expectations of their sensory consequences (Jeannerod 1988; von Holst 1954; von Holst and Mittelstaedt 1950). These expectations would be "subtracted" from the incoming sensory information, thus highlighting any remaining unpredicted sensations, which were assumed to arise from external sources. In this way, efference copy was hypothesized to enable the central nervous system (CNS) to distinguish "self" from "non-self" sources of sensory input.

But for such a scheme to work, the sensory consequences of motor actions must already be known. This knowledge is assumed to be learned from past experience in a "forward model" of the associations between motor commands and their sensory consequences. However, what was not appreciated in earlier accounts of this process is that, even after the forward model is learned, there is a limit to how well the sensory consequences of actions can be predicted. All neural commands to the body's muscle systems include an unavoidable amount of unpredictable noise (Harris and Wolpert 1998), resulting in self-generated sensory feedback that unavoidably deviates somewhat from target expectations. In this case, such unpredicted deviations should not be considered "non-self," but indicate motor disturbances requiring corrective action.

Thus, in addition to filtering out self-generated sensations, the efference copy process also has a possible role in feedback control. In fact, the two roles appear to be at odds with each other: how could the CNS know whether to interpret a deviation from expected feedback as arising from an external source or from internal motor noise needing correction? Part of the answer, at least for auditory feedback, is that auditory processing appears to also involve complex processes of auditory stream segregation, in which the auditory input is effectively split into separate auditory "streams," each containing only the audio signal from a single putative source in the environment (Bregman 1990). We use such processes to isolate a single voice from many others (the so-called "cocktail party effect," Cherry 1953) and it is likely we use the same processes to isolate our own voice from others' voices.

Further consideration of auditory stream segregation is beyond the scope of this chapter, but there is a simpler way that has been proposed for how deviations from expected feedback could be used for both feedback control and distinguishing self- from non-self-generated sensations: assume small deviations are from self-generated motor noise, while large deviations are from external sources (Burnett et al. 1998; Heinks-Maldonado, Nagarajan, and Houde 2006; Houde et al. 2002). This may be a feasible approach for well-learned motor skills like speaking, since high consistency (low noise) behavior is one of the chief characteristics of skilled motor performance (Rosenbaum, Carlson, and Gilmore 2001). It may also partly explain why compensation for auditory feedback perturbations tends to be smaller for larger feedback perturbations. For example, Burnett et al. (1988) found nearly complete compensation was found for 25 cent pitch perturbations and only 10% compensation for 250 cent perturbations. We will return to this issue later in this chapter and consider other factors that may contribute to compensation being incomplete, but here we note that if subjects considered larger perturbations to be externally generated, it would be reasonable for them to refrain from compensating for their effects. This explanation may also account for why speakers tend to be less impaired by DAF as feedback delays are increased past 200–300 ms (Fairbanks 1955): at larger delays, speakers may increasingly consider the auditory feedback as not arising from their own productions. (Note however, that it does not necessarily explain why increasing feedback delay from 0 to 200–300 ms has the opposite effect and increasingly disturbs a speaker's production.) A non-speech analog of this situation can be seen when subjects tickle their own hand using a robot that delays the tickle action (Blakemore, Wolpert, and Frith 1998, 1999). With increasing delay, subjects report a more ticklish sensation, as expected if the delay created mismatch between a sensory prediction derived from the tickle action and the actual somatosensory feedback. Finally, if the DAF effect is reduced because the delayed feedback is no longer considered self-produced, then altering audio feedback in other ways that make it seem not self-produced should also decrease the DAF effect. This hypothesis was tested by Toyomura and Omori (2005), who found that the disfluent effects of DAF were lessened if audio feedback was also pitch-shifted to sound like a different speaker.

13.2.2 Adaptation and the maintenance of speech motor control

The compensatory phenomena described above show that, when the timescales of the speech behavior allow for it (i.e., suprasegmental rates), auditory feedback does appear to be used for online corrections to speech output. But as we will discuss below, at the timescale of segmental production (10–12 phonemes per second, Levelt 1999) the delays inherent in processing auditory feedback are too long to allow for moment-by-moment online control. Given these constraints, how does auditory feedback affect the production of segments? The answer appears to be: indirectly. Even after acquiring speech production, speakers use auditory feedback to maintain their speech production motor skill. This can be seen in the gradual deterioration of intelligibility of deafened adults' speech (Cowie and Douglas-Cowie 1992) and it can be seen in the laboratory setting in the phenomenon of speech sensorimotor adaptation (speechSA). SpeechSA refers to the changes induced in speech output over repeated utterances produced while hearing altered feedback. These long-term changes can be shown to be retained in any subsequent absence of auditory feedback (i.e., with hearing blocked by masking noise) and are analogous to similar phenomena seen in visuomotor adaptation studies of arm movements (Wolpert and Ghahramani 2000).

The original experiment demonstrating speechSA (Houde and Jordan 1998) used whispered speech, but the same adaptation effects it found were subsequently also shown for voiced speech and its basic design is seen in the many speechSA experiments that have come after it. In the experiment, subjects received audio feedback during their productions of "train" words ("pep," "peb," "bep," and "beb"). The train words were all bilabial CVC syllables with /ɛ/ as the vowel. During production, subjects heard feedback, which was processed by DSP to alter formant frequencies in a gradual fashion to some maximum value, which was then held there for one hour. Depending on the subject group, the maximum formant shift caused subjects to hear their productions of /ɛ/ as either /i/ or /ɑ/. To varying degrees, most subjects changed production of /ɛ/ to compensate for the feedback alteration. That is, subjects gradually shifted their productions of /ɛ/ to oppose the shift of formants in their feedback; for example, if formants were shifted toward /i/ in their feedback, they shifted their produced formants toward /ɑ/. This had the effect of making the altered feedback sound more like /ɛ/ again.

Throughout the experiment, train word trials with altered feedback were interleaved with trials in which subjects produced "test" words with feedback blocked by masking noise. One test word was also a train word ("pep"). As a train word, subjects changed this word's production to compensate for the altered feedback. Such production changes were largely retained when the word was produced as a test word with feedback blocked. Thus, the altered feedback not only induced subjects to compensate, it induced subjects to adapt their productions. Three other test words ("peg," "gep," and "teg") shared the same vowel as the train words, but varied the consonant context. The production of /ɛ/ was also adapted in these words, showing that adaptation of /ɛ/ generalized to different contexts. The remaining test words ("peep," "pip," "pap," and "pop") had different vowels. Their productions also changed somewhat during the experiment, showing that the adaptation of /ɛ/ also partially generalized to other vowels.

Since the original experiment, many other studies have shown that speakers exhibit speechSA in their production of formants in voiced speech (e.g., Katseff, Houde, and Johnson 2012; MacDonald, Goldberg, and Munhall 2010; Purcell and Munhall 2006a). Due to the much louder volume of voiced speech, it becomes difficult to block audio feedback completely with a safe level of masking noise. Thus, few of these studies have attempted to assess adaptation directly, by showing that compensation is retained in productions made with feedback blocked. Instead, most studies use indirect methods to infer adaptation has occurred: they show that compensation for the altered feedback develops over many trials, at a rate slower than the ramp-up of the feedback alteration, and that the compensation developed during the experiment takes many trials to disappear ("washout") after the feedback alteration has been removed. Using these indirect methods, sensorimotor adaptation has also been demonstrated in the production of pitch (Jones and Munhall 2000) and in the production of fricatives (Shiller et al. 2009).

13.2.3 Conscious control of compensation for altered auditory feedback

The processing of auditory feedback during speaking does not appear to be a consciously mediated attention-dependent process. In most auditory feedback adaptation experiments, the feedback alteration is gradually introduced and subjects increasingly compensate to keep pace with this increasing alteration. In these experiments, many subjects report not being aware of any change in their auditory feedback, even though they were measurably compensating (Houde and Jordan 2002; Purcell and Munhall 2006a). To explore this issue further, Munhall et al. (2009) conducted a formant adaptation experiment with three different groups of subjects: (1) subjects were not told about the altered feedback, (2) subjects were told to ignore any changes they heard in their feedback, and (3) subjects were given a lecture about what would happen in the experiment and told to avoid responding to the altered feedback. All subjects groups compensated equally for the altered feedback, regardless of their conscious awareness of it.

Automatic compensation is observed in experiments where pitch feedback is briefly altered. Unlike most formant adaptation experiments where the feedback alteration is gradual, transient pitch perturbations are abrupt and quite noticeable. But does conscious awareness confer the ability to consciously control one's reaction to the feedback perturbation? Hain et al. (2000) did an experiment to address this question. Subjects phonated while their pitch feedback was occasionally and transiently perturbed. Different groups of subjects were given different instructions: upon hearing the perturbation, they should (1) oppose the pitch alteration in their production, or (2) follow the alteration, or (3) avoid responding to the alteration. The authors found that instructions to subjects had little effect on the early responses to the perturbations, which generally started roughly 200 ms after perturbation onset and were mostly compensatory. Subjects' later responses (>300 ms latency) better matched what they were instructed to do.

Zarate and colleagues extended the results of the Hain et al. (2000) study with two studies that showed how training could increase the degree of conscious control over the pitch perturbation response. In their first study, subjects who either had or had not acquired extensive vocal voice/singing training responded to long (starting 1 sec after phonation onset, then lasting the rest of the trial) alterations in the pitch of their auditory feedback. Throughout the experiment, subjects were instructed to either ignore or oppose (i.e., compensate for) the pitch alteration. Both singers and non-singers compensated similarly, but musicians were significantly more able to avoid compensating in the "ignore" condition (Zarate and Zatorre 2008). In a follow-up study, singers were tested on their ability to refrain from compensating for large (200 cent) and small (25 cent) pitch perturbations (100 cents = 1/12 octave). They were much less able to avoid compensating for the small perturbations (Zarate, Wood, and Zatorre 2010).

13.2.4 Relation between auditory feedback and speech timing

Speakers are highly sensitive to the time of arrival of their auditory feedback. As mentioned above, DAF of roughly 100–200 ms (comparable to the production time of a syllable) will disrupt fluency, causing speakers to exhibit "stuttering"-like behavior and slow down their speaking rate (Lee 1951; Yates 1963). Even smaller feedback delays (e.g., a sub-syllabic 50 ms delay), which generally do not induce disfluencies, nevertheless cause speakers to slow down their speaking rate (Black 1951; Stuart et al. 2002).

Why does DAF alter speakers' speech? According to the efference copy hypothesis, incoming feedback is compared with a motor/frontal-derived prediction of the expected feedback. As we will discuss more below, there are delays inherent in conveying incoming feedback to the CNS, so for proper time alignment, the prediction must be delayed by a time that precisely matches the incoming feedback delay. Presumably, this delay is part of what is learned as speakers associate their motor actions with the resulting feedback. Thus, in some sense, even unaltered feedback is a kind of DAF, but at a delay that speakers have learned to accommodate. Without such accommodation the time misalignment creates false feedback prediction "errors." These errors drive erroneous corrective actions that disrupt ongoing articulatory control.

A prediction of the efferent copy hypothesis is that, with time, speakers will form new associations between actions and their sensory consequences, including the new artificial delay. These associations will allow them to adapt to a given feedback delay, becoming less disfluent and speed up their speaking rate. Indeed, several studies have reported that speakers can adapt to DAF (Fillenbaum 1965; Winchester, Gibbons, and Krebs 1959). Other studies report more mixed results. For example, one study found that extended exposure to DAF reduced disfluencies but resulted in no speech rate increase (Tiffany and Hanley 1956). Support for the efference copy account is also complicated by evidence that speakers "adapt" to DAF by consciously employing strategies such as listening for their own bone-conducted speech (Katz and Lackner 1977). Also at odds with the hypothesis is evidence that DAF does not affect the production of individual speech sounds (i.e., speakers don't mispronounce a phoneme with DAF), but usually disrupts the sequencing of speech sounds (Perrier 2006), or disrupts speech rhythm (Kaspar and Rubeling 2011).

Recently, Cai et al. (2011) have used altered formant feedback to undertake a more nuanced examination of how auditory feedback is involved in speech timing. By dynamically altering formants as a function of where a speaker is in their production of a diphthong syllable, Cai et al. were able provide a "local" version of DAF: one which provided speakers with the illusion that they had reached a specific target either earlier or later than expected, without altering the apparent timing of other targets. Cai et al. found that speakers made within-syllable adjustments (speeding up or slowing down) for these timing changes and also changed the timing of the next syllable to accommodate their within-syllable adjustments. The results suggest that, rather than operating only a high-level syllabic sequencing level of speech production, auditory feedback also partly controls moment-by-moment timing.

This possible role of auditory feedback in controlling the low-level timing of individual phoneme targets is also supported by a study that altered feedback of the apparent voice onset time (VOT) that speakers heard in their production of stop consonants. The study used voice-triggered playback to provide subjects with the audio of one consonant when they produced another. When they played out a voiced version (short VOT, "dip") of an unvoiced consonant that subjects were producing ("tip"), subjects compensated by lengthening their produced VOT (Mitsuya, Macdonald, and Munhall 2009).

13.2.5 *Somatosensation and auditory feedback processing*

It is likely that audition interacts with somatosensation during speech production. Indeed, this interaction has been suggested as an explanation for why compensation for altered audio feedback is usually not complete. In the audio feedback alteration experiments, the CNS is receiving two types of feedback: auditory and somatosensory. If the CNS does not compensate at all for the altered audio feedback, its somatosensory feedback reports that production is fully on target, while its auditory feedback reports that production is off target. On the other hand, if the CNS compensates fully, the two feedback sources report the opposite production situation. Thus, no matter how precise the speech production system may be, there is no amount of compensation the CNS can produce that will resolve the mismatch between audition and somatosensation. To compensate at all, the CNS is forced to decide how much mismatch it is willing to tolerate in each of the senses.

A similar problem is faced by the CNS when it must compensate for altered visual feedback in a reaching task. An alteration creates a visual target error with no proprioceptive error. A model that successfully predicts behavior in this situation is one where the two sense modalities are weighed to create an integrated estimate, or percept, of the true arm position that is then compared with the target (Sober and Sabes 2005). In this estimation, each sense is weighted according to the estimated reliability of each sense. Thus if vision is considered more accurate that somatosensation, then the contribution of vision to the perceived targeting error will be large and there will be a large compensation response to a visual alteration.

If this understanding of the CNS response to visual feedback information is applied to predict speech motor responses to altered auditory feedback, then we would have both audition and somatosensation being combined to make an integrated percept of the estimated speech target error. To combine the two senses, each percept would be weighted according to its expected accuracy, or reliability, in reporting the true speech output. From this model, several predictions can be made. First, if perceived uncertainty in somatosensation is increased, the estimate of speech output should rely more heavily on audition and speech target errors created by altering auditory feedback would be perceived to be bigger, resulting in greater compensation. For example, numbing the articulators should increase uncertainty in somatosensory feedback, which should then increase compensations for altered auditory feedback. Such an effect has indeed been observed: Larson et al. (2008) tested what happens to the pitch feedback perturbation response if anesthetic is sprayed on the vocal folds and found that this resulted in larger compensatory pitch responses.

The view that auditory and somatosensory feedback merge to create an integrated percept also suggests that auditory feedback alterations may affect somatosensation. This possibility was tested in a study by Champoux, Shiller, and Zatorre (2011), who modulated the amplitude of subjects' auditory feedback during the production of voiced and unvoiced sounds. They found that 16 Hz amplitude modulation of the auditory feedback during the production of voiced sounds consistently induced a "throbbing sensation" for subjects at their lips.

Another prediction of the merged feedback model is that if the CNS has a fixed tolerance for somatosensory mismatch, but is always striving for minimal mismatch (i.e., maximal precision) in auditory feedback, then compensation should be more complete for smaller audio feedback alterations that do not require the compensatory articulations to deviate much from the somatosensory target. We recently explore this possibility and find it to be the case: in an experiment where F1 was altered between 50 and 250 Hz, mean percent compensation across subjects increased from roughly 50% for a 250 Hz F1 shift to essentially 100% for a 50 Hz F1 shift (Katseff et al. 2012). Other recent studies have also found this pattern of more compensation for smaller formant shifts (MacDonald et al. 2010) and analogous results have been found in studies of responses to pitch feedback perturbations, where complete compensation was found for small (25 cent) pitch perturbations (Burnett et al. 1998).

There is some evidence, however, that feedback processing during speaking is not always a simple weighting of somatosensory and auditory feedback. Several previous studies have shown that speakers will compensate for a somatosensory feedback alteration, even if the alteration has no acoustic consequences (Nasir and Ostry 2006, 2008, 2009; Tremblay, Houle, and Ostry 2008; Tremblay, Shiller, and Ostry 2003), but if auditory and somatosensory feedback perturbations are pitted against each other, does auditory feedback take primacy? A study by Feng, Gracco, and Max (2011) addressed this question. In the experiment, subjects spoke while either their auditory or somatosensory feedback, or both types of feedback were altered. The auditory alteration was a shift up of F1, while the somatosensory alteration was an external force that acted to either close or open the jaw. Since tongue height (and, roughly speaking, also jaw height) varies inversely with F1, compensating for the jaw closing alteration (i.e., lowering the jaw) would work against compensating for the F1 raising (i.e., raising the jaw to lower F1). In this situation, Feng et al. found subjects chose to compensate for the F1 raising at the expense of compensating for the jaw closing. In fact, subjects always compensated for the F1 shifts, regardless of jaw alteration, but only compensated for the jaw alteration when F1 was not altered, or when the jaw compensation raised the jaw and thus also helped compensate for the F1 raising. In the Feng et al. experiment, it seems auditory feedback takes priority over somatosensory feedback.

But what happens if speakers are simultaneously exposed to both somatosensory and auditory feedback alterations that are not pitted against each other? This question was addressed in a recent study by Lametti, Nasir, and Ostry (2012). Like Feng et al. (2011), Lametti et al. used an adaptation paradigm involving exposure to simultaneous somatosensory and auditory feedback alterations. But whereas the Feng et al. study was designed to force subjects to choose which sensory alteration to compensate for, the Lametti et al. study was designed to avoid any interaction between the two sense modalities. Thus, the somatosensory alteration was a velocity-dependent radial pull of the jaw – one that the authors had previously shown has minimal acoustic consequences but that speakers compensate for (Tremblay et al. 2003), while the auditory alteration was an F1 shift that can be compensated for by a change in tongue height. Subjects not only compensated for both feedback alterations, they also adapted their productions. Although the feedback alterations were abruptly introduced, subjects' maximal compensation developed over successive trials. Adaption varied drastically across subjects. Some subjects adapted only to the somatosensory alteration, some only to the auditory alteration and others partially adapted to both. In addition, the degree to which a subject adapted to the somatosensory alteration was inversely correlated ($R=0.54$, $p<0.001$) with the degree to which he/she adapted to the auditory alteration. The results suggest that speakers, to some extent, choose between which sense modality they attend to while speaking.

13.3 Modeling the role of auditory feedback in speech production

Early models of feedback's role in speaking were heavily influenced by the advent of cybernetic theory (Wiener 1948) and the discovery of the DAF effect (Lee 1950). Following these developments, Fairbanks (1954) proposed a model of speech motor control based on feedback control. A key element of Fairbanks's model was a "comparator" which subtracted sensory feedback (including auditory feedback) from a target "input signal," creating an "error signal" which was used in the control of the vocal tract articulators. However, various phenomena discussed above (e.g., speech in the absence of auditory feedback) suggest that speech motor control is not entirely dependent on sensory feedback. Indeed, even Fairbanks did not propose a model of speech motor control based exclusively on feedback. In his model, the "error signal" output of his feedback control subsystem does not drive the vocal tract directly. Instead it is first combined with the "input signal" (the output of a feedforward control subsystem) by a "mixer" element to create the "effective driving signal" which directly controls the vocal tract. This combination of feedback and feedforward control subsystems is similar in design to that of the current Directions into Velocities of Articulators (DIVA) model of speech motor control (Guenther 1995; Guenther, Ghosh, and Tourville 2006; Guenther, Hampson, and Johnson 1998; Guenther and Vladusich 2012), although the feedforward control subsystem in DIVA is implemented as an internal feedback loop, which we will describe further below.

But have we yet completely ruled out feedback control as the basis for controlling speaking? Based on what we have covered above, it could still be argued that speech could be controlled by a combination of auditory and somatosensory feedback, since somatosensory feedback is always available, even with deafness, or with audition blocked by masking noise. But experiments have shown that somatosensory nerve block impacts only certain aspects of speech (e.g., lip rounding, fricative constrictions) and even for these, the impact is not sufficient to prevent intelligible speech (Scott and Ringel 1971). Thus, it appears that intelligible speech is possible in the absence of sensory feedback in general, which is difficult to explain with any pure feedback control model.

Beyond this, however, there are also more basic difficulties with modeling the control of speech as being based on sensory feedback. In biological systems, sensory feedback is noisy, due to environment noise and the stochastic firing properties of neurons (Kandel, Schwartz, and Jessell 2000). Furthermore, as we alluded to above, an even more significant problem is that sensory feedback is delayed. There are several obvious reasons why sensory feedback to the CNS is delayed (e.g., by axon transmission times and synaptic delays, Kandel et al. 2000), but a less obvious reason involves the time needed to process raw sensory feedback into features useful for monitoring speech. For example, in the auditory domain, there are several key features of the acoustic speech waveform that are important for discriminating between speech utterances. For some of these features, like pitch, spectral envelope, and formant frequencies, signal processing theory dictates that the accuracy in which the features are estimated from the speech waveform depends on the duration of the time window used to calculate them (Parsons 1987). In practice, this means such features are estimated from the acoustic waveform using sliding time windows with lengths on the order of 30–100 ms in duration. Such integration-window-based feature estimation methods are slow to respond to changes in the speech waveform and thus effectively will introduce additional delays in the detection of such changes. Consistent with this theoretical account, studies show that response latencies of auditory areas to changes in higher-level auditory features can range from 30 ms to over 100 ms (Cheung et al. 2005; Godey et al. 2005; Heil 2003). A particularly relevant example is the long (~100 ms) response latency of neurons in a recently discovered area of pitch-sensitive neurons in auditory cortex (Bendor and Wang 2005). As a result, while auditory responses can be seen within 10–15 ms of a sound at the ear (Heil and Irvine 1996; Lakatos et al. 2005), there are important reasons to suppose that the features needed for controlling speech are not available to the CNS until a significant time (~30–100 ms) after they are peripherally present. This is a problem for feedback control models, because direct feedback control based on delayed feedback is inherently unstable, particularly for fast movements (Franklin, Powell, and Emami-Naeini 1991).

Feedback control models can be considered the most extreme implementation of the efference copy hypothesis, where the motor-derived prediction functions as the target output and comparison with this target/prediction results in a prediction error that directly drives the motor control output. In current speech motor control models, the efference copy/feedback prediction process is still used to create a correction, but that correction does not directly generate output controls. Instead, it is a contributing factor in the generation of output controls. These models retain the concept of feedback control but put the feedback loop inside the CNS, where processing delays are minimal, with actual sensory feedback forming a slower, possibly delayed and intermittent, external loop that updates the internal feedback loop (Guenther and Vladusich 2012; Hickok, Houde, and Rong 2011; Houde and Nagarajan 2011; Price, Crinion, and Macsweeney 2011; Tian and Poeppel 2010).

13.4 Neural pathways of auditory feedback processing

From anatomical studies it appears that auditory feedback makes contact with speech motor control at both subcortical and cortical locations. On each side of the CNS, the auditory pathway from the ear reaches the cochlear nucleus and extends through the superior olivary complex and the lateral lemniscus to the inferior colliculus (IC) (Webster 1992). The IC potentially provides auditory feedback control of vocalization with its projection to the periaqueductal gray (PAG) (Burnett et al. 1998; Jürgens 1993, 2002), but also projects through the medial geniculate nucleus to auditory cortex (AC) (Webster 1992). In each hemisphere, auditory feedback goes from AC to facial and laryngeal motor cortex (M1) by at least three pathways: (1) via the pontine nuclei (Glickstein 1997) to the auditory region of the cerebellum (Huang et al. 1991) and back to M1 (Ghez and Thach 2000); (2) via the facial area of the putamen (Yeterian and Pandya 1998), then through the globus pallidus and motor thalamus and back to M1 (Alexander and Crutcher 1990); and (3) via a network of higher auditory and prefrontal cortical areas, to premotor areas (Kaas and Hackett 1998; Petrides and Pandya 1988), which connect directly with M1 (Dum and Strick 2005; Greenlee et al. 2004). We will have much more to say about this last pathway in the sections that follow.

13.4.1 Speech-sensitive regions of auditory cortex

Auditory input arrives through sensory thalamus into primary auditory cortex (AI) located in the Heschl's gyrus (HG) (Rauschecker and Scott 2009). Subsequently, auditory processing occurs in several higher-order auditory belt and parabelt regions located posterior (dorsal) and anterior (ventral) to HG in the superior temporal plane. These higher-order areas are sensitive to more spectro-temporally complex sounds including speech (Obleser and Kotz 2011; Obleser et al. 2010; Rauschecker and Scott 2009) and there is an active debate about the roles of the dorsal and ventral regions (Obleser et al. 2010; Okada et al. 2010). Engagement of these superior temporal regions in processing speech during listening has been extensively documented. These regions are more activated during processing of speech stimuli than when processing noise (Jancke et al. 2002; Obleser et al. 2010; Rimol et al. 2005; Zatorre et al. 1992) and other non-speech sounds (Belin 2006; Belin et al. 2000; Benson et al. 2006; Uppenkamp et al. 2006; Whalen et al. 2006). Recent imaging studies suggest that it is the processing of speech and not the acoustic structure of speech that is responsible for the activation in these regions (Dehaene-Lambertz et al. 2005; Liebenthal et al. 2010; Mottonen et al. 2006; Scott et al. 2006). Higher-order auditory areas in turn project both lateral-anteriorly and lateral-posteriorly along the superior temporal sulcus (STS) and to the medial temporal gyrus (MTG).

Several studies on phonetic perception suggest that categorization of highly familiar sound patterns are mediated by left mSTS just ventral to HG, whereas left pSTS plays a role in transient representation of relevant sound features that provide the basis for identifying newly acquired sound categories (Golestani and Zatorre 2004; Liebenthal et al. 2010) and in transient storage and retrieval of phonological sequences (Hickok et al. 2011; Indefrey and Levelt 2000). Further downstream in superior temporal gyrus (STG), Dewitt and Rauschecker (2012) suggest processing of short time-scale patterns is consistently localized to left mid-STG, whereas activation associated with integration of phonemes into temporal complex patterns is consistently localized to left anterior STG. Mid-anterior STG is implicated in invariant representations of phonetic forms, preferring phonemes to environmental sounds. The bilateral STG regions, together with more inferior STS/MTG regions, also exhibit greater activity when listening to speech compared with noise, consistent with them being speech sensitive. Speech versus non-speech activation differences are highly variable along STS (Liebenthal et al. 2010).

The degree to which auditory speech processing is lateralized is a matter of some debate. There is a general debate about the exact division of labor between left and right hemispheres in many auditory tasks. Most researchers agree that the mSTS bilaterally activates for speech and other complex sounds (Binder et al. 1996; Hall, Hart, and Johnsrude 2003; Hall et al. 2002; Seifritz et al. 2002; Wessinger et al. 2001), but that the more posterior and anterior STS regions tend to activate more on the left for lexical and categorization tasks. Indeed, many of the studies of auditory cortex discussed above emphasize the dominance of the left hemisphere, but in certain tasks (e.g., pitch perception, music perception, and speaker recognition) the right hemisphere may have an advantage (Johnsrude, Penhune, and Zatorre 2000; Mathiak et al. 2002; Zatorre 2001; Zatorre et al. 1992). Some have said the right is involved in emotion processing, while others have found less laterality in this respect (Kotz et al. 2003) and instead emphasize a short temporal/poor frequency versus long temporal/good frequency differentiation between left and right (Johnsrude et al. 1997; Poeppel 2003; Zatorre, Belin, and Penhune 2002).

13.4.2 Speech-sensitive regions of frontal/motor cortex

Several regions in frontal cortex involved in speech production are implicated in auditory feedback processing. Many are activated in speech perception. These include primary motor cortex (M1), the final cortical output to laryngeal muscles

(Simonyan and Horwitz 2011; Simonyan et al. 2009), as well as other traditional speech motor planning regions such as PMC and regions in the IFG, preSMA, and SMA. Callan et al. (2004) suggest that ventral PMC including opercular part of Broca's area is influential in facilitating speech perception performance in noise, suggesting that motor areas are recruited to predict upcoming speech sounds' more difficult tasks. Wilson and Iacoboni (2006) showed that producibility of sounds varies activity in STG, and motor areas show slightly greater activity for non-native speech sounds when compared to native sounds. Meister et al. (2007) show that rTMS of PMC impairs phoneme discrimination in noise whereas Sato, Tremblay, and Gracco (2009) showed slowing of phoneme discrimination. Peeva et al. (2010) suggest left vPMC is the site for syllable-level perceptual representations. In contrast, others (McGettigan et al. 2012) find pPT/vSMG to be a key region for phonological working memory and have audiomotor templates. Price et al. (2011) showed that silent speech activates both vPMC and pPT/vSMG. Papoutsi et al. (2009) show that activity in posterior pars opercularis, PMC, IFG, and preSMA/SMA is increased for production of low- versus high-frequency nonwords and others have shown increased PMC, IFG, and SMA activation for sequence and syllable complexity (Bohland and Guenther 2006). Many of these regions are also implicated in speech compensation (Tourville et al. 2008; Toyomura et al. 2007; Zarate et al. 2010).

13.4.3 The dual stream hypothesis

As alluded to above, within auditory cortex, even in other primates, there appear to be at least two distinct pathways, or streams, of auditory processing. The concept of multiple sensory processing streams gained most attention when it was advanced as an organizational principle of the visual system, with a dorsal "where" stream leading to parietal cortex that is concerned with object location and a ventral "what" stream leading to the temporal pole concerned with object recognition (Mishkin, Ungerleider, and Macko 1983). Subsequently, studies of the auditory system found a match to this visual system organization. Neurons responding to auditory source location were found in a dorsal pathway leading up to parietal cortex and neurons responding to auditory source type were found in a ventral pathway leading down toward the temporal pole (Rauschecker and Tian 2000). More recent evidence, however, has refined the view of the dorsal stream's task to be one of sensorimotor integration. The dorsal visual stream was found to be closely linked with motor control systems (e.g., reaching, head and eye movement control) (Andersen 1997; Rizzolatti, Fogassi, and Gallese 1997), while, in humans, the dorsal auditory stream was found to be closely linked with the vocal motor control system. In particular, a variety of studies have implicated the posterior STG (Zheng, Munhall, and Johnsrude 2010) and the superior parietal temporal area (Spt) (Buchsbaum, Hickok, and Humphries 2001; Hickok et al. 2003) as serving feedback processing specifically related to speech production. Consistent with this, studies of stroke victims have shown a double dissociation between ability to perform discreet production-related perceptual judgments and ability to understand continuous speech that depends on lesion location (dorsal and ventral stream lesions, respectively) (Baker, Blumstein, and Goodglass 1981; Miceli et al. 1980).

Overall, these studies have led to refined looped and "dual stream" models of speech processing (Hickok et al. 2011; Hickok and Poeppel 2007; Rauschecker and Scott 2009) with a ventral stream serving speech comprehension and a dorsal stream serving feedback processing related to speaking. Yet, although clear distinctions are seen between anterior-ventral and posterior-dorsal auditory processing streams, the specific function and degree of specialization of each stream, particularly in the context of speech perception in humans, remains highly debated (Belin and Zatorre 2000; Binder et al. 2000; Hickok and Poeppel 2007; Liebenthal et al. 2010; Scott 2006). Both pathways also make contact with frontal and premotor areas. The white matter tracts of the extreme capsule and uncinate fasciculus connect the mid- and anterior-STG/STS with the pars triangularis (PTr) and ventral opercular (vOp) areas of Broca's region (Friederici 2011; Saur et al. 2008). However, the principal pathways from auditory to the frontal/motor cortices supporting auditory feedback processing appear to favor the dorsal pathway. The arcuate fasciculus and more generally, the superior longitudinal fasciculus, link dorsal stream areas (pSTS/STG, pPT, vSMG, Spt) to the premotor areas (PMv and PMd) and frontal areas (PTr, vOp, dOp; all fields of Broca's region) implicated in speech production (Friederici 2011; Glasser and Rilling 2008; Schmahmann et al. 2007; Upadhyay et al. 2008). Some (Wise et al. 2001) have postulated the presence of two dorsal streams. One stream is hypothesized to connect Broca's region with pSTS and play a major role in the transient representation of the temporal structure of phonetic sequences. This stream is described as an interface between phoneme perception and long-term lexical memory. A second dorsal stream is hypothesized to link premotor areas to auditory areas in the temporoparietal junction and it is this stream which is thought to be most involved in enabling auditory feedback to interact with lower-level speech motor control (Hickok and Poeppel 2007).

13.4.4 *Disruptions of the dorsal processing stream*

When the dorsal stream is disrupted, a number of speech sensorimotor disorders appear to result (Hickok et al. 2011). Conduction aphasia is a neurological condition resulting from stroke in which production and comprehension of speech is preserved but the ability to repeat speech sound sequences just heard is impaired (Geschwind 1965). Conduction aphasia appears to result from damage to area Spt in the dorsal auditory processing stream (Buchsbaum et al. 2011). Consistent with this, the impairment is particularly apparent in the task of repeating nonsense speech sounds, because when the sound sequences do not form meaningful words, the intact speech comprehension system (the ventral stream) cannot aid in remembering what was heard.

More speculatively, stuttering may also result from impairments in auditory feedback processing in the dorsal stream. It is well known that altering auditory feedback (e.g., altering pitch (Howell, El-Yaniv, and Powell 1987), masking feedback with noise (Maraist and Hutton 1957), and DAF (Soderberg 1968) can make many persons who stutter speak fluently. Evidence for dorsal stream involvement in these fluency enhancements comes from a study relating DAF-induced fluency to structural MRIs of the brains of persons who stutter (Foundas et al. 2004). The planum temporale (PT) is an area of temporal cortex encompassing dorsal stream areas like Spt and the study found that right PT was aberrantly larger than left PT in those stutterers whose fluency was enhanced by DAF. Several other anatomical studies have also implicated dorsal stream dysfunction in stuttering, including studies showing impaired white matter connectivity in this region (Cykowski et al. 2010), as well as aberrant gyrification patterns (Foundas et al. 2001).

Temporary disruptions of the dorsal stream have also been shown to rather directly affect auditory feedback processing. In a recent study, Shum et al. (2011) used repetitive transcranial magnetic stimulation (rTMS) of the inferior parietal lobe (near the Spt region) to inhibit its activity as subjects spoke while exposed to altered formant feedback. The authors found that rTMS of this region did in fact reduce the degree that subjects compensated for the altered feedback.

13.4.5 Neural activity during auditory feedback processing

In the previous discussion, the likely neural substrate of auditory feedback processing for speech was proposed based on the functional properties of different cortical areas and their anatomical connectivities. More specific definition of this substrate has required more direct investigations of neural activity during the actual processing of auditory feedback during production. These studies have not only helped reveal specific cortical regions that process feedback, but have also provided more evidence about how auditory feedback is processed.

13.4.5.1 Neural activity during normal auditory feedback processing The response of a subject's auditory cortices to his/her own self-produced speech is significantly smaller than their response to similar, but externally produced speech (e.g., tape playback of the subject's previous self-productions). This effect, which we call speaking-induced suppression (SIS), has been seen using positron emission tomography (PET) (Hirano et al. 1996; Hirano, Kojima, et al. 1997; Hirano, Naito, et al. 1997), electroencephalography (EEG) (Ford and Mathalon 2004; Ford et al. 2001), magnetoencephalography (MEG) (Curio et al. 2000; Houde et al. 2002), and electrocorticography (ECoG) (Greenlee et al. 2011). An analog of the SIS effect has also been seen in non-human primates (Eliades and Wang 2003, 2005, 2008). Our own MEG experiments have shown that the SIS effect is only minimally explained by a general suppression of auditory cortex during speaking and that this suppression is not happening in the more peripheral parts of the CNS (Houde et al. 2002). We have also shown that the observed suppression goes away if the subject's feedback is altered to mismatch his/her expectations (Heinks-Maldonado et al. 2006; Houde et al. 2002), as is consistent with some of the PET study findings.

Taken together, the studies of the SIS phenomenon suggest that production-specific feedback processing involves comparison of incoming feedback with a feedback prediction derived from motor efference copy, which is very consistent with the efference copy hypothesis discussed in previous sections of this chapter. Indeed, a recent study has found that the level of functional connectivity between Broca's area and auditory cortex (i.e., a neural correlate of efference copy) just prior to speech onset predicted the level of SIS observed (Chen et al. 2011). Further evidence for the hypothesis comes from a test of the prediction that if SIS depends on a precise match between feedback and prediction, then precise time alignment of prediction with feedback would be critical for complex rapidly changing productions (e.g., rapidly speaking "ah-ah-ah") and less critical for slow or static productions (e.g., speaking "ah"). Assuming a given level of time alignment inaccuracy, the prediction/feedback match should therefore be better (and SIS stronger) for slower, less dynamic productions, which is what we found in a recent study (Ventura, Nagarajan, and Houde 2009).

13.4.5.2 Neural responses to altered auditory feedback Functional imaging studies examining speaking with audio feedback alterations have identified a number of cortical areas that are potentially involved in processing auditory feedback. These studies used blood flow based imaging methods (fMRI or PET) and localized activity by contrasting trials subjects spoke with altered feedback with unaltered feedback trials. A variety of feedback alterations have been investigated, including pitch shifts (Fu et al. 2006; McGuire, Silbersweig, and Frith 1996; Parkinson et al. 2012; Toyomura et al. 2007; Zarate et al. 2010; Zarate and Zatorre 2008), DAF (Hashimoto and Sakai 2003; Hirano, Kojima, et al. 1997), formant shifts (Tourville et al. 2008) and replacement of the voiced feedback with noise modulated by the amplitude envelope of the voiced feedback (Zheng et al. 2010).

The results of these studies all tended to support the hypothesized role of the dorsal speech processing stream in processing auditory feedback. All studies found the STG to be more active when feedback was altered, with some studies localizing activity to the mid-STG (Fu et al. 2006; Hirano, Kojima, et al. 1997; McGuire et al. 1996; Tourville et al. 2008) or mid-to-post STG (Hashimoto and Sakai 2003; Parkinson et al. 2012) and most studies finding the posterior STG (pSTG) region particularly responsive to altered feedback (Hashimoto and Sakai 2003; Takaso et al. 2010; Tourville et al. 2008; Zarate et al. 2010; Zarate and Zatorre 2008; Zheng et al. 2010). Nearby the pSTG, many studies also found the ventral supramarginal gyrus (vSMG) more active in altered feedback trials (Hashimoto and Sakai 2003; Tourville et al. 2008; Toyomura et al. 2007). These results especially implicate the sylvian-parietal-temporal (Spt) region in auditory feedback processing, but, contrary to the lesion studies, do not show a predominant role for the left hemisphere. Most studies found bilateral activations and the one study finding this region active in only a single hemisphere found it on the right side (Toyomura et al. 2007). Further away from the Spt region in the parietal lobe, a few studies also found responses in the SMG (Zarate and Zatorre 2008) and intraparietal sulcus (IPS) (Toyomura et al. 2007; Zarate and Zatorre 2008). Only one study found activity in auditory areas (anterior STG, MTG) of the ventral speech processing stream (Fu et al. 2006). Taken together, these results address the question posed by Levelt (1989) about whether the same areas involved in speech perception are also involved in speech feedback monitoring. From the neural evidence, the answer appears to be: partly. In particular, comparison of the speech-sensitive auditory regions with the auditory regions activated by altered feedback shows an overlap in the areas of dorsal speech processing stream but very little overlap in the areas of the ventral speech processing stream.

In contrast to auditory regions, frontal and motor regions have not always shown more activity in altered feedback trials. Dorsal premotor cortex (PMd) (Hirano, Kojima, et al. 1997; Toyomura et al. 2007; Zarate and Zatorre 2008) and areas around the ventral premotor cortex (PMv)/inferior frontal gyrus (IFG, Broca's region) (Hashimoto and Sakai 2003; Tourville et al. 2008; Toyomura et al. 2007; Zarate and Zatorre 2008) have been found active in many speaking tasks (Price 2010). Though hemispheric dominance results are mixed. For PMd, two of three studies found only left hemisphere activation (Hirano, Kojima, et al. 1997; Toyomura et al. 2007), while for PMv/IFG, two of four studies found only right hemisphere activation (Tourville et al. 2008; Toyomura et al. 2007). Other frontal regions found to be active in the studies include the left anterior cingulated cortex (ACC) (Zarate and Zatorre 2008), a region known to be involved in cognitive error monitoring and reinforcement learning (Cohen 2008; Gehring and Knight 2000); the bilateral pre-supplementary motor area (preSMA) (Zarate and Zatorre 2008), a region involved in sequential and self-generated behaviors (Passingham 1995; Romo and Schultz 1987; Tanji 2001); the bilateral anterior insula (Zarate and Zatorre 2008), a region implicated in the left hemisphere as involved with apraxia of speech (Dronkers 1996); and the right cerebellum (Tourville et al. 2008), a subcortical structure strongly implicated in learning sensorimotor associations (Imamizu et al. 2000; Wolpert, Miall, and Kawato 1998).

Complementing the feedback alteration studies are a set of studies examining how blocking or reducing auditory feedback with masking noise affects brain areas active during speaking. A number of contrasts have been examined. First, considering only areas more active during speaking than listening, researchers found areas most active when feedback was not blocked included a number of bilateral motor areas (ACC, SMA, anterior insula, dorsal motor cortex) as well as subcortical structures (pons, thalamus, and basal ganglia) (Christoffels, Formisano, and Schiller 2007; van de Ven, Esposito, and Christoffels 2009). On the other hand, the areas more active when feedback was blocked with noise were around the mid-to-post STG, largely bilaterally (Christoffels et al. 2007; van de Ven et al. 2009). These STG areas were also shown to have activity correlated with the level of masking noise used (Christoffels et al. 2011).

Several of the studies of neural responses to altered auditory feedback have also found an interesting result that, in some sense, is the opposite of the SIS effect described above. In response to altered feedback, some auditory cortical areas have an enhanced response, compared to their response to hearing the same altered feedback when passively listening (Behroozmand et al. 2009; Zheng et al. 2010).

This effect has been called speech perturbation response enhancement (SPRE) and has been seen in an event-related potential study based on EEG (Behroozmand et al. 2009), as well as an fMRI study which localized the effect to the dorsal speech processing stream SPT region (left pSTG, left vSMG, right mSTG) (Zheng et al. 2010). More recently, SPRE was demonstrated in an MEG study (Kort, Nagarajan, and Houde 2014) and also in an ECoG study which suggested a functional connection between SPRE and feedback control of speaking (Chang et al. 2013). The ECoG study found that auditory electrodes exhibiting SPRE were the ones whose perturbation responses were most correlated with subjects' compensations.

The SPRE phenomenon is interesting because it takes the efference copy hypothesis a step further. According to the efference copy account, SPRE should not exist. The hypothesis predicts that in both the speaking and listening conditions, alteration of the auditory input by an external device is equally unpredicted and should generate equal neural responses. But what if there was more to predicting feedback than representing what input is predicted? If a sensory prediction also included a probabilistic confidence in what was predicted, then SPRE could be an expression of the probabilistic "surprise" in a deviation from the prediction. In this modified efference copy account, in both speaking and listening, there is a prediction of continuation of hearing unaltered feedback. However, the level of prediction confidence is likely to be greater during speaking (when the speaker has control over what he/she is hearing) than during listening (when the speaker has no control). If confidence in a prediction modulated the neural "surprise" response to a prediction error, then we might indeed expect a greater surprise response during speaking resulting in SPRE.

13.5 Summary

In this chapter, we began by considering how auditory feedback is not only critical to learning to speak, but is also important to both the online control of speaking and the maintenance of the speaking motor skill. The efference copy hypothesis was introduced to explain the compensation responses speakers make to auditory feedback perturbations and the phenomenon of sensorimotor adaptation was described. We also discussed how auditory feedback affects the timing of the production of speech and we discussed how interactions between somatosensation and auditory feedback may partly explain why compensation for altered auditory feedback tends to be incomplete and why there are individual variations in speakers' responses to altered auditory feedback.

Next, we considered the challenges of modeling how auditory feedback is processed during speaking. We discussed how a pure feedback control model can be considered the most extreme implementation of the efference copy hypothesis, with a feedback comparison directly driving output control, but how such a control model was unlikely in light of the feedback phenomena described earlier and especially given the delays inherent in processing auditory feedback. However, we also discussed how the efference copy hypothesis lives on in current models of speech motor control, with auditory feedback prediction errors being calculated in slower, external feedback loops that indirectly modify the behavior of internal feedback control loops.

Finally, we considered what is known about the neural substrate of auditory feedback processing, beginning with a discussion of the basic pathways where afferent auditory information makes contact with efferent motor control in the central nervous system. We then discussed what has been learned from perceptual studies about what regions of auditory and frontal/motor cortex are sensitive to speech. From there, we moved on to discuss an important organizing concept for describing auditory speech processing: the dual stream hypothesis and how the dorsal stream (posterior auditory cortex, the sylvian-temporal-parietal region and premotor cortex) appears to be largely responsible for processing auditory feedback. In particular, we discussed how disruption of the dorsal stream leads to disabilities that may be related to auditory feedback processing deficits and how functional neuroimaging studies reveal dorsal stream activations in response to auditory feedback alterations. In the process, we discussed two neurophysiological phenomena related to auditory feedback processing. Early in the section, we described speaking-induced suppression (SIS) of responses to auditory feedback and how it constituted further evidence for the efference copy hypothesis. Later, we described the speech perturbation response enhancement (SPRE) phenomena and how it suggested a probabilistic interpretation of the efference copy hypothesis that includes measures of confidence in feedback predictions.

REFERENCES

Alexander, Garrett E. and Michael D. Crutcher. 1990. Functional architecture of basal ganglia circuits: Neural substrates of parallel processing. *Trends in Neurosciences* 13(7): 266–271.

Andersen, Richard A. 1997. Multimodal integration for the representation of space in the posterior parietal cortex. *Philosophical Transactions of the Royal Society Series B: Biological Sciences* 352(1360): 1421–1428.

Baker, Errol, Sheila E. Blumstein, and Harold Goodglass. 1981. Interaction between phonological and semantic factors in auditory comprehension. *Neuropsychologia* 19(1): 1–15.

Bauer, Jay J., Jay Mittal, Charles R. Larson, and Timothy C. Hain. 2006. Vocal responses to unanticipated perturbations in voice loudness feedback: An automatic mechanism for stabilizing voice amplitude. *Journal of the Acoustical Society of America* 119(4): 2363–2371.

Behroozmand, Roozbeh, Laura Karvelis, Hanjun Liu, and Charles R. Larson. 2009. Vocalization-induced enhancement of the auditory cortex responsiveness during voice F0 feedback perturbation. *Clinical Neurophysiology* 120(7): 1303–1312.

Belin, Pascal. 2006. Voice processing in human and non-human primates. *Philosophical Transactions of the Royal Society Series B: Biological Sciences* 361(1476): 2091.

Belin, Pascal and Robert J. Zatorre. 2000. "What", "where" and "how" in auditory cortex. *Nature Neuroscience* 3(10): 965–966.

Belin, Pascal, Robert J. Zatorre, Phillippe Lafaille, Pierre Ahad, and Bruce Pike. 2000. Voice-selective areas in human auditory cortex. *Nature* 403(6767): 309–312.

Bendor, Daniel and Xiaoqin Wang. 2005. The neuronal representation of pitch in primate auditory cortex. *Nature* 436(7054): 1161–1165.

Benson, Randall R., Matthew Richardson, Doug H. Whalen, and Song Lai. 2006. Phonetic processing areas revealed by sinewave speech and acoustically similar non-speech. *NeuroImage* 31(1): 342–353.

Binder, Jeffrey R., Julie A. Frost, Thomas A. Hammeke, Stephen M. Rao, and Robert W. Cox. 1996. Function of the left planum temporale in auditory and linguistic processing. *Brain* 119(4): 1239–1247.

Binder, Jeffrey R., Julie A. Frost, Thomas A. Hammeke, Patrick S. Bellgowan, Jane A. Springer, Jacqueline N. Kaufman, and Edward T. Possing. 2000. Human temporal lobe activation by speech and nonspeech sounds. *Cerebral Cortex* 10(5): 512–528.

Black, John W. 1951. The effect of delayed side-tone upon vocal rate and intensity. *Journal of Speech and Hearing Disorders* 16: 56–60.

Blakemore, Sarah J., Daniel M. Wolpert, and Chris D. Frith. 1998. Central cancellation of self-produced tickle sensation. *Nature Neuroscience* 1(7): 635–640.

Blakemore, Sarah J., Daniel M. Wolpert, and Chris D. Frith. 1999. The cerebellum contributes to somatosensory cortical activity during self-produced tactile stimulation. *NeuroImage* 10(4): 448–459.

Bohland, Jason W. and Frank H. Guenther. 2006. An fMRI investigation of syllable sequence production. *NeuroImage* 32(2): 821–841.

Bregman, Albert S. 1990. *Auditory Scene Analysis: The Perceptual Organization of Sound*. Cambridge, MA: MIT Press.

Buchsbaum, Bradley, Gregory Hickok, and Colin Humphries. 2001. Role of left posterior superior temporal gyrus in phonological processing for speech perception and production. *Cognitive Science* 25(5): 663–678.

Buchsbaum, Bradley R., Juliana Baldo, Kayoko Okada, Karen F. Berman, Nina Dronkers, Mark D'Esposito, and Gregory Hickok. 2011. Conduction aphasia, sensory-motor integration and phonological short-term memory – an aggregate analysis of lesion and fMRI data. *Brain and Language* 119(3): 119–128.

Burnett, Theresa A., Jill E. Senner, and Charles R. Larson. 1997. Voice F0 responses to pitch-shifted auditory feedback: A preliminary study. *Journal of Voice* 11(2): 202–211.

Burnett, Theresa A., Marcia B. Freedland, Charles R. Larson, and Timothy C. Hain. 1998. Voice F0 responses to manipulations in pitch feedback. *Journal of the Acoustical Society of America* 103(6): 3153–3161.

Cai, Shanqing, Satrajit S. Ghosh, Frank H. Guenther, and Joseph Perkell. 2011. Focal manipulations of formant trajectories reveal a role of auditory feedback in the online control of both within-syllable and between-syllable speech timing. *Journal of Neuroscience* 31(45): 16483–16490.

Callan, Daniel E., Jeffrey A. Jones, Akiko M. Callan, and Reiko Akahane-Yamada. 2004. Phonetic perceptual identification by native- and second-language speakers differentially activates brain regions involved with acoustic phonetic processing and those involved with articulatory-auditory/orosensory internal models. *NeuroImage* 22(3): 1182–1194.

Champoux, Francois, Douglas M. Shiller, and Robert J. Zatorre. 2011. Feel what you say: An auditory effect on somatosensory perception. *PLoS ONE* 6(8): e22829.

Chang, Edward F., Caroline A. Niziolek, Robert T. Knight, Srikantan S. Nagarajan, and John F. Houde. 2013. Human cortical sensorimotor network underlying feedback control of vocal pitch. *Proceedings of the National Academy of Sciences, USA* 110(7): 2653–2658.

Chang-Yit, Rudolph, Herbert L. Pick, and Gerald M. Siegel. 1975. Reliability of sidetone amplification effect in vocal intensity. *Journal of Communication Disorders* 8(4): 317–324.

Chen, Chi-Ming, Daniel H. Mathalon, Brian J. Roach, Idil Cavus, Dennis D. Spencer, and Judith M. Ford. 2011. The corollary discharge in humans is related to synchronous neural oscillations. *Journal of Cognitive Neuroscience* 23(10): 2892–2904.

Cherry, E. Colin. 1953. Some experiments on the recognition of speech, with one and with two ears. *The Journal of the Acoustical Society of America* 25(5): 975–979 doi:10.1121/1.1907229. ISSN 0001-4966.

Cheung, Steven W., Srikantan S. Nagarajan, Christoph E. Schreiner, Purvis H. Bedenbaugh, and Andrew Wong. 2005. Plasticity in primary auditory cortex of monkeys with altered vocal production. *Journal of Neuroscience* 25(10): 2490–2503.

Christoffels, Ingrid K., Elia Formisano, and Niels O. Schiller. 2007. Neural correlates of verbal feedback processing: An fMRI study employing overt speech. *Human Brain Mapping* 28(9): 868–879.

Christoffels, Ingrid K., Vincent van de Ven, Lourens J. Waldorp, Elia Formisano, and Niels O. Schiller. 2011. The sensory consequences of speaking: Parametric neural cancellation during speech in auditory cortex. *PLoS ONE* 6(5): e18307.

Cohen, Michael X. 2008. Neurocomputational mechanisms of reinforcement-guided learning in humans: A review. *Cognitive Affective and Behavioral Neuroscience* 8(2): 113–125.

Cowie, Roddy and Ellen Douglas-Cowie. 1992. *Postlingually Acquired Deafness: Speech Deterioration and the Wider Consequences*. Berlin: Mouton de Gruyter.

Curio, Gabriel, Georg Neuloh, Jussi Numminen, Veikko Jousmaki, and Riitta Hari. 2000. Speaking modifies voice-evoked activity in the human auditory cortex. *Human Brain Mapping* 9(4): 183–191.

Cykowski, Matthew D., Peter T. Fox, Roger J. Ingham, Janis C. Ingham, and Donald A. Robin. 2010. A study of the reproducibility and etiology of diffusion anisotropy differences in developmental stuttering: A potential role for impaired myelination. *NeuroImage* 52(4): 1495–1504.

Dehaene-Lambertz, Ghislaine, Christophe Pallier, Willy Serniclaes, Liliane Sprenger-Charolles, Antoinette Jobert, and Stanislas Dehaene. 2005. Neural correlates of switching from auditory to speech perception. *NeuroImage* 24(1): 21–33.

Dewitt, Iain and Josef P. Rauschecker. 2012. Phoneme and word recognition in the auditory ventral stream. *Proceedings of the National Academy of Sciences, USA* 109(8): E505–514.

Dronkers, Nina F. 1996. A new brain region for coordinating speech articulation. *Nature* 384(6605): 159–161.

Dum, Richard P. and Peter L. Strick. 2005. Frontal lobe inputs to the digit representations of the motor areas on the lateral surface of the hemisphere. *Journal of Neuroscience* 25(6): 1375–1386.

Eliades, Steven J. and Xiaoqin Wang. 2003. Sensory-motor interaction in the primate auditory cortex during self-initiated vocalizations. *Journal of Neurophysiology* 89(4): 2194–2207.

Eliades, Steven J. and Xiaoqin Wang. 2005. Dynamics of auditory-vocal interaction in monkey auditory cortex. *Cerebral Cortex* 15(10): 1510–1523.

Eliades, Steven J. and Xiaoqin Wang. 2008. Neural substrates of vocalization feedback monitoring in primate auditory cortex. *Nature* 453(7198): 1102–1106.

Elman, Jeffrey L. 1981. Effects of frequency-shifted feedback on the pitch of vocal productions. *Journal of the Acoustical Society of America* 70(1): 45–50.

Fairbanks, Grant. 1954. Systematic research in experimental phonetics: 1. A theory of the speech mechanism as a servosystem. *Journal of Speech and Hearing Disorders* 19(2): 133–139.

Fairbanks, Grant. 1955. Selective vocal effects of delayed auditory feedback. *Journal of Speech and Hearing Disorders* 20(4): 333–346.

Feng, Yongqiang, Vincent L. Gracco, and Ludo Max. 2011. Integration of auditory and somatosensory error signals in the neural control of speech movements. *Journal of Neurophysiology* 106(2): 667–679.

Fillenbaum, Samuel. 1965. Adaptation with constant and variable delay in auditory feedback. *Psychonomic Science* 3(2): 45–46.

Ford, Judith M. and Daniel H. Mathalon. 2004. Electrophysiological evidence of corollary discharge dysfunction in schizophrenia during talking and thinking. *Journal of Psychiatric Research* 38(1): 37–46.

Ford, Judith M., Daniel H. Mathalon, Theda Heinks, Sontine Kalba, William O. Faustman, and Walton T. Roth. 2001. Neurophysiological evidence of corollary discharge dysfunction in schizophrenia. *American Journal of Psychiatry* 158(12): 2069–2071.

Foundas, Anne L., Angela M. Bollich, David M. Corey, Megan Hurley, and Kenneth M. Heilman. 2001. Anomalous anatomy of speech-language areas in adults with persistent developmental stuttering. *Neurology* 57(2): 207–215.

Foundas, Anne L., Angela M. Bollich, J. Feldman, David M. Corey, Megan Hurley, Lisa C. Lemen, and Kenneth M. Heilman. 2004. Aberrant auditory processing and atypical planum temporale in developmental stuttering. *Neurology* 63(9): 1640–1646.

Franklin, Gene F., J. David Powell, and Abbas Emami-Naeini. 1991. *Feedback Control of Dynamic Systems*, 2nd edn. Reading, MA: Addison-Wesley.

Friederici, Angela D. 2011. The brain basis of language processing: From structure to function. *Physiological Review* 91(4): 1357–1392.

Fu, Cynthia H., Goparlen N. Vythelingum, Michael J. Brammer, et al. 2006. An fMRI study of verbal self-monitoring: Neural correlates of auditory verbal feedback. *Cerebral Cortex* 16(7). 969–977.

Gehring, William J. and Robert T. Knight. 2000. Prefrontal-cingulate interactions in action monitoring. *Nature Neuroscience* 3(5): 516–520.

Geschwind, Norman. 1965. Disconnexion syndromes in animals and man, Part II. *Brain* 88(3): 585–644.

Ghez, Claude and William T. Thach. 2000. The cerebellum. In E.R. Kandel, J.H. Schwartz, and T.M. Jessell (eds.), *Principles of Neural Science*, 4th edn, 832–852. New York: McGraw-Hill.

Glasser, Matthew F. and James K. Rilling. 2008. DTI tractography of the human brain's language pathways. *Cerebral Cortex* 18(11): 2471–2482.

Glickstein, Mitchell. 1997. Mossy-fibre sensory input to the cerebellum. *Progress in Brain Research* 114: 251–259.

Godey, Benoit, Craig A. Atencio, Ben H. Bonham, Christoph E. Schreiner, and Steven W. Cheung. 2005. Functional organization of squirrel monkey primary auditory cortex: Responses to frequency-modulation sweeps. *Journal of Neurophysiology* 94(2): 1299–1311.

Golestani, Narly and Robert J. Zatorre. 2004. Learning new sounds of speech: Reallocation of neural substrates. *NeuroImage* 21(2): 494–506.

Greenlee, Jeremy D., Adam W. Jackson, Fangxiang Chen, Charles R. Larson, Hiroyuki Oya, Hiroto Kawasaki, Haiming Chen, and Matthew A. Howard III. 2011. Human auditory cortical activation during self-vocalization. *PLoS ONE* 6(3): e14744.

Greenlee, Jeremy D., Hiroyuki Oya, Hiroto Kawasaki, Igor O. Volkov, Olaf P. Kaufman, Christopher Kovach, Matthew

A. Howard, and John F. Brugge. 2004. A functional connection between inferior frontal gyrus and orofacial motor cortex in human. *Journal of Neurophysiology* 92(2): 1153–1164.

Guenther, Frank H. 1995. Speech sound acquisition, coarticulation and rate effects in a neural network model of speech production. *Psychological Review* 102(3): 594–621.

Guenther, Frank H. and Tony Vladusich. 2012. A neural theory of speech acquisition and production. *Journal of Neurolinguistics* 25(5): 408–422.

Guenther, Frank H., Satrajit S. Ghosh, and Jason A. Tourville. 2006. Neural modeling and imaging of the cortical interactions underlying syllable production. *Brain and Language* 96(3): 280–301.

Guenther, Frank H., Michelle Hampson, and Dave Johnson. 1998. A theoretical investigation of reference frames for the planning of speech movements. *Psychological Review* 105(4): 611–633.

Hain, Timothy C., Theresa A. Burnett, Swathi Kiran, Charles R. Larson, Shajila Singh, and Mary K. Kenney. 2000. Instructing subjects to make a voluntary response reveals the presence of two components to the audio-vocal reflex. *Experimental Brain Research* 130(2): 133–141.

Hall, Deborah A., Heledd C. Hart, and Ingrid S. Johnsrude. 2003. Relationships between human auditory cortical structure and function. *Audiology and Neurotology* 8(1): 1–18.

Hall, Deborah A., Ingrid S. Johnsrude, Mark P. Haggard, Alan R. Palmer, Michael A. Akeroyd, and A. Quentin Summerfield. 2002. Spectral and temporal processing in human auditory cortex. *Cerebral Cortex* 12(2): 140–149.

Harris, Christopher M. and Daniel M. Wolpert. 1998. Signal-dependent noise determines motor planning. *Nature* 394(6695): 780–784.

Hashimoto, Yasuki and Kuniyoshi Sakai. 2003. Brain activations during conscious self-monitoring of speech production with delayed auditory feedback: An fMRI study. *Human Brain Mapping* 20(1): 22–28.

Heil, Peter. 2003. Coding of temporal onset envelope in the auditory system. *Speech Communication* 41(1): 123–134.

Heil, Peter and Dexter R. Irvine. 1996. On determinants of first-spike latency in auditory cortex. *Neuroreport* 7(18): 3073–3076.

Heinks-Maldonado, Theda H. and John F. Houde. 2005. Compensatory responses to brief perturbations of speech amplitude. *Acoustics Research Letters Online* 6(3): 131–137.

Heinks-Maldonado, Theda H., Srikantan S. Nagarajan, and John F. Houde. 2006. Magnetoencephalographic evidence for a precise forward model in speech production. *Neuroreport* 17(13): 1375–1379.

Hickok, Gregory and David Poeppel. 2007. The cortical organization of speech processing. *Nature Reviews Neuroscience* 8(5): 393–402.

Hickok, Gregory, John Houde, and Feng Rong. 2011. Sensorimotor integration in speech processing: computational basis and neural organization. *Neuron* 69(3): 407–422.

Hickok, Gregory, Bradley Buchsbaum, Colin Humphries, and Tugan Muftuler. 2003. Auditory-motor interaction revealed by fMRI: Speech, music and working memory in area Spt. *Journal of Cognitive Neuroscience* 15(5): 673–682.

Hirano, Shigeru, Hisayoshi Kojima, Yasushi Naito, et al. 1996. Cortical speech processing mechanisms while vocalizing visually presented languages. *Neuroreport* 8(1): 363–367.

Hirano, Shigeru, Hisayoshi Kojima, Yasushi Naito, et al. 1997. Cortical processing mechanism for vocalization with auditory verbal feedback. *Neuroreport* 8(9–10): 2379–2382.

Hirano, Shigeru, Yasushi Naito, Hidehiko Okazawa, et al. 1997. Cortical activation by monaural speech sound stimulation demonstrated by positron emission tomography. *Experimental Brain Research* 113(1): 75–80.

Houde, John F. and Michael I. Jordan. 1998. Sensorimotor adaptation in speech production. *Science* 279(5354): 1213–1216.

Houde, John F. and Michael I. Jordan. 2002. Sensorimotor adaptation of speech I: Compensation and adaptation. *Journal of Speech, Language, and Hearing Research* 45(2): 295–310.

Houde, John F. and Srikantan S. Nagarajan. 2011. Speech production as state feedback control. *Frontiers in Human Neuroscience* 5: 82.

Houde, John F., Srikantan S. Nagarajan, Kensuke Sekihara, and Michael M. Merzenich. 2002. Modulation of the auditory cortex during speech: An MEG study. *Journal of Cognitive Neuroscience* 14(8): 1125–1138.

Howell, Peter, Nirit El-Yaniv, and David J. Powell. 1987. Factors affecting fluency in stutterers when speaking under altered auditory feedback. In H.F. Peters and W. Hulstijn (eds.), *Speech Motor Dynamics in Stuttering*, 361–369. New York: Springer.

Huang, Chi-ming, Guolong Liu, Bo-Yi Yang, Hao Mu, and Chie-Fang Hsiao. 1991. Auditory receptive area in the cerebellar hemisphere is surrounded by somatosensory areas. *Brain Research* 541(2): 252–256.

Imamizu, Hiroshi, Satoru Miyauchi, Tomoe Tamada, Yuka Sasaki, Ryousuke Takino, Benno Putz, Toshinori Yoshioka, and Mitsuo Kawato. 2000. Human cerebellar activity reflecting an acquired internal model of a new tool. *Nature* 403(6766): 192–195.

Indefrey, Peter and Willem J.M. Levelt. 2000. The neural correlates of language production. In M.S. Gazzaniga (ed.), *The New Cognitive Neurosciences*, 845–865. Cambridge, MA: MIT Press.

Jancke, Lutz, Torsten Wustenberg, Henning Scheich, and Hans-Jochen Heinze. 2002. Phonetic perception and the temporal cortex. *NeuroImage* 15(4): 733–746.

Jeannerod, Marc. 1988. *The Neural and Behavioural Organisation of Goal-directed Movements*. Oxford: Oxford University Press.

Johnson, Cynthia I., Herbert L. Pick, Jr., Sharon R. Garber, and Gerald M. Siegel. 1978. Intensity of guitar playing as a function of auditory feedback. *Journal of the Acoustical Society of America* 63(6): 1930–1932.

Johnsrude, Ingrid S., Virginia B. Penhune, and Robert J. Zatorre. 2000. Functional specificity in the right human auditory cortex for perceiving pitch direction. *Brain* 123(1): 155–163.

Johnsrude, Ingrid S., Robert J. Zatorre, Brenda A. Milner, and Alan C. Evans. 1997. Left-hemisphere specialization for the processing of acoustic transients. *Neuroreport* 8(7): 1761–1765.

Jones, Jeffrey A. and Kevin G. Munhall. 2000. Perceptual calibration of F0 production: Evidence from feedback perturbation. *Journal of the Acoustical Society of America* 108(3): 1246–1251.

Jürgens, Uwe. 1993. A comparison of the neural systems underlying speech and nonspeech vocal utterances. Paper presented at the Annual Meeting of the Language Origins Society, Saint Petersburg, Russia.

Jürgens, Uwe. 2002. Neural pathways underlying vocal control. *Neuroscience Biobehavioral Reviews* 26(2): 235–258.

Kaas, Jon H. and Troy A. Hackett. 1998. Subdivisions of auditory cortex and levels of processing in primates. *Audiology and Neurotology* 3(2–3): 73–85.

Kandel, Eric R., James H. Schwartz, and Thomas M. Jessell. 2000. *Principles of Neural Science*, 4th edn. New York: McGraw-Hill.

Kaspar, Kai and Hartmut Rubeling. 2011. Rhythmic versus phonemic interference in delayed auditory feedback. *Journal of Speech, Language, and Hearing Research* 54(3): 932–943.

Katseff, Shira, John Houde, and Keith Johnson. 2012. Partial compensation for altered auditory feedback: A tradeoff with somatosensory feedback? *Language and Speech* 55(2): 295–308.

Katz, Douglas I. and James R. Lackner. 1977. Adaptation to delayed auditory feedback. *Perception and Psychophysics* 22(5): 476–486.

Kawahara, Hideki. 1993. Transformed auditory feedback: Effects of fundamental frequency perturbation. *Journal of the Acoustical Society of America* 94(3): 1883.

Kort, Naomi S., Srikantan S. Nagarajan, and John F. Houde. 2014. A bilateral cortical network responds to pitch perturbations in speech feedback. *NeuroImage* 86: 525–535.

Kotz, Sonja A., Martin Meyer, Kai Alter, Mireille Besson, D. Yves von Cramon, and Angela D. Friederici. 2003. On the lateralization of emotional prosody: An event-related functional MR investigation. *Brain and Language* 86(3): 366–376.

Lakatos, Peter, Zsuzsanna Pincze, Kai-Ming Fu, Daniel C. Javitt, George Karmos, and Charles E. Schroeder. 2005. Timing of pure tone and noise-evoked responses in macaque auditory cortex. *Neuroreport* 16(9): 933–937.

Lametti, Daniel R., Sazzad M. Nasir, and David J. Ostry. 2012. Sensory preference in speech production revealed by simultaneous alteration of auditory and somatosensory feedback. *Journal of Neuroscience* 32(27): 9351–9358.

Lane, Harlan and Bernard Tranel. 1971. The Lombard sign and the role of hearing in speech. *Journal of Speech and Hearing Research* 14(4): 677–709.

Lane, Harlan, Jane Wozniak, Melanie Matthies, Mario Svirsky, Joseph Perkell, Michael O'Connell, and Joyce Manzella. 1997. Changes in sound pressure and fundamental frequency contours following changes in hearing status. *Journal of the Acoustical Society of America* 101(4): 2244–2252.

Larson, Charles R., Kenneth W. Altman, Hanjun Liu, and Timothy C. Hain. 2008. Interactions between auditory and somatosensory feedback for voice F-0 control. *Experimental Brain Research* 187(4): 613–621.

Lee, Bernard S. 1950. Some effects of side-tone delay. *Journal of the Acoustical Society of America* 22: 639–640.

Lee, Bernard S. 1951. Artificial stutter. *Journal of Speech and Hearing Disorders* 16(1): 53–55.

Levelt, Willem J.M. 1989. *Speaking: From Intention to Articulation*. Cambridge, MA: MIT Press.

Levelt, Willem J.M. 1999. Models of word production. *Trends in Cognitive Sciences* 3(6): 223–232.

Levitt, Harry, H. Stromberg, C. Smith, and Toni Gold. 1980. The structure of segmental errors in the speech of deaf children. *Journal of Communication Disorders* 13(6): 419–441.

Liebenthal, Einat, Rutvik Desai, Michael M. Ellingson, Brinda Ramachandran, Anjali Desai, and Jeffrey R. Binder. 2010. Specialization along the left superior temporal sulcus for auditory categorization. *Cerebral Cortex* 20(12): 2958–2970.

Lombard, Etienne. 1911. Le signe de l'élévation de la voix. *Annales des maladies de l'oreille, du larynx, du nez, et du pharynx* 37: 101–119.

MacDonald, Ewen N., Robyn Goldberg, and Kevin G. Munhall. 2010. Compensations in response to real-time formant perturbations of different magnitudes. *Journal of the Acoustical Society of America* 127(2): 1059–1068.

Maraist, Jean Ann and Charles Hutton. 1957. Effects of auditory masking upon the speech of stutterers. *Journal of Speech and Hearing Disorders* 22(3): 385–389.

Mathiak, Klaus, Ingo Hertrich, Werner Lutzenberger, and Hermann Ackermann. 2002. Functional cerebral asymmetries of pitch processing during dichotic stimulus application: A whole-head magnetoencephalography study. *Neuropsychologia* 40(6): 585–593.

McGettigan, Carolyn, Andrew Faulkner, Irene Altarelli, Jonas Obleser, Harriet Baverstock, and Sophie K. Scott. 2012. Speech comprehension aided by multiple modalities: Behavioural and neural interactions. *Neuropsychologia* 50(5): 762–776.

McGuire, Philip K., David A. Silbersweig, and Christopher D. Frith. 1996. Functional neuroanatomy of verbal self-monitoring. *Brain* 119(3): 907–917.

Meister, Ingo G., Stephen M. Wilson, Choi Deblieck, Allan D. Wu, and Marco Iacoboni. 2007. The essential role of premotor cortex in speech perception. *Current Biology* 17(19): 1692–1696.

Mesgarani, Nima and Edward F. Chang. 2012. Selective cortical representation of attended speaker in multi-talker speech perception. *Nature* 485(7397): 233–236.

Miceli, Gabriele, Guido Gainotti, Carlo Caltagirone, and Carlo Masullo. 1980. Some aspects of phonological impairment in aphasia. *Brain and Language* 11(1): 159–169.

Mishkin, Mortimer, Leslie G. Ungerleider, and Kathleen A. Macko. 1983. Object vision and spatial vision: Two cortical pathways. *Trends in Neurosciences* 6: 414–417.

Mitsuya, Takashi, Ewen N. Macdonald, and Kevin G. Munhall. 2009. Auditory feedback and articulatory timing. *Journal of the Acoustical Society of America* 126(4): 2223.

Mottonen, Riikka, Gemma A. Calvert, Iiro P. Jaaskelainen, Paul M. Matthews, Thomas Thesen, Jyrki Tuomainen, and Mikko Sams. 2006. Perceiving identical sounds as speech or non-speech modulates activity in the left posterior superior temporal sulcus. *NeuroImage* 30(2): 563–569.

Munhall, Kevin G., Ewen N. Macdonald, Stacie K. Byrne, and Ingrid Johnsrude. 2009. Talkers alter vowel production in response to real-time formant perturbation even when instructed not to compensate. *Journal of the Acoustical Society of America* 125(1): 384.

Nasir, Sazzad M. and David J. Ostry. 2006. Somatosensory precision in speech production. *Current Biology* 16(19): 1918–1923.

Nasir, Sazzad M. and David J. Ostry. 2008. Speech motor learning in profoundly deaf adults. *Nature Neuroscience* 11(10): 1217–1222.

Nasir, Sazzad M. and David J. Ostry. 2009. Auditory plasticity and speech motor learning. *Proceedings of the National Academy of Sciences, USA* 106(48): 20470–20475.

Niziolek, Caroline A. 2010. The role of linguistic contrasts in the auditory feedback control of speech. PhD thesis, Massachusetts Institute of Technology.

Obleser, Jonas and Sonja A. Kotz. 2011. Multiple brain signatures of integration in the comprehension of degraded speech. *NeuroImage* 55(2): 713–723.

Obleser, Jonas, Amber M. Leaver, John Vanmeter, and Josef P. Rauschecker. 2010. Segregation of vowels and consonants in human auditory cortex: Evidence for distributed hierarchical organization. *Front Psychology* 1: 232.

Okada, Kayoko, Feng Rong, Jon Venezia, et al. 2010. Hierarchical organization of human auditory cortex: Evidence from acoustic invariance in the response to intelligible speech. *Cerebral Cortex* 20(10): 2486–2495.

Oller, D. Kimbrough and Rebecca E. Eilers. 1988. The role of audition in infant babbling. *Child Development* 59(2): 441–449.

Papoutsi, Marina, Jacco A. de Zwart, J. Martijn Jansma, Martin J. Pickering, James A. Bednar, and Barry Horwitz. 2009. From phonemes to articulatory codes: An fMRI study of the role of

Broca's area in speech production. *Cerebral Cortex* 19(9): 2156–2165.

Parkinson, Amy L., Sabina G. Flagmeier, Jordan L. Manes, Charles R. Larson, Bill Rogers, and Donald A. Robin. 2012. Understanding the neural mechanisms involved in sensory control of voice production. *NeuroImage* 61(1): 314–322.

Parsons, Thomas W. 1987. *Voice and Speech Processing*. New York: McGraw-Hill.

Passingham, Richard E. 1995. *The Frontal Lobes and Voluntary Action*. Oxford: Oxford University Press.

Peeva, Maya G., Frank H. Guenther, Jason A. Tourville, et al. 2010. Distinct representations of phonemes, syllables and supra-syllabic sequences in the speech production network. *NeuroImage* 50(2): 626–638.

Perrier, Pascal. 2006. About speech motor control complexity. In J. Harrington and M. Tabain (eds.), *Speech Production: Models, Phonetic Processes and Techniques*, 13–26. New York: Psychology Press.

Petrides, Michael and Deepak N. Pandya. 1988. Association fiber pathways to the frontal cortex from the superior temporal region in the rhesus monkey. *Journal of Comparative Neurology* 273(1): 52–66.

Poeppel, David. 2003. The analysis of speech in different temporal integration windows: Cerebral lateralization as "asymmetric sampling in time." *Speech Communication* 41(1): 245–255.

Price, Cathy J. 2010. The anatomy of language: A review of 100 fMRI studies published in 2009. *Annals of the New York Academy of Sciences* 1191: 62–88.

Price, Cathy J., Jenny T. Crinion, and Mairead Macsweeney. 2011. A generative model of speech production in Broca's and Wernicke's areas. *Frontiers in Psychology* 2: 237.

Purcell, David. W. and Kevin G. Munhall. 2006a. Adaptive control of vowel formant frequency: Evidence from real-time formant manipulation. *Journal of the Acoustical Society of America* 120(2): 966–977.

Purcell, David W. and Kevin G. Munhall. 2006b. Compensation following real-time manipulation of formants in isolated vowels. *Journal of the Acoustical Society of America* 119(4): 2288–2297.

Rauschecker, Josef P. and Sophie K. Scott. 2009. Maps and streams in the auditory cortex: Nonhuman primates illuminate human speech processing. *Nature Neuroscience* 12(6): 718–724.

Rauschecker, Josef P. and Biao Tian. 2000. Mechanisms and streams for processing of "what" and "where" in auditory cortex. *Proceedings of the National Academy of Sciences, USA* 97(22): 11800–11806.

Rimol, Lars M., Karsten Specht, Susanne Weis, Robert Savoy, and Kenneth Hugdahl. 2005. Processing of sub-syllabic speech units in the posterior temporal lobe: An fMRI study. *NeuroImage* 26(4): 1059–1067.

Rizzolatti, Giacomo, Leonardo Fogassi, and Vittorio Gallese. 1997. Parietal cortex: From sight to action. *Current Opinion in Neurobiology* 7(4): 562–567.

Romo, Ranulfo and Wolfram Schultz. 1987. Neuronal activity preceding self-initiated or externally timed arm movements in area 6 of monkey cortex. *Experimental Brain Research* 67(3): 656–662.

Rosenbaum, David A., Richard A. Carlson, and Rick O. Gilmore. 2001. Acquisition of intellectual and perceptual-motor skills. *Annual Review of Psychology* 52: 453–470.

Ross, Mark and Thomas G. Giolas. 1978. *Auditory Management of Hearing-Impaired Children: Principles and Prerequisites for Intervention*. Baltimore, MD: University Park Press.

Sato, Marc, Pascale Tremblay, and Vincent L. Gracco. 2009. A mediating role of the premotor cortex in phoneme segmentation. *Brain Language* 111(1): 1–7.

Saur, Dorothee, Bjorn W. Kreher, Susanne Schnell, et al. 2008. Ventral and dorsal pathways for language. *Proceedings of the*

National Academy of Sciences, USA 105(46): 18035–18040.

Schmahmann, Jeremy D., Deepak N. Pandya, Ruopeng Wang, et al. 2007. Association fibre pathways of the brain: Parallel observations from diffusion spectrum imaging and autoradiography. *Brain* 130(3): 630–653.

Scott, Cheryl M. and Robert L. Ringel. 1971. Articulation without oral sensory control. *Journal of Speech and Hearing Research* 14(4): 804–818.

Scott, Sophie K. 2006. Language processing: The neural basis of nouns and verbs. *Current Biology* 16(8): R295–296.

Scott, Sophie K., Stuart Rosen, Harriet Lang, and Richard J.S. Wise. 2006. Neural correlates of intelligibility in speech investigated with noise vocoded speech – a positron emission tomography study. *Journal of the Acoustical Society of America* 120(2): 1075–1083.

Seifritz, Erich, Fabrizio Esposito, Franciszek Hennel, et al. 2002. Spatiotemporal pattern of neural processing in the human auditory cortex. *Science* 297(5587): 1706–1708.

Shiller, Douglas M., Marc Sato, Vincent L. Gracco, and Shari R. Baum. 2009. Perceptual recalibration of speech sounds following speech motor learning. *Journal of the Acoustical Society of America* 125(2): 1103–1113.

Shum, Mamie, Douglas M. Shiller, Shari R. Baum, and Vincent L. Gracco. 2011. Sensorimotor integration for speech motor learning involves the inferior parietal cortex. *European Journal of Neuroscience* 34(11): 1817–1822.

Simonyan, Kristina and Barry Horwitz. 2011. Laryngeal motor cortex and control of speech in humans. *The Neuroscientist* 17(2): 197–208.

Simonyan, Kristina, John Ostuni, Christy L. Ludlow, and Barry Horwitz. 2009. Functional but not structural networks of the human laryngeal motor cortex show left hemispheric lateralization during syllable but not breathing production. *Journal of Neuroscience* 29(47): 14912–14923.

Smith, Clarissa R. 1975. Residual hearing and speech production in deaf children. *Journal of Speech and Hearing Research* 18(4): 795–811.

Sober, Samuel J. and Philip N. Sabes. 2005. Flexible strategies for sensory integration during motor planning. *Nature Neuroscience* 8(4): 490–497.

Soderberg, George A. (1968). Delayed auditory feedback and stuttering. *Journal of Speech and Hearing Disorders* 33(3): 260–267.

Stuart, Andrew, Joseph Kalinowski, Michael P. Rastatter, and Kerry Lynch. 2002. Effect of delayed auditory feedback on normal speakers at two speech rates. *Journal of the Acoustical Society of America* 111(5): 2237–2241.

Takaso, Hideki, Frank Eisner, Richard J. Wise, and Sophie K. Scott. 2010. The effect of delayed auditory feedback on activity in the temporal lobe while speaking: A positron emission tomography study. *Journal of Speech, Language, and Hearing Research* 53(2): 226–236.

Tanji, Jun. 2001. Sequential organization of multiple movements: Involvement of cortical motor areas. *Annual Review of Neuroscience* 24(1): 631–651.

Tian, Xing and David Poeppel. 2010. Mental imagery of speech and movement implicates the dynamics of internal forward models. *Frontiers in Psychology* 1: 166.

Tiffany, William R. and Clair N. Hanley. 1956. Adaptation to delayed sidetone. *Journal of Speech and Hearing Disorders* 21(2): 164–172.

Tourville, Jason A., Kevin J. Reilly, and Frank H. Guenther. 2008. Neural mechanisms underlying auditory feedback control of speech. *NeuroImage* 39(3): 1429–1443.

Toyomura, Akira and Takashi Omori. 2005. Auditory feedback control during a sentence-reading task: Effect of other's voice. *Acoustical Science and Technology* 26(4): 358–361.

Toyomura, Akira, Sachiko Koyama, Tadao Miyamaoto, et al. 2007. Neural correlates of auditory feedback control in human. *Neuroscience* 146(2): 499–503.

Tremblay, Stephanie, Guillaume Houle, and David J. Ostry. 2008. Specificity of speech motor learning. *Journal of Neuroscience* 28(10): 2426–2434.

Tremblay, Stephanie, Douglas M. Shiller, and David J. Ostry. 2003. Somatosensory basis of speech production. *Nature* 423(6942): 866–869.

Upadhyay, Jaymin, Kevin Hallock, Mathieu Ducros, Dae-Shik Kim, and Itamar Ronen. 2008. Diffusion tensor spectroscopy and imaging of the arcuate fasciculus. *NeuroImage* 39(1): 1–9.

Uppenkamp, Stefan, Ingrid S. Johnsrude, Dennis Norris, William Marslen-Wilson and Roy D. Patterson. 2006. Locating the initial stages of speech-sound processing in human temporal cortex. *NeuroImage* 31(3): 1284–1296.

van de Ven, Vincent, Fabrizio Esposito, and Ingrid K. Christoffels. 2009. Neural network of speech monitoring overlaps with overt speech production and comprehension networks: A sequential spatial and temporal ICA study. *NeuroImage* 47(4): 1982–1991.

Ventura, Maria I., Srikantan S. Nagarajan, and John F. Houde. 2009. Speech target modulates speaking induced suppression in auditory cortex. *BMC Neuroscience* 10: 58.

von Holst, Erich W. 1954. Relations between the central nervous system and the peripheral organs. *British Journal of Animal Behaviour* 2: 89–94.

von Holst, Erich W. and Horst Mittelstaedt. 1950. Das Reafferenzprinzip. *Naturwissenschaften* 37: 464–476.

Webster, Douglas B. 1992. An overview of mammalian auditory pathways with an emphasis on humans. In D.B. Webster, A.N. Popper, and R.R. Fay (eds.), *The Mammilian Auditory Pathway: Neuroanatomy*, vol. 1, 1–22. New York: Springer-Verlag.

Wessinger, C.M., J. VanMeter, Biao Tian, J. Van Lare, J. Pekar, and Josef P. Rauschecker. 2001. Hierarchical organization of the human auditory cortex revealed by functional magnetic resonance imaging. *Journal of Cognitive Neuroscience* 13(1): 1–7.

Whalen, Doug H., Randall R. Benson, Matthew Richardson, et al. 2006. Differentiation of speech and nonspeech processing within primary auditory cortex. *Journal of the Acoustical Society of America* 119(1): 575–581.

Wiener, Norbert. 1948. *Cybernetics: Control and Communication in the Animal and the Machine*. New York: John Wiley & Sons, Inc.

Wilson, Stephen M. and Marco Iacoboni. 2006. Neural responses to non-native phonemes varying in producibility: Evidence for the sensorimotor nature of speech perception. *NeuroImage* 33(1): 316–325.

Winchester, Richard A., Edward W. Gibbons, and Donald F. Krebs. 1959. Adaptation to sustained delayed sidetone. *Journal of Speech and Hearing Disorders* 24(1): 25–28.

Wise, Richard J., Sophie K. Scott, S. Catrin Blank, Cath J. Mummery, Kevin Murphy, and Elizabeth A. Warburton. 2001. Separate neural subsystems within "Wernicke's area." *Brain* 124(1): 83–95.

Wolpert, Daniel M. and Zoubin Ghahramani. 2000. Computational principles of movement neuroscience. *Nature Neuroscience* 3: 1212–1217.

Wolpert, Daniel M., R. Chris Miall, and Mitsuo Kawato. 1998. Internal models in the cerebellum. *Trends in Cognitive Sciences* 2(9): 338–347.

Yates, Aubrey J. 1963. Delayed auditory feedback. *Psychological Bulletin* 60(3): 213–232.

Yeterian, Edward H. and Deepak N. Pandya. 1998. Corticostriatal connections of the superior temporal region in rhesus monkeys. *Journal of Comparative Neurology* 399(3): 384–402.

Zarate, Jean Mary and Robert J. Zatorre. 2008. Experience-dependent neural substrates involved in vocal pitch regulation during singing. *NeuroImage* 40(4): 1871–1887.

Zarate, Jean Mary, Sean Wood, and Robert J. Zatorre. 2010. Neural networks involved in voluntary and involuntary vocal pitch regulation in experienced singers. *Neuropsychologia* 48(2): 607–618.

Zatorre, Robert J. 2001. Neural specializations for tonal processing. *Annals of the New York Academy of Sciences* 930: 193–210.

Zatorre, Robert J., Pascal Belin, and Virginia B. Penhune. 2002. Structure and function of auditory cortex: Music and speech. *Trends in Cognitive Sciences* 6(1): 37–46.

Zatorre, Robert J., Alan C. Evans, Ernst Meyer, and Albert Gjedde. 1992. Lateralization of phonetic and pitch discrimination in speech processing. *Science* 256(5058): 846–849.

Zheng, Zane Z., Kevin G. Munhall, and Ingrid S. Johnsrude. 2010. Functional overlap between regions involved in speech perception and in monitoring one's own voice during speech production. *Journal of Cognitive Neuroscience* 22(8): 1770–1781.

14 Speech Production in Motor Speech Disorders
Lesions, Models, and a Research Agenda

GARY WEISMER AND JORDAN R. GREEN

14.1 Introduction

The term "motor speech disorders" typically encompasses all speech production problems resulting from neurological lesions, excluding those difficulties in spoken language production classically associated with aphasia, or major sensory deficits (such as hearing impairment). The two major subdivisions of motor speech disorders are dysarthria on the one hand, and apraxia of speech (AOS) on the other. In this chapter, we consider how these motor speech disorders affect spoken language production independently (in theory) from effects of other neurological conditions with which they often coexist, such as aphasia and sensory deficits (e.g., hearing loss).

The definitions of dysarthria and AOS are not without controversy (for reviews see McNeil, Robin, and Schmidt 2009; Rosenbek, Kent, and LaPointe 1984; Ziegler 2002). The classical definition of dysarthria is due to Darley, Aronson, and Brown (1975: 2), by way of Grewel (1957) and Peacher (1950). The dysarthria(s) are a *group* of neurologically-based speech disorders "due to disturbances in muscular control of the speech mechanism resulting from impairment of any of the basic motor processes involved in the execution of speech." This definition is noteworthy both for what it includes and what it leaves out. Included in the definition is the idea that dysarthria occurs when weakness, paresis, and/or incoordination within the speech mechanism interfere with the production of speech. In this classic view of dysarthria, the unique movement deficits resulting from specific neurological diseases and/or lesion locations engender distinctive, abnormal articulatory, voice, and resonance characteristics. In this chapter, we consider how lesion and imaging studies have been important for advancing knowledge about the neural basis of dysarthria and apraxia of speech, but we also challenge the underlying assumption of simple mappings between lesion sites, neurological signs, and dysarthric speech characteristics.

The controversy concerning the definition and conceptual view of dysarthria is relatively recent. In contrast, controversy regarding the nature of, and in some cases the very existence of AOS has a long history. Apraxia as a neurological phenomenon, of course, is not controversial, at least with respect to the existence of the disorder. When a patient has difficulty performing skilled movement in the absence of evidence of muscle weakness or paralysis, sensory dysfunction, cognitive and/or motivational deficits, and/or cerebellar or basal ganglia disorders that might otherwise "explain" the loss of movement skill, a patient may be diagnosed with apraxia (Heilman and Watson 2008). According to Heilman and Watson, apraxia is a problem of movement representations, which may be affected directly by a brain lesion; alternatively, the representations may be intact but disconnected from the regions of the brain that execute the represented movements. As reviewed by McNeil et al. (2009), AOS is a disorder in which there is a problem with the selection and sequencing of programming units for voluntarily produced speech. These definitions underscore a fundamental issue with our current understanding of AOS – they are based on speculation about processes (i.e., movement representations and programming) for which there is little scientific consensus or evidence (anatomic or behavioral).

One of the goals of this chapter is to consider what is known about the speech production deficit in motor speech disorders, including both dysarthria and apraxia of speech, and how the current empirical knowledge can be squared with existing models and theories of speech production. We also consider what *should be* known to develop a model, and perhaps eventually a theory, of motor speech disorders.

In this chapter, we consider two different perspectives on speech production deficits. One perspective focuses on the structures and/or mechanisms associated with normal speech production and motor speech disorders. This perspective, which is consistent with the classic, Mayo view of motor speech disorders, is a driving force underlying contemporary lesion and imaging studies of speech production (see Duffy 2005). Below we review what is known about these components, based on imaging work in normal speakers and lesion studies. The other perspective is concerned exclusively with processes. In this view, pathologies are studied for the way in which they perturb the coordinative organization of speech behaviors. In the case of speech production, such behaviors may include (but are not limited to) the magnitude and sequencing of articulatory, laryngeal, and respiratory gestures to produce intelligible speech. In the case of motor speech disorders, the magnitude and sequencing of speech gestures are clearly perturbed, but the nature of these perturbations and how they map onto a speech intelligibility deficit are largely unknown.

Although to our knowledge, models of spoken language processing have rarely been leveraged to simulate or explain the neuronal basis of dysarthria, we anticipate rapid progress in this area because of the recent swell of interest in the neurologic basis of human communication. For these models to be useful in explaining the dysarthrias, they will need to account for the varying effects that neurologic damage have on speech mechanism function. The resulting models may have a number of important clinical implications. For example, they would be useful for predicting the therapeutic and adverse effects of deep brain stimulation, transcranial magnetic stimulation, and novel drug interventions. They may also be useful for modeling and predicting the biologically plausible adaptations that occur in response to neurologic impairment at the neurologic, physiologic, and behavioral levels.

The scientific melding of these approaches is obviously preferable to a continuation of the separate pathways these two lines of inquiry have, for the most part, followed to date (Bohland, Bullock, and Guenther 2010, is a good example of an initial attempt to join the two approaches). Our suggestions, outlined below, for merging these two complementary perspectives in a projected research program should be considered as a hypothesis for the future of research in motor speech disorders.

14.2 Nervous system structures, speech motor control, and motor speech disorders

The following section considers the findings from research that has attempted to map particular brain structures to specific aspects of speech production. We focus attention on both *speech planning* (alternately called programming or preparation) and *speech execution*. The execution stage is particularly interesting because hypotheses regarding the effects of disruptions to this pathway on speech are well entrenched in the scientific literature and in clinical practice (see below), but at the same time it has largely been glossed over by models of spoken language. Knowledge about the neural basis of the dysarthrias has been derived primarily from studies of neurogenic movement disorders. The widely used classification system developed by Darley et al. (1975) classifies the dysarthrias into distinct subtypes (e.g., spastic, flaccid, hypokinetic, hyperkinetic, ataxic, and mixed), which parallel the subtypes of movement disorders used for decades to characterize motor problems in the limbs and trunk. For speech, this classification system is intended to provide an explanatory framework based on assumed causal linkages between the location of neuroanatomic lesions, resulting movement disruptions, and resulting speech characteristics.

In one of the largest lesion studies on dysarthria, Urban and colleagues (2006) investigated the speech of 62 consecutive patients with dysarthria 72 hours post isolated infarction. Strokes were distributed widely across the speech motor execution pathway: striatocapsular (46.8%), base of pons (24.2%), ventral motor cortex (14.5%), and the remainder in cerebellum. Over 89% of the strokes occurred in the left hemisphere; right-sided strokes were associated with a less severe form of dysarthria. In general, articulatory errors and slowed speaking rate were more prominent in left-hemisphere lesions; whereas prosodic disturbances were more closely associated with right-hemisphere lesions (Benke and Kertesz 1989). Independent of lesion topography, lesions to the left hemisphere were more commonly associated with a severe dysarthria than lesions to the right hemisphere (Urban et al. 2006). A similar profile of the speech characteristics of stroke patients whose brain damage was confined to the pathway between the cortex and cranial nerve nuclei, or to the basal ganglia or cerebellum, was reported by Kumral et al. (2007). These studies underscore what has been known for many decades, that the basic components of the speech motor execution network include the motor cortex and corticobulbar tract, insula, basal ganglia, cerebellum, and cranial nerve pathways. The tendency in both studies for the more severe dysarthrias (or even the occurrence of dysarthria with such lesions) to be associated with left-side damage is interesting for modeling efforts that include laterality effects.

What follows is a brief review of the neural structures that are thought to underlie the planning and execution phases of speech production.

14.2.1 Upper motor neuron tract (corticobulbar)

The corticobulbar tract is the primary descending pathway that exerts cortical control over the speech musculature. Approximately 40% (Porter and Lemon 1993) of the tract's fibers originate in pyramidal cells of the primary motor cortex (M1). M1 cells receive inputs from many sources including the peripheral somatosensory pathways via brainstem, cerebellar, and subcortical nuclei, subcortical regions (i.e., basal ganglia and cerebellum), and many other cortical regions including premotor cortex, prefrontal cortex, Broca's area, and limbic cortex. Based on what is known about M1, it is no surprise that dysarthria has been associated with lesions to most regions of the left corticobulbar tract including the ventral portion of M1 (Ichikawa and Kageyama 1991), the corona radiata (Ozaki et al. 1986), and the internal capsule (Chamorro et al. 1991; Ichikawa and Kageyama 1991).

The function of M1 and its somatotopic organization are still poorly understood. Imaging studies show ventral regions of M1 that are loosely segregated by articulator with some overlap (Takai, Brown, and Liotti 2010). Classical descriptions portray M1 as the cortical access point to single muscles. Support for this assertion is based on early studies showing that direct electrical stimulation of M1 resulted in isolated muscle twitches or simple movements such as protrusion of the tongue (Penfield and Jasper 1954; Rothwell et al. 1987). These findings spurred a flurry of research aimed toward identifying what motor parameters might be encoded by M1 neurons. This research showed that M1 encoded many parameters including force, and movement direction, extent, and speed (Cheney and Fetz 1980; Evarts 1968; Fu, Suarez, and Ebner 1993; Georgopoulos et al. 1982; Kakei, Hoffman, Strick 1999; Kalaska, Cohen, Hyde, and Prud'homme 1989; Moran and Schwartz 1999).

The assertion that M1 encodes only simple kinematic and dynamic variables has, however, been challenged by more recent intracortical M1 stimulation techniques, which have evoked complex, coordinated multiple muscle group (Porter and Lemon 1993) and multiple joint movements (Graziano et al. 2002). A series of studies by Graziano and colleagues (2002; Cooke et al. 2003; Cooke and

Graziano 2004) suggest that the duration of M1 simulation also affects the complexity of motor responses with short stimulation trains only evoking isolated muscle twitches and longer trains (i.e., 500 ms or longer) resulting in complex, functional movements such as bringing the hand to the mouth coupled with mouth opening (Graziano et al. 2002).

From a movement disorders perspective, lesions to the corticobulbar tract are predicted to produce speech symptoms caused by spastic paresis of vocal tract muscles. Spastic paresis is characterized by hypertonus, hyper-reflexia, and weakness, among other symptoms. Spasticity is thought to engender a strain-strangled voice; and slowed and reduced articulatory movements (see Darley et al. 1975 for a summary of relevant perceptual data and Platt, Andrews, and Howie 1980, for segmental analyses; Ackermann et al. 1997, for movement data; and Ziegler and von Cramon 1986, for acoustic data). However, as suggested by Ackermann et al. (1997), the articulatory deficits due to corticobulbar damage – such as reduced rate and extent of articulatory movement – are also characteristics associated with other motor speech disorders due to, for example, Parkinson's and cerebellar disease.

In summary, as pointed out many years ago by Ziegler and von Cramon (1986), mapping "typical" aspects of muscle spasticity onto speech production symptoms is far from simple; only weak causal connections have been established between corticobulbar damage, speech muscle spasticity, and speech symptoms. The functions of M1 cells, which are the origin of the corticobulbar pathway, continue to be debated. The varying functions of M1 and its complex role in movement need to be taken into account when understanding the effect of M1 lesions on articulatory control problems. Neural models of speech impairment also will need to account for both the location and size of lesions in the corticobulbar tract.

14.2.2 Insula and supplementary motor area

As reviewed by Ackermann and Riecker (2010b), the function of the left insular cortex in speech production is controversial. Lesion studies are difficult to interpret because damage restricted to the intrasylvian cortex is rare. Functional imaging studies in neurologically normal speakers suggest that the anterior insula, together with its connections to adjacent, frontal opercular cortex as well as the supplementary motor area (SMA), are functionally linked with the complexity of phonetic sequence production (see review of relevant evidence in Park, Iverson, and Park 2011). The phonetic complexity effect (see below), plus the effect of SMA lesions on spontaneity of verbal behavior (Jonas 1981) explain the theoretical link between this part of brain circuitry for speech production and preparation and coordination of articulatory sequences (Ackerman and Riecker 2010a, 2010b). By extension, the insula and SMA have been implicated as a neural substrate of apraxia of speech (e.g., Dronkers 1996).

The use of phonetic complexity as a litmus test for normal and disordered planning processes is burdened by the absence of experiments having control groups of speakers with lesions in brain regions typically associated with speech disorders *other* than apraxia of speech. Especially relevant to this concern is the negative effect of phonetic complexity on the speech of adults with persistent stuttering (and no detectable lesion by imaging) and the claim from fMRI work that *basal ganglia* structures are responsible for this planning deficit (see review in Howell 2010). Phonetic complexity has also been invoked as a trigger for involvement of the cerebellum in speech timing: greater demand for interarticulator coordination is thought to recruit greater cerebellar involvement in the speech timing task, and patients with cerebellar disease may only show speech timing deficits when the coordination demand is high (see review in Schirmer 2004). Patients with the hypokinetic type of dysarthria (and, presumably, basal ganglia disease) have also been shown to produce speech reaction times consistent with a pre-articulatory processing or planning deficit (Spencer and Rogers 2005). Taken together, these data suggest substantial ambiguity concerning the "location" of speech programming processes in the brain. Phonetic complexity experiments in which multiple groups of speakers with different "types" of motor speech disorder (or different, documented lesion types), perhaps including persons with persistent stuttering, who experience the same set of speech production conditions and are imaged in the same way, are required to get a better handle on the notion of planning versus execution and their relationship to nervous system components of the speech motor control system.

14.2.3 Basal ganglia

Damage to one or more components of the basal ganglia clearly affects speech production, as evidenced by dysarthrias in Parkinson's disease (Kim, Kent, and Weismer 2011), Huntington's disease (Ludlow, Connor, and Bassich 1987), and the athetoid type of cerebral palsy (Neilson and O'Dwyer 1984). At least two other general findings also implicate lesions to basal ganglia structures as having the potential to disrupt speech motor control. First, Deep Brain Stimulation (DBS) of the subthalamic nucleus, an increasingly common treatment for Parkinson disease, often worsens dysarthric symptoms even when limb symptoms improve (see reviews in Tripoliti and Limousin 2010; and Weismer, Yunusova, and Bunton 2012). Second, a large clinical study of frequent symptoms in dementia associated with small-vessel disease, in which lesions are likely restricted to basal ganglia structures and associated white matter, showed approximately 43% of affected patients to have dysarthria (Staekenborg et al. 2008). It is important to point out that many individuals in these patient groups may have had damage in regions of the brain outside the basal ganglia as well, but the implication of a link between basal ganglia and speech motor control is supported by the converging nature of the data reviewed above. As suggested by Peach and Tonkovich (2004), damage restricted to basal ganglia structures may also be associated with the symptoms of apraxia of speech.

When patients with presumed basal ganglia disease are studied using speech movement or acoustic methods, abnormalities in speech planning (see above), speaking rate/segmental durations, speech rhythm, movement extent and speed (and the related acoustic measures, formant transition extent and slope), and contrasts between segmental "targets" are observed (see reviews in Kim et al. 2011; and Liss et al. 2009). These abnormal speech characteristics, however, vary as much within disease groups as they do across disease groups (Weismer and Kim 2010).

Ackermann and Riecker (2010a), using a functional connectivity analysis of fMRI data, place basal ganglia structures in what they term the "Executive Loop" of the speech motor control network, which presumably does not contribute substantially to speech planning processes. The review above suggests either that basal ganglia structures are involved in both preparation and execution processes in speech production, or that the distinction between the two processes is illusory.

14.2.4 Cerebellum

The cerebellum has been implicated in almost all aspects of speech production including motor planning (Spencer and Rogers 2005), execution (Riecker et al. 2005), sensorimotor feedback integration and monitoring (e.g., Golfinopoulos et al. 2011; Tourville, Reilly, and Guenther 2008), speech perception (Mathiak et al. 2002), and cognitive/linguistic functions (see Murdoch 2010). Most research on cerebellar damage and speech function has been conducted on individuals identified as having an ataxic dysarthria due to cerebellar lesions that vary in severity, location, and etiology (i.e., stroke, tumor, or degenerative diseases such as Friedreich's ataxia).These investigations have identified a constellation of speech abnormalities that characterize ataxic dysarthria, which include a slowed speaking rate, reduced articulatory precision, harsh voice quality, and prosodic disturbances (Darley, Aronson, and Brown 1969a, 1969b; Duffy 1995). Although these speech characteristics considerably overlap with other types of dysarthria and are highly variable across those affected, ataxic dysarthria is widely considered a distinct (easily recognizable) type of dysarthria (Weismer and Kim 2010). Several authors have emphasized that speech timing abnormalities and articulatory inconsistency are defining characteristics of ataxic dysarthria (Ackermann et al. 1992; Spencer and Slocomb 2007; Ziegler and Wessel 1996). Few investigators, however, have taken on the challenge of disambiguating articulatory timing abnormalities from other potential articulatory control problems such as articulatory inconsistency, which is thought to be a defining characteristic of AOS (Croot 2002; and see below).

The topographic basis of ataxic dysarthria is still relatively unexplored and poorly understood (Ackermann 2008). A notable limitation of the extant literature is the absence of well-controlled studies accounting for the specific location and severity of the cerebellar lesion. One of the few existing focal lesion studies on speech revealed that dysarthria tended to occur with damage to the upper paravermal area of the right cerebellar hemisphere and the superior portion of the left cerebellar hemisphere (Urban et al. 2003). In addition, Ackermann et al. (1992) examined 12 persons with cerebellar infarcts in either the posterior inferior cerebellar artery or the superior cerebellar artery. All participants who exhibited dysarthria had lesions that extended into the paravermal region of the superior cerebellar portion. The authors identified inconsistent articulatory deficits and slowed speech tempo as the most common abnormal speech features. In a longitudinal study of seven subjects with a progressive hereditary ataxia, Sidtis and colleagues (2010) observed significant declines in cerebellar blood flow in the inferior, mid, and superior cerebellum. These decreases coincided with a putatively compensatory increase in blood flow to Broca's area.

Although the number of lesion studies on speech production is limited, recent neuroimaging studies on healthy talkers are beginning to elucidate the cerebellar regions essential for speech production. Ackerman (2008) proposed separate roles for the inferior and superior regions of the cerebellar hemispheres, with the superior and inferior regions involved in speech motor preparation and execution, respectively; in addition, each region is considered to be part of distinct corticocerebellar pathways. Ghosh, Tourville, and Guenther (2008) identified increased localized activity specifically in the left superior paravermal regions during the production of consonant-vowel syllables as compared to production of isolated vowels. These findings underscore the possibility that the role of the cerebellum in speech is load-dependent or speaking-task specific. Additional support for this assertion comes from a study by Riecker and colleagues (2005), who observed increased hemodynamic activity in both hemispheres of the cerebellum only when syllables rates exceeded 2.5 Hz. The authors concluded that the cerebellum plays a role in regulating speaking rate. This conclusion is also supported by prior behavioral data showing that the speaking rate of persons with ataxic dysarthria is normal, whereas their maximum repetition rate is slowed (Ziegler and Wessel 1996).

Overall, neuroimaging findings support a functional topography within the cerebellum and suggest that the contribution of the cerebellum to speech motor control varies depending on the complexity of the speaking task, speaking rate, and possibly propositional load. The task-dependent response of the cerebellum underscores the importance of using well-controlled speaking tasks in imaging and clinical investigations of ataxic speech. These studies require control groups comprised of speakers with other forms of neurogenic disease and speech disorders, to ensure that the task-specific hypothesis can be accepted or rejected for the specific case of cerebellar disease. For example, speaking-task effects on the dysarthria in Parkinson's disease are well known (see discussion in Weismer 1984; and Kempler and Van Lancker 2002) but are also considered to be a signature characteristic of AOS (McNeil et al. 2009). Perhaps any disruption of central nuclei and pathways for speech production causes greater sensitivity to task demands, with the nature and degree of the speech deficit depending on the location and extent of damage. Teasing out specific mechanisms requires the careful use of control groups in addition to neurologically normal speakers.

14.2.5 *Cranial nerve pathway: Cranial nerve nuclei, cranial nerves, neuromuscular junction, and muscle*

The cranial nerve pathway consists of the cranial nuclei in the brainstem, their axons, the neuromuscular junction, and muscle fibers. A large number of neuromuscular disorders can affect these different components of the cranial nerve pathway. These disorders, broadly referred to as cranial nerve palsies, have the potential to alter sensation significantly and limit the activation of speech muscles as a result of flaccid paresis or paralysis.

Cranial nerve nuclei in the brainstem provide the final common neuronal pathway to the speech muscles. These nuclei are major neural integration centers receiving inputs not only from descending corticobulbar fibers, but also from other cortical (e.g., premotor cortex, SMA, primary somatosensory cortex) and subcortical structures (e.g., amygdala, cingulate, and striatum), afferent fibers, and brainstem central pattern generators. Cranial nerve nuclei containing motor neurons for speech muscles are primarily located in the pons and medulla, with sensory nuclei for head and neck structures found throughout the brainstem.

In general, lesions to the cranial nerve motor nuclei, their axons, or muscles result in a flaccid hemiparesis of speech muscles. Flaccid paresis is typically characterized by weakness, hypotonus (or normal tone), and atrophy of affected muscle tissue. The impact on speech will vary considerably, however, depending on the location and extent of damage, and on which speech subsystems are affected.

The articulatory characteristics of persons with brainstem or peripheral nerve disease have not been studied very carefully, most likely because it is difficult to assemble groups of speakers who share sharply defined neuropathologies. In addition, brainstem disease rarely involves just one motor nucleus associated with speech musculature (see, e.g., Kameda et al. 2004), and is most often unilateral. Despite these difficulties, there is great value in studying lower motor neuron effects on articulatory behavior using physiological and acoustic techniques, because the data may serve as a kind of neuropathological baseline against which the effects on speech of lesions in the cortex, basal ganglia, cerebellum, and corticobulbar tract can be compared.

14.2.6 *Components of the speech motor control system: Conclusions*

A brief review of the components of the speech motor control system suggests continuing effort to identify regions of the nervous system responsible for specific characteristics of speech production. The review reflects a strategy consistent with the Mayo Clinic notion of motor speech disorders wherein different speech disorders result from lesions in different locations in the brain. Taken together, these findings underscore the need for more research on the pathophysiologic and anatomic basis of dysarthric syndromes, particularly as imaging technologies allow for fine-grained distinctions in brain processes and speech motor behaviors. Two very challenging, but necessary aspects of this work are the identification of participant groups with relatively well-defined neural lesions and the identification of speaking tasks that elicit the relevant speech motor processes.

The framing of motor speech impairments within a classic movement disorders perspective, however, has several significant limitations: (1) It is often inconsistent with behavioral data; a significant number of speech symptoms are remarkably similar across different dysarthria types (Weismer and Kim 2010; Kim et al. 2011); (2) the goals of speech movements are drastically different from those for limb movements; (3) the anatomic and biomechanic characteristics of each speech subsystem are unique and specialized to meet the varying demands of speech, chewing, swallowing, breathing, and facial expression; and (4) an approach narrowly focused on lesions and their symptoms fails to account for important interactions between speech motor control, linguistic processing, and perceptual processes. Regarding point 3, within the cranial system, there is considerable diversity of biomechanical mechanisms and muscle types. Cranial muscles differ from limb muscles in their architecture, innervations, contractile protein profile, mitochondrial content, and aging patterns (Kent 2004). These differences have significant implications for how lesions resulting in spasticity, for example, may differentially affect speech and limb behaviors. Regarding point 4, multiple imaging studies are now revealing complex interactions between the speech execution centers (such as primary motor cortex) and those used for speech perception and language processing (i.e., Wernicke's area). For example, under some conditions, the speech motor neural network may be used to facilitate lexical and phonologic retrieval (Hickok and Poeppel 2004; Pulvermüller, 2010). The implications for these interactions on the manifestation of dysarthria, which is commonly considered a motor execution disorder, are unexplored.

Several significant caveats must be considered when attempting to link motor pathway lesions to speech symptomatology. For the same isolated lesion, individual patterns of speech impairment are to be expected because of across-talker differences in adaptations to the motor control deficit (see Kent et al. 2000). In addition, even fairly localized lesions often tend to result in multiple deficits related to cognitive, language, motor, and sensory impairments (Arboix et al. 1991; Fisher 1982; Ichikawa and Kageyama 1991; Orefice et al. 1999; Ozaki et al. 1986; Tohgi et al. 1996); all these factors influence speech performance (Green and Nip 2010). These issues should not discourage critical efforts to understand the effects of focal lesions on speech, but rather should emphasize the many factors (e.g., biologic, study design, talker characteristics) that currently challenge the expectation for one-to-one mappings between brain lesions and speech behaviors.

14.3 Speech production processes: Data, models, and theories of motor speech disorders

As reviewed above, it is useful to break the "minimal network for speech motor control" (Bohland and Guenther 2006) into its hypothesized components to determine how each component might contribute to the products of speech motor control. These "products" can be considered on a coarse scale, such as the general ability to match an actual output of the speech mechanism to an *expected* output, and in the case of errors to recalibrate the system. Such match-and-correct mechanisms may apply to a broad variety of speech products, including voice pitch, vowels, consonants, syllabic forms, and so forth. The products may also be defined at a more fine-grained level, such as quantitative estimates of the target regions for vowels and the patterning and magnitude of somatosensory consequences of lingual consonant production.

The flipside of exciting model-building and theorizing efforts are the often messy and difficult-to-interpret experimental data obtained from persons with motor speech disorders; and the uncertain relations between those data and the models and theories under development. Below we summarize findings from several studies on persons with motor speech disorders, and consider the fit between these findings and two well-known models/theories of speech production.

At the level of speech movements, the most consistent finding is that motions of the lip/jaw complex (as well as decomposed lower lip and jaw motions) as well as the tongue tend to be smaller and slower (have reduced speed) than those of properly matched controls (e.g., Ackerman et al. 1997; Forrest, Weismer, and Turner 1989; Green et al. 2013; Hirose et al. 1981; Hirose, Kiritani, and Sawashima 1982; Kuruvilla, Murdoch, and Goozée 2007; Mefferd, Green, and Pattee 2012; Weismer 1997; Weismer et al. 2012; Yunusova, Weismer, and Lindstrom 2011). Under certain conditions, and especially in speakers with amyotrophic lateral sclerosis (Yunusova et al. 2010) or cerebral palsy (Kent, Netsell, and Bauer 1975; Nip 2013), motions of the lips and jaw may actually be larger than normal, possibly reflecting compensation to early stages of speech motor impairment. Some data show tongue displacements and speeds in persons with traumatic brain injury (TBI) to be similar to those of neurologically normal speakers (Kuruvilla et al. 2007) and *greater* in persons with Parkinson's disease than normal controls (e.g., Wong, Murdoch, and Whelan 2011). The compensation argument could be invoked for these greater tongue displacements and speeds in speakers with PD, because older data show a reduction in speech-related jaw motions in speakers with dysarthria associated with PD (Forrest et al. 1989). In the Wong et al. (2011) study, the tongue and jaw motions were not decoupled, so it is impossible to determine if jaw motions were also reduced relative to their neurologically normal control group.[1]

Although speech movement data taken as a whole suggest smaller displacements and lower speeds in persons with dysarthria as compared to controls (Weismer 1997), with reduction of movement and speed becoming more prominent with increasing severity of dysarthria (Green et al. 2013; Weismer et al. 2012), the conflicting findings summarized here suggest the need for a more integrated approach to speech movement research in motor speech disorders. The available speech movement data, and interpretations of the movement control problem in dysarthria, are derived from a wide range of speech material types, including repeated syllables (diadochokinesis) either self- or externally-timed (compare Ackerman et al. 1997 to Mefferd et al. 2012), to a single vowel-stop gesture (e.g., Bartle et al. 2006; Kuruvilla et al. 2007), to vocalic gestures (Yunusova et al. 2008) and connected passages spanning multiple breath groups (Weismer et al. 2012). In many of these studies, speech intelligibility data were not reported, or were described using a coarse classification system (e.g., "normal," "mild," "moderate," "severe"); in some studies at least a portion of the neurologically impaired speakers had no perceptually identifiable speech disorder.

Interestingly, most speech acoustic data obtained from persons with motor speech disorders are consistent with a general reduction of movement extent and speed. Weismer and Kim (2010) and Kim et al. (2011) have reviewed speech acoustic data obtained from speakers with various types of dysarthria (where "types" means those specified in the Mayo system). Reduction of the acoustic vowel space and of the frequency range covered for second formant (F2) transitions for diphthongs and semivowels, are common observations for speakers with dysarthria, regardless of dysarthria type or underlying disease process. Moreover, speakers with dysarthria have a tendency to produce less distinctive acoustic contrasts (such as between voiced and voiceless stops, or between apical versus palatal fricatives) when compared to properly matched controls. Because acoustic measures used to make these observations can be mapped back to articulatory position and movement measures, at least in an ordinal fashion (Stevens 2000), speech acoustic data suggest reduction of movement as a prominent, albeit coarse, description of dysarthria (Weismer et al. 2012). A small amount of data from speakers diagnosed with AOS suggest the same coarse-grained description of movement reduction, especially for formant transition extents and slopes (Kent and Rosenbek 1983; Liss and Weismer 1994) but perhaps not for vowel "target" formant frequencies (Jacks, Mathes, and Marquardt 2010).

Whereas speech movement reduction is frequent in speakers with motor speech disorders, and especially with increasing severity of the disorder, other aspects of speech movement deterioration may have equal importance in persons with neurological disease. The coordination of speech movements to achieve a vocal tract shape consistent with a desired acoustic signal is of obvious theoretical and practical significance. Coordination is not always an easy phenomenon to define, and the concept is not easy to map back to a particular measurement. For example, speech coordination is sometimes viewed as a coarse-grained phenomenon whose cumulative effect across an utterance can be captured with a summary measure such as the spatiotemporal index (STI: see Smith et al. 2000; and Grimme et al. 2011: 16, for a claimed link between loss of coordination and increased variability). In the STI perspective, each utterance has an underlying, prototype template for temporal and spatial aspects of its production. When actual utterances are repeated many times and their normalized temporal and spatial characteristics measured and indexed relative to an empirically derived estimate of the hypothesized template, deviations from the template, summed across repetitions, provide an index of spatiotemporal stability. A key contributor to such instability is presumably utterance-to-utterance fluctuation in coordination control for the multiple gestures required to execute the utterance. A recent example of this reasoning can be found in Walsh and Smith (2011), wherein speakers with Parkinson's disease were reported to have greater STI values for cumulative lip aperture in phrase-level material (that is, cumulative across the phrase), when compared to neurologically normal control participants. This greater variability was interpreted as reflecting a significant degree of lip and jaw incoordination – whose combined motions create variation in aperture – among participants with PD, as compared to controls. A more fine-grained approach to articulatory coordination in speakers with dysarthria was taken by Weismer, Yunusova, and Westbury (2003; see Alfonso and Baer 1982; and Perkell et al. 1993, for precedents in neurologically normal speakers) who examined simultaneous labial and lingual motions for the production of /u/ in sentence productions. Both labial protrusion and lingual backing can produce the desired low second formant frequency (F2) associated with /u/; the experimental question was whether or not speakers with PD or amyotrophic lateral sclerosis (ALS) coordinated these movements differently, in terms of relative timing, when compared to normal speakers. Somewhat surprisingly, speakers with PD timed the labial and lingual gestures for /u/ very similarly to the timing observed for normal speakers. Speakers with ALS had more noise in this timing relationship, but the differences from the normal pattern were small. Normal lip and jaw coordination has similarly been reported in speakers with dysarthria due to head injury (Bartle et al. 2006).

Coordination among articulators, and even within a single articulator, is sometimes subsumed under the general heading of *coarticulation*. Coarticulation, often defined as the influence of one segment's articulatory characteristics on the articulatory characteristics of a nearby segment (where "nearby" means adjacent or near-adjacent phonemes, or within some relatively brief temporal window), is the result of coordinated relationships among and within articulators. Because specific coarticulations, and presumably specific patterns of coordination in time and space, are potentially as many as there are phonetic contexts, one popular theoretical proposal has been to imagine a store of highly practiced, frequently used syllables as precompiled articulatory "packages" (the mental syllabary) whose off-the-shelf articulatory specifications reduce the storage, retrieval, and execution demands on a speaker. In speakers with apraxia of speech, predictions of error patterns and error frequency that follow from the mental syllabary perspective are not particularly accurate (Ziegler, Staiger, and Aichert 2010).

Determining the impact of articulatory dyscoordination on speech is very difficult. As pointed out by Urban et al. (2006: 774), a paretic structure can contribute to the appearance of coordination problems, perhaps in precisely the same way as a "planning" disorder disrupts the spatial and temporal relationships among articulators. Speakers with AOS, for example, may exhibit increased movement coupling between the front and back of the tongue (Bartle-Meyer et al. 2009). Is this increase in coupling due to a primary disease effect (i.e., a decreased ability to differentially control tongue regions due to spasticity) or an adaptation to preserve speech (i.e., a simplification control strategy)? Similarly, for the speakers with ALS in Weismer et al. (2003), who evidenced dyscoordination between labial and lingual gestures meant to lower F2 for production of /u/, was the aberrant pattern related to weakness, change in the command sequencing from M1, or even true programming adjustments of a compensatory nature? And, in terms of coordinative dysfunction, how are we to interpret the larger STIs in Parkinsonian utterances as compared to control utterances (Walsh and Smith 2011)? To the extent that coarticulation reflects inter- and intra-articulatory coordination, do coarticulatory patterns, normal or abnormal, reveal planning versus low-level peripheral effects (see Whalen 1990, for an opinion concerning normal speakers)? Empirical and theoretical work on temporal and spatial characteristics of multi-articulatory behavior, and the relationship of that behavior to speech acoustic events, is in a fairly primitive stage for motor speech disorders, and perhaps even for neurologically normal speech. In the current opinion, this is a high-priority research need in motor speech disorders.

14.3.1 *Speech production models/theories and motor speech disorders*

Bernstein and Weismer (2000) argued that speech production and perception models/theories should have the capacity to predict and/or explain data from *any* speaker or listener, regardless of his or her status as "normal" or communicatively impaired. Bernstein and Weismer noted the trend of speech production models/theories being developed and refined for "normal" speakers, with minimal attention paid to speakers with communicative disorders. In addition to the argument that data from persons with speech disorders should fall within the predictive or explanatory domain of "normal" speech production models/theories, Bernstein and Weismer argued that models/theories could be refined by incorporating knowledge of speech production data from persons with speech production disorders.

Following Bernstein and Weismer (2000), our current interest is in evaluating the fit of data from motor speech disorders to speech production models/theories. To focus our discussion, we posed the following two questions: Are data from persons with motor speech disorders accounted for, even in a preliminary way, by existing models/theories (or frameworks, as clarified below)? How do these data contribute to model/theory development? To address these questions, we consider the axioms of a hypothetical theory of speech production that in combination may account for several findings in both healthy and speech disordered populations. The relevance of Articulatory Phonology (AP) to motor speech disorders is then considered. The larger point to be made is twofold. First, data from speakers with motor speech disorders must make contact with theories based on normal speech production. Second, normal speech production theory, whatever its form, cannot simply be grafted onto speech production phenomena in motor speech disorders – rather data from speech motor control deficits can inform the "normal" theories.

14.3.2 *An example of a speech production theory*

Consider the following two statements as axioms of a hypothetical theory of speech motor control.

Statement #1: A component of speech motor control, vested in specific brain regions and mechanisms, is the time-varying acoustic signal generated by a changing vocal tract configuration.

Statement #2: The act of producing speech involves an internal model of linkages between vocal tract movements (and perhaps movements of other speech structures) and their sensory consequences, as well as real-time comparison between the *actual* linkage and the *expected* linkage.

Either of these two axioms (pulled from a thread in the speech research literature extending at least back to Fairbanks (1954), through studies such as Scott and Ringel (1971) and Lindblom, Lubker, and Gay (1979) to contemporary literature including Guenther (2006) and Bohland et al. (2010)) could, in principle, be posited in the absence of the other (for example, the "sensory consequences" mentioned in the second axiom need not include the auditory channel). Nor are either of the axioms obvious, at least when viewed through the historical lens of speech research (see, e.g., MacNeilage 1970, for a view of speech motor control that does not include vocal tract output as a component of the control). Taken together, the two axioms seem to "explain" (what a theory is supposed to do) a variety of experimental phenomena that are fairly disparate in the sense of not being logically interrelated or consequences of one another. For example, the relatively recent demonstration of adjustments of phonatory or articulatory behavior when either vocal fundamental frequency or vowel formant frequencies are altered and delivered back to the speaker's ear in near real time (see, e.g., Houde and Nagarajan, this volume, Chapter 13) is explained by the combination of the two axioms, especially because feedback-induced articulatory behaviors are almost always adjusted to offset (compensate for) the altered feedback. A second experimental phenomenon, related to this first one but not required by it, is the maintenance for a short period of time of the new, feedback-induced linkage between articulatory behavior and acoustic output (axiom #2), even after removal of the altered feedback. Third, an unpublished set of data[2] indicated that for within-speaker comparisons, articulatory positions for "mimed" (no phonation and associated respiratory control) vowels were different from the positions for the same vowels produced with phonation. A related finding is that during whispered speech (where acoustic feedback is attenuated), talkers tended to mark the difference between the voiced cognates /p/ and /b/ by increasing both the extent and speed of maximum lip opening for whispered /b/; in contrast, no kinematic differences were observed between the sounds during voiced speech (Higashikawa et al. 2003). When taken together, these findings are predicted by the combination of the two axioms stated above, wherein the acoustic output of the vocal tract is an essential component of speech motor control by virtue of a learned linkage between articulatory positions/gestures and their associated acoustic output. The fourth set of experimental findings consistent with the two axioms above is found in the fairly extensive literature on the prediction, among adult speakers with dysarthria, of *speech* measures (such as speech intelligibility measures) from oromotor, *nonspeech* behaviors (such as ability to generate "normal" maximum forces or maintain submaximal forces over some short period of time with "normal" variability around the force target). In fact, there is no prediction: oromotor, nonspeech measures do not seem to be a good conduit to understanding a person's *speech* motor control deficit (Weismer 2006; Ziegler, 2003). If the speech acoustic signal is considered an integral component of speech motor control, rather than something produced by the control, this negative finding is not surprising.

This example of how two broad axioms can be invoked to explain several disparate experimental findings is impressive, but can be considered only as the beginning of an adequate theory of speech production; many well-known phenomena cannot be accounted for solely with the conceptual apparatus of these two statements. Because there is no sophisticated theory of speech motor control, but there are relatively sophisticated models, we turn now to a consideration of how two models developed from considerations of normal speech production may be applied to data from speakers with motor speech disorders. We also consider why these models may need to be revised in light of their relative lack of success in accounting for data from speakers with motor speech disorders.

14.3.3 Articulatory Phonology (AP)

Articulatory phonology, a well-known model/theory of speech production, includes independent articulatory gestures which are combined along the time axis to produce specific sounds (Hoole and Pouplier, this volume, Chapter 7, for further details). This combination results in the relative overlap of adjacent gestures. Byrd (1996), following Bell-Berti and Krakow (1991) and Munhall and Löfqvist (1992), argued that the "sliding" of articulatory gestures in time was influenced by speaking rate. As rate increases, adjacent gestures on different "tiers" of the gestural score slide together; the opposite happens as speaking rate decreases. The model makes more than the qualitative prediction of gestures moving relative to each other with changes in speaking rate; predictions can be extended to the quantitative domain, because the variable, mutual sliding of adjacent articulatory gestures should have graded acoustic results for carefully selected sound sequences (see Browman and Goldstein 1990: 352–353). A direct example of these quantitative predictions is illustrated in Figure 14.1. Here a spectrogram of the utterance "Put a bell" is shown

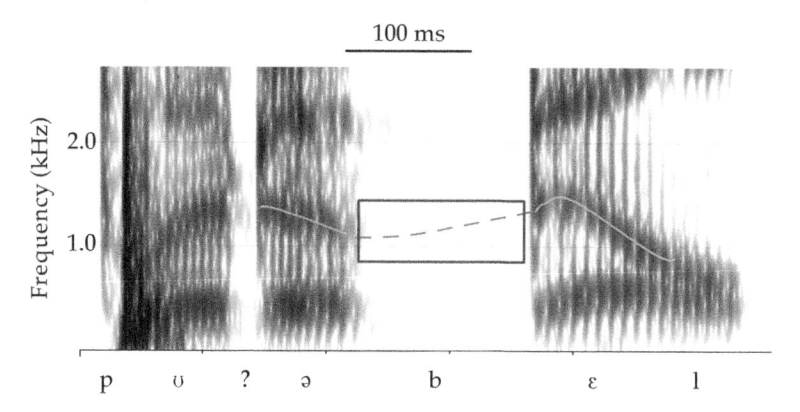

Figure 14.1 Spectrogram of the utterance "Put a bell," showing the labial closure gesture as a rectangle (left edge = onset, right edge = offset), F2 tracks for the preceding and following vowels (continuous line), and extrapolated F2 track (dashed line) "hidden" by the labial closure. Different phasings of the labial closure relative to the ongoing tongue gesture change the measurable F2 offset (at schwa-/b/ interface) and F2 onset (at /b/-/eh/ interface).

with the labial gesture for /b/ shown as a rectangle extending from the final glottal pulse of the schwa to the burst of /b/. The left edge of this rectangle is the onset of labial closure, the right edge the release of the closure. The tongue gestures for the schwa preceding the /b/ closure, and the /eh/ following the closure, are depicted by second formant (F2) transitions, shown as tracks superimposed on the F2s. Under the assumption that the tongue gesture throughout a VCV sequence, where C = bilabial stop, is more or less continuous but whose potential acoustic consequences during the bilabial gesture are largely "hidden" by the labial closure (Engstrand 1988; Löfqvist and Gracco 1999), the estimated F2 transition connecting the schwa and /eh/ is illustrated by the dotted line whose temporal extent is equivalent to that of the labial closure. This gestural score-like model shows that as the phasing of the labial closure is changed relative to either the preceding schwa or following /eh/, the point in time at which the lingual gesture is first (or last) "covered" by the labial gesture determines the F2 frequency at the boundary of the vowel and /b/. For example, continuous "leftward" sliding of the labial closing gesture into the schwa (or rightward sliding of the schwa tongue gesture, "underneath" the labial stop gesture), with all else held constant, results in a continuously increasing F2 off (the F2 at the boundary between the schwa and the /b/). Similarly, rightward sliding of the labial closure gesture into the /eh/ results first in increasing F2 on values, and after approximately 20 ms, deceasing F2 on values.

These are interesting, quantitative model predictions for motor speech disorders, in which abnormally slow, and occasionally abnormally rapid, speaking rates are a prominent characteristic. Are, for example, the F2 onsets and offsets surrounding a /b/ in sequences such as "Put a bell" disrupted by speaking rate abnormalities in dysarthria or apraxia of speech? The question seems especially relevant because adult speakers with certain types of motor speech disorder (such as apraxia of speech, or ataxic dysarthria) have been described in perceptual terms as producing a "scanning" type of connected speech. "Scanning" speech refers to equal marking of each syllable, or even each sound as if it were paced by a metronome beat. Consequently, the normally smooth coordination and overlap of succeeding speech sounds is lost by a pulling apart of contiguous gestures. In other words, scanning speech can be hypothesized as the perceptual result of the sliding apart of component articulatory gestures for a sound sequence; the reduction of overlap produced by such sliding may be a direct (or partial) result of the slow rates observed in many motor speech disorders.

A prior question is whether or not the acoustic predictions of systematic, rate-induced variation in formant offset and onset frequencies hold for normal speakers. Both Tjaden and Weismer (1998), and Weismer and Berry (2003) studied the covariation of F2 on and F2 off measures and speaking rate in VCV sequences produced by young adult speakers. When C = bilabial stop, the relative independence of the vocalic lingual gesture and labial consonantal gesture offers the best scenario for a systematic result of rate-induced gesture sliding. The results of these experiments were only partially consistent with the predictions of the gesture sliding model. Specifically, the effects were fairly consistent, strong, and in the correct direction for the F2 off measure, but not for the F2 on measure. The partial confirmation of the model was that gestures were, in fact, pulled apart with decreased speaking rate, but not symmetrically around a V1CV2 sequence. The lack of effects for the CV portion of the sequence may have do to with the often-hypothesized, integrated production mechanisms for CV, as compared to VC sequences (see review of relevant information in Hall 2010: 822–825). Perhaps the lingual gesture for V1 and the labial C gesture have greater flexibility for mutual phasing than the C and V2 gestures.

Relative gesture overlap among articulators can also be described as coarticulation, or interarticulator coordination. The few relevant, published studies on neuromotor speech disorders have not produced strong evidence of articulatory dyscoordination (see, e.g., Bartle et al. 2006; Hertrich and Ackermann 1999; Weismer et al. 2003; Tjaden and Wilding 2005). This finding is somewhat surprising because loss of neuromotor integrity, whatever the underlying cause, is thought to result in some form of dyscoordination when complex movements of any kind are examined, even if dyscoordination is not assumed to be a core neurological sign of a particular disorder (Cantiniaux et al. 2010; Poizner et al. 1995; and see discussion above of STI). The phasing of articulatory gestures for a variety of speech samples and for a reasonable number of speakers is still poorly understood, because sufficient data have not been reported.

14.3.4 DIVA/GODIVA

A simplified version of the GODIVA model is shown in Figure 14.2. This schematic is based closely on versions of DIVA and GODIVA presented in Guenther (2006), Guenther, Ghosh, and Tourville (2006), Bohland et al. (2010), Peeva et al. (2010), and Perkell (2012). The boxes show processes, and, when appropriate, neuroanatomical regions where those processes are thought to "reside." The arrows show information flow between processes (and their putative regions). For example, the box labeled "speech sound map" shows a process of speech sound representation, in syllabic units, located in the lateral ventral premotor cortex (lvPMC) of the left hemisphere (parts of Brodmann areas 44 and 6). These are the sounds-to-be-produced plus their abstract "plan" for articulatory behavior. In the older literature on AOS (e.g., Martin 1974; Buckingham 1986; Rosenbek et al. 1984; Ziegler 2009), this process and its location within the left hemisphere were at the center of the controversy regarding whether AOS is a motor speech disorder or an aphasia. The controversy, put simply, was whether speakers diagnosed with AOS had defective representations. Those who believed the representations were correct but were realized (produced) inaccurately because of a programming disorder regarded the problem as a motor speech disorder. Those who thought the representation was incorrect, with the erroneous output mirroring the damaged representation, regarded the disorder as an aphasia. GODIVA appears to hold the tacit assumption of representations as always correct; GODIVA also seems to locate the programming of the represented syllables in the same tissue as the representations, although it is possible to view the projections from the speech sound map to the artic velocity/position maps (downward-pointing arrow,

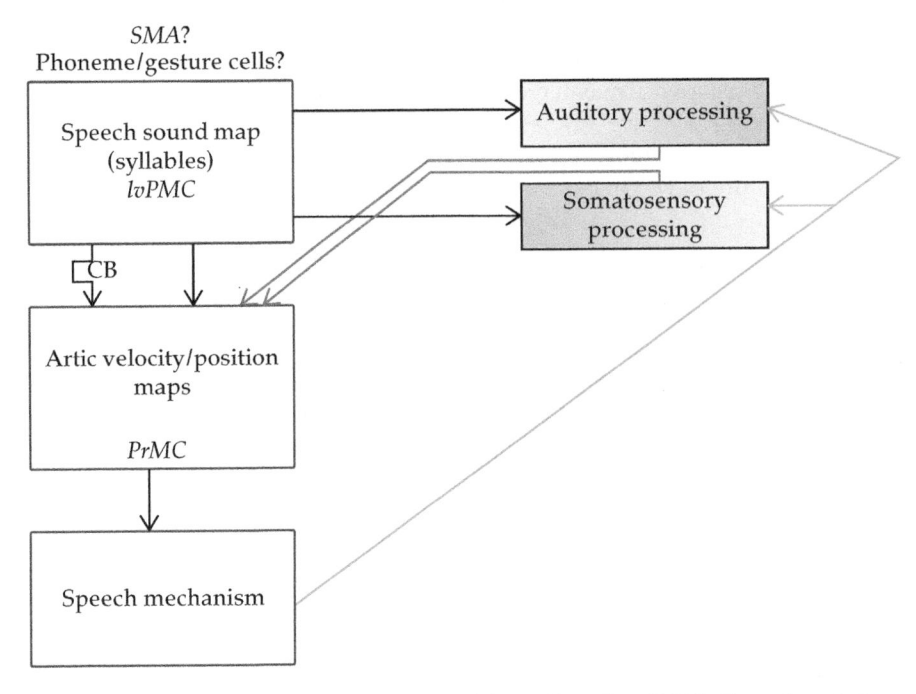

Figure 14.2 Simplified DIVA model. Adapted from Guenther (2006), Guenther et al. (2006), Bohland et al. (2010), and Peeva et al. (2010).

Figure 14.2) as "containing" the program (see Perkell 2012). The lvPMC is a region where lesions may produce articulatory symptoms that are consistent with a diagnosis of AOS, at least in adults (see, e.g., Mohr et al. 1978; and Alexander, Naeser, and Palumbo 1990; compare these reports to the lesion locations claimed to produce apraxia of speech described by Ogar et al. 2006). These symptoms include slow speaking rate, inconsistent speech-sound errors across multiple attempts of the same syllables and/or words, a tendency for increasing phonetic complexity to induce more articulatory errors and/or modification of articulatory behavior (see Laganaro et al. 2012), and difficulty initiating speech – "groping" for correct articulatory positions – as well as dysfluency and self-correction of produced errors with multiple attempts to "get it right."

GODIVA has two major outputs from the speech sound map. One is to the primary motor cortex, and specifically the ventral region containing cortical motor neurons for head and neck structures. This output is shown as the rightmost arrow pointing downward from the speech sound map to the box labeled "Artic Velocity/position maps." The second output from the speech sound map is in the form of expectations, predictions, or "targets" concerning the sensory consequences of executing the components of the plan. This output is shown in Figure 14.2 as two arrows directed from the speech sound map to boxes labeled "Auditory Processing" and "Somatosensory Processing." In GODIVA, these projections carry a model of the auditory and somatosensory consequences of the planned, *successful* action; the information is stored as "here-is-how-it-should-be" form.

Two reasonable questions are, what is the structure of the information concerning expected consequences, and how does the model come to know their "correct" (and by implication, incorrect) forms? The answers to these questions are interdependent, and based fully on feedback pathways shown in Figure 14.2 as arrows from the speech mechanism to the "Auditory Processing" and "Somatosensory Processing" boxes. The act of moving articulators as the vocal folds vibrate produces an acoustic signal, as well as tactile, proprioceptive, and baroceptive (at least) information, all of which presumably combine to form a multidimensional, unified concept of a "correct" phonetic region. The comparison between prediction and realization allows error detection and on-line correction and adjustment of the calibration (prediction) parameters (arrows delivering information from the comparators to the primary motor cortex). The calibrations are plastic, and even when well learned can be adjusted by information from the comparison process. Experimental demonstrations of such nearly-immediate recalibrations have been reported for vowels, fricatives, and voice fundamental frequency (Perkell 2012).

Does DIVA have the potential to contribute to an understanding of dysarthria, and/or apraxia of speech? Putting aside the controversy and details, for the moment, of unique roles for different parts of what Bohland and Guenther (2006) have called the "minimal network" for speech motor control, let us follow Ackermann and Riecker (2010a) and assume the SMA, lvPMC, and anterior insula jointly play a role in preparation and initiation of articulatory sequences. Damage to any one of these areas, or to tracts connecting them, may affect a patient's ability to start speaking, as manifested either by a simple delay in initiation of articulatory movements or by the more complicated "groping" behaviors often considered as diagnostic of AOS (McNeil et al. 2009). Of greater interest, perhaps, is the influence of phonetic content on articulatory behaviors when a patient has a lesion in this planning part of the speech motor network (Ackermann and Riecker 2010a). The intertwined representation, planning, and initiation functions of the preparative component of the network suggest specific predictions of variation in articulatory behavior with variations in phonetic complexity of experimental utterances. These conclusions about the speech motor planning networks, however, are challenged by findings from studies also showing the negative effects of phonetic complexity on speech disorders such as stuttering and the absence of experimental comparisons across multiple types of neuromotor speech disorders (e.g., apraxia versus dysarthria).

The simplest and most general inference from DIVA to the planning difficulties mentioned above, is that damage to the cortical tissue of the lvPMC and/or insula interferes with the ability to "unpack" a readied string of syllables (or phonemes), or results in a breaking apart of the "off-the-shelf" (precompiled) gesture ensembles (assumed, in at least one popular theoretical formulation, to be available for frequently occurring syllables; see Roelofs 2002). Presumably, difficulty of either kind could cause a delay in initiation of an articulatory sequence and/or the occurrence of articulatory errors classified as substitutions.

This general inference, and the more specific details of matching the claimed speech production phenomena of AOS with the DIVA model, present some challenges both to modelers and observers of actual speech production data from patients diagnosed with this disorder. One claim from the AOS literature is that some patients, some of the time, self-correct initiation errors and perhaps even errors produced after initiation, and even converge on the correct articulatory gestures (inferred from perceptual evaluation) over a series of attempts. Another claim is the tendency for errors and initiation difficulties to increase with increased phonetic complexity of the sequence to be produced. A third claim is the one related to articulatory groping, or more generally a delayed initiation of speech when a patient is asked to say something. It is reasonable to ask how DIVA might account for these phenomena and to question the prevailing views about the characteristics that uniquely define AOS.

One approach to seeking answers to these questions is to examine the GODIVA model shown in Figure 14.2 and predict what might happen if there are "breaks" in components of its speech motor control network. For this discussion, we emphasize that DIVA is currently a model of this "higher-level" ("preparative," in Ackermann and Riecker's 2010b terms) part of speech motor control. In DIVA, there is a firewall between the preparative or planning part of speech motor control and the execution component. When the sequence prepared in DIVA arrives at the "lower-level" part of the model – what Ackermann and Riecker call the "Executive Loop" – the sensitivity to factors such as phonetic complexity ends. The interface between the higher-level and lower-level parts of the speech motor control circuitry is, in DIVA, roughly at the boundary between the lvPMC and the M1 regions, the latter responsible for control of orofacial, laryngeal, and respiratory musculature. One interesting prediction that seems to follow from this "firewall" is the attenuation of phonetic complexity effects in *dysarthria*. The ideal comparison group in such a study would be patients with damage to the corticobulbar tract because lesions associated with Parkinson's and cerebellar disease have often been assumed to result in some degree of "higher-level" effects on speech (Spencer and Rogers 2005).

14.3.4.1 Damage to lvPMC In GODIVA, the output plan for an articulatory sequence may include temporal ordering and phasing (Bohland et al. 2010: 1507); units of these processes are generally syllable-sized (Peeva et al. 2010). Damage to the *representation* of the phonological syllable(s) could, in principle, either destroy the representation or make it unreliable. A destroyed representation seems unlikely for persons diagnosed with AOS because most of these patients do produce speech, even if they hesitate to initiate utterances, and errors are typically (but not exclusively) related in lawful ways to the "target" syllables and segments (see Rosenbek et al. 1984: 14; Miller 2002, for summaries of the error types produced by persons diagnosed with AOS). A partially destroyed representation is more difficult to conceptualize, at least in terms of how it might affect speech production behaviors. For example, it could be argued that some *disruption* of the representation makes it more difficult to access (or, in the language of connectionist thinking, raises activation thresholds), leading to the initiation problems and possibly augmented effects of phonetic complexity on initiation time and/or segmental errors.

14.3.4.2 Damage to projections from lvPMC to auditory and somatosensory cortex

When executed, the speaker expects the phonological sequence and plan for its motor program to result in certain signal (acoustic and somatosensory) characteristics. In the neurologically normal adult, these expectations are fine-tuned over the thousands of iterations of speech motor acts (see Ziegler et al. 2010: 4, for conservative estimates of typical speech iterations). Some theorists have argued that such extensive fine-tuning results in a kind of phonological-to-articulatory hard wiring, or binding, for frequently produced syllable shapes (Levelt, Roelofs, and Meyer 1999). Perhaps less well-known are the theoretical (and practical) difficulties with this view of speech motor control as applied to the case of AOS; an excellent discussion of these problems is presented in Ziegler et al. (2010).

What happens if the comparison of expected and actual consequences produces a significant error? A range of disparities between the two sources of information is tolerable but there are thresholds for error tolerance that when exceeded result in speech errors. A series of elegant studies in neurologically normal speakers has shown that experimental modifications of either auditory or sensory feedback result in speakers making corrective adjustments to their output (see Perkell 2012). These measurable output adjustments show drift over time (both during the altered feedback and after it is withdrawn), suggesting fine-tuned modifications of the consequence "model" carried by the dashed arrows in Figure 14.2. Even though the "consequence model" is based on thousands of speech-event iterations, the speech motor control system is sufficiently sensitive and plastic to change its calibrations, even for subtle changes in the match between expected and actual consequences.

Within the DIVA framework, what might be a reasonable expectation for speech motor control problems when there is damage to the neuroanatomical substrates of these calibration pathways (the existence of such pathways has been reviewed by Turken and Dronkers 2011; and Hickok and Poeppel, 2004, 2007)?

Let us assume that damage to either the lvPMC or tracts connecting the frontal to posterior zones can disturb the calibration model and its ability to be used for comparison to the auditory and somatosensory data entering the system as a result of vocal tract movements. The calibration model can, in theory, either be destroyed, or damaged but with some of its information presumably available for comparison to incoming data. In the event of damage to the model, articulatory groping at the onset of an attempt to speak that, in some cases, is followed by an awareness of the groping (as evidenced by restarts and frustration) would be expected. It is as if the map is there, but the locations and directions are unmarked. In the rare case of a patient who has a stroke and suffers extensive perisylvian damage and remains mute for a long period of time (Brendel et al. 2010), or for the remainder of his or her life, perhaps the muteness is explained by the missing model.

Some patients with perisylvian damage in regions associated with AOS are mute at the beginning of their speech recovery (Mohr et al. 1978) but gradually or sometimes rapidly regain the ability to produce correct articulatory sequences; muteness has even been suggested as the most severe manifestation of AOS (see Ziegler et al. 2010: 18). The patient who regains the ability to produce articulatory sequences during the acute phase of recovery clearly has some calibration information available; perhaps this is the kind of speaker likely to converge on a correct sound production over several attempts. Precisely how a partially damaged calibration model leads to repeated attempts that converge on correct production is unclear. One hypothesis is that the repeated attempts prime the model in the correct direction, but more natural data on self-generated corrections, and more detail in a model such as DIVA on how the calibration model may fluctuate and be primed by erroneous attempts, are required to develop these notions.

14.3.4.3 Damage to correction signals Which of the classic AOS speech production symptoms might be explained if damage occurs at the comparison site(s), or in the projections from the comparison site(s) to the primary motor cortex (i.e., the lightly shaded arrows in Figure 14.2)? For the sake of simplicity, let us assume normal function of the comparison site, with the problem located in the tracts carrying the correction signals to the primary cortex. These signals adjust the feedforward model, the empirical evidence for which is not only the on-line adjustments made to subtly altered feedback but the "afterimage" of the new model even after an experimentally induced feedback error has been withdrawn (Perkell 2012). AOS speech symptoms such as sensitivity to utterance complexity and successive errors converging on a correct form do not seem easily inferred from the loss of ability to correct a mismatch between actual and calibration data. A case could be made for groping as consistent with the inability to compare actual with calibration model data, but groping is one of those symptoms potentially explainable in lots of different ways.

14.4   Summary and conclusions

In this chapter, we have discussed speech motor control in persons with motor speech disorders. Traditionally, motor speech disorders have been partitioned into "planning" disorders on the one hand, and "execution" disorders on the other. The boundary between these terms, apraxia of speech ("planning") and dysarthria ("execution"), has been drawn both neuroanatomically and behaviorally. Clinical and experimental data reviewed above show the boundary to be poorly defined, for both the anatomical and behavioral domains. We suggest that the current absence of clear mappings between brain regions and specific speech motor control processes, and their varying dissolution in neurological disease, is partially due to incomplete experimental evaluation of functional speech production deficits in motor speech disorders (e.g., comparisons between groups of speakers with expected planning deficits to those with expected, straightforward execution deficits). Another challenge to establishing causal linkages between structure and function is that the system is truly a *system*. Perhaps only under the most restrictive, clinically unusual conditions, as in the case of very focal lesions, can clear mappings be established between brain anatomy and speech production phenomena in motor speech disorders.

We presented a view of motor speech disorders in which two types of knowledge accumulation have served as templates for scientific advance. The first template is the lesion/function or imaging/function line of inquiry. The second type seeks to identify speech production deficits in motor speech disorders without specific reference to lesion location, to document presumably abnormal movement and coordination processes and compare them to those of normal participants. A reason to value this latter approach is the empirical gray area, noted above, between planning and execution disorders of speech production, as well as the more recent documentation of substantial *commonalities* in speech production deficits of speakers with a variety of dysarthria types, and even between dysarthria and apraxia of speech. These commonalities are still based on a very small amount of data; the phenomenology of speech production in motor speech disorders must be more firmly established so that we know what the models and theories of speech production are trying to model or explain, whether tied strongly to neuroanatomy (e.g., DIVA) or primarily concerned with processes (e.g., Articulatory Phonology).

At the outset of this chapter, we said that we would offer suggestions for a research pathway to join the best aspects of the two templates. Our suggestions, which emerge as logical (even prosaic) conclusions from the considerations presented above, are as follows. First, a consortium of scientists interested in developing an understanding of speech motor control disorders should be organized to develop and propose a multicenter study to document speech production phenomena in relatively large populations of persons with diverse motor speech disorders. The details should include uniform imaging, speech movement, speech acoustic, and speech intelligibility measures, across the several research sites involved in the work. A set of criteria should be developed for the identification of underlying disease (a fairly easy task) and the diagnosis of type and severity of speech motor control deficit (both somewhat more difficult tasks). The pooling of participants across the several sites should produce large enough N's to make both within-group (e.g., variation in speech severity) and cross-group (either cross-disease or cross-type) comparisons and possible interactions meaningful in quantitative terms. Initially, the work should be designed for a small number of groups likely to yield the greatest theoretical payoff. Following the discussion presented above, these groups might be limited to persons with bilateral upper motor neuron disease, Parkinson's disease, and damage to lvPMC. Careful design of speech samples for manipulation of speaking rate, phonetic complexity, and coarticulatory demands (perhaps partially redundant with complexity) can lead to experiments conducted during imaging, whereas a broader set of speech samples should be collected outside the imaging environment, for broad and deep knowledge of speech movement characteristics in these groups. Multivariate analysis strategies should be planned for an understanding of the interrelationships among these different kinds of data, but especially to get a better handle on levels of activity in the different components of the minimal network for speech motor control and experimental effects of phonetic complexity, rate, and so forth.

We are technique and idea rich, but data poor. We would suggest that the above sketch of a research program would contribute to solving the latter problem while exploiting the former. A 10-year research program following several focused conferences to set criteria and designs, as described above, seems a realistic path for continuing research in motor speech disorders.

NOTES

1 It should be pointed out that the data in Wong et al. (2011) showing greater displacements (and speeds) in persons with Parkinson's disease and dysarthria (PD-D), versus persons with Parkinson's disease who are not dysarthric (PD-ND), are confounded by differences in speaker sex across the two groups and cannot be reasonably interpreted as showing a real tendency for dysarthria to be characterized by greater movements than normal. Six of the eight speakers in the PD-D group were male, and five of the seven speakers in the PD-ND group were female. Simpson (2001) showed for neurologically normal speakers that males typically have larger and faster tongue motions than females, so the small gesture displacement and speed differences between dysarthric and non-dysarthric speakers with PD, reported by Wong et al. (2011), may reflect some degree of sex confound across the two groups (and possibly across their control group, whose sex distribution is unspecified and impossible to infer from the report).
2 These data were produced toward the end of the 1970s by Dr. C.K. Chuang who at that time was working in the Speech Motor Control Laboratories, University of Wisconsin-Madison; the study should be repeated with contemporary methods.

REFERENCES

Ackermann, Hermann. 2008. Cerebellar contributions to speech production and speech perception: Psycholinguistic and neurobiological perspectives. *Trends in Neurosciences* 31: 265–272.

Ackermann, Hermann and Axel Riecker. 2010a. Cerebral control of motor aspects of speech production: Neurophysiological and functional imaging data. In B. Maassen and P. Van Lieshout (eds.), *Speech Motor Control: New Developments in Basic and Applied Research*, 117–134. Oxford: Oxford University Press.

Ackermann, Hermann and Axel Riecker. 2010b. The contribution(s) of the insula to speech production: A review of the clinical and functional imaging literature. *Brain Structure and Function* 214: 419–433.

Ackermann, Hermann, Matthias Vogel, Dirk Petersen, and Michael Poremba. 1992. Speech deficits in ischaemic cerebellar lesions. *Journal of Neurology* 239: 223–227.

Ackermann, Hermann, Ingo Hertrich, Irene Daum, Gabriele Scharf, and Sybille Spieker. 1997. Kinematic analysis of articulatory movements in central motor disorders. *Movement Disorders* 12: 1019–1027.

Alexander, Michael P., Margaret A. Naeser, and Carole Palumbo. 1990. Broca's area aphasias: Aphasia after lesions including the frontal operculum. *Neurology* 40: 353–362.

Alfonso, Peter J. and Thomas Baer. 1982. Dynamics of vowel articulation. *Language and Speech* 25: 151–173.

Arboix, Adria, Juan Massons, Montserrat Oliveres, and F. Titus. 1991. Isolated dysarthria. *Stroke* 22: 531.

Bartle, Carly J., Justine V. Goozée, Dion Scott, Bruce E. Murdoch, and Mili Kuruvilla. 2006. EMA assessment of tongue–jaw co-ordination during speech in dysarthria following traumatic brain injury. *Brain Injury* 20: 529–545.

Bartle-Meyer, Carly J., Justine V. Goozée, Bruce E. Murdoch, and Jordan R. Green. 2009. Kinematic analysis of articulatory coupling in acquired apraxia of speech post-stroke. *Brain Injury* 23: 133–145.

Bell-Berti, Fredericka and Rena Arens Krakow. 1991. Anticipatory velar lowering: A coproduction account. *Journal of the Acoustical Society of America* 90: 112–123.

Benke, Thomas and Andrew Kertesz. 1989. Hemispheric mechanisms of motor speech. *Aphasiology* 3: 627–641.

Bernstein, Lynne E. and Gary Weismer. 2000. Basic science at the intersection of speech science and communication disorders. *Journal of Phonetics* 28: 225–232.

Bohland, Jason W. and Frank H. Guenther. 2006. An fMRI investigation of syllable sequence production. *NeuroImage* 32: 821–841.

Bohland, Jason W., Daniel Bullock, and Frank H. Guenther. 2010. Neural representations and mechanisms for the performance of simple speech sequences. *Journal of Cognitive Neuroscience* 22: 1504–1529.

Brendel, Bettina, Ingo Hertrich, Michael Erb, Axel Lindner, Axel Riecker, Wolfgang Grodd, and Hermann Ackermann. 2010. The contribution of mesiofrontal cortex to the preparation and execution of repetitive syllable productions: An fMRI study. *NeuroImage* 50: 1291–1230.

Browman, Catherine P. and Louis Goldstein. 1990. Tiers in articulatory phonology with some implications for casual speech. In J. Kingston and M.E. Beckman (eds.), *Between the Grammar and Physics of Speech*, 341–376. Cambridge: Cambridge University Press.

Buckingham, Hugh W. 1986. The scan-copier mechanism and the positional level of language production: Evidence from phonemic paraphasia. *Cognitive Science* 10: 195–217.

Byrd, Dani. 1996. A phase window framework for articulatory timing. *Phonology* 13: 139–169.

Cantiniaux, Stephanie, Marianne Vaugoyeau, Daniele Robert, Christine Horrelou-Pitek, Julien Mancini, Tatiana Witjas, and Jean-Philippe Azulay. 2010. Comparative analysis of gait and speech in Parkinson's disease: Hypokinetic or dysrhythmic disorders. *Journal of Neurology, Neurosurgery and Psychiatry* 81: 177–184.

Chamorro, Angel, Ralph L. Sacco, Jay P. Mohr, Mary A. Foulkes, Carlos S. Kase, Thomas K. Tatemichi, and Daniel B. Hier. 1991. Clinical-computed tomographic correlations of lacunar infarction in the Stroke Data Bank. *Stroke* 22: 175–181.

Cheney, Paul D. and Eberhard E. Fetz. 1980. Functional classes of primate corticomotoneuronal cells and their relation to active force. *Journal of Neurophysiology* 44: 773–791.

Cooke, Dylan F. and Michael S.A. Graziano. 2004. Sensorimotor integration in the precentral gyrus: Polysensory neurons and defensive movements. *Journal of Neurophysiology* 91: 1648–1660.

Cooke, Dylan F., Charlotte S.R. Taylor, Tirin Moore, and Michael S.A. Graziano. 2003. Complex movements evoked by microstimulation of the ventral intraparietal area. *Proceedings of the National Academy of Sciences, USA* 100: 6163–6168.

Croot, Karen. 2002. Diagnosis of AOS: Definition and criteria. *Seminars in Speech and Language* 23: 267–280.

Darley, Frederic L., Arnold E. Aronson, and Joe R. Brown. 1969a. Differential diagnostic patterns of dysarthria. *Journal of Speech and Hearing Research* 12: 246–269.

Darley, Frederic L., Arnold E. Aronson, and Joe R. Brown. 1969b. Clusters of deviant speech features in the dysarthrias. *Journal of Speech and Hearing Research* 12: 462–496.

Darley, Frederic L., Arnold E. Aronson, and Joe R. Brown. 1975. *Motor Speech Disorders*. Philadelphia, PA: W.B. Saunders.

de Lafuente, Victor and Ranulfo Romo. 2004. Language abilities of motor cortex. *Neuron* 41: 178–180.

Dronkers, Nina F. 1996. A new brain region for coordinating speech articulation. *Nature* 384: 159–161.

Duffy, Joseph R. 1995. Why differential diagnosis? *Special Interest Division 2, Newsletter* 5: 2–6.

Duffy, Joseph R. 2005. *Motor Speech Disorders: Substrates, Differential Diagnosis and Management*. St. Louis, MO: Elsevier Mosby.

Engstrand, Olle. 1988. Articulatory correlates of stress and speaking rate in Swedish VCV utterances. *Journal of the Acoustical Society of America* 83: 1863–1875.

Evarts, Edward V. 1968. Relation of pyramidal tract activity to force exerted during voluntary movement. *Journal of Neurophysiology* 31: 14–27.

Fairbanks, Grant. 1954. Systematic research in experimental phonetics. I: A theory of the speech mechanism as a servosystem. *Journal of Speech and Hearing Disorders* 19: 133–140.

Fisher, C. Miller. 1982. Lacunar strokes and infarcts: A review. *Neurology* 32: 871–876.

Forrest, Karen, Gary Weismer, and Greg S. Turner. 1989. Kinematic, acoustic and perceptual analyses of connected speech produced by Parkinsonian and normal geriatric adults. *Journal of the Acoustical Society of America* 85: 2608–2622.

Fu, Qing-Gong, Jose I. Suarez, and Timothy J. Ebner. 1993. Neuronal specification of direction and distance during reaching movements in the superior precentral premotor area and primary motor cortex of monkeys. *Journal of Neurophysiology* 70: 2097–2116.

Georgopoulos, Apostolos P., John F. Kalaska, Roberto Caminiti, and Joe T. Massey. 1982. On the relations between the direction of two-dimensional arm movements and cell discharge in primate motor cortex. *Journal of Neuroscience* 2: 1527–1537.

Ghosh, Satrajit S., Jason A. Tourville, and Frank H. Guenther. 2008. A neuroimaging study of premotor lateralization and cerebellar involvement in the production of phonemes and syllables. *Journal of Speech, Language, and Hearing Research* 51: 1183–1202.

Golfinopoulos, Elisa, Jason A. Tourville, Jason W. Bohland, Satrajit S. Ghosh, Alfonso Nieto-Castanon, and Frank H. Guenther. 2011. fMRI investigation of unexpected somatosensory feedback perturbation during speech. *NeuroImage* 55: 1324–1338.

Graziano, Michael S.A., Charlotte S.R. Taylor, Tirin Moore, and Dylan F. Cooke. 2002. The cortical control of movement revisited. *Neuron* 36: 349–362.

Green, Jordan R. and Ignatius S.B. Nip. 2010. Organization principles in the development of early speech: Catalysts, constraints and synergy. In B. Maaseen and P.H.H.M. Van Lieshout (eds.), *Speech Motor Control: New Developments in Basic and Applied Research*, 171–188. Oxford: Oxford University Press.

Green, Jordan R., Yana Yunusova, Mili S. Kuruvilla, et al. 2013. Bulbar and speech motor assessment in ALS: Challenges and future directions. *Amyotrophic Lateral Sclerosis and Frontotemporal Degeneration* 14: 494–500.

Grewel, Fritz. 1957. Classification of dysarthrias. *Acta Psychiatrica Scandinavica* 32: 325–337.

Grimme, Britta, Susanne Fuchs, Pascal Perrier, and Gregor Schöner. 2011. Limb versus speech motor control: A conceptual review. *Motor Control* 15: 5–33.

Guenther, Frank H. 2006. Cortical interaction underlying the production of speech sounds. *Journal of Communication Disorders* 39: 350–365.

Guenther, Frank H., Satrajit S. Ghosh, and Jason A. Tourville. 2006. Neural modeling and imaging of the cortical interactions underlying syllable production. *Brain and Language* 96: 280–301.

Hall, Nancy. 2010. Articulatory phonology. *Language and Linguistics Compass* 4/9: 818–830.

Heilman, Kenneth M. and Robert T. Watson. 2008. The disconnection apraxias. *Cortex* 44: 975–982.

Hertrich, Ingo and Hermann Ackermann. 1999. Temporal and spectral aspects of coarticulation in ataxic dysarthria: An acoustic analysis. *Journal of Speech, Language, and Hearing Research* 42: 367–381.

Hickok, Gregory and David Poeppel. 2004. Dorsal and ventral streams: A framework for understanding aspects of the functional anatomy of language. *Cognition* 92: 67–99.

Hickok, Gregory and David Poeppel. 2007. The cortical organization of speech processing. *Nature Reviews: Neuroscience* 8: 393–402.

Higashikawa, Masahiko, Jordan R. Green, Christopher A. Moore, and Fred D. Minifie. 2003. Lip kinematics for /p/ and /b/ production during whispered and voiced speech. *Folia Phoniatrica et Logopaedica* 55: 17–27.

Hirose, Hajime, Shigeru Kiritani, and Masayuki Sawashima. 1982. Patterns of dysarthric movement in patients with amyotrophic lateral sclerosis and pseudobulbar palsy. *Folia Phoniatrica* 34: 106–112.

Hirose, Hajime, Shigeru Kiritani, Tatsujiro Ushijima, Hirohide Yoshioka, and Masayuki Sawashima. 1981. Patterns of dysarthric movement in patients with Parkinsonism. *Folia Phoniatrica* 33: 204–215.

Howell, Peter. 2010. Behavioral effects arising from the neural substrates for atypical planning and execution of word production in stuttering. *Experimental Neurology* 225: 55–59.

Ichikawa, Kiyoshi and Yasunori Kageyama. 1991. Clinical anatomic study of pure dysarthria. *Stroke* 2: 809–812.

Jacks, Adam, Katey A. Mathes, and Thomas P. Marquardt. 2010. Vowel acoustics in adults with apraxia of speech. *Journal of Speech, Language, and Hearing Research* 53: 61–74.

Jonas, Saran. 1981. The supplementary motor region and speech emission. *Journal of Communication Disorders* 14: 349–373.

Kakei, Shinji, Donna S. Hoffman, and Peter L. Strick. 1999. Muscle and movement representations in the primary motor cortex. *Science* 285: 2136–2139.

Kalaska, John F., Dan A.D. Cohen, Martha L. Hyde, and Michel Prud'Homme. 1989. A comparison of movement direction-related versus load direction-related activity in primate motor cortex, using a two-dimensional reaching task. *Journal of Neuroscience* 9(6): 2080–2102.

Kameda, Wataru et al. 2004. Lateral and medial medullary infarction: A comparative analysis of 214 patients. *Stroke* 35: 694–699.

Kempler, Daniel and Diana Van Lancker. 2002. Effect of speech task on speech intelligibility in dysarthria: A case study of Parkinson's disease. *Brain and Language* 80: 449–464.

Kent, Ray D. 2004. The uniqueness of speech among motor systems. *Clinical Linguistics and Phonetics* 18: 495–505.

Kent, Raymond D. and John C. Rosenbek. 1983. Acoustic patterns of apraxia of speech. *Journal of Speech and Hearing Research* 26: 231–249.

Kent, R.D., R. Netsell, and L.L. Bauer. 1975. Cineradiographic assessment of articulatory mobility in the dysarthrias. *Journal of Speech and Hearing Disorders*, 40: 467–480.

Kent, Ray D., Jane F. Kent, Gary Weismer, and Joseph R. Duffy. 2000. What dysarthrias can tell us about the neural control of speech. *Journal of Phonetics* 28: 273–302.

Kim, Yunjung, Raymond D. Kent, and Gary Weismer. 2011. An acoustic study of the relationships among neurologic disease, dysarthria type and severity of dysarthria. *Journal of Speech, Language, and Hearing Research* 54: 417–429.

Kumral, Emre, Mehmet Çelebisoy, Nese Çelebisoy, Diler Hulya Canbaz, and Cem Çalli. 2007. Dysarthria due to supratentorial and infratentorial ischemic stroke: A diffusion-weighted imaging study. *Cerebrovascular Diseases* 23: 331–338.

Kuruvilla, Mili, Bruce Murdoch, and Justine Goozée. 2007. Electromagnetic articulography assessment of articulatory function in adults with dysarthria following traumatic brain injury. *Brain Injury* 21: 601–613.

Laganaro, Marina, Michele Croisier, Odile Bagou, and Frederic Assal. 2012. Progressive apraxia of speech as a window into the study of speech planning processes. *Cortex* 48: 963–971.

Levelt, Willem J.M., Ardi Roelofs, and Antje S. Meyer. 1999. A theory of lexical access in speech production. *Behavioral and Brain Sciences* 22: 1–38.

Lindblom, Bjorn, James Lubker, and Thomas Gay. 1979. Formant frequencies of some fixed-mandible vowels and a model of speech motor programming by predictive simulation. *Journal of Phonetics* 7: 147–161.

Liss, Julie M. and Gary Weismer. 1994. Selected acoustic characteristics of contrastive stress production in control geriatric, apraxic and ataxic dysarthric speakers. *Clinical Linguistics and Phonetics* 8: 45–66.

Liss, Julie M., Laurence White, Sven L. Mattys, Kaitlyn Lansford, Andrew J. Lotto, Stephanie M. Spitzer, and John N. Caviness. 2009. Quantifying speech rhythm abnormalities in the dysarthrias. *Journal of Speech, Language, and Hearing Research* 52: 1334–1352.

Löfqvist, Anders and Vincent L. Gracco. 1999. Interarticulator programming in VCV sequences: Lip and tongue movements. *Journal of the Acoustical Society of America* 105: 1864–1876.

Ludlow, Christy L., Nadine P. Connor, and Celia J. Bassich. 1987. Speech timing in Parkinson's and Huntington's disease. *Brain and Language* 32: 195–214.

MacNeilage, Peter F. 1970. Motor control of the serial ordering of speech. *Psychological Review* 77: 182–196.

Martin, A. Damien. 1974. Some objections to the term apraxia of speech. *Journal of Speech and Hearing Disorders* 39: 53–64.

Mathiak, Klaus, Ingo Hertrich, Wolfgang Grodd, and Hermann Ackermann. 2002. Cerebellum and speech perception: A functional magnetic resonance imaging study. *Journal of Cognition Neuroscience* 14: 902–912.

McNeil, Malcolm R., Donald A. Robin, and Richard A. Schmidt. 2009. Apraxia of speech. In M.R. McNeil (ed.), *Clinical Management of Sensorimotor Speech Disorders*, 2nd edn, 249–268. New York: Thieme.

Mefferd, Antje S., Jordan R. Green, and Gary Pattee. 2012. A novel fixed-target task to determine articulatory speed constraints in persons with amyotrophic lateral sclerosis. *Journal of Communication Disorders* 45: 35–45.

Miller, Nick. 2002. The neurological basis of apraxia of speech. *Seminars in Speech and Language* 23: 223–230.

Mohr, Jay P., Michael S. Pessin, Sydney Finkelstein, H. Harris Funkenstein, Gary W. Duncan, and Kenneth R. Davis. 1978. Broca aphasia: Pathologic and clinical. *Neurology* 28: 311–324.

Moran, Daniel W. and Andrew B. Schwartz. 1999. Motor cortical representation of speed and direction during reaching. *Journal of Neurophysiology* 82: 2676–2692.

Munhall, Kevin and Anders Löfqvist. 1992. Gestural aggregation in speech: Laryngeal gestures. *Journal of Phonetics* 20: 111–126.

Murdoch, Bruce E. 2010. The cerebellum and language: Historical perspectives and review. *Cortex* 46: 858–868.

Neilson, Peter D. and Nicholas J. O'Dwyer. 1984. Reproducibility and variability of speech muscle activity in normal and cerebral palsied subjects: EMG findings. *Journal of Speech and Hearing Research* 27: 502–517.

Nip, Ignatius S.B. 2013. Kinematic characteristics of speaking rate in individuals with cerebral palsy: A preliminary study. *Journal of Medical Speech-Language Pathology* 20: 88–94.

Ogar, Jennifer, Sharon Willock, Juliana Baldo, David Wilkins, Carl Ludy, and Nina Dronkers. 2006. Clinical and anatomical correlates of apraxia of speech. *Brain and Language* 97: 343–350.

Orefice, Giuseppe, Nina A. Fragassi, Roberta Lanzillo, Annalisa Castellano, and Dario Grossi. 1999. Transient muteness followed by dysarthria in patients with pontomesencephalic stroke. Report of two cases. *Cerebrovascular Diseases* 9: 124–126.

Ozaki, Isamu, Masayuki Baba, Shoko Narita, Muneo Matsunaga, and Kazuo Takebe. 1986. Pure dysarthria due to anterior internal capsule and/or corona radiata infarction: A report of five cases. *Journal of Neurology, Neurosurgery & Psychiatry* 49: 1435–1437.

Park, Haeil, Gregory K. Iverson, and Hae-Jong Park. 2011. Neural correlates in the processing of phoneme-level complexity in vowel production. *Brain and Language* 119: 158–166.

Peach, Richard K. and John D. Tonkovich. 2004. Phonemic characteristics of apraxia of speech resulting from subcortical hemorrhage. *Journal of Communication Disorders* 37: 77–90.

Peacher, William G. 1950. The etiology and differential diagnosis of dysarthria. *Journal of Speech and Hearing Disorders* 15: 252–265.

Peeva, Maya G., Frank H. Guenther, Jason A. Tourville, Alfonso Nieto-Castanon, Jean-Luc Antonn, Bruno Nazarian, and F.-Xavier Alario. 2010. Distinct representation of phonemes, syllables and supra-syllabic sequences in the speech production network. *NeuroImage* 50: 626–638.

Penfield, Wilder and Herbert Jasper. 1954. *Epilepsy and the Functional Anatomy of the Human Brain*. Boston, MA: Little, Brown.

Perkell, Joseph S. 2012. Movement goals and feedback and feedforward control mechanisms in speech production. *Journal of Neurolinguistics* 25: 382–407.

Perkell, Joseph S., Melanie L. Matthies, Mario A. Svirsky, and Michael I. Jordan. 1993. Trading relations between tongue body raising and lip rounding for the vowel /u/: A pilot "motor equivalence" study. *Journal of the Acoustical Society of America* 93: 2948–2961.

Platt, Larry J., Gavin Andrews, and Pauline M. Howie. 1980. Dysarthria of adult cerebral palsy. II: Phonemic analysis of articulation errors. *Journal of Speech and Hearing Research* 23: 41–55.

Poizner, Howard, MaryAnn Clark, Alma S. Merians, Beth Macauley, Leslie J. Gonzalez Rothi, and Kenneth M. Heilman. 1995. Joint coordination deficits in limb apraxia. *Brain* 118: 227–242.

Porter, Robert and Roger N. Lemon. 1993. *Corticospinal Function and Voluntary Movement*. Oxford: Oxford University Press.

Pulvermüller, Friedemann. 2010. Brain embodiment of syntax and grammar:

Discrete combinatorial mechanisms spelt out in neuronal circuits. *Brain and Language* 112: 167–179.

Riecker, Axel, Klaus Mathiak, Dirk Wildgruber, Michael Erb, Ingo Hertrich, Wolfgang Grodd, and Hermann Ackermann. 2005. fMRI reveals two distinct cerebral networks subserving speech motor control. *Neurology* 64: 700–706.

Roelofs, Ardi. 2002. Spoken language planning and the initiation of articulation. *Quarterly Journal of Experimental Psychology* 55: 465–483.

Rosenbek, John C., Ray D. Kent, and Leonard L. LaPointe. 1984. Apraxia of speech: An overview and some perspectives. In J.C. Rosenbek, M.R. McNeil, and A.E. Aronson (eds.), *Apraxia of Speech*, 1–72. San Diego, CA: College-Hill Press.

Rothwell, John C., Philip D. Thompson, Brian L. Day, Jeremy P. Dick, Teruhiko Kachi, Janet M. Cowan, and Charles D. Marsden. 1987. Motor cortex stimulation in intact man. I: General characteristics of EMG responses in different muscles. *Brain* 110: 1173–1190.

Schirmer, Annett. 2004. Timing speech: A review of lesion and neuroimaging findings. *Cognitive Brain Research* 21: 269–287.

Scott, Cheryl M. and Robert L. Ringel. 1971. Articulation without oral sensory control. *Journal of Speech and Hearing Research* 14: 804–818.

Sidtis, John J., Stephen C. Strother, Ansam Groshong, Ansam Naoum, David A. Rottenberg, and Christopher Gomez. 2010. Longitudinal cerebral blood flow changes during speech in hereditary ataxia. *Brain and Language* 114: 43–51.

Simpson, Adrian P. 2001. Dynamic consequences of differences in male and female vocal tract dimensions. *Journal of the Acoustical Society of America* 109: 2153–2164.

Smith, Anne, Michael Johnson, Clare McGillem, and Lisa Goffman. 2000. On the assessment of stability and patterning of speech movements. *Journal of Speech, Language, and Hearing Research* 43: 277–286.

Spencer, Kristie A. and Margaret Rogers. 2005. Speech motor programming in hypokinetic and ataxic dysarthria. *Brain and Language* 94: 347–366.

Spencer, Kristie and Dana Slocomb. 2007. The neural basis of ataxic dysarthria. *The Cerebellum* 6: 58–65.

Staekenborg, Salka S., Wiesje M. van der Flier, Elisabeth C. van Straaten, Roger Lane, Frederik Barkhof, and Philip Scheltens. 2008. Neurological signs in relation to type of cerebrovascular disease in vascular dementia. *Stroke* 39: 317–322.

Stevens, Kenneth N. 2000. *Acoustic Phonetics*. Cambridge, MA: MIT Press.

Takai, Osamu, Steven Brown, and Mario Liotti. 2010. Representation of the speech effectors in the human motor cortex: Somatotopy or overlap? *Brain and Language* 113: 39–44.

Tjaden, Kris and Gary Weismer. 1998. Speaking-rate-induced variability in F2 trajectories. *Journal of Speech, Language, and Hearing Research* 41: 976–989.

Tjaden, Kris and Gregory E. Wilding. 2005. Effect of rate reduction and increased loudness on acoustic measures of anticipatory coarticulation in multiple sclerosis and Parkinson's disease. *Journal of Speech, Language, and Hearing Research* 48: 261–277.

Tohgi, Hideo, Shigeki Takahashi, Hiroaki Takahashi, Koichiro Tamura, and Hisashi Yonezawa. 1996. The side and somatotopical location of single small infarcts in the corona radiata and pontine base in relation to contralateral limb paresis and dysarthria. *European Neurology* 36: 338–342.

Tourville, Jason, Kevin Reilly, and Frank Guenther. 2008. Neural mechanisms underlying auditory feedback control of speech. *NeuroImage* 39: 1429–1443.

Tripoliti, Elina and Patricia Limousin. 2010. Electrical stimulation of deep brain structures and speech. In B. Maassen and P. Van Lieshout (eds.), *Speech Motor Control: New Developments in Basic and Applied Research*, 297–313. Oxford: Oxford University Press.

Turken, A. Umit and Nina F. Dronkers. 2011. The neural architecture of the language comprehension network: Converging evidence from lesion and connectivity analysis. *Frontiers in Systems Neuroscience* 5: 1–20.

Urban, Peter Paul, Juergen Marx, Stefan Hunsche, et al. 2003. Cerebellar speech representation: Lesion topography in dysarthria as derived from cerebellar ischemia and functional magnetic resonance imaging. *Archives of Neurology* 60: 965–972.

Urban, Peter Paul, Roman Rolke, Susanne Wicht, Annerose Keilmann, Peter Stoeter, Hanns C. Hopf, and Megan Dieterich. 2006. Left hemispheric dominance for articulation: A prospective study on acute ischaemic dysarthria at different localizations. *Brain* 129: 767–777.

Walsh, Bridget and Anne Smith. 2011. Linguistic complexity, speech production and comprehension in Parkinson's disease: Behavioral and physiological indices. *Journal of Speech, Language, and Hearing Research* 54: 787–802.

Weismer, Gary. 1984. Articulatory characteristics of Parkinsonian dysarthria. In M.R. McNeil, J.C. Rosenbek, and A. Aronson (eds.), *The Dysarthrias: Physiology, Acoustics, Perception, Management*, 101–130. San Diego, CA: College-Hill Press.

Weismer, Gary. 1997. Motor speech disorders. In W.J. Hardcastle and J. Laver (eds.), *The Handbook of Phonetic Sciences*, 191–219. Oxford: Blackwell.

Weismer, Gary. 2006. Philosophy of research in motor speech disorders. *Clinical Linguistics and Phonetics* 20: 315–349.

Weismer, Gary and Jeff Berry. 2003. Effects of speaking rate on second formant trajectories of selected vocalic nuclei. *Journal of the Acoustical Society of America* 113: 3362–3378.

Weismer, Gary and Yunjung Kim. 2010. Classification and taxonomy of motor speech disorders: What are the issues? In B. Maassen and P.H.H.M. Van Lieshout (eds.), *Speech Motor Control: New Developments in Basic and Applied Research*, 229–241. Oxford: Oxford University Press.

Weismer, Gary, Yana Yunusova, and Kate Bunton. 2012. Measures to evaluate the effects of DBS on speech production. *Journal of Neurolinguistics* 25: 74–94.

Weismer, Gary, Yana Yunusova, and John R. Westbury. 2003. Interarticulator coordination in dysarthria: An X-ray microbeam study. *Journal of Speech, Language, and Hearing Research* 46: 1247–1261.

Whalen, Doug. 1990. Coarticulation is largely planned. *Journal of Phonetics* 18: 3–35.

Wong, Min Ney, Bruce E. Murdoch, and Brooke-Mai Whelan. 2011. Lingual kinematics in dysarthric and nondysarthric speakers with Parkinson's disease. *Parkinson's Disease*, 1–8.

Yunusova, Yana, Gary G. Weismer, and Mary J. Lindstrom. 2011. Classification of vocalic segments from articulatory kinematics: Healthy controls and speakers with dysarthria. *Journal of Speech, Language, and Hearing Research* 54: 1302–1311.

Yunusova, Yana, Gary Weismer, John R. Westbury, and Mary J. Lindstrom. 2008. Articulatory movements during vowels in speakers with dysarthria and healthy controls. *Journal of Speech, Language, and Hearing Research* 51(3): 596–611.

Yunusova, Yana, Jordan R. Green, Mary J. Lindstrom, Laura J. Ball, Gary L. Pattee, and Lorne Zinman. 2010. Kinematics of disease progression in bulbar ALS. *Journal of Communication Disorders* 43: 6–20.

Ziegler, Wolfram. 2002. Psycholinguistic and motor theories of apraxia of speech. *Seminars in Speech and Language* 23: 231–243.

Ziegler, Wolfram. 2003. Speech motor control is task-specific: Evidence from dysarthria and apraxia of speech. *Aphasiology* 17(1): 3–36.

Ziegler, Wolfram. 2009. Modelling the architecture of phonetic plans: Evidence from apraxia of speech. *Language and Cognitive Processes* 24: 631–661.

Ziegler, Wolfram and Detlev von Cramon. 1986. Spastic dysarthria after acquired brain injury: An acoustic study. *British Journal of Disorders of Communication* 21: 173–187.

Ziegler, Wolfram and Karl Wessel. 1996. Speech timing in ataxic disorders: Sentence production and rapid repetitive articulation. *Neurology* 47: 208–214.

Ziegler, Wolfram, Anja Staiger, and Ingrid Aichert. 2010. Apraxia of speech: What the deconstruction of phonetic plans tells us about the construction of articulate language. In B. Maassen and P. Van Lieshout (eds.), *Speech Motor Control: New Developments in Basic and Applied Research*, 3–21. Oxford: Oxford University Press.

15 Process-Oriented Diagnosis of Childhood and Adult Apraxia of Speech (CAS and AOS)

BEN MAASSEN AND HAYO TERBAND

15.1 Setting the stage

In order to appreciate the complexity of speech motor control, the reader is invited to visualize professional ice dancing. Assuming this is not your daily practice, the following impressions probably impose themselves. First, the skating is fluent, rapid, and complex. Second, from the perspective of the perceiver/watcher, it is extremely difficult to describe or to remember what the ice-dancing person is doing. Third, from the perspective of the producer, it is hard to understand how the ice dancer is able to remember this sequence of thousands of complex movements; it is like playing the piano without a music score.

Speaking is a skill at least as complex as ice dancing, which we practice as a daily routine. If listening to speech in a language not known to the listener (e.g., Japanese), the first striking feature is the fluency, speed, and complexity. Second, the listener will not be able to remember or repeat the utterances. Third, the listener has a hard time understanding how the foreign-language speaker is able to produce these rapid sound sequences in such a fluent manner. We ourselves are always impressed hearing 4-year-olds speaking Japanese fluently.

What can we learn from these performances about the human motor system? From the fluency of the movements we can derive that skating and speech production are under the influence of open-loop, rather than closed-loop, control. The ice dancer produces the series of axel jumps and haircutter spins in an open-loop fashion, which is obvious because any correction that needs ice contact during the axel jump is impossible. Furthermore, a feedback-controlled servo-system that starts calculating the next movement on the basis of the outcome of the previous

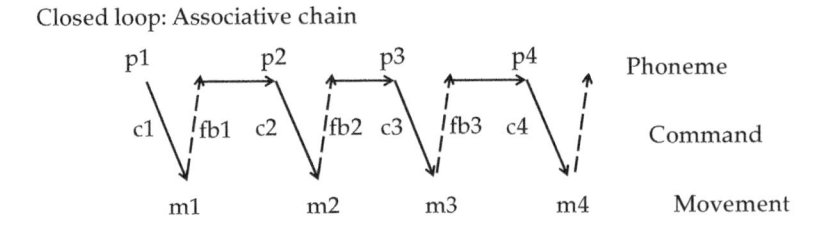

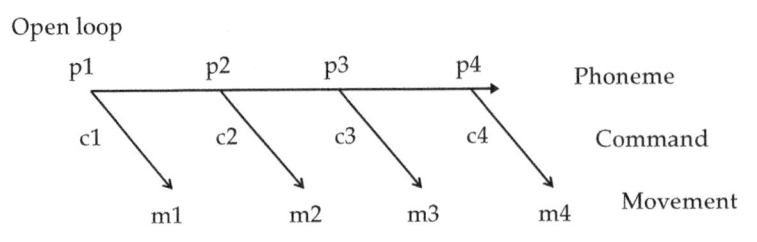

Figure 15.1 Diagrams of the associative chain model (top) and open-loop "comb model" (bottom). For explanation see text.

movement could never produce the rapid sequences required. Figure 15.1 (top) shows a closed-loop effector model producing the series of phonemes p1 to p4, for example, the word /stɪk/ ("stick"). Phoneme p1 (/s/) evokes command c1 resulting in movement m1. Somatosensory and auditory feedback fb1 informs the motor system about the current incomplete alveolar constriction of the tongue tip during /s/, then starts calculating the command to produce the next phoneme /t/, resulting in the command (c2) for a very small closing gesture (m2). Be aware that c2 and m2 would be drastically different if p1 was not /s/ but /ə/ (utterance: "a tick"). The alveolar position of /t/ is fed back to the motor system (fb3), compared to the next target /ɪ/ (p3) to calculate the specific tongue-lowering gesture. In closed-loop models commands are calculated on-line, based on the difference between current position of the articulators (as signaled by fb_n) and the target state for the next phoneme p_{n+1}. Considering that the lower limit of simple reaction latencies, such as pressing a button as soon as a light switches on, is approximately 100 ms, it is clear that a closed-loop model would be way too slow for speaking (up to 30 phonemes per second) or playing the piano. In contrast, in the open-loop model plotted in Figure 15.1 (bottom), the commands c1 to c4 for the production of phonemes p1 to p4 are calculated in advance, such that the motor program runs off more are less automatically. Exactly how far speakers plan ahead – a syllable, a word, a phonological phrase? – is still a matter of debate, but a prerequisite for being able to plan ahead is practice, much practice, as every pianist knows and most speakers have forgotten.

Complex performances indicate that there must be a hierarchy in representation. All primates produce some natural communicative oral gestures, but during evolution only homo sapiens was able to develop not only more complex and more diverse oral gestures, but also a hierarchical structure to control these: language. It is because of language that speech has become the most complex motor performance humans perform; in parallel, further refinement of the basic oral gestures has taken place during the evolutionary process.

All models of speech production – or any motor performance for that matter – adopt a hierarchy of control. One could (and should) dispute about which model gives the best account of all speech phenomena (Levelt 1989; van der Merwe 1997; Guenther, Hampson, and Johnson 1998; Goldstein and Fowler 2003), but all speech production models agree on a preparatory psycholinguistic process of producing a sequence of one or more word forms (a phrase) stored in some short-term memory (buffer), followed by a process that calculates (process of encoding; transcoding; planning; programming) the speech movements that must be made in order to articulate the sequence (phrase). Also, all models agree that the calculations themselves from stored word forms to actual movements are hierarchically structured.

The decision of the ice dancer to perform an axel jump, rather than a haircutter spin, is like lexical selection of a word in speaking. From that decision onward, the exact execution of the jump is determined by a series of processing steps, such as: determining the current position on the ice track, the current body posture and speed, and the target position after the jump. From these calculations at the outset, the body movements can be calculated to position the body in the optimal posture to make the jump, and the jumping movement itself. The execution of these movements is the final step; the precise parameter settings of the movements (precise force and speed) must then be determined. These could not be specified in advance, because they depend on factors such as the local (square cm) ice conditions, and the sharpness of the blade at the position where it makes contact to the ice. Setting these parameters is generally referred to as being part of execution.

Thus, leaving out all the details of dispute, speech production models agree on the following stages: (1) selecting lexical elements (word forms), and putting these into a memory buffer, somehow organized in phrases; (2) transforming the phrases into specifications for articulatory movements; (3) executing those movements, thereby taking current circumstances into account.

15.2 Behavioral characteristics of verbal apraxia

Let us now turn to Apraxia of Speech (AOS) and Childhood Apraxia of Speech (CAS). All definitions specify stage (2) as the underlying deficit. Thus, Darley, Aronson, and Brown (1975) gave the following definition of AOS, as compared to dysarthria: "an articulatory disorder resulting from impairment, as the result of *brain damage*, of the capacity to *program* the *positioning* of speech musculature and the *sequencing* of muscle movements for the *volitional* production of phonemes. The speech musculature does not show significant weakness, slowness, or incoordination when used for reflex and automatic acts" (639). Definitions of CAS also focus on the transformation process from linguistic code to specifications of articulatory movements. Thus, Hayden (1994) defined CAS as "a disorder of the ability to translate phonemic and linguistic codes *to articulatory movements*"; Maassen, Nijland, and van der Meulen (2001) and McNeil and Kent (1990) as: "an impairment in the mechanism for *motor planning* and/or *motor programming* of speech production"; and Smith and colleagues (1994) as: "a *neurologically based* disorder in the ability to program movements for speech volitionally."

Finally, the comprehensive technical report developed by the American Speech-Language-Hearing Association Ad Hoc Committee on Childhood Apraxia of Speech gives the following definition:

> *Childhood apraxia of speech (CAS)* is a neurological childhood (pediatric) speech sound disorder in which the precision and consistency of movements underlying speech are impaired in the absence of neuromuscular deficits (e.g., abnormal reflexes, abnormal tone). CAS may occur as a result of known neurological impairment, in association with complex neurobehavioral disorders of known or unknown origin, or as an idiopathic neurogenic speech sound disorder. The core impairment in *planning and/or programming spatiotemporal parameters of movement sequences* [our italics] results in errors in speech sound production and prosody.
> (ASHA 2007)

As far as the underlying speech production process is concerned, this definition also indicates the planning of speech movements.

15.3 Clinical definitions and diagnosis

Although definitions of AOS and CAS refer to the underlying deficit, clinical differential diagnostic and clinical classification procedures are not based on these definitions, but rather on speech and language symptoms assessed at the behavioral level. Thus, in clinical diagnosis behavioral symptoms such as the "errors in speech sound production and prosody" and "the precision and consistency of movements underlying speech" are assessed. Furthermore, information regarding etiological factors "known neurological impairment [or] complex neurobehavioral disorders of known or unknown origin" is collected based on the personal history and a physical examination.

Remarkably, however, no direct assessments are conducted to assess "the core impairment in planning and/or programming spatiotemporal parameters of movement sequences," which can be considered the diagnostic marker of CAS at the processing level. All other characteristics, the speech symptoms that are the result of the core deficit and the neurological mechanisms or genetic endowment that underlie it, can be considered secondary to defining CAS. The clinical importance is that all other characteristics might not be unique for CAS: speech symptoms might be similar across different processing deficits (slow speech rate is such a general, non-specific characteristic), and underlying neurological or genetic deficits might also cause other processing impairments (e.g., oral or limb apraxia) and other behavioral symptoms than just CAS (e.g., word-sequencing difficulties).

We can conclude that apparently clinical practice is not very successful in transforming major parts of the definition of CAS into diagnostic procedures, especially those parts that refer to underlying speech production mechanisms. What then, are the clinical tools available, and how successful have they been so far? The first series of studies have been conducted to make an inventory of speech symptoms of CAS, following several approaches.

15.3.1 Diagnostic characteristics based on AOS in adults

The first studies of AOS started from the contrast with dysarthria, and the first studies of CAS approached the speech disorder from the perspective of AOS. The following line of reasoning was followed. Since the definition of AOS by Darley et al. (1975) refers to the underlying programming deficit, as compared to motor execution deficit in dysarthria, speech characteristics have been described that have a certain face-validity of reflecting these deficits. Thus, place-of-articulation errors were hypothesized to reflect "an impairment ... of the capacity to program the *positioning* of speech musculature" and anticipations, perseverations, and metathetic errors were hypothesized to reflect "the *sequencing* of muscle movements." In addition, inconsistency in apraxic speech might be related to the specific difficulty with "the *volitional* production of phonemes."

Despite the face-validity these symptoms may have, no methods are available to directly validate the mechanisms causing a particular symptom. Therefore, studies have been conducted in which speech symptoms of clinically defined patients with "pure" AOS were studied. However, this unavoidably introduced a circularity since the study participants are diagnosed in part based on their speech motor behavior while the study sets out to investigate that same speech motor behavior.

15.3.2 Diagnostic characteristics used by clinicians

Two extensive studies aiming to define the diagnostic characteristics of CAS have been conducted based on clinical judgments by speech-language pathologists. In the first study 30 diagnostic features of developmental apraxia of speech were identified from the literature, and it was investigated to what extent these characteristics applied to a total number of 50 children with pediatric speech sound disorder (McCabe, Rosenthal, and McLeod 1998). The major finding was that many characteristics regarded as diagnostic for developmental dyspraxia occur in the general speech-impaired population. The authors suggest as possible interpretation the syndromatic nature of CAS, which implies no specific pathognomonic features of CAS, and a large overlap with other childhood speech disorders.

The second study presented the criteria to diagnose CAS used by 75 speech-language pathologists (Forrest 2003). Although 50 different characteristics were identified, 6 of these characteristics accounted for more than half the responses.

These 6 characteristics (such as increasing difficulty with increased utterance length) also are found in other speech-sound disorders. The authors concluded that the diagnostic criteria of CAS are ambiguous, suggesting that no single deficit is used among clinicians.

15.3.3 Diagnostic markers

Shriberg and colleagues (Shriberg 2003; Shriberg et al. 2003a, 2003b) proposed a research program on the etiological origins of child speech-sound disorders of unknown origin, and thereby adopted a classificatory framework that posits six putative subtypes. The clinical aim was to find diagnostic markers that clinicians and clinical researchers can use for classification. Two such diagnostic markers could be identified that each encompass several diagnostic features. The first is the coefficient of variation ratio, which quantifies temporal regularity in speech, and corresponds with the isochrony, syllable segregation, scanning speech, and staccato-like rhythmic quality. The 15 children with suspected CAS had higher coefficient of variation ratios than 30 children with moderate to severe speech delay, and 30 children with normal speech acquisition (Shriberg et al. 2003b). The second diagnostic marker was the lexical stress ratio, that quantifies the acoustic correlates of stress in two-syllabic words (Shriberg et al. 2003a). It turned out that 5 out of 11 children with suspected CAS had an extreme value on lexical stress ratio in a distribution composed of 35 children in total. It is noteworthy that the diagnostic markers for CAS identified are both related to suprasegmental rather than phonemic aspects of speech.

15.3.4 Consensus definition

Three segmental and suprasegmental features that are consistent with a deficit in the planning and programming of movements for speech have gained some consensus among investigators in apraxia of speech in children: (1) inconsistent errors on consonants and vowels in repeated productions of syllables or words; (2) lengthened and disrupted coarticulatory transitions between sounds and syllables; and (3) inappropriate prosody, especially in the realization of lexical or phrasal stress. Also with respect to diagnostic markers, we can ask the question about the underlying mechanism.

The basic question to diagnose CAS therefore is *not*: what are the speech (and possibly other) symptoms that belong to the diagnostic category CAS?, *but*: how can we demonstrate that the child with speech sound disorder (SSD) has a deficit at the level of speech motor planning and programming? If we had the diagnostic tool to make this assessment, the gold standard for CAS would be available, against which all other studies on CAS could be validated. For a particular child, if defective speech motor planning and programming could be demonstrated, the diagnosis speech apraxia is valid. If in addition, for this child, *all* speech phenomena can be explained on the basis of a planning/programming deficit, the diagnosis pure CAS would be valid. In this chapter we advocate this approach as the only way to break through the circularity of having to diagnose a pure case of CAS in order to study the characteristics of CAS.

15.4 Challenges in defining the underlying deficit

Speech symptoms are ambiguous with respect to the underlying deficit: a particular symptom can be caused by different deficits. In a recent overview, Kent (2004) questioned the modularity of motor control processes and argued that "speech, or any motor behavior, is best viewed as a cognitive–motor accomplishment" (3). Speech motor processes cannot be clearly distinguished from cognitive processes because of the interdependent interaction with higher-order psycholinguistic processes. In the case of impaired speech systems, this applies even more due to adaptive and compensatory mechanisms. For instance, difficulties in phonological encoding may influence speech motor control processes. This is not only due to degraded input (e.g., underspecified or noisy) causing an altered output, but also because the speech motor process itself is likely to adapt to the deviant circumstances and/or compensate for the impediments. For example, slow speech rate is a general, non-specific feature of speech motor control disorders, irrespective of the underlying deficit and whether or not it occurs as primary symptom or as compensatory response (Duffy 1995, 2010; Weismer and Kim 2010).

In the course of speech acquisition/development a particular deficit can have effects on other processing levels. This developmental interaction between the different cognitive levels of processing constitutes a fundamental challenge in isolating the underlying deficit of developmental disorders. Both in normal as in disordered development, cognitive functional networks are the outcome of development rather than the starting point and the progression to the adult system is a gradual and continuous process comprising interactions between emerging functional networks (Karmiloff-Smith 2006; Karmiloff-Smith, Scerif, and Ansari 2003; Karmiloff-Smith and Thomas 2003). Phonological representations are dynamic, multilayered structures that besides lexical and auditory information, also contain sensorimotor and somatosensory information (Edwards et al.1999; Maassen, Nijland, and Terband 2010; Perrier 2005). As a result, a specific underlying impairment on one cognitive level also affects the development on adjacent levels, meaning that a particular deficit can disrupt the processing at other levels, and thereby cause indirect symptoms. For example, we know that a specific speech-motor impairment can interrupt the development of the lexicon, the phonological system, and auditory processing (Crary, Landess, and Towne 1984; Marion, Sussman, and Marquardt 1993). Due to this developmental interaction there is a strong association between different developmental speech disorders at the behavioral level. "Pure" cases are very rare and the differences between developmental speech disorders are a matter of degree of involvement rather than an issue of diagnostic categories (Terband and Maassen 2010).

15.5 Neuropsychological approach: Test batteries

Speaking is a complicated process comprising a series of sequential and parallel subprocesses. Since the seminal publication by Levelt (1989), much research has been conducted focusing on the sequential psycholinguistic processing steps in speech production. Speaking starts with conceptualizing a preverbal message, either from memory or from perception, like in picture naming. The next stage is formulating a sentence, a process driven by the two steps of lexicalization: selecting a *lemma*, containing meaning and grammatical information, and the corresponding *lexeme* or *word-form*, which forms the input for the next stage of phonological encoding. Phonological encoding entails specifying the sequence of speech sounds together with their *syllabic* and *prosodic* structure. Syllables are the basic units of articulo-motor planning and programming; execution is the final process of actually performing the articulatory movements resulting in an acoustic speech signal.

The speaker continuously monitors his/her own speech, not only at the level of lexical selection and formulation, but also at the lower levels of the *phonetic plan* and during *motor programming*, in addition to external self-monitoring after the utterance has been produced. It has been theorized that many dysfluencies in speech in fact are *covert repairs*, resulting from interventions by the internal self-monitoring system that detects and corrects an error before it is overtly produced (Postma, Kolk, and Povel 1990). The internal self-monitoring at the level of motor programming allows the speaker to fine-tune articulatory movements upon, for instance, an external distortion like speaking while smoking a pipe (in phonetics known as "pipe-speech"; Kent 1983).

This processing model gives a conceptual basis to analyze speech disorders and pinpoint the underlying deficit, and thereby forms the basis for a process-oriented diagnostic classification. Much research has been conducted to validate the model against natural speech production data, see for instance Levelt, Roelofs, and Meyer (1999). However, studies that systematically apply this or a similar model to AOS (Ziegler 2005) or CAS (Maassen et al. 2010; Nijland 2009; Nijland et al. 2003b; Nijland, Maassen, and van der Meulen 2003a) are scarce. Above, we saw that there is general consensus that CAS is a disorder of transforming an abstract phonological code into movements of the articulators. In Levelt's extended model, the underlying deficit can thus be localized at the level of phonetic planning, and/or motor programming, and/or motor execution, including internal and external self-monitoring systems. The question then becomes: how can we clinically assess the contribution of separate processing stages to the symptom profile? One approach to tackle this question is the construction of a test battery comprising a set of speech tasks that each require different steps in the production process. By comparing speech performances obtained from such a battery, the clinician can determine which processing steps function normally and which are disrupted.

Figure 15.2 gives a schematic diagram of such a test battery, consisting of four tasks: picture naming, word and non-word imitation, and maximum repetition

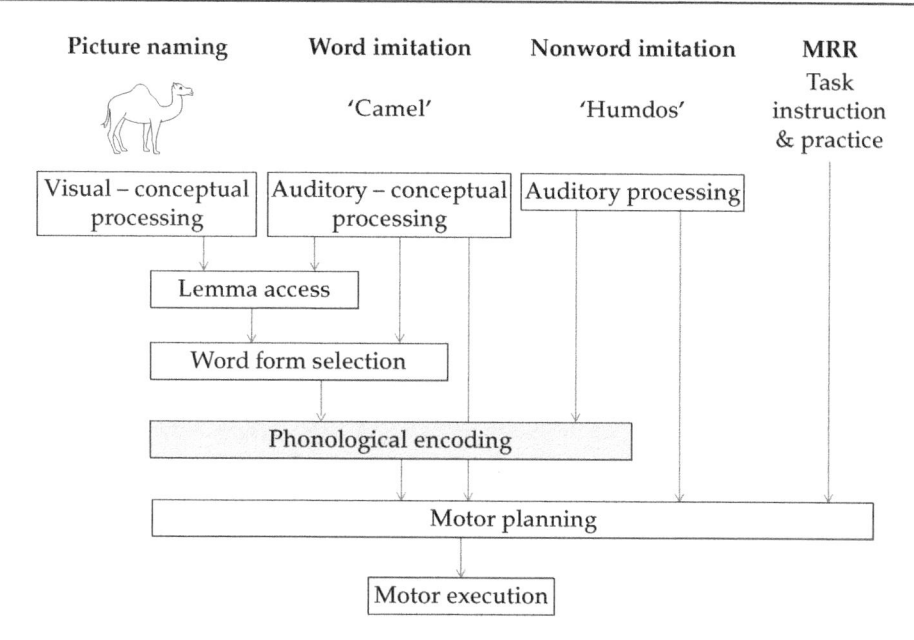

Figure 15.2 Decomposition of speech tasks, indicating which processes are involved in which tasks. For explanation see text.

rate (MRR). In picture naming, the whole chain of processes is involved, from preverbal visual-conceptual processing, to lemma access, word-form selection, phonological encoding, motor planning, and articulation (motor execution). In the word-imitation task, the production process of word-form selection is more strongly accessed than in the picture-naming task: not only from the lemma, if the speaker has this lemma stored in her lexicon and recognized meaning of the presented word, but also directly from the auditory channel. In contrast, imitation of non-words cannot make use of the lexicon for the obvious reason that the lexicon by definition does not contain non-words, and thus directly addresses the phonological encoding system, provided the speaker is able to analyze the phonological structure of the non-word, or directly addresses the motor planning system. In the latter case, non-word imitation is similar to imitation of non-speech sounds. Finally, in the MRR task, also known as diadochokinesis, the speaker is requested to produce monosyllabic sequences like /pʌpʌpʌ, tʌtʌtʌ, kʌkʌkʌ/ and multisyllabic sequences like /pʌtʌkʌ/ as fast as possible. MRR tasks are purely motor tasks, and do not require any knowledge of words, syllables, or phonemes.

The most detailed and comprehensive test battery for speech assessment in children to our knowledge is the Madison Speech Assessment Protocol (MSAP; Shriberg et al. 2010). The MSAP comprises 25 tests and tasks each requiring a different aspect of speech production. Thus, in addition to the Goldman-Fristoe Test of Articulation, the Woodcock-Johnson III Tests of Achievement, and the Kaufman Brief Intelligence Test (2nd edn.), tasks are administered to assess word and non-word production (Challenging Word Task, Non-word Repetition Task), vowel production (Vowel tasks), production of particular consonants (Rhotic and Sibilants Task), syllable production (Syllable Repetition Task), stress patterns (Lexical Stress Task, Emphatic Stress Task), and utterances (Speech Phrases Task, Conversational Speech Sample). This test battery yields a full description of all aspects of speech production, scaled on the dimensions labeled Competence, Precision, and Stability, which is extremely useful for clinical purposes as description of determinants of communicative ability and intelligibility of speech. In that sense, these descriptive dimensions can be considered orthogonal to the process-oriented orientation adopted in this chapter. The descriptive and process-oriented approaches are complementary: combining quantitative descriptions of speech performance as in the MSAP with analyses of subprocesses by systematically comparing processes, yields an assessment procedure that quantifies relative strength of processes.

Following the same paradigm, the Computer Articulation Instrument (CAI) has been developed and is currently normalized for Dutch. The CAI consists of a battery of speech production tasks based on a series of studies in children with developmental and acquired speech sound disorders (Thoonen 1998; Nijland 2003). Applying a naming task, word and non-word repetition, and diadochokinetic tasks, obtained measures allow for differential diagnosis of phonological disorder, dysarthria, and childhood apraxia of speech. Further steps are the addition of objective (acoustic) measurements of speech production, the addition of different speaking conditions, and the implementation of a process analysis of the assessment battery outcomes.

15.6 Tests with experimental manipulations that affect processes separately

In the past decades, the symptomatology of childhood apraxia of speech has been charted to a large extent, and systematically knowledge has been gathered about the underlying processes, covering a variety of aspects of speech production and perception, and the relation between these two. New techniques and research paradigms played an important role. In this paragraph, we will shortly review a number of studies from our own research line that contributed in this respect.

First, Thoonen (1998) focused on the differential diagnosis between children with CAS and children with spastic dysarthria and provided an objective and quantitative description of speech characteristics in children with CAS. Based on a feature analysis of phonological errors in consonants, Thoonen and colleagues came to the conclusion that the underlying cognitive deficit is a processing rather than a representational deficit that emerges during the stage of phonological encoding (Thoonen et al. 1994). Nijland (2003) took this idea further and focused on the differences between CAS and Phonological Disorder (PD). By means of fine-grained acoustic measurements, she investigated speech motor characteristics in different phonological contexts (same sequences of speech sounds, but with different syllable boundaries) and different articulatory circumstances (articulatory compensation for a bite-block). The results confirmed and further specified the findings of Thoonen, indicating that the underlying deficit in CAS resides in the difficulty to transform an abstract phonological code into motor speech commands.

Subsequently, this line was continued and Terband (2011) focused on sensorimotor information processing in CAS. In this we used a combination of acoustic and kinematic measurements and neurocomputational modeling. The results provide important insight into the mechanisms that are involved in developmental speech-sound disorders and into the relation between primary deficits, derived, or consequential deficits, and how these express themselves in symptomatology. Auditory perception impairments have been found in children with CAS (e.g., Groenen et al. 1996; Maassen, Groenen, and Crul 2003; Marion et al. 1993; Nijland 2009), and more in general, many studies have shown that in children with developmental speech disorders, there is a close relation between perceptual acuity and production symptoms (e.g., Edwards et al. 1999; Edwards, Fox, and Rogers 2002; Groenen et al. 1996; Maassen et al. 2003; Marion et al. 1993; Nijland 2009; Raaymakers and Crul 1988). Our modeling studies provide valuable insight into the exact nature of this relation. A series of computer simulations showed that a motor programming deficit predominantly leads to deterioration on the phonological level (phonemic mappings) if auditory self-monitoring was intact, and on the systemic level (systemic mapping) if auditory self-monitoring was impaired. These findings indicate a close relation between quality of auditory self-monitoring and the involvement of phonological vs. motor processes in children with developmental speech disorders. Furthermore, these results exemplify *how* an impairment that apparently resides on the phonological level (stored representations) could actually have a motoric origin (Terband 2011; Terband et al. 2014), which was previously found in behavioral studies (Crary et al. 1984; Edwards et al. 1999; Marion et al. 1993).

Furthermore, in the past years some insight was gathered into possible adaptive or compensatory strategies. First, fine-grained analyses of the kinematics and dynamics of articulatory movements suggested that both SSD and subtype CAS used the same adaptive strategy where possible, that is, increase movement amplitude as a strategy to increase articulatory stability (Terband et al. 2011). Larger movement amplitudes involve a stronger neural signal, which is less susceptible to interference of noise and makes it easier to maintain a stable coordination between efferent and afferent signals in rhythmic movements (e.g., Beek, Peper, and Daffertshofer 2002; Kelso et al. 1998; Van Lieshout 2004; Williamson 1998). Second, a modeling study indicated that slowing down articulation might be used as an adaptive strategy (Terband and Maassen 2010; Terband et al. 2009). Slow speech rate is a recurrent characteristic in CAS (ASHA 2007; Hall, Jordan, and Robin 2007; Maassen et al. 2010; Ozanne 2005), and in motor speech disorders in general (Duffy 1995, 2010; Weismer and Kim 2010). A first series of computer simulations indicated that four of the key phonetic characteristics of CAS (increased coarticulation, speech-sound distortion, searching articulatory behavior, and increased token-to-token variability) might result from an overreliance on sensory feedback control due to impaired feedforward control (Terband et al. 2009). In theory, such disadvantageous consequences of overreliance on feedback could be neutralized by giving the speaker ample opportunity to make use of sensory feedback, such as by slowing down articulation. A second series of simulations indicated that slowing down articulation has a facilitating effect on the learning of motor commands in circumstances of CAS/overreliance on feedback control (Terband and Maassen 2010).

15.7 Implications for management (diagnostic procedure)

Therapeutic intervention methods for SSD are aimed at different parts of the speech production process. Current diagnostic instruments are output-oriented tests of speech performance, yielding a behavioral description of speech symptoms, and therefore do not match the requirements for intervention. To get concrete indications for targeted treatment requires the step from behavioral diagnostics and classification to process-oriented diagnostics (Terband and Maassen 2012). The analysis of the processes and processing deficits that underlie speech disorders can be achieved through the implementation of experimental methodology in clinical instruments. In other words, through objective measurements of speech in systematically varied speech tasks under systematically varied speaking conditions.

The current assessment protocols Computer-Articulation Instrument (CAI; Maassen et al., in press) and the MSAP (Shriberg et al. 2010) are already a large step in this direction. They already provide the necessary variety of speech tasks (picture naming, word and non-word repetition, diadochokinesis). The analysis of the CAI and MSAP are based on phonetic transcription, perceptual judgment, and limited acoustic analysis, which is an important addition to previous articulation tests since it objectifies the analysis and creates the possibility to take context into account. Furthermore, the outcome of these assessment batteries is a *speech performance profile*, describing profiles of symptoms to characterize disorders rather than focusing on single diagnostic markers. From this, it is only one step further to a *speech processing profile* describing the processing deficits that underlie the different skills and symptoms.

First, the analysis of speech output can be objectified further by using acoustical analysis, through which the speech signal can be analyzed without the intervention of a listener. Acoustic measurements enable the analysis and quantification of speech characteristics that cannot be perceived by ear, such as vowel quality, coarticulation, and variability. Second, the different parameters should be analyzed in different contexts. More specifically, we mean the systematic and controlled variation of speaking conditions and instructions, such as a rate instruction (increase or decrease articulation rate), practice (repeated utterances to determine the learning effect), auditory feedback masking (by applying noise through headphones), and articulatory perturbation (e.g., by fixating a pencil between lower and upper jaw). Based on the results of a particular test, a subsequent test or condition is then administered, finally leading to the identification of the impaired underlying process. For example, a high variability in vowel quality (excluding dysarthria) points at a problem in motor programming. Subsequently, the question rises whether the stored motor programs are deviant themselves, or that the problem stems from the parameterization and execution. This makes a fundamental difference for treatment. A method to investigate this is to present masking noise through headphones during speech and compare the acoustical realization of speech sounds in the conditions with and without auditory self-monitoring. If there is a difference in the acoustical realization of speech sounds between the conditions with and without auditory self-monitoring, the problem is in the stored motor programs. In the case where there is no difference, the problem is in the parameterization and execution of the motor programs.

However, more important than a ready-to-go instrument is the implementation in clinical practice; a method has no merit if people cannot work with it. This particularly applies in the case of *speech processing profiles*. The step from a behavioral to a process-oriented diagnostics and treatment planning requires a different way of thinking. Speech pathologists are well educated, but are used to think and work according to a model of diagnostic classification, oriented on speech output skills and symptoms, and plan treatment according to the corresponding protocol. The introduction of a process-oriented approach starts with the education and training of professionals, providing them with the theoretical background and the clinical skills to utilize and interpret an instrument based on *speech processing profiles*.

15.8 Implications for management (treatment)

What is particularly striking is that the possibilities in the treatment of speech-sound disorders appear to be ahead of diagnostics. A wide variety of different treatment techniques has been developed for the children that experience speech difficulties to help them through the acquisition process, each focusing at different parts of the speech production chain. The bottleneck lies in the assessment and treatment planning: clear criteria to determine which treatment is the most suitable are lacking. The current diagnostic instruments consist of output-oriented tests of speech performance that assess knowledge and skills (e.g., sentence formulation, lexicon, phonological awareness, phoneme inventory, percentage consonants correct). This yields a behavioral description of symptoms that suffices to give directions for treatment of relatively isolated speech difficulties that are not symptomatic for more complex underlying deficits, but is insufficient as a basis for diagnostic classification, treatment program and possibly referral to special education. Because a behavioral description gives no direct information with respect to the underlying impairment, it does not match the requirements for intervention. To get more specific indications for targeted treatment requires a step from behavioral diagnostics and classification to process-oriented diagnostics (Terband and Maassen 2012). A process-oriented approach holds important advantages for the diagnosis and treatment of pediatric speech disorders. The switch from perceptually based classification related to behavioral symptoms to a more dynamic process analysis allows for a treatment planning tailored to the specific needs of the individual. Process-analysis offers direct leads for treatment aimed at the specific underlying impairment and offers a better starting point to evaluate and adjust the therapeutic approach in the course of the speech disorder. A more purposeful treatment would render therapy more effective and efficient, yielding better outcome and increased quality of life. Furthermore, a more effective and efficient treatment may reduce the necessary length of therapy, thus leading to a reduction of health care costs.

15.9 Conclusion

Since the critical review of Guyette and Diedrich (1981), the debate about the reality of CAS as a diagnostic entity has provided a constant threat to research into developmental speech disorders. To be able to investigate the mechanisms underlying CAS, "pure" cases are necessary that are selected based on unambiguous criteria. Unambiguous selection criteria, however, are only available as a result of research, rendering a chicken-and-egg situation. This practical-diagnostic circularity is a result of the behavioral, symptom-oriented approach that is employed. McNeil, Pratt, and Fosset (2004) noted a similar situation with respect to AOS. There are clear ideas and theories about what apraxia is and what the underlying deficits are, but the progress of research is being held back by "the lack of a comprehensive and clear definition that leads to an agreed-upon set of criteria for subject selection" (McNeil et al. 2004: 389–390). Although the symptomatology is unclear, we can conclude that from the perspective of the underlying cognitive and neurological processes, it is possible to describe a specific speech-motor core deficit. Additionally, cases have been reported of children with specific speech-motor impairments (see, e.g., ASHA 2007 for an overview).

The speech production models have been around for quite some time. Recent research has further refined these models by adding developmental aspects and computational implementations. In addition, tools (acoustic, kinematic, brain imaging) have become available that enable a close monitoring of the speech production process. Together, this allows for fine-tuning diagnosis by (more) directly demonstrating the underlying deficit. In addition, current technological aids provide better opportunities to make these procedures clinically available.

REFERENCES

ASHA. 2007. American Speech-Language-Hearing Association Ad Hoc Committee on Childhood Apraxia of Speech, position statement. http://www.asha.org/policy/PS2007-00277/, accessed December 6, 2014.

Beek, Peter J., C.E. Peper, and Andreas Daffertshofer. 2002. Modeling rhythmic interlimb coordination: Beyond the Haken-Kelso-Bunz model. *Brain and Cognition* 48(1): 149–165.

Crary, Michael A., Susan Landess, and Roger Towne. 1984. Phonological error patterns in developmental verbal dyspraxia. *Journal of Clinical Neuropsychology* 6(2): 157–170.

Darley, Frederic L., Arnold E. Aronson, and Joe R. Brown. 1975. Apraxia of speech: Impairment of motor speech programming. In F.L. Darley, A.E. Aronson, and J.R. Brown (eds.), *Motor Speech Disorders*, 250–287. Philadelphia, PA: W.B. Saunders.

Duffy, Joseph R. 1995. *Motor Speech Disorders: Substrates, Differential Diagnosis and Management*. St. Louis, MO: Mosby.

Duffy, Joseph R. 2010. Distinguishing among motor speech disorders is important: The role of speech pathology in neurologic diagnosis. In B. Maassen and P. Van Lieshout (eds.), *Speech Motor Control: New Developments in Basic and Applied Research*, 271–282. Oxford: Oxford University Press.

Edwards, Jan, Robert A. Fox, and Catherine L. Rogers. 2002. Final consonant discrimination in children: Effects of phonological disorder, vocabulary size and articulatory accuracy. *Journal of Speech, Language, and Hearing Research* 45(2): 231–242.

Edwards, Jan, Marios Fourakis, Mary E. Beckman, and Robert A. Fox. 1999. Characterizing knowledge deficits in phonological disorders. *Journal of Speech, Language, and Hearing Research* 42(1): 169–186.

Forrest, Karen. 2003. Diagnostic criteria of developmental apraxia of speech used by clinical speech-language pathologists. *American Journal of Speech-Language Pathology* 12(3): 376–380.

Goldstein, Louis and Carol A. Fowler. 2003. Articulatory phonology: A phonology for public language use. In N.O. Schiller and A.S. Meyer (eds.), *Phonetics and Phonology in Language Comprehension and Production: Differences and Similarities*, 6th edn. Berlin: Mouton de Gruyter.

Groenen, Paul, Ben Maassen, Thom Crul, and Geert Thoonen. 1996. The specific relation between perception and production errors for place of articulation in developmental apraxia of speech. *Journal of Speech and Hearing Research* 39(3): 468–482.

Guenther, Frank H., Michelle Hampson, and Dave Johnson. 1998. A theoretical investigation of reference frames for the planning of speech movements. *Psychological Review* 105: 611–633.

Guyette, Thomas and William M. Diedrich. 1981. A critical review of developmental apraxia of speech. In N.J. Lass (ed.), *Speech and Language: Advances in Basic Research and Practice*, vol. 5, 1–49. New York: Academic Press.

Hall, Penelope, Linda Jordan, and Donald Robin (eds.). 2007. *Developmental Apraxia of Speech: Theory and Clinical Practice*, 2nd edn. Austin, TX: Pro-ed.

Hayden, Deborah A. 1994. Differential diagnosis of motor speech dysfunction in children. *Clinics in Communication Disorders* 4: 119–141.

Karmiloff-Smith, Annette. 2006. The tortuous route from genes to behavior: A neuroconstructivist approach. *Cognitive, Affective and Behavioral Neuroscience* 6(1): 9–17.

Karmiloff-Smith, Annette and Michael Thomas. 2003. What can developmental disorders tell us about the neurocomputational constraints that shape development? The case of Williams syndrome. *Developmental Psychopathology* 15(4): 969–990.

Karmiloff-Smith, Annette, Gaia Scerif, and Daniel Ansari. 2003. Double dissociations in developmental disorders? Theoretically misconceived, empirically dubious. *Cortex* 39(1): 161–163.

Kelso, J.A. Scott, Armin Fuchs, R. Lancaster, Tom Holroyd, Douglas Cheyne, and Harold Weinberg. 1998. Dynamic cortical activity in the human brain reveals motor equivalence. *Nature* 392: 814–818.

Kent, Raymond D. 1983. The segmental organization of speech. In P.F. MacNeilage (ed.), *The Production of Speech*, 57–89. New York: Springer-Verlag.

Kent, Raymond D. 2004. Models of speech motor control: Implications from recent developments in neurophysiological and neurobehavioral science. In B. Maassen, R. Kent, H.F.M. Peters, P.H.H.M. Van Lieshout, and W. Hulstijn (eds.), *Speech Motor Control in Normal and Disordered Speech*, 1–28. Oxford: Oxford University Press.

Levelt, Willem J.M. 1989. *Speaking: From Intention to Articulation*. Cambridge, MA: MIT Press.

Levelt, Willem J.M., Ardi Roelofs, and Antje Meyer. 1999. A theory of lexical access in speech production. *Behavioral and Brain Sciences* 22: 1–75.

Maassen, Ben, Paul Groenen, and Thom Crul. 2003. Auditory and phonetic perception of vowels in children with apraxic speech disorders. *Clinical Linguistics and Phonetics* 17(6): 447–467.

Maassen, Ben, Lian Nijland, and Hayo Terband. 2010. Developmental models of Childhood Apraxia of Speech. In B. Maassen and P. Van Lieshout (eds.), *Speech Motor Control: New Developments in Basic and Applied Research*, 243–258. Oxford: Oxford University Press.

Maassen, Ben, Lian Nijland, and Sjoeke van der Meulen. 2001. Coarticulation within and between syllables by children with developmental apraxia of speech. *Clinical Linguistics and Phonetics* 15: 145–150.

Maassen, Ben, Lenke van Haaften, Sanne Diepeveen, Bert de Swart, Sjoeke van der Meulen, and Lian Nijland. In press. *Computer Articulatie-Instrument (CAI)*. Amsterdam: Boom test uitgevers.

Marion, Michelle J., Harvey M. Sussman, and Thomas P. Marquardt. 1993. The perception and production of rhyme in normal and developmentally apraxic children. *Journal of Communication Disorders* 26(3): 129–160.

McCabe, Patricia, Joan B. Rosenthal, and Sharynne McLeod. 1998. Features of developmental dyspraxia in the general speech-impaired population? *Clinical Linguistics and Phonetics* 12: 105–126.

McNeil, Malcolm R. and Raymond D. Kent. 1990. Motoric characteristics of adult apraxic and aphasic speakers. In G.R. Hammond (ed.), *Cerebral Control of Speech and Limb Movements*, 349–386. Amsterdam: North-Holland.

McNeil, Malcolm R., Sheila Pratt, and Tepanta R.D. Fosset. 2004. The differential diagnosis of apraxia of speech. In B. Maassen, R. Kent, H.F.M. Peters, P.H.H.M. Van Lieshout, and W. Hulstijn (eds.), *Speech Motor Control in Normal and Disordered Speech*, 389–414. Oxford: Oxford University Press.

Nijland, Lian. 2003. Developmental apraxia of speech: Deficits in phonetic planning and motor programming. PhD dissertation, University of Nijmegen, The Netherlands.

Nijland, Lian. 2009. Speech perception in children with speech output disorders. *Clinical Linguistics and Phonetics* 23(3): 222–239.

Nijland, Lian, Ben Maassen, and Sjoeke van der Meulen. 2003a. Evidence of motor programming deficits in children diagnosed with DAS. *Journal of Speech, Language and Hearing Research* 46. 437–450.

Nijland, Lian, Ben Maassen, Sjoeke van der Meulen, Fons Gabreëls, Floris W. Kraaimaat, and Rob Schreuder. 2003b. Planning of syllables by children with developmental apraxia of speech. *Clinical Linguistics and Phonetics* 17: 1–24.

Ozanne, Anne. 2005. Childhood apraxia of speech. In B. Dodd (ed.), *Differential Diagnosis and Treatment of Children with Speech Disorder*, 2nd edn. London: Whurr.

Perrier, Pascal. 2005. Control and representations in speech production. *ZAS Papers in Linguistics* 40: 109–132.

Postma, Aalbert, Herman Kolk, and Dirk-Jan Povel. 1990. Speech planning and execution in stutterers. *Journal of Fluency Disorders* 15: 49–59.

Raaymakers, Emile M. and Thom A. Crul. 1988. Perception and production of the final /s-ts/ contrast in Dutch by misarticulating children. *Journal of Speech, Language, and Hearing Research* 53(3): 262–270.

Shriberg, Lawrence D. 2003. Diagnostic markers for child speech-sound disorders: Introductory comments. *Clinical Linguistics and Phonetics* 17: 501–505.

Shriberg, Lawrence D., Thomas F. Campbell, Heather B. Karlsson, Roger L. Brown, Jane L. McSweeny, and Connie J. Nadler. 2003a. A diagnostic marker for childhood apraxia of speech: The lexical stress ratio. *Clinical Linguistics and Phonetics* 17: 549–574.

Shriberg, Lawrence D., Jordan R. Green, Thomas F. Campbell, Jane L. McSweeny, and Alison R. Scheer. 2003b. A diagnostic marker for childhood apraxia of speech: The coefficient of variation ratio. *Clinical Linguistics and Phonetics* 17: 575–595.

Shriberg, Lawrence D., Marios Fourakis, Sheryl D. Hall, et al. 2010. Perceptual and acoustic reliability estimates for the Speech Disorders Classification System (SDCS). *Clinical Linguistics and Phonetics* 24: 825–846.

Smith, Beverly, Thomas Marquardt, Michael Cannito, and Barbara Davis. 1994. Vowel variability in developmental apraxia of speech. In J.A. Till, K.M. Yorkston, and D.R. Beukelman (eds.), *Motor Speech Disorders: Advances in Assessment and Treatment*, 81–89. Baltimore, MD: Paul H. Brookes.

Terband, Hayo. 2011. Speech motor function in relation to phonology: Neurocomputational modeling of disordered development. PhD dissertation, University of Groningen, The Netherlands.

Terband, Hayo and Ben Maassen. 2010. Speech motor development in Childhood Apraxia of Speech (CAS): Generating testable hypotheses by neurocomputational modeling. *Folia Phoniatrica et Logopaedica* 62: 134–142.

Terband, Hayo and Ben Maassen. 2012. Spraakontwikkelingsstoornissen: Van symptoom- naar procesdiagnostiek. *Logopedie en Phoniatrie* 7–8: 229.

Terband, Hayo, Ben Maassen, Frank H. Guenther, and Jonathan Brumberg. 2009. Computational neural modeling of Childhood Apraxia of Speech (CAS). *Journal of Speech, Language, and Hearing Research* 52(6): 1595–1609.

Terband, Hayo, Ben Maassen, Frank H. Guenther, and Jonathan Brumberg. 2014. Auditory-motor interactions in pediatric motor speech disorders: Neurocomputational modeling of disordered development. *Journal of Communication Disorders* 47: 17–33.

Terband, Hayo, Ben Maassen, Pascal H.H.M. Van Lieshout, and Lian Nijland. 2011. Stability and composition of functional synergies for speech movements in children with developmental speech disorders. *Journal of Communication Disorders* 44(1): 59–74.

Thoonen, Geert. 1998. Developmental apraxia of speech in children: Quantitative assessment of speech characteristics. PhD dissertation, University of Nijmegen, The Netherlands.

Thoonen, Geert, Ben Maassen, Fons Gabreels, and Rob Schreuder. 1994. Feature analysis of singleton consonant errors in developmental verbal dyspraxia (DVD). *Journal of Speech and Hearing Research* 37(6): 1424–1440.

van der Merwe, Anita. 1997. A theoretical framework for the characterization of pathological speech sensorimotor control. In M.R. McNeil (ed.), *Clinical Management of Sensorimotor Speech Disorders*, 1–25. New York: Thieme Medical Publishers.

Van Lieshout, Pascal H.H.M. 2004. Dynamical systems theory and its application in speech. In B. Maassen, R. Kent, H.F.M. Peters, P.H.H.M. Van Lieshout, and W. Hulstijn (eds.), *Speech Motor Control in Normal and Disordered Speech*, 51–82. Oxford: Oxford University Press.

Weismer, Gary and Yunjung Kim. 2010. Classification and taxonomy of motor speech disorders: What are the issues? In B. Maassen and P. Van Lieshout (eds.), *Speech Motor Control: New Developments in Basic and Applied Research*, 229–242. Oxford: Oxford University Press.

Williamson, Matthew M. 1998. Neural control of rhythmic arm movements. *Neural Networks* 11: 1379–1394.

Ziegler, Wolfram. 2005. A nonlinear model of word length effects in apraxia of speech. *Cognitive Neuropsychology* 22: 1–21.

FURTHER READING

ASHA. 2007. American Speech-Language-Hearing Association Ad Hoc Committee on Childhood Apraxia of Speech, technical report. http://www.asha.org/policy/TR2007-00278.htm, accessed December 14, 2014. Technical paper giving research background for the position paper on the diagnosis and underlying deficits related to Childhood Apraxia of Speech.

Forrest, Karen. 2003. Diagnostic criteria of developmental apraxia of speech used by clinical speech-language pathologists. *American Journal of Speech-Language Pathology* 12(3): 376–380. Publication giving an overview of speech symptoms and diagnostic criteria of CAS, as they are used and motivated by speech-language pathologists.

Guenther, F.H. and J.S. Perkell. 2004. A neural model of speech production and its application to studies of the role of auditory feedback in speech. In B. Maassen, R. Kent, H.F.M. Peters, P.H.H.M. Van Lieshout, and W. Hulstijn (eds.), *Speech Motor Control in Normal and Disordered Speech*, 29–50. Oxford: Oxford University Press. DIVA (Directions Into Velocities of Articulators) is a neurocomputational model of speech production; altering parameters of the model can induce symptoms of stuttering, AOS, or CAS.

Kent, Raymond D. 2004. Models of speech motor control: Implications from recent developments in neurophysiological and neurobehavioral science. In B. Maassen, R. Kent, H.F.M. Peters, P.H.H.M. Van Lieshout, and W. Hulstijn (eds.), *Speech Motor Control in Normal and Disordered Speech*, 1–28. Oxford: Oxford University Press. A general overview of models of speech motor control, especially the hierarchical organization of control at the linguistic sentence level, the phonological level, and the level of articulation planning and execution.

Maas, E., D.A. Robin, S.N. Austermann Hula, S.E. Freedman, G. Wulf, K.J. Ballard, and R.A. Schmidt. 2008. Principles of Motor Learning in Treatment of Motor Speech Disorders, American Journal of Speech-Language Pathology, 17(3), 277-298. Tutorial providing an understanding of how the motor system learns and how principles of motor learning, derived from studies of nonspeech motor skills, may be incorporated into treatment for motor speech disorders.

Maassen, Ben, Lian Nijland, and Hayo Terband. 2010. Developmental models of Childhood Apraxia of Speech. In B. Maassen and P. Van Lieshout (eds.), *Speech Motor Control: New Developments in Basic and Applied Research*, 243–258.

Oxford: Oxford University Press. Gives background on developmental aspects of speech motor control and speech motor disorders, with focus on CAS.

McNeil, Malcolm R., Sheila Pratt, and Tepanta R.D. Fosset. 2004. The differential diagnosis of apraxia of speech. In B. Maassen, R. Kent, H.F.M. Peters, P.H.H.M. Van Lieshout, and W. Hulstijn (eds.), *Speech Motor Control in Normal and Disordered Speech*, 389–414. Oxford: Oxford University Press. Gives background on aspects of speech motor control and acquired speech motor disorders, and the lack of specificity of clinical characteristics of AOS and other speech sound disorders in adults.

Shriberg, L.D. 2010. A neurodevelopmental framework for research in Childhood Apraxia of Speech. In B. Maassen and P.H.H.M. Van Lieshout (eds.), *Speech Motor Control: New Developments in Basic and Applied Research*, 259–270. Oxford: Oxford University Press. This chapter sketches an outline of a research framework that includes distal (genetic, neurological) and proximal (deficit at the level of phonological or motoric processing) causes of CAS.

Terband, Hayo and Ben Maassen. 2010. Speech motor development in Childhood Apraxia of Speech (CAS): Generating testable hypotheses by neurocomputational modeling. *Folia Phoniatrica et Logopaedica* 62: 134–142. Paper illustrating a modeling approach in which a computational neural model of speech acquisition and production is utilized in order to find the neuromotor deficits that underlie the diversity of phonological and speech-motor symptoms of CAS.

Weismer, Gary and Yunjung Kim. 2010. Classification and taxonomy of motor speech disorders: What are the issues? In B. Maassen and P. Van Lieshout (eds.), *Speech Motor Control: New Developments in Basic and Applied Research*, 229–242. Oxford: Oxford University Press. Weismer and Kim argue strongly for a taxonomy of motor speech disorders, that not only represents the differential diagnostic characteristics, but – more importantly – includes the common symptoms that are present across neurogenic deficits.

Part IV Sequencing and Planning

16 Central Tenets of the Frame/Content Theory of Evolution and Acquisition of Speech Production

PETER F. MACNEILAGE

16.1 Introduction: The intellectual context

Speech is the most important movement control system (action system) to have evolved in humans, and, in affording us language, it has been at center stage in our rise to the pinnacle of life forms. Placing it in an appropriate perspective needs to be one of the main tasks in our attempt to understand our species. It is often featured, along with right-handedness, in conceptions of the evolution of specializations of the left cerebral hemisphere in humans. These conceptions have been, for the most part, totally anthropocentric (see MacNeilage, Rogers, and Vallortigara 2009 for a recent exception). But, as Dobzhansky (1973) correctly noted: "Nothing in biology makes sense except in the light of evolution" (125). The cornerstone of our understanding of evolution is Darwin's (1859) theory of evolution by natural selection. Furthermore, the central tenet of this theory is descent with modification. To make biological sense of speech, in terms of what the evolutionary biologist, Ernst Mayr (1982) has called "ultimate causes," we need to understand how it has evolved its most distinctive properties by descent with modification of pre-speech capabilities.

This paper is a status report on the only systematic attempt to understand how speech, as an action system, evolved by natural selection – the Frame/Content (F/C) theory of evolution and the acquisition of speech production. Key sources include *The Origin of Speech* (MacNeilage 2008) and the following papers: MacNeilage, Studdert-Kennedy, and Lindblom 1984; MacNeilage and Davis 1990a; Davis and MacNeilage 1995; MacNeilage 1998; MacNeilage and Davis 2000, 2001; MacNeilage 2011, 2012, 2013.

Why is there only one theory of the evolution of speech? The answer lies primarily in anthropocentrism. Even now that Darwinian theory has been basically accepted, we still tend to regard ourselves as a breed apart. In the case of speech, as with other human capabilities, we tend want to believe that this apartness arises from de novo evolutionary developments in the cognitive domain, such as a left hemisphere specialization for sequencing, or analyticity, or, more recently, generativity (Corballis 1991). Such developments do not involve the necessary scenario of descent with modification.

In the case of speech, we certainly have some encouragement for anthropocentrism. There is no close parallel to speech in our nearest primate relatives, or anywhere else in the animal kingdom. But two main philosophical traditions relating to the attempt to understand the human mind have contributed to the problem of our understanding of speech. The first and most prestigious tradition is the one that asserts that we simply possess mind in advance of its use. This tradition is exemplified by Plato and Descartes and, with respect to speech/language, by Chomsky (see MacNeilage 2008: chapters 1 and 2). The other tradition is the position of the English associationists, particularly Locke and Hume, who asserted that the mind is built from experience. Neither of these approaches has paid any attention to what we *do*, even though evolution is primarily about what we successfully or unsuccessfully do, leading Huxley (1863/2005) to conclude that "the great end of life is not knowledge but action." A consequence of these philosophical traditions, and of the choice of the sensory/perceptual discipline of psychophysics as basis for early psychology is that, as Rosenbaum (2005) puts it, motor control is the "Cinderella of Psychology" (308). Most interest in speech within psychology has been devoted to speech perception. In the field of linguistics, since Saussure (1915/1959) made the distinction between linguistic form and substance, phonetics, the study of substance, has taken on Cinderella status by being only of interest insofar as it throws light on the underlying abstract form, an attitude that lies at the center of modern Chomskyan generative linguistics (see MacNeilage 2008: chapters 1, 2, 11, and 12). Thus the topic of speech production can be regarded as lying at the point of intersection of several lacunae, making clear why this volume is the first handbook of speech production ever published.

16.2 The evolution of syllabic "frames"

In the light of these traditions, coupled with the absence of a specific precedent, how can we best come to understand the evolution of speech production? In the present case, the impetus came from a landmark 1951 paper by Karl Lashley called "The Problem of Serial Order in Behavior." The problem is how any sequence of events is ordered in the time domain. He presented a critique of the prevailing behavioristic conception of serial ordering in which each response was considered to be the stimulus for the next. His critique centered on serial ordering errors of speech in which speech segments (consonants and vowels) were misplaced in an otherwise correct utterance. He noted that spoonerisms such as saying "my queer old dean" for "my dear old queen" showed that the serial ordering of speech was determined by something other than the actual units themselves.

Lashley's observation gave rise to a class of "competitive queuing" models of output (see Bohland, Bullock, and Guenther 2010 for a brief review) in which the level of temporary activation of representations of the units determines their queuing priorities, and therefore the serial ordering of their output. But what lies behind the achievement of the correct sequence of activation of these units? Part of the answer is a syllable structure constraint, revealed by the fact that consonants and vowels, even when incorrectly placed, go into consonantal and vocalic positions in syllable structure respectively. Examples involving spoonerisms are "dancy fress" for "fancy dress," "odd hack" for "ad hoc," and "dad bet" for "bad debt." Three other main error types, namely addition errors, shift errors, and substitution errors, also obey this constraint (see Shattuck-Hufnagel 1979 for an error classification). The nature of the ordering mechanism is captured by the "frame/content" metaphor (Levelt 1992) according to which segmental "content" elements are inserted into syllable structure "frames."

Although Lashley himself did not systematically consider the syllable structure constraint on speech errors, this constraint is of fundamental significance to our understanding of the serial ordering of modern speech, and to the evolution of speech. To see where this significance lies, we must look to another Lashley insight. He hypothesized that timing mechanisms, such as rhythm generators, may play an important role in serially ordered behaviors because of their capacity to integrate separate strands of central neural activity. In the domain of animal action, rhythm can be defined as "movement or fluctuation marked by the regular recurrence or natural flow of related elements" (Merrian-Webster 2000).

The syllable is the core element of speech rhythmicity. Kohler's (2009) précis of 70 years of his research on speech rhythm describes the parameters that create rhythmicity of speech: "recurring patterns of fundamental frequency, syllable duration, syllabic energy, spectral dynamics generate a regular recurrence of waxing and waning prominence profiles across syllable chains over time" (11). Rhythmicity at the level of individual syllables, determined primarily by their duration, derives basically from a regularly timed alternation between a relatively closed mouth for the consonantal component and a relatively open mouth for the vowel. This biphasic rhythmic alternation is produced by an elevation-depression cycle of mandibular oscillation. The resultant consonant-vowel (CV) form is, with a single exception (Breen and Pensalfini 1999), present in all languages, and it tends to be the dominant syllable form in individual languages, though syllables with more consonants on each side of the vowel are often encountered, as, for example, in the English language.

There are two important evolutionary properties of biphasic movement cycles such as that one associated with the syllable, which make them important in our effort to understand the evolution of speech. The first is noted in MacNeilage (2008):

> In fact, biphasic cycles seem to be the main way that the animal kingdom performs any kind of action that requires more than a single discrete act. Examples of biphasic cycles in nature are legion. Consider locomotion in the three available media – water, land, and air. Swimming, walking, running, hopping, writhing on the ground like a snake, flying – all involve biphasic cycles. Animals also use the biphasic cycle in breathing, scratching, digging, copulating, vomiting, shaking off bodily impediments, tail-wagging – even in their heartbeat.
>
> (90)

Thus, in centering on a biphasic cycle, speech can be seen to conform with evolutionary orthodoxy.

The second important property of biphasic cycles is revealed by the way they are distributed in phylogeny. Biphasic cycles show that nature is extremely conservative. Once a particular cyclicity has first developed, evolution tends to use it over and over again in modified form for different purposes. Jacob (1977) captured this generalized property with a metaphor. Evolution characteristically operates in the mode of a tinker, tinkering existing machinery into use for new purposes. For example, a biphasic cycle underlying fin movement in fish was adapted for terrestrial locomotion when tetrapods (ground-dwelling quadrupeds) made their transition from an aquatic medium (Cohen 1988). And many tetrapods have the ability to dig and scratch, which involves modifications of the biphasic cycles that originally evolved for limb use in locomotion – modifications for operations on the environment, and on their own body respectively.

16.3   The neurobiology of biphasic cycles

In the area of comparative neurobiology of action the production of biphasic cycles in general is considered to be controlled by neurophysiological entities known as Central Pattern Generators (CPGs). A CPG is defined as "any network within the CNS that coordinates a motor behavior or part thereof" (Grillner 2006: 751). Grillner notes that

> We know in all animals, vertebrates or invertebrates, movements are controlled by CPG networks that *determine appropriate sequences of muscle activation*. Each animal is endowed with a broad repertoire of CPGs located in different regions of the central nervous system, and available for differential activation, thus providing animals with a distinctive set of solutions to accommodate their widely divergent patterns of behavior.
>
> (751, my italics)

A similar progression in the history of the use of CPGs for food processing to the progression observed for locomotion can be envisaged in the evolution of mammals. As part of selection for increasing food processing and ingestion in newly evolving warm-blooded mammals, about 200 million years ago, an oscillatory CPG controlling the mandible for chewing, sucking, and licking was utilized, and in various taxonomic groups, an increasing ability to modulate the biphasic cycle for special processing purposes, especially those related to chewing, has followed.

A key hypothesis of the frame/content theory of the evolution of speech is that the evolution of syllables involved a further modification of the CPG mechanisms of control of chewing/sucking/licking for communicative purposes, perhaps particularly mechanisms associated with chewing. The widespread existence of visuofacial communicative cyclicities in higher primates – lipsmacks, tonguesmacks, teeth chatters – all of which involve rhythmic mandibular oscillation, supports this hypothesis (Redican 1975). Combining visuofacial communicative cyclicities with the already existing vocalization abilities of our ancestors may well have led to the first syllabic forms. If this pattern of close-open alternation was the basic articulatory pattern of the simple initial phases of speech, and was present before a separate capacity to control consonants and vowels evolved from it, there may never have been an opportunity for vowels and consonants to get mixed up with each other in the evolution of the control program for serial ordering.

An understanding of why the evolution of separable consonants and vowels from the mandibular cycle is a plausible possibility can be gained by considering a proposal by Georgopoulos and Grillner (1989) regarding the evolution of manual function, particularly reaching/grasping. They suggest that in primates "the precise forelimb movements used to position the limb at will and to grasp different objects are very similar to, and have evolved from, those used to position the limb accurately during locomotion" (1210). Thus they propose in this case that the ability to make single discrete movements may have evolved from single phases of a locomotor cyclicity. A similar progression may have occurred in the evolution of speech. Note though that while the ability to grasp would have entailed increases in the capacity of the distal component of the cycling limb itself – the hand – the ability to make separable consonants and vowels would have primarily entailed increases in the capacity of the organ "riding" on the mandibular cycle, namely the tongue.

A perspective on the possibility that the evolutionary sequence of events was the syllable first, and then differentiation of segments from it, can be gained by considering the opposite possibility, as suggested by Ohala (2008). He argues that the reason consonants and vowels tend to alternate with each other is not because of a pre-existing rhythmic mouth close-open cyclicity but because such an alternation is necessary to provide syntagmatic (serial) perceptual contrasts required as speech evolved to communicate more and more separable meanings.

If the origin of speech lay in the serial organization of initially separable discrete units, it would seem likely that the serial ordering errors we would expect to see in speech would be like the ones we see in typing, which we know to be produced by a sequence of discrete keystrokes. But typing errors reveal no syllable structure constraint. Instead consonant and vowel letters reverse with each other in typing errors as often as would be expected from their relative frequencies in letter production (MacNeilage 1985). The syntagmatic contrast hypothesis is somewhat less parsimonious than the hypothesis that the syllable cycle came first, because one would need an additional later evolving control property to account for the existence of the syllable structure constraint on speech production errors. Furthermore, it would seem unlikely that one of the major subcategories of consonants – stop consonants, /d/, /d/, /g/, and /p/, /t/, and /k/ in English – would have ever been available as discrete sounds for subsequent combination with vowels because they do not occur independently of vowels in modern speech. We will see later that consonants, and the vowels that follow them, tend not to have the syntagmatic perceptual *contrasts* that Ohala's perspective would expect them to have. Instead we find the opposite tendency – a tendency for syntagmatic perceptual *similarity* arising from syntagmatic motor similarity.

16.4 Babbling as syllabic frames

The likelihood that rhythmic protosyllables may have been the original basis for the articulatory component of speech is enhanced by the existence of the phenomenon of babbling. Babbling can be defined as "one or more instances of a rhythmic alternation of a closed and open mouth, produced by a mandibular elevation/depression cycle, accompanied by vocal fold vibration, and linguistically meaningless, though giving the perceptual impression of a consonant-vowel (CV) sequence" (MacNeilage 2013). An example of a babbled utterance is "bababa." Babbling tends to begin rather suddenly at about eight months of age (van der Stelt and Koopmans-van Beinum 1986) and to continue for a few months after the first words are spoken, about five months later. It is of interest that speech-like activity in infants does not begin in a manner similar to the manner in which speech first evolved, contrary to what might have been expected from Ohala's perspective. There is no sign of an early process in which we begin to put consonant-like sounds and vowel-like sounds together to form CV syllables.

Dolata, Davis, and MacNeilage (2008) confirmed findings that the modal rate of syllable production in babbling is about three CV cycles per second. These cycles are highly rhythmic, as can easily be noted by the casual listener. The standard deviation of intersyllabic durations in babbling infants was 24 ms. Thus, two-thirds of the intervals ranged from $\frac{1}{40}$th of a second less than the mean CV duration, to $\frac{1}{40}$th of a second more. The rate of syllable production gradually increases with the infant's development, leading eventually to a rate of about five syllables per second in adult speech (Greenberg 1999).

Although the term "babbling" has the inappropriate connotation of disorganized and even inappropriate behavior, it is instead the relatively organized framework on which an infant's first words are based (MacNeilage 1997, 2008). For example, most of an infant's first word errors can be described as approximations to the correct word in the form of instances of preferred babbling patterns.

16.5 Neurobiological aspects of the syllable

Strong evidence that a rhythmic syllabification propensity remains basic to speech across the life span is supported by repeated observations of three instances of repetitive speech automatisms involving the Supplementary Motor Area (SMA) whereby neurological patients tend to involuntarily produce rhythmic sequences of a single specific CV syllable (MacNeilage and Davis 2001: MacNeilage 2008) These so-called "non-meaningful recurrent utterances" have been observed in three kinds of studies: (1) as a result of electrical stimulation of the SMA (e.g., Penfield and Welch 1951), (2) as a result of irritative lesions affecting the SMA (Jonas 1981), and (3) in a class of global aphasics who, in addition to widespread damage to lateral cortical language areas, have additional subcortical damage to the basal ganglia, leaving the SMA as the only major brain region available for speech production (Brunner et al. 1982).

Further evidence for the fundamental role of syllabic rhythmic organization in speech comes from studies which have identified endogenous cortical rhythms which are associated with speech-related functions. Giraud et al. (2007) found a 3–6 Hz power band in the lower part of the motor cortex which, they maintain, "offers a direct neural underpinning for the F/C theory of speech that assumes that syllables are phylogenetically and ontogenetically determined by natural mandibular cycles occurring at about 4 Hz" (1132). They consider that overall, their findings "emphasize the role of common cortical oscillatory frequency bands for speech production and perception and thus provide a brain-based account for the phylogenetic emergence and shaping of speech from available neural substrates" (1133).

Similar conclusions regarding the fundamental role of syllabic rhythmic organization in modern on-line brain function for both production and perception, perhaps originating in the phylogeny of production, are reported in a study by Morrillon et al. (2010). They observed that during viewing of a movie involving two participants lecturing, "activity in auditory cortex synchronizes with left-dominant input from the motor cortex at frequencies corresponding to syllabic but not phonemic speech rhythms" (18688). They conclude that "Our results support theories of language lateralization that posit a major role for intrinsic hardwired perceptuomotor processing in syllable parsing and are compatible ... with the view that speech arose from 'syllable-sized vocalizations'" (18688).

Evidence for a central role of the syllable in perception in particular comes from a study of the intelligibility of speech into which various silent intervals were introduced. It was concluded that "optimum intelligibility is achieved when the syllable rhythm is within the range of high frequency theta brain rhythms (6–12Hz) comparable with the rate at which segments and syllables are articulated in conversational speech" (Ghitza and Greenberg 2009).

Returning to the issue of the phylogenetic basis of the syllable, important behavioral evidence in support of the claim that syllables evolved from lipsmacks, has recently been provided by Morrill et al. (2012) in their paper "Monkey Lipsmacking Develops Like Speech." In this developmental study of the dynamics of lipsmacks in macaque monkeys they explicitly tested the F/C hypothesis that syllables evolved from lipsmacks. They found that neonatal monkeys produce lipsmacks at the rate of about three per second, the rate reported earlier for syllable production in infant babbling, while adult monkeys produced lipsmacks at the rate of about five per second, the rate of syllable production in adult speech. The similarity of these repetition rates for neonatal and adult lipsmacks, on the one hand, and for babbling and speech on the other, is highly suggestive evidence that speech might well have evolved from lipsmacks.

The behavioral evidence suggesting an evolutionary relation between lipsmacks and syllable frames also fits with an increasing body of comparative neurobiological evidence from studies of the anterior insula. The insula is a region of cerebral cortex lying deep within the lateral sulcus (sylvian fissure), intermediate between the superior medial surface and the inferior medial surfaces of the sulcus. The initial indication that the anterior insula might be involved in the evolution of speech derived from a study of "Apraxia of Speech" (Ackerman and Riecker 2010). Apraxia of speech (AOS) is "a syndrome assumed to reflect impaired higher order aspects of speech motor control, i.e. the 'planning' of the respective vocal tract movement sequences" (420). In a surprising finding, Dronkers (1996) reported that the only area of brain damage common to a group of patients with apraxia of speech was the anterior region of the insula in the dominant hemisphere. Ackerman and Riecker (2010) summarize subsequent imaging studies that confirm the role of the anterior insula in the planning of speech production. They conclude that the region is "sensitive to phonetic-linguistic structure of verbal utterances" (419), and they particularly emphasize a study in which haemodynamic activity in the region is sensitive to the complexity of syllable structure.

Ackerman and Riecker (2010) observed that

> considering ... the well-established participation of the anterior insula in the phylogenetically rather old perceptual-motor functions such as feeding-related behavior ... it is a bit bewildering that 'motor planning' of speech (Dronkers, 1996) or 'motor articulatory planning' (Nestor, 2003), capacities unique to our species, might depend on the rostral, i.e. 'paralimbic' component of intrasylvian cortex.
>
> (420)

However, far from being bewildering, it is exactly what would be expected if one believes that the articulatory capabilities of speech evolved from food ingestion capabilities. Numerous imaging studies have shown involvement of the insula in both swallowing and chewing. The specific involvement of the insula in the motor action of human chewing, as distinct from effects of gustatory and olfactory input concurrent with the chewing of the object, is indicated by a study in which electrical stimulation of the insula of epileptic patients produced chewing movements (Ostrovsky et al. 2000).

In the present context it is interesting to note that Ostrovsky et al. also reported the elicitation of "lipsmacks" in one patient. These might have been instances of pure frames unaccompanied by phonation. Thus frames, or frame-like actions, may have had a phylogenetic precursor in insular cortex. A further confirmation of a phylogenetic relation between lipsmacks and syllables is found in a study by Caruana et al. (2011) who reported that stimulation of the insula elicited lipsmacks in monkeys. These lipsmacks were dependent on social context, occurring only when the monkey was face to face with the experimenter, an interpersonal circumstance that could presumably have been carried over to humans. The fundamental role of lipsmacks in monkey communication is emphasized by the finding of Ferrari et al. (2009) that they are already present in neonatal monkeys, in interactions with their mothers. It may also be of interest, in the light of the possibility that lipsmacks derived from chewing, that the lipsmacks elicited by Caruana et al. sometimes terminated in chewing movements.

Additional evidence that ingestive actions and lipsmacks may have been precursors to speech comes from the discovery of mirror neurons in area F5 of monkey premotor cortex, an area of inferior posterior frontal cortex considered to be homologous to Broca's area, which of course plays a key role in human speech production (Ferrari et al. 2003). Mirror neurons are neurons which discharge during a particular action, and also when an animal observes another animal performing the same action, suggesting they could have played a crucial role in the evolution of the human ability to learn speech. Summarizing Ferrari et al.'s (2003) study of F5, MacNeilage (2008) notes that they

> found that 11 of 12 "communicative mirror neurons" – neurons that responded to species-specific communicative gestures made by the experimenters – also discharged during the making of ingestive actions by the monkey. The neurons were perceptually sensitive to communicative gestures of lip-smacking, teeth chatter, lip protrusion, tongue protrusion, and lip and tongue protrusion together. Associated ingestive actions were sucking, grasping with lips, chewing, reaching with tongue, and grasping with mouth. (The 12th neuron, which responded to the communicative gesture of lip protrusion, was active during the animal's production of another communicative gesture – lip-smacking.)
>
> (2008: 177)

Ferrari et al. concluded: "In general there was a good correlation between the motor features of the effective observed (communicative) action and those of the effective executed (ingestive) action" (2003: 1709). The authors considered these findings to be consistent with the contention from F/C theory that ingestive actions may have been precursors to the subsequent oral communicative role of this region. In their own words, "Ingestive actions are the basis on which communication is built" (1713).

One final property of the mandibular cycle points to its important role in integration of the newly evolving articulatory component of speech with the phonatory (laryngeal) and respiratory components, which have long played a central role in the evolution of vocalization. McClean and Tasko (2002) recorded the acoustic signal and the movements of the upper lips, lower lips, tongue, mandible, rib cage, and abdomen while 14 participants repeated a simple test utterance at varying rates and vocal intensities. They found that the action of the mandible was more highly correlated with indices of laryngeal and respiratory function than were the other articulatory structures (tongue and lips). Such a finding is consistent with Lashley's proposal that rhythm generators play a role in integrating separate strands of neural activity.

16.6 Syllable frames: Descent with modification

What might have been the historic origin of selection pressures that resulted in ingestive mandibular cyclicities forming the articulatory component of protosyllables? As to the origin of lipsmacks themselves, van Hooff (1967) has suggested that they may have evolved their communicative status from cyclical ingestive movements elicited during a manual-grooming event. Animals looking forward to finding a food item, such as a salt grain, in an individual instance of grooming, might have begun chewing movements in anticipation of such a discovery.

Selection pressure for mandibular cyclicities with phonation may have been exerted in the pre-speech context of the evolution of "vocal grooming," a substitute for actual hands-on grooming when ancestral troop sizes got too large for the latter to remain effective, as suggested by Dunbar (1996). More generally, the ability to do these motor frames, and more importantly to imitate them, may have been just one offshoot of the evolution of a general-purpose mimetic ability. This capability to recreate the observed actions of others, almost as salient and unique in humans as is speech, is evident in modern human music, dance, opera, movies, games, sports, etc. According to Donald (1999), this capability may have evolved well before speech as an adaptive response to pressures for social communication, and pressures related to the maintenance of sociocultural stability.

16.7 Babbling and the origin of speech

The rhythmic nature of babbling and the predominance of the virtually universal CV syllable in babbling can provide key evidence regarding the basic nature of serial ordering of speech. But could the investigation of babbling and early words which have babbling-like patterns throw any further light on the details of what the first speech-like vocalizations of hominins were like? For the past two decades a research project focused on this question has been conducted by Barbara Davis and myself. We have investigated the internal structure of babbling episodes, which consist primarily of a single CV, or of a series, usually constituted by repetitions of the same CV. The latter is referred to as "reduplicative babbling."

Prior to this research it had been established that the consonants of babbling are primarily labial (lip), or coronal (tongue front) stop consonants and nasals, whereas vowels are primarily in the lower left quadrant of the vowel space – mid and low, front and central vowels (see MacNeilage and Davis 1990a for a summary). Our research began with the question of whether there were any tendencies for particular consonants and vowels to co-occur, thus perhaps indicating what the characteristic original intrasyllabic serial organization patterns might have been.

This research focused on stop consonants, the most frequently occurring consonants, using a simple classification of the place of consonantal articulation (labial, coronal, and dorsal), as well as a simple division of the vowel space into three along a front-back dimension (front, central, back). In these studies we used extremely large databases, typically involving data of over 1000 CV syllables per infant studied.

In an initial case study of a single American infant (Davis and MacNeilage 1990) we found tendencies toward three particular consonant-vowel co-occurrences: (1) coronal (front) consonants tended to occur with front vowels; (2) dorsal (back) consonants tended to occur with back vowels; (3) labial (lip) consonants tended to co-occur with central vowels. In a subsequent case study of another American infant (Davis and MacNeilage 1994), we confirmed the existence of the first and third patterns, but there were too few dorsal consonants and back vowels to test for their co-occurrence, a result which is often observed babbling. In a third study we found all three of these patterns to be present in the babbling of six American infants (Davis and MacNeilage 1995). A fourth study showed these patterns to be present at strengths approximately equal to those observed in babbling (about 30% above chance expectations) in a study of the first words of 10 American infants (Davis, MacNeilage, and Matyear 2002). We also found similar CV co-occurrence patterns when nasals and glides (MacNeilage, Davis, and Matyear 1997), and when fricatives and liquids (Gildersleeve-Neumann, Davis, and MacNeilage 2000) were considered in addition to stop consonants.

A relatively large number of other studies have confirmed, for the most part, the existence of these three patterns in 11 language environments representing a number of widely separated language families: American English, Brazilian Portuguese, Dutch, French, Japanese, Korean, Mandarin Chinese, Quichua, Romanian, Serbian, Swedish, Tunisian Arabic, and Turkish (de Boysson-Bardies 1993; Chen and Kent 2005; Gildersleeve-Neumann, Davis, and MacNeilage 2013; Giulivi et al., 2011; Lee, Davis, and MacNeilage 2007; Kern and Davis 2009; Oller and Steffans 1994; Teixeira and Davis 2002; Tyler and Langsdale 1996; Vihman 1992; Zlatic et al. 1997). Only the coronal-front vowel co-occurrence was found in Romanian and in Dutch, in the Kern and Davis (2009) study. Occasional other null findings or instances of a preference for one or another of the six other possible CV patterns in these studies, neither of which occur very frequently, may often be attributed to the use of relatively small databases, or the use of different vowel classifications (see Davis and MacNeilage 2002 for an earlier review of these studies and Lee, Davis, and MacNeilage 2007 for a more recent review). Of the six non-predicted patterns, the tendency for labials to co-occur with back vowels is the most frequent one.

The three preferred CV co-occurrence patterns have also been observed in infants with input and output deficits. McCaffrey et al. (2000) and von Hapsburg, Davis, and MacNeilage (2008) have observed them in hearing impaired American infants, though Schauwers, Govaerts, and Gillis (2008) did not observe them in hearing impaired Dutch infants. Stout, Hardin-Jones, and Chapman (2011) observed them in American infants with cleft lip and palate.

Why are these three particular forms favored? The coronal-front and dorsal-back patterns are consistent with the possibility that the tongue tends to stay in either a front or a back position in the mouth during the CV alternation, doing nothing specific to the consonant or the vowel. The third pattern suggests that when the tongue is not involved in forming the consonant it tends to occupy the same position in the mouth throughout the CV alternation, presumably its rest position.

These three patterns are, of course, observable not only in single CVs, but in sequences of them as well. As already mentioned, babbling tends to be reduplicative. It was long believed that while babbling was primarily reduplicative in the earlier stages of babbling (7–10 months) it then became predominantly variegated, meaning that the consonants and/or vowels were not the same in successive syllables (Oller 1980; Stark 1980). On the face of it this belief would seem logical as variegated syllable sequences are typical of languages, and in the course of speech acquisition infants would be expected to become more capable of producing them. However in an early study of six infants (Davis and MacNeilage 1995), and in two earlier studies (Smith, Brown-Sweeney, and Stoel-Gammon 1989; Mitchell and Kent 1990) data did not support this hypothesis. For example we found that about 50% of pairs of syllables were reduplicative and 50% were variegated in both halves of the babbling period (Davis and MacNeilage 1995). In addition we found that infants did not increase the amount of variation in the first word period (12–18 months) relative to the babbling period (Davis et al. 2002).

If variegation cannot be taken as an index of increasing developmental versatility in these early stages, how should it be characterized? In 1990 Davis and I made the prediction that most of the intersyllabic variation in babbling might be primarily attributable to the movement of the mandible, just as intrasyllabic variation is (Davis and MacNeilage 1990). It might primarily involve the vertical dimension rather than the horizontal one, in that most consonantal variation might relate to the degree of constriction of the vocal tract, controlled by amount of mandibular elevation, rather than to the place of articulation, and most vowel variation might be in vowel height, controlled by amount of mandibular depression, rather than in the front-back axis of the vowel space. This has proven to be the case. These predictions have been confirmed for American infants in both babbling (Davis and MacNeilage 1995) and for first words (Davis et al. 2002). In addition, both these predictions in babbling episodes that involve later developing consonants – fricatives, affricates, and liquids have also been confirmed (Gildersleeve-Neumann et al. 2000). It was also found for both vowels and consonants by Lee et al. (2007) in the babbling stage of Korean infants, and for vowels, though not consonants, in the infants' first words. In addition it was found for vowels but not consonants in the babbling of Quichua infants (Gildersleeve-Neumann, Davis, and MacNeilage 2013). It seems possible that at least some of this variation might be adventitious or random, rather than goal-directed, under the voluntary control of the infant.

In summary, the babbling stage of speech acquisition, and even the first word stage, can be characterized by "Frame Dominance" (Davis and MacNeilage 1995), being mainly a result of a "frame" produced by mandibular oscillation, with a minimum of active articulation produced by the tongue or other articulators during an utterance.

Finding this highly impoverished initial infant output pattern caused us to wonder whether the vocal output of the first hominin speakers would have been any different. We believe that the proto-syllabic mode was primarily one of "pure frames," namely of alternations between labials and central vowels with minimal independent tongue movement, and only perhaps with an option of producing a nasalized ("mamama") or an oral ("bababa") utterance.

The three CV co-occurrence patterns can be regarded as the main property of the serial order of babbling beyond the CV form itself. To better understand the significance of these patterns we looked at whether they are also present in modern languages. Some earlier work by Locke (1983) and by Janson (1986) suggested that modern languages might have some favored CV patterns. We looked at CV co-occurrences in the dictionary counts of 10 diverse languages (English, Estonian, French, German, Hebrew, Japanese, New Zealand Maori, Quichua, Spanish, and Swahili). Focusing on stops and nasals, we looked at CVC words, CVCV words, and words that began with a CVCV sequence. Pooling the results from the CVC and CVCV forms we found coronal-front, dorsal-back, and labial-central CV patterns in about 75% of the cases. Eight out of the 10 languages had the dorsal-back pattern while 7 out of 10 languages had the coronal-front and labial-central patterns (MacNeilage et al. 2000). In a study of 14 other languages a similar result was obtained by Rousset (2003). Note that the coronal-front and dorsal patterns indicate syntagmatic motor similarity and therefore syntagmatic perceptual similarity. They are the opposite of the coronal-back and dorsal-front patterns which would have been expected to have evolved according to Ohala's syntagmatic perceptual contrast hypothesis.

The finding that the three CV co-occurrence patterns are usually present in languages suggests that they were probably present in the first words of early humans. Because these patterns have a strongly inertial nature they must have been present in vocal output for as long as the close-open alternation has been present, suggesting that the biomechanically constrained alternations might even have preceded the origin of speech. That is, the patterns might have been present before concepts and sound patterns were paired to form the first words.

16.8 Babbling as an innate pattern

Having considered the basic properties of babbling it is now important to view it in the broader context of naturally occurring action patterns in general. An evolutionary perspective on babbling can be enhanced by a consideration of the discipline of Ethology – the science of naturally occurring behavior, historically non-human behavior. A central phenomenon in this field is the "fixed action pattern," a species-wide stereotyped movement or movement complex, often called "innate" as it can exhibit basic properties independent of experience. More recently these patterns have been incorporated into the broader category of "motor mechanisms" (Hogan, 2001: 230) with less, but still some, emphasis on innateness. Eibl-Eibesfeldt (1989), in a discussion of these patterns, draws attention to their "form constancy" (25–32). Prominent examples of such patterns, which are often extraordinarily complex, are rodent grooming, mud bathing, food caching, and courtship rituals (Fentress and Gadbois 2001). Mouse grooming, for instance involves four phases, all repeated several times, with some constancy in both the individual phases, and in the order of phases (Berridge et al. 2005).

There are innumerable instances of such innate adaptive motor patterns, both in vertebrates and in invertebrates. Davis and Richards (2000) point out that with respect to communicative movements in particular "A common and predictable feature of such intentional display movements is rhythmic (oscillatory) repetition" (1). They cite examples including male mallard ducks bobbing their heads up and down to a female, spiders waving their palps up and down as a form of courtship, Sceloporus lizards identifying one another from push-ups, and chimpanzees swaying from side to side as either a threat, or for courtship. One property of many of these patterns is that they manifest themselves prior to being used for an adaptive purpose. For example, the action pattern of pecking in young chicks can be observed before it is used for ingesting food objects. It seems appropriate to regard babbling as a fixed action pattern, and to conclude that it evolved as an innate basis for speaking. It certainly has the stereotypy and the form constancy that is characteristic of fixed action patterns, as well as the oscillatory character that communication patterns often possess. It is also like other innate patterns in that it appears prior to its eventual use for communication. It is well known that infants do not typically accompany babbling with eye contact with a potential receiver, or with any sign that they are trying to evoke a response.

The term "innate" has had a vexed history in science. Indeed, Fitch (2012) has suggested that we avoid the term in the domain of language evolution in particular. However, I believe it is of value to retain the term with respect to babbling, focusing on one specific connotation. It is that babbling has action characteristics that are not consistently present in language environments and these characteristics must, therefore, at least to some degree, emanate from the infant. Two particular characteristics are relevant: one observable in babbling in general, and the other observed in the development of babbling in one specific type of language environment. The first, already mentioned, is the high degree of *rhythmicity* with which successive syllables are produced. This rhythmicity is clearly present from the beginning of babbling onward. It does not develop gradually, as it would if it were being learned. Moreover, while it could be argued that a regular intersyllabic rhythm might be auditorily available to the infant listener in languages like Spanish, in which successive syllables tend to have similar durations, it is certainly not available in a very large number of languages, such as English, in which successive syllables are typically not similar to each other in duration.

A second indication of a partial independence of babbling structures from input is that the three favored consonant-vowel co-occurrence patterns can be present in babbling even when they are not favored in the language being learned, which, as already indicated, is sometimes the case. For example, all three patterns have been found in the babbling of Korean infants even though none of the patterns was consistently favored in either a dictionary count of Korean words, a sample of speech addressed to adults, or a sample of speech addressed to infants (Lee et al. 2007). This finding reinforces the conclusion stated earlier that the patterns are apparently the result of species-wide biomechanical constraints likely to also have been present in early human speakers.

It is pertinent to add the observation by Thelen (1981) that babbling is far from unique as an infant rhythmic behavior. Instead, it is simply one of a wide variety of repetitive rhythmic movements characteristic of infants in the first few months of life. These rhythmic movements include "kicking, rocking, waving, bouncing, banging, rubbing, scratching, swaying" (1981: 238). Thelen believed that such "rhythmic stereotypies are transition behavior between uncoordinated behavior and complex coordinated motor control." She also maintained that the patterns are innate because she described them as "phylogenetically available to the immature infant" (253). In her view, "rhythmical patterning originating as *motor programs essential for movement control* ... are 'called forth', so to speak, during the long period before full voluntary control develops in order to serve adaptive needs later met by goal-corrected behavior" (253, my italics).

16.9 The evo-devo perspective and babbling

When considering the origin of babbling, the new discipline of evolutionary developmental biology (Evo-Devo) seems to have something to offer. Proponents of this discipline have successfully shown that changes in the roles played by regulatory genes in affecting the timing, or the strength, of expression of other genes during development, can have profound phylogenetic effects by producing differences in animal groups descending from a common ancestor. This conceptual framework goes beyond the classical genetic conception that evolution of form is directly specified by genes. Although work in this relatively new domain is mainly focused on the evolution of animal morphology – body shape and pattern – such as the structure of forelimbs during the transition from aquatic to land animals (Shubin, Tabin, and Carroll 2009), there is no reason why similar processes would not have consequences for animal *behavior*. Developmental changes, resulting in the developmental patterns we see today, may have evolved from the fixation of babbling in the human infant developmental ethogram (behavioral repertoire), with desirable consequences for the attainment of adult behavior in subsequent generations.

Babbling today certainly does not appear to be a work in progress. Even though we have no way of determining exactly how long ago the first words were spoken, nothing about babbling suggests that it might not have been available from the very beginning of words.

As Goodman and Coughlin (2000) point out in their introduction to a special issue on developmental evolutionary biology: "Certainly the old maxim 'ontogeny recapitulates phylogeny' could be the evo-devo battle cry" (4425). If so, the F/C theory fits nicely within the discipline. They go on to suggest that "a more apt saw would be 'altering ontogeny formulates new phylogeny'"(4425). If we apply this conception to language, an alteration in the developmental program for vocal communication in earlier hominins might have made available to them the basic underpinning of the sound patterns to be used in the production of their first words.

16.10 Achieving variegation: The first words of infants

If speech started out favoring syllable reduplication, as the F/C theory suggests, how did it proceed toward evolving variegation as the favored pattern? Looking at how *infants* begin to intentionally variegate their output intersyllabically may help us understand how they developed for hominins. The most well-known pattern of early variegation in infants is for them to begin a word with a labial consonant and follow it, after the vowel, with a coronal consonant, as in "bado" for "bottle" (Ingram 1974). One study of the first words of 10 infants showed 9 of them having this tendency, with a mean preference ratio of LC over CL patterns of 2.55:1 (MacNeilage et al., 1999).

This labial-coronal (LC) effect appears to be a self-organizational consequence of the simultaneous operation of three factors in first word production (MacNeilage and Davis 2000). First, "pure" frames, those with labial consonants and central vowels, may be easier to produce than frames with coronals and front vowels because the latter involves the addition of a tongue fronting movement, whereas the former only involves pure frame production. Second, an addition to the functional load associated with vocalization in the babbling stage occurs at the first word stage when an infant has to produce a specific vocal episode motivated by a particular lexical concept, rather than simply producing an output episode from their small vocal repertoire. This produces a generalized bias in first words toward increasing use of pure frames, with their labial-central pattern. We have found a tendency for use of more labial than coronal consonants in first words even though the opposite was true in pre-speech babbling (MacNeilage et al. 1997). Third, the initiation of action is a separable functional role of motor systems (Gazzaniga and Heatherton 2003), and as the serial output pattern becomes more complex, the initiation may become more difficult. As a consequence of these three factors, a tendency may arise, in instances in which infants are simulating an adult word with intercyclical variegation, for them to begin the simulation with the easier pure frame pattern and then add a tongue movement to the next frame.

In order to fully understand the LC pattern it is necessary to look at whether it is also favored in the world's languages just as the three CV co-occurrence preferences are. A study of the occurrence of stops and nasals in CVC words, CVCV words, and words beginning with a CVCV sequence in 10 languages showed that the LC preference was found in every language except in Japanese. The mean ratio of LC to CL patterns was remarkably high in these languages (2.3:1) (MacNeilage et al. 1999). This ratio is almost as high as the infant ratio of 2.55:1. Rousset (2003) has also found that this pattern is predominant in her sample of 14 languages. It appears that the same factors that may produce the LC effect in a self-organizational manner in infants may have been at work in earlier hominids. However, while modern infants have a language model of this form to copy, hominins had to invent it.

We have characterized the overall developmental progression of speech acquisition as "frames, then content" (MacNeilage and Davis 1990b). We have not studied this progression, which is basically one from reduplication to variegation, beyond the exploration of the LC effect. One obvious possibility is that infant speech errors might provide valuable information regarding the supposed progression from the frame stage to the frame/content stage. Fortunately a large-scale study of speech errors during speech acquisition is available. Jaeger (2005) has analyzed 1383 speech errors made by three infants/children within the age range of 1–5 years. In a summary of her findings she states that "An extremely valuable heuristic in which to frame this discussion is the 'Frames, then Content' developmental progression proposed by MacNeilage and Davis (1990b)" (214). Her conclusion from an analysis of these errors is that "The discussion ... regarding the developmental pathways taken by children toward the learning of phonology is completely consistent with MacNeilage and Davis's (1990b) model of language acquisition" (219).

16.11 The invention of the first words

The question about the origin of speech that most people find primary is *How did sound patterns become paired with concepts?* This question is a daunting one because it is generally true that, except for onomatapoeic forms, there is an *arbitrary* relation between concepts and sound patterns in modern languages. A dog doesn't look like "dog." Nor does it look like "chien," etc. The present day arbitrariness of the concept-sound relation makes it difficult to see how some *natural* process originally resulted in pairing concepts with words, even though there must originally have been one.

According to F/C theory (see MacNeilage 2008: chapter 7), this pairing may have first occurred in the parent/infant communicative dyad in the form of parental terms (e.g., "mama" and "papa"). And the words, from the beginning, must have had the frame-stage properties – properties shown to exist (see MacNeilage 2008: chapter 7) in both modern baby-talk words compiled by Ferguson (1964), and parental terms in language proper compiled by Murdock (1959). But equally importantly, we are guided here by the fact that this is the only instance of a systematic relation between particular concepts and particular sounds in the world's languages that is not onomatopoetic or otherwise iconic. In more than two-thirds of documented instances, words for the female parent today in widely differing languages, tend to contain nasal consonants while words for the male parent do not (e.g., "mother, "father"; see Murdock 1959).

Why would such a systematic relationship between concepts and sounds exist in this domain in particular? Falk (2004) and others suggest that the first word might have been created when a mother responded to the kind of nasalized infant demand vocalization that is still evident today (Goldman 2001). This pre-babbling vocalization, a nasalized alternation between glottal stops and vowels, roughly translated as *"mama,"* may have been understood by mothers as meaning "this sound stands for me." Then, a phonetically contrasting non-nasal form for the male parent may have been created (e.g., "papa"). Additional words may then have been created, eventually leading to the epochal "nominal insight" that vocal patterns can stand for things, which would allow intentional word invention (McShane 1979). There have no doubt been long-standing and intense selection pressures for parent-infant communication. In addition, evidence from historical linguistics that the baby-talk/parental-terms domain has been continually active across recorded linguistic history in terms of continued coinage of new terms (see MacNeilage 2008: chapter 7), both constitute evidence that parental terms may well have been the first words. In short, parental baby talk terms may be "living fossils" constituting the "missing link" between pre-linguistic and linguistic hominins (see Bancel and Matthey de l'Etang 2013 for a current review.)

16.12 F/C theory and articulatory phonology

The most well-known conception of the organization of adult speech production is that of Articulatory Phonology (AP) (Browman and Goldstein 1992). This conception has been suggested as an alternative to the F/C conception of speech phylogeny and speech ontogeny in several papers by Studdert-Kennedy over the past decade or so (e.g., Studdert-Kennedy 1998, 2012), and most recently as an alternative to the F/C conception of ontogeny by a group of authors holding the AP perspective (Giulivi et al. 2011; Whalen et al. 2011). (See MacNeilage and Davis 2011 for a detailed response to the latter critique.) According to the AP conception, six units called "gestures" are the irreducible minimal units or "atoms" of speech, and with respect to serial organization, these atoms are considered to be concatenated to form spoken words according to universal principles of motor coordination.

Imagine what a momentous discovery this would be if it were, in fact, found to be true. The atoms of physics and chemistry are the basic components of all matter, and are cornerstones of theory in the physical sciences. They are well defined, even though not totally understood, and finite in number – 118 in a current count. Unfortunately, there is no analog to this state of affairs in phonetics, and that fact alone would seem to remove AP from serious consideration as a general theory of speech production. The actual state of affairs becomes clear when we consider the treatment of the tongue in AP. Although there is no doubt that the tongue is a single organ, to AP it is made up of *three* organs, which constitute three of the proposed total of six gestural atoms. To consider the scope of the claim, Maddieson (1984), in a study of 317 languages, found a total of 768 segment types – 558 consonants and 210 vowels. With the exception of 31 consonantal segments (about 4%) which were either purely labial or purely glottal, all of these segment types involved tongue positioning. One other factor should also be noted. Tongue shapes for individual segments are subject to coarticulation, which means that the actual achievement of any tongue position for a segment must be contingent on the tongue position for at least one previous segment, and probably on tongue position for the next segment as well (see MacNeilage and DeClerk 1969 for examples). Surprisingly, although the claim that the tongue consists of three organs in now two decades old, no systematic approach has been made to show how this extraordinary complexity can be encompassed by the action of these three organs. In fact it is not at all clear how one would go about substantiating this claim.

There is another major flaw in the AP conception when it is applied to the phylogeny and ontogeny of speech production. It is that the conception does not encompass change, in either the deep time of phylogeny, or in the shallow time of ontogeny. First, with respect to phylogeny, Studdert-Kennedy provides no consideration of how these gestures attained functional independence in hominins, when they lacked such independence in ancestral forms, except for brief references to the attempts of others to evoke self-organization in the context of increases in the size of the message set (Studdert-Kennedy 2012). With respect to ontogeny, neither critique actually has a developmental component in the sense that they deal with changes in the nature of the gestures. They do not provide any account of the progression of gestures from immature to mature status. Studdert-Kennedy acknowledges the existence of an initial frame stage in development, but goes on to assert that gestures subsequently emerge, apparently fully formed, and the process of development is only the process of arranging them appropriately in the time domain, independently of frames. He does not consider the conception of the LC effect as the first major step from reduplication toward variegation, nor the evidence from Jaeger's (2005) studies that segmental elements emerge from frame structures.

Studdert-Kennedy's conception of gesture development, though like the other AP group's contention in assuming they do not develop across time but instead enter the repertoire fully formed, is diametrically opposed to the position of other AP proponents with respect to the question of serial organization. Though Studdert-Kennedy considers that the infant lacks an ability to serially organize gestures when they first emerge, AP proponents have historically asserted there are natural laws of coordination which demand that gestures for the consonant and the following vowel are triggered simultaneously, and they apparently expect these laws to be operative in full form at the beginning of the babbling stage. This perspective is in stark contrast to the F/C conception which asserts that there are no substantial independent control contributions to the consonant and the vowel in CV syllables – at least in those syllables which exhibit the three CV co-occurrence patterns.

In summary, there are two aspects of the AP perspective that disqualify it as a viable alternate to the F/C conception of the evolution and acquisition of speech. First, the central claim of AP, that speech is made with six gestures, three of which involve tongue organs, has not been established. Second, the AP perspective does not encompass change, and therefore does not seem to be an appropriate approach to either phylogeny, or to ontogeny, where change is the main concern.

16.13 Summary and implications

The frame/content theory is the only theory of the evolution and acquisition of speech production, perhaps our most important action capability. It has two main parts. The first is that a syllable "frame" produced by mandibular oscillation is the main initial basis for both the evolution and the acquisition of speech. The second is that the main subsequent development in both evolution and acquisition of speech has been the emergence of the ability to independently insert segmental content (consonants and vowels) into frame structures. It provides a unified account of a large number of salient properties of modern speech and its acquisition, and of comparative behavioral and neurobiological aspects of vocal/auditory communication in primates in general. Perhaps its main promise for the future lies in two domains; First, it serves as a guide to the further understanding of how speech evolved by descent with modification, particularly at the neurobiological level. Second, it suggests that the most rewarding approach to the acquisition of speech will be to further understand how content gradually becomes differentiated from frames. Of special interest in this regard will be further studies of infant speech errors, and of the time course of development of intersegmental versatility in individual infants.

REFERENCES

Ackermann, Hermann and Axel Riecker. 2010. The contribution(s) of the insula to speech production: A review of the clinical and functional imaging literature. *Brain Structure and Function* 214: 419–433.

Bancel, Pierre J. and Alain Matthey de l'Etang. 2013. Brave new words. In Claire Lefebvre, Bernard Comrie, and Henri Cohen (eds.), *New Perspectives on the Origins of Language*, 333–378. Amsterdam: John Benjamins.

Berridge, Kent C., J. Wayne Aldridge, Kimberly R. Houchard, and Zhuang Xiaoxi. 2005. Sequential super-stereotypy of an instinctive fixed action pattern in hyperdominergic mice: A model of obsessive-compulsive disorder and Tourette's. *BMC Biology* 3: 4.

Bohland, Jason W., Daniel S. Bullock, and Frank H. Guenther. 2010. Neural representations and mechanisms for the performance of simple speech sequences. *Journal of Cognitive Neuroscience* 22: 1504–1529.

Breen, Gava and Rob Pensalfini. 1999. Arrernte: A language with no syllable onsets. *Linguistic Inquiry* 30: 1–26.

Browman, Cathe P. and Louis M. Goldstein. 1992. Articulatory Phonology: An overview. *Phonetica* 49: 155–180.

Brunner, Richard J., Hans H. Kornhuber, Eva Seemuller, Gerhard Suger, and Claus W. Wallesch. 1982. Basal ganglia participation in language pathology. *Brain and Language* 16: 281–299.

Caruana, Fausto., Ahmed Jazzini, Beatrice Sbriscia-Fioretti, Giacomo Rizzolatti, and Vittorio Gallese. 2011. Emotional and social behaviors elicited by electrical stimulation of the insula in the macaque monkey. *Current Biology* 21: 1–5.

Chen, Li-Mei and Raymond D. Kent. 2005. Consonant-vowel co-occurrence patterns in Mandarin-learning infants. *Journal of Child Language* 32: 507–534.

Cohen, Avis H. 1988. Evolution of the vertebrate central pattern generator for locomotion. In Avis H. Cohen, Serge Rossignol, and Sten Grillner (eds.), *Neural Control of Rhythmic Movements*, 129–166. New York: John Wiley & Sons, Inc.

Corballis, Michael C. 1991. *The Lopsided Ape: Evolution of the Generative Mind*. Oxford: Oxford University Press.

Darwin, C. 1859. *On the Origin of Species*. London: John Murray.

Davis, Barbara L. and Peter F. MacNeilage. 1990. The acquisition of correct vowel production: A quantitative case study. *Journal of Speech and Hearing Research* 33: 16–27.

Davis, Barbara L. and Peter F. MacNeilage. 1994. Organization of babbling: A case study. *Language and Speech* 37: 341–355.

Davis, Barbara L. and Peter F. MacNeilage. 1995. The articulatory basis of babbling. *Journal of Speech and Hearing Research* 38: 1199–1211.

Davis, Barbara L. and Peter F. MacNeilage. 2002. The internal structure of the syllable. In Talmy Givón and Bertram F. Malle (eds.), *The Evolution of Language out of Prelanguage*, 135–154. Amsterdam: John Benjamins.

Davis, Barbara L., Peter F. MacNeilage, and Christine L. Matyear. 2002. Acquisition of serial complexity in speech production: A comparison of phonetic and phonological approaches. *Phonetica* 59: 75–107.

Davis, James W. and Whitman A. Richards. 2000. Relating categories of animal motion. Ohio State University, Dept. of Communication and Information Science, Technical Report OSU-CISRC-11/00-TR 25.

de Boysson-Bardies, Benedict. 1993. Ontogeny of language-specific syllabic productions. In Benedict de Boysson-Bardies, Scania de Schonen, Peter Jusczyk, Peter F. MacNeilage, and John Morton (eds.), *Developmental Neurocognition: Speech and face Processing in the First Year of Life*, 353–363. Dordrecht: Kluwer.

Dobzhansky, Theodosius. 1973. Nothing in biology makes sense except in the light of evolution. *The American Biology Teacher* 35: 125–129.

Dolata, Jill, Barbara L. Davis, and Peter F. MacNeilage. 2008. Characteristics of the rhythmic organization of babbling: Implications for an amodal linguistic rhythm. *Infant Behavior and Development* 31: 422–431.

Donald, Merlin. 1999. Preconditions for the evolution of protolanguages. In Michael C. Corballis and Stephen E.G. Lea (eds.), *The Descent of Mind: Psychological Perspectives on Hominid Evolution*, 138–154. Oxford: Oxford University Press.

Dronkers, Nina F. 1996. A new brain region for coordinating speech articulation. *Nature* 384: 159–161.

Dunbar, Robin I.M. 1996. *Grooming, Gossip and the Evolution of Language*. Cambridge, MA: Harvard University Press.

Eibl-Eibesfeldt, Irenäus. 1989. *Human Ethology*. New York: Aldine de Gruyter.

Falk, Dean. 2004. Prelinguistic evolution in early hominins: Whence motherese. *Behavioral and Brain Sciences* 27: 491–503.

Fentress, John C. and Simon Gadbois. 2001. The development of action sequences. In Elliott Blass (ed.), *Handbook of Behavioral Neurobiology*, vol. 13, 393–431. New York: Kluwer Academic/Plenum Publishers.

Ferguson, C.A. 1964. Baby talk in 6 languages. *American Anthropologist* 66: 103–114.

Ferrari, Pier F., Vittorio Gallese, Giacomo Rizzolatti, and Leonardo Fogassi. 2003. Mirror neurons responding to the observation of ingestive and communicative mouth movements in the monkey ventral premotor cortex. *European Journal of Neuroscience* 17: 1703–1714.

Ferrari, Pier F., Annika Paukner, Consuel Ionica, and Stephen J. Suomi. 2009. Reciprocal face-to-face communication between rhesus macaque mothers and their newborn infants. *Current Biology* 19: 1768–1772.

Fitch W. Tecumseh. 2012. Innateness in language: A biological perspective. In Maggie Tallerman and Kathleen R. Gibson (eds.), *Encyclopedia of Language Evolution*, 143–156. Oxford: Oxford University Press.

Gazzaniga, Michael S. and Todd F. Heatherton. 2003. *Psychological Science*. New York: Norton.

Georgopoulos, Apostolos P. and Sten Grillner. 1989. Visual-motor coordination in reaching and locomotion. *Science* 245: 1209–1210.

Ghitza, Oded and Steven Greenberg. 2009. On the possible role of brain rhythms in speech perception: Intelligibility of time-compressed speech with periodic and aperiodic insertions of silence. *Phonetica* 66: 113–126.

Gildersleeve-Neumann, Christina E., Barbara L. Davis, and Peter F. MacNeilage. 2000. Contingencies governing production of fricatives, affricates and liquids in babbling. *Applied Psycholinguistics* 21: 341–363.

Gildersleeve-Neumann, Christina. E., Barbara L. Davis, and Peter F. MacNeilage. 2013. Syllabic patterns in the early vocalizations of Quichua children. *Applied Psycholinguistics* 34(1): 111–134.

Giraud, Anne-Lisa, Andreas Kleinschmidt, David Poeppel, Torben Lund, Richard S.J. Frackowiak, and Helmut Laufs. 2007. Endogenous cortical rhythms determine cerebral specialization for speech perception and production. *Neuron* 56: 1127–1134.

Giulivi, Sara, Douglas H. Whalen, Louis M. Goldstein, Hosung Nam, and Andrea G. Levitt. 2011. An articulatory phonology account of preferred consonant-vowel combinations. *Language Learning and Development* 7: 202–225.

Goldman, Herbert I. 2001. Parental reports of "MAMA" sounds in infants: An exploratory study. *Journal of Child Language* 28: 497–506.

Goodman, Corey S. and Bridget C. Coughlin. 2000. Introduction: The evolution of evo-devo biology. *Proceedings of the National Academy of Sciences, USA* 97: 4424–4425.

Greenberg, Steven. 1999. Speaking in shorthand: A syllable-centric perspective for understanding pronunciation variation. *Speech Communication* 29: 159–176.

Grillner, Sten. 2006. Biological pattern generation: The cellular and computational logic of networks in motion. *Neuron* 52: 751–766.

Hogan, Jerry A. 2001. Development of behavioral systems. In Elliot Blass (ed.), *Handbook of Behavioral Neurobiology*, vol. 13, 229–279. New York: Kluwer Academic/Plenum Publishers.

Huxley, Thomas H. 1863/2005. *Collected Essays of Thomas Huxley: Man's Place in Nature and Other Anthropological Essays*. Whitefish, MT: Kessinger Publishing.

Ingram, David. 1974. Fronting in infant phonology. *Journal of Child Language* 1: 233–241.

Jacob, François. 1977. Evolution and tinkering. *Science* 196: 1161–1166.

Jaeger, Jeri. 2005. *Kids Slips: What Young Children's Slips of the Tongue Reveal About Language Development*. Mahwah, NJ: Lawrence Erlbaum Associates.

Janson, Tore. 1986. Cross-linguistic trends in the frequency of CV sequences. *Phonology Yearbook* 3: 179–195.

Jonas, Saran. 1981. The supplementary motor region and speech emission. *Journal of Communication Disorders* 14: 349–373.

Kern, Sophie and Barbara L. Davis. 2009. Emergent complexity in early vocal acquisition: Cross-linguistic comparisons of canonical babbling. In Iona Chitoran, Christophe Coupé, Egidio Marisco, and Francois Pellegrino (eds.), *Approaches to Phonological Complexity, Phonology and Phonetics Series*, 353–376. Berlin: Mouton de Gruyter.

Kohler, Klaus. 2009. Editorial: Whither speech rhythm research. *Phonetica* 66: 5–14.

Lashley, Karl. S. 1951. The problem of serial order in behavior. In Lloyd A. Jeffress (ed.), *Cerebral Mechanisms in Behavior: The Hixon Symposium*, 112–136. New York: John Wiley & Sons, Inc.

Lee, Soyoung, Barbara L. Davis, and Peter F. MacNeilage. 2007. "Frame dominance" and the serial organization of babbling and first words in Korean-learning infants. *Phonetica* 64: 217–236.

Levelt, Willem J.M. 1992. Accessing words in speech production: Stages, processes and representations. *Cognition* 48: 1–22.

Locke, John L. 1983. *Phonological Acquisition and Change*. New York: Academic Press.

MacNeilage, Peter F. 1985. Serial ordering errors in speech and typing. In Victoria A. Fromkin (ed.), *Phonetic Linguistics*, 193–201. New York: Academic Press.

MacNeilage, Peter. F. 1997. Acquisition of speech. In William J. Hardcastle and John Laver (eds.), *Handbook of Phonetic Sciences*, 301–322. Oxford: Blackwell Publishing.

MacNeilage, Peter F. 1998. The frame/content theory of evolution of speech production. *Behavioral and Brain Sciences* 21: 499–548.

MacNeilage, Peter F. 2008. *The Origin of Speech*. Oxford: Oxford University Press.

MacNeilage, Peter F. 2011. Lashley's problem of serial order and the problem of acquisition and evolution of speech. *Cognitive Critique* 3: 49–86.

MacNeilage, Peter F. 2012. The evolution of phonology. In Maggie Tallerman and Kathleen R. Gibson (eds.), *The Handbook of Language Evolution*, 423–434. Oxford: Oxford University Press.

MacNeilage, Peter F. 2013. Sound patterns and conceptual content of the first words. In Claire Lefebvre, Bernard Comrie, and Henri Cohen (eds.), *New Perspectives on the Origins of Language*, 301–332. Amsterdam: John Benjamins.

MacNeilage, Peter F. and Barbara L. Davis. 1990a. Acquisition of speech production: The achievement of segmental independence. In William J. Hardcastle and Alain Marchal (eds.), *Speech Production and Speech Modeling*, 55–68. Dordrecht: Kluwer.

MacNeilage, Peter F. and Barbara L. Davis. 1990b. Acquisition of speech production: Frames, then content. In Marc Jeannerod (ed.), *Attention and performance XIII: Motor representation and control*, 453–476. Hillsdale, NJ: Lawrence Erlbaum Associates.

MacNeilage, Peter F. and Barbara L. Davis. 2000. On the origin of the internal structure of word forms. *Science* 288: 527–531.

MacNeilage, Peter F. and Barbara L. Davis. 2001. Motor mechanisms in speech ontogeny: Phylogenetic, neurobiological and linguistic implications. *Current Opinion in Neurobiology* 11: 696–700.

MacNeilage, Peter F. and Barbara L. Davis. 2011. In defense of the "frames, then content" (FC) perspective on speech acquisition: A response to two critiques. *Language Learning and Development* 4: 234–242.

MacNeilage, Peter F. and Joseph L. DeClerk. 1969. On the motor control of co-articulation in CVC syllables. *Journal of the Acoustical Society of America* 45: 1217–1233.

MacNeilage, Peter F., Barbara L. Davis, and Christine L. Matyear. 1997. Babbling and first words: Phonetic similarities and differences. *Speech Communication* 22: 269–277.

MacNeilage, Peter F., Michael G. Studdert-Kennedy, and Björn Lindblom. 1984. Functional precursors to language and its lateralization. *American Journal of Physiology* 246 (*Regulatory, Integrative and Comparative Physiology* 15): R912–914.

MacNeilage, Peter F., Lesley J. Rogers, and Giorgio Vallortigara. 2009. Origins of the left and right brain. *Scientific American*, July: 60–67.

MacNeilage, Peter F., Barbara L. Davis, Ashlynn Kinney, and Christine L. Matyear. 1999. Origin of serial output complexity in speech. *Psychological Science* 10: 459–460.

MacNeilage, Peter F., Barbara L. Davis, Ashlynn Kinney, and Christine L. Matyear. 2000. The motor core of speech: A comparison of serial organization patterns in infants and languages. *Child Development* 71: 153–163.

Maddieson, Ian. 1984. *Patterns of Sounds*. Cambridge: Cambridge University Press.

Mayr, E. 1982. *The Growth of Biological Thought*. Cambridge, MA: Belknap Press.

McCaffrey, Helen L., Barbara L. Davis, Peter F. MacNeilage, and Deborah von Hapsburg. 2000. Effects of multichannel cochlear implantation on the organization of early speech. *The Volta Review* 101: 5–29.

McClean, Michael D. and Stephen M. Tasko. 2002. Association of orofacial with laryngeal and respiratory motor output during speech. *Experimental Brain Research* 146: 481–489.

McShane, John. 1979. The development of naming. *Linguistics* 17: 879–905.

Merriam-Webster. 2000. *Merriam-Webster's Collegiate Dictionary*, 10th edn. Springfield, MA: Merriam-Webster Inc.

Mitchell, Pamela R. and Raymond D. Kent. 1990. Phonetic variation in multisyllable babbling. *Journal of Child Language* 17: 247–265.

Morrill, Ryan J., Annika Paukner, Pier F. Ferrari, and Asif Ghazanfar. 2012. Monkey lipsmacking develops like human speech. *Developmental Science* 15(4): 557–568.

Morrillon, Benjamin, Katia Lehongre, Richard S.J. Frackowiak, Antoine Ducorps, Andreas Kleinschmidt, David Poeppel, and Anne-Lise Giraud. 2010. Neurophysiological origin of human brain asymmetry for speech and language. *Proceedings of the National Academy of Sciences, USA* 107: 18688–18693.

Murdock, George P. 1959. Cross-language parallels in parental kin terms. *Anthropological Linguistics* 1: 1–5.

Nestor, Peter J., Naida L. Graham, Tim D. Fryer, Guy B. Williams, Karolyn Patterson, and John R. Hodges. 2003. Progressive non-fluent aphasia is associated with hypometabolism centered on the left anterior insula. *Brain* 126: 2406–2418.

Ohala, John J. 2008. The emergent syllable. In Barbara L. Davis and Kristina Zajdó (eds.), *The Syllable in Speech Production*, 1–28. New York: Lawrence Erlbaum Associates.

Oller, D. Kimbrough. 1980. The emergence of speech sounds in infancy. In Grace Yeni-Komshian, James. F. Kavanagh, and Charles A. Ferguson (eds.), *Child Phonology*, vol. 1, *Production*, 93–112. New York: Academic Press.

Oller, D. Kimbrough and Michelle L. Steffans. 1994. Syllables and segments in infant vocalizations and young child speech. In Mehmet Yavas (ed.), *First and Second Language Phonology*. San Diego, CA: Singular Publishing Group.

Ostrovsky, Karine, Jean Isnard, Philippe Ryvlin, Marc Guénot, Catherine Fischer, and François Mauguière. 2000. Functional mapping of the insular cortex:

Clinical implication in temporal lobe epilepsy. *Epilepsia* 41: 681–686.

Penfield, Wilder and Keasley Welch. 1951. The supplementary motor area of the cerebral cortex: A clinical and experimental study. *AMA Archives of Neurology and Psychiatry* 66: 289–317.

Redican, William K. 1975. Facial expressions in nonhuman primates. In Lawrence A. Rosenblum (ed.), *Primate Behavior: Developments in Field and Laboratory Research*, vol. 4, 103–194. New York: Academic Press.

Rosenbaum, David. A. 2005. The neglect of motor control in the science of mental life and behavior. *American Psychologist* 60: 308–317.

Rousset, Isobelle. 2003. From lexical to syllabic organization: Favored and disfavored co-occurrences. In *Proceedings of the 15th International Congress of Phonetics*, 2705–2708. Barcelona: Autonomous University of Barcelona.

Saussure, Ferdinand de. 1915/1959. *Course in General Linguistics*, trans. Charles Bally and Albert Sechehaye. New York: Philosophical Library.

Schauwers, Karen, Paul J. Govaerts, and Stephen Gillis. 2008. Co-occurrence patterns in the babbling of children with a cochlear implant. In Barbara L. Davis and Kristina Zajdó (eds.), *The Syllable in Speech Production*, 187–204. New York: Lawrence Erlbaum Associates.

Shattuck-Hufnagel, Stefanie. 1979. Speech errors as evidence for a serial ordering mechanism in speech production. In William E. Cooper and Edward C.T. Walker (eds.), *Sentence Processing: Psycholinguistic Studies Presented to Merrill Garrett*, 295–342. Hillsdale, NJ: Lawrence Erlbaum Associates.

Shubin, Neil, Cliff Tabin, and Sean Carroll. 2009. Deep homology and the origins of evolutionary novelty. *Nature* 457: 818–823.

Smith, Bruce L., Sharon Brown-Sweeney, and Carol Stoel-Gammon. 1989. A quantitative analysis of reduplicated and variegated babbling. *First Language* 9: 175–189.

Stark, Rachel E. 1980. Features of infant sounds: The emergence of cooing. In Grace Yeni-Komshian, James. F. Kavanagh, and Charles A. Ferguson (eds.), *Child Phonology*, vol. 1, *Production*, 73–92. New York: Academic Press.

Stout, Gwendolyn, Mary Hardin-Jones, and Kathy L. Chapman. 2011. An analysis of the frame-content theory in babble of 9-month-old babies with cleft lip and palate. *Journal of Communication Disorders* 44: 584–594.

Studdert-Kennedy, Michael G. 1998. The particulate origins of language generativity: From syllable to gesture. In James R. Hurford, Chris Knight, and Michael. G. Studdert-Kennedy (eds.), *Approaches to the Evolution of Language*, 202–221. Cambridge: Cambridge University Press.

Studdert-Kennedy, Michael G. 2012. The emergence of phonetic form. In Maggie Tallerman and Kathleen R. Gibson (eds.), *The Oxford Handbook of Language Evolution*, 417–422. Oxford: Oxford University Press.

Teixeira, Elizabeth R. and Barbara L. Davis. 2002. Early sound patterns in the speech of two Brazilian Portuguese speakers. *Language and Speech* 45: 179–204.

Thelen, Esther. 1981. Rhythmical behavior in infants: An ethological perspective. *Developmental Psychology* 17: 237–257.

Tyler, Ann A. and Teru E. Langsdale. 1996. Consonant-vowel interaction in early phonological development. *First Language* 16: 159–191.

van der Stelt, Jeanette M. and Florian J. Koopmans-van Beinum. 1986. Early stages in the development of speech movements. In Björn Lindblom and Rolf Zetterström (eds.), *Precursors of Early Speech*, 37–50. New York: Stockton Press.

van Hooff, Jan A.R.A.M. 1967. The facial displays of the catarrhine monkeys and apes. In Desmond Morris (ed.), *Primate Ethology*, 7–68. London: Weidenfeld and Nicolson.

Vihman, Marilyn. 1992. Early syllables and the construction of phonology. In Charles Ferguson, Lise Menn, and Carol Stoel-Gammon (eds.), *Phonological Development: Models, Research, Implications*, 393–422. Timonium, MD: York Press.

von Hapsburg, Deborah, Barbara L. Davis, and Peter F. MacNeilage. 2008. Frame dominance in infants with hearing loss. *Journal of Speech, Language, and Hearing Research* 51: 306–320.

Whalen, Douglas H., Sara Giulivi, Louis M. Goldstein, Hosung Nam, and Andrea G. Levitt. 2011. Response to MacNeilage and Davis, and Oller. *Language Learning and Development* 7: 243–249.

Zlatic, Larisa, Peter F. MacNeilage, Christine Matyear, and Barbara L. Davis. 1997. Babbling of twins in a bilingual (English/Serbian) environment. *Applied Psycholinguistics* 18: 453–469.

17 The Acquisition of Temporal Patterns

MELISSA A. REDFORD

17.1 Introduction[1]

Speech can be defined in terms of the signal, as a time-varying acoustic waveform. We associate speech segments with abrupt spectral or amplitude changes in that waveform. Some of the variation in the temporal aspects of segments can be ascribed to the inherent durations of different articulatory configurations. Other variation is contextually driven. For instance, the order in which segments are sequenced has consequences for coarticulation, which has consequences for segmental duration. The relative speed with which segment sequences are executed also interacts with coarticulation, and so with patterns of segmental duration. Still other variation is linguistically specified. For example, at the segmental level, different languages will use different patterns of inter-articulatory timing to execute the "same" sound (e.g., Spanish /p/ is more similar to English /b/ than English /p/). At the suprasegmental level, there is prosody, which has extensive effects on segmental durations through reduction and lengthening processes. The focus of this chapter is on the acquisition of temporal patterns that are defined by all of these influences. In keeping with the continuity hypothesis, we assume that the motor factors that constrain the shape of pre-speech vocalizations also influence the realization of temporal patterns in children's fluent speech. That said, we recognize that the transition from vocal play and imitation (pre-speech) to concept-driven communication (speech) represents an important discontinuity in development. We propose that this transition marks the development of a speech plan; a representation that guides speech action. Overall, our thesis is that the acquisition of temporal patterns reflects motor skill development; but some patterns are planned, in that they reflect remembered speech action (i.e., stored acoustically-linked articulatory schema), while others emerge during fluent speech from the practiced execution of serially ordered schemas (i.e., multi-word plans). Our thesis structures the content presented in this chapter, which is a review of research on early vocalizations, first words, and developmental changes in children's fluent speech.

17.2 Early sound patterns

The human drive to communicate is overwhelming. Several innate features scaffold the development of speech and, by extension, language acquisition. One of these features is the ability to act and react in an interpersonal context (Trevarthen 1979; Trevarthen and Aitken 2001). Relevant to speech are infants' different facial expressions and vocalizations (acting) combined with adjustments of these based on feedback from another (reacting). Human neonates will also initiate facial movement (e.g., tongue protrusion) with the expectation of a response from their interlocutor (Nagy and Molnar 2004). Another feature that scaffolds the development of communication is the innate ability and drive for infants to imitate facial expressions and movements (Maratos 1973; Meltzoff and Moore 1977). Importantly, the innate capacity for imitation is not restricted to the visual modality. Kuhl and Meltzoff (1996), for example, have shown that infants as young as 12 weeks of age shift their vocal productions in the direction of an auditory, speech-like stimulus. This ability suggests that an auditory-to-articulatory map, critical to the acquisition of target speech sounds, begins to be established early in development. Of course, attempting the production of target speech sounds also requires that they are represented in memory. Thus, a final feature necessary to scaffold speech acquisition is the innate ability to attend to and rapidly learn extended sound patterns (Saffran, Aslin, and Newport 1996). It is presumably this feature that allows the newborn infant to differentiate the rhythms of his mother's language from those of another language (Nazzi, Bertoncini, and Mehler 1998) in addition to enabling the older infant to recognize and extract recurrent sub-sequences (e.g., "words") from extended, fluent speech input (Saffran et al. 1996).

The innate drive to communicate coupled with remarkable imitative and perceptual learning abilities is presumably what pushes the infant to experiment with vocalization. By 2 months of age, infants make a variety of sounds. Most of these are reflexive and either communicate basic needs (i.e., cries) or have no discernible communicative function (i.e., grunts). A few sounds appear, however, to be speech-like. These deliberate vocalizations are the quasi-vowel-like sounds that define the so-called cooing stage of early vocal development (Stark 1980). From the point of view of production, the coo is significant in that it demonstrates the coupling of an articulatory posture with phonation. Specifically, the "coo" or "goo" quality of these sounds suggests a somewhat retracted tongue position. Unlike speech, the tongue is stationary during vocalization and only one dimension (height) of one articulator (tongue dorsum) is engaged to modify the sound across different repetitions (Oller 2000). It is also not clear that the modifications are deliberate in any way. That said, assuming the infant makes a connection between the modifications (based on somatosensory feedback) and the experience of different acoustics, this earliest stage of pre-speech vocalization will provide the foundation for the auditory-to-articulatory mapping that is required for spoken language acquisition.

By 4 months of age, infants' vocal experimentation expands to include a wider variety of sounds (Stark 1980). Some of these new sounds involve the lips as articulators (e.g., raspberries), but most involve changes in pitch or voice quality (e.g., squealing, song-like play, and whispers). Again, there is little evidence of supraglottal articulatory movement or of coordination between articulators in service of achieving a particular sound. There is, however, change over time within the course of a single vocalization. Specifically, infants will vary vocal fold tension and glottal closure during a vocal bout to achieve a variety of melodic patterns (Papoušek and Papoušek 1981; Hsu, Fogel, and Cooper 2000). They can also apparently exercise deliberate control over laryngeal movements, sufficient to imitate melodic contours that a parent produces (Papoušek and Papoušek 1989; Gratier and Devouche 2011). The continuous and deliberate changes in laryngeal posture to meet some acoustic target represents a significant step forward in the acquisition of speech. This stage also likely provides the foundation for the acquisition of language-specific intonation patterns.

At around 7 months of age, infants begin to coordinate phonation with opening and closing movements in the supraglottal vocal tract to produce speech-like sequences of proto-syllables; namely, regular alternations between consonant- and vowel-like sounds. This is the so-called canonical babbling stage (Stark 1980), the final pre-speech stage of vocal play, and a critical stage in the initial acquisition of articulatory timing and coordination (Davis and MacNeilage 1995; MacNeilage, Davis, and Matyear 1997; Oller 2000). Although babbling appears to replicate the basic phonological structure of spoken language, it is substantially different from speech in that the syllabic sequences are highly redundant (reduplicative); for example, *bababa*. An infant might also produce sequences with some variability in vowel height or consonantal manner changes (Davis and MacNeilage 1995), but do not expect to hear an infant produce a speech-like sequence that requires multiple place and manner changes (e.g., *bisogremu*).

The hallmark redundancy of babbling reflects immature control over the individual movements of the supraglottal articulators and over the coordination of their movements. The supraglottal articulator over which infants appear to first gain control is the jaw, as measured by trial-to-trial variability in movement. For example, Green, Moore, and Reilly (2002) showed that jaw movement during infant babbling and adult speech is similarly stable, but upper and lower lip movements are much more variable in infant babbling and in 2-year-old speech than in adult speech. Although there is no equivalent kinematic studies of tongue movement in infants and very young children, the assumption is that control over our most versatile speech articulator takes an especially long time to develop (Green and Nip 2011). What is also clear from kinematic studies is that coordinated supraglottal articulatory movement (i.e., of lip and jaw or of tongue and jaw) remains immature until early adolescence and continues to be refined through late adolescence (e.g., Walsh and Smith 2002; Cheng et al. 2007). This protracted development of speech motor skills has implications for the acquisition of temporal patterns at both the word and phrase level, as we will see below.

Early control over jaw movements coupled with the slow development of coordinated movement is consistent with the Frame/Content account of the sound patterns in babbling and first words (MacNeilage and Davis 1990; Davis and MacNeilage 1995; MacNeilage et al. 1997; see also MacNeilage, this volume, Chapter 16). In this account, the serial alternation of consonants and vowels in babbling and first words is driven mainly by jaw movement: an infant chooses a tongue position and then raises and lowers the jaw to achieve an alternation between vocal tract closure (consonant) and opening (vowel). When the tongue is advanced, the alternation yields the percept of an extended sequence of alternating front consonants and vowels (e.g., *dididi*); when retracted, a sequence of alternating back consonants and vowels (e.g., *gugugu*); and when in a neutral position, a sequence of labial consonants and central vowels (e.g., *bababa*). MacNeilage and Davis's work has shown that these co-occurrence patterns provide a good description of the perceived sound patterns of babbling. These same patterns also characterize early word productions (MacNeilage et al. 1997).

The similarities between patterns observed during the canonical babbling stage and first words strongly suggest that the motor skills gained during babbling provide the foundation for early attempts at producing words. These attempts in turn provide the foundation for the acquisition of fluent speech, and so for the acquisition of the complex temporal patterns that arise from multiple articulatory and linguistic influences.

17.3 First words

Typically developing children usually attempt their first words by 12 months of age. We acknowledge that the notion of "word" may strike some as a bit tricky. In particular, linguists will point out that word-like units in an agglutinative language, such as Finnish, are comprised of many individual units, each with a separate and unique meaning. In these languages, words are more akin to the English sentence than to the English word, which very often represents a correspondence between a sound pattern and an indivisible meaning. Yet, when we talk about first words in acquisition, the bias derived from our experience with English words is perfectly acceptable. Children – even Finnish children – do not attempt utterances that combine or layer individual meanings. Instead, they produce units that conventionalize a relationship between a sound pattern and a meaning, one that is recognized by the caregiver or others as communicative. So, for example, "uh-oh" counts as a word when learned and repeated in an appropriate context: a child drops a food item on the floor that he is supposed to eat, mom picks it up and hands it back to the child, child drops it again, and the game continues with "uh-oh"s all around. Vihman and colleagues (1985: 402–408), writing for linguists, carefully elaborate on this lay (and perhaps English-centric) understanding of a word. Some of their discussion is worth quoting because it also makes two central points more relevant to our interest in motor skill development; namely, that the sound patterns of first words are distant approximations of adult targets and that children utter these with intentionality. Vihman et al. (403) explain that:

> Before we credited a child with a spontaneous use of a word, we required that he or she produce a phonetic form that was a recognizable attempt at the adult word, given frequent child-reduction rules (cf. Ingram, 1974, 1979). In addition, the child had to use the word appropriately, with an apparently intentional meaning that was plausible in terms of the adult meaning or use of the word and commonly occurring child-semantic rules, such as over-extension of *doggy* to cats and other animals (cf. Clark, 1973).

With regard to "child-reduction rules," Vihman et al. (1985) are referring to processes like reduplication, fronting, and other simplifications. For example, a 12- to 14-month-old child is likely to produce "guk" for "duck" or "ditty" for "kitty," patterns that recall the redundancies and simplified syllable structure of babbling. Vihman and colleagues in fact carefully documented the sound pattern similarities between babbled utterances and first words. Their study corpus was obtained from a set of 10 children, whom they observed and recorded weekly over a 7-month period starting when the children were just 9 months of age and only babbling. Vihman and colleagues found that individual children had specific sound preferences in their babbled utterances. These same sound preferences then appeared in their first words. There were also consistent dependencies between first words and babbled utterances, when these overlapped in developmental time.

A more general way to think of the sound pattern similarities across the pre-speech and early speech period is in terms of continuity. Vihman et al. (1985) were among the first to articulate the *continuity hypothesis* for speech sound acquisition: that babbling and first words reflect different developmental stages in the continuous acquisition of the sound patterns of language. Their work also helped to define the current view that the same immature motor skills that shape babbling patterns also shape the patterns observed in first words (Vihman 1996; MacNeilage et al. 1997; Davis, MacNeilage, and Matyear 2005; Nip, Green, and Marx 2009). Reduplicated forms, for example, can be produced by exploiting the open-close cycle of the jaw, requiring minimal intra-utterance movement of the other supraglottal articulators (MacNeilage et al. 1997; Davis et al. 2005). Similarly, the simpler syllable structures of early words reduce the number of supraglottal articulatory movements within a single open-close jaw cycle. As such, these structures stand in contrast to the more complex forms that adults produce, which require repositioning lip, tongue, and/or velum movement and coordinating these with the downward or upward movements of the jaw (see, e.g., Redford 1999).

In spite of the evidence that the sound patterns in babbling and first words are both shaped by the still limited speech motor skills of the young child, it is important to recognize that Vihman et al.'s (1985) definition alludes also to a critical difference between babbling and first words. Whereas babbling is content free and a feature of relaxed play, first words have meaning and are uttered with communicative intent. This difference suggests that an important *discontinuity* in the acquisition of speech and language occurs around a child's first birthday: the transition from speech-like vocal behavior that has no specific goal to behavior that is goal directed.

Goal-directed behavior requires that the to-be-achieved targets are represented in memory with a sufficiently detailed motor plan to be realized again and again in the same way. How are these targets represented in first word production? McCune and Vihman (1987) hypothesized that children might initially rely on the "vocal-motor schemes" established during babbling to produce first words, which we will refer to as schemas. These schemas are the acoustic-articulatory memories of the child's preferred sound patterns; that is, those patterns that the child produced over and over again during babbling. McCune and Vihman hypothesized that a child might select one of their preferred schemas to attempt a proximal word target, thus associating the schema with meaning. Different stored schemas could be associated with different meanings by perceptually matching the stored forms to ambient perceptual targets. The schemas may then serve as initial word representations. We propose that this is what happens, and that the schemas are then continually modified over developmental time in order to more and more closely match the ambient target. The refinement process results in more sophisticated speech motor skills. At the same time, different moments in the development of these skills are reflected in the revised schemas that guide behavior.

Children's extension of acoustically linked articulatory schemas to word production requires the deliberate selection of a stored representation to match a specific perceptual target in order to convey a specific concept in a specific moment in time. In this way, children's first words mark the transition from unplanned speech-like motor behavior to behavior that is guided by a plan. According to McCune and Vihman (1987), the relevant representation is essentially an abstract articulatory specification for the production of a sound pattern associated with meaning. This kind of representation recalls the gestural scores of Articulatory Phonology (Browman and Goldstein 1992), which are also thought of both as speech motor plans and as lexical representations. Assuming continuity in development, we suggest that the acoustically linked articulatory schemas of early childhood are the lexical representations activated during speech planning and execution throughout life. Again, what changes over developmental time is the extent to which these schemas code actions that enable the speaker to produce acoustics that match perceptual representations built up from the ambient language input.

The acoustically linked articulatory schemas that we imagine as the phonological aspect of lexical representation clearly include temporal information because they include information about sequential articulatory action. Consider, for example, the near minimal pairs that a child might produce in attempting the words *powder*, [pʰaʊdɚ], and *spider*, [spaɪdɚ]. The child would likely simplify the cluster in *spider* so that the two words would be produced as *powder* and *pider*. Written like this, one might think that the child produces the same "p" in both words; but this is not the case. Consistent with the perceptual input, *pider* will be rendered with an unaspirated /p/, [paɪdɚ], and *powder* with an aspirated /p/, [pʰaʊdɚ] (see, e.g., Redford and Gildersleeve-Neumann 2007). That is, the representation that guides the child's speech action is a plan that the child has built, within the parameters of his or her motor abilities, to approximate a whole-word perceptual target. In order to achieve this best approximation, the plan must include detailed information about articulatory timing. In the present case, that would be information about the relative timing of voice onset after the release of stop closure. Given that laryngeal control is achieved relatively early and coupled with supraglottal articulatory action during the pre-speech phase of development, this is the kind of temporal information that the child could incorporate into an early lexical representation. In the next two sections, we consider the acquisition of temporal patterns that emerge above the level of a single word.

17.4 Multi-word utterances

In the previous section, we introduced the concept of a plan that guides speech action. Although this plan may initially be just a single schema, guiding the production of a single word, we hypothesize that the plan expands with mean length of utterance in development. Specifically, as children's linguistic and cognitive capacities grow, their default speech plan becomes a sequence of schemas, each associated with a single word. Multi-word speech plans are hypothesized to account for the fact that fluent speech is defined by a smooth temporal flow from one word to another, with strong junctures (e.g., pauses) occurring only to define or delimit conceptually coherent sequences of words. Although the structure and extent of the plan that governs continuous speech is an area of active research (see, e.g., Shattuck-Hufnagel, this volume, Chapter 19), we concur with the view in the adult literature that the plan extends over at least the length of one intonational phrase (Keating and Shattuck-Hufnagel 2002; Krivokapić 2007; Choe and Redford 2012). An intonational phrase is defined by a continuous intonational contour and is delimited by strong junctures, often pauses, at the beginning and end of its realization.

So, our proposal is that an intonational phrase defines the temporal extent of the speech plan in development, just as in adult speech. This proposal is supported by the characterization of early language production as holophrastic (see, e.g., Tomasello 2003: 36–40): it has long been observed that children at the one-word stage of language acquisition utter each word with a particular intonational contour and, often, the same word with different intonational contours. The intonationally inflected single word productions of early child language has led to the notion that, with every word, the child tries to convey – in some sense – the information of a sentence (= a holophrase). Whatever its relation to sentences, holophrastic speech is consistent with the view that speech action is guided by a plan defined by a coherent intonational contour. Clearly the number of words that are incorporated under this contour increases with developmental time. To wit, the child moves from the one-word stage to producing an average of two words per utterance, then three, then four, and so on (Brown 1973). The developmental increases in phrase length reflect a child's linguistic knowledge and increasing cognitive capacity, but also an ability to execute increasingly long and complex action sequences.

The remainder of this chapter addresses the acquisition of temporal patterns associated with fluent speech, that is, the execution of multi-word speech plans. More specifically, we review developmental changes in speech rate, and the acquisition of language rhythm. These two phenomena, rate and rhythm, together subsume all articulatory and linguistic influences on the complex temporal patterns of speech. The review of rate is meant to underscore the protracted development of speech motor skills, with increasing rate tied to advances in skill. The review of rhythm acquisition will be used to argue that some global temporal patterns emerge fortuitously with the development of speech motor skills while others are themselves the targets of acquisition.

17.4.1 Speech rate: Speaking versus articulation

Speech rate is measured as the number of syllables per second or words per minute that an individual produces. The clinical literature makes a distinction between speaking rate and articulation rate following Miller, Grosjean, and Lomanto (1984; see, e.g., Tsao and Weismer 1997; Hall, Amir, and Yairi 1999; Flipsen 2002; Tsao, Weismer, and Iqbal 2006): speaking rate includes pauses; articulation rate does not. Speaking rate is thought to reflect language planning processes; articulation rate, purer motor processes. However, the distinction is not totally clear cut. Speaking rate incorporates articulation rate, and articulation rate can be modified by the speaker to achieve different communicative goals.

Both speaking and articulation rate continue to increase throughout childhood and into early adolescence (Kowal, O'Connell, and Sabin 1975; Sabin et al. 1979; Smith, Sugarman, and Long 1983; Haselager, Slis, and Rietveld 1991; Walker et al. 1992; Hall et al. 1999; Flipsen 2002). Kowal and colleagues, who investigated speaking rate in 168 American-English-speaking children, present data from narrative tasks that indicate an increase in rate until 13 or 14 years old (8th grade), with the most substantial increases occurring between 5 and 8 years old (kindergarten through 2nd grade). For example, Kowal et al. (1975) report speaking rates of 2.15 syllables per second (SD=.75 syll/sec) in 5- and 6-year-old speech, 2.86 syllables per second (SD = .53 syll/sec) in 7- and 8-year-old speech, and 3.84 syllables per second (SD=.52 syll/sec) in 17- and 18-year-old speech. We have found similarly small increases in articulation rate over the same developmental period in a corpus of spontaneous narratives produced by 68 children and their parents. Our data indicate mean rates of 3.16 syllables per second (SD=0.43 syll/sec) in 5-year-old speech, 3.49 syllables per second (SD = 0.51 syll/sec) in 7-year-old speech, and 4.13 syllables per second (SD=0.67 syll/sec) in adult speech. Mean articulation rates in our sample of 6-year-old speech are 3.38 syllables per second (SD=0.57 syll/sec), not significantly different from either the 5-year-old or 7-year-old rates. The articulation rates we find in our corpus are consistent with the developmental changes in articulation rates reported for Dutch-speaking school age children (Haselager et al. 1991) and for American-English-speaking pre-school age children (Walker et al. 1992; Hall et al. 1999; Flipsen 2002).

The parallelism between developmental increases in speaking rate and articulation rate suggests a correlation between the two. Robb and colleagues (2003) have confirmed this correlation in pre-school Australian-English-speaking children, age 2–4 years. Sabin et al. (1979) also found that speaking and articulation rates were significantly correlated in their data. In spite of this, they advocated for treating the two quite differently. Citing Lenneberg (1967), Sabin et al. argued that "speech rate is limited by the 'cognitive aspects of language' rather than simply (by) the physical ability to articulate speech" (46), and pointed to task-dependent differences in pause frequency and duration. Like Goldman-Eisler (1968) before them, Sabin et al. found higher rates of pausing when speakers retold a previously read narrative than when they produced spontaneous narratives based on cartoon sequences. As in Goldman-Eisler (1968), the task-dependent differences were attributed to different demands on cognitive processing. The idea is that certain kinds of language (e.g., spontaneous narratives) require more time to formulate than others (e.g., retold narratives), and that this processing time is reflected in the amount of pausing that occurs. Sabin and colleagues suggested that developmentally related changes in pausing could be understood in the same way. In particular, their idea was that children spend more time formulating an utterance than adults.

Sabin et al.'s (1979) measure of pause frequency and duration was calculated as a function of language produced (i.e., per 100 syllables). Such a measure leaves open the possibility that pauses are more frequent and longer in younger children's speech compared to older children's speech, not because of differences in formulation time, but because younger children produce shorter utterances on average than older children. When pause frequency is assessed as the number of pauses per unit time and pause duration in terms of absolute duration, the developmental effect on pause frequency and duration disappears (Redford 2013): children pause for as much time as adults when speaking, even though they produce less speech over time than adults. That said, the effect of spontaneous telling versus retelling on pause frequency and duration is as robust in children as in adults (ibid.). Children and adults also pause for more time before longer utterances than before shorter utterances, and before discourse markers and other conceptual junctures than elsewhere (ibid.). Overall, these findings support the idea of an association between pausing and language formulation, but not the idea that children require more time to formulate language. Instead, the findings suggest that pause frequency is negatively correlated with developmental changes in mean utterance length.

Changes in mean utterance length are usually attributed to the acquisition of syntax, with longer utterances indicative of more complex syntactic structures (see, e.g., Brown 1973; Tomasello 2003). But utterance length is also likely to be conditioned by speech motor skills and non-language cognitive factors. With respect to speech motor skills, it is clear that multi-word utterances require the ability to effectively instantiate planned actions, one after another and without interruption. The difficulty of this task increases with the size of the plan (see, e.g., Maassen and Terband, this volume, Chapter 15), which means that immature motor skills could limit the size of the plan. With respect to non-language cognitive factors, it seems likely that working memory is involved in speech planning, which means that working memory capacity could also limit the size of the plan. One could even imagine an interaction between the "physical ability to articulate speech" and working memory capacity: slower articulation rates increase the amount of time that a plan must be held in working memory, which could lead either to the premature decay of elements not yet executed in the plan or to an accommodation in the planning process, such that fewer elements are prepared for execution at any one time. Although even a partial review of the working memory literature is outside the scope of this chapter, this novel hypothesis for developmentally related changes in mean length of utterance is consistent with theories that emphasize temporal constraints (e.g., processing speed and memorial decay) over task switching (i.e., executive control) to explain developmental changes in working memory capacity (cf. Towse, Hitch, and Hutton 1998; Gathercole et al. 2004). It also aligns well with the robust finding of a close relationship between speech rate and number of words recalled in studies of child and adult working memory (see Hitch and Towse 1995).

17.4.2 Articulation rate and speech motor skills

Rapid, stable, and efficient execution of complex movement sequences requires extensive practice, which continues to improve over many years (Schmidt and Lee 2005). It is likely for this reason that children's articulation rates are slower than adults' until early adolescence.

Every speech posture is achieved by the precise spatial-temporal coordination of articulators to achieve an acoustic target – a specific phone or segment – that is embedded in a sequence of such targets, whose order defines the sound/movement pattern of a particular word. Although motor constraints on coordination are particularly apparent in the production of early sound patterns and first words, kinematic evidence suggests that adult-like performance is not achieved until adolescence (e.g., Walsh and Smith 2002; Cheng et al. 2007). In the acoustic domain, the protracted acquisition of postural control is reflected in the slow decrease of segmental durations over developmental time (Smith 1978; Kent and Forner 1980; Lee, Potamianos, and Narayanan 1999). For example, Lee et al. (1999), who reported data from 56 adults and 436 children between the ages of 5 and 17 years, found that segmental durations are longer in younger children's speech compared with older children's speech, and that adult norms are not attained until age 12. Recall that Kowal et al.'s (1975) data indicated that adult speaking rates (pause inclusive) are not attained until age 13 or 14. Thus, the Lee et al. results are in strikingly parallel to the Kowal et al. findings, underscoring the important contribution of articulation to speaking rate.

The longer segmental durations of child speech compared to adult speech are frequently discussed in conjunction with temporal variability, which is also greater in child speech compared to adult speech (Tingley and Allen 1975; Kent and Forner 1980; Smith et al. 1983; Lee et al. 1999). Temporal variability refers to variation in the duration of a linguistic unit (segment, syllable, or word) across repetitions of the unit when other linguistic, cognitive, and social factors are held constant. Of course, variation in duration will be proportional to the mean, especially when measured in standard deviations. For this reason, Kent and Forner (1980) proposed that temporal variability may be larger in child speech than in adult speech only because mean durations are larger. Smith et al. (1983) and Smith (1992) referred to this proposal as the statistical artifact hypothesis, and argued against it.

In a first study, Smith et al. (1983) asked 5-, 7-, and 9-year-old children as well as a group of adults to repeat a sentence multiple times at a normal speech rate (i.e., their default rate) and at slow and fast rates. Phrase and syllable durations were found to vary systematically as a function of age and speech rate, but there was no interaction between these factors. Next, Smith et al. investigated temporal variability as a function of speech rate using a mean normalized measure of variation, namely, the coefficient of variation. The results were that temporal variability was higher in 5- and 7-year-old children's speech than in 9-year-old children's speech. Older children's speech was in turn more variable than adults' speech. Temporal variability was also higher at slower and faster speaking rates than at default speaking rates across speakers regardless of age, suggesting independence between absolute duration and variability. In a later study, Smith (1992) directly examined the relationship between duration and temporal variability in children's speech, aged 2 to 9 years. He found that in spite of overall decreases in both duration and variability with age, intra-subject correlations between the measures were relatively low. The combined results suggest that developmental decreases in temporal variability, though correlated with decreases in segmental duration, reflect the development of different motor skills than those required to achieve a specific linguistic target. The distinction may be one of coordinating independent articulators through time (i.e., articulatory timing) versus independently controlling individual articulators to achieve a target (i.e., articulatory coordination).

The explanation that different motor control processes underlie changes in variability and duration also makes sense of the finding that variability is higher at non-default speech rates (Smith et al. 1983). Whereas individual targets do not change with speech rate, voluntary manipulations of rate entail changes in the sequential timing of articulatory action, which also has consequences for articulatory coordination. For example, we know from studies of intra-speaker rate control in adults that fast speech is achieved primarily through vowel reduction, and especially through the temporal compression of stressed vowels (Gay 1978, 1981). These changes may or may not result from direct control. Direct control over rate implies that a clock-like mechanism, extrinsic to the representations underlying speech production, drives the rate with which each sound target embedded in a sequence is executed. Indirect control over rate implies that changes follow from the manipulation of parameters within the speech production system (see also Fowler 1980).

Whether control is direct or indirect, the child must acquire a strategy for executing speech movements more rapidly in time. The adult literature makes clear that at least two strategies are available (e.g., Ostry and Munhall 1985; Adams,

Weismer, and Kent 1993; Matthies et al. 2001). Some speakers decrease articulatory displacement (e.g., increase damping) at faster rates of speech, resulting in incomplete target attainment. Others increase movement velocity (e.g., increase stiffness), thereby maintaining targets even at fast rates of speech. Children presumably acquire the ability to manipulate both displacement and velocity, even if they choose to manipulate just one to effect changes in speech rate. Children also presumably gain more and more fine-grain temporal control over changes in articulatory displacement and velocity during the protracted development of speech motor skills, and use this control to meet communicative demands. It is this modulatory control, along with practice of basic articulatory timing patterns, that allows for the emergence of prosodically related temporal patterns.

17.4.3 *Prosodically related temporal patterns*

Insofar as the speech plan guides the production of multi-word utterances, it encodes both the order of words in a phrase as well as the articulatory timing information that is part of the phonological specification of the word. Whereas just this information may be sufficient to realize language-specific phonetic and phonemic patterns at different rates, it is not sufficient to account for prosodically related temporal patterns, which introduce variable lengthening and shortening (reduction) unequally across the phrase. To make this point explicitly, let us consider a few seconds of speech produced by a 5-year-old American-English-speaking boy. The speech was collected in a narrative task that children completed with their caregiver. This task used wordless picture books (Mercer Mayer's frog stories) to elicit fluent, structured spontaneous speech (see Redford 2013 for task details). The transcribed extracted speech sample shown below has been rendered in normal orthography and syllabified (txt tier). Slashes indicate pauses. The numbers below each syllable show approximate syllable and pause durations in milliseconds (dur tier). The various notations above the text show a trained analyst's judgment of weak ("x") and strong ("X") prominences at the level of the phrase and of weak (")") and strong ("))") prosodic phrase boundaries (pros tier; see Breen et al. 2012 for details regarding labeling).

pros:		x))			))?	X					X?))	)?
txt:	/	and	/	he	was	try-	ing		to	get	the	frog	but
dur:	1530	565		789	218	154	495	161	91	211	80	471	299
pros:		X?	)?				X?		)			x))	
txt:	he	could-	n't	be's	it	just	jumped	up	to	the	branch	/
dur:	279	175	178	271	131	349	366	198	196	83	323	1944
pros:	x))			)?	X		x		))				x
txt:	and	/	he	was	ver-	ry	mad	at	/	<teh>	/	so
dur:	566	1069	73	176	272	117	258	151	837	270	621	327

The snippet illustrates well the temporal variability of naturally produced speech in relation to the phrase-level coding of rhythm. Note, for example, that the stressed syllable of the main verb "try" is over three times as long as the auxiliary that precedes it, even though both syllables are comprised of just three phonemes each. Note also that some lexical items, such as "he" and "to," are realized with substantially different absolute durations in the same grammatical context, while another, "was," is realized with substantially similar durations in two different grammatical contexts. Finally, note the relatively long syllables in the vicinity of a boundary judgment, and that only these relatively longer syllables are heard as most prominent.

How are these prosodically related temporal patterns acquired? To answer this question, let us first introduce the notion of rhythm more completely.

17.4.4 What is speech rhythm?

Rhythm is best defined with respect to alternations in prominence (Liberman and Prince 1977; Hayes 1984), a perceptually-based linguistic construct (Terken and Hermes 2000; Arvaniti 2009). The acoustic-phonetic study of rhythm, which had been more or less abandoned after extensive arguments about the psychological reality of isochrony (equally timed stresses), was reinvigorated when Ramus, Nespor, and Mehler (1999) and Grabe and Low (Low, Grabe, and Nolan 2000; Grabe and Low 2002) introduced a few simple, interval-based measures that seemingly differentiated languages on the basis of their perceived rhythm pattern (see Cummins, this volume, Chapter 8 for a discussion of these measures and their historical context). The researchers who introduced these measures interpreted their results to support the so-called rhythm class hypothesis, which provided the original impetus for the isochrony debate. The rhythm class hypothesis states that languages belong to one of three rhythm classes: stress-timed, syllable-timed, and mora-timed. Stress-timed languages, such as English and Russian, have lexical stress (e.g., the verb, to *reCORD* versus the noun, *REcord*), syllable- and mora-timed languages do not. Mora-timed languages make extensive use of gemination (phonologically long consonants and vowels), stress- and syllable-timed languages do not.

Although dissatisfaction with the interval-based measures of rhythm abounds (see, e.g., Arvaniti 2009), the measures clearly capture something about speech rhythm, which is evident even in our snippet above. Duration is also the key correlate of lexical stress in English (Terken and Hermes 2000; Kochanski et al. 2005). For example, the unstressed vowel /ə/ in the verb "record" is likely to be shorter than the stressed vowel /ɛ/ in the noun "record" when produced by the same speaker under the same conditions. The stressed vowel in both the verb and noun is also likely to be significantly longer than the unstressed vowel in the same word. The duration contrast is due to the fullness of the stressed vowel and to the short, centralized quality of the vowel in the unstressed syllable. This quality of unstressed vowels in stress-timed languages like English and Russian has been referred to as "reduced." The phonological notion of reduction assumes that an underlying full vowel is transformed at some point during the production process, which is why it surfaces as a reduced version of itself. Whereas such a transformation may have occurred over historical time, we do not think that it occurs during production. In our view, the central quality and length of the unstressed vowel is available in the acoustic waveform and is thus the target of acquisition. As a target of acquisition, it becomes represented directly as part of the articulatory timing pattern of the word when children have gained the motor skills necessary to produce consecutive vowels of different lengths.

In a stress-timed language, lexically-based differences in vowel length co-occur with complex syllables structures. This means that stress-timed languages also allow for long and short sequences of consonants intervocalically. By contrast, syllable structures are simpler in syllable- and mora-timed languages. Thus, stress-timed languages are differentiated from syllable- and mora-timed languages by higher variability in vocalic and consonantal interval durations and relatively lower proportions of total vocalic to total consonantal interval durations.

17.4.5 Rhythm acquisition

A few studies have applied interval-based rhythm measures to child speech and language (Grabe, Post, and Watson 1999; Bunta and Ingram 2007; Sirsa and Redford 2011; Payne et al. 2012). These studies generally confirm an observation that Allen and Hawkins (1978) originally made; namely, that children's speech is more syllable-timed than adult speech. For example, Grabe et al. (1999) and Bunta and Ingram (2007) find that children acquire the distinctive rhythm pattern of a syllable-timed language earlier than they do a stress-timed language. Even so, Payne and colleagues showed that language-specific rhythm differences can be detected in early child speech. They also showed that, though more vocalic than adult speech, children's speech is also not exactly syllable-timed.

Payne et al. (2012) used several interval-based rhythm measures to compare the rhythm patterns produced by 27 children acquiring either English, Catalan, or Spanish in a cross-sectional study of 2-, 4-, and 6-year-old speech. For comparative purposes, they also analyzed the speech produced by the children's parents. The findings for adult speech were that English and Spanish were well distinguished by all measures: English vocalic and consonantal interval durations were more variable than in Spanish, and the proportion of vowel to total duration was lower in English than in Spanish. Catalan tended to cluster with Spanish, but was more similar to English on certain measures. The findings for child speech mirrored the findings for adult speech and the cross-linguistic differences were evident by age 2. Nonetheless, children's speech did differ from adult speech along a number of dimensions across all three languages. In keeping with the idea that child speech is more syllable-timed than adult speech, the proportion of vowel to total duration was higher and variability in vowel durations was lower in child compared to adult speech, though this difference disappeared by age 6. Children's speech was also characterized by more variability in consonant durations than adult speech, and this difference persisted even at age 6.

In discussing their findings, Payne et al. (2012) suggested that persistent differences in the rhythms of child and adult speech might reflect an interaction between developing phonological and phonetic abilities. In particular, they suggested that the finding of higher variability in consonant durations might emerge from simplifications of syllable structure as well as from immature postural control and sequencing abilities. Insofar as cluster simplification and other processes that change syllable shape also have their origins in immature speech skills, we might conclude that speech rhythm is influenced by many of the same factors that account for slower speech rates in children compared to adults.

Whereas Payne et al. (2012) concentrate on the finding of cross-linguistic differences in the speech rhythms of very young children, Grabe et al. (1999) concentrate on the differential rate at which different language rhythms are acquired. Grabe et al. investigated speech of 6 mother–child dyads. Half of the dyads were English speakers and half were French speakers. Children in both groups were 4 years of age. Using a variety of temporal measures, including the interval-based measure of sequential vowel durations (PVI-V), Grabe et al. found that the French-speaking children had acquired the syllable-timed pattern of their language, but the English-speaking children had not acquired the stress-timed pattern of their language. A study by Bunta and Ingram (2007), though focused on the acquisition of rhythm by Spanish-English bilinguals, also indicated that Spanish monolinguals acquire the syllable-timed rhythm pattern of their language prior to English monolinguals. In particular, the rhythm patterns of Spanish-speaking children did not differ from Spanish-speaking adults at 4½ years of age, but those of English-speaking children did differ from English-speaking adults at this age. We found similar differences in the rhythm patterns of 5- and 8-year-old monolingual English speakers (Sirsa and Redford 2011). Younger children were found to have lower normalized vocalic PVI scores on average than older children.

Overall, studies on the acquisition of rhythm suggest that syllable-timed patterns are acquired before stress-timed patterns, and that the English stress-timed pattern may not be fully acquired until age 6 or 7. Whereas it is likely that the vocalic nature of early child speech can be accounted for largely in terms of simplified syllable structures, these simplifications originate from immature motor skills, codified by the stored acoustically-linked articulatory schemas that guide speech action. Similarly, the higher variability in consonant durations and lower nPVI-V scores in 5-year-old speech are also likely due to immature motor skills, albeit at the level of on-line articulatory timing control.

17.4.6 Rhythmic groupings and speech motor skills

One might expect that the protracted acquisition of stress-timing can be explained by the delayed acquisition of lexical stress. However, several acoustic-phonetic studies on the implementation of lexical stress in English suggest instead that stress is acquired fairly early (Pollock, Brammer and Hageman 1993; Kehoe, Stoel-Gamon, and Buder 1995; Schwartz et al. 1996). For example, Kehoe et al. (1993) found no measurable differences in the acoustic marking of stress in familiar words produced by 2-year-old children (+/− 6 months) and adults. Pollock et al. (1993) also found that 2-year-old children use duration to distinguish stressed and unstressed syllables, but the other correlates of lexical stress, fundamental frequency and intensity, are not used appropriately until age 3. Still, if the duration patterns associated with lexical stress are acquired so early, then the protracted acquisition of a stress-timed rhythm, as measured by changes in the sequential variation in vowel durations, is unlikely to be explained in terms of the acquisition of lexical stress.

It turns out that in spite of the early marking of lexical stress, 2-year-olds and adults do not produce unstressed syllables in the same way. Kehoe and colleagues found that unstressed syllables were 55% longer in children's speech than in adults' speech, even though the relative difference between stressed and unstressed syllable durations was not different. Schwartz et al. (1996) found that even the relative difference of stressed and unstressed syllables within a word was smaller in 2-year-old than adult speech, and attributed this smaller difference to relatively longer unstressed syllables in child speech compared to adult speech. Pollock et al. (1993) found that unstressed syllable durations decreased over developmental time, but stressed syllable durations stayed the same. Relatedly, kinematic data indicates that even older children (4+ years of age) are more variable in their production of unstressed syllables compared to stressed syllables (Goffman 1999), suggesting that reducing unstressed syllables may require more advanced motor skills than producing stressed syllables. Ballard et al. (2012) have recently advanced a similar argument based on acoustic evidence, showing that 7-year-olds continue to deviate from adults in their realization of weak-strong syllable sequences. The suggestion that shorter durations are especially hard for children to realize is consistent with the notion that efficient and reduced movements are characteristic of expert motor control (e.g., Green et al. 2000, 2002), and with data showing that young children make relatively larger amplitude speech movements than adults (Riely and Smith 2003).

Unstressed syllable (vowel) reduction is also a feature of phrasal stress patterns. Function words like "a" and "the" in English, when cliticized (attached) to a following noun, are particularly reduced. This is evident even from the short snippet of speech presented in section 17.4.3 above; there, "the" is less than one-third the length of the following monosyllabic nouns it determines. The perceptual effect of cliticization is the creation of a so-called clitic group or prosodic word, such that a phrase like "The boy walked the dog" with five orthographic words is produced with just three prosodic words (i.e., [the boy] [walked] [the dog]). Allen and Hawkins (1978) may have been the first to observe that young English-speaking children do not reduce function words to the same extent as adults. Further, they suggested that it was the less reduced function words of child speech that contributed to the percept that children's spoken English is more syllable-timed than adult English. Allen and Hawkins's evidence was largely transcription-based, but Goffman (2004) provided some acoustic and kinematic evidence for the idea. Goffman's interest was in whether or not the morphosyntactic status of the unstressed syllable affected its production. Accordingly, she compared lexically unstressed syllables to function word syllables in child and adult speech. She found that adults reduce unstressed syllables in a function+content word phrase (e.g., "a *bab*") more than they do in a disyllabic word (e.g., "*abab*"). Children, between 4 and 7 years of age, did not differentiate between unstressed syllables as a function of morphosyntactic status.

Further evidence for the idea that the slow acquisition of function word vowel reduction provides the key to explaining the late acquisition of English rhythm comes from our study of rhythm acquisition in 5- and 8-year-olds (Sirsa and Redford 2011). As previously noted, we found that, on average, 5-year-old speech had lower nPVI-V scores than 8-year-old speech. In order to understand why this might be, we took a number of more specific temporal measures on the children's speech. These included a measure of the relative duration of lexically stressed and unstressed vowels, a measure of the relative duration of function and content word vowels in determiner noun phrases with monosyllabic nouns, and a measure of phrase-final lengthening. We then used these measures to predict nPVI-V scores and found that only the measure of function-to-content word vowel duration accounted for a significant amount of the variance: higher function-to-content word vowel duration ratios (i.e., less reduced function word vowels) predicted lower nPVI-V scores. The relationship between function word vowel reduction in determiner noun phrases and adult-like rhythm production was very strong; it accounted for 46% of the variance in nPVI-V scores.

In sum, unstressed vowel reduction is acquired slowly, perhaps because smaller, faster speech movements are a feature of motor expertise, which children only develop over a long period of time. The unstressed vowels of function words are even more reduced than the unstressed vowels of di- or multisyllabic content words in adult speech. This could be why adult-like function word vowel reduction is acquired especially late and contributes the most to explaining the immature English rhythm patterns of school-age children, as measured by the variability in sequential vowel durations.

17.4.7 *Temporal modulation in service of meaning*

If unstressed vowel reduction is tied to the development of speech motor skills, as we argue above, then the prosodic words that result from the reduction of function words adjacent to content words are not themselves the target of acquisition, but instead emerge fortuitously with faster, more fluent speech. That said, the semantically light nature of the specific items that are reduced suggests that motor skills alone cannot provide a complete picture of prosodic word acquisition. Before concluding this chapter, we must underscore that meaning also matters to the acquisition of temporal patterns. For example, children must learn that only certain syllables within a word and certain lexical items within a phrase can be reduced without sacrificing speech intelligibility. The role of meaning in the acquisition of temporal patterns is even more evident when we consider lengthening processes.

In English and many other languages, lengthening is one of several acoustic cues used to mark focus (a grammatical category related to information structure) and utterance-final boundaries. These types of lengthening are known as accentual lengthening and phrase-final lengthening, respectively. The domain of accentual lengthening in English is primarily the stressed syllable (Turk and White 1999), but lengthening effects are also observed at the prosodic word level

(Turk and Sawusch 1997; Turk and White 1999). In the snippet presented in section 17.4.3, accentual lengthening occurred on the words "trying," "jumped," and "very." Note that the length of the stressed syllables in these words was especially long relative to the surrounding syllables. The domain of phrase-final lengthening may be somewhat less extensive: lengthening effects are especially notable on ultimate syllables of the phrase, whether these are lexically stressed or not (Turk and Shattuck-Hufnagel 2007). Lengthening effects can also extend to non-final syllables in phrase-final multisyllabic words, but only if these are lexically stressed (ibid.).

Even though there is some evidence that pre-speech vocalizations replicate accentual and phrase-final lengthening patterns of the language (de Boysson-Bardies, Sagart, and Durand 1984; Robb and Saxman 1990), it is equally clear that their semantic-pragmatic functions must also be acquired. Acquiring these functions necessitates coordinating the modulation of F0 with patterns of lengthening. Although there is very little acoustic-phonetic study on the acquisition of focus marking, some careful acoustically-based transcription work by Ajou Chen (Chen and Fikkert 2007; Chen 2011a) suggests that, at a minimum, the intonational marking of focus is not fully developed in Dutch-speaking children until after age 8. Chen (2011b) argues that younger children, aged 2 and 3, have trouble just with the phonetic realization of the complex tonal patterns associated with focus marking; and that older children struggle with the form-to-function mapping, confusing topic and focus marking. As for phrase-final lengthening, there is some indication that it may originate in physiological constraints (Robb and Saxman 1990), but Snow (1994) has shown that its linguistic aspect is not fully acquired until three months after the onset of combinatorial speech; a finding he then uses to highlight the challenges inherent to coordinating supraglottal articulatory timing and F0 patterns.

In addition to marking focus and utterance boundaries, lengthening is also used to indicate utterance-internal junctures. Speakers' implicit knowledge of this function is demonstrated when they are asked to disambiguate a potentially ambiguous sequence. For example, the most natural way to disambiguate the scope of "old" in the sentence "The old men and women stayed home" is to lengthen "men" relative to "and women," assuming the speaker wants to indicate that the scope of "old" is restricted to "men" (Lehiste 1973). Lengthening is also used to mark ambiguous word boundaries. For example, Christie (1977) showed that listeners use consonantal duration to distinguish between minimal pair sentences such as "help us *n*ail" versus "help a *sn*ail." Redford and Gildersleeve-Neumann (2007) found that pre-school children have trouble instantiating this specific cue to word boundaries. We compared the production of /s/+sonorant and /s/+stop offset-onset and onset cluster sequences (*this nail* versus *bitty snail*; *nice top* versus *I stop*) in 20 pre-school children, aged 3 and 4 years, with their parents' production. Whereas all children produced the primary cue to juncture in the /s/+stop sequences – the presence versus absence of stop aspiration – even 4-year-olds could not reliably distinguish singleton sonorant onsets from /s/+sonorant clusters in two-word phrases. This differential acquisition of the juncture cues is in line with the distinction in this chapter between articulatory timing patterns at the level of the word versus those at the level of the phrase: the allophonic cue to juncture (+/− aspiration) is a pattern that is acquired and represented with the lexical items; the lengthening pattern, by contrast, requires focal control over lengthening at a boundary.

In sum, certain aspects of rhythm may emerge with the extensive practice required to efficiently execute extended movement sequences (i.e., multi-word plans) and from the development of control over the parameters that affect movement amplitude and velocity. However, when phrase-level temporal patterns are tied to meaning, they become – like words – the targets of acquisition. The challenges inherent to the acquisition of meaningful, phrase-level temporal patterns lies first in their coordination with separately generated intonational patterns, and second in their context-dependency. Unlike the patterns that guide word production, phrase-level temporal patterns cannot be learned and stored directly. Instead, they must be abstracted based on an understanding of the semantic-pragmatic context and generated based on a plan that marks out specific stretches as requiring a change in the parameters affecting movement amplitude and velocity, and thus time.

17.5 Summary

The present chapter examined the role that motoric factors play in the acquisition of the complex temporal patterns that characterize spoken language. We began by reviewing the motoric constraints that so clearly influence pre-speech vocalizations and early word production. In keeping with the continuity hypothesis, we proposed that the motor constraints that are evident in pre-speech also influence the later acquisition of temporal patterns at every level of linguistic analysis. However, an important discontinuity between pre-speech and speech was also noted; namely, the transition from vocal play and imitation to concept-driven communication. This transition marks the development of a speech plan, which guides speech action and represents what the child has learned about the structure of language. The temporal patterns that are produced from the first word stage onward thus reflect an interaction between motor skill development and the representation of language. This interaction presents a significant challenge, frequently overlooked by those who study speech and language acquisition: the challenge of distinguishing variance in performance due to immature motor skills from variance due to immature linguistic representations. Our review of rate and rhythm was motivated by this challenge and by the hypothesis that the acquisition of linguistic representation interacts with motor skill development. For example, we suggested that increases in the size of the speech plan may depend in part on developmental changes in the ability to rapidly attain sequences of different articulatory postures. We also argued that rhythm, though a linguistic construct, is not phonology-driven. Instead, we proposed that practice with different articulatory timing routines and the development of control over increasing movement efficiency is manifested as age-related differences in the realizations of stressed and unstressed syllables at the word and phrase levels. Increasing movement efficiencies over developmental time results ultimately in the emergence of prosodic words. Finally, we acknowledged a critical role for meaning in the acquisition of temporal patterns. In addition to encoding inter- and intra-articulatory timing at the level of the (stored) word, the speech plan must specially mark stretches in the plan for focal changes in timing so that context-dependent temporal patterns are appropriately realized.

NOTE

1   This work was supported by Award Number R01HD061458 from the Eunice Kennedy Shriver National Institute of Child Health and Human Development (NICHD). The content is solely my responsibility and does not necessarily reflect the views of NICHD. I am grateful to Zahra Foroughifar, Jeffery Kallay, and Paul Olejarczuk for reading and commenting on an early version of the chapter.

REFERENCES

Adams, Scott G., Gary Weismer, and Raymond D. Kent. 1993. Speaking rate and speech movement velocity profiles. *Journal of Speech and Hearing Research* 36: 41–54.

Allen, George D. and Sarah Hawkins. 1978. The development of phonological rhythm. In Alan Bell and Joan Bybee Hooper (eds.), *Syllables and Segments*, 173–185. Amsterdam: North-Holland Publishing.

Arvaniti, Amalia. 2009. Rhythm, timing, and the timing of rhythm. *Phonetica* 66: 46–63.

Ballard, Kirrie J., Danica Djaja, Joanne Arciuli, Deborah G.H. James, and Jan van Doorn. 2012. Developmental trajectory for production of prosody: Lexical stress contrastivity in children ages 3 to 7 years and in adults. *Journal of Speech, Language, and Hearing Research* 55: 1822–1835.

Breen, Mara, Laura C. Dilley, John Kraemer, and Edward Gibson. 2012. Inter-transcriber agreement for two systems of prosodic annotation: ToBI (Tones and Break Indices) and RaP (Rhythm and Pitch). *Corpus Linguistics and Linguistic Theory* 8: 277–312.

Browman, Catherine P. and Louis M. Goldstein. 1992. Articulatory Phonology: An overview. *Phonetica* 49: 155–180.

Brown, Roger. 1973. *A First Language: The Early Stages*. Cambridge, MA: Harvard University Press.

Bunta, Ferenc and David Ingram. 2007. The acquisition of speech rhythm by bilingual Spanish- and English-speaking 4- and 5-year-old children. *Journal of Speech, Language, and Hearing Research* 50: 999–1014.

Chen, Ajou. 2011a. Tuning information packaging: Intonational realization of topic and focus in child Dutch. *Journal of Child Language* 38: 1055–1083.

Chen, Ajou. 2011b. The developmental path to phonological focus-marking in Dutch. In S. Frota, E. Gorka, and P. Prieto (eds.), *Prosodic Categories: Production, Perception and Comprehension*, 93–109. Dordrecht: Springer.

Chen, Ajou and Fikkert, Paula. 2007. Intonation of early two-word utterances in Dutch. In J. Trouvain and W.J. Barry (eds.), *Proceedings of the 16th International Congress of Phonetic Sciences (ICPhS 2007)*, 315–320.

Cheng, Hei Yan, Bruce E. Murdoch, Justine V. Goozée, and Dion Scott. 2007. Electropalatographic assessment of tongue-to-palate contact patterns and variability in children, adolescents, and adults. *Journal of Speech, Language, and Hearing Research* 50: 375–392.

Choe, Wook Kyung and Melissa A. Redford. 2012. The distribution of speech errors in multi-word prosodic units. *Laboratory Phonology* 3: 5–26.

Christie, William M. 1977. Some multiple cues for juncture in English. *General Linguistics* 17: 212–222.

Clark, Eve. 1973. What's in a word? On the child's acquisition of semantics in his first language. In T.E. Moore (ed.), *Cognitive Development and the Acquisition of Language*, 65–110. New York: Academic Press.

Davis, Barbara L. and Peter F. MacNeilage. 1995. The articulatory basis of babbling. *Journal of Speech, Language, and Hearing Research* 38: 1199–1211.

Davis, Barbara L., Peter F. MacNeilage, and Christine L. Matyear. 2005. Acquisition of serial complexity in speech production: A comparison of phonetic and phonological approaches to first word production. *Phonetica* 59: 75–107.

de Boysson-Bardies, Bénédicte, Laurent Sagart, and Catherine Durand. 1984. Discernible differences in the babbling of infants according to target language. *Journal of Child Language* 11: 1–15.

Flipsen, Peter. 2002. Articulation rate and speech-sound normalization failure. *Journal of Speech, Language, and Hearing Research* 46: 724–737.

Fowler, Carol. 1980. Coarticulation and theories of extrinsic timing. *Journal of Phonetics* 8: 113–133.

Gathercole, Susan E., Susan J. Pickering, Benjamin Ambridge, and Hannah Wearing. 2004. The structure of working memory from 4 to 15 years of age. *Developmental Psychology* 40: 177–190.

Gay, Thomas. 1978. Effect of speaking rate on vowel formant movements. *Journal of the Acoustical Society of America* 63: 223–230.

Gay, Thomas. 1981. Mechanisms in the control of speech rate. *Phonetica* 38: 148–158.

Goffman, Lisa. 1999. Prosodic influences on speech production in children with specific language impairment and speech deficits. *Journal of Speech, Language, and Hearing Research* 42: 1499–1517.

Goffman, Lisa. 2004. Kinematic differentiation of prosodic categories in normal and disordered language development. *Journal of Speech, Language, and Hearing Research* 47: 1088–1102.

Goldman-Eisler, Freida. 1968. *Psycholinguistics: Experiments in Spontaneous Speech*. London: Academic Press.

Grabe, Esther and Ee Ling Low. 2002. Durational variability in speech and the rhythm class hypothesis. *Papers in Laboratory Phonology* 7: 515–546.

Grabe, Esther and Paul Warren. 1995. Stress shift: Do speakers do it or do listeners hear it? *Papers in Laboratory Phonology* 4: 95–110.

Grabe, Esther, Brechtje Post, and Ian Watson. 1999. The acquisition of rhythmic patterns in English and French. In *Proceedings of the 14th International Congress of Phonetic Sciences, (ICPhS-99)*, 1201–1204.

Gratier, Maya and Emmanuel Devouche. 2011. Imitation and repetition of prosodic contour in vocal interaction at 3 months. *Developmental Psychology* 47: 67–76.

Green, Jordan R. and Ignatius S.B. Nip. 2010. Some organization principles in early speech development. In B. Maassen and P. Van Lieshout (eds.), *Speech Motor Control: New Developments in Basic and Applied Research*, 171–188. Oxford: Oxford University Press.

Green, Jordan R., Christopher A. Moore, and Kevin J. Reilly. 2002. The sequential development of lip and jaw control for speech. *Journal of Speech, Language, and Hearing Research* 45: 66–79.

Green, Jordan R., Christopher A. Moore, Masahiko Higashikawa, and Roger W. Steeve. 2000. The physiological development of speech motor control: Lip and jaw coordination. *Journal of Speech, Language, and Hearing Research* 43: 239–255.

Hall, Kelly D., Ofer Amir, and Ehud Yairi. 1999. A longitudinal investigation of speaking rate in preschool children who stutter. *Journal of Speech, Language, and Hearing Research* 42: 1367–1377.

Haselager, G.J.T., I.H. Slis, and A.C.M. Rietveld. 1991. An alternative method of studying development of speech rate. *Clinical Linguistics and Phonetics* 5: 53–63.

Hayes, Bruce. 1984. The phonology of rhythm in English. *Linguistic Inquiry* 15: 33–74.

Hitch, Graham J. and John N. Towse. 1995. Working memory: What develops. In F.E. Weinert and W. Schneider (eds.), *Memory Performance and Competencies: Issues in Growth and Development*, 3–21. Mahwah, NJ: Lawrence Erlbaum Associates.

Hsu, Hui-Chin, Alan Fogel, and Rebecca B. Cooper. 2000. Infant vocal development during the first 6 months: Speech quality and melodic complexity. *Infant and Child Development* 9: 1–16.

Ingram, David. 1974. Phonological rules in young children. *Journal of Child Language* 1: 49–64.

Ingram, David. 1979. Phonological patterns in the speech of young children. In P. Fletcher and M. Garman (eds.), *Language Acquisition*, 133–148. Cambridge: Cambridge University Press.

Keating, Patricia and Stefanie Shattuck-Hufnagel. 2002. A prosodic view of word form encoding for speech production. *UCLA Working Papers in Phonetics* 101: 112–156.

Kehoe, M., Carol Stoel-Gammon, and Eugene H. Buder. 1995. Acoustic correlates of stress in young children's speech. *Journal of Speech and Hearing Research* 38: 338–350.

Kent, Raymond D. and L.L. Forner. 1980. Speech segment durations in sentence recitations by children and adults. *Journal of Phonetics* 8: 157–168.

Kochanski, Greg, Esther Grabe, John Coleman, and Burton Rosner. 2005. Loudness predicts prominence: Fundamental frequency lends little. *Journal of the Acoustical Society of America* 118: 1038–1054.

Kowal, Sabine, Daniel C. O'Connell, and Edward J. Sabin. 1975. Development of temporal patterning and vocal hesitations in spontaneous narratives. *Journal of Psycholinguistic Research* 4: 195–207.

Krivokapić, Jelena. 2007. Prosodic planning: Effects of phrasal length and complexity on pause duration. *Journal of Phonetics* 35: 162–179.

Kuhl, Patricia K. and Andrew N. Meltzoff. 1996. Infant vocalizations in response to speech: Vocal imitation and developmental change. *Journal of the Acoustical Society of America* 100: 2425–2438.

Lee, Sungbok, Alexandros Potamianos, and Shrikanth Narayanan. 1999. Acoustics of children's speech: Developmental changes of temporal and spectral parameters. *Journal of the Acoustical Society of America* 105: 1455–1468.

Lehiste, Ilse. 1973. Rhythmic units and syntactic units in production and perception. *Journal of the Acoustical Society of America* 54: 1228–1234.

Lenneberg, Eric H. 1967. *Biological Foundations of Language*. New York: John Wiley & Sons, Inc.

Liberman, Mark and Allen Prince. 1977. On stress and linguistic rhythm. *Linguistic Inquiry* 8: 249–336.

Low, Ee Ling, Esther Grabe, and Francis Nolan. 2000. Quantitative characterisations of speech rhythm: "Syllable-timing" in Singapore English. *Language and Speech* 43: 377–401.

MacNeilage, Peter F. and Barbara L. Davis. 1990. Acquisition of speech production: Frames, then content. In Marc Jeannerod (ed.), *Attention and Performance XIII: Motor Representation and Control*, 453–476. Hillsdale, NJ: Lawrence Erlbaum Associates.

MacNeilage, Peter F., Barbara L. Davis, and Christine L. Matyear. 1997. Babbling and first words: Phonetic similarities and differences. *Speech Communication* 22: 269–277.

Maratos, Olga. 1973. The origin and development of imitation in the first six month of life. PhD thesis, University of Geneva.

Matthies, Melanie, Pascal Perrier, Joseph S. Perkell, and Majid Zandipour. 2001. Variation in anticipatory coarticulation with changes in clarity and rate. *Journal of Speech, Language, and Hearing Research* 44: 340–353.

McCune, Lorraine and Marilyn Vihman. 1987. Vocal motor schemes. *Papers and Reports on Child Language Development* 26: 72–79.

Meltzoff, Andrew N. and M. Keith Moore. 1977. Imitation of facial and manual gestures by human neonates. *Science* 198(4312): 75–78.

Miller, Joanne L., François Grosjean, and Concetta Lomanto. 1984. Articulation rate and its variability in spontaneous speech: A reanalysis and some implications. *Phonetica* 41: 215–225.

Nagy, Emese and Peter Molnar. 2004. Homo imitans or homo provocans? Human imprinting model of neonatal imitation. *Infant Behavior and Development* 27: 54–63.

Nazzi, Thierry, Josiane Bertoncini, and Jacques Mehler. 1998. Language discrimination by newborns: Toward an understanding of the role of rhythm. *Journal of Experimental Psychology: Human Perception and Performance* 24: 756–766.

Nip, Ignatius S.B., Jordan R. Green, and David B. Marx. 2009. Early speech motor development: Cognitive and linguistic considerations. *Journal of Communication Disorders* 42: 286–298.

Oller, D. Kimbrough. 2000. *The Emergence of the Speech Capacity*. Mahwah, NJ: Lawrence Erlbaum Associates.

Ostry, David J. and Kevin G. Munhall. 1985. Control of rate and duration of speech movements. *Journal of the Acoustical Society of America* 77: 640–648.

Papoušek, Mechthild and Hanuš Papoušek. 1981. Musical elements in the infant's vocalization: Their significance for communication, cognition, and creativity. In L.P. Lipsitt and C.K. Rovee-Collier (eds.), *Advances in Infancy Research*, vol. 1, 163–224. Norwood, NJ: Ablex.

Papoušek, Mechthild and Hanuš Papoušek. 1989. Forms and functions of vocal matching in interactions between mothers and their pre-canonical infants. *First Language* 9: 137–158.

Payne, Elinor, Brechtje Post, Luïsa Astruc, Pilar Prieto, and Maria del Mar Vanrell. 2012. Measuring child rhythm. *Language and Speech* 55: 203–229.

Pollock, Karen E., Diane M. Brammer, and Carlin F. Hageman. 1993. An acoustic analysis of young children's productions of word stress. *Journal of Phonetics* 21: 183–203.

Ramus, Franck, Marina Nespor, and Jacque Mehler. 1999. Correlates of linguistic rhythm in the speech signal. *Cognition* 73: 265–292.

Redford, Melissa A. 1999. An articulatory basis for the syllable. PhD dissertation, University of Texas.

Redford, Melissa A. 2013. A comparative analysis of pausing in child and adult storytelling. *Applied Psycholinguistics* 34: 569–589.

Redford, Melissa A. and Christina E. Gildersleeve-Neumann. 2007. The acquisition of two phonetic cues to word boundaries. *Journal of Child Language* 34: 815–843.

Riely, Rachel R. and Anne Smith. 2003. Speech movements do not scale by orofacial structure size. *Journal of Applied Physiology* 94: 2119–2126.

Robb, Michael P. and John H. Saxman. 1990. Syllable durations of pre-word and early word vocalizations. *Journal of Speech and Hearing Research* 33: 583–593.

Robb, Michael, Harvey Gilbert, Viki Reed, and Amanda Bisson. 2003. A preliminary study of speech rates in young Australian English-speaking children. *Contemporary Issues in Communication Science and Disorders* 30: 84–91.

Sabin, Edward J., Edward J. Clemmer, Daniel O'Connell, and Sabine Kowal. 1979. A pausological approach to speech development. In A. Siegman, and S. Feldstein (eds.), *Of Speech and Time: Temporal Speech Patterns in Interpersonal Contexts*, 35–55. Hillsdale, NJ: Lawrence Erlbaum Associates.

Saffran, Jenny R., Richard N. Aslin, and Elissa L. Newport. 1996. Statistical learning by 8-month-old infants. *Science* 274: 1926–1928.

Schmidt, Richard A. and Timothy D. Lee. 2005. *Motor Control and Learning: A Behavioral Emphasis*, 5th edn. Champaign, IL: Human Kinetics.

Schwartz, Richard G., Kakia Petinou, Lisa Goffman, Gerri Lazowski, and Christine Cartusciello. 1996. Young children's production of syllable stress: An acoustic analysis. *Journal of the Acoustical Society of America* 99: 3192–3200.

Sirsa, Hema and Melissa A. Redford. 2011. Towards understanding the protracted acquisition of English rhythm. In W.-S. Lee and E. Zee (eds.), *Proceedings from the 17th International Congress of Phonetic Sciences, (ICPhS-11)*, 1862–1865.

Smith, Bruce. 1978. Temporal aspects of English speech production: A developmental perspective. *Journal of Phonetics* 6: 37–67.

Smith, Bruce L. 1992. Relationships between duration and temporal variability in children's speech. *Journal of the Acoustical Society of America* 91: 2165–2174.

Smith, Bruce L., Michael D. Sugarman, and Steven H. Long. 1983. Experimental manipulation of speaking rate for studying temporal variability in children's speech. *Journal of the Acoustical Society of America* 74: 744–749.

Snow, David. 1994. Phrase-final syllable lengthening and intonation in early child speech. *Journal of Speech and Hearing Research* 37: 831–840.

Stark, Rachel E. 1980. Stages of speech development in the first year of life. In G. Yeni-Komshian, J. Kavanagh, and C. Ferguson (eds.), *Child Phonology*, vol. 1: *Production*, 73–90. New York: Academic Press.

Terken, Jacques and Dik Hermes. 2000. The perception of prosodic prominence. In G. Bruce and M. Horne (eds.), *Prosody, Theory and Experiment: Studies Presented to Gösta Bruce*, 89–127. New York: Springer.

Tingley, Beth M. and George D. Allen. 1975. Development of speech timing control in children. *Child Development* 46: 186–194.

Tomasello, Michael. 2003. *Constructing a Language: A Usage-Based Theory of Language Acquisition*. Cambridge, MA: Harvard University Press.

Towse, John N., Graham J. Hitch, and Una Hutton. 1998. A reevaluation of working memory capacity in children. *Journal of Memory and Language* 39: 195–217.

Trevarthen, Colwyn. 1979. Communication and cooperation in early infancy: A description of primary intersubjectivity. In M. Bullowa (ed.), *Before Speech: The Beginning of Interpersonal Communication*, 321–347. Cambridge: Cambridge University Press.

Trevarthen, Colwyn and Kenneth J. Aitken. 2001. Infant intersubjectivity: Research, theory, and clinical applications. *Journal of Child Psychology and Psychiatry* 42: 3–48.

Tsao, Ying-Chiao and Gary Weismer. 1997. Interspeaker variation in habitual speaking rate: Evidence for a neuromuscular component. *Journal of Speech, Language, and Hearing Research* 40: 858–866.

Tsao, Ying-Chiao, Gary Weismer, and Kamran Iqbal. 2006. Interspeaker variation in habitual speaking rate: Additional evidence. *Journal of Speech, Language, and Hearing Research* 49: 1156–1164.

Turk, Alice E. and James R. Sawusch. 1997. The domain of accentual lengthening in American English. *Journal of Phonetics* 25: 25–41.

Turk, Alice E. and Stefanie Shattuck-Hufnagel. 2007. Multiple targets of phrase-final lengthening in American English words. *Journal of Phonetics* 35: 445–472.

Turk, Alice E. and Laurence White. 1999. Structural influences on accentual lengthening in English. *Journal of Phonetics* 27: 171–206.

Vihman, Marilyn. 1996. *Phonological Development: The Origins of Language in the Child*. Oxford: Blackwell.

Vihman, Marilyn May, Marlys A. Macken, Ruth Miller, Hazel Simmons, and Jim Miller. 1985. From babbling to speech: A re-assessment of the continuity issue. *Language* 61(2): 397–445.

Walker, Jean F., Lisa M.D. Archibald, Sharon R. Cherniak, and Valerie G. Fish. 1992. Articulation rate in 3- and 5-year-old children. *Journal of Speech and Hearing Research* 35: 4–13.

Walsh, Bridget and Anne Smith. 2002. Articulatory movements in adolescents: Evidence for protracted development of speech motor control processes. *Journal of Speech, Language, and Hearing Research* 45: 1119–1133.

18 Insights for Speech Production Planning from Errors in Inner Speech

GARY S. DELL AND GARY M. OPPENHEIM

18.1 Introduction[1]

In her 1971 paper, "Speech Errors as Linguistic Evidence," Victoria Fromkin made the case that speech errors are a product of linguistic knowledge. Linguistic units of all sizes can slip, and the resulting slips are profoundly sensitive to linguistic constraints. Phonological errors, in particular, involve the substitution, addition, or deletion of single phonological segments (e.g., "auditory feedback" → "audif…," an anticipatory substitution of /f/ for /t/), multi-segment syllabic constituents (e.g., "sweater drying" → "dreater swying," an exchange of onset clusters /sw/ and /dr/), or phonological features (e.g., "clear blue" → "glear plue," an exchange of voicing). In an overwhelmingly large percentage of these slips, the resulting strings create well-formed segments and segment sequences. Thus, phonological slips implicate a production process in which discrete phonological units are retrieved and ordered in accordance with linguistic rules.

In this chapter, we investigate the kinds of phonological errors that Fromkin was talking about. But our slips are not actual slips of the *tongue*, that is, audible slips produced in audible speech. They are slips of inner speech, the soundless mental speech that one generates when thinking, reading, or mentally rehearsing a list.

Although most people are aware of their inner speech, few consider the possibility that it could have slips in it. But it clearly does. Researchers who know something about speech errors have noticed such slips in themselves (and sometimes write about them, e.g., Hockett 1973; Meringer and Meyer 1895, cited in MacKay 1992). Moreover, it is easy to demonstrate to the nonexpert that such slips exist. Simply ask them to say in their mind something like "thirty-seven silver thistles" and to listen closely to what they "hear." Most will then report making a slip such as "thilver." Experimental studies of such slips use just this technique. Participants imagine tongue twisters, often in time with a metronome, and report the errors that they hear. When these inner slips are compared with the slips that occur when the material is spoken aloud, researchers report that the internal errors have much in common with actual slips (Dell 1978; Dell and Repka 1992; Postma and Noordanus 1996). The commonalities between inner and overt slips suggest, first, that internal speech is generated in much the same way as overt speech and, second, that errors specifically emerge from the planning of speech, rather than its articulatory implementation.[2] Here, we discuss the implications of this unusual source of data for theories of production, with a focus on some recent inner-slip studies that question both of these conclusions. We begin, though, with the issue of the extent to which overt phonological slips involve abstract units.

18.2 Gradient effects in phonological errors

Fromkin's (1971) claim that phonological errors are slips of discrete linguistic units was anticipated in earlier error studies (e.g., MacKay 1970; Nooteboom 1969; Wells 1951) and echoed in later work (e.g., Dell 1986; Garrett 1975; Shattuck-Hufnagel 1979; Stemberger 1992). When researchers, however, began to examine the articulatory and phonetic properties of slips, the discreteness claim came under fire (Frisch and Wright 2002; Goldrick and Blumstein 2006; Mowrey and MacKay 1990). We now know that phonological slips, at least those generated in the laboratory, often consist of the blending of the articulatory properties of the target and substituting segments resulting in nondiscrete or "gradient" errors. For example, the production of the /t/ in "top cop" sometimes exhibits an intrusion of tongue-dorsum raising (e.g., as in /k/), creating an articulatory mix that is neither a pure /t/ or /k/ (Goldstein et al. 2007; Pouplier 2007). To take another example, Frisch and Wright (2002) examined the acoustics of utterances of tongue twisters with lots of /s/'s and /z/'s. Occasionally, the uttered consonant's duration would be typical of, say, /s/, while its degree of voicing would be more like that of /z/. Thus, slips do not always involve discrete substitutions of linguistic units resulting in the production of well-formed segments (see also Pouplier 2008; Pouplier and Goldstein 2010).

How should we think about these nondiscrete errors? First, it is important to note that, although articulatory blends clearly occur, phonetic and articulatory analyses of errors also clearly support the conclusion that many, if not most, phonological errors are well described as discrete substitutions that are phonologically well formed (e.g., Frisch 2007; Goldrick and Blumstein 2006). For example, Frisch and Wright's (2002) s-z study found that, when an /s/ was produced erroneously, it was more likely to slip to something like a canonical /z/ than to an /s/-/z/ mix. Given this, one could attempt to retain the classic perspective illustrated in Fromkin's paper. On this view, errors occur at various levels of the system, with discrete well-formed errors occurring at abstract linguistic levels, and articulatory blends at a motor execution level. This approach is exemplified by the production model of Levelt, Roelofs, and Meyer (1999). In that model, there is a hard and fast distinction between the phonological encoding of an utterance and the subsequent retrieval of its phonetic/articulatory representation. During phonological encoding, strings of abstract segments are retrieved and assigned to syllables. Then, these syllabified strings are transformed into syllable-sized articulatory representations that guide motor execution. Given this model, we can associate the nondiscrete errors with the articulatory level and well-formed linguistic slips with the earlier phonological encoding level. One point against such a proposal, though, is the finding that the supposed articulatory-level errors are affected by abstract linguistic properties such as whether a discrete segment substitution would create a word or a nonword (Frisch and Wright 2002; Goldrick and Blumstein 2006; Goldrick et al. 2011; McMillan, Corley, and Lickley 2009). For example, the fact that "zit" exists as a lexical item on its own makes "sit" more likely to admit the intrusion of articulatory aspects of the onset /z/. Thus, the intrusion reflects information that would not be considered a property of the articulatory level. Of course, one could theorize that the articulatory level *is* lexically sensitive indirectly through an ability to record common motor patterns.

The alternative is to change the way that we think about the distinction between the linguistic and the motor levels. One approach is to preserve the notion of specifically linguistic units and constraints, but to allow for gradience in them, for example, as a result of computations under time pressure (e.g., Smolenksy, Goldrick, and Mathis 2014). A second, more radical, approach is to eliminate the distinction between the levels altogether. For example, in Articulatory Phonology (Browman and Goldstein 1992), production is carried out by a single complex system whose primitives are articulatory units called *gestures*. A gesture itself is a dynamically organized set of actions that achieves an articulatory goal, for example, a lip closure gesture. A low-dimensional description of this system could correspond to a linguistic characterization, with discrete segments corresponding to gestural molecules. But, even so, these "segments" are not abstract units that are strung together to form syllables and words. Instead, these units are specified for their gestural content, and represented as temporally coordinated assemblies of these gestures.

Given this background, we now turn to our central question. What happens when we remove articulation from language production? This is the essence of inner speech; it is speech production, but without movement or sound. The nature of inner speech, just like the nature of overt speech, can be revealed by looking at its slips.

18.3 Subphonemic attenuation in inner speech

Phonological errors exhibit a number of regularities that are informative about the speech planning process. We are concerned with two such effects. First, the *phonemic similarity effect* is the tendency for a substituting segment to be similar to the segment that it replaces (MacKay 1970; Shattuck-Hufnagel and Klatt 1979). For example, every phonological system considers /r/ and /l/ to be more similar (e.g., sharing more features) than /r/ and /b/, so everything else being equal, "reef" would slip to "leaf" more often than it would slip to "beef." This effect is often explained by proposing that subphonemic features participate in production planning at the level at which segmental errors occur (Dell 1986; Goldrick 2008; see, however, Shattuck Hufnagel and Klatt 1979). Second, the *lexical bias effect* is the tendency for phonological slips to create words over nonwords (Baars, Motley, and MacKay 1975). So, "reef" would be more likely slip to the word "leaf" than "wreath" would to the nonword "leath." Lexical bias requires that the production process make contact with lexical representations, either during segment planning, as proposed in interactive accounts of lexical bias (e.g., Dell 1986), or afterward during prearticulatory monitoring (e.g., Baars et al. 1975).

Oppenheim and Dell (2008) used the phonemic similarity and lexical bias effects as tools to probe the nature of inner speech. Like other inner speech error experiments, they elicited inner and overt errors from the paced recitation of tongue twisters. Participants either said aloud or imagined saying four-word tongue twisters that manipulated onset similarity and the lexicality of potential slip outcomes. Table 18.1 illustrates these manipulations. As they attempted the tongue twisters in time with a metronome, participants reported their errors. Inner slips, of course, have to be self-reported and so the same requirement was placed on overt slips. Thus, the errors necessarily reflect any reporting bias that arises from the speakers' conception of their errors. This bias, though, applies to the overt as well as the inner slips and hence any differences between them cannot be attributed to the fact that errors are reported rather than being directly recorded.

As expected, Oppenheim and Dell (2008) found that the lexical bias effect and the phonemic similarity effect were present in the reported overt speech errors. These are robust error effects, having been demonstrated many times in natural error corpora as well as in experiments. Inner slips, however, were completely insensitive to phonemic similarity; slips involving similar onsets were no more likely than those with dissimilar onsets (see Figure 18.1a). Inner speech did show the lexical bias effect, though, so the lack of a phonemic similarity effect cannot be due to some general lack of systematicity in inner slips. Instead, Oppenheim and Dell, following

Table 18.1 Example tongue twister set from Oppenheim and Dell (2008) manipulating onset similarity and outcome lexicality on the third word (the outcome of the slip on the third word is given after the → sign).

	Similar onsets	*Dissimilar onsets*
Word outcome	lean reed *reef* leech → **leaf**	bean reed *reef* beech → **beef**
Nonword outcome	lean reed *wreath* leech → **leath**	bean reed *wreath* beech → **beath**

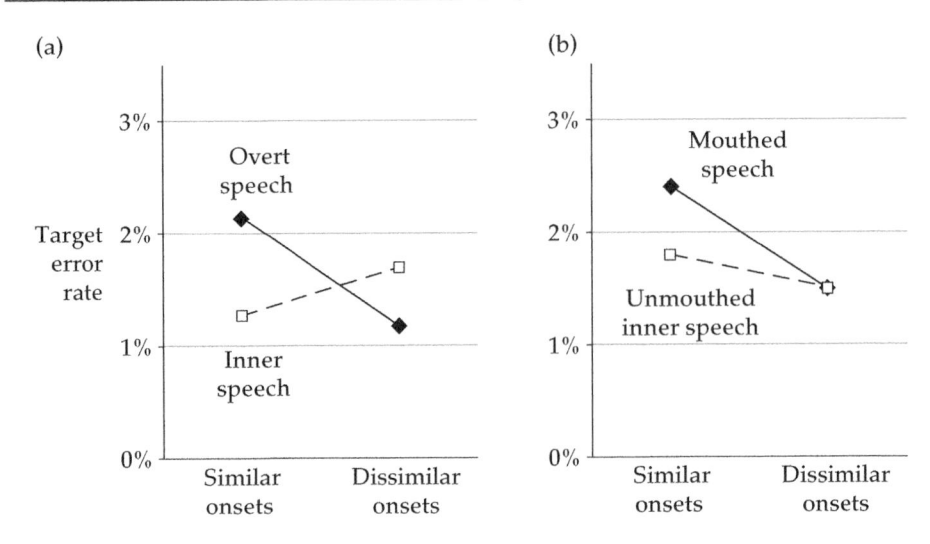

Figure 18.1 Target error distributions contrasting the phonemic similarity effects (a) in inner and overt speech (Oppenheim and Dell 2008) and (b) in inner and silent mouthed speech (Oppenheim and Dell 2010).

a related proposal by Wheeldon and Levelt (1995), proposed that inner speech is "impoverished," specifically that it is attenuated at a subphonemic level.

The subphonemic attenuation hypothesis starts with the view that phonological planning in production entails multiple processing levels, including at least a lexical, segmental, and sub-segmental (e.g., featural) level. Overt production fully engages all of these levels. The lexical bias effect has been thought to arise because of a lexical influence on segmental selection. In Dell's (1986) model of production, the activation of segments that form a word, whether correctly or in error, is reinforced because the activated segments send activation to the word level, which in turn reinforces the activation of those segments. The phonemic similarity effect can be attributed to the influence of the sub-segmental level. For example, the same kind of interactive spreading activation that hypothetically allows lexical units to affect segmental selection, would allow features to affect segment selection. When activation spreads back from features to segments, it increases the activation of an incorrect segment that shares features with the target segment, thus increasing the chance that the incorrect one will replace the target (see Figure 18.2).

Given this multi-level architecture, the presence of a robust lexical bias effect in inner speech suggests the engagement of the lexical and segmental levels. The segmental level is involved because the errors in question are segment substitutions (e.g. reef → beef), and the lexical level is revealed in the tendency for the slips to create words. The lack of a phonemic similarity effect then suggests that the sub-segmental level is not participating to the extent that it does in overt speech. This is the subphonemic attenuation hypothesis for inner speech. In the model illustrated in Figure 18.2, this hypothesis can be implemented by reducing

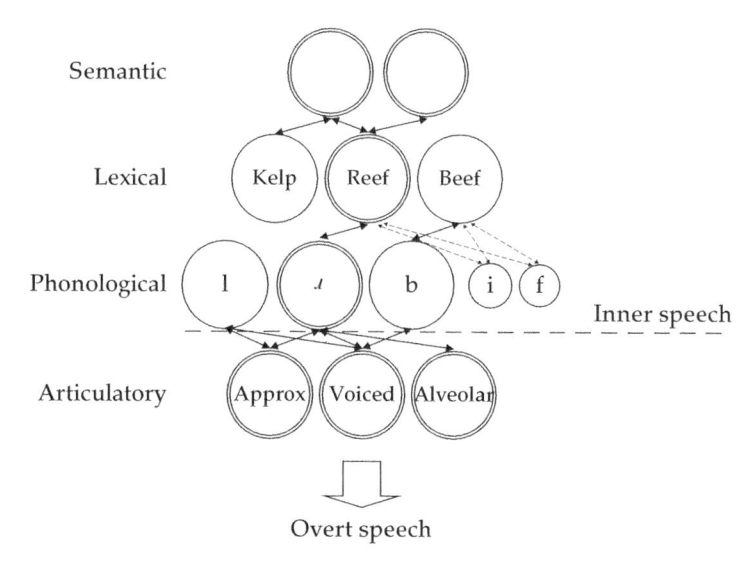

Figure 18.2 Illustration of Dell's (1986) spreading activation model of language production, as adapted to inner speech. The subphonemic attenuation hypothesis holds that portions below the dotted line have less influence in inner speech.

the influence of the features on the spreading activation process, for example, by reducing the connection strengths to and/or from the features.

18.4 Putting some articulation in inner speech

Although inner slips, to a first approximation, look like overt slips, it thus appears that there is at least one difference: the phonemic similarity effect is stronger in overt speech. Why is this? The subphonemic attenuation hypothesis is simply a statement that subphonemic features play less of a role in inner speech. But is that because the articulation is not planned in sufficient detail for subphonemic features to matter (because there is no overt articulation)? Or could it be that the weakened similarity effect in inner speech is seen because the lack of auditory output impacts which inner slips are detected? Perhaps substitutions of similar phonemes cannot be so easily "heard" in one's mind. Oppenheim and Dell (2010) attempted to address this issue by looking at slips in articulated inner speech, that is, soundless, but "mouthed" speech. Articulation of a sort is present because the participant is instructed to move their mouth just as if they were saying the words, but without making any sound.

Specifically, Oppenheim and Dell (2010) compared slips in mouthed inner speech to those in unarticulated inner speech, using the same methods as in their earlier study. For unarticulated inner slips, the results replicated the pattern found in the earlier study: there was lexical bias, but little similarity effect. Mouthing, however, restored the similarity effect (see Figure 18.1b). This pattern invites two conclusions. First, it suggests that the weakened similarity effect in unarticulated inner speech is not just due to the absence of sound, and specifically, that this effect is not a byproduct of difficulties in detecting soundless slips. More importantly, the result shows that internal speech is not uniform. It can vary in the extent to which subphonemic detail is present. By requiring that the inner speech have soundless articulation, the resulting inner slips behave just like overt slips with respect to the influence of phonemic similarity.

Oppenheim and Dell (2010) characterized the variability of inner speech as "flexible abstraction." The idea was that inner speech is a cognitive tool that speakers develop and use in service of particular goals. Depending on why speakers are using inner speech, it can be more or less abstract.[3] For example, trying to remember a shopping list may evoke a fairly abstract inner voice, as the only goal is to remember the contents of the list. But an actress mentally rehearsing her big speech might well be concerned with how things will sound and so the mental practice might more thoroughly represent the speech's articulatory details. In this light, an experiment using tongue-twister material might naturally elicit inner speech with some subphonemic detail. Even so, the similarity effect was increased when the inner speech included some silent articulation.

The idea that inner speech's subphonemic detail is typically attenuated was contested in a series of studies by Corley, Brocklehurst, and Moat (2011). They replicated Oppenheim and Dell's (2008) manipulations in a comparison between overt and inner recitations of tongue twisters. They replicated the findings of lexical bias in both overt and inner slips. And they replicated the strong effect of phonemic similarity on overt errors. However, unlike Oppenheim and Dell, they also found a reliable similarity effect in inner speech errors. There are two ways to think about this result. First, we can take it as evidence for the claim that inner speech is variable in the degree to which it is attenuated. Perhaps Corley et al.'s experiments induced participants to generate a less abstract form of inner speech than Oppenheim et al.'s participants used. For instance, Corley et al.'s participants could have articulated their inner speech to some extent, or simply been motivated to form more detailed imagery. This interpretation is consistent with the findings of Oppenheim and Dell (2010). Alternately, one could conclude, as Corley et al. did, that inner speech is generally not as abstract as originally thought, and hence that the subphonemic attenuation hypothesis may not be true. In the next section, we consider all of the data on this question, and summarize some meta-analyses and modeling studies from Oppenheim (2012).

18.5 Is the subphonemic attenuation hypothesis correct? A consideration of how speech-error effects vary with overall error rates

Given the apparent flexibility of inner speech production, the crucial test of the subphonemic attenuation hypothesis is not whether *any* effect of phonemic similarity can be found in inner speech. What matters is whether the similarity effect in unarticulated inner speech is *typically* as large as that in overtly articulated speech. The effect in overtly articulated speech is especially important because its size varies considerably from experiment to experiment. For instance, using the same stimuli, each overtness condition in Corley et al.'s Experiment 3 elicited a similarity effect that was approximately 80% larger than that of the corresponding condition in Oppenheim and Dell's (2010) study. Such variation means that a simple main effect of similarity in inner speech, when considered in isolation, may not reveal much about whether inner speech involves attenuated subphonemic processing. Attenuation must be evaluated relative to an appropriate baseline, that is, the similarity effect for inner slips in a particular experiment must be compared to the corresponding effect for overt slips in the same experiment.

Statistically reconsidering all of the published data on the question, Oppenheim (2012) confirmed the subphonemic attenuation claim. Although some experiments showed larger *main* effects of similarity than others, the similarity effects in unarticulated inner speech were consistently weaker. In fact, when considering inner speech effects relative to their corresponding overt effects, Corley et al.'s data neatly converged with Oppenheim and Dell's, estimating that the similarity effect in unarticulated inner speech is consistently about 40% smaller than that in overtly articulated speech (an odds ratio of 1:1.6). Thus the demonstration that similarity effects *can* be found in inner speech remains compatible with the broader claim that inner speech typically incorporates less subphonemic detail.

While this explanation seems satisfying on its own, it raises another question: why would the similarity of two phonemes – which should remain constant across replications with the same stimuli – affect error distributions more strongly in one experiment than in another? Such variation, it turns out, naturally emerges from the fact that speech errors are, as Freud (1901/1958) noted, *overdetermined*: many factors conspire to determine if and how production will go astray (see Dell 1986 for review). For instance, we know that similarly articulated phonemes are more likely to interact in slips, reflecting the underlying structure of the speech planning system. But because slips occur so rarely, researchers routinely use externalities – factors like time pressure and phonological priming that are not directly of theoretical interest – to boost their overall incidence. The externalities are thought to work together with the structure of the speech planning system to elicit the desired, or target, errors, meaning that each target error concurrently reflects multiple causes – that is, it is overdetermined.

One consequence of overdetermination is that when one factor promotes errors more, other factors matter less. In terms of the similarity effect, this makes phoneme selection like a player tossing darts at a dartboard (Figure 18.3). In this analogy, shared features set the layout of the dartboard. The target phoneme occupies the bullseye and phonemes that share more features with it sit closer to the center. We can visualize the probability distribution function for phoneme selection as a normal distribution centered on the bullseye. Externalities like time pressure and priming modulate the variance in the distribution, generally making production less precise. With minimal variance, few productions lie beyond the target phoneme boundary (offering little data with which to robustly estimate

/r/ /l/ /b/

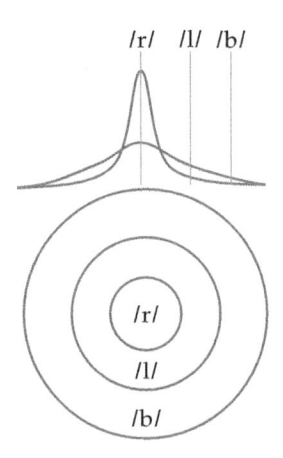

Figure 18.3 Slips of the tongue are overdetermined, so when one factor drives error production more, other factors matter less. With very accurate production, most phoneme selections hit the bullseye, but even misses still tend to get close, boosting the ratio of /l/ to /b/ outcomes. With less accurate production, misses stray more widely, lessening the ratio of /l/ to /b/ outcomes.

error effects), but those that do overrepresent similar phonemes. In Figure 18.3, for example, with minimal variance, erroneous /r/ attempts should be much more likely to result in /l/ (closer to the bullseye) than /b/ (further away). As variance increases, not only do fewer productions lie within the bullseye, but errorful productions are generally less focused on the target, and consequently show less dramatic similarity effects, in terms of the ratio of /l/ to /b/ outcomes. Thus, the similarity effect is a consequence of the fact that, even when production goes astray, it is usually more right than wrong. Consequently, as production degrades, yielding higher overall error rates, its errors grow more egregious, resembling the target utterance less and therefore yielding weaker similarity effects.[4]

This association between the strength of the similarity effect and overall error rate explains much of the observed variation in the similarity effects across inner speech experiments, including a puzzle of how Corley et al. could find similarity effects in inner speech that were comparable in odds-size to those that Oppenheim and Dell found in articulated speech. In both inner and overt speech, stronger odds-ratio similarity effects are empirically associated with experiments where production was more accurate overall, eliciting fewer errors (the fact that the lines in Figure 18.4 slope downward). This association is predicted by the assumption that, when extraneous factors boost the incidence of phoneme errors overall, the similarities of interacting phonemes matter less in determining error outcomes. The principle of overdetermination thus explains why and how similarity effects *should* vary in size, both in inner and overt speech. The crucial point, though, is that although the similarity effects vary across experiments, they are consistently greater in articulated speech than in unarticulated inner speech (the "articulated" line and its corresponding points are higher than the "unarticulated" ones in

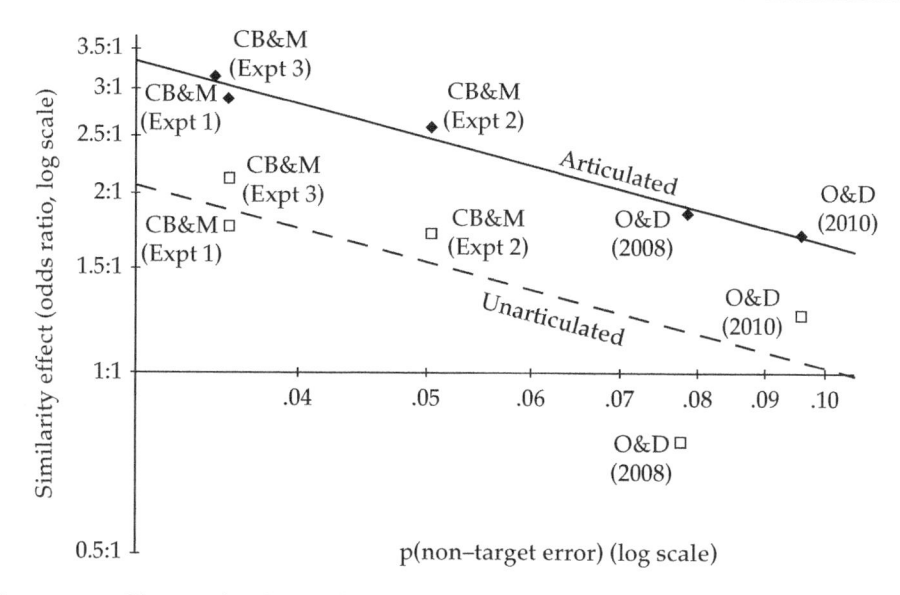

Figure 18.4 Plotting the observed similarity effects in Oppenheim and Dell's (2008, 2010) and Corley et al.'s (2011) experiments against the experiments' respective non-target error rates shows that both inner and overt speech show stronger similarity effects when production is more accurate, but overt articulation leads to stronger similarity effects overall. Black diamonds represent overtly articulated speech; open squares represent unarticulated inner speech. Based on data reported in Oppenheim (2012).

Figure 18.4). To sum up, the principle of overdetermination of errors and the subphonemic attenuation hypothesis together account for all of the variation in the size of the similarity effect in these experiments.

18.6 The nature of attenuation in inner speech

The fact that we experience internal slips of the tongue that seem to be a lot like overt slips had led to the conclusion that overt articulation does not play a causal role in speech errors. Both this fact and the conclusion from it must be modified. With regard to the fact, although inner slips are indeed like overt slips, they are considerably less sensitive to phonemic similarity than overt slips when the inner speech is unarticulated, that is, when there is no "mouthing." So, inner slips can follow different laws than overt slips. We must also set aside the conclusion that articulation does not matter to slips. Clearly it does, as the strength of the phonemic similarity effect reflects the extent to which the speech involves overt articulation (whether soundless or not).

Given this revision, let us return to the issue that we started with. What do speech errors tell us about the relation between linguistic abstractions and their motoric realizations? The data supporting the subphonemic attenuation hypothesis can be thought of as dissociating abstract linguistic planning from more phonetic or articulatory planning. You get one result when the processing is occurring at the more abstract level (unarticulated inner speech) and a different result when the processing involves motoric planning (articulated inner speech and overt speech). This way of thinking is consistent with Fromkin's classic linguistic perspective on speech errors, at least insofar as it allows for phonological errors to occur at abstract linguistic levels. Moreover, it is consistent with neuropsychological studies of aphasic language production that also find related dissociations. For example, Buchwald and Miozzo (2011) studied two English-speaking patients who tended to delete /s/ from onset clusters such as /sp/ in "spin." One patient's productions of the remaining voiceless stop (e.g., /p/) were aspirated. "Spin," for example, would be spoken much like the word "pin." This suggests that the /s/ deletion occurred at an abstract phonological level because, after /s/ is gone, /p/ is now in a position that requires aspiration according to English phonology. In contrast, the other patient's stops were, after /s/ deletion, produced without aspiration (e.g., [p°ɪn]). We can explain these unaspirated forms by locating the deletion of the /s/ at a later level than for the previous patient. Thus the data motivate two levels, one more abstract than the other (see also Goldrick and Rapp 2007 for other phonological/phonetic dissociations in aphasic production error patterns).

Although these studies support the idea of unarticulated inner speech as a mental traversal of strings of abstract phonological segments, there is one property of inner speech that we have not yet considered that stands in the way of such a conclusion. This is that inner speech seems to occur in real time. It both sounds like speech and it feels like talking. To convince yourself of this, try to say "big tip" over and over a few times to yourself, and then compare by saying "loose rose." You will have the impression that you can go through the "big tip" utterances more quickly. In fact, you would find the same result if you were to repeatedly say these aloud. "Big" and "tip" are short compared to "loose" and "rose," even though they have the same number of phonological segments.[5] In this way, inner speech resembles auditory imagery of, for example, music. If you imagine a section of a song that you know well from a recording, your imagined construction of it will likely take about the same amount of time as the real thing. Of course, you could speed it up or slow it down on purpose, but the relative temporal properties are present.

If inner speech is experienced in real time, the temporal dynamics that underlie overt articulation must be realized during its generation. It cannot consist of the scanning of abstract segments such that the vowels of "rose" and "big" would take the same amount of time. This suggests that there may be a role for something like Articulatory Phonology (Browman and Goldstein 1992) in explaining the nature of inner speech. Recall that in Articulatory Phonology there is no traditional segmental representation. Instead, word forms are represented as temporally coordinated sets of gestures. The key is that the representation specifies the relative timing of the gestures. So, what would inner speech correspond to? The simplest answer is that it would consist of running through the gestural plan, while inhibiting muscle movements. As we have seen, though, this is too simple. It is inconsistent with the evidence for abstraction in inner speech, as demonstrated by the weaker phonemic similarity effect in unarticulated inner speech errors. By some means or other, the gestural plan that is internally run through must be associated with a relative loss of the similarity relations among consonants.

One possibility is that the long-period aspects of timing are fully preserved when gestural plans are internally executed. For example, timing that controls syllable length would be fully present (cf. Filik and Barber 2011). The representation of more rapid gestures, though, may be attenuated. This proposal reminds us of another domain that is associated with attenuated rehearsal that nonetheless occurs in real time, namely dance. As a dancer learns and rehearses, he will often "mark" instead of dance. Marking consists of going through the motions in real time ("marking" comes from "marking time"), but with greatly reduced gestures. Sometimes gestures may be eliminated or substituted for with some kind of symbol. For example, a jump with spread legs may be skipped during marking, but a hand gesture mimicking the spread legs would be substituted at the appropriate time. This strikes us as a useful metaphor for inner speech, one that seems compatible with its temporal and (flexibly) abstract nature. Like a dancer who is marking, an inner speaker generates something that preserves the temporal outline of the full overt activity, but attenuates and eliminates aspects of the activity, sometimes substituting a component of the activity with something that symbolizes that component.

Clearly, the field is moving away from the classical notion of phonemes as abstract beads on a string. Phonemes have been recharacterized as goals for articulation (e.g., Guenther 1995; Hickok 2012), gestural molecules (Browman and Goldstein 1992), and attractor states for distributed representations (e.g., Goldrick 2008; Smolensky et al. 2014). However, as the field develops a more nuanced view of production units, our inner speech work suggests that it must retain a distinction between a level of word-form representation where sensory and motor details matter less, and a later level where they matter more.

More generally, a consideration of inner speech along with other forms of reduced rehearsal or practice may help explain the relation between the planning and the execution of behavioral sequences. Ultimately, we hope to learn how the seemingly unique linguistic aspects of speech and speech errors that Fromkin (1971) studied are situated within a general theory of serially ordered behavior.

NOTES

1. This work was supported by NIH DC000191 and HD44458.
2. For instance, MacKay (1992: 125) interpreted inner speech error patterns as suggesting that, "contrary to popular belief, overtly produced tongue twisters result in errors at the phonological level but not at the articulatory or muscle movement level," and hence, "tongue twister errors must have nothing to do with the tongue."
3. The degree of abstraction is also presumably influenced by other factors such as expertise (as in other domains of motor imagery, e.g., Guillot et al. 2008) and task difficulty (Hardyck and Petrinovich 1970; Marvel and Desmond 2011).

4 Of course, with human-subjects research, the major challenge typically lies in collecting enough target errors to estimate effect sizes and support robust statistical analyses. Lower error rates are problematic in that they provide fewer errors in a given number of trials, thereby supplying statistical analyses with less data and greater vulnerability to sampling error. Thus successful speech error research requires finding a balance between too much randomness and too few data.

5 Baddeley, Thomson, and Buchanan (1975) showed that people's short-term memory spans were greater for words like "big" than for words like "rose," thus implicating a role for word duration in memory. It is possible that this finding is due to the use of inner speech as a rehearsal mechanism, but this is not a necessary conclusion from the study. It could instead be due to the effects of duration during overt recall.

REFERENCES

Baars, Bernard J., Michael T. Motley, and Donald G. MacKay. 1975. Output editing for lexical status in artificially elicited slips of the tongue. *Journal of Verbal Learning and Verbal Behavior* 14: 382–391.

Baddeley, Alan, Neil Thomson, and Mary Buchanan. 1975. Word length and the structure of short-term memory. *Journal of Verbal Learning and Verbal Behavior* 14: 575–589.

Browman, Catherine P. and Louis Goldstein. 1992. Articulatory Phonology: An overview. *Phonetica* 49: 155–180.

Buchwald, Adam and Michele Miozzo. 2011. Finding levels of abstraction in speech production: Evidence from sound-production impairment. *Psychological Science* 22: 1113–1119.

Corley, Martin, Paul H. Brocklehurst, and H. Susannah Moat. 2011. Error biases in inner and overt speech: Evidence from tongue twisters. *Journal of Experimental Psychology: Learning, Memory, and Cognition* 37: 162–175.

Dell, Gary S. 1978. Slips of the mind. In *The Fourth LACUS Forum 1977*, 69–75. Columbia, SC: Hornbeam Press.

Dell, Gary S. 1986. A spreading-activation theory of retrieval in sentence production. *Psychological Review* 93: 283–321.

Dell, Gary S. and Renee J. Repka. 1992. Errors in inner speech. In Bernard J. Baars (ed.), *Experimental Slips and Human Error: Exploring the Architecture of Volition*, 237–262. New York: Plenum.

Filik, Ruth and Emma Barber. 2011. Inner speech during silent reading reflects the reader's regional accent. *PLoS ONE* 6: e25782.

Freud, Sigmund. 1901/1958. *The Psychopathology of Everyday Life*, trans. A.A. Brill. New York: New American Library.

Frisch, Stefan A. 2007. Walking the tightrope between cognition and articulation: The state of the art in the phonetics of speech errors. In Carson T. Schutze and Victor S. Ferreira (eds.), *The State of the Art in Speech Error Research: Proceedings of the LSA Institute Workshop*, 155–172. Cambridge, MA: MIT Press.

Frisch, Stefan and Richard Wright. 2002. The phonetics of phonological speech errors: An acoustic analysis of slips of the tongue. *Journal of Phonetics* 30: 139–162.

Fromkin, Victoria A. 1971. The non-anomalous nature of anomalous utterances. *Language* 47: 27–52.

Garrett, Merrill F. 1975. The analysis of sentence production. In Gordon H. Bower (ed.), *The Psychology of Learning and Motivation: Advances in Research and Theory*, 133–177.

Goldrick, Matthew A. 2008. Does like attract like? Exploring the relationship between errors and representational structure in connectionist networks. *Cognitive Neuropsychology* 25: 287–313.

Goldrick, Matthew A. and Sheila Blumstein. 2006. Cascading activation from phonological planning to articulatory processes: Evidence from tongue twisters. *Language and Cognitive Processes* 21: 649–683.

Goldrick, Matthew A. and Brenda Rapp. 2007. Lexical and post-lexical phonological representations in spoken production. *Cognition* 102: 219–260.

Goldrick, Matthew, H. Ross Baker, Amanda Murphy, and Melissa Baese-Berk. 2011. Interaction and representational integration: Evidence from speech errors. *Cognition* 121: 58–72.

Goldstein, Louis, Marianne Pouplier, Larissa Chen, Elliot Saltzman, and Dani Byrd. 2007. Dynamic action units slip in speech production errors. *Cognition* 103: 386–412.

Guenther, Frank H. 1995. Speech sound acquisition, coarticulation, and rate effects in a neural network model of speech production. *Psychological Review* 102: 594–621.

Guillot, Aymeric, Christian Collet, Vo A. Nguyen, Francine Malouin, Carol Richards, and Julien Doyon. 2008. Functional neuroanatomical networks associated with expertise in motor imagery. *NeuroImage* 41: 1471–1483.

Hardyck, Curtis D. and Lewis F. Petrinovich. 1970. Subvocal speech and comprehension level as a function of the difficulty level of reading material. *Journal of Verbal Learning and Verbal Behavior* 9: 647–652.

Hickok, Gregory. 2012. Computational neuroanatomy of speech production. *Nature Reviews Neuroscience* 13: 135–145.

Hockett, Charles F. 1973. Where the tongue slips, there slip I. In Victoria A. Fromkin (ed.), *Speech Errors as Linguistic Evidence*. The Hague: Mouton.

Levelt, Willem J.M., Ardi Roelofs, and Antje S. Meyer. 1999. A theory of lexical access in speech production. *Behavioral and Brain Sciences* 22: 1–38.

MacKay, Donald G. 1970. Spoonerisms: The structure of errors in the serial order of speech. *Neuropsychologia* 8: 323–350.

MacKay, Donald G. 1992. Constraints on theories of inner speech. In D. Reisberg (ed.), *Auditory Imagery*, 121–149. Hillsdale, NJ: Erlbaum.

Marvel, Cherie L. and John E. Desmond. 2011. From storage to manipulation: How the neural correlates of verbal working memory reflect varying demands on inner speech. *Brain and Language* 120: 42–51.

McMillan, Corey T., Martin Corley, and Robin Lickley. 2009. Articulatory evidence for feedback and competition in speech production. *Language and Cognitive Processes* 24: 44–66.

Meringer, Rudolf and Carl Mayer. 1895. *Versprechen und Verlesen*. Stuttgart: G.J. Göschen.

Mowrey, Richard A. and Ian R.A. MacKay. 1990. Phonological primitives: Electromyographic speech error evidence. *Journal of the Acoustical Society of America* 88: 1299–1312.

Nooteboom, Sieb G. 1969. The tongue slips into patterns. In A.G. Sciarone, A.J. van Essen, and A.A. van Raad (eds.), *Leyden Studies in Linguistics and Phonetics*, 114–132. The Hague: Mouton.

Oppenheim, Gary M. 2012. The case for subphonemic attenuation in inner speech: Comment on Corley, Brocklehurst, and Moat (2011). *Journal of Experimental Psychology: Learning, Memory, and Cognition* 38: 502–512.

Oppenheim, Gary M. and Gary S. Dell. 2008. Inner speech slips exhibit lexical bias, but not the phonemic similarity effect. *Cognition* 106: 528–537.

Oppenheim, Gary M. and Gary S. Dell. 2010. Motor movement matters: The flexible abstractness of inner speech. *Memory and Cognition* 38: 1147–1160.

Postma, Albert and Catharina Noordanus. 1996. Production and detection of speech errors in silent, mouthed, noise-masked, and normal auditory feedback speech. *Language and Speech* 39: 375–392.

Pouplier, Marriane. 2007. Tongue kinematics during utterances elicited with the SLIP technique. *Language and Speech* 50: 311–341.

Pouplier, Marianne. 2008. The role of a coda consonant as error trigger in repetition tasks. *Journal of Phonetics* 36: 114–140.

Pouplier, Marianne and Louis Goldstein. 2010. Intention in articulation: Articulatory timing in alternating consonant sequences and its implications for models of speech production. *Language and Cognitive Processes* 25: 616–649.

Shattuck-Hufnagel, Stephanie. 1979. Speech errors as evidence for a serial-ordering mechanism in sentence production. In William E. Cooper and Edward C.T. Walker (eds.), *Sentence Processing: Psycholinguistic Studies Presented to Merrill Garrett*, 295–342. Hillsdale, NJ: Lawrence Erlbaum Associates.

Shattuck-Hufnagel, Stephanie and Dennis H. Klatt. 1979. The limited use of distinctive features and markedness in speech production: Evidence from speech error data. *Journal of Verbal Learning and Verbal Behavior* 18: 41–55.

Smolenksy, Paul, Matthew Goldrick, and Donald Mathis. 2014. Optimization and quantization in gradient symbol systems: A framework for integrating the continuous and the discrete in cognition. *Cognitive Science* 38(6): 1102–1138.

Stemberger, Joseph P. 1992. The reliability and replicability of naturalistic speech error data: A comparison with experimentally induced errors. In Bernard J. Baars (ed.), *Experimental Slips and Human Error: Exploring the Architecture of Volition*, 195–215. New York: Plenum.

Wells, Rulon. 1951. Predicting slips of the tongue. *Yale Scientific Magazine* 3: 9–30.

Wheeldon, Linda R. and Willem J.M. Levelt. 1995. Monitoring the time course of phonological encoding. *Journal of Memory and Language* 34: 311–334.

19 Prosodic Frames in Speech Production

STEFANIE SHATTUCK-HUFNAGEL

19.1 Introduction

Questions about how speakers plan and produce an utterance have long been posed by cognitive scientists, linguists, practitioners of speech synthesis, clinicians, and teachers of second languages. For example, what kinds of information are represented during the planning and implementation processes? what types of cognitive mechanisms are involved? And, what set of factors must be included in this planning process, to account for the pervasive, extensive, and highly systematic patterns of phonetic variation in word forms across different contexts that are observed in continuous communicative speech? At one time in the mid-twentieth century, the dominant psychological approach to speech production modeled the act of speaking an utterance in terms of a sequence of learned stimulus-response links, in which each word served as the stimulus for the following word which was produced as the response (Skinner 1957). In such a model, the speaker needs to know almost nothing about the overall structure of the utterance, or even about the upcoming words, in order to produce the current word, because the stimulus for each word is the preceding word (with the exception of the initial word, which requires a different stimulus mechanism). An alternative view, which emerged with Karl Lashley's seminal paper "The Problem of Serial Order in Behavior" (1951) and flowered in the 1970s and 1980s, is that the speaker generates a global planning frame for each utterance, and thus formulates a structure that specifies at least some aspects of the entire message, early on in the planning process (Garrett 1975; Shattuck-Hufnagel 1982; Levelt 1989; Levelt, Roelofs, and Meyer 1999; Bock 1990; Bock and Loebell 1990).

While cognitive science has come a long way from the former view, investigators who model speech production processing have not fully adopted the latter. That is, there is not general acceptance of the idea that a speaker generates an abstract planning frame, in the sense of a representation of the structure of an

---

The Handbook of Speech Production, First Edition. Edited by Melissa A. Redford.
© 2015 John Wiley & Sons, Inc. Published 2019 by John Wiley & Sons, Inc.

utterance that is independent of the full specification of its contents. While it is accepted that speakers do not plan and produce one word at a time, the nature and extent of the more global aspects of utterance planning are not fully understood. In this chapter we review the evidence that, early on in the planning process, speakers know something about the larger structure of an utterance they plan to produce, suggesting a positive answer to the question (1) Does the weight of the evidence suggest that a speaker plans ahead? In the succeeding sections we address questions like (2) Does this evidence suggest that the speaker generates a structural planning frame that is at least somewhat independent of its contents? (3) Does that planning frame correspond to prosodic structure? (4) What can we learn about planning frames from the speech behavior of children who are learning to talk, of people who use sign language, and of speakers with atypical speech capacities, such as aphasia, as well as from comparing error patterns across different languages?

As will become clear, most of the evidence presented here is drawn from studies of the production of English utterances, and it remains to be determined how far the findings can be generalized to different languages, especially those with different prosodic structures. Toward the end of the chapter, we evaluate several current models of speech production planning in light of their capacity to account for these observations.

19.2 What is the evidence that speakers plan ahead?

Some of the most compelling evidence that speakers plan ahead (i.e., that they represent/compute some aspects of the utterance beyond the current word) comes from a particular type of speech error that involves the early production of an element that belongs later in the utterance:

- *whenever I sew the button **off**, it comes **on*** for *whenever I sew the button **on**, it comes **off*** (where the error units are words);
- *in**telephon**ing **stall**s* for *in**stall**ing **telephone**s* (where the error units are morphemes);
- ***dr**etter *sw*ying* for *sweater drying* (where the error units are onset clusters);
- *feak and weeble* for *weak and feeble* (where the error units are single phonemic segments).

The class of errors considered here can be distinguished on the one hand from disfluencies, which interrupt the smooth and timely articulation of a planned utterance with perceptually salient repetitions, silences, interruptions, or lengthenings; and on the other hand from the fluent production of utterances generated by a speaker using a non-standard grammar. That is, the types of errors discussed here are distinct from disfluencies, which are prosodic in nature (although the detection and/or correction of constituent-based errors may also lead to prosodic disfluencies), and they are also distinct from the use of a grammar that is different from that of the observer. Instead, speech errors of the type used as evidence here correspond to largely fluent renditions of an output utterance that departs from what is inferred to be the speaker's well-formed morphosyntactic intention. In addition, with only a few exceptions, we restrict the discussion here to evidence from a particular type of speech errors: interaction errors. An interaction error is one in which a target segment occurs in a location within the utterance that is different from what is inferred to be its target location, so that there is an interaction between a segment's target location and a different location in the utterance. Other error types, such as the substitution of a non-target word from the lexicon, and their implications for the production process, will not be discussed extensively here.

Interaction errors generally involve linguistic units such as whole words, morphemes, or their individual phonemic constituents,[1] and have been well documented in a number of error corpora collected by listening to ongoing ambient speech (e.g., for American English: Fromkin 1971, Shattuck 1975; for German: Meringer and Mayer 1895/1978, Berg 1992; for Dutch: Nooteboom 1973; for Finnish: Hokkanen, 1995; for Spanish: del Viso 1992). As Lashley (1951) pointed out, errors with an anticipatory component demonstrate that the speaker has access to at least some information about later parts of the utterance, at the moment in time when an earlier target word is being articulated. While anticipatory errors collected in corpora may be ambiguous as to the nature of the error unit (i.e., because of the hierarchical nature of linguistic structure, it is often uncertain whether a particular error like *cat the cat* for *pat the cat* involves a word, an individual sound segment, or an individual articulatory gesture), they unambiguously indicate the fact that the speaker has generated a representation of the later element at the point in time when the earlier element would be expected to occur.

A number of different types of speech errors show such an anticipatory characteristic. In addition to complete exchanges (like those illustrated above), in which a later constituent changes places with an earlier one, other types of interaction errors with an anticipatory component include:

- complete anticipatory substitutions (such as *a **gas** of gas* for *a **tank** of gas* or *p**h**onal phonology* for *t**onal** phonology*);
- anticipatory additions (such as *k**l**um to fly* for *come to fly*); and
- incomplete or interrupted errors (like *sye – **try** to see*).[2]

Errors that involve some kind of anticipatory component have been estimated to make up as many as 75% of sound-level errors (Shattuck-Hufnagel 1987; Schwartz et al. 1994), and the fact that they occur must be accounted for in an adequate model of the speech planning process. It is true that the sheer anticipatory nature of such errors doesn't necessarily require that speakers preplan an utterance frame independent of its contents, since they might arise from the simple early activation of target words intended for later production. However, we will see below that the further claim that a structural planning framework is generated is supported by other systematic aspects of spontaneous speech error patterns, as well as by additional behavioral data elicited experimentally.

A second line of evidence that speakers plan ahead is that certain aspects of the beginning of an utterance or phrase vary systematically with aspects of the remainder of the utterance. This suggests the speaker's behavior is influenced by aspects of the upcoming utterance even before articulation of the first word begins. For example, Fuchs et al. (2008) report that speakers take a deeper breath before a longer utterance. While it is logically possible that the causality here goes in the other direction (i.e., that speakers produce longer utterances as a result of having taken a deeper breath), the relationship is at least consistent with the speaker having some idea of how long the upcoming utterance will be. Another observation with similar implications is that speakers begin longer utterances at a higher pitch (Ladd 2008). Since F0 often declines over an utterance (particularly if it is a statement), and moreover seems to decline toward a fixed F0 near the bottom of the speaker's range, the fact that a speaker begins at a higher pitch for a longer utterance leaves room for this declination to unfold over the longer time required, and so to reach the same end-point pitch while maintaining about the same rate of change. Finally, there is evidence that it takes longer to initiate the production of longer and/or more complex utterances, in the sense that they are preceded by longer pause/initiation times (Krivokapić 2007; Wheeldon and Lahiri 2002). All of these lines of evidence suggest that the speaker is planning at least some global aspects of the upcoming material during a time period that precedes the beginning of articulation. This supports the hypothesis that a speaker generates at least some structural representation of the later parts of the utterance, early in the planning process.

Given these observations, it is natural to ask about the nature of the speech plan representation; that is, just exactly what does the speaker know about the upcoming parts of an utterance, and/or about the utterance as a whole, as he or she begins to talk? The observations cited so far suggest that speakers know something about the individual phonological elements that are included in at least some of the words of the upcoming utterance, and something about the length of the utterance, either about its temporal duration or about the number of elements it contains. But what is the evidence that this foreknowledge takes the form of a structured planning frame that is represented independently of its eventual word and sound segment content? In the next section we consider the evidence for this claim.

19.3 Do speakers generate a structured planning frame represented independently of its contents?

The most compelling evidence that speakers generate an independently represented planning frame rather than simply retrieving lexical items (with their constituent phonemic sounds) ahead of time knowing something about the overall duration or item count of the utterance, comes from a particular fact about interaction errors. When a target word or other linguistic element either is displaced from its intended location or is reduplicated so that it appears twice in the utterance, it does not reappear in a random location. Instead, it appears in a location that is structurally similar to its original target location. This structural similarity constraint on interaction errors is not only characteristic of exchange errors, of the type that we have seen above, but also of other types of interaction errors, including anticipations and incomplete errors (also illustrated above), and perseveration errors such as *play the pliano* for *play the piano*. In all of these types of errors, a displaced or reduplicated element appears not in some random location, but in a structural slot that is similar to its target location. Specifically, a displaced noun reappears in a slot where a noun should go, and a preposition where a preposition should go (Garrett 1975); similarly, a displaced word-onset consonant reappears in an onset consonant slot, a vowel in a nucleus slot, and a word-final consonant in a final slot (Shattuck-Hufnagel 1979).

Thus, what is almost never observed in spoken errors that involve an interaction between target elements/locations in an utterance is the appearance of a displaced or reduplicated target element in a random location. For example, it is common to observe errors such as *The yard in the front tree* for *The tree in the front yard*, or *The cack of the bar* for *The back of the car*, but not errors such as **The yard in tree the front* or **The _ack of the carb*. These examples illustrate a second characteristic of interaction errors which is revealed most clearly by exchanges: there must be a mechanism for representing a structural location even when its target content element has moved to a different location, so that that slot will be available to receive the displaced element. Similarly, there must be a selection mechanism to ensure that the displaced element can be inserted into that preserved slot. Shattuck-Hufnagel (1975, 1979, 1992) proposed a slot+filler process which provides a "slot-maintaining" mechanism (preserving a target location to receive a displaced target segment), and a "scan-copy" mechanism to select the target element to fill it. This model will be discussed further and compared with other current models in section 19.6 below. One of its key principles, that slot structures are represented independent of slot contents, is illustrated not only by the first and second parts of an exchange error, but also by the constraints exhibited by both anticipatory and perseveratory substitution errors.

To sum up, interaction error patterns appear to follow two separate constraints, which suggest an important aspect of the planning representation of an utterance: both the Position Similarity Constraint (by which interacting segments occupy similar positions) and the Independent Frame Constraint (by which target slots are maintained when their target contents move elsewhere) are consistent with the view that speakers generate a structural planning frame, and that a structural frame exists independent of its contents, because its slots can be filled by other (displaced) elements from similar locations. (A third constraint, the Onset Error Preference Constraint, proposed by Fromkin (1971), appears to hold most strongly for exchange errors (Shattuck-Hufnagel 1987).) Given these constraints, the question then arises, what is the nature of this structural planning frame?

19.4 Does the planning frame correspond to prosodic structure?

A wide variety of evidence supports the view that speakers generate a hierarchical prosodic structure as part of the process of planning and producing an utterance, and that this prosodic structure is separate from the morphosyntactic structure of the sentence that underlies that utterance (see Shattuck-Hufnagel and Turk 1996 for a review of literature in support of the separation). In this section we summarize some of this evidence, and then present arguments to support the view that this prosodic structure provides the planning frame argued for in section 19.3.

During the early decades of modern linguistics, prosody was largely viewed as a set of acoustic parameters, that is, F0, amplitude, and duration, whose variation was governed by syntactic structure (see, e.g., Klatt 1976). The last quarter of the twentieth century, however, saw the emergence of a theory of prosodic structure as an entity separate from (although closely related to) morphosyntactic structure. This view of prosody proposed a hierarchy of constituents, from the utterance through intonational phrases, prosodic (or phonological) phrases to lower-level constituents such as feet, syllables, and morae (Hayes 1984; Selkirk 1984; Nespor and Vogel 1986; and relatedly Beckman and Pierrehumbert 1986). In some models, each of these constituents was hypothesized to have a head (Beckman and Edwards 1994), and as a result, prosodic theory provided a hierarchy of both constituents and prominences.

Armed with this theoretical description of the constituents and relative prominences in spoken utterances, investigators began to study the acoustic correlates of these structures in recorded speech. The results of these studies revealed a significant role for prosodic structure in governing the phonetic realization of spoken utterances. For example, it is prosodic structure rather than syntactic structure that influences the degree of phrase-final lengthening (Ferreira 1993, 2007; Price et al. 1991), which in turn reflects the hierarchical structure of prosodic constituents (Wightman et al. 1992), with greater degrees of lengthening for higher-level constituents. Moreover, prosodic structure has been shown to govern many aspects of structure-based phonetic variation, such as glottalization (manifested as irregular pitch periods) at the beginnings and ends of intonational phrases and at pitch accents (Henton and Bladon 1986; Pierrehumbert and Talkin 1992; Dilley, Shattuck-Hufnagel, and Ostendorf 1996; Redi and Shattuck-Hufnagel 2001), and the degree of tongue contact during an onset /n/ (Fougeron and Keating 1995) known as "initial strengthening." Such phenomena have been observed not only in English but in a range of languages: see Keating et al. (2003) for initial strengthening in prosodic constituents in French, Korean, and Taiwanese; Fougeron (2001) for strengthening of constituent-onsets in French; Jun (1993) for the duration of VOT in Korean at Accentual Phrase boundaries; and Shih (1997) for tone sandhi in Mandarin. Finally, prosodic structure has been shown to govern phonological as well as phonetic variation. For example, intonational phrasing governs the placement of pitch accents within a polysyllabic word, giving, for example, nuclear main-stress accent in *MassaCHUsetts* but phrase-initial early accent in *MAssachusetts paRADES* (Bolinger 1986; Shattuck-Hufnagel, Ostendorf, and Ross 1994).

The accumulating evidence that prosodic structure governs much of contextual phonetic variation has inspired the hypothesis that the influence of morphosyntactic structure on phonetics is indirect, via its influence on prosodic structure. On this view, the many different ways in which a given underlying sentence can be "prosodified" result in many different patterns of articulatory/acoustic variation, and these differences can be understood as the result of different paths through the universe of possible prosodic structures from a single morphosyntactic sentence. Thus, for the study of prosody it is no longer sufficient to ask "how would you say this sentence?" but instead "how did the speaker produce this sentence in this particular utterance?"

In sum, there is increasing evidence that speakers generate prosodic structure for their utterances, independent of (although influenced by) the morphosyntactic structure of the intended sentence, and that these structures govern not only the traditional "prosodic parameters" of F0, amplitude and duration, but also a substantial portion of systematic structure-governed phonetic variation in word forms (in addition to other factors that influence systematic phonetic variation not addressed here, including word frequency, speaking rate, and speaking style). Although this evidence does not necessarily mean that the utterance-specific prosodic structure corresponds to the planning frame that was argued for in section 19.3, if the planning frame *is* prosodic in nature, it would help to explain one of the most mysterious aspects of sound-level errors. It has long been a puzzle why serial ordering errors occur at the sound level at all, because the serial order of a word's sound segments must be specified in its lexical entry. That is the case because the order of the segments is contrastive; that is, the serial order of segments is what distinguishes among sets of words such as *act, cat, tack*. But if serial order is specified in the lexicon, why and how do the sounds of words become misordered in speech? A solution to this puzzle would be provided if errors occur during the process of integrating the information in the morphosyntactic specification of the sentence (which distinguishes this sentence from all other sentences of the language), with the prosodic specification of the intended utterance of that sentence which is currently being planned. Such a model has been proposed by Keating and Shattuck-Hufnagel (2002), who suggest that speech production planning includes the generation of an abstract content-free prosodic structure as a "spine" for each utterance; this model will be discussed further, along with other models of the production planning process, in section 19.6 below.

Briefly, the planning frame envisioned in Keating and Shattuck-Hufnagel's (2002) conceptual model of speech production is a prosodic representation of the planned utterance. Following the lead of Levelt and colleagues (Levelt 1989; Levelt et al. 1999), this conceptual model adopts the mechanism of successive partial transfers of information from a morphosyntactic representation to the planning frame. However, the prosodic planning frame proposed by Keating and Shattuck-Hufnagel has several substantial differences from Levelt et al.'s approach: (1) it spans at least an intonational phrase, or perhaps more, as opposed to the Prosodic Word frame of Levelt et al., (2) it is dynamic, in the sense that it is highly abstract at the onset of the planning process (i.e., represents the utterance at the level of the Intonational Phrase), and changes step by step from an abstract representation of this high-level prosodic structure of an utterance (which is determined largely by the syntactic structure) toward a representation that is specified in terms that can drive the articulatory motor system, and (3) it is represented independent of its contents, rather than as a way of grouping existing elements as in the Levelt et al. model. As a result, it is capable of accounting for the pattern of interaction errors that we observe in error corpora. In the Keating and Shattuck-Hufnagel model, the structural representation of the forthcoming utterance is not fixed at the onset of the planning process, but evolves in terms of both its structure and its content, from a general representation at the highest prosodic levels to a detailed specification of the words, sounds, lower level prosodic structure, and plan for the phonetic implementation of the utterance, expanding and becoming more quantitative with every step. An important aspect of this model is that the phrasal prosody of an utterance is not constructed by stringing together the lexical prosody of its words. Instead, there is another level of representation, or more accurately a hierarchy of additional levels, that includes lexical-level prosody for the individual words but also phrase-level prosody for the phrases of the utterance. Thus, it is termed a Prosody First model, in contrast to Prosody Last models in which phrase-level prosodic structure is imposed on the sequence of lower-level constituents late in the planning process.

A different line of evidence for the prosodic planning frame is presented by Croot and her colleagues, based on extensive experimental elicitation of tongue twister errors (Croot, Au, and Harper 2010). They report that the patterns of speech errors elicited by the word strings of tongue twisters that have repetitive alternating patterns of onset consonants, like *den ton tuck dial* and *den ton dial tuck*, can be systematically manipulated by changing the prosodic structure of the utterance, for example, by varying the phrasal position and prominence of the target words. This provides evidence to support the view that information about prosodic phrasing and grouping is available at the moment in the planning process when sound-level errors occur, as would be the case in Keating and Shattuck-Hufnagel's (2002) Prosody First model. Interestingly, Croot and colleagues note that onset consonants of words produced with pitch accents in these experiments are protected against sound-level errors, as are words in phrase-onset position, and they postulate two different planning mechanisms for these two patterns. Both of these protective mechanisms are consistent with a prosodic planning frame.

Additional evidence that the planning frame contains prosodic constituents comes from Choe and Redford (2010), who found that errors increase across a prosodic phrase as it unfolds in time, and that position in the prosodic constituent had various other effects on segmental errors.

In addition to the arguments that the sheer availability of the prosodic structure of an utterance makes it a good candidate for the planning frame proposed in section 19.3 above, that such a planning frame (with an associated serial ordering mechanism) would provide an account of interaction errors, and that prosodic information (i.e., information about prominence and word grouping) is available at the point in production processing where speech errors occur, there is also evidence for a prosodic planning representation from other aspects of speech behavior that reflect the operation of the planning process for typical fluent error-free speech. For example, as noted in section 19.2 (where it was cited as evidence for planning ahead), data reported by a number of investigators suggests that the length of a phrase or other constituent determines, for example, prior pausing behavior and F0 at onset. What makes these findings relevant to the question of whether the planning frame is prosodic is that in many cases it appears that the length and complexity of that constituent is measured in prosodic constituents (Krivokapić 2007; Watson and Gibson 2004; Wheeldon and Lahiri 1997; Ferreira 1993). That is, phrases with a greater number of prosodic sub-constituents or more complex prosodic structures are the ones that require more planning time.

The relevance of length in prosodic elements or complexity of prosodic structure to the speaker's pausing behavior supports the proposal argued for in section 19.3: that speakers generate a planning frame in terms of prosodic structure. But what about the claim that this planning structure is, initially at least, represented independently of its morphosyntactic content? Recall that this was proposed by Shattuck-Hufnagel (1992 inter alia), along with a serial ordering mechanism to fill the slots in the framework with the appropriate words and sounds, in order to account for observed constraints on the misordering of planned elements in interaction errors. A line of behavioral evidence that further supports the hypothesis that prosodic structure might be represented separately from its contents, rather than as a grouping and prominence structuring imposed on the morphosyntactic sequence, comes from the observation that many speakers can perform a reiterant imitation of the prosody of a stimulus utterance which contains completely different phonemic content (Nakatani, O'Connor, and Aston 1981; Larkey 1983). That is, speakers can produce a reiterant version of an utterance that has recognizably the same prosody as the original target utterance, replacing the target syllables with successive productions of a single syllable, for example, /ma/ or /sa/. Thus, the target sentence *My name is Stefanie* can be produced *Ma ma ma Ma-ma-ma*, and the phrasing and prominence structure of the target and reiterant utterances sound recognizably similar. Although not all speakers can do this task reliably, the fact that at least some speakers are able to separate the prosodic structure of an utterance from its morphosyntactic content, and can use that structure to guide the production of a different (and meaningless) phonological string, suggests that speakers can represent the accent structure and constituent structure of an utterance separately from the words they were realized on.

In sections 19.2–4 we have examined evidence and arguments from the behavior of typical adult speakers, largely of English but with some supporting evidence from speakers of other languages, in support of the view that speakers generate an abstract planning frame for an utterance, that this planning frame corresponds to prosodic structure, and that it is represented independent of its contents. In the next section we review evidence from other types of speakers.

19.5 What can we learn about planning frames from other behavioral domains?

Most of the evidence and arguments considered in sections 19.2–4 are drawn from patterns of behavior in typical adult speakers. However, it is reasonable to ask whether evidence for the representation of structured planning frames can also be found in the behavior of child speakers who are still learning to produce utterances; of speakers whose language production skills have been damaged by an event in adulthood; and of those who use signed languages. In this section, we examine evidence from these three domains which, although not offering as direct and compelling support as the evidence from speech errors and behavioral experiments described above, nevertheless provide some support for the hypothesis that speakers form abstract structural planning frames to guide the production of their utterances.

19.5.1 Evidence that the child learns to generate a planning frame

We have argued that speakers generate phrase-level planning frames and that these planning frames correspond to the prosodic structure that speakers must generate in any case, in order to derive the prosodic phrasing and accent specifications for a spoken utterance, with its resulting systematic context-driven phonetic variation. A number of proposed accounts of non-adult-like aspects of child speech are consistent with this view; that is, they offer evidence that planning an utterance involves the representation of more structure than simply a string of word forms, and that the process of learning to talk includes learning to generate these frames.

One line of evidence that children form prosodic phrasal planning structures well before they produce fluent multi-word utterances comes from the work of Branigan (1979). He found that at a certain stage of development, children produced what appeared to adult listeners to be a sequence of single-word utterances (separated by pauses), but which actually had the prosodic structure of a single three-word utterance. Evidence for this interpretation was the observation that the first two words did not show signs of phrase- or utterance-final lengthening or final F0 fall, while the third word did show these cues to the end of a prosodic constituent. This observation is consistent with work by Snow (1994, 1997) showing that very young children have mastered the skill of cueing the ends of prosodic constituents by lengthening their final elements (see Turk and Shattuck-Hufnagel 2007 for a discussion of final lengthening in adult speech).

The production of multi-word utterances in which the successive words are prosodically integrated but separated by pauses is reminiscent of covert contrast in the segmental domain. Covert segmental contrast involves the production by children of systematically different parameter values which reliably signal distinctive feature contrasts but cannot be easily perceived by adult listeners, because the two sets of values fall within the range that adult speakers use to signal just one member of the contrast (Macken and Barton 1980; Scobbie et al. 2000; Gibbon and Scobbie 1997). This phenomenon has been widely reported as a characteristic of the developmental course of phonology and of the phonology-to-phonetics mapping in some children, and has recently been proposed as an alternative view of traditionally described segmental substitutions during development (Richtsmeier 2010). Branigan's (1979) data provide evidence for a covert prosodic contrast between three successive single-word utterances versus a prosodically integrated three-word utterance interrupted by pauses. This raises the question of whether a similar phenomenon may mask the development of the child's ability to generate a prosodic frame to govern the planning of utterances. That is, children at this stage may be generating a larger planning frame for their three-word sequences, and signaling it with duration and F0 cues, but the insertion of pauses between the words may make it difficult for adult listeners to perceive this evidence.

More direct evidence for the possibility that children generate prosodic frames that are larger than a single word and that systematically govern their productions comes from work by Gerken (1994, 1996) and by Demuth and colleagues (Demuth and Tremblay 2008; Demuth and McCullough 2009), showing that phrase-level metrical structure constrains the production of function elements in early child productions. It has long been noted that children who are just beginning to produce multi-word utterances and use syntactic morphemes such as articles and syllabic markers for plural and past forms often show extreme variability in their productions. That is, some utterances include these syntactic markers while others do not, often within the same day or even the same conversation, and in the absence of an approach to production planning that includes prosodic structure it is not easy to formulate a model that predicts such variable use of these constituents. Interestingly, however, evidence from children learning English suggests that such elements are omitted in precisely those contexts where they can't be fitted into a strong-weak metrical structure. For example, a two-year-old might be more likely to produce the article in *[Tom] [pushed the] [zebra]* than in *[Tom] [pushes the] [zebra]*, because in the former case the article *the* fits into the structure of a strong-weak foot (Gerken 1996).

Such observations suggest that the child speaker formulates a prosodic framework consisting of prosodic constituents that at some level license a sequence of strong+weak elements, but not a sequence of strong+weak+weak elements. When a given syntactic morpheme fits the strong+weak framework, it can be produced; when it does not, it is omitted from the utterance. This discovery goes a long way toward accounting for the variation in the appearance of certain syntactic morphemes in child speech at a certain stage of language development; it also provides some evidence that children who are still learning to speak are nevertheless formulating a prosodic frame that governs the words they produce.

The nature of the prosodic structure implicated by the results on morpheme omission is metrical, and it is not immediately clear that this kind of structure fits comfortably into the now-traditional Prosodic Hierarchy of Utterance, Intonational

Phrase, Intermediate Intonational Phrase, and so on proposed by Hayes (1984), Selkirk (1984), Nespor and Vogel (1986), and others. Interestingly, there is an aspect of speech errors in English that also implicates a type of phrase-level metrical regularity constraint in adult speech production planning. Cutler (1980) noted that when speakers omit a syllable from a longer derived word such as *photography*, it often creates a more regular metrical pattern within the utterance. Kelly and Bock (1988) make a related argument in ascribing the asymmetrical distribution of stress patterns for nouns vs. verbs in English to the influence of preferred metrical patterns. The question of how phrase-level metrical structures interact with other prosodic structures in the Prosodic Hierarchy is clearly in need of further investigation.

19.5.2 Evidence for planning frames in the pattern of errors produced by adult speakers of languages other than English

One of the most interesting questions about speech production planning is how differently this process unfolds for speakers of different languages, and how the representations that are generated are influenced by the grammatical characteristics of the language. While there are scattered studies of error patterns in different languages (see references in section 19.3 above), not much work on this specific issue has emerged. However, the few studies that have appeared suggest that there may be different constraints on sound-level error patterns in different languages that reflect differences in the preferred structures for syllables or morphemes. For example, Garcia-Albea, del Viso, and Igoa (1989) have shown that the constraints on segment-level errors in Spanish are different from those in English. That is, Spanish shows no evidence of the word-onset preference or word-based similarity constraints that are so powerful in English; the Position Similarity Constraint on interaction errors for Spanish is better described in terms of the syllable than of the word. Clearly, additional work focused on this question is needed if we are to understand the role of prosodic frames in speech production processing. It is possible that the question of what light can be shed on inter-language processing differences by speech errors will be easier to address in the future than it was in the past, because of the availability of large samples of continuous conversational speech which are increasingly being collected, providing a rich source of speech errors whose prosodic context can be analyzed.

19.5.3 Evidence for planning frames in the pattern of errors produced by users of sign language

If the generation of a phrase- or utterance-level planning framework with little or at least incomplete specification of its contents is characteristic of speech production, then it makes sense to ask whether it is also characteristic of utterances produced in languages that use a different modality, such as sign languages. While few studies have addressed this question directly, a groundbreaking set of studies by Klima and Bellugi and their colleagues (e.g., Bellugi, Klima, and Siple 1975; Newkirk et al. 1980) describe some tantalizing analyses from a small corpus of errors observed in signed utterances. Klima and Bellugi and their colleagues were mostly concerned with showing that signs are not unitary elements, but rather are defined by a set of contrastive features, such as hand-shape, location, and movement. As a result, they focused on the fact that sign errors can substitute one of these sign features for another. Of particular interest for us here, however, is the observation that interaction errors in sign, as in speech, provide evidence for early activation of information about an utterance (as argued for spoken utterances in section 19.2), and for at least some degree of representation of structural slots for the upcoming signs (as in section 19.3). Moreover, a small number of the errors in their corpus take the form of exchanges; that is, they show the characteristic that we observe in spoken errors: the later target location of the displacing element in the first part of the exchange error is preserved for the later insertion of the displaced element. In this sense they support the same arguments as do the exchanges that occur in spoken utterances. But because signs combine their meaning-contrasting features with much greater temporal overlap than do words in speech, these signed errors do not provide the same kind of evidence for the generation of a minimally contentful phrase-level planning framework that spoken exchange errors do. For example, it is harder to find evidence for a position similarity constraint, since the elements of a sign are realized in the same temporal and structural position.

In sum, there is some evidence in the behavior of children, of speakers of languages other than English, and to some extent of signers, for the hypothesis that language users generate a structure-based planning frame for their utterances. Another population of language users whose behavior might provide a test of this hypothesis is found in adult speakers who have developed difficulty with speech production as the result of injury or disease. For a number of such clinical populations, there is evidence that providing a planning framework in the form of a rhythmic or intonational scaffold can result in improved speech production. In the next subsection we review some of this tantalizing, though as yet inconclusive, evidence.

19.5.4 *Evidence that generating a rhythmic and/or intonational framework is a clinically effective intervention for some kinds of speech production disabilities*

Many different disease and injury processes can result in challenges to the fluent production of speech. These include some types of aphasia (in which brain injury can result in difficulty with speaking), Parkinson's disease (in which there is loss of fluency in some actions), dysarthria (in which the neurological system controlling speech articulation is damaged), and stuttering, among others. For each of these conditions, there are reports that treatment providing a rhythmic or rhythmic/intonational scaffold for an utterance can, for some patients, result in measurably improved speech production. For example, for some speakers who develop severe aphasia as the result of brain damage that compromises their ability to produce speech, an intervention method known as Melodic Intonation Therapy (Helm-Estabrooks, Morgan, and Nicholas 1989; Norton et al. 2009; Zipse et al. 2012) has been reported to be effective (see Zumbansen, Peretz, and Hébert 2014 for a critical review).

This method was inspired by the observation that some speakers who experience difficulty in speaking conversationally after neurological damage to the dominant hemisphere can nevertheless produce song. Melodic Intonation Therapy involves a sequence of treatment steps, built around the therapist guiding the non-dominant hand of the patient to tap out the rhythm of simple utterances likely to be of use in daily life, such as *I want a cup of coffee*, while the patient produces the speech using just two pitch levels, with the higher one for accented syllables. In some cases this treatment has been reported to lead to improvements in spontaneously generated speech, and it is possible that this is due, at least in part, to the provision of a simple prosodic framework for the utterance, so that the speaker does not have to compute the complex timing and intonation contours required by typical spoken prosody.

A second type of speech production problem that can be addressed by providing a rhythmic framework is dysarthria. Treatment here sometimes involves encouraging the patient to tap on spatially regular marks on a board, as they produce speech. Again, it is possible that the provision of a regular timing framework for the speech via temporally regular motor activity by the hand somehow relieves the production planning system of some of the burden of generating this framework, facilitating the speech production. It must be said that the mechanism for this facilitation is somewhat mysterious, since typical speech is not temporally regular, but it is possible that there is a path to speech timing that invokes periodic or quasi-periodic temporal structure (Goldstein et al. 2007; but see Turk and Shattuck-Hufnagel 2013). It is also possible that much of the benefit from treatments like this arises from the simple slowing down of the speech; a controlled study comparing the effects of slowing vs. the provision of a regular timing framework would be useful in evaluating these mechanism that underlies the usefulness of these treatments.

A third type of speech problem that has been found to benefit from external provision of a temporally regular framework is stuttering (Brady 1971). In some cases a speaker who stutters is able to speak more fluently when listening to a metronome, although it is reported that this method eventually loses its effectiveness. In view of the reported effectiveness of Melodic Intonation Therapy discussed above, it is interesting that some speakers who stutter when speaking conversationally find that they can maintain a professional career as singers, with little or no interference in their singing onstage.

There is also a small amount of evidence suggesting that a pre-supplied rhythmic and/or melodic structure aids in learning the phonology (or perhaps the phonology-phonetic mapping) of a second language. Hagen, Kerkhoff, and

Gussenhoven (2011) report that speakers of Dutch who are producing English are judged to have more native-like English accents by native speakers of English when they sing, than when they speak. Relatedly, Geiser, Shattuck-Hufnagel, and Gabrieli (2011) report that, for speakers of English who are learning German, and are asked to imitate strongly rhythmicized vs. more typically timed German utterances, there is some improvement in the phonological match for the rhythmicized tokens. Taken together with often-heard anecdotal reports that second language learners experience greater ease in producing their new language when singing simple folk songs than when speaking more conversationally, these preliminary findings suggest at least that controlled experiments are needed in order to tease out the relative contributions of (a) provision of a timing pattern, (b) provision of an intonational pattern, and (c) producing the speech more slowly.

Finally, returning to child speakers, there is an interesting line of evidence that links certain types of developmental speech and language problems, particularly those related to phonological acquisition, to the child's ability to find and entrain to a beat in auditory stimuli (Goswami 2011). Goswami relates this correlation to brain mechanisms that involve ongoing oscillation patterns, and notes the presence of substantial neural connections between the auditory processing regions and the motor control regions of the human brain. This observation is particularly tantalizing in view of recent reports that non-human species who can entrain to an external auditory stimulus, that is, who can organize their motor activity so that successive movements are timed to occur "on the beat" of that stimulus, appear to be limited to those who must learn a vocal communication system (Schachner et al. 2011; Patel et al. 2009). (This ability is to be distinguished from the ability to organize temporally regular motor activity, as in walking or flying, which is widespread among species and does not require entrainment to the timing of an external stimulus.)

In sum, there are thought-provoking hints in the literature of an important link between the ability to entrain to an auditory stimulus, the ability to generate a "prosodic plan," and the ability to learn and use a vocal communication system. The precise nature of this potential link remains to be explored, but to the extent that it exists, it would be consistent with the view that speakers generate a prosodic framework for their spoken utterances.

19.6 Evaluating current models of speech production planning

In this section we briefly review several current models of the speech planning process, in light of their capacity to incorporate a phrase- or utterance-level prosodic planning frame. We also consider studies of other motor activities which, like speech, involve both serial ordering and hierarchical organization, and at least one relevant model which has emerged from that line of investigation.

As noted by Pfau (2000) in his extensive review of the speech error literature, after Lashley's seminal 1951 paper, Fromkin (1971) was the first modern investigator to consider what speech error constraints might reveal about the process of speech planning for production. She was primarily interested in error evidence that supports the role of linguistic elements in speech processing, arguing for example that the occurrence of errors that involve the misordering of individual phonemic segments shows that speakers represent these linguistic units during the production planning process, rather than words as wholes. She proposed a conceptual model of the overall speech planning process in terms of neurological processing. Garrett (1975, 1980), also drawing on error evidence, proposed a model which emphasized the separation of word-level versus sound-level processing. He noted that word interaction errors often involve words of the same form class from target sites in two different syntactic phrases, while sound interactions often involve sounds from words of different form classes in the same syntactic phrase, and argued that this difference in constraints on interacting elements suggests a separation between word-level processing and sound-level processing. In contrast to these investigators, Dell (1986) and Dell and colleagues (1997) focused largely on what sound-level errors might tell us about the process of activating lexical items during production.

As noted earlier, the most thoroughly worked out model of speech production planning in the literature is the one proposed by Levelt and colleagues (Levelt 1989: Bock and Levelt 1994; Levelt et al. 1999; Levelt 2001). In contrast to other proposals, this model covers the entire process of formulating and producing an utterance of a sentence, and distinguishes a number of separate sub-processes, which generate a sequence of increasingly specific representations as the production process unfolds. With respect to word form encoding, the Levelt, Roelofs, and Meyer (LRM99) model involves a lemma level, which is abstract; it specifies the grammatical role(s) that a word can fill in a sentence, and provides the storage address for retrieving the phonological specification of the word, but it does not contain any phonological information about word form. Thus, the early-stage syntactic processor in the LRM99 model already postulates abstract representations for the structure of the sentence. The positional level envisioned by Ferreira and Engelhardt (2006) as coming from the "phrasal frames" that are retrieved with the target words has the same characteristic. Two lines of evidence from spoken errors support the hypothesis of abstract syntactic planning frames: (1) the lack of serial ordering errors among the grammatical morphemes that define these frames (e.g., function words seldom if ever exchange), and (2) the nature of "spellout errors" for these morphemes (e.g., pronoun errors such as *She told him* → *He told her*, but not → **Him told she*; Garrett 1975). The latter line of evidence is consistent with the hypothesis that, at the moment when such pronoun "exchange" errors occur, the representation of these functional elements in the frame specifies their grammatical role but not their number or gender, and does not include their phonological specification; this is specified later, to fit the new post-ordering-error location of the gender and number information for the pronouns in the planning frame.

Ferreira and Engelhardt (2006), discussing the Bock and Levelt (1994) or BL version of the LRM99 model, note that

> the BL model of production assumes a non-lexical view of syntactic structure. In BL, trees are conceptualized as "control hierarchies" which contain no lexical content but instead coordinate the insertion of lexical material which is retrieved and assembled separately (BL pp. 947–948).
>
> (2006: 71)

Drawing on Garrett's distinction between the assignment of words to their grammatical functions in the sentence and their "linearization" into a serially ordered sequence, Levelt et al. (1999) postulate a two-stage syntactic processor (see Ferreira and Engelhardt 2006). That is, the syntactic plan is generated in two separate stages, the first stage creating a representation that represents hierarchical relations but not necessarily linear order, and a second stage in which linearization within phrases takes place. The output is then organized into Prosodic Words (PWds), for phonological and phonetic encoding, one PWd at a time. At this point the sequence of phonological elements within the PWd is fixed, and the relevant syllable-sized articulatory plans can be retrieved from their long-term store. At a later stage, the higher-level prosodic structure is imposed on this string of PWds, as proposed in the earlier 1989 model. Thus, the basic treatment of phonological and phonetic processing in LRM99 is that the phrase-level phonological plan for the utterance involves first stringing together individual smaller units, PWds, which are specified phonologically; then encoding these units phonetically; and finally imposing a phrase-level prosodic shape on the resulting phonetically specified string of PWds.

Two major insights from Levelt's work are relevant for us here: the planning process must involve phrase-level prosody (Levelt 1989), and not all of the stored information about a target word need be transferred from the lexicon to the utterance plan at the same time (Levelt et al. 1999). The significance of phrase-level prosody for speech planning is that this aspect of an utterance can't be fully accounted for in terms of the morphosyntactic structure of the underlying sentence, but requires a hierarchical constituent structure of its own. As noted in section 19.4, the hierarchy of prosodic constituents specified for an utterance is influenced by, but separate from, its morphosyntactic structure, and must be included in the planning process because it governs much of the contextual variation in the phonological and phonetic (i.e., articulatory and acoustic) shapes of words. In the LRM99 model, this phrase-level prosody is imposed on an existing string of lower-level constituents (PWds), for which the articulatory plans are already worked out, providing no obvious mechanism for prosodically governed phonetics.

Keating and Shattuck-Hufnagel (2002) note several difficulties with the post-syntactic processes suggested in LRM99, including the lack of a mechanism to account for segmental interaction errors (which primarily occur between segments in different PWds, a pattern which is impossible if phonological planning takes place one PWd at a time). They propose a different role for phrase-level prosody in the planning process. Instead of imposing phrase-level prosodic structure late in the planning process, they argue for a Prosody First model, in which the planned utterance begins with a prosodic representation at the highest, most abstract level. This prosodic representation expands and becomes specified in greater and greater detail, as the relevant information is transferred from the morphosyntactic representation of the sentence to the prosodic specification of the utterance, one step at a time. On the Prosody First view, this dynamically changing prosodic planning frame supports the generation of more detailed specifications at each step. As a result, the prosodic structure serves as a bridge from the abstract grammatical representation of a sentence to the more quantitative specifications required by the sensory-motor systems that control the articulatory tract in order to produce the desired acoustic outcome. In a slightly different vein, Ferreira and Engelhardt (2006) note that prosodic structures are flatter than syntactic ones, allowing prosody to serve as an interface between deeply hierarchical and recursive syntactic/semantic representations and the sequential speech channel through which articulation must take place. As discussed earlier, Croot and colleagues (2010) have provided evidence from experimentally induced sound-level speech errors that at least some aspects of phrase-level grouping and accentual prosodic structure are available at the planning stage when sound-level errors occur, offering support for a Prosody First approach.

19.7 Unanswered questions and future work

We have argued that a number of lines of evidence suggest that speakers generate a phrase-level structural plan for an utterance; that this plan is abstract in form and changes dynamically during the planning process, specifying its elements in greater and greater detail as the planning process unfolds; and that this abstract planning framework corresponds to prosodic structure. This view is supported by evidence from speech error patterns, by experimental evidence from reaction time and priming studies, and by evidence that systematic phonetic variation is governed by prosodic structure. Somewhat more indirectly, it is compatible with certain aspects of language development, of speech-language pathologies, and of the effectiveness of certain intervention methods which have prosodic components. However, it is clear that many questions remain to be resolved, including the following.

19.7.1 *How do languages differ in the types of prosodic planning frames that their speakers generate?*

While speech error corpora collected by listening to ongoing speech in a number of languages reveal error patterns that are compatible with the general claim that linguistic elements serve as error units and are serially ordered into an abstract phrase-level planning frame, some of the details of the observed error patterns differ across languages. This is not unexpected if the planning frame is prosodic, since the prosodies of different languages are known to differ, but it will be important to test the Prosody First hypothesis across languages, and to determine how the proposed prosodic structure of each language might influence its error patterns. It is even possible that the constraints on errors (as well as patterns of systematic phonetic variation) can help to test alternative views of prosodic structure. Additional useful information about the planning frame might come from studies of speech pathologies (and effective prosody-related treatments) across languages (see Seki and Sugishita 1983 for an example of Melodic Intonation Therapy adjusted to the prosodic aspects of Japanese); from cross-language studies of phonological development, both prosodic and segmental, and its pathologies; and from more comprehensive studies of sign language errors.

19.7.2 What are the dynamic characteristics of the unfolding planning process?

We are only at the initial stages of addressing questions like: Which aspects of a potential planning frame govern which aspects of planning? At what point in the process do the abstract slots contain specifications for which type of information? Precise answers to these critical questions will require implementing a model of the planning process, a goal which was substantially advanced by Levelt et al.'s (1999) report of Roelofs' (1997) implementation of their model. However, this implementation was not designed to take the final steps in the process, that is, to produce acoustic wave forms corresponding to spoken utterances. Since then, evidence has accumulated that systematic patterns of detailed acoustic variation, often below the level of conscious perceptual access, play a significant role in speech processing, both on the input and the output side, and that prosodic structure (in the form of phrasing and prominence) is an important factor governing this variation. As a result, an important criterion for a speech planning model is that it can generate context-appropriate phonetic forms at this level of detail. A future implementation of a planning model that includes a speech synthesis component will be required to determine how appropriately the model generates these forms.

19.7.3 Do different types of language production elicit different types of prosodic planning frames?

In view of the fact that typical conversational speech does not exhibit reliable surface temporal regularity (although see Dilley 1997 and the extensive body of recent work on comparative perceived speech rhythms across languages for evidence that it sometimes exhibits *perceived* temporal regularity, and Turk and Shattuck-Hufnagel 2013 for a critical review of this evidence), it is particularly interesting to find evidence that temporal regularity in various forms can be helpful in speech production. As noted earlier, it is possible that speech timing is generated differently for different speaking modes, for example, conversational sentences vs. word lists; typical speech vs. song vs. the recitation of poetry vs. rhythmically regular repetitive speech. Further investigation of these possibilities may shed light on the nature of the planning frame, and how it might vary across speaking circumstances.

19.7.4 Which aspects of the planning process result in which types of error?

It may be important to distinguish among different levels of processing at which different types of sound-level errors can occur; for example, errors which occur during the lexical retrieval process (Dell 1986), during the motor implementation process (Goldstein et al. 2007), and during the integration of planning elements with an abstract structural planning frame, hypothesized to be prosodic in nature (Shattuck-Hufnagel 1992; Keating and Shattuck-Hufnagel 2002). Relatedly, how far ahead is the planning frame constructed (and how might this vary with speaking circumstances)? Which levels of prosodic structure govern which aspects of phonological and phonetic planning? And, when two elements of a planned utterance interact, suggesting that both of them are actively represented, is it the case that all of the intervening elements have also been activated?

One particularly vexing question about the planning frame concerns errors which add or omit phonemic segments. As argued above, exchange errors (as well as certain aspects of anticipatory and perseveratory substitutions) suggest strongly that the planning frame specifies a number of serially ordered segmental slots for the phrase or utterance, because pairs of interacting segments are usually targeted for similar structural slot positions, and displaced segments almost always appear in the target location that served as the source of the displacing segment. But there are certain types of sound-level errors that appear to insert segments into locations without a target slot, or remove segments (leaving empty slots), as in apparent single-segment shifts such as *tie grow-strips* → *try g_o-strips* and, to the listening ear at least, such changes do not lead to disfluent-sounding productions. Experimental investigation of when and why the number of segmental target slots can be changed in an error may shed some light on this aspect of the planning frame; see, for example, Stemberger (1990) on the prevalence of /r/ and /l/ targets in such errors in English.

These are potentially fruitful times for the investigation of how speakers generate planning frames, what kinds of planning frames they generate, and how planning frames might change during the planning process and vary across speaking circumstances. There are large corpora of digitized speech just waiting to be analyzed for their error patterns; a variety of theories and models of the planning process to be tested, using error patterns, reaction times, and acoustic/articulatory-phonetic data; and on the horizon, brain imaging methods and speech synthesis systems to test these models even more comprehensively and searchingly. It is to be hoped that the next decade will see many of our most pressing questions in this domain convincingly answered.

NOTES

1 Articulatory measures (Goldstein et al. 2007) have documented the fact that repetitive alternating temporally periodic tongue twisters (like *top cop top cop top cop ...*) can elicit articulatory intrusions in which the constriction gestures for both the target and the intrusion onset consonants (in this example, /t/ and /k/) occur in onset position; they have also demonstrated that these gestural intrusions can be gradient, so that in some cases only one of the constrictions is perceived. This finding has been interpreted as casting some doubt on the claim that sound-level errors in typical communicative speech involve the substitution of one linguistic element for another. But recent results (Shattuck-Hufnagel et al. 2013) suggest that errors that occur during the production of more typical sentence structures (like *The top cop saw a cop top*) are less likely to be gestural intrusions, and more likely to be whole-segment substitutions. This evidence is consistent with the view that, while errors made during the production of tongue twisters reveal important characteristics of the speech planning and production mechanisms, the types of errors they most frequently elicit may be significantly different from the types that occur more frequently in spoken sentences, and so should be interpreted with care as evidence for the nature of the typical speech production process. Moreover, one possible interpretation of this difference is that typical speech production involves the generation of a multilayered hierarchical planning frame, whereas the production of a repetitive alternating periodic tongue twister may be planned in a very different way.

2 An incomplete error like *sye – try to see*, if completed, might have taken the form of either a full exchange (e.g., *sye to tree*) or an anticipatory substitution/addition (e.g., *sye to see*). Shattuck-Hufnagel (1987) has argued that a substantial proportion of incomplete errors correspond to the first half of an exchange error, while the rest correspond to the first half of an incomplete anticipatory substitution. Evidence for this possibility comes from the asymmetry in word position for exchanges vs. anticipatory substitutions at the sound-segment level; that is, exchanges tend to occur between word-onset consonants (Fromkin 1971), while anticipatory substitutions are more evenly spread across position in the word (Shattuck-Hufnagel 1987). Interestingly, the position preference for incomplete errors is somewhere in between. Because these two error types are governed by different position preference constraints, it is possible that they occur at different stages in the utterance planning process, or by different mechanisms. In other words, sound-level errors may occur at more than one level in the production planning process. A second line of evidence that supports this view is the difference between error patterns elicited by repetitive alternating temporally periodic tongue twisters vs. by sentences, described in note 1; this difference in error types suggests a second kind of distinction between two error-producing processes, i.e., sentence-level phonological planning and articulatory implementation of that plan. The possibility that sound-level errors can occur at various levels in the utterance-planning process is ripe for future investigation (see section 19.7).

REFERENCES

Beckman, Mary E. and Jan Edwards. 1994. Articulatory evidence for differentiating stress categories. *Papers in Laboratory Phonology* 3: 7–33.

Beckman, Mary and Janet Pierrehumbert. 1986. Intonational structure in Japanese and English. *Phonology Yearbook* 3: 5–70.

Bellugi, Ursula, Edward S. Klima, and Patricia Siple. 1975. Remembering in signs. *Cognition* 3: 93–125.

Berg, Thomas. 1992. Productive and perceptual constraints on speech-error correction. *Psychological Research* 54: 114–126.

Bock, J.K. 1990. Structure in language: Creating form in talk. *American Psychologist* 45: 1221–1236.

Bock, J.K. and W.J.M. Levelt. 1994. Language production: Grammatical encoding. In M.A. Gernsbacher (ed.), *Handbook of Psycholinguistics*, 945–984. San Diego, CA: Academic Press.

Bock, Kathryn and Helga Loebell. 1990. Framing sentences. *Cognition* 35: 1–39.

Bolinger, Dwight. 1986. *Intonation and Its Parts: Melody in Spoken English*. Stanford, CA: Stanford University Press.

Brady, John. 1971. Metronome-conditioned speech retraining for stuttering. *Behavior Therapy* 2(2): 129–150

Branigan, George. 1979. Some reasons why successive single word utterances are not. *Journal of Child Language* 6: 411–422.

Choe, Wook Kyung and Melissa A. Redford. 2012. The distribution of speech errors in multi-word prosodic units. *Laboratory Phonology* 3: 5–26.

Croot, Karen, Claudia Au, and Amy Harper. 2010. Prosodic structure and tongue twister errors. *Laboratory Phonology* 10: 433–459.

Cutler, Anne. 1980. Syllable omission errors and isochrony. In H.W. Dechert and M. Raupach (eds.), *Temporal Variables in Speech: Studies in Honour of Frieda Goldman-Eisler*, 183–190. The Hague: Mouton.

Dell, Gary S. 1986. A spreading-activation theory of retrieval in sentence production. *Psychological Review* 93: 283–321.

Dell, Gary S., Myrna F. Schwartz, Nadine Martin, Eleanor M. Saffran, and Deborah A. Gagnon. 1997. Lexical access in aphasic and nonaphasic speakers. *Psychological Review* 104: 801–838.

del Viso, Susana. 1992. *Errores espontáneos del habla y producción del lenguaje*. Madrid: Editorial de la Universidad Complutense de Madrid.

Demuth, Katherine and Elizabeth McCullough. 2009. The prosodic (re)organization of children's early English articles. *Journal of Child Language* 36: 173–200.

Demuth, Katherine and Annie Tremblay. 2008. Prosodically-conditioned variability in children's production of French determiners. *Journal of Child Language* 35: 99–127.

Dilley, Laura. 1997. Some factors influencing duration between syllables judged perceptually isochronous. *Journal of the Acoustical Society of America* 102: 3205–3206.

Dilley, Laura, Stefanie Shattuck-Hufnagel, and Mari Ostendorf. 1996. Glottalization of word-initial vowels as a function of prosodic structure. *Journal of Phonetics* 24: 423–444.

Ferreira, Fernanda. 1993. Creation of prosody during sentence production. *Psychological Review* 100: 233–253.

Ferreira, Fernanda. 2007. Prosody and performance in language production. *Language and Cognitive Processes* 22: 1151–1177.

Ferreira, Fernanda and Paul E. Engelhardt. 2006. Syntax and production. In M. Traxler and M.A. Gernsbacher, *Handbook of Psycholinguistics*, 61–91. London: Academic Press.

Fougeron, Cecile. 2001. Articulatory properties of initial segments in several prosodic constituents in French. *Journal of Phonetics* 29: 109–135.

Fougeron, Cecile and Patricia A. Keating. 1995. Demarcating prosodic groups with articulation. *Journal of the Acoustical Society of America* 97: 3384.

Fromkin, Victoria A. 1971. The non-anomalous nature of anomalous utterances. *Language* 47: 27–52.

Fuchs, Susanne, Phil Hoole, Dominique Vornwald, Anne Gwinner, Hristo Velkov, and Jelena Krivokapic. 2008. The control of speech breathing in relation to the upcoming sentence. In *Proceedings of the 8th International Seminar on Speech Production*, 77–80.

García-Albea, José E., Susana del Viso, and José M. Igoa. 1989. Movement errors and levels of processing in sentence production. *Journal of Psycholinguistic Research* 18: 145–161.

Garrett, Merrill F. 1975. The analysis of sentence production. In G.H. Bower (ed.), *The Psychology of Learning and Motivation*, vol. 9, 133–177. San Diego, CA: Academic Press.

Garrett, Merrill F. 1980. Levels of processing in sentence production. In B. Butterworth (ed.), *Language Production*, vol. 1, 177–220. London: Academic Press.

Geiser, Eveline, Stefanie Shattuck-Hufnagel, and John D.E. Gabrieli. 2011. Temporal regularity in speech perception: Is regularity beneficial or deleterious? *Journal of the Acoustical Society of America* 130: 2568.

Gerken, LouAnn. 1994. A metrical template account of children's weak syllable omissions from multisyllabic words. *Journal of Child Language* 21: 565–565.

Gerken, LouAnn. 1996. Prosodic structure in young children's language production. *Language* 72: 683–712.

Gibbon, Fiona and James M. Scobbie. 1997. Covert contrasts in children with phonological disorder. *Australian Communication Quarterly*, 13–16.

Goldstein, Louis, Marianne Pouplier, Larissa Chen, Elliot Saltzman, and Dani Byrd. 2007. Dynamic action units slip in speech production errors. *Cognition* 103: 386–412.

Goswami, Usha. 2011. A temporal sampling framework for developmental dyslexia. *Trends in Cognitive Sciences* 15(1): 3–10.

Hagen, Marinda, Joop Kerkhoff, and Carlos Gussenhoven. 2011. Singing your accent away, and why it works. In *Proceedings of the 17th International Congress of Phonetic Sciences*, 799–802.

Hayes, Bruce. 1984. The phonology of rhythm in English. *Linguistic Inquiry* 15: 33–74.

Helm-Estabrooks, Nancy, Alisa Ruggiero Morgan, and Marjorie Nicholas. 1989. *Melodic Intonation Therapy*. Chicago, IL: Riverside Publishing Company.

Henton, Caroline and Anthony Bladon. 1986. Creak as a sociophonetic marker. In L. Hyman and C.N. Li (eds.), *Language, Speech and Mind: Studies in Honor of Victoria Fromkin*, 3–29. London: Routledge.

Hokkanen, Tapio. 1995. Puheentuotoksen mallit ja suomen nominintaivutuksen morfosyntaktinen koodaus. Unpublished licentiate thesis, General Linguistics, University of Joensuu, Finland.

Jun, Sun-Ah. 1993. The phonetics and phonology of Korean prosody. PhD dissertation, Ohio State University.

Keating, Patricia and Stefanie Shattuck-Hufnagel. 2002. A prosodic view of word form encoding for speech production. *UCLA Working Papers in Phonetics* 101: 112–156.

Keating, Patricia A., Taehong Cho, Cecile Fougeron, and Chai-Shune Hsu. 2003. Domain-initial strengthening in four languages. *Papers in Laboratory Phonology* 6: 145–163.

Kelly, Michael and Kathryn Bock. 1988. Stress in time. *Journal of Experimental Psychology: Human Perception and Performance* 14: 381–403.

Klatt, Dennis. 1976. Linguistic uses of segmental duration in English: Acoustic and perceptual evidence. *Journal of the Acoustical Society of America* 59: 1208–1221.

Krivokapić, Jelena. 2007. Prosodic planning: Effects of phrasal length and complexity on pause duration. *Journal of Phonetics* 35: 162–179.

Ladd, D. Robert. 2008. *Intonational Phonology*. Cambridge: Cambridge University Press.

Larkey, Leah S. 1983. Reiterant speech: An acoustic and perceptual validation. *Journal of the Acoustical Society of America* 73: 1337–1345.

Lashley, Karl Spencer. 1951. The problem of serial order in behavior. In L.A. Jeffress (ed.), *Cerebral Mechanisms in Behavior*, 112–135. New York: John Wiley & Sons, Inc.

Levelt, Willem J.M. 1989. *Speaking: From Intention to Articulation*. Cambridge, MA: MIT Press.

Levelt, Willem J.M. 2001. Spoken word production: A theory of lexical access. *Proceedings of the National Academy of Sciences, USA* 98: 13464–13471.

Levelt, Willem J.M., Ardi Roelofs, and Antje S. Meyer. 1999. A theory of lexical access in speech production. *Behavioral and Brain Sciences* 22: 1–38.

Macken, Marlys A. and David Barton. 1980. The acquisition of the voicing contrast in English: A study of voice onset time in word-initial stop consonants. *Journal of Child Language* 7: 41–74.

Meringer, Rudolf and Carl Mayer. 1895/1978. *Versprechen und Verlesen: Eine psychologisch-linguistische Studie*. New edition with an introductory article by Anne Cutler and David Fay. Amsterdam: John Benjamins Publishing.

Nakatani, Lloyd H., Kathleen D. O'Connor, and Carletta H. Aston. 1981. Prosodic aspects of American English speech rhythm. *Phonetica* 38: 84–105.

Nespor, Marina, and Irene Vogel. 1986. *Prosodic Phonology*. Dordrecht: Foris.

Newkirk, Don, Edward S. Klima, Carlene C. Pedersen, and Ursula Bellugi. 1980. Linguistic evidence from slips of the hand. In V. Fromkin, *Errors in Linguistic Performance: Slips of the Tongue, Ear, Pen, and Hand*, 165–197. New York: Academic Press.

Nooteboom, Sieb G. 1973. The tongue slips into patterns. In V. Fromkin (ed.), *Speech Errors as Linguistic Evidence*, 144–156. Berlin: Walter de Gruyter.

Norton, Andrea, Lauryn Zipse, Sarah Marchina, and Gottfried Schlaug. 2009. Melodic intonation therapy. *Annals of the New York Academy of Sciences* 1169: 431–436.

Patel, Aniruddh D., John R. Iversen, Micah R. Bregman, and Irena Schulz. 2009. Studying synchronization to a musical beat in nonhuman animals. *Annals of the New York Academy of Sciences* 1169: 459–469.

Pfau, Roland. 2000. Features and categories in language production. PhD dissertation, Johann Wolfgang Goethe-University, Frankfurt/Main.

Pierrehumbert, Janet, and David Talkin. 1992. Lenition of /h/ and glottal stop. *Papers in Laboratory Phonology* 2: 90–117.

Price, Patti J., Mari Ostendorf, Stefanie Shattuck-Hufnagel, and Cynthia Fong. 1991. The use of prosody in syntactic disambiguation. *Journal of the Acoustical Society of America* 90: 2956–2970.

Redi, Laura, and Stefanie Shattuck-Hufnagel. 2001. Variation in the realization of glottalization in normal speakers. *Journal of Phonetics* 29: 407–429.

Richtsmeier, Peter T. 2010. Child phoneme errors are not substitutions. *Toronto Working Papers in Linguistics* 33: 1–13.

Roelofs, Ardi. 1997. The WEAVER model of word-form encoding in speech production. *Cognition* 64: 249–284.

Schachner, Adena, Timothy F. Brady, Irene Pepperberg, and Marc D. Hauser. 2009. Spontaneous motor entrainment to music in multiple vocal mimicking species. *Current Biology* 19: 831–836.

Schwartz, Myrna F., Eleanor M. Saffran, Diane E. Bloch, and Gary S. Dell. 1994. Disordered speech production in aphasic and normal speakers. *Brain and Language* 47: 52–88.

Scobbie, James M., Fiona Gibbon, William J. Hardcastle, and Paul Fletcher. 2000. Covert contrast as a stage in the acquisition of phonetics and phonology. *Papers in Laboratory Phonology* 5: 194–207.

Seki, K. and M. Sugishita. 1983. [Japanese-applied melodic intonation therapy for Broca aphasia]. *No to shinkei = Brain and Nerve* 35: 1031–1037.

Selkirk, Elisabeth. 1984. *Phonology and Syntax: The Relation Between Sound and Structure*. Cambridge, MA: MIT Press.

Shattuck, Stefanie. 1975. Speech errors and sentence production. PhD dissertation, Massachusetts Institute of Technology.

Shattuck-Hufnagel, Stefanie. 1979. Speech errors as evidence for a serial order mechanism in sentence production. In W.E. Cooper and E.C.T. Walker (eds.), *Sentence Processing*, 295–342. Hillsdale, NJ: Lawrence Erlbaum Associates.

Shattuck-Hufnagel, Stefanie. 1982. Three kinds of speech error evidence for the role of grammatical elements in processing. In L. Obler and L. Menn (eds.), *Exceptional Language and Linguistics*, 133–142. San Diego, CA: Academic Press.

Shattuck-Hufnagel, Stefanie. 1987. The role of word-onset consonants in speech production planning: New evidence from speech error patterns. In E. Keller and M. Gopnik (eds.), *Motor and Sensory Processes of Language*, 17–51. Hillsdale, NJ: Lawrence Erlbaum Associates.

Shattuck-Hufnagel, Stefanie. 1992. The role of word structure in segmental serial ordering. *Cognition* 42: 213–259.

Shattuck-Hufnagel, Stefanie and Alice E. Turk. 1996. A prosody tutorial for investigators of auditory sentence processing. *Journal of Psycholinguistic Research* 25: 193–247.

Shattuck-Hufnagel, Stefanie, Mari Ostendorf, and Ken Ross. 1994. Stress shift and early pitch accent placement in lexical items in American English. *Journal of Phonetics* 22: 357–388.

Shattuck-Hufnagel, Stefanie, Cathy Bai, Mark Tiede, Argyro Katsikis, Marianne Pouplier, and Louis Goldstein. 2013. A comparison of speech errors elicited by sentences and alternating repetitive tongue twisters. *Journal of the Acoustical Society of America* 134: 4166.

Shih, Chilin. 1997. Mandarin third tone sandhi and prosodic structure. In Wang Jialing and Norval Smith (eds.), *Studies in Chinese Phonology*, 81–123. Berlin: Mouton de Gruyter.

Skinner, Burrhus Frederic. 1957. *Verbal Behavior*. New York: Appleton-Century-Crofts.

Snow, David. 1994. Phrase-final syllable lengthening and intonation in early child speech. *Journal of Speech, Language, and Hearing Research* 37: 831–840.

Snow, David. 1997. Children's acquisition of speech timing in English: A comparative study of voice onset time and final syllable vowel lengthening. *Journal of Child Language* 24: 35–56.

Stemberger, Joseph. 1990. Wordshape errors in language production. *Cognition* 35: 123–157.

Turk, Alice E. and Stefanie Shattuck-Hufnagel. 2007. Multiple targets of phrase-final lengthening in American English words. *Journal of Phonetics* 35: 445–472.

Turk, Alice E. and Stefanie Shattuck-Hufnagel. 2013. What is speech rhythm? A commentary inspired by Arvaniti & Rodriquez, Krivokapić, and Goswami & Leong. *Journal of Laboratory Phonology* 4(1): 93–118.

Watson, Duane and Edward Gibson. 2004. The relationship between intonational phrasing and syntactic structure in language production. *Language and Cognitive Processes* 19: 713–755.

Wheeldon, Linda and Aditi Lahiri. 1997. Prosodic units in speech production. *Journal of Memory and Language* 37: 356–381.

Wheeldon, Linda R. and Aditi Lahiri. 2002. The minimal unit of phonological encoding: Prosodic or lexical word. *Cognition* 85: B31–B41.

Wightman, Colin W., Stefanie Shattuck-Hufnagel, Mari Ostendorf, and Patti J. Price. 1992. Segmental durations in the vicinity of prosodic phrase boundaries. *Journal of the Acoustical Society of America* 91: 1707–1717.

Zipse, Lauryn, Andrea Norton, Sarah Marchina, and Gottfried Schlaug. 2012. When right is all that is left: Plasticity of right-hemisphere tracts in a young aphasic patient. *Annals of the New York Academy of Sciences* 1252: 237–245.

Zumbansen, Anna, Isabelle Peretz, and Sylvie Hébert. 2014. Melodic intonation therapy: Back to basics for future research. *Frontiers in Neurology* 5: 7.

20 Fluency and Disfluency

ROBIN J. LICKLEY

20.1 Introduction

Speech production involves a remarkably complex combination of processes. Prior to articulation, it involves rapid interactions of processes of utterance planning, formulation, and motor planning for execution whose timing requires close coordination. During articulation, motor commands activating several muscle systems need to ensure that respiratory, phonatory, and articulatory gestures are timed in such a way as to produce an acoustic signal that adequately conveys the intended message both quickly and smoothly. Although it seems crucial to successful communication, fluency is an aspect of speech and language that is largely overlooked within mainstream linguistics, where the focus is on language competence, rather than spoken performance, and where fluency is the unmentioned default consequence of following the rules. This study of speech and language from a relatively static viewpoint stands in contrast to the study of the mechanisms of speech production, which presents a dynamic view. The *failure* to maintain the flow in overt speech, through error and repair and through hesitation, has been the focus of a growing number of studies within speech production. But an overarching definition of fluency (and of disfluency) is hard to come by and there exists confusion in the use of terminology. This chapter explores the notion of fluency in typical speech production and attempts to add some clarity.

20.2 Meanings of fluency

An intuitive definition of fluency in speech is based on a listener's perception of what they are hearing. This is reflected in typical dictionary entries for "fluency," which refer to "smoothness of flow"; a listener would presumably consider speech that does not sound as if it flows smoothly to be lacking in fluency. So, in attempting

---

The Handbook of Speech Production, First Edition. Edited by Melissa A. Redford.
© 2015 John Wiley & Sons, Inc. Published 2019 by John Wiley & Sons, Inc.

to explain what fluency means, we begin with a fairly loose definition and one that takes a listener's perspective. But this chapter is about fluency in speech *production*, so we need to consider more than simply the perception of flow. There may not always be a perfect match between the flow of the processes underlying speech production and the listener's perception of fluency. An utterance that is perceived as fluent may still have contained hitches during the production processes. Minor disturbances in the flow of overt speech are easily missed by the listener, and may be detectable only on close inspection of the acoustic signal (Bard and Lickley 1998; Lickley 1995). When minor difficulties at planning and formulation stages are resolved sufficiently quickly, there may be no disturbance at all to the flow of speech at the acoustic output level. So fluency can be seen as multidimensional: *planning fluency* in speech production entails smoothness of flow within and between a range of planning levels; *surface fluency* in articulated speech entails a smooth flow from one sound to the next and between the words that make up phrases and sentences; and *perceived fluency* is what gives a listener the impression that the speech that they are listening to has been produced smoothly.

The main focus of this chapter will be fluency in typical, healthy adult speech production. But the notion of fluency is also crucial in considering atypical cases, such as the speech of people with difficulties arising from pathology and the issues affecting the speech production of people learning a new language. In such cases, fluency can be affected in a number of ways and for different reasons. As a result, the word "fluency" is applied in numerous contexts and interpreted in a variety of ways. There is some overlap between uses of the word in atypical and in typical cases, but there are is also scope for confusion, so before we move on to considering issues in typical fluency, we will look at some fluency-related issues arising in atypical speech, first in some pathological cases and then in second-language learning.

20.3 Fluency in speech pathology

In this brief discussion of fluency within speech pathology, we focus on three areas; aphasia and the two so-called disorders of fluency, stuttering and cluttering. There is no intention here to relate the fluency problems associated with pathological disorders of speech and language to the etiologies of the disorders; the purpose is simply to highlight usages of the word and potential confusions that arise.

20.3.1 Aphasia

Aphasia refers to a broad range of speech and language difficulties that result from brain damage. When a person's speech production is affected by aphasia, there are a number of ways in which their fluency can be affected. In this short discussion, we focus not so much on description of the impact of aphasia on fluency, but on two ways in which the word fluency is applied in the diagnosis of aphasia; in the Verbal Fluency Test and in the categorical distinction between fluent and non-fluent aphasias.

While interactive communication in conversation may be the natural setting for speech production, the term "fluency" is also used to refer to smoothness of a specific type in certain non-conversational speaking tasks. The Verbal Fluency Test is one such task. This is a psychological test, frequently used with people whose speech has been affected by brain damage, in which participants are required to produce a list of words of a specific category within a set time frame (usually 60 seconds). In a semantic version of the test, participants are asked to list words from a given semantic category (e.g., animals or household objects; Goodglass and Kaplan 1972); in a phonological version of the task, participants are asked to list words beginning with a specific letter (Benton and Hamsher 1976). The tests often form part of a clinical neuropsychological battery, since performance on these tests is known to vary with severity and type of brain damage (Brickman et al. 2005). Thus, in this context, "fluency" refers not to the flow of words in connected speech, but to smoothness in a specific task in language production. Fluency in this task depends on the ability of the speaker to access and encode items of vocabulary according to given criteria within a time limit. The measure of fluency is simply the number of correct items named within that time. Clearly, the ability to access words in a mental lexicon, and to do so within time limits, is a prerequisite for producing flowing speech in general, so it might be expected that people who score poorly on a Verbal Fluency Test would also show impaired fluency in speech production in more typical speaking situations. The most likely form of this failure of fluency would be hesitation when trying to access words.

People with anomic aphasia, in particular, would be expected to perform poorly on a verbal fluency test and therefore display very hesitant speech, since the defining characteristic of anomia is to have difficulties in accessing the lexicon. But, rather confusingly, anomic aphasia falls into the more general class of "Fluent Aphasia" in the view of the influential Boston School (Goodglass and Kaplan 1972: Goodglass, Kaplan, and Baresi 2001). Under this nomenclature, the word "fluent" has a rather different definition: "fluent aphasia is associated with easy articulation, facility with the patterns of sentence structure, but with difficulty in word finding and errors of word and sound substitution" (Goodglass et al. 2001: 7).

The speech of a person with "fluent aphasia" may still contain evidence of extreme difficulty with accessing the lexicon, manifested, for example, by hesitations or abandoned sentences, and syntactic irregularities, as well as smoothly uttered nonsensical speech containing phonological paraphasias and neologisms (Edwards 2005). Non-fluent aphasia, on the other hand, is associated with articulation difficulties, and characterized by speech that is slow and labored. Under the Boston School classification system, then, "fluency" refers to the smooth flow of movement of speech articulators. The Verbal Fluency Test does not test the same kind of fluency as referred to in this fluent/non-fluent distinction; it tests the smooth, easy flow of activation at a lexical level. Perceived fluency can be affected in both fluent and non-fluent aphasia, although the difficulties at the planning fluency level and the manifestations at the surface level may differ between the two types.

In practice, it is hard to pin down a standard, lucid, definition of fluency in aphasia; clinicians find it difficult to distinguish fluent from non-fluent cases (Gordon 1998), and the employment of the distinction between fluent and non-fluent cases is not universally accepted (Poeck 1989). "Fluent" in this clinical area means something along the lines of "relatively smooth speech, compared to other cases of aphasia which present with a lack of capacity to string together more than a couple of words." That there is scope for such terminological confusion to have a wider impact is evident where researchers have used the term "verbal fluency" to refer to the flow of (typical) speech, rather than to naming (e.g., Daneman 1991) or to both naming ability and the flow of speech (Day 1977).

20.3.2 Disorders of fluency

The clinical field known as "disorders of fluency" embodies in its name an assumption that there exists something well defined (fluency) that is disordered in the case of its two main exemplars, stuttering and cluttering. For the most part, in the case of stuttering, "typical fluency" would be seen as a therapy goal. Here, typical fluency means not so much perfectly smooth speech with no hesitations, repairs, repetitions (etc.), as speech that does not contain the blocks, repetitions, prolongations, and the associated tensions and gestures that characterize stuttered speech. So a definition of "fluency" in the context of stuttering may include phenomena like hesitations, repetitions, and error repairs amongst "fluent" behaviors (Wingate 1988), since these form part of typical non-stuttered speech. In analysis of speech in this field, a distinction is often made between "stuttering-like disfluencies" (Yairi and Ambrose 1992) and "typical disfluencies," though this usage is not universally accepted (Wingate 2002).

The other major "disorder of fluency," cluttering, presents problems first and foremost because it is hard for researchers to agree on a definition (Lickley 2010). For some authors, the principal feature of cluttering is its very rapid, and thus incomprehensible, speech (St. Louis et al. 2007); for others, the disorder also entails various disfluent features (including stuttering-like disfluencies), and speech that is generally disorganized on a discourse level (Daly 2006; Ward 2006). The more conservative definition begs the question of whether cluttering can be said to be a disorder affecting *fluency*, unless the definition of fluency makes reference to speech rate, as, for example, Starkweather's definition does (Starkweather 1987). But it is also generally accepted that, in addition to a high articulation rate, the disorder often manifests with prosodic irregularities involving unusual patterns of pausing. As for the potential atypicality of fluency in cluttering, a recent study suggests that people who clutter do not differ significantly from a typical population in the types and frequencies of their disfluencies (Myers et al. 2012).

We have discussed just two general areas where pathological disorders affecting communication require reference to the notion of fluency. Of course, there are many other speech disorders where we might talk about fluency at a number of levels of production, but full discussion of these could fill a whole book. The purpose of this subsection was simply to highlight two key areas where different perspectives on fluency are important and where the word "fluency" receives a variety of definitions. This also serves to re-emphasize the difficulty of giving a universal definition of fluency in speech.

20.4 Fluency in second-language learning

Probably the most common usage of the word "fluency" makes reference to a speaker's perceived ability in speaking a second language. But what does it mean to be fluent in a language?

Definitions of fluency in the field of language learning typically refer to what can happen to disturb the flow of speech as a result of a lack of full proficiency in the target language. Such problems in proficiency include accessing vocabulary, formulating syntactically correct phrases, preparing motor commands for articulatory sequences, and the intrusion of errors, at various levels (syntactic, lexical, phonological, articulatory), from the speaker's first language. The resulting speech may have its rhythm broken up by silent pauses and other indications of hesitation (e.g., prolongations, ums and uhs). These features are apparent in definitions of fluency in this field. Thus Fillmore writes that fluency is "simply the ability to talk at length with few pauses" (1979: 93) and Lennon suggests that native-like fluency entails producing speech "at the tempo of native speakers, unimpeded by silent pauses and hesitations" (1990: 390).

There are many other views of fluency, and Segalowitz (2010) provides a detailed critical review of approaches to fluency in this field. Recognizing the need for a multidimensional approach to the notion of fluency in second-language learning, he proposes distinctions between cognitive fluency, utterance fluency, and perceptual fluency. Under Segalowitz's definitions, *cognitive fluency* refers to the smoothness of the processes of planning that lie behind the act of speaking; *utterance fluency* refers to the acoustically measurable speech that results from the planning stages; *perceptual fluency* refers to the listener's perspective on the perceived smoothness of a speaker's production processes.[1]

Language learners may aspire to become fluent (or proficient) in a language, and this may entail achieving cognitive fluency in constructing spoken utterances in their target language that result in perceptually fluent speech. However, in order for a language learner to reach a level of proficiency that matches native speakers, it may also be reasonable for the learner to aspire to reach native-speaker levels of *dis*fluency, by acquiring appropriate native-like hesitation and by being prone to native-like speech error and repair, which they can then repair efficiently ("repair fluency" Tavakoli and Skehan 2005). So, in some sense, the goal is similar to that of a person who stutters; to achieve typical levels of speech fluency, rather than the faultlessly smooth speech of an "ideal" speaker.

This brief excursion into speech pathology and second-language learning served to illustrate that the word "fluency" is used in many different ways in work related to speech production. In most cases, fluency is set in a context where the concept is required in order to provide a baseline of some kind against which to compare speech or processing that is not fluent. It is important to take into account these different usages, and to understand their habitual usages. As illustrated above, it is easy to assume, wrongly, that fluency (or disfluency) has some universally accepted central meaning.

20.5 Typical speech

In the cases above, there is a contrast to be drawn between what is fluent and what is not within atypical cases of speech production. The notion of fluency and a definition of the word is important because fluency may be seen as a target, whether for therapeutic intervention or for learning and teaching.

In contrast, research involving typical speech and language suggests little need to define fluency, because failures of fluency are seen as peripheral. Within descriptive linguistics, the unspoken default scenario is that the ideal output is fluent. The emphasis is on competence in executing the rules of language, rather than performance in the real world, where things can go awry. The result of following the rules should be fluent speech. So an "ideal" speaker will devise a faultless plan, instantly find the words to fit the message and the syntactic rules to order the words, activate the required syllables and phonemes in the correct order, and send motor commands to the respiratory, phonatory, and articulatory systems to coordinate their actions and produce output with the appropriate timing, phrasing, and intonation.

If we consider speech production within standard cognitive models, the word "fluency" can be used to refer to smoothness of flow at several different levels of production, broadly matching the generally accepted levels proposed within language production models (e.g., Garrett 1980; Levelt 1989). For the most part, these levels of production range from the process of making general decisions about what to say and how to say it, through deciding which words to use and ensuring that the words combine in structures that are compatible with syntactic rules of the language being spoken and with appropriate prosody, to phonological encoding and articulation of speech sounds.

There is a further dimension to fluency that is easily overlooked. In much of the literature, whether mainstream linguistics or psycholinguistics, the focus has been on individual sentences and the individual speaker, as if speech occurs in monologue. But of course speech usually takes place in a communicative scenario, involving two or more participants collaborating to reach a communicative goal. So, our discussion of fluency should also take into account discourse. To achieve fluency in discourse, in addition to producing "perfect" sentences, speakers also need to fit their speech into the context of the conversation in which they are engaged. This entails not only taking into account the relevant discourse information, the conversational setting, and other speakers' needs, but also timing their speaking turns to ensure optimal conditions for communicating their message.

Perfect performance in all the above aspects of speech production may result in output that could be said to be produced fluently. However, given the complexity of the task, with its multiple levels of processing, the involvement of several different forms of memory, the potential disruption in an interactive setting, and the need to produce a lot of output in a short time span, it is unsurprising that the system can break down, and it often does, resulting in frequent instances of disfluency.

In the next section, we focus on typical speech production, and in particular on what can go wrong, resulting in the phenomena commonly referred to as "disfluencies" (hesitations, repetitions, and error-repair sequences).

20.6 Disfluency: When fluency breaks down

The word "disfluency" has been used increasingly in the literature on speech production and perception in recent decades, but its usage dates back at least to Johnson's (1961) listing of types for stuttered and typical speech. A number of PhD dissertations focusing on typical speech have "disfluency" in the title (to name but a few: Lickley 1994; Shriberg 1994; Bailey 2004; Eklund 2004; MacGregor 2008; Collard 2009; Schnadt 2009; Miller 2010; Brocklehurst 2011; Finlayson 2014). The academic disciplines from which these works emanated are varied, and this is reflected in the many contributions to an international interdisciplinary conference series DiSS (Disfluency in Spontaneous Speech), which, since 1999, has brought together researchers from all over the world to discuss the implications for various disciplines of what happens when fluency fails. The fact that so many researchers regularly use the word gives the impression that there is some accepted definition of disfluency on which a fairly large body of researchers agrees. However, given the problems that we have observed in pinning down a definition for the word "fluency", it will come as no surprise to the reader that agreement on a definition of the word "disfluency" is lacking, and there are various issues surrounding its use. We will return to these issues once we have explored the phenomena in more depth.

Is fluent speech the norm? If a speaker can produce a stream of spontaneous speech without having second thoughts about whether they are conveying the correct message at the right time, without spotting and reacting to an inaccuracy in the message or an error in its production, without struggling to find the right words and getting the sounds right, and without being interrupted by another speaker or some other distraction, then that stream of speech is likely to be completed smoothly, without interruption or revision – fluently, in other words. However, both casual observation and corpus studies of unrehearsed speech suggest that such fluency is the exception, rather than the rule. Disfluencies occur at an average rate of around 6 per 100 fluent words (Bortfeld et al. 2001; Eklund 2004; Fox Tree 1995; Shriberg 1994). Longer utterances attract more disfluencies (Oviatt 1995; Shriberg 1994), as do more complex ones (Lickley 2001; Shriberg 1994). In an analysis taking into account the length and type of utterance (dialogue move) in a task-oriented dialogue corpus, Lickley (2001) reports that of the longer and more cognitively demanding utterances (where speakers were generating instructions) more than 43% contained disfluencies. While speakers may vary in the frequency of disfluencies in their speech, everyone is disfluent some of the time. So, it is unusual for any speaker to talk spontaneously for long with perfectly fluent speech.

The phenomena that we are calling "disfluencies" can be described from different points of view. One focuses on the forms that they take; another emphasizes the functions of the phenomena within speech production. A formal account describes the patterns of words and syntactic units that disfluencies display. A functional account is based on assumptions about the planning processes involved in speech production and it allows us to describe disfluencies with reference to these processes: It makes reference to what goes awry in the planning and execution of speech. There is often some overlap between formal and functional descriptions.

In the next sections we first look at the forms that disfluencies can take and then consider the functions that they perform.

20.7 Formal description of disfluency

Studies dating back to the late 1950s provide various formal categorizations of "disturbances" (Mahl 1956), or "hesitation phenomena" (Blankenship and Kay 1964; Maclay and Osgood 1959). Mahl's categories of disturbances include:

- "ah"
- Sentence correction
- Sentence incompletion
- Repetition of words
- Stutter (referring to repetition of part words)
- Intruding incoherent sound
- Tongue slip
- Omission of words or parts of words

Mahl's main interest was in exploring differences between typical and schizophrenic speech, and the last three categories above may reflect the interest in pathological cases more than typical cases.

Maclay and Osgood's (1959) categories match the first four of Mahl's with in addition the following "hesitations":

- Filled pause
- Non-retraced false start
- Repeat (covering Mahl's repetition of words and stutter)

Maclay and Osgood also include the categories *retraced false start* and *unfilled pause*. Blankenship and Kay (1964) largely follow Mahl's classification, omitting, like Maclay and Osgood, the last three categories, but adding *word change* and *non-phonemic lengthening of phonemes*.

With studies focusing on comparison between stuttered and non-stuttered speech, Johnson (1961) published a list of eight categories of "disfluency":

- Interjections of sounds, syllables, words, or phrases (including, for example, "uh" and "well")
- Part-word repetitions
- Word repetitions
- Phrase repetitions
- Revisions
- Incomplete phrases
- Broken words
- Prolonged sounds

For some critical discussion of these classifications again from the stuttering literature, see Wingate (1988, 2002).

The advent of speech technology, and the associated need for natural speech data from which to develop models, led to a huge growth in the availability of large digitally recorded corpora of natural speech. Naturally enough, speech technologists are interested in handling disfluent speech, and this interest has facilitated a number of studies involving annotation of large amounts of speech data. Such annotation schemes need to be well defined formally and capable of labeling patterns in a reliable manner. Annotation schemes employed by Shriberg (1994), Heeman (1997), Lickley (1998), and Eklund (2004), have a consensus on several features (see Table 20.1 for some examples). Within all their corpora, the following basic forms are annotated:

- Filled pauses (e.g., um, uh)
- Repetitions (of part-words, whole words, phrases)
- Substitutions (where a part-word, word, or string of words is replaced by another word or string)
- Insertions (where a speaker repeats a string, but adds a word or more)
- Deletions (where a speaker abandons the utterance mid-stream)

Like Maclay and Osgood (1959), these authors categorize all forms of repetition as one group, although sub-categorization by repetition length is also included in their annotation schemes. Substitutions and Insertions match up with Maclay and Osgood's *retraced false starts*, while Deletions match their *non-retraced false starts*. So, while there are a number of different systems for naming and describing the forms of disfluency that can occur, some consensus seems to have developed over the past decade or two.

In repetitions, substitutions, insertions, and deletions, some part of the speaker's utterance is, in effect, replaced or rejected. Levelt (1983) provides a way to describe the structure of such utterances, and some of his terminology is in regular use. The string that is replaced is referred to as the *Reparandum* (marked in Table 20.1 by words in *italics*) and the string that is replacing it, the *Repair*. Any

Table 20.1 Examples of major structural disfluency types. Examples all taken from the HCRC Map Task Corpus (Anderson et al. 1991), where interlocutors discuss a route through maps. Reparanda are in *italic font*. Abandoned words are terminated with a hyphen. Measurable silent pause durations are given in milliseconds.

Repetitions

R1	Straight up *f-* from there
R2	Continue to *just* (38 ms) just above the telephone box
R3	When you're about level *with the b-* (70 ms) with the bottom of the waterfall

Substitutions

S1	Have you got *a* – some gorillas on the left
S2	So you're *going* aiming towards the yacht club (no pause)
S3	*You're doing* you're continuing that U shape (no pause)
S4	Have you got some stones *at the left hand s-* on the left hand side (no pause)

Insertions

I1	so you're going down *to* just to the bottom
I2	*That's probably* – do you think that's probably the same (no pause)
I3	*to the mona-* just to the monastery
I4	we're about six centimeters *from the edge of the page* from the right hand edge of the page (no pause)

Deletions

D1	Do a sort of U shape *for* and the bottom of the U shape should be about 3 centimeters long
D2	Now you're heading back up *sort of two thir-* have you got allotments?
D3	Draw a line towards the yacht club for about three centimeters *underneath where the* – (22 ms) – if you drew a line right across the bottom of the page

words that come after the *Repair* are denoted *the Continuation*. Repair can take time, although it is common for it to occur rapidly; the time between the end of the Reparandum and start of the Repair is referred to as the *Editing Phase*. The moment at which the speaker stops can be termed the *Interruption Point*. Often, a speaker starts a word but stops before the word is completely articulated: the incomplete word can be termed a *Fragment* (Examples R1, R3, S4, I3, and D2 in Table 20.1 contain fragments at the interruption point).

20.8 Functional description of disfluency

A formal description makes no assumptions about what lies behind the failures of fluency. One functional view of the same phenomena is that introduced by Levelt in his description of self-repairs of errors at various levels of planning in a corpus of Dutch speech. The corpus consisted of monologues where speakers described a network of colored dots (Levelt 1983). Levelt's focus is on repair types, and he provides a classification of self-repair strategies used by speakers as well as a general structural description of phases in self-repair. He also relates error and repair to stages of speech production. Repair assumes that something has gone wrong during the process of planning an utterance and that the mistake must be corrected. The most important and most numerous types in Levelt's classification are named *Appropriateness Repairs*, *Error Repairs*, and *Covert Repairs*.

Appropriateness repairs are required when a speaker realizes that there is something in the message that has been prepared that is correct but needs to be amended for the purposes of optimal communication (Levelt 1983: 51–53). The information may be ambiguous (AA-Repairs), it may need to be better specified (AL-Repairs), or it may need to be made more cohesive with the context (AC-Repairs). Error repairs correct errors that are made at a lexical, syntactic, or phonological level (Levelt's EL-, ES-, and EF-Repairs; 1983: 53–54).

Levelt makes a fundamental distinction between overt and covert error. An overt error is an error that is spoken. A covert error is an error that has been made at some point in the planning process but has been detected and corrected by the speaker before it is articulated. So *Covert Repairs* (C-Repair; Levelt 1983: 55) are repairs that are hypothesized to have taken place after an error occurred during planning but before the error was articulated, so that the error is never heard. According to Levelt's model of speech production (1989), speakers are able to monitor a plan before motor commands are sent to the articulators, so that it is theoretically possible for a lexically and phonologically specified plan to be checked for accuracy and rejected before it reaches the articulatory mechanism. Levelt (1983) suggests that covert repairs may be realized by editing terms (like *uh*) or repetition of one or more lexical items. In developing their *Covert Repair Hypothesis*, Postma and colleagues (Postma, Kolk, and Povel 1990, 1991; Postma and Kolk 1993) list filled and silent pauses, repeated part words, whole words and strings of words, prolonged sounds and abrupt interruptions ("blocks") as manifestations of covert repair.[2]

Additional repair types discussed by Levelt are D-Repairs, which address the question "Do I want to say this now?" (1983: 51), and repairs of prosodic errors. Levelt finds none of the latter in his corpus, but an example of a prosodic repair would be the following: "The BBC should never campaign: It can an*a*- it can analyze campaigns." In this example, the speaker commenced a word with an unstressed initial syllable and a stressed second syllable (possibly *analysis*) and replaced it with a word with initial stress. Levelt also proposes R-Repairs, a catch-all category for repairs that defy other categorizations.

Now that we have in place some of the terminology used to refer to typical disfluencies we will take a closer look at the nature of these disfluencies. We begin with the simplest forms, hesitations (represented by silent pause, prolongation, filled pauses, repetitions), where speakers just delay continuation of the message, and then the more complex forms, repairs, where speakers retrace and alter something that they have said. We consider how and why such disfluencies arise in natural speech, and the role that they play in conversation.

20.9 Hesitations

How do we hesitate in speech? Hesitation usually involves the temporary suspension of flowing speech. It may be achieved by stopping altogether and remaining silent for a moment, by prolonging a syllable, by producing a filled pause or a lexical filler, or by repeating the onset of the current phrase. It may also be achieved overtly in a phrase openly expressing the speaker's uncertainty. Combinations of these phenomena are normal.

20.9.1 Silent pause

The simplest way to hesitate would seem to be just to stop talking and pause silently. But of course, *fluent* speech contains silence. A basic question might be: What duration of silence constitutes a silent pause? A second question is: Can we distinguish between fluent and hesitant silent pauses?

To attempt to address the duration question, we can consider what durations of silence do reliably occur in fluent running speech. At one extreme, there is usually a moment of silence during the closure phase of stop consonants. This can vary from immeasurably short to relatively long, depending on various prosodic and contextual factors. In an experiment where subjects were asked to read out specially designed sentences, the mean closure duration in English word-final stops (/p, b, t, d, k, g/) varied from around 30 ms to around 250 ms with phrase-final stops being significantly longer than others (Luce and Charles-Luce 1985). At the other extreme might be the pauses that can occur between turns in dialogue, which can average less than half a second (Bard, Aylett, and Lickley 2002; Bull and Aylett 1998). But turns regularly overlap in time, without negative consequences for the interaction.

From these extremes and the variability that they display, it is evident that a definite value for what constitutes a silent pause, whether fluent or hesitant, is likely to be elusive. In early work that has remained influential, Goldman-Eisler (1958a, 1958b, 1961) proposed that any within-sentence breaks in phonation shorter than 250 ms could be accounted for by the time required for articulatory adjustments during normal speech production, and suggested that pauses shorter than 250 ms should not be included in studies that addressed the cognitive processes involved in hesitation. While many accepted and adopted this figure (Beattie 1979; Boomer 1965; Butterworth 1980; Greene and Cappella 1986), others challenged this threshold as too high. Martin (1970), for example, preferred to use a lower threshold of 50 ms in his perception experiments. More recently, Eklund (2004) reports a minimum of between 70 and 90 ms for "unfilled pauses" annotated in his study of Swedish dialogues. Why posit an absolute lower threshold at all? The idea has been challenged. Butcher's (1981) study (on German speech) showed that what is perceived by listeners as an excessive pause depends not on absolute duration, but on prosodic context. Breaks inserted between tone groups were detected by 75% of listeners when they were 220 ms long, but breaks *within* tone groups were detected by the same percentage of listeners when they were only 80 ms. Setting definite limits can cause problems: Campione and Véronis (2002) demonstrate that setting a lower threshold for pause duration can distort the view of pause distribution characteristics in corpus studies. It seems that for the first question ("How long is a pause?"), a flexible approach is necessary and no absolute figure can sensibly be defined.

To address the second question, how to differentiate a fluent pause from one which is hesitant, we need first to have some idea of what factors sanction pausing during speech production. Intuitively, one would assume that the likelihood of a fluent pause would vary according to position in the structure of the utterance. Between a determiner and a noun (e.g., *the _ likelihood*), a pause would be highly unlikely; between two phrases (e.g., *between these extremes _ there is potential*), a pause would be more acceptable, even though it would be by no means obligatory. It has been proposed that both prosodic and syntactic structure may determine how likely a fluent pause can be between words, with boundaries between larger structural units allowing pauses of longer duration than those between smaller units. Indeed, attempts to model the probability of pause between words have differentiated between inter-word intervals on the bases of both prosodic and syntactic structure (e.g., Cooper and Paccia-Cooper 1980; Gee and Grosjean 1983; Watson and Gibson 2004). But Ferreira (1993, 2007) shows that there is not a straightforward relationship between syntactic and prosodic structure. She proposes a distinction between pause that is licensed by prosodic (rather than syntactic) structure and hesitation pause that is a function of planning demands. According to Ferreira, the duration of a prosodic pause is dependent on the prior prosodic unit and licensed by the prosodic rules of the language. Hesitation, on the other hand, is a performance characteristic, a function of difficulty in planning the next phrase, which varies with the (syntactic) complexity of that phrase, amongst other factors.

Ferreira's work provides a neat explanation of how fluent and disfluent pauses may come about for different reasons. Distinguishing between them is still a problem in analyzing speech. Absolute durations of fluent and hesitant pauses are elusive – there is no simple acoustic definition, which is one reason why it is difficult for people annotating speech corpora to give reliable measures of silent pause. Nakatani and Hirschberg (1994) take a pragmatic approach, relying on the subjective perceptual judgment of their independent labelers in identifying silent pauses where there is repair, versus where there is none and the pause is not classed as hesitant. Eklund (2004) also uses his own subjective perceptual judgment in annotating "unfilled" pauses in his corpora. If inter-rater reliability is built in to the annotation process, this perceptual method is probably currently the safest approach.

20.9.2 Prolongation

So far, we have talked about silent pause as if it occurs in the absence of any other phenomena that could contribute to the production and perception of pause. Of course, when they pause, people do not just stop abruptly and remain silent.

Where "fluent" silent pause is sanctioned by prosodic structure, it is likely to be preceded by a prolonged syllable (Boomer 1965; Cooper and Paccia-Cooper 1980; Ferreira 1993), and the same may apply to a hesitant pause (Bell et al. 2003): prolongation and silence are part of the same phenomenon. In fact, Duez, working with French speech, observed that what people perceived as pause was often not realized as silence at all, but as syllabic lengthening (Duez 1993). As with silent pause, people may use prolongation when they hesitate. As with silent pause, there is a question over how long a syllable needs to be before it can be considered prolonged in a manner that can be considered hesitant. In some cases, a planned hesitant prolongation can have an impact on the sounds of the prolonged word. In English, certain function words (e.g., *the*, *a*, *and*, *that*) may be pronounced with a strong rather than a weak vowel (Bell et al. 2003), as well as being prolonged. In English, hesitant prolongation is usually word-final, though there may be exceptions, and evidence of word-initial prolongation for hesitation has been reported for Swedish (Eklund 2001). So prolongation, usually of final syllables, can form part of a hesitation, but, for the same reasons as for silent pause, it is often hard to distinguish a hesitant from a fluent prolongation.

20.9.3 Filled pauses

Filled pauses are also usually produced alongside silent pause and prolongation. There is, though, less difficulty in distinguishing *um* and *uh* and their various alternative pronunciations from fluent words, and for this reason frequency counts are more reliable. Their frequency varies from corpus to corpus: Bortfeld et al. (2001) report 2.6 filled pauses per 100 words in their corpus of experimental dialogues; Shriberg's (1994) three corpora vary between 1.6 and 2.2 filled pauses per 100 words; Eklund (2004) gives an overall figure of 3.6 per 100 words, varying between 2.2 and 4.4 per 100 words across the five Swedish corpora that he examines; for the Corpus of Spontaneous Japanese, Maekawa (2004) reports a rate of filled pauses as high as 7.23 for 528 male speakers in spontaneous monologue. Filled pause rates also vary from speaker to speaker, within speakers performing the same task. In the HCRC Map Task Corpus (Anderson et al. 1991), I can report an overall frequency of filled pauses of 1.3 per 100 words and per speaker ranging from 0.18 to 6.6 per 100 words for 64 speakers.

The forms that filled pauses can take vary across languages. It seems fairly common for filled pauses to have at least two forms in a given language, including both a prolonged vowel sound and a vowel (usually) followed by a nasal. Some languages are reported as also having filled pauses that have lexical form, in addition to prolonged vowels (e.g., ano, eeto in Japanese: Watanabe 2009). For Mandarin Chinese, Tseng (2006) comments that it is difficult to differentiate between discourse particles and filled pauses. The same probably applies to a large number of languages. In English, lexical fillers (such as *I mean*, *like*, and *kind of*) have been classed (alongside repetitions) as filled pauses by some authors (Maclay and Osgood 1959; Zellner 1994).

Filled pauses are commonly assumed to be close in quality to the mid-central vowel *schwa* (e.g., Clark and Fox Tree 2002; Shriberg 2001; Tottie 2011; Wingate

1988) but this may be an overgeneralization. To give two examples, in standard British English, the nasal-final filled pause *um* rhymes with *thumb*; in accents of Scottish English the equivalent filled pause rhymes with *them*. Filled pause vowels also differ from the typical unstressed English *schwa* in their durations. Compared with short, unstressed words like *a* and *the*, and, in fact, compared with lexically stressed vowels in fluent speech, *um* and *uh* tend to be very long (Shriberg 2001). In the HCRC Map Task Corpus, the mean duration of all *uh/eh* filled pauses is 316 ms, compared to 74 ms for the word *a*; *um/ehm* has a mean duration of 424 ms, compared to 107 ms for *an* and 176 ms for *and*. Similar filled pause durations are reported for other corpora (O'Connell and Kowal 2005).

Having a vowel with a duration that is considerably greater than both similar short function words, and many stressed syllables, it almost as though filled pauses could have similar prosodic status to stressed vowels in English. But it is in the area of prosody relating to pitch that filled pauses blend most with their surroundings, rather than standing out. In analysis of corpora in American and British English, Shriberg and Lickley's (1993) findings showed that the fundamental frequency of filled pauses in the middle of clauses tended to be closely related to the frequency of their surrounding sounds. As an example, the pitch on the filled pause in a phrase like *the uh middle* would typically follow the low and fairly flat tone of the preceding word, *the*. In that sense, *uh* seems to lend continuity to the speech, rather than interrupting it. Note that, in claiming that *uh/um* are signals produced intentionally by a speaker to signal to their listener that they are in trouble, Clark and Fox Tree (2002) misinterpret Shriberg and Lickley's (1993) findings to mean that the low pitch of mid-clause filled pauses makes them stand out from the stream of speech. Quite the opposite is true; filled pauses typically have low pitch in mid-clause, because their pitch fits in with that of the surrounding unstressed syllables. Unlike lexically stressed syllables in English words, filled pauses never attract a pitch accent. These facts are not really compatible with the speaker intending to use the filled pause as a signal.

20.9.4 *Repetition*

When speakers pause in the middle of saying something, then start again, they often restart by backtracking by one or two words and repeating them with a fluent continuation. So repetition can be classed as a hesitation phenomenon. Of course, people also repeat words in fluent, non-hesitant speech, either because some words need to be repeated in order to convey the intended message (e.g., *my phone number is four four four two zero three three*) or for rhetorical purposes, like emphasis (e.g., *that was a very, very exciting movie*). What makes the "fluent" uses of repetition sound fluent, rather than hesitant, is their prosody. A phone number is usually produced with a stylized phrasing pattern and intonation contour: A hesitant repetition of a digit in a phone number would most likely repeat the pitch level as well as the word itself; it would also likely be accompanied by silent pause and/or prolongation. An intensifier (*very*) repeated for rhetorical effect would likely be intensified itself by use of emphatic pitch, and produced in an uninterrupted sequence, like a pair of non-identical adverbs, whereas a hesitant repetition of the same words would be accompanied by other hesitation phenomena. There is a relatively restricted set of words that can be repeated for rhetorical purposes; disfluent repetitions may have a freer distribution. However, corpus studies of English have shown that the words most likely to be repeated are function words (Clark and Wasow 1998; Fox and Jasperson 1995; Lickley 1994; Maclay and Osgood 1959; Shriberg 1994). In Lickley's (1994) corpus, 96% of repeated words were function words; Clark and Wasow (1998) report 25.2 function word repetitions per 1000 words, versus 2.4 per 1000 for content words. Words like *the* and *I* are rarely repeated for fluent rhetorical reasons, but are frequently repeated disfluently.

Acoustic and prosodic analysis provides support for the claim that disfluent repetition may perform more than one function. At the start of this section, we introduced the idea of repetition being used to resume speech after hesitating. Hieke (1981) differentiates between such *retrospective* repetitions, which enable a speaker to resume continuity after a break and *prospective* repetitions, which themselves buy time as the speaker deals with planning demands like lexical search. An acoustic prosodic analysis of repetition lent support to Hieke's ideas (Plauché and Shriberg 1999; Shriberg 1995) and further analysis on over 800 utterances containing repetitions of *I* and *the*, using a hierarchical clustering of prosodic features, led to the conclusion that three types could be distinguished on the basis of pause lengths and syllable prolongations (Plauché and Shriberg 1999). Two of these types corresponded to Hieke's retrospective and prospective repeats; the third type corresponded to *covert repairs*, as introduced by Levelt (1983). We will return to covert repairs later.

Repetitions are among the most frequent types of disfluency (Branigan, Lickley, and McKelvie 1999; Lickley 1994; Shriberg 1994). Just as prosodic information can help to distinguish fluent from disfluent cases of repetition, different types of disfluent case can also be distinguished.

20.9.5 *Why hesitate?*

Before producing an utterance in spontaneous speech, we need to plan. There are several factors that can affect the level of difficulty in planning. Some of these concern overall planning at a prelinguistic stage; others are related to language factors; others may come from articulation.

At the conceptual level, fluency may be affected by the difficulty inherent in the length and structure of the utterance being planned, or because the speaker is not certain of what to say or how to say it. A long and complex utterance may require more time to prepare than a short and simple one. For example, if your friend asks you for instructions on how to make chocolate brownies, you may need to pause a while to think. Assuming you know the recipe, you would need to recall a list of several ingredients and prepare a complex sequence of instructions. If you are asked for instructions on how to boil an egg, you will probably need less time to consider this relatively simple recipe. So, cognitive complexity of an utterance plan can affect the time required to plan it, and this can mean that a speaker needs to buy time while preparing to speak. It has long been known that utterances that are longer and cognitively more demanding elicit more hesitation (Goldman-Eisler 1968; Good and Butterworth 1980; Maclay and Osgood 1959). Experimental studies suggest that speakers' initiation times for sentences vary with length (Holmes 1988) and complexity, in a way that reflects incremental sentence planning (Ferreira 1991). It has also been shown that initiation time for a prepared sentence varies with the prosodic complexity of the sentence (Wheeldon and Lahiri 1997). We might expect the increased initiation times produced via experimental manipulations in the laboratory to be reflected in more natural speaking situations by hesitation phenomena.

Hesitation can also reflect a speaker's indecision or uncertainty. Uncertainty can arise when a speaker is making decisions about the general message or about the information required to make the message adequate to convey an appropriate meaning. In experiments with quiz questions, it has been shown that hesitation is greater where people feel less certain about the answer (Brennan and Williams 1995; Smith and Clark 1993). The search of memory for an answer to a factual question can be matched by a physical search. In the HCRC Map Task Corpus, filled pauses are more likely before the answer "no" than before the answer "yes" in response to a question about the presence of a landmark on the respondent's map (*Do you have a xxx on your map?*), simply because it takes longer to search the map visually for a landmark that is not there (Lickley 2001).

At the lexical level, it is well known that speakers struggle to access some words more than others. Why would this be? One explanation is that words with which a speaker is more familiar will be easier to produce fluently, because they are more easily recalled than less familiar words. It is well known from laboratory experiments that words that occur more *frequently* in everyday language use are more quickly retrieved (Oldfield and Wingfield 1965). In experiments with single-word picture naming, pictures with higher-frequency names were named 50–100 ms quicker than those with low frequency names (Jescheniak and Levelt 1994). But other measures of familiarity, such as the extent to which people agree on the name for a noun (Hartsuiker and Notebaert 2010) and the age at which words are typically acquired (Morrison, Ellis, and Quinlan 1992) seem closer to an individual's experience of words than a global frequency measure, even if they correlate closely with frequency. If such measures of familiarity have ecological validity, then we might expect speakers to be more likely to hesitate as they recall lower-frequency words. Hartsuiker and Notebaert's (2010) experiment demonstrated that people are less fluent and hesitate more often when they planned sentences containing words with lower name agreement (and therefore more competing lexical candidates for selection), in a network task. We might then ask whether we hesitate more often before low-frequency words. However, most speech does not happen in response to stimuli in a psycholinguistics laboratory, and we do not habitually throw random picture names in to conversation. The topic of conversation and the speakers involved impose some restrictions on the words that are likely to be required. Further restrictions are imposed by local discourse context. In conversation, many words are predictable, given these contextual constraints. To address this kind of issue, early studies of hesitation in running speech examined the probability of words in context and suggested that there was a relationship between the predictability of a word in its context and the likelihood of hesitation before that word – hesitation was more likely before less likely words (Goldman-Eisler 1958a, 1958b; Lounsbury 1954; Tannenbaum, Williams, and Hillier 1965). Of course, less likely words in context are also less frequent words in general. But with word frequency controlled, an effect of contextual probability on fluency is still apparent (Beattie and Butterworth 1979).

In addition to factors relating to familiarity that affect accessibility of words, the *form* of the word can also have an effect on the time that it takes for a speaker to begin to produce it. The length in syllables of Dutch words in a picture-naming task, was found to relate to reaction time (Severens et al. 2005); similar results were found for a number of other languages (Bates et al. 2003). If effects found in picture-naming experiments are valid for conversational speech, it may be that longer words are more likely to be preceded by hesitation than shorter words.

Problems in commencing production of a word may arise as a result of factors external to the word itself that affect a speaker's ability to start the word. A large number of experiments have investigated interference effects from other words on the time taken by participants to begin a target word. The results seem contradictory. In some cases, prime words whose onsets are phonologically similar to the target appear to cause delays or errors in the target words (e.g., O'Seaghdha and Marin 2000; Wheeldon 2003), while in other cases, a facilitatory effect has been found (e.g., Meyer and Schriefers 1991; Schnur, Costa, and Caramazza 2006; Schriefers 1999; Smith and Wheeldon 2004). However, since these experiments are rarely performed in anything like everyday speaking situations, it is hard to gauge whether the delays observed could have any equivalence to hesitation in typical speech. Recent work makes an attempt to bridge this gap. In a study where unscripted sentences were elicited via description of the action in short video clips, Jaeger and colleagues found that when adjacent content words had shared phonological onsets (e.g., *hand the hammer*), there was a tendency for more hesitation and lower speech rate on these words, compared to instances where there was no shared onset (Jaeger, Furth, and Hilliard 2012).

To summarize, speakers may hesitate over lexical access because they have trouble accessing words that are less familiar to them, or are less appropriate in their discourse context, or have more rivals for selection. They may also need to pause if there are other words being planned alongside the target word that share phonological onset with the target. Many mainstream, psycholinguistic studies that address lexical access measure the relative timings of responses consisting of one isolated word to pictures representing one word, often alongside distractors or primes of one word. It is hard to relate such findings directly to spontaneous speech.

Does the articulatory difficulty inherent in a word have an impact on the likelihood of hesitation on that word? This is an area with relatively little relevant research. One recent study suggests that the amount of time that it takes to prepare a given syllable depends partly on the structure of the syllable and partly on the initial sound (Mooshammer et al. 2012). While it is tempting to suggest that this could have an impact of hesitation in spontaneous speech, once again, it is important to consider whether the responses elicited in laboratory conditions bear any relationship to what might happen in rapid connected speech.

So far, we have only very briefly considered the idea that hesitation may result from error during the speech production process. Overt speech errors are usually repaired and the repair disrupts the flow of speech, creating the type of disfluency that we have referred to as repairs. Production errors may also be detected and repaired before they have been articulated. According to Levelt (1983) and others, the only manifestation of such *covert* errors will be the kinds of hesitation phenomena that we have been discussing (see note 2). There remains also the possibility that covert errors may be covertly repaired with no effect on surface fluency at all.

Of course, a speaker may also require time to repair overt errors, so hesitation phenomena may occur alongside repair. However, the common assumption that speakers "mark" error repairs with filled pauses is not supported by evidence. Corpus studies have reported that only 6–10% of repairs and repetitions have filled pauses in the editing phase (Lickley 1994; Nakatani and Hirschberg 1994; Shriberg 1994). Lickley reports only 10.6% and Shriberg fewer than 20% of filled pauses in their corpora occurring in repairs or repetitions. The concept that there is often little need for the speaker to hesitate during repair is reinforced by the observation that there is often no gap at all between a cut-off and a repair (Blackmer and Mitton 1991).

We have discussed some factors internal to the speech production system that can induce hesitation, but we should note that external factors matter, too. When a speaker is distracted by another task, as often happens in natural speaking situations, the division of attention means that there is less focus on planning an utterance and a greater likelihood of filled pauses and repetitions (Oomen and Postma 2001).

It is worth noting that filled pauses may serve functions other than simply hesitation. If uttered with relatively high pitch at the start of a speaking turn, *um* may signal an intention to speak, or a request for attention, as in *"um, excuse me!"* Over half a century ago, it was suggested that speakers may use filled pauses (and repetitions, though this is rarely reported) to hold the floor, or prevent another speaker from interrupting (Maclay and Osgood 1959), and this has often been cited as if it were a robust research finding, rather than the somewhat speculative comment that it actually was. Casual observation that this is not typically the case, is supported by a failure to find supporting evidence (e.g., Cook and Lalijee 1970; Lallgee and Cook 1969).

20.10 Repairs

20.10.1 Forms and functions

We have already introduced the main types of repair forms. As can be seen from the examples in Table 20.1, in producing Substitutions and Insertions, speakers retrace to a place in the original utterance and the repair repeats the structure of the reparandum and may include repetition of one or more of the words while replacing or amending others. In Deletions, the speaker abandons the current plan and starts anew. As described earlier, Levelt's (1983) scheme ascribes functions to repairs. In this section, we briefly show how the main formal repair types illustrated in Table 20.1 map on to the main functional categories provided by Levelt, and we discuss how they represent solutions to problems at different levels of processing.

The major repair structures illustrated in Table 20.1 almost map on in a one-to-one manner to the functional categories that Levelt (1983) describes (Table 20.2). The main exception is Substitutions, which can map on to two repair types.

Levelt's *appropriateness repairs* represent cases where a speaker backtracks to amend the specificity of what they have said. Most cases of the formal type Insertion correspond to appropriateness repairs, as they simply add to the reparandum to align it better with the speaker's intended meaning. It is also possible for a Substitution to be an appropriateness repair, for example when one word is substituted by another that is more specific in meaning (e.g., *going* replaced by *aiming* in example S2, Table 20.1). But Substitutions are also the typical form for *error repairs*, whether lexical, syntactic, or phonological, so a word or a sound may substitute for another, erroneous, word or sound (see all error repair examples in Table 20.2). Levelt's *D-Repairs*, which represent cases where the speaker has decided to reorder their overall plan, correspond to the Deletions in Table 20.1.

How do the forms and functions of repairs relate to processes in speech production? Levelt's repair categories can be mapped on to processes in his (1989) model of speech production. Since *appropriateness* errors normally originate in the overall plan, rather in processes of formulation, we can think of their repairs as being conceptually based (Blackmer and Mitton 1991). An exception might be the case of one word substituting for another with similar meaning, which involves a correction at the level of lemma selection. Levelt's *D-Repairs* involve major shifts in the plan and can thus also be seen as conceptually based. *Error* repairs, correcting errors of lexical selection, syntax, and phonology, are mostly associated with the formulation processes (classed as "production-based repairs" by Blackmer and Mitton 1991). The distinction may be important in considering the predictions that

Table 20.2 Examples of Levelt's (1983) Appropriateness Repairs and Error Repairs.

Appropriateness Repair	
Ambiguity (AA)	we arrive at the airport – Heathrow airport – around noon
Specification (AL)	the museum is near the town hall – just across the square from the town hall
Contextual (AC)	turn to the left – to your left
Error Repair	
Lexical	John Donne's famous explanation uh exclamation
Syntactic	he was really welcomed with them – by them with open arms
Phonological	Glomal – global warming

a model of speech production might make as to the speed at which repair may take place. Finally, *covert repairs* may emanate from appropriateness or error repairs at the conceptual or formulation stages.

20.10.2 *The fluency of the repair process*

Although we have classified repairs as types of disfluency, we can still consider the smoothness of the processes of repair as a form of planning fluency. In order for repair to take place, a speaker must in some sense detect that there is a problem, must stop the current utterance and must plan and execute an adequate repair. If repair had to wait until the speaker stopped, if planning of the repair had to start from scratch, and if the process of planning a new word were as lengthy as suggested on the basis of picture naming tests (Indefrey and Levelt 2004) then repair could be a very tedious process. But it is not. Corpus analysis reveals that the time that elapses between a speaker stopping after an error and resuming speech with a repair is usually very short and is frequently zero (Blackmer and Mitton 1991). Some of the repairs presented in Table 20.1 contain no pause at the interruption point. If there is no pause between cut-off and repair, when was the repair planned? The speaker must have planned the repair while still articulating the words in the reparandum. As we suggested above, the point in the production process at which an error occurs may have an impact on the time that it takes for a speaker to construct a repair. If a speaker has to begin from scratch in constructing a new utterance, we might expect a longer delay before speaking resumes: this may be the case in Levelt's *D-Repairs*. If a new word is required to add greater specificity to a phrase or to replace a less appropriate word, then that should have implications for the amount of time it takes to produce the repair. If the lemma and lexical form for a word have been selected correctly but a phonological error has slipped in because of interference from another word in the utterance (e.g., *bood book* for *good book*), then if the mental representation of the correct form is still activated, it should take little time to produce a repair. To summarize, *D-Repairs* and *appropriateness repairs* should take longer to carry out than *error repairs*. In Blackmer and Mitton's (1991) corpus analysis, which measured error-to-repair and cut-off-to-repair times in repairs in conversational speech, *D-Repairs* and *appropriateness repairs* were combined into the category of *Conceptually Based Repairs* and error-to-repair times for *error repairs* (*Production Based Repairs* in their classification) were indeed significantly shorter. The less that there is to repair, the smoother, or more fluent, the repair process.

So, while a failure of what we have called "planning fluency" (or "cognitive fluency" to recall Segalowitz 2010) may lie behind the production of an error, the processes of error detection and repair are usually very smooth. As already noted, the inclusion of a filled pause before repair is the exception, rather than the rule, so there seems to be no great need to play for time. It has been suggested that, in producing repairs, speakers have a preference for fluency over accuracy (Seyfeddinipur, Kita, and Indefrey 2008). By *fluency*, these authors mean that speakers prefer not to hesitate for too long when they need to repair. Instead of interrupting their speech as soon as they detect an error and then stalling while a repair is planned, it is suggested that they can delay the interruption, continuing to speak, until they are ready with a repair. Their evidence from cut-off-to-repair times argues against Levelt's Main Interruption Rule (Levelt 1983, 1989; Nooteboom 1980), which suggests that speakers interrupt their flow when they detect trouble and then commence the process of planning the subsequent repair during the editing phase. Instead, they claim, speakers maintain some fluency in their self-corrections, by minimizing the delay between cut-off and repair.

If the act of halting speech to produce a repair depends on the speaker's readiness to enact the repair rather than to factors related to linguistic structure, then we would expect the point at which speakers interrupt their flow not to respect linguistic conventions. And, indeed, there is no obvious pattern to interruption. Speakers do not wait for a convenient phrase boundary. In fact speakers frequently interrupt their speech during a word or a syllable or even a phonetic segment (for example, during the closure phase of a stop consonant). Reports of how frequently this happens vary between corpora, with Nakatani and Hirschberg (1994) reporting as many as 73% of reparanda in their data ending in fragments, Shriberg (1994, 2001) reporting around 60% for one corpus (involving human-computer interaction) and 20–25% for others (human-human interaction), and Lickley (dialogue, 1994) 36%. In the HCRC Map Task dialogue corpus (Anderson et al. 1991), I can report that around 40% of Insertions and Substitutions have fragment-final reparanda, with Deletions having fewer, at 32% (Repetitions, 34%). Levelt (1983) reports 7% of appropriateness reparanda versus 23% of error reparanda ending in a word fragment in his corpus of monologues. The considerable variation between corpora has yet to be explained, though speaking styles surely differ between dialogue and monologue and between human-human interaction and human-computer interaction.

Although the point of interruption seems to be unpredictable, it should be noted that the figures still suggest a tendency to halt at the end of a word, rather than at some random position. Levelt (1983) suggests that speakers may tend to interrupt a word if that word is itself erroneous. More recent work suggests that this may be particularly true of potential non-words which would result from phonological speech errors. It has long been noted that phonological speech errors are more likely to result in real words being fully realized than in non-words being uttered (e.g., Baars, Motley, and MacKay 1975; Dell 1986; Hartsuiker, Corley, and Martensen 2005), the phenomenon known as the lexical bias effect. One explanation for this, which adds partial support to Levelt's position, is that prearticulatory monitoring, matching the planned output against lexical items, results in non-words being rejected and interrupted before they can be fully realized more often than erroneous real words, at least in an experimental setting which elicits errors via spoonerisms (Nooteboom 2005). But there is also evidence that words may simply be interrupted because a repair has already been prepared. In arguing that speakers prefer fluency over accuracy when they make repairs, Seyfeddinipur et al. (2008) show that the cut-off-to-repair interval following mid-word interruptions is significantly shorter than after less abrupt interruptions. This, they suggest, is because most of the replanning required for repair is complete when speakers interrupt mid-word. They propose that this evidence, too, argues against the accuracy-focused Main

Interruption Rule, and in favor of an account that assumes speakers strive to maintain some impression of fluency during the process of repairing errors. This Delayed Interruption for Planning hypothesis of Seyfeddinipur et al. and Nooteboom's (2005) account of lexical bias are not necessarily incompatible. If an erroneous nonword has been halted because the correct version has played a part in the detection of the error, then the repair is in effect ready at the interruption point.

When a speaker stops with a full word, there are phonetic and therefore acoustic consequences. If the interruption is not abrupt, there may be prolongation of the final syllable of the reparandum. Shriberg (2001) suggests that this prolongation is different from typical phrase- and sentence-final lengthening and that its intonation also differs, in that it does not display the boundary tones that are characteristic of phrase and sentence boundaries. Shriberg (2001), Nakatani and Hirschberg (1994), and Plug (2011) give descriptions of the acoustic-phonetic properties of reparanda, the editing phase and repairs, which will not be detailed here. It is worth mentioning that, although there are acoustic features in reparanda that can be detected on close inspection, they may not always be perceptually salient. Listeners are not often able to detect that a repair is about to occur, when they have heard the full reparandum (Lickley and Bard 1998).

We have discussed some features of the reparandum and the editing phase that contribute a degree of fluency to this otherwise disfluent act. What of the repair section? Again, other authors give thorough accounts of phonetic and prosodic aspects of repair (Nakatani and Hirschberg 1994; Plug 2011; Shriberg 2001). We focus on one prominent aspect. It seems to be a common misapprehension that speakers tend to mark a repair with a prosodic accent, perhaps to convey to the listener that they have made a mistake and they are correcting it. In the vast majority of repairs, this is not the case. There is some evidence that where there is an error that contrasts semantically with the intended message (e.g., *left* for *right*, *no* for *yes*) a speaker may signal the importance of the correction by marking the repair prosodically (Levelt and Cutler 1983), typically with emphatic stress. However, three decades and many large speech corpora later, the idea that prosodic marking is typical in repair has proven difficult to replicate (e.g., Plug 2011). Most of the evidence points to the conclusion that speakers do their best to bury the error, when it is not catastrophic, and get on with communicating, to allow a perception of fluency, despite their planning problems.

20.11 Conclusion

This chapter has mainly addressed the notion of fluency in typical speech production. The word "fluency" is used in many different ways and fluency is a crucial aspect not only of typical speech but also of speech pathology and second language learning. To understand how speech can be produced fluently and what levels of production are important for fluent speech, it is important to consider what can go wrong in the processes that underlie speech production. To this end, a large portion of the chapter has focused on just that – disfluency. Without disfluency, there would perhaps be no reason to discuss fluency. We have considered how and why speech can become disfluent, referring to levels of processing in a standard model of production. Hesitation and errors can arise at any level of speech production. Given the number of ways that things can go wrong while producing speech, whether spontaneously or in laboratory experiments, it is unsurprising that speech output is rarely perfectly fluent for long.

We have seen that fluency of a speech is a concept that is important in different disciplines. We can also see that within each area there is a lack of agreement over what fluency actually is and that, between areas, the meanings may overlap, but they may also differ in many respects. It is unlikely that there will ever be consensus on the words that people use to refer to the phenomena. The notion of fluency, and therefore of disfluency, needs to be considered at different levels. We have discussed how the disfluencies that we hear in speech, whether hesitations or repairs, can originate with problems at a number of levels of planning for speech production, from conceptualization, through syntactic and morphophonological encoding, to articulation. We can also therefore refer to fluency at these different levels and assume that fluency in planning will result in fluent output. We know that some errors in production can be detected and corrected by the speaker before they are articulated and that this may result in audible disfluency of some kind. But is also possible that speech output may be unaffected. So it is conceivable that the speaker can continue to articulate fluently, despite there having been some minor disfluency in the planning processes. So it seems necessary to be able to talk about fluency (and therefore disfluency) on at least two levels: *planning fluency* (referring to smoothness of the internal processes) and *surface fluency* (referring to smoothness of overt speech). We might wish to specify further for levels of planning fluency, but it is useful to begin with one general category. As for surface fluency, there is also reason to consider a division. It is possible that what is perceived by typical listeners, under typical listening conditions, as fluent speech, still contains minor disfluencies that are not disruptive enough to affect the impression of fluency (Bard and Lickley 1998). For this reason, I suggest that a distinction should be made between what the listener perceives – *perceived fluency* – and what the speaker actually produced – *surface fluency* – since minor *surface disfluencies* may only be noticeable on close inspection of the speech signal, under ideal listening conditions. Fluency (and disfluency) are features of speech production at several levels, that affect perception of the speech in different ways. No single definition can suffice.

NOTES

1 The difficulties arising in planning, the surface forms, and the perception of "fluency" in a second-language speaker differ somewhat from a typical native speaker's performance, so I deliberately avoid using Segalowitz's (2010) terms in my coining of *planning, surface,* and *perceived* fluency (section 20.2).
2 These authors call this set of phenomena "disfluencies," making a distinction between disfluencies, repairs, and uncorrected errors (Postma et al. 1990).

REFERENCES

Anderson, Anne H., Miles Bader, Ellen G. Bard, et al. 1991. The HCRC Map Task Corpus. *Language and Speech* 34: 351–366.

Baars, Bernard J., Michael T. Motley, and Donald G. MacKay. 1975. Output editing for lexical status in artificially elicited slips of the tongue. *Journal of Verbal Learning and Verbal Behavior* 14: 382–391.

Bailey, Karl G.D. 2004. Disfluent speech and the visual world: An application of the visual world paradigm to the study of spoken language comprehension. PhD dissertation, Michigan State University.

Bard, Ellen Gurman and Robin J. Lickley. 1998. Disfluency deafness: Graceful failure in the recognition of running speech. In *Proceedings of the 20th Annual Meeting of the Cognitive Science Society*, 108–113.

Bard, Ellen Gurman, Matthew Aylett, and Robin J. Lickley. 2002. Towards a psycholinguistics of dialogue: Defining reaction time and error rate in a dialogue corpus. In Proceedings of the Sixth Workshop on the Semantics and Pragmatics of Dialogue (EDILOG 2002), 29–36.

Bates, Elizabeth, Simona D'Amico, Thomas Jacobsen, et al. 2003. Timed picture naming in seven languages. *Psychonomic Bulletin & Review* 10: 344–380.

Beattie, Geoffrey W. 1979. Planning units in spontaneous speech: Some evidence from hesitation in speech and speaker gaze direction in conversation. *Linguistics* 17: 61–78.

Beattie, Geoffrey W. and Brian L. Butterworth. 1979. Contextual probability and word frequency as determinants of pauses and errors in spontaneous speech. *Language and Speech* 22: 201–211.

Bell, Alan, Daniel Jurafsky, Eric Fosler-Lussier, Cynthia Girand, Michelle Gregory, and Daniel Gildea. 2003. Effects of disfluencies, predictability, and utterance position on word form variation in English conversation. *Journal of the Acoustical Society of America* 113: 1001.

Benton, Arthur L. and Kerry Hamsher. 1976. *Multilingual Aphasia Examination*. Iowa City, IA: AJA Associates.

Blackmer, Elizabeth R. and Janet Mitton. 1991. Theories of monitoring and the timing of repairs in spontaneous speech. *Cognition* 39: 173–194.

Blankenship, Jane and Christian Kay. 1964. Hesitation phenomena in English speech: A study in distribution. *Word* 20: 360–372.

Boomer, Donald S. 1965. Hesitation and grammatical encoding. *Language and Speech* 8: 148–158.

Bortfeld, Heather, Silvia D. Leon, Jonathan E. Bloom, Michael F. Schober, and Susan E. Brennan. 2001. Disfluency rates in conversation: Effects of age, relationship, topic, role, and gender. *Language and Speech* 44: 123–147.

Branigan, Holly, Robin J. Lickley, and David McKelvie. 1999. Non-linguistic influences on rates of disfluency in spontaneous speech. In *Proceedings of the 14th International Congress of Phonetic Sciences (ICPhS)*, 387–390.

Brennan, Susan E. and Maurice Williams. 1995. The feeling of another's knowing: Prosody and filled pauses as cues to listeners about the metacognitive states of speakers. *Journal of Memory and Language* 34: 383–398.

Brickman, Adam M., Robert H. Paul, Ronald A. Cohen, et al. 2005. Category and letter verbal fluency across the adult lifespan: Relationship to EEG theta power. *Archives of Clinical Neuropsychology* 20: 561–573.

Brocklehurst, Paul H. 2011. The roles of speech errors, monitoring, and anticipation in the production of normal and stuttered disfluencies. PhD dissertation, University of Edinburgh.

Bull, Matthew and Matthew Aylett. 1998. An analysis of the timing of turn-taking in a corpus of goal-oriented dialogue. In *Proceedings of the 5th International Conference on Spoken Language Processing (ICSLP)*, 1175–1178.

Butcher, Andrew. 1981. Aspects of the speech pause: Phonetic correlates and communicative functions. PhD dissertation, Christian Albrechts Universität zu Kiel, Germany.

Butterworth, Brian. 1980. Evidence from pauses in speech. In Brian Butterworth (ed.), *Language Production*, vol. 1, 155–176. London: Academic Press.

Campione, Estelle and Jean Véronis. 2002. A large-scale multilingual study of silent pause duration. *Speech Prosody* 2002: 199–202.

Clark, Herbert H. and Jean E. Fox Tree. 2002. Using *uh* and *um* in spontaneous speaking. *Cognition* 84: 73–111.

Clark, Herbert H. and Thomas Wasow. 1998. Repeating words in spontaneous speech. *Cognitive Psychology* 37. 201–242.

Collard, Philip. 2009. Disfluency and listeners' attention: An investigation of the immediate and lasting effects of hesitations in speech. PhD dissertation, University of Edinburgh.

Cook, Mark and Mansur Lalijee. 1970. The interpretation of pauses by the listener. *British Journal of Social and Clinical Psychology* 9: 375–376.

Cooper, William E. and Jean M. Paccia-Cooper. 1980. *Syntax and Speech*. Cambridge, MA: Harvard University Press.

Daly, David A. 2006. Predictive Cluttering Inventory (PCI). http://www.mnsu.edu/comdis/isad10/papers/daly10/dalycluttering2006R.pdf, accessed December 9, 2014.

Daneman, Meredyth. 1991. Working memory as a predictor of verbal fluency. *Journal of Psycholinguistic Research* 20: 445–64.

Day, Ruth S. 1977. Verbal fluency and the language-bound effect. In Charles J. Fillmore, Daniel Kempler, and William S.-Y. Wang (eds.), *Individual Differences in Language Ability and Language Behavior*, 57–84. New York: Academic Press.

Dell, Gary S. 1986. A spreading-activation theory of retrieval in sentence production. *Psychological Review* 93: 283.

Duez, Danielle. 1993. Acoustic correlates of subjective pauses. *Journal of Psycholinguistic Research* 22: 21–39.

Edwards, Susan. 2005. *Fluent Aphasia*. Cambridge: Cambridge University Press.

Eklund, Robert. 2001. Prolongations: A dark horse in the disfluency stable. ISCA Tutorial and Research Workshop (ITRW) on Disfluency in Spontaneous Speech (DiSS 01), 5–8.

Eklund, Robert. 2004. Disfluency in Swedish human-human and human-machine travel booking dialogues. PhD dissertation, University of Linköping, Sweden.

Ferreira, Fernanda. 1991. Effects of length and syntactic complexity on initiation times for prepared utterances. *Journal of Memory and Language* 30: 210–233.

Ferreira, Fernanda. 1993. Creation of prosody during sentence production. *Psychological Review* 100: 233–253.

Ferreira, Fernanda. 2007. Prosody and performance in language production. *Language and Cognitive Processes* 22: 1151–1177.

Fillmore, Charles. 1979. On fluency. In Charles J. Fillmore, Daniel Kempler, and William S.-Y. Wang (eds.), *Individual Differences in Language Ability and Language Behavior*, 85–101. New York: Academic Press.

Finlayson, Ian R. 2014. Testing the roles of disfluency and rate of speech in the coordination of conversation. PhD dissertation, Queen Margaret University, Edinburgh.

Fox, Barbara A. and Robert Jasperson. 1995. A syntactic exploration of repair in English conversation. In Philip W. Davis (ed.), *Descriptive and Theoretical Modes in the Alternative Linguistics*, 77–134. Amsterdam: John Benjamins.

Fox Tree, Jean E. 1995. The effects of false starts and repetitions on the processing of subsequent words in spontaneous speech. *Journal of Memory and Language* 34: 709–738.

Garrett, Merrill F. 1980. Levels of processing in sentence production. In Brian Butterworth (ed.), *Language Production*, vol. 1. London: Academic Press.

Gee, James P. and François Grosjean. 1983. Performance structures: A psycholinguistic and linguistic appraisal. *Cognitive Psychology* 15: 411–458.

Goldman-Eisler, Frieda. 1958a. The predictability of words in context and the length of pauses in speech. *Language and Speech* 1: 226–231.

Goldman-Eisler, Frieda. 1958b. Speech production and the predictability of words in context. *Quarterly Journal of Experimental Psychology* 10: 96–106.

Goldman-Eisler, Frieda. 1961. A comparative study of two hesitation phenomena. *Language and Speech* 4: 18–26.

Goldman-Eisler, Frieda. 1968. *Psycholinguistics: Experiments in Spontaneous Speech*. Academic Press: New York.

Good, David A. and Brian L. Butterworth. 1980. Hesitancy as a conversational resource: Some methodological implications. In Hans-Wilhelm Dechert and Manfred Raupach (eds.), *Temporal Variables in Speech: Studies in Honour of Frieda Goldman-Eisler*, 145–152. The Hague: Mouton.

Goodglass, Harold and Barbara Kaplan. 1972. *The Assessment of Aphasia and Related Disorders*. Philadelphia, PA: Lea and Febiger.

Goodglass, Harold, Barbara Kaplan, and Barbara Baresi. 2001. *The Assessment of Aphasia and Related Disorders*. London: Lippincott, Williams and Wilkins.

Gordon, Jeanne K. 1998. The fluency dimension in aphasia. *Aphasiology* 12: 673–688.

Greene, John O. and Joseph N. Cappella. 1986. Cognition and talk: The relationship of semantic units to temporal patterns of fluency in spontaneous speech. *Language and Speech* 29: 141–157.

Hartsuiker, Robert J. and Lies Notebaert. 2010. Lexical access problems lead to disfluencies in speech. *Experimental Psychology (formerly Zeitschrift für Experimentelle Psychologie)* 57: 169–177.

Hartsuiker, Robert J., Martin Corley, and Heike Martensen. 2005. The lexical bias effect is modulated by context, but the standard monitoring account doesn't fly: Related beply to Baars et al. 1975. *Journal of Memory and Language* 52: 58–70.

Heeman, Peter A. 1997. Speech repairs, intonational boundaries and discourse markers: Modeling speakers' utterances in spoken dialog. PhD dissertation, University of Rochester, NY.

Hieke, Adolf E. 1981. A content-processing view of hesitation phenomena. *Language and Speech* 24: 147.

Holmes, Virginia M. 1988. Hesitations and sentence planning. *Language and Cognitive Processes* 3: 323–361.

Indefrey, Peter and Willem J.M. Levelt. 2004. The spatial and temporal signatures of word production components. *Cognition* 92: 101–144.

Jaeger, T. Florian, Katrina Furth, and Caitlin Hilliard. 2012. Phonological overlap affects lexical selection during sentence production. *Journal of Experimental Psychology: Learning, Memory and Cognition* 38: 1439.

Jescheniak, Jorg D. and Willem J.M. Levelt. 1994. Word frequency effects in speech production: Retrieval of syntactic information and of phonological form. *Journal of Experimental Psychology: Learning, Memory, and Cognition* 20: 824–843.

Johnson, Wendell. 1961. Measurements of oral reading and speaking rate and disfluency of adult male and female stutterers and nonstutterers. *Journal of Speech and Hearing Disorders* 7: 1–20.

Lallgee, Mansur G. and Mark Cook. 1969. An experimental investigation of the function of filled pauses in speech. *Language and Speech* 12: 24–28.

Lennon, Paul. 1990. Investigating fluency in EFL: A quantitative approach. *Language Learning* 40: 387–417.

Levelt, Willem J.M. 1983. Monitoring and self-repair in speech. *Cognition* 14: 41–104.

Levelt, Willem J.M. 1989. Speaking: From Intention to Articulation. Cambridge, MA: MIT Press.

Levelt, Willem J.M. and Anne Cutler. 1983. Prosodic marking in speech repair. *Journal of Semantics* 2: 205–217.

Lickley, Robin J. 1994. Detecting disfluency in spontaneous speech. PhD dissertation, University of Edinburgh.

Lickley, Robin J. 1995. Missing disfluencies. In *Proceedings of the International Congress of Phonetic Sciences (ICPhS)*, vol. 4, 192–195.

Lickley, Robin J. 1998. *HCRC Disfluency Coding Manual*. Edinburgh: Human Communication Research Centre Technical Report TR-100, University of Edinburgh.

Lickley, Robin J. 2001. Dialogue moves and disfluency rates. In *Proceedings of Disfluency in Spontaneous Speech (DiSS)*, 93–96.

Lickley, Robin J. 2010. Towards a data-based definition of cluttering. International Cluttering Online Conference, http://www.mnsu.edu/comdis/ica1/papers/lickleyc.html, accessed December 9, 2014.

Lickley, Robin J. and Ellen G. Bard. 1998. When can listeners detect disfluency in spontaneous speech? *Language and Speech* 41: 203–226.

Lounsbury, Floyd G. 1954. Transitional probability, linguistic structure and systems of habit-family hierarchies. In Charles E. Osgood and Thomas A. Sebeok (eds.), *Psycholinguistics: A Survey of Theory and Research Problems*, 93–101. Baltimore, MD: Williams and Wilkins.

Luce, Paul A. and Jan Charles-Luce. 1985. Contextual effects on vowel duration, closure duration, and the consonant/vowel ratio in speech production. *Journal of the Acoustical Society of America* 78: 1949.

MacGregor, Lucy J. 2008. Disfluencies affect language comprehension: Evidence from event-related potentials and recognition memory. PhD dissertation, University of Edinburgh.

Maclay, Howard and Charles E. Osgood. 1959. Hesitation phenomena in spontaneous English speech. *Word* 15: 19–44.

Maekawa, Kikuo. 2004. Design, compilation and some preliminary analyses of the Corpus of Spontaneous Japanese. In Kiyoko Yonemada and Kikuo Maekawa (eds.), *Spontaneous Speech: Data and Analysis*, 87–108. Tokyo: The National Institute for Japanese Language.

Mahl, George F. 1956. Disturbances and silences in the patient's speech in psychotherapy. *Journal of Abnormal and Social Psychology* 53: 1–15.

Martin, James G. 1970. On judging pauses in spontaneous speech. *Journal of Verbal Learning and Verbal Behaviour* 9: 75–78.

Meyer, Antje S. and Herbert Schriefers. 1991. Phonological facilitation in picture-word interference experiments: Effects of stimulus onset asynchrony and types of interfering stimuli. *Journal of Experimental Psychology: Learning, Memory, and Cognition* 17: 1146–1160.

Miller, Timothy A. 2010. Generative models of disfluency. PhD dissertation, University of Minnesota.

Mooshammer, Christine, Louis Goldstein, Hosung Nam, Scott McClure, Elliot Saltzman, and Mark Tiede. 2012. Bridging planning and execution: Temporal planning of syllables. *Journal of Phonetics* 40(3): 374–389.

Morrison, Catriona M., Andrew W. Ellis, and Philip T. Quinlan. 1992. Age of acquisition, not word frequency, affects object naming, not object recognition. *Memory & Cognition* 20: 705–714.

Myers, Florence L., Klaas Bakker, Kenneth O. St. Louis, and Lawrence J. Raphael. 2012. Disfluencies in cluttered speech. *Journal of Fluency Disorders* 37: 9–19.

Nakatani, Christine H. and Julia Hirschberg. 1994. A corpus-based study of repair cues in spontaneous speech. *Journal of the Acoustical Society of America* 95: 1603–1616.

Nooteboom, Sieb G. 1980. Speaking and unspeaking: Detection and correction of phonological and lexical errors in spontaneous speech. In Victoria A. Fromkin (ed.), *Errors in Linguistic Performance: Slips of the Tongue, Ear, Pen and Hand*, 87–95. New York: Academic Press.

Nooteboom, Sieb G. 2005. Lexical bias revisited: Detecting, rejecting and repairing speech errors in inner speech. *Speech Communication* 47: 43–58.

O'Connell, Daniel C. and Sabine Kowal. 2005. Uh and um revisited: Are they interjections for signaling delay? *Journal of Psycholinguistic Research* 34: 555–576.

Oldfield, Robert C. and Arthur Wingfield. 1965. Response latencies in naming objects. *Quarterly Journal of Experimental Psychology* 17: 273–281.

Oomen, Claudy C.E. and Albert Postma. 2001. Effects of divided attention on the production of filled pauses and repetitions. *Journal of Speech, Language, and Hearing Research* 44: 997–1004.

O'Seaghdha, Padraig G. and Joseph W. Marin. 2000. Phonological competition and cooperation in form-related priming: Sequential and nonsequential processes in word production. *Journal of Experimental Psychology: Human Perception and Performance* 26: 57.

Oviatt, Sharon. 1995. Predicting spoken disfluencies during human-computer interaction. *Computer Speech and Language* 9: 19–35.

Plauché, Madelaine and Elizabeth Shriberg. 1999. Data-driven subclassification of disfluent repetitions based on prosodic features. In *Proceedings of the International Congress of Phonetic Sciences (ICPhS)*, vol. 2, 1513–1516.

Plug, Leendert. 2011. Phonetic reduction and informational redundancy in self-initiated self-repair in Dutch. *Journal of Phonetics* 39: 289–297.

Poeck, Klaus 1989. Fluency. In Chris Code (ed.), *The Characteristics of Aphasia*, 23–32. Hove, UK: Lawrence Erlbaum.

Postma, Albert and Herman Kolk. 1993. The covert repair hypothesis: Prearticulatory repair processes in normal and stuttered disfluencies. *Journal of Speech and Hearing Research* 36(3): 472–487.

Postma, Albert, Herman Kolk, and Dirk-Jan Povel. 1990. On the relation among speech errors, disfluencies and self-repairs. *Language and Speech* 1: 19–29.

Postma, Albert, Herman Kolk, and Dirk-Jan Povel. 1991. Disfluencies as resulting from covert self-repairs applied to internal speech errors. In Herman F.M. Peters, Wouter Hulstijn, and C. Woodruff Starkweather (eds.), Speech Motor Control and Stuttering, 141–147. Amsterdam: Elsevier Science.

Schnadt, Michael 2009. Lexical influences on disfluency production. PhD dissertation, University of Edinburgh.

Schnur, Tatiana T., Albert Costa, and Alfonso Caramazza. 2006. Planning at the phonological level during sentence production. *Journal of Psycholinguistic Research* 35: 189–213.

Schriefers, Herbert. 1999. Phonological facilitation in the production of two-word utterances. *European Journal of Cognitive Psychology* 11: 17–50.

Segalowitz, Norman. 2010. Cognitive Bases of Second Language Fluency. New York: Routledge.

Severens, Els, Sven Van Lommel, Elie Ratinckx, and Robert J. Hartsuiker. 2005. Timed picture naming norms for 590 pictures in Dutch. *Acta Psychologica* 119: 159–187.

Seyfeddinipur, Mandana, Sotaro Kita, and Peter Indefrey. 2008. How speakers interrupt themselves in managing problems in speaking: Evidence from self-repairs. *Cognition* 108: 837–842.

Shriberg, Elizabeth. 1994. Preliminaries to a theory of speech disfluencies. PhD dissertation, University of California, Berkeley.

Shriberg, Elizabeth. 1995. Acoustic properties of disfluent repetitions. In *Proceedings of the International Congress of Phonetic Sciences*, vol. 4, 384–387.

Shriberg, Elizabeth. 2001. To "errrr" is human: Ecology and acoustics of speech disfluencies. *Journal of the International Phonetic Association* 31: 153–69.

Shriberg, Elizabeth and Robin J. Lickley. 1993. Intonation of clause-internal filled pauses. *Phonetica* 50: 172–179.

Smith, Mark and Linda Wheeldon. 2004. Horizontal information flow in spoken sentence production. *Journal of Experimental Psychology: Learning, Memory, and Cognition* 30: 675–686.

Smith, Vicki L. and Herbert H. Clark. 1993. On the course of answering questions. *Journal of Memory and Language* 32: 25–38.

St. Louis, Kenneth O., Florence Myers, Klaas Bakker, and Lawrence Raphael. 2007. Understanding and treating cluttering. In Edward G. Conture and Richard F. Curlee (eds.), *Stuttering and Related Disorders of Fluency*, 297–325. New York: Thieme.

Starkweather, C. Woodruff. 1987. *Fluency and Stuttering*. Englewood Cliffs, NJ: Prentice Hall.

Tannenbaum, Percy H., Frederick Williams and Carolyn S. Hillier. 1965. Word predictability in the environments of hesitations. *Journal of Verbal Learning and Verbal Behavior* 4: 134–140.

Tavakoli, Parvaneh and Peter Skehan. 2005. Strategic planning, task structure, and performance testing. In Rod Ellis (ed.), *Planning and Task Performance in a Second Language*, 239–277. Amsterdam: John Benjamins.

Tottie, Gunnel. 2011. Uh and um as sociolinguistic markers in British English. *International Journal of Corpus Linguistics* 16: 173–197.

Tseng, Shu-chuan. 2006. Repairs in Mandarin conversation. *Journal of Chinese Linguistics* 34: 80.

Ward, David. 2006. *Stuttering and Cluttering: Frameworks for Understanding and Treatment*. Hove, UK: Psychology Press.

Watanabe, Michiko. 2009. *Features and Roles of Filled Pauses in Speech Communication: A Corpus-Based Study of Spontaneous Speech*. Tokyo: Hituzi Syobo Publishing.

Watson, Duane and Edward Gibson. 2004. The relationship between intonational phrasing and syntactic structure in language production. *Language and Cognitive Processes* 19: 713–755.

Wheeldon, Linda. 2003. Inhibitory form priming of spoken word production. *Language and Cognitive Processes* 18: 81–109.

Wheeldon, Linda and Aditi Lahiri. 1997. Prosodic units in speech production. *Journal of Memory and Language* 37: 356–381.

Wingate, Marcel, E. 1988. *The Structure of Stuttering*. New York: Springer.

Wingate, Marcel, E. 2002. *Foundations of Stuttering*. San Diego, CA: Academic Press.

Yairi, Ehud and Nicoline Ambrose. 1992. A longitudinal study of stuttering in children: A preliminary report. *Journal of Speech, Language, and Hearing Research* 35: 755.

Zellner, Brigitte. 1994. Pauses and the temporal structure of speech. In Eric Keller (ed.), *Fundamentals of Speech Synthesis and Speech Recognition*, 41–62. Chichester: John Wiley & Sons Ltd.

Part V Language Factors

21 Insights from the Field

DIDIER DEMOLIN

21.1 Introduction

Describing the processes of speech production necessitates mastering and understanding a number of domains linked to the generation of sounds in human languages. The speech signal is time varying. There are anatomical differences between speakers, and articulatory strategies also differ within and between speakers. The vocal tract is a 3D tube which is not easily accessible to study. The voice source, which excites the vocal tract, is even less accessible to study. All these points are well-known facts for those who investigate speech production. The complexity of the speech process and the types of measurements needed to study it can become an even greater challenge for those acquiring data in the field. Even so, there are a number of techniques for investigating speech production which can be used in field situations. Other methods, such as those that track the movement of multiple articulators (EMA, MRI), remain laboratory-bound for the moment. The aim of this chapter is to show that even with the limitations presented by the field situations, data from the field provides an essential contribution to understanding the principles of speech production and the variety of sounds that are produced in human languages.[1]

21.1.1 Fieldwork

Roughly speaking, phonetic fieldwork has two main objectives. The first is to describe the sound system of a particular language or to understand the production of some particular phenomenon linked to the production of speech. The second is to look for unfamiliar sounds, features or phenomena using a particular measurement technique. Fieldwork can therefore be defined differently according to various perspectives. One is to consider any kind of data collection outside the laboratory to be fieldwork. Another viewpoint defines fieldwork as data collection from undescribed or poorly described languages. Sometimes there are opportunities to further an investigation of data originally collected in the field by bringing subjects to the laboratory. Tabain (2011) offers a good illustration of this practice with her electropalatographic study of Central Arrente consonants. Combining work in the field with laboratory work using investigation tools not available in the field deepens some aspects of the research undertaken. This chapter will consider data from the field and laboratory to demonstrate how fieldwork provides data and observations that contribute to new testable hypotheses by adding new evidence to the understanding of speech production.

21.1.2 *From impressionistic data to quantified data*

Any researcher doing fieldwork is confronted, sooner or later, with the following basic question: how best to describe (sometimes unknown) speech sounds in a reliable way? This question implies a need to understand how they are produced, and what are the best primitives, gestures, and/or features necessary to describe the sounds. Any phonetician doing fieldwork is also confronted with a second question connected to the first: how to quantify data? The rapid development and miniaturization of research tools and the development of computational techniques makes this enterprise much easier than it was before. Quantifying data allows fieldworkers to address another fundamental question: what are the patterns of variation in the phenomena being studied?

21.1.3 *Equipment and measurement tools*

A lot of equipment to record data in the field is now available to answer the basic questions that confront a fieldworker. These include tools available to collect acoustic, aerodynamic, and articulatory data. The choice of a particular measurement technique often depends on the research undertaking and, of course, on the research budget available. Apart from acoustic measurements, which are now routine in the analysis of speech data whether they come from the field or the laboratory, a number of additional techniques are available for the measurement and quantification of field data.

If the precision is accurate (e.g., up to 1 mbar for pressure), the use of aerodynamic measurement allows the researcher to deduce articulatory movements in the vocal tract with great precision. Acoustic cues and features may also be deduced from changes of flow and pressure in the vocal tract. Despite the fact that measuring intraoral pressure (Po) can be invasive at times, aerodynamic measurement is one of the most reliable and powerful techniques speech scientists have to describe and understand the behavior and the production of speech sounds. While the old kymograph contributed to the description of sounds from languages in sometimes very remote areas, it could hardly be considered a portable tool, and not much had been used prior to Ladefoged's (1968) equipment for his work on West African languages. Bringing speakers to a laboratory is not always possible, and if one wishes to record data from speakers in remote areas, reliable and portable equipment is a necessity. Such tools are now available and change the way that phoneticians do fieldwork. This leads to new challenges for fieldworkers such as being able to interpret aerodynamic data right in the field and being able to quickly pose new questions based on that interpretation. Reference values (such as maxima, minima, and mean for pressure and flow) are also required for the phenomena to those studied, along with a basic understanding of the physical principles involved in the aerodynamics of speech. When these challenges are overcome, the integration of aerodynamic parameters in models of speech production leads to a better understanding of the phenomena which are studied.

Ultrasound is another technique used for linguistic description that can also reveal a number of things about the articulatory mechanisms involved in speech production. Ultrasound is ideal for fieldwork because the machines are portable and because data collection is non-invasive. Lingual ultrasound is used to measure constriction location and tongues shape directly. Recently a lot of ultrasound research has been undertaken in fieldwork studies, revealing a number of new and interesting features of speech production. For example, ultrasound has been used to measure constriction locations in click consonants (Miller 2013) and doubly articulated stops (Hudu, Miller, and Pulleyblank 2009). Ultrasound has revealed that the articulation of Arabic guttural and emphatic sounds are produced with more subtle tongue root and tongue dorsum retraction mechanisms than previously thought (Al Solami 2013; Lapinskaya 2013). Esling and Moisik (2012) have extended the use of ultrasound technique beyond investigations of lingual articulation. For example, Bird et al. (2013) show the usefulness of the technique to visualize the laryngeal vocal tract. Ultrasound images of the lower vocal tract may also be compared to oral-endoscopic videos of the vocal tract. Laryngoscopic studies are also sometime possible in the field as shown by Esling and Harris (2005) and by Edmonson and Esling (2006) in their study of different throat valves and their functioning in tone, vocal register, and stress. A guide for laryngoscopic fieldwork has been proposed by Edmonson et al. (2011).

Electroglottography (EGG), recorded synchronously with audio waveform, measures the impedance at the glottis, that is, the contact between the vocal folds, while the acoustic recording shows short time-pressure variations produced by the opening and closure of the glottis. The technique is useful, although not often used, to study phenomena related to what is generally called laryngealization or glottalization phenomena and to other speech events involving the contact or not of the vocal folds. The important thing to bear in mind is that the EGG technique essentially transduces the vocal fold contact area. Accordingly, it should not be referred to "closing" or "opening" gestures of the glottis but rather to "contacting" and "decontacting" phases of the vibratory cycle. That is, EGG is sensitive to covert changes in contact area during glottal closure, and reflects the growth and loss of contact area along the length of the vocal folds as glottal closure and opening succeed each other (Baken and Orlikoff 2000). There are, however, degrees of contact. Over the course of the "closed" phase of each glottal cycle, the contact of the vocal folds varies from minimal (valley represented in the signal) to maximal (represented by a peak in the signal) as contact involves more of the vertical dimension of the vocal folds (Hayward 2001).

Electromyography (EMG) is also portable and quite accessible when used to study muscle activity with contact electrodes that are not invasive. Lips are an excellent candidate for study using this technique, but the activity of other muscles where the contact is easy and straightforward, like the masseter (to study jaw activity), can also be undertaken.

Finally, video techniques are also quite easy to use in the field. Data recorded using a mirror set at a 45° angle of the face allows recording of lips and jaw (Ladefoged 2003; Ladefoged and Maddieson 1996). Reflective markers set at various places along the cheeks, jaw, lips, and under the tongue also provide excellent data on the muscular activity involved in speech production (Demolin, Ngonga, and Soquet 2002). The use of high-speed video might be limited at times because of light requirements, but the high speed is not usually necessary to study the external muscles involved in speech production.

21.1.4 Speech production and the international phonetic alphabet

To explain phenomena related to speech production and their variation in the world's languages, we have to consider that phonetic and phonological systems are open systems and there is no a priori reason to believe that they are based on a universal inventory of features or elements. The only true limits on sound systems are those defined by physics, the vocal tract morphology, and by constraints on audition as well as those on cognition and the brain. One key element to understanding the diversity of sound systems is understanding variation in the production mechanism and the constraints acting on sound production. The way the results of sound pattern variation are processed in perception, integrated, and categorized in phonetic and phonological systems also has to be considered. Understanding human language sound systems depends crucially on the explanation of possible variation, specifically, the source of the variation, its propagation, and transmission.

Linguistic description relies on the notion of a universal phonetic space defined by discrete elements that do not reference time. Presumed discreteness at the phonetic level guarantees a discrete interpretation of structure at all other levels of language. The assumption of discreteness also implies that there is a sharp division between language and speech, which is a continuous event. Port and Learey (2005) emphasize that linguistics has wrongly presumed that speech can always be translated with discrete elements similar to letters, and work in phonetics demonstrates that there exists no universal inventory of phonetic objects. Indeed some phonetic characteristics of languages depend on intrinsic temporal patterns. In particular, the same sound categories of languages can be very different one from the other due to differences in timing (see, e.g., Cho, this volume, Chapter 22). Overlapping categories across languages also argue against discretization. For example, languages divide the possible continuum of consonant place of articulation in very different ways, but in almost the same number of ways as they divide the continuous tonal or vowel space. Why do we then imagine that there are discrete places of articulations for consonants? Phonological features as they are specified in formal models have multiple realizations in real phonetic parameters: it is impossible to specify all the phonetic aspects of languages if we imagine that each phonological feature denotes values on a single physical scale. The complexity of the phonetic phenomena demonstrated by language-specific data shows that the phonology of human languages can vary in ways almost impossible to measure. The phonological features that are typically used to classify sounds only provide information about the phonetic phenomena when supplemented with a number of ad hoc specifications.

Cross-linguistic data from many languages illustrate many of these points. With regard to timing, acoustic data show that articulatory movements associated with clicks in Khoisan languages are slower in the case of some clicks compared to others (Traill 1985). Kinematic measures of Amharic geminated ejective fricative consonants compared to other singleton ejective fricatives show differences in the velocity and control of gestures (Demolin 2002). With regard to place of articulation, comparisons between retroflexed fricative consonants across languages (Mandarin, Dravidian languages, and Namtrik from Colombia) leads one to wonder if there are, in a general phonetic sense, places of articulation that can be used to describe the production of retroflex sounds. In fact the comparisons indicate that retroflexion might be better considered a manner of articulation, suggesting that the relevance of a retroflex place of articulation should be reconsidered.

The following sections exemplify how a detailed understanding of the speech production mechanism supports the view that no universal, discrete set of features is adequate to describe phonetic systems in the world's languages. The sections are developed around four themes: coordination of articulatory gestures; place and manner of articulation; challenging models and theories; refining the description of speech sounds.

21.2   Coordination of articulatory gestures

Sounds observed in the world's languages which are less central or common than the set found in most languages often require understanding the coordination of articulatory gestures to be described with accuracy. Impressionistic data based on auditory phonetic transcriptions are only approximations of the physical reality and need to be substantiated by objective production data. Very often the information obtained shed new light on speech production abilities and variations in human languages.

21.2.1   Glottalic consonants

The role played by the larynx in the production of glottalic consonants is reasonably well known (Catford 1977; Ladefoged and Maddieson 1996). Data from different languages raise questions about possible differences in the amplitude of larynx displacement and how larynx displacement is coordinated with voicing and oral gestures. For example, Bird and colleagues (2013) suggested a strong-weak distinction for ejectives that depends on larynx displacement such that strong ejectives are associated with a large amplitude displacement, and weak ejectives with a small amplitude displacement. This suggests that speakers manipulate and control gestures in ways not previously understood. Each time new data come into the field, more subtle features of speech production are discovered. Consider, for example, Fulfulde (Niger-Congo, Atlantic), a language spoken across the Sahel from Senegal in the West to Sudan in the East. The language has many dialects. Previous descriptions (e.g., Boly 1984) clearly indicated three implosives, /ɓ, ɗ, ʄ/, in the language. However some problems remain unsolved in the description of these consonants. Indeed it is still unclear how to account for what Boly (1984) described as voiced geminated implosives and for the possible occurrence of voiceless implosives in the language. Data discussed here focus on the dialect spoken in the Douentza area (Mali).

In order to understand how implosive sounds are produced, we recently recorded several Fulfulde speakers using an EVA2 portable machine, which allows for the synchronous recording of acoustic, aerodynamic (intra-oral pressure and oral airflow), and EGG information.[2] The recorded Fulfulde data included single stops and implosives at the same place of articulation and also the sounds that have been described as voiced geminated stops and voiced geminated implosives. Several parameters were measured: the duration of the whole closure based on acoustic and aerodynamic parameters; the maximum value of intraoral pressure (positive and negative); and the duration of negative intraoral pressure for the implosives. Data obtained with acoustic and aerodynamic parameters were then compared to the EGG recordings, in order to interpret the contacting and decontacting phases of the glottis during the production of these sounds (Cissé, Demolin, and Vallée 2011; Demolin 2011). Boly's (1984) observations of contrasts between single modal stops and implosives was confirmed. Occurrences of geminated voiced stops were also confirmed. However, the description of voiced geminated implosives should be modified. Instead, these should be described as geminated voiceless implosives. When compared to geminated voiceless stops that have a clear positive VOT at the end, the sounds described until now as voiced geminated implosives are acoustically characterized by a long voiceless closure followed by a short pre-voicing occurring at the end of the consonant. This pre-voicing corresponds to the larynx's elevation following the lowering phase that is characteristic of implosive consonants. Modifying the description of Fulfulde geminated implosives in this way fits with previously described voiceless implosives in languages such as Seerer Singandum (Faye 1979), Quiché languages (Pinkerton 1986), Lendu (Demolin 1995), Seerer (MacLaughlin 2005), Ese Ejja (Vuillermet and Demolin 2006). It would therefore seem that the production of voiceless implosives follows a similar pattern wherever they are encountered in the world's languages. The production of these rather rare glottalic consonants requires a lowering movement of the larynx, but with a closed glottis. The lowering is followed by rapid rising of the larynx, which is accompanied by voicing. The gesture involved (i.e., the coordination of different articulators) in the production of these consonants suggest that speakers have some control on the coordination between the lowering movement of the larynx and the glottis closure. Note that this detailed description of sound production relies on tools such as aerodynamic transducers and EGG without which it would be difficult to characterize in details the parameters involved and their timing.

21.2.2 Overlap of articulatory gestures

In some Bantu languages such as Shona (Doke 1931) and particularly Rwanda, the sequence [m]-[ŋ] can be realized as: [mŋ], [mᵊŋ], [mʘŋ], [mʘg], and the sequence [n]-[ŋ] as [n!ŋ], [nᵊŋ]. These variations come from differences in the timing and coordination of the labial, alveolar, and velar gestures involved in the production of these nasal consonants. When gestures overlap in the front-back nasal sequence, and when the anterior constriction is released before the posterior velar closure, a burst appears. This is in fact a click burst, but with weaker intensity compared to Khoisan clicks. The click bursts are homorganic to the first nasal. If the two gestures involved in the front-to-back nasal sequence do not overlap, and if a small delay occurs before the velar closure, then a small vocoid [ᵊ] appears between the two nasal consonants. The slight negative airflow that occurs in the middle of the [mʘŋ], [n!ŋ] nasal clusters and after the bilabial nasal in the sequence [mʘg] is the consequence of cavity expansion between the two closures. Data show that after the beginning of the velar, which triggers a gradual increase of intraoral pressure (Po, up to 3.5 hPa), there is a gradual increase of nasal airflow. At the same time oral airflow becomes gradually negative (down to 0.98 dm^3/s). This reflects a lowering and backing movement of the tongue anticipating the following vowel [a]. The last part of the velar articulation is voiceless and has a slightly aspirated release. When vocoids occur after bilabial or alveolar nasals, there is always an increase of oral airflow before the realization of the velar nasal for which there is no oral airflow. Sometimes oral airflow can even become negative. This too reflects the backing movement of the tongue which is required to articulate the velar nasal.

Bursts and vocoids appear in other complex consonant sequences in Rwanda. For example, the word for "dog" /imbga/ has several possible free variants [imʘga], [imᵊga], [imbga]. The main difference between the three variants comes from the overlap or separation between the lip and tongue body (TB) gestures. In the first case, the release of the bilabial nasal occurs before the velar. This is a mechanism similar to the production of clicks. The aerodynamic data, even in the absence of oral pressure measurements independent from Po, confirm this point as a slight negative airflow is observed between the bilabial nasal and the velar stop. The emergent burst is similar to the bursts that have been mentioned a number of times in the literature on stop sequences in Indo-European languages (e.g., Marchal 1987; Ohala 1995). The Rwandan case is therefore not so uncommon. What is a little unusual is that it involves nasal sequences. The second case is accounted for by an earlier release of the bilabial nasal, before velar closure takes place. During this short interval of time, a vocoid emerges. The third case has a velum closure preceding the bilabial closure and the start of the velar closure.

Variations in Rwanda could contribute to our understanding of diachronic processes observed in Bantu languages. The timing patterns described above are similar to what happens in Eastern dialects of Shona where /imga/ has the following variants: [ibɣa], [imᵊga], [imbga], [imϴga] (Doke 1931). Note that these variants also reflect a process of velarization which is a well-known evolution from Proto Bantu: *ɲ–bua > m-bwa> m-bya > m-bga. Thus, data from Rwanda reflect phenomena not limited to the language. The occurrence of clicks homorganic to the first nasal in a cluster, where the first is bilabial or alveolar in place of articulation and the second velar, might be confused with stop bursts. This is because click bursts produced in Rwanda nasal clusters are of a weaker intensity than those found in other click languages. The emergence of small vocoids in complex nasals due to timing and coordination of articulatory gestures found in Rwanda's complex consonant sequences could trigger resyllabification processes.

21.2.3 *Timing of articulatory gestures*

Amharic, a Semitic language spoken in Ethiopia, has a set of fricative and affricate geminates, both plain and ejective, in its phonological inventory. One important question about these consonants is their characterization by features. Ladefoged and Maddieson (1996: 92) remind us that unlike a sequence, geminates cannot be separated by an epenthetic vowel or any other interruption. Amharic's set of geminates provides an interesting case to test these claims, particularly the claim, again by Ladefoged and Maddieson (1996: 92), who say that geminate affricates are very clearly different from an affricate sequence. Geminates are expected to have one long stop closure followed by one fricative portion.

In Amharic there are interesting findings about the difference between ejectives and plain fricatives (Demolin 2002). The coordination of the glottal gestures (closure and opening) differs in the two cases. Ejective fricatives are characterized by a glottal closure at the start, contrary to what happens with plain fricatives where there is glottal opening. Compared to the constant noise of plain fricatives, frication noise increases toward the end of ejective fricatives. This is due to the elevation of the larynx, which is necessary to produce the ejective. In the case of the fricative ejective in [k'is':il] the larynx rise is delayed. Producing a geminate ejective fricative seems to require this delay as the air resources within the oral cavity cannot be extended (see Demolin 2002 for more details).

Other important differences between plain and ejective geminate affricates and fricatives in Amharic involve the coordination of glottal and oral gestures. For instance, the voice onset times (VOT) for plain and ejective velar stops are different. The ejective has an interval of time corresponding to a VOT with no noise. This suggests that the glottis is still closed at the release of the oral constriction. A similar coordination between glottal and oral gestures happens at the end of the fricatives. There is a glottal lag at the end of the ejective fricatives due to continued glottal closure at constriction release. A similar effect of the closed glottis can be seen comparing the starts of plain and ejective fricatives. Experiments involving measures of Ps showed a drop in subglottal air pressure (Ps) at the start of plain fricatives that is due to the wider glottal opening necessary to increase the volume velocity of airflow and thus generate the frication noise. This shows up as a drop of Ps simultaneous to an increase in oral airflow. This effect is not seen in ejective fricatives, as the glottis is closed. The comparison confirms that frication in ejective fricatives is produced only with the air available in the oral cavity between the sealed glottis and the constriction.

Phenomena such as these raise fundamental questions about the control and coordination of articulatory gestures, and notably about the kind and degree of control that speakers exert on articulations. The data about Amaharic affricates, plain and ejective, confirm Ladefoged and Maddieson's (1996) claims about the unity of geminates. It is specifically the increase in duration of the stop that makes the main difference between these sounds, rather than an increase in the duration of frication noise.

21.2.4 Glottalic vowels

Nasa Yuwe, a language spoken in the Cauca region of Colombia, displays vowel characteristics related to phonation types that are typologically unusually and not described in phonetic detail. Rojas Curieux (1998) describes a complex vowel system based on four qualities [i, e, a, u], which can be oral, nasal, aspirated, and glottalized (or *interruptas* in Rojas Curieux's terms). Oral and nasal also contrast for length. Glottal vowels are particularly interesting because they are clearly distinguished from laryngealized vowels (i.e., vowels produced with creaky or pressed voice). Glottal vowels are produced with a sharp closure at the end of the vowel. Perceptually they sound like vowels followed by a glottal stop, but the perceptual feature belongs to the vowel and not to a potentially following glottal stop. Acoustic, aerodynamic, and EGG data clearly show that there is an abrupt interruption of the signal at the end of vowel, which is accompanied by an interruption of the oral airflow. The EGG signal confirms that there is complete contact between the vocal folds starting at the end of the vowel. This observation has been made on several subjects showing that the articulation is reproduced across speakers and is not idiosyncratic. This type of vowel is encountered before voiceless stops which are produced with a glottal closure and before sonorants. The interesting feature here is that glottalic vowels must distinguished from laryngealized vowels, and might therefore represent a distinct phonation type.

Some other South American languages show phenomena which could be produced by a similar mechanism, but which has no phonological relevance. For example, the bursts observed at the end of vowels in languages like Karitiana (Demolin and Storto in press) and Dâw. These bursts reflect a closing gesture that often occurs when the vowel precedes a voiceless stop. Such phenomena are also encountered at times in English and in French when either a glottal closure or a voiceless stop follows the vowel. What make languages like Nasa Yuwe, and maybe other South American languages, special is that the vocal folds' contact at the end of vowels is controlled to produce a specific phonological feature that is pertinent to the vowel category.

21.2.5 Gestures and whistled sounds

Sardinian, a Romance language spoken on the island of Sardinia, shows some complex features resulting from a unique coordination of articulatory gestures. Contini (1987) describes whistled lateral consonants (transcribed as [L]) in this language. This consonant can be voiceless or voiced depending on the following consonant. What is particularly interesting about this sound is the way it is articulated. Contini (1987) distinguishes three articulatory types depending on the position of the apex, which can be (a) lowered and positioned against the lower incisors with the tongue bunched and in contact with the postalveolar region; (b) in interdental position; or (c) horizontal and in contact with the upper incisor. In all cases, the tongue dorsum is in contact with the two sides of the hard palate from the front teeth (or the postalveolar region) up to the first molars. In the three types of variants the airflow is unilateral. Friction is produced by a narrow passage situated to the back of the last molars. This is suggested by palatographic data and by films made of the lips movements. In addition, these consonants show a unilateral stretch of the lips well marked in the context of front vowels. This particular coordination of gestures is quite unusual and cannot be made randomly. Whatever the diachronic reasons are to account for the occurrence of these sounds, they show a quite complex coordination of lips and tongue gestures to produce a specific acoustic output, a whistled or strident sound. The acoustic features are an intense frication noise with energy concentrated between 2200 and 4000 Hz, around F3 and F4 of the vowels in contact. This rather unusual sound shows that languages sometimes require a complex coordination of articulatory gestures, that must come together in short periods of time.

Whistled sounds are also encountered with alveolar and palatal fricatives. Bantu languages from the Southeast, like Shona and Changana, have been described as having such sounds (Doke 1931; Shosted 2006a; Janson and Engstrand 2001). Whistled fricatives have also been reported at times in South American varieties of Spanish (Chile and Peru). Kamsa, a language spoken in Colombia, which has such sounds has been studied using ultrasound, aerodynamic, and acoustic recordings. Results show that to produce the very acute frication noise accompanied by a slightly decreasing resonance around 2700 Hz, speakers make a pre-palatal or post-alveolar constriction with the tongue tip posited just behind the teeth, but no contact, and the lips making a small aperture with a very slight protrusion. This articulatory configuration makes a narrow channel between the two constrictions (pre-palatal or post-alveolar and alveolar) generating the frication noise. A high-frequency resonance is produced by the small tube between the two constrictions. This seems to vary a little with the Shona whistling fricatives where there is extreme lip rounding combined with the lateral alveolar gesture.

Altogether, whistled sounds from Sardinian to Kamsa provide good examples of the complex control that is necessary to produce a particular acoustic output.

21.3 Place and manner of articulation

When looking at the IPA (2006), one can notice that it has reserved space on the chart for sounds that are either deemed impossible or are not yet known. Fieldwork data potentially provides the opportunity to identify such sounds. The relevance of the place and manner of articulation categories according to which the IPA chart is organized can also be discussed with reference to field data from many languages. Two examples will be discussed here, the occurrence of a uvular tap and descriptions of retroflex consonants.

21.3.1 Uvular tap

This description of an uvular tap comes from Kalapalo, a dialect of Kuikuro, which is a language belonging to one of the two Southern branches of the Carib family, known as Upper Xingu Carib (Meira and Franchetto 2005). The two main dialectal variants of Upper Xingu Carib languages, Kuikuro and Kalapalo, are spoken in the Kuikuro villages and in the Kalapalo, Nahukwá, and Matipu villages, respectively. The variants can be distinguished by differences in lexicon and, especially, by differences in their prosodic structures (Franchetto 2001, 2005). Phonologically, the Upper Xingu Carib language has a set of characteristics that are unique in the family, such as frequent dorsal consonants, lenition processes, and the absence of syllabic coda.

As a result of his 1887 expedition to the Upper Xingu, the German ethnographer Karl von den Steinen presented two word lists of a Carib language that he called Nahuquá. In this list he used the symbol r and λ to transcribe: "a sound complicated to pronounce, between gl and ri, always forming a syllable equivalent to r followed by a reduced vowel" (von den Steinen 1940: 662). This sound is not represented in the IPA, but we are describing it as an uvular tap/flap, temporarily transcribed [ř] (Demolin, Franchetto, and Fausto in press). Note that the absence of such a sound on the IPA chart suggests that a tap or flap at this place of articulation is possible but not yet found. The field data indicate that the IPA should be revised to state that an uvular tap is possible.

The Kuikuro uvular tap is characterized by a short closure that lasts on average 39 msec (N = 200, SD = 3.6). This sound is described as a tap because it is made by a brief contact between the tongue dorsum that strikes the back uvular region, most of the time steadily and sometimes in passing. The short duration of the tap is clearly identifiable in intervocalic position. The burst at the end of the articulation also indicates a momentary closure in the vocal tract. The features correspond to the definition of taps and flaps proposed by Catford (1977), Ladefoged and Maddieson (1996), and in the Handbook of the International Phonetic Association (HIPA 1999). There are some variations in the realization of this sound that may sound uvular, velar, and palatal. It may even sound like an approximant due to coarticulation processes.

Place of articulation for this sound was established from two sets of data: acoustic and articulatory (using ultrasound). Formant transitions into and out of the tap situated between identical central and back vowels [i-i, o-o, u-u] helped to identify the constriction location. These transitions show a clear convergence of F4 and F5. Fant (1960) and Vaissière (2007) have demonstrated that the convergence of F2/F3 and F4/F5 transitions identify a constriction in the palatal-velar and uvular regions. Constrictions made between the palatal and velar place of articulation correspond to the convergence of F2 and F3 and a more posterior constriction, around the uvular place of articulation, corresponds to a convergence of F4 and F5. Nomograms derived from Fant's (1960) second three-parameter VT model show that F4 rises and F5 lowers with a pharyngeal constriction. However, in the present case, most of the taps were produced in the context of a rising F4 transition only, suggesting an uvular constriction. This suggestion is confirmed by ultrasound recordings, which show that there is indeed an uvular place of articulation for these taps. When realized between front vowels [i-i] taps are rather more palatal or velar due to the coarticulation with the front vowels, as confirmed by a convergence of F2 and F3.

The posterior articulation of the tap/flap in Carib languages may shed light on diachronic processes in the region and in the world's languages more generally. Engstrand, Frid, and Lindblom (2007) observe that rhotic place of articulation may be ambiguous enough to be misperceived forcing an articulatory reinterpretation. Specifically, changes from coronal to dorsal place of articulation for rhotics may be phonetically motivated. The evidence from Carib languages supports this hypothesis, with convergence in the F2/F3 region the perceptual source of the diachronic change. The fact that the Kuikuro uvular tap/flaps occur primarily in front to back sequences of vowels rather than the contrary favors the lowering of F3 and its approximation with F2. This contributes to what Engstrand and his colleagues call an ambiguous rhotic that can be reinterpreted as a short backward closure.

We have no comparable acoustic data from other Carib languages to support the hypothesis of a diachronic reinterpretation for rhotic place of articulation from the coronal region to the dorsal region. However, some interesting variations produced by two of the eldest Kuikuro informants are suggestive. These speakers realized a variant [l] in the word [ilo] where the other speakers were producing a clear uvular tap/flap. The interesting fact about this word is that the variant was produced between a high front and back vowel. Coarticulation between a high front vowel and an alveolar tap makes the initial transition different compared to a transition going from a back vowel tap to a back vowel where F2, F3, F4, and F5 may converge after the tap, suggesting a more backward place of articulation. We believe that the [l] variant of the eldest Kuikuro speakers might be a remaining trace of the coronal to dorsal sound change process that occurred in the history of Kuikuro and Carib languages. If true, then the story of the uvular tap in this language sheds light on a well-known sound change in rhotic consonants by providing clues to explain the source of the change.

21.3.2 *Retroflex consonants*

Retroflex consonants are found in many languages. Their variability in the world's languages makes them difficult to compare. Ladefoged and Maddieson (1996) note that the term retroflex has been used for a variety of different articulations. These consonants are usually described as articulations in which the tip of the tongue is curled up, but the place of articulation and the tongue shape vary greatly from one language to the other. Languages like Tamil and Telugu are called sub-apical retroflex, while Hindi is an apical retroflex language (Ladefoged and Baskararao 1983). The description of retroflex using dynamic techniques, such as ultrasound, is adding more data regarding retroflex articulation and its variation.

As noted, the place of retroflex articulation varies significantly from one language to another, ranging from alveolar, post-alveolar, retroflex, and palatal. There are also different manners of retroflex articulation, including stop, nasal, tap, fricative, and approximant. This great variability does not mean, however, that similarities in retroflex articulation cannot be found between very different languages. For example, fieldwork data reveal that there is a remarkable similarity between retroflex fricatives of Namtrik, an Indian language spoken in Colombia, and the Beijing dialect of Mandarin (Ladefoged and Wu 1984). In these two languages, the articulation is not made with the tip of tongue being curled up, like in Dravidian languages. Instead, the sound is produced with an elevated upper surface of the tongue blade, making it more laminal than canonical retroflex. Also, the place of articulation is post-alveolar rather than alveolar.

Other comparisons between languages like Anong (Thurgood 2009), Komi-Permyak (Kochetov and Lobanova 2007), Mandarin, and Polish (Nowak 2006) suggest that the spectral shapes of retroflex fricatives in these languages pattern well with Namtrik. All show a significant lowering of F3. But the variety suggests that this acoustic feature, which characterizes retroflexion, might be due to different articulatory strategies. In spite of the similarity in retroflex articulation between divergent languages, the cross-linguistic variability suggests that retroflex is a rather vague term with respect to place of articulation. The variability also suggest that the class of sounds might be better understood to reflect a mode of articulation.

21.4 Challenging models and theories

Well-established theories like the acoustic theory of speech production (Fant 1960) provide powerful frameworks to study the variety of speech sounds found in the world's languages, as do aerodynamic laws like the Boyle-Marriott law or Pascal's principle. Sometimes data from the field support these well-established principles, and sometimes they challenge them. This is illustrated in the following sections with reference to (a) nasalized fricatives, which appear to challenge aerodynamic principles, (b) the absence of a rounding feature, which may be understood with reference to genetically linked differences in orofacial musculature, and (c) the shape of vowel systems that lack high back vowels but nonetheless conform to the theory of adaptive dispersion (Lindblom 1986).

21.4.1 Nasal features and nasalized fricatives

Observations made in Guarani and several other South American languages (Storto and Demolin 2012) show nasal harmony phenomena and the occurrence of nasalized fricatives. In Guarani, nasal harmony produces cross-segmental spans of nasalization. Nasal spreading in the word is initiated in two different ways (1) bidirectionally from a nasal vowel in a stressed syllable (phonemic nasal vowels only appear in stressed syllables in Guarani) and (2) from a nasal consonant to a stressed syllable. Spreading is blocked by a stressed syllable containing an oral vowel (Gregores and Suarez 1967). Nasal spans are produced with a lowered velum and are usually described as having a [+ nasal] phonological feature extending across a number of segments. However, aerodynamic data from Guarani show that nasal airflow is quite variable in nasal spans, suggesting either that the velum opening varies or that some other phenomenon is at play in nasal harmony phenomena.

There are three different patterns of nasal airflow in Guarani defined by the amount of nasal airflow: weak and strong for nasal vowels, and intermediate for nasal consonants. Does this correspond with three velum apertures? If so how can this be proved? The data are equivocal with respect to the first question. Yes, there are three velum positions in Guarani – fully closed for voiceless stops, "loosely" closed for nasal vowels and fricatives, and open for nasal consonants – but these positions do not explain the difference between weak and strong nasal vowels. Instead, the three different patterns of nasal airflow can be explained in the following way.

In Guarani, "weak nasal vowels" and nasalized fricatives are made with a small or "loose" velum opening (i.e., with some air leakage). The weak nasal vowel appears in the context of sonorants. The "strong nasal vowel" occurs when a nasal vowel precedes a voiceless stop or fricative. In these cases, there is a strong peak of nasal airflow at the end of the vowel due to the sequencing of velum closure made after the oral closure for the stops and after the glottal opening gesture for the voiceless fricatives. This sequence of oral closure and "late" velum closure gesture triggers a strong peak of nasalization at the end of the vowel since all the airflow goes through the nose at this time. Strong nasal vowels also appear before the alveolar tap. In nasalized stretches within words, the velum is lowered for the production of nasal consonants. Vowels in the vicinity show nasal airflow somewhere between the weak and strong pattern.

The pattern of weak and strong nasalized vowels, nasalized fricatives, and oral stops and fricatives suggests that phonetic implementation is governed by certain constraints which limit the range of possible realizations; within this range, the speaker regularly controls aspects of articulation to maximize the perceptibility of particular features (Kingston and Diehl 1994). Guarani shows that a complex relation between the sequencing of velic gestures and their acoustic output explains nasal harmony found in this, and possibly other, South American languages.

Guarani data are also interesting because they challenge claims made by Ohala and Ohala (1983) about difficulties in the realization of nasalized fricatives. Ohala and Ohala proposed that: "The velic closure must be closed (i.e., the soft palate must be elevated) for an obstruent articulated further forward than the point where the velic valve joins nasal cavity and the oral cavity." They argue that voiced nasalized fricatives, such as those mentioned by Schadeberg (1982), may be frictionless continuants (i.e., [v] → [ṽ]), and are skeptical about the existence of voiceless nasalized fricatives, such as those described in Guarani and the Appelcross dialect of Scots Gaelic (Tenes 1973), suggesting that these must be determined instrumentally. Shosted (2006b) predicted that if nasalized, voiceless fricatives should have a flattened spectrum compared to their oral counterpart, [s] → [θ], [x] → [ɦ], [ɣ] → [ɦ]. Although Ohala and Ohala insights for voiced nasalized fricatives are borne out in Guarani, since they turn frictionless approximants, the data from Guarani challenge their skepticism and the prediction from Shosted's model. Even when there is a clear nasal airflow during the realizations of voiceless nasalized fricatives, the acoustic output is like an oral fricative.

Bell-Berti (1993) showed that the production of perceptually appropriate nasal/oral segment distinctions requires that a speaker manipulates the size of the velopharyngeal port, either to prevent or to enhance the acoustic aerodynamic coupling of the oropharyngeal tract. This also means that for oral segments, the area of the port must only be sufficiently small so that the nasal cavities will not be acoustically coupled to the oral cavity. The nasal airflow must also be sufficiently small so that no audible turbulence occurs in the nasal cavities. Note that the velopharyngeal port does not need to be completely closed for successful oral articulations to occur. So long as the area of the velopharyngeal port is no greater that about 20mm^2, a perceptually oral segment may be produced (Bell-Berti 1993). This is shown in Figure 21.1 for the Guarani word

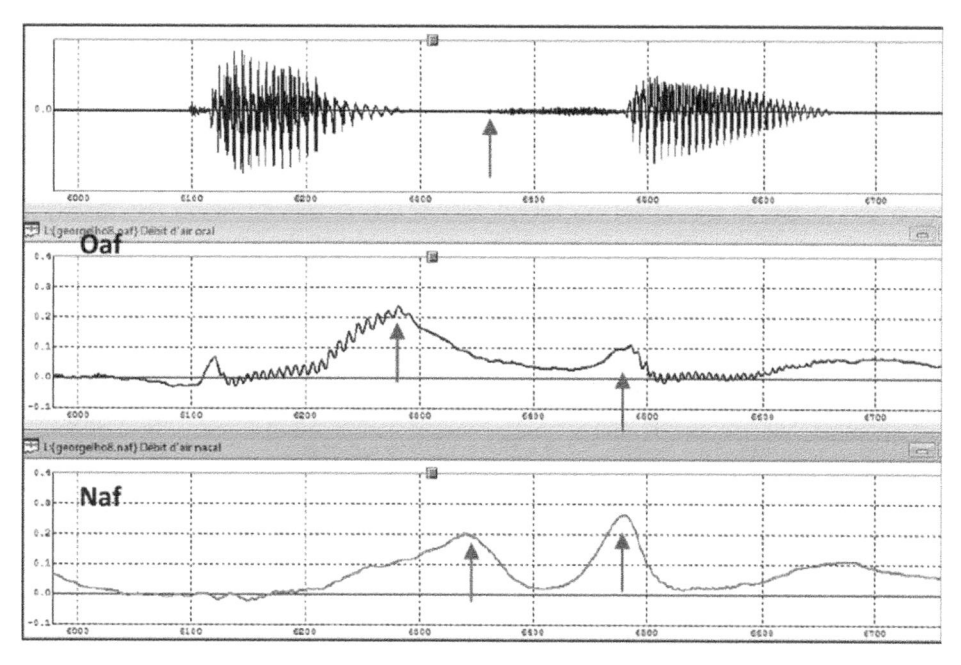

Figure 21.1 Audio wave form, oral airflow (Oaf) and nasal airflow (Naf) in dm^3/s for the word [kãsõ] "trouser" in Guarani. Arrows indicate the beginning of the frication noise on the audio waveform; the initial peak of Oaf at the beginning of the fricative and the release of the alveolar constriction; the initial peak of Naf after which the velum closes and the second peak at the end of the fricative.

"trouser" where there is nasal airflow (Naf) during the whole constriction of [s]. After the first nasal vowel [ã] there is a peak of oral airflow (Oaf) accounting for the glottal opening at the beginning of the fricative. At the same time Naf continues to increase, indicating that there is air going through the velum. This prevents frication noise to start. Only when Naf diminishes, does frication start, and Naf then remains weak when there is frication noise. The two final peaks of Oaf and Naf show that when the constriction is released Oaf increases with Naf since the velum is not completely closed.

21.4.2 Lip rounding

Variations and regularities found in the sound systems of human languages might be due at least in part to the intrinsic properties of the orofacial motor system. Variability across humans could have initiated differences in articulatory gestures across languages. Properties shared by all human orofacial motor systems could have been the basis for articulatory and motor trends observed in various languages.

Lip gestures are good candidates for the investigation of potential links between anatomical variability in human orofacial muscular and variability of the sound systems across languages. A number of anatomical studies have demonstrated significant differences in facial muscles that could be at the origin of differences in speech specific lip gestures, such as lip protrusion and lip rounding. Brosnahan (1961) and Catford (1977), discussing aspects of anthropophonetic variations, and quoting studies of Huber (1931), mention that the risorius muscle is found in about 20% of Australians and Melanesians, 60% of Africans, 75–80% of Europeans, and over 80% of Chinese and Malays. More recently, Pessa et al. (1998) showed that as many as 22 of their 50 subjects lacked this muscle. Even if based on rather small samples of data, these studies suggest that this genetically linked anatomical feature manifests as an orderly and constant increase over successive sections of populations of the African-European-Asian land mass. Pessa et al. (1998) also found that the zygomaticus major presented a bifid structure with two insertions points in 17 of their 50 subjects. The presence of these two insertion points could be responsible for the dimple in the cheeks that can be seen in a number of humans when smiling (Schmidt and Cohn 2001). These observations confirm that significant interspeaker differences exist in facial muscles that are likely to determine variations in face shaping and orofacial gestures in mimics and speech production. In so far as these differences are genetically linked and define group level characteristics, they could contribute to differences in sound production.

Fieldwork data on possible links between anatomical variability across humans and variations in articulatory and acoustical characteristics of human languages has been gradually accumulating. Ladefoged (1984) showed that differences between the vowel systems of Yoruba and Italian could have a biological (i.e., anatomical) basis. Ladefoged noted the existence of small differences in formant values between Yoruba and Italian, which have otherwise very similar seven-vowel systems.

He noted that these differences are consistent with anatomical differences generally observed between Africans and Europeans.

> Some of the differences between the two languages are due to the shapes of the lips of Italian as opposed to Yoruba speakers. ... with the exception of /i/ and to a lesser extent /e/, the second formant is lower for the Italian vowels than for the Yoruba vowels. These differences are precisely those that one would expect if Yoruba speakers, on the whole, used a larger mouth opening than that used by the Italian. ... The possibility of overall differences in mouth opening is certainly compatible with the apparent facial differences between speakers of Yoruba and Italian.
>
> (1984: 85–86)

More recently Storto and Demolin (in press) found that in Karitiana, a Tupi language spoken in Brazil, none of their five subjects showed lip rounding and protrusion while producing the vowel [o]. Additional contact EMG measurements showed no activity when electrodes were put at the rim of the lips when speakers were producing the vowel [o]. In spite of this, the first and second formant values for this vowel were 459 Hz and 1056 Hz (N = 250), respectively, which corresponds to F1/F2 values for mid-back or mid-high back rounded vowels in the acoustic space. A perceptual test with Portuguese and French speakers showed that these listeners had no difficulty identifying the Karitiana [o] as corresponding to the mid-high back rounded vowel [o] in their languages. Note that contact EMG measures taken on Portuguese and French speakers showed clear electric activity for the production of [o].

Assuming that the absence of lip rounding in Karitiana and its presence in Portuguese and French is due to group differences in underlying orofacial musculature, the data suggest that small anatomical differences can influence the shape of sound patterns found in the world's languages. It would be interesting to simulate [o] production based on the assumption of anatomical differences in speakers to further investigate the link between this factor and sound systems (Staveness et al. 2013). It must also be acknowledged, though, that sociocultural and historical factors are likely the prime factors that contribute to how sounds are produced and categorized in a language and to the transmission of these sounds across many generations.

21.4.3 Vowel systems without high back vowels

Karitiana has a vowel system with five vowel qualities (see Storto 1999 and Storto and Demolin in press for more details). The absence of the high back vowel is a typological rarity, but it is not unique in the world's languages. Crothers (1978) reports five languages where such systems can be found. Maddieson (1984) and Lindblom (1986) have also noted that a system /i, a, o, ɛ, ɨ/, although rare, exists in the world's languages. The latter system is comparable to what is found in Karitiana.

Lindblom (1986) proposed a theory of adaptive dispersion to account for preferred vowel systems in the world's languages. To test the theory, he developed a numerical model based on maximal and sufficient contrasts and derived different optimal vowel systems. The derived optimal systems were then compared to the typologically most common vowel systems described in Crothers (1978) and Vallée (1994). There was good agreement between the model results and one common five-vowel system, [i, ɛ, a, ɔ, u] (C_1 in Lindblom's tables), when simulations were based on loudness density (L-prediction) and auditory filter (F-prediction) functions. However, Crothers also describes a second, less common system, [i, ɛ, a, ɨ, o] (C_2 in Lindblom's tables), which is the one observed for Karitiana and other Tupi languages. Following Lindblom's proposition, we accept that even if the C_2 system is not as frequent as the C_1 system, it is nonetheless optimal in models where the criterion of sufficient contrast is introduced.

McDonough, Ladefoged, and George (1993) have discussed acoustic data from Navajo vowels, showing that its four-quality vowel system (where length and nasality are distinctive) also lacks /u/. In Navajo, however, there is a slightly higher realization of short /o/ when compared to short /e/ (and virtually no difference in the height of the mid-long vowels). In Karitiana, one sees no rising of the vowel /o/ above the level of the mid-front vowel /e/, as might have been expected by a theory that predicts compensatory effects to fill in "gaps" in the system. Another point of comparison that could be made between Karitiana and Navajo is that in both one finds greater differences (less overlap) between the mid-back vowels than between the front vowels. In Karitiana, however, these greater differences are also observed for high central vowels. McDonough et al. (1993) and McDonough and Austin-Garrison (1994) argue that this increase in variance in back vowels cannot be seen as a compensatory effect. They consider that, in a parallel with Japanese, the Navajo system is skewed, with front vowels showing overlap and back vowels showing no overlap. In Karitiana, we also have a skewed system, with central and back vowels showing little overlap.

In sum, the rarity of systems without /u/ does not constitute a counterexample to the theory of adaptive dispersion. The principle of sufficient contrast, which defines the theory, requires enough distance between vowels in a system. Skewed systems like those found in Karitiana and Navajo perfectly meet this requirement. Therefore, if one talks about "compensation effects" for the lack of a vowel in a system, one must define what is compensating for what. We saw, on the one hand, that there is a wider variation in the quality of back vowels in languages like Navajo, which has a skewed system without /u/. Navajo also has a slightly higher realization of short /o/ when compared to short /e/. Karitiana, on the other hand, is a skewed system, but there is less variation in the back vowels and rising of the mid-back vowels. Instead, it has a wider distribution for /o/ in the F2 axis and for high central /ɨ/ in the F1 (long vowels) or F2 (short vowels) axis. This shows that greater differences between vowels do not follow directly from the absence of the back vowel /u/. In Karitiana the space for /u/ is simply empty. That is, a skewed system like Karitiana is stable, there is no evidence that the shape of the vowel system is compensating for the lack of the typologically frequent vowel /u/.

21.5 Variation in the production of sounds

21.5.1 Voice onset time

Voicing is found in virtually all languages, but it is used differently from one language to another. Particularly notable are differences in the degree or the duration of voicing that characterizes two or three different VOT categories in a language. Many languages, including French, Spanish, Dutch, Tamil, Wa'ikhana, or Portuguese, have voiced stop consonants that are produced with substantial pre-voicing. These contrast with voiceless stop consonants that are produced with a short lag between consonant release and the onset of voicing. Other languages, including English and Kotiria, have voiced consonants that are produced with a short-lag onset. Their voiceless counterparts are produced with a long-lag VOT (aspirated consonants). Hay (2005: 7) suggests that languages with two stops along the voicing continuum tend not to have a (voice) distinction that contrasts pre-voiced stops with aspirated long-lag voiceless stops. It seems rather that these languages choose VOT categories that are immediately adjacent on the continuum.

Data from fieldwork studies contribute to our understanding of variation in VOT categories. Kanincin, a dialect of the Bantu language Ruwund, shows a very interesting distinction between voiced and voiceless stops defined by the set of acoustic features that usually contribute to a distinction between the two stop categories; namely, the duration of closure and of preceding vowels, a negative VOT contrasting with a positive VOT, and the presence or absence of voicing. In this language, sounds that are identified by native speakers as voiceless show decreasing voicing toward the end of the closure. Contrasting voiced stops show a high intensity of voicing sometimes even with a slight increase in voicing toward the end of the closure, suggesting that these are implosives. Since it seems quite unlikely that a voice-voiceless distinction would be made based on voicing intensity, other features that contribute to the distinction were explored. Measurements of the duration between voiceless and voiced stops at the bilabial and alveolar places of articulation showed that closure duration was almost equivalent for the two stop categories. The slightly greater duration of voiced stops was not statistically different from the duration of voiceless stops. This leaves the possibility that the distinction is made using postive VOT in spite of the fact that voicing occurs during closure for stops perceived as voiceless or as voiced. The difference is that voicing ends before closure release in stops heard as voiceless, but continues in those heard as voiced. A single experiment where the positive VOT is removed from the voiceless stops shows that without this feature, what is heard in Kanincin as a voiceless stop is then heard as voiced consonants. This shows that listeners track the positive VOT to make the distinction between voiceless and voiced stops in this language even though both are produced with voicing during closure.

21.5.2 Laryngeal features

Numerous glottalization phenomena are observed in South American languages. Fieldwork investigations on this topic must move beyond the view that attributes a weakly defined "glottalization" or "laryngealization" feature to the voice source. New data provides empirical evidence that the constriction of the epilaryngeal tube constitutes an integral part of laryngeal articulations. The epilaryngeal source posited by new models of phonation is employed by phonology to create distinctions.

The data that contribute to a reappraisal of laryngeal features come from fieldwork research in Dâw, Pirahã, Kotiria, Wanano, Juruna, and from Brazil (Stenzel 2007; Stenzel and Demolin 2012). In these languages, sounds perceptually similar to glottal stops or other glottalic phenomena occur within and around the edges of vowels. From a descriptive point of view, the easiest case to identify and transcribe is the creaky voiced character of vowels that occur before or after glottal stops [V̰ʔ, ʔV̰]. More complicated are cases where two consecutive vowels are distinguished by the creaky character of the first or second [V̰V, VV̰], often at a syllabic boundary. The most complicated case is when two identical vowels (or sometimes two different vowels) are separated by a creaky transition or by a rapid falling/rising pattern in the source, realized between two consecutive pulses. Although these transitions have sometimes been described as glottal stops, they are fully voiced sounds phonetically, albeit with a lower intensity and sometimes creaky character than a vowel. Similarly complicated patterns have been described by Gerfen and Baker (2005) for Coatzospan Mixtec and by Ladefoged and Maddieson (1996) for Gimi, a Papua New Guinea language. Recent work by Moisik (2013) and Moisik and Esling (2011) suggests that these laryngealized transitions between vowels might be due to constriction of the epilaryngeal tube. This suggestion would account in a natural way for the creaky character of the transitions and/or for the variable dip in amplitude and F0 between two identical vowels.

Esling's (2005) Laryngeal Articulator Model (LAM) establishes that there are canonical relationships among three components of laryngeal constriction: larynx raising, lingual retraction, and intrinsic laryngeal muscle constriction. Based on LAM, Moisik and Esling (2011) suggest revising the set of laryngeal features to include a feature representing epilaryngeal constriction. This feature [± constricted epilarynx tube (± cet)], is not only precise, but has acoustic connotations due to the invocation of a tube concept. In addition to [± cet], Moisik and Esling retain the features [± spread glottis] and [± stiff] from Halle and Stevens's (1971) model. Spread glottis is used to represent glottal aperture, and stiffness to represent pitch and internal vocal fold tension for some articulations (as in glottal stops). The feature [± cet] has two possible interpretations depending on place of articulation: when linked with [Glottal], it indicates ventricular incursion, that is, constriction of the lower margin of the epilaryngeal tube; when dominated by [Epilaryngeal], it denotes aryepiglotto-epiglottal constriction. Finally, Moisik and Esling (2011) argue that while larynx height is not a distinctive feature, it is an important component for describing the laryngeal-pharyngeal state.

In Moisik and Esling's (2011) view, phonation is a parameter that can result in four states: no phonation, glottal-level phonation, epilaryngeal phonation, and a mix of glottal and epilaryngeal phonation. The new features they propose to account for these four states have consequences for the description of both glottal stops and creaky voice in languages like Kotiria and Wa'ikhana, as they describe these qualities as more than glottal-level activity whereas Gordon and Ladefoged (2001) only identify two states, no phonation and glottal-level phonation. In so far as the ventricular folds play a critical role in the production of glottal stop and creaky voice through ventricular incursion (Edmonson and Esling 2006), Mosik and Esling (2011) argue strongly for abandoning the traditional practice of using the feature [+ constricted glottis] to characterize them. The important point is that ventricular insertion is intermediary between simple glottal adduction and the hermetic sealing of the larynx that characterizes an aryepiglotto-epiglottal (pharyngeal) stop. These facts are reflected in the phonologies of Kotiria and Wa'ikhana where glottal stops alternate with creaky voice phonation.

A detailed understanding of laryngeal articulation is useful for understanding other aspects of the phonetics and phonologies in languages. Consider, for example, the phonetic aspects of aspiration in Kotiria and Wa'ikhana. In Kotiria, there is a clear contrast between initial voiceless stops with almost no VOT (never > than 4 ms in our data) and strongly aspirated stops, which have an average of 92.6 ms. Compared to Kotiria aspiration, Wa'ikhana initial voiceless stops have only moderate VOT that differs according to place of articulation. In both Kotiria and Wa'ikhana, all voiceless consonants are preaspirated in medial position in root morphemes. Thus, in C_2 position in a $(C_1)VC_2V$ sequence, there are predictably the variants [^{h}p, ^{h}t, ^{h}k, ^{h}s, ^{h}tʃ]. The preaspirated affricate in Kotiria corresponds to preaspirated velar /k/ in Wa'ikhana, reflecting a velar palatalization process. The phonetic characteristics of intervocalic, root internal, preaspirated voiceless stops in Kotiria and Wa'ikhana are different in total duration and in the duration of preaspiration with durations slightly greater in Kotiria than in Wa'ikhana. However, the average duration in both languages for intervocalic, root internal, preaspirated voiceless stops approximates known data for the duration of geminated consonants in other languages (Ladefoged and Maddieson 1996). The long duration of root internal preaspirated consonants in the languages suggests that a wider glottal opening at the start of the voiceless creates preaspiration. This suggestion is compatible with what is already known about differences in fricative noise for singleton and geminate voiceless fricatives. A wider glottal opening facilitates the generation of frication noise, but a voiceless geminated fricative requires relatively high intraoral pressure (Po) over a longer period of time to sustain frication, thus requiring an even wider glottal opening. A wider glottal opening gesture would lead naturally to more substantial aspiration at the beginning of stop consonant articulation.

A final phonological process in Kotiria is worth mentioning as it too is linked to the assumption of a wider glottal opening gesture for preaspirated voiceless stops. A number of roots in Kotiria have both post and preaspirated consonants (e.g., C^{h}V^{h}C). In such roots, the intervening vowel is partially or completely devoiced, likely because of the post- and preaspirated sequence. Postaspiration of the initial consonant is the result of a glottal opening gesture. Since the duration of the postaspiration is quite long (about 92.6 ms on average) and the duration of the vowel occurring before the (long) preaspirated consonant is quite short – as expected based on an analogy with voiceless geminated consonants – the conditions are set for the voicing in the vowel to be extinguished. The vowel itself is then perceived only by virtue of the higher resonances of the vocal tract. These data from South American languages corroborate similar processes described in recent studies of Scottish Gaelic (Gordeeva and Scobbie 2010; Nance and Stuart-Smith 2013).

21.5.3 Variation in rhotic consonants

Earlier it was noted that rhotic consonants are a class of sounds in the world's languages marked by particularly large variation in their articulation and resulting sound shapes. Dialectological studies made, for example, in Dutch (Van de Velde and Van Houdt 2001) and Brazilian Portuguese (Barbosa and Albano 2004) show a spectrum of sound that ranges from alveolar and uvular trills to fricatives, approximants, and taps. Thus these consonants are defined neither by a single place of articulation nor by a single manner of articulation. Most of the world's languages have one or two rhotics in their sound inventory, but others like Dutch and Brazilian Portuguese have many more. Data from as yet undescribed languages might uncover still new variation, but an investigation of variation in the articulation of these consonants within a single language (i.e., dialectological variation) may help to shed some light on the development of particular variants or on changes from one variant to another. Even if one important reason for sound change is in "errors" of perception (Ohala 1981), the source of the variability is to be found in the speech production mechanism. The question of interest here, then, is to understand whether or not there are any particular reasons for the variability of rhotics.

Lindblom and Lubker (1985), among others, have shown that speakers are less accurate in their articulation of vowel the further posterior the articulation. In languages that have a rhotic trill and/or a tap at an alveolar place of articulation, most variants would seem to be produced either in the posterior or the anterior portion of the vocal tract. When a language has uvular trills, it seems to manifest as one of several variants: voiceless trills or voiceless fricative or voiced fricatives. Some of these variants might be explained by coarticulation, similar to what has been shown for vowels. Some of these changes imply lenition, but not from a weakening of the gestures involved in the production of /r/, but rather from a change in the timing of the gestures involved. For example, Lawson, Stuart-Smith, and Scobbie (2008) showed that in the case of surface variability in their realization, articulatory data show /r/ gestures present but delayed relative to voicing. It is these kinds of detailed observations and data that will be necessary to eventually model the many different phenomena associated with rhotic consonants.

21.6 Conclusion

Fieldwork studies have significantly contributed to the understanding of speech production by detailing the variety of speech sounds that are possible in the world's languages. The fact that portable tools for studying the details of speech production are now much more easily available than before means that we can expect an increasing number of studies to provide additional and more detailed data from many different speech production phenomena. In this chapter, a number of phenomena from various languages were discussed with reference to basic articulatory processes and the models and theories that have been used to understand such processes. But much more work is needed. For example, we need more experimental work on different known phonation types to better understand their primitives and patterns of variation that languages can exploit (Garellek and Keating 2011). The same is true for syllables and syllable complexity. A diversity of data is needed to better understand how these units and their complexity relate to the control of jaw movements (see, e.g., MacNeilage, this volume, Chapter 16). Similarly, the asymmetry between syllable onsets and offset in relation to opening and closure gestures needs to be better understood (Carissimo-Bertola, Vallée, and Chitoran 2014; Vallée, Rossato, and Rousset 2009) and data from many of the world's languages is critical to this understanding. New data from many different languages is also important for understanding secondary articulations, such as palatalization or velarization, which were not addressed in the present chapter. In brief, additional instrumental data from understudied languages, gathered in the field or in the laboratory, is still needed to fully understand what the human speech production mechanism is capable of, and what fundamentals underlie the phonological systems of the world's languages and their change through time.

NOTES

1 This chapter owes much to exchanges and discussions with: Ibrahima Cissé, Cyrille Ngulinzira, Solange Ngulinzira, Moges Yigezu, Sergio Hassid, Tulio Rojas Curieux, Esteban Diaz, Geny Gonzales, Michel Contini, Bruna Franchetto, Carlos Fausto, Kunué Kalapalo, Mutua Kuikuro, Xiu Ming, Leonardo Lancia, Dami Bas, Waldemar Ferreira, Ian Staveness, Yohan Payan, Pascal Perrier, Mohammad Nazari, Bernard Teston, Luciana Storto, Luiz Karitiana, Inacio Karitiana, Kristine Stenzel, William Kamsa, Christfred Naumann, Scott Moisik, Clothilde Chabiron, Christophe Savariaux, John Kingston, Eleonora Albano, Nathalie Vallée, Hans Van de Velde, and Melissa Redford.
2 Aerodynamic recordings presented in this chapter were made using the Physiologia workstation (Teston and Galindo 1990) for sections 21.2.1 and 21.2.3 or with the portable EVA2 for sections 21.2.1 and 21.4.1 (the two systems, though of differing ages, are essentially the same). The systems were linked to a data collection system equipped with different transducers. Oral airflow measurements were taken with a small flexible silicon mask placed against the mouth; nasal airflow by two plastic tubes connected to each nostril by a small silicon olive. Intraoral pressure was recorded with a small flexible

plastic tube (ID 2 mm) inserted through the nasal cavity into the oro-pharynx. Acoustic recordings were made via a High Fidelity microphone set on the hardware equipment connecting the transducers to the computer. Subglottal pressure (Ps) was measured (timing of articulatory gestures in section 21.2.3) with a needle (ID 2 mm) inserted in the trachea. The needle was placed after local anesthesia with 2% Xylocaine, including the subglottal mucosa. The tip of the needle was inserted, right under the cricoid cartilage. EGG recordings were made using the Glottal enterprise system.

REFERENCES

Al Solami, M. 2013. Arabic emphatics and gutturals. In *Ultrafest VI Programme and Abstracts, 44*. Edinburgh: Queen Margaret University.

Baken, Ronald J. and Robert F. Orlikoff. 2000. *Clinical Measurements of Speech and Voice*. San Diego, CA: Singular Publishing Group.

Barbosa, Plínio A. and Eleonora C. Albano. 2004. Brazilian Portuguese. *Journal of the International Phonetic Association* 34(2): 227–232.

Bell-Berti, Fredericka. 1993. Understanding velic motor control: Studies of segmental context. In M.K. Huffman and R.A. Krakow (eds.), *Phonetics and Phonology*, vol. 5: *Nasals, Nasalization, and the Velum*, 63–85. San Diego, CA: Academic Press.

Bird, Sonya, Scott Moisik, John Esling, and P. Jacobs. 2013. Laryngeal contributions to weak vs. strong ejectives. In *Ultrafest VI Programme and Abstracts*, 20–21. Edinburgh: Queen Margaret University.

Boly, Aliou. 1984. Description du Fulfulde parlé dans le Liptako (Haute-Volta). Doctoral dissertation, Université Stendhal-Grenoble III.

Brosnahan, Leonard F. 1961. *The Sounds of Language: An Inquiry into the Role of Genetic Factors in the Development of Sound Systems*. Cambridge : W. Heffer and Sons.

Carissimo-Bertola, Manon, Nathalie Vallée, and Ioana Chitoran. 2014. Labial-Coronal vs. Labial-Vélaire: Étude du phasage des gestes en français. In *XXXièmes Journées d'études sur la parole (JEP2014), Le Mans*.

Catford, John C. 1977. *Fundamental Problems in Phonetics*. Edinburgh: Edinburgh University Press.

Cissé, Ibrahima, Didier Demolin, and Nathalie Vallée. 2011. The acquisition of plosives and implosives by a Fulfulde-speaking child aged from 5 to 10;29 months. In *Proceedings of the 17th International Congress of Phonetic Sciences, Hong Kong*, 500–503.

Contini, Michel. 1987. *Etude de géographie phonétique et de phonétique instrumentale du sarde*. Torino: Edizioni dell'Orso.

Crothers, John. 1978. Typology and universals of vowel systems. In J. Greenberg (ed.), *Universals of Human Language*, vol. 2, 93–152. Stanford, CA: Stanford University Press.

Demolin, Didier. 1995. The phonetics and phonology of glottalized consonants in Lendu. *Papers in Laboratory Phonology* 4: 368–385.

Demolin, Didier. 2002. The search for primitives in phonology and the explanation of sound patterns: The contribution of fieldwork studies. *Papers in Laboratory Phonology* 7: 355–434.

Demolin, Didier. 2011. Aerodynamic constraints on the shape and dynamics of phonological systems. In *Proceedings of the 17th International Congress of Phonetic Sciences, Hong Kong*.

Demolin, Didier and Luciana Storto. (in press). Temporal coordination of glottalic gestures in Karitiana. In

M. Coller (ed.), *Laryngeal Features in Amazonian Languages*. Leiden: Brill.

Demolin, Didier, Bruna Franchetto, and Carlos Fausto. (in press). Uvular taps in Kuikuro. *Journal of the International Phonetic Association*.

Demolin, Didier, Hubert Ngonga, and Alain Soquet. 2002. Phonetic characteristics of an exploded palatal implosive in Hendo. *Journal of the International Phonetic Association* 32(1): 1–17.

Doke, Clement M. 1931. *A Comparative Study in Shona Phonetics*. Johannesburg: University of Witwatersrand Press.

Edmonson, Jerold A. and John H. Esling. 2006. The valves of the throat and their functioning in tone, vocal register, and stress: Laryngoscopic case studies. *Phonology* 23: 157–191.

Edmonson, Jerold A., Yueh-chin Chang, Feng-fan Hsieh, and Hui-chuan Huang. 2011. Laryngoscopic fieldwork: A guide. In *Proceedings of the 17th International Congress of Phonetic Sciences, Hong Kong*, 88–91.

Engstrand, Olle, Johan Frid, and Björn Lindblom. 2007. A perceptual bridge between coronal and dorsal /r/. In M.-J. Sole, P.S. Beddor, and M. Ohala (eds.), *Experimental Approaches to Phonology*, 54–71. Oxford: Oxford University Press.

Esling, John H. 2005. There are no back vowels: The laryngeal articulator model. *Canadian Journal of Linguistics* 50: 13–44.

Esling, John H. and Jimmy G. Harris. 2005. States of the glottis: An articulatory phonetic model based on laryngoscopic observations. In William J. Hardcastle and Janet M. Beck (eds.), *A Figure of Speech: A Festschrift for John Laver*, 347–383. Mahwah, NJ: Lawrence Erlbaum.

Esling, John H. and Scott R. Moisik. 2012. Laryngal aperture in relation to larynx height change: An analysis using simultaneous laryngoscopy and laryngeal ultrasound. In Dafydd Gibbon, Daniel Hirst, and Nick Campbell (eds.), *Rhythm, Melody and Harmony in Speech: Studies in Honor of Wiktor Jassem*, 117–128. Poznan: Polskie Towarzystwo Fonetyczne.

Faye, Waly C. 1979. Étude morphosyntaxique du Sereer Singandum (région de Jaxaaw-Naaxar). Doctoral sissertation, Université de Grenoble.

Fant, Gunnar. 1960. *Acoustic Theory of Speech Production*. The Hague: Mouton.

Franchetto, Bruna. 2001. Linguas e historia no Alto Xingu. In B. Franchetto and M. Heckenberger (eds.), *Os povos do Alto Xingu*, 111–156. Rio de Janeiro: Editora da UFRJ.

Franchetto, Bruna. 2005. Processos fonologicos em Kuikuro: uma visao autosegmental. In Leo Wetzels (eds.), *Estudos fonológicos das línguas indígenas brasileiras*, 53–84. Rio de Janeiro: Editora UFRJ.

Garellek, Marc and Patricia Keating. 2011. The acoustic consequences of phonation and tone in Jalapa Mazatec. *Journal of the International Phonetic Association* 41(2): 185–206.

Gerfen, Chip and Kirk Baker. 2005. The production and perception of laryngealized vowels in Coatzospan Mixtec. *Journal of Phonetics* 33: 311–334.

Gordeeva, Olga B. and James M. Scobbie. 2010. Pre-aspiration as a word-final voice in Scottish English fricatives. In Susanne Fuchs, Martine Toda, and Marzena Zygis (eds.), *Turbulent Sounds: An Interdisciplinary Guide*, 167–208. Berlin: Walter de Gruyter.

Gordon, Matthew and Peter Ladefoged. 2001. Phonation types: A cross-linguistic overview. *Journal of Phonetics* 29: 383–406.

Gregores, Emma and Jorge A. Suarez. 1967. *A Description of Colloquial Guarani*. The Hague: Mouton.

Halle, Morris and Kenneth N. Stevens. 1971. A note on laryngeal features. *MIT Quarterly Progress Report* 101: 198–212.

Hay, Jessica S.F. 2005. How auditory discontinuities and linguistic experience affect the perception of speech and non-speech in English- and Spanish-speaking listeners. PhD dissertation, University of Texas at Austin.

Hayward, Katrina. 2001. *Experimental Phonetics*. London: Longman.

HIPA. 1999. *Handbook of the International Phonetic Association*. Cambridge: Cambridge University Press.

Huber, Ernst. 1931. *Evolution of Facial Musculature and Facial Expression*. Baltimore, MD: Johns Hopkins Press.

Hudu, Fusheini, Amanda Miller, and Douglas Pulleyblank. 2009. Ultrasound imaging and theories of tongue root phenomena in African languages. In P.K. Austin, O. Bond, M. Charette, D. Nathan, and P. Sells (eds.), *Proceedings of Conference on Language Documentation and Linguistics Theory 2*, 153–163. London: SOAS.

IPA. 2006. The international phonetic alphabet revised to 2005. *Journal of the International Phonetic Association* 36(1): 135.

Janson, Tore and Olle Engstrand. 2001. Some unusual sounds in Changana. *Lund University Department of Linguistics Working Papers* 49: 74–77.

Kingston, John and Randy Diehl. 1994. Phonetic knowledge. *Language* 40: 419–454.

Kochetov, Alexei and Alevtina Lobanova. 2007. Komi-Permyak coronal obstruents: Acoustic contrats and positional variation. *Journal of the International Phonetic Association* 37(1): 51–82.

Ladefoged, Peter. 1968. *A Phonetic Study of West African Languages*. Cambridge: Cambridge University Press.

Ladefoged, Peter. 1984. "Out of chaos comes order": Physical, biological, and structural patterns in phonetics. In *Proceedings of the Tenth International Congress of Phonetic Sciences*, 83–95.

Ladefoged, Peter. 2003. *Phonetic Data Analysis*. Oxford: Blackwell.

Ladefoged, Peter and P. Baskararao. 1983. Non-quantal aspects of consonant production: A study of retroflex sounds. *Journal of Phonetics* 11: 291–302.

Ladefoged, Peter and Ian Maddieson. 1996. *The Sounds of the World's Languages*. Oxford: Blackwell.

Ladefoged, Peter and Zongji Wu. 1984. Places of articulation: An investigation of Pekingese fricatives. *Journal of Phonetics* 12: 267–278.

Lapinskaya, Natalia. 2013. An exploratory ultrasound investigation of emphatic articulation in Cairene Arabic. *Ultrafest VI Programme and Abstracts*, 67–68. Edinburgh: Queen Margaret University.

Lawson, Eleanor, Jane Stuart-Smith, and James M. Scobbie. 2008. Articulatory insights into language variation and change: Preliminary findings from an ultrasound study of derothacisation. In *Selected Papers from NWAV 36: Special Issue of Pennsylvania Working Papers in Linguistics* 36: 102–110. Philadelphia, PA: The Penn Linguistics Club.

Lindblom, Björn. 1986. Phonetic universals in vowel systems. In J.J. Ohala and J.J. Jaeger (eds.), *Experimental Phonology*, 13–44. Orlando, FL: Academic Press.

Lindblom, Björn and James Lubker. 1985. The speech homunculus and a problem of phonetic linguistics. In V.A. Fromkin (ed.), *Phonetic Linguistics*, 169–192. Orlando, FL: Academic Press.

MacLaughlin, Fiona. 2005. Voiceless implosives in SeereerSiin. *Journal of the International Phonetic Association* 35(2): 201–214.

Maddieson, Ian. 1984. *Pattern of Sounds*. Cambridge: Cambridge University Press.

Marchal, Alain. 1987. Des clics en français? *Phonetica* 44: 30–37.

McDonough, Joyce and Martha Austin-Garrison. 1994. Vowel enhancement and dispersion in the vowel space of Western Navajo: A study of traditional Navajo speakers. *UCLA Working Papers in Phonetics* 87: 93–104.

McDonough, Joyce, Peter Ladefoged, and Helen George. 1993. Navajo vowels and phonetic universal tendencies. *UCLA Working Papers in Phonetics* 84: 143–150.

Meira, Sergio and Bruna Franchetto. 2005. The Southern Cariban languages and the Cariban family. *International Journal of American Linguistics* 71(2): 127–190.

Miller, Amanda L. 2013. Estimating lingual cavity volume in click consonant production from combined lingual ultrasound and palatographic data. In *Ultrafest VI Programme and Abstracts*, 35–37. Edinburgh: Queen Margaret University.

Moisik, Scott R. 2013. The epilarynx in speech. PhD dissertation, University of Victoria, BC.

Moisik, Scott R. and John Esling. 2011. The "whole larynx" approach to laryngeal features. In *Proceedings of the 17th International Congress of Phonetic Sciences, Hong Kong*, 1406–1409.

Nance, Claire and Jane Stuart-Smith. 2013. Pre-aspiration and post-aspiration in Scottish Gaelic stop consonants. *Journal of the International Phonetic Association* 43(2): 129–152.

Nowak, Pawel. 2006. The role of vowel transition and frication noise in the perception of Polish fricative sibilants. *Journal of Phonetics* 34(2): 139–152.

Ohala, John J. 1981. The listener as a source of sound change. In C.S. Masek, R.A. Hendrick, and M.F. Miller (eds.), *Papers from the Parasession on Language and Behavior*, 178–203. Chicago, IL: Chicago Linguistic Society.

Ohala, John J. 1995. A probable case of clicks influencing the sound patterns of some European languages. *Phonetica* 52: 160–170.

Ohala, John J. and Manjari Ohala. 1993. The phonetics of nasal phonology: Theorems and data. In M.K. Huffman and R.A. Krakow (eds.), *Nasals, Nasalization, and the Velum*, 225–249. San Diego, CA: Academic Press.

Pessa, Joel, Vikram Zadoo, Earl K. Adrian, Jr., Cheng Yuan, Jason Aydelotte, and Jaime Garza. 1998. Variability of the midfacial muscles: Analysis of 50 hemifacial cadaver dissections. *Plastic and Reconstructive Surgery* 102: 1888–1893.

Pinkerton, Sandra. 1986. Quichean (Mayan) glottalized and nonglottalized stops: A phonetic study with implications for phonological universals. In J.-J. Ohala and J.-J. Jaeger (eds.), *Experimental Phonology*, 125–139. Orlando, FL: Academic Press.

Port, Robert F. and Adam P. Leary. 2005. Against formal phonology. *Language* 81(4): 927–964.

Rojas Curieux, Tulio. 1998. *La lengua páez: una visión de su gramática*. Santafé de Bogota: Ministerio de Cultura.

Schadeberg, Thilo. 1982. Nasalization in Umbundu. *Journal of African Languages and Linguistics* 4: 109–132.

Schmidt, Karen L. and Jeffrey F. Cohn. 2001. Human facial expressions as adaptations: Evolutionary questions in facial expression research. *Yearbook of Physical Anthropology* 44: 3–24.

Shosted, Ryan K. 2006a. Just put your lips together and blow? Whistled fricatives in Southern Bantu. In H.C. Yehia, D. Demolin, and R. Laboissière (eds.), *Proceedings of ISSP 2006: 7th International Seminar on Speech Production*, 565–572.

Shosted, Ryan K. 2006b. The aeroacoustics of nasalized fricatives. PhD dissertation, University of California, Berkeley.

Stavness, Ian, Mohammad A. Nazari, Pascal Perrier, Didier Demolin, and Yohan Payan. 2013. Effects of oribicularis oris and jaw position on lip shape: A biomechanical modeling study of the effects of the orbicularis oris muscle and jaw posture on lip shape. *Journal of Speech, Language, and Hearing Research* 56(3): 878–890.

Stenzel, Kristine. 2007. Glottalization and other suprasegmental features in Wanano. *International Journal of American Linguistics* 73(3): 331–366.

Stenzel, Kristine and Didier Demolin. 2012. Traços laringais em Kotiria e Wa'ikhana (Tukano Oriental). In Gisela Collischonn and Leda Bisol (eds.), *Fonologia: Teoria e perspectivas – Anais do IV Seminario Internacional de Fonologia*. Porto Alegre: PURS.

Storto, Luciana. 1999. Aspects of Karitiana grammar. PhD dissertation, MIT.

Storto, Luciana and Didier Demolin. 2012. The phonetics and phonology of South American languages. In L. Campbell and V. Grondona (eds.), *The Indigenous Languages of South America: A Comprehensive Guide*, 331–390. Berlin/Boston: De Gruyter Mouton.

Storto, Luciana and Didier Demolin. (in press). Phonetics and phonology of Karitiana. *Mémoires de l'Académie Royale des Sciences d'outre mer de Belgique*.

Tabain, Marija. 2011. Electropalatography data from Central Arrente: A comparison of the new articulate palate with the standard Reading palate. *Journal of the International Phonetic Association* 43(3): 343–367.

Tenes, Elmar. 1973. *The Phonemic Analysis of Scottish Gaelic: Based on the Dialect of Applecross, Ross-Shire*. Hamburg: Helmut Buske.

Teston, Bernard and Benoit Galindo. 1990. Design and development of a workstation for speech production analysis. In *Proceedings of VERBA90: International Conference on Speech Technology, Rome*, 400–408.

Thurgood, Ela. 2009. Coronal contrast in Anong. *Journal of the International Phonetic Association* 39(1): 53–66.

Traill, Anthony. 1985. *Phonetic and Phonological Studies of !Xóõ Bushman*. Hamburg: Helmut Buske.

Vaissière, J. 2007. Area functions and articulatory modelling as a tool for investigating the articulatory, acoustic, and perceptual properties of sounds across languages. In M.-J. Sole, P. Beddor, and M. Ohala (eds.), *Experimental Approaches to Phonology*, 175–191. Oxford: Oxford University Press.

Vallée, Nathalie. 1994. Les systèmes vocaliques: de la typologie aux prédictions. Thèse de doctorat, Université Stendhal, Grenoble.

Vallée, Nathalie, Solange Rossato, and Isabelle Rousset. 2009. Favored syllabic patterns in the world's languages and sensori-motor constraints. In F. Pellegrino, E. Marsicoa, I. Chitoran, and C. Coupé (eds.), *Approaches to Phonological Complexity*, 111–140. Berlin: Mouton de Gruyter.

Van de Velde, Hans and Roeland Van Houdt. (eds.) 2001. *'r-atics: Sociolinguistic, Phonetic and Phonological Characteristics of /r/*. Bruxelles: ILVP.

von den Steinen, Karl. 1940. *Entre os Aborigenes do Brasil Central*, trans. Egon Schaden. São Paulo: Departamento de Cultura (collected articles from *Revista do Arquivo* 34–58).

Vuillermet, Marine and Didier Demolin. 2006. Voiceless implosives: A comparison between American and African languages. Paper presented to the International Rara and Rarissima Conference: Collecting and Interpreting Unusual Characteristics of Human Language, Leipzig, Germany.

22 Language Effects on Timing at the Segmental and Suprasegmental Levels

TAEHONG CHO

22.1 Introduction

A number of timing patterns recur in a myriad of languages. For example, low vowels are widely observed to be longer than high vowels (Lindblom 1968; Lehiste 1970; Lisker 1974; Keating 1985; Maddieson 1997, inter alia); vowels are longer before voiced than before voiceless consonants (Halle and Stevens 1967; Chen 1970; Lisker 1974; Maddieson and Gandour 1977; Maddieson 1997, inter alia); and voice onset time (VOT) is generally longer for velar stops, intermediate for coronal stops, and shortest for labial stops (Fischer-Jørgensen 1954; Peterson and Lehiste 1960; Maddieson 1997; Cho and Ladefoged 1999; Ladefoged and Cho 2001, inter alia). These universally observable timing patterns are often thought to have come about due to physiological and biomechanical constraints on production. An extreme version of this mechanistic view was crystallized in the Sound Patterns of English (SPE) tradition (Chomsky and Halle 1968) where the phonetic component was not considered as part of the grammar and was thus treated as something "physical" or "automatic" that can be studied outside the realm of linguistics. Convergent evidence accumulated over the past several decades suggests, however, that recurrent timing patterns are likely under a speaker's control (e.g., Keating 1985, 1990; Kingston and Diehl 1994; Maddieson 1997; Cho and Ladefoged 1999; Ladefoged and Cho 2001). Many non-contrastive and gradient (or scalar) aspects of speech, which were once considered to be beyond the speaker's control (i.e., as low-level biomechanical phenomena), are now understood as part of the grammar governed by the phonetic rules of a given language – the native speaker's "phonetic knowledge" (see Kingston and Diehl 1994).

Language-specific phonetic knowledge is something that a native speaker acquires in order to sound like other members of the ambient speech community. That is, while language sounds may be grouped "phonologically" together and labeled in the same way, say, as a "voiceless aspirate," the sounds are never

---

The Handbook of Speech Production, First Edition. Edited by Melissa A. Redford.
© 2015 John Wiley & Sons, Inc. Published 2019 by John Wiley & Sons, Inc.

pronounced in exactly the same way across languages (e.g., Cho and Ladefoged 1999). Rather, the same phonological label is physically realized in phonetic detail according to language-specific phonetic rules. This chapter is concerned with these cross-linguistic phonetic differences with special reference to variation in speech timing at both the segmental and suprasegmental levels. The structure of the chapter will be as follows. First, the notion of language-specific phonetic rules and phonetic arbitrariness will be briefly introduced, taking variation in VOT as an example (section 22.2). Second, cross-linguistically recurrent patterns of segmental speech timing will be discussed with reference to language-specific phonetic rules that are assumed to operate in the phonetic component of the grammar of individual language (section 22.3). Third, variation in speech timing at the suprasegmental level will be discussed with respect to cross-linguistic differences in two aspects of the phonetics-prosody interface (section 22.4). Finally, a brief conclusion will follow with some implications for language effects on speech timing (section 22.5).

22.2 Phonetic arbitrariness and language-specific phonetic rules

One source of evidence for language-specific phonetic rules comes from unexplained language variation in temporal values for the same phonemic categories. For example, Cho and Ladefoged (1999) investigated differences in voice onset time (VOT) values for voiceless stops across 18 languages, and found not only that languages differed in their choice of values for the voiceless unaspirated and aspirated stop categories, but also that the specific values were not accounted for by general phonetic principles such as ease of articulation and contrast maximization (e.g., Lindblom 1986, 1990). The cross-language data on voiceless velar stops shown in Figure 22.1 help to make this point.

Figure 22.1 shows that VOT values vary from around 28 ms to 80 ms in 11 languages that lack an aspiration contrast (gray bars). The wide VOT distribution not only makes it hard to determine where to draw a line between phonetically unaspirated and aspirated stops across languages, it is also at odds with the principle of maximal articulatory ease. The "low-cost" option for languages with no phonological contrast between unaspirated and aspirates stops would be to use a single, simplest articulatory gesture for the voiceless sound (Docherty 1992). This would predict similar VOT values for languages. But the values that have been actually observed appear to be arbitrary.

With respect to the principle of contrast maximization, the prediction is that languages with a contrast between unaspirated and aspirated stops should have polarized VOT values in order to maximize their perceptual distinctiveness (as discussed in Keating 1984). The white (unaspirated and aspirated) bars in Figure 22.1 show that some languages obey the principle of contrast maximization (e.g., Khonoma Angami), but others do not (e.g., Hupa) in that the difference

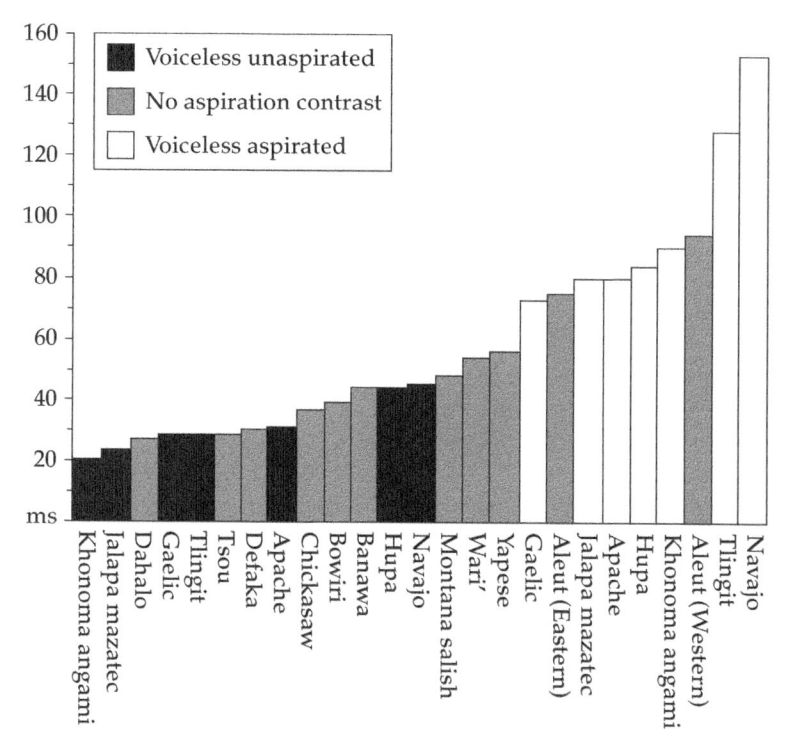

Figure 22.1 Mean VOTs (ms) for voiceless velar stops in 18 languages (adapted from Cho and Ladefoged 1999 and Ladefoged and Cho 2001).

between unaspirated and aspirated voiceless stops is not as large as it could be (i.e., Khonoma Angami).

To account for cross-language variation in VOT values, Cho and Ladefoged (1999) proposed Articulatory VOT as a phonological feature defined in terms of differences in intergestural timing (see Hoole and Pouplier, this volume, Chapter 7) between the initiation of the articulatory gesture responsible for the release of a closure and the initiation of the laryngeal gesture responsible for vocal fold vibration. In this way, Articulatory VOT was abstracted away from the traditional phonetic definition of VOT, which is directly measurable as an interval between the stop release to voicing onset along the acoustic dimension. Following Keating (1985, 1990) and Cohn (1993), Cho and Ladefoged (1999) assumed that phonology sets a modal VOT value associated with the phonemic category (e.g., voiceless unaspirated or aspirated stops), and a language-specific rule assigns target Articulatory VOT values. The assigned Articulatory VOT target values are phonetically realized by universal phonetic implementation rules which are generally subject to the physical laws. The implication is that the phonetic component in a model of language is divided into two domains: one governed by the grammar and the other by the physical laws.

22.3 Language effects on speech timing at the segmental level

22.3.1 Vowel duration differences before voiced versus voiceless obstruents

One of the most common recurrent temporal patterns across languages is variation in vowel duration as a function of voicing in the following obstruent consonant: vowels are longer before voiced than before voiceless obstruents (Peterson and Lehiste 1960; Halle and Stevens 1967; Chen 1970; Lisker 1974; Maddieson and Gandour 1977; Keating 1985; Maddieson 1997, inter alia). Under the assumption that this pattern is driven by universally applicable mechanical factors, Chen (1970) concluded that aerodynamic factors triggered different consonantal closing movement speeds at the V-to-C transition. His explanation was as follows: A voiceless stop is produced with an open glottis through which air flows relatively unimpeded. The airflow creates resistance to constriction formation. In order to overcome the resistance, more articulatory effort is required. The resulting forceful articulation induces faster articulatory movement and hence a more rapid target attainment of the consonantal closing gesture. (See below for further discussion on this and alternative explanations.)

Whereas the widespread postvocalic voicing effect on vowel duration may be due originally to physiological and biomechanic factors, it has long been observed that languages differ in the degree to which the effect is realized. In particular, the effect is substantially larger in English than in other languages (e.g., Chen 1970; Keating 1985; Maddieson 1997; de Jong 2004; Solé 2007). Fromkin (1977) argued that universal phonetic conventions might account for the effect of postvocalic voicing on vowel duration in most languages, but the exaggerated effect in English suggests a phonological rule. A study on English and Arabic by de Jong and Zawaydeh (2002) supports Fromkin's proposal. They found that the duration of accented vowels was longer in both English and Arabic than the duration of unaccented vowels, but the amount of accent-induced lengthening effect was significantly larger before a voiced than before a voiceless consonant in English but not in Arabic. In a similar vein, Solé (2007) showed that English differed from Catalan in terms of how vowel duration was modulated as a function of speaking rate. As the speaking rate decreased, vowels before voiced obstruents became much longer than vowels before voiceless obstruents in English, whereas the size of the consonant voicing effect on the preceding vowel in Catalan remained stable across speaking rates. Solé proposed that a vowel duration ratio be used as a metric for determining whether the lengthening effects are controlled versus mechanical. When controlled, the speaker aims to keep the vowel duration ratio (e.g., between different speaking rate conditions) constant such that longer vowels are lengthened more, and shorter vowels are lengthened less in absolute terms, independently of the "extrinsic" vowel duration differences. When the effect is mechanically driven, overall changes in absolute vowel durations should be similar regardless of the context in which it is occurring.

Just as English chooses to exaggerate the effect of postvocalic voicing on vowel duration, a language may also choose not to participate at all in this recurrent sound pattern. Keating (1985) discusses the examples of Polish and Czech, neither of which show systematic vowel duration changes as a function of voicing in the following consonant. Keating points out that the absence of an effect of postvocalic voicing on vowel duration in Polish appears arbitrary, but that the effect in Czech might be explained in terms of functional load. Czech employs a phonological vowel-length (quantity) contrast so vowel duration variation might be reserved just for the vowel quantity contrast, and thus the cross-linguistic pattern of longer vowels before voiced consonants and shorter vowels before voiceless ones is suppressed. Related to this point, it is interesting to note that although Arabic also employs a vowel quantity contrast, it still shows the consonant voicing effect on the preceding vowel duration (de Jong and Zawaydeh 2002). This could indicate that languages may differ in terms of whether vowel duration is exclusively used to convey phonological quantity (like Czech) or whether the quantity contrast gives way partially to the physiologically preferred pattern (like Arabic). Whether arbitrary or due to an interaction with other phonological contrast, the facts of Polish and Czech suggest that vowel duration be specified in the grammar in much the same way as the exaggeration of the effect in English should be.

Thus far, we have observed three types of languages according to the extent to which consonantal voicing influences preceding vowel duration:

Type 1: consonantal voicing is phonetically encoded by the preceding vowel duration (as in English);
Type 2: consonantal voicing is not phonetically manifested in the preceding vowel duration (as in Polish and Czech);
Type 3: consonantal voicing influences the preceding vowel duration in physiologically preferred ways (as in Catalan and Arabic).

Both Type 1 and Type 2 are the cases in which the degree of the consonantal voicing effect on the preceding vowel duration should be specified in the phonetic component of the grammar of the language, regardless of whether the effect is exaggerated or suppressed. What of Type 3 cases?

Although some might argue that Type 3 cases can be attributed to phonetic implementation rules that are automatically supplied by universal phonetic conventions (Chen 1970; Fromkin 1977), Keating (1985: 124) argues: "It appears that the role of the phonetics is to provide a pattern that might be preferred. Within any one language, however, vowel duration is controlled by the grammar, even though it is a low-level phonetic phenomenon." Loosely speaking, the rationale for this view is that if vowel duration is a controllable parameter, and the consonant voicing effect on vowel duration is indeed controlled by speakers in some languages (such as English, Polish, and Czech), it is also likely to be controlled by speakers of other languages as well, even if the pattern can be explained by physiological or mechanical facts. Similar arguments have been advanced by Maddieson (1997).

22.3.2 Height-related vowel duration

Another recurrent temporal pattern across languages is variation in vowel duration due to vowel height: low vowels (e.g., /æ/ and /ɑ/) are longer than high vowels (e.g., /i/ and /u/) (Lindblom 1968; Lehiste 1970; Lisker 1974; Keating 1985; Maddieson 1997, inter alia). This effect is often thought to be due to the mechanical constraints that are imposed on vowel articulation by jaw movement. The jaw, which is mechanically linked to the tongue, is required to move farther to go from a consonantal constriction to a lower vowel (and back again) than for a higher vowel. All other things being equal, greater displacements take more time than smaller displacements, so the lower jaw position for low vowels results in longer vowels compared to the higher jaw position for high vowels (Lindblom 1968). However, even such an apparently mechanically-driven timing pattern can be thought of as being modulated by a language-specific phonetic rule (Keating 1985; Maddieson 1997). For example, Maddieson (1997) points out that the magnitude of the vowel duration difference observed in Swedish vowels (reported in Lindblom 1968) was actually less than one might have expected from the differences in jaw height, which allows for the possibility that even so-called intrinsic timing effects may be controlled by the speaker. Westbury and Keating (1980) tested this possibility in an electromyographic (EMG) study. They examined the force input to the jaw-lowering muscle, the anterior belly of the digastric (ABD), for different vowels. They hypothesized that if the height-related vowel duration difference was due purely to differences in the rate at which the jaw attains its final position, the force input to the ABD will remain constant regardless of vowel height. Westbury and Keating found, however, that low vowels were produced with longer EMG durations and higher EMG amplitudes than high vowels, suggesting that the speaker deliberately modulated the force input to ABD as a function of vowel height. Regarding this finding, Keating (1985: 120) suggested that "if vowel duration is a controllable parameter, it is in principle available for language-specific manipulation." Again, language-specific manipulation of height-related vowel duration may well be carried out by language-specific phonetic rules before motor commands are issued.

If the duration differences observed for vowel height are due to language-specific rules rather than to mechanical factors, then we should in principle be able to find language effects on the vowel duration difference due to vowel height. For example, there may be a language that has a *shorter* low vowel and a *longer* high vowel rather than the other way around. Cho and Ladefoged (1999) commented that such a case might arise if a language lost a phonemic contrast based on duration, but kept just the long high vowels and short low vowels. Assuming that this pattern violates naturalness considerations, such a language could be more difficult to learn, but it would provide evidence that vowel duration is controllable by a language-specific phonetic rule. Additional evidence for language-specific rules could come from languages (or dialects) with similar vowel inventories that nonetheless show subtle but significantly varying degrees of "intrinsic" vowel duration differences. For example, two languages may have comparable magnitude of jaw lowering movement for vowels, but the actual height-related vowel duration difference may not be comparable. Just as a language (such as English) might use vowel duration as a cue to the voicing status of a following obstruent, so too could height-related variation in vowel duration be deliberately exaggerated by the speaker in a language to provide a cue to height contrast.

A recent study by Solé and Ohala (2010) was precisely aimed at testing the hypothesis that languages might use height-related vowel duration differentially (as a controllable parameter), and that this might provide a cue to the vowel height contrast. Using Solé's (2007) ratio metric (see 22.3.1), they compared the relative duration of high, mid, and low vowels in American English, Catalan, and Japanese at slow, normal, and fast rates of speech. The results showed that height-related vowel duration differences were not adjusted to speaking rate differences in Japanese, which was interpreted as indicating that this aspect of vowel duration in Japanese may be attributable to differences in jaw displacement. However, the results for American English and Catalan showed that vowel duration ratios across height remained more or less constant across rates. These results were interpreted to suggest that height-related vowel duration differences are deliberately manipulated (or controlled) by the speakers of these languages as a secondary feature to enhance the height contrast. Solé and Ohala (2010) also asked Catalan listeners to categorize an ambiguous sound as /e/ and /ɛ/ while varying the duration of the stimulus. The results showed that /e/ responses increased and received higher goodness rating scores as the duration of the ambiguous vowel became shorter, lending support to their argument that Catalan listeners exploit height-related vowel durations as cues to the vowel-height contrast. Based on these results, Solé and Ohala concluded that languages may differ in the use of the "intrinsic" vowel duration differences in that they may be controlled by the speaker. Again, even the mechanically explainable effect found in Japanese could still be controlled by the speaker, even if it is a preferred pattern derived from biomechanical constraints (cf. Keating 1985).

22.4 Language effects on speech timing at the suprasegmental level

In the previous section, it was discussed how cross-linguistically recurrent timing patterns at the segmental level, which may derive from physiological and biomechanical factors, differ from language to language or from variety to variety in fine phonetic detail. These kinds of cross-linguistic differences were taken to be due to language-specific phonetic rules that are assumed to operate in the grammatical component of individual languages. In the present section, the hypothesis is extended to the suprasegmental level under the rubric of the phonetics-prosody interface.

The reader may be familiar with the term phonetics-phonology interface, which refers to how abstract "phonological" structure (usually at the word level) informs, or is informed by, detailed phonetic patterns (e.g., Keating 1988, 1996; Hume and

Johnson 2001; Hayes, Kirchner, and Steriade 2004; Kingston 2007; Cohn 2007). Similarly, the phonetics-prosody interface refers to how abstract "prosodic structure" influences the phonetic implementation of sound categories, and how the fine-grained phonetic detail in turn informs higher-level prosodic structure (e.g., Beckman 1996; Keating et al. 2003; Cho 2006; Cho, McQueen, and Cox 2007; Byrd and Choi 2010; Krivokapić and Byrd 2012). To understand the phonetics-prosody interface, a brief introduction of prosodic structure is in order.

Prosodic structure can be defined as "a hierarchically organized structure of phonologically defined constituents and heads" (Beckman 1996: 19), reflecting both constituent-based and prominence-based prosodic hierarchies of an utterance (see Shattuck-Hufnagel and Turk 1996 for a review). The prosodic structure of an English utterance (i.e., *The monkey hid eight banana chips*) is depicted in Figure 22.2. As can be seen, the level of a prosodic constituency is higher at the top of the figure than at the bottom, with lower constituents combined to form immediately higher ones in a hierarchically nested way. Specifically, one or more syllables are grouped into a prosodic (or phonological) word (PWd); one or more prosodic words combine to form the Intermediate (Intonational) Phrase (ip); and finally one or more Intermediate Phrases are clustered to form the Full Intonational Phrase (IP), which is the highest prosodic unit assumed in the influential prosodic models, such as the one proposed by Beckman and Pierrehumbert (1986).

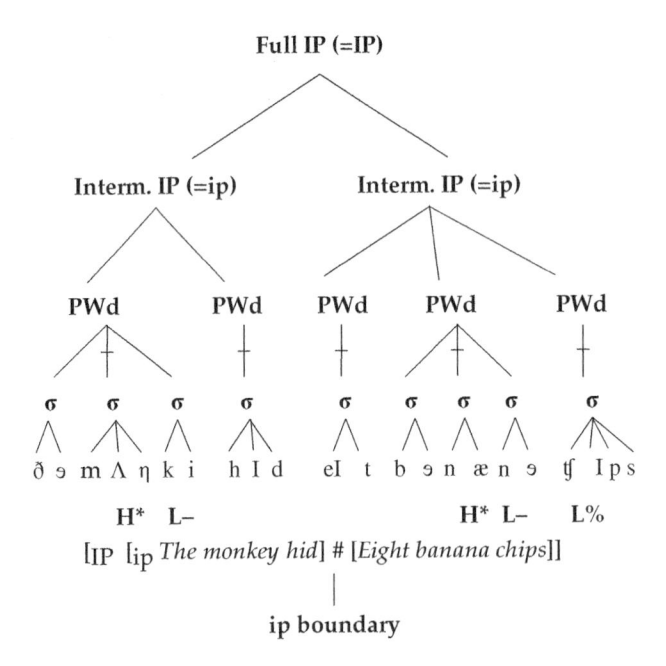

Figure 22.2 A prosodic structure of *The monkey hid eight banana chips*. Dashes in the association line between PWd and the syllable (σ) tier indicate stressed syllables as in Keating and Shattuck-Hufnagel (2002); H* refers to an H-tone pitch accent associated with stressed syllables.

The prosodic constituents shown in Figure 22.2 are also referred to as prosodic domains as they often serve as domains of certain intonational patterns as well as applications of phonological rules (cf. Selkirk 1984, 1995; Jun 1998). The prosodic structure in the figure also reflects some aspects in the relative prominence of prosodic constituents. A lexically stressed syllable is marked by a dash in the association line between PWd and the syllable (σ) tier (following Keating and Shattuck-Hufnagel 2002), indicating the greater prominence of these syllables compared to unstressed syllables. The pitch accented syllables (i.e., lexically stressed syllables receiving a phrase-level stress) are marked by H* (as in *monkey* and *banana*), indicating that these are more prominent than the rest in the phrase. Finally, the prosodic structure includes tonal markings of constituent boundaries such as phrase tones (e.g., L- or H-) and boundary tones (e.g., L% or H%), which, together with the pitch accents, describe the overall tune of the utterance.

Prosodic structure thus serves two functions relevant to speech production: boundary marking, i.e., the hierarchical grouping of prosodic constituents; and prominence marking, i.e., the relative prominence among prosodic constituents. In the following subsections, cross-linguistic timing patterns will continue to be discussed in the context of prosodic structure with special reference to how languages may differ in the temporal dimensions of boundary marking, and in the timing of tonal targets that signal structural prominence. We begin with the latter topic.

22.4.1 Timing of tonal targets with the segmental string

The phonetics-prosody interface is incorporated into theories of Intonation Phonology (Bruce 1977; Pierrehumbert 1980; Pierrehumbert and Beckman 1988; Ladd 1996), which were at the vanguard of bridging the categorical and gradient aspects of speech sounds. One of the most important contributions of Intonational Phonology was to understand gradient fundamental frequency (F0) events (i.e., the acoustic correlate of pitch) as resulting from organized phonological patterns. The F0 events were mapped onto categorical phonological representations referred to as tones (or tonal targets). The whole gradient F0 pattern across a segmental string could then be understood as the phonetic interpolation between tonal targets (Pierrehumbert 1980). It should be evident from this description that Intonation Phonology makes an assumption first formalized in Autosegmental Phonology (Goldsmith 1976, 1990), namely, that phonological processes can be confined to separate tiers in a representation. In Intonation Phonology the tonal components are realized in a tier that is independent of the segmental tier, which is an important assumption of the Autosegmental Metrical theory of intonation (AM theory) (Bruce 1977; Pierrehumbert 1980; Pierrehumbert and Beckman 1988; Ladd 1996). An important theoretical question for speech production is thus how the underlying tones constituting the intonational structure of an utterance in one tier are "associated" with the segmental string in another tier. For example, in Figure 22.2, the starred H tone (H*) is associated with the stressed syllables [mʌŋ] in *monkey* and [næ] in *banana*. The primary association specifies the mapping of an accent to a syllable, but it does not specify the actual tone-segment mapping, or, which specific segment the tone is linked to. Given that the component tone in Figure 22.2 is monotonal (H), and given that the tonal target is generally realized during the vowel of the syllable (as the vowel often serves as a tone bearing unit), specifying the association between a tone and a syllable may seem redundant. However, when an accent is bitonal (e.g., L+H), the association becomes crucial. In English, for example, the bitonal sequence of L and H is often distinguished between L+H* and L*+H (e.g., Beckman and Pierrehumbert 1986), with the assumption that the starred tone is associated with the nucleus of the accented syllable, so that the F0 peak of L+H* is realized during the vowel, while the F0 peak of L*+H may be delayed, possibly realized during the following consonant or the onset of the following vowel. This captures the autosegmental nature of the tone-segment association, in that both bitonal accents are identical in tonal composition but differ only in the way the component tones are "timed" (or "aligned") with the segmental string.

Categorical descriptions of tone-segment associations are certainly useful, but they do not capture the details of how a tonal target is phonetically "aligned" with the segmental string, and they fail to reflect the important fact that the same tonal pattern can be realized differently from language to language or from variety to variety of the same language (e.g., Arvaniti, Ladd, and Mennen 2000; Atterer and Ladd 2004; Ladd et al. 2009; see also Ladd 2008: chapter 5 for a review). For example, Figure 22.3 shows that the F0 peak for a prenuclear accentual rise (L+H) occurs relatively later in Southern German than in Northern German, and later in Northern

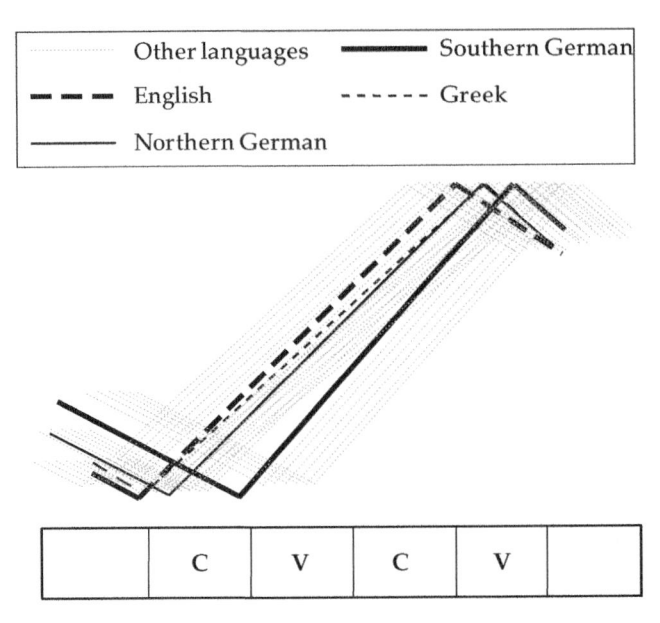

Figure 22.3 Degree of tone-segment alignment for a bitonal L+H sequence across languages (adapted from Atterer and Ladd 2004). Fine lines have been added here to refer loosely to possible F0-alignment patterns for other languages which employ an L+H sequence.

German than in English (Atterer and Ladd 2004); and F0 peaks for both prenuclear and nuclear pitch accents are aligned later in Dutch (Dutch data are not shown in Figure 22.3) than in English (Ladd et al. 2009). (Note that when more than two pitch accents occur within an intonationally defined prosodic domain such as the Intermediate Intonational Phrase in English, the last pitch accent, which is generally the most prominent, is referred to as "nuclear" and the rest as "prenuclear".) Similarly, small but systematic tone-segment alignment differences have been found between varieties of English: both nuclear and prenuclear peaks are aligned later in Scottish Standard English (SSE) than in Southern British English (RP) (Ladd et al. 2009); and certain accentual F0 peaks come later in an American English variety spoken by Southern Californians than in a variety spoken by Minnesotans (Arvaniti and Garding 2007).

The cross-linguistic and cross-dialectal differences in tone-segment alignment for a comparable accent type clearly suggest that the categorical descriptions of tone to segment alignment do not suffice to capture language-specific phonetic details. So how can the detailed phonetic alignment be properly captured in linguistic descriptions of the tone-segment alignment for a given language? One way is to appeal to the notion of *segmental anchoring* (see Ladd 2008).

Segmental anchoring refers to a phenomenon that tonal targets such as F0 valleys and peaks for L and H tones are consistently aligned with specific locations or landmarks in the segmental structure, while the slope and the duration of the pitch movement (for a rise or a fall) are adjusted to keep the F0 valley and the peak "anchored" to the specified segmental landmarks. Segmental anchoring landmarks were initially defined in terms of syllable structure such as the beginning and the end of the stressed syllable (e.g., Arvaniti et al. 1998; Ladd, Mennen, and Schepman 2000). Subsequent studies, however, have cast doubt on the syllable-based interpretation of segmental anchoring, showing that, for example, the alignment pattern can be directly conditioned by phonetic vowel length (e.g., in Dutch, Schepman, Lickley, and Ladd 2006) or by the presence or absence of the coda consonant in the accented syllable with no specific reference to syllable boundaries (e.g., in Spanish, Prieto and Torreira 2007).

Converging evidence now suggests that segmental anchors cannot be defined in a unified way. Rather, these vary from language to language or from variety to variety of the same language. To account for the cross-linguistic differences in segmental anchoring, Ladd (2006, 2008) made the analogy to cross-linguistic variation in VOT of stops (as in Cho and Ladefoged 1999). Both VOT and segmental anchoring involve relative timing between laryngeal and supralaryngeal gestures. Just as languages may choose a target VOT value along the VOT continuum that can be expressed in terms of intergestural timing, so can they take on any of a continuum of alignment possibilities. Different alignment possibilities can again be expressed quantitatively using the notion of relative timing between laryngeal and supralaryngeal gestures. Ladd argued that segmental anchoring is best understood in these terms rather than as associations between categories on different phonological tiers.

The schematized tone-segment alignment patterns shown in Figure 22.3 for English, German, and Greek were originally meant to illustrate cross-linguistic differences in segmental anchors in the acoustic dimension as expressed by CVCV. The same degree of variation, however, could also be expressed in terms of articulatory anchors, in which case CVCV would be translated into gestural landmarks such as the onset and the target of the gestures or other kinematic landmarks. Some recent studies have endeavored to test whether the tone-segment alignment is better captured with articulatory anchors rather than acoustic anchors. For example, Mücke et al. (2009) examined tonal alignment for the L+H tonal sequence in two varieties of German (Northern vs. Southern) by looking at both acoustic and articulatory (kinematic) data. They looked at whether the H peak is better described as anchored to an articulatory landmark (e.g., the constriction target for the consonantal gesture for /n/ or /m/ in CVNV), or to an acoustic landmark (e.g., the acoustic onset of /n/ or /m/ or the onset of the following vowel). For prenuclear pitch accents, they found that articulatory anchoring provided a better description of the data than segmental (acoustic) anchoring. However, the effect was not robust: the articulatory anchoring pattern was not necessarily more stable in its timing than the segmental anchoring pattern. Similarly, D'Imperio, Nguyen, and Munhall (2003) and D'Imperio et al. (2007) have shown in articulatory studies in Neopolitan Italian that F0 peaks are better mapped on to kinematically defined articulatory anchors (e.g., the peak velocity or the zero velocity corresponding to the tongue tip lowering and raising gestures and the lip opening and closing gestures) than on to acoustically defined anchors. But it was also noted that articulatory anchoring was not necessarily more stable in timing than acoustic anchoring. Moreover, D'Imperio et al.'s (2007) French data did not show any clear evidence favoring articulatory anchoring over acoustic anchoring.

In all, the nature of tone-segment alignment remains unresolved. If tone-segment alignment is indeed better captured in terms of gestural coordination than by acoustic events, the first question that must be answered is what gesture or gestures in the supralaryngeal dimension should be coordinated with the laryngeal gestures that are responsible for an F0 peak or valley. Answering this question alone requires numerous empirical cross-linguistic studies, as languages may differ not only in terms of timing between laryngeal and supralaryngeal gestures, but also in terms of what supralaryngeal gesture should be involved.

With what criteria can we then determine that a supralaryngeal gesture is to be coordinated with a specific laryngeal gesture? While most acoustically-based tone-segment anchoring studies have generally relied on the synchrony between F0 peaks and valleys and segmental landmarks (as the term "anchoring" implies), another important criterion (perhaps more important than synchrony) may be stability of intergestural timing. If a language-specific phonetic rule modulates tone-segment alignment for a given tonal sequence, and if it can be successfully accounted for in terms of gestural coordination, then the rule could be expressed in terms of a phasing angle, or something equivalent, which would specify the timing between the two gestures. If intergestural timing matters, the principle of synchrony (i.e., two events should be synchronized or occur near each other in time) becomes less important, and the stability in relative timing between events more so.

It remains to be seen how languages differ in employing synchrony and stability to define tone to segment alignment. Also of continuing interest is whether or not the tone-segment alignment is under speaker control, and, if so, how this can be incorporated into the phonetic grammar of the language. In all, much more work is certainly called for in order to develop our understanding of the timing between tonal and segmental events.

22.4.2 Variation in timing at prosodic boundaries

Another important issue at the phonetics-prosody interface concerns how the prosodic structure of a given utterance is expressed through fine phonetic detail as *prosodic strengthening*. The term "prosodic strengthening" describes the spatial and/or temporal expansion of articulatory gestures that occurs at landmark locations such as prosodic domain edges and syllables with prominence (e.g., Cho 2005, 2008; Cho and McQueen 2005). In this subsection, I will continue to discuss language effects on timing at the suprasegmental level by focusing on cross-linguistic temporal patterns associated with boundary marking, looking at how languages are similar or dissimilar in marking the boundaries of prosodic structure (junctures) in the temporal dimension.

22.4.2.1 Preboundary (domain-final) lengthening One of the most consistent phonetic correlates of prosodic structure is the pattern of temporal modification of segments near the end of a prosodic constituent before a prosodic boundary, a phenomenon often referred to as domain-final lengthening or preboundary lengthening (e.g., Edwards, Beckman, and Fletcher 1991; Wightman et al. 1992; Gussenhoven and Rietveld 1992; Berkovits 1993; Byrd 2000; Cambier-Langeveld 2000; Byrd, Krivokapić, and Lee 2006; Cho 2006; Turk and Shattuck-Hufnagel 2007). In particular, segments are longer in IP-final position than in non-IP-final or IP-medial position. This pattern exists across languages. Given its recurrence across languages, the natural explanation is that it is driven by physiological and biomechanical factors. For example, one account is that final lengthening emerges as a byproduct of the natural physical tendency to decelerate movement before its cessation (e.g., Lindblom 1968). Others have expanded this account to suggest that supralaryngeal movement may slow down (decline) over the course of an utterance (Fowler 1988; Vayra and Fowler 1992; Berkovits 1993; Krakow, Bell-Berti, and Wang 1995; Tabain 2003).

The notion of movement declination across a sentence is analogous to the robust observation of F0 declination across an utterance. All other things being equal, F0 will fall over the course of an utterance, presumably because subglottal pressure declines over the course of an utterance (Cohen, Collier, and 't Hart 1982; Cooper and Sorenson 1981; Pierrehumbert 1979). This decline also has consequences for acoustic amplitude (Gelfer 1987).

The physiological explanation for F0 and amplitude declination assumes that declination occurs as the passive consequence of speaking, rather than due to control by the speaker. Shadle (1997) also points out that the cause of F0 declination remains unresolved: F0 can be affected by activities of both respiratory and laryngeal muscles, but it is not clear which is involved in producing declination, especially because subglottal pressure can also be modulated by laryngeal muscle activity.

In line with the possibility that F0 declination is under speaker control, many researchers have suggested that preboundary lengthening is an active process, not a physiological one. The preferred explanation is that speakers lengthen at the right edge of a prosodic boundary in order to cue juncture location (e.g., Edwards et al. 1991; Beckman and Edwards 1994; Byrd 2000; Byrd and Saltzman 2003; Cho 2006). Substantial evidence exists to show that preboundary lengthening serves as a perceptual cue to upcoming prosodic boundaries, and that this cue facilitates speech comprehension (see Christophe et al. 2004; Cho et al. 2007; Tyler and Cutler 2009; Kim and Cho 2009; Kim, Broersma, and Cho 2012).

This view of preboundary lengthening is further supported by the fact that preboundary lengthening varies in its extent from language to language, just like VOT values and F0-segment alignment patterns vary from language to language. For example, the domain of preboundary lengthening in Hebrew is the phrase-final disyllabic word (Berkovits 1993), but preboundary lengthening in English has generally been observed only during the final syllable or rhyme of a phrase-final word (e.g., Klatt 1975; Edwards et al. 1991; Wightman et al. 1992; Byrd and Saltzman 2003).

Preboundary lengthening also interacts with other prosodic factors. A recent study by Turk and Shattuck-Hufnagel (2007) showed that a primary stressed syllable also undergoes small but significant lengthening, even if it is non-final. In particular, preboundary lengthening was shown to extend to a stressed antepenultimate syllable, even though the intervening penultimate unstressed syllable does not undergo lengthening. This kind of interaction with stress has also been observed in other languages. The particulars of the patterns are somewhat different from those of English. For example, in Italian, preboundary lengthening was found to extend to a non-final stressed syllable only when the stressed syllable was penultimate, but not when it was antepenultimate (D'Imperio 2011). In Northern Finnish, preboundary lengthening also extends to the non-final stressed syllable in disyllabic words (Nakai et al. 2008), but the effect is constrained by phonological vowel quantity: preboundary lengthening of a phonemically long vowel was restricted when it occurred next to a syllable with another long vowel. Nakai et al. (2008) interpreted this finding as due to syntagmatic constraints. When a long vowel is adjacent to a short vowel, the long vowel may be freely lengthened phrase-finally, which would have an effect of enhancing its syntagmatic contrast with the preceding short vowel (e.g., enhancement of the short-long syntagmatic contrast), but when two adjacent vowels are both long, excessive lengthening of the second vowel would make the preceding long vowel sound relatively short, blurring the long-long syntagmatic contrast.

Japanese, which has a vowel quantity contrast like Finnish, but does not employ a lexical stress system like English, presents yet another pattern of preboundary lengthening; one that interacts with the moraic structure of the final syllable. Only the last mora undergoes preboundary lengthening (Shepherd 2008). This assertion is based on the finding that the degree of preboundary lengthening is proportionally larger for a short vowel (with one mora) than for a long vowel (with two moras).

The cross-linguistic patterns of preboundary lengthening indicate, without a doubt, that preboundary lengthening is a universal phenomenon. However, the degree of preboundary lengthening varies across languages, showing language specificity in terms of its domain as well as in the way that it interacts with other phonological factors of the language such as stress and vowel quantity. These cross-linguistic differences lend support to the view that preboundary lengthening is controlled by the speaker and so must be specified in the phonetic grammar of the language.

22.4.2.2 Postboundary (domain-initial) lengthening In addition to marking the end of a prosodic domain, domain-initial position is marked in production by temporal and spatial expansion (e.g., Pierrehumbert and Talkin 1992; Fougeron and Keating 1997; Cho and Keating 2001, 2009; Fougeron 2001; Keating et al. 2003; Kuzla, Cho, and Ernestus 2007, inter alia). In particular, electropalatography (EPG) studies have demonstrated that the strength of consonant articulation, as reflected in the amount of oral constriction and seal (closure) duration, increases in a cumulative way as the domain that contains the consonant becomes larger from PWd to IP (e.g., Fougeron and Keating 1997; Keating et al. 2003; Cho and Keating 2001, 2009). This kind of domain-initial strengthening pattern has also been observed in the acoustic dimension, and across languages. For example, aspirated stops are produced with longer VOTs in domain-initial than in domain-medial position in English (Cho and Keating 2009), Korean (Jun 1993, 1995; Cho and Jun 2000; Cho and Keating 2001), Japanese (Onaka 2003; Onaka et al. 2003), Taiwanese (Hsu and Jun 1998; Hayashi, Hsu, and Keating 1999), and French (Fougeron 2001). The effect of initial position on VOT is thought to be a consequence of strengthening the glottal abduction gesture (Pierrehumbert and Talkin 1992; cf. Cooper 1991). This idea is supported by results from a fiberscopic study of laryngeal position in Korean, which found larger glottal apertures in AP-initial position than in AP-medial position in Korean (Jun, Beckman, and Lee 1998). (Here AP refers to the Accentual Phrase, which is an intermediate level of prosodic domain assumed in a prosodic model of Korean; Jun 1993, 1995).

Cho and Keating (2001) suggested that domain-initial strengthening (and lengthening) may result from the close relationship between space and time in action. The proposal was that domain-initial position is allotted with enough time to execute an articulatory action, so the articulatory target is fully attained. In contrast, less time is allotted to domain-medial articulations, resulting in articulatory undershoot for that position. An alternative proposal, advanced by Fougeron (1999; Fougeron and Keating 1997), is that domain-initial strengthening involves "articulatory force" (cf. Straka 1963), which can be defined as "the amount of energy necessary to the realization of all the muscular effort involved in the production of a consonant" (Delattre 1940, translated). Whatever the mechanism, both proposals assume that strengthening is under speaker control.

The scope of domain-initial strengthening in English has been generally assumed to be confined to the initial syllable, and particularly to initial consonants in CV (Fougeron and Keating 1997; Barnes 2002; Cole et al. 2007; Cho and Keating 2009). Cho and Keating (2009) reported, though, that strengthening processes were often observable during the following vowel; for example, the vowel intensity was greater in CV in domain-initial than domain-medial position, but only when the syllable was not accented. Magnetometer studies of vowel tongue positions, vowel-to-vowel tongue movements, and lip opening movements also showed provide evidence for domain-initial strengthening effects on the vowel in an initial CV sequence (e.g., Cho 2005, 2006, 2008; Byrd 2000). Results accumulated so far, however, clearly suggest that at least the acoustic duration of the vowel in the initial sequence does not undergo domain-initial lengthening in English.

Barnes (2002) suggested that the V in an initial CV sequence is not lengthened because vowel duration in English is reserved for marking lexical and phrasal stress. This explanation is, however, at odds with results from a kinematic study we recently conducted. Kim and Cho (2012) showed that lip opening duration from a schwa to /æ/ was longer IP-initially than IP-medially for the vowel-initial word "add" but not for the consonant-initial word "pad." The suggestion is that weak domain-initial effects on the vowel in a CV sequence is not due to an interaction with stress, but rather is due to the scope of the effect, which may be only adjacent to the boundary. This suggestion is further supported by acoustic data that we have recently analyzed in our lab. We have found that the vowel in an initial CV sequence in English does not undergo domain-initial lengthening even when the initial vowel is not stressed as in "banal" or "panache." We have also explored the possibility that the domain-initial strengthening may be extended to a stressed syllable in iambic words (e.g., "banal" and "panache"), given that the locus of preboundary (final) lengthening is extended to a non-initial stressed syllable as was discussed above (e.g., Turk and Shattuck-Hufnagel 2007). Our preliminary analyses have shown no boundary effect on the strength of the non-initial stressed syllable, indicating that the scopes for boundary-related lengthening are different between preboundary and postboundary positions.

Languages other than English also show domain-initial lengthening effects on initial consonants, as noted above. However, little is known about how languages differ in the way domain-initial lengthening is realized. That said, we recently conducted an acoustic study comparing communicatively driven (in a clear speech mode) versus prosodically driven strengthening effects in Korean (Cho, Lee, and Kim 2011). The finding is that domain-initial lengthening in Korean can spread to the second syllable of the initial word, which is clearly different from what has been found with English and other languages. Cho et al. ascribed the apparent cross-linguistic difference to language-specific prosodic systems. Korean, without lexical stress and pitch accent, appears to have a greater degree of freedom for spatio-temporal expansion than English, as its domain of influence is not restricted by the lexical prominence system. We also noted that preboundary effects were more robust in Korean than in English, which was again taken to be due to a lack of interference from lexical stress.

While more work is certainly needed to make solid generalizations, what appears to have emerged from the work conducted to date is that boundary-induced lengthening (both before and after the boundary) interacts with the prominence system of the language, and that the complexity of the interaction differs across languages. As was the case with preboundary lengthening, the strong evidence that domain-initial lengthening occurs across languages suggests that it is a universal tendency, but the cross-language differences indicate that its phonetic implementation is controlled by the speaker in language-specific ways, which must be learned.

22.4.2.3 Pi-gesture as a device modulating boundary-related lengthening The previous two subsections were devoted to discussion on how languages may differ in implementing preboundary and postboundary lengthening, which signals junctures in the prosodic structure of speech. This section is devoted to addressing how prosodic structure influences the detailed timing of individual articulators. Recall that cross-linguistic variation in timing at the segmental level was discussed in terms of language-specific differences in intergestural timing, which is specified in the grammar of individual languages. Cross-linguistic differences in preboundary and postboundary lengthening may also be captured by assuming that timing between gestures is modulated in language-specific ways. In the remainder of this section, I will discuss one proposal for how this can be represented within the framework of Articulatory Phonology (Browman and Goldstein 1990, 1992) and computationally implemented in the related Task Dynamic model (Saltzman and Munhall 1989; see also Mücke, Grice, and Cho 2014 for a commentary with respect to dynamics of articulation and prosodic structure).

Byrd and her colleagues have proposed that boundary-induced lengthening can be understood in terms of the influence of a so-called "π-gesture" that is governed by prosodic constituency in the task dynamics model (Saltzman 1995; Byrd et al. 2000; Byrd 2000, 2006; Byrd and Saltzman 2003; Byrd et al. 2006). The π-gesture is defined as an abstract "prosodic" gesture that does not have a constriction task, and therefore is not actually realized in terms of vocal tract constrictions. Based on the important assumptions in Articulatory Phonology that gestures are active over a temporal interval and that their activation intervals overlap in time, the π-gesture also overlaps with constriction gestures in time. The effect of a π-gesture is to pace constriction gestures, by modulating the rate of the clock that controls the articulatory activation of gestures. The π-gesture slows the clock at a prosodic juncture, and so the articulatory movement at the juncture is also slowed down. The π-gesture has a domain of influence which waxes and wanes with its activation box. Peak activation is anchored to a prosodic boundary, and so the effect of this gesture is strongest at a juncture and weaker as it gets farther away from the boundary in both directions.

When the π-gesture is overlapped with the timing of consonant and vowel gestures, the configuration captures the frequently reported asymmetry between preboundary and postboundary lengthening in English that was described above (robust lengthening of preboundary V and strengthening of postboundary) so long as we assume a preboundary vowel and a postboundary consonant. It also predicts initial lengthening effects on vowels adjacent to the boundary, which has also been observed (Kim and Cho 2011).

As noted earlier, there is some evidence that postboundary lengthening may be pervasive into the vocalic articulation in initial CV sequences (Byrd 2000; Cho 2006, 2008; Byrd et al. 2006). For example, Byrd et al. (2006) reported that the articulatory opening movement for a vowel was lengthened after a boundary in CV sequences, though not in all speakers. Similarly, Cho (2006, 2008) showed that domain-initial CV lip opening movement and V-to-V tongue movement across a boundary (V#CV) were lengthened more in IP-initial position compared to IP-medial position. These results suggest that domain-initial effects on duration may be gradient in nature, varying as a function of distance from the boundary (Cho 2008; Cho and Keating 2009). This gradient pattern is consistent with the π-gesture activation curve, which increases before the boundary and decreases thereafter.

If it is accurate to model boundary effects as due to gradient activation, then the question arises as to how far the π-gesture extends around prosodic junctures. The answer to this question may be different for different languages, and requires that scope be specified in the representation.

In all, cross-linguistic differences in boundary-related timing patterns are likely best understood in terms of two parameters. The first parameter is the coordination of the π-gesture with constriction gestures. The default might be to anchor the π-gesture at the prosodic boundary, but other coordination patterns are also possible in principle (Byrd and Saltzman 2003). As schematized in the top half of Figure 22.4, a π-gesture activation curve may be shifted to the left or to the right as its coordination

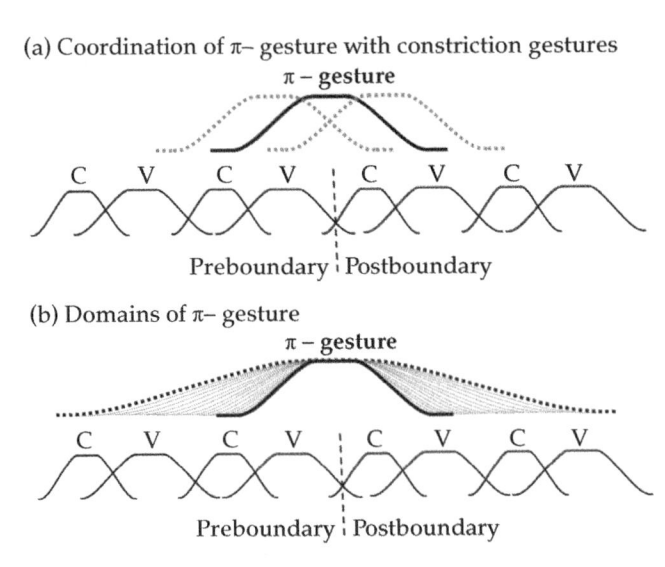

Figure 22.4 Hypothetical schema for variation in the coordination of a π-gesture with constriction gestures (a) and for its variable domains (b) that may differ within and across languages.

with constriction gestures varies. A left-shifted curve will result in extended preboundary lengthening while its domain over postboundary lengthening will be reduced. The opposite will be true when the curve is shifted to the right.

The second parameter is the scope of the π-gesture. That is, the activation interval of a π-gesture itself may vary, stretching or shrinking depending on the boundary strength within a language as well as across languages. It is theory-internally possible that a language that shows a relatively larger stretch of a boundary-related lengthening has a longer activation interval of the π-gesture in its prosodic system. The bottom half of Figure 22.4 shows a hypothetical continuum of activation intervals for a π-gesture along which individual languages may fall.

If one combines the two parameters illustrated in Figure 22.4, various language-specific patterns can be captured. Recall that Korean shows quite extensive postboundary lengthening (up to the second syllable), while preboundary lengthening appears to be limited to the final syllable (Cho et al. 2011). This particular language-specific pattern could arise if the activation interval of a π-gesture extends over three syllables and its center is shifted to the right of the boundary (by approximately one syllable). The progressive preboundary lengthening throughout a disyllable word in Hebrew (Berkovits 1993) could be described by a π-gesture whose scope is extended to the left. This can be achieved either by shifting the π-gesture to the left or by stretching it. If Hebrew turns out to show an extended postboundary lengthening pattern up to the second syllable of an initial word (just like the preboundary lengthening pattern), it can be taken to have an overall extended π-gesture symmetrically covering two syllables before and after the juncture. On the other hand, if Hebrew has only a limited postboundary lengthening effect, like English, then the pattern would be a mirror of the proposed Korean pattern; the activation interval would be stretched over three syllables, but shifted to the left of the boundary.

The π-gesture model thus provides possible ways of capturing boundary-related lengthening that varies within and across languages. The model has certainly advanced our understanding of effects of prosodic structure on speech timing. There are, however, some questions that remain unresolved. One important question is what factors influence the scope of a π-gesture and its coordination with constriction gestures. Consider, for example, the previously described interactions between lengthening and strengthening patterns and other prosodic factors, such as stress. An important challenge for the π-gesture model is to determine how these other prosodic factors interact with the π-gesture and how much each factor should be weighted in the model (see Katsika, Krivokapić, Mooshammer, Tiede and Goldstein, 2014 for a related discussion).

22.5 Conclusion

This chapter introduced a number of cross-linguistically recurrent patterns in speech timing at the segmental and the suprasegmental level. The goals were to show the extent to which timing patterns may vary from language to language or from variety to variety, and to argue that such variation is best accounted for by language-specific phonetic rules that operate in the grammar of individual languages. In particular, whereas many of the patterns we considered in this chapter likely have their origins in physiological or biomechanical constraints imposed on the human speech production and perception systems, fine-grained phonetic details suggest that none of the putative universal timing patterns can be accounted for in their entirety by physiological/biomechanical factors. Converging evidence for extensive variation in the patterns suggests that the putative universals are internalized into the grammars of individual languages in language-specific ways. These language-specific phonetic rules apply at a fairly late stage in speech production where speech timing is fine-tuned before production. This fine-tuning process can be understood in dynamical terms. This framework includes intergestural timing schemes as well as timing coordination and overlap between the segmental and suprasegmental tiers. In sum, we conclude that language variation, whether phonetic or phonological, is due to the grammar.

REFERENCES

Arvaniti, Amalia and Gina Garding. 2007. Dialectal variation in the rising accents of American English. *Laboratory Phonology* 9: 547–576.

Arvaniti, Amalia, D. Robert Ladd, and Ineke Mennen. 2000. What is a starred tone? Evidence from Greek. *Papers in Laboratory Phonology* 5: 119–131.

Atterer, Michaela and D. Robert Ladd. 2004. On the phonetics and phonology of "segmental anchoring" of F0: Evidence from German. *Journal of Phonetics* 32: 177–197.

Barnes, Jonathan A. 2002. Positional neutralization: A phonologization approach to typological patterns. PhD dissertation, University of California, Berkeley.

Beckman, Mary E. 1996. The parsing of prosody. *Language and Cognitive Processes* 11: 17–67.

Beckman, Mary E. and Jan Edwards. 1994. Articulatory evidence for differentiating stress categories. *Papers in Laboratory Phonology* 3: 7–33.

Beckman, Mary E. and Janet B. Pierrehumbert. 1986. Intonational structure in Japanese and English. *Phonology Yearbook* 3: 255–309.

Berkovits, Rochele. 1993. Utterance-final lengthening and the duration of final-stop closures. *Journal of Phonetics* 21: 479–489.

Browman, Catherine, Louis Goldstein. 1990. Tiers in articulatory phonology, with some implications for casual speech. *Papers in Laboratory Phonology* 1: 341–376.

Browman, Catherine and Louis Goldstein. 1992. Articulatory Phonology: An overview. *Phonetica* 49: 155–180.

Bruce, Gosta. 1977. *Swedish Word Accents in Sentence Perspective*. Lund: Gleerups.

Byrd, Dani. 2000. Articulatory vowel lengthening and coordination at phrasal junctures. *Phonetica* 57: 3–16.

Byrd, Dani. 2006. Relating prosody and dynamic events: Commentary on the papers by Cho, Navas and Smiljanić. *Laboratory Phonology* 8: 549–561.

Byrd, Dani and Susie Choi. 2010. At the juncture of prosody, phonology, and phonetics: The interaction of phrasal and syllable structure in shaping the timing of consonant gestures. *Laboratory Phonology* 10: 31–59.

Byrd, Dani and Elliot Saltzman. 2003. The elastic phrase: Modeling the dynamics of boundary-adjacent lengthening. *Journal of Phonetics* 31: 149–180.

Byrd, Dani, Jelena Krivokapić, and Sungbok Lee. 2006. How far, how long: On the temporal scope of prosodic boundary effects. *Journal of the Acoustical Society of America* 120: 1589–1599.

Byrd, Dani, Abigail Kaun, Shrikanth Narayanan, and Elliot Saltzman. 2000. Phrasal signatures in articulation. *Papers in Laboratory Phonology* 5: 70–88.

Cambier-Langeveld, Tina. 2000. Temporal marking of accent and boundaries. PhD dissertation, University of Amsterdam.

Chen, Matthew. 1970. Vowel length variation as a function of the voicing of the consonant environment. *Phonetica* 22: 129–159.

Cho, Taehong. 2005. Prosodic strengthening and featural enhancement: Evidence from acoustic and articulatory realizations of /a, i/ in English. *Journal of the Acoustical Society of America* 117(6): 3867–3878.

Cho, Taehong. 2006. Manifestation of prosodic structure in articulation: Evidence from lip kinematics in English. *Laboratory Phonology* 8: 519–548.

Cho, Taehong. 2008. Prosodic strengthening in transboundary V-to-V lingual movement in American English. *Phonetica* 65: 45–61.

Cho, Taehong and Sun-Ah Jun. 2000. Domain-initial strengthening as featural enhancement: Aerodynamic evidence from Korean. *Chicago Linguistics Society* 36: 31–44.

Cho, Taehong and Patricia A. Keating. 2001. Articulatory and acoustic studies of domain-initial strengthening in Korean. *Journal of Phonetics* 29: 155–190.

Cho, Taehong and Patricia Keating. 2009. Effects of initial position versus prominence in English. *Journal of Phonetics* 37: 466–485.

Cho, Taehong and Peter Ladefoged. 1999. Variation and universals in VOT: Evidence from 18 languages. *Journal of Phonetics* 27: 207–229.

Cho, Taehong and James M. McQueen. 2005. Prosodic influences on consonant production in Dutch: Effects of prosodic boundaries, phrasal accent and lexical stress. *Journal of Phonetics* 33: 121–157.

Cho, Taehong, Yoonjeong Lee, and Sahyang Kim. 2011. Communicatively driven versus prosodically driven hyper-articulation in Korean. *Journal of Phonetics* 39(3): 344–361.

Cho, Taehong, James M. McQueen, and Ethan A. Cox. 2007. Prosodically driven phonetic detail in speech processing: The case of domain-initial strengthening in English. *Journal of Phonetics* 35: 210–243.

Chomsky, Noam and Morris Halle. 1968. *The Sound Pattern of English*. New York: Harper and Row.

Christophe, Anne, Sharon Peperkamp, Christophe Pallier, Eliza Block, and Jacques Mehler. 2004. Phonological phrase boundaries constrain lexical access: I. Adult data. *Journal of Memory and Language* 51: 523–547.

Cohen, Antonie, Rene Collier, and Johan 't Hart. 1982. Declination: Construct or intrinsic feature of speech pitch? *Phonetica* 39: 254–273.

Cohn, Abigail C. 1993. Nasalization in English: Phonology or phonetics. *Phonology* 10: 43–81.

Cohn, Abigail C. 2007. Phonetics in phonology and phonology in phonetics. *Working Papers of the Cornell Phonetics Laboratory* 16: 1–13.

Cole, Jennifer, Heejin Kim, Hansook Choi, and Mark Hasegawa-Johnson. 2007. Prosodic effects on acoustic cues to stop voicing and place of articulation: Evidence from Radio News speech. *Journal of Phonetics* 35: 180–209.

Cooper, Andre M. 1991. Glottal gestures and aspiration in English. PhD dissertation, Yale University.

Cooper, William and John Sorensen. 1981. *Fundamental Frequency in Sentence Production*. Heidelberg: Springer.

D'Imperio, Mariapaola. 2011. Prosodic hierarchy and articulatory control:

Evaluating the pi-gesture hypothesis in Italian EMA data. Handout from a talk presented at the Speech Production Workshop, Venice International University, October 2011.

D'Imperio, Mariapaola, Noel Nguyen, and Kevin G. Munhall. 2003. An articulatory hypothesis for the alignment of tonal targets in Italian. In *Proceedings of the 15th ICPhS, Barcelona, Spain*, 253–256.

D'Imperio, Mariapaola, Robert Espesser, Helene Loevenbruck, Caroline Menezes, Noel Nguyen, and Pauline Welby. 2007. Are tones alinged with articulatory events? Evidence from Italian and French. *Laboratory Phonology* 9: 577–608.

de Jong, Kenneth. 2004. Stress, lexical focus and segmental focus in English: Patterns of variation in vowel duration. *Journal of Phonetics* 32: 493–516.

de Jong, Kenneth and Bushra Zawaydeh. 2002. Comparing stress, lexical focus, and segmental focus: Patterns of variation in Arabic vowel duration. *Journal of Phonetics* 30: 53–75.

Delattre, Pierre C. 1940. La force d'articulation consonantique en français. *The French Review* 14: 220–232.

Docherty, Gerald J. 1992. *The Timing of British English Obstruents*. Berlin: Foris.

Edwards, Jan E., Mary E. Beckman, and Janet Fletcher. 1991. The articulatory kinematics of final lengthening. *Journal of the Acoustical Society of America* 89: 369–382.

Fischer-Jørgensen, Eli. 1954. Acoustic analysis of stop consonants. *Miscellanea Phonetica* 2: 42–59.

Fougeron, Cécile. 1990. Prosodically conditioned articulatory variation. *UCLA Working Papers in Phonetics* 97: 1–73.

Fougeron, Cécile. 2001. Articulatory properties of initial segments in several prosodic constituents in French. *Journal of Phonetics* 29: 109–135.

Fougeron, Cécile and Patricia A. Keating. 1997. Articulatory strengthening at edges of prosodic domains. *Journal of the Acoustical Society of America* 106: 3728–3740.

Fowler, Carol. 1988. Periodic dwindling of acoustic and articulatory variables in speech production. *PAW Review* 3: 10–13.

Fromkin, Victoria A. 1977. Some questions regarding universal phonetics and phonetic representations. In A. Juilland (ed.), *Linguistic Studies Offered to Joseph Greenberg on the Occasion of his Sixtieth Birthday*, 365–380. Saratoga, CA: Anma Libri.

Gelfer, Carole. 1987. A simultaneous physiological and acoustic study of fundamental frequency declination. PhD dissertation, City University of New York.

Goldsmith, John. 1976. *Autosegmental phonology*. PhD dissertation, MIT.

Goldsmith, John. 1990. *Autosegmental and Metrical Phonology*. Oxford: Blackwell.

Gussenhoven, Carlos and Antonius C.M. Rietveld. 1992. Intonation contours, prosodic structure and preboundary lengthening. *Journal of Phonetics* 20: 283–303.

Halle, Morris and Kenneth N. Stevens. 1967 On the mechanism of glottal vibration for vowels and consonants. *Quarterly Progress Report of the Research Laboratory of Electronics, MIT* 85: 267–271.

Hayashi, Wendy, Chai-Shune Hsu, and Patricia Keating. 1999. Domain-initial strengthening in Taiwanese: A follow-up study. *UCLA Working Papers in Phonetics* 97: 152–156.

Hayes, Bruce, Robert Kirchner, and Donca Steriade (eds.). 2004. *Phonetically Based Phonology*. Cambridge: Cambridge University Press.

Hsu, Chai-Shune K. and Sun-Ah Jun. 1998. Prosodic strengthening in Taiwanese: Syntagmatic or paradigmatic? *UCLA Working Papers in Phonetics* 96: 69–89.

Hume, Elizabeth V. and Keith Johnson (eds.). 2001. *The Role of Speech Perception in Phonology*. San Diego, CA: Academic Press.

Jun, Sun-Ah. 1993. The phonetics and phonology of Korean prosody. PhD dissertation, Ohio State University.

Jun, Sun-Ah. 1995. Asymmetrical prosodic effects on the laryngeal gesture in Korean. *Papers in Laboratory Phonology* 4: 235–253.

Jun, Sun-Ah. 1998. The accentual phrase in the Korean prosodic hierarchy. *Phonology* 15(2): 189–226.

Jun, Sun-Ah, Mary E. Beckman, and Hyuck-Joon Lee. 1998. Fiberscopic evidence for the influence on vowel devoicing of the glottal configurations for Korean obstruents. *UCLA Working Papers in Phonetics* 96: 43–68.

Katsika, Argyro, Jelena Krivokapić, Christine Mooshammer, Mark Tiede, and Louis Goldstein. 2014. The coordination of boundary tones and its interaction with prominence. *Journal of Phonetics* 44: 62–82.

Keating, Patricia A. 1984. Phonetic and phonological representation of stop consonant voicing. *Language* 60: 286–319.

Keating, Patricia A. 1985. Universal phonetics and the organization of grammars. In V.A. Fromkin (ed.), *Phonetic Linguistics: Essays in Honor of Peter Ladefoged*, 115–132. Orlando, FL: Academic Press.

Keating, Patricia A. 1988. The phonology-phonetics interface. In F. Newmeyer (ed.), *Linguistics: The Cambridge Survey*, vol. 1: *Grammatical Theory*, 281–302. Cambridge: Cambridge University Press.

Keating, Patricia A. 1990. Phonetic representations in a generative grammar. *Journal of Phonetics* 18(3): 321–334.

Keating, Patricia A. 1996. The phonology–phonetics interface. In U. Kleinhenz (ed.), *Interfaces in Phonology*, 262–278. Berlin: Akademie Verlag.

Keating, Patricia A. and Stephanie Shattuck-Hufnagel. 2002. A prosodic view of word form encoding for speech production. *UCLA Working Papers in Phonetics* 101: 112–156.

Keating, Patricia A., Taehong Cho, Cécile Fougeron, and Chai-Shune Hsu. 2003. Domain-initial strengthening in four languages. *Papers in Laboratory Phonology* 6: 145–163.

Kim, Sahyang and Taehong Cho. 2009. The use of phrase-level prosodic information in lexical segmentation: Evidence from word-spotting experiments in Korean. *Journal of the Acoustical Society of America* 125(5): 3373–3386.

Kim, Sahyang and Taehong Cho. 2011. Articulatory manifestation of prosodic strengthening in English /i/ and /ɪ/. *Phonetics and Speech Sciences* 3(4): 13–21. (Journal of the Korean Society of Speech Sciences.)

Kim, Sahyang and Taehong Cho. 2012. Prosodic strengthening in the articulation of English /æ/. *Studies in Phonetics, Phonology and Morphology* 18(2): 321–337. (Published by The Phonology-Morphology Circle of Korea.)

Kim, Sahyang, Mirjam Broersma, and Taehong Cho. 2012. The use of prosodic cues in processing an unfamiliar language. *Studies in Second Language Acquisition* 34(3): 415–444.

Kingston, John. 2007. The phonetics-phonology interface. In P. de Lacy (ed.), *The Cambridge Handbook of Phonology*, 401–434. Cambridge: Cambridge University Press.

Kingston, John and Randy L. Diehl. 1994. Phonetic knowledge. *Language* 70: 419–454.

Klatt, Dennis H. 1975. Vowel lengthening is syntactically determined in connected discourse. *Journal of Phonetics* 3: 129–140.

Krakow, Rena A., Fredericka Bell-Berti, and Q. Emily Wang. 1995. Supralaryngeal declination: Evidence from the velum. In F. Bell-Berti and J.J. Raphael (eds.), *Producing Speech: Contemporary Issues: For Katherine Safford Harris*, 333–354. New York: AIP Publishing.

Krivokapić, Jelena and Dani Byrd. 2012. Prosodic boundary strength: An articulatory and perceptual study. *Journal of Phonetics* 40: 430–442.

Kuzla, Claudia, Taehong Cho, and Mirjam Ernestus. 2007. Prosodic strengthening of German fricatives in duration and assimilatory devoicing. *Journal of Phonetics* 35: 301–320.

Ladd, D. Robert. 1996. *Intonational Phonology*. Cambridge: Cambridge University Press.

Ladd, D. Robert. 2006. Segmental anchoring of pitch movements: Autosegmental association or gestural coordination? *Rivista di linguistica* 18: 19–38.

Ladd, D. Robert. 2008. *Intonational Phonology*, 2nd edn. Cambridge: Cambridge University Press.

Ladd, D. Robert, Ineke Mennen, and Astrid Schepman. 2000. Phonological conditioning of peak alignment in rising pitch accents in Dutch. *Journal of the Acoustical Society of America* 107: 2685–2696.

Ladd, D. Robert, Astrid Schepman, Laurence White, Louise M. Quarmby, and Rebekah Stackhouse. 2009. Structural and dialectal effects of pitch peak alignment in two varieties of British English. *Journal of Phonetics* 37: 145–161.

Ladefoged, Peter and Taehong Cho. 2001. Linking linguistic contrasts to reality: The case of VOT. In N. Gronnum and J. Rischel (eds.), *Travaux du cercle linguistique de Copenhague*, vol. 31, 212–223. Copenhagen: C.A. Reitzel.

Lehiste, Ilse. 1970. *Suprasegmentals*. Cambridge, MA: MIT Press.

Lindblom, Björn. 1968. Temporal organization of syllable production. *Speech Transmission Laboratory Quarterly Progress Status Report* 2–3: 1–5.

Lindblom, Björn. 1986. Phonetic universals in vowel systems. In J.J. Ohala and J.J. Jaeger (eds.), *Experimental Phonology*, 13–44. Orlando, FL: Academic Press.

Lindblom, Björn. 1990. Explaining phonetic variation: A sketch of the H and H theory. In W.J. Hardcastle and A. Marchal (eds.), *Speech Production and Speech Modeling*, 403–440. Dordrecht: Kluwer Academic.

Lisker, Leigh. 1974. On "explaining" vowel duration variation. *Glossa* 8: 233–246.

Maddieson, Ian. 1997. Phonetic universals. In J. Laver and W.J. Hardcastle (eds.), *The Handbook of Phonetic Science*, 619–639. Oxford: Blackwell.

Maddieson, Ian and Jack Gandour. 1977. Vowel length before aspirated consonants. *Indiana Linguistics* 38: 6–11.

Mücke, Doris, Martine Grice, and Taehong Cho. 2014. More than a magic moment: Paving the way for dynamics of articulation and prosodic structure. *Journal of Phonetics* 44: 1–7.

Mücke, Doris, Martine Grice, Johannes Becker, and Anne Hermes. 2009. Sources of variation in tonal alignment: Evidence from acoustic and kinematic data. *Journal of Phonetics* 37(3): 321–338.

Nakai, Satsuki, Sari Kunnari, Alice Turk, Kari Suomi, and Riikka Ylitalo. 2008. Utterance-final lengthening and quantity in Northern Finnish. *Journal of Phonetics* 37: 39–45.

Onaka, Akiko. 2003. Domain-initial strengthening in Japanese: An acoustic and articulatory study. In *Proceedings of the 15th International Congress of Phonetic Sciences, Barcelona, Spain*, 2091–2094.

Onaka, Akiko, Catherine Watson, Sallyanne Palethorpe, and Jonathan Harrington. 2003. An acoustic analysis of domain-initial strengthening effect in Japanese. In S. Palethorpe and M. Tabain (eds.), *Proceedings of the 6th International Seminar on Speech Production*, Sydney, 201–206.

Peterson, Gordon E. and Ilse Lehiste. 1960. Duration of syllable nuclei in English. *Journal of the Acoustical Society of America* 32(6): 693–703.

Pierrehumbert, Janet. 1979. The perception of fundamental frequency declination. *Journal of the Acoustical Society of America* 66: 363–369.

Pierrehumbert, Janet. 1980. The phonology and phonetics of English intonation. PhD dissertation, MIT.

Pierrehumbert, Janet and Mary Beckman. 1988. *Japanese Tone Structure*. Cambridge, MA: MIT Press.

Pierrehumbert, Janet and David Talkin. 1992. Lenition of /h/ and glottal stop. *Papers in Laboratory Phonology* 2: 90–117.

Prieto, Pilar and Francisco Torreira. 2007. The segmental anchoring hypothesis revisited: Syllable structure and speech rate effects on peak timing in Spanish. *Journal of Phonetics* 35: 473–500.

Saltzman, Elliot. 1995. Intergestural timing in speech production: Data and modeling. In *Proceedings of the XIIIth International Congress of Phonetic Sciences*, vol. 2, 84–91.

Saltzman, Elliot and Kevin G. Munhall. 1989. A dynamical approach to gestural patterning in speech production. *Ecological Psychology* 1: 333–382.

Schepman, Astrid, Robin Lickley, and D. Robert Ladd. 2006. Effects of vowel length and "right context" on the alignment of Dutch nuclear accents. *Journal of Phonetics* 34: 1–28.

Selkirk, Elisabeth. 1984. *Phonology and Syntax: The Relation Between Sound and Structure*. Cambridge, MA: MIT Press.

Selkirk, Elisabeth. 1995. Sentence prosody: Intonation, stress, and phrasing. In J.A. Goldsmith (ed.), *The Handbook of Phonological Theory*, 550–569. Oxford: Blackwell.

Shadle, Christine H. 1997. The aerodynamics of speech. In W.J. Hardcastle and J. Laver (eds.), *The Handbook of Phonetic Sciences*, 33–64. Oxford: Blackwell.

Shattuck-Hufnagel, Stefanie and Alice E. Turk. 1996. A prosody tutorial for investigators of auditory sentence processing. *Journal of Psycholinguistic Research* 25(2): 193–247.

Shepherd, Michael A. 2008. The scope and effects of preboundary prosodic lengthening in Japanese. *USC Working Papers in Linguistics* 4: 1–14.

Solé, María-Josep. 2007. Controlled and mechanical properties in speech. In M.J. Solé, P.S. Beddor, and M. Ohala (eds.), *Experimental Approaches to Phonology*, 302–321. Oxford: Oxford University Press.

Solé, Maria-Josep and John Ohala. 2010. What is and what is not under the control of the speaker: Intrinsic vowel duration. *Laboratory Phonology* 10: 607–655.

Straka, Georges. 1963. La division de sons du langage en voyelles et consonnes peut-elle être justifiée? *Travaux de linguistique et de littérature, Université de Strasbourg* 1: 17–99.

Tabain, Marija. 2003. Effects of prosodic boundary on /aC/ sequences: Articulatory results. *Journal of the Acoustical Society of America* 113: 2834–2849.

Turk, Alice E. and Stefanie Shattuck-Hufnagel. 2007. Multiple targets of phrase-final lengthening in American English words. *Journal of Phonetics* 35(4): 445–472.

Tyler, Michael D. and Anne Cutler. 2009. Cross-language differences in cue use for segmentation. *Journal of the Acoustical Society of America* 126: 367–376.

Vayra, Mario and Carol Fowler. 1992. Declination of supralaryngeal gestures in spoken Italian. *Phonetica* 49: 48–60.

Westbury, J. and P. Keating. 1980. Central representation of vowel duration. *Journal of the Acoustical Society of America* 67 (Suppl. 1): S37(A).

Wightman, Colin W., Stefanie Shattuck-Hufnagel, Mari Ostendorf, and Patti J. Price. 1992. Segmental durations in the vicinity of prosodic phrase boundaries. *Journal of the Acoustical Society of America* 91: 1707–1717.

23 Cross-Language Differences in Acquisition

JAN R. EDWARDS, MARY E. BECKMAN, AND BENJAMIN MUNSON

Pour l'étude du langage enfantin en général, une observation brute, même très complète, a encore un inconvénient. Elle ne suffit pas à distinguer clairement les particularités de l'enfant observé. L'individualité, chez l'adulte, n'affecte pas le système linguistique, qui est imposé socialement; elle se réfugie dans l'équilibre particulier des ressource du lexique, la manière d'utiliser les possibilités de la phrase, le débit, la mimique, rarement dans certains détails de l'articulation; elle se marque surtout au choix des choses dites. Chez l'enfant non encore adapté au langage normal, tout contient une part d'individuel, depuis l'articulation de chaque son du langage jusqu'au sens donné aux mots. Un fait observé chez l'enfant n'est bien utilisable pour le linguiste d'une part, le psychologue de l'autre, que si la part originale de l'individu peut y être délimitée, ce qui ne se réalise bien que par des comparaisons nombreuses. Ceci fait désirer, malgré toutes les difficultés, que les observations sur les enfants se multiplient en toutes langues, et doit encourager les linguistes et les amateurs de linguistique à observer les enfants – particulier leurs enfants – même lorsqu'ils ne peuvent pas le faire complètement. (Cohen 1925: 111)

[For studying child language in general, a single set of raw observations, no matter how thorough, still has a drawback. It is not sufficient for clearly distinguishing the idiosyncrasies of the child observed. Individuality, in an adult, does not affect the linguistic system, which is imposed socially; it retreats to the particular balance among lexical resources, the way in which one uses possible sentences, rate, gesture, and rarely in certain details of articulation; it is marked above all in the choice of what is said. In the child not yet adapted to language norms, everything contains an element of individuality, from the articulation of each sound of the language to the meaning assigned to words. A fact observed in a child can only be used by the linguist on the one hand or by the psychologist on the other, if the part that is unique to the individual can be delimited, which is something that can be accomplished only by making many comparisons. This makes it desirable, despite the difficulties, *for observations of children to be multiplied in all languages, and it should encourage linguists and amateur linguists to observe children – particularly their own children – even if they cannot do so thoroughly.]*

23.1 Introduction[1]

Researchers have long been interested in comparing phonological acquisition across children learning different first languages (e.g., Cohen 1925; Locke 1983). Although children with typical phonological development can follow variable paths as their early vocalizations converge to the norms of their speech community (e.g., Ferguson 1979; Vihman 1993), they do begin learning to talk with the same constraints on production and perception, regardless of what language (or languages) to which they are exposed. In order to produce speech that is intelligible to other members of their speech community, children must acquire progressively more fine-grained phonetic control. Certain speech sound contrasts are more difficult than others (e.g., the /s/:/ʃ/ contrast requires more fine-grained motor control than the /p/:/m/ contrast), so researchers have hypothesized that early-acquired contrasts generally are ones that place relatively lesser demands on the talker/listener, while late-acquired contrasts place relatively greater ones.

Such reasoning has led researchers to propose that similarities in phonological acquisition across children learning different first languages should tell us something about pan-species constraints on what kinds of sound system are easiest to maintain in language transmission. In his influential monograph on child language, aphasia, and phonological universals, Jakobson (1941) proposed specific phonetic bases for generalizations that had been noted in the literature to that time (e.g., by Jespersen 1922). While our explanations have evolved considerably since then, many of the generalizations still stand. For example, across languages, children generally acquire stops and nasals before fricatives and liquids, and voiceless unaspirated stops before both voiceless aspirated stops and prevoiced stops. Moreover, these earlier acquired sound types also are ones that tend to occur in the phoneme inventories of more languages (e.g., Lindblom and Maddieson 1988).

More recently, a growing number of differences in phonological acquisition across languages have also been identified. For example, in a cross-language longitudinal study of consonants transcribed in babbling and early words, de Boysson-Bardies and Vihman (1991) found a dominance of labial sounds at the earliest recording sessions for the French- and English-learning children, but a dominance of lingual sounds for the Japanese- and Swedish-learning children. Moreover, there was a subsequent decrease in labials relative to linguals (particularly dentals) in the productions of the English-learning children, but not in the French-learning children. Examples of cross-language differences for later-acquired sounds include the earlier acquisition of the affricate /ts/ in Cantonese relative to Greek, the earlier acquisition of the non-sibilant fricative /θ/ in Greek relative to English (Edwards and Beckman 2008a), and the earlier acquisition of

/s/ in English relative to Japanese (Li, Edwards, and Beckman 2009). Some of these differences are context specific. For example, /t/ is generally more accurate than /tʃ/ in both English- and Japanese-speaking toddlers, but for Japanese children, /t/ is less accurate than /tʃ/ in the context of /i/ (Edwards and Beckman 2008a).

Presumably, these cross-linguistic differences must be attributed to language-specific factors, such as differences in phoneme frequency in the earliest words that children learn or in the lexicon in general. Thus, Vihman et al. (1994) related the early dominance of labials in French-speaking children and of dentals in Swedish-speaking children to the differences in counts of labial-initial versus dental-initial content words in speech directed to the children. Similarly, Edwards and Beckman (2008a) related the earlier acquisition of /ts/ in Cantonese relative to Greek to the much higher type frequency of this affricate in the Cantonese lexicon as compared to Greek (/ts/ is almost as frequent as /t/ in Cantonese, while it is a very low-frequency sound in Greek). The same explanation holds for the earlier acquisition of /θ/ in Greek relative to English.

Differences in consonant-vowel (CV) sequence frequency can also help to explain differences in accuracy within and across languages. For example, Edwards and Beckman (2008a) relate the differences between /ti/ and /tʃi/ for Japanese- versus English-speaking children to the extremely low type frequency of /ti/ in Japanese. Similarly, Monnin et al. (2011) examined acquisition of /t/ and /k/ in different vowel contexts by children acquiring French and Drehu, an Austronesian language spoken in New Caledonia. They found that child speakers of both languages produced /k/ more accurately before /u/ than before /i/, in keeping with the predictions of the Frame/Content Theory developed by MacNeilage and colleagues (Davis, MacNeilage and Matyear 2002; other earlier literature reviewed in MacNeilage, this volume, Chapter 16). However, contra the predictions of Frame/Content Theory, the French-speaking children (but not the Drehu-speaking children) also produced /t/ more accurately before /u/ than before /i/, a difference that Monnin and colleagues relate to the high frequency of /tu/ relative to /ti/ in French.

This approach of looking for differences in phoneme frequency and phoneme sequence frequency to explain exceptions to developmental universals was our primary focus when we began the παιδολογος (paidologos) project in 2003. This project was a systematic, large-scale cross-language comparison of accuracy in productions of lingual obstruents by children from 2 to 5 years (approximately 100 children in each language) elicited using a picture-prompted auditory word repetition task (Edwards and Beckman 2008b). The comparison began with recordings of children acquiring Cantonese, English, Greek, or Japanese and has been extended in collaboration with other researchers to Korean, two varieties of Mandarin Chinese, Taiwanese, two varieties of French, and Drehu. We were interested in identifying language-specific differences in phonological acquisition that were related to differences in phoneme frequency or phoneme sequence frequency across languages.

Differences in frequency, however, cannot explain all of the cross-linguistic differences that we investigated. For example, they cannot account for the later acquisition of /s/ relative to /ʃ/ in Japanese but not in English, as /s/ is a higher-frequency sound than /ʃ/ in both languages. A secondary focus, therefore, was to look also at finer-grained phonetic differences in how the sounds are produced by adult speakers and how children's immature productions are assimilated to the community norms for the phonetic cues for each relevant contrast (Beckman, Yoneyama, and Edwards 2003). One of the most important lessons that we learned from the παιδολογος project is that we would have missed a great deal of what was interesting in our data if we had focused only on cross-linguistic differences in order of phoneme acquisition assessed using phonetic transcriptions, and explanations that focused solely on differences in phoneme frequency across languages.

In this chapter, we will present data from the παιδολογος project and from other cross-language studies to illustrate three important reasons why studies that rely solely on phonetic transcription as data and cross-linguistic frequency differences as explanations are overly simplistic. The first reason is that cross-linguistic differences in production begin very early in life, well before children produce speech sounds correctly. The second reason is that there is daunting cross-linguistic variation in what is ostensibly the "same" sound, which affects not just details of production but also the community-specific norms for what can be perceived as a "correct" production of the sound. This makes it difficult to generalize about speech sound acquisition across languages when studies use native speaker transcriptions as the sole measure of speech-sound acquisition. Finally, there is more to phonological development than learning to produce speech sounds that adults will recognize in terms of the lexical contrasts of the language. Children also need to acquire sociophonetic competence if they are to be able to quickly and accurately parse the variation they hear, as well as to produce the subtle differences that convey different speaker attributes, such as gender, socioeconomic status, and ethnicity, among others.

23.2 When do cross-language differences in production begin?

It is by now well established that there are extensive cross-linguistic differences in fine phonetic detail in adult speech. That is, sounds that are transcribed with the same phonetic symbol in cross-language comparisons of phoneme inventories and phonotactics are not the same when examined using finer-grained analysis tools than IPA transcription. For example, the vowel transcribed as /i/ is not as high and front in American English or Dutch as it is in German, Swedish, or Danish, and the vowel transcribed as /u/ is not as back in American English as it in German or French (e.g., Disner 1983; Flege 1987). The voicing contrast in Hungarian, Dutch, Polish, French, and Swedish differentiates stops with short-lag voice onset time (VOT) from stops with voicing lead, even in word-initial position, whereas the "same" contrast in German and English differentiates stops with long-lag VOT from stops with short-lag VOT (e.g., Lisker and Abramson 1964; Keating 1984; Flege 1987; Stoel-Gammon, Williams, and Buder 1994). The consonants transcribed as /t/ and /d/ are dental and typically laminal in French (Dart 1998) or Swedish (Stoel-Gammon et al. 1994), but alveolar and typically apical in American English (Dart 1998), and the consonants transcribed as /ʈ/ and /ɖ/ in Hindi are not nearly so retroflex as the "same" sounds in Tamil or Telegu (Ladefoged and Bhaskararao 1983). Similarly, although both English and Japanese have a sibilant fricative contrast, /s/ in English is alveolar and often apical (Dart 1998) and /ʃ/ also is apical and typically rounded, while /s/ in Japanese is dental and typically laminal and /ʃ/ is an alveolopalatal produced with spread lips (Toda and Honda 2003).

23.2.1 Early differences

These cross-linguistic differences are known to influence early infant speech perception (e.g., Kuhl et al. 1992 for Swedish versus English /i/, Mattock et al. 2010 for French versus English VOT), and a growing literature suggests that language-specific phonetic detail is acquired quite early in production as well. For example, Stoel-Gammon et al. (1994) found systematic cross-linguistic differences in fine phonetic detail of productions of /t/ by a sample of 10 Swedish- and 10 American-English-speaking 30-month-old children. They found that the children already were producing language-specific differences in VOT, burst intensity, and burst spectral diffuseness in their /t/ productions, measures that systematically differentiated between the unaspirated laminal dental /t/ of Swedish productions and the aspirated apical alveolar /t/ of English productions by a control group of 20 adults (10 per language). We found similar results when comparing peak frequencies for stop burst spectra in productions of /k/ (and /kʲ/) across languages. In adult productions, the dorsal stops of English are less palatalized (less "acute") before front vowels or /j/ and less rounded and backed (less "grave") before /u/ and /o/ by comparison to the "same" sounds of Greek, and we observed this cross-language difference in productions by English- and Greek-speaking children as young as 24 months (Arbisi-Kelm et al. 2009).

Stoel-Gammon and colleagues looked at 30-month-old children because /t/ is acquired by that age by the majority of typically developing children in both languages, and the question that they were asking was, "Do children begin by 'hitting the right target' for their language, or do they share some default place of articulation and then acquire the language-specific target with increased exposure to the language and practice" (1994: 150). The results for dorsal stops in the παιδολογος project are noteworthy, then, because /k/ is typically acquired somewhat later than /t/ by English-speaking children, and "fronting" errors (transcribed [t] for /k/ substitutions) are not unusual in the speech of typically developing 24-month-olds. Moreover, while /k/ before back vowels is error free in productions by Greek-speaking children at an age when some English-speaking ones make [t] for /k/ substitutions in that context, "fronting" errors for the palatalized allophone are not uncommon in either group at this age. In other words, the evidence is against any "unmarked" universal default place for these "young" consonants. Even before the variable productions of children within a speech community converge on a pattern that reliably differentiates /k/ from /t/, the "undifferentiated lingual gesture" (Gibbon 1999) is one that is aimed toward "the right target" for the ambient speech community.

23.2.2 Fricative place contrasts

For "older" consonants that tend to be acquired late across languages as well, we often found language-specific patterns in production before children had reliably mastered a particular contrast, that is, before productions were identified consistently as accurate by native speaker/transcribers. For example, Li (2008) observed systematic cross-linguistic differences between English and Japanese /ʃ/ and /s/ productions, even by the 2-year-olds. At this age, transcribed accuracy rates were below 50% for both fricatives for both languages, and they were especially low for Japanese, where fewer than 10% of /s/ targets and only 20% of /ʃ/ targets were transcribed as correct. Figure 23.1 shows mean values for three acoustic measures that differentiate /s/ from /ʃ/ in adult productions plotted against age for English and Japanese-acquiring children. The distribution of means for /s/ and /ʃ/ for most of the youngest children show considerable overlap in both English and Japanese. Note, however, that the region of overlap differs between the two languages; the means for the Japanese-speaking children have lower (more /ʃ/-like) centroid frequencies whereas means for the English-speaking children have higher (more /s/-like) values. That is, we see differences between 2-year-old English and Japanese speakers for these two sibilant fricatives, even though the majority of productions of both sounds were transcribed as incorrect by the native-speaker transcribers.

This difference in fine phonetic detail is reflected also in the transcribed substitution patterns (Li 2008: Tables 6.2 and 6.3). For English-learning children, the most frequently transcribed substitutions were "fronting" errors: [s] for /ʃ/ and [θ] for /s/. For Japanese-learning children, they were "palatalization" and "stopping" errors: [ç] for /s/ and [tç] for /ʃ/. The only one of these patterns that is predicted by a frequency difference between the target consonant and the transcribed substitution is the [s] for /ʃ/ substitution transcribed for the English-learning children. A question that naturally arises, then, is how to explain such differences.

In an earlier paper (Beckman et al. 2003), we suggested that the different accuracy rates and stereotypical error patterns might be related to two other differences between the two languages. First, there is a difference in lingual fricative phoneme inventory. In English, /s/ and /ʃ/ contrast with dental /θ/, whereas in Japanese, they contrast with palatal /ç/. Second, there are different sequential constraints. In particular, although /s/ in Japanese is more frequent than /ʃ/ overall, it is restricted to the contexts of following back vowels /a/, /o/, /u/, and also /e/ (which has the lowest type frequency of the five vowels). In contrast, /ʃ/ occurs very frequently before /i/, less frequently before /a/, /o/, and /u/, and before /e/ in only a small number of words such as /ʃeriː/ "sherry" which are unlikely to be among the words that young children learn. In English, on the other hand, /s/ and /ʃ/ have no such dependencies. Rather, both sibilants are attested

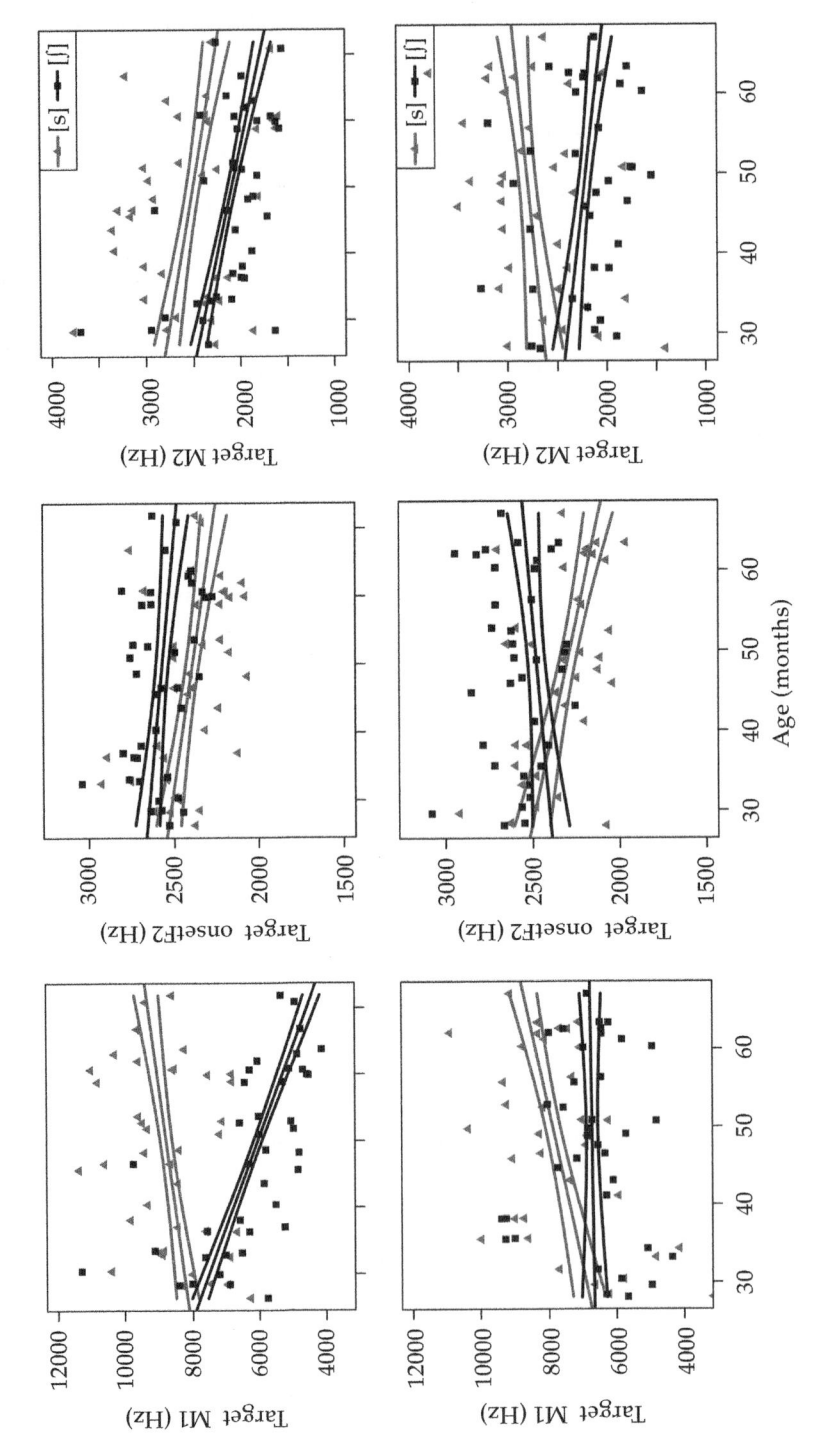

Figure 23.1 Child-by-child mean values for centroid frequency in a spectrum taken from the middle of the frication interval, F2 frequency at the onset of the vowel, and standard deviation for the fricative spectrum in productions of /s/ (triangles and gray regression lines) and of /ʃ/ (squares and black regression lines) plotted against age in months for English-speaking (top plots) and Japanese-speaking (bottom plots) children. Adapted from Li (2008: Figure 6.3), with permission.

before all of the many more vowels of English. We further noted that there are many more English words beginning with a lingual obstruent followed by a front vowel than a lingual obstruent before a back vowel. We speculated (Beckman et al. 2003: 26) that these facts "might conspire to induce a difference in 'basis of articulation' (Heffner, 1950) between the two languages."

More recently, the advent of easier-to-obtain articulatory measures has begun to provide instrumental support for this long-standing idea of a "basis of articulation" or "articulatory setting" (Honikman 1964) specific to each target language (see review of this concept in Laver 1978). Wilson and colleagues (Wilson 2006; Wilson, Horiguchi and Gick 2007) use Ultrasound in combination with Optotrack to examine tongue and lip postures during inter-sentence pauses. They note consistently higher tongue tip postures for English speakers relative to both French and Japanese speakers. Following our earlier speculation, we wonder whether this "high front" articulatory setting for English might be related to the very high (type and token) frequencies for front vowels in the language. In an early cross-language comparison of formant frequencies measured in babbling productions by 10-month-olds, de Boysson-Bardies et al. (1989) found a concentration of values in the high-front region for English-learning infants, by comparison to Arabic-, French-, and Cantonese-learning infants. They related the differences in formant distributions to cross-language differences in vowel token frequencies in running speech. The difference between English- and French-learning 10-month-olds was replicated in a cross-sectional study by Rvachew et al. (2006). That is, Rvachew and colleagues found that 10-month-olds had a smaller vowel space than older infants for both languages, but centered differently. Plots of mean values across ages showed a developmental expansion of the vowel space in both languages, but in different dimensions, in keeping with the different starting points. If the fine-grained phonetic differences for sibilant fricative place in English- versus Japanese-learning children are related to a difference in habitual tongue posture that begins to be set in place in preverbal babbling, we might expect to see cross-language differences in babbling for features that define other late contrasts as well.

23.2.3 *Stop voicing contrasts*

Indeed, other researchers have observed language-specific fine phonetic detail for some consonant sounds much earlier than 24 months, in vocalizations of infants before they have begun to produce any words at all. For example, Whalen, Levitt, and Goldstein (2007) examined VOT in initial stops in babbled utterances of French- and English-acquiring 9- and 12-month-old infants. They found that the French-learning infants produced a much higher proportion of initial stops with voicing lead than did the English-learning infants. This is despite the fact that French word-initial prevoiced stop consonants are not transcribed as being produced correctly until much later in word productions. That is, at 30 months (an age when English-speaking children begin to have good control of the contrast between aspirated /p, t, k/ and unaspirated /b, d, g/ in their language), French-speaking children are transcribed as either substituting the voiceless stop or as producing "filler" syllables – preceding homorganic nasals or vowels "that are easily perceived as one of the indefinite articles *un* or *une*" by the transcriber (Allen 1985: 41).

Kewley-Port and Preston (1974) also found very few prevoiced stops in their longitudinal studies of English-learning children (see also Macken and Barton 1980), and their explanation for this pattern predicts the early "substitution" of voiceless unaspirated stops for prevoiced stops in French. The build-up of oral air pressure during stop closure inhibits voicing even when the vocal folds are adducted, so producing truly voiced stops (i.e., with audible voicing during the oral constriction) requires the child to perform other maneuvers, such as expanding the pharynx or making a "leaky" naso-pharyngeal closure to allow the oral air pressure to vent. The French children's production of filler syllables, then, seems to be a reflex of the latter maneuver, which is then interpreted (and reinforced) as a meaningful morpheme where appropriate, thus explaining the early mastery of determiners by French-learning children (see Demuth and Tremblay 2008 and literature reviewed there).

In the παιδολογος data, we found two more patterns in the acquisition of the voicing contrast in languages that have been described as being like French in contrasting "true" voiced stops with voiceless unaspirated stops. Word-initial voiced stops produced by the Greek-speaking children systematically showed pronounced prevoicing, and unlike in French, even the 24-month-old children were transcribed as making virtually no voicing errors. By contrast, very few of the voiced stops produced by the Japanese-speaking children showed any prevoicing, and there were many instances of transcribed substitutions of [t] for target /d/ and [k] for /g/. Kong, Beckman, and Edwards (2012) explain the difference between the Greek and Japanese patterns in terms of the different community norms, which are complicated because of sound changes in progress in both communities.

Specifically, in native Greek words, the voiced stops developed fairly recently from nasal-plosive clusters (see, e.g., Arvaniti and Joseph 2004), and in the standard variety today, voiced stops show voicing lead, as in French, but they differ from French in that they can be pronounced with more or less strong prenasalization (Arvaniti and Joseph 2000). Kong and colleagues developed a measure of degree of nasal venting, based on a study by Burton, Blumstein, and Stevens (1992). By this measure, many adult productions showed evidence of some nasal venting, and the children's productions showed even more clear signs of nasal venting to produce long voicing lead. Because prenasalized stops are an accepted allophonic variant, when Greek-learning children use nasal venting, they are not transcribed as producing a preceding indefinite article as the French-acquiring children are.

In Tokyo Japanese also, there are at least two variant realizations of the contrast, due to a sound change in progress (Takada 2011). For some speakers, particularly male and older adult speakers, it is a contrast between prevoiced and short-lag stops. However, for younger female adult speakers, many voiced stops have short-lag VOT values and the voiceless stops have VOT values intermediate between short- and long-lag VOT values (as noted also by Riney et al. 2007). Note that this sound change is distinct from the better-known older sound change, whereby [ŋ] is no longer produced as an allophone of /g/ by most Tokyo Japanese speakers today. The older [ŋ]~[g] alternation may explain why Yasuda (1970) noted virtually no errors for /g/ in the 3-year-old children she studied, in marked contrast to the high error rates for /g/ and /d/ in Kong et al. (2012). Presumably, children must be learning to control other cues in addition to VOT in order to make the voicing contrast today. Kong and colleagues suggest that this presumed greater complexity might explain why the Japanese-learning children in the παιδολογος database were transcribed as making more voicing errors than either the Greek- or the English-learning children.

In Seoul Korean, another language that had traditionally been described as contrasting short-lag and intermediate-lag VOT values, one cue to this contrast is a difference between modal and breathy voice, as noted by Kong and colleagues (Kong, Beckman, and Edwards 2011; Holliday and Kong 2011) among others. One measure of breathy voice quality is the difference in power between the first and second harmonic (H1-H2), a measure that has been correlated with contrastive breathy voice in many languages (e.g., Miller 2007 for Ju | 'hoansi vowels and consonants, Gordon and Ladefoged 2000 for a review of earlier studies for other languages with contrastive breathy voice on vowels or consonants). Kong et al. (2012) found that H1-H2 values were systematically higher for voiceless than for voiced stops produced by adult Japanese speakers. However, they also found this to be true for productions by adult English speakers. Therefore, in order to assess whether there are fine-grained phonetic differences between Japanese and English in the use of voice quality, and to see whether these differences might explain the later acquisition of the voicing contrast in Japanese-learning children relative to English-learning children, it is necessary to adopt more sensitive behavioral measures of the community norms. We describe these measures in the next section.

23.3 Using perception tasks to assess differences in community norms

As the results reviewed in the previous section make clear, when children's productions are examined using the same acoustic measures that have been applied in documenting the extent of differences in adult productions, no exact comparisons are possible. Even when the two languages being compared have ostensibly the "same" inventory (e.g., a two-way contrast in sibilant fricative place or a two-way contrast between prevoiced and voiceless stops) the children are never really acquiring the "same" sounds. This means that, in order to assess perceived production accuracy relative to the community norms, we also need to supplement accuracy as gauged by the phonetic symbol assigned by a transcriber with finer-grained measures. Recently child language researchers have begun to develop such measures by designing perception tasks to elicit accuracy judgments for children's productions of target sounds from samples of naïve listeners from each target community.

For example, Li et al. (2011) extracted CV stimuli from a large subset of the same productions of English and Japanese words beginning with /ʃ/ and /s/ examined in Li et al. (2009). Li and colleagues presented these stimuli (N = 200 for each language) twice, in two different blocks, to 19 English-speaking listeners (tested in Minneapolis) and 20 Japanese-speaking listeners (tested in Tokyo). In one block, listeners said whether a stimulus was an acceptable production of /ʃ/ and, in the other, whether it was an acceptable production of /s/. The target consonant was defined in the instructions at the beginning of the block in terms of orthographic categories appropriate for the language and illustrated with sample words, such as *shape* for the "sh" category for the English-speaking listeners and さる /saru/ "monkey" for the "さ行" ("s") category for the Japanese. The data were analyzed separately by both listener and speaker language. A token was judged to be classified as /ʃ/ if 70% or more of the listeners answered "yes" in the "sh" block and "no" in the "s" block. Conversely, it was judged to be /s/ if 70% of the listeners answered "yes" in the "s" block and "no" in the "sh" block. The stimuli were plotted in a two-dimensional space defined by the centroid frequency of a spectrum taken over the middle 40 ms of the fricative (as in the left panels in Figure 23.1) and the F2 frequency of the following vowel at its onset (as in the middle panels of Figure 23.1). Li et al. (2009) had shown earlier that the first of these measures discriminates between the two fricatives in productions by those English-speaking children who were transcribed by the English-speaker phonetician as having a contrast, and that the two measures together discriminate between the two fricatives in productions by those Japanese-speaking children who were transcribed by the Japanese phonetician as having a contrast. In the naïve English-speaking listeners' classifications of the children's productions in the Li et al. (2011) study, the /s/ stimuli occupied a larger area in this space than the /ʃ/ stimuli. For the Japanese-speaking listeners, the relationship was the opposite: the /ʃ/ space was larger than the /s/ space. Li and colleagues argue that these cross-linguistic differences in perception might be part of the explanation for the cross-linguistic differences in acquisition. When faced with a sound intermediate between /s/ and /ʃ/, Japanese listeners are more apt to call it "sh" while English-speaking listeners are more apt to call it "s."

An even more sensitive measure can be obtained by asking listeners to provide a rating along a continuous visual analog scale (VAS, Massaro and Cohen 1983), instead of a simple yes/no response. Kong et al. (2012) used this method to elicit goodness ratings for CV stimuli extracted from English- and Japanese-speaking children's productions of words beginning with /t/, /k/ versus /d/, /g/. They analyzed the responses by building models that regressed the ratings against VOT alone, or against VOT and either fundamental frequency or H1-H2 (after transforming the acoustic measures into z-scores to be able to compare the regression coefficients directly). Adding H1-H2 values to a model that differentiated between voiced and voiceless stops significantly improved the model fit for the productions of Japanese- but not English-speaking adults. Adding H1-H2 values to the model significantly improved the model fit for the productions of Japanese- but not English-speaking children. These results suggest that children learning Japanese must learn to control voice quality in addition to VOT in order to be recognized as making a distinction between voiced and voiceless stops by adults in the ambient speech community.

An added advantage of the VAS design is that it elicits a continuous response that is simultaneously listener-specific and stimulus-specific. This means that it can be used in combination with other responses, to begin to understand the social dynamics of the input that children receive during acquisition. For example, Julien and Munson (2012) elicited productions of target English words beginning with /s/ versus /ʃ/ in both a casual and a clear speech style from 22 English speakers, to provide a baseline measure of each speaker's range for the hypoarticulation/hyperarticulation continuum. The same subjects then participated in a "listen-rate-say" task, in which they listened to CV stimuli extracted from English-speaking children's productions of these words, rated the initial sound of each stimulus on a VAS scale from "s" to "sh," and then said the target word as a model for the child. The results suggest that English-speaking adults in this particular speech community, at least, hyperarticulate speech in response to listening to a child's production that they perceive to be inaccurate.

More recently, we have begun to use VAS ratings also to explore cross-linguistic differences in vowel perception, as a first step in building models of how pre-verbal infants might use responses from adults in the ambient community in the "imitation game" (de Boer 2000; Plummer 2014). Figure 23.2 illustrates the kinds of difference that we are finding, showing a small part of the results from an experiment in which adult native speakers of Cantonese (N = 15), English (N = 21), Greek (N = 20), Japanese (N = 21), and Korean (N = 20) categorized 6 sets of 38 synthetic vowels created with an articulatory synthesizer (Boë and Maeda 1997) to simulate the vocal tract and voice source of a very young infant (in the block shown in the figure), or of a 2-year-old, 4-year-old, or 10-year-old child, or of a 16-year-old or 21-year-old man (see Plummer et al. 2013 for more complete results). Cantonese- and English-speaking listeners categorized each stimulus by clicking on any of 11 keywords representing the monophthongal vowels in each language (e.g., Cantonese 歡 /fun/ and English *soup* /sup/ for the "shared" phoneme /u/). Listeners for the other languages categorized by clicking on a symbol or symbol string that unambiguously represented a (short monophthongal) vowel in isolation (e.g., Korean 우, Japanese う, Greek ου for the "shared" phoneme /u/), choosing among 7 vowels (Korean-speaking listeners) or among 5 vowels (Greek- and Japanese-speaking listeners).

The first panel of Figure 23.2 shows the location in the vowel formants space of the stimuli simulating infant productions (see Ménard et al. 2009 for further details). The remaining panels of the figure show some of the categorization results, separately by adult listener language. In each, the size of the symbol is proportional to the percentage of listeners for that language who categorized the stimulus as /u/. Consider first the results for the adult Japanese listeners. Stimuli in the high-mid portion of the vowel space were just as likely to be identified as う as stimuli in the high-back portion. This is consistent with the description of the Japanese /u/ as an unrounded [ɯ]. Contrast this pattern with the stimuli labeled *soup* in English and ου in Greek. Both English and Greek have only two high vowels, /i/ and /u/, and adult listeners in both of these languages labeled a large

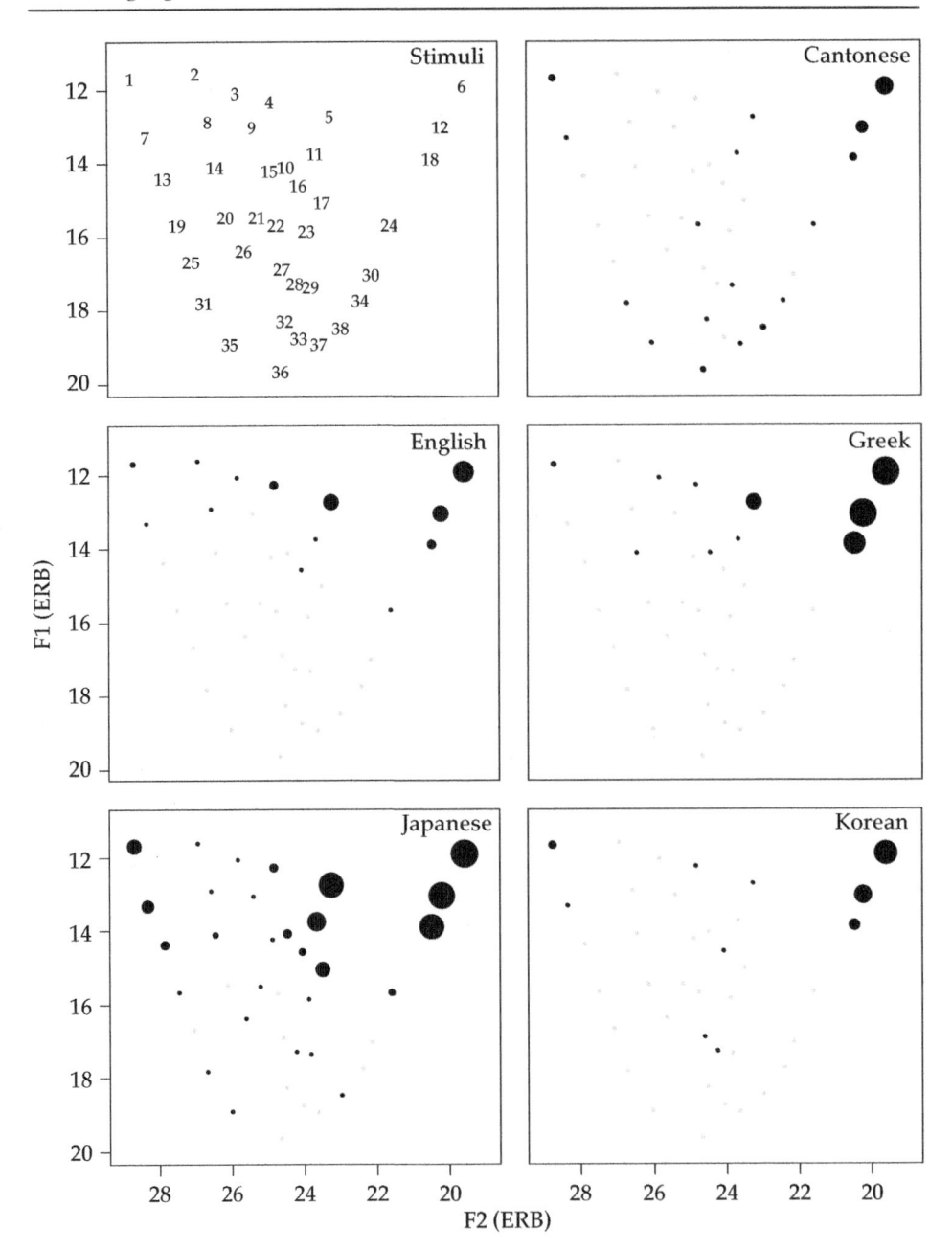

Figure 23.2 Stimuli synthesized with an articulatory synthesizer scaled to represent an infant's vocal tract (top left) and proportion of listeners who identified each one as /u/ in a cross-language vowel perception experiment.

set of non-front high vowels as /u/, albeit not as many as the Japanese did. (The same pattern held for the Texas dialect English-speaking listeners' responses to these stimuli in Ménard et al. 2009.) Finally, contrast both patterns to the very few stimuli that were labeled as 우 by the Korean- or as 歡 by the adult Cantonese-speaking listeners. Korean has three high vowels, /i/, /i/, and /u/. Many of the stimuli that English, Greek, and Japanese listeners identified as /u/ (i.e., responding with *soup*, ου, or う) were identified as /i/ by adult speakers of Korean. Cantonese has a different set of three high vowels, /i/, /y/, and /u/. Moreover, the type frequency of /u/ in Cantonese is lower than that of many of the other languages because of a phonotactic prohibition against /u/ after any of the dental consonants /t, tʰ, s, ts, tsʰ, n, l/. Presumably, these two factors are responsible for Cantonese speakers' unwillingness to identify many synthesized vowels as /u/. (The same pattern holds for the adult French-speaking listeners' responses to the similar synthetic stimuli in Ménard, Schwartz, and Boë 2004, and it mirrors the differences between the English- versus French-dominant listeners' categorization of the natural vowel tokens in Rvachew et al. 2008: Figure 3.) These findings emphasize that categories such as /u/ can be associated with very different patterns of perception across languages that ostensibly share this phoneme.

Cross-linguistic differences in perception like those described in the previous paragraph may underlie some cross-linguistic differences in the acquisition of speech sounds. For a hypothetical illustration of how cross-linguistic differences in perception might influence acquisition, consider children's acquisition of the vowel /u/. Imagine that a child were saying a word such as Cantonese /kʰu:⁵⁵ŋa:²¹/ "braces," English *cougar*, French /kuto/ "knife," Greek /kukla/ "doll," Japanese /kutsu/ "shoes," or Korean /kutu/ "shoes," and produced a sound in the high central region of the vowel space – something near to stimulus number 5 – for the vowel in the first syllable of the word. If this child were acquiring English, Greek, or Japanese, the token might well be recognized as a correct token of /u/. If this same child were acquiring Cantonese, French, or Korean, the very same token would not be recognized as correct. Rvachew et al. (2008) present acoustic and perceptual evidence that /u/ is acquired earlier in English than in French. If we were to find, similarly, that /u/ is acquired earlier in Greek and Japanese than it is in Cantonese and Korean, then we should consider the possibility that these apparent cross-language differences in production are due, at least in part, to cross-language differences in adults' perception of children's productions. That is, different speech community norms for carving up the acoustic-phonetic space map differently onto the distribution of sounds that children are producing.

23.4 Variation conditioned by position and by social categories

In other future applications of these methods, we plan to begin to explore the effects of cross-language differences in positional variants of more challenging contrasts, to see how these affect acquisition. For example, children who are acquiring Tokyo Japanese must not only learn to produce the contrast between /ʃi/ and /ʃu/, but they must also learn to recognize and reproduce this contrast even before voiceless stops, in words such as /ʃika/ "deer" and /ʃukudai/ "homework," where these CV sequences are often produced with no voiced interval to carry the distinct resonances of the [i] versus [ɯ] contrast, so that the vowel posture must be deduced from the effects on the frication spectrum (Beckman and Shoji 1984). Imaizumi, Hayashi, and Deguchi (1995) show that at least some adults adjust their productions of vowels in syllables such as these in talking to children, particularly to children with hearing impairment, so that there is a voiced interval to carry the vowel formants. We could use the "listen-rate-say" task to see whether comparable adjustments can be induced in adults just in case they rate a child's production as being a less acceptable production of the syllable.

Another such positional effect involves word-medial /d/ for children who are learning English or Japanese. In American English, /d/ and /t/ contrast with each other but not with [ɾ]. However, children who are learning American English master both stops in word-medial position relatively late, because most longer words that they are learning are trochees, and foot-medial position is a prosodic environment where both /t/ and /d/ are typically produced as [ɾ] (see Klein and Altman 2002 and literature reviewed there). This flap consonant is very similar to the difficult /r/ phoneme of Japanese, which is one of the last sounds to be mastered by Japanese-learning children. In word-medial position, the Japanese /r/:/d/ contrast is perceptually difficult as well, and /r/:/d/ confusions are attested even in school-age children (Otuka 2005). Children who are learning American English do not need to differentiate [ɾ] from [d] as phonemes, but they do need to learn whether words such as *Daddy* and *water* have medial /d/ or /t/, in order to be able to map from the usual variant to the "correct" hyperarticulate variant as they begin to command the distinction between casual and careful speech styles. Again, we could use the "listen-rate-say" task to see whether adult speakers in the two different speech communities behave differently in accommodating to young children's difficulties with [d] and [ɾ] in word-medial position.

The example of position-specific flapping (and neutralization of the /d/:/t/ contrast) in English drives home the point that children must amass a substantial body of knowledge about systematic sources of variation in production, and they must exploit this knowledge in real-time speech perception. One substantial source of variation relates to social categories: At least some of the variability in speech sounds occurs because the phonetic characteristics of sounds are manipulated in a way that conveys attributes about speakers. These attributes can be highly individual (i.e., distinctive pronunciations that allow people to identify a familiar talker), or they can relate to group-level characteristics, be they macro-sociological categories such as race, age, and gender, or local structures like social cliques in schools.

Researchers have begun to document how children learn to produce socially meaningful variation in language, such as the difference between the careful-speech register of American English in which medial /t/ and /d/ are differentiated and the casual-speech register in which they are neutralized to a flap. Redford and Gildersleeve-Neumann (2009), examined the production and perception of these two registers in typically developing 3- to 5-year-old children. They found that even the youngest children produced speech that adults perceived as more accurate in careful speech than in conversational speech (a result that is replicated in a perception study and accompanying acoustic analyses by Syrett and Kawahara 2014). However, the difference in rated accuracy of words produced in careful versus conversational styles was larger for adults than for 5-year-olds, and larger for 5-year-olds than for younger children. Redford and Gildersleeve-Neumann's results show that careful and casual speech styles become more distinct between ages 3 and 5, and control of the distinction continues to develop as children become adults.

Consider next the acquisition of one of the most widely studied social categories, gender. Docherty et al. (2006) show that girls acquiring the variety of English spoken in the Tyneside region of Northeast England begin to produce a gendered variant, preaspiration in medial stop consonants, sometime between 42 and 48 months of age. They also show that this gender variation is correlated with differences in the early input; mothers of girls produce the preaspirated variant more in talking to their babies relative to mothers of boys.

Another case of early socially relevant gender differentiation comes from the παιδολογος database. Li and colleagues (Li 2008; Li et al. 2008) examined the development of the three-way sibilant fricative contrast in a dialect of Dongbei (northeast) Mandarin spoken in Songyuan City. In the speech of young adults, /s/ has a higher centroid frequency than both /ɕ/ and /ʂ/, while /ʂ/ has a higher F2 onset frequency than both /s/ and /ɕ/. Sociolinguistic studies of Mandarin dialects spoken in Beijing and further north have documented the emergence of a so-called "feminine accent" variant of alveolopalatals, a systematically higher centroid frequency for /ɕ/ and /tɕ/ relative to /ʂ/ and /tʂ/ for younger women relative to older women and men (see Hu 1991; Li 2005, and even earlier literature reviewed in Li 2005). Presumably, this mimics the effect of having a smaller vocal tract and thus sounding more "feminine" (or child-like). Li examined spectral characteristics of the three Mandarin fricatives by 2-, 3-, 4-, and 5-year-old boys and girls in Songyuan. She found that the centroid frequencies of 2- and 3-year-old boys' and girls' productions of /ɕ/ and /ʂ/ were not different. However, there was a significant gender difference by fricative interaction for the centroids of 4- and 5-year-old children's productions, such that girls produced a larger difference between /ɕ/ and /ʂ/ than did boys. Li interprets this finding as potential evidence for acquisition of the feminine-accented variant of /ɕ/ by the age of 4.

By contrast, Kong et al. (2012) found no gender differentiation for voiced stops in Japanese. As described in section 23.2, Japanese voiced stops are generally produced by adult males and older speakers with prevoicing but by adult females and younger speakers with short-lag VOT. Kong, Yoneyama, and Beckman (2014) show that lack of prevoicing in adult males is associated with less masculine-sounding voices. However, Kong and colleagues found very high rates of the short-lag variant among 2- to 5-year-old boys as well as girls. This is likely due to the difficult intrinsic aerodynamic demands of producing prevoicing. That is, the short-lag variant that is associated with female speakers who are leading this sound change in progress is also an "easier" sound that occurs "naturally" as a characteristic early misarticulation of voiced stops in languages such as French. As Li et al. (2008) note, these findings suggest that socially meaningful phonetic variation could be acquired early, but evidence for or against acquisition must be interpreted carefully, taking more general constraints into account.

Roberts (1994) makes a similar point in her study of the acquisition of phonological and morphological constraints on socially meaningful variation in the production of coda /t/ and /d/ in American English. Roberts studied preschool children in Philadelphia and found that the children deleted coda /t/ and /d/ less often before a vowel than before a following consonant, a pattern that could be due simply to the easier perceptual parsing of the stop closure in prevocalic positions. However, Roberts also found that the children deleted /t/ and /d/ less often before a pause, a pattern that is characteristic of Philadelphia, which differentiates it from the New York pattern. Of course, Roberts's argument would have been even stronger if she had been able to compare productions by preschool children acquiring the New York dialect.

Imaizumi, Fuwa, and Hosoi (1999) is a good example of how cross-dialect comparison (like cross-language comparison) can help differentiate developmental differences from sociophonetic differences. Imaizumi and colleagues looked at vowel devoicing in productions of words such as /kitsutsuki/ "woodpecker" elicited from three groups of speakers of the Tokyo dialect and of the Osaka dialect. There were age differences in both dialects, with the adults producing more devoiced vowels than the 5-year-olds and the 5-year-olds producing more devoiced vowels than the 4-year-olds. These age differences could reflect differences in the input, if speech directed to younger children differs from speech directed to older children in the direction expected from the results of Imaizumi et al. (1995). Also, the Osaka speakers showed much lower rates of vowel devoicing than the Tokyo speakers, confirming earlier research. Moreover, the cross-dialect difference was attested for all three age groups.

In other related work, Roberts and Labov (1995) suggest a "critical period" for the acquisition of regional variation in the contexts for a split of /æ/ into a "tensed" low-mid falling diphthong contrasting with the original "lax" monophthong that characterizes many dialects of the northeastern United States. Young children of parents who had moved to Philadelphia as adults acquired the Philadelphia pattern, rather than the pattern of their parents' native dialect. The older siblings of these children either showed a mixed pattern or their parents' pattern. This finding is in accord with the much older observation that children of immigrants generally grow up producing the community language with the appropriate regional accent, rather than the foreign accent of their parents, particularly if they are very young when the parents immigrated or are born after the immigration.

Within-child (as opposed to within-family) comparisons provide evidence that children of immigrants may be learning to command socially meaningful variation when they learn to speak like their peers. In a study of vowels produced by children of immigrants and close neighboring friends, Khattab (2007) found that the children produced variants more like the Arabic-accented immigrant parents' speech when talking with the parents or when caricaturing their parents' speech as compared to when talking with the non-immigrant neighbors.

Baron-Cohen and Staunton (1994) uncovered an interesting exception to the general rule that children learn to control the accent of their peers and not (just) that of their parents. They compared the speech of children with autism to that of their siblings with typical language development. Half of the children had mothers who were non-native speakers of English, while half had native English-speaking mothers. All children had grown up in England and attended school with native English-speaking peers. Based on ratings by naïve listeners, most of the children with autism (83%) who had non-native English-speaking mothers were judged to speak "like their mother," while most of their siblings with typical language development (88.5%) were judged to speak "like their peer group." In this case, the comparison between neurotypical children and children with autism provides the control for interpreting the general rule as evidence of the early development of socially meaningful variation in regional accent or foreign accent.

Comparisons across groups within a language community also can help in interpreting evidence of gender differentiation. In addition to control of specific gendered sounds, children also learn control of more global aspects of speech production that let them sound progressively more like the adults in the ambient speech community who share their gender identity. Naïve adults can reliably differentiate between the speech of boys and girls in their own language community, even for children as young as 4 years (Perry, Ohde, and Ashmead 2001), and evidence is beginning to emerge suggesting that this differentiation results from learned control rather than from the subtle differences in vocal tract size and shape recently documented by Vorperian et al. (2011). For example, Munson and Baylis (2007) found that 3- to 7-year-old boys with phonological disorder were rated to sound less "boy-like" (more "girl-like") than their typically developing age peers. Furthermore, boys with Gender Identity Disorder or GID (a clinical label sometimes given when individuals display behavior that is not expected for their sex, such as having opposite-sex peer preferences, preferences for opposite-sex typed toys, and, in some cases, overt gender dysphoria) have less masculine-sounding speech than age-matched boys whose gender development was deemed to meet cultural expectations. Crocker and Munson (2006) examined the characteristics of the speech of 5- to 13-year-old boys clinically identified as having GID. A perception test with content-neutral speech samples showed that even the youngest boys with GID were rated to sound less masculine relative to boys with typical gender development. Acoustic analysis further suggested that this difference was due to the production of specific gender-marked variants of sounds, rather than to overall characteristics such as average fundamental frequency or the spacing of the ensemble of vowels in the F1/F2 space. These findings suggest that boys with GID learn specific gendered speech variants early in life, perhaps as the result of selective attention to specific adult models.

23.5 Summary and conclusion

In this chapter we have reviewed studies comparing children's productions across languages and across varieties within a language. These studies illustrate the three points with which we began. First, even before they begin to produce vocalizations that are reliably recognized as words by the ambient speech community, children's productions reflect language-specific norms. Second, adults perceive children's productions in terms of language-specific perceptual norms. Finally, children must learn to produce socio-indexical characteristics that let them signal their identities and their social affiliations.

In the last half century, there has been much attention to the interplay between universal constraints and language-specificity in regards to the first two points, the production and perception of lexical contrasts. The fact that human language is also used to signal group affiliation may be deeply embedded in the evolution of the species. Fitch (2004) reviews research on cases of non-human animal communication where subgroups of species produce distinctive vocalizations to mark themselves as kin. For example, in large breeding colonies, seal pups produce vocalizations that are sufficiently distinct that when their mothers return from hunting for food they can recognize and locate their kin even in very large groups. Socially indexed phonetic variation serves an analogous purpose, as anyone who has discerned a familiar regional accent among a large crowd of people can attest.

The data that we have discussed drive home two important methodological points that we are far from the first to make. The first point concerns the measures that we use to study children's production. Far more phonetic variation exists, both across and within languages, than simple IPA-style transcriptions would suggest. In some cases, the cross-language variation explains cross-linguistic differences in patterns of acquisition that would be difficult to understand if only IPA transcriptions were used. In particular, the studies described in section 23.2 show that there are cross-linguistic differences in children's earliest productions, even before they have mastered particular contrasts. Moreover, the studies described in section 23.3 show that adults in different speech communities may interpret children's productions differently even when they are phonetically the same. For example, when French children and Greek children both use nasal venting to produce strong prevoicing, their productions are perceived as following different developmental trajectories on the way to mastering the "same" difficult voicing contrast.

The second methodological point concerns the appropriate control comparisons. Taken together, the results in sections 23.2 and 23.3 make it clear why we need to compare across languages in order to make sensible models of the development course that children follow as they learn to produce speech. The results also make it clear why we need to exercise caution in interpreting evidence that very young children have acquired socially meaningful variation. That is, it is not enough simply to show that children's productions vary in ways that reflect the variation within the society into which they are born. If Northeastern Mandarin-speaking girls' productions of /ç/ and /tç/ differ from boys' productions of these sounds, it does not necessarily mean that they have chosen to mark themselves as little women. It could simply mean that their mothers and other caretakers use the "feminine accent" more in talking to them. Similarly, it is not surprising that children growing up in Tokyo show higher devoicing rates than children growing up in Osaka. Children acquire the production patterns that let them match the sound patterns that they hear. The studies described in section 23.4 that compare productions by neurotypical children to productions by children with autism, or that compare productions by a single child when talking to different addressees or in different styles, allow us to see this point especially clearly.

Taken together, then, the studies reviewed in all three of these sections help us to appreciate better the true complexities of speech production and the importance of the social group at all stages of language acquisition. The results in section 23.4, especially, suggest that the acquisition of socially meaningful phonetic variation cannot be taken for granted – children gradually learn to vary their productions in ways that let them control how they mark their identities as members of a particular speech community in terms of gender, social class, and regional accent. In contrast to the relatively large literature on stylistic variation in other linguistic variables, such as word choice (Andersen 1990), we know remarkably little about children's acquisition of socio-indexical phonetic variation. In fact, we do not even know at what age children's voices are as recognizable as adult voices. We might ask whether the fact that all mothers turn to look for their child on the playground when they hear a child cry "mommy" is because they are such good caregivers, or is it simply because young children's voices are not individually recognizable? When we contrast this to what the seal pups (do not) need to learn to be individually identifiable, it helps us begin to understand how kin selection may have acted as a ratchet in driving the evolution of greater and greater complexity and cultural diversity that spoken language enabled.

NOTE

1 This work was supported in part by NIH grant R01 DC02932 and NSF grant BCS0729140 to Jan Edwards, by NSF grant BCS0729277 to Benjamin Munson, and by NSF grant BCS0729306 to Mary E. Beckman. We also gratefully acknowledge the contributions of Tim Arbisi-Kelm, Eunjong Kong, and Fangfang Li.

REFERENCES

Allen, George D. 1985. How the young French child avoids the pre-voicing problem for word-initial voiced stops. *Journal of Child Language* 12: 37–46.

Andersen, Elaine S. 1990. *Speaking with Style: The Sociolinguistic Skills of Children*. London: Routledge.

Arbisi-Kelm, Timothy, Mary E. Beckman, Eun Jong Kong, and Jan Edwards. 2009.

Production of dorsal places of articulation by children and adult speakers of four languages. Paper presented at the Annual Meeting of the Linguistics Society of America, January 8–11, San Francisco, CA.

Arvaniti, Amalia and Brian D. Joseph. 2000. Variation in voiced stop prenasalisation in Greek. *Glossologia* 11–12: 131–166.

Arvaniti, Amalia and Brian D. Joseph. 2004. Early Modern Greek /b d g/: Evidence from rebétika and folk songs. *Journal of Modern Greek Studies* 22: 73–94.

Baron-Cohen, Simon and Ruth Staunton. 1994. Do children with autism acquire the phonology of their peers? An examination of group identification through the window of bilingualism. *First Language* 14: 241–248.

Beckman, Mary E. and Atsuko Shoji. 1984. Spectral and perceptual evidence for CV coarticulation in devoiced /si/ and /syu/ in Japanese. *Phonetica* 41: 61–71.

Beckman, Mary E., Kiyoko Yoneyama, and Jan Edwards. 2003. Language-specific and language-universal aspects of lingual obstruent productions in Japanese-acquiring children. *Journal of the Phonetic Society of Japan* 7(2): 18–28.

Boë, Louis-Jean and Shinji Maeda. 1997. Modélisation de la croissance du conduit vocal. Éspace vocalique des nouveaux-nés et des adultes. Conséquences pour l'ontegenèse et la phylogenèse. In *Journées d'Études Linguistiques: la voyelle dans tous ces états*, 98–105. Nantes: Université de Nantes.

Burton, Martha W., Sheila E. Blumstein, and Kenneth N. Stevens. 1992. A phonetic analysis of prenazalized stops in Moru. *Journal of Phonetics* 20(1): 127–142.

Cohen, Marcel. 1925. Sur les langages successifs de l'enfant. In *Mélanges linguistiques offerts à M.J. Vendryes*, 109–127. Paris: Champion.

Crocker, Laura and Benjamin Munson. 2006. Speech characteristics of gender-nonconforming boys. Paper presented at the Conference on New Ways of Analyzing Variation in Language, Columbus, OH.

Dart, Sarah N. 1998. Comparing French and English coronal consonant articulation. *Journal of Phonetics* 26: 71–94.

Davis, Barbara L., Peter F. MacNeilage, and Christine L. Matyear. 2002. Acquisition of serial complexity in speech production: A comparison of phonetic and phonological approaches. *Phonetica* 59: 75–107.

de Boer, Bart. 2000. Self-organization in vowel systems. *Journal of Phonetics* 28(4): 441–465.

de Boysson-Bardies, Bénédicte and Marilyn May Vihman. 1991. Adaptation to language: Evidence from babbling and first words in four languages. *Language* 67(2): 297–319.

de Boysson-Bardies, Bénédicte, Pierre Hallé, Laurent Sagart, and Catherine Durand 1989. A crosslinguistic investigation of vowel formants in babbling. *Journal of Child Language* 161: 1–17.

Demuth, Katherine and Annie Tremblay. 2008. Prosodically-conditioned variability in children's production of French determiners. *Journal of Child Language* 35: 99–127.

Disner, Sandra Ferrari. 1983. Vowel quality: The relation between universal and language-specific factors. PhD dissertation, University of California Los Angeles (UCLA Working Papers in Phonetics 58.)

Docherty, Gerard, Paul Foulkes, Jenny Tillotson, and Dominic Watt. 2006. On the scope of phonological learning: Issues arising from socially-structured variation. *Laboratory Phonology* 8: 393–421.

Edwards, Jan and Mary E. Beckman. 2008a. Some cross-linguistic evidence for modulation of implicational universals by language-specific frequency effects in phonological development. *Language Learning and Development* 42: 122–156.

Edwards, Jan and Mary E. Beckman. 2008b. Methodological questions in studying consonant acquisition. *Clinical Linguistics and Phonetics* 22(12): 939–958.

Ferguson, Charles A. 1979. Phonology as an individual access system: Some data from language acquisition. In Charles J. Fillmore, Daniel Kempler, and William S.-Y. Wang (eds.), *Individual Differences in Language Ability and Language Behavior*, 189–201. New York: Academic Press.

Fitch, W. Tecumseh. 2004. Kin Selection and "mother tongues": A neglected component in language evolution. In D. Kimbrough Oller and Ulrike Griebel (eds.), *Evolution of Communication Systems: A Comparative Approach*, 275–296. Cambridge, MA: MIT Press.

Flege, James Emil. 1987. The production of "new" and "similar" phonemes in a foreign language: Evidence for the effect of equivalence classification. *Journal of Phonetics* 15: 47–65.

Gibbon, Fiona E. 1999. Undifferentiated lingual gestures in children with articulation / phonological disorders. *Journal of Speech, Language, and Hearing Research* 42: 382–397.

Gordon, Matthew and Peter Ladefoged. 2001. Phonation types: A cross-linguistic overview. *Journal of Phonetics* 29: 383–406.

Heffner, Roe-Merrill Secrist. 1950. *General Phonetics*. Madison, WI: University of Wisconsin Press.

Holliday, Jeffrey J. and Eun Jong Kong. 2011. Dialectal variation in the acoustic correlates of Korean stops. In *Proceedings of the XVIIth International Congress of Phonetic Sciences*, 878–881.

Honikman, Beatrice. 1964. Articulatory settings. In David Abercrombie, D.B. Fry, P.A.D. MacCarthy, N.C. Scott, and J.L.M. Trim (eds.), *In Honour of Daniel Jones: Papers Contributed on the Occasion of His Eightieth Birthday*, 73–84. London: Longman.

Hu, Mingyang. 1991. Feminine accent in the Beijing vernacular: A sociolinguistic investigation. *Journal of the Chinese Language Teachers Association* 26: 49–54.

Imaizumi, Satoshi, Kiyoko Fuwa, and Hiroshi Hosoi. 1999. Development of adaptive phonetic gestures in children: Evidence from vowel devoicing in two different dialects of Japanese. *Journal of the Acoustical Society of America* 106(2): 1033–1044.

Imaizumi, Satoshi, Akiko Hayashi, and Toshisada Deguchi. 1995. Listener adaptive characteristics of vowel devoicing in Japanese dialogue. *Journal of the Acoustical Society of America* 98(2): 768–778.

Jakobson, Roman. 1941. *Kindersprache, Aphasie und allgemeine Lautgesetze*. Uppsala: Almqvist and Wiksell. Translated by Allan R. Keiler as *Child Language: Aphasia and Phonological Universals*. The Hague: Mouton, 1968.

Jespersen, Otto. 1922. *Language: Its Nature, Development, and Origin*. London: George Allen & Unwin.

Julien, Hannah and Benjamin Munson. 2012. Modifying speech to children based on their perceived phonetic accuracy. *Journal of Speech, Language, and Hearing Research* 55(6): 1836–1849.

Keating, Patricia A. 1984. Phonetic and phonological representation of stop consonant voicing. *Language* 60(2): 285–319.

Kewley-Port, Diane and Malcolm S. Preston. 1974. Early apical stop production: A voice onset time analysis. *Journal of Phonetics* 2: 195–210.

Khattab, Ghada. 2007. Variation in vowel production by English-Arabic bilinguals. *Laboratory Phonology* 9: 383–410.

Klein, Harriet B. and Elaine K. Altman. 2002. The acquisition of medial /t, d/ allophones in bisyllabic contexts. *Clinical Linguistics and Phonetics* 16(3): 215–232.

Kong, Eun Jong, Mary E. Beckman, and Jan Edwards. 2011. Why are Korean tense stops acquired so early? The role of acoustic properties. *Journal of Phonetics* 39: 196–211.

Kong, Eun Jong, Mary E. Beckman, and Jan Edwards. 2012. Voice onset time is necessary but not always sufficient to describe acquisition of voiced stops: The cases of Greek and Japanese. *Journal of Phonetics* 40: 725–744.

Kong, Eun Jong, Kiyoko Yoneyama, and Mary E. Beckman. 2014. Effects of a sound change in progress on gender-marking cues in Japanese. Paper presented to the 14th Conference on Laboratory Phonology, Tokyo, Japan.

Kuhl, Patricia K., Karen A. Williams, Francisco Lacerda, Kenneth N. Stevens, and Björn Lindblom. 1992. Linguistic experience alters phonetic perception in infants by 6 months of age. *Science* 255(5044): 606–608.

Ladefoged, Peter and Peri Bhaskararao. 1983. Non-quantal aspects of consonant production: A study of retroflex consonants. *Journal of Phonetics* 11(3): 291–302.

Laver, John. 1978. The concept of articulatory settings: An historical survey. *Historiographia Linguistica* 5(1/2): 1–14.

Li, Fangfang. 2005. An acoustic study on feminine accent in the Beijing Dialect. In Qian Gao (ed.), *North American Conference on Chinese Linguistics*, vol. 17, 219–224. Los Angeles: GSIL Publications.

Li, Fangfang. 2008. The phonetic development of voiceless sibilant fricatives in English, Japanese and Mandarin Chinese. PhD dissertation, Ohio State University.

Li, Fangfang, Jan Edwards, and Mary E. Beckman. 2009. Contrast and covert contrast: The phonetic development of voiceless sibilant fricatives in English and Japanese toddlers. *Journal of Phonetics* 37: 111–124.

Li, Fangfang, Eunjong Kong, Mary E. Beckman, and Jan Edwards. 2008. Adult acoustics and developmental patterns for gender-marked phonetic variants in Mandarin fricatives and Japanese stops. Paper presented to the 11th Conference in Laboratory Phonology, Wellington, New Zealand.

Li, Fangfang, Benjamin Munson, Jan Edwards, Kiyiko Yoneyama, and Kathleen Hall. 2011. Language specificity in the perception of voiceless sibilant fricatives in Japanese and English: Implications for cross-language differences in speech-sound development. *Journal of the Acoustical Society of America* 129(2): 999–1011.

Lindblom, Björn and Ian Maddieson. 1988. Phonetic universals in consonant systems. In Larry M. Hyman and Charles N. Li (eds.), Language, Speech, and Mind: Studies in Honor of Victoria A. Fromkin, 62–78. New York: Routledge.

Lisker, Leigh and Arthur S. Abramson 1964. A cross-language study of voicing in initial stops: Acoustic measurements. *Word* 20(3): 384–422.

Locke, John L. 1983. *Phonological Acquisition and Change*. New York: Academic Press.

Macken, Marlys A. and David Barton. 1980. The acquisition of the voicing contrast in English: A study of voice onset time in word-initial stop consonants. *Journal of Child Language* 7: 41–74.

Massaro, Dominic W. and Michael M. Cohen. 1983. Categorical or continuous speech perception: A new test. *Speech Communication* 2: 15–35.

Mattock, Karen, Linda Polka, Susan Rvachew, and Madelaine Krehm. 2010. The first steps in word learning are easier when the shoes fit: Comparing monolingual and bilingual infants. *Developmental Science* 13(1): 229–243.

Ménard, Lucie, Jean-Luc Schwartz, and Louis-Jean Boë. 2004. Role of vocal tract morphology in speech development: Perceptual targets and sensorimotor maps for synthesized French vowels from birth to adulthood. *Journal of Speech, Language, and Hearing Research* 47(5): 1059–1080.

Ménard, Lucie, Barbara L. Davis, Louis-Jean Boë, and Johanna-Pascale Roy. 2009. Producing American English vowels during vocal tract growth: A perceptual categorization study of synthesized vowels. *Journal of Speech, Language, and Hearing Research* 525: 1268–1285.

Miller, Amanda L. 2007. Guttural vowels and guttural co-articulation in Ju|'hoansi. *Journal of Phonetics* 35(1): 56–84.

Monnin, Julia, Hélène Loevenbruck, Mary E. Beckman, and Jan Edwards. 2011. Vowel context and frequency effects in dorsal and coronal acquisition in Drehu and French. Paper presented to the 9th International Seminar on Speech Production. Montreal.

Munson, Benjamin and Adriane L. Baylis. 2007. Gender typicality in the speech of children with phonological disorder. Paper presented to the Symposium for Research on Child Language Disorders, Madison, WI.

Otuka, Noboru. 2005. Articulation development and phonological perception. *Nihon University Graduate School of Social and Cultural Studies Journal* 6: 150–160. [In Japanese.]

Perry, Theodore L., Ralph N. Ohde, and Daniel H. Ashmead. 2001. The acoustic bases for gender identification from children's voices. *Journal of the Acoustical Society of America* 109(6): 2988–2998.

Plummer, Andrew R. 2014. The acquisition of vowel normalization during early infancy: Theory and computational framework. PhD dissertation, Ohio State University.

Plummer, Andrew R., Lucie Ménard, Benjamin Munson, and Mary E. Beckman. 2013. Comparing vowel category response surfaces over age-varying maximal vowel spaces within and across language communities. In *InterSpeech2013*, 421–425.

Redford, Melissa A. and Christina E. Gildersleeve-Neumann. 2009. The development of distinct speaking styles in preschool children. *Journal of Speech, Language, and Hearing Research* 52: 1434–1448.

Riney, Timoth James, Naoyuki Takagi, Kaori Ota, and Yoko Uchida. 2007. The intermediate degree of VOT in Japanese initial voiceless stops. *Journal of Phonetics* 35: 439–443.

Roberts, Julia Lee. 1994. Acquisition of variable rules: (-t, d) deletion and (ing) production in preschool children. PhD dissertation, University of Pennsylvania.

Roberts, Julia Lee and William Labov. 1995. Learning to talk Philadelphian: Acquisition of short *a* by preschool children. *Language Variation and Change* 7: 101–112.

Rvachew, Susan, Abdulsalam Alhaidary, Karen Mattock, and Linda Polka. 2008. Emergence of the corner vowels in the babble produced by infants exposed to Canadian English or Canadian French. *Journal of Phonetics* 36: 564–577.

Rvachew, Susan, Karen Mattock, Linda Polka, and Lucie Ménard. 2006. Developmental and cross-linguistic variation in the infant vowel space: The case of Canadian English and Canadian French. *Journal of the Acoustical Society of America* 120(4): 2250–2259.

Stoel-Gammon, Carol, Karen Williams, and Eugene Buder 1994. Cross-language differences in phonological acquisition: Swedish and English /t/. *Phonetica* 51: 146–158.

Syrett, Kristen and Shigeto Kawahara. 2014. Production and perception of listener-oriented clear speech in child language. *Journal of Child Language* 41(6): 1373–1389.

Takada, Mieko. 2011. *Nihongo no goto heisaon no kenkyu: VOT no kyojiteki bunpu to tsujiteki henka* [Research on the word-initial stops of Japanese: Synchronic distribution and diachronic change in VOT]. Tokyo: Kurosio.

Toda, Martine and Kiyoshi Honda 2003. An MRI-based cross-linguistic study of sibilant fricatives. Paper presented to the 5th International Seminar on Speech Production.

Vihman, Marilyn May. 1993. Variable paths to early word production. *Journal of Phonetics* 21: 61–82.

Vihman, Marilyn May, Edwin Kay, Bénédicte de Boysson-Bardies, Catherine Durand, and Ulla Sundberg. 1994. External sources of individual differences? A cross-linguistic analysis of the phonetics of mothers' speech to

1-year-old children. *Developmental Psychology* 30(5): 651–662.

Vorperian, Houri K., Shubing Wang, E. Michael Schimek, Reid B. Durtschi, Ray D. Kent, Lindell R. Gentry, and Moo K. Chung. 2011. Developmental sexual dimorphism of the oral and pharyngeal portions of the vocal tract: An imaging study. *Journal of Speech, Language, and Hearing Research* 54(4): 995–1010.

Whalen, Douglas H., Andrea G. Levitt, and Louis M. Goldstein 2007. VOT in the babbling of French- and English-learning infants. *Journal of Phonetics* 35: 341–352.

Wilson, Ian Lewis. 2006. Articulatory settings of French and English monolingual and bilingual speakers. PhD dissertation, University of British Columbia.

Wilson, Ian, Naoya Horiguchi, and Brian Gick. 2007. Japanese articulatory setting: The tongue, lips and jaw. Presentation to Ultrafest IV, New York University. https://files.nyu.edu/ld43/public/PEPLab/presentations/WilsonHoriGickUF4.pdf, accessed December 11, 2014.

Yasuda, Akiko. 1970. Articulatory skills in three-year-old children. *Studia Phonologica* 5: 52–71. [In Japanese.]

24 Effects of Language on Motor Processes in Development

LISA GOFFMAN

24.1 Introduction[1]

While language acquisition is a very broad topic, research over the last 40 years has primarily been framed in the tradition in which language mechanisms are viewed as relatively domain specific. That is, much effort has been devoted to understanding how children acquire the phonological structure (e.g., Bernhardt and Stemberger 1998; Velleman and Vihman 2007), words (e.g., Hollich, Hirsh-Pasek, and Golinkoff 2000), and grammatical structures (e.g., Radford 1990) of their native language(s). Language systems are often considered to develop independently of other cognitive systems (Fodor 1983). However, it has become apparent that, when considering language effects in acquisition, a critical issue concerns how speech is mediated by language and cognitive domains.

One longstanding exception to the more modularist view is the interactionist perspective of Elizabeth Bates and her colleagues. These researchers turned to considerations of other cognitive and motor components of development, primarily to understand why children show individual differences in their early acquisition of words and sentences (e.g., Bates, Bretherton, and Snyder 1988; Bates et al. 1994). Individual differences in early language acquisition, such as those observed in children who first learn single words compared with those who first learn larger prosodic structures, reveal how underlying mechanisms of language learning can be teased apart. Factors such as cognitive style and temperament, as well as developmental rate, are argued to influence early language acquisition; in many ways this perspective runs counter to a domain-specific view.

Another theoretical perspective makes an alternative interactionist case, now explicitly for the role of motor and sensory experience on language and cognitive acquisition (e.g., Thelen and Smith 1994; Iverson 2010). Working from a dynamical systems, or "embodied cognition" perspective these researchers actively "reject modularity" (Thelen and Smith 1994: 36), claiming instead that cognition, including language, develops dynamically as a child engages in sensory and motor interactions with the world. Some of the most compelling examples from this perspective draw analogies to language from work on reaching (Corbetta and Snapp-Childs 2009) and the A-not-B error (Spencer, Smith, and Thelen 2001). Reaching is not simply the acquisition of a visually guided search nor is the solution to the A-not-B problem simply the result of improvements in memory or in object representation. The A-not-B problem is an excellent example of how a strictly cognitive interpretation may be questioned. In this task, the infant is repeatedly shown an object hidden in location A. The infant successfully searches for the object in location A over the course of several trials. The object is then moved to a new location B. Surprisingly, the infant continues to search in location A. Spencer et al. (2001) argue that infants, children, and even adults commit the A not B error, and that this problem, that had been viewed as related to a cognitive variable (e.g., conceptualization of an object) should be reconfigured instead to reflect dynamic interactions across a number of factors, such as the number of prior repetitions of a behavior, the child's motor skill, and the context in which the behavior occurred.

My purpose here is not to provide an in-depth view of these competing perspectives, but only to demonstrate that, though there is little question that the more domain-specific view is dominant in framing how research on language acquisition has been approached, there have long been powerful suggestions that motor and other factors also play a crucial role in how children approach the language learning task.

Complementing behavioral findings, increasingly sophisticated neuroimaging techniques have produced compelling evidence that motor and language processing are interconnected. Relations between language capacity and action have received particular attention and, over the last several years, it has become apparent that conventional divisions of language and action do not explain either neurophysiological or behavioral observations of adults or children's language processing (for reviews, see Arbib 2006; Diamond 2000; Kent 2004). Numerous lines of evidence demonstrate shared neural substrates for speech-language and other motor behaviors (e.g., Arbib 2006; Pulvermüller 2005; Pulvermüller et al. 2006; Jancke et al. 2006). Especially relevant for the language and motor domains is Broca's area, which plays a role in translating complex hierarchical functions into serial outputs, both linguistic and non-linguistic (Arbib 2006; Greenfield 1991). This anatomical area is important for the acquisition of skills involving both the hand and the mouth.

Other sites involved in motor control, including the basal ganglia and the cerebellum, similarly participate in cognitive as well as language functions. The mirror neuron system, which includes Broca's area, suggests that motor imagery and performance share neural substrates. That is, neurons in the same cortical region fire whether a monkey or a human is producing or is merely observing a movement (Rizzolatti 2005). Even in adults, with their relatively localized functions, there is evidence for common neural machinery that is used for language and action (e.g., Pulvermüller 2005). For example, comprehension of action words also activates somatotopic regions in the motor system. These associations between language and action are beginning to be exploited by treatment programs for adults with aphasia (e.g., Buccino, Soldkin, and Small 2006; Pulvermüller and Berthier 2008).

Empirical work in language acquisition has been rather slow to follow these theoretical shifts. Perhaps the most compelling case comes from children with specific language impairment (SLI), the quintessential developmental language disorder. Children with SLI are defined by their difficulties with language that are not explained by other cognitive, motor, or behavioral factors (Leonard 2014). Consistent with the findings from adults, there is an abundance of behavioral evidence and some emerging neurophysiological evidence that limb motor deficits co-occur with the developmental language impairments that define SLI. Jancke et al. (2006) found that children with language impairments exhibit performance decrement with manual tasks, such as tapping and peg moving. Critically, neuroanatomical studies reveal that these children also show decreased white matter in a network of structures in the left hemisphere (e.g., motor cortex, premotor cortex, planum polare on the superior temporal gyrus).

Numerous behavioral studies of children with SLI further support that the traditional dichotomy between language and limb motor control should be reconsidered. In group studies, children with SLI show impaired motor performance on standardized tests of motor skill (reviewed in Hill 2001; Zelaznik and Goffman 2010). The assessment of specific skills reveals a number of deficits across several dimensions of limb motor control (see Hill 2001). For example, fine motor skills requiring spatiotemporal precision (e.g., copying shapes) are correlated with receptive language abilities (Schwartz and Regan 1996). Children with SLI also perform more slowly on a peg moving task (Bishop and Edmundson 1987; Powell and Bishop 1992) and are less able to imitate gestures, such as miming brushing their teeth and saluting (Hill 1998). In their manual gestures, children with SLI produce errors in the implementation of a sequence of actions, though not in the conceptualization of these actions (Hill, Bishop, and Nimmo-Smith 1998). These children also show persistence of associated hand movements while performing fine motor tasks (Noterdaeme et al. 1988). We have found that children with SLI show speech motor deficits (Goffman 1999, 2004; Goffman, Heisler, and Chakraborty 2006). As with language, not all areas of motor skill are equally disrupted, suggesting that motor impairment may show some of the specific patterns of performance that are observed in the language domain. For instance, in a simple timing task, children with SLI are similar to their age matched peers (Zelaznik and Goffman 2010).

Hypotheses explaining the motor deficit in SLI are varied and rather nonspecific, often suggesting slowed processing or neuromaturational variables as the cause. Perhaps the most specific idea to emerge is Ullman and Pierpont's (2005) procedural deficit hypothesis, in which they delineate those specific cognitive processes that underlie deficits observed in limb motor and language domains. According to this view, children with SLI show deficits in cross-domain tasks that are related to the procedural memory system, the brain system that underlies the acquisition and implementation of skills involved in the production of motor and language sequences. The procedural memory system is "the brain system that is implicated in ... the learning of new, and the control of long-established motor and cognitive skills" (Ullman and Pierpont 2005: 401).

Procedural memory deficits are particularly salient to disorders of syntactic processing. Yet other areas of language processing involving the lexicon could remain unaffected by procedural memory deficits, because they are supported by declarative memory systems. In accordance with their view of the procedural memory system, Ullman and Pierpont suggest that impairments in "grammar, lexical retrieval, and the non-linguistic functions that depend on these" (2005: 405) should be present in children with SLI. Critically, they predict broad deficits in limb motor as well as language tasks requiring speeded or complex sequential movements.

In sum, motor influences on language development have been documented, but are not well understood, especially when considering normal acquisition. What is clear is that speech processes are not modular. In the remainder of this chapter, I shall review some of the major findings about normal language and motor development, and suggest how these results may relate to yet another hypothesis related to language processing. In the end, the hypothesis put forward here is one in which there are specific interactions between aspects of language and motor processing.

24.2 Language and motor interactions in infants and toddlers

Motor effects on language acquisition are perhaps most obvious in infancy, during babbling and the transition to first words. The repeated canonical syllables observed in babbling show continuity with the sounds and syllable structures appearing in first words (Vihman et al. 1985). MacNeilage and Davis (2000) and MacNeilage, this volume, Chapter 16, in their frame content model, make the case that these early sound and syllable patterns are biomechanically determined. There is a tendency for infants to produce co-occurring sound patterns of front consonants and central vowels, alveolar consonants and front vowels, and back consonants and back vowels. This is referred to as the "frame" and is argued to arise from the mandibular oscillations of the jaw that occur with chewing as well as with sound production. It is only later in development that young children separate elements of the frame, to produce differentiated consonant and vowel sequences. It is in this period of early speech production that motor influences on language are most apparent.

Even in this early period, however, interpretations of these posited interactions between language and motor domains are not without controversy. Moore, Green, and their colleagues (e.g., Green et al. 1997; Moore 2004) have collected electromyographic and kinematic data from infants and young children engaged in chewing, as well as in vocalization and speech production. The dominant result from their research is that the organization of muscle activity is reciprocal during chewing (i.e., alternating activation of jaw opening and jaw closing muscles), with co-activation observed during vocalization and speech (Green et al. 1997). These findings contradict the frame content model in that, at the periphery, the organization for chewing and speech do not overlap. While these perspectives are not easily reconcilable at the present time, there remains evidence that early speech production is at least influenced by biases of the motor system, whether or not these are tied to chewing or other feeding behaviors.

There are other sources of evidence for language and motor interactions, though these are less directly tied to articulation. Iverson along with Thelen and others have long argued that language should be viewed in the "context of the body in which the developing language system is embedded" (Iverson 2010: 230). The child's interactions with the world change based on motor skill development, thus influencing cognitive and language domains. According to the dynamical systems perspective, "order, discontinuities, and new forms emerge precisely from the complex interactions of many heterogeneous forces" (Thelen and Smith 1994: 37). There is some evidence that motor skill and language production are intricately connected in early environmental and social interactions.

Correlational studies have demonstrated that aspects of motor development and early expressive and receptive language use are associated. For example, Alcock and Krawczyk (2010) reported on a group of 21-month-old toddlers who engaged in experimental tasks assessing their use of meaningful and meaningless gesture as well as of a series of simple and more complex oral motor skills (e.g., blowing; opening mouth, protruding tongue, and closing mouth). This study revealed that imitation of oral movements was associated with parent reports of expressive vocabulary on the MacArthur-Bates Communicative Development Inventories (CDI; Fenson et al. 2007). Gesture was not related to spoken language. It is notable that prior work has shown that gesture links to expressive vocabulary, but these other studies have tended to emphasize toddlers who were late talkers, and thus at risk for language impairment (Thal and Bates 1988).

A second correlational study focused on fine grained articulatory analysis of infants and toddlers speech production in relation, again, to expressive vocabulary performance on the CDI (Nip, Green, and Marx 2009). These children were longitudinally followed from 9–21 months, with a motion capture system employed to record their speech movements. The speed and amplitude of these movements correlated with their performance on the CDI, again suggesting connections between speech motor and language processing.

24.3 Language and motor interactions in the production of complex language models

The studies reviewed thus far have focused on general indices of relationships between vocabulary growth and motor skill in very young children. When turning to more detailed accounts of how motor and language domains interact, it becomes apparent that models of language processing and of motor control use entirely different constructs to explain how humans produce speech; the terminology incorporated into the models themselves almost precludes interaction, though obviously language and articulation ultimately must be integrated to provide a coherent explanation of speech production (Goffman 2010; Smith and Goffman 2004; Hickok 2012). Traditional models of language production are concerned with conceptualization and with lexical, syntactic, and phonological processing (e.g., Bock 1995; Garrett 1980; Levelt 1989; Levelt, Roelofs, and Mayer 1999). Using an entirely different framework, models of motor control, including speech motor control, investigate how the motor cortex interacts with the cerebellum and the brainstem to drive pools of motor neurons that ultimately lead to articulatory movement and how sensory feedback may influence such motor control processes (e.g., Guenther 2002; Hickok 2012). Models of language and of motor control simply do not employ the same descriptive and explanatory constructs even though it is true that, without exception, language is expressed through movement.

Within these two broad classes of theory, language processing and motor control, attempts have been made to reconcile how language and speech motor processing interact in speech production (e.g., Hickok 2012; Levelt et al. 1999). Both of these types of theoreticians agree that only the lowest levels of language processing, the syllable and segment, are connected to articulation. Generally, it is at these final levels of language processing (in particular the production of the syllable) that the linkage to movement occurs.

Levelt's (Levelt et al. 1999) speech production model emphasizes multiple processing components, including conceptual, grammatical and lexical (lemma), phonological, and phonetic. The syllable is proposed as the point of translation to articulation. The syllabary is a repository of frequently occurring syllables in a given language. This inventory of syllables can be rapidly drawn on during the online production of speech (Cholin, Levelt, and Schiller 2006; Levelt and Wheeldon 1994).

Guenther's DIVA model (Guenther 2002; Tourville and Guenther 2011) also emphasizes the syllable. The DIVA model is a neural network that learns sounds and syllables and incorporates sensorimotor representations, including auditory and somatosensory. This model is explicitly applied to development, in that the network initially learns in a "babbling" phase during which tactile, proprioceptive, and auditory feedback transform random articulatory movements to "learned" speech sounds. Babbling is described as the acquisition of "the relationship between motor commands and their sensory consequences" (Tourville and Guenther 2011: 966). Children first acquire syllables as they map auditory and somatosensory targets to movement. Following the acquisition of a repertoire of syllables comes an imitation phase (also loosely aligned with observations from child development) in which, relying on auditory and somatosensory feedback, the sound and syllable repertoire is tuned. Quite clearly, the DIVA model focuses on the level of the syllable and segment. Although Guenther and his colleagues are moving into prosodic components of phonology, higher language levels are deliberately not addressed in the DIVA model.

In an opinion piece, Hickok (2012) has explicitly presented an approach to reconciling hierarchical models of language and articulatory processing. His account shares many features with Guenther's DIVA model and with MacNeilage and Davis's frame-content model. That is, auditory targets are mapped to close-open movement trajectories (i.e., the frame) and somatosensory targets to finer-grained phonetic components (i.e., the content). Once again, all of these models have in common that the syllable and perhaps the segment are the locus of interaction.

There is an alternate perspective, in which there are interactions between articulation and language across broader domains than the syllable and the segment. For example, in exemplar-based models, specific tightly coupled interactions are proposed across lexical and phonetic processing levels (Pierrehumbert 2001). This view has been delineated by Goldrick and his colleagues, as applied to interactions across lexical, phonological, and phonetic domains. Adult talkers, in their speech errors, show fine-grained lexical effects at a phonetic level of analysis. There are signatures, or traces, in the phonetic output that reflect a number of lexical factors. For example, errors in nonwords contain increased traces compared with words (Goldrick and Blumstein 2006; McMillan, Corley, and Lickley 2009). Further, frequency effects are observed, with low-frequency words showing increased articulatory precision compared with high-frequency words (Bell et al. 2009; Gladfelter and Goffman 2013). These results, along with others, support a model of production that includes interactions at least between the lexicon and articulation. Our view of development is consistent with this "leakier" perspective, in which there are specific tightly coupled interactions across motor, language, and perhaps even other cognitive levels of processing.

With the exception of DIVA, all of the models reviewed address adult speech and language processing. It seems essential, especially when considering development, to work from a model in which components of processing may emerge and interact (perhaps differentially) over time. This framework, in which the classic components may interact, will form the basis of the more detailed treatment of language and motor interactions that will follow. But first, it is necessary to discuss methodological approaches that allow consideration of the motor aspects of language processing. It is partly the result of a methodological divide that language and articulatory models are so disconnected, and some discussion of methods is necessary. I will note that neuroimaging methods are beyond the scope of this chapter, though they promise to play an increasingly critical role as they become able to address production processes in children.

24.4 Methodological approaches

Classically, phonetic and orthographic transcription has served as the primary tool of the child language researcher who is interested in speech production. Other psycholinguistic paradigms have emerged, such as priming and reaction time, with some application to children (e.g., Leonard et al. 2000). From these behavioral tools, the traditional components of production, including sentences, words, prosodic structure, and phonetic contrasts, can be studied.

There are well-documented limitations to transcription, most critically the reliance on the bias of the listener (Munson et al. 2010). Transcription data may not reveal how new contrasts emerge for young children. In research on covert contrasts, children who are typically developing as well as those with speech and language disorders often mark phonetic distinctions that are not overtly apparent through perceptually-based transcription (Scobbie et al. 2000; Weismer, Dinnsen, and Elbert 1981). Similarly, grammatical morphemes may initially be marked covertly (Owen and Goffman 2007; Theodore, Demuth, and Shattuck-Hufnagel 2011). Acoustic analyses may reveal these covert contrasts. Children differentiate linguistic categories in their speech production that are not apparent through perceptually-based transcription.

Of course, the purpose of the present chapter is to discuss how articulatory and language levels interact. Therefore, it is important to include articulatory kinematic analyses and what they may potentially reveal. While articulatory components may be inferred from acoustic analysis, direct measures are needed to understand how movement (kinematic analysis) and muscle activity (electromyographic analysis; EMG) are organized for the production of speech. Several methodologies are available, including movement tracking, which in children focuses on lip and jaw movement (Goffman 2004; Green, Moore, and Reilly 2002; Grigos 2009; Smith and Zelaznik 2004). Tongue movement is an even more essential component of the articulatory complex, but to date is rather difficult to measure from children. Researchers have recently made great headway with ultrasound (e.g., Ménard et al. 2012) and, for slightly older children, electromagnetic articulography (EMA) (e.g., Murdoch, Cheng, and Goozée 2012). However, to date the majority of work looking at language and articulatory interactions in young children has focused on lip and jaw kinematics.

Several sorts of data can be derived from movement tracking, usually obtained from lip and jaw movement trajectories that correspond with children's productions of words and sentences. One standard measure is of amplitude, duration, and velocity of articulatory movements (see top panel of Figure 24.1). For example, the displacement and duration of a movement corresponding to a strong or a weak syllable may be directly measured. In addition, the structure and stability of speech movements can be determined as a child or adult produces multiple renditions of a specific word or sentence target (see lower three panels of Figure 24.1). In this methodology, articulatory movement trajectories are time- and amplitude-normalized. Standard deviations are obtained at prescribed intervals across the normalized trajectories, and the sum of these standard deviations serves as an index of variability. Smaller sums reveal more stable productions (Smith et al. 1995; Smith et al. 2000). With some background regarding methods, I now turn to data.

24.5 Global description of developmental change

The most general finding from a number of studies of the articulatory components of speech production is that the development of the speech motor system is extraordinarily protracted (Nip et al. 2009; Sharkey and Folkins 1985; Smith and Goffman 1998; Smith and Zelaznik 2004; Walsh and Smith 2002). While segmental

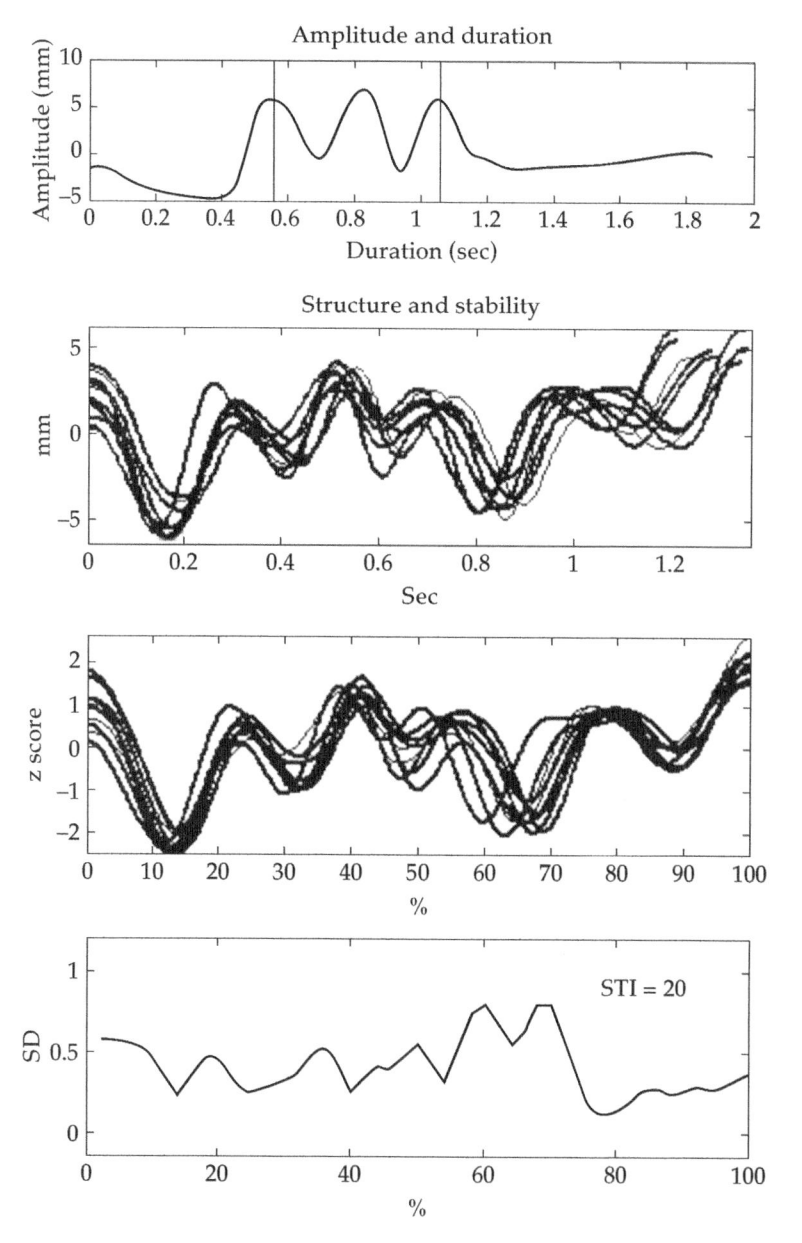

Figure 24.1 Methodological illustration. On the top panel is a movement trajectory for the phrase "Em's a baboon." From this displacement record the duration and amplitude of movement associated with the unstressed article and the weak syllable of the following noun can be determined. On the lower panels is an illustration of an articulatory variability index (Smith et al. 1995). In the second panel are 10 non-normalized productions of the sentence "Bobby's pupup is falling" obtained from a 4-year-old child. The next panel shows these same productions, now time- and amplitude-normalized. The bottom panel shows the spatiotemporal variability index (STI), which is the sum of standard deviations obtained at 2% intervals across the normalized record. In this case, the STI is 20.

substitution errors that are identifiable based on phonetic transcription typically resolve by the early school years (Smit et al. 1990), articulatory movements do not become adult-like, in duration or variability, until late adolescence (Smith and Zelaznik 2004; Walsh and Smith 2002).

In early development, Green and his colleagues (2000, 2002) have shown that jaw movements stabilize prior to lip movements. Larger ballistic components of movement (Kent 1992) are thought to be easier to acquire than more finely adjusted components, with the jaw providing the frame (MacNeilage and Davis 2000) and thus showing a faster maturational course. Overall, there is an intriguing disjunct between speech motor development and linguistic categories, with slower development observed, for example, in the movements used to implement segments than in the perceived accuracy of these segments.

Equipped with some theoretical and methodological frameworks, researchers are just beginning to tackle the question of how children implement articulatory movements to produce differentiable phonetic, prosodic, lexical, and syntactic categories. For the remainder of this chapter, I will consider current evidence that emphasizes interfaces among each of these language levels and articulation; or directly consider the language-motor interface in the strictest sense. Figure 24.2 serves as an illustration of processing levels along with hypothesized interactions.

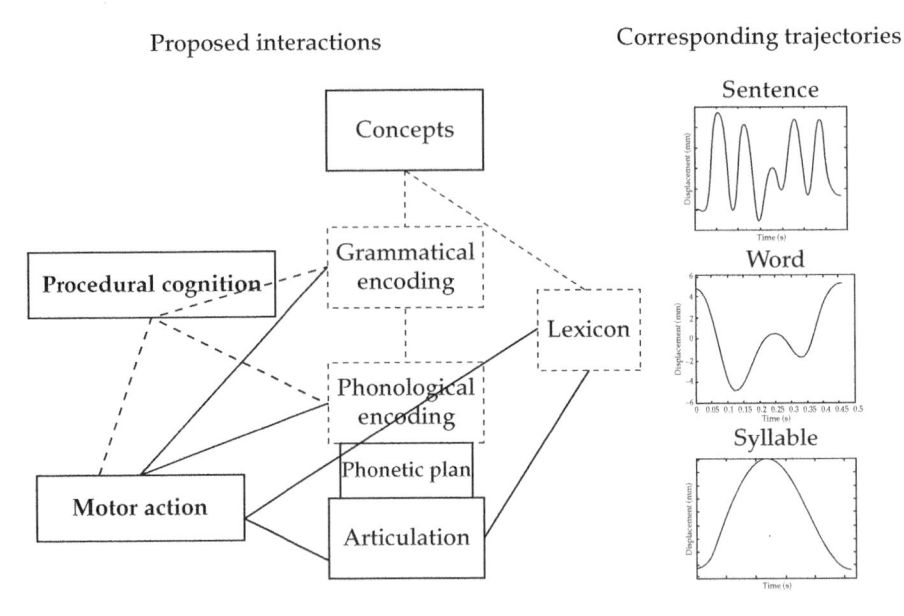

Figure 24.2 Illustration of potential linguistic and extra-linguistic interactions within an interactive and developmental model of speech production. Note that traditionally modular elements of grammar, phonology, and the lexicon are proposed to interact directly with procedural cognition (proposed interactions shown in dotted lines) and with motor action (shown in continuous lines). On the right are articulatory movement trajectories, of lower lip and jaw movement, extracted at sentence, word, and syllable levels.

Articulatory trajectories associated with three primary components of language processing (i.e., grammar, words, and syllables) are also depicted.

24.6 Segmental interactions with articulation

As previously discussed, the most basic building blocks of speech production are thought to be segments and syllables. Models that attempt to link articulatory and language levels tend to emphasize the segment and the syllable. Cholin et al. (2006) describe the mental syllabary, a stored repository of syllables prepared for movement implementation. The DIVA model (Guenther 2002) and Hickok's (2012) recent hierarchical state feedback control model also focus on mapping somatosensory and auditory targets to phonemes and syllables. The majority of work considering interactions between language and action occur at the syllable-articulatory interface, which is as expected in a modular, top-down theory.

Infants perceive subtle distinctions that occur within syllables (e.g., [pa] vs. [ba]) (Eimas et al. 1971). However, the physical manifestation of these distinctions is far more protracted in production. A fundamental developmental question involves how children implement the movements associated with segmental contrasts. With the perceptual system developing so early, it is hypothesized that the initial mapping is between auditory targets and somatosensory-driven movement trajectories (Guenther 2002; Tourville and Guenther 2011). Several researchers have employed acoustic evidence in an attempt to understand how the production of differentiated segments within syllables develops. Because the most direct approach to this problem of understanding how children begin to specify the production of phonetic units is through kinematic analysis (Goldstein et al. 2007), only direct articulatory evidence will be considered here.

Grigos, Saxman, and Gordon (2005) investigated the acquisition of the voicing contrast, before, during, and after mastery. Children were followed longitudinally from 18–26 months, during the acquisition of the /p/ and /b/ contrast. The voicing contrast is described canonically as the timing relationship between laryngeal vibration and articulatory movement. Grigos and her colleagues asked whether there are clues in supralaryngeal articulatory movement patterns that mark the emergence of the voicing contrast. Findings were that developmental changes occurred in movement displacement and velocity. However, there was no differentiation of lip opening or closing amplitude, duration, or velocity across voicing contrasts. Grigos (2009) also showed that variability shifted as a function of learning.

Goffman and Smith (1999) used a slightly different strategy to study changes in movement patterning of supralaryngeal articulatory movements. Children (aged 4–7 years) and adults all produced sentences that included medial words that were minimal pairs (i.e., "Bob saw fan/van/ban/pan/man again"). A pattern recognition procedure was used to assess whether there were differentiated lower lip and jaw movements used to produce the closing-opening movements associated with these fricative and stop consonants (e.g., the lip movement into and out of the

[p] in "pan"). Lip movements were time- and amplitude-normalized, then velocity profiles were subjected to a pattern recognition routine. All groups, including the youngest children, produced articulatory movements that patterned differently even across a voicing contrast (e.g., [p] vs. [b] and [f] vs. [v]). While a similar degree of articulatory differentiation was seen across age groups, as in the Grigos study (Grigos et al. 2005), variability showed the expected decrease with development. Children were able to attain the same degree of differentiation as adults, even through a noisier, more variable speech production system. Further, once it has stabilized in these slightly older children, the voicing contrast does not arise simply through changes in timing across the articulatory and voice onset components. Rather, the articulatory complex itself is differentially controlled to achieve this segmental contrast.

These two kinematic studies focused on the structure of the syllable. However, it has long been known that there are coarticulatory effects, with segments influencing speech production beyond the bounds of the syllable. Most developmental work has been acoustic, and findings reveal that children show broader coarticulatory effects than adults, resulting in the suggestion that the word rather than the syllable may be the basic organizing unit (Nittrouer, Studdert-Kennedy, and McGowan 1989). Recasens (2002) reported that, even for adults, coarticulatory effects extend across multiple syllables and even words. In a study that included 5-year-old children and adults, we (Goffman et al. 2008) tested the breadth of coarticulatory effects in articulatory movement. Speakers produced the phrase "Mom put the man/moon, beet/boot, geese/goose in the box." All of these phrases contained minimal pairs that included a difference between a rounded and an unrounded vowel. This simple vowel change influenced how children and adults organized the entire sentence; a rounded vowel in the medial position affected the lip movement trajectory from the initial word "Mom" to the final word "box." Once again, children were more variable, but produced the same linguistic distinctions as adults.

Based on these segmental findings, two core tenets may be questioned. First, production of a segmental voicing or manner contrast is not just the result of changes in coordination across components (e.g., velar, laryngeal, and articulatory) of the articulatory complex. The organization of the constituent structure of articulatory trajectories is distinct. Second, the syllable and segment do not appear to be the only organizing units for speech production. A simple change at the level of the segment influences the movement organization of an entire phrase or sentence. It seems that broader units need to be considered.

24.7 Lexical interactions with articulation

As described above, some investigators suggest that there is interactivity between articulatory and lexical language processes (Baese-Berk and Goldrick 2009; Frisch and Wright 2002; Goldrick and Blumstein 2006; McMillan et al. 2009). Neighborhood density influences vowel space, with expansion observed in words that are from high- compared with low-density neighborhoods (Munson and Solomon 2004).

Baese-Berk and Goldrick (2009) showed that voice onset time was longer when words had neighbors that were minimal pairs. Like vowel space, voice onset time varied as a function of lexical neighborhood effects. Goldrick and colleagues (2011) followed up on this result showing that low lexical frequency facilitates phonetic levels of processing.

Other work with adults has compared words to nonwords. Errors on tongue twisters showed different effects when the elicited errors resulted in real words compared with nonwords (Goldrick and Blumstein 2006; Frisch and Wright 2002). One prior study looked directly at movement, using electropalatographic data to assess articulatory variability (McMillan et al. 2009). Similar to the acoustic findings, these investigators showed that there was more articulatory variability in nonword than word productions. Transcription data revealed a similar effect, with more substitution errors in real words.

In children, it has been established that lexical and phonological factors interact (Storkel and Lee 2011; Goffman, Schwartz, and Marton 1996). Children acquire words with high frequency phonotactic structure more easily than those with low frequency structure (Storkel and Lee 2011). Neighborhood density also influences the learning of novel words, with words in sparse neighborhoods learned more readily by preschool children than those in dense neighborhoods (Munson, Swenson, and Manthei 2005).

We have considered interactions between lexical and articulatory components of processing in young children (Heisler, Goffman, and Younger 2010; Gladfelter and Goffman 2013). We included measures of articulatory variability and transcription accuracy to evaluate whether word status influences articulatory components of production. In our first study (Heisler et al. 2010) we asked whether manipulation of a semantic cue would influence articulatory variability. Young children (aged 4–6 years), both those developing language typically and those with specific language impairment (SLI), produced four novel word strings, well controlled for neighborhood density and phonotactic frequency. Two of these strings were assigned a visual referent over the course of learning and two were not. Lip and jaw movements were recorded during a pre- and post-test. More standard measures of comprehension and production accuracy were also obtained. In this paradigm, the children first produced the nonwords multiple times during a pre-test phase while looking at a checkerboard pattern. During a learning phase, two of the words were assigned a visual referent and two were presented only with a checkerboard pattern. Children listened but did not speak during this learning phase. A post-test was conducted that was identical to the pre-test, again with the children looking only at a checkerboard pattern.

Findings showed that articulatory variability decreased following the learning, but only when the visual referent was assigned to the novel word. In the condition in which the children only saw the checkerboard during the learning phase, no change in articulatory variability was observed in the post-test. Transcription results showed no difference between the visual referent and nonword conditions. Thus, the effects were driven by an articulatory-lexical interaction rather than other factors that may influence phonetic accuracy. Similar to the studies of adults (Goldrick et al. 2011; McMillan et al. 2009), we found that in young children, both typically developing and language impaired, lexical and motor implementation components are not independent. These processing levels appear to be closely linked as suggested by Goldrick and others. It is unclear whether lexical or deeper semantic effects drove these results, and this is the focus of ongoing studies.

24.8 Articulatory precision in the production of lexical stress

Articulatory data reveal differences in precision when an individual talker produces various linguistic targets. Increased precision has been observed when adults produce words compared with nonwords (McMillan et al. 2009). Tourville and Guenther (2011: 970) state "clear and stressed speech involve the use of smaller, more precise sensory targets." Differences in precision also occur across different prosodic targets. In our earliest kinematic work, we assessed children's productions of iambic and trochaic word forms (Goffman 1999; Goffman and Malin 1999). Children produced novel two-syllable words that were segmentally identical, but differed in prosodic foot structure, with one iambic, or weak-strong (e.g., [pʌˈpəp]) and one trochaic, or strong-weak (e.g., [ˈpʌpəp]). These words were assigned discrete novel visual referents. Two sorts of kinematic measures were obtained, one of the rhythmic structure of the words, or of the relative amplitude and duration of movements associated with weak compared with strong syllables. The second measure was of articulatory variability of iambic and trochaic words. Not surprisingly, the initial weak syllables in iambs were produced with smaller and shorter movements than the initial strong syllables in trochees. Amplitude and duration are kinematic correlates of stress. Further, the weak syllables in iambs are produced with especially small and short movements, even compared with the weak syllables in trochees. This is consistent with Prince's (1990) notion that there are asymmetries between the prosodic contrast observed in iambs and trochees, with contrast exaggerated in the iambic environment. Relatively equal amplitude and duration were observed between strong and weak syllables in the trochaic compared with the iambic context.

The less intuitive result in this work was that iambs were not only produced with more contrast, but with decreased variability. To return to the notion of precision, iambs were produced, even by 4-year-old children both with and without language impairment, with increased precision compared with trochees. There is substantial evidence that iambs are more difficult for children to acquire, since these unfooted weak syllables are omitted for a protracted time period (Demuth 2003; Gerken 1994a, 1994b; Kehoe 1998; Schwartz and Goffman 1995; Snow 1998). In addition, in English iambic nouns are much lower frequency than trochaic (Cutler and Carter 1987). For these reasons, it is initially surprising that more precision is observed in iambs.

Our initial explanation for the increased precision in iambs was that the more frequently occurring and rhythmically unmodulated trochee could rely on the earlier developing articulatory movement patterns observed in babbling (Goffman 1999). More recently, we have argued that neighborhood density influences not only segmental but also prosodic aspects of production (Gladfelter and Goffman 2013). Iambs reside in sparser neighborhoods, and thus experience reduced competition. Increased precision follows. Within-participant differences in precision, both at a single time point and with learning over time, provide a window into implicit learning that influences language and articulation.

24.9 Syntactic and morphological interactions with articulation (sequencing)

24.9.1 Sentential stress

Prosodic distinctions do not only occur within words, but also incorporate grammatical morphemes and even broader sentential units. Acoustic studies have demonstrated that children may mark grammatical morphemes covertly, even when they are not transcribed as accurate (Owen and Goffman 2007; Theodore et al. 2011). In the kinematic domain (Goffman 2004; Goffman and Westover 2013), an important question is whether morphosyntactic status influences the structure of the syllable. Is the inventory of highly frequent syllables, as proposed by Cholin et al. (2006), modified by prosodic foot structure? In one study that used nonce words, adults produced distinct articulatory structures when a weak syllable occurred in a noun as compared to a function word (Goffman 2004). Children, on the other hand, were not sensitive to this distinction and produced movements of similar structure in both grammatical contexts.

In a second study (Goffman and Westover 2013), now using real rather than novel words, children also showed systematic differences in articulatory structure across grammatical contexts. These results suggest that the syllable is not the sole interface between language processing and articulation; syllables systematically vary as a function of their linguistic environment. These results are consistent with those supporting increased interactivity across processing levels (e.g., Goldrick et al. 2011; McMillan et al. 2009), with components above the syllable and even the word systematically influencing the structure of articulatory output.

Grigos and Patel (2007) evaluated differences in articulatory control when children (aged 4, 7, and 11 years) produced interrogative and declarative sentences. Four-year-olds produced differentiated movements between declarative and interrogative forms. Four-year-olds produced longer movements in declaratives than interrogatives. The older children showed more specific distinctions, lengthening only in the utterance final position (which is where lengthening is supposed to occur to mark this prosodic distinction). Spatially, larger amplitude jaw movements were observed in declarative compared with interrogative utterances across all three age groups. The weak-strong sequence associated with a content+function word was differentiated even in 4-year-old children. That is, the final article+noun sequences in the sentences "Show Bob a bot" and "Show pop a pot" were both produced differently when in an interrogative than a declarative prosodic environment. These results further support that sentential level prosodic distinctions also directly interact with articulatory components of language production.

24.9.2 Manipulations of length, and syntactic complexity

In a series of studies, Smith and colleagues (MacPherson and Smith 2012; Maner, Smith, and Grayson 2000; Sadagopan and Smith 2008) have demonstrated that sentence length and complexity influence articulatory coordination variability. For example, MacPherson and Smith (2012) asked children to produce sentences that varied in both length (e.g., "The birds and the butterflies played" vs. "The birds and the butterflies played by the pond") and complexity (e.g., "The birds and the butterflies played"; simple conjunction vs. "The birds that saw butterflies played"; complex relative clause). Children showed higher levels of articulatory variability in longer sentences. Children who were typically developing also were more variable in complex compared with simple sentences that were matched for length. These studies as a whole suggest that there are close links between syntactic levels of language processing and articulatory implementation. Other manipulations of load, such as generating a sentence through a priming rather than an imitation paradigm (Brumbach and Goffman 2014) or including a novel word without a visual referent (Heisler et al. 2010) also lead to increased articulatory variability. Overall, along with the well-established links between the syllable and articulation, it appears that lexical and morphosyntactic components of language processing interact directly with speech output.

24.10 Conclusions and a return to models

I set out in this chapter to address the question of how language effects in acquisition are mediated via motor and cognitive domains. The interactionist view of development has a long history (e.g., Bates et al. 1988; Thelen and Smith 1994), and recently it has become increasingly apparent that there are interactions between language and motor processing. Empirical work elaborating on these interactions has been slow, particularly as applied to young children, and limited by both methodological and conceptual constraints.

We, along with several other research groups, hypothesize specific and targeted interactions among language, motor, and cognitive domains; maturational explanations appear insufficient for explaining the current evidence. In Figure 24.2, we delineate several of our predicted connections. These go beyond the syllable as the locus of the interface between language and articulation. We and others have identified specific linkages between lexical, prosodic, and grammatical processing and speech output. In addition, though not the focus of this chapter, we concur with Ullman and Pierpont (2005) that aspects of movement and cognition, perhaps related to the procedural learning system, may underlie some of the observed cross-domain interactions.

It is still too early in the collection of an empirical base to determine unequivocally how language and speech motor interactions unfold over the course of development. However, it seems most likely, based on what is known at this time, that there is far more interactivity than is proposed by models that focus on the interface between the syllable and articulatory implementation. The structure of articulatory movement is also systematically modulated as a function of semantic, prosodic, and syntactic cues.

An intriguing finding to date is that, while children irrefutably produce noisy and unstable speech movements, they show the same differentiated production units as adults. Based on the present results, it seems possible that, like perception, the representations that form the backbone of production are in place quite early in development; however, the child does not have the ability to implement linguistic distinctions with sufficient precision to cross a critical perceptual threshold. This possibility has significant implications for our view of perceptually-based transcription and of intervention for children who are not developing language as they should.

NOTE

1 I am grateful to Janna Berlin, Bill Saxton, Anne Smith, and Howard Zelaznik for invaluable assistance with many phases of this work. This research was supported by the National Institutes of Health (National Institute of Deafness and other Communicative Disorders) grant DC04826.

REFERENCES

Alcock, Katherine J. and Kirsty Krawczyk. 2010. Individual differences in language development: Relationship with motor skill at 21 months. *Developmental Science* 13: 677–691.

Arbib, Michael A. 2006. *Action to Language via the Mirror Neuron System*. Cambridge: Cambridge University Press.

Baese-Berk, Melissa and Matthew Goldrick. 2009. Mechanisms of interaction in speech production. *Language and Cognitive Processes* 24: 527–554.

Bates, Elizabeth, Inge Bretherton, and Lynn Snyder. 1988. *From First Words to Grammar: Individual Differences and Dissociable Mechanisms*. Cambridge: Cambridge University Press.

Bates, Elizabeth, Virginia Marchman, Donna Thal, et al. 1994. Developmental and stylistic variation in the composition of early vocabulary. *Journal of Child Language* 21: 85–123.

Bell, Alan, Jason M. Brenier, Michelle Gregory, Cynthia Girand, and Dan Jurafsky. 2009. Predictability effects on durations of content and function words in conversational English. *Journal of Memory and Language* 60: 92–111.

Bernhardt, Barbara Handford and Joseph Paul Stemberger. 1998. *Handbook of Phonological Development from the Perspective of Constraint-Based Nonlinear Phonology*. San Diego, CA: Academic Press.

Bishop, Dorothy V.M. and Andrew Edmundson. 1987. Specific language impairment as a maturational lag: Evidence from longitudinal data on language and motor development. *Developmental Medicine and Child Neurology* 29: 442–459.

Bock, Kathryn. 1995. Sentence production: From mind to mouth. In J.L. Miller and P.D. Eimas (eds.), *Speech, Language, and Communication: Handbook of Perception and Cognition*, 2nd edn., 191–216. San Diego, CA: Academic Press.

Brumbach, Andrea D. and Lisa Goffman. 2014. Interaction of language processing and motor skill in children with specific language impairment. *Journal of Speech, Language, and Hearing Research* 57: 158–171.

Buccino, Giovanni, Ana Soldkin, and Steven L. Small. 2006. Functions of the mirror neuron system: Implications for neurorehabilitation. *Cognitive Behavioral Neurology* 19: 55–63.

Cholin, Joana, Willem J.M. Levelt, and Niels O. Schiller. 2006. Effects of syllable frequency in speech production. *Cognition* 99: 205–235.

Corbetta, Daniela and Winona Snapp-Childs. 2009. Seeing and touching: The role of sensory-motor experience in the development of infant reaching. *Infant Behavior and Development* 32: 44–58.

Cutler, Anne and David M. Carter. 1987. The predominance of strong initial syllables in the English vocabulary. *Computer Speech and Language* 2: 133–142.

Demuth, Katherine. 2003. The status of feet in early acquisition. In *Proceedings of the 15th International Congress of Phonetic Sciences (ICPhS), Universidad Autonima de Barcelona*, 151–154.

Diamond, Adele. 2000. Close interrelation of motor development and cognitive development and of the cerebellum and prefrontal cortex. *Child Development* 71: 44–56.

Eimas, Peter D., Einer R. Siqueland, Peter Jusczyk, and James Vigorito. 1971. Speech perception in infants. *Science* 171: 303–306.

Fenson, Larry, Virginia Marchman, Donna Thal, Philip Dale, Steven Reznick, and Elizabeth Bates. 2007. *MacArthur-Bates Communicative Development Inventories (CDIs)*, 2nd edn. Baltimore, MD: Brookes.

Fodor, Jerry A. 1983. *The Modularity of Mind*. Cambridge, MA: MIT Press.

Frisch, Stefan A. and Richard Wright. 2002. The phonetics of phonological speech errors: An acoustic analysis of slips of the tongue. *Journal of Phonetics* 30: 139–162.

Garrett, Merrill F. 1980. Levels of processing in sentence production. In B. Butterworth (ed.), *Language Production*, vol. 1: *Speech and Talk*, 177–220. London: Academic Press.

Gerken, LouAnn. 1994a. A metrical template account of children's weak syllable omissions from multisyllabic words. *Journal of Child Language* 21: 565–584.

Gerken, LouAnn. 1994b. Young children's representation of prosodic phonology: Evidence from English-speakers' weak syllable productions. *Journal of Memory and Language* 33: 19–38.

Gladfelter, Allison and Lisa Goffman. 2013. The influence of prosodic stress patterns and semantic depth on novel word learning in typically developing children. *Language, Learning, and Development* 9: 151–174.

Goffman, Lisa. 1999. Prosodic influences on speech production in children with specific language impairment: Kinematic, acoustic, and transcription evidence. *Journal of Speech, Language, and Hearing Research* 42: 1499–1517.

Goffman, Lisa. 2004. Kinematic differentiation of prosodic categories in normal and disordered language development. *Journal of Speech, Language, and Hearing Research* 47: 1088–1102.

Goffman, Lisa. 2010. Dynamic interaction of motor and language factors in development. In B. Maassen, P.H.H.M. Van Lieshout, R. Kent, and W. Hulstijn (eds.), *Speech Motor Control: New Developments in Applied Research*. Oxford: Oxford University Press.

Goffman, Lisa and Caren Malin. 1999. Metrical effects on speech movements in children and adults. *Journal of Speech, Language, and Hearing Research* 42: 1003–1115.

Goffman, Lisa and Anne Smith. 1999. Development and phonetic differentiation of speech movement patterns. *Journal of Experimental Psychology: Human Perception and Performance* 25: 649–660.

Goffman, Lisa and Stefanie Westover. 2013. Interactivity in prosodic representations in children. *Journal of Child Language* 40: 1032–1056.

Goffman, Lisa, Lori Heisler, and Rahul Chakraborty. 2006. Mapping of prosodic structure onto words and phrases in children's and adults' speech production. *Language and Cognitive Processes* 21: 25–47.

Goffman, Lisa, Richard G. Schwartz, and Klara Marton. 1996. Information level and young children's phonological accuracy. *Journal of Child Language* 23: 337–347.

Goffman, Lisa, Anne Smith, Lori Heisler, and Michael Ho. 2008. Coarticulation as an index of speech production units in children and adults. *Journal of Speech, Language, and Hearing Research* 51: 1424–1437.

Goldrick, Matthew and Sheila E. Blumstein. 2006. Cascading activation from phonological planning to articulatory processes: Evidence from tongue twisters. *Language and Cognitive Processes* 21: 649–683.

Goldrick, Matthew, H. Ross Baker, Amanda Murphy, and Melissa Baese-Berk. 2011. Interaction and representational integration: Evidence from speech errors. *Cognition* 121(1): 58–72.

Goldstein, Louis, Marianne Pouplier, Larissa Chen, Elliot Saltzman, and Dani Byrd. 2007. Dynamic action units slip in speech production errors. *Cognition* 103: 386–412.

Green, Jordan R., Christopher A. Moore, and Kevin J. Reilly. 2002. The sequential development of jaw and lip control for speech. *Journal of Speech, Language, and Hearing Research* 45: 66–79.

Green, Jordan R., Christopher A. Moore, Masahiko Higashikawa, and Roger W. Steeve. 2000. The physiologic development of speech motor control: Lip and jaw coordination. *Journal of Speech, Language, and Hearing Research* 43: 239–255.

Green, Jordan R., Christopher A. Moore, Jacki L. Ruark, Paula R. Rodda, Wendy T. Morvée, and Marcus J. VanWitzenburg. 1997. Development of chewing in children from 12 to 48 months: Longitudinal study of EMG patterns. *Journal of Neurophysiology* 77: 2704–2727.

Greenfield, Patricia M. 1991. Language, tools, and brain: The ontogeny and phylogeny of hierarchically organized sequential behavior. *Behavioral and Brain Sciences* 14: 531–595.

Grigos, Maria I. 2009. Changes in articulator movement variability during phonemic development: A longitudinal study. *Journal of Speech, Language, and Hearing Research* 52: 164–177.

Grigos, Maria I. and Rupal Patel. 2007. Articulator movement associated with the development of prosodic control. *Journal of Speech, Language, and Hearing Research* 50: 119–130.

Grigos, Maria I., John H. Saxman, and Andrew M. Gordon. 2005. Speech motor development during the acquisition of the voicing contrast. *Journal of Speech, Language, and Hearing Research* 48: 739–752.

Guenther, Frank. 2002. Neural control of speech movements. In A. Meyer and N. Schiller (eds.), *Phonetics and Phonology in Language Comprehension and Production:*

Differences and Similarities. Berlin: Mouton de Gruyter.

Heisler, Lori, Lisa Goffman, and Barbara Younger. 2010. Lexical and articulatory interactions in children's language production. *Developmental Science* 13: 722–730.

Hickok, Gregory. 2012. Computational neuroanatomy of speech production. *Nature Reviews Neuroscience* 13: 135–145.

Hill, Elisabeth L. 1998. A dyspraxic deficit in specific language impairment and developmental coordination disorder? Evidence from hand and arm movements. *Developmental Medicine and Child Neurology* 40: 388–395.

Hill, Elisabeth L. 2001. Non-specific nature of specific language impairment: A review of the literature with regard to concomitant motor impairments. *International Journal of Language and Communication Disorders* 36: 149–171.

Hill, Elisabeth L., Dorothy V.M. Bishop, and Ian Nimmo-Smith. 1998. Representational gestures in developmental coordination disorder and specific language impairment: Error types and the reliability of ratings. *Human Movement Science* 17: 655–678.

Hollich, George J., Kathy Hirsh-Pasek, and Roberta Golinkoff. 2000. *Breaking the Language Barrier: An Emergentist Coalition Model for the Origins of Word Learning*. New York: John Wiley & Sons, Inc. (Monographs of the Society for Research in Child Development 65(3), series no. 262).

Iverson, Jana. 2010. Developing language in a developing body: The relationship between motor development and language development. *Journal of Child Language* 37: 229–261.

Jancke, Lutz, Thomas Siegenthaler, Sabine Preis, and Helmuth Steinmetz. 2006. Decreased white-matter density in a left-sided fronto-temporal network in children with developmental language disorder: Evidence for anatomical anomalies in a motor-language network. *Brain and Language* 102: 91–98.

Kehoe, Margaret. 1998. Support for metrical stress theory in stress acquisition. *Clinical Linguistics and Phonetics* 12: 1–23.

Kent, Ray D. 1992. The biology of phonological development. In C.A. Ferguson, L. Menn, and C. Stoel-Gammon (eds.), *Phonological Development: Models, Research, Implications*, 65–90. Timonium, MD: York Press.

Kent, Ray D. 2004. Models of speech motor control: Implications from recent developments in neurophysiological and neurobehavioral science. In B. Maassen, R. Kent, H. Peters, P. Van Lieshout, and W. Hulstijn (eds.), *Speech Motor Control in Normal and Disordered Speech*, 3–28. Oxford: Oxford University Press.

Leonard, Laurence B. 2014. *Children with Specific Language Impairment*, 2nd edition. Cambridge, MA: MIT Press.

Leonard, Laurence B., Carol A. Miller, Bernard Grela, Audrey L. Holland, Erika Gerber, and Marcia Petucci. 2000. Production operations contribute to the grammatical morpheme limitations of children with specific language impairment. *Journal of Memory and Language* 43: 362–378.

Levelt, Willem J.M. 1989. *Speaking: From Intention to Articulation*. Cambridge, MA: MIT Press.

Levelt, Willem J.M. and Linda Wheeldon. 1994. Do speakers have access to a mental syllabary? *Cognition* 50: 239–269.

Levelt, Willem J.M., Ardi Roelofs, and Antje S. Meyer. 1999. A theory of lexical access in speech production. *Behavioral and Brain Sciences* 22: 1–75.

MacNeilage, Peter F. and Barbara L. Davis. 2000. On the origin of internal structure of word forms. *Science* 288: 527–531.

Maner, Kimberly Jones, Anne Smith, and Liane Grayson. 2000. Influences of utterance length and complexity on speech motor performance in children and adults. *Journal of Speech, Language, and Hearing Research* 43: 560–573.

McMillan, Corey T., Martin Corley, and Robin J. Lickley. 2009. Articulatory evidence for feedback and competition in speech production. *Language and Cognitive Processes* 24: 44–66.

MacPherson, Megan K. and Anne Smith. 2013. Influences of sentence length and syntactic complexity on the speech motor control of children who stutter. *Journal of Speech, Language, and Hearing Research* 56: 89–102.

Ménard, Lucie, Jérôme Aubin, Mélanie Thibeault, and Gabrielle Richard. 2012. Comparing tongue shapes and positions with ultrasound imaging: A validation experiment using an articulatory model. *Folia Phoniatrica et Logopaedica* 64: 64–72.

Moore, Christopher A. 2004. Physiological development of speech production. In B. Maassen, R. Kent, H. Peters, P. Van Lieshout, and W. Hulstijn (eds.), *Speech Motor Control in Normal and Disordered Speech*, 191–209. Oxford: Oxford University Press.

Munson, Benjamin and Nancy Pearl Solomon. 2004. The effect of phonological neighborhood density on vowel articulation. *Journal of Speech, Language, and Hearing Research* 47(5): 1048–1058.

Munson, Benjamin, Cyndie L. Swenson, and Shayla C. Manthei. 2005. Lexical and phonological organization in children: Evidence from repetition tasks. *Journal of Speech, Language, and Hearing Research* 48: 108–124.

Munson, Benjamin, Jan Edwards, Sarah K. Schellinger, Mary E. Beckman, and Marie K. Meyer. 2010. Deconstructing phonetic transcription: Covert contrast, perceptual bias, and an extraterrestrial view of vox humana. *Clinical Linguistics and Phonetics* 24: 245–260.

Murdoch, Bruce E., Hei Yan Cheng, and Justine V. Goozée. 2012. Developmental changes in the variability of tongue and lip movements during speech from childhood to adulthood: An EMA study. *Clinical Linguistics and Phonetics* 26: 216–231.

Nip, Ignatius S.B., Jordan R. Green, and David B. Marx. 2009. Early speech motor development: Cognitive and linguistic considerations. *Journal of Communication Disorders* 42: 286–298.

Nittrouer, Susan, Michael Studdert-Kennedy, and Richard S. McGowan. 1989. The emergence of phonetic segments: Evidence from the spectral structure of fricative-vowel syllables spoken by children and adults. *Journal of Speech and Hearing Research* 32: 120–132.

Noterdaeme, M., H. Amorosa, M. Ploog, and G. Scheimann. 1988. Quantitative and qualitative aspects of associated movements in children with specific developmental speech and language disorders and in normal pre-school children. *Journal of Human Movement Studies* 15(4): 151–169.

Owen, Amanda and Lisa Goffman. 2007. Covert marking of grammatical inflections in children with specific language impairment. *Clinical Linguistics and Phonetics* 21: 501–522.

Pierrehumbert, Janet. 2001. Exemplar dynamics: Word frequency, lenition and contrast. In J. Bybee and P. Hopper (eds.), *Frequency and the Emergence of Linguistic Structure*, 137–157. Amsterdam: John Benjamins.

Powell, R.P. and Dorothy V.M. Bishop. 1992. Clumsiness and perceptual problems in children with specific language impairment. *Developmental Medicine and Child Neurology* 34: 755–765.

Prince, Alan. 1990. Quantitative consequences of rhythmic organization. In M. Ziolkowski, M. Noske, and K. Denton (eds.), *Papers from the 26th Regional Meeting of the Chicago Linguistic Society: The Parasession on the Syllable in Phonetics and Phonology*, 355–398. Chicago, IL: Chicago Linguistic Society.

Pulvermüller, Friedemann. 2005. Brain mechanisms linking language and action. *Nature Reviews Neuroscience* 6(7): 576–582.

Pulvermüller, Friedemann and Marcelo L. Berthier. 2008. Aphasia therapy on a neuroscience basis. *Aphasiology* 22: 563–599.

Pulvermüller, Friedemann, Martina Huss, Ferath Kherif, Fermin Moscoso del Prado Martin, Olaf Hauk, and Yury Shtyrov. 2006. Motor cortex maps articulatory features of speech sounds. *Proceedings of the National Academy of Sciences, USA* 103: 7865–7870.

Radford, Alan. 1990. *Syntactic Theory and the Acquisition of English Syntax: The Nature of Early Child Grammars of English.* Oxford: Basil Blackwell.

Recasens, Daniel. 2002. An Ema study of VCV coarticulatory direction. *Journal of the Acoustical Society of America* 111: 2828–2841.

Rizzolatti, Giacoma. 2005. The mirror neuron system and its function in humans. *Anatomic Embryology* 210: 419–421.

Sadagopan, Neeraja and Anne Smith. 2008. Developmental changes in the effects of utterance length and complexity on speech movement variability. *Journal of Speech, Language, and Hearing Research* 51: 1138–1151.

Schwartz, Marcelle and Vivian Regan. 1996. Sequencing, timing, and rate relationships between language and motor skill in children with receptive language delay. *Developmental Neuropsychology* 12: 255–270.

Schwartz, Richard G. and Lisa Goffman. 1995. Metrical patterns of words and production accuracy. *Journal of Speech and Hearing Research* 38: 876–888.

Scobbie, James M., Fiona Gibbon, William J. Hardcastle, and Paul Fletcher. 2000. Covert contrasts as a stage in the acquisition of phonetics and phonology. *Papers in Laboratory Phonology* 5: 194–207.

Sharkey, Susan G. and John W. Folkins. 1985. Variability of lip and jaw movements in children and adults: Implications for the development of speech motor control. *Journal of Speech and Hearing Research* 28: 8–15.

Smit, Ann Bosma, Linda Hand, Joseph Freilinger, John E. Bernthal, and Ann Bird. 1990. The Iowa articulation norms project and its Nebraska replication. *Journal of Speech and Hearing Disorders* 55: 779–798.

Smith, Anne and Lisa Goffman. 1998. Stability and patterning of speech movement sequences in children and adults. *Journal of Speech, Language, and Hearing Research* 41: 18–30.

Smith, Anne and Lisa Goffman. 2004. Interaction of motor and language factors in the development of speech production. In B. Maassen, R. Kent, H. Peters, P. Van Lieshout, and W. Hulstijn (eds.), *Speech Motor Control in Normal and Disordered Speech*, 225–252. Oxford: Oxford University Press.

Smith, Anne and Howard N. Zelaznik. 2004. The development of functional synergies for speech motor coordination in childhood and adolescence. *Developmental Psychobiology* 45: 22–33.

Smith, Anne, Michael Johnson, Clare McGillem, and Lisa Goffman. 2000. On the assessment of stability and patterning of speech movements. *Journal of Speech, Language, and Hearing Research* 43: 277–286.

Smith, Anne, Lisa Goffman, Howard N. Zelaznik, Goangshiuan Ying, and Clare McGillem. 1995. Spatiotemporal stability and patterning of speech movement sequences. *Experimental Brain Research* 104: 493–501.

Snow, David. 1998. A prominence account of syllable reduction in early speech development: The child's prosodic phonology of tiger and giraffe. *Journal of Speech, Language, and Hearing Research* 41: 1171–1184.

Spencer, John P., Linda B. Smith, and Esther Thelen. 2001. Tests of a dynamic systems account of the A-not-B error: The influence of prior experience on the spatial memory abilities of two-year-olds. *Child Development* 72: 1327–1346.

Storkel, Holly L. and Su-Yeon Lee. 2011. The independent effects of phonotactic probability and neighborhood density on lexical acquisition by preschool children. *Language and Cognitive Processes* 26: 191–211.

Thal, Donna and Elizabeth Bates. 1988. Language and gesture in late talkers. *Journal of Speech and Hearing Research* 31: 115–123.

Thelen, Esther and Linda Smith. 1994. *A Dynamic Systems Approach to the Development of Cognition and Action*. Cambridge, MA: MIT Press.

Theodore, Rachel M., Katherine Demuth, and Stefanie Shattuck-Hufnagel. 2011. Acoustic evidence for positional and complexity effects on children's production of plural -s. *Journal of Speech and Hearing Research* 54: 539–548.

Tourville, Jason A. and Frank H. Guenther. 2011. The DIVA model: A neural theory of speech acquisition and production. *Language and Cognitive Processes* 26: 952–981.

Ullman, Michael T. and Elizabeth I. Pierpont. 2005. Specific language impairment is not specific to language: The procedural deficit hypothesis. *Cortex* 41: 399–433.

Velleman, Shelley L. and Marilyn M. Vihman. 2007. Phonology development in infancy and early childhood: Implications for theories of language learning. In M.C. Pennington (ed.), *Phonology in Context*, 25–50. Basingstoke: Palgrave Macmillan.

Vihman, Marilyn May, Marlys A. Macken, Ruth Miller, Hazel Simmons, and Jim Miller. 1985. From babbling to speech: A re-assessment of the continuity issue. *Language* 61: 397–445.

Walsh, Bridget and Anne Smith. 2002. Articulatory movements in adolescents: Evidence for protracted development of speech motor control processes. *Journal of Speech, Language, and Hearing Research* 45: 1119–1133.

Weismer, Gary, Daniel Dinnsen, and Mary Elbert. 1981. A study of the voicing distinction associated with omitted, word final stops. *Journal of Speech and Hearing Disorders* 46: 320–327.

Zelaznik, Howard N. and Lisa Goffman. 2010. Motor abilities and timing behavior in children with specific language impairment. *Journal of Speech, Language, and Hearing Research* 53: 283–293.

Index of Authors

Abberton, Evelyn, 41
Abbink, Jan Hendrik, 95
Abbs, James A., 226, 254, 256, 257
Abd-el-Malek, Shafik, 61
Abel, Jennifer, 189, 193
Abercrombie, D., 159, 161–2
Abramson, Arthur S., 142
Abry, Christian, 188
Ackermann, Hermann, 96, 302, 304, 305, 317, 318, 360
Aichert, Ingrid, 310
Alcock, Katherine J., 559
Alfonso, Peter J., 69
Al-Hayani, A., 85
Al-Hoqail, Rola A., 82
Alipour, Fariborz, 53
Allen, George D., 392, 394
Allen, J., 170
Altman, Elaine K., 544
Ambrose, Nicoline, 448
Andersen, Elaine S., 549
Anderson, D.L., 86–8
Andrade, Cláudia R.F. de, 99
Andrews, G., 168
Aoba, Tsuneo, 113
Arbib, Michael A., 166, 556
Arbisi-Kelm, Timothy, 534
Archontaki, Maria, 82
Aronson, Arnold E., 298, 333
Arvaniti, Amalia, 166, 515, 538
Ashby, W. Ross, 191

Ashmead, Daniel H., 547
Aslin, Richard N., 380
Aston, Carletta H., 427
Asu, E., 165
Atterer, Michaela, 515
Au, Claudia, 426
Auer, Edward T., 261
Austin-Garrison, Martha, 494
Au-Yeung, J., 170
Aylett, Matthew, 456

Baddeley, Alan, 415n
Bae, Youkyung, 110
Baer, Thomas, 67, 69, 70, 72
Baese-Berk, Melissa, 567
Bailly, Gérard, 242
Baken, R.J., 112, 125n
Baker, Herbert K., 118
Ballard, Kirrie J., 394
Banzett, Robert B., 15
Barber, Carroll G., 189
Barber, Paul, 183
Barbosa, Adriano V., 181, 187, 189
Bard, Ellen Gurman, 446, 456, 468
Baresi, Barbara, 447
Barlow, Steven M., 98, 99–100, 252
Barnes, Jonathan A., 520
Baron-Cohen, Simon, 547
Barry, W.J., 159, 172
Bartle-Meyer, Carly J., 310
Baskararao, P., 489

The Handbook of Speech Production, First Edition. Edited by Melissa A. Redford.
© 2015 John Wiley & Sons, Inc. Published 2019 by John Wiley & Sons, Inc.

Bates, Elizabeth, 462, 555, 559
Baylis, Adriane L., 547
Beckman, M., 163
Beckman, Mary E., 9, 424, 512, 513, 519, 531–3, 535–7, 538, 539, 544, 545–6
Behroozmand, Roozbeh, 284, 285
Bell, Alan, 458, 561
Bell-Berti, Fredericka, 115, 116, 313, 491–2
Bellugi, Ursula, 431
Bendor, Daniel, 277
Benke, Thomas, 301
Bennett, Janice W., 100
Bennett, William D., 17
Bentsianov, Boris, 83, 85
Beňuš, Stefan, 147
Bergeson, T., 159
Berkovits, Rochele, 518, 523
Bernardis, Paolo, 203
Bernstein, Lynne E., 261, 311
Bernstein, Nikolaj A., 135, 240
Berridge, Kent C., 366
Berry, David A., 38–9, 53–4
Berry, Jean K., 20
Berry, Jeff, 314–15
Bertinetto, P.M., 163
Bertoncini, Josiane, 380
Bianchini, Esther M.G., 99
Billings, Dumont, 201
Bird, Sonya, 479, 482
Black, Leo F., 20
Blackmer, Elizabeth R., 463, 464, 465
Blakemore, Sarah J., 270
Blankenship, Jane, 452
Blazek, Barbara, 209
Blitzer, Andrew, 83, 85
Bloom, Paul, 2
Blumstein, Sheila E., 201, 561, 567
Bock, J.K., 434, 435
Bode, Frederick R., 19
Boë, Louis-Jean, 541
Boer, Bart de *see* de Boer, Bart
Bohland, Jason W., 300, 307, 315–16, 317, 318, 355
Boly, Aliou, 482
Bombien, Lasse, 141, 142, 143, 146
Bortfeld, Heather, 458
Bose, Arpita, 101
Bouchard, M.-Eve, 208

Boysson-Bardies, Bénédicte de, 163, 531, 537
Braak, Heiko, 26
Brady, John, 432
Branigan, George, 428–9
Breen, Gava, 355
Bregman, Albert S., 269
Brendel, Bettina, 319
Brennan, Susan E., 461
Brocklehurst, Paul H., 410
Brosnahan, Leonard F., 492
Browman, Catherine P., 4, 100, 138, 139, 147, 148–9, 150, 166, 184, 203, 313, 370, 384, 406, 414, 521
Brown, Joe R., 298, 333
Brown, Roger, 385
Brown-Sweeney, Sharon, 364
Bruce, Gosta, 513
Brugman, Peter, 90–1
Brumbach, Andrea D., 570
Brunner, Richard J., 359
Bryan, A. Charles, 17
Buchanan, Mary, 416n
Buchsbaum, Bradley R., 281
Buchwald, Adam, 414
Bull, Matthew, 456
Bull, M.C., 171
Bullock, Daniel, 300, 355
Bundy, Emily, 121
Bunta, Ferenc, 392, 393
Bunton, Kate, 26, 303
Bunz, H., 168
Burnett, Theresa A., 268, 270
Burton, Harold, 16
Butcher, Andrew R., 138, 456–7
Butler-Browne, Gill S., 251
Byrd, Dani, 138, 145–6, 166, 203, 521, 522
Bzoch, Kenneth R., 113, 126n

Cai, Shanqing, 273–4
Callan, Daniel E., 192, 280
Campione, Estelle, 457
Cano-de-la-Cuerda, Roberto, 14
Carissimo-Bertola, Manon, 499
Carney, Patrick J., 116
Carpenter, Roger H.S., 182
Carré, René, 72
Carter, John N., 180, 194n
Caruana, Fausto, 361
Cassell, J., 172

Catford, John C., 188, 487, 492
Cathiard, Marie-Agnes, 188
Cerny, Frank J., 16
Chakraborty, Rahul, 557
Champoux, François, 261, 275
Chandrasekaran, Bharath, 23
Chang, Edward F., 269, 285
Chang-Yit, Rudolph, 268
Chapman, Kathy L., 364
Charles-Luce, Jan, 456
Chen, Ajou, 396
Chen, Chi-Ming, 283
Chen, Matthew, 508, 509
Cheung, Steven W., 277
Chiba, Tsutomu, 60, 75
Chistovich, Ludmilla, 144
Chitoran, Ioana, 145–6, 499
Cho, Taehong, 9, 480, 506–7, 510, 519, 520, 522, 523
Choe, Wook Kyung, 426
Cholin, Joana, 565
Chomsky, Noam, 2, 190–1, 354, 505
Christie, William M., 396
Christoffels, Ingrid K., 284
Chuang, C.K., 322n
Cissé, Ibrahima, 482
Clark, Herbert H., 459, 460, 461
Classé, A., 159–60
Clément, Philippe, 72
Cocks, N., 167
Cohen, Avis H., 356
Cohen, Dan A.D., 255
Cohen, Henri, 208
Cohen, Marcel, 530–1
Cohn, Abigail, 138
Cohn, Jeffrey F., 492
Cole, Ronald A., 201
Collins, David F., 257
Collins, Maryann, 24
Condon, W.S., 169
Connor, Nadin P., 256
Contini, Michel, 486
Cooke, Dylan F., 301–2
Cooper, Sybil, 251
Cooper, William E., 201
Corballis, Michael C., 354
Corbetta, Daniela, 556
Cordo, Paul, 250
Corley, Martin, 410, 411–13, 561

Coughlin, Bridget C., 368
Coulter, David C., 261
Counihan, Donald T., 113–14
Couper-Kuhlen, E., 171
Cowan, Robert S., 261
Cowie, Roddy, 270
Cramon, Detlev von see von Cramon, Detlev
Crary, Michael A., 337, 341
Crocker, Laura, 547
Croot, Karen, 426, 436
Crothers, John, 493, 494
Cummins, Fred, 7, 161, 168–9, 172, 391
Curio, Gabriel, 202
Curtis, Cindy, 124
Cutler, Anne, 166, 430, 467
Cykowski, Matthew D., 282

Daegling, David J., 86, 88
Dalby, J., 162–3
Dalston, Rodger D., 121, 122–3
Daly, David A., 448
Dang, Jianwu, 73, 74
Daniele, J., 172
Darley, Frederic L., 298, 300, 333, 335
Darling, Meghan, 23, 25, 26–7
Darwin, Charles, 353
Dauer, R.M., 162
Davies, Colin J., 180
Davies, Joel C., 89
Davis, Barbara L., 208, 358, 359, 362–3, 364, 365, 368, 369, 370, 381, 382, 532, 558, 561, 564
Davis, James W., 366
de Andrade, Cláudia R.F., 99
de Boer, Bart, 541
de Boysson-Bardies, Bénédicte, 163, 531, 537
de Jong, Kenneth, 160, 163, 508, 509
De Nil, Luc, 100
De Troyer, Andre, 22
DeClerk, Joseph L., 371
Deguchi, Toshisada, 544
Dekle, Dawn J., 261
Del Tredici, Kelly, 26
del Viso, Susana, 430
Delattre, Pierre C., 519
Dell, Gary S., 8, 407–10, 411–13, 434, 438
Dellwo, V., 165
Demolin, Didier, 9, 481, 482, 484, 485, 489, 493, 496

Demuth, Katherine, 429
dePaula, Hugo, 183
Derrick, Donald, 261
Descartes, René, 354
Dewitt, Iain, 279
Diedrich, William M., 344
Diehl, Randy L., 204, 490, 505
Dilley, Laura, 437
D'Imperio, Mariapaola, 516, 518
Ding, Ruiying, 95–6
Diogo, Rui, 83
Dobzhansky, Theodosius, 353
Docherty, Gerard J., 149, 545
Doke, Clement M., 483, 484
Dolata, Jill, 358
Donald, Merlin, 362
Donnelly, Martin J., 122
Douglas-Cowie, Ellen, 270
Draper, M.H., 15
Dromey, Christopher, 98, 99
Dronkers, Nina F., 319, 360
Druker, David, 41
DuBois, Arthur, 111, 125n
Duez, Danielle, 458
Duffy, Joseph R., 337
Dunbar, Robin I.M., 362
Dunn, Hugh K., 60

Edin, Benoni B., 254, 255, 256
Edizer, Mete, 82
Edmonson, Jerold A., 479, 497
Edwards, Jan R., 9, 341, 424, 531–3, 538, 539
Edwards, Susan, 447
Eibl-Eibesfeldt, Irenäus, 366
Eigsti, Inge-Marie, 181–2
Eilers, Rebecca E., 119
Eimas, Peter D., 565
Eklund, Robert, 456, 457, 458
Ekman, Paul, 187
Ellis, Andrew W., 461
Ellsworth, Phoebe, 187
Elman, Jeffrey L., 268
Elstner, W., 210, 211
Emami-Naeini, Abbas, 277
Emanuel, Floyd W., 113–14
Engelhardt, Paul E., 434–5, 436
Engstrand, Olle, 488
Enright, Paul L., 20

Erdle, Christa, 209
Eriksson, Per-Olof, 251
Ertmer, David J., 208, 209
Esling, John H., 479, 496–7
Esposito, Fabrizio, 284
Essick, Gregory K., 255
Estep, Meredith, 98

Fadiga, L., 169
Fairbanks, Grant, 270, 276–7
Falk, Dean, 370
Fant, Gunnar, 43, 51, 60, 72, 190, 191, 229, 488, 489
Fausto, Carlos, 487
Feldman, Anatol G., 91
Feng, Yongqiang, 238–9, 275
Fentress, John C., 366
Ferguson, C.A., 369
Ferrari, Pier F., 361
Ferreira, Fernanda, 434–5, 436, 457, 461
Fikkert, Paula, 396
Fillmore, Charles, 449
Finnegan, Eileen M., 25
Fitch, W. Tecumseh, 71, 366, 548
Flanagan, James L., 43, 52, 53
Fletcher, Harvey, 60
Flipsen, Peter, 387
Fogassi, Leonardo, 201
Folkins, John W., 68, 250
Formisano, Elia, 284
Forner, L.L., 389
Forrest, Karen, 335–6
Fossett, Tepanta R.D., 344
Fougeron, Cecile, 424, 519
Foundas, Anne L., 282
Fourcin, Adrian J., 41
Fowler, Carol A., 163, 166, 169, 200, 202, 232, 261
Fox, Robert A., 204–5
Fox Tree, Jean E., 459
Franchetto, Bruna, 487
Frank, N. Robert, 19
Frankel, Steven H., 47
Frankish, C., 160
Franklin, Gene F., 277
Freud, Sigmund, 411
Frid, Johan, 488
Friesen, Wallace V., 187
Frisch, Stefan A., 405, 567

Frith, Chris D., 270
Fromkin, Victoria A., 404, 405, 423, 434, 508, 509
Fu, Cynthia H., 284
Fuchs, Susanne, 7, 133, 135, 422
Fujimura, Osamu, 70, 139, 140, 232
Fukase, Hitoshi, 86
Fulcher, Lewis P., 53
Furth, Katrina, 462
Furukawa, Kazunori, 240
Fuwa, Kiyoko, 546

Gabrieli, John D.E., 433
Gadbois, Simon, 366
Gafos, Adamantios I., 146
Galantucci, Bruno, 200, 202
Galindo, Benoit, 499n
Gallese, Vittorio, 201
Galves, A., 165
Galvin, Karyn L., 261
Gandevia, Simon C., 257
García-Albea, José E., 430
Garding, Gina, 515
Garellek, Marc, 499
Garrett, Merrill F., 423, 434, 435
Gay, Thomas, 232–3, 238, 389
Gazzaniga, Michael S., 368
Geiser, Eveline, 433
Gentilucci, Maurizio, 203
George, Helen, 494
Georgopoulos, Apostolos P., 357
Gerken, LouAnn, 429
Geschwind, Norman, 281
Geumann, Anja, 135
Ghahramani, Zoubin, 271
Gharb, Bahar B., 85
Ghitza, Oded, 359
Ghosh, Satrajit S., 204, 205, 305, 315–16
Gibbon, D., 165
Gibbon, Fiona E., 535
Gibellino, Francesca, 19
Gick, Bryan, 138, 140, 141, 145, 261, 537
Giedd, Jay, 71
Gildersleeve-Neumann, Christina E., 121, 363, 364, 396–7, 545
Gillis, Stephen, 363–4
Giraud, Anne-Lisa, 359
Gladfelter, Allison, 561, 567, 569
Godey, Benoit, 277

Goffman, Lisa, 9, 98, 209, 394, 557, 560, 561, 565–6, 567, 569, 570
Goldfarb, W., 167
Goldman, Herbert I., 370
Goldman, Michael D., 15
Goldman-Eisler, Freida, 387, 456
Goldrick, Matthew, 561, 567
Goldsmith, John, 513
Goldstein, Louis M., 4, 67, 100, 138, 139, 143, 144, 145–6, 147–9, 150, 166, 184, 203, 313, 370, 384, 406, 414, 432, 438, 439n, 521, 523, 537–8, 565
Gomi, Hiroaki, 255–6
Goodglass, Harold, 447
Goodman, Corey S., 368
Goodwin, Guy M., 250
Gopal, Hundrai S., 207
Gordeeva, Olga B., 498
Gordon, Andrew M., 565
Gordon, Matthew, 497, 539
Goswami, Usha, 433
Govaerts, Paul J., 363–4
Grabe, Esther, 165, 391, 392, 393
Graber, Thomas M., 113
Gracco, Vincent L., 137, 144, 238–9, 257–8, 275, 280
Grayson, Liane, 98, 570
Graziano, Michael S. A., 301–2
Green, Jordan R., 5, 8, 97, 98, 99, 381, 558–9, 564
Greenberg, Steven, 358, 359
Greenfield, Patricia M., 556
Gregores, Emma, 490
Grewel, Fritz, 298
Grigos, Maria I., 565, 569–70
Grill, Stephen E., 254
Grillner, Sten, 168, 356, 357
Grosjean, Francois, 24
Guenther, Frank H., 204, 205, 212, 231, 300, 305, 307, 315–16, 317, 355, 560, 561, 565, 568
Guérin, Bernard, 72
Gussenhoven, Carlos, 433
Gut, U., 165
Guyette, Thomas, 344

Hagen, Marinda, 432–3
Hain, Timothy C., 272
Haken, H., 168

Hall, Kelly D., 387
Halle, Morris, 190–1, 496, 505
Hallett, Mark, 254
Hanawa, Soshi, 95
Handelman, Chester S., 118
Hanley, Clair N., 273
Hannam, Alan G., 88–9, 91
Hapsburg, Deborah von *see* von Hapsburg, Deborah
Hardin-Jones, Mary, 364
Harper, Amy, 426
Harris, Christopher M., 269
Harris, Jimmy G., 479
Harshman, Richard, 67
Hartsuiker, Robert J., 461
Haselager, G.J.T., 387
Hauser, Marc D., 80
Hawkins, Sarah, 392, 394
Hay, Jessica S.F., 495
Hayashi, Akiko, 544
Hayden, Deborah A., 334
Hayes, Bruce, 430
Heatherton, Todd F., 368
Heilman, Kenneth M., 299
Heinks-Maldonado, Theda H., 282
Heisler, Lori, 557, 567–8, 570
Hermes, Dik, 391
Hertrich, Ingo, 96
Hickok, Gregory, 281, 307, 319, 560, 561, 565
Hieke, Adolf E., 460
Higashikawa, Masahiko, 312
Hiiemae, Karen M., 96
Hill, Elisabeth L., 557
Hill, Harold, 186
Hilliard, Caitlin, 462
Hinton, Geoffrey E., 193
Hirano, Minoru, 34, 36, 53
Hirano, Shigeru, 284
Hirschberg, Julia, 457, 466
Hixon, Thomas J., 15, 16, 20–2, 23, 25, 36, 114, 115, 116, 118, 119–21, 126n
Hoffman, Eric A., 72
Hoffman, Henry T., 25
Hogan, Jerry A., 366
Hoit, Jeannette D., 15, 16, 20–2, 23, 27, 36, 121, 125n
Holliday, Jeffrey J., 539
Hollien, Harry, 52
Holmes, Virginia M., 461

Holst, Erich W. von, 269
Holt, Lori L., 204
Honda, Kiyoshi, 6, 61, 69, 70, 73, 74, 209–10, 252
Honda, Masaaki, 236–7, 256
Honikman, Beatrice, 537
Hooff, Jan A.R.A.M. van, 362
Hoole, Philip, 7, 135, 141, 142, 143, 146, 149, 150, 313
Horiguchi, Naoya, 537
Horn, Berthold K.P., 187, 189
Hosoi, Hiroshi, 546
Houde, John, 7, 8, 271, 282, 283, 285, 312
House, Arthur S., 115
Howell, P., 170
Huber, Ernst, 492
Huber, Jessica E., 6, 23, 24, 25, 26–7
Hughes, Marie Olive, 226
Hume, David, 354
Hunnicutt, M., 170
Hutchinson, J.M., 121
Hutters, Birgit, 142
Huxley, Thomas, 354
Hwang, Kun, 81, 85
Hwang, SeHo, 81
Hyatt, Robert E., 20

Igoa, José M., 430
Imaizumi, Satoshi, 544, 546
Indefrey, Peter, 465–6
Ingervall, Bengt, 81–2
Ingram, David, 368, 392, 393
Isard, S., 163
Ishizaka, Kenzo, 44, 52, 53
Ito, Takayuki, 7–8, 230–1, 255–6, 257, 259, 260–1
Iverson, Jana, 559

Jacks, Adam, 309
Jacob, François, 356
Jaeger, Jeri, 369, 371
Jaeger, T. Florian, 462
Jakobson, Roman, 190, 531
Jancke, Lutz, 557
Janson, Tomas, 81–2
Janson, Tore, 365
Jasper, Herbert, 301
Jeannerod, Marc, 269
Jescheniak, Jorg D., 461

Jessell, Thomas M., 277
Jiang, Jack Jiaqi, 47
Johansson, Roland S., 252, 254, 256
Johnson, Wendell, 453
Jonas, Saran, 302, 359
Jones, D., 160
Jones, Jeffrey A., 185–6, 234–5, 238
Jordan, Michael I., 271
Joseph, Brian D., 538
Jozan, Gregoire, 182, 183
Julien, Hannah, 541
Jun, Sun-Ah, 424, 519

Kahane, Joel C., 68
Kajiyama, Masato, 60, 75
Kakita, Yakita, 70
Kalaska, John F., 255
Kandel, Eric R., 277
Kaplan, Barbara, 447
Kasowski, Stanley, 60
Kaspar, Kai, 273
Kataoka, Ryuta, 116–17
Katseff, Shira, 275
Katsika, Argyro, 523
Katz, Douglas I., 273
Kawahara, Hideki, 268
Kawahara, Shigeto, 545
Kawakami, Shigehisa, 89
Kawato, Mitsuo, 240
Kay, Christian, 452
Keating, Patricia, 424, 425–6, 435–6, 438, 499, 506, 507, 509, 510, 513, 519, 520, 522
Keele, Steven W., 3
Kehoe, M., 393, 394
Keidar, Anat, 52
Keller, E., 170
Kelsen, Steven G., 19
Kelso, J.A. Scott, 100, 135, 136, 168, 170, 226–7, 230, 241
Kent, Raymond D., 80, 116, 118, 307, 309, 334, 337, 338, 364, 389, 564
Kerkhoff, Joop, 432–3
Kern, Sophie, 363
Kertez, Andrew, 301
Kewley-Port, Diane, 538
Khattab, Ghada, 547
Kim, D.J., 81
Kim, Sahyang, 520, 522
Kim, Yunjung, 304, 307, 309, 337

Kingston, John, 490, 505
Kita, Sotaro, 465–6
Kitamura, Tatsuya, 73, 75
Klatt, D., 170
Klein, Harriet B., 544
Klich, Richard J., 23–4
Klima, Edward S., 431
Kluender, Keith R., 204
Knight, R., 167
Knudson, Ronald J., 17
Kobayashi, Noriko, 209–10
Kochanski, Greg, 391
Kochetov, Alexei, 140–1
Kohler, Evelyne, 201
Kohler, Klaus, 355
Kojima, Hisayoshi, 284
Kolk, Herman, 338, 455
Kollia, H. Betty, 136–7
Kolta, Arlette, 95
Kong, Eun Jong, 538, 539, 540–1, 545–6
Koolstra, Jan Harm, 89, 90, 91
Koopmans-van Beinum, Florian J., 358
Korfage, Joannes A.M., 90–1
Kort, Naomi S., 285
Kowal, Sabine, 386, 388, 459
Kozhevnikov, Valerii A., 144
Krakow, Rena A., 116, 137–9, 143, 313
Krawczyk, Kirsty, 559
Kristofferson, A.B., 170
Krivokapić, Jelena, 422, 523
Kubo, Masayoshi, 240
Kubota, Kinziro, 95, 251
Kuhl, Patricia K., 380
Kühnert, Barbara, 146
Kuiper, K., 159
Kummer, Ann, 118, 122, 124
Kumral, Emre, 301
Kuratate, Takaaki, 179, 180, 184–5, 188
Kurths, J., 171

Laboissière, Rafael, 91–2, 242
Labov, William, 546
Lackner, James R., 273
Ladd, D. Robert, 422, 513, 514, 515
Ladefoged, Peter, 15, 67, 141, 478, 484, 485, 487, 488–9, 492–3, 494, 497, 506–7, 510, 539
Lahiri, Aditi, 422, 461
Lallouache, Mohamed-Tahar, 188
Lamarre, Y., 251

Lametti, Daniel R., 239, 258, 276
Landess, Susan, 337
Landgraf, Lorinda, 52
Lane, Harlan, 209
Lanteri, Celia J., 22
Large, E.W., 166
Larkey, Leah S., 427
Larson, Charles R., 250, 268, 275
Lashley, Karl S., 1–2, 4–5, 8, 354–5, 419, 421
Latash, M., 168
Lawson, Eleanor, 498
Leary, Adam P., 480
Lee, Hyuck-Joon, 519
Lee, Linda, 124
Lee, ShuJin, 83–4
Lee, Soyoung, 364, 367
Lee, Sungbok, 388
Lee, Yoonjeong, 520
Legerstee, Maria, 203
Lehiste, Ilse, 163, 396
Lemon, Roger N., 301
Lennartson, Bertil, 251
Lenneberg, Eric H., 387
Leonard, T., 172
Levelt, Willem J.M., 284, 319, 338, 355, 406, 408, 425–6, 434, 435, 437, 453–5, 460, 461, 463, 464–5, 466, 467, 560
Levison, Henry, 17
Levitt, Andrea G., 537–8
Levitzky, Michael G., 15, 16
Li, Fangfang, 532, 535, 540, 545, 546
Li, H., 69
Li, Sheng, 47
Liberman, Alvin M., 159, 166, 202
Lickley, Robin J., 8, 9, 446, 451–2, 456, 459, 460, 461, 463, 466, 468, 561
Lieberman, Philip H., 80, 86
Liljencrants, Johan, 52
Limousin, Patricia, 303
Lindblom, Björn, 488, 489, 493–4, 498
Lisker, Leigh, 142
Liss, Julie M., 304, 309
Liu, Antang, 83–5
Liu, Jianmin, 96
Lloyd James, A., 161
Locke, John, 354
Locke, John L., 365
Löfqvist, Anders, 100, 134, 137, 143, 144, 149–50, 209–10, 313

Lotto, Andrew J., 204
Low, Ee Ling, 165, 391
Lowell, Soren Y., 52
Lubker, James F., 110, 115, 170, 498
Lucas, Sally Anne, 211
Luce, Paul A., 456
Lulich, Steven M., 73
Lund, James P., 95, 251
Luschei, Erich S., 25

Maasen, Ben, 8, 334, 337, 341, 342, 343, 387
MacDonald, Ewen N., 275
MacDonald, John, 188, 200, 260
MacKay, Donald G., 415n
Macko, Kathleen A., 280
Maclay, Howard, 452, 453, 463
MacLeod, Alison, 213
MacNeilage, Peter F., 6, 8, 93, 97–8, 353, 354, 356, 358, 359, 361, 362–3, 364, 365, 368, 369, 370, 371, 381, 382, 532, 558, 561, 564
MacPherson, Megan K., 570
Maddieson, Ian, 141, 371, 484, 485, 487, 488, 493, 497, 509, 510
Maeda, Shinji, 67, 70, 72, 206, 226, 541
Maekawa, Kikuo, 458
Mağden, Orhan, 82
Mahl, George F., 452
Mahshie, James M., 41
Malin, Caren, 568
Maner, Kimberly J., 98, 570
Mansell, Anthony L., 17
Marcus, S., 160
Marin, Stefania, 144–5
Marion, Michelle J., 337, 341
Marquardt, Thomas P., 309, 337
Martin, James G., 456
Marx, David B., 559
Marzullo, Ana Carolina de Miranda, 100
Masegi, Toshiaki, 95, 251
Mathes, Katey A., 309
Matsudaira, M., 44, 52
Matsuo, Kolchiro, 96
Matthews, Peter B.C., 250
Matthies, Melanie L., 205
Mattingly, I.G., 166
Matyear, Christine L., 363, 532
Max, Ludo, 167, 238–9, 275
Mayo, Robert, 114, 116–17, 120, 123
Mayr, E., 353

McCabe, Patricia, 335
McCaffrey, Helen A., 208, 363
McClean, Michael D., 99, 251, 361–2
McCloskey, D. Ian, 250
McCullough, Elizabeth, 429
McCune, Lorraine, 384
McDonough, Joyce, 494
McDowell, Margaret A., 16
McGarr, Nancy S., 143, 209–10
McGettigan, Carolyn, 280
McGowan, Richard S., 566
McGurk, Harry, 188, 200, 260
McKerns, David, 126n
McLeod, Sharynne, 335
McMillan, Corey T., 561, 567, 568
McNeil, Malcolm R., 299, 305, 317, 334, 344
McShane, John, 370
McWilliams, Betty Jane, 111
Mead, Jere, 15, 19
Meguid, E.M.A., 82
Mehler, Jacques, 163–5, 166, 380, 391
Meira, Sergio, 487
Meister, Ingo G., 280
Meltzoff, Andrew N., 380
Ménard, Lucie, 7, 207, 212–13, 541–3
Mermelstein, Paul, 67
Mesgarani, Nima, 269
Meulen, Sjoeke van der, 334
Meyer, Antje S., 319, 406, 434
Miller, Amanda L., 539
Miller, Nick, 318
Mills, Anne E., 210–11
Miozzo, Michele, 414
Mishkin, Mortimer, 280
Mitchell, Heather L., 27
Mitchell, Pamela R., 364
Mitra, Subhobrata, 134
Mittelstaedt, Horst, 269
Mittman, Charles, 19
Mitton, Janet, 463, 464, 465
Moat, H. Susannah, 410
Mohr, Jay P., 319
Moisik, Scott R., 479, 496–7
Mokhtari, Parham, 72, 73
Moll, Kenneth L., 110, 113, 114, 115, 116
Mongeau, Luc, 47, 53
Monnin, Julia, 532
Moore, Christopher A., 98, 257, 381, 558–9
Moore, Paul, 37

Mooshammer, Christine, 135, 146, 462, 523
Morgan, J.L., 166
Morrill, Ryan J., 359–60
Morrillon, Benjamin, 359
Morrison, Catriona M., 461
Morrison, Judith A., 208
Morton, J., 160
Möttönen, Riikka, 201, 261
Mrayati, Mohammed, 72
Mu, Liancai, 68–9
Mücke, Doris, 516
Muller, Eric M., 100
Munhall, Kevin G., 7, 100, 150, 178, 182–3, 185–6, 188–9, 203, 206, 234–5, 236, 238, 272, 313, 516, 521
Munson, Benjamin, 9, 541, 547
Murdock, George P., 369–70
Murray, Ann D., 118
Mussa-Ivaldi, Ferdinando A., 242
Myers, Florence L., 448

Nagarajan, Srikantan S., 283, 285
Nakai, Satsuki, 518
Nakatani, Christine H., 457, 466, 467
Nakatani, Lloyd H., 427
Nam, Hosung, 144
Namasivayam, Aravind Kumar, 100
Nasir, Sazzad M., 239, 258, 276
Nazzi, Thierry, 380
Neilson, Peter D., 250, 252
Nelson, Winston L., 206
Nerbonne, M.A., 121
Nespor, Marina, 163–5, 391, 430
Newport, Elissa L., 380
Nguyen, Noel, 516
Nigro, Georgia, 201
Nijland, Lian, 334, 340–1
Nil, Luc de, 100
Nip, Ignatius S.B., 381, 559
Nittrouer, Susan, 566
Nolan, Francis, 165, 391
Nooteboom, Sieb G., 466, 467
Nordin, Magnus, 254
Norton, A., 170
Notebaert, Lies, 461

O'Connell, Daniel C., 459
O'Connor, Kathleen D., 427

O'Dell, M., 162–3
O'Dwyer, Nicolas J., 250
Ogar, Jennifer, 316
Ohala, John J., 357, 358, 490–1, 498, 511
Ohala, Manjari, 490–1
Ohde, Ralph N., 547
Öhman, Sven E., 144
Oldfield, Robert C., 461
Oller, D. Kimbrough, 119, 364, 380
Oomen, Claudy C.E., 463
Oppenheim, Gary M., 8, 407–10, 411–13
Orliaguet, Jean-Pierre, 229
Orlikoff, Robert F., 112, 125n
Osborne, George, 118
Osgood, Charles E., 452, 453, 463
Osindero, Simon, 193
Ostrovsky, Karine, 360–1
Ostry, David J., 90, 91–2, 194n, 230–1, 239, 251, 256, 257, 258, 259, 260–1, 276
Otuka, Noboru, 544
Ouellet, Christine, 208
Owens, Elmer, 209

Palmer, Jeffrey B., 96
Papoutsi, Marina, 280
Parsons, Thomas W., 277
Patel, A., 172
Patel, Aniruddh D., 433
Patel, Rupal, 569–70
Paul, R., 167
Payne, Elinor, 392–3
Peach, Richard K., 303
Peacher, William G., 298
Peck, Christopher C., 88–9, 91
Peeva, Maya G., 280, 315–16, 318
Pelletier, Cathy A., 96–7
Penfield, Wilder, 301
Pensalfini, Rob, 355
Perkell, Joseph S., 67, 180, 204, 205, 206, 209, 212, 226, 315–16, 319, 320
Perrier, Pascal, 7, 133, 135, 229, 242, 273
Perry, Theodore L., 547
Pessa, Joel, 492
Peterson-Falzone, Sally, 124
Pfau, Roland, 434
Pfitzenmeyer, Pierre, 19, 20
Pick, Herbert L., 268
Pierpoint, Elizabeth I., 557–8, 570
Pierrehumbert, Janet, 512, 513, 561

Pike, K.L., 161
Pikovsky, A., 171
Pinker, Steven, 2
Pitts, Teresa, 28
Plato, 354
Plauché, Madelaine, 460
Plavcan, J. Michael, 86
Plug, Leendert, 467
Plummer, Andrew R., 541
Poeck, Klaus, 448
Poeppel, David, 307, 319
Polgar, George, 17
Pollack, Irwin, 178, 181, 200, 260
Pollock, Karen E., 393–4
Popovich, Frank, 86–8
Port, Robert F., 161, 162–3, 168–70, 480
Porter, Robert, 301
Postma, Aalbert, 338, 455, 463, 468n
Pouplier, Marianne, 7, 134, 143, 144, 145, 147, 313
Povel, Dirk-Jan, 338, 455
Powell, J. David, 277
Pratt, Carol A., 257
Pratt, Sheila, 344
Preston, Malcolm S., 538
Price, Patti J., 24
Prince, Alan, 147, 159
Prochazka, Arthur, 257
Prost, Véronique, 211
Prud'homme, Michel J., 255
Pulvermüller, Friedemann, 307, 556
Purcell, David W., 236, 238

Quinlan, Philip T., 461

Rahn, Douglas A., 14
Ramig, Lorraine O., 98, 99
Rampazzo, Antonio, 85
Ramus, Franck, 163–5, 391
Rasch, R., 161
Rath, Erick M., 99–100
Rauschecker, Josef P., 279, 280
Recasens, Daniel, 566
Redford, Melissa A., 8, 387, 390, 393, 395, 396–7, 426, 544–5
Redican, William K., 357
Reed, Charlotte M., 261
Refshauge, Kathryn M., 257
Reilly, Kevin J., 98, 231, 381

Richards, Whitman A., 366
Richtsmeier, Peter T., 429
Riecker, Axel, 302, 304, 305, 317, 318, 360
Riely, Rachel R., 98, 99, 394
Riess Jones, M., 166
Ringel, Robert L., 277
Ringqvist, Torsten, 19
Rizzolatti, Giacomo, 166, 201, 556
Robb, Michael P., 387, 396
Robert-Ribes, Jordi, 200, 207
Roberts, Julia Lee, 546
Robinson, K.L., 121
Rodella, Luigi F., 86, 92, 93
Roelofs, Ardi, 317, 319, 406, 434, 437
Rogers, Carolyn R., 80, 82
Rogers, Lesley J., 353
Rogers, Margaret, 303
Rojas Curieux, Tulio, 485
Rosenbaum, David A., 354
Rosenbek, John C., 309, 318
Rosenblum, M., 171
Rosenthal, Joan B., 335
Rossato, Solange, 499
Rothenberg, Martin, 41, 43, 51
Rothwell, John C., 301
Rousset, Isobelle, 365, 369, 499
Rubeling, Hartmut, 273
Rubin, Philip, 67, 179–80, 254
Rvachew, Susan, 537, 543

Sabes, Philip N., 274
Sabin, Edward J., 387
Sadagopan, Neeraja, 25, 27, 570
Saffran, Jenny R., 380
Saltzmann, Elliot, 100, 134, 135, 137, 144, 150, 166, 203, 240, 521, 522
Samlan, Robin A., 54
Sams, Mikko, 201, 261
Sander, L.W., 169
Sanders, Ira, 68–9
Sanguineti, Vittorio, 91–2
Santana, M., 169
Sapienza, Christine M., 20–2, 23, 25, 28
Sasaki, Clarence T., 118
Sato, Marc, 280
Saussure, Ferdinand de, 354
Savariaux, Christophe, 229, 233–4, 238
Sawusch, James R., 396
Saxman, John H., 396, 565

Schachner, Adena, 433
Schadeberg, Thilo, 490
Schauwers, Karen, 363–4
Scherer, Ronald C., 47
Schiller, Niels O., 284
Schmidt, Karen L., 492
Scholte, Tom, 181
Scholz, John P., 239–40
Schöner, Gregor, 239–40
Schunk, Brian G., 187, 189
Schwartz, C. E., 213
Schwartz, James H., 277
Schwartz, Jean-Luc, 205, 212, 242
Schwartz, Myrna F., 421
Schwartz, Richard G., 394
Scobbie, James M., 498
Scott, Cheryl M., 277
Scott, D., 163
Scott, S.K., 160
Seccombe, Leigh M., 26
Segalowitz, Norman, 449, 465, 468n
Seki, K., 437
Selkirk, Elisabeth, 430
Senner, Jill E., 268
Serrurier, Antoine, 98
Sessle, Barry J., 95
Severeid, Larry R., 116
Severens, Els, 462
Seyfeddinipur, Mandana, 465–7
Shadle, Christine H., 180, 517–18
Shadmehr, Reza, 242
Shaiman, Susan, 100, 257–8
Shattuck-Hufnagel, Stefanie, 8–9, 355, 385, 396, 421, 423, 424, 425–6, 427, 428, 432, 433, 435–6, 437, 438, 439n, 512, 513, 518, 520
Shaw, Jason A., 146
Shepherd, Michael A., 519
Sherrill, D.L., 17
Shih, Chilin, 424
Shiller, Douglas M., 258, 261, 275
Shockley, K., 169
Shoji, Atsuko, 544
Shosted, Ryan K., 491
Shriberg, Elizabeth, 458, 459, 460, 463, 466, 467
Shriberg, Lawrence D., 208, 336, 339, 342
Shum, Mamie, 282
Sidtis, John J., 305

Siegel, Gerald M., 268
Siemionow, Maria, 85, 92
Sihvonen, Toni, 201, 261
Simko, J., 172
Simpson, Adrian P., 322n
Siple, Patricia, 431
Sirsa, Hema, 393, 395
Skehan, Peter, 449
Skinner, Burrhus F., 2, 419
Skipper, Jeremy I., 202
Slaughter, Kate, 69
Sly, Peter D., 22
Smit, Ann Bosma, 564
Smith, Anne, 98, 99, 251, 257, 309, 310, 394, 560, 564, 565–6, 570
Smith, Beverly, 334
Smith, Bruce L., 364, 389
Smith, Linda, 555, 556, 559
Smith, Vicki L., 461
Smolensky, Paul, 147
Snapp-Childs, Winona, 556
Snow, David, 396, 428
Sober, Samuel J., 274
Sokoloff, Alan J., 69
Solé, María-Josep, 508, 511
Solomon, Nancy P., 27
Sorkin, John D., 15
Spencer, John P., 556
Spencer, Kristie A., 303
Sperry, Elizabeth E., 23–4
Sproat, Richard, 139, 140
St. Louis, Kenneth O., 448
Staekenborg, Salka S., 303
Staiger, Anja, 310
Stål, Per, 250
Stark, Rachel E., 364, 380, 381
Starkweather, C. Woodruff, 167, 448
Stathopoulos, Elaine T., 6, 20–2, 23, 25, 27
Staunton, Ruth, 547
Steele, Catriona M., 96–7, 100
Steele, J., 159–60
Steinen, Karl von den, 487
Stelt, Jeanette M. van der see van der Stelt, Jeanette M.
Stenzel, Kristine, 496
Stevens, Kenneth N., 44, 60, 72, 115, 232, 496
Stoel-Gammon, Carol, 364, 534
Storto, Luciana, 485, 489, 493
Story, Brad H., 6, 49–50, 51, 52, 53, 54, 72, 73

Story, Robin Seider, 209–10
Stout, Gwendolyn, 364
Strife, Janet L., 124
Stuart-Smith, Jane, 498
Stucchi, Natale, 203
Studdert-Kennedy, Michael G., 371, 566
Suarez, Jorge A., 490
Subtelny, J. Daniel, 118
Sugishita, M., 437
Sumby, William H., 178, 181, 200, 260
Summerfield, Quentin, 191, 213
Sundberg, Johan, 72, 75
Sussman, Harvey M., 337
Suzuki, Ryoji, 240
Svirsky, Mario A., 209
Syrdal, Ann K., 207
Syrett, Kristen, 545

Tabain, Marija, 478
Takada, Mieko, 538–9
Takano, Sayoko, 69, 252
Takemoto, Hironori, 61, 69, 73, 74
Talkin, David T., 53
Tamura, Fumiyo, 96
Tasko, Stephen M., 99, 361–2
Tavakoli, Parvaneh, 449
Teh, Yee-Whye, 193
Terband, Hayo, 8, 337, 341, 342, 343, 387
Terken, Jacques, 391
Teston, Bernard, 499n
Thal, Donna, 559
Thelen, Esther, 170, 367, 555, 556, 559
Thom, Stacey A., 119
Thomander, Lars, 254
Thomas, K., 211
Thompson, Amy E., 114, 116, 119–20
Thompson, Gordon W., 86–8
Thomson, Neil, 415n
Thomson, Scott L., 47
Thoonen, Geert, 340
Thornell, Lars-Eric, 251
Tian, Biao, 280
Tiede, Mark, 256, 523
Tiffany, William R., 273
Titze, Ingo R., 36, 37, 38–9, 43, 44, 45, 47, 49–50, 51, 52, 53–4, 72
Tjaden, Kris, 314–15
Tobey, Emily A., 208–9
Tohkura, Yoh'ichi, 188–9

Tolep, Kenneth, 19
Tonkovich, John D., 303
Tourville, Jason A., 204, 231, 284, 305, 315–16, 560, 565, 568
Towne, Roger, 337
Toyomura, Akira, 283, 284
Traill, Anthony, 481
Trehub, S., 159
Tremblay, Annie, 429
Tremblay, Pascale, 280
Tremblay, R. E., 238, 259
Tremblay, Stéphanie, 235–6, 258
Tripoliti, Elina, 303
Trost, Judith E., 124
Trouvain, J., 159, 172
Trulsson, Mats, 252
Tsao, Cheng-Chi, 240
Tseng, Shu-chuan, 458
Tuller, Betty, 135, 226–7, 230, 241
Turgeon, Christine, 209
Turk, Alice E., 395–6, 424, 428, 432, 437, 512, 518, 520
Turken, A. Umit, 319
Turvey, Michael T., 135, 200
Tye-Murray, Nancy, 208–9

Ullman, Michael T., 557–8, 570
Ungerleider, Leslie G., 280
Urban, Peter Paul, 300–1, 304, 310

Vaissière, J., 488
Vallée, Nathalie, 482, 494, 499
Vallino, Linda D., 111
Vallortigara, Giorgio, 353
Van de Ven, Vincent, 284
Van den Berg, Janwillem, 44
Van der Bilt, Andries, 93–5, 97
Van der Meulen, Sjoeke, 334
Van der Stelt, Jeanette M., 358
Van Eijden, Theo M.G.J., 90–1
Van Hooff, Jan A.R.A.M., 362
Van Lieshout, Pascal H.H.M., 6, 96–7, 98, 100, 101
Vatikiotis-Bateson, Eric, 7, 90, 178, 179–80, 181–2, 185, 186–7, 194n, 206, 254
Ventura, Maria I., 283
Véronis, Jean, 457
Vick, Jennell C., 209
Vihman, Marilyn, 382–4, 531, 532, 558

Villacorta, Virgilio M., 204
Vinyard, Christopher J., 98
Viso, Susana del *see* del Viso, Susana
Vitkovich, Melanie, 183
Viviani, Paolo, 203
Vogel, Irene, 430
von Cramon, Detlev, 302
von den Steinen, Karl, 487
von Hapsburg, Deborah, 363
von Holst, Erich W., 269
Vorperian, Houri K., 118, 547
Vos, J., 161

Wagner, P., 165, 172
Walker, Jean F., 387
Walsh, Bridget, 309, 310, 564
Wang, Qi Emily, 139
Wang, Xiaoqin, 277
Wang, Yu-Tsai, 24
Ward, David, 448
Warner-Czyz, Andrea D., 208
Warren, Donald W., 111, 124, 125n, 126n
Wasow, Thomas, 460
Watkins, Kate E., 202
Watson, Peter J., 27
Watson, Robert T., 299
Weismer, Gary, 5, 8, 16, 36, 303, 304, 307, 309, 310, 311, 312, 314–15, 337
Weng, Tzong R., 17
Wenk, B., 166
Wessel, Karl, 305
Westbury, John R., 61, 310, 510
Whalen, Doug H., 202, 310, 537–8
Wheeldon, Linda R., 408, 422, 461
White, Laurence, 395
Whitteridge, David, 15
Wiggs, Melissa, 124
Williams, Maurice, 461
Williams, William N., 110
Williamson, Matthew M., 98
Wilson, Ian Lewis, 537
Wing, A.M., 170
Wingate, Marcel E., 448, 453
Wingfield, Arthur, 461
Winkworth, Alison L., 23
Wise, Richard J., 281
Wlodarczak, M., 172
Wodicka, George R., 53
Wolpert, Daniel M., 269, 270, 271

Wolstencroft, Jay J., 23
Wong, Min Ney, 322n
Wood, Sean, 272
Woodward, Mary F., 189
Wright, Richard, 405, 567
Wroe, Stephen, 94
Wu, Zongji, 489

Yairi, Ehud, 448
Yano, Sumio, 181–2
Yaruss, J.S., 167
Yasuda, Akiko, 539
Yates, Cambell C., 111
Yehia, Hani C., 179–81, 182, 184–5, 186–7, 191, 193, 254
Yoneyama, Kiyoko, 533, 545–6
Yoshioka, Hirohide, 143
Young, Lisa H., 117

Younger, Barbara, 567
Yudman, E.M., 167
Yunosova, Yana, 303, 310

Zajac, David J., 6, 114, 116–17, 119, 120, 121, 123, 125n
Zanartu, Matias, 53
Zarate, Jean Mary, 272, 283
Zatorre, Robert J., 261, 272, 275, 283
Zawaydeh, Bushra, 508, 509
Zelaznik, Howard N., 557, 564
Zeman, Kirby L., 17
Zemlin, Willard R., 36, 41, 85, 86, 89, 90, 92
Zhang, Futang, 88–9, 91
Zheng, Zane Z., 284, 285
Ziegler, Wolfram, 302, 305, 310, 312, 319, 320
Zsiga, Elizabeth C., 140

Index of Subjects

References to tables, figures and notes are given as, for example, 62t, 81f, 499n.

abdominal muscles, 15, 19–20, 27
accentual lengthening, 395–6
acoustic signal, 6, 7, 41–4, 70–5, 179–81, 230, 234–8, 478–9, 487–8
   boundary effects, 73–4
   and velopharyngeal function, 109–25
acoustic theory, 6, 489–95
adaptation, 270–2
adenoids, 118
aerodynamics, 109, 111–25, 478–9, 499n
affricates, 484–5, 531–2
age-related differences
   breathing, 14, 17–22, 23–4, 25
   jaw movement, 100–1
   Parkinson's disease, 25–7, 167–8, 303–4
   velopharyngeal function, 120–1
alveolar ridge, 86
American English, 137–9, 141, 544–5, 546
American Speech-Language-Hearing Association (ASHA), 334
Amharic (Semitic language), 484–5
amyotrophic lateral sclerosis (ALS), 308, 310
anatomy, 16–20, 80–93
anesthesia, 230–1
animal studies, 82, 86–8, 168, 201–2, 280, 359–60, 361
anthropocentrism, 354
aphasia, 432, 446–8

apraxia of speech, 8, 299, 301, 305, 309, 310–11, 315–20, 331–44
Arabic (Semitic language), 479, 509, 547
Arrernte (Pama-Nyungan language), 138
articulators, 3–4, 59–76, 478–80
   coordination *see* coordination
   developmental changes, 71, 97–101, 114, 118–21
   jaw and lips, 6, 79–101, 135–8, 206, 209–10, 212–13, 359–62, 492–3
   larynx, 34–6, 481–3
   modeling of, 67–70, 91–2
   tongue, 60–5, 67–70, 96–7, 135, 148, 209–10, 251–2
   velopharyngeal port (VP port), 109–25, 489–92
   vocal folds, 6, 34–55
Articulatory Phonology, 4, 7, 8, 143–8, 166, 184, 192–4, 313–15, 370–2, 384
arytenoid cartilages, 34
aspiration, 141–2, 261, 497–8
ataxic dysarthria, 304–5
attenuation, 406–15
auditory cortex, 278–9, 280–6
auditory feedback, 7–8, 98–9, 115–16, 178–94, 200–14, 267–86
   altered feedback experiments, 230–1, 236, 238–9, 242, 267–86

The Handbook of Speech Production, First Edition. Edited by Melissa A. Redford.
© 2015 John Wiley & Sons, Inc. Published 2019 by John Wiley & Sons, Inc.

modeling of, 276–8
visual feedback, 274
Auditory Theory of Speech Perception, 204–5
auditory-visual speech processing, 7, 169–70, 178–94, 200–14
autism, 547
Autosegmental Phonology, 513

babbling, 97–8, 208, 210–11, 358, 362–8, 380–2, 383, 558–9, 560–1
language-specific factors, 537
back vowels, 493–5
Bantu languages, 483–4
basal ganglia, 301, 303–4
Beijing dialect (Mandarin Chinese), 489
Bernouilli effect, 44, 49
bilabial consonants, 112
biphasic movement cycles, 355–8
bite-block experiments, 203–4, 228–9, 232–3, 241
blindness *see* visual impairment
blood supply, 82–3, 92
body language, 172
body size, 13, 16–17
boundary effects, 73–4, 148, 394–7, 424–5, 517–22, 569–70
brain, 7, 8
brainstem, 26, 95, 98–9, 356–8
breathing control, 26
central pattern generator, 95, 98–9, 356–8
feedback control mechanisms, 268–86
lateralization, 279
mirror neurons, 201–2, 361, 556–7
Parkinson's disease, 25–7
plasticity, 211, 225
breathing, 13–28
effects of disease on, 14, 25–7
measurement of respiratory patterns, 20–5
Broca's area, 280, 281, 283, 284, 305, 361, 556–7
buccinator, 81f, 94–5, 250

Cantonese (Sino-Tibetan language), 139, 531–2, 537, 541–3
Carib languages, 487–8
Catalan (Indo-European language), 392–3, 508, 509, 511
categorical perception, 279

central nervous system (CNS), 7, 8
breathing control, 26
central pattern generator, 95, 98–9, 356–8
feedback control mechanisms, 268–86
lateralization, 279
mirror neurons, 201–2, 361, 556–7
Parkinson's disease, 25–7
plasticity, 211, 225
cerebellum, 301, 304–5
cerebral palsy, 303, 308
Chebchev filters, 183
chewing, 8, 93–5, 96, 98, 357, 360, 558–9
childhood apraxia of speech (CAS), 331–44
children, physical development, 16–19, 20–5, 71, 81–2, 118–20, 123–4, 126n, 547
chimpanzee, 82
choral speaking, 169–70
cleft lip/palate, 116, 118, 121–5, 126n
clicks, 483–4
clinical conditions (disordered speech), 5, 298–322, 446–9
amyotrophic lateral sclerosis (ALS), 308, 310
aphasia, 432, 446–8
apraxia of speech, 8, 299, 301, 305, 309, 310–11, 315–20, 331–44
cerebral palsy, 303, 308
cleft lip/palate, 116, 118, 126n
diagnosis, 110, 250, 299, 315–16, 317, 318–19, 332–43, 446–8
dysarthria, 8, 298–9, 300–7, 308–10, 322n, 432
fluency disorders, 167–8, 280–2, 432–3, 448–9
hearing and visual impairments, 207–13, 258, 261–2, 267–8
Parkinson's disease, 14, 25–7, 167–8, 303–4, 309–10, 322n
pulmonary fibrosis, 14
specific language impairment (SLI), 557–8
stroke victims, 280–1, 300–1
treatment, 303, 343–4, 431–3
cliticization, 394–5
cluttering, 448
coarticulation *see* coordination
cochlear implants, 208–9
coda timing patterns, 139–40, 144, 145–6
cognitive rhythms, 172n

compensation, 268–70
computational models, 49–51, 52–4, 170
   articulators, 67–70, 91–2
   limitations, 193–4
   see also theory
Computer Articulation Instrument (CAI), 340
consonants, 112–14, 135, 137–43, 481–5, 486–92, 531–2, 534–9
   perturbation studies, 234–5
coordination, 3, 6–7, 99–101, 133–214
   developmental changes, 97–101, 379–98, 562–70
   internal model hypothesis, 242
   language-specific factors, 481–6, 516
   laryngeal-oral coordination, 134, 137, 141–3, 148–51
   motor speech disorders, 300–7, 313–15
   multiple segments, 143–51, 483–4
   perturbation studies, 7–8, 100–1, 203–4, 227–43
   rhythm, 7, 148, 158–72
   single segments, 134–43
   spatiotemporal coordination, 192–4
corticobulbar tract, 301–2
Coupled Oscillator Model of Syllable Structure (COMS), 143–8
cover-body model, 37–8, 49–50, 53
cranial nerves, 85, 92, 301, 305–6
creaky voice, 496, 497
cricoarytenoid muscle, 35
cricoid cartilage, 34, 35f
cricothyroid muscle, 35f
cross-language studies, 9, 477–571
   acquisition, 530–49
   phonetic fieldwork, 477–99, 500n
   phonetics-prosody interface, 511–23
   sequencing and planning, 436–7, 458–9
   timing patterns, 137–41, 143–51, 161–6, 391–7, 505–24
Czech (Indo-European language), 509

deafness *see* hearing impairment
Deep Brain Stimulation, 303
dementia, 303
dental prosthesis experiments, 234–5
devoicing, 148–9
digastric muscle, 61f, 63t, 64–5
digital signal processing (DSP), 267, 268
direct realism theory, 202–3

disfluency, 9, 167–8, 432–3, 448–9, 451–68
disordered speech, 5, 298–322, 446–9
   amyotrophic lateral sclerosis (ALS), 308, 310
   aphasia, 432, 446–8
   apraxia of speech, 8, 299, 301, 305, 309, 310–11, 315–20, 331–44
   cerebral palsy, 303, 308
   cleft lip/palate, 116, 118, 126n
   diagnosis, 110, 250, 299, 315–16, 317, 318–19, 332–43, 446–8
   dysarthria, 8, 298–9, 300–7, 308–10, 322n, 432
   fluency disorders, 167–8, 280–2, 432–3, 448–9
   hearing and visual impairments, 207–13, 258, 261–2, 267–8
   Parkinson's disease, 14, 25–7, 167–8, 303–4, 309–10, 322n
   pulmonary fibrosis, 14
   specific language impairment (SLI), 557–8
   stroke, 280–1, 300–1
   treatment, 303, 343–4, 431–3
DIVA/GODIVA model, 315–20, 560–1
Dongbei dialect (Mandarin Chinese), 545
dorsal processing stream, 280–2
Drehu (Austronesian language), 532
dual stream hypothesis, 280–1
duration, 390–2, 459, 508–11
Dutch speakers of English, 433
dynamical systems models, 170–1
dysarthria, 8, 298–9, 300–7, 308–10, 322n, 432

efference copy hypothesis, 269–70, 273, 277–8
eigenmodes, 38–9
elderly people
   breathing, 14, 17–22, 23–4, 25
   jaw movement, 100–1
   Parkinson's disease, 25–7, 167–8, 303–4
   velopharyngeal function, 120–1
electroglottograph (EGG), 41, 479–80, 482, 485, 500n
electromyography (EMG), 70, 241, 480, 493, 510, 562
emphysema, 14
English (Indo-European language), 137–9, 141, 391–7, 508, 509, 511, 520–3, 531–2, 537, 538, 539, 541–3, 544–5, 568–70

epiglottic vallecula, 71, 72f, 73
errors, 8–9, 355, 451–68, 534–9
 exchange errors, 423, 431, 434–5, 438, 439n
 inner speech errors, 404–15
 interaction errors, 421–39
 prosodic frames, 419–39
 repair strategies, 9, 451–4, 463–8
 second language learners, 430, 433
 sign language errors, 430–1
 tongue twister errors, 405–15, 426, 439n, 567
ethical issues, research methods, 111, 479
ethology, 365–7
evolutionary theory, 2, 8, 80, 86, 87, 353–72
exchange errors, 423, 431, 434–5, 438, 439n
eye movements, 181–2, 183–4

F0 (fundamental frequency), 38, 120–1, 180–1, 183, 234, 514–15, 517–18
Facial Action Coding System (FACS), 187–8
facial skin, role in speech motor control, 230–1, 248–62
feedback, 7–8, 98–9, 115–16, 178–94, 200–14, 267–86
 altered feedback experiments, 230–1, 236, 238–9, 242, 267–86
 modeling of, 276–8
 visual feedback, 274
feet (stress feet), 148, 162, 568–9
females
 anatomy and physiology, 99–101, 116, 126n
 breathing, 15, 17, 19–23, 24, 26–7
 developmental changes, 16–19, 20–5, 71
 'feminine' speech styles, 545–6, 547
 formants, 75
 Parkinson's disease, 26–7, 322n
fieldwork, 9, 477–99, 500n
filled pauses, 458–9
film and video recordings, 37, 97
Finnish (Uralic language), 382, 518
first words, 368–70, 382–5, 559
flaps, 544–5
fluency, 445–68
 disorders, 167–8, 280–2, 448–9
 repair strategies, 9, 451–4, 463–8
 rhythm, 166–8
foot (stress foot), 148, 162, 568–9
force field perturbation studies, 230, 235–6, 238–9, 242

formants, 42–4, 70–5, 206–7, 226, 235–6, 487–8, 537
 altered feedback experiments, 270–6
 singers, 75, 181, 270–6
Frame/Content theory, 353–72, 532, 558–9
French (Indo-European language), 138, 207, 212–13, 226, 233–4, 458, 532, 537–8, 541–3
frequency effects, 462, 566–9
fricatives, 124–5, 142–3, 484–5, 486, 489–92, 535–6
frontal cortex, 279–80
Fulfulde (Niger-Congo language), 482–3
functional residual capacity, 15–16
fundamental frequency, 38, 120–1, 180–1, 183, 234, 514–15, 517–18
fusion illusion (McGurk effect), 188–90, 200, 201, 260, 261

Gaussian filters, 183
gaze, 181–2, 183–4
gemination, 482, 484–5
gender identity, 545–6, 547
genioglossus, 61f, 62t, 63, 68–9, 70
geniohyoid (muscle), 61f, 63t, 64
Georgian (Kartvelian language), 145–6, 147–8
German (Indo-European language), 143, 145, 146, 210–11, 456–7, 514–16
 second language learners, 433
gestures and body language, 172
glottal flow, 15, 20, 23, 25, 27, 44–52, 496–8
glottalic consonants, 481–3, 497
glottalic vowels, 485–6
glottis, 34–5, 39–41, 45–7, 73, 479–80
GODIVA model, 315–20, 560–1
gorilla, 87
gradient effects (speech errors), 405–6
Greek (Indo-European language), 531–2, 534, 538, 541–3
Guarani (Tupian language), 489–92

head movement, 179–81, 183, 184–6
hearing impairment, 207–10, 258, 261–2, 267–8
height (vowels), 61, 69, 73, 74, 114–16, 188, 206, 493–5
Heschl's gyrus, 278
hesitations, 456–63
Hindi (Indo-European language), 141–2, 489, 534

hot-wire anemometers, 113
hyoglossus, 61f, 62t, 64, 70
hyoid bone, 61f, 63–4
hypopharynx, 6, 70, 71, 72–3, 74

immigrants, 546–7
implosives, 482–3
infants
    babbling, 97–8, 208, 210–11, 358, 362–8, 380–2, 383, 558–9, 560
    effect of hearing and visual impairments on, 207–8, 210–11
    speech perception, 203, 534
    velopharyngeal function, 118, 119, 126n
inferior colliculus, 278
inflated palate task, 236–7
innate behavior patterns, 365–7
inner speech errors, 404–15
insula, 301, 302–3, 360–1
interaction errors, 421–39
International Phonetic Alphabet (IPA), 9, 480–1
Intonational Phonology, 513
intonational phrase, 385–6, 424–33, 512
intraglottal pressure, 44–52
IPA (International Phonetic Alphabet), 9
isochrony, 159–66
Italian (Indo-European language), 492–3, 518

Japanese (Altaic language), 162–3, 179–82, 184–6, 237–8, 511, 518–19, 532, 533, 538–9, 540–3, 544, 545–6
jaw, 6, 8, 61, 79–80, 86–95, 96–8, 99, 100–1, 135–7, 209–10, 360–2, 562–4
    anatomy and physiology, 86–93
    perturbation studies, 203–4, 228–9, 232–3, 235–6

Kalapalo (Upper Xingu Carib dialect), 487–8
Kanincin dialect (Ruwund), 495
Karitiana (Tupi language), 493–5
kinematics
    breathing cycle, 14–16
    jaw and lips, 89–92, 99–101, 562–4
    multimodal speech, 178–94, 203, 209
    vocal fold vibration, 36–41
Korean (Altaic language), 519–20, 539, 541–3
Kotiria (Tucanoan language), 497–8
kymographs, 160, 478

language acquisition, 2–3, 5, 8, 358, 530–49
    apraxia of speech, 8, 331–44
    autism, 547
    babbling, 97–8, 208, 210–11, 358, 362–8, 380–2, 383, 537, 558–9, 560
    breathing, 16–19, 20–5
    cross-language studies, 9, 530–49
    effect of anatomical and physical development on, 16–19, 20–5, 71, 115–16, 118–20, 123–4
    effect of hearing and visual impairments on, 207–9, 210–11, 267
    first words, 368–70, 382–5, 534–5, 559
    and motor control, 2–3, 9, 97–101, 530–49, 555–71
    prosody, 9, 379–98, 428–30
    role of auditory feedback, 115–16, 124
    theoretical models, 5, 8, 9
language hierarchies, 1–2
language-specific factors, 9, 477–571
    acquisition, 530–49
    phonetic fieldwork, 477–99, 500n
    phonetics-prosody interface, 511–23
    sequencing and planning, 436–7, 458–9
    timing patterns, 137–41, 143–51, 161–6, 391–7, 505–24
laryngealization, 496–8
laryngeal-oral coordination, 134, 137, 141–3, 148–51
larynx, 34–6, 481–3, 496–8
    developmental changes, 71, 120–1
    modeling of, 72–5
    subglottal pressure, 15, 20, 23, 25, 44–9, 485, 500n, 517–18
lateral consonants, 139–40, 143, 148
learning tasks, 258–60
lengthening, 395–7, 457–8, 518–23, 569–70
lesion studies, 298–322
lexical access, 462, 566–9
lexical bias effect, 407, 408, 409, 410
lexical frequency, 144–5, 567
lexical stress, 336, 391, 393–7, 568–9
limb studies, 254–5, 256–7
lips, 6, 79–86, 93, 94–6, 97–101, 135–8, 203–4, 253, 359–61, 362, 562–4
    anatomy and physiology, 80–6, 492–3
    boundary effects, 73–4
    developmental changes, 81–2, 97–101
    rounding, 206, 212–13, 226, 229, 492–3

lip-tube experiment, 233–4
liquids, 115, 138–9, 145, 148
lung-thorax unit, 14–16
   anatomical and physical developmental changes, 13, 16–25
   effects of disease on, 25–7

macaque, 201, 361
MacArthur-Bates Communication Development Inventories (CDI), 559
Madison Speech Assessment Protocol (MSAP), 339–40
magnetic resonance imaging (MRI), 65, 68, 72f, 110, 118, 141, 192, 283, 285, 304
magnetoencephalography (MEG), 282
males
   anatomy and physiology, 99–101, 116, 126n
   breathing, 15, 17, 19–23, 26–7
   developmental changes, 16–19, 20–5, 71
   formants, 75
   'masculine' speech styles, 545–6, 547
   Parkinson's disease, 26–7, 322n
mandible (jaw), 6, 8, 61, 79–80, 86–95, 96–8, 99, 100–1, 135–7, 209–10, 360–2, 562–4
   anatomy and physiology, 86–93
   perturbation studies, 203–4, 228–9, 232–3, 235–6
mandibular nerve, 85
masseter, 87f, 90–1, 95, 98
maxillary nerve, 85–6
McGurk effect, 188–90, 200, 201, 260, 261
medial pterygoid (muscle), 87f, 90–1
medial temporal gyrus, 279
Melodic Intonation Therapy, 432
memory, 242, 280, 281, 333, 338, 380, 384, 388, 416n, 451, 461, 556, 557–8
mesopharynx, 70–1
minority languages, 9, 477–99
mirror neurons, 201–2, 361, 556–7
mora-timing, 162–3, 391
motion studies, 179–81
motor control, 2–4, 9, 225–344
   chewing, 8, 93–5, 96, 98, 357, 360, 558–9
   developmental changes, 97–101, 379–98, 555–71
   evolutionary theory, 8, 353–72
   interaction with language skills, 555–71
   internal model hypothesis, 242
   mirror neurons, 201–2, 361, 556–7
   motor equivalence, 225–43
   motor goals, 3, 7–8, 213, 226–7, 232–8
   orofacial cutaneous function, 230–1, 248–62
   stuttering, 167–8, 281–2, 432–3, 448
   swallowing, 95–7, 360
motor cortex, 279–80, 301–3
Motor Theory of Speech Perception, 166, 202
movement, measurement issues, 183–8, 194n, 195n
MRI (magnetic resonance imaging), 65, 68, 72f, 110, 118, 141, 192, 283, 285, 304
mucosal wave, 37, 38–9, 44–5, 50f, 52–3, 54
multimodal speech, 7, 169–70, 178–94, 200–14
   altered feedback experiments, 230–1, 236, 238–9, 242, 267–86
muscles, 34–6
   breathing, 15, 19–20, 27
   effects of disease on, 27
   jaw, 88–92, 251
   lips and face, 80–3, 85–6, 249–52, 492–3
   pharynx, 65–7
   tongue, 60–5
   see also vocal folds
music, 158–9, 169–70, 172
mylohyoid (muscle), 61f, 63t

Namtrik (Barbacoan language), 489
Nasa Yuwe (isolate), 485–6
nasal cavity, 109
nasal consonants, 112–14, 137–8, 489–92
nasalization, 115–17, 143, 490, 492
Nasometer, 121
nasopharynx (adenoids), 118
Navajo (Athabaskan language), 494
neighborhood density, 462, 566–8
nervous system
   brain *see* brain
   cranial nerves, 85, 92, 301, 305–6
   facial nerves, 84–6, 252–3, 270, 274–6
   jaw, 92–3, 95
   sensory nerves, 85–6, 95, 270, 274–6, 277
   spinal nerves, 15
nonce words, 569

oblique muscles, 15
obstruent consonants, 112–13, 124
onset timing patterns, 143–4, 145, 147
   measurement issues, 160–1

Optotrak, 194n
oral consonants, 112–14
oral motor functions *see* chewing; speech motor control
orbicularis oris, 80–1, 85, 94, 96, 202, 241, 250, 253
orofacial cutaneous function, 230–1, 248–62
orofacial landmarks, 183–4, 186–8

PACT (perception for action control theory), 213
paidologos project, 532, 533
palatalization, 140–1
palatoglossus, 62t
palatopharyngeus, 61f, 66t, 67
Pan troglodytes (chimpanzee), 82
parent-child interaction, 369–70
Parkinson's disease, 14, 25–7, 167–8, 303–4, 309–10, 322n
pauses, 456–63
P-center, 160–1
perception for action control theory (PACT), 205, 213
perception tasks, 539–43
perioral reflex, 253
perturbation studies, 7–8, 100–1, 203–4, 227–43
pharynx, 61, 65–7, 74
Philadelphia English, 546
phonation, 34–55, 495–8
phonemic similarity effect, 406–15
phonetics, 9
phonetics-prosody interface, 511–23
phrase-final lengthening, 396–7, 426–7, 428–9, 569–70
physiology, 16–20, 80–93
piriform fossa, 71, 72f, 73, 74, 75
place-order effects, 145–6, 147–8
planning and sequencing, 2–5, 8–9, 353–468, 569–70
 breathing, 23–5
 hesitations, 456–63
 language-specific factors, 436–7
 motor speech disorders, 300–7, 331–44
 prosodic frames, 419–39
 speech errors, 9, 404–15, 419–39, 451–68
plasticity, 7, 211, 225
plosives, 112, 113–14, 122–4, 135, 141–3, 497, 537–9

pneumotachography, 112, 114, 117, 121
Polish (Indo-European language), 509
prediction-error-correction principle, 240–1, 242
premotor cortex, 201–2, 284, 286, 315, 361
pressure-flow method, 111–12, 114, 120, 125n
primates, 82, 86–8, 280, 361
procedural memory, 557–8
prolongation, 457–8
prosody, 8–9
 acquisition, 379–98
 boundary effects, 148, 394–7, 424–5, 517–22, 569–70
 breath groups, 24
 frames, 419–39
 intonational phrase, 385–6, 424–33
 phonetics-prosody interface, 511–23
 rhythm, 7, 158–72, 355, 359, 390–7, 431–3, 438
 sign language, 430–1
 see also timing
pulmonary fibrosis, 14

radiography (X-rays), 37, 91, 110, 232–3
recall tasks, 416n
recoil pressure, 14–15, 17–19, 25
rectus abdominus, 15
reduction, 394–5
redundancy, role in perception, 7, 189, 190–2
reflexes, 249–52, 253, 256, 257
regional dialects, 546–7
reliability, research methods, 111–12, 183–4, 416n, 561–2
repair strategies, 9, 451–4, 463–8
repetition, 459–60
research questions
 coordination, 141, 150–1, 171–2
 language acquisition, 569–70
 motor control, 239, 321–2, 344, 569–70
 sequencing and planning, 372, 436–9, 451
 speech mechanism, 28, 55, 101, 125
 speech perception, 190–4
residual capacity, 15–16, 17
resonance, 6, 7, 42–4, 70–5, 230, 234–8, 487–8
 fundamental frequency, 38, 180–1, 183, 234, 514–15, 517–18
respiratory system *see* breathing
retroflex consonants, 488–9
rhotacization, 141, 143

rhotic consonants, 498
rhythm, 7, 148, 158–72, 355, 359, 390–7, 431–3, 438
risorius (muscle), 81f, 85, 250, 492–3
Romanian (Indo-European language), 144–5
rounding, 206, 210, 212–13, 226, 233–4, 492–3
Russian (Indo-European language), 140–1, 162, 391
Rwanda (Bantu language), 483–4

saliva, 93, 94, 95, 101n
salpingopharyngeus, 66t, 67
Sardinian (Indo-European language), 486
second language learning, 430, 449–50
self-sustaining oscillation, 36, 44–52
sensory nerves, 85–6, 95, 270, 274–6, 277
    see also feedback
septum, 61f
sequencing and planning, 2–5, 8–9, 353–468, 569–70
    breathing, 23–5
    hesitations, 456–63
    language-specific factors, 436–7
    motor speech disorders, 300–7, 331–44
    prosodic frames, 419–39
    speech errors, 9, 404–15, 419–39, 451–68
Serbo-Croat (Indo-European language), 140
sex differences, 99–101, 116, 126n
    breathing, 15, 17, 19–23, 24, 26–7
    developmental changes, 16–19, 20–5, 71
    formants, 75
    gendered speech styles, 545–6, 547
    Parkinson's disease, 26–7, 322n
Shona (Bantu language), 483–4
sibilants, 234–5
sidetone amplification effect, 268
sign language errors, 430–1
silent pause, 456–7
singing, 75, 181, 270–6, 432–3
skin, role in speech motor control, 230–1, 248–62
Slovak (Indo-European language), 147
sociolinguistic variation, 543–7
Sound Pattern of English (Chomsky and Halle), 190
source-filter model, 42–4
South American languages, 493–5, 496–8
Spanish (Indo-European language), 392–3
spatiotemporal coordination, 192–4

speaker-listener dyads, 7, 169, 171–2, 369–70
specific language impairment (SLI), 557–8
speech breathing *see* breathing
speech cycling experiments, 168–9
speech errors, 8–9, 355, 451–68, 534–9
    exchange errors, 423, 431, 434–5, 438, 439n
    inner speech errors, 404–15
    interaction errors, 421–39
    and prosodic frames, 419–39
    repair strategies, 9, 451–4, 463–8
    second language learners, 430, 433
    sign language errors, 430–1
    tongue twister errors, 405–15, 426, 439n, 567
speech motor control, 2–4, 8, 9, 225–344
    developmental changes, 97–101, 379–98, 555–71
    evolutionary theory, 353–72
    internal model hypothesis, 242
    mirror neurons, 201–2, 361, 556–7
    motor equivalence, 225–43
    motor goals, 3, 7–8, 213, 226–7, 232–8
    orofacial cutaneous function, 230–1, 248–62
    stuttering, 167–8, 281–2, 432–3, 448
    see also chewing
speech pathology, 5, 298–322, 446–9
    amyotrophic lateral sclerosis (ALS), 308, 310
    aphasia, 432, 446–8
    apraxia of speech, 8, 299, 301, 305, 309, 310–11, 315–20, 331–44
    cerebral palsy, 303, 308
    cleft lip/palate, 116, 118, 126n
    diagnosis, 110, 250, 299, 315–16, 317, 318–19, 332–43, 446–8
    dysarthria, 8, 298–9, 300–7, 308–10, 322n, 432
    fluency disorders, 167–8, 280–2, 432–3, 448–9
    hearing and visual impairments, 207–13, 258, 261–2, 267–8
    Parkinson's disease, 14, 25–7, 167–8, 303–4, 309–10, 322n
    pulmonary fibrosis, 14
    specific language impairment (SLI), 557–8
    stroke victims, 280–1, 300–1
    treatment, 303, 343–4, 431–3

Index of Subjects

speech perception, 7, 115–16, 178–94, 200–14, 260–2
  categorical perception, 279
  cross-language studies, 163–6, 539–48
  fluency, 445–6, 451–2, 468
  measurement issues, 160–1
  sociolinguistic variation, 543–7
  Tadoma method, 261–2
speech production, definition, 1–5
speech rate, 386–90
speech SA (sensorimotor adaptation) studies, 270–2
speech sound disorder (SSD), 336–7, 341–2, 343–4 *see also* apraxia of speech
SPIN studies (SPeech-In-Noise), 182–3
spinal nerves, 15
stop consonants, 112, 113–14, 122–4, 135, 141–3, 497, 537–9
stress, 7, 158–72, 336, 355, 391, 393–7, 568–70
stress-timing, 161–6, 391–7
stroboscopic techniques, 37
stroke victims, 280–1, 300–1, 304–5
stuttering, 167–8, 281–2, 432–3, 448
styloglossus, 61f, 62t, 63–4, 69, 70
stylohyoid (muscle), 63t, 64–5
stylopharyngeus, 66t, 67
subglottal pressure, 15, 20, 23, 25, 44–51, 485, 500n, 517–18
subphonemic attenuation hypothesis, 406–15
superior temporal gyrus, 279
superior temporal sulcus, 279
supralaryngeal articulators, 59–76
  coordination, 3, 6–7, 133–51
  jaw, 79–80, 86–95, 96–8, 99, 100–1
  lips, 79–86, 93, 94–6, 97–101
  tongue, 60–5, 67–70, 96–7, 135, 148, 209–10, 251–2
  velopharyngeal port (VP port), 109–25
swallowing, 95–7, 360
Swedish (Indo-European language), 232–3, 456, 458, 510, 531–2, 534
syllable structure, 137–41, 143–51, 355–60, 362–8, 560–1, 565–6
syllable-timing, 161–6, 391–3
synchronous speech task, 169–70
syntactic theory, 1–2

Tadoma communication method, 261–2
talking head animations, 184–6
Tamil (Dravidian language), 489
taps, 487–8, 498
task dynamics model, 521–3
Telugu (Dravidian language), 489
temporal alignment problem, 188–90
temporalis (muscle), 87f, 90–1
theory, 1–5
  acoustic theory, 115–16, 489–95
  Articulatory Phonology, 4, 7, 8, 143–8, 166, 184, 192–4, 313–15, 370–2, 384
  auditory feedback, 276–8
  Auditory Theory of Speech Perception, 204–5
  COMS model, 143–8
  direct realism theory, 202–3
  DIVA/GODIVA model, 315–20, 560–1
  dual stream hypothesis, 280–1
  efference copy hypothesis, 269–70, 273, 277–8
  evolutionary theory, 2, 8, 80, 86, 87, 353–72
  Frame/Content theory, 353–72, 532, 558–9
  innate behavior patterns, 365–7
  internal model hypothesis, 242
  LRM99 model, 434–6, 560
  motor speech disorders, 307–21, 343–4
  Motor Theory of Speech Perception, 166, 202
  perception for action control theory (PACT), 213
  phonetics-prosody interface, 511–23
  rhythm class hypothesis, 161–6
  rhythm theory, 7, 158–72
  role of motor control in language development, 555–71
  self-sustaining oscillation models, 44–52
  source-filter models, 42–4
  speech planning, 433–6
  subphonemic attenuation hypothesis, 406–15
  syntax, 1–2
  task dynamics model, 521–3
  see also computational models
thyroarytenoid muscle, 34, 35f, 36
thyroid cartilage, 34, 35f

timing, 9, 133, 158–72, 273–4, 379–98, 438
  coda timing patterns, 139–40, 144, 145–6
  language-specific factors, 137–41,
    143–51, 161–6, 505–24, 569–70
  modeling of, 170–1
  tone-segment alignment, 513–17
  turn-taking, 171–2
tongue, 60–5, 96–7, 135, 148, 209–10, 251–2
  modeling of, 67–70
tongue twister errors, 405–15, 426,
    439n, 567
trachea, 35f
transcription, 9, 160, 480–1, 561–2
transmission-line model (vocal tract), 72–3
transverse abdominus, 15
trills, 145, 498
tube models (vocal tract), 6, 71–2, 73
Tupi languages, 493–5
turn-taking, 171–2

ultrasound, 479
uncontrolled manifold (UCM), 239–40
utterance length, 23–5, 426–7
uvular tap, 487–8

validity, 185, 335, 416n, 461–2
vallecula, 71, 72f, 73
velarization, 139–40
velopharyngeal port (VP port), 109–25
  developmental changes, 118–21
  observation and measurement, 110–12,
    114, 489–92
velum, 136–7, 138–9
Verbal Behavior (Skinner), 2
vertical phase difference, 37
video recordings, 37, 97

videofluoroscopy, 126n
visual feedback, 274
visual impairment, 210–13, 261–2
vital capacity, 16, 17, 18–20
vocal folds, 6, 34–55
  modeling of, 36, 37–8, 44–54
vocal intensity, 24–5, 27
vocal process, 34, 35f
vocal tract, 35f, 41–4, 59–76, 226
  aerodynamics, 109, 111–25, 230
  developmental changes, 71, 80
  individual differences, 206–7
  modeling of, 6, 47–51, 60, 67–70, 71–5
voice onset time (VOT), 142, 146, 495,
    506–7, 515, 537–9
voiceless consonants, 148–50
vowel systems, 492–5
vowels
  articulation, 61, 67–70, 73, 74, 114–17,
    188, 205–6, 211, 212–13, 485–6, 498
  duration, 390–2, 459, 508–11
  formants, 42–4, 70–5, 206–7
  nasalization, 115–17, 143, 490, 492
  perturbation studies, 226, 232–4

Wa'ikhana (Tukanoan language), 497–8
whistles, 486
words (prosodic words), 148, 394–6
working memory, 280, 388

X-rays, 37, 91, 110, 232–3

Yoruba (Niger-Congo language), 492–3

zygomaticus major (muscle), 81f, 85, 250,
    492–5

Printed and bound by CPI Group (UK) Ltd, Croydon, CR0 4YY
06/02/2023